1628

10,000
JOKES, TOASTS & STORIES

10,000
JOKES, TOASTS
& STORIES

EDITED BY

LEWIS AND FAYE COPELAND

ARRANGED BY SUBJECT AND
COMPLETELY INDEXED FOR
READY REFERENCE

Doubleday & Company, Inc.
GARDEN CITY, NEW YORK

INTRODUCTION

IN COMPILING this large collection of jokes and other forms of brief humor, the editors had a double purpose in mind. One was to present our heritage of humor to the seekers of reading entertainment for their own pleasure and relaxation. The other was to make easily available to public speakers and others the funny stories and witty sayings they need to brighten their addresses and illustrate their arguments.

Carrying out this twofold plan, the book has been divided into eleven principal parts containing in all 126 major classifications. A comprehensive index at the back of the book enables the reader to find what he wants, classified not only according to a great variety of subjects but also according to abstract qualities such as conceit, encouragement, gratitude, resourcefulness, tact, etc.

Acknowledgment is here made to the legion of story-tellers and wits everywhere, the product of whose humor and originality has traveled from person to person, from one public print to another, and—from one generation to another. For the good joke is ageless. Even the oldest joke is always new to some, and, cleverly embellished and properly modernized, the chestnut often becomes the latest gag of the comedians of stage and radio.

They say no joke is really new but has its origin in the hinterlands of another day, the product of some distant unnamed jokesmith. So here is our salute to all the merry company of wits who have made it their happy business to concoct the food of laughter!

LEWIS COPELAND
FAYE COPELAND

CONTENTS

PART I

THE AMERICAN SCENE

The American Scene 1
Art 38
Music 43
Literature 49
Editors and Reporters 53
Hotels 56
Restaurants 61
Boarding Houses 72
Barbers 74
Automobiles 77
Buses and Street Cars 91
Railroads 94
Aboard Ships 100
Soldiers and Sailors 103
Police and Prisoners 113
Insane Persons 120
Drunks 123
Tramps 133
Rural 140
Western 171
Loony Laws 178
Americans Abroad 181

PART II

LOVE, COURTSHIP AND MARRIAGE

The Dear Ladies 187
Love and Courtship 197

MARRIED LIFE 226
MOTHERS-IN-LAW 277
DIVORCE 279
BACHELORS AND SPINSTERS 281

PART III

HOME AND SCHOOL HUMOR

BABIES 283
THE LITTLE DARLINGS—AND DEVILS 288
FAMILY HUMOR 331
SCHOOL CHILDREN AND TEACHERS 334
SUNDAY SCHOOLS 353
SERVANTS 361

PART IV

COLLEGE WIT AND HUMOR

IN THE CLASSROOM 373
ABSENT-MINDED PROFESSORS 384
COLLEGE LIFE 387
FLAMING YOUTH 391
ATHLETICS 404
BACK HOME 405

PART V

THE BUSINESS WORLD

OFFICES 411
STENOGRAPHERS 416
OFFICE BOYS 418
EFFICIENCY EXPERTS 421
DRUG STORES 421
GROCERS AND BUTCHERS 423
MISCELLANEOUS STORES 426
REAL ESTATE 437
INSURANCE 439
BANKS 441
STOCK BROKERS 443

SALESMEN 444
WORKING-MEN 447
MISCELLANEOUS BUSINESS 449

PART VI

THE PROFESSIONS

LAWYERS 459
DOCTORS 484
DENTISTS 499
PREACHERS 501
POLITICIANS 518
FAMOUS MEN 532

PART VII

ENTERTAINMENT AND SPORTS

BROADWAY 567
HOLLYWOOD 575
CIRCUSES AND SHOW BUSINESS 581
STAGE AND RADIO GAGS 584
GOLF 603
BRIDGE 610
HUNTING 612
FISHING 614
BASEBALL 622
BOXING 623
HORSE RACING 625
SPORTS IN GENERAL 626
TALL STORIES 629

PART VIII

QUOTATION DICTIONARY

PART IX

RACES AND NATIONS

ENGLISH 684
SCOTCH 707

IRISH 728

FRENCH 751

GERMAN 753

SWEDISH 757

CHINESE 758

OTHER NATIONS 761

PART X

MISCELLANEOUS HUMOR

COMIC DICTIONARY 765

WITTY SAYINGS 775

WISECRACKS 779

LINCOLN STORIES 795

EPITAPHS 805

    AMERICAN 805

    BRITISH 809

    SUGGESTED 816

HUMOROUS ERRORS 817

    HEADLINES 817

    TEXT OF STORIES 819

    CHURCH ANNOUNCEMENTS 832

    VARIED ANNOUNCEMENTS 833

    ADVERTISEMENTS 834

    WANT ADS 837

    SIGNS 841

BONERS 842

HOWLERS 847

PUNS 850

"YOU TELL 'EM" PUNS 867

CONUNDRUMS 869

PART XI

HUMOR IN VERSE

COMIC POEMS 881

COMIC SHORT VERSE 905

COMIC VERSE CHAINS 913

Nonsense Poems 915
Parodies 926
Limericks 939
Edward Lear's Limericks 950
Little Willies 956
Western Dialect Verse 959
Miscellaneous Dialect Verse 968
Irish Dialect Verse 977

PART XII

TOASTS FOR ALL OCCASIONS

Toasts to Men 983
Toasts to Women 984
Toasts to Love, Courtship and Marriage 990
Toasts to Friends 992
Toasts to Good Fellowship 994
Toasts on Fortune and Prosperity 996
Patriotic Toasts 996
Toasts of Sentiment and Good-Will 998
Toasts to Hosts and Guests 1001
Toasts in General 1001
Stories About Toasts 1005
Index 1008

PART I

THE AMERICAN SCENE

THE AMERICAN SCENE

[1]

A New Yorker was traveling west in a Pullman when a group of chamber of commerce boosters from Kansas City, Mo., boarded the train and began to praise their city to the New Yorker, telling him of its beautiful boulevards, large industrial establishments, and its wonderful possibilities. Finally the New Yorker became tired and said the only thing that would improve their city would be to make it a seaport.

The enthusiastic Kansas Citians laughed at him and asked how they could make it a seaport, being so far from the ocean.

The New Yorker replied that it would be a very easy task.

"The only thing that you will have to do," said he, "is to lay a two-inch pipe from your city to the Gulf of Mexico. Then if you fellows can suck as hard as you can blow you will have it a seaport inside half an hour."

[2]

"Doctor," she said loudly, bouncing into the room, "I want you to say frankly what's wrong with me."

He surveyed her from head to foot. "Madam," he said at length, "I've just three things to tell you.

"First, your weight wants reducing by nearly fifty pounds.

"Second, your beauty would be improved if you used about one tenth as much rouge and lipstick.

"And third, I'm an artist—the doctor lives on the next floor."

[3]

Mrs. Green had recently acquired a dog and was proudly demonstrating his good points to a friend.

"I know he's not what you would call a pedigree dog," she said, "but no tramp or beggar can come near the house without his letting us know about it."

"What does he do?" asked her friend. "Bark the house down?"

"No; he crawls under the sofa."

[4]

Bore — "Talking about Africa makes me think of the time——"

Bored One — "Good gracious, you're quite right. I had no idea it was so late. Goodby."

[5]

"When I see you I always think of Smith."

"But I am not in the least like Smith."

"Oh, yes. You both owe me $100."

[6]

His wife asked him to copy a radio recipe. He did his best, but got two stations at once. And this is what he wrote down:

"Hands on hips, place one cup of flour on your shoulder, raise knees and depress toes; mix thoroughly in one-half cup of milk, repeat six times. Inhale quickly one-half teaspoon of baking powder, lower the legs and mash two hard-boiled eggs in a sieve; exhale breath naturally and sift in a bowl. Attention! Lie flat on the floor and roll in the whites of two eggs backward and forward until it comes to a boil. In ten minutes remove from fire and rub smartly with a rough towel. Breathe naturally, dress in warm flannels and serve with tomato soup."

[7]

Henry Brown arrived late at the country club dance, and discovered that in slipping on the icy pavement outside, he had torn one knee of his trousers.

"Come into the ladies' dressing room, Henry," said his wife. "There's no one there and I'll pin it up for you."

Examination showed that the rip was too large to be pinned. A maid furnished needle and thread and was stationed at the door to keep out intruders, while Mr. Brown removed his trousers. His wife went busily to work.

Presently at the door sounded excited voices.

"We must come in, maid," a woman was saying. "Mrs. Jones is ill. Quick, let us in."

"Here," said the resourceful Mrs. Brown to her terrified husband, "get into this closet for a minute."

She opened the door and pushed her husband through it just in time. But instantly, from the opposite side of the door, came loud thumps and the agonized voice of Mr. Brown demanding that his wife open it at once.

"But the women are here," Mrs. Brown objected.

"Oh, damn the women!" yelled Mr. Brown. "I'm out in the ballroom."

[8]

Aunt—"Can you explain radio to me, Arthur?"

Arthur—"Well, if you had a very long dog, reaching from New York to Chicago, and you trod on its tail in New York, it would bark in Chicago. That's telegraphy; and radio is precisely the same only without the dog."

[9]

"Did you set a steel trap on your front porch?"

"Yeh, the wolf had better not come to my door."

"Well, you've caught a bill collector."

[10]

Jill, accompanied by her dog, is out walking.

She meets Jack, who invites her to the matinee.

Jill is willing—but what to do with the dog?

Jack suggests taking it to the police station.

Jill does so, pretending she has found it.

Matinee enjoyed.

Jack now calls at police station and claims "lost" dog.

Is told he must leave $2 reward for the finder, does so.

Jill then drops in and as "finder" receives the $2. All square.

[11]

A family living in an apartment house in the suburbs of a large city had a cat to which they were very much attached. One day the cat got sick and finally died. As there was no rear yard to their home in which to bury the cat, father was forced to wrap the cat up in a newspaper and take it with him, being carefully reminded by mother to toss the bundle from the train window when en route to his work.

Father placed his bundle upon the baggage rack over his seat, but struck up a conversation with a fellow commuter and forgot to toss the bundle out the window. He took the package on to his office, thinking that he would dispose of it on his way home that evening. But again he got to talking to someone on the train, forgot about the cat, and still had the bundle under his arm when he arrived home. His wife scolded him about it and father promised to take care of the matter the next day. But once more his memory failed him. When for the third time he arrived home still carrying the bundle, poor mother became quite angry.

"You've got to dispose of that cat right now," said she. "Put it in the furnace right now as the fireman is seldom there at this hour."

Well, father decided perhaps he'd better take it to the basement and put it in the furnace, but as he lifted the bundle from a table it fell open, and lo and behold there was—a boiled ham!

[12]

"Do you live within your income?"

"Good heavens, no! It's all I can do to live within my credit."

[13]

"Can you name an animal that has eyes and cannot see; legs and cannot walk, but can jump as high as the Empire State Building?" asked the life of the party.

Everybody racked his brains during a period of deep silence, and racked in vain. Finally, they gave it up and demanded the solution.

"The answer," he said, "is a wooden horse. It has eyes and cannot see, and legs and cannot walk."

"Yes," the company agreed. "But how does it jump as high as the Empire State Building?"

"The Empire State Building," the humorist explained, "can't jump."

[14]

"Johnson is so conceited."

"Yes, on his last birthday he sent a telegram of congratulation to his mother!"

[15]

The story is told of the Kentucky colonel who had an argument with the devil. The devil said that no one had a perfect memory. But the colonel maintained that there was an Indian on his plantation who never forgot anything. The colonel agreed to forfeit his soul to the devil if the Indian ever forgot anything.

The devil went up to the Indian and said: "Do you like eggs?" The Indian replied, "Yes." The devil went away.

Twenty years later the colonel died. The devil thought, "Aha, here's my chance." He came back to earth and presented himself before the Indian. Raising his hand, he gave the tribal salutation, "How."

Quick as a wink the Indian replied, "Fried."

[16]

"What's the idea of the Greens having French lessons?"

"They have adopted a French baby, and want to understand what she says when she begins to talk."

[17]

"You can't imagine what things are like out in the arctic regions," the explorer was telling a group of friends.

"Oh, I don't know," said one. "Even if we haven't seen it we can imagine what it feels like."

"I doubt it. It's impossible until you've really seen it; until you've stood there, a small, insignificant atom, surrounded by vast stretches of white—"

"Yes, I know. I've been like that."

"Really? Where was that, may I ask?"

"First time I appeared at a formal dinner in a stiff dress shirt."

[18]

She (looking through family album)—"Doesn't dad look funny in those suspenders?"

He (a practical soul)—"Yes, but he'd look a darned sight funnier without them."

[19]

Tabloid Biography:
High chair,
High school,
High stool,
High finance,
High hat,
"Hi, Warden!"

[20]

She (to Cousin John, who has just returned from the tropics)— "O John, dear, how kind of you to bring me this dear little monkey! How thoughtful you are! But—but it is just like you!"

[21]

Hobbs—"I really believe you have stopped your worrying. What brought about the change?"

Dobbs (cheerfully)—"My troubles are more real than they used to be."

[22]

"Oh, yes," said Mrs. Lowell-Cabot, proudly, "we can trace our ancestors back to—to—well, I don't know exactly who, but we've been descending for centuries."

[23]

"Since he lost his money, half his friends don't know him any more."

"And the other half?"

"They don't know yet that he has lost it."

[24]

"I'm getting old."

"Having rheumatism?"

"Worse than that. I'm having reminiscences."

[25]

Wilson—"Col. Becker says it's his rule 'Never to take a drink when you feel as if you need one'; and old Browning says 'Never take a drink except when you need one.' Now what is a fellow going to do?"

Manson—"Follow both rules, and you'll be all right."

[26]

"You say he left no money!"

"No. You see he lost his health getting *wealthy,* and then lost his wealth trying to get *healthy.*"

[27]

"Why didn't you deliver that message as instructed?" a man asked his servant.

"I did th' best I could, sir."

"The best you could! Why, if I had known I was going to send a donkey, I would have gone myself."

[28]

Two young men had been invited out to dinner by their employer. During the course of the meal the conversation drifted into channels which got the young friends into rather deep water for them.

"Do you care for Omar Khayyam?" asked their host, at one point during the dinner, thinking to discover the literary tastes of the young men.

"Pretty well," the one addressed replied, "but, personally, I prefer Chianti."

The subject was abandoned, but on the way home the other said to his chum:

"Why don't you simply say you don't know when you're asked something you don't understand? Omar Khayyam isn't a wine, you idiot. It's a kind of cheese."

[29]

At a dance the young lady had just been introduced to her partner. By way of making conversation, she said, as they waltzed around the ballroom floor:

"Who is that terribly ugly man sitting over there?"

Her partner looked at the man she indicated.

"Why, that's my brother!" he exclaimed.

"Oh, you must excuse me," said the lady, in embarrassment, and added apologetically, "I really hadn't noticed the resemblance."

[30]

Antiquarian—"This vase is 2,000 years old. Be very careful in carrying it."

Moving Man—"You can depend on me, professor; I'll be as careful of it as if it were new!"

[31]

A young fellow once offered to kiss a Quakeress. "Friend," said she, "thee must not do it."

"O, *by Jove!* but I must," said the youth.

"Well, friend, as thee hast *sworn,* thee may do it, but thee must not make a practice of it."

[32]

The following admonition was addressed by a Quaker to a man who was pouring forth a volley of ill language against him:

"Have a care, friend, thou mayest run *thy face* against *my fist.*"

[33]

Smith was relating his experiences in South America.

"I was taking my usual morning dip when I spotted three gladiators making for me, so I had to swim for my life!"

"You mean navigators—something like a crocodile?" interposed Jones.

"Well, what are gladiators?"

"Gladiators? Why, they're a sort of flower grown from bulbs."

[34]

Harry Jones was a prominent member of a fraternal lodge. At the breakfast table he was relating to his wife an incident that occurred at the lodge the previous night. The president of the lodge offered a silk hat to the brother who could stand up and truthfully say that during his married life he had never kissed any woman but his own wife. "And, would you believe it, Helen?—not a one stood up."

"Harry," his wife said, "why didn't you stand up?" "Well," he replied, "I was going to, but I know I look like hell in a silk hat."

[35]

"He said you were what?"

"Laconic."

"What does that mean?"

"Dunno. But I gave him one on the nose to be on the safe side."

[36]

A gentleman was much surprised when the good-looking young lady greeted him by saying, "Good evening." He could not remember ever having seen her before.

She evidently realized that she had made a mistake, for she apologized, and explained:

"Oh, I'm so sorry. When I first saw you I thought you were the father of two of my children."

She walked on while the man stared after her. She did not realize, of course, that he was unaware of the fact that she was a school teacher.

[37]

A man who stuttered was asked why he did so.

"It's my p-p-p-peculiarity," he answered. "Everybody has s-s-s-some p-p-p-peculiarity."

"I don't have any," said the questioner.

"Don't y-y-y-you s-s-stir your c-c-c-coffee with your r-r-r-right hand?"

"Yes, of course."

"Th-that's your p-p-p-peculiarity. Most p-p-p-people use a s-s-s-poon!"

[38]

We stood awed at the beauty of the great canyon. Not a member of the party spoke; speech was inadequate for such a spectacle as this.

"Well," broke out the wit of the company, "isn't it gorgeous?"

It was such fun to shove him off the edge.

[39]

"Your apartment is just as cute as ever. Don't you just adore it?"

"Naw. I'm moving."

"Why, what's come over you?"

"An opera singer."

[40]

An elderly man put a dime on the Salvation Army drum, then asked the girl in charge:

"What do you do with this money?"

"Give it to the Lord."

"How old are you, young lady?"

"Nineteen."

"I'm eighty-seven," said the man as he recovered his dime from the drum. "You don't need to bother; I'll more likely see the Lord before you do."

[41]

A man dreamed that he had died and that he found himself in a vast expanse where he was exceedingly comfortable. He rested for awhile and then, becoming somewhat bored, he shouted out, "Is there anybody here?"

In a moment a white-robed attendant appeared and asked, "What do you want?"

"What can I have?" was the answer.

"You can have whatever you want," replied the attendant.

"Well, then bring me something to eat."

"What do you want to eat?" asked the attendant. "You can have anything you want."

And so they brought him just what he wanted, and he went on eating and sleeping and having a glorious time. He wanted something more and asked for games. He went on getting everything he wanted whenever he asked for it, but at last he got more than a little bored and summoned the attendant and said:

"I want something to DO!"

"I am sorry, but that is the only thing we cannot give you here."

And the man said, "I am sick and tired of it; I'd rather go to hell!"

"Where do you think you are?!" exclaimed the attendant.

[42]

"What happened after you were thrown out of the side exit on your face?"

"I told the usher I belonged to a very important family."

"So what?"

"He begged my pardon, asked me in again and threw me out of the front door."

[43]

Father (impressively)—"Suppose I should be taken away suddenly, what would become of you, my boy?"

Irreverent Son—I'd stay here. The question is, What would become of you?"

[44]

"John has an umbrella that has been in his possession for twenty years."

"That's long enough. He ought to return it."

[45]

A very valuable dachshund, owned by a wealthy woman, was run over.

The policeman detailed a man to tell the woman of her misfortune.

"But break the news gently," he said. "She thinks a lot of this dog."

The man rapped on the mansion door and, when the woman appeared, he said: "Sorry, lady, but part of your dog has been run over."

[46]

An income tax repayment claim had been made for $60.00, but the taxpayer had miscalculated the amount, for actually $90.00 was due to him. A check for this amount was sent, and this is how he acknowledged it:

"Dear Sir,—I am now seventy years of age. At last I believe in Santa Claus."

[47]

Gardener—"This is a tobacco plant in full flower, madam."

Dear Old Lady—"How very interesting! And how long will it be before the cigars are ripe?"

[48]

"Say, what's that building there?"

"Where?"

"You looked too late. It's gone."

[49]

An Englishman who had been visiting a Kentucky Colonel living in New York City, decided to go to Virginia to spend the winter. After he had been away for a couple of weeks he wrote enthusiastically to his southern friend in New York:

"Oh, I say, old top, you never told me that the South was anything like I've found it, and so different to the North. Why, man, it's God's country!"

The Colonel, a voluntary exile from Kentucky, promptly wired back:

"Of course it is. You didn't suppose God was a Yankee, did you?"

[50]

"Can you tell me how to get to the Postoffice?"

"That's just where I want to go. Let's work together. You go south, and I'll go north, and we'll report progress every time we meet."

[51]
"But why did you buy a dachshund for the children?"
"So that they can all pet him at once."

[52]
Weather Man—"Put down rain for a certainty this afternoon."
Assistant—"Are you positive, sir?"
Weather Man—"Yes, indeed. I've lost my umbrella. I'm planning to play golf, and my wife's giving a lawn-party."

[53]
"I wonder why it is that fat men are always good-natured?"
"Probably because it takes them so long to get mad clear through."

[54]
"After all, what is the difference between the rich man and the poor man?"
"The rich man has acute laryngitis and the poor man has a cold."

[55]
Landlady (in the year 2000)— "And this is the bathroom."
Modern Miss—"Yes. Now show me the television arrester."

[56]
"Brown volunteered to lend me money."
"Did you take it?"
"No. That sort of friendship is too good to lose."

[57]
In a certain mining town, there was a competition to see who could eat the most in the shortest time. One man easily outdistanced all the other competitors. During the time allowed, he put away a beefsteak, a pound of sausages, a hefty meat pie and about a yard of suet pudding. For this remarkable performance he was roundly feted and, of course, he was adjudged the winner.

Just as he was about to leave the scene of his glory, he turned round and said, "I say, you fellows, don't let my wife know or I won't get any dinner."

[58]
Anxious that his meeting should go off quietly, the temperance reformer had hired an ex-prizefighter to keep order. Now he was speaking in glowing words:
"What is it that we all want when we get home tired from work? What do we long for to lighten our burdens, to gladden our hearts, and to bring a smile of true happiness to our lips?"
When he paused for effect, the ex-prizefighter butted in:
"And the first man who says 'a drink' goes out on his ear!"

[59]
"Here's one name on the committee that I never heard of."
"Oh, that's probably the person who actually does the work."

[60]
Diogenes was looking for an honest man in New York. "What luck?" asked the wayfarer. "Oh, pretty fair," replied Diogenes. "I still have my lantern."

[61]
Smith was sitting down to breakfast one morning when he was astounded to see in the paper an announcement of his own death.
He rang up his friend Jones at once. "Hello, Jones!" he said. "Have you seen the announcement of my death in the paper?"
"Yes," replied Jones. "Where are you speaking from?"

[62]
"Have any of your family connections ever been traced?"
"Yes, they traced an uncle of mine as far as Canada once."

[63]
Chairman (finishing eulogistic speech)—"Our dear old friend here has lived amongst us for forty years, is living with us now, and, he says, hopes to live amongst us for many years to come. Gentlemen, I can only add that we are looking forward to burying him here."

[64]
A speaker talking for more than two hours, said to his audience, "I'm sorry I spoke so long—you see, I haven't got a watch with me."
"Yes," shouted one in the audience, "but there's a calendar back of you."

[65]
The speaker was getting tired of being interrupted.
"We seem to have a great many fools here tonight," he said. "Wouldn't it be advisable to hear one at a time?"
"Yes," said a voice. "Get on with your speech."

[66]
"So you have been cured of your insomnia? It must be an immense relief."
"You've said it. Why, I lie awake half the night thinking how I used to suffer from it."

[67]
The bored youth turned to his partner at a dinner party. "Who is that strange-looking man over there, who stares at me so much?"
"Oh, that's Professor Jenkins," she replied brightly. "You know, the famous expert on insanity."

[68]
If a Hottentot tot taught a Hottentot tot to talk e'er the tot could totter, ought the Hottentot tot be taught to say aught, or naught, or what ought to be taught her?
If to hoot and to toot a Hottentot tot be taught by a Hottentot tutor, should the tutor get hot if the Hottentot tot hoot and toot at the Hottentot tutor?

[69]
Noah was surprised to see three camels coming up the gangway. "Hey!" he shouted, "one of you will have to stay ashore."
"Not me," said the first ship of the desert, "I am the camel so many people swallow while straining at a gnat."
"I," said the second, "am the camel whose back is broken by the last straw."
"And I," said the third and last, "am the camel which shall pass through the eye of a needle sooner than a rich man shall enter the kingdom of heaven."
Noah scratched his head in perplexity. Finally, deciding that posterity could ill spare any of these and would be lost for illustrations without them, he let them all come aboard.

[70]
Interviewer—"Do you believe that the younger generation is on the road to perdition?"
Octogenarian—"Yes, sir; I've believed that f'r nigh onto 60 years!"

[71]
City Slicker—"What does your son do?"
Farmer—"He's a bootblack in the city."
City Slicker—"Oh, I see, you make hay while the son shines."

[72]

A boastful Englishman was holding forth on the merits of his watch to friends in New York City. At last one of the Americans decided he could stand it no longer.

"That's nothing," he interrupted. "I dropped my watch into the Hudson a year ago, and it's been running ever since."

The Englishman looked taken aback.

"What!" he exclaimed, "the same watch?"

"No," he replied, "the Hudson."

[73]

Mayor—"I never saw the park littered so with paper as it is this morning. How do you account for it?"

Superintendent—"The Park Commissioner had leaflets distributed yesterday asking people not to throw paper about."

[74]

"What makes your next-door neighbor so unpopular?"

"He's fixed his lawn-mower so you have to drop a nickel in the slot to make it go."

[75]

The objector to temperance spoke bitterly. "Water has killed more people than liquor ever did."

"You are raving," declared the teetotaler. "How do you make that out?"

"Well, to begin with, there was the flood!"

[76]

"Hullo, Brown. Are you using your lawn-mower this afternoon?"

"Yes, I'm afraid I am."

"Splendid! Then you won't be wanting your tennis racket—I've broken mine!"

[77]

"Were any of your boyish ambitions ever realized?"

"Yes. When my mother used to cut my hair I often wished I might be bald-headed."

[78]

"I'd be much better off if they'd put that sign on the mail box."

"What sign?"

"Post no bills."

[79]

Maiden Aunt — "And what brought you to town, Henry?"

Henry—"Oh, well, I jus' come to see the sights, and I thought that I'd call on you first."

[80]

"Where are you going in such a hurry?" asked Mrs. Jones.

"Over to Bill Brown's house," said Mr. Jones. "He has just telephoned to ask if I could lend him a corkscrew, and I'm taking it myself."

"Couldn't you send it?"

"Mrs. Jones," said Mr. Jones, in cutting tones, "the question you asked me shows why most women are unfit to lead armies and make quick decisions in business deals involving millions. When the psychological moment arrives they don't know what to do with it."

[81]

The Bore—"I passed by your place yesterday."

The Bored—"Thanks, awfully!"

[82]

"Do Englishmen understand American slang?"

"Some of them do. Why?"

"My daughter is to be married in London, and the earl has cabled me to come across."

[83]

Soon after a society woman obtained a cat from the Humane Society she telephoned back to say they would not keep it. "I'm awfully sorry," she said, "It's a dear, and we are fond of it, but the cat is a bird killer, and we just can't have a bird killer.

"I'm sure my husband would be glad to make a contribution to the Humane Society for your trouble in taking the cat back," she added, "but he is up north shooting deer."

[84]

"Where is that beautiful canary-bird of yours that used to sing so clearly and sweetly?"

"I had to sell him. My son left the cage on the radio set and he learned static."

[85]

Downstairs—"Didn't you hear me pounding on the ceiling?"

Upstairs—"Oh, that's all right. We were making a lot of noise ourselves."

[86]

The quack was selling an elixir which he declared would make men live to a great age.

"Look at me," he shouted. "Hale and hearty, I'm over 300 years old."

"Is he really as old as that?" asked a listener of the youthful assistant.

"I can't say," replied the assistant. "I've only worked for him for 100 years."

[87]

"Lay down, pup, lay down," ordered the man. "Good doggie, lay down, I say."

"You'll have to say 'lie down,' Mister," declared a small bystander. "That's a Boston terrier."

[88]

A lady going from home for the day locked everything up well, and for the grocer's benefit wrote on a card: "All out. Don't leave anything." This she stuck on the door. On her return home, she found her house ransacked and all her choicest possessions gone. To the card on the door was added: "Thanks! We haven't left much."

[89]

"Wife home from the mountains, Jim?"

"Just got back."

"Didn't she stay longer than usual?"

"Yes. Couldn't afford to leave there while there were so many servants to tip. She had to stay until most of them were gone."

[90]

A hint, if properly managed, may be given without offending.

"Are you still bothered by those relatives of yours who come down from town to eat a big Sunday dinner and never invite you in return?" asked Mrs. Smith.

"No," said the unfortunate victim, "they finally took the hint."

"What did you say to them?" asked Mrs. Smith eagerly.

"Nothing was said," explained the other, "but we served sponge cake every time they came."

[91]

Judge—"Too old! Why, I could give you twenty years."

Friend — "Now, now, Judge. Don't start talking shop!"

[92]

"There is talk that the next war will be fought with radio."

"Well, I'm in training. I've faced some terrible programs."

[93]

Bob—"Aren't you coming in swimming?"

Bertha—"I can't. A moth ate my bathing suit."

Bob—"The little rascal. He must have been on a diet."

[94]

On a rainy day recently a lady in a mink coat got on a Madison Avenue bus. "I don't suppose I've ridden on a bus in two years," she said to the conductor, a gloomy fellow, as she paid her fare. "I ride in my own car," she explained.

"You don't know how we've missed you," the conductor said.

[95]

"Bragson claims to have been born with a gold spoon in his mouth."

"If he was, I'll bet it had somebody else's initials on it."

[96]

"I gave that man fifty cents for saving my life."

"What did he do?"

"Gave me back twenty cents change."

[97]

"Mr. Jones," began the timid-looking young man, "er—ah—that is, can—er—I—will you—"

"Why, yes, my boy, you may have her," smiled the girl's father.

The young man gasped.

"What's that? Have whom?" he asked.

"My daughter, of course," replied Jones. "That's what you mean. You want to marry her, don't you?"

"Why, no," said the young man. "I just wanted to know if you could lend me $25.00.

"Certainly not!" said Jones, sharply. "Why, I hardly know you."

[98]

After having listened, at a Christmas dinner, to Jones' stale jokes, Smith said: "I say, Jones, the Christmas turkey is luckier than we are."

"In what way?"

"He isn't stuffed with chestnuts until after he is dead."

[99]

The blacksmith was instructing a novice in the way to treat a horseshoe.

"I'll bring the shoe from the fire and lay it on the anvil. When I nod my head you hit it with this hammer."

The apprentice did exactly as he was told, but he'll never hit a blacksmith again!

[100]

A speaker was lecturing on Forest Reserve. "I don't suppose," said he, "that there is a person in the house who has done a single thing to conserve our timber resources."

Silence ruled for several seconds and then a meek voice from the rear of the hall timidly retorted: "I once shot a woodpecker."

[101]

Pretty Girl—"It must have taken a lot of courage to rescue me as you did."

Fireman—"Yeh. I had to knock down three other guys who wanted to do it."

[102]

"How does that clock go that you won at the fair?"

"Fine—it does an hour in fifty minutes."

[103]

"If you join our lodge you will be buried with music."

"That's no inducement for me. I'm not a bit musical."

[104]

Lecturer—"Of course, you all know what the inside of a corpuscle is like."

Chairman—"Most of us do, but you'd better explain it for the benefit of them as have never been inside one."

[105]

As the doorman ran down to open the limousine door, he tripped and rolled down the last four steps.

"For heaven's sake, be careful," cried the club manager, "they'll think you're a member."

[106]

Years ago there was an old man who lived at the edge of the Grand Canyon, and who used to tell tourists that he had dug out the big cleft in the ground, and had wheeled away the dirt in a wheelbarrow. He told the tale once to a young girl from the East.

"I don't believe it!" she said, indignantly.

"Why don't you believe it?" he asked.

"Well, you might have dug it out, as you say, and wheeled the dirt away in a wheelbarrow—but what did you do with the dirt?"

[107]

First Kangaroo — "Annabelle, where's the baby?"

Second Kangaroo—"My goodness, I've had my pocket picked."

[108]

Fortune Teller—"You are about to be discovered by a big movie producer and will soon be a star."

Mamie—"But that's the same thing you told my friend Rosa."

Fortune Teller—"I can't help it. You girls won't be satisfied with anything less nowadays."

[109]

Old Aunt (despondently)—"Well, I shall not be a nuisance to you much longer."

Nephew (reassuringly)—"Don't talk like that, aunt; you know you will."

[110]

She—"This is an ideal spot for a picnic."

He—"It must be. Fifty million insects can't be wrong."

[111]

Sir Walter Raleigh, with a flourish, spreads his new cloak over the mud-puddle. Newsreel cameras click, and a man in the crowd faints.

"It's his tailor," whispers the jealous Essex to Queen Elizabeth. "Walt hasn't paid for that cloak."

[112]

The aviation instructor, having delivered a lecture on parachute work, concluded:

"And if it doesn't open—well, gentlemen, that's what is known as 'jumping to a conclusion.'"

[113]

Brown (proud of his lineage)—"If you can pop in tomorrow evening I'll show you my family tree."

Smith—"Sorry, but I've promised to look at Robinson's cabbages."

[114]

A man who was criticized for not having a Bible in the house, excused himself by saying that there was not a word in the Bible that wasn't in his dictionary.

[115]

Howell—"A good deal depends on the formation of early habits."

Powell—"I know it; when I was a baby my mother hired a woman to wheel me about, and I have been pushed for money ever since."

[116]

Gushing Young Thing—"It was wonderful of you to drop ten thousand feet in a parachute. Do tell me your sensation."

Bored Aviator—"Oh—er—it was just a kind of sinking feeling."

[117]

"Once a friend of mine and I agreed that it would be helpful for each of us to tell the other all our faults."

"How did it work?"

"We haven't spoken for five years."

[118]

Pestor (looking up from his newspaper)—"I say, Jim, what is the Order of the Bath?"

Nestor (embracing the opportunity)—"Well, as I've experienced it, it's too cold; then you're short a towel; then you step on the soap, and, finally, the telephone bell rings!"

[119]

A man was tuning in on the radio, when he got a sudden twinge of pain in his back.

"I believe I'm getting lumbago!" he exclaimed.

"What's the use," answered his wife, "You won't understand a word they say."

[120]

A lecturer who was speaking on the drink question. "Now, supposing I had a pail of water and a pail of beer on this platform, and then brought on a donkey; which of the two would he take?"

"He'd take the water," came a voice from the gallery.

"And why should he take the water?" asked the lecturer.

"Because he's an ass," came the reply.

[121]

Professor—"Now this plant belongs to the Begonia family."

Visitor—"Ah, yes, and you're looking after it for them while they're away on holiday?"

[122]

"Is that a real diamond?"

"Well, very nearly."

[123]

MEN ONLY READ THIS

Out of ninety thousand women there will be eighty-nine thousand, nine hundred and ninety-four who will read this. The other six will be blind.

[124]

A man was happy because he had done three good deeds the day before. He had met a poor woman on the street, who was weeping and who held a sickly-looking child in her arms. Inquiry showed that she was weeping because she was convinced that her unbaptized child was dying.

"But," said the man, "why don't you have the child baptized?"

"Because I have no money, and the fee for baptism is one dollar," said the woman.

Whereupon the good Samaritan handed the woman a ten dollar bill, gave her his address so that she could bring back the change—which she did return—and went his way.

"That is one good deed," said a friend. "Now for the other two."

"Oh," observed the man of three good deeds, "they're all three in that one. First, I relieved the sorrows of a weeping woman; second, I assured the child of eternal salvation; and third, I got rid of that counterfeit ten dollar bill I'd been carrying for more than a year."

[125]

"He claims to be related to you and says he can prove it."

"The man's a fool."

"That may be a mere coincidence."

[126]

"Don't you think a real friend ought to feel sympathetic when one needs money?"

"I think a good many friends in such cases are touched."

[127]

"Why is it, Bob," asked George of a very stout friend, "that you fat fellows are always good natured?"

"We have to be," answered Bob. "You see, we can't either fight or run."

[128]

Miss Gushin—"It must be wonderful to be a parachute jumper. I suppose you've had some terrible experiences."

Parachutist (fed up)—"Yes, miss, terrible. Why, once I came down where there was a sign, 'Keep Off the Grass.'"

[129]

We arise in the morning, contact a cake of soap briefly, a shaving brush more extensively. We contact a pair of eggs, a street-car conductor, and finally the office. There is an unpleasant contact with a bill collector. He says he must contact some money. Later, perhaps, we contact a customer or two. When the shades of night have contacted the earth, we contact dinner, and pass the evening contacting poor bridge hands.

And so to bed.

Our fathers had all these experiences, but they didn't know how to describe them.

[130]

"Can you operate a typewriter?"

"Yes, sir, I use the Biblical system."

"I never heard of it."

"Seek and ye shall find."

[131]

"You look depressed, my friend. What are you thinking of?"

"My future."

"What makes it seem so hopeless?"

"My past."

[132]

"Doesn't it madden you when a girl is slow about getting ready to go to dinner with you?"

"Yes, the longer she takes the hungrier she gets."

[133]

Married Granddaughter—"Tom and I have arranged our holiday. We're going to hike."

Grandma—"It's wonderful how popular that place has become. Everybody seems to be going there nowadays."

[134]

According to an old superstitious belief, the wearing of a turquoise would preserve one from injury by falling. A medieval king who wore a turquoise ring asked his jester one day:

"What do you think would happen if I jumped off the highest part of the castle with this ring on my finger?"

The jester replied with a ready wit worthy of his office, "The turquoise, my lord, would probably not be hurt."

[135]

"Do you summer in the country?"

"No, I simmer in the city."

[136]

Young Girl—"Yes! I feel an intense longing to do something for others."

Friend—"Just whom do you mean by others?"

"Well, I suppose almost anybody outside of my immediate family."

[137]

A country woman was walking along a city street when she was amazed to see a man take pigeon after pigeon out of a hamper, look at his watch and then project the birds into the air.

"Hey, mister," she cried, running up to him, "you might give me one for my little Johnny before you throw them all away."

[138]

Cynic—"The owner of young chickens must quit counting them when he has 3,000."

Wiseguy—"No doubt. Solomon stopped a long time before that."

[139]

A gold-digger had died and all her worldly possessions, including a parrot, were being auctioned off. "What am I offered for this beautiful bird?" said the auctioneer.

"One bean," bid a bystander.

"Two bucks," roared another.

"Make it five, Daddy," croaked the parrot, "an' I'll give you a kiss."

[140]

A skeptic who was badgering a simple-minded old man about a miracle and Balaam's ass, finally said: "How is it possible for an ass to talk like a man?"

"Well," replied the honest old believer, with meaning emphasis, "I don't see why it ain't as easy for an ass to talk like a man as it is for a man to talk like an ass."

[141]

Handwriting Expert—"This specimen indicates patience, indulgence, kindness. . . ."

Client—"That's fine! It's the writing of the tailor I have selected to make my new suit."

[142]

A young wife, wishing to announce the birth of her first child to a friend in a distant city, telegraphed:

"Isaiah 9:6."

Which passage begins, "For unto us a child is born, unto us a son is given."

Her friend, not familiar with the Scriptures, said to her husband:

"Margaret evidently has a boy who weighs nine pounds and six ounces, but why on earth did they name him Isaiah?"

[143]

"Was it hot where you spent your vacation last summer?"

"Terrible, and no trees! We took turns sitting in each other's shadow!"

[144]

A truck driver was indulging in a burst of profanity which shocked the lady passing by. She regarded him reprovingly, as she demanded:

"My man, where did you learn such awful language?"

"Where did I learn it?" the truck driver repeated. "Huh! I didn't learn it, it's a gift."

[145]

Englishman (patronizingly) — "Your school facilities are excellent, I am told."

American (suavely) — "Well, I should say. See the Smithsonian Institution over there? Think of a building like that just to educate the Smiths."

[146]

"He's a nice little horse (I saw him myself) and the dealer says I may have him for a song. Would you advise me to buy him?"

"That depends upon your eye for a horse and his ear for music."

[147]

"It is hard, indeed," said the melancholy gentleman, "to lose one's relatives."

"Hard?" snorted the gentleman of wealth. "Hard? It is impossible!"

[148]

A young man fell into a state of coma, but recovered before his friends had buried him. One of them asked what it felt like to be dead.

"Dead," he exclaimed. "I wasn't dead, and I knew I wasn't dead, because my feet were cold, and I was hungry."

"But how did that make you sure?"

"Well, I knew that if I were in heaven I shouldn't be hungry, and if I were in the other place my feet wouldn't be cold."

[149]

"Jack hasn't come home. Am worried. Is he spending the night with you?" wired Smith's wife to five of his lodge brothers.

Soon after the husband arrived home, and before long a messenger boy came in with five replies to the wires his wife had sent. They all read:

"Yes, Jack is spending the night with me."

[150]

"You don't seem to realize on which side your bread is buttered."

"What does it matter? I eat both sides!"

[151]

"My ancestors came over in the Mayflower."

"It's lucky they did; the immigration laws are a little stricter now."

[152]

"I'm just a young fellow that is struggling to make ends meet."

"Well, if you're so badly bent financially it ought to be easy for you."

[153]

"Do you know any reliable rule for estimating the cost of living?"

"Yes. Take your income—whatever that may be—and add 25 per cent."

[154]

A wager was laid that it was a Yankee peculiarity to answer one question by another. To sustain the assertion a down-Easter was interrogated. "I want you," said the bettor, "to give me a straight-forward answer to a plain question."

"I kin do it, mister," said the Yankee.

"Then why is it that New Englanders always answer a question by asking one?"

"Du they?" was the Yankee reply.

[155]

A well-known speaker lectured to the members of a literary society, and at the end of his address the secretary approached him with a check. This he politely refused, saying that it might be devoted to some charitable purpose.

"Would you mind," asked the secretary, "if we add it to our special fund?"

"Not at all," said the speaker. "What is the special fund for?"

"To enable us to get better lecturers next year."

[156]

A New Yorker who is a combination of Albert Einstein, the great mathematician, and Rube Goldberg, creator of nutty cartoons, worried a good deal over making out his income-tax return, until he finally hit upon a simple formula, which he now offers free of charge to any who may be perplexed in the future.

He listed as dependents one blonde wife, a sedan car, three goldfish, and two children. He then multiplied his grandfather's age by six and seven-eights, subtracting his telephone number. Next he added the size of his hat and subtracted the number of his car. After these preliminaries, the rest was easy.

Deducting $1,000 for keeping his wife a blonde for the whole year, he divided the remainder by the number of lodges he belonged to, multiplied by the number of electric lights in the house, divided by the size of his collar.

This gave his gross income, which, after dividing by his chest measurement, and subtracting his blood-pressure, gave the net amount owed to the Government.

[157]

New Iceman—"Say, what do you think? The guy in that house threw me out because I tried to kiss the cook this morning."

Milkman—"I think the lady of that house does her own cooking."

[158]

"He drove straight to his goal," said the orator. "He looked neither to the right nor to the left, but pressed forward, moved by a definite purpose. Neither friend nor foe could delay him nor turn him from his course. All who crossed his path did so at their own peril. What would you call such a man?"

"A truck driver," shouted some one from the audience.

[159]

Jane—"Jack was at the masquerade last night, but I couldn't tell him from Adam."

John—"My heavens! Did they dress like that?"

[160]

A tourist was enjoying the wonders of California as pointed out by a native.

"What beautiful grapefruit," he said, as they passed through a grove of citrus-trees.

"Oh, those lemons are a bit small owing to a comparatively bad season," explained the Californian.

"What are those enormous blossoms?" questioned the tourist a little bit farther on.

"Just a patch of dandelions," answered the guide.

Presently they reached the Sacramento River.

"Ah," said the tourist, "some one's radiator is leaking."

[161]

Mrs. Petty—"I'm going to enter Fido in the dog show next month."

Friend—"Do you think he will win many prizes?"

"No, but he'll meet some very nice dogs."

[162]

Two rabid Californians, during a heavy rain-storm in Los Angeles, watched the downpour with embarrassed expressions. Finally, after a deep silence, one said to the other:

"Boy, some terrible weather certainly blows in from Nevada, doesn't it?"

[163]

Hostess—"This is Captain Banks, who has just returned from a trip to the Arctic regions."

Pretty Guest—"Oh, do come nearer the fire. You must be cold."

[164]

"Did you take your usual two weeks' camping trip this year?"

"No; we just left our house doors open, removed the window screens, and got the same effect."

[165]

"That means fight where I come from!"

"Well, why don't you fight then?"

"'Cause I ain't where I come from."

[166]

A Boston spinster was shocked at the language used by workmen repairing telephone wires near her home, so she wrote to the Telephone Company. The manager immediately asked the foreman on the job to make a report and here's what the foreman said:

"Me and Spike Williams were on this job. I was up the pole and accidentally let the hot lead fall on Spike—and it went down his neck. Then Spike looked up at me and said: 'Really, Harry, you must be more careful.'"

[167]

Jones—"Well, how are you getting on in your new eight-room house?"

Smith—"Oh, not so badly. We furnished one of the bedrooms by collecting soap coupons."

Jones—Didn't you furnish the other seven rooms?"

Smith—"We can't. They're full of soap."

[168]

A farmer on his first visit to New York came out of the Grand Central Station into the confusion of Forty-second Street, and after standing somewhat bewildered for a few minutes walked over to a traffic officer and said, "Mister, I want to go to Central Park."

"All right," said the officer. "You can go this time, but don't you ever, ever ask me again."

[169]

Old Lady (to parachutist)—"I really don't know how you can hang from that silk thing. The suspense must be terrible."

Parachutist—"No, mum; it's when the suspense ain't there that it's terrible."

[170]

Tourist (in Yellowstone Park)—"Those Indians have a blood-curdling yell."

Guide—"Yes, ma'am; every one of 'em is a college graduate!"

[171]

Nephew—"Thanks very much for the present."

Aunt—"Oh, that's nothing to thank me for!

Nephew—"That's what I thought, but mother told me to thank you just the same."

[172]

"I've got a pretty distasteful job before me," remarked the genealogist. "Mrs. Newrich employed me to look up her family-tree, and I've got to inform her that one of her relatives was electrocuted."

"Why worry about that?" said his friend. "Just write that the man in question 'occupied the chair of applied electricity at one of our public institutions.'"

[173]

At an examination of a class in first aid, a member was asked:

"What would you do if you found a man in a fainting condition?"

"I'd give him some brandy," was the answer.

"And if there were no brandy?"

"I'd promise him some."

[174]

"No, Nora," Grandpa Burns nodded sadly, "girls are not the same nowadays, unfortunately." His granddaughter smiled. She had heard this so many times. "No," went on the old man, "you never see a girl blush nowadays. When I was a young man it was different."

"Oh, granddad!" exclaimed the girl, "What ever did you say to them?"

[175]

"So Joe was the life of the party?"

"Yeah. He was the only one who could talk louder than the radio."

[176]

Hampton—"Dinwiddow told me his family is a very old one. They were one of the first to come across."

Rhodes—"The grocer told me yesterday that now they are the last to come across."

[177]

Old Lady (at the zoo)—"Is that a man-eating lion?"

Fed-up Keeper—"Yes, lady, but we're short of men this week, so all he gets is beef."

[178]

"All that I am I owe to my mother."

"Why don't you send her 30 cents and square the account."

[179]

Man (at telephone)—"Zander! Zander! Z! Z! No, not C! ABCDEF GHIJKLMNOPQRSTUVWXYZ!!"

[180]

He—"Don't you hate people who talk behind your back?"

She—"Yes, especially at the movies."

[181]

"What is the weather like?"

"It's so cloudy I can't see."

[182]

"How many cigars do you smoke a day?"

"About ten."

"What do they cost you?"

"Twenty cents apiece."

"My, that's two dollars a day. How long have you been smoking?"

"Thirty years."

"Two dollars a day for thirty years is a lot of money."

"Yes, it is."

"Do you see that office building on the corner?"

"Yes."

"If you had never smoked in your life you might own that fine building."

"Do you smoke?"

"No, never did."

"Do you own that building?"

"No."

"Well, I do."

[183]

Jones—"How do you spend your income?"

Smith—"About 30 per cent for shelter, 30 per cent for clothing, 40 per cent for food and 20 per cent for amusement."

Jones—"But that adds up to 120 per cent."

Smith—"That's right."

[184]

Jones—"Sorry, old man, that my hen got loose and scratched up your garden."

Smith—"That's all right, my dog ate your hen."

Jones—"Fine! I just ran over your dog and killed him."

[185]

"What a lot of friends we lose through their borrowing money from us."

"Yes, it is touch and go with most of them."

[186]

Floridan (picking up a melon)—"Is this the largest apple you can grow in your State?"

Californian—"Stop fingering that grape."

[187]

"What do you take for your insomnia?"

"A glass of wine at regular intervals."

"Does that make you sleep?"

"No, but it makes me satisfied to stay awake."

[188]

"My laundry sends back my shirts with different buttons sewed on them."

"You don't know when you are well off. My laundry sends back my buttons with different shirts sewed on them."

[189]

Caleb—"Why don't you get a job and go to work? You know that worry kills more people than work does."

Loafer—"Yes, I've heard all that but the trouble with me is that nothing worries me so much as work. I'd rather loaf and let other people do the worrying."

[190]

Neighbor—"Did I bring your lawn mower back last month?"

Indignant Householder — "No, you did not."

Neighbor—"Now what'll I do? I wanted to borrow it again."

[191]

"Well, I did my good deed today, made at least a hundred people more cheerful."

"How was that?"

"I chased my hat when the wind blew it down the street."

[192]

"Have you seen my dog this morning, Mr. Smith?"

"Seen him! I should think I have. He came in here, stole a leg of pork, bit me in the foot, then tripped a customer into a crate of eggs."

"Did he really? Well, I wonder if you would mind putting this 'Lost' notice in your window?"

[193]

A Boston citizen, whose supply of water had been turned off because he wouldn't pay his bills, wrote to the Water Department as follows:

"In the matter of shutting off the water on unpaid bills, your company is fast becoming a regular crystallized Russian bureaucracy, running in a groove and deaf to the appeals of reform. There is no use of your trying to impugn the verity of this indictment by shaking your official heads in the teeth of your own deeds.

"If you will persist in this kind of thing, a widespread conflagration of the populace will be so imminent that it will require only a spark to let loose the dogs of war in our midst. Will you persist in hurling the corner stone of our personal liberty to your wolfish hounds of collectors, thirsting for its blood? If you persist, the first thing you know you will have the chariot of a justly indignant revolution rolling along in our midst and gnashing its teeth as it rolls.

"If your rascally collectors are permitted to continue coming to our doors with unblushing footsteps, with cloaks of hypocritical compunction in their mouths, and compel payment from your patrons, this policy will result in cutting the wool off the sheep that lays the golden egg, until you have pumped it dry—and then farewell, a long farewell, to our vaunted prosperity."

[194]

Two men, who were visiting a Museum, were seen standing in front of an Egyptian mummy, over which hung a placard bearing the inscription: "B. C. 1187."

Both visitors were much mystified thereby.

"What do you make of that, Jim?"

"Well," said Jim, "I dunno; but maybe it was the number of the motor-car that killed him."

[195]

"You say he's 94, never looked at a girl in his life, and doesn't smoke, drink, or gamble?"

"Aye—beats me why he wanted to live so long."

[196]

"Hello, Frank, I thought you were dead?"

"Oh," said Frank, "they did get a story around that I was dead, but it was another man. I knew it wasn't me as soon as I heard of it."

[197]

A Westerner was visiting New York. Walking on a side street late one evening, he was held up by a bandit.

"Give me your money, or I'll blow out your brains!"

"Blow away," said the man from the West. "You can live in New York without brains, but not without money."

[198]

"Hello!" exclaimed Jenkins, as he met his friend Jones. "You're looking a bit off color. Anything wrong?"

"I'm afraid there is," replied Jones. "I've had to give up drinking, smoking, and gambling."

"Well, I must say that's all to your credit," commended Jenkins.

"Oh, no, it isn't!" snapped Jones. "It's due to my lack of credit."

[199]

"Are you going to the flower show?"

"No, it's too much trouble. I think I'll stay home and get it over the radio."

[200]

Adam and Eve were naming the animals of the earth when along came a rhinoceros.

Adam—"What shall we call this one?"

Eve—"Let's call it a rhinoceros."

Adam—"Why?"

Eve—"Well, because it looks more like a rhinoceros than anything we've named yet."

[201]

Here are some things about elevators I'd like to have cleared up:

Why starters always send a car up just as I am about to step in.

Why you have to face the front

of the car instead of forming congenial groups in the rear.

Why my voice always breaks when I give my floor number.

Whether big buildings hire operators to fit uniforms, or buy uniforms to fit operators.

Why the big woman in the back always gets out on the mezzanine floor.

Whether you should leave the elevator quickly after your cigarette has burned through the large man's gaberdine suit.

Whether I could run one of the things.

[202]

"Yes, my dear, I have lost Azor, my precious little dog!"

"But you must put an advertisement in the papers!"

"The poor little pet can't read!"

[203]

An Alabama man was talking with a man from Maine:

"As near's I can see," said the Alabaman, "there ain't much difference atweens we-uns and you-uns, 'cept that we-uns reckon an' you-uns guess."

"That's 'bout all, neighbor," replied the Maine man, " 'cept that we can guess a plaguy sight better than you can reckon!"

[204]

An inexperienced speaker arose in confusion after dinner and murmured stumblingly:

"M-m-my f-f-friends, when I came here tonight only God and myself knew what I was about to say to you—and now only God knows!"

[205]

The man of the house finally took all the disabled umbrellas to the repairer's. Two days later, on his way to his office, when he got up to leave the street car, he absentmindedly laid hold of the umbrella belonging to a woman beside him, for he was in the habit of carrying one. The woman cried "Stop thief!" rescued her umbrella and covered the man with shame and confusion.

That same day, he stopped at the repairer's, and received all eight of his umbrellas duly repaired. As he entered a street car, with the unwrapped umbrellas tucked under his arm, he was horrified to behold glaring at him the lady of his morning adventure. Her voice came to him charged with a withering scorn:

"Huh! Had a good day, didn't you!"

[206]

A man took down his telephone receiver and while he was waiting for a chance to call the operator, heard this conversation on a party line:

"Hello."

"Hello."

"That you, Jake?"

"Yep, this is Jake."

"It don't sound like Jake."

"Well, this is Jake speaking all right."

"Are you sure this is Jake?"

"Sure, this is Jake!"

"Well, listen, Jake. This is Henry. Lend me fifty dollars."

"All right. I'll tell him when he comes in."

[207]

Said a jaded guest at a formal function to the man next to him:

"Gee, this thing is a bore; I'm going to beat it!"

"I would, too," said the other, "but I've got to stay. I'm the host!"

[208]

Shoemaker—"Here are the boots for your new polar expedition. Were you satisfied with the boots I made for the last trip?"

Explorer—"Quite. They were the best boots I ever ate on a polar expedition."

[209]

A guide, showing an old lady through the Zoo, took her to a cage occupied by a kangaroo.

"Here, madam," he said, "we have a native of Australia."

"Good gracious," she replied, "and to think my sister married one of them."

[210]

"Papa, what is the person called who brings you in contact with the spirit world?"

"A bartender, my boy."

[211]

"I just dreamed I had a job."

"You look tired."

[212]

"I have just heard that my sister has a baby. They don't say what sex and so I don't know whether I am an uncle or aunt."

[213]

Him—"Hurry, dear, we'll be late for the theatre."

Her—"I'm trying my reducing machine; I'll be ready in a hundred shakes."

[214]

"Statistics show," declared the bespectacled woman lecturer, "that the modern, common-sense style of woman's dress has reduced accidents on the street-cars by 50 per cent."

"Why not do away with accidents altogether?" piped a masculine voice from the rear of the hall.

[215]

A New York business man visiting Salt Lake City strolled about the city and made the acquaintance of a little Mormon girl.

"I'm from New York," he said to her. "I suppose you do not know where New York is?"

"Oh, yes, I do," answered the little girl eagerly. "Our Sunday-school has a missionary there."

[216]

Said the chairman of a certain society at its annual meeting: "In most kindred associations half the committee does all the work, whilst the other half does nothing. I am pleased to place on record that in the society over which I have the honor to preside it is just the reverse."

[217]

Here are a few Famous Last Words:

"Gimme a match, I think my gas tank is empty."

"Gosh, wife, these biscuits are tough."

"Let's see if it's loaded."

"You can make it easy, that train isn't coming fast."

"What, your mother going to stay another month?"

"Lemme have that bottle, I'll try it."

"Sure I was out with your wife, what about it?"

"Say, who's boss of this joint, anyhow?"

"If you knew anything you wouldn't be a traffic cop."

"Y-e-s, dear, I l-o-s-t m-y p-a-y g-a-m-b-l-i-n-g."

"Just watch me dive from that bridge."

"Step on her, boy, we're only going seventy-five."

[218]
"My grandfather lived to be nearly ninety and never used glasses."

"Well, lots of people prefer to drink from a bottle."

[219]
Col. Southblood—"Yes, suh, he got mad an' called me a derned old bareface scoundrel."

Col. Bluegrass—"Well, he's slightly mistaken, suh. You've got a goatee an' mustache."

[220]
A man bet ten dollars that he could ride the fly-wheel in a saw-mill, and as his widow paid the bet she remarked, "William was a kind husband, but he didn't know much about fly-wheels."

[221]
Government Examiner—"How did you come to mark this man's paper 101 per cent.? Don't you know that nothing can be more perfect than 100 per cent.?"

New Assistant—"Yes, but this man answered one question we didn't ask."

[222]
A miserly man was approached by a friend who did his best to per-suade him to dress more in accor-dance with his station in life. "I'm surprised," said the friend, "that you should allow yourself to be-come shabby."

"But I'm not shabby," said the miser.

"Oh, but you are," said his friend. "Remember your father. He was always neatly dressed. His clothes was always well tailored and of the best material."

"Why!" shouted the other, tri-umphantly, "these clothes I'm wear-ing were father's!"

[223]
Attendant—"Do you wish to con-sult Woosung Portung, the great Chinese mystic?"

Woman—"Yes, tell him his mother is here from The Bronx."

[224]
Jones was always trying to bor-row money, and his friends had begun to avoid him.

One morning he tackled an ac-quaintance in the street before the latter had a chance to escape.

"I say, old man," began Jones, "I'm in a terrible fix. I want some money badly, and I haven't the slightest idea where on earth I'm going to get it from."

"Glad to hear it, my boy," re-turned the other promptly. "I was afraid that you might have an idea you could borrow it from me."

[225]
A census clerk, in scanning over the form to see if it had been prop-erly filled up, noticed the figures 120 and 112 under the headings, "Age of Father, if living," and "Age of Mother, if living."

"But your parents were never so old, were they?" asked the aston-ished clerk.

"No," was the reply, "but they would have been, if living."

[226]
"Yes," said the boastful young man, "my family can trace its an-cestry back to William the Con-queror."

"I suppose," remarked his friend, "you'll be telling us that your an-cestors were in the Ark with Noah?"

"Certainly not," said the other. "My people had a boat of their own."

[227]

"Is a ton of coal very much, papa?"

"That depends, my son, on whether you are shoveling or buying it."

[228]

Jones—"The Chinese make it an invariable rule to settle all their debts on New Year's day."

Smith—"So I understand, but, then, the Chinese don't have a Christmas the week before."

[229]

He had been sitting next to her at the dinner table for the last hour and was deeply admiring her beautiful arms and shoulders.

"Do you know," she said suddenly, "I've been in misery for a week. Sometimes I could almost scream with pain!"

"Why, what's the matter?" he exclaimed sympathetically.

"I was vaccinated last week and it has taken dreadfully."

His eyes fell and his gaze was curious. But he saw no scar. "Why, where were you vaccinated?" he asked impetuously.

She raised her eyebrows and smiled sweetly. "In New York."

[230]

"Thirty years ago," said the man who had traveled to the end of the earth and most of the way back, "I started out, alone, unaided, without friends to help me along, with the intention of making the world pay me the living that it owes me. My only allies were a dollar bill and a determination to make a million more. Today" (and he threw out his chest proudly) "I still have the determination and fifty cents in change."

[231]

A religious and charitable woman noticed a very down-and-out sort of man standing at the corner of the street near her residence.

One morning she took compassion on him, pressed a dollar into his hand and whispered, "Never despair."

Next time she saw him he stopped her and handed her nine dollars.

"What does this mean?" she asked.

"It means, ma'am," said the man, "that 'Never Despair' won at 8 to 1."

[232]

"Did the patent medicine you purchased cure your aunt?"

"Mercy, no. On reading the circular that was wrapped around the bottle she got two more diseases."

[233]

The lady was visiting the aquarium. "Can you tell me whether I could get a live shark here?" she asked an attendant.

"A live shark? What could you do with a live shark?"

"A neighbor's cat has been eating my goldfish, and I want to teach him a lesson."

[234]

"Did you give the mayor my note?" a man asked of the messenger.

"Yes, sir, but there ain't no use sendin' that man any notes. He's blind as a bat."

"Blind? How do you know? That's news to me."

"Course he's blind. Twice he asked me where my hat was, and there it was in plain sight on my head all the time. Yes, sir, he's blind as a bat!"

[235]
Sherlock Holmes—"Ah, Watson, I see you have on your winter underwear."

Watson — "Marvelous, Holmes, marvelous! How did you ever deduce that?"

Sherlock—"Well, you've forgotten to put on your trousers."

[236]
His relatives telephoned to the nearest florist's. The ribbon must be extra wide, with "Rest in Peace" on both sides, and if there was room, "We Shall Meet in Heaven."

The florist was away and his new assistant handled the job. There was a sensation when the flowers turned up at the funeral. The ribbon was extra wide, indeed, and on it was the inscription:

"Rest in peace on both sides, and, if there is room, we shall meet in heaven."

[237]
A man in Chicago was grumbling about the heat. Said another, who had just returned from a trip through the South:

"Hot! Boy, you don't know what hot is. One day this week in Mississipi I saw a dog chasing a cat and they were both walking."

[238]
A local forecaster of the weather was so often wrong in his predictions that he became the laughing stock of the community. He, therefore, asked headquarters to transfer him to another station.

A brief correspondence ensued. "Why," asked headquarters, "do you wish to be transferred?"

"Because," the forecaster promptly replied, "the climate doesn't agree with me."

[239]
Mr. Brown was sitting down to breakfast one morning when he was astounded to see in the paper an announcement of his death. He rang up his friend Smith.

"Hello, Smith," he said, "have you seen the announcement of my death in the paper?"

"Er—yes," replied Smith, "where are you talking from?"

[240]
Belle—"If I were you, Percy, I should tell him just what I think of him."

Percy—"How can I? The cad has no telephone."

[241]
A census-taker working in lower New York on the East Side, came to a tenement that was literally crowded with children, and observing a woman bending over a washtub he addressed her as follows:

"Madam, I am the census-taker; how many children have you?"

"Well, lemme see," replied the woman, as she straightened up and wiped her hands on her apron. "There's Mary and Ellen and Delia and Susie and Emma and Tommy and Albert and Eddie and Charlie and Frank and——"

"Madam," interrupted the census man, "if you could just give me the number——"

"Number!" she exclaimed, indignantly. "I want you to understand that we ain't got to numberin' 'em yet. We ain't run out o' names!"

[242]
Friend—"Was your uncle's mind vigorous and sane up to the very last?"

Heir—"I don't know—the will won't be read until tomorrow."

[243]
Missionary—"Why do you look at me so intently?"
Cannibal—"I am the food inspector."

[244]
A gentleman feeling a bit fed up with life decided to commit suicide by hanging himself. A friend came into the room and discovered him standing with a rope round his waist, and he inquired what he was trying to do. The gentleman told him he was taking his own life.
"But," said his friend, "why have you the rope round your waist?"
"Well," said the man, "when I tied it round my neck it was choking me."

[245]
He—"If you'll give me your telephone number I'll call you up sometime."
She—"It's in the book."
He—"Fine! What's your name?"
She—"That's in the book, too."

[246]
"Those girls look exactly alike. Are they twins?"
"Oh, no. They merely went to the same plastic surgeon."

[247]
"Have you noticed how Ashton drops his aspirates?"
"It's nothing to the way he drops his vowels. I've got more than a dozen of his I. O. Us."

[248]
"We go away for our holidays every third year."
"What do you do the other years?"
"The first one we talk of last year's holiday, and the next year we discuss plans for the following year."

[249]
"Hello, Brown! Have you seen Smith lately? I've been looking for him high and low for the last three months."
"Well, those are the places. He's been dead about that long."

[250]
Stranger—"I've come out here to make an honest living."
Native—"Well, there's not much competition."

[251]
A man called at a village post-office for a registered letter which he knew would be awaiting him. The letter was there, but the clerk demurred at handing it over, as he had no means of identifying the caller. The caller took a photograph of himself from his pocket, remarking:
"I think that ought to satisfy you as to who I am."
The clerk looked long and earnestly at the portrait, and then said:
"Yes, that's you, right enough. Here's your letter."

[252]
"Thankful! What have I to be thankful for? I can't pay my bills."
"Then, man alive, be thankful you aren't one of the creditors."

[253]
First Mosquito—"Why are you making such a fuss?"
Second Ditto — "Whoopee! I passed the screen test."

[254]
"I don't know how to fill out this question."
"What is it?"
"It says, 'Who was your mother before she was married?' and I didn't have any mother before she was married."

[255]

A southerner, with the intense love for his own section of the country, attended a banquet. The next day a friend asked him who was present. With a reminiscent smile he replied: "An elegant gentleman from Virginia, a gentleman from Kentucky, a man from Ohio, a bounder from Chicago, a fellow from New York, and a galoot from Maine."

[256]

"Yes," said the cheerful one, telling of a harrowing experience, "we had reached the place where we had eaten the last dog."

"It must have been terrible!" exclaimed the fair listener.

"It was," he said; "they didn't even have mustard to put on it, and it was at least twenty miles to the next stand."

[257]

"Of course you entertained during the social season?"

"Well," answered Mr. Newrich, "mother and the girls didn't think much of me as an entertainer, but I overheard several visitors say I was one of the most amusin' people that ever broke in."

[258]

Here is a question that stumps all applicants for jobs in the New York Fire Department:

"What piece of fire apparatus won't go up a one-way street?"

No applicant has ever answered it correctly.

The answer is: "A fireboat."

[259]

A party of young men were camping, and to avert annoying questions they made it a rule that the one who asked a question that he could not answer himself had to do the cooking.

One evening, while sitting around the fire, one of the boys asked: "Why is it that a groundsquirrel never leaves any dirt at the mouth of its burrow?"

They all guessed and missed. So he was asked to answer it himself.

"Why," he said, "because it always begins to dig at the other end of the hole."

"But," one asked, "how does it get to the other end of the hole?"

"Well," was the reply, "that's your question."

[260]

Here are some of the questions and answers overheard at the Bureau of Naturalization:

"Where is Washington?"

"He's dead."

"I mean the Capital of the United States."

"Oh, they loaned it all to Europe."

"Do you promise to support the Constitution?"

"Me? How can I? I've a wife and six children to support."

[261]

"Who was that pretty little thing I saw you with last night?"

"Will you promise not to tell my wife?"

"Surely, I promise."

"Well, it was my wife."

[262]

A wag asked his friend, "How many knaves do you suppose live in this street besides yourself?"

"Besides myself!" replied the other. "Do you mean to insult me?"

"Well, then," said the first, "how many do you reckon including yourself?"

[263]

Host (doing the honors)—"And that is a portrait of my great-great-grandfather."

Visitor—"Wonderful! Why, he doesn't look any older than you!"

[264]

Two young men were in earnest conversation on matters regarding the fair sex.

"How could you be so deceitful as to tell Miss Woodly she was pretty?" asked Clarence.

"I wasn't deceitful at all," replied Charles.

"But, my dear man," said Clarence, "you don't mean to say you think she is actually pretty?"

"Of course not," replied his companion. "What I told her was that she was as pretty as she could be."

[265]

"When are you going on your vacation?"

"I don't know. I've got to wait until the neighbors get through using my suit case."

[266]

"Don't you agree that Time is the greatest healer?"

"He may be—but he's certainly no beauty specialist."

[267]

Smith (reading statistics)—"Do you know that every time I breathe, a man dies?"

Jones—"Why don't you sterilize your mouth?"

[268]

He—"I saved a lot of money to-day."

She—"That's fine. How did you do it?"

He—"Instead of suing a man for what he owed me, I let him have it."

[269]

"That speaker certainly made a hit."

"What did he talk about?"

"About five minutes."

[270]

Officer (to man pacing sidewalk at three a. m.)—"What are you doing here?"

Gentleman—"I forgot my key, officer, and I'm waiting for my children to come home and let me in."

[271]

Brown—"Back to town again? I thought you were a farmer."

Green—"You made the same mistake I did."

[272]

Two deacons once disputing about a proposed new graveyard, one remarked:

"I'll never be buried in that ground as long as I live!"

"What an obstinate man!" said the other.

"If my life is spared, I will!"

[273]

"Porter can read three languages."

"What are they?"

"Magazines, sporting pages and railroad time-tables."

[274]

"There's nothing like cheerfulness. I admire anyone who sings at his work."

"How you must love a mosquito!"

[275]

Smith (after telling a whopper) —"I assure you, Jones, if I hadn't seen it myself I wouldn't have believed it."

Jones — "Ha — h'm — well, you know, I didn't see it."

[276]
At Brooklyn Bridge—"Madam, do you want to go to Brooklyn?"
"No, I have to."

[277]
Excitable Party (at telephone)—"Hello? Who is this? Who is this, I say?"
Man at Other End—"Haven't got time to guess riddles. Tell me yourself who you are."

[278]
"I hear that they belong to the early settlers."
"Well, you wouldn't think so if you could see the bill collectors climbing the front steps."

[279]
Smith—"I keep hearing the word 'Idiot.' I hope you are not referring to me."
Jones—"Don't be so conceited. As if there are no other idiots in the world!"

[280]
The amateur gardener, who loved to experiment with plants, sat locked in his room. He refused to take any food all day, and his wife finally insisted on being let in.
"You must tell me what's on your mind," she said, firmly. "You've been here brooding all day, and I must know what's wrong."
The gardener sighed heavily.
"It's just that one of my pet experiments didn't turn out the way I expected. Remember the time I crossed a potato with an onion?"
"Yes, yes," coaxed the anxious wife, "What happened?"
The gardener shook his head sadly.
"No good," he murmured, sinking his head on to his eyes. "All I got was a potato with watery eyes!"

[281]
A local citizen was walking down town one morning when a stranger addressed him: "Do you know where the post office is?"
"Yes," answered the citizen, affably, and walked on without further reply. After proceeding for about ten steps he looked back, and inquired in his turn, "Why? Did you want to know?"
"No," replied the stranger, with great earnestness, and then, the account having been balanced, the two walked away in opposite directions.

[282]
Jones—"Good evening, old man. Thought I'd drop in and see you about the umbrella you borrowed from me last week."
Brown—"I'm sorry, old man, but I lent it to a friend of mine. Were you wanting it?"
Jones—"Well, not for myself, but the fellow I borrowed it from says the owner wants it."

[283]
"So you and your neighbor are not on speaking terms?"
"No. My neighbor sent me a can of oil to use on my lawn mower when I started to cut the grass at six in the morning."
"And what did you do?"
"I sent it back and told him to use it on his wife when she started singing at eleven at night."

[284]
"Do you remember that couple we met on the steamer we took such a violent fancy to—I mean the couple we invited to visit us?"
"Yeah. You don't mean to say—"
"Yes, the idiots are actually coming!"

[285]
"Well, I must be going."
"Don't let me keep you if you really must be going," said his bored host.
"Yes, I really must go. But, really, I did enjoy our little visit. Do you know when I came in here I had a headache, but now I have lost it entirely."
"Oh, it isn't lost," was the patient reply. "I've got it now."

[286]
"Do you know what it is to go before an audience?"
"No. I spoke before an audience once, but most of it went before I did."

[287]
"Have any of your childhood hopes been realized?"
"Yes. When mother used to pull my hair I wished that I didn't have any."

[288]
"Whaddaya consider the height of human incompetence?"
"How about a drum-major with an inferiority complex?"

[289]
"How was the scenery on your trip?"
"It ran largely to tooth-paste and smoking tobacco."

[290]
Cries for help had attracted Fred's attention. A big man was beating a much smaller individual.
"Leave him alone!" shouted Fred, who threw himself into the fray and knocked out the big man with a well-timed uppercut.
"Thanks," said the little man after he had pulled himself together. "Now, look here, you share this $50 I took off him."

[291]
The preacher came along and wrote upon the signboard: "I pray for all."
The lawyer wrote underneath: "I plead for all."
The doctor added: "I prescribe for all."
The plain citizen wrote: "I pay for all!"

[292]
"I fought a tough battle to get into society in Boston, but I finally managed it."
"I imagine you had to keep your chin up."
"No, just my nose!"

[293]
"I dreamed last night that I had invented a new type of breakfast food and was sampling it when—"
"Yes, yes; go on."
"I woke up and found a corner of the mattress gone!"

[294]
A lady had just purchased a postage stamp at a substation. "Must I stick it on myself?" she asked.
"Positively not, madam," replied the postal clerk. "It will accomplish more if you stick it on the envelope."

[295]
"Glad to see you, old man. Can you lend me five dollars?"
"Sorry, but I haven't a cent with me today."
"And at home?"
"They're all very well, thank you, very well."

[296]
First New Englander—"So you had an operation on your nose?"
Second New Englander—"Yes, it was getting so I could hardly talk through it."

[297]
"You're what is called a self-made man?"
"Yes, I suppose I am."
"Your wife and daughters must be proud of you."
"They're about as proud of me as they would be of a home-made dress."

[298]
"You didn't roll your own cigarets before. Why do you do so now?"
"Because the doctor told me I needed a little exercise."

[299]
Fire Chief (putting recruit through his paces)—"We have only one fire engine. Now, suppose we are called away to a fire and you are left in charge of the station. Another fire breaks out several miles away. What would you do about the second fire?"
Recruit—"I'd endeavor to keep it alight, sir, until you got back."

[300]
New Yorker (incredulously)—"And you mean to say that in California you have 365 days of sunshine a year?"
Man from Los Angeles—"Exactly so, sir, and that's a mighty conservative estimate."

[301]
"What is it about a dachshund that you don't care for?"
"They make such a draft when they come into a room. They always keep the door open so long."

[302]
He—"Going to have dinner anywhere tonight?"
She (eagerly)—"Why, no, not that I know of."
He—"Gee, you'll be awfully hungry by morning!"

[303]
"The word 'reviver' spells the same backwards and forwards," said the frivolous man. "Can you think of another?"
The serious man scowled. "Tut-tut!" he cried contemptuously.
And they rode on in silence.

[304]
They had just turned the corner from one of the most beautiful of steep valleys.
She exclaimed: "What a beautiful gorge that was!"
"Yes, it wasn't bad," he replied, his mind flashing back, unromantically, to the restaurant in the hollow, "but I could have done with a bit more apple pie."

[305]
A lady traveling through California for the first time saw a fig tree. She said to the guide, "My good man, what kind of a tree is that?"
"Lady, that is a fig tree."
"Oh, no, it can't be a fig tree," she said.
"Yes, ma'am, that's a fig tree."
"Oh," said the lady, "I thought the leaves were larger than that."

[306]
Smith—"You mustn't take offense if I speak to you about something I have had on my mind for some time, just a little habit of yours."
Jones—"Certainly not."
Smith—"Nobody has ever had the nerve to tell you before. And you are such a splendid, noble fellow."
Jones—"Yes, yes."
Smith—"You're one of those fellows who never really know what is being said to them; you're always pursuing some train of thought. Anyone can tell half the time you

are not listening by the far-away look in your eyes. You've offended a lot of people. Of course, it's terribly rude—only you don't know it. You mustn't any more, old chap (putting his hands on Jones's shoulder). Promise me you'll quit."

Jones (obliged to face him)— "Just what were you saying?"

[307]

A young man wise beyond his years paused before answering a widow who had asked him to guess her age.

"You must have some idea," she said.

"I have several ideas," said the young man, with a smile. "The only trouble is that I hesitate whether to make you ten years younger on account of your looks, or ten years older on account of your intelligence."

[308]

"Animals do not know what it is to be superstitious," declares a clergyman. But we have yet to hear of a mouse that will pass a black cat on a Friday.

[309]

"Purely by accident, I have made one of the greatest discoveries," said the scientist.

"May I ask what it was?"

"I found," said the scientist, "that by keeping a bottle of ink handy you can use a fountain pen just like any other pen—without all the trouble of filling it."

[310]

A man walked into a pool parlor and said: "I will give a dollar to the laziest man here."

Man lying on billiard table: "Roll me over, buddy, and stick it in my back pocket."

[311]

A newly-married couple were entertaining and among the guests was one whose conduct was rather flippant. At supper he held up on his fork a piece of meat which had been served him, and in a vein of intended humor, remarked, "Is this pig?"

"To which end of the fork do you refer?" asked a quiet-looking man sitting at the other end of the table.

[312]

"Friend," said one immigrant to another, "America is a grand country to settle in. They don't hang you here for murder."

"What do they do to you?" the other immigrant asked.

"They kill you," was the reply, "with elocution."

[313]

The prim old lady was given the first glass of beer she ever had. After sipping it for a moment she looked up with a puzzled air.

"How odd!" she murmured. "It tastes just like the medicine my husband has been taking for the last twenty years."

[314]

Mrs. Newrich—"I want you to teach my son a foreign language."

Professor — "Certainly, madam, French, German, Russian, Italian, Spanish—?"

Mrs. Newrich—"Which is the most foreign?"

[315]

"Major, I see two cocktails carried to your room every morning, as if you had some one to drink with."

"Yes, sir; one cocktail makes me feel like another man; and, of course, I'm bound to treat the other man."

[316]

First Southerner—"Were you in New York long enough to feel at home?"

Second Southerner—"Yes, sir; why, I got so I could keep my seat in the cars with a lady standing and not even think about it."

[317]

"Can you tell me how to get to Adams Street?"

"What's that, stranger? I'm a little deaf."

"I beg your pardon?"

"I said I'm a little deaf. I didn't hear you."

"You don't say! I'm deaf too."

"That's too bad! Now, what was it you wanted?"

"Can you tell me how to get to Adams Street?"

"Sure. You go down this way for four blocks and then turn to your right. It's the third street down."

"That's Adams Street, is it?"

"Oh! No. Excuse me, old man. I thought you said Adams Street."

"No, I said Adams Street."

"Never heard of it. Sorry, stranger."

[318]

"A fine youngster," said the elderly man to the young mother, sitting opposite him on the train. "I hope you will bring him up to be an upright and conscientious man."

"Yes," smiled the fond mother, "but I'm afraid it's going to be a bit difficult, as——"

"Oh, nonsense," continued the adviser; "as the twig is bent so is the tree inclined."

"I know it," agreed the mother; "but this twig is bent on being a girl, and we are inclined to let it go at that."

[319]

He was genuinely enthusiastic about the virtues of temperance, but his face made people doubt him.

Toward the close of his lecture, he squared his shoulders, held his rather large head erect, and said: "I have lived in this town all my life. In this town there are fifty-five public houses, and I am proud to say that I have never been in one of them!"

Then came a voice from the back: "Which one is that?"

[320]

A man threw a nickel towards the blind man's cup. The coin missed and rolled along the pavement, but the man with the dark glasses quickly recovered it.

"But I thought you were blind?"

"No, I am not the regular blind man, sir," he said. "I'm just taking his place while he's at the movies."

[321]

Hewitt—"You don't seem to think much of him."

Jewett—"If he had his conscience taken out it would be a minor operation."

[322]

Medium—"I see a great loss—the loss of your husband."

Minnie—"But he has been dead five years."

Medium—"Then you will lose your umbrella."

[323]

"So you really think your memory is improving under treatment. You remember things now?"

"Well, not exactly, but I have progressed so far that I can frequently remember that I have forgotten something, if I could only remember what it is."

[324]
Uncle and niece stood watching the young people dance about them.
"I'll bet you never saw any dancing like that back in the 'nineties, eh, uncle?"
"Once — but the place was raided!"

[325]
"I heard your daughter speaks Esperanto. Does she speak it fluently?"
"Just like a native."

[326]
An Englishman was being shown the sights along the Potomac. "Here," remarked the American, "is where George Washington threw a dollar across the river."
"Well," replied the Englishman, "that is not very remarkable, for a dollar went much further in those days than it does now."
The American would not be worsted, so after a short pause, he said: "But Washington accomplished a greater feat than that. He once chucked a sovereign across the Atlantic."

[327]
"I'm glad to find you as you are," said the old friend. "Your great wealth hasn't changed you."
"Well," replied the candid millionaire, "it has changed me in one thing. I'm now 'eccentric' where I used to be impolite, and 'delightfully witty' where I used to be rude."

[328]
"If you are tired of dancing, let us sit down and have a little tête-à-tête."
"No, thank you. After such a big supper I really couldn't eat a thing."

[329]
Liberal Young Man — "I see there's some talk in this state upon the question of abolishing capital punishment. Would you vote to abolish it?"
Old Stuffed Shirt — "I would not. Capital punishment was good enough for my ancestors, and it's good enough for me!"

[330]
"That is Black Mountain?"
"Yes, sir—highest mountain about Lake George."
"Any story or legend connected with that mountain?"
"Lots of 'em. Two lovers once went up that mountain, and never came back again."
"Indeed! Why, what became of them?"
"Went down on the other side."

[331]
Two old sailors were sitting in what evidently had been their favorite barroom. The old place had been completely modernized and refurnished. Both old tars fell to reminiscing on the good old days. Said one old salt:
"I suppose it's all right, Bill, these new-fashioned trappings, but I miss the old spittoon."
"Yes," answered the other, "you always did, Jim."

[332]
"I have an awfully hard time catching people's names when I'm introduced," said one.
"So do I," said the other, "but I found a clever way to get around the awkwardness of asking to have the name repeated. I just ask, 'Do you spell your name with an *e* or an *i*?' It usually works splendidly."
"I know. I heard about that be-

fore. It worked with me, too, until once I met a girl I wanted to know better. Now she won't even look at me."

"Why is that?"

"Well, when I was introduced to her, I didn't catch her name, so I asked whether she spelled it with an *e* or an *i*."

"What was her name?"

"Hill."

[333]

"What did the Puritans come to this country for?" asked a Massachusetts teacher of a class in American history.

"To worship in their own way, and make other people do the same." was the reply.

[334]

A famous man once arrived in a big city and it is said that he was kissed by two thousand girls in two hours. When queried upon the matter, he commented somewhat mischievously: "I'd much rather have had my pick of the two thousand girls and kissed her alone for two hours."

[335]

"Come, come, come," said one who was wide-awake to one who was fast asleep, "Get up, get up; don't you know it's the early bird that catches the worm?"

"Serves the worm right," said the grumbling sleeper; "worms shouldn't get up before the birds do."

[336]

She—"Where did you get that umbrella?"

He—"It was a gift from sister."

She—"You told me you hadn't any sisters."

He—"I know—but that's what's engraved on the handle."

[337]

A man boasted of having eaten forty-nine boiled eggs.

"Why did you not eat one more and make it fifty?" asked one of his listeners.

"Humph, do you want a man to make a hog of himself just for one egg?"

[338]

"More than 5,000 elephants go each year to make our piano keys."

"Really? Well, it's remarkable what those beasts can be trained to do."

[339]

The lady of uncertain age simpered at the gentleman of about the same age who had offered her his seat in the car.

"Why should you be so kind to me?" she asked.

"My dear madam, because I myself have a mother and wife and a daughter."

[340]

A young couple that had received many valuable wedding presents established their home in a suburb. One morning they received in the mail two tickets for a popular show in the city, with a single line:

"Guess who sent them."

The pair had much amusement in trying to identify the donor, but failed in the effort. They duly attended the theater, and had a delightful time. On their return home late at night, still trying to guess the identity of the unknown host, they found the house stripped of every article of value. And on the bare table in the dining-room was a piece of paper on which was written in the same hand as the enclosure with the tickets.

"Now you know!"

3

[341]
"Here comes the parade, and your Aunt Helen will miss it. Where is she?"
"She's up-stairs waving her hair."
"Mercy! Can't we afford a flag?"

[342]
Reformer (to prostrated man)—"And so this is the work of rum, is it?"
Prostrated Man—"No, sir; this is the work of a banana-skin, sir."

[343]
"I've got a new idea. Fortune in it."
"What now?"
"It's an alarm clock that emits the delicious odors of frying bacon and fragrant coffee."

[344]
St. Peter—"And here is your golden harp."
Newly Arrived American—"How much is the first payment?"

[345]
"Did you ever hear from the $10 our neighbor Jones borrowed from you?"
"Every night. He used the money for a down payment on a radio set!"

[346]
"Is your dog intelligent?"
"Very. When I say to him, 'Come here or don't come here, just as you please,' he comes or he doesn't come, as he pleases."

ART

[347]
Critic—"The picture of the horse is good, but where is the wagon?"
Artist—"Oh, the horse will draw that."

[348]
Struggling Artist (being dunned for rent and endeavoring to put a bold front on things)—"Let me tell you this—in a few years' time people will look up at this miserable studio and say, 'Cobalt, the artist, used to work there'!"
Landlord—"If you don't pay your rent by tonight, they'll be able to say it tomorrow!"

[349]
First Artist—"Well, old man, how's business?"
Second Artist—"Oh, splendid! Got a commission this morning from a millionaire. Wants his children painted very badly."
First Artist (pleasantly)—"Well, my boy, you are the very man for the job."

[350]
Artist—"This is my latest picture. It's called 'Builders at Work.' It's very realistic."
Friend—"But they really aren't at work."
Artist—"Of course—that's the realism."

[351]
Artist—"Now, here's a picture—one of my best, too—I've just finished. When I started out I had no idea what it was going to be."
Friend—"After you got through, how did you find out what it was?"

[352]
A gentleman wishing to settle a point or two on art approached the information desk of a certain public library.
"Where," he asked, "shall I find something on Correggio and his 'Flight Into Egypt'?"
"Everything about aviation in Room 121," responded the clerk.

[353]

Artist—"That, sir, is a cow grazing."

Visitor—"Where is the grass?"

Artist—"The cow has eaten it."

Visitor—"But where is the cow?"

Artist—"You don't suppose she'd be fool enough to stay there after she'd eaten all the grass, do you?"

[354]

Auctioneer—"What am I offered for this beautiful bust of Robert Burns?"

Man in Crowd—"That ain't Burns . . . that's Shakespeare."

Auctioneer—"Well, folks, the joke's on me. That shows what I know about the Bible."

[355]

"How do you account for your success as a futuristic painter?"

"I use a model with the hiccoughs."

[356]

A cynic was standing in front of an exhibition of local art talent labeled, "Art Objects."

"Well," he announced to the attendant in charge, "I should think Art would object, and I can't say that I blame her."

[357]

"You say that I am the first model you ever kissed?"

"Yes."

"And how many models have you had before me?"

"Four. An apple, two oranges, and a vase of flowers."

[358]

Friend—"Why have you the general in such a peculiar pose?"

Sculptor—"You see, it was started as an equestrian statue, and then the committee found they couldn't afford the horse."

[359]

Mrs. Newrich had given the landscape artist carte blanche and he was showing her over the formal garden.

"What is that?" she asked. He told her it was a sundial. "What's a sundial?" He patiently explained how the sun moving through the heavens cast a shadow which is recorded on the dial, indicating the time of day. Mrs. Newrich beamed with interest.

"My goodness," she exclaimed, "these modern inventions! What will they be thinking of next?"

[360]

Critic—"Ah! And what is this? It is superb! What soul! What expression!"

Artist—"Yeah? That's where I clean the paint off my brushes."

[361]

"I painted something for last year's academy."

"Was it hung?"

"Yes, near the entrance where everybody could see it."

"Congratulations! What was it?"

"A board saying, 'Keep to the left.'"

[362]

"And this beautiful jar," said Jones, proudly exhibiting his treasures. "It cost me $50."

"Well, well, $50!" said his friend. "I suppose they threw in the marmalade."

[363]

"I don't like these photos at all," he said, "I look like an ape."

The photographer, famous for his wit as well as for his art, favored him with a glance of lofty disdain.

"You should have thought of that before you had them taken," was his reply as he turned back to work.

[364]

The painter was required to render an itemized bill for his repairs on various pictures in a convent. The statement was as follows:

Corrected and renewed the Ten Commandments 6.00

Embellished Pontius Pilate and put a new ribbon on his bonnet 3.06

Put a new tail on the rooster of St. Peter and mended his bill 4.08

Put a new nose on St. John the Baptist and straightened his eye 2.06

Replumed and gilded the left wing of the Guardian Angel 5.06

Washed the servant of the High Priest and put carmine on his cheeks 2.04

Renewed Heaven, adjusted ten stars, gilded the sun and cleaned the moon 8.02

Reanimated the flames of Purgatory and restored some souls 3.06

Revived the flames of Hell, put a new tail on the devil, mended his left hoof and did several odd jobs for the damned 4.10

Put new spatter-dashes on the son of Tobias and dressing on his sack 2.00

Rebordered the robe of Herod and readjusted his wig 3.07

Cleaned the ears of Balaam's ass, and shod him 2.08

Put earrings in the ears of Sarah 5.00

Put a new stone in David's sling, enlarged Goliath's hand and extended his legs 2.00

Decorated Noah's Ark 1.20

Mended the shirt of the Prodigal Son, and cleaned the pigs 1.00
53.83

[365]

Critic—"By George, old chap, when I look at one of your paintings I stand and wonder—"
Artist—"How I do it?"
Critic—"No; why you do it."

[366]

Mr. Babbitt (looking at a well-known picture)—"'Van Dyke, by Himself.' What a silly thing to put there; anyone could see that there is no one with him."

[367]

Guest—"That's an artistic rug. May I ask how much it cost you?"
Host—"Two thousand dollars. Two hundred for it and the rest for furniture to match."

[368]

"And this, I suppose, is one of those hideous caricatures you call modern art."
"Nope, that's just a mirror."

[369]

Cubist—"The gentleman, whose portrait this is, has come and asked me to alter his nose a little."
Friend—"And that makes you cross?"
Cubist—"No, but I can't remember where I put the nose."

[370]

Niece (in the picture gallery)—"Aunt Sarah, this is the famous 'Angelus,' by Millet."
Aunt Sarah—"Well, I never! That man had the nerve to copy the calendar that has hung in our kitchen for a dozen years or more."

[371]

"Have you seen how Slaminoff, the critic, has massacred my last painting?"
"Don't mind him—he just repeats, like a parrot, what everyone else is saying."

[372]

Father—"This is the sunset my daughter painted. She studied painting abroad, you know."

Friend—"Ah, that accounts for it! I never saw a sunset like that in this country."

[373]

Visitor (to butler who is showing him through the picture gallery)— "That's a fine portrait! Is it an old master?"

Butler—"No, that's the old missus."

[374]

Whistler once undertook to get a fellow artist's work into the autumn salon. He succeeded, and the picture was hung. But the painter, going to see his masterpiece with Whistler on varnishing day, uttered an exclamation of dismay.

"Good Heavens!" he cried, "you're exhibiting my picture upside down."

"Hush!" said Whistler. "The committee refused it the other way."

[375]

Peck—"Do you think you can make a good portrait of my wife?"

Artist—"My friend, I can make it so lifelike you'll jump every time you see it."

[376]

"Do you make life-size enlargements of snapshots?"

"That's our specialty."

"Fine; here's a picture I took of the Grand Canyon."

[377]

"Why did they hang that picture?"

"Perhaps they couldn't find the artist."

[378]

Artist—"Whatever success I have had, I owe it all to the telephone."

Friend—"How's that?"

Artist—"Well, while I was waiting for them to give me the right number I practiced drawing on a pad."

[379]

Art Editor—"Now, what we need for our next magazine cover is a girl wearing one of those religious gowns."

Artist—"What do you mean, a religious gown?"

Art Editor—"Oh, you know, one of these lo and behold."

[380]

A well-known Royal Academician who noticed a drawing of a fish by a pavement-artist asked the man what sort of fish it was supposed to be.

"A shark, sir!"

"But you've never seen a shark," said the R.A.

"That's true, sir," the man agreed: "but then, don't some of those Academy chaps paint angels?"

[381]

An artist famous for painting animals was motoring through Iowa, when he saw a very animated looking bull. Thinking he would like to take him on canvas, he got permission of the owner. In due time he produced an excellent likeness of the bull, which he sold for five hundred dollars. On seeing the farmer a year later, he told him he had sold the picture of his bull for five hundred dollars.

"Good Lord!" exclaimed the old farmer, "why I would have sold two real bulls for less than that one imitation of yours."

[382]

A painter of the "impressionist" school is now confined in a lunatic asylum. To all persons who visit him he says, "Look here; this is the latest masterpiece of my composition." They look, and see nothing but an expanse of bare canvas. They ask, "What does that represent?"

"That? Why, that represents the passage of the Jews through the Red Sea."

"Beg pardon, but where is the sea?"

"It has been driven back."

"And where are the Jews?"

"They have crossed over."

"And the Egyptians?"

"Will be here soon. That's the sort of painting I like; simple, suggestive, and unpretentious."

[383]

There was a wealthy amateur who prided himself on his skill in landscape painting, although his canvases were really little more than daubs.

Once he invited a couple of critics to look at his pictures. One of the visitors paused in front of the pictures. "Here's one you ought to call 'Home,' " he said.

"Why?" asked the painter.

"Because there's no place like it," said the critic.

[384]

"Is this a picture of you?"

"Yes. That's me."

"That's bad grammar."

"I know it. It's a bad picture, too."

[385]

Mrs. Newrich—"And the portrait will be real pretty?"

Artist—"Of course. You won't know yourself."

[386]

Photographer—"Please look pleasant, lady, and in a few moments you may resume your natural expression."

[387]

She—"I hear you are a great artist."

He—"I hope to be. I've only just started."

She—"What are you doing?"

He—"Well, I'm living in a studio and growing whiskers."

[388]

First Man (in art museum)—"Hello! Here's the Mona Lisa."

Second Man—"Aw, come on! That dame's smile reminds me of my wife's when she thinks I'm lying."

[389]

A rich but ignorant Englishman once went to the famous painter Turner and ordered a painting. When it was finished he refused to pay the price that the painter demanded.

"What," he said, "all that money for a square yard of canvas and a little paint!"

"Oh," replied Turner, "if it's just paint and canvas that you want, here's a half-used tube, and over in the corner you will find some canvas. I won't charge you much for them."

[390]

Patron—Do you ever draw pictures in the nude?

Artist—No, I usually wear a smoking jacket.

[391]

"Did you visit the art galleries when you were in New York."

"We didn't need to. Our daughter paints."

MUSIC

[392]

It was an opening appearance of the Philadelphia Symphony Orchestra, with Stokowski at his most majestic. The music was crashing and thunderous, when suddenly there fell an abrupt and complete silence, beginning a brief but absolute rest in the music.

Out of the stilly night there came a high-pitched feminine voice, full of reproach. "But," it said, "I always fry mine in lard."

[393]

"I can't think why they make so much fuss about Miss Smith's voice. Miss Jones has a much richer voice."

"Yes, but Miss Smith has a much richer father."

[394]

"Sir," the great violinist said to the host, Mr. Newrich, "the instrument I shall use at your gathering is over two hundred years old."

"Oh, that's all right! I wouldn't worry," returned the host; "no one'll ever know the difference."

[395]

Visitor—"Your son is making good progress with his violin. He is beginning to play quite nice tunes."

Host—"Do you really think so? We were afraid that we'd merely got used to it."

[396]

"What is your occupation?"

"I used to be an organist."

"And why did you give it up?"

"The monkey died."

[397]

"They tell me you love music."

"Yes, but never mind; keep on playing."

[398]

One of the briefer musical criticisms appeared in the local paper: "An amateur string quartet played Brahms here last evening. Brahms lost."

[399]

Vocalist—"I'm going away to study singing."

Friend—"Good! How far away?"

[400]

"Did you ever hear anything so beautiful?" exclaimed the daughter of the house, as she turned a new swing record on the Victrola.

"No," replied her father. "The nearest thing I ever heard to it was when a truck loaded with empty milk cans had a collision with another truck that was loaded with hogs."

[401]

"My daughter has arranged a little piece for the piano."

"Good! It's about time we had a little peace!"

[402]

Friend—"So you were asked for an opinion of that amateur's playing. What do you think of it?"

Master Musician—"He plays in the true spirit of Christian charity."

Friend—"What do you mean?"

Master Musician—"His right hand does not know what his left hand is doing."

[403]

"Why do you prefer Wagner?"

"Because he composes about the only kind of music one can hear above the conversation."

[404]

"Call that a Caruso record? The man is singing in German."

"Yes, sir. The record has been translated."

[405]

An old man at an evening function bowed his head and wept quietly but copiously while a young woman rendered the plaintive ballad, "My Old Kentucky Home."

The hostess tiptoed up to him and inquired tenderly: "Pardon me, are you a Kentuckian?"

"Nay, madam," the tearful one replied, "I'm a musician."

[406]

"Did you know that I had taken up story-writing as a career?"

"No. Sold anything yet?"

"Yes; my watch, my saxophone and my overcoat."

[407]

"Why do you go on the balcony when I sing? Don't you like to hear me?"

"It isn't that. I want the neighbors to see that I'm not beating my wife."

[408]

"Do you sing and play much?" a young man asked the pretty girl who was carelessly thrumming the keys of the piano.

"Only to kill time," she replied.

"You've got a fine weapon, I must admit," ventured the young man.

[409]

One of the guests turned to a man by his side to criticize the singing of the woman who was trying to entertain them.

"What a terrible voice! Do you know who she is?"

"Yes," was the answer. "She's my wife."

"Oh, I beg your pardon. Of course, it isn't her voice, really. It's the stuff she has to sing. I wonder who wrote that awful song?"

"I did," was the answer.

[410]

Dinner was a little late. A guest asked the hostess to play something. Seating herself at the piano, the good woman executed a Chopin nocturne with precision. She finished, and there was still an interval of waiting to be bridged. In the grim silence she turned to an old gentleman on her right and said:

"Would you like a sonata before going in to dinner?"

He gave a start of surprise and pleasure as he responded briskly:

"Why, yes, thanks! I had a couple on my way here, but I could stand another."

[411]

"My wife used to play the piano a lot, but since the children came she doesn't have time."

"Children are a comfort, aren't they?"

[412]

She—"I'm continually breaking into song?"

He—"You wouldn't have to break in if you'd get the key."

[413]

Two ladies were attending a concert or something at the Civic Auditorium. Seated in the parquet, they looked about them.

"Nice building," said one lady. "What style of architecture is it?"

"I'm not quite sure," said the other lady, "but I think it's Reminiscence."

[414]

"She sang that song in a haunting manner."

"Do you think so?"

"Yes, there was just the ghost of a resemblance to the original air."

[415]

Agent (to newly rich client, engaging talent for her "At Home") —"What about Madame D'Oprano?"

Client—"Is she good?"

Agent—"Good? Why, she's a great virtuosa."

Client—"Never mind about her morals. Can she sing?"

[416]

Man (to neighbor)—"I wish you would sell that dog. Yesterday my daughter had to stop her singing lesson because your dog was whining all the time."

Neighbor—"I'm sorry. But your daughter began it."

[417]

"My daughter is having her voice cultivated."

"Is it improving?"

"It's growing stronger. She used to be heard only two apartments away. Now we get complaints from away off in the next building."

[418]

Next-door Neighbor's Little Boy —"Father says could you lend him your victrola, for tonight?"

Victrola Enthusiast—"Have you a party on?"

Little Boy—"Oh, no; Father only wants to go to bed."

[419]

The hostess was talking to one of her guests as the two sat on the lawn listening to a chimes recital.

"Beautiful, aren't they?" remarked the hostess.

"Pardon?" inquired the guest.

"I say, they're beautiful, aren't they?"

"I'm sorry," roared the guest, "but I can't hear a word for those damned chimes."

[420]

"That tenor of ours has a marvelous voice. He can hold one of his notes for half a minute."

"That's nothing! I have held one of his notes for two years."

[421]

"Do you know the motive in that Russian composition they are playing?"

"By the sound I should judge it was revenge."

[422]

"That's a difficult number the baritone is struggling with!"

"Difficult? I would to God it were impossible!"

[423]

Musical Student—"That piece you just played is by Mozart, isn't it?"

Hurdy-gurdy Man—"No, by Handel."

[424]

Manager—"Are you sure you are qualified to lead a swing orchestra?"

Applicant—"Absolutely. I've had two nervous breakdowns, was shellshocked in France, and I live in an apartment above a family with twelve noisy children."

[425]

"I hear you and your neighbor are on the outs. What happened?"

"Well, my kids are taking music lessons, and the other day he sent over an ax with a note saying, 'Try this on your piano!'"

[426]

"What did you hear at the Opera yesterday?"

"All sorts of things. Smith is going bankrupt, Mrs. Brown has dyed hair, the Whites are having a divorce."

[427]

"You say your son plays the piano like Paderewski?"

"Yes. He uses both hands."

[428]

"Excuse me," said the detective as he presented himself at the door of the music academy, "but I hope you'll give me what information you have, and not make any fuss."

"What do you mean?" was the indignant inquiry.

"Why, you see, we got a tip from the house next door that somebody was murdering Wagner, and the chief sent me down here to work on the case."

[429]

"What do you find the most difficult thing on the piano?"

"To pay the instalments."

[430]

"It must be terrible for an opera singer to realize that he can never sing again."

"Yes; but it's much more terrible if he doesn't realize it."

[431]

"What's that prima donna angry about?"

"Oh, some well-meaning critic said she sang like a siren. The only siren she knows anything about is the whistle they use on a steamboat."

[432]

Singer—"Don't you think the audience shows feeling when I sing?"

Critic—"You bet. They're feeling for their hats and coats."

[433]

Soprano—"Did you notice how my voice filled the hall last night?"

Contralto—"Yes, dear; in fact, I noticed several people leaving to make room for it."

[434]

"Doesn't that soprano have a large repertoire?"

"Yes, and that dress she has on makes it look worse."

[435]

"That girl across the hall has a singular voice."

"Thank heaven it isn't plural."

[436]

"I want to do something that will draw out the conversational abilities of my guests."

"That's easy. Give a musicale."

[437]

"What a nuisance!" exclaimed a man at a concert, as a young fop in front of him kept talking in a loud voice to a lady at his side.

"Did you refer to *me*, sir?" threateningly demanded the fop.

"Oh, no; I meant the musicians there, who keep up such noise with their instruments that I can't hear your conversation."

[438]

"What has become of the big man who used to beat the bass drum?" asked the private of the drum-major.

"He quit us about three months ago."

"Good drummer, too, wasn't he?"

"Yes, very good; but he got so fat that when he marched he couldn't hit the drum in the middle."

[439]

"But," protested the new arrival, as St. Peter handed him a golden trumpet, "I can't play this instrument; I never practised while on earth."

"Of course you didn't," chuckled the saint. "That's why you are here."

[440]

"That last little thing of yours was charming," said the gushing hostess. "I loved it's wild abandon. Was it your own composition?"

"No, madam," scowled the lion of the evening. "I was putting a new string on my violin."

[441]

"My daughter can do anything with the piano."

"Could she lock it up and drop the key in the river?"

[442]

"George sang at the Glee club concert last night."

"Say, that's rich. Why that guy can't sing. Who egged him on?"

"I don't know, but he's looking for the guy that egged him off."

[443]

Composer—"Well, how did you like my new operetta?"

Critic—"Very much. One of the finest things Strauss ever composed."

[444]

"I see by the paper that the concert we attended last night was a tremendous success."

"Yes, I had no idea we enjoyed it half so much at the time."

[445]

First Music Critic—"I wasted a whole evening by going to that new pianist's concert last night!"

Second Music Critic—"Why?"

First Music Critic—"His playing was above criticism!"

[446]

Two movie actresses went to the opera. One actress said to the other:

"If you close your eyes, can't you just imagine you're home at the radio?"

[447]

Aspiring Vocalist — "Professor, do you think I will ever be able to do anything with my voice?"

Perspiring Teacher — "Well it might come in handy in case of fire or shipwreck."

[448]

On the concert program of one of the larger orchestras, not so many weeks ago, was Beethoven's "Leonore" overture, the two climaxes of which are each followed by a trumpet passage offstage.

The first climax came, but not a sound emanated from the trumpet.

The conductor, considerably annoyed, went on to the second.

Again there was silence.

This time, the overture being finished, he rushed into the wings. There he found the trumpet player still arguing with the house fireman.

"I tell you, you can't play that thing back here!" the latter was saying. "There's a concert going on!"

[449]

A violinist was bitterly disappointed with the account of his recital printed in the paper of a small town.

"I told your man three or four times," complained the musician to the owner of the paper, "that the instrument I used was a genuine Stradivarius, and in his story there was not a word about it, not a word."

Whereupon the owner said with a laugh:

"That is as it should be. When Mr. Stradivarius gets his fiddles advertised in my paper under ten cents a line, you come around and let me know."

[450]

"Does he talk sense?"

"Sense? His sanest remark would be too foolish for a popular song title."

[451]

Host—"Mr. Jenkins, I'm sure, will now help us out with a little song."

Jenkins—"I'm sorry but I never vocalize except in my bath."

"Oh, that's all right, I'll warn them you're out of practice."

[452]

"Sir, would you give five dollars to bury a saxophone player?"

"Here's thirty dollars; bury six of 'em."

[453]

In reply to an advertisement for an organist who could also teach music, the following epistle was received:

"Gentlemen: In reply to your ad. for a music teacher and organist, either lady or gentleman, will say that I have been both for several years, and I am sure I can handle the job."

[454]

"So you've been singing in the church choir?"

"Yes."

"What part?"

"Well, I sang first base when I went in, but they changed it after they heard my voice."

"What did you sing after that?"

"Short stop."

[455]

"Have you ever speculated on why you are so popular in your neighborhood?"

"No, except that I told my neighbors that I always played the saxophone when I got lonely."

[456]

Servant (delivering message)— "Mr. Jones sends his compliments to Mr. Brown with the request that he shoot his dog, which is a nuisance in the neighborhood."

Brown—"Give Mr. Brown's compliments to Mr. Jones, and ask him to kindly poison his daughter or burn up her piano."

[457]

He—"By the way, I met Dupont. His wife is very hoarse and can't sing."

She—"Oh, what about inviting them both to dinner to-night?"

[458]

They were having a musical evening, and the hostess asked the celebrated basso to sing another song. "I'm afraid it's too late," he replied. "I should disturb the people in the neighboring house."

"And a good thing, too," replied the lady. "They poisoned our dog last week."

[459]

"My daughter's music lessons are a fortune to me."

"How is that?"

"They enabled me to buy the neighbors' houses at half price."

[460]

"So that is a popular song he's singing?"

"It was before he sang it."

[461]

"Madame, I'm the piano-tuner."

"I didn't send for a piano-tuner."

"I know it, lady; the neighbors did."

[462]

Musician (after much pressing) —"Well, all right, since you insist. What shall I play?"

Host—"Anything you like. It is only to annoy the neighbors."

LITERATURE

[463]
Author—"I'm convinced that the publishers have a conspiracy against me."
Friend—"What makes you think so?"
Author—"Ten of them have refused the same story."

[464]
"Your narrative is too highly colored," remarked the editor, returning the bulky manuscript.
"In what way?" inquired the disappointed author.
"Why," replied the editor, "in the very first chapter you make the old man turn purple with rage, the villain turn green with envy, the hero turn white with anger, the heroine turn red with blushes, and the coachman turn blue with cold."

[465]
Author—"I once got ten dollars a word."
Editor—"Hmm! How was that?"
Author—"I talked back to the judge."

[466]
"Don't you find writing a thankless job?"
"On the contrary, everything I write is returned to me with thanks."

[467]
"If Shakespeare were here today he would be looked on as a remarkable man."
"Yes, he'd be more than 300 years old."

[468]
Two men were hotly discussing the merits of a book. Finally, one of them, himself an author, said to the other: "No, John, you can't appreciate it. You never wrote a book yourself."
"No," retorted John, "and I never laid an egg, but I'm a better judge of an omelet than any hen."

[469]
"Sir, I have all the gems of English literature in my library."
"Yes, and I notice that they are uncut gems."

[470]
"Pa, what is a rare volume?" asked Clarence.
"It's a book that comes back after you have loaned it," replied Pa.

[471]
"How did you compile your great dictionary?" the lexicographer was asked.
"Oh, it was something like having a quarrel with one's wife—one word led to another."

[472]
Critic—"Your work seems a little raw."
Poet—"It oughtn't to be. It's been roasted enough."

[473]
"At last," said the novelist, "I have written something that will be accepted by any magazine."
"What is it?" asked a friend.
"A check for a year's subscription."

[474]
An up-and-coming business man tried to read Shakespeare. After struggling with a page for an hour he submitted it to his secretary, with the anxious question:
"What do you make of that?"
"Not a blamed thing," said the secretary.
"Thank God!" exclaimed the business man. "I thought I was going mad!"

[475]

"Jenks, the famous ghost-writer, has finally achieved the ultimate in success."

"And what is that?"

"He has another ghost-writer write his ghost-writing for him."

[476]

"Who is your favorite classic novelist?"

"Thackeray."

"Great Scott!"

"Some think so; still I prefer Thackeray."

[477]

Old Lady (to librarian)—"Will you please look up my card and see if I've read 'The Mystery of the Purple Tower?'"

[478]

"I desire no remuneration for this poem," said the office visitor. "I merely submit it as a compliment."

"Then, my dear sir, allow me to return the compliment," replied the editor with true journalistic courtesy.

[479]

"John, take that ink away from the baby."

"Eh?"

"He's too young to write a novel."

[480]

"My husband is merely a manufacturer of waste-baskets," sighed the woman with aspirations. "It seems such a prosy occupation."

"On the contrary, there is really much poetry in waste-baskets," replied the unappreciated bard.

[481]

"The scene beggared description."

"Never mind," said the editor, "borrow a few adjectives and go on with it."

[482]

"H'm," the publisher murmured. "Your handwriting's so indistinct I can hardly read these poems of yours. Why didn't you type them before bringing them to me?"

"Type 'em?" the would-be poet gasped. "D'you think I'd waste my time writing poetry if I could type?"

[483]

Author—"Well, sir, the upshot of it was that it took me ten years to discover that I had absolutely no talent for writing literature."

Friend—"You gave up?"

Author—"Oh, no; by that time I was too famous."

[484]

Addressing the new class concerning the merits of shorthand, the instructor said:

"It is a matter of record that it took the poet Gray seven years to write his famous poem, 'Elegy in a Country Churchyard.' Had he been proficient in stenography, he could have done it in seven minutes. We have had students who have written it in that length of time."

[485]

Young Lady—"Your novel has a charming ending."

Author—"What do you think of the opening chapters?"

Young Lady—"I have not got to them yet!"

[486]

An author once praised another writer very heartily to a third person. "It is very strange," was the reply, "that you speak so well of him, for he says that you are a charlatan."

"O," replied the other, "I think it very likely that both of us may be mistaken."

[487]
Mrs. Methuselah—"Did you have anything in the mail, dear?"
Methuselah—"Nothing but another brochure from the 'Book-of-the-Century' people."

[488]
Mrs. Middlebrow (to famous author)—"I'm so delighted to meet you! It was only the other day I saw something of yours, about something or other, in some magazine."

[489]
A novelist who writes stories that are perhaps too good to be "best sellers" was asked by a little girl the meaning of the word penury. "Penury, my child," was the answer, "means the wages of the pen."

[490]
Customer—"I would like a book, please."
Bookseller—"Something light?"
Customer—"That doesn't matter —I have my car with me."

[491]
Editor—"Did you write this poem yourself?"
Contributor—"Yes, every line of it."
Editor—"Then I'm glad to meet you, Edgar Allan Poe, I thought you were dead long ago."

[492]
"Your wife looks stunning tonight. Her gown is a poem."
"What do you mean, poem?" replied the struggling author. "That gown is two poems and a short story."

[493]
Literary Hostess — "And you really have never written a book! How quaint!"

[494]
Ambitious Author — "Hurray! Five dollars for my latest story, 'The Call of the Lure!'"
Fast Friend—"Who from?"
Ambitious Author—"The express company. They lost it."

[495]
A friend came to call on a well-known poet. The poet's wife met him at the door, with her finger to her lips.
"Hush!" she said. "Don't make any noise. He's up-stairs, having a poem."

[496]
"Why is it," asked the persistent poet, "that you always insist that we write on one side of the paper only? Why not on both?"
"One side of the paper, madame," replied the cynical editor, "is in the nature of a compromise."
"A compromise?"
"A compromise. What we really desire, if we could have our way, is not one, or both, but neither."

[497]
Hostess—"I sometimes wonder if there is anything vainer than you authors about the things you write."
Author—"There is, madam; our efforts to sell them."

[498]
Husband (after the theater)— "But, dear, what did you object to?"
Wife—"Why, the idea of you bellowing 'Author! Author!' at a Shakespearian drama!"

[499]
"Where did you get the plot of your second novel?"
"From the film version of my first!"

[500]

A famous author was traveling in a train with two very talkative women. Having recognized him from his published portraits, they opened fire upon him in regard to his novels, praising them in a manner which was unendurable to the sensitive author. Presently the train entered a tunnel, and in the darkness the novelist raised the back of his hand to his lips and kissed it soundingly. When light returned he found the two women regarding one another in icy silence. Addressing them with great suavity, he said, "Ah, ladies, the one great regret of my life will be that I shall never know which of you it was that kissed me!"

[501]

Landlady—"Just when are you going to pay your arrears of room rent?"

Hard-up Author—"As soon as I receive the check which the publisher will send me if he accepts the novel I am about to commence when I have found a suitable subject and the necessary inspiration."

[502]

A struggling author had called on a publisher to inquire about a manuscript he had submitted.

"This is quite well written," admitted the publisher, "but my firm only publishes work by writers with well-known names."

"Splendid!" shouted the caller in great excitement. "My name's Smith!"

[503]

"My son seems anxious for a literary career."

"What are you going to do with him?"

"Have him study to be a doctor."

[504]

"So you're planning to write a real down-to-earth story?"

"Sure, it's about a parachute jumper!"

[505]

"Which of your works of fiction do you consider the best?"

"My last income-tax return."

[506]

Poet—"Do you think I should put more fire into my poetry?"

Editor—"No, quite the reverse."

[507]

Author—"The style of writing that you do must be very hard work."

Layman—"Well, it is; but what made you think of it?"

Author—"Why, it makes me tired to read it."

[508]

"Milton's 'Paradise Lost' is a noble poem, isn't it?"

"Grand."

"Did you ever read it?"

"No. Have you read it?"

"No."

[509]

"I'm going out to buy a book."

"A book!"

"Yes, my husband bought me the most adorable reading-lamp yesterday."

[510]

Editor—"Historically, this story is incorrect."

Author—"But hysterically it is one of the best things I have ever done."

[511]

"They have just dug up the corner-stone of an ancient library in Greece, on which is inscribed '4000 B. C.'"

"Before Carnegie, I presume."

[512]
Young Thing—"I wonder why they call it free verse?"
The Poet—"That's simple. Did you ever try to sell any?"

[513]
A Bostonian and his wife took opposite sides in the Shakespeare-Bacon controversy, the woman being sure that the plays were written by Shakespeare, while the man was equally sure that they were the work of Bacon.

"When I get to Heaven," said the woman, "I am going to ask Shakespeare whether he really wrote the plays."

"But suppose that he is not in Heaven?" said the husband.

"Then you can ask him, my dear."

[514]
He (poet)—"Didn't you know that poets were born?"
She—"No. I always considered them as the ones that bore."

[515]
Writer—"How much board will you charge me for a few weeks while I gather material for my new country novel?"
Hiram—"Five dollars a week unless we have to talk dialect. That's $3 extra."

[516]
Editor—"Say, this story can't be printed. It says here that the heroine was nude."
Author—"That's all right. I cover her with remorse in the next paragraph."

[517]
The Poet—"Dash it—I can't find that sonnet anywhere. Emily must have thrown it into the fire."
His Wife—"Don't be absurd, Peter. The child can't read."

[518]
She—"I hope your recent marriage has turned out a great success."
He—"Oh, quite; I've already made three plays out of my wife's past."

[519]
Old Lady (to librarian)—"I'd like a nice book."
Librarian—"Here's one about the cardinal."
O. L.—"I'm not interested in religion."
L.—"But this is a bird."
O. L.—"I'm not interested in his private life, either."

[520]
Poet—"Burglars broke into my house last night."
Friend—"Yes? What happened?"
Poet—"They searched through every room, then left a $5 bill on my bureau."

EDITORS AND REPORTERS

[521]
Customer—"I inserted an advertisement for my lost dog in the paper here. Has anything been heard of it? I offered a reward."
Office Boy—"Sorry, all the editors and reporters are out looking for the dog."

[522]
Would-Be Advertiser—"Are you certain that advertisements in your paper bring results?"
Country Editor — "Absolutely. Why, the last time a man advertised a lost dog, the dog walked in while the man was writing out the advertisement."

[523]

Dear Editor—"One night I came home and found my wife in the arms of a man who owes me money. Have I grounds for divorce?"

Answer—"The man was just paying a little interest to your wife."

[524]

"Is the editor in?"

"He's somewhere about," said the office boy.

"Tell him a friend wants to see him."

"You live here, don't you?"

"No."

"All right, I'll tell him. He says he ain't got no friends in this town."

[525]

The reporter was sent to write up a charity ball. Next day the editor called him to his desk.

"Look here, what do you mean by this? 'Among the most beautiful girls was Henry Lewis Bottomley.' Why, you crazy idiot! Old Bottomley isn't a girl—and besides he's one of our principal stockholders."

"I can't help that," returned the realistic reporter. "That's where he was."

[526]

Curious ideas about anatomy prevail in the press. It was stated the other day that a colonel was recently "shot in the ticket office." Another paper says a man was "shot in the suburbs," "He kissed her passionately upon her reappearance," "She whipped him upon his return," "He kissed her back," "Mr. Jones walked in upon her invitation," "She seated herself upon his entering," "We thought she sat down upon her being asked," "She fainted upon his departure."

[527]

The oldest inhabitant had celebrated his hundredth birthday and the reporter of a local paper called on him for an interview. Having congratulated the old fellow, the reporter asked a few questions.

"To what do you attribute your longevity?" he inquired.

The centenarian paused a moment and then, holding up his hand and ticking off the items on his fingers, began: "I never smoked, drank alcoholic liquors, or overate, and I always rise at six in the morning."

"But," protested the reporter, "I had an uncle who acted in that way, yet he only lived to be eighty. How do you account for that?"

"He didn't keep it up long enough," was the calm reply.

[528]

The telegraph-editor of a Denver newspaper complained to a country correspondent who omitted names in his stories. He wrote the man that if he neglected this essential detail in his next yarn he would be discharged.

A few days later the editor got this dispatch:

"Como, Colorado, June 8—A severe storm passed over this section this afternoon and lightning struck a barbed-wire fence on the ranch of Henry Wilson, killing three cows —their names being Jessie, Bossie, and Buttercup."

[529]

"Can you make anything out of the news from Europe?"

"Easiest thing in the world. I only read the newspapers every other day. In this way I get a connected story of one side or the other and avoid the denials."

[530]

"And what," asked the chief of the Cannibal Islands, in his kindest tones, "was your business before you were captured by my men?"

"I was a newspaper man," answered the captive.

"An editor?"

"No, merely a sub-editor."

"Cheer up, young man! Promotion awaits you. After dinner you shall be editor-in-chief."

[531]

"My gosh, Bill," groaned the managing editor of the tabloid, "nothing scandalous has happened in twenty-four hours. What'll we do for the front page?"

"Aw, don't get discouraged, Steve," the city editor comforted. "Something'll happen. I've still got faith in human nature."

[532]

One of the veteran reporters on a city newspaper died, after having served for many years at fire headquarters. The men in the fire department liked him very much, and raised a fund for a floral piece for the funeral. They gave the money to a florist, and told him to get up something appropriate.

The florist made up a piece in the shape of a gigantic fire badge. And across it, in big red letters, he put: "Admit within fire lines."

[533]

Editor—"You wish a position as a proofreader?"

Applicant—"Yes, sir."

"Do you understand the requirements of that responsible position?"

"Perfectly, sir. Whenever you make any mistakes in the paper, just blame 'em on me, and I'll never say a word."

[534]

The reporter who had accompanied the special train to the scene of the wreck, hurried down the embankment and found a man who had one arm in a sling, a bandage over one eye, his front teeth gone, and his nose knocked four points to starboard, sitting on a piece of the locomotive and surveying the horrible ruin all about him.

"Can you give me some particulars of this accident?" asked the reporter, taking out his notebook.

"I haven't heard of any accident, young man," replied the disfigured party stiffly.

He was one of the directors of the railroad.

[535]

Cub Reporter—"I'd like some advice, sir, on how to run a newspaper."

Editor—"You've come to the wrong person, son. Ask one of my subscribers."

[536]

Editor—"Did you ever write anything before?"

Authoress—"Oh, yes, I wrote a confession story once."

Editor—"Did the editor send it back?"

Authoress—"No, he came all the way from New York to San Francisco to meet me."

[537]

This letter exemplifies the power of the press:

"Dear Editor: Thursday I lost a gold watch which I valued very highly. Immediately I inserted an ad in your lost-and-found column and waited. Yesterday I went home and found the watch in the pocket of another suit. God bless your paper."

[538]

Irate Caller—"You spoiled my article by a misprint."

Editor—"I'm very sorry. What did we get wrong?"

Caller—"A proverb I employed. You printed it, 'A word to the wife is sufficient.'"

[539]

Subscriber—"Is it ever permissible for a young woman to ask a man she has never met to call at her home?"

Editor—"Yes; if she asks him to call for the laundry."

[540]

Editor—"Does it pay to advertise in my paper? Well, I should say it does. Look at Smith, the grocer, for instance. He advertised for a boy last week, and the very next day Mrs. Smith had twins—both boys."

[541]

Country Policeman (at scene of murder)—"You can't come in here."

Reporter—"But I've been sent to do the murder."

"Well, you're too late; the murder's been done."

[542]

A newspaper reporter bent over a badly injured passenger in the train wreck.

"I am going fast," the wounded one said feebly.

"Cheer up, my brave fellow," said the reporter, "how do you spell your last name?"

[543]

An angry subscriber called to see "the scoundrel who wrote the libelous article" about him.

"You'll have to be patient," said the office boy. "He's out attending the funeral of the man who called to get satisfaction yesterday."

[544]

A shiftless and unemployed New York newspaper man approached an old friend, and said:

"What do you think? I have just received the prize insult of my life. A paper down in Ohio offered me a job."

"Do you call that an insult?"

"Not the job, but the salary. They offered me fifteen dollars a week."

"Well," said the friend, "fifteen dollars a week is better than nothing."

"Fifteen a week—hell!" exclaimed the newspaperman. "I can borrow more than that right here in New York."

[545]

Reporter—"Madam, you may recollect that we printed yesterday your denial of having retracted the contradiction of your original statement. Would you care to have us say that you were misquoted in regard to it?"

[546]

Reporter—"Why all the gloom?"

Editor—"I received a letter yesterday informing me that I was the beneficiary of a large bequest; and in the rush I replied, 'Your contribution is returned with thanks.'"

HOTELS

[547]

Irate Guest—"Look here, the rain is simply pouring through the roof of my bedroom."

Summer Hotel Proprietor—"Absolutely according to our prospectus, sir. Running water in every room."

[548]

"So you are the new girl," said the young smart aleck to the new waitress in his hotel. "What shall we call you?"

"Pearl, sir."

"The Pearl of Great Price?"

"No, sir, the Pearl cast before swine."

[549]

"Isn't this resort a good place for men to come who have asthma?"

"Yes, the girls here are so dumb they can't tell it from passion."

[550]

A New York club had replaced its male staff with young and, in some cases, pretty waitresses.

One day a member who had been strongly opposed to the change arrived at the club for lunch.

"How's the duck?" he asked an attractive waitress, rather gruffly.

"Oh, I'm fine!" she replied, perkily. "And how's the old pelican himself?"

[551]

Guest—"Do you run a bus between the hotel and the railway station?"

Manager—"No, sir."

Guest—"That's strange. All my friends said you would get me coming and going."

[552]

Hotel Page—"Telegram for Mr. Neidspondiavanci, Mr. Neidspondiavanci!"

Mr. Neidspondiavanci—"What initial please?"

[553]

"Last night a man at the hotel wanted to bet he could whip anybody in the lobby."

"My word!"

"The elevator boy took him up."

[554]

A commercial traveler, on leaving a certain hotel, said to the proprietor: "Pardon me, but with what material do you stuff the beds in your establishment?"

"Why," said the landlord, proudly, "with the best straw to be found in the whole country!"

"That," returned the traveler, "is very interesting. I now know whence the straw came that broke the camel's back."

[555]

Hotel Maid (to new arrival)— "The proprietress says, madam, that she will move your dressing-table, alter the position of your bed, let you have another blanket, and provide some wedges for your windows, stop the clock striking on the landing, and give you a separate table at the window—but she says you'll have to take the weather as you find it."

[556]

He (in hotel dining-room)—"A scientist says that what we eat we become."

She (seizing the menu)—"Let's order something rich."

[557]

Hotel Keeper—"Here are a few views of our hotel for you to take with you, sir."

"Thanks, but I have my own views of your hotel."

[558]

Two travelers arrived at the hotel and were shown a rather dingy room.

"What," said one, "does this pig-sty cost?"

Promptly the proprietor replied: "For one pig, two dollars; for two pigs, three dollars."

[559]

Guest—"Does the water always come through the roof like that?"

Hotel Keeper—"No, sir, only when it rains."

[560]

"I tell you that I won't have this room," protested the old lady to the bell-boy, who was conducting her. "I ain't going to pay my good money for a pig-sty with a measly little foldin' bed in it. If you think that jest because I'm from the country—"

Profoundly disgusted, the boy cut her short. "Get in, mum, get in. This ain't your room, this is the elevator."

[561]

A tall, gaunt-looking person recently entered a hotel in a town where several fires had occurred and applied for a room at a price which entitled him to lodging on the top floor of the house. Among his belongings the proprietor noticed a coil of rope, and asked what it was for.

"That's a fire escape," said the man, "I carry one with me so I can let myself down from the window without troubling anyone."

"Good plan," said the landlord, "but guests with fire escapes like that pay in advance at this hotel."

[562]

A farmer who went to a large city to see the sights engaged a room at a hotel and before retiring asked the clerk about the hours for meals.

"We have breakfast from 7 to 11, dinner from 12 to 3, and supper from 6 to 8," explained the clerk.

"Look here," inquired the farmer in surprise, "what time am I goin' to see the town?"

[563]

Bell Hop—"Did you ring, sir?"

Irate Guest—"No, I was tolling. I thought you were dead."

[564]

The prosperous, pompous business man was staying at a small country hotel, and as he entered the breakfast-room in the morning the only other visitor rose from his seat.

"Sit down, sit down!" boomed the great man condescendingly.

"Why?" asked the other, surprised. "Can't I get the marmalade from the next table?"

[565]

The hotel clerk was growing impatient as the prospect took so long to read the names on the register. "Just sign on that line, please," said the clerk.

The prospect was indignant and retorted: "Young man, I'm too old a hand to sign anything without readin' it."

[566]

Patron—"May I have some stationery?"

Hotel Clerk (haughtily)—"Are you a guest of the house?"

Patron—"Hell, no. I am paying twenty dollars a day."

[567]

Departing Guest—"Enjoyed ourselves? Oh yes! What I'm upset about is leaving your hotel so soon after I've bought it."

[568]

Two traveling salesmen, having a few hours in a small town, decided to dine at the village hotel.

One of them turned to the pretty waitress and asked:

"How's the chicken?"

"Oh, I'm all right," she blushed. "How are you?"

[569]
Lady—"Can you give me a room and bath?"
Clerk—"I can give you a room, madam, but you will have to take your own bath."

[570]
The noise of an all-night poker game in the next hotel room kept a tired tourist from sleeping. At 3 A.M. he started to pound on the wall hoping to silence the revellers.
"Hey," shouted one of the gamblers, "this is a hell of a time to be hanging pictures."

[571]
The hotel-clerk was astonished to see a guest parading through the foyer in a pair of pajamas.
"Here, what are you doing?"
The guest snapped out of it and apologized:
"Beg pardon. I'm a somnambulist."
"Well," sneered the clerk, "you can't walk around here like that, no matter what your religion is."

[572]
Guest—"And the flies are certainly thick around here?"
Hotel Manager—"Thick? What can you expect for two dollars a day? Educated ones?"

[573]
"Look here," said the irate traveling man to the small-town hotelkeeper, "don't you know that rollertowels in hotels have been prohibited in this State for three years?"
"Sure," replied the hotel man, "but that there towel was put up before the law was passed."

[574]
"We are taking in boarders this summer."
"Have they found it out yet?"

[575]
"But," protested the vacationist, "your advertisement states that the hotel is only five minutes from the station. It took me nearly an hour to reach here."
"Ah," said the boarding-house keeper, "you've been walking. We don't cater to pedestrians."

[576]
A very thin man met a very fat man in the hotel lobby.
"From the looks of you," said the fat man, "there might have been a famine."
"Yes," was the reply, "and from the looks of you, you might have caused it."

[577]
First Guest—"I'm sure I don't know why they call this hotel the Palms, do you? I've never seen a palm anywhere near the place."
Second Guest—"You'll see them before you go. It's a pleasant little surprise the whole staff keeps for the guests on the last day of their stay."

[578]
Mr. Brown had just registered and was about to turn away when the clerk asked:
"Beg pardon, but what is your name?"
"Name!" echoed the indignant guest. "Don't you see my signature there on the register?"
"I do," returned the clerk calmly. "That is what aroused my curiosity."

[579]
Hotel Manager (to new guest)—"I shall have to ask you to pay in advance. Your luggage is too—er—emotional."
Guest—"Emotional?"
"Yes—easily moved."

[580]

"I've solved the mystery of what a hotel means when it advertises 'rooms $1 and up.'"

"What is it?"

"I got one of the dollar rooms and was up all night."

[581]

"My dear sir, you flatter me by lingering to hear the remainder of my tale when the other passengers dashed away at the sound of the dinner-bell," said the long-winded tourist to his one remaining listener.

"What! Has the dinner-bell rung?" asked the other, as he jumped to his feet and dashed toward the dining-room.

[582]

A page passed through the lobby of the exclusive hotel.

"Young man," remonstrated the manager, sternly, "you should know that it is against the rules of this hotel for an employe to whistle while on duty."

"I'm not whistling, sir," replied the employe. "I'm paging somebody's dog."

[583]

The manager of an hotel, finding that a guest had departed without paying his hotel bill, wrote him:

"My dear Mr. Smythe: Will you please send the amount of your bill, and oblige," etc.

To this Mr. Smythe wrote politely:

"My dear Mr. Manager: The amount of my bill is a hundred and ten dollars. Yours respectfully."

[584]

Daughter—"Did you hear, dad, they have just caught the biggest hotel-thief in New York?"

Dad—"What hotel did he run?"

[585]

The British Ambassador walked briskly into the foyer of a magnificent Washington hotel, and stopped for a moment to speak with one of the bright-buttoned servitors in the lobby. After he walked on, an assistant manager who had noted the incident, went over to the boy and said, "What did the Ambassador want?"

"I don't know," answered the bell-hop. "He couldn't speak English."

[586]

Hotel Clerk—"I hope you enjoyed your stay with us, sir."

Departing Guest—"Well, the bed was too hard, the price too high, the food was lousy, the service slow, there's too much noise, but, by gad, I certainly enjoyed your ice water."

[587]

The country boy who had "made good" in New York asked his old mother to come to the metropolis. He gave the old lady the best room in the hotel—one with a private bath adjoining. The next morning the boy asked:

"Did you have a good night's rest?"

"Well, no, I didn't," she replied. "The room was all right, and the bed was pretty. But I couldn't sleep very much, for I was afraid someone would want to take a bath, and the only way to it was through my room!"

[588]

Two lady school-teachers from Brooklyn, spending their sabbatical year exploring western Canada, stopped at a small and old-fashioned hotel in Alberta recently.

One of the pair was inclined to

be worrisome when traveling, and she couldn't rest until she had made a tour of the corridors to hunt out exits in case of fire. The first door she opened, unfortunately, turned out to be that of the public bath, occupied by an elderly gentleman taking a shower.

"Oh, excuse me!" the lady stammered, flustered. "I'm looking for the fire escape." Then she ran for it.

To her dismay, she hadn't got far along the corridor when she heard a shout behind her and, looking around, saw the gentleman, wearing only a towel, running after her. "Where's the fire?" he hollered.

[589]

The train was approaching Podunk. "Say," a passenger accosted his neighbor, "do you know Podunk well?"

"Yes, sir. Very well. I come here at least twice a year."

"Well, what hotel would you recommend?"

"Try the Smith hotel."

"Do you always stop there?"

"No, but I have stopped at all the others."

[590]

"I shall have to put you fellows in the same room," said the hotel keeper.

"That's all right," the guests replied.

"Well, I think," said the host, "you'll have a comfortable night. It's a featherbed."

At two o'clock in the morning one of the guests awoke his companion.

"Change places with me, Dick," he groaned. "It's my turn to lie on the feather."

[591]

A man met another in a hotel lobby. While not remembering who he was, feeling certain that he was acquainted with him, held out his hand and said: "I am sure I have met you somewhere."

"No doubt," was the reply, "I have been there often."

RESTAURANTS

[592]

A customer sat down at a table in a smart restaurant and tied a napkin around his neck. The scandalized manager called a waiter and instructed him, "Try to make him understand, as tactfully as possible, that that's not done."

Said the thoughtful waiter to the customer: "Pardon me, sir. Shave or haircut, sir?"

[593]

"I'm sorry," said the diner, who hoped to get away with it, "but I haven't any money to pay for that meal."

"That's all right," said the cashier. "We'll write your name on the wall and you can pay the next time you come in."

"Don't do that. Everybody who comes in will see it."

"Oh, no, they won't. Your overcoat will be hanging over it."

[594]

They laughed when the waiter spoke to me in Greek, but their laughter changed to astonishment at my ready reply:

"I wanna roasta bif san'wich, str-r-romberry pie, two cup skaw-fee."

[595]
"No," snapped the old man, as he scanned the menu. "I won't have any mushrooms, waiter. I was nearly poisoned by them last week."
The waiter leaned confidingly across the table.
"Is that really so, sir?" he said, blandly. "Then I've won my bet with the cook."

[596]
Diner—"Waiter, how was this steak cooked?"
Waiter—"Smothered in onions, sir."
"Well, it died hard."

[597]
The sad-looking man had been waiting a long time for his order. Finally his waiter approached, and said:
"Your fish will be coming in a minute or two now, sir."
The sad man looked interested. "Tell me," he said, "what bait are you using?"

[598]
Diner—"Waiter, this soup is spoiled."
Waiter—"Who told you?"
Diner—"A little swallow."

[599]
A discouraged restaurant patron called solemnly for pen and ink.
"What are you going to do?" the waiter inquired.
"Well, I've given up all hope of ever seeing that dinner I ordered, so I want to make a will leaving it to my heirs and assigns, forever."

[600]
Waiter—"Yes, sir, we're very up to date. Everything here is cooked by electricity."
Diner—"I wonder if you would mind giving this steak another shock?"

[601]
A man went into a restaurant and called for a glass of whisky and water. Having tasted it, he exclaimed:
"Which did you put in first, the whisky or the water?"
"The whisky, of course," the waiter replied.
"Ah, well," said the man, "perhas I'll come to it by and by."

[602]
"Bill told me to go over to that new restaurant if I wanted some good roast beef."
"And?"
"It was a bum steer."

[603]
After placing an order for a Swiss cheese sandwich, the customer changed his mind. "Would it be possible to change his order to an American cheese sandwich" he asked.
"Naturalize that Swiss," called the counterman to the cook.

[604]
He had been trying to secure the attention of a waiter for ten minutes, but at last got up from his chair and, going to the cashier's desk, demanded to see the manager.
"What for?" asked the girl.
"I've got a complaint."
"Complaint?" retorted the girl, haughtily. "This is a restaurant, not a hospital."

[605]
A man hurried into a quick-lunch restaurant and said: "Give me a ham sandwich."
"Yes, sir," said the waiter, reaching for the sandwich; "will you eat it or take it with you?"
"Both," was the unexpected but obvious reply.

[606]
"Are you the waiter who took my order?"

"Yes, sir."

"H'm, still looking well, I see. How are your grandchildren?"

[607]
Restaurant Patron (crossly)— "Waiter, what are those black specks in my milk?"

Waiter—"I dunno, suh—unlessen dey's some ob dem vitamins dey's talkin' so much about."

[608]
Customer—"What does this mean? There's a fly in the bottom of my tea-cup!"

Waitress—"How do I know? I'm a waitress, not a fortune-teller!"

[609]
Waiter—"Would you mind settling your bill, sir? We're closing now."

Irate Patron—"But, hang it all, I haven't been served yet."

"Well, in that case, there'll only be the cover charge."

[610]
A well-known, but shy, actor, dropped into a Broadway restaurant very early the other morning.

He sat at a table and waited—and waited. Three waiters, at a table in the rear, were earnestly playing pinochle. Finally, after long minutes, the proprietor sauntered through and caught the situation at a glance.

"That's how it is!" he roared. "I got three waiters and they can't even wait on one lousy customer!"

[611]
Patron—"Do you serve fish here?"

Waiter—"Certainly, we cater to everyone."

[612]
"Now, girls," said the restaurant manager, "I want you all to look your best to-day. Add a little dab of powder to your cheeks and take a bit more care with your hair."

"Something special on?" asked the head waitress.

"No," informed the manager. "The beef's tough."

[613]
A man, in his carefree bachelor days, had been very fond of a Washington restaurant which specialized in waffles with honey. Year after year he had journey to the place to get the delectable viand; so, when he finally married, he decided to take his wife there, in order to share the pleasure with her. He did not tell her what was coming; merely ordering an excellent meal, with two orders of waffles.

The meal came, the waffles came: but there were two small pitchers of near-maple syrup, and no honey.

He called the waitress over, and whispered, loud enough for his wife to hear: "Where's my honey?"

The waitress beamed intelligently. "She's on her vacation now, sir," was her answer.

[614]
"We have everything on the menu today, sir," the waitress said.

"So I see," the customer said. "How about a clean one?"

[615]
The owner of the restaurant walked menacingly toward his cashier.

"I see," he barked, "that you're a little behind in your accounts."

"Oh, no," answered the cashier, happily. "The restaurant's behind— I'm a few bucks to the good!"

[616]

Diner—"Waiter, didn't you hear me say 'Well done'?"

Waiter (ignoring pale pink steak)—"Yes, sir; thank you very much, sir. It's seldom we get any thanks, sir."

[617]

Waitress—"Tea or coffee?"

Customer — "Coffee, without cream."

Waitress—"You'll have to take it without milk. We have no cream."

[618]

"My friend laughed when I spoke to the waiter in French, but the laugh was on him. I told the waiter to give him the check."

[619]

Restaurant Version—One man's meat is another man's croquette.

[620]

"You say you served in France?" said the restaurant manager, as he sampled the new cook's first soup.

"Yes, sir. Officer's cook for two years and wounded twice."

"You're lucky, man. It's a wonder they didn't kill you."

[621]

"Yes, I know fish is brain food, but I don't care so much for fish. Hain't there some other brain food?"

"Well, there's noodle soup."

[622]

"Did you ever hear an after-dinner speech that was really worth while?"

"Only once. Last night I dined with an old acquaintance and he said: 'Waiter, bring me the check.' "

[623]

"Waiter, have you forgotten me?"

"Oh, no, sir, you are the stuffed calf's head."

[624]

Diner—"Waiter, this soup is cold. Bring me some that's hot."

Waiter—"What do you want me to do? Burn my thumb?"

[625]

Irate Diner—"Hey, waiter! This soup tastes like dish water!"

Waiter—"How do you know?"

[626]

Diner—"See here, where are those oysters I ordered on the half shell?"

Waiter—"Don't get impatient, sah. We're dreffle short on shells; but you're next, sah."

[627]

"No soup, please; I just had my suit cleaned."

[628]

Waitress — "Two-minute eggs, sir? I thought you always wanted them three minutes."

Breakfaster—"I know, but I've decided to sleep a little longer mornings."

[629]

Diner—"Waiter, the portions seem to have got a lot smaller lately."

Waiter—"Just an optical illusion, sir. Now that the restaurant has been enlarged, they look smaller—that's all."

[630]

Waiter (to patron who has been kept waiting for some time)—"What is it you wish, sir?"

Patron—"Well, what I originally came in for was breakfast but if dinner is ready now, I'll take supper."

[631]

Diner—"Waiter, it's been half an hour since I ordered that turtle soup."

Waiter—"Yes, but you know how turtles are."

[632]

A Georgia Congressman had put up at an American-plan hotel in New York. When, upon sitting down at dinner the first evening of his stay, the waiter obsequiously handed him a bill of fare, the Congressman tossed it aside, slipped the waiter a dollar bill, and said, "Bring me a good dinner."

The dinner proving satisfactory, the Southern member pursued this plan during his entire stay in New York. As the last tip was given, he mentioned that he was about to return to Washington.

Whereupon, the waiter, with an expression of great earnestness, said: "Well, sir, when you or any of your friends that can't read come to New York, just ask for Dick."

[633]

Diner—"What on earth is this broth made from, waiter? Surely it isn't chicken broth?"

Waiter—"Well, sir, it's chicken broth in its infancy. It's made out of the water the eggs were boiled in."

[634]

"Do you like spinach?"

"No, and I'm glad I don't like it, for if I did, I'd eat it, and I hate the darned stuff.

[635]

"Waiter, these are very small oysters."

"Yes, sir."

"And they don't appear to be very fresh."

"Then it's lucky they're small, ain't it, sir?"

[636]

Customer—"Is there any soup on the bill of fare?"

Waiter—"No, sir; there was, but I wiped it off."

[637]

Diner—"There's something wrong with these hot dogs."

Waiter—"Well, don't tell it to me; I'm only a waiter, not a veterinarian."

[638]

Customer—"I haven't come to any ham in this sandwich yet."

Waiter—"Try another bite."

Customer (taking huge mouthful)—"Nope, none yet."

Waiter—"Dog-gone it! You must have gone right past it."

[639]

"Smith," said the restaurant manager to a waiter, "why did that man from table No. 5 leave so suddenly?"

"Well, sir," said the waiter, "he sat down and asked for sausages, and I told him we were out of them; but if he would care to wait a few minutes I could get the cook to make some."

"Well," said the manager, "what then?"

"I went to the kitchen," resumed the waiter, "and accidentally trod upon the dog's tail, and of course it yelped out. And suddenly the man got up and left."

[640]

"What's the difference between valor and discretion?"

"Well, to go to a swell restaurant without tipping the waiter would be valor."

"I see. And discretion?"

"That would be to dine at a different restaurant the next day."

[641]

Diner—"Waiter, take this coffee away. It's like mud."

Waiter—"Well, it was ground this morning."

[642]

"Give me a glass of milk and a muttered buffin."

"You mean a buffered muttin."

"No, I mean a muffered buttin."

"Why not take doughnuts and milk?"

[643]

Diner—"Waiter, I was here yesterday and had a steak."

Waiter—"Yes, sir; will you have the same today?"

Diner—"Well, I might as well, if no one else is using it."

[644]

Waiter—"These are the best eggs we have had for years."

Diner—"Well, bring me some you haven't had so long."

[645]

"You sometimes find a pearl in an oyster stew," remarked the waiter, pleasantly.

But the customer only grunted: "I'm looking for oysters."

[646]

"Waiter, did I leave an umbrella here, yesterday?"

"What kind of an umbrella?"

"Oh, any kind. I'm not fussy."

[647]

A man eating dinner in a restaurant found that he could not possibly cut his steak, no matter how he jabbed at it. He said to the waiter at last, "You'll have to take this steak back and get me another piece. I can't even begin to cut it."

"Sorry sir," replied the waiter, examining the steak closely, "I can't take this back now. You've bent it."

[648]

"Why do you call this an enthusiastic stew?"

"Because the cook put everything he had into it."

[649]

The lonely stranger entered a restaurant in New York.

"May I take your order?" the sprightly waitress inquired.

"Yes," he replied. "Two eggs and a kind word."

The waitress brought the eggs and was moving away when the stranger stopped her. "What about the kind word?" he said.

The waitress leaned over and whispered, "Don't eat the eggs."

[650]

Waitress—"Oh, I'm sorry I spilled water all over you."

Patron—"That's perfectly all right, the suit was too large anyway."

[651]

"Look here, Waiter, I just found a collar-button in my soup."

"Oh, thank you, sir. I have been looking all over for it."

[652]

Guest—"Why does your dog sit there and watch me eat?"

Hotel Host—"I can't imagine, unless it's because you have the plate he usually eats from."

[653]

Customer—"What's this in my soup?"

Waiter—"Don't ask me, sir. I don't know one insect from another."

[654]

"Some people would kick anywhere but in a football game," snorted the restaurant proprietor. "I can't see what them epicures has got to complain about with this soup."

"They wouldn't have no grouch coming, sir," explained the waiter, tactfully, "if only the cook would admit it's soup. He says it's coffee."

[655]

"Very sorry, Mr. Brown, but the coffee is exhausted," the landlady announced.

"Not at all surprised," came back Mr. Brown. "I've seen it growing weaker and weaker every morning."

[656]

Customer—"Why do they call this course 'pièce de resistance'?"

Waiter—"Wait till you try it."

[657]

Customer—"I'll have some raw oysters, not too large nor too small, not too salty nor too fat. They must be cold and I want them quickly!"

Waiter—"Yes sir. With or without pearls?"

[658]

Diner to Headwaiter—"By the way, did that fellow who took our order leave any family?"

[659]

Customer—"What's wrong with these eggs?"

Waitress—"Don't ask me; I only laid the table."

[660]

A middle-aged bachelor was in a restaurant at breakfast, when he noticed this inscription on the egg:

"To whom it may concern: Should this meet the eye of some young man who desires to marry a farmer's daughter, eighteen years of age, kindly communicate with—."

After reading this, he made haste to write to the girl, offering marriage, and in a few days received this note:

"Your note came too late. I am married now and have four children."

[661]

"Waiter, there's a fly on my pretzel!"

"Yes, out on a bender, sir."

[662]

Diner—"Have you any wild duck?"

Waiter—"No, sir, but we can take a tame one and irritate it for you."

[663]

"Why are you washing your spoon in your finger bowl?"

"So I won't get egg all over my pocket."

[664]

Customer—"Is this tea or coffee? It tastes exactly like kerosene."

Waiter—"If it tastes like kerosene, it's positively tea—because our coffee tastes like turpentine."

[665]

"I say, waiter, the flowers on this table are artificial, aren't they?"

"Yes, sir. That's the worst of running a vegetarian restaurant—if we use real flowers, the customers eat them."

[666]

Customer (viciously attacking a piece of chicken)—"This must be an incubator chicken."

Waiter—"Why?"

Customer—"No chicken with a mother could be so tough."

[667]

Waiter—"Did I bring you a menu?"

Customer—"If you did, I ate it."

[668]

"Waiter, there's a fly in my jelly!"

"Are you sure, sir?"

"Yes. Why?"

"He seems to be in rather a jam, sir."

[669]

She (dining)—"Seems to me we won't hear so much jazz in the restaurants."

He—"No, and as a consequence we hear more soup."

[670]

Waiter — "Zoup, sir? Zoup? Zoup?"

Customer—"I don't know what you're talking about."

Waiter—"You know what hash is? Well, zoup is looser."

[671]

Angry Customer (in restaurant) —"Hey, I've found a tack in this doughnut."

Waiter—"Why the ambitious little thing! I'll bet he thinks it is a tire."

[672]

He was studying the menu as the waitress came to take his order.

"Have you frog's legs?" he asked.

"No. It's my rheumatism that makes me walk this way."

[673]

"Roast beef," said a jolly customer to waiter."

"How will you have it, sir?"

"Well done, thou good and faithful servant."

[674]

"My girl is the luckiest person in restaurants! She's always finding money under plates."

[675]

Affable Waiter—"How did you find that steak, sir?"

Guest—"Oh, quite accidentally. I moved that piece of potato and there it was, underneath."

[676]

"Waiter, an hour ago I ordered some lamb chops. Have you forgotten them, or have I had them?"

[677]

"Bring me another sandwich, please."

"Will there be anything else?"

"Yes, a paper weight. The last sandwich blew away."

[678]

Waiter (to professor of English) —"Did you say pudden, sir?"

Enraged Diner—"I did not—and I hope I never shall."

[679]

The second course of the table d'hôte was being served.

"What is this leathery stuff?" demanded the diner.

"That, sir, is filet of sole," replied the waiter.

"Take it away," said the diner, "and see if you can't get me a nice, tender piece from the upper part of the boot."

[680]

Diner—"Do you serve crabs here?"

Waiter—"We serve anyone; sit down."

[681]

"Why did you give that check room girl a dollar tip?"

"Look at the hat she gave me!"

[682]

Irate Diner—"Say, Waiter, just look at that chicken. Why, it's nothing but skin and bones!"

Waiter—"Well, what do you want on it, feathers?"

[683]

Guest—"Look here! How long must I wait for the half-portion of duck I ordered?"

Waiter—"Till somebody orders the other half. We can't go out and kill half a duck."

[684]

"Are you Donald Vance?" he asked the young man beside the cloak rack in the restaurant.

"No," was the surprised reply.

"Well, I am," came the frosty rejoinder, "and that is his overcoat you are putting on."

[685]

Head Waiter—"Would monsieur prefer Spanish, French, or Italian cooking?"

Customer — "I don't mind—I want a boiled egg."

[686]

"Waiter, what kind of meat is this?"

"Spring lamb, sir."

"Is that so; I've been chewing on one of the springs for an hour!"

[687]

"Waiter."

"Yes, sir."

"Have you ever been to the zoo?"

"No, sir."

"Well, you'd sure get a kick out of watching the turtles zip by."

[688]

"Yes sir, Guiseppe goes to great lengths to please his restaurant patrons."

"In what way?"

"With spaghetti."

[689]

A very fussy diner entered a restaurant.

"Now, waiter, I want a nice chop," he said. "I want there to be a little fat on one side. I don't want the chop to be underdone, nor do I want it to be burnt. I want it just right, with plenty of gravy. Now, you'll tell your chef exactly what I require, won't you?"

"Certainly, sir," said the waiter, whereupon he shouted down the speaking-tube that connected with the lower regions: "One chop, Joe."

[690]

Taxi-Driver — "Cup of coffee, doughnuts, and some griddle cakes."

Waitress—"Cylinder oil, couple of non-skid, and an order of blow-out patches."

[691]

A doctor who was called to a small country town to extract an appendix, missed the last train back, stayed over night in a miserable hotel, and was waited on at breakfast by a sallow and cadaverous country girl. Said she:

"Boiled tongue, stewed kidneys, fried liver."

Said he:

"Hang your symptoms! Bring me something to eat!"

[692]

Some day we hope to see a waiter with enough of what it takes to lay the check face-up on the table.

[693]

A man went into a restaurant and had a "sizzling platter" of sole. On the way to the cashier's desk he happened to notice how the item was entered on his check: "1 sizzling soul."

[694]

Waiters, of course, are not in a position to snap back at ill-bred guests; but one English head waiter once made the perfect retort to an uncouth customer:

"My position, sir," he said, "does not allow me to argue with you; but if it ever came to a choice of weapons, I would choose grammar."

[695]

Inspector—"We notice a sign outside your restaurant that you are serving rabbit stew today. Is it all rabbit?"

Proprietor—"No, not exactly—it has a little horsemeat also in it."

Inspector—"How much horsemeat?"

Proprietor—"Fifty-fifty, one horse and one rabbit."

[696]

Diner—"You advertised that this restaurant is under new management, but I see the same manager is still here."

Waiter—"Yes, sir, but he got married yesterday."

[697]

A big buck Indian had just ordered a ham sandwich at a restaurant and was peering between the slices of bread when he turned and said to the waiter: "Ugh, you slice 'em ham?"

The waiter replied: "Yes, I sliced the ham."

"Ugh," grunted the Indian. "You darn near miss 'em."

[698]

"This inn must go back to Revolutionary days," said the diner, evidently a Westerner, visiting New England for the first time.

"Very old, sir," said the proprietor. "Would you like to hear some of the stories connected with the place?"

"I would, indeed," replied the tourist. "Tell me the legend of that curious old mince pie the waiter just brought in."

[699]

Diner—"What sort of pudding is this?"

Waitress—"We call it college pudding, sir. Like it?"

Diner—"No. I'm afraid there's an egg in it that ought to have been expelled."

[700]

"Waiter, my lobster is without a claw. How is that?"

"Well, sir, they are so fresh that they fight with each other in the kitchen."

"Take this one away, and bring me one of the winners."

[701]

"That's a tactful waitress. Yesterday she said to me as I was leaving: 'Please remind me tomorrow that you didn't pay your bill today.'"

[702]

A retired printer went into the restaurant business.

"This is an outrage—there's a needle in this soup!" cried one of his customers.

"Merely a typographical error, sir," said the aforetime typo suavely. "Should have been noodle."

[703]

"Bring me a plate of hash," said the diner.

The waiter walked over to the kitchen elevator. "Gent wants to take a chance," he called down the speaking tube.

"I'll have some hash, too," said a second customer.

The waiter picked up the tube again. "Another sport," he yelled.

[704]

Diner—"Here, waitress, take this chicken away: it's as tough as a paving-stone."

Waitress—"Maybe it's a Plymouth Rock, sir."

[705]

Waiter (in London restaurant)—"Your coffee, sir; it's special from South America, sir."

Diner (sarcastically)—"Oh, so that's where you've been?"

[706]

Waitress—"Pardon me, but was yours 'ham and beans' or 'ham and eggs?'"

Diner (who has been waiting thirty minutes)—"Why ask me now?"

Waitress—"Because we're all out of ham."

[707]
Customer—"Are these the Swedish sardines that you have given me?"
Waiter—"Now, as to that I couldn't say, for they were past speaking when we opened the box."

[708]
"I want this meal put on the cuff."
"Sure, I'll throw the whole thing in your lap, if you want."

[709]
"Waiter, there is a hair in my soup."
"Blonde or red. We're missing a waitress."

[710]
Waitress—"Have you given your order?"
Customer—"Yes, but I should like to change it to an entreaty."

[711]
Customer—"By Jove, I am glad to see you back. Has the strike been settled?"
Waiter—"What strike, sir?"
Customer — "Oh, come, now. Where have you been since you took my order?"

[712]
Man—"I'll have a scotch and soda."
Waitress—"Straight or with ginger ale?"

[713]
Jones (at lunch counter)—"Will you pass the limburger?"
Brown—"Oh, yes. Certainly."
Smith—"I pass, too."

[714]
"I must have a holiday," said the pretty cashier of a restaurant. "I'm not looking my best."
"Ridiculous," said the manager.
"It isn't ridiculous; the men are beginning to count their change."

[715]
Restaurant Manager (to orchestra conductor)—"I wish you'd display a little more tact in choosing the music. We've got the National Association of Umbrella Manufacturers here this evening, and you've just played 'It Ain't Gonna Rain No More!'"

[716]
"Fill her up," said the absent-minded motorist to the waiter, as he parked himself in the restaurant with his sweetie.

[717]
No matter how many times a year Uncle Eli goes to the city, he just can't seem to get used to city ways, especially around restaurants. As a result, he often gets into embarrassing predicaments. Just the other day a waitress in a Washington café set his order before him. Picking up the small portion of steak, Eli examined it critically and said: "Yep, that's exactly what I want. Bring me some of it."

[718]
"Do you want a steak for a dollar or a dollar and a half?" demanded the waiter in the restaurant.
"What's the difference?" inquired the tourist.
"You get a sharp knife with the dollar and a half steak," explained the waiter.

[719]
"This is a cottage pudding."
"Whew—I think I got a piece of shingle in my mouth."

[720]
MENU IN THE VERNACULAR
Duck Soup
Cold Shoulder   *Good Eggs*
Dead Beets   *Kale*
Applesauce

[721]

"What's yours?"

"Coffee and rolls, my girl."

One of those iron-heavy, quarter-inch, thick mugs of coffee was pushed over the counter. The fastidious person seemed dazed. He looked under the mug and over it.

"But where is the saucer?" he inquired.

"We don't give no saucers here. If we did some low-brow'd come pilin' in an' drink out of his saucer, an' we'd lose a lot of our swellest trade."

[722]

"Waiter!"

"Yes, sir."

"What's this?"

"It's bean soup, sir."

"No matter what it's *been*. What is it now?"

[723]

Guest — "My word, but I'm thirsty."

Waiter—"Wait a minute and I'll get you some water.

Guest—"I said thirsty, not dirty."

[724]

A one-armed man entered a restaurant at noon and seated himself at a lunch-counter, next to a man, who evidently was of the inquisitive type. The one-armed man paid no attention to him but kept on eating with his one hand. Finally the inquisitive one could stand it no longer, and said: "I beg your pardon, sir, but I see you have lost an arm."

The one-armed man picked up his empty sleeve with his hand and peered anxiously into it. "Bless my soul!" he exclaimed, looking up with great surprise. "I do believe you're right."

[725]

It was Dorothy's first time out with a young man. She knew nothing of how to order in a café. But Jim, her escort, took charge of things. When they sat down at the table, the waiter came for the order. "Two beers," said the escort. The innocent damsel thought a moment and made her decision— "I'll follow you, Jim, I'll take two beers also."

[726]

A restaurant patron whose patience was rewarded at the end of fifty-five minutes said he would like to add to the meal some roquefort cheese and crackers.

"And while you are away," he said to the waitress, "would you mind dropping me a postal card every now and then?"

BOARDING HOUSES

[727]

"It looks like rain," said the boarding house hasher as he set a bowl of soup in front of one of his boarders.

"Yes, it does," he replied, getting a whiff of it, "but it smells a little like soup."

[728]

"How do you boarders find your meals?"

"With a magnifying glass."

[729]

Landlady—"What do you think the poet meant when he said, 'The substance of things hoped for, the evidence of things unseen?'"

Boarder—"Hash, probably."

[730]

Landlady—"What are you grumbling about?"

Boarder—"You advertised this place ten dollars a week for bed and board."

Landlady—"Well, isn't this so?"

Boarder—"But I find they are one and the same thing."

[731]

If all the boarders in all the boarding houses were placed side by side at a table, they would still reach.

[732]

Boarder—"Ah, your steak is like the weather this evening, madam, rather raw."

Landlady—"Indeed? By the way, your account is like the weather, too, unsettled."

[733]

Landlady—"So Mr. Newboard has found something fresh to complain about this morning."

Maid—"No, mum, it's the eggs."

[734]

A tenant had not paid his room rent for several weeks. Something was always happening that took his ready money, and tomorrow was going to be the day. Finally came the breaking point.

"See here," said the landlord, "I'll meet you half way. I'm ready to forget half of what you owe me."

"Great! I'll meet you!" replied the impecunious one. "I'll forget the other half."

[735]

Landlady (discussing world's troubles)—"I suppose we must be prepared for anything these days."

Boarder (eying his helping)—"Yes—or at any rate for hardly anything!"

[736]

Oldtime Boarder (to newcomer) —"I say, old man—I don't think I'd touch the rice pudding if I were you—there was a wedding in this street yesterday."

[737]

"There!" said Jones, as he wrathfully pushed away the pie which his landlord had just served him, "that stuff ain't fit for a pig to eat, and I ain't going to eat it."

[738]

"Henrietta," said a lady to her new girl, "when there's bad news—particularly family afflictions—always let the boarders know it before dinner. It may seem strange to you, Henrietta, but such things make a great difference in the eating in the course of a year."

[739]

"Have you much variety at your boarding-house?"

"Yes, we have three different names for the meals."

[740]

Landlady—"I think you had better board elsewhere."

Boarder—"Yes, I often have."

Landlady—"Often had what?"

Boarder—"Had better board elsewhere."

[741]

Doctor—"You are suffering from indigestion. Drink a glass of hot water every morning."

Patient (star boarder)—"I have been doing that for months, doctor, only my landlady calls it coffee."

[742]

New Guest—"Has this boarding-house any special advantage?"

Regular Boarder—"Yes, you'll find it quite safe to bathe directly after a meal!"

[743]

A man was complaining of the lack of warmth in the boarding-house in which he was staying.

"In the daytime it is bad enough," he said, "but at night I frequently wake up and hear my teeth chattering on the dressing table."

BARBERS

[744]

Customer—"Your dog seems very fond of watching you cut hair."

Barber—"It ain't that; sometimes I snip off a bit of a customer's ear."

[745]

Customer—"Where is the other barber you formerly had here? The one who used to tell the funny stories?"

Barber—"He got too ambitious. He started to illustrate his funny stories with cuts."

[746]

Biff (twice nicked by the barber's razor)—"Hey barber, gimme a glass of water."

Barber—"What's wrong, sir, hair in your mouth?"

Biff—"Naw, I wanna see if my neck leaks."

[747]

"Talk about torture!"

"Yes?"

"Nothing worse than sitting in a barber's chair with your mouth full of lather watching the boy trying to give another customer your new Panama hat."

[748]

"I have a hair-raising story."

"Tell it to some baldheaded man."

[749]

Barber—"And how did you find the razor?"

Customer—"Didn't know I was being shaved."

Barber—"Very glad, I'm sure, sir."

Customer—"Thought I was being sandpapered."

[750]

"Your hair is thinning, sir. Ever try our hair preparations?"

"No, I can't blame it on that."

[751]

A screwball raced into a barber shop.

"Gimme a haircut," he ordered. "And make it snappy."

"Certainly," replied the barber. "Just sit right down here."

"Never mind," said the nut. "I'll stand."

"Come, come," smiled the barber. "Why don't you sit down?"

"I'm sorry," explained the nut. "But I'm in a hurry!"

[752]

Baldheaded Gent—"You ought to cut my hair cheaper, there's so little of it."

Barber—"Oh, no. In your case we don't charge for cutting the hair, we charge for having to search for it."

[753]

"Does the razor hurt, sir?" inquired the barber, anxiously.

"Can't say," replied the victim, testily, "but my face does."

[754]

Barber—"Try a little hair-restorer, sir?"

Customer—"Why don't you use it? You're bald."

Barber—"I represent before using. My brother at the next chair represents after using."

[755]

There were dark shadows under his eyes as he sank into the barber's chair.

"Haircut, please," he replied to the barber's polite greeting.

"Then please sit up a bit," said the barber. "You're rather far down in the chair for a haircut."

"Then give me a shave," murmured the man wearily.

[756]

Client — "The periodicals you have here are full of detective and mystery stories."

Barber — "Yes, sir; my clients' hair stands on end and is easier to cut."

[757]

He swung wide the massive portal and strode briskly in. Instantly six uniformed men spring to attention. He fiercely tore open his shirt collar and jerked off his coat. His glaring eyes became narrow slits as he turned and stood facing them. Not a thing stirred in the tense silence. Each of their anxious faces showed expectancy and suspense. He picked his man and advanced two paces. His look was keen, and his voice was stern — "I want a shave and a haircut," he said.

[758]

Stranger (after being ruthlessly butchered by a rural barber for five minutes) — "Are you interested in poetry?"

Barber (astonished) — "No, sir."

Stranger — "Indeed. I thought that you might be trying to give an imitation of the 'Man with the Hoe.'"

[759]

"What's the matter with Briggs?"

"He was getting shaved by a lady barber when a mouse ran across the floor."

[760]

"Your hair wants cutting badly, sir," said a barber insinuatingly to a customer.

"No, it doesn't," replied the man in the chair; "it wants cutting nicely. You cut it badly last time."

[761]

The old barber was giving the new barber a few last minute instructions before he shaved his first customer:

"All right, John. Be careful and don't cut yourself!"

[762]

Customer — "Just look at that! I look as if I had been in a slaughter house instead of a barber shop! How much do I owe you?"

Barber — "Twelve cents, sir."

Customer — "Twelve! How come such a funny price?"

Barber — "Cut rate, sir, cut rate!"

[763]

Joan — "Do you know anything about surgery?"

John — "Oh yes, I shave myself."

[764]

Youth — "Barbah, how long will I have to wait for a shave?"

Barber (glancing at him) — "Oh, about two years."

[765]

Barber — "Well, my little man, and how would you like your hair cut?"

Small Boy — "If you please, sir, just like father's, and don't forget the little round hole at the top where the head comes through."

[766]

Customer — "Do you think that long hair makes a man look intellectual?"

Barber — "Not when his wife finds it on his coat; it then makes him look foolish."

[767]

"Why do you always insist on talking about the weather to your barber?"

"You wouldn't have me talk about anything as exciting as politics to a man who is handling a razor, would you?"

[768]

Bill—"Can you shave yourself as well as a barber can shave you?"

Jim—"I think so, but the trouble is I hate to talk to myself."

[769]

"Shall I go over your face again?" asked the barber.

"I don't mind your going over it," replied the man in the chair, "but please don't go under the skin like you did the first time."

[770]

"Will you have anything on your face when I've finished?"

"I don't know, but I hope you'll at least leave my nose."

[771]

The customer was being shaved in a country town to which he was a visitor, when the barber cut his cheek.

The man was all apologies, and to give the cut a chance to close up, he placed a piece of tissue paper over the gash.

When the shave was finished the customer—to the great surprise of the barber—handed over a substantial tip.

"That's all right," said the victim, with a smile of forgiveness; "I don't often get shaved by a man who deals in three trades."

"Three trades?" queried the puzzled barber.

"Yes," came the sarcastic reply—"barber, butcher, and paperhanger."

[772]

"Can you shave me with my collar on?" asked the bald-headed, always-in-a-hurry customer as he jumped into the barber's chair.

"Sure thing," answered the barber as he tucked a towel under his chin, "and I can cut your hair with your hat on."

[773]

Barber (entertaining his customer as usual)—"Your hair is getting very gray, sir."

Customer—"I'm not surprised. Hurry up."

[774]

What barbers listen to every day:

"Could you also trim the hair a little while you shave the neck?"

"You should gimme half price—I'm nearly bald."

"What do you do with all the hair you cut?"

"Gimme the same haircut you gave me last year."

"A once-over. Twice."

[775]

"So you think I'm a good barber. Well, I suppose I inherited that."

"Was your father a barber?"

"No. He was a famous orator."

[776]

A gentleman having his hair cut, was asked by the garrulous barber "how he would have it done?"

"If possible," replied the gentleman, *"in silence."*

[777]

"I just got back from a funeral," ventured the barber as a starter.

The tired business man opened his eyes, cleared the lather out of the corner of his mouth and in a biting tone retorted:

"You ought to be blamed glad to get back—a good many people don't."

[778]

"You needn't worry about my cutting you," said the barber reassuringly to a nervous customer. "We pay every patron we cut ten cents for every slip that draws blood. Why, sometimes customers go away from here with a lot of our money."

[779]

"How do you like your hair cut?" asked the barber, who was anxious to please.

"Off," replied the customer, who was a man of few words.

[780]

Talkative Barber (about to lather) —"Do you mind shutting your mouth, sir?"

Tired Customer—"No—do you?"

[781]

"My instructor in English told me not to say 'hair-cut.' "

"How's that?"

"He said it was a barbarism."

[782]

"Where's the barber who worked on the next chair?" asked the old customer as he was getting a shave.

"Hadn't you heard about Bill?" said the barber. "It was a very sad case. He grew nervous and despondent over poor business, and one day when a customer said he didn't care for a massage he suddenly went out of his mind and slashed the customer's throat. He is in the asylum for the criminal insane now. Will you be having a massage, sir?"

"Sure, go ahead!" said the customer.

[783]

Barber—"You are losing your hair fast, sir. Are you doing anything to save it?"

Customer—"Yes; I'm getting a divorce."

AUTOMOBILES

[784]

The Scandinavian had just arrived in California, delighted with the way his new car withstood the trials and tribulations of the trip.

"How are the roads, Eric?"

"Vell, dis guy Lincoln was uh great engineer, but dat Frenchman De Tour he vas no road-builder at all."

[785]

Policeman (producing notebook) —"Name, please."

Motorist—"Aloysius-Alastair-Cyprian-"

Policeman (putting book away) —"Well, don't let me catch you again."

[786]

Mother—"What did your father say when you smashed the new car."

Son—"Shall I leave out the swear words?"

Mother—"Yes, of course."

Son—"He didn't say a word."

[787]

Woman Learning to Drive—"But I don't know what to do!"

Her Husband—"Just imagine that I'm driving."

[788]

"How do you get along without a speedometer?"

"Well, when I get to driving 15 miles an hour my fenders start to rattle; at 25 the windows rattle; at 30 the motor starts knocking—and that's as fast as she'll go!"

[789]

Timid Wife (to husband who has fallen asleep at the wheel)—"I don't mean to dictate to you, George, but isn't that bill-board coming at us awfully fast?"

[790]

Sheriff—"Did you catch the auto thief?"

Deputy—"He was a lucky bird. We had chased him only a mile when our 500 miles was up and we had to stop and change the oil."

[791]

"Look at that fellow; driving from one side of the road to the other. Is he drunk, or a beginner?"

"No; he's a frankfurter salesman calling on the trade."

[792]

Doctor (taking visitor round asylum)—"This room is reserved for auto maniacs."

Visitor—"But the room is empty —are there no patients?"

Doctor—Yes, they are all under the beds repairing."

[793]

Recent reports from the authorities show that seventy-five per cent of the accidents in automobiles are due to drivers hugging too close to the curves.

[794]

"But how will I know when I come to the crossroads?"

"You can't miss the place. It has only four filling stations."

[795]

"Lady," said the traffic officer, who had motioned her to stop, "how long do you expect to be out?"

"What do you mean by that question?" she demanded indignantly.

"Well," he replied sarcastically, "there are a couple of thousand other drivers who would like to use this street after you get through with it."

[796]

Reckless Driver—"Hear those cylinders knocking?"

Timid Passenger—"It's not the cylinders, it's my knees."

[797]

Auto Dealer—"How about that car I sold you? Everything going satisfactorily?"

Undertaker—"Well, it did give me a little trouble at first. I used it for a mourning vehicle, you know, to carry the mourners and friends, and they didn't like to be shook up in their grief. But now I'm using it as a hearse, and I haven't had any complaints so far."

[798]

"Has your baby learned to walk yet?"

"Heavens, no! Why, he's just learning to drive the car."

[799]

Two men in a car went right past the traffic lights when they were red, and were stopped by a policeman.

"I'm sorry, Officer," said the driver, thinking quickly. "I happen to be a doctor and I'm taking a patient to the asylum in a hurry."

The policeman was suspicious —but the passenger was just as quick. Looking up at the constable with a seraphic smile, he whispered: "Kiss me, darling!"

They got away with it!

[800]

Perfection will be reached when the automobile can be made fool-in-the-other-car-proof.

[801]

Son—"Tomorrow is Dad's birthday; what shall we do for him?"

Daughter—"We might let him have his car for a change."

[802]

"Now, we're all set to drive, Mrs. Smith. Just turn the jigger over and push on the hickey with your left hand and pull down on the other little jim-crack with your right, then press down the doodad with your foot and pull the thing-umbob at the same time, and when it starts you push down on the doo-funny with your left foot and yank the umptydiddy back, then let up on the foot dingus and put your other foot on the hickey-madoodle; and don't forget to push down on the hootnanny every time you move the whatyoumaycallit, and you'll be hunky-dory, see?"

[803]

"Why is your car painted blue on one side and red on the other?"

"It's a great scheme. You should hear the witnesses contradicting each other."

[804]

"Jones expects 100 per cent. disability on his accident-insurance policy. He says he is completely incapacitated by the loss of a thumb."

"What's his vocation?"

"He's a professional hitch-hiker."

[805]

A man who was motoring along a country road offered a stranger a lift. The stranger accepted. Shortly afterward the motorist noticed that his watch was missing.

Whipping out a revolver which he happened to be carrying, he dug it into the other man's ribs and exclaimed: "Hand over that watch!"

The stranger meekly complied before allowing himself to be booted out of the car. When the motorist returned home he was greeted by his wife.

"How did you get on without your watch?" she asked. "I suppose you know that you left it on your dressing-table?"

[806]

Second-hand Car Salesman (on trial ground)—"This car is sound in every part."

Prospective Buyer—"So I hear."

[807]

"Clarence," she called. He stopped the car and looked around.

"I am not accustomed to call my chauffeurs by their first name, Clarence. What is your surname?"

"Darling, mum."

"Drive on, Clarence."

[808]

An elderly lady of very prim and severe aspect was seated next a young couple, who were discussing the merits of their motor cars.

"What color is your body?" asked the young man of the girl at his side, meaning of course, the body of her motor car.

"Oh, mine is pink. What is yours?"

"Mine," replied the man, "is brown."

This was too much for the old lady. Rising from the table, she exclaimed:

"When young people come to asking each other the color of their bodies at a dinner-party, it is time I left the room."

[809]

A motorist was helping his extremely fat victim to rise. "Couldn't you have gone around me?" growled the victim.

"Sorry," said the motorist, sadly. "I wasn't sure whether I had enough gasoline."

[810]
Chauffeur—"This, madame, is the hand brake—it's put on very quickly, in case of an emergency."
Madame—"I see—something like a kimono."

[811]
"Even in Bible times a blowout was a great annoyance," writes J. B., "for do we not read in Isaiah XXIII, 5: 'They shall be sorely pained at the report of Tyre'?"

[812]
Filling-station Attendant—"Here comes another I. W. W. customer."
Patron—"What's that?"
Attendant—"A motorist who wants only Information, Wind and Water."

[813]
Auto Salesman—"Yes, sir, this car is absolutely the very last word."
Customer—"Good! I'll take it. My wife loves it."

[814]
Policeman—"How did you knock him down?"
Motorist—"I didn't! I pulled up to let him go across and he fainted."

[815]
"I've just got rid of my saxophone in part exchange for a new car."
"I didn't think they accepted things like that for a car."
"Well, this case was an exception. The dealer happened to be our next-door neighbor."

[816]
"Motoring is surely a great thing. I used to be fat and sluggish before the motoring craze, but now I'm spry and energetic."
"I didn't know you motored."
"I don't. I dodge."

[817]
Salesman—"Yes, sir, of all our cars, this is the one we feel confident and justified in pushing."
Prospective Customer—"That's no good to me. I want one to ride in."

[818]
The candidate for a chauffeur's job was being examined by the car owner.
He got along all right until the questioner asked whether he had traveled much in other States.
The applicant had.
"All right, let's see you fold this road map."

[819]
The fair motorist was speeding through the sleepy village when a policeman stepped out on the road in front of her and forced her to stop.
"What have I done?" she asked innocently.
"You were traveling forty miles an hour," replied the policeman, taking out his notebook.
"Forty miles an hour!" echoed the fair motorist. "Why, I haven't been out an hour!"
The policeman scratched his head with his pencil before replying. "Go on, then. That's a new one on me."

[820]
Traffic Cop—"Now, Miss, what gear were you in at the time of the accident?"
Demure Miss—"Oh, I had on a black beret, tan shoes, and a tweed sports dress."

[821]
Irate Motorist (in a hurry when stopped by traffic officer)—"Well, what is it? Are you going to give me a ticket or sell me one?"

[822]

"What would your wife say if you bought a new car?"

" 'Look out for that traffic-light! Be careful now! Don't hit that truck! Why don't you watch where you're going? Will you never learn?' And a lot more like that."

[823]

"Going to a fire?" asked the traffic officer sarcastically to the speeding motorist.

"W-well, not exactly," answered the motorist. "Just trying to prevent one."

"Yes, and how were you going to do that?"

"Well, the boss said that's what he'd do if I were late again, and I was hurrying to get to the office in time."

[824]

"Didn't you claim when you sold me this car that you would replace anything that broke or was missing?"

"Yes, sir. What is it?"

"Well, I want four front teeth and a collar bone."

[825]

An auto-manufacturer has just completed a million-dollar proving-ground to give his car the acid test in staying power and endurance. It seems a much simpler method would be to let a friend take it over the week-end.

[826]

It's funny a woman who can spot a blonde hair on your coat at ten paces can't see a pair of garage doors.

[827]

"Is your wife having any success in learning to drive a car?"

"Well, the road is beginning to turn when she does."

[828]

Customer—"I've come back to buy the car I was looking at yesterday."

Salesman—"Fine. Now tell me, what was the one dominating thing that made you buy this car?"

Customer—"My wife."

[829]

A girl was driving in her new car when something went wrong with the engine. The traffic light changed from green to red and back to green and still she could not get the car to budge. The traffic cop came up.

"What's the matter, miss?" he inquired. "Ain't we got colors you like?"

[830]

A man was taking an examination for an auto-driving license, and one of the questions asked was:

"What would you do if the driver of a car ahead moved arm up and down?"

"Man or woman?" asked the applicant.

[831]

First Motorist—"I dreamed last night that I died and went to hell."

Second Motorist—"How did you know it was hell?"

First Motorist—"There were forty fireplugs on every block."

[832]

Motor Cop (after hard chase)— "Why didn't you stop when I shouted back there?"

Driver (with only five dollars, but presence of mind)—"I thought you just said, 'Good morning, Senator.' "

Cop—"Well, you see, Senator, I wanted to warn you about driving fast through the next township."

[833]
Officer (to couple in parked auto)—"Don't you see that sign, 'Fine for parking'?"
Driver—"Yes, Officer, I see it and heartily agree with it."

[834]
Battered Motorist (waking up)—"Where am I? Where am I?"
Nurse—"This is number 127."
Motorist—"Room or cell?"

[835]
Judge—"Why did you run down this man in broad daylight on a perfectly straight stretch of road?"
Prisoner—"Your Honor, my windshield was almost totally obscured with Safety First stickers."

[836]
A fellow in the machine shop who had the habit of driving somewhat faster than the law allowed was hailed before a local justice, who imposed a fine of $15. The autoist drew a roll of bills and laid a sum of money on the desk and started to leave the room.
"Here!" the justice called. "There is $30 here."
"That's all right. Keep it. I am going out of town faster than I came in."

[837]
A policeman who had stopped a motorist for dangerous driving, and was taking down the particulars, kept putting the point of his pencil in his mouth.
"Why is it necessary to moisten your pencil?" the motorist asked.
"To make the case look blacker," replied the policeman.

[838]
"Is he a good driver?"
"Well, when the road turns the same time he does, it's just a coincidence."

[839]
Defendant—"I was not going forty miles an hour—not twenty—not even ten—in fact, when the officer came up I was almost at a standstill."
Judge—"I must stop this or you will be backing into something. Twenty-five dollars."

[840]
"Well, miss," said the traffic cop to the perfectly sweet motorist, "I suppose you know why I stopped you?"
"Don't tell me," she replied, "let me guess. Yes, I know! You're lonely."

[841]
When better autos are built, the rear seat driver will be enclosed in a sound-proof case.

[842]
Hell, for garage mechanics, will be a land of abundant grease and no steering wheels to wipe it on.

[843]
"What are you doing there?" asked a policeman of a woman who had stopped her automobile near a busy street corner.
"Parking my car," she replied. "I thought this would be a good place. The sign there reads, "Safety Zone.'"

[844]
"Think of those Spaniards going 3,000 miles on a galleon!"
"Aw, forget it. Yuh can't believe all yuh hear about them foreign cars."

[845]
Traffic Cop—"Use your noodle, lady! Use your noodle!"
Lady—"My goodness! Where is it? I've pushed and pulled everything in the car."

[846]

"I wonder why there are so many more auto wrecks than railway accidents?"

"That's easy. Did you ever hear of the fireman hugging the engineer?"

[847]

A budding journalist was told never to use two words where one would do. He carried out this advice in his report of a fatal accident in the following manner:

"John Jones struck a match to see if there was any gasoline in his tank. There was. Age sixty-five."

[848]

"How far do you get on a gallon?"

"All depends on what's in the gallon."

[849]

Cop—"What'ya mean goin' fifty miles an hour?"

Pretty Motorist—"My brakes don't work and I was hustling to get home before I had an accident."

[850]

If you can start out on an automobile trip with the certainty of knowing where you are going—

If you don't have to stop every five minutes to look at your gas and oil—

If you make every turn and detour correctly according to the road map—

If you are driving along at just the right speed for comfort and safety—

If you're certain that there isn't a squeak or rattle in the old bus—

Look around, old top: She's either asleep or she's fallen out somewhere!

[851]

A miss in the car is worth two in the engine.

[852]

Policeman (after the collision)—"You saw this lady driving toward you. Why didn't you give her the road?"

Motorist—"I was going to, as soon as I could discover which half she wanted."

[853]

"Are you saving up anything for a rainy day?"

"Yes, in a little while I expect to have enough to buy a new top for my old auto."

[854]

"How much do you still owe on your car?"

"Only a grudge against the man who sold it to me."

[855]

The Joneses were entertaining friends.

"I think I shall get a car this year," said Mr. Jones. "I haven't decided what make, but it's no use getting a cheap one. I suppose I could get a serviceable affair for three thousand or so?"

While the company was gasping at the careless mention of such a sum, the host's youngest son remarked: "And will that funny little man with the black whiskers call every week, like he did when you bought my bike, Dad?"

[856]

"What are the town fathers debating?"

"Whether to keep up the good roads and fine the motorists for speeding, or maintain a mudhole and charge them for hauling 'em out."

[857]

Wife (in back seat)—"Henry, dear! You mustn't drive so fast!"

Husband—"Why not?"

Wife—"The motor policeman who has been following us won't like it."

[858]

"It was very romantic. He proposed to her in the automobile."

"Yes?"

"And she accepted him in the hospital."

[859]

"What is the name of your automobile?"

"I don't know."

"You don't know? What do your folks call it?"

"Oh, as to that, Father always says 'The Mortgage'; brother Tom calls it 'The Fake'; Mother, 'My Limousine'; Sister, 'Our Car'; Grandma, 'That Peril'; the chauffeur, 'Some Freak,' and our neighbors, 'The Limit.' "

[860]

Policeman—"Didn't you hear me call you to stop?"

Driver—"I didn't know it was you. I thought it was someone I'd run over."

[861]

"Honestly, now, you would never have thought this car of mine was one I had bought secondhand, would you?"

"Never in my life. I thought you had made it yourself."

[862]

Judge—"Speeding, eh? How many times have you been before me?"

Speeder—"Never, your Honor. I've tried to pass you on the road once or twice, but my car will do only fifty-five."

[863]

"Now that you have a new auto I suppose you are out all the time."

"You bet! I was out $50 on repairs last week."

[864]

Traffic Judge, 1960—"Wrong side of the cloud, eh? Fifty dollars and costs."

[865]

"I see you're letting your little son drive the car."

"Yes, he's still too young to be trusted as a pedestrian."

[866]

"What's become of that hit-and-run driver?"

"He's now doing his stunt on the prison baseball team."

[867]

A man pinned under his car was being questioned by a policeman.

"Married?"

"No. This is the worst fix I've ever been in."

[868]

Defendant—"The things the prosecutor don't know about driving a car, your Worship, would fill a book."

Judge—"And it seems to me, young man, the things you don't know about it would fill a hospital."

[869]

"I turned the way I signaled," said the lady, indignantly, after the crash.

"I know it," retorted the man. "That's what fooled me."

[870]

First Auto Mechanic—"Which do you prefer, leather or fabric upholstery?"

Second Auto Mechanic—"I like fabrics; leather is too hard to wipe your hand on."

[871]

"How did your father know we went out in the car yesterday?"

"Quite simple! Remember that stout gentleman we ran into? That was Father."

[872]

Lady (at busy corner)—"Isn't it wonderful how a single policeman can dam the flow of traffic?"

Her Escort—"Yes, but you should hear some of the motorists that are held up."

[873]

"All this talk about back-seat drivers is bunk. I've driven a car for ten years and I've never had a word from behind."

"What sort of car?"

"A hearse."

[874]

"What's happened, George?" she asked her husband, who had got out of the car to investigate.

"Puncture," he said briefly.

"You ought to have been on the lookout for this," was the helpful remark. "You remember the guide warned you there was a fork in the road."

[875]

The other day I heard of one of these new small-sized autos speeding fifty miles an hour on one of our main highways. And every fifty feet the little trinket would hop right up in the air about five feet. A motor cop finally overtook the midget-motor and brought it to a stop.

"What's the big idea of that car jumpin' that a-way?" asked the cop.

The driver answered:

"Why, Officer, there's nothing wrong with the car. You see!—I've got—hic—the hiccups!"

[876]

Policeman—"As soon as I saw you come around the bend I said to myself, 'Forty-five at least.' "

Lady Driver—"How dare you? It's this hat that makes me look so old."

[877]

Salesman—"What kind of car would you like, madam, four, six or eight cylinders?"

Timid Customer—"Couldn't I begin with one?"

[878]

Auto Tourist—"I clearly had the right of way when this man ran into me, and yet you say I was to blame."

Local Officer—"You certainly were."

Autoist—"Why?"

Local Officer—"Because his father is Mayor, his brother is Chief of Police and I go with his sister."

[879]

She—"You certainly do keep your car nice and clean."

He—"It's an even deal—my car keeps me clean, too."

[880]

The Prospective Purchaser—"I'm afraid your make of car does not suit us. My fiancée can not reach the brakes and the steering-wheel at the same time."

The Salesman—"But, sir, the car is perfect. Why not try a new girl?"

[881]

His Boss—"Dodson, I found this long blonde hair on the back seat of my limousine. My wife's hair is black."

Chauffeur—"I'll give you an explanation, sir."

Boss — "Explanation nothing! What I want is an introduction."

[882]

"Hello, Jones! Got a new car?"

"Yes. I went into a garage to use the phone, and I didn't like to come away without buying something."

[883]

"She is one of those worm-style motorists."

"What do you mean, worm-style?"

"A worm never gives any signal which way it will turn."

[884]

"Did you have the car out last night?"

"Yes, Dad; I took some of the boys for a run round."

"Well, tell them I've found two of their lipsticks!"

[885]

"How long did it take your wife to learn to drive?"

"It will be ten years in September."

[886]

Magistrate—"Witness says you neither slowed down nor tried to avoid the pedestrian."

Motorist—"I took all precautions. I blew my horn and cursed him."

[887]

Lady Driver (after collision)— "But I insist it was my fault."

Gentleman Driver—"No, my dear lady, it was my fault. I could tell your car was being driven by a woman at least 300 feet away and I could easily have driven over into the field and avoided this."

[888]

Southern Californian (home from a vacation trip out of the State)— "Ah-h-h! Doesn't the old bus ride nice, now that we've got the tires filled again with this wonderful Los Angeles air?"

[889]

The genteel motorist had just pulled into the gasoline-station for the inevitable gasoline. That being over, the attendant was going through his little ritual.

"Check the oil, sir?"

"Now, it's O. K."

"Got enough water in the radiator?"

"Yep, filled up."

"Anything else, sir?"

"Yes, would you please stick out your tongue so I can seal this letter?"

[890]

Traffic Cop—"Say, you, get going—what's the matter with you?"

Motorist—"I'm just fine, thank you, but I think my engine's dead."

[891]

Motorist—"I've had it a whole year and I haven't paid a cent for repairs or upkeep on my car since I bought it."

Friend—"Yes, so the man at the service station tells me."

[892]

Customer—"I want some hinges for the end wall of my garage."

Hardware Clerk—"That's a funny place to put them."

Customer—"I know, but my wife can't always stop the car."

[893]

Judge—"You admit you drove over this man with a loaded truck?"

Driver—"Yes, your honor."

Judge—"And what have you to say in your defense?"

Driver—"I didn't know it was loaded."

[894]

Guest—"Gosh, I wish I could afford a car like this!"

Owner—"So do I."

[895]

"It's absurd for this man to charge us ten dollars for towing us three miles."

"That's all right; he's earning it —I have my brakes on."

[896]

"Does she know much about cars?"

"Naw. She thinks you cool the motor by stripping the gears."

[897]

Cop—"Didn't you hear me yell for you to stop?"

Motorist—"No, sir."

Cop—"Didn't ya hear me whistle?"

Motorist—"No, sir."

Cop—"Didn't ya see me signal?"

Motorist—"No, sir."

Cop—"Well, I guess I'd better go home. I don't seem to be doing much good around here."

[898]

A motorcycle policeman was about to write up a ticket charging a motorist with speeding, when a woman in the back seat who could restrain herself no longer, began this tirade:

"There! Didn't I tell you to watch out? But you kept right on speeding all morning, getting out of line, not blowing your horn, passing stop streets, and everything else. Didn't I tell you you'd get caught? Didn't I? Didn't I?"

"Who is this woman?" asked the officer, with pencil poised.

"My wife," said the motorist grimly.

"Drive on, my friend!" exclaimed the officer, pityingly, as he proceeded to tear up the ticket. "Drive on—and may the Lord have mercy on you!"

[899]

Prospective Customer—"What's the difference between this new model and last year's car?"

Efficient Salesman—"Well, the automatic cigarette lighter is about an inch nearer the steering-wheel."

[900]

Policeman—"Miss, you were doing sixty miles an hour!"

She—"Oh, isn't that splendid! I only learnt to drive yesterday."

[901]

Constable—"Let me see your driving license."

Girl—"Well, as a matter of fact, Officer, I don't happen to have it on me, but if it will save you any bother I can assure you it's very much like any other old driving license."

[902]

A mother was taking her young son for a ride in the car. On their way home, the lad asked:

"Mother, where are all the infernal idiots?"

"Why, Son," she replied, "they only happen to be on the highway when your father is driving."

[903]

Motorist who always insists on his rights, just regaining consciousness: "I had the right of way, didn't I?"

His disgusted passenger—"Yeah, but the other fellow had the truck."

[904]

Motorist—"How far is it to the next town?"

Native—"Nigh on to five miles as the crow flies."

Motorist—"Well, how far is it if a damned crow has to walk and carry an empty gasoline can?"

[905]

The shortest perceptible unit of time is the difference between the moment the traffic light changes and the boob behind you honks for you to go.

[906]

A hard-driving taxi-driver ignored a red signal, threatened the traffic policeman's knees, missed the street island by a hair, and grazed a bus, all in one dash.

The policeman hailed him, then strolled over to the taxi, pulling a big handkerchief from his pocket *en route.*

"Listen, cowboy!" he growled. "On the way back I'll drop this and see if you can pick it up with yer teeth."

[907]

"You sold me a car two weeks ago."

"Yes, sir."

"Tell me again all you said about it then. I'm getting discouraged."

[908]

"Some of you pedestrians walk as if you owned the streets."

"Yes, and some of you motorists drive around as if you owned your cars."

[909]

Policeman—"Did you get the number of that car that knocked you down, madam?"

Victim—"No, but the hussy that was driving it wore a three-piece tweed suit, lined with Canton crape, and she had on a periwinkle hat, trimmed with artificial cherries."

[910]

The decrepit old car drove up to the toll-bridge.

"Fifty cents," cried the gateman.

"Sold," replied the driver.

[911]

Judge—"The traffic officer says you got sarcastic with him."

Motorist—"But I didn't intend to be. He talked to me like my wife does, and I forgot myself and answered, 'Yes, my dear.'"

[912]

Dialogue at the scene of an automobile crash:

"Hello, old man! Have an accident?"

"No thanks, I've just had one!"

[913]

"Your doctor's out here with a flat tire."

"Diagnose the case as flatulency of the perimeter and charge him accordingly," ordered the garage man. "That's the way he does."

[914]

"Jones always strikes me as an indolent sort of chap."

"Indolent? Why that fellow is so lazy he always runs his automobile over a bump to knock the ashes off his cigar."

[915]

Motor Cop—"You were doing forty, ma'am."

Pretty Thing—"Forty—oh, was I? Well, you were doing as much yourself—so there!"

[916]

A man was trying to teach his nervous little wife to drive a car. They were out on a narrow country road, and the wife had been at the wheel for only a short time when she exclaimed:

"Take the wheel, Bill! Here comes a telephone pole."

[917]

"Are you a back seat driver?"

"Indeed I'm not. I sit right here where I can grab the wheel if he doesn't do what I tell him."

[918]

A woman motorist was driving along a country road when she noticed a couple of repairmen climbing telephone poles.

"Fools!" she exclaimed to her companion, "they must think I never drove before."

[919]

She was having her first driving lesson and her husband was the teacher. Suddenly, finding herself faced with a difficult traffic problem, she lost her head.

"Tell me quickly," she cried. "What do I do now?"

Hubby seized his chance.

"Oh," he replied, quietly, "just imagine that I'm driving and do what you'd say I should do."

[920]

Guide—"This, sir, is the leaning tower of Pisa."

Tourist—"Pisa! Let me think. No, that doesn't sound like the contractor's name who built my garage, but it looks like his work."

[921]

Two truck drivers were all snarled up in the traffic at a busy intersection. One lost his temper and yelled at the other:

"Why don't you look where you're going, you great, big, cross-eyed, bow-legged, knock-kneed dumb-bell!"

The other driver, smiling sweetly, said: "You're nice looking, too, buddy."

[922]

Mrs. Thompson (learning to drive)—"Henry, that little mirror up there isn't set right."

Thompson—"Isn't it?"

Mrs. Thompson—"No; I can't see anything but the car behind."

[923]

Motorist—"These chickens in the road cause a lot of accidents."

Farmer—"But not as many as the chickens beside the driver."

[924]

"You say that you have driven a car for ten years and never had a back seat driver?" inquired the weak-chinned gentleman.

"Yeah," asserted the sad-faced man, "I drive a hearse."

[925]

Wife (at busy crossing)—"Now remember, Herbert, the brake is on the left—or is it the right—but don't——"

Husband—"For heaven's sake stop chattering. Your job is to smile at the policeman!"

[926]

"What is the best thing to do when the brakes of one's car give way?" asks a motorist. Hit something cheap.

[927]

Father (with new car)—"Can't understand what's wrong. It went all right when I drove it down yesterday."

Bobbie—"Yes; but yesterday it was new, Daddie."

[928]

"At times my wife seems to be trying to be an angel."

"You mean when she wants something from you?"

"No; when she drives the car."

[929]

A motorist speeding along a highway at 80 miles an hour was stopped by a policeman. "Was I driving too fast?" asked the motorist apologetically.

"Hell no," replied the policeman. "You were flying too low."

[930]
Old Gentleman—"I see that in London a man is run over every half-hour."
Old Lady—"Poor fellow!"

[931]
"That fellow's driving his car so carefully that I think he must be a new driver."
"No, he just paid cash for the car."

[932]
"I can't see why they have a man to steer from the rear of the fire department's ladder truck," said Mrs. Tellum.
"Well, it's a necessary thing, I suppose," replied Mrs. Backseat, "but I agree with you that it's not a man's work."

[933]
"Where's old Bill been lately? I haven't seen him for months."
"What? Haven't you heard? He's got three years for stealin' a car."
"What did he want to steal a car for? Why didn't he buy one an' not pay for it, like a gentleman!"

[934]
"Has your wife learned to drive the car yet?"
"Yes, in an advisory capacity."

[935]
"You almost struck that pedestrian!"
"I don't care," blurted the reckless motorist, "I haven't time now to go back and try again!"

[936]
"Mommer, what becomes of an automobile when it gets too old to run any more?"
"Why, somebody sells it to your pa, dearie, for a used car good as new."

[937]
"Are you sure you have shown me all the principal parts of this car?" asked the fair prospective purchaser.
"Yes, madam, all the main ones," replied the dealer.
"Well, then, where is the depreciation? Tom told me that was one of the biggest things about a car."

[938]
Herbert—"Arthur hasn't been out one night for three weeks."
Flora—"Has he turned over a new leaf?"
"No; he's turned over a new car."

[939]
"What happened to your face?"
"Had a little argument with a fellow about driving in traffic."
"Why didn't you call a cop?"
"He was a cop."

[940]
"Bothered much by hitch hikers when you're out riding?"
"Not now. Tried a new plan. As soon as I get out of town I show the sign 'Taxi' on my car."

[941]
Woman Driver—"Can you fix this fender so my husband will never know I bent it?"
Garage Mechanic—"No, but I can fix it so that you can ask him in a few days how he bent it."

[942]
He was the only witness to the car accident. The cop asked his name. "John Smith," he said.
"Give us your real name," ordered the cop.
"Well," said the witness, "put me down as William Shakespeare."
"That's better," said the cop, "you can't fool me with that Smith stuff."

[943]
Automobile dealer—"This car is a real buy. The engine runs so smoothly you can't hear it; knee action doesn't let you feel a thing; with its perfect combustion there are no odors for you to smell; and as for speed—you can't see."
Prospect—"My gosh, how do you know whether you brought it along or left it at home?"

[944]
Valet (to Master)—"Sir, your car is at the door."
Master—"Yes, I hear it knocking."

[945]
"I want a chauffeur who can think quickly in an emergency."
Applicant—"That's me, sir! I never smashed a car yet that I couldn't think up an A-1 excuse in five seconds."

[946]
Husband—"I've got to get rid of my chauffeur; he's nearly killed me four times."
Wife—"Oh, give him another chance."

[947]
"What model is his car?"
"It's not a model; it's a horrible example."

[948]
"I'm not sure I quite understand those knee-action wheels."
"Why, it's like this—the wheels give. So if you run over a pedestrian, you hardly feel it."

[949]
A tourist stopped his car on the road and asked a country boy how far it was to Smithville.
The boy replied: "It's 24,999 miles the way you're goin', but if you turn around it ain't but four."

[950]
"What part of the car causes the most accidents?"
"The nut that holds the wheel."

[951]
"The horn on your car must be broken."
"No, it's just indifferent."
"Indifferent! What do you mean?"
"It just doesn't give a hoot."

[952]
Policeman—"How did the accident happen?"
Motorist—"My wife fell asleep in the back seat."

[953]
A man and his wife were driving back into town after an evening at a roadhouse. Suddenly the wife spoke up: "What're you doing? Watch out for those cars. You're too close!"
"Are you nuts?" asked the husband.
"Nuts? hoddya get that way?"
"Well," said the husband, "you're driving."

BUSES AND STREET CARS

[954]
A lady much above the usual size was trying to enter a street car. A passenger, who was waiting to get off, began to laugh at her futile efforts.
"If you were half a man, you'd help me on this street car," snapped the fat lady.
The passenger retorted, "Madam, if you were half a lady, you wouldn't need any help."

[955]

Jane (discussing operas with friend in street car)—"I simply love Carmen."

Conductor (blushing)—"Try the motorman, Miss. I'm a married man."

[956]

Mavis—"How did Simpson meet his death?"

Mann—"A man behind him in the street-car shot him for turning the page of his newspaper too quickly."

[957]

When a group of women got on the car, every seat was already occupied. The conductor noticed a man who seemed to be asleep, and, fearing that he might miss his stop, he nudged him and said:

"Wake up!"

"I wasn't asleep," the man protested.

"Not asleep? But you had your eyes closed."

"I know. I just hate to look at ladies standing up in a crowded car."

[958]

The girl stopped the car and promptly got on, but the motorman had no sooner started the car than she asked him anxiously:

"Will this car take me to the football game?"

"No, miss."

"But you have an announcement of the game on the front of the car," she said, as though that were sufficient reason for the car to be going to the game.

"I know, miss. We also have an announcement of Boston baked beans back in the car there, but this car certainly don't go to Boston!"

[959]

The large lady was trying desperately to get on the trolley car, but the narrow space between the seats seemed too much for her.

"Why not try sideways, lady?" the conductor suggested helpfully.

" 'Cause I ain't got no sideways!" she expostulated.

[960]

Muggins—"Yes, I'm living out in the country now. It certainly has its inconveniences."

Buggins—"What do you miss most?"

Muggins—"The last train home at night."

[961]

The suburban train was ploughing through the snow. After countless stops, it at last came to a dead halt, and all efforts to start it again were fruitless.

In the small hours of the morning one of the passengers, numb with cold, crawled out of his compartment and floundered through the snow to the nearest telegraph office.

"Will not be at the office today," he wired to his boss. "Not home yesterday yet."

[962]

Woman with satchel enters streetcar, sits down.

Enters conductor, asks fare.

Women opens satchel, takes out purse, shuts satchel, opens purse, takes out dime, shuts purse, opens satchel, puts in purse, shuts satchel.

Offers dime, receives nickel.

Opens satchel, takes out purse, shuts satchel, opens purse, puts in nickel, closes purse, opens satchel, puts in purse, closes satchel.

Stop the car, please.

[963]

"I see you carrying home a new kind of breakfast food," said the first commuter.

"Yes," admitted the second commuter, "I was missing too many trains. The old brand required three seconds to prepare. You can fix this new brand in a second and a half."

[964]

"John," said the commuter's wife, "what train does Mr. Jones take to town?"

"He takes the one after mine."

"If he takes the train after yours, how do you know what train he takes?"

"Because that's the one I take."

[965]

First Commuter—"Why are you at the station at this unearthly hour?"

Second Commuter—"Well, you see, I can never remember all the things I've forgotten till I get to the station, so I have to allow for plenty of time to go back for them."

[966]

"One-two-three-four-five," said a street-car passenger counting out the pennies.

"Aw, I can't take them!" cried the conductor.

"Then give 'em to the company," said the passenger.

[967]

"I noticed you got up and gave that lady your seat in the bus the other day."

"Since childhood I have respected a woman with a strap in her hand."

[968]

"How far is your new house from the station?"

"Only a five-minute walk if you run."

[969]

A very pretty but extremely slender girl entered a street car and managed to seat herself in a narrow space between two men. Presently a portly colored mammy entered the car, and the pretty miss, thinking to humiliate the men for lack of gallantry, arose.

"Aunty," she said, with a wave of her hand toward the place she had just vacated, "take my seat."

"Thank you, missy," replied the colored woman, smiling broadly, "but which gen'man's lap was you sittin' on?"

[970]

"Pardon me, does this train stop at Tenth Street?"

"Yes; watch me and get off one station before I do."

"Thank you."

[971]

A woman visitor to the city entered a taxicab. No sooner was the door closed than the car leaped forward violently, and afterward went racing wildly along the street, narrowly missing collision with innumerable things. The passenger, naturally enough, was terrified. She thrust her head through the open window of the door, and shouted at the taxi driver.

"Please, be careful, sir! I'm nervous. This is the first time I ever rode in a taxi."

The driver yelled in reply, without turning his head:

"That's all right, ma'am. It's the first time I ever drove one!"

[972]

"There's no danger in riding in these subways, is there?"

"I should say so. The last time I tried them I found myself in Brooklyn."

[973]

A Washington car conductor, born in London and still a cockney, has succeeded in extracting thrills from the alphabet—imparting excitement to the names of the national capitol's streets. On a recent Sunday morning he was calling the streets thus:

"Haitch!"

"High!"

"Jay!"

"Kay!"

"Hell!"

At this point three prim ladies picked up their prayer-books and left the car.

[974]

Conductor—"Did you get home all right last night, sir?"

Passenger—"Of course; why do you ask?"

Conductor—"Well, when you got up and gave the lady your seat last night, you were the only two in the car."

[975]

"Was the train crowded when you came home?"

"No, I had a strap all to myself."

[976]

A thin man resented the lateral pressure of a fat man on the same seat with him in a street car.

He said—"They ought to charge by weight in these cars."

"If they did, sonny," said the fat man, "you'd have to walk. They couldn't afford to stop for you."

[977]

Man (having given up his seat in the street car)—"I beg your pardon."

The Girl—"I didn't speak!"

The Man—"Sorry, I'm sure. I thought you said 'thank you'."

[978]

Passenger—"Does this bus stop at the Ritzmore Hotel?"

Conductor—"No, sir. We leave it in the barn at night."

[979]

Passenger—"Conductor, we are like sardines here. Can't you prevent our being crushed?"

Conductor—"Certainly, sir. Number off the passengers and then make the even numbers breathe in while the odd numbers breathe out."

[980]

The bus was full but a large lady elbowed her way in.

Lady—"Two fares, please. One for me and one for my husband outside."

Conductor—"Can't your husband pay his own fare. How am I to know which is your husband?"

Lady—"Impudence! I shall complain to the company."

Conductor — "Calm yourself, madam. I can imagine what your husband is like."

RAILROADS

[981]

"Going far?" asked the talkative little man on the train.

"Only to Springfield," replied the other, who hated talking to strangers and wished to nip this one in the bud. "I am a commercial artist. My age is forty-six. I am married. I have a son of twenty. He is at Harvard. My father died last January. He was on the Stock Exchange. Mother is still living. I have a niece with red hair. Our cook's name is Bridget. Is there anything else?"

[982]

It is said that on an Oregon railroad there is much dispute over the proper pronunciation of the town called Eurelia. The brakemen who call the stations, however, always have to resort to their own judgment. On one of the trains, one day, so the story goes, a brakeman opened the door at one end of the car and called out:

"You're a liar!" which was his version of how to yell Eurelia.

Immediately afterward another brakeman opened the door at the other end of the car and yelled:

"You really are!" and he was calling the same station, Eurelia.

[983]

Old Lady—"Is this the train to Chicago?"

Trainman—"Yes, ma'am."

Old Lady—"Are you sure it goes to Chicago?"

Trainman—"Well, ma'am, the station-agent, the engineer, the fireman, the conductor, and the waiters in the dining car say it goes to Chicago, and that is all I know."

[984]

A woman with a small boy asked the information clerk what time the train left for Bingham.

"Theven thithty-theven," was the reply.

The woman went away, but soon came back to ask the same question.

"Theven thithty-theven," the clerk said again.

Still a third time the woman came back, after a lapse of ten or fifteen minutes.

"At theven thithty-theven," said the clerk. "You hath lotht the train now, madam, I'm thorry. It letht at theven thithty-theven, ath I told you, and ith the latht that thtopth at Bingham."

"Oh, that's all right," said the woman. "I didn't want the train anyway, only my little boy likes so well to hear you say 'seven fifty-seven.'"

[985]

"The time-table says that this train will arrive at nine-ten and it's half an hour late now," complained the traveler at the small-town railroad station.

"Well, 'taint ten yet, is it?" the agent countered.

[986]

A man bought the only remaining sleeping car space. An old lady next to him in line burst into tears, wailing that it was of vital importance that she have a berth on that train. Gallantly the man sold her his ticket, and then strolled to the telegraph office. His message read:

"Will not arrive until tomorrow. Gave berth to an old lady just now."

[987]

A pedantic bore forced himself upon a fellow traveler aboard a transcontinental train, and made a great parade of his learning. The traveler stood it as long as he could, and at length, looking at him gravely, said: "My friend, you and I know all that is to be known."

"How is that?" said the bore, pleased with what he thought a complimentary association.

"Why," said the traveler, "you know everything except that you are a fool, and I know that."

[988]

"Conductor, at which end of the car do I get off?"

"Either one, madam. Both ends stop at the same time."

[989]

The train came to a sudden grinding stop, causing the passengers to jump. "What has happened, conductor?" cried a nervous old lady.

"Nothing much. . . . We ran over a cow."

"Was it on the track?"

"No," replied the disgusted conductor, "we chased it into a barn."

[990]

The train had stopped on the line and the conductor was tired of answering stupid questions.

"What's the matter, conductor?" came yet another query.

"The signalman up in the tower has got red hair," replied the conductor, "and we can't get the engineer to pass the tower."

[991]

Inquirer—"When is the next train to Albany?"

Stationmaster—"Twelve o'clock, sir."

Inquirer—"What, isn't there one before that?"

Stationmaster—"No, sir, we never run one before the next."

[992]

"Conductor! Help me off the train."

"Sure."

"You see, I'm stout and I have to get off the train backwards; the porter thinks I'm getting on and gives me a shove on again. I'm five stations past my destination now."

[993]

A woman inquired of a Negro porter the time of the train to Chicago. She then went to a white man and asked him.

The porter went to the white man afterwards and said, with a

smile, "Perhaps she will believe it, now she has got in black and white."

[994]

Grandma Jackson and her young grandson were riding on a train. Grandma had dozed and suddenly she sat up. "What was that station the conductor called?" she asked the boy.

"He didn't announce any station; he just put his head in the door and sneezed."

"Get the bundles together quickly," said grandma. "This is Oshkosh."

[995]

A midget belonging to a circus got on the sleeper at Chicago to go to New York. He had an upper berth. He went into the diner and drank a large cup of coffee. About two hours later the man in the lower berth rang violently for the porter.

"Porter!" he exclaimed. "I can't sleep. Someone is pacing overhead."

[996]

Passenger (to negro porter)— "What time do we get to New York, George?"

Porter—"We is due to get there at 1:15, unless you has set your watch by Eastern time, which would make it 2:15. Then, of co'se, if you is goin' by daylight saving time, it would be 3:15, unless we is an hour an' fifty minutes late— which we is."

[997]

"I want to return to the city on a late train," said the stranger at the small town ticket office.

"Well," responded the agent, "I'd recommend Number 7. She's usually as late as any of 'em."

[998]

Visitor (in early morning, after week-end, to chauffeur)—"Don't let me miss my train."

Chauffeur—"No danger, sir. The missus said if I did, it'd cost me my job."

[999]

Conductor—"Do you mind if I put your bag out of the way, sir? People coming in are falling over it."

Traveler—"You leave it where it is. If nobody falls over it I shall forget it's there."

[1000]

A woman traveling by train was talking with the man in the next seat. In describing her holiday, she said that she had visited San Jose. "You pronounce that wrong," said the man. "It is San Hosay. In California you should pronounce all J's as H's. When were you there?"

The woman thought a minute, then answered, "In Hune and Huly."

[1001]

A fat man made a mad rush through the gate for the rear platform of a departing train. As he came back perspiring and frowning, the gateman said:

"Just missed her, eh?"

"Oh, no!" the exhausted one replied. "I was only chasing her out of the station!"

[1002]

A lady in the centre seat of the parlor car heard the request of a fellow-passenger directly opposite asking the porter to open the window, and, scenting a draft, she snapped testily:

"Porter, if that window is opened, I shall freeze to death."

"And if the window is kept closed," returned the other passenger, "I shall surely suffocate."

The poor porter stood absolutely puzzled between the two fires.

"Say, boss," he finally said to a traveling salesman seated nearby, "what would you do?"

"Do!" echoed the traveler. "Why, man, that is a very simple matter; open the window and freeze one lady. Then close it and suffocate the other."

[1003]

Tom—"Have you ever been in a railway accident?"

Dick—"Yes, once when I was in a train and we went through a tunnel I kissed the father instead of the daughter."

[1004]

Conductor—"Sorry, madam, but we have learned that the station where you intend to get off has been burned to the ground."

Lady—"That's all right; they'll probably have it rebuilt by the time this train gets there."

[1005]

Politician—"Can you give my friend a job on your railway?"

Manager—"But he cannot talk English."

Politician—"Well, then, give him a job calling out trains."

[1006]

A lecturer aboard a Southern train was complaining about the slowness of the train to the conductor.

"Well, if yer don't like it," the conductor finally blurted out, "why in thunder don't yer git out an' walk?"

"I would," the lecturer blandly replied, "but you see the committee doesn't expect me until this train gets in."

[1007]

"We were bounding along," said a recent traveler on a local South African single-line railway, "at the gate of about seven miles an hour, and the whole train was shaking terribly. I expected every moment to see my bones protruding through my skin. Passengers were rolling from one end of the car to the other. I held on firmly to the arms of the seat. Presently we settled down a bit quieter; at least, I could keep my hat on, and my teeth didn't chatter.

"There was a quiet looking man opposite me. I looked up with a ghastly smile, wishing to appear cheerful, and said:

"'We are going a bit smoother, I see.'

"'Yes,' he said, 'we're off the track now.'"

[1008]

"Here!" said a man angrily to the railway official. "I got a cinder in my eye from one of your engines, and it cost me five dollars for a doctor to have it taken out and the eye dressed. What are you going to do about it?"

"Nothing, my dear sir, nothing," the official replied suavely. "We have no further use for the cinder and you are quite welcome to it. From a legal point of view, the cinder was not yours, and no doubt you could be proceeded against for removing our property. But we will take no steps in the matter."

[1009]

Inquirer (at Philadelphia Station)—"Where does this train go?"

Brakeman—"This train goes to New York in ten minutes."

Inquirer—"Goodness! That's going some!"

[1010]

Railroad Agent—"Here's another farmer who is suing us on account of his cows."

Official—"One of our trains has killed them, I suppose?"

Agent—"No, he claims our trains go by so slow that the passengers lean out the windows and milk the cows when they go by."

[1011]

They tell about a very ordinary sort of fellow who got suddenly rich by striking oil, and who got awfully swell-headed and pompous, always trying to impress those with whom he came in contact with his great importance.

One day he rushed into the railway station, laid a twenty-dollar bill down at the ticket-seller's window, and said:

"Gimme a ticket."

"Where to?" asked the ticket-agent.

"Anywhere. It doesn't make no difference," said the newly rich guy. "I got business all over."

[1012]

An elderly lady in one of the railway coaches inquired of the fresh young trainman what the train was stopping for.

"Engine was out late last night, ma'am," he grinned, "so she's got a thirst on her this morning. They're givin' her a drop o' water."

"Sure it's water?" the old lady asked.

"If you'll wait a second, ma'am, I'll inquire whether they're givin' 'er hard cider."

"Never mind, young man," came the answer, "but I thought, perhaps, by the way we have been dragging along she was run on sloe gin."

[1013]

First Traveler (cheerily)—"Fine day, isn't it?"

Second Ditto (haughtily)—"Sir! You have the advantage of me. I don't know you."

First Ditto—"Humph! I fail to see the advantage."

[1014]

Confused passenger (nervously fumbling through his pockets)— "I'm afraid I've lost my ticket."

Irate conductor—"Why, man alive, you're foolish. You couldn't lose a ticket a yard long."

"The hell I couldn't. You don't know me. I lost a bass drum once."

[1015]

"Let me off at the next stop, conductor, I thought this was a lunch-wagon."

[1016]

The Baltimore & Ohio R. R. Co.,
Pittsburgh, Pa.
Gentlemen:

Why is it that your switch engine has to ding and dong and fizz and spit and pant and grate and grind and puff and bump and chug and hoot and toot and whistle and wheeze and howl and clang and growl and thump and clash and boom and jolt and screech and snarl and snort and slam and throb and roar and rattle and hiss and yell and smoke and smell and shriek all night long when I come home from a hard day at the boiler works and have to keep the dog quiet and the baby quiet so my wife can squawk at me for snoring in my sleep?

Yours,

[1017]

A lady seated herself in a train, containing a solitary traveling salesman.

After a while the traveler said, politely: "Excuse me, miss, but ——"

"If you speak or annoy me, I'll pull the train cord," snapped the girl.

Whenever he attempted to speak, the girl threatened to give the alarm.

At last the train slowed up at a station and the traveler rose to his feet.

"I don't care whether you like it or not," he said, "but I want that torn bag of strawberries you've been sitting on for the last six miles."

[1018]

Father—"Are there half fares for children?"

Conductor—"Yes, under fourteen."

Father—"That's all right. I've only five."

[1019]

"What good," asked the angry would-be passenger, "are the figures set down in these railway timetables?"

"Why," patiently explained the genial agent, "if it weren't for them figures we'd have no way of findin' out how late the train is."

[1020]

Trainman—"This train goes to Philadelphia and points west."

Old Lady—"Well, I want a train that goes to Altoona and I don't care which way it points."

THE AMERICAN SCENE

ABOARD SHIPS

[1021]
A Mississippi River steamboat was stopped in the mouth of a tributary stream, owing to a dense fog. An inquisitive passenger inquired of the captain the cause of the delay.

"Can't see up the river," was his laconic reply.

"But I can see the stars overhead," the passenger replied sharply.

"Yes," came back the captain, "but unless the boilers bust, we ain't going that way."

[1022]
First Shark—"What's that funny two-legged thing that just fell in the water?"

Second Shark—"Dunno, but I'll bite."

[1023]
The two men were adrift in an open boat and it looked bad for them. Finally one of them, frightened, began to pray.

"O Lord," he prayed, "I've broken most of Thy commandments. I've been a hard drinker, but if my life is spared now I'll promise Thee never again——"

"Wait a minute, Jack," said his friend. "Don't go too far. I think I see a sail."

[1024]
"Yes," said the captain of the steamboat to the nervous passenger. "I've been running boats on this river so long I know where every snag and sandbar is."

Just then the boat struck a submerged snag with such force that it shivered from stem to stern.

"There!" said the pilot, "that's one of them now!"

[1025]
The skipper of a tramp steamer, in writing up the log recording an eventful day, rounded off his task with the entry: "Mate intoxicated." To the mate, who indignantly protested on reading it, the skipper retorted: "Well, it's true, ain't it?"

On the following day it was the mate's duty to write up the log, and he completed his account with "Skipper sober."

The captain stared at it for a moment, then exploded.

"Well, it's true, ain't it?" was the mate's rejoinder.

[1026]
Captain—"There's a tramp steamer."

Passenger—"Oh, do you ever give them anything?"

[1027]
"My dear old fellow! What's the matter? The sea's like a duck-pond!"

"I know, old boy—but I've taken six—different—remedies."

[1028]
Captain (receiving the new middy)—"Well, boy, the old story, I suppose—fool of the family sent to sea?"

Boy—"Oh, no, sir. That's all changed since your day."

[1029]
"My husband is particularly liable to sea-sickness, captain," said the woman.

The skipper nodded. "I've heard of the complaint before, ma'am," he said.

"Could you tell him what to do in case of an attack?" asked the woman.

"'Taint necessary, ma'am," replied the skipper. "He'll do it."

[1030]

The nervous passenger approached the captain timidly.

"What would happen," she asked, "if we struck a large iceberg?"

"The iceberg would pass along as if nothing had happened," replied the captain.

And the old lady was very much relieved.

[1031]

A steward stood at the gangway of the liner and kept shouting for the benefit of arriving passengers: "First-class to the right! Second-class to the left."

A young woman stepped daintily aboard with a baby in her arms. As she hesitated before the steward he bent over her and said in his chivalrous way: "First or second?"

"Oh!" said the girl, her face as red as a rose. "Oh, dear, it's—it's not mine."

[1032]

As the boat was sinking. The captain lifted his voice to ask: "Does anybody know how to pray?"

One man spoke confidently in answer:

"Yes, Captain, I do."

"That's all right then," he declared. "You go ahead and pray. The rest of us will put on life-belts. They're one short."

[1033]

"Can't something be done for that ship in distress?" asked an old lady at the seaside.

"It's all right, mam. We sent a line to the crew to come ashore," said the surfman.

Old Lady (excitedly)—"Good gracious! Must they have a formal invitation?"

[1034]

"What is the difference between valor and discretion?"

"Well, to travel on an ocean liner without tipping would be valor."

"I see."

"And to come back on a different boat would be discretion."

[1035]

Willie, accompanied by father and mother, was crossing the ocean. Father and mother were both very seasick, but Willie was immune. Throughout the trip he had been annoying the passengers. Finally his mother, turning to the father, said, in a very weak voice, gasping between each word: "Father—I wish—you'd—speak—to—Willie."

Father, turning a sea-green face toward that rampant youngster, spoke in a languid voice: "Howde-do, Willie?"

[1036]

As customary, the reporters and photographers greeted the great incoming liner and went hunting for personages. The first lady they encountered was the most beautiful woman they had ever seen. Immediately they surrounded her, and inquired her name.

The lady smiled sweetly and spoke as follows:

"Does it matter? Who would be interested in it?"

"But surely you will pose for us?" said the photographers.

"I think not," replied the lady. "You will not care for my picture when I tell you what I am not."

"What you are not!" exclaimed the reporters, puzzled.

"Yes, what I am not," said she. "I am not separated from my husband, I haven't divorced him, nor do I intend to divorce him. I am not going to spend the season at my place on Long Island. This is not the latest costume from Paris. I brought back no strange pet with me, not even a French count. That I am not an actress you have, of course, gathered long since. I have not been studying any art in Paris. And, in addition, I wouldn't think of sitting for my photograph with one knee on top of the other."

The reporters and the photographers put on their hats and proceeded along the deck.

[1037]

On a Great Lakes boat a woman passenger came out of her cabin, and saw one of the sailors pumping out the vessel. Nearby was one of the ship's officers. The woman went to him and said, "I see that you have a well on board."

"Oh, yes, madam," he replied, "we always carry one for the use of the passengers."

"That is very good," she said. "I don't like that nasty lake water."

[1038]

Wife (to seasick husband)— "Look, John, over there. Such a big ship!"

Husband—"I don't want to see any ships. Call me when you see a bus."

[1039]

"I'm planning to travel on one of those stabilized steamships."

"It will cost you more."

"Maybe, but expenses aren't what I have to keep down on my sea trips."

[1040]

Lady—"Could I see the captain?"

First Mate — "He's forward, Miss."

Lady Passenger—"I'm not afraid. I've been out with college boys.".

[1041]

A tourist, on his way to Europe, was experiencing seasickness for the first time. Calling his wife to his bedside, he said in a weak voice: "Jennie, my will is in the National Bank. Everything is left to you, dear. My various stocks you will find in my safe-deposit box." Then he said, fervently: "And Jennie, bury me on the other side. I can't stand this trip again, alive or dead."

[1042]

A master of a ship called out, "Who is below?"

A boy answered, "Will, sir."

"What are you doing?"

"Nothing, sir."

"Is Tom there?"

"Yes," said Tom.

"What are *you* doing?"

"Helping Will, sir."

[1043]

"What did the seasick man say when you asked him if you could bring him anything else?"

"He said, 'Bring me an island.' "

[1044]

Sea Captain—"There is no hope! The ship is doomed! In an hour we will all be dead!"

Seasick Passenger—"Thank Heaven!"

[1045]

The poor fellow was a light green in color as he leaned miserably over the rail near the bows.

"Sick?" asked someone walking jauntily by.

"Not a bit of it!" the suffering man plucked up enough spunk to reply. "I'm just hanging over the rail here to see how the captain cranks the darn thing."

[1046]

"How many fathoms?" asked the captain.

"Can't touch bottom, sir," was the answer.

"Well, consarn you, how near do you come to it?" the captain shot back.

[1047]

A Bostonian, who was making his first trip on a steamboat on the lower Mississippi, was much interested in watching the alligators from the upper deck. As an unusually large specimen showed his rusty back, the Bostonian asked the captain, "Is the alligator an amphibious animal?"

"Amphibious hell!" replied the captain. "He'd bite your leg off in a minute!"

SOLDIERS AND SAILORS

[1048]

The soldier asked for a furlough, so that he might get married.

"How long have you known the girl?" his superior asked.

"A week."

"Why, my lad, that's hardly long enough. I suggest that you wait a couple of months, and then, if you still want to get married, I'll grant you a furlough."

In two months the soldier was back, reminding his superior of his promise.

"So you still want to get married? My, my! I didn't suppose that a young man would stay interested in the same girl for such a long time nowadays."

"I know, sir. But it isn't the same girl, sir."

[1049]

"No," growled the quartermaster, "you can't have a new pair of shoes. The pair you have are not worn out."

"Not worn out," cried the recruit, "I don't know about that. Why, if I step on a dime I can feel if it's heads or tails."

[1050]

A soldier sought shelter in the cook's tent during a dust storm that swept over the camp during war maneuvers. He noticed that the lid of the soup kettle was awry, permitting dust to blow into the soup, and undertook to call the cook's attention to it.

"If you'd put the lid more firmly on that kettle, we wouldn't get so much dust and dirt with our soup," he said tartly.

"See here, my lad," said the cook angrily, "your business is to serve your country."

"Quite right. My business is to serve my country," the soldier answered, "but not to eat it."

[1051]

Marine Corporal (at party)—"Do you know that ugly sap of an officer standing over there? He's the meanest egg I have ever seen."

She—"Do you know who I am? I am that officer's daughter."

Corporal—"Do you know who I am?"

She—"No."

Corporal—"Thank goodness."

[1052]

Navy Bill—"What sports do you like best?"

Hollywood Katie—"Those who are free with their money and know when to say good night and go home."

[1053]

Soldier—"The bullet struck my head and went careening into space."

Friend—"You're being candid about it, anyway."

[1054]

A small boy, leading a donkey, passed by an army camp. A couple of soldiers wanted to have some fun with the lad.

"What are you holding on to your brother so tight for, sonny?" said one of them.

"So he won't join the army," the youngster replied, without blinking an eye.

[1055]

She—"You're the nicest boy that I have ever met."

He—"Tell it to the Marines."

She—"I have—to dozens of them."

[1056]

Stella—"My, your heart's beating like a drum."

Soldier—"Yeah, that's the call to arms."

[1057]

It was during World War II. The army transport was several days out of New York, and running without lights in the submarine zone. Some of the fellows were having a little sociable game of poker. In the midst of some friendly kicking and re-kicking, there was a mighty impact against the boat. All was quiet for a moment and then a voice rang out:

"We're torpedoed!"

All the card players but one jumped to their feet.

"Hold on, fellows!" shouted the one who remained seated. "You can't leave me now, I've got four aces!"

[1058]

A soldier wore size 14 shoes. One day he walked from camp to a nearby town over a muddy road. His first stop was at a bootblack's, where he mounted the stand and presented his enormous hobnails for a shine. The little bootblack sighed as he went bravely to work, but his supply of lubricating fluid was speedily exhausted. He stopped, straightened up and called to another bootblack:

"Say, Bob, lend me a spit. I've got an army contract!"

[1059]

Says Jack: "What made you go into the army, Tom?"

"Well," replied Tom, "I had no wife, and I loved war. What made you join the army, Jack?"

"Well," he replied, "I had a wife, and I loved peace, so I went to the war."

[1060]

Recruiting Officer—"What's the good of coming here and saying you're only seventeen years old! Go and walk around that yard and come back and see if you're not nineteen."

[1061]

"Remember, my son," said his mother as she bade him good-by, "when you get to camp try to be punctual in the mornings, so as not to keep breakfast waiting."

[1062]

Sergeant (speaking to raw recruit trying to drill)—"What was your occupation before entering the army?"

Rookie—"Traveling salesman, sir."

Sergeant—"Stick around; you'll get plenty of orders here."

[1063]

Recruit—"Shall I mark time with my feet, sir?"

Lieutenant (sarcastically)—"My dear fellow, did you ever hear of marking time with your hands?"

Recruit—"Yes, sir! Clocks do it."

[1064]

"How perfectly splendid to think you're one of the heroes who went over there to die for your country!"

"Like hell, I did, ma'am! I went over to make some other guy die for his."

[1065]

Passing a hand over his forehead, the worried drill-sergeant paused for breath as he surveyed the knock-kneed recruit. Then he pointed a scornful finger. "No," he declared, "you're hopeless. You'll never make a soldier. Look at you now. The top 'alf of your legs is standin' to attention, an' the bottom 'alf is standin' at ease!"

[1066]

Two veterans were boasting about their old outfits.

"Why, our company was so well drilled," said one, "that when we presented arms all you could hear was slap, slap, click."

"Pretty fair," said the other. "But when our company presented arms you could hear slap, slap, jingle."

"Jingle?" said the other. "What did that?"

"Oh, just our medals."

[1067]

Cheerful One (to newcomer, on being asked what the trenches are like)—"If yer stands up yer get sniped; if yer keeps down yer gets drowned; if yer moves about yer gets shelled; and if yer stands still yer gets court-martialed for frost-bite."

[1068]

"Why are the mules so well taken care of?"

"Because they have the biggest pull in the army."

[1069]

Soldier—"I'm hungry enough to eat a horse."

Corporal—"That's what we're getting in ten minutes."

[1070]

Artillery Commander—"Fire at Will!"

Recruit—"Where's Will?"

[1071]

"So," sobbed Illma Vaselineovitch, "Ivan Ninespotski died in battle! Do you say he uttered my name as he was dying?"

"Part of it," replied the returned soldier; "part of it."

[1072]

A sailor went dashing down the float to a boat just as it was pulling out. The boat had moved off three or four yards, and he jumped and fell, hitting athwart with the back of his head. For several minutes he lay stunned. When he came to, the boat was several hundred yards from shore. He looked back, blinked a time or two, and shouted: "Boy! Oh, boy; can I jump?"

[1073]

Back in 1917 a father and his small son were on a train. Across the aisle were seated two soldiers. Pointing to one of them, the boy asked:

"Daddy, what's he goin' to do?"

"Capture the Kaiser," the father replied.

The little boy pondered the matter for a moment, and then asked:

"Well, what's the other one going to do?"

[1074]

From a sailor's letter to his wife: "Dear Jane,—I am sending you a postal order for $5, which I hope you may get—but you may not—as this letter has to pass the Censor."

[1075]

Commander — "Now, suppose you are on your post one dark night. Suddenly a person appears from behind and wraps two arms around you. What will you call then?"

Cadet—"Let go, Honey."

[1076]

Conductor—"Can't you see the sign 'No Smoking?'"

Sailor—"Sure, mate, that's plain enough. But there are so many dippy signs here. Looka there, one says, 'Wear Nemo Corsets.' So I ain't paying attention to any of them."

[1077]

Scene: Army barracks.
Characters: Two soldiers.
"Got a pen I can borrow?"
"Sure thing, Pal."
"Some paper, too?"
"Guess so."
"Going past the mail-box when you go out?"
"Uh-huh!"
"Wait till I finish this letter."
"O. K."
"Lend me a stamp."
"Yeh."
"What is your girl's address?"

[1078]

Henderson—"Why are you in the air force now? I thought you were in the cavalry."

Peterson—"I got transferred."
"Why was that?"
"Well, after an airplane throws you out, it doesn't generally walk over and bite you."

[1079]

Captain—"Is there any difference between a fort and a fortress?"

Stude—"I should imagine a fortress would be more difficult to silence."

[1080]

Officer—"Now tell me, what is your idea of strategy?"

Stude—"It's when you're out of ammunition, but keep right on firing."

[1081]

Sergeant—"Did you shave this morning, Smith?"

Rookie—"Yes, Sir."

Sergeant — "Well, next time stand closer to the razor."

[1082]

To disobey a command of a colonel is to invite disaster, as many a green rookie had learned.

One morning on a tour of inspection a colonel stopped at the kitchen of one of the companies in his command, where he met two K. P.'s with a large soup kettle.

"Here, you K. P.," he bellowed. "Let me taste that soup." One of the men hurried back after a large spoon, which he handed respectfully to the colonel.

The officer plunged the ladle into the pot, took a mouthful of the steaming liquid, and smacked his lips critically. Then he let out a howl that could be heard at G. H. Q. half a mile away.

"Soup, you blasted fool, do you call that soup?" he roared.

"No, sir, colonel, that's just some dish water we was carrying out."

[1083]

"Once upon a time there were two sailors. Now there are gobs of them."

[1084]

A soldier in battle, happening to *bow,* a cannon-ball passed over his head, and took off that of the soldier who stood behind him.

"You see," said he, "that a man never loses *by politeness."*

[1085]

"When I was a little child," the sergeant sweetly addressed his men after an exhaustive two hours of drilling, "I had a set of wooden soldiers. There was a poor boy in the neighborhood, and after I had been to Sunday School one day and listened to a stirring talk on the beauties of charity, I was softened enough to give them to him. Then I wanted them back and cried, but my mother said, 'Don't cry, sonny, some day you'll get your wooden soldiers back.'

"And, believe me, you thick-headed bums, that day has come."

[1086]

An American doughboy and a French poilu were parting at the end of World War I.

"Au revoir!" said the poilu.

"What does that mean?" asked the doughboy.

"That's good-bye in French."

"Well, carbolic acid!" cried the doughboy.

"What does that mean?" the French soldier asked.

"That's good-bye in any language!" said the American.

[1087]

Sergeant—"What is the first thing to do when cleaning a rifle?"

Private—"Look at the number."

Sarge—"And what has that to do with it?"

Buck—"To make sure I'm cleaning my own gun."

[1088]

A captain's suspicions were aroused by a private whom he saw peering eagerly under the porch of a house in Puerto Rico, near the army camp.

"What are you doing there?" he demanded, in his gruffest tones.

"Why, sir," said the soldier, saluting, "I'm only trying to catch a chicken which I've just bought."

The lieutenant stooped and caught sight of a pair of fine fowls.

"There are two chickens under there," he exclaimed, excitedly; "I bought the other one. Catch 'em both."

[1089]

"What's the matter with you?" asked the major of a private who reported sick.

"I've got a pain in my abdomen," said the private.

"Your abdomen!" exclaimed the officer. "You mean your stomach. Don't you know that only second lieutenants have abdomens?"

[1090]

Corporal—"They say that girl you introduced me to is pretty hard, eh?"

Sergeant—"Hard is right. It would take a diamond to make an impression on her."

[1091]

Two soldiers were engaged in trench digging practice. It was a very hot day and both felt pretty tired.

"Do you remember the big posters saying, 'Enlist and see the world,'" asked one.

"Yes," replied his companion, "but why?"

"Well, I didn't know we had to dig clear through it in order to see it."

[1092]

A lady was visiting a training camp. She saw a recruit going around the parade ground with a sharp-pointed stick spearing cigarette butts and paper. Stopping him, she asked:

"Doesn't that sort of work fatigue you a great deal?"

"Oh, no," replied the soldier. "I was born to it. My father used to harpoon whales."

[1093]

A number of Legionnaires were seated around a table in a crowded restaurant when a much hurried waitress spilt a bowl of hot soup all over a chaplain. The good man spluttered, tried to control his anger, and finally sounded off with:

"Come, come! One of you sinful comrades say something appropriate!"

[1094]

A naval officer fell overboard. He was rescued by a deck hand. The officer asked how he could reward him.

"The best way, sir," said the gob, "is to say nothing about it. If the other fellows knew I'd pulled you out, they'd chuck me in."

[1095]

Officer (examining recruit)—"Have you any scars on you?"

Recruit—"No sir, but I can give you a cigarette."

[1096]

An old man was making his first visit to an army post. He watched two sentries passing and repassing each other in silence.

After several minutes he stepped up to them as they were passing and said:

"Come now, boys, why not make up and be friend?"

[1097]

"Where did you get that turkey?" asked the colonel of a Texas regiment, to one of his amiable recruits, who came into camp with a fine bird.

"Stole it," was the laconic reply.

"Ah," said the colonel, triumphantly, to a bystander, "you see my boys may steal, but they won't lie."

[1098]

The wife and daughter of Lieutenant Berry were halted by a sentry on duty, who had orders to allow no one to enter by that gate.

"Sorry, but you will have to go around to the main gate."

"Oh, but we're the Berrys."

"Lady, I don't care if you're the cat's meow! You can't go through this gate."

[1099]

"Bang!" went the rifles at the maneuvers. "Oo-oo!" screamed the pretty girl—a nice, decorous, surprised little scream. She stepped backward into the arms of a young man.

"Oh!" said she, blushing. "I was frightened by the rifles. I beg your pardon."

"Not at all," said the young man. "Let's go over and watch the artillery."

[1100]

"Halt," yelled the sergeant to a new squad of recruits. But one of them marched on.

"Here, Jones, what were you doing before you joined the Army?" yelled the sergeant.

"A horse driver, sir," replied Jones.

When the squad was marching again the sergeant cried: "Squad halt! Jones, whoa."

[1101]
Sailor—"Don't bother me. I am writing to my girl."
Marine—"But why are you writing so slowly?"
Sailor—"She can't read very fast."

[1102]
A sailor's enlistment in the navy expired. A friend gob asked him what he thought of the sea.
"Just this much," he said. "I'm going to put an oar over my shoulder and start walking inland—and I'm going to keep on walking and walking and walking until some one stops me and asks, 'What's that thing you've got over your shoulder?' Then I'm going to settle right down there until I die."

[1103]
Sergeant (bursting in during dinner)—"Any complaints?"
Timid Doughboy—"If you please, the meat's terribly funny."
Sergeant—"Well, then, laugh."

[1104]
An officer on board a battleship was drilling his men.
"I want every man to lie on his back, put his legs in the air, and move them as if he were riding a bicycle," he explained. "Now begin!"
After a short effort, one of the men stopped.
"Why have you stopped, Cassidy?" asked the officer.
"If you plaze," was the reply, "Oi'm free-wheeling."

[1105]
Two of Uncle Sam's sailors, retiring from the sea, purchased a small saloon in a country town. The place was painted inside and out, being closed for that purpose.
The villagers, after a few days,

gathered outside the place and one of them knocked at the door. A window opened, and one of the former sailors inquired the reason for the gathering outside.
"We want to know when you are going to open up," was the reply.
"Open up?" retorted the man at the window, "we bought this place for ourselves!"

[1106]
"What must a man be that he shall be buried with military honors?"
"He must be a Captain."
"Then I lose the bet."
"What did you bet?"
"I bet he must be dead."

[1107]
Captain—"What are you scratching your head for, Private Honeywell?"
Draftee—"Guess ah got 'rithmetic bugs."
Captain—"What are arithmetic bugs?"
Draftee—"Cooties."
Captain—"Why do you call them arithmetic bugs?"
Draftee—"Because they add to mah misery, subtract from mah pleasure, divide mah attenshun, and multiply like the dickens."

[1108]
"And there, son, you have the story of your dad during World War II."
"Yes, Dad, but why did they need all the other soldiers?"

[1109]
Visitor—"Are you the Executive Officer? I have a grandson serving on board."
Any Exec—"Yes, madam. He's away on leave just now attending your funeral."

[1110]

Private Shepherd had been in the Army a week when his sergeant asked:

"What do you think of the Army as far as you've gone?"

"I may like it after awhile," he replied, "but just now I think there's too much drilling and fussing around between meals."

[1111]

"Mr. Congressman," said an American major, "I always observe that those persons who have a great deal to say about being ready to shed their last drop of blood, are amazingly particular about the first drop."

[1112]

A young naval student was being put through the paces by an old sea-captain. "What would you do if a sudden storm sprang up on the starboard?"

"Throw out an anchor, sir."

"What would you do if another storm sprang up aft?"

"Throw out another anchor, sir."

"And if another terrific storm sprang up forward, what would you do?"

"Throw out another anchor."

"Hold on," said the Captain, "where are you getting all your anchors from?"

"From the same place you're getting your storms, sir."

[1113]

During World War II some of our soldiers were billeted with the English, and they taught the English boys poker. One Englishman picked up his hand and said, "I don't know your poker game, but I'll wager a pound."

An enlisted man looked at his hand and found he had four aces. He said, "I don't know much about your money, but I'll see your pound, and raise you a ton."

[1114]

A Civil War soldier telling his mother of the terrible rifle fire at Chickamauga, was asked by her why he did not get behind a tree. "Tree!" said he. "There wasn't enough for the officers!"

[1115]

Captain—"Did you enjoy your leave, lieutenant?"

Paymaster—"Yes, but there's nothing like the feeling of a good desk under your feet again."

[1116]

Lady—"How were you wounded, my kind man?"

Soldier—"By a shell, lady."

Lady—"Did it explode?"

Soldier—"No. It crept up close and bit me."

[1117]

A sergeant was drilling raw recruits.

"Right turn!" he cried. Then followed quickly, "Left turn!" Again "Right turn!"

One rookie left the ranks and started off towards the barracks.

"Hey, you!" yelled the sergeant. "Where are you going?"

"I've had enough," replied the recruit in a disgusted tone. "You don't know your own mind for two minutes runnin'!"

[1118]

His friend was worrying. "Tell me all about it. Get it off your chest."

"I wish I could," groaned the sailor. "I've got the name Maude tattooed there, and I'm engaged to marry Bertha."

[1119]

"I want a shave," said the disgruntled Sergeant as he climbed into the barber's chair. "No haircut, no shampoo, no rum, witch hazel, hair tonic, hot towels or face massage. I don't want the manicurist to hold my hand, nor the bootblack to handle my feet. I don't want to be brushed off, and I'll put on my coat myself. I just want a plain shave, with no trimmings. Understand that?"

"Yes, sir," said the barber quietly. "Lather, sir?"

[1120]

Sergeant—"What would you do if an appeal came through for volunteers?"

Recruit—"I would step aside and let them pass."

[1121]

"Keep on fighting, boys," said the general, "never say die. Never give up till your last shot is fired. When it is fired, then run. I'm a little lame so I'm starting now."

[1122]

Officer (just bawled out)—"Not a man in this division will be given liberty this afternoon."

Voice—"Give me liberty or give me death!"

Officer—"Who said that?"

Voice—"Patrick Henry."

[1123]

"Want to leave me, Mary? I thought you were quite comfortable. What is it for—something private?"

"No, ma'am, it's a sergeant."

[1124]

A new volunteer at a national guard encampment who had not quite learned his business, was on sentry duty, one night, when a friend brought a pie from the canteen.

As he sat on the grass eating pie, the major sauntered up in undress uniform. The sentry, not recognizing him, did not salute, and the major stopped and said:

"What's that you have there?"

"Pie," said the sentry, good-naturedly. "Apple pie. Have a bite?"

The major frowned.

"Do you know who I am?" he asked.

"No," said the sentry, "unless you're the major's groom."

The major shook his head.

"Guess again," he growled.

"The barber from the village?"

"No."

"Maybe"—here the sentry laughed—"maybe you're the major himself?"

"That's right. I am the major," was the stern reply.

The sentry scrambled to his feet.

"Good gracious!" he exclaimed. "Hold the pie, will you, while I present arms!"

[1125]

Barber—"Haven't I shaved you before, sir?"

Customer—"No, I got that scar in France."

[1126]

Sergeant—"Why is it important not to lose your head in an attack?"

Recruit—"Because that would leave no place to put the helmet."

[1127]

"What were you in the war?" he asked.

"A private," the veteran answered.

And Diogenes blew out his lamp and went home.

[1128]

A soldier went to his colonel and asked for leave to go home to help his wife with the spring house-cleaning.

"I don't like to refuse you," said the colonel, "but I've just received a letter from your wife saying that you are no use around the house."

The soldier saluted and turned to go. At the door he stopped:

"Colonel, there are two persons in this regiment who handle the truth loosely, and I'm one of them. I'm not married."

[1129]

Mess Cook—"Did you say you wanted those eggs turned over?"

Hard-bitten Gob—"Yeah, to the Museum of Natural History."

[1130]

She—"So you were hurt in the war? Where were you wounded?"

He—"Lady, I was hit in the Dardanelles."

She—"How dreadful!"

[1131]

The debutante was surrounded by an admiring crowd of officers of the nearby military post. Mama was standing near by enjoying her daughter's social success. The discussion was over the quarrel of the day before between two brother officers.

"What was the *casus belli?*" asked the fair debutante.

"Maud!" exclaimed mama, in a shocked voice, "how often have I told you to say stomach?"

[1132]

The first officer called a deck-hand to him and said, "Go below and break up that crap-game." The sailor disappeared below and remained for the better part of an hour. Upon his return his superior officer demanded: "Did you succeed in breaking up that game?"

"Yes, sir," replied the gob.

"Well, what in thunder took you so long?"

"Well, sir," the sailor replied, "I had only two bits to start with!"

[1133]

Old Lady to Old Tar—"Excuse me. Do those tattoo marks wash off?"

Old Tar—"I can't say, lady."

[1134]

Gob (writing a letter, to mate sitting on bunk)—"Hey, Joe, take yer shirt off. I want to see how yer spell Matilda."

[1135]

"I'll never forget Christmas in 1930. I spent the whole day peeling spuds."

"What happened?"

"Our sergeant asked me what I wanted for Christmas and I told him the truth."

"What did you tell him?"

"A new sergeant."

[1136]

A soldier was having refreshments at one of the army canteens when a friend joined him.

"Hullo, Bill," he said. "What have you got there, tea or coffee?"

"They didn't say," he replied sadly.

[1137]

"Raise the right leg and hold it at right angle to the body," commanded the sergeant.

A recruit raised his left leg by mistake, so that it was extended close to the right leg of the file at the left.

"Who's that raising both legs?" called out the sergeant severely.

[1138]
Vice Admiral Kerr (addressing the middies of the *St. Vincent*)—"If you are fortunate enough to die while on active service, it provides you with a beautiful funeral, headed by a wonderful band."

[1139]
The old soldier was telling of his thrilling adventures on the field of battle.

"Then," he said, "the surgeons took me up and laid me in the ammunition wagon, and—"

"Look here," said one of his listeners, "you don't mean the ammunition wagon! You mean the ambulance."

"No," he insisted, "I was so full of bullets that they decided I ought to go in the ammunition wagon."

[1140]
A rookie passing the mess hall, asked the cook:

"What's on the menu tonight?"

"Oh, we have thousands of things to eat tonight."

"What are they?"

"Beans!"

[1141]
The recruit, on maneuvers for the first time, heard the sound of an approaching horse in the darkness.

"Halt! Who goes there?" he challenged.

"Commanding officer," came the reply.

"Dismount, sir, and advance to be recognized," called the recruit.

The officer did so, and the recruit saluted smartly and said: "Proceed, sir."

As he remounted, the C.O. asked, "By the way, who posted you here?"

"No one, sir," said the recruit. "I'm just practicing."

[1142]
The regiment was trekking through the desert: it was arid and parched and not a drop of water was to be found. One recruit sat sadly on a stone, his head in his hands.

"What's the matter with him?" asked the sergeant.

"Home sickness," said Private Smith.

"We've all got that."

"Yes, but his is worse than for most of us—his father owns a saloon!"

[1143]
Corporal—"Squad's right!"
Rear Rank—"After all these years he admits it."

[1144]
Captain—"Coward, why did you run when the battle began?"
Private—"Captain, that was no battle. It looked like a plain shell game to me."

[1145]
A general and a colonel were walking down the street. They met many privates, and each time the colonel would salute he would mutter, "The same to you."

The general's curiosity soon got the better of him, and he asked: "Why do you always say that?"

The colonel answered: "I was once a private and I know what they are thinking."

POLICE AND PRISONERS

[1146]
The town of Plunkville has a regulation against bare legs on the street. Flesh-colored hose were a problem. They solved that nicely

by watching for the seam. Then came seamless hose.

"How can I tell whether these girls have bare legs or not?" was the plaint of a policeman on guard.

"Pinch 'em," was the only suggestion he got.

[1147]

Visitor—"And you always did your daring robberies single-handed? Why didn't you have a pal?"

Prisoner—"Well, sir, I wuz afraid he might turn out to be dishonest."

[1148]

Minister (calling on inmate of prison)—"Remember, that stone walls do not a prison make, nor iron bars a cage."

"Well, they've got me hypnotized then; that's all."

[1149]

A man who was wanted by the police had been photographed in six different positions and the pictures were circulated among the police.

The chief in a small town wrote headquarters a few days later, saying:

"I duly received the pictures of the six miscreants whose capture is desired. I have arrested five of them; the sixth is under observation and will be taken soon."

[1150]

Two bandits were holding up a train; one fellow, a big man, walks in at one end of the sleeping car, and a little fellow walks in at the other end of the car.

The big fellow says, "Don't be alarmed; we're not going to hurt anybody; we're going to rob the men, and we're going to kiss the women."

The little fellow says, "Aw, Bill,

we don't want to hurt these women's feelings; all we want here is money."

There was an old maid in one of the sections, and she stood up on her feet and said, "Say, young feller, you shut up and mind your own business; the big fellow's robbing this train."

[1151]

"My good man," said the kindly lady uplifter, "I hope that since you have come here you have had time for meditation and have decided to correct your faults."

"I have that, mum," replied the prisoner. "Believe me, the next job I pull, this baby wears gloves."

[1152]

Some people are never satisfied. For example, the prisoner who complained of the books the chaplain gave him to read.

"Nutt'n but continued stories," he grumbled. "An' I'm to be hung next Tuesday."

[1153]

Magistrate (to prisoner)—"What is your name?"

Prisoner—"S-s-sam   S-s-sissons, S-s-sir."

Magistrate—"Where do you live?"

Prisoner—"S-s-seventy seven S-s-surrey street. S-s-sir."

Magistrate (to policeman)—"Officer, what is this man charged with?"

Officer—"Begorry, yer honor. Oi think he must be charged with soda wather."

[1154]

"You admit having broken into the same dress shop four times. What did you steal?"

"A dress for my wife, but she made me change it three times."

[1155]
Burglar at home to young son—
"I did not spank you for taking the jam, my boy, but for leaving your fingerprints."

[1156]
The eminent alienist recognized the thug who was holding him up. "Look here," he protested, "I'm your benefactor. Don't you recall that I once saved you from a life sentence by proving you crazy?"

"Sure, I remember you now," the thug said as he continued his work. "And ain't holdin' up your benefactor a crazy thing to do?"

[1157]
A prosperous gangster, having arrived to dine with some of his friends, discovered that he had forgotten to bring his gun. He telephoned to his valet, and the following conversation took place:

Gangster—"Say, George, I want you to hurry along here with my gun."

Valet—"Your what?"

Gangster—"My gun."

Valet—"I still can't hear."

Gangster—"My gun, G-U-N, gun, 'G' for 'justice,' 'U' for 'Europe,' and 'N' for 'pneumonia'."

[1158]
Two burglars had broken into a clothing store and were busy sorting out some suits when one of them saw one marked $125.00.

"Bert, look at the price of that one," he said. "Why, it's downright robbery, ain't it?"

[1159]
Fred Flatfoot—"We'd better keep 'Fingers' Tortelli under surveillance."

Donald Dick—"Yeah and we'd better keep watching him, too."

[1160]
In the office of the prison warden a notorious crook was being divested of the contents of his pockets. As each article was removed, it was carefully examined, listed and then placed temporarily on a nearby desk. Among the articles was a badly tarnished silver dollar.

The prisoner pointed to the dull-looking coin and in a suppliant tone asked the warden:

"Would you mind letting me keep that with me?"

"Why?" asked the warden.

"Oh, just a little sentiment, I suppose," the prisoner explained. "You know, it's the first dollar I ever stole."

[1161]
Convict (just arrived)—"This is an old-fashioned prison. Why don't they get some up-to-date machinery?"

Guard—"What do you mean?"

Convict—"Well, it's just like it was when I was here twenty years ago—we still crack rocks by hand."

[1162]
Citizen—"I've nothing—and my watch has only sentimental value."

Bandit—"Fork it over. I feel like a good cry, anyway."

[1163]
Bandit (to bank teller)—"Get a move on, you! Don't you know I can only park my car out there for ten minutes?"

[1164]
Social Worker—"And what is your name, my good man?"

The Convict—"999."

Social Worker—"O, but that's not your real name."

Convict—"Naw, that's only me pen name."

[1165]

The Blankville moving picture theatre installed a burglar alarm in the box office. In case of robbery, all the girl selling tickets had to do was to press a pedal sunk in the floor behind her foot. This rang a bell rigged up in police headquarters.

About two days after the burglar alarm had been installed, a gunman poked a pistol through the window of the box office and, in usual gunman fashion, demanded the cash therein. The girl, before handing over the money, pressed her foot on the pedal. At this point, however, the phone began to ring, and as the girl reached over to answer it the man grabbed the phone himself and lifted the receiver.

"This is the Police Department," the irate voice at the other end of the wire said. "Say, do you know you've got your foot on the pedal that rings the alarm over here?"

[1166]

Gangster—"Come on! Let's figure up how much we made on this job."

Accomplice—"Hell, no! I'm tired. Let's wait and look in the morning papers."

[1167]

"What brought you here, my man?" asked the prison visitor.

"Just plain absent-mindedness," replied the prisoner.

"Why, how could that be?"

"I forgot to change the engine number of the car before I sold it."

[1168]

Police Chief—"How's that murder story?"

Cop—"The same old bunk! They catch the murderer in the end!"

[1169]

Sergeant—"Are you married?"

Prisoner—"No, sir."

Officer—"He's a liar, Sergeant. When we searched him we found in his pockets a clipped recipe for curing croup, a sample of silk, and two unposted letters in a woman's handwriting a week old."

[1170]

Timid Householder (resourcefully, after discovering two burglars at work)—"D-d-don't take any n-notice of me—I'm only walking in my s-s-sleep."

[1171]

The policeman's son was learning music.

"How many beats are there to the bar in this piece of music, Dad?"

"Fancy asking a policeman a question like that," said the boy's mother. "If you asked your daddy how many bars there were to the beat he might have been able to tell you!"

[1172]

"Did you give that mug the third degree?" asked the police chief.

"Yes. We browbeat and badgered him with every question we could think of."

"What did he do?"

"He dozed off and merely said now and then: 'Yes, my dear, you are perfectly right.'"

[1173]

Visitor—"What terrible crime has this man committed?"

Jailer—"He has done nothing. He merely happened to be passing when 'Gyp the Blood' tried to kill a man, and he is held in prison as a witness."

"Where is 'Gyp the Blood?'"

"He is out on bail."

[1174]
Policeman (calling up precinct) —"A man has been robbed down here, and I've got one of them."
Chief—"Which one have you?"
Policeman—"The man that was robbed."

[1175]
Officer—"I ketched this here guy pinchin' bananas off a fruit-stand."
Magistrate—"Aha! 'personating an officer! Two years."

[1176]
First Prisoner—"What are you in for?"
Second Prisoner—"Want to be a warden, so I thought I'd start from the bottom."

[1177]
Visitor (at the jail)—"Poor man! What are you locked up here for?"
Prisoner (wearily)—"I suppose they think I'd get out if I wasn't."

[1178]
Guard—"Sir, the prisoners are rioting again."
Warden — "What's the matter now?"
Guard—"The chef used to cook for a fraternity."

[1179]
Police Sergeant—"Have you caught that burglar yet?"
Cop—"No, but we've got him so scared that he doesn't dare show himself when we're around."

[1180]
A social worker, visiting a prison, was much impressed by the melancholy attitude of one man she found.
"My poor man," she sympathized, "what is the length of your term?"
"Depends on politics, lady," replied the melancholy one. "I'm the warden."

[1181]
A Missouri county grand jury once passed the following resolutions:
Resolved, that the present jail is insufficient, and that another ought to be built.
Resolved, that the materials of the old jail be used in constructing the new one.
Resolved, that the old jail shall not be taken down until the new one is finished.

[1182]
"Great new improvement, this, the Police Department is installing. They're going to make every policeman wear rubber heels from now on, while he's on duty."
"What in the world for?"
"To keep them from waking each other up."

[1183]
A burglar was one night engaged in stowing a good haul of plunder in his bag when he was startled by a touch on the shoulder, and, turning his head, he beheld a venerable, mild-eyed clergyman gazing sadly at him.
"Oh, my brother," groaned the reverend gentleman, "wouldst thou rob me? Turn, I beseech thee—turn from thy evil ways. Return those stolen goods and depart in peace, for I am merciful and forgive. Begone!"
And the burglar, only too thankful at not being given into custody of the police, obeyed and slunk swiftly off.
Then the good old man carefully and quietly packed the plunder into another bag and walked softly (so as not to disturb the slumber of the inmates) out of the house and away into the silent night.

[1184]

Visitor—"Why are you here, my poor man?"

Prisoner—"I'm a victim of dat unlucky 13, lady."

Visitor—"Indeed! How's that?"

Prisoner — "Twelve jurors and one judge."

[1185]

Old Lady (visiting State Prison) —"I suppose, my poor man, it was poverty brought you to this."

Counterfeiter—"On the contrary, mum, I was just coining money."

[1186]

Prisoner—"The judge sent me here for the rest of my life."

Prison Guard—"Got any complaints?"

Prisoner—"Do you call breaking rock with a hammer a rest?"

[1187]

Burglar—"Get ready to die. I'm going to shoot you."

Victim—"Why?"

Burglar—"I've always said I'd shoot anyone who looked like me."

Victim—"Do I look like you?"

Burglar—"Yes."

Victim—"Then shoot."

[1188]

The lane was dark and deserted, and Jones was suddenly accosted by two men, the bigger of whom said politely: "Excuse me, sir—I wonder if you could oblige me with the loan of a penny?"

"Why—er—yes, I think so," replied Jones. "But may I ask for what purpose you require it?"

"Oh, certainly, sir," the other replied. "My pal and I wish to toss the coin to decide our little argument as to which of us shall have your watch, and which your wallet!"

[1189]

"What do they mean by 'the city's pulse?'"

"Oh, I suppose it has something to do with the policemen's beats."

[1190]

A wayfaring man was gagged and bound to a tree. A passer-by removed the gag and heard the poor victim's story of how he had been left there absolutely helpless after the thugs had taken everything but his watch.

"You are sure you are unable to make a move?" asked the passer-by.

"I am unable to make a move," the unhappy man groaned.

"In that case," said the stranger, "I think I'll help myself to the watch."

[1191]

"But how did the police spot you in your woman's disguise?"

"I passed a milliner's shop without looking in at the window."

[1192]

Guard (to prisoner about to be electrocuted)—"Have you any last words?"

Prisoner—"Yeah, I'd like to offer my seat to a lady."

[1193]

Welfare Worker—"And have you any plans for the future when your sentence expires?"

The Incorrigible—"Yus. I've got the plans of two joolers and a post-office to start with."

[1194]

A murderer who was being led to the gallows, saw a crowd of people running on before.

"Don't be in such a hurry," said he to them. "I can assure you nothing will be done *without me.*"

[1195]

Two expert pickpockets were strolling along the road together.

Every now and then one of them would stop, take out his watch and look at it.

His companion began to get annoyed.

"I say, Jim," he said, "what's up with you? Why d'yer keep looking at your ticker? Ain't it going, or something?"

"I'm not looking at it to see the time," said the other; "I'm looking at it to make sure that it's still there!"

[1196]

Prison Warden—"I've had charge of this prison for ten years. We're going to celebrate. What kind of a party do you boys suggest?"

Prisoners—"Open house."

[1197]

"See? My dog will come when I blow this police whistle."

"I wonder whether we could train the police to do that?"

[1198]

"Excuse me, sir, do you happen to have seen a policeman anywhere about here?"

"I am sorry, but I have not seen a sign of one."

"All right, hurry up and give me your watch and pocketbook then."

[1199]

Warden—"We must set you to work. What can you do?"

Forger—"Give me a week's practise and I will sign your checks for you."

[1200]

"I am at your service, ma'am," the burglar said when the lady of the house caught him stealing her silver.

[1201]

"Modern science cost me a year of my life."

"A badly managed operation?"

"No, my finger-prints were responsible."

[1202]

At a busy corner a traffic officer saw an old lady beckon to him. He held up two dozen cars, trucks and taxicabs to get to her side and inquire, "What is it, ma'am?"

The old lady smiled and put her hand on his arm. "Officer," she said in a soft voice, "I just want to tell you that your number is the number of my favorite hymn."

[1203]

First Burglar — "I need eyeglasses."

Second Burglar — "What makes you think so?"

First Burglar — "Well, I was twirling the knobs of a safe and a dance-orchestra began to play."

[1204]

An old offender being asked whether he had committed all the crimes he was charged with, answered, "I have done still worse! I suffered myself to be *apprehended*."

[1205]

The young policeman was undergoing his examination. "Now assume," said the examiner, "that you are accosted by a charming young lady late one evening, who tells you that a strange man has embraced and kissed her. What would you do?"

The young policeman did not hesitate long. "I should—er—endeavor to reconstruct the crime with the young lady's assistance," he replied.

INSANE PERSONS

[1206]

A student of Social Research visited a local insane asylum. In one of the cells sat a man whose only garment was a hat.

"My good man," cried the interested student, "that's no way to be sitting around. Why don't you put some clothes on?"

"Because," replied the inmate sadly, "nobody ever comes to see me."

"But," said the student, "why do you wear a hat?"

The nut shrugged his shoulders. "Oh," he exclaimed "somebody *might* come."

[1207]

A lunatic was sitting in his cell, playing solitaire. Another nut was watching. Finally the kibitzer spoke up.

"Wait a minute!" he cried. "I just caught you cheating yourself!"

The first nut placed a finger to his lips.

"Shh," he whispered. "Don't tell anybody—but, for years, I've been cheating myself at solitaire."

"You don't say," said his amazed pal. "Don't you ever catch yourself cheating?"

The first nut shook his head.

"Naw," he returned proudly. "I'm too clever!"

[1208]

A doctor came up to a patient in an insane asylum, slapped him on the back, and said: "Well, old man, you're all right. You can run along and write your folks that you'll be back home in two weeks as good as new."

The patient went off gayly to write his letter. He had it finished and sealed, but when he was licking the stamp it slipped through his fingers to the floor, lighted on the back of a cockroach that was passing, and stuck. The patient hadn't seen the cockroach—what he did see was his escaped postage stamp zigzagging aimlessly across the floor to the baseboard, wavering up over the baseboard, and following a crooked track up the wall and across the ceiling. In depressed silence he tore up the letter he had just written and dropped the pieces on the floor.

"Two weeks! Hell!" he said. "I won't be out of here in three years."

[1209]

Two inmates of an asylum had been given a hammer and one nail. One of the inmates had placed the nail head first against the wall and started hammering. Seeing that he was getting no appreciable results, he said to his companion:

"The bird who made this nail is crazy. He put the point on the wrong end."

"Oh, no!" replied the other. "You're the one that's crazy—this nail goes in the opposite wall."

[1210]

A number of visitors in an insane asylum were being shown around by an employe.

"You see that man over there, he thinks he is the Lord," said the employe.

One of the visitors then asked the insane one whether he really made the earth in seven days.

The nut looked at him contemptuously, and said as he walked away, "I'm not in the mood to talk shop!"

[1211]

Visitor to asylum—"Why do you say you are George Washington? The last time I was here you said you were Napoleon Bonaparte."

Inmate—"Yes, that's true, but that was by my first wife."

[1212]

A fool, a barber, and a bald-headed man were travelling together. Losing their way, they were forced to sleep in the open air; and, to avert danger, it was agreed to watch by turns.

The first lot fell on the barber, who, for amusement, shaved the fool's head while he was sleeping. He then awoke him, and the fool, raising his hand to scratch his head, exclaimed: Here's a pretty mistake; you have awakened the old bald-headed man instead of me."

[1213]

Nurse (in insane asylum)—"There is a man outside who wants to know if we have lost any male inmates."

Doctor—"Why?"

Nurse—"He says that someone has run off with his wife."

[1214]

A man was being examined in lunacy proceedings.

"Who was our first President?" asked his lawyer.

"Washington."

"Right; and who was our second President?"

"John Adams."

"Correct."

There was a pause. "He's doing splendidly," whispered a friend of the lawyer. "Why don't you keep on?"

"I ain't sure who was the third President myself."

[1215]

A stranger mistook an insane asylum for a college. Realizing his mistake he said to a guard:

"I suppose after all there isn't much difference between them."

"Oh yes, there is," replied the guard. "In this place you've got to show improvement before you can get out."

[1216]

An inmate of the asylum who was pushing a wheelbarrow upside down was stopped by a visitor who asked: "What's the idea?"

"I'm not crazy," was the retort. "Yesterday they filled it with bricks."

[1217]

A passenger in an airplane was far up in the sky when the pilot began to laugh hysterically.

Passenger—"What's the joke?"

Pilot—"I'm thinking of what they'll say at the asylum when they find out I have escaped."

[1218]

A visitor who was being shown over a lunatic asylum inquired of his guide what method was employed to discover when the inmates were sufficiently recovered to be discharged.

"Well," replied he, "you see, it's this way. We have a big trough of water and we turn on the tap. We leave it running and tell them to bail out the water with pails until they have emptied the trough."

"How does that prove it?" asked the visitor.

"Well," said the guide, "the ones who are not crazy will turn off the tap."

"Well I declare. I never would have thought of that," said the visitor.

[1219]

A nut was smoking a cigarette—but he was placing the lighted end in his mouth. A passerby watched the nut for a moment, and then couldn't stand it any longer.

"Hey, you!" he shouted. "What's the idea of putting a lighted cigarette in your mouth?"

The nut shrugged.

"It's the best I can do," he sighed. "I can't afford a cigar."

[1220]

A farmer was passing the insane asylum with a load of fertilizer. An inmate called through the fence, "What are you hauling?"

"Fertilizer," replied the farmer.

"What are you going to do with it?"

"Put it on my strawberries."

"And we put cream on ours, and they say we're crazy," the inmate countered.

[1221]

Two pipe-smokers were conversing in an opium-den.

One said casually: "I've just decided to buy all the diamond and emerald mines in the world."

The second dreamy gent considered this seriously for a few moments, and then murmured softly: "I don't know that I care to sell."

[1222]

A lady visiting an asylum displayed a great interest in one old man particularly. "And how long have you been here, my man?" she inquired.

"Twelve years," was the answer.

"Do they treat you well?"

"Yes."

After addressing a few more questions to him the visitor passed on. She noticed a smile broadening on the face of her attendant, and on asking the cause heard with consternation that the old man was none other than the medical superintendent. She hurried back to make apologies. How successful she was may be gathered from these words: "I am sorry, doctor. I will never be governed by appearances again."

[1223]

"Why are you so sad?" a friend asked a man whose aunt had just died. "You never appeared to care much for the poor old lady."

"I didn't," admitted the sad man, "but I was the means of keeping her in a lunatic asylum during the last five years of her life. She has left me all her money, and now I've got to prove that she was of sound mind!"

[1224]

A distinguished visitor to an insane asylum went to the telephone and found difficulty in getting his connection. Exasperated, he shouted to the operator:

"Look here, girl, do you know who I am?"

"No," was the calm reply, "but I know *where* you are."

[1225]

Visitor—"I suppose you have to be constantly on the alert to prevent the escape of lunatics."

Attendant—"Yes; nearly all of them are just crazy to get out."

[1226]

A non compos mentis patiently held a fish pole and line in his asylum retreat.

"What are you fishing for, my man?" asked a visitor.

"Suckers," he said, without looking up.

"Caught any?"

"You're the ninth!"

[1227]

A party of visitors were being shown over a large lunatic asylum. The doctor who acted as guide paused before a cell in which a man sat nursing a large doll which was dressed in the gay and gaudy costume of an up-to-date young lady.

"This poor fellow," explained the doctor, "has a very sad history. See how he is bending over that doll and fondling it so tenderly. He spends most of his time like that. He was engaged to a girl, of whom he was very fond. She jilted him, however, and married another man, while this one lost his reason over the affair."

The visitors were much touched, and uttered various expressions of sympathy.

They passed to the next cell, which was barred and thickly padded.

"And this," resumed the doctor, "is the other man."

[1228]

"Dear me!" said the lady to the superintendent of the insane asylum, "what a vicious look that woman has we passed just now in the corridor. Is she dangerous?"

"Yes, at times," replied the superintendent evasively.

"But why do you allow her such freedom?"

"Can't help it."

"But isn't she an inmate and under your control?"

"No, she's neither under my control nor an inmate. She's my wife."

[1229]

A minister of the Gospel was conducting religious services in an asylum for the insane. His discourse was suddenly interrupted by one of the inmates crying out wildly:

"I say, have we got to listen to this tommyrot?"

The minister, surprised and confused, turned to the keeper and said:

"Shall I stop speaking?"

The keeper replied:

"No, no; keep right on, that won't happen again. That man has only one sane moment every seven years."

[1230]

Patient (at lunatic asylum)— "We like you better than the last doctor."

New Doctor (flattered)—"How is that?"

Patient—"You seem more like one of us."

[1231]

A young mill hand was sent to a state asylum. After he had been there for a few weeks, a fellow worker visited him.

"Hello, Jim!" he said. "How are you getting along?"

"I'm gettin' on fine," said the patient.

"Glad to hear it. I suppose you'll be comin' back to the mill soon?"

"What!" exclaimed Jim. "Do you think I'd leave a big, fine house like this and a grand garden to come back and work in a mill? You must think I am crazy!"

DRUNKS

[1232]

"Waiter—hic—bring me a dish o' prunes."

"Stewed, sir?"

"Thash none o' your bishness."

[1233]

"What are you doing?"

"I am playing a game."

"What is the game called?"

"The game is called Mississippi."

"How do you play the game called Mississippi?"

"Well, first you take a long, tall glass, and fill it up with some delightful mixture, like 68c whiskey. Then you get a partner. This partner is your opponent. How can a partner be an opponent? A partner can be an opponent in this game because I invented it myself, and I made my own rules up as I went along.

"Then you and your partner-opponent start playing the game called 'Mississippi.' First you take a sip. Then your partner takes a sip. Then you take a sip. Then your partner takes a sip. Then you take a sip. And so on. And the first one to say Mississippi is a sissy."

[1234]

A drunk searching diligently along the edge of the pavement and the gutter was approached by an officer who said:

"What are you looking for?"

"I just lost fifty cents."

"Where did you lose it?"

"About a half a block down the street."

"Well, why are you looking for it here?" asked the impatient officer.

"Oh," replied the drunk, "the light's much better here."

[1235]

Drunk (stopping street car)— "Say—thish car go to Fortieth Street?"

Conductor—"Yes."

Drunk—"Well, g'bye an' God blesh you."

[1236]

Thoughtful Friend—"My good man, why don't you take the street-car home?"

Illuminated One—"Sh no ushe. My wife wouldn't let me keep it in the houshe."

[1237]

"One drink always makes me dizzy."

"Really?"

"Yes — and it's usually the eigh'h."

[1238]

"Was my husband intoxicated when he came home last night, Polly?"

"I didn't notice anything, ma'am. He only asked for a mirror to see who he was."

[1239]

Two intoxicated gentlemen wandered into a public dance hall. One asked the location of the cloak room and was told to take the first door to the right and to go down three steps. Due to the liquor-logged condition of his brain, he got the elevator door by mistake and fell five stories to the basement. His friend watched his sudden departure and leaning through the door called out:

"What are you doing down there?"

After a short pause the answer came floating up the shaft:

"Hanging up my coat. Look out for that first step—it's an awful one."

[1240]

She-sez—"I have no sympathy for a man who gets drunk every night."

He-sez — "A man who gets drunk every night doesn't need sympathy."

[1241]

A northern gentleman was being entertained by a southern colonel on a fishing-trip. It was his first visit to the South, and the mosquitoes were so bothersome that he was unable to sleep, while at the same time he could hear his friend snoring audibly.

The next morning he approached the old darky who was doing the cooking.

"Jim," he said, "how is it the colonel is able to sleep so soundly with so many mosquitoes around?"

"I'll tell yo', boss," the darky replied, "de fust part of de night de kernel is too full to pay any 'tenshum to de skeeters, and de last part of de night de skeeters is too full to pay any 'tenshum to de kernel."

[1242]

Drunk (to bartender) — "Hey, gimmie a horse's neck."

Second Drunk — "I'll have a horse's tail. There's no use killing two horses."

[1243]

The drunk hailed a cab and fell into the back seat.

"Shay, driver," he ordered, "drive me around the block a hundred times."

The driver was startled, but he obliged just the same. Around and around the block they went. And on the sixty-fifth trip, the stew leaned forward.

"Step on it, buddy," he hiccoughed. "I'm in a hurry."

[1244]

Cop—"Say, fellow, do you know who I am?"

Drunk—"I can't shay ash I do, but if you'll tell me where you live, I'll help you home."

[1245]

A good woman, seeing a man emerge from a saloon, said:

"I am sorry to see you *come* out of such a place."

"Why, madam, would you have me stay there all night."

[1246]

"Jack was held up on the way home last night."

"Yeh, that's the only way he could have got home."

[1247]

Wife—"What do you mean by getting in at this hour?"

Hubby—"'Sall right, m'love. I just hurried home 'cause I thought you might be lonesome, but I shee your twin shister's staying with you."

[1248]

Mrs. (sternly to husband arriving at 3)—"What does the clock say?"

Mr. (genially)—"It shay 'ticktock,' an' the li'l doggies shay 'bow-bow,' an' the li'l pshy-cat shay 'meow-meow.' "

[1249]

Drunk (looking down at moon's reflection in water)—"Say, what's that I see down there?"

Cop—"It's the moon."

Drunk—"Well, how did I get way up here?"

[1250 [

Judge—"Rastus, you are here for intoxication."

Rastus—"Fine, Jedge; bring on the intoxication."

[1251]

A great drinker being at table, they offered him grapes at dessert.

"Thank you!" said he, pushing back the plate; "I don't take my wine in pills!"

[1252]

"Your ticket," emphatically declared the conductor to the intoxicated passenger after examining the latter's ticket, "is for Decatur, and this train is on the St. Louis line, which doesn't go through Decatur."

"Good heavensh!" exclaimed the intoxicated one. "Have you told 'sh engineer?"

[1253]

An old soak, well known to the police, was brought up before a magistrate who knew him well. He recognized "his honor" familiarly.

"John Jones," said the magistrate, with severity, "you are charged with habitual drunkenness; what have you to offer in excuse for your offense?"

"Habitual thirst, your honor."

[1254]

A drunk was swaying back and forth on the sidewalk when the cop stepped up and asked him what he was doing and where he lived.

"Right there," he said, pointing to a house, "but I rang the bell and nobody answered."

"How long ago was that?"

"About three hours ago."

"Well, why don't you try them again?"

"Aw, to hell with 'em—let 'em wait."

[1255]

When intoxicated, a Frenchman wants to dance; a German to sing; a Spaniard to gamble; an Englishman to eat; an Italian to boast; a Russian to be affectionate; an Irishman to fight; and an American to make a speech.

[1256]

Festive One—"Whash yer looking for?"

Policeman—"We're looking for a drowned man."

Festive One—"Whash yer want one for?"

[1257]

"Is that you, Charles?" called an angry wife at two in the morning.

"Zash me, my dear."

"Here I've been standing at the head of the stairs these two hours. Oh, Charles, how *can* you?"

"Shtandin' on your head on th' shtairs! My dear, I'm shprized. How *can* I? My dear, I can't. Two hours, too! 'Strornary woman!"

[1258]

Wife (with newspaper) *to husband*—"Here is another powerful temperance moral:

"Young Spillers got into a boat and shoved out into the river, and as he was intoxicated, he upset the boat, fell into the river and was drowned.

"Now, sir (addressing her husband), if he had not drunk whisky he would not have lost his life."

Husband—"Let me see. He fell into the river, didn't he?"

Wife—"Of course he did."

Husband—"Didn't die until he fell in?"

Wife—"James, you are positively silly. Of course he didn't die until he was drowned."

Husband—"Then it was the water that killed him."

[1259]

"One swallow does not make a summer."

"Very true, but several swallows of liquor frequently make a fall."

[1260]

On a pleasant Sunday afternoon an old German and his youngest son were seated in the village inn. The father had partaken liberally of the beer, and was warning his son against the evils of intemperance.

"Never drink too much, my son. A gentleman stops when he has enough. To be drunk is a disgrace."

"Yes, Father, but how can I tell when I have enough or am drunk?"

The old man pointed with his finger.

"Do you see those two men sitting in the corner. If you should see four men there, you would know that you were drunk."

The boy looked long and earnestly. After a time, in puzzled tones, he said:

"Yes, Father, but—but—there is only one man in that corner."

[1261]

Counsel (to police witness)— "But if a man is on his hands and knees in the middle of the road, does that prove he is drunk?"

Policeman—"No, sir, it does not, but this one was trying to roll up the white line."

[1262]

A man met a stranger from the West who lived in the same town where the new acquaintance had a brother who had made good in mining. They had a convivial glass or two together.

"If you meet my brother when you return, do you mind telling him that you fell in with me? Tell him things have not gone as well with me as they have with him. In fact, I'm rather up against it,

and a little brotherly lift wouldn't come amiss. Understand?"

After a few more potations, the Easterner said: "Shay, if you shee anything of my brother out there tell him you met me an' I'm all right. D'ye get me, old sport?"

There followed other libations. Then—" 'F you see anything of my brother out there, an' he needs help, tell him to draw on me. Will yuh?"

[1263]

"But this officer says that while you were in a drunken state you tried to climb a lamp-post."

"Yes, I did, your honor, but three crocodiles had been following me about all night, and they were getting on my nerves."

[1264]

"Shay, pardon me, offisher, but where am I?"

"You're on the corner of Broadway and Forty-second Street."

"Cut out the details. What town am I in?"

[1265]

There are five stages of Brandy and Water.

The first is "Brandy and Water."

The second is "Branny and Warwer."

The third, "Bran Warr."

Fourth, "Brraorr."

And the fifth, Collapse.

[1266]

An intoxicated gentleman asked a pedestrian, "I shay, which ish the other shide of the shtreet?"

"Why, over there," was the answer.

"Shtrange. I was jus' over there an' a gen'l'm'n shaid it wash over here."

[1267]

"Are you positive that the defendant was drunk?"

"No doubt," growled Officer Kelly.

"Why are you so almighty certain about it?"

"Well, anyhow," replied Kelly, "I saw him put a penny in the patrol box on Fourth Street and then he looked up at the clock on the Presbyterian Church and roared, 'Gawd, I've lost fourteen pounds' weight'."

[1268]

A citizen who prided himself on being something of a good Samaritan was passing an apartment house in the small hours of the morning when he noticed a man leaning limply against the doorway.

"What's the matter," he asked, "Drunk?"

"Yup."

"Do you live in this house?"

"Yup."

"Do you want me to help you upstairs?"

"Yup."

With much difficulty he half dragged, half carried the drooping figure up the stairway to the second floor.

"What floor do you live on?" he asked. "Is this it?"

"Yup."

Rather than face an irate wife who might, perhaps, take him for a companion more at fault than her spouse, he opened the first door he came to and pushed the limp figure in.

The good Samaritan groped his way downstairs again. As he was passing through the vestibule he was able to make out the dim outlines of another man, apparently in a worse condition than the first one.

"What's the matter?" he asked. "Are you drunk, too?"

"Yep," was the feeble reply.

"Do you live in this house, too?"

"Yep."

"Shall I help you upstairs?"

"Yep."

The good Samaritan pushed, pulled, and carried him to the second floor, where this second man also said he lived. He opened the same door and pushed him in.

As he reached the front door he discerned the shadow of a third man, evidently worse off than either of the other two. He was about to approach him when the object of his solicitude lurched out into the street and threw himself into the arms of a passing policeman.

"Off'shur! Off'shur! Fer Heav'n sake, Off'shur," he gasped, "protec' me from that man. He's done nothin' all night long but carry me upstairs and throw me down th' elevator shaf'."

[1269]

Mrs. Jones—"Look, dear, how picturesque; the Browns are bringing in a Yule log."

Mr. Jones—"Yule log my eye; that's Brown."

[1270]

"Seen Jones 'bout here 'n the lash hour an' half?"

"Yes, he was here."

"Ja notice whether I was with him?"

[1271]

"Shay, Offisher, wheresh th' corner?"

"You're standing on it."

"'S no wonder I couldn't find it!"

[1272]

"Is there any alcohol in cider?"

"Inside whom?"

[1273]

"I left a bottle of Scotch in the train this morning.

"Was it turned into the lost and found department?"

"No, but the fellow who found it was."

[1274]

The man rushed excitedly into the smoking car. "A lady has fainted in the next car! Has anybody got any whisky?" he asked.

Instantly a half-dozen pints and half-pints were thrust out to him. Taking the nearest one, he turned the bottle up and took a big drink, then, handing the bottle back, said, "Thank you. It always did make me feel sick to see a lady faint."

[1275]

The very convivial gentleman left his club happy, but somewhat dazed. On his homeward journey, made tackingly, he ran against the vertical iron rods that formed a circle of protection for the trunk of a tree growing by the curb. He made a tour around the barrier four times, carefully holding to one rod until he had a firm grasp on the next. Then, at last, he halted and leaned despairingly against the rod to which he held, and called aloud for succor:

"Hellup! hellup! Somebody let me out!"

[1276]

Policeman (to intoxicated man who is trying to fit his key to a lamp-post)—"I'm afraid there's nobody home there tonight."

"Mus' be. Mus' be. Theresh a light upstairsh."

[1277]

There is a saloon in Brooklyn which has three entrances. Casey enters and the bartender refuses to serve him because he is intoxicated. After an argument Casey leaves the saloon and soon discovers the second entrance. He goes in and looks at the bartender with considerable surprise and again calls for a drink and is again refused. He leaves, but soon comes back through the third entrance. He walks up to the bar unsteadily and looking the bartender in the face says disgustedly, "Say, do you own all the saloons in town?"

[1278]

Magistrate—"What gave you the impression that the prisoner was worse for drink?"

Policeman—"Well, sir, he engaged in a heated argument with a taxi driver."

"But that doesn't prove anything."

"Well, sir, there was no taxi driver there at all!"

[1279]

A retired colonel had been advised by his doctor that if he did not give up whiskey it would shorten his life.

"Think so?" asked the colonel.

"I am sure of it, colonel. If you stop drinking I am sure it will prolong your days."

"Come to think of it, I believe you are right about that, Doctor," said the colonel. "I went twenty-four hours without a drink six months ago, and I never put in such a long day in my life."

[1280]

"Was Bill drunk last night?"

"I dunno, but he was trying to get his pants off over his head."

[1281]

Two drunks were babbling about cradle days as they leaned heavily against the bar.

"You know," said one, "when I was born I only weighed a pound and a half and that's a fac'."

"You don't shay," said the other. "Did you live?"

"Did I live!" exclaimed the first. "Shay, man, you ought to shee me now!"

[1282]

"What did you get drunk for, in the first place?"

"I didn't get drunk in the first place. I got drunk in the last place."

[1283]

A man was fumbling at his keyhole in the small hours of the morning. A policeman saw the difficulty and came to the rescue.

"Can I help you to find the keyhole, sir?" he asked.

"Thash all right, old man," said the other cheerily, "you jusht hol' the housh shtill and I can manage."

[1284]

Two befuddled visitors to the Kentucky Derby approached a hotel desk to register. One of them attempted to tell the clerk what they wanted, but in vain. Finally the other said:

"Jush a minute. What we wansh ish a bed with two rooms."

"I think what you want," said the clerk, "is a room with two beds."

This met with the approval of the men, and a few minutes later—fully dressed—they were stretched out on the same bed.

"Shay, Jack, there's somebody in my bed."

"Shinsh you mention it, old man, there'sh somebody sleeping in mine too."

"What'sh you say les' kick 'em out."

There were sounds of a terrific struggle.

"Shay, Jack," one of them panted. "I got mine out."

"Good boy! But, I can't handle mine—he pushed me out."

"Thash all right, pal, you jush come an' sleep with me."

[1285]

"I managed to get drunk on cider last night."

"You must have found it rather hard."

[1286]

The temperance lecturer had rented a hall for the evening, and he was discoursing on the Rum Evil.

"Now, supposing I had a pail of water and a pail of beer on this platform, and then brought on a donkey; which one of the two would he take?"

"He'd take the water," came a voice from the gallery.

"And why should he take the water?" asked the lecturer.

"Because he's an ass," came the reply.

[1287]

First Drunk—"Say, know what time it is?"

Second Drunk—"Yeah."

First Drunk—"Thanks."

[1288]

"Hi, there," bellowed a policeman to an inebriated citizen, "you can't stand there in the street."

"Yes, I can, orfsher," retorted the citizen proudly. "Don't you worry 'bout me. I been standin' here an hour an' ain't fell off yet."

[1289]
Drunk—"Shay, call me a cab, willya?"

Bystander—"My good man. I'm not a doorman, I am a naval officer."

Drunk—"Awright, then call me a boat, gota get home."

[1290]
The highly inebriated individual halted before a solitary tree, and regarded it as intently as he could, with the result that he saw two trees. His attempt to pass between these resulted in a near-concussion of the brain. He reeled back, but presently sighted carefully, and tried again, with the like result. When this had happened a half-dozen times, the unhappy man lifted up his voice and wept.

"Lost—lost!" he sobbed. "Hopelessly lost in an impenetrable forest!"

[1291]
The old farmer was driving home from town, after having imbibed rather freely. In descending a hill, the horse stumbled and fell, and either could not, or would not, get to its feet again. At last, the farmer spoke savagely:

"Dang yer hide, git up thar—or I'll drive smack over ye!"

[1292]
A man had to make a train trip on the morning after a heavy night. Still nursing a hangover, he 'phoned the ticket office and reserved two seats in the chair car.

"But why two seats?" asked a fellow sufferer.

"Because," he explained, "old Colonel Remorse will be right there with me, and I may as well make him comfortable."

[1293]
A mouse chanced on a pool of whiskey that was the result of a leaking barrel. It had had no previous experience with liquor, but now, being thirsty, it took a sip of the strange fluid, and then retired into a hole to think. After some thought, it returned to the pool, and took a second sip of the whiskey. It then withdrew to its hole to think some more. Presently, it issued forth and drew near the pool for the third time. It drank again, this time long and deep. Nor did it retreat to its hole. Instead, it climbed on a soap box, stood on its hind legs, bristled its whiskers, and squeaked:

"Whee! Now bring on that dam' cat!"

[1294]
Swell Souse—"Where was I last night, Thompson?"

Valet—"I couldn't say, sir, but your bank manager has rung up to ask if it's all right to pay out a check of yours written on your dress collar."

[1295]
A man standing at the bar was drinking by himself. Every few minutes he would let out a laugh and then say, "Aw nertz." This had been going on for some time, when the bartender finally asked:

"What's the idea? You laugh, and then say, 'Aw nertz!'"

"Oh," explained the stew, "you see I'm telling jokes to myself, and I've heard those before."

[1296]
Policeman—"Have an accident, sir?"

Reveler (who has collided with lamp post)—"No, thauksh—just had one."

[1297]

An Irishman encountered a lady who had been ill, and made gallant inquiries.

"I almost died," she explained. "I had ptomaine-poisoning."

"And is it so?" the Irishman gushed. And he added in a burst of confidence: "What with that, ma'am, and delirium tremens, a body these days don't know what he dare eat or drink."

[1298]

A drunk standing at a bar ordered a cocktail, drank it, then started chewing and swallowing the glass up to the stem. A drunk standing next to him was watching the procedure. After eating five glasses that way right up to the stem, he noticed the fellow looking at him.

"Who you looking at—what is this to you?"

"Nothing," came the drunken reply, "But you don't know how to eat those glasses—why do you leave the stem? That's the best part."

[1299]

A deputy sheriff was sent to take an inventory of the property in a house. When he did not return for three hours, the sheriff went after him, and found him asleep on a lounge in the living room of the house. He had made a brave effort with his inventory, however: he had written down, "Living room. 1 table. 1 sideboard. 1 full bottle whiskey." Then the "full" had been crossed out, and "half full" substituted. Then this was overlined, and "empty" put in its place. At the bottom of the page, in wobbly writing, was written: "1 revolving carpet."

[1300]

Magistrate—"You are charged with being drunk. Have you anything to say?"

Culprit—"I've never been drunk in my life, sir, and never intend to be, for it always makes me feel so bad in the morning."

[1301]

The Lord Mayor of London had been dining pretty well, and Mr. Choate, Ambassador to England, was seeing his Lordship to the door.

"Now, your Lordship, if you will allow me to advise you," said Mr. Choate, "when you get to the sidewalk curb you will see two hansoms. Take the one to the right: the one to the left doesn't exist."

[1302]

As a drunk staggered his way homeward he pondered the ways of concealing his condition from his wife. "I'll go home and read," he decided. "Whoever heard of a drunken man reading a book?"

Later his wife heard a noise in the library. "What in the world are you doing in there?" she asked.

"Reading, my dear," he replied cheerfully.

"You old idiot!" she said as she looked in at the library door, "shut up that valise and come to bed."

[1303]

A drunken guest fell down the hotel stairs, and, on striking the landing reproachfully apostrophized himself with:

"If you'd been a waitin' to come downstairs, why'n thunder didn't you say so, you wooden-headed old fool an' I'd a come with you and showed you the way."

[1304]

A gentleman pretty well perfumed picked up the telephone: "Hello! Hic! Hello!"

"Hello!" returned the operator.

"Hello!"

"Hello!"

"My gosh!" said the gentleman, "how this thing echoes."

[1305]

He was doing his best to fit his key into the lock, singing a happy song meanwhile. After a time a head looked out of the window above.

"Go away, you fool," cried the man upstairs. "You're trying to get into the wrong house."

"Fool yourself!" shouted back the man below. "You're looking out of the wrong window."

[1306]

A drunkard was asked if he had ever met a certain gentleman, also notorious for his drinking habits.

"Know him!" was the reply. "I should say I do! Why, I got him so drunk one night it took three hotel porters to put me to bed."

[1307]

When the Kentucky colonel was in the North, some one asked him if the Kentuckians were in fact very bibulous.

"No, suh," the colonel declared. "I don't reckon they're mo' than a dozen Bibles in the whole state."

[1308]

A drunk finally finds the keyhole and enters into the house, where he stumbles around looking for lights. Wife pipes up: "That you, Henry?" No answer. A big crash of glass. "Henry! What in the world are you doing?"

"Teaching your goldfish not to bark at me."

[1309]

After-dinner orator who imbibed too freely—"It's in the wonderful insight inter 'uman nature that Dickens gets the pull over Thackeray; but on t'other hand, it's in the brilliant shafts of satire, t'gether with a keen sense o' humor, that Thackens gets the pull on Dickery. It's just this: Thickery is the humorist, and Dackens is the satirist. But, after all, it's 'bsurd to instoot any comparison between Dackery and Thickens."

TRAMPS

[1310]

Lady (to tramp)—"If you're begging a favor you might at least take your hands out of your pockets."

Tramp—"Well, the truth is, lady, I'm beggin' a pair o' suspenders."

[1311]

Lady—"Can't you find work?"

Tramp—"Yessum; but everyone wants a reference from my last employer."

Lady—"And can't you get one?"

Tramp—"No, mum. You see, he's been dead twenty-eight years."

[1312]

Tramp—"Can you help an unfortunate wanderer? I've lost my leg."

Irate Old Gentleman—"Well, I haven't got it. Why don't you advertise for it?"

[1313]

Tramp—"Could you give a poor fellow a bite?"

Housewife—"I don't bite myself, but I'll call the dog."

[1314]
First Hobo (surveying stream of pleasure seekers)—"I hate holidays."
Second Hobo—"Yes, makes yer feel common when nobody ain't workin'."

[1315]
Tramp—"Madam, I have seen better days."
Madam—"So have I, but I have no time to discuss the weather with strangers."

[1316]
Old Maid—"But why should a great strong man like you be found begging?"
Wayfarer—"Dear lady, it is the only profession I know in which a gentleman can address a beautiful woman without an introduction."

[1317]
Tramp—"Lady, I'm almost famished."
Housewife—"Here's a cent. But how did you fall so low?"
Tramp—"I had your fault. I was too extravagant."

[1318]
"Buddy, coudja spare a dime?"
"No, but come along and I will buy your breakfast."
"Hell, I've et three breakfasts now trying to get a dime!"

[1319]
Policeman (to tramp sitting on top of oak tree)—"Hey! What are you doing up there?"
Tramp—"I don't know; I must have sat on an acorn."

[1320]
Charitable Lady—"But, my good man, there must be many generous persons in the world."
Beggar—"Yes, ma'am, but they never have any money."

[1321]
The housewife passed a handout to the disreputable hobo standing at her back door, and as she did so she remarked curtly:
"Eat it outside, if you don't mind."
"If I don't mind?"
"Yes, that's what I said."
"Why, bless yer ma'am, I don't mind. I'm used to it. When I was at home and in clover, as it were, it was me daily custom, when donnin' me dress suit, to announce to me valet, 'Parkins, don't await dinner fer me tonight. I'm dinin' out.'"

[1322]
Lethargic Larry—"Say, dese railroad police got a tough life, ain't dey—always trampin' a beat."
Ossified Oscar—"Yeah, and when dey ain't doin' dat, dey gotta be beatin' a tramp."

[1323]
Lady (to tramp who had been commissioned to find her lost poodle)—"The poor little darling, where did you find him?"
Tramp—"Oh, a man 'ad 'im, miss, tied to a pole, and was cleaning the windows wiv 'im!"

[1324]
Lady—"You seem able-bodied and healthy. You ought to be strong enough to work."
Tramp—"True enough, lady. And you seem beautiful enough to be in the movies, but evidently you prefer the simple life."

[1325]
"Ever bothered with tramps out your way?"
"No; I have a sign on the gate reading: 'We are vegetarians, but our dog isn't.'"

[1326]
The two tramps were stretched out on the green grass. Above them was the warm sun, beside them was a babbling brook. It was a quiet, restful, peaceful scene.

"Boy," mused the first tramp contentedly, "right now I wouldn't change places with a guy who owns a million bucks!"

"How about five million?" asked his companion.

"Not even for five million," drowsed the first tramp.

"Well," persisted his pal, "how about ten million bucks?"

The first tramp sat up.

"That's different," he admitted. "Now you're talking real dough!"

[1327]
"I 'aven't 'ad a bite for days," said a tramp to the landlady of the George and the Dragon. "D'yer think you could spare me one?"

"Certainly not!" bellowed the landlady.

"Thank yer," said the tramp and slouched off; but a few minutes later he was back.

"What d'yer want now?" asked the landlady.

"Could I have a few words with George?" queried the tramp.

[1328]
"Boss, will you give me a dime for a sandwich?"

"Let's see the sandwich."

[1329]
Housewife—"Look here, my man, why do you always come to my house to beg?"

Tramp — "Doctor's orders, madam."

Housewife—"Doctor's orders?"

Tramp—"He told me that when I found food that agreed with me I should stick to it."

[1330]
The housewife gave the tramp a large piece of pie on condition that he would saw some wood. The tramp retired to the woodshed, but presently he reappeared at the back door of the house with the piece of pie still intact save for one mouthful bitten from the end.

"Madam," he said respectfully to the wondering woman, "if it's all the same to you, I'll eat the wood, and saw the pie."

[1331]
"Gimme a dime for a cup of coffee?" asked the hobo of the plain-clothes man.

"Do you ever work?" said the plain-clothes man.

"Now and then."

"What do you do?"

"This and that."

"Where?"

"Oh, here and there."

The plain-clothes man took him to the police station.

"When do I get out of here?" wailed the hobo.

"Sooner or later," growled the desk sergeant.

[1332]
"What are you doing there, Bo?"

"I'm writing a letter to my brother out in Leavenworth."

"Go on, Bo; you know you don't know how to write."

"That don't make no difference; me brother don't know how to read."

[1333]
Lady—"But didn't I give you a cake last week?"

Beggar—"Yes, ma'am."

Lady—"And you are here again?"

Beggar—"Yes, ma'am, your cake was nothing to me. I used to be a sword swallower."

[1334]

First Tramp—"What would you do if you won the first prize in the big Sweepstakes?"

Second Tramp—"I'd have the park benches upholstered."

[1335]

Two old timers of the road were discussing the power of will as their mulligan simmered over the campfire.

"When I was twenty I made up my mind to get rich," one of them said.

"But you never got rich."

"No. By the time I was twenty-one I decided it was easier to change my mind."

[1336]

"Out of work, are you? Then you're just in time. I've a cord of wood to be cut up and I was just going to send for a man to do it."

"That so, mum? Where does he live? I'll go and get him."

[1337]

Old Lady (to mendicant)—"But —my good man, your story has such a hollow ring."

"Yes, missis—that's the natural result of speaking with an empty stummick."

[1338]

Lady (after tramp finished eating)—"It's merely a suggestion. The wood-pile is in the back yard."

Tramp—"You don't say. What a splendid place for a wood-pile."

[1339]

Housewife (to tramp)—"I know you. You are one of the tramps that I gave a pie to last summer."

Tramp—"You are right, madam. You gave it to three of us. I am the sole survivor."

[1340]

Beggar—"It isn't that I'm afraid to work, ma'am, but there ain't much doing now in my particular line."

Lady of the House—"Why, what are you?"

Beggar—"A window-box weeder, ma'am."

[1341]

Householder — "You're a big, healthy man; why don't you go to work?"

Tramp—"Madam, I'll tell you my trouble. I'm an unhappy medium."

Householder — "Whatever that is."

Tramp—"I'm too heavy for light work and too light for heavy work."

[1342]

"Well, make it short," snapped the housewife as she answered the knock of the ragged individual at her back door.

The tramp took a deep breath, and blurted:

"Will you, ma'am, give me a drink of water, because I'm so hungry I don't know where to stay tonight?"

[1343]

Beggar—"Say, buddy, can you give me two dollars for coffee?"

Citizen—"I thought you always asked for ten cents for a cup of coffee."

Beggar—"Yeah, I know, but I'm putting all my begs in one ask-it."

[1344]

A tramp applied at the back door of a farm house and asked for help.

"Madam," he said to the farmer's wife, "would you help a poor man out of his troubles?"

"Certainly," said she. "Would you rather be shot or hit with an ax?"

[1345]
Lady—"I should think you would be ashamed to beg in this neighborhood."
Tramp—"Don't apologize for it, ma'am, I've seen worse."

[1346]
Lady—"You would stand more chance of getting a job if you would shave and make yourself more presentable."
Tramp—"Yes, lady. I found that out years ago."

[1347]
"My poor fellow," said the lady, "here is a quarter for you. Goodness gracious, it must be dreadful to be lame, but just think how much worse it would be if you were blind."
"Yer right, lady," agreed the beggar, "when I was blind I was always getting counterfeit money."

[1348]
"Say, boss," said the husky tramp, "kin ye tell me where I kin git fifteen cents for a bed?"
"Certainly," answered the kind philanthropist, "Bring the bed to me, and if it's worth fifteen cents I'll buy it."

[1349]
Millionaire (to a beggar)—"Be off with you this minute!"
Beggar—"Look 'ere, mister; the only difference between you and me is that you are makin' your second million, while I am still workin' at my first."

[1350]
Tramp—"But, lady, every Christmas for twenty-five years I've received something from this house —since before you were born."
Miss Fortyodd—"Oh, well, that's different. I'll see what I can do."

[1351]
Lady of the House — "What caused you to become a tramp, my man?"
Ragged Rogers—"The fam'ly physician, mum."
Lady of the House—"The family physician? Why, how in the world could the family physician have been the cause?"
Ragged Rogers—"Well, it was him, and none other, mum. He advised me to take long walks after me meals, an' I've been walkin' after 'em ever since."

[1352]
Persistent Tramp (successful at last)—"Thank yer, lady. Is there anything I can do by way of return?"
Housewife (shortly) — "Yes — don't."

[1353]
"But I couldn't give you enough work to keep you occupied."
"Missus, you'd be surprised wot a little it takes to keep me occupied."

[1354]
Housewife—"You can earn your dinner if you'll chop up that pile of wood."
Tramp—"Let me see the menu first."

[1355]
Two hungry tramps were wandering in the woods. "Just think, Bill, if I had a big fat slice of ham, I'd have a ham sandwich, if I only had two slices of bread!"

[1356]
Tramp—"The lady next door has given me a piece of home-made cake. Won't you give me somethin' too?"
Lady—"Yes, I'd better give you a digestive tablet."

[1357]

It was a hobo college track meet. A late comer saw six contestants in track suits walking very slowly. "That's the slowest walking race I ever saw," said the late comer. "Walking race, nothing," explained another spectator, "that's the one-hundred-yard dash."

[1358]

"Madam," remarked the ragged wayfarer with the bandaged eye, "I was not always as you see me now."

"I know it," replied the stern visaged woman at the back door. "The last time you were here you had on a deaf-and-dumb sign."

[1359]

"Kind lady," remarked the weary wayfarer, "can you oblige me with something to eat?"

"Go to the woodshed and take a few chops," replied the kind lady.

[1360]

The cultured maid servant announced to her mistress, wife of the profiteer:

"If you please, ma'am, there's a mendicant at the door."

The mistress sniffed contemptuously:

"Tell him there's nothing to mend."

[1361]

"Please, ma'am, could you spare me an old coat?"

"But, my good man, the one you are wearing is nearly new."

"I know, ma'am, but it's this coat that's ruining my profession."

[1362]

First Hobo—"What's worryin' yer, Bill?"

Second Hobo—"I found a recipe for home-made beer an' I ain't got no home."

[1363]

"Have you ever done a lick of work?" demanded the angry housewife of the tramp.

"Lady," he retorted, "if you think asking dames like you for a bite to eat ain't work you's don't know what work is."

[1364]

"Some men have no hearts," said the tramp. "I've been a tellin' that feller I am so flat busted that I have to sleep outdoors."

"Didn't that make him come across?" asked the other.

"Naw. He told me he was a-doin' the same thing, and he had to pay the doctor for tellin' him to do it."

[1365]

The grizzled old beggar had chopped his quota of stovewood and the kind lady had admitted him to the kitchen for his meal. She was an inquisitive person, and while the tramp made away with all the food placed before him, she set up an endless line of questioning.

"And what was your occupation before you fell into this sad plight, my man?" she asked.

"I was a sailor, mum," said the bum between mouthfuls.

"Oh, a sailor. Well, you must have had some exciting adventures then?"

"That I did, mum. Why once, mum, I was shipwrecked on the coast of South Africa, and there I came across a tribe of wild women, who had no tongues."

"Mercy!" exclaimed the inquisitive woman. "Why how could they talk, then?"

"They couldn't, mum," replied the man, reaching for his hat and the last piece of bread on the plate, "That's what made them wild."

[1366]

Tramp—"Lady, won't you help a poor man that lost his family and all his property in the Florida flood?"

Lady—"Why, you are the same man that lost his family in the Galveston flood and was shellshocked during the war."

Tramp—"Ain't it so, lady? I'm the unluckiest guy on the face of the earth."

[1367]

Old Lady (to tramp)—"Why don't you work? Hard work never killed any one."

Tramp—"You're wrong, lady. I lost both of my wives that way."

[1368]

"Tramps are so lazy, it's a wonder they do not get tired when they talk to each other."

"You forget that most of their conversation is idle gossip."

[1369]

Lady—"Have you ever been offered work?"

Tramp — "Only once, madam. Aside from that, I've met with nothing but kindness."

[1370]

"I haven't averaged more than one meal a day all this week, lady."

"Oh, are you trying to reduce, too?"

[1371]

Beggar—"Madam, I have not seen a piece of meat for weeks."

Lady—"Mary, show this poor man a mutton chop."

[1372]

Old Lady—"If you really want work—Farmer Gray wants a right-hand man."

Wanderer—"Jus' my luck, lidy—I'm left-'anded!"

[1373]

The beggar wore his most pathetic expression and wept a crocodile tear.

"Please, sir, won't you give me a loaf of bread for my wife and family?"

The kind man patted him on the shoulder.

"No, no, my poor fellow," he said, sympathetically, "I would not deprive you of your wife and family for anything."

[1374]

Tramp—"Have you a piece of cake, lady, to give a poor man who hasn't had a bite to eat for two days?"

Lady—"Cake? Isn't bread good enough for you?"

Tramp—"Ordinarily, yes, ma'am, but this is my birthday."

[1375]

Cook—"Why, you're the same man I gave a piece of mince-pie to yesterday!"

Tramp—"Yus, but I 'ardly expected to find the same cook 'ere today!"

[1376]

First Hobo—"I'm like the poet, I long for the wings of a dove."

Second Ditto—"Huh! Right now I'd rather have the breast of a chicken, 'long with a couple'a drumsticks."

[1377]

Weary Willie, who wa_ out of a job, as usual, rapped timidly at Mrs. Murphy's kitchen door. The lady, angry at being interrupted at her washing, flung open the door, and glowered at him. "Did you wish to see me?" she bellowed.

Weary Willie backed down the steps and said meekly, "Well, if I did, I got my wish, thank you."

[1378]

The tramp, brought into court charged with vagrancy, replied to the magistrate's questioning:

"My God! I ain't had no chance to git a damn' job."

"Here! Here! What kind of language is that to use in a court room!" exclaimed the bailiff, springing to his feet. "For one thing you used a double negative, and besides that you're old enough to know that 'ain't' is incorrect."

[1379]

"These trousers may be useful to you," said the kind old lady. "All they need is a little mending."

"That's all right, mum," said the tramp. "I'll call back in half an hour."

RURAL

[1380]

A kind-hearted farmer told the forlorn lad whose load of hay had overturned in the road, to forget his troubles and come in and have dinner with his family. It would be time enough to right the hayrick after a good meal.

The boy demurred; said he didn't think his father would like it.

But the farmer persisted and won. Coming out from the repast the boy said he felt better and expressed his appreciation of the hospitality. At the same time, he was sure his father wouldn't like it.

"Nonsense!" said the host. "By the way," he added, "where is your father?"

"He's under the hay!" said the boy.

[1381]

Tourist—"And to what do you owe your great age, my dear sir?"

Old Resident—"Wal, I dunno yit. I'm dickering with two or three patent medicine concerns."

[1382]

Traveler—"I want to buy a toothbrush."

Storekeeper—"Sorry, brother, but our line of summer novelties ain't in yet."

[1383]

The farmer whose pig was killed by an automobile was raving mad.

"Don't worry," said the motorist, trying to pacify the bereaved owner, "I'll replace your pig."

"You can't," growled the farmer, "you ain't fat enough."

[1384]

Lightning knocked over three men who were sitting on boxes in front of Sawyer's store. One of them was knocked senseless; the other two exclaimed, "Leggo! I'm comin' right home!"

[1385]

Northern Visitor (in Georgia)— "I see you raise hogs almost exclusively about here. Do you find that they pay better than corn and potatoes?"

Native (slowly)—"Wal, no; but yer see, stranger, hawgs don't need no hoeing."

[1386]

Little Mary was visiting her grandmother in the country. Walking in the garden, she chanced to see a peacock, a bird she had never seen before. After gazing in silent admiration, she ran quickly into the house and cried out: "Oh, granny, come and see! One of your chickens is in bloom."

[1387]

Uncle Ezra—"So Eph Hoskins has gone to Palm Beach! I wonder if there'll be enough going on to suit him."

Uncle Eben—"Wal, Eph ain't taking no chances. He's took his checkerboard along with him."

[1388]

"I read of the terrible vengeance inflicted upon one of their members by a band of robbers in Arkansas last week."

"What did they do? Shoot him?"

"No, they tied him upon the railroad tracks."

"Awful! And he was ground to pieces, I suppose?"

"Nothing like it. The poor fellow starved to death waiting for the next train."

[1389]

"Your cow just got into my field and ate up all my vegetables."

"All right. I'll send you over a quart of milk."

[1390]

At Bill Jones's funeral the doctor and the undertaker were conversing in low tones.

"Too bad," said the undertaker, "that poor Bill's wife wasn't with him when he passed away. How did it happen she wasn't?"

"Mrs. Jones," the doctor whispered, "had hitched up and driven into town to get her mourning outfit at the time it happened."

The undertaker, with a bitter smile, turned away to supervise the wealthy farmer's funeral procession. "Hold on, gentlemen; this won't do," he said sternly; "where is the sixth pallbearer?"

"He's upstairs," another pallbearer explained, "proposing to the widow."

[1391]

"Mr. Perkins left his umbrella again. I do believe he'd lose his head if it were loose."

"I dare say you're right. I heard him say only yesterday that he was going to Colorado for his lungs."

[1392]

"You know," said John Perkins, "It used to be said that anybody could farm—that about all that was required was a strong back and a weak mind, but now'-days, to be a successful farmer a feller must have a good head and a wide education in order to understand the advice ladled out to him from all sides by city men and to select for use that which will do him the least damage."

[1393]

The farmer's mule had just balked in the road when the country doctor came by. The farmer asked the physician if he could give him something to start the mule. The doctor said he could, and, reaching down into his medicine case, gave the animal some powders. The mule switched his tail, tossed his head and started on a mad gallop down the road. The farmer looked first at the flying animal and then at the doctor.

"How much did that medicine cost, Doc?" he asked.

"Oh, about fifteen cents," said the doctor.

"Well, give me a quarter's worth, quick! I've got to ketch that mule."

[1394]

Traveler—"How's the train service here?"

Small Town Native—"Wal, they advertise one train a day, but you and me know them advertisements exaggerate."

[1395]

A couple of farmers out in Ioway were discussing the drought. One fellow had some wheat which he managed to harvest.

"The drought sure has made the wheat short this year."

"Short? Say, I had to lather mine to mow it!"

[1396]

"Is your boy Josh ambitious?"

"Yes," replied Farmer Perkins. "He's plannin' to be so rich an' successful that already he's beginnin' to look on me as a sort o' poor relation."

[1397]

An old farmer was once asked by a young man how it was he had become so rich.

"It is a long story," said the old man, "and while I am telling it we might as well save the candle." And he put it out.

"You need not tell the story," said the youth. "I understand."

[1398]

Hotel Clerk—"Why don't you wipe the mud off your shoes when you come in here?"

Kentucky Mountaineer—"What shoes?"

[1399]

"How has your potato crop turned out, old chap?" asked one ardent amateur gardener of his neighbor.

"Splendid, old man," replied the other; "some are as big as marbles, some as big as peas, and, of course, quite a lot of little ones."

[1400]

Speaker—"Nothing that is false ever does anybody any good."

Old Man (in audience)—"Yer're wrong, stranger. I have false teeth and they do me a lot of good."

[1401]

The motor-car was a thing unheard of to a Kentucky mountaineer in an out-of-the-way community, and he was astounded one day when he saw one go by without any visible means of locomotion. His eyes bulged, however, when a motor-cycle followed and disappeared like a flash round a bend in the road.

"Great guns!" he said, turning to his son. "Who'd 'a' s'posed that thing had a colt."

[1402]

"Well, Ezri, how'd jer make out with yer boarders this year?"

"Fine! Best season I ever had. There was seven, all told—three couples in love an' a dyspeptic."

[1403]

"How did old man Perkins git all cut up like that?"

"Wal, he took a trip down to the City here last week, and he was gittin' shaved by one of them lady barbers when a mouse ran across the floor."

[1404]

A tourist in the mountains of Tennessee was talking with an old mountaineer who complained considerably about hard times.

"Why, man," said the tourist, "you ought to be able to make money shipping green corn to the northern market."

"Yes, I oter," was the sullen reply.

"You have the land, I suppose, and can get the seed."

"Yes, I guess so."

"Then why don't you do this?

"No use, stranger," sadly replied the cracker, "the old woman is too lazy to do the plowin' and plantin'.'"

[1405]

Visitor—"How does the land lie out this way?"

Native—"It ain't the land that lies; it's the real-estate agents."

[1406]

"What became of the hired man you got from the city?"

"He crawled under a mule to see why it didn't go."

[1407]

Two backwoodsmen knock on door of cabin.

"Howdy, Joe; me and Ed just found the body of a dead man over there in the holler, and we thought maybe it was you."

"What'd he look like?"

"He was about your build, and—"

"Did he have on a flannel shirt?"

"Yup."

"With red and white checks?"

"No, it was plain gray."

(Closing the door)—"Nope, it wasn't me."

[1408]

A farmer drove up to the bank, hitched his horse to the post and carefully muzzled the animal with a feed bag. He then went around to the back of his wagon and took out of it a chicken with a piece of string tied to one leg. With the string he fastened the chicken to the hitching post, so that it could pick up the oats dropped from the horse's nosebag.

[1409]

"What is the principal occupation of this town?"

"Wall, boss," the man answered, yawning, "in winter they mostly sets on the east side of the house and follers the sun around to the west, and in summer they sets on the west side and follers the shade around to the east."

[1410]

Hiram had walked four miles over the Great Smokies to call on his lady fair. For a time they sat silent on a bench by the side of her log cabin, but soon the moon, as moons do, had its effect and Hiram slid closer to her and patted her hand.

"Mary," he began, "y'know I got a clearin' over thar and a team an' wagon an' some hawgs an' cows, an' I 'low to build me a house this fall an'—"

Here he was interrupted by Mary's mother who had awakened.

"Mary," she called in a loud voice, "is that young man thar yit?"

Back came the answer: "No, maw, but he's gittin' thar."

[1411]

A farmer came into the village railway station with his wife and approached the ticket window. He addressed the station agent:

"Say, Mister, has the three-ten train gone yet?"

"The three-ten train left a quarter of an hour ago."

"And how soon will the four o'clock train be along, do you think?"

"It'll be quite a while before that train is due."

"Air there any passenger trains before then?"

"No."

"Any freights?"

"No."

"No trains at all?"

"None."

"Are you sure?"

"Certainly, I'm sure!" bawled the exasperated ticket-agent.

"Then, Sophie," said the old farmer, turning to his wife, "now I reckon we can cross them tracks."

[1412]

Farmer Perkins (reading from newspaper to his wife)—" 'It is estimated that the recent dinner given by Mrs. Copley was served at a cost of at least ten dollars a plate.' What must the victuals have cost?"

Mrs. Perkins—"Land's sake, Joshua! and such folks always has a different plate for everything they eat."

[1413]

Dad had been ill for several weeks but was still keenly interested in the way the farm work was being carried on.

"Dave," he said, " 'ow are th' cows goin'?"

"Not too bad," Dave vouchsafed. "Gettin' about ten gallons a day."

"Ain't so bad," Dad agreed. " 'Ow much skim milk are we sellin'?"

"Nine gallons a day, Dad."

"How much cream?"

"Three gallons an' a bit, Dad."

The man in the bed did a bit of complicated mental addition. Then his smile vanished. "Wot the hell are you doin' with the rest?" he demanded.

[1414]

They went out buggy-riding. The young man ventured to ask for a kiss. The girl was much surprised —as all young ladies affect to be when such a request is made—and asked him what good it would do him.

"Oh," replied the young man, "it would make one feel so gay and lively."

"Well, Charley, if as you say, a kiss is apt to make one feel so gay and lively, I think if we expect to get home before morning you had better get out at once and kiss the old horse."

[1415]

A farmer was delivering vegetables to a public sanitarium. A patient saluted him.

"You're a farmer, ain't yuh?"

The farmer allowed that he was.

"I used to be a farmer once," said the guest of the State.

"Did yuh?"

"Yes. Say, stranger, did yuh ever try bein' crazy?"

The farmer never had, and started to move on.

"Well, you oughta try it," was the ex-farmer's parting shot. "It beats farmin' all hollow."

[1416]

"It's a strange thing, Jim," said the farmer to one of his men, "yer allus late of a morning and yer living right on the farm. Now Bill Brown, who lives two miles away, is allus on time."

"There's nothing funny about that," retorted Jim. "If Bill's late in the morning he can hurry a bit, but if I'm late, I'm here."

[1417]

"Your house is on fire," shouted a passing motorist to a thick-bearded mountaineer.

"Ah knows it, stranger," nodded the mountaineer.

"Then why aren't you doing something about it?" cried the excited stranger.

"Ah am," drawled the mountaineer. "Ever since the fire started, Ah bin prayin' fer rain."

[1418]

First Hen—"That big rooster has been making love to me."

Second Hen—"Did you give him any encouragement?"

First Hen—"Just egged him on a bit."

[1419]

Mr. Backwoods had called for the first time to escort Miss Bumpkin to the weekly prayer meeting. An excess of timidity and self-consciousness reduced both to the point of absolute silence until at last and with visible effort, as the "meeting house" is neared, the gallant summons all his courage:

"Do you like stewed rabbit?" he hazards.

"Yes," returns the maiden, coyly.

Again silence, until on the return journey the home lights are sighted, when, with another mighty effort the resourceful swain asks feelingly:

"Ain't the gravy nice?"

And yet there are those that maintain that country folks sometimes seem at a loss for conversational topics.

[1420]

"Now, Silas," said the teacher, "if there were eleven sheep in a field and six jumped the fence, how many would there be left?"

"None," replied Silas.

"Why, but there would," said she.

"No, ma'am, there wouldn't," persisted he. "You may know arithmetic, but you don't know sheep."

[1421]

"An Arkansas local weekly soliloquizes thus:

" 'Some of our exchanges are publishing as a curious item a statement to the effect that a horse in Iowa pulled the plug out of the bunghole of a barrel for the purpose of slacking his thirst.' We do not see anything extraordinary in the occurrence. Now, if the horse had pulled the barrel out of the bunghole and slacked its thirst with the plug, or if the barrel had pulled the bunghole out of the plug and slacked its thirst with the horse, or if the plug had pulled the horse out of the barrel and slacked its thirst with the bunghole, or if the bunghole had pulled the thirst out of the horse and slacked the plug with the barrel, or if the barrel had pulled the horse out of the bunghole and plugged its thirst with a slake, it might be worth while to make some fuss over it."

[1422]

A farmer, on his way to town in his wagon, overtook a peddler with a heavy pack on his back. The kind-hearted farmer pulled up his horse and offered the wayfarer a ride, which was gratefully accepted.

After a while the farmer noticed that the peddler kept his pack on his back. "Why don't you relieve yourself of that load, and put it in the back of the wagon?" he asked.

"Well," said the peddler, "you have been so kind to me, and I noticed that your horse did not seem particularly strong, so I thought I would take some of the load myself."

[1423]

Poor old Hiram! He went up to New York determined to make his living pulling some skin games on innocent strangers. However, the first fellow he tried to sell the Brooklyn Bridge to turned out to be the owner of the darned thing, and if Hiram hadn't paid him ten dollars to keep quiet the man would have had him arrested.

[1424]

Country Girl—"Mr. Jones, I'd like you to meet Mr. Gush."

Village Postmaster—"How do you do, Mr. Gush, you certainly write a mean love letter."

[1425]
When the train stopped at the little Southern station, the tourist from the North sauntered out and gazed curiously at a lean animal with scraggy bristles which was rubbing itself against a scrub-oak.

"What do you call that?" he asked curiously of a native.

"Razorback hawg, suh."

"What is he doing rubbing himself against that tree?"

"He stropping hisself, suh; jes' stropping hisself."

[1426]
Two city fellows vacationing in the country hired a horse and buggy for a little outing. Upon reaching their destination, the horse was unharnessed and permitted peacefully to graze while the men fished for an hour or two.

When they were ready to go back, a difficulty at once presented itself, inasmuch as neither of the city fellows knew how to reharness the horse. Every effort in this direction met with dire failure, and the worst problem was properly to adjust the bit. The horse himself seemed to resent the idea of going into harness again.

Finally one of the friends, in great disgust, sat down in the road. "There's only one thing we can do," Bill," said he.

"What's that?" asked Bill.

"Wait for the foolish beast to yawn!"

[1427]
A boy left the farm and got a job in the city. He wrote a letter to his brother who elected to stick to the farm, telling of the joys of city life, in which he said:

"Thursday we autoed out to the Country Club where we golfed un-til dark. Then we motored to the Beach for the week-end."

The brother on the farm wrote back:

"Yesterday we buggied to town and baseballed all the afternoon. Then we went to Ned's and pokered until morning. Today we muled out to the cornfield and ge-hawed until sundown. Then we suppered and piped for awhile. After that we staircased up to our room and bedsteaded until the clock fived."

[1428]
"Which weeds are the easiest weeds to kill?" asked the city chap of the farmer.

"Widow's weeds," replied the farmer; "you have only to say 'wilt thou' and they wilt."

[1429]
The editor of the poultry-journal received a letter from a woman reader. It read: "How long should a hen remain on the eggs?"

The editor replied: "Three weeks for chickens and four weeks for ducks."

Three weeks passed, and the editor again received a letter from the reader. "Thank you very much for your kind advice," it read. "The hen remained on the eggs for three weeks, and there were no chickens hatched, and, as I did not care for ducks, I took her off the nest and sold the eggs."

[1430]
A good-for-nothing city idler had inherited a country grocery store. He was taking his ease alongside the counter in his favorite chair when a customer came in and asked for a dozen apples. "I can't wait on you today," said the ex-city man. "Come in some time when I'm standing up."

[1431]

An older farmer was moodily regarding the ravages of the flood.

"Hiram," yelled a neighbor, "your pigs were all washed down the creek."

"How about Thompson's pigs?" asked the farmer.

"They're gone, too."

"And Larsens?"

"Yes."

"Humph!" ejaculated the farmer cheering up. " 'Taint as bad as I thought."

[1432]

A farmer was trying to sell his horse. After exercising it, he exclaimed to his prospective buyer: "Don't you admire his coat?"

"Coat's all right," said the prospect, "but I dont care for the pants!"

[1433]

A man walking on a country road noticed that a farmer was having trouble with his horse. It would start, go slowly for a short distance, and then stop again. Thereupon the farmer would have great difficulty in getting it started. Finally the traveler approached and asked, solicitously:

"Is your horse sick?"

"Not as I knows of."

"Is he balky?"

"No. But he is so danged 'fraid I'll say whoa and he won't hear me, that he stops every once in a while to listen."

[1434]

"To what do you attribute your remarkable health?"

"Well," replied the old farmer, "I reckon I got a good start on most people by bein' born before germs was discovered, thereby havin' less to worry about."

[1435]

Hiram—"Waal, Si, I planted a mess o' turnips in th' garden, an' what d'ye think cum up?"

Cyrus—"Dunno, what?"

Hiram—"A flock o' hogs, and 'et 'em."

[1436]

A farmer returned from the city to tell of the wonders of the taxicab.

"They calls 'em taxidermy cabs," he said, "because they skin ye."

[1437]

"Say, mister, what time is it?"

" 'Bout Tuesday, I'd say."

"No, what hour? I have to catch a train."

"Aw, Tuesday's close enough. There an't no train 'til Saturday, anyhow."

[1438]

"Old man," asked the traveling salesman of Rock Ridge's only cab driver, "why in hell did they put this depot so far from town?"

"Wall, stranger," answered the driver, "I dunno ez I kin say, unlessn they wanted to get the depot jest ez close ez possible to the railroad."

[1439]

A business man was showing his farmer friend the city. During the course of the day's excursion they entered a cafe, one of the exclusive sort with bar. As the pair approached, the bartender uttered the usual, "What'll you have gents?"

To the amazement of the farmer his friend said: "Make mine a sidecar, buddy."

"How about you, mister?" The bartender pointed at the farmer.

"Oh!" exclaimed the hayseed triumphantly. "I'll have just a plain horse and buggy."

[1440]

A backwoods mountaineer one day found a mirror which a tourist had lost.

"Well, if it ain't my old dad," he said as he looked in the mirror. "I never knowed he had his pitcher took."

He took the mirror home and stole into the attic to hide it. But his actions didn't escape his suspicious wife. That night while he slept she slipped up to the attic and found the mirror.

"Hum-um," she said, looking into it, "so that's the old hag he's been chasin'."

[1441]

A farmer in great need of extra hands at haying time finally asked Si Smith, who was accounted the town fool, if he could help him out.

"What'll ye pay?" asked Si.

"I'll pay you what you're worth," answered the farmer.

Si scratched his head a minute, then answered decisively:

"I'll be *durned* if I'll work for that!"

[1442]

"There'll be one good thing when the season's over," remarked the farmer who took summer boarders. "I can shave this bunch of spinach off my chin and pull my trouser legs out of my boots."

[1443]

Uncle Ezra—"So ye just got back from New York! What's the difference between the city and the country?"

Uncle Eben—"Wal, in the country you go to bed feeling all in and get up feeling fine, and in the city you go to bed feeling fine and get up feeling all in."

[1444]

Two parsons were having lunch at a farm during the progress of certain anniversary celebrations. The farmer's wife cooked a couple of chickens, saying that the family could dine on the remains after the visitors had gone. But the hungry parsons wolfed the chickens bare.

Later the farmer was conducting his guests round the farm, when an old rooster commenced to crow *ad lib*. "Seems mighty proud of himself," said one of the guests.

"No wonder," growled the farmer, "he's got two sons in the ministry."

[1445]

A westerner entered a saloon with his wife and six-year-old boy. He ordered two straight whiskies.

"Hey, pa," said the kid, "ain't ma drinking?"

[1446]

Missus—"Don't bring any more of that milk. It's positively blue."

Farmer—"It ain't our fault, lady, it's these long dull evenings that make the cows depressed."

[1447]

Egg Peddler (to wife)—"Sufferin' snakes, Mandy, you sold the wrong eggs to that last woman."

Wife—"How so?"

Peddler—"You sold her some of that lot we dated August 20, and it's only August 10 now."

[1448]

"After another season," said Farmer Perkins, "I guess we'll have a chef for the summer boarders."

"What's a chef?" asked Mrs. Perkins.

"A chef is a man with a big enough vocabulary to give the soup a different name every day."

[1449]

"My old man made a scarecrow so natural that it frightened every single crow off the farm."

"That's nothing! I made one that scared 'em so much they brought back the corn they stole last year."

[1450]

Visitor—"What became of that other windmill that was here last year?"

Native—"There was only enough wind for one, so we took it down."

[1451]

When riding near a farm orchard two city motorists stopped the car, stepped out, climbed the wall, and gathered half a peck of rosy apples. Thinking lightly of their "prank," they slowed down as they went by the farmhouse and called out to the farmer:

"We helped ourselves to your apples, old man. Thought we'd tell you."

"Oh, that's all right," the farmer called back, "I helped myself to your tools while you were in the orchard."

[1452]

In Arkansas, where many of the natives take life easy, a man and his wife were one day sitting on the porch when a funeral procession passed the house. The man was seated in a chair which was tilted back on its hind legs against the side of the house, and he was engaged in whittling a piece of wood. As the procession proceeded, he said:

"I reckon ole man Perkins havin' about the biggest funeral that's ever been held around hyear, Samantha."

"A purty good-sized one, is it, Josh?" queried the wife, making no effort to move.

"You betcher!" Josh answered.

"I certainly would like to see it," said the woman. "It's a shame I ain't facin' that way."

[1453]

The stingy farmer was scoring the hired man for carrying a lighted lantern to call on his best girl.

"The idea!" he exclaimed. "When I was courtin', I never carried no lantern; I went in the dark."

"Yes," said the hired man, sadly, "and look what you got."

[1454]

Truck Farmer—"Have you had any experience at gardening?"

Applicant—"Sure thing. I was a waiter in a city roof-garden for a whole month."

[1455]

"What's coming off out in front there?" asked the proprietor of the general store.

"A couple o' fellers from Blue Ridge swapped mules," replied the clerk, "and now each is accusing the other of skinning him."

"Well, then, why don't they trade back?"

"I reckon they are both afraid of getting skinned again."

[1456]

"I've got a cow I want to sell you, Charlie."

"Yes? Would she fit into my Guernsey herd?"

"No; I dunno as she would."

"Does she give lots of milk?"

"No; I can't say as she gives lots of milk, but I can tell you this: She's a kind, gentle, good natured old cow, and if she's got any milk she'll give it to you."

[1457]

"What was your plum-crop like?"

"Well, a heavy storm blew down 50 per cent. of it, and we'd hardly gathered that when another wind blew down the rest."

"Bad luck! Could you do anything with them?"

"Well, my wife ate one and I ate the other."

[1458]

Visiting a Southern State, a man from the North was walking along a road when he met a farmer accompanied by a drove of hogs. They stopped to chat, and the Northerner asked:

"Where are you taking those hogs?"

"I'm turning them loose in the woods to feed on the acorns," said the farmer.

"We don't do that in the North; we pen them up and feed them corn."

"What for?"

"Why," answered the Northerner, "that gets them fat so much faster. It saves time."

The Southerner answered: "Aw, what's time to a hog?"

[1459]

In Missouri, where they raise more mules than in any other place in the world, a farmer died, leaving behind seventeen mules and three sons. In his will he disposed of his mules as follows: One-half to the eldest son, one-third to the next, and one-ninth to the youngest.

The administrator who went to divide the property drove a span of mules out to the farm, but when he went to divide the seventeen into halves, thirds and ninths he found it was impossible with live mules.

Mules not being very valuable at the time, he unhitched one of his own, putting it with the seventeen, making eighteen, which he proceeded to divide as follows:

One-half, or nine, to the eldest son.

One-third, or six, to the next son.

One-ninth, or two, to the youngest.

Adding up nine, six, two, he found that it made seventeen, so he hitched up his own mule and went away rejoicing.

[1460]

"A farmer was driving a load of hay down a road and when he came to the bridge, he found that last summer's flood had washed it away, and he had no way of crossing the river. How did he get the load of hay over the river?"

"Ya got me."

"He sat down on the bank and thought it over."

[1461]

"Guess I'll hit the hay," said the farmer, as he slipped off the barn.

[1462]

"How's times?" inquired a tourist.

"Oh, pretty tolerable," responded the old native who was sitting on a stump. "I had some trees to cut down, but a cyclone come along and saved me the trouble."

"Fine."

"Yes, and then the lightning set fire to the brush pile and saved me the trouble of burnin' it."

"Remarkable. But what are you going to do now?"

"Oh, nothin' much. Jest waitin' for an earthquake to come along and shake the potatoes out of the ground."

[1463]

The new farm hand was awakened at 4:00 A. M. by the farmer, who announced that they were going to cut oats.

"Are they wild oats?"

"No, why?"

"Then why do you have to sneak up on them in the dark?"

[1464]

Farmer—"This is a dogwood tree."

Tourist—"How can you tell?"

Farmer—"By its bark."

[1465]

A farmer complained to the proprietor of the village store that a ham which he had purchased there was not good.

"Why that ham is all right, Zeke," insisted the storekeeper.

"No, it ain't, Si. That ham's spoiled."

"Why how could that ham be spoiled," continued the storekeeper, "when it was only cured last week?"

"Wall, Si, that ham may have been cured last week, but it's got a relapse now, and they ain't no doubt about it."

[1466]

"Got any medicine?" asked a boy, entering the village drug store.

"Yes, lots of it. What do you want?" inquired the clerk.

"Oh, it don't make any difference, so that it's something lively. Dad is fearful bad."

[1467]

A stranger on horseback came to a river with which he was unfamiliar. The traveller asked a youngster if it was deep.

"No," replied the boy, and the rider started to cross, but soon found that he and his horse had to swim for their lives.

When the traveller reached the other side he turned and shouted: "I thought you said it wasn't deep?"

"It isn't," was the reply; "it only takes grandfather's ducks up to their middles!"

[1468]

A certain train on the Southern railroad had been late every day for years, but one day it rolled into the depot exactly on the dot. The surprised and pleased passengers got together and made up a handsome purse for the engineer and presented it to him with an eloquent speech, commending him for being at last on time.

The engineer refused the purse sadly, saying: "Gentlemen, it breaks my heart to do this, for I sho' do need the money. But this heah is yesterday's train."

[1469]

Aunt Hetty—"Sakes alive! I don't believe no woman could ever been so fat."

Uncle Hiram—"What y' readin' now, Hetty?"

Aunt Hetty—"Why, this paper tells about an Englishwoman that lost two thousand pounds."

[1470]

Old Hen—"Let me give you a piece of good advice."

Young Hen—"What is it?"

Old Hen—"An egg a day keeps the ax away."

[1471]

Lost Balloonist—"Ahoy, where am I?"

Farmer—"Heh, heh, you can't fool me, by gum. Yer right up there in that little basket—giddap, Susie!"

[1472]

The family ne'er-do-well, returning home after adventuring for many years in the West, told his father, a Vermont farmer, about buying a silver mine in Colorado for $1000—all the money he could scrape together.

"I knew they'd rope you in!" exclaimed the old man. "So you were ass enough to buy a humbug mine."

"Yes, but I didn't lose anything. I formed a company, and sold half the stock to a Vermont man for $10,000."

"Y-you did," gasped the old man as he turned white. "I'll bet I'm the one who bought it."

[1473]

They were lost in a snow-storm: "Oh, look, George! There's a chicken, so we must be near a farm."

"That's not a chicken. That's the weathercock on the township school house."

[1474]

Farmer Haye—"That Jones boy who used to work for you wants me to give him a job. Is he steady?"

Farmer Seede—"Well, if he was any steadier he'd be motionless."

[1475]

"How's Abel Jones getting on with that school-teacher he's calling on now?"

"Well, every time he goes to see her she keeps him an hour longer for being naughty."

[1476]

"The horse you sold me last week is a fine animal, but I can't get him to hold his head up."

"Oh, it's because of his pride. He'll hold it up as soon as he's paid for."

[1477]

A salesman at the village store was trying to persuade a farmer to buy a bicycle.

"I'd rather spend my money on a cow," he said.

"But think," insisted the salesman, "what a fool you'd look like riding about on a cow."

"Not half such a fool as I'd look trying to milk a bicycle," answered the farmer.

[1478]

"What is the difference between a practical and a theoretical farmer?"

"A theoretical farmer," answered Farmer Perkins, "is one that insists on tryin' to make a livin' off the farm, an' a practical one jes' faces the inevitable an' turns the place over to summer boarders."

[1479]

A near-sighted man lost his hat in a strong wind. He gave chase. A woman screamed from a near-by farmhouse:

"What are you doing there?"

"Getting my hat," he replied.

"Your hat," exclaimed the woman. "That's our little black hen you're chasing."

[1480]

"You told me you hadn't any mosquitoes," said the summer boarder, reproachfully.

"I hadn't," replied Farmer Homespun. "Them you see floatin' around come from Si Perkins's place. They ain't mine."

[1481]

Mountaineer (to three-year-old son)—"Ezry, quit pointin' that thar gun at yore little brother. Hit might go off and kill one of them chickens he's playin' with."

[1482]

"Has that expert in farm relief been of assistance to you?"

"Some," answered Farmer Perkins. "He showed me where I can put a good golf course on my land as soon as I can afford to play the game."

[1483]

A farmer wrote to a rural paper to ask "how long cows should be milked."

"Why the same as short cows, of course," advised the editor.

[1484]

City man (vacationing on farm) —"Do insects ever get in your corn out here?"

Farmer—"Yeh, but we just fish 'em out and drink it anyway."

[1485]

City visitor—"Mr. Farmer, why are you running that steam roller over your field?"

Farmer—"I'm going to raise mashed potatoes this year."

[1486]

A few days after a farmer had sold a pig to a neighbor he chanced to pass the neighbor's place, where he saw their little boy sitting on the edge of the pig-pen watching its new occupant.

"How d'ye do, Johnny," said he; "how's your pig today?"

"Oh, pretty well, thank you," replied the boy. "How's all your folks?"

[1487]

When he told his parents he had secured a job at the blacksmith shop, they laughed, and said:

"You surely don't mean to tell us that a little fellow like you can shoe horses."

"No," said the boy, "but I can shoo flies."

[1488]

The farmer was so discourteous as to pass by a very good friend of his deceased wife, who promptly reprimanded him.

"Mr. Stubbs, I am surprised! You didn't even tip your hat to me."

"I know, Mrs. Green. You're a widow an' I'm a widower, but my poor wife ain't been dead more'n two weeks, an' I ain't started lookin' at the wimmin yet."

[1489]

When a village idiot blossomed out all of a sudden in new clothes, the neighbors wondered at his prosperity.

"What's happened to you?" asked one of them.

"I won the first prize in the lottery," he answered.

"How did you come to guess the lucky number?"

"Well, three times running I dreamed of seven; so I figured it out that three times seven are twenty-four, and I bought ticket number 24. It won the first prize."

"Why, you blamed fool, three times seven is twenty-one, not twenty-four."

"Gosh, is that so?" said the village idiot. "Well, twenty-four won, anyway."

[1490]

An old man approached the ticket wagon on the circus grounds and asked for three seats for the afternoon performance.

"Sorry, but we're sold out," the ticket seller told him.

"You mean to say you haven't even three seats you can sell me?"

"That's about the situation."

"Well," said the old man, "I call that derned poor management."

[1491]

Lady—"What is that peculiar odor I get from that field?"

Farmer—"That's fertilizer."

Lady—"Oh, for the land's sake!"

Farmer—"Yes, lady."

[1492]

"I've been spending a holiday at a watering place."

"Why, Harry told me you were on a farm."

"Yes, a dairy-farm."

[1493]

"Were the farmers out your way hard hit by the storm?"

"Were they! Filling-station receipts fell off 50 per cent."

[1494]

A rural tragedy in rhymed prose: Mule in a barnyard, lazy and sick. Boy with a pin on the end of a stick. Boy jabbed mule—mule gave a lurch—(services Monday at the M. E. Church).

[1495]

Farmer—"I've arranged so as not to be caught by any drought this summer."

Friend—"What have you done?"

Farmer—"Planted onions and potatoes in alternate rows. The onions will make the potatoes' eyes water and so irrigate the soil."

[1496]

"You are charged with selling adulterated milk," said the judge.

"Your Honor, I plead not guilty."

"But the testimony shows that it is 25 per cent water."

"Then it must be high-grade milk," returned the plaintiff. "If your Honor will look up the word 'milk' in your dictionary you will find that it contains from 80 to 90 per cent water. I should have sold it for cream!"

[1497]

A city man was driving through a village when he saw a man amusing a crowd with the antics of his trick dog. The city man pulled up and said: "My dear man, how do you manage to train your dog that way? I can't teach mine a single trick."

The villager glanced up with a simple rustic look and replied: "Well, you see, it's this way; you have to know more'n the dog or you can't learn him nothin'."

[1498]

"Did you make any money on your tobacco crop this year?"

"Yes, I made just enough to keep my boy Josh in cigarets for another year."

[1499]

The visitor from the city stopped in at the general store of the village, and inquired:

"Have you anything in the shape of automobile tires?"

"Yep," the store-keeper answered briskly, "life-preservers, invalid cushions, funeral wreaths, doughnuts, an' sich."

[1500]

A commercial traveler having missed the bus found himself with two hours to spend in Brushville. He approached an ancient porter.

Traveling Man—"Got a picture show here?"

Porter—"No."

Traveling Man—"A pool room, or library?"

Porter—"No."

Traveling Man—"Well, how on earth do you amuse yourselves?"

Porter—"We go down to the grocery store in the evenings. They have a new bacon slicer."

[1501]

"How did you make your neighbor keep his hens in his own yard?"

"One night I hid a half-dozen eggs under a bush in my garden, and next day I let him see me gather them. I wasn't bothered after that."

[1502]

A farmer was the owner of a prize Jersey heifer. A stranger, having admired the animal browsing on the hillside, drove around the hill to the farmer's home, and asked:

"How much will you take for your cow?"

The farmer scratched his head for a moment, and then said: "Look-a-here, be you the tax-assessor, or has she been killed by the railroad?"

[1503]

Farmer (to new hired hand)— "Where's that mule I told you to take out and have shod?"

New Hand—"Did you say 'shod'? I thought you said 'shot.' I've just been buryin' her."

[1504]

A lady complained to her milkman of the quality of milk he sold her.

"Well, mum," said the milkman, "the cows don't get enough grass feed this time o' year. Why them cows are just as sorry about it as I am. I often see 'em cryin'—regular cryin', mum—because they feel as how their milk don't do 'em credit. Don't you believe it, mum?"

"Oh, yes, I believe it," responded his customer; "but I wish in future you'd see that they don't drop their tears into our can."

[1505]

Bill Brown kept a general store at Farlington. One day he set off for New York to buy a lot of goods. The goods were shipped immediately; and as Bill had lingered in New York sightseeing, they reached Farlington before him. The goods, in an enormous packing-case, were hauled to the general store by the local teamster. Mrs. Brown came out to see the box unloaded, and suddenly, with a piercing shriek, tottered and fell.

"Oh, what's the matter, ma'am?" cried the drayman.

Mrs. Brown, her eyes blinded with tears, pointed to the packing-case, whereon was stenciled in large black letters: "BILL INSIDE."

[1506]

Seth Smith was reckoned the laziest man in the village. So tired had the authorities become of contributing to his support that they decided to confine him to a living tomb. Accordingly he was prepared for burial. The hearse was an old ramshackle country wagon.

As the strange cortége moved along some old resident asked, "Who is it?"

"Why, Seth Smith, who is too lazy to get anything to live on, so we are going to bury him alive."

"I'll give him a bushel of corn," said one.

"So will I," said another.

Slowly raising his head, Seth asked:

"Is the corn shelled, neighbor?"

"No, you'll have to shell it yourself."

Gently replacing his head, he said: "Drive on, boys, drive on."

[1507]

Farmer—"I never see such a season. My corn isn't an inch high!"

Neighbor—"An inch? Why the sparrows have to kneel down to eat mine."

[1508]

"Can you tell me how far it is to Ridge Town," a motorist said to a mountaineer.

The mountaineer's lips moved in answer, but no sound reached the driver's ears.

"What's the matter with you?" he inquired. "Can't you talk?"

"Yes, I kin talk," whispered the mountaineer, "but the fact is, stranger, land is so poor in these parts that I kain't even raise my voice."

[1509]

The summer boarder asked: "Why is it that old hog keeps trying to come into my room? Do you think he has taken a fancy to me?"

Little Willie explained it. He whispered: "Why, that's his room during the winter."

[1510]

A town guy said to a farmer: "You ought to be getting along all right. You have your own milk, butter, eggs, meat and vegetables. You have enough to eat and a place to sleep. That's a lot."

"Uh, huh," assented the farmer. "But you come around about eight-nine months from now and you will see the fattest, sleekest, nakedest farmer you ever beheld."

[1511]

A farmer had an argument with his hired man.

A break in the pasture fence was discovered, and some hair was found sticking to one of the splintered rails.

"Black heifer," said the farmer.

"Red heifer," said the hired man.

Right after breakfast the following morning the hired man quit.

"Too durn much argying here to suit me," he explained.

[1512]

An old farmer was complaining bitterly to the minister of the terribly bad weather for the crops, when the latter reminded him that he had much to be grateful for, all the same.

"And remember," said the good man, "Providence cares for all. Even the birds of the air are fed each day."

"Yep," replied the farmer, darkly, "off my corn."

[1513]

"Ezra," ordered the farmer, "all the clocks in the house have run down. Wish you'd hitch up and ride down to the junction and find out what time it is."

"I ain't got a watch. Will you lend me one?"

"Watch! Watch! What d'ye want a watch fer? Write it down on a piece of paper."

[1514]

Come-to-grief airman—"I was trying to make a record."

Farmer—"Well, you've made it. You be the first man in these parts who climbed down a tree without having to climb up it first."

[1515]

A farmer, just arrived in town, was walking across the street and happened to notice a sign on a hardware store, "Cast Iron Sinks."

He stood for a minute and then said, "Any fool knows that."

[1516]

An old farmer and his wife drove to market one very wet day when large pools of water had formed in the roadway between the farm and the town. On the return journey he met an old friend.

"And how are you today?" was the friendly greeting.

"Very well, thank you," answered the farmer.

"How is the missus?" continued the friend.

"Fine," answered the farmer. "She's behind there"—jerking his thumb toward the back of the wagon.

"She's not there!" exclaimed the astonished friend.

The old farmer turned and looked over his shoulder. Then he coolly replied:

"Humph! That accounts for the splash."

[1517]

Joshkins—"That drought cost us over 5,000 bushels of wheat."

His Wife—"Yes, but there is no evil without some good and you know that during that dry spell we could at least get some salt out of the shakers."

[1518]

A farmer had returned home after a visit to a large city. Someone asked him what he thought of the big city.

"It's a fine place, all right, but the folks there ain't honest," he replied.

"Not honest! Where'd you get that idea?"

"Wa-al, I bought a paper of pins there labeled 'Five Hundred Pins for Ten Cents,' and coming home on the train I counted them: they were eleven short."

[1519]

While the train was waiting on a side track down in Georgia, one of the passengers walked over to a cabin near the track, in front of which sat a cracker dog, howling. The passenger asked a native why the dog was howling.

"Hookworm," said the native. "He's lazy."

"But," said the stranger, "is hookworm so painful?"

"Nope," responded the talkative native.

"Why, then, should the dog howl?"

"Jes' lazy."

"But why does laziness make him howl?"

"Wal," said the Georgian, "thet blame fool dawg is settin' on a sandburr, an' he's too tarnation lazy to git off, an' he jes' sets thar an' howls 'cause it hurts."

[1520]

"Which way to Rock Ridge?" asked a motorist of a dejected looking man perched on a fence near a ramshackle farmhouse.

The native languidly waved his hand toward the right.

"Thanks," said the motorist. "How far is it?"

" 'Tain't so very far," was the drawling reply. "When you get there, you'll wish it was a durn sight farther."

[1521]

At a village concert at which the local blacksmith was chairman, a vocalist was loudly encored after singing "The Village Blacksmith."

As he was about to respond to the encore, the chairman whispered: "When you sing that again, put in a verse about me repairing automobiles."

[1522]

Mrs. Perkins—"What'll we contribute to the minister's donation-party?"

Farmer Perkins—"Wal, I dunno, Hannar! Taters is 'way up, pork is 'way up, fowl is 'way up—we'll save money by giving him money."

[1523]

When an old farmer was asked if hot weather was really good for the cotton crop he replied: "Well, somebody said so at that time and it was too hot for anybody to deny it and that's how the damned idea got started."

[1524]

Up in Maine a motorist came across a lonely hut and interviewed the proprietor with a view to writing up the locality.

"Whose house is this?" he asked.

"Moggs."

"What in the world is it built of?"

"Logs."

"Any animals natural to the locality?"

"Frogs."

"What sort of soil have you?"

"Hogs."

"How about the climate?"

"Fogs."

"What do you live on chiefly?"

"Hogs."

"Have you any friends?"

"Dogs."

[1525]

A doctor was trying to check an epidemic in a village. Visiting a family, he asked:

"Are you taking precautions to prevent spread of contagion?"

"Yes, sir, doctor," replied the head of the family. "We've even bought a sanitary cup and we all drink from it."

[1526]

Having enjoyed the previous summer at a farm in the country, John Jones wrote to the farmer and asked if he might have the same accommodations for the coming August. "But," he added in his letter, "I wish you'd move that pig-pen out back of the house. It was right under my windows last year and was most obnoxious."

Shortly Mr. Jones received the farmer's reply, assuring him of the same accommodations, and adding by way of explanation: "As to that there pig-pen, don't let that worry you. We ain't had no hogs on this farm since you went away last year."

[1527]

Friend—"Why are you so jubilant?"

Country Editor—"I just received another fine contribution from Farmer Brown's pen."

Friend—"Huh—what was it?"

Country Editor—"A fine fat pig on subscription."

[1528]

"Your methods of cultivation are hopelessly out of date," said the youthful agricultural college graduate to the old farmer. "Why, I'd be astonished if you got even ten pounds of apples from that tree."

"So would I," replied the farmer. "It's a pear tree."

[1529]

An optimistic Kansas farmer, on seeing some clouds floating by, remarked:

"Well I guess we are going to have some rain."

"Aw!" said his pessimistic neighbor, an ex-railroad man, "those are just empties coming back from Illinois."

[1530]

"Speaking of railroad service in Arkansas," said a traveling salesman, "one day I was waiting for a train in a small town there. One hour, two hours, three hours passed, but no train pulled in. I was about to negotiate for a vehicle to drive me to the place I wished to make, when the station agent said: 'I wouldn't go to that trouble, sir. The train'll be along soon now.'

"What makes you think so?"

" 'Well,' he answered, 'I'm pretty certain of it. Here comes the conductor's dog now.' "

[1531]

A young city girl was vacationing in the country and became friendly with a farmer boy. One evening as they were strolling across a pasture they saw a cow and calf rubbing noses in the accepted bovine fashion.

"Ah," said the farmer boy, "that sight makes me want to do the same."

"Well, go ahead," said the girl, "it's your cow."

[1532]

Country Constable — "Pardon, miss, but swimming is not allowed in this lake."

City Flapper—"Why didn't you tell me before I undressed?"

Constable—"Well, there ain't no law against undressin'."

[1533]

A couple of farmers from Ohio visited New York, and were shown about the city by a New Yorker. He showed them the Empire State Building, and said:

"There, what do you rubes think about that?"

"Seems to me," said one of the Westerners, "that you folks here in New York are the real 'rubes,' and not we."

"How do you make that out?"

"Well, out where we come from, the folks know all about New York, but you people here seem to know mighty little about our State."

[1534]

"Now, my boys," said the philosophical farmer to his sons, "don't ever spekerlate on a gamble or jus' sit around a-waitin' fer somethin' to turn up. You might just as well go an' sit down on a rock in the middle o' the pasture with a pail 'twixt yer legs an' wait for a cow to back up to yer to be milked!"

[1535]

The town's religious zealot, passing Farmer Jones on horseback, called:

"Brother, have you made your peace with God?"

He didn't hear and inquired:

"What say?"

The question was repeated. Farmer Jones drawled:

"We ain't come to no open break yit!"

[1536]

"How did you find things down on the farm this summer? Crops good, I hope."

"Well, father did fairly well on his barbecue, but he just about broke even on his gasoline and oil."

[1537]

"So you are undertaking to keep bees?"

"Yes," answered Farmer Jones. "I don't want to miss anything, and I've been stung every other way there is."

[1538]

The farmer's rosy-cheeked, bobbed-haired daughter came striding along the lane from the farmhouse. She was clad in grimy overalls; from the pockets bulged bunches of cottonwaste and sundry tools. One hand carried a bag of tools, the other a wrench.

"Where are you going, my pretty maid?" jokingly asked the squire's son, who met her.

"I'm going a-milking, sir," she said.

The squire's son looked surprised.

"But the tools—what are they for?" he asked.

"Trouble," sighed the girl, "with that dashed new milking machine that father has just installed in the cowshed."

[1539]

A city girl visiting her uncle on the farm was watching a cow chewing her cud.

"Pretty fine cow, that," said her uncle as he came by.

"Yes," said the girl, "but doesn't it cost a lot to keep her in chewing-gum?"

[1540]

Friend—"Remember, Si, every cloud has a silver lining."

Si Perkins—"It would be better if they also had a lining of arsenic. Then the rain would spray our crops with insecticide as well as moisten them."

[1541]

Farmer Jones kept summer boarders. One of these, a school-teacher, hired him to drive her to the various points of interest around the country. He pointed out this one and that, at the same time giving such items of information as he possessed.

The school-teacher, pursing her lips, remarked, "It will not be necessary for you to talk."

When her bill was presented, there was a five-dollar charge marked "Extra."

"What is this?" she asked, pointing to the item.

"That," replied the farmer, "is for sass. I don't often take it, but when I do, I charge for it."

[1542]

"Is a chicken big enough to eat when it's two weeks old?"

"Of course not!"

"Then how does it manage to live?"

[1543]

Uncle Silas (visiting city relatives who use electrical appliances for cooking at the table)—"Well, I swan! You make fun of us for eatin' in the kitchen. I don't see as it makes much difference whether you eat in the kitchen or cook in the dining-room."

[1544]

"How did Blank lose the fingers of his right hand?"

"Put them in the horse's mouth to see how many teeth he had."

"And then what happened?"

"The horse closed his mouth to see how many fingers Blank had."

[1545]

"We be pretty well for old folks," the old lady said. "Josiah, my husband, ain't had an ailin' for fifty years, 'cept last winter. An' I ain't never suffered but one day in my life, an' that was when I took some of the medicine Josiah had left over, just so's it wouldn't go to waste."

[1546]

A farmer had 10 employees on his farm, and as none of them was as energetic as the farmer thought he should be, he hit upon a plan which he believed would cure them of their lazy habits.

"Men," he said one morning, "I have a nice, easy job for the laziest man on the farm. Will the laziest man step forward?"

Instantly 9 of the men stepped forward.

"Why don't you step to the front with the rest," inquired the farmer of the remaining one.

"Too much trouble," came the reply.

[1547]

While a farm girl was milking a cow, a bull tore across the meadow toward her. The girl did not stir, but continued milking. Observers, who had run to safety, saw to their amazement that the bull stopped dead within a few yards of the girl, turned round and walked sadly away. "Weren't you afraid?" asked everyone.

"Certainly not," said the girl. "I happened to know this cow is his mother-in-law."

[1548]

Two gentlemen were traveling in one of the hill counties of Kentucky not long ago, bound on an exploration for pitch pine. They had been driving for two hours without encountering a human being, when they came in sight of a cabin in a clearing. It was very still. The hogs lay where they had fallen, the thin claybank mule grazed round and round in a great circle, to save the trouble of walking, and one lean, lank man, whose garments were the color of the claybank mule, leaned against a tree and let time roll by.

"Wonder if he can speak?" said one traveler to the other.

"Try him," said his companion.

"How do you do?" said the Northerner.

"Howdy," remarked the Southerner languidly.

"Pleasant country."

"Fur them that likes it."

"Lived here all your life?"

The Southerner spat pensively in the dust.

"Not yit," he said.

[1549]

Miranda edged to the ticket window to secure information.

"I say, young man, what time does the next train arrive and how long does it wait here?"

"From two to two to two-two," was the prompt reply.

"Well, I declare!" Miranda exclaimed. "Be you the whistle?"

[1550]

The Vicar—"So you like country life. Are your hens good layers?"

Mabel (fresh from town)—"Topping! They haven't laid a bad egg yet."

[1551]

"How's your farm work coming?"

"Oh, fine! Got the billboard and hotdog stand painted, and the filling station stocked full of gas."

[1552]

Mrs. Heigho—"Old Jonas Hardscrabble fell plumb off th' roof of his house while he wuz shingling it."

Mrs. Whyso—"Didn't his wife feel awful?"

"Awful is no name for it—he fell right into her bed of sweet peas."

[1553]

A tourist in the Kentucky mountains one day observed a woman dousing the reclining figures of two ragged and bearded men with water.

The tourist stopped his car and asked what she was doing that for.

"Keeps the flies off'n 'em," she explained.

[1554]

Summer Boarder — "What a beautiful view that is!"

Farmer — "Maybe. But if you had to plow that view, harrow it, cultivate it, hoe it, mow it, fence it and pay taxes on it, it would look derned ornery."

[1555]

A countryman started off to the city on a train. There was a sheriff across the aisle and a man in handcuffs.

"What's wrong with him?" he asked.

"Bugs," said the sheriff, pointing to the prisoner's head. "He's crazy."

"Bugs in his head and his hands handcuffed," said the man. "No wonder he's crazy!"

[1556]

Grandpappy Morgan, a hillbilly of the Ozarks, had wandered off into the woods and failed to return for supper, so young Tolliver was sent to look for him. He found him standing in the bushes.

"Gettin' dark, Grandpap," the tot ventured.

"Yep."

"Suppertime, Grandpap."

"Yep."

"Airn't ye hungry?"

"Yep."

"Wal, air ye comin' home?"

"Nope."

"Why ain't ye?"

"Can't."

"Why can't ye?"

"Standin' in a b'ar trap."

[1557]

The one-ring circus was visiting a town in the hills. The folks there recognized all the instruments of the band except the slide trombone.

One old settler watched the player for quite some time, then, turning to his son, said:

"Don't let on that you're watching him. There's a trick to it; he ain't really swallerin' it."

[1558]

A farmer married a girl from a town, and found on the return from the honeymoon that she had not the slightest idea of farm work. So he took her out to the barn to break her in at milking the cows.

But the big animals scared her, and she said:

"I don't think I'll be able to milk those big cows, Josh. Couldn't we just start with one of the calves?"

[1559]

The farmer had watched the motorist working on his second-hand car for about an hour.

"What are you looking at?" asked the motorist. "Is this the first motor-car you ever saw?"

"No," was the dry reply, "but it's very much like it."

[1560]

A six-weeks-old calf was nibbling at the grass in the yard, and was viewed in silence for some minutes by the city girl.

"Tell me," she said, turning impulsively to her hostess, "does it really pay you to keep as small a cow as that?"

[1561]

The Sunday drivers had picked the farmer's fruit and his flowers, and their car was full of plunder. Pointing to an unexplored highway, they inquired of the farmer:

"Shall we take this road back to the city?"

"You might as well," replied the farmer, "you've got almost everything else!"

[1562]

Si—"Yes sir, Zeke, as sure as I sit here now, I shot that old doublebarrel in that flock of ducks and I brung down five of them."

Zeke (unconcernedly)—"Didn't I ever tell you about me huntin' frogs the other night, fired at one, then five hundred croaked."

[1563]

The tourist from the East had stopped to change tires in a desolate region of the far South. "I suppose," he remarked to a native onlooker, "that even in these isolated parts the bare necessities of life have risen tremendously in price."

"Y'er right, stranger," replied the native gloomily, "an' it ain't worth drinkin' when ye get it."

[1564]

A city man once had occasion to stop at a country home where a tin basin and a roller-towel on the back porch sufficed for the family's ablutions. For two mornings the "hired man" of the household watched in silence the visitor's efforts at making a toilette under the unfavorable auspices, but when on the third day the tooth-brush, nail-file, whisk-broom, etc., had been duly used and returned to their places in the traveler's grip,

he could suppress his curiosity no longer, so boldly put the question: "Say, Mister, air you always that much trouble to yo'se'f?"

[1565]

Little Johnny, a city boy in the country for the first time, saw the milking of a cow.

"Now you know where the milk comes from, don't you?" he was asked.

"Sure!" replied Johnny. "You give the cow some breakfast food and water and then drain the crankcase."

[1566]

"That new farm-hand is terribly dumb."

"How's that?"

"He found some milk bottles in the grass and insisted he had found a cow's nest."

[1567]

Willie's little sister came to the schoolroom door and handed the following note in to the teacher:

"Teacher, please excuse Willie— he caught a skunk."

[1568]

An untimely frost effectually completed the mischief done earlier by the insect enemies of Mr. Perkins's potatoes. The tops of the plants, which had served as pasturage for the pests, were entirely destroyed, and with them Mr. Perkins's hopes of a crop. He was not selfish, however, and could think of others in the hour of adversity. In the afternoon he was accosted at the post-office by a friend.

"Hello, Perkins! How's everything up to the corners?"

"Trouble enough, Williamson, trouble enough!" was the gloomy response. "Ten million potato-bugs, and nothing for 'em to eat!"

[1569]

A backwoods woman, the soles of whose feet had been toughened by a lifetime of shoelessness, was standing in front of her cabin fireplace one day when her husband addressed her.

"You'd better move your foot a mite, maw; you're standing on a live coal."

Said she, nonchalantly: "Which foot, paw?"

[1570]

"You remember when you cured my rheumatism a year ago, don't you, Doctor?" asked the patient, "and told me not to get myself wet?"

"Yes, Ephraim," replied the doctor.

"Well, I just wanted to ask you if you think it's safe for me to take a bath now?"

[1571]

The farmer came back to the farm, after a weekend in the city. The hired man met him at the station in the Ford.

"How's everything?"

"Oh, so-so."

"Anything much happen?"

"Nothing to speak of. The dog limps a little."

"Zat so? How'd that happen?"

"The horse was kinder crazy, running out of the stable, half singed, an' kicked it."

"Half singed?"

"Yeah. When the barn burnt down, and all the hay and stock got burnt, except the horse—an' I had to shoot him later, he was so singed."

"How'd the barn catch?"

"A few sparks from the house, I reckon. That was what woke me —one of yore darters screaming on the second story that the house was afire."

"Humm! House went too! Save anything?"

"Oh yes. When I woke, the whole kitchen end wuz blazin', but I still could unlock the front stairway, and got the folks out. But I remembered yore barrel of applejack in the shed behind the kitchen, and I knew you didn't want nothing to happen to that. When I got her out, it was too late to save the two girls, or the three boys, or the baby, or even yore wife. I suppose yer maw an' paw got crisped right off. But I saved the applejack."

"Well, that's something. Anything else happen?"

"That wuz all. It wuz a pretty quiet weekend."

[1572]

"Now, John, suppose there's a load of hay on one side of the river and a jackass on the other side, and no bridge, and the river is too wide to swim, how can the jackass get to the hay?"

"I give it up."

"Well, that's just what the other jackass did."

[1573]

"I would like a straw with this lemonade," said the lady at the table.

"Hey?" ejaculated the waiter, who was hard of hearing.

"No; straw, I said."

[1574]

Silas — "Say, paw, I can't get these 'rithmetic examples. Teacher said something 'bout findin' the greatest common divisor."

Paw (in disgust) — "Great Scott! Haven't they found that thing yet? Why, they were huntin' for it when I was a boy."

[1575]

A country school board was visiting a school, and the principal was putting his pupils through their paces.

"Who signed Magna Charta, Robert?" he asked, turning to one boy.

"Please, sir, 'twasn't me," whimpered the youngster.

The teacher, in disgust, told him to take his seat; but an old tobacco-chewing countryman on the board was not satisfied; so, after a well-directed aim at the cuspidor, he said: "Call that boy back. I don't like his manner. I believe he did do it."

[1576]

"Josh," said Farmer Wilkins to his son, "I wish, if you don't mind, you'd eat off by yourself instead of with the summer boarders."

"Ain't my society good enough for 'em?"

"Your society's all right, but your appetite sets a terrible example."

[1577]

She was in Alaska looking over a fox farm. After admiring a beautiful silver specimen, she asked her guide, "Just how many times can the fox be skinned for his fur?"

"Three times, madam," said the guide gravely. "Any more than that would spoil his temper."

[1578]

Little Willie, being a city boy, had never seen a cow. While on a visit to his grandmother he walked out across the fields with his cousin John. A cow was grazing there, and Willie's curiosity was greatly excited.

"Oh, Cousin John, what is that?" he asked.

"Why, that is only a cow," John replied.

"And what are those things on her head?"

"Horns," answered John.

Before they had gone far the cow mooed long and loud.

Willie was astounded. Looking back, he demanded, in a very fever of interest:

"Which horn did she blow?"

[1579]

A certain Kansas farmer was observed by his wife to be unusually pensive. "A penny for your thoughts!" she remarked.

"I was thinking, my dear," he said, "what epitaph I should put on your tombstone."

As his spouse was in perfect health, naturally, she resented this undue thoughtfulness.

"Oh, that's very simple," she responded briskly. "Just put 'Wife of the Above.'"

[1580]

The hired man on a farm went on his first trip to the city. He returned wearing a scarf pin set with at least four carats bulk radiance. The jewelry dazzled the village belles, and excited the envy of the other men. His employer bluntly asked if it was a real diamond.

"Wall, if it ain't," answered the hired man, "I've been skun out o' four bits."

[1581]

"How are the roads in this section?"

"Fine," replied Farmer Perkins. "We've abolished bad roads."

"Big job, wasn't it?"

"Not at all. Wherever the going is 'specially hard we don't call it a 'road.' We call it a detour."

[1582]

An up-state farmer went to a circus for the first time and stood before the dromedary's cage, gaping at the strange beast within. He remained there in wondering silence long after the main show began, examining every detail of the misshapen legs, the cloven hoofs, the sleepy eyes, and the mounded back of the dromedary. For some time he continued to gaze. Then the skeptical farmer turned away with an air of disgust.

"Hell, there ain't no such animal."

[1583]

A farmer was losing his patience and temper trying to drive two mules into a field, when the local parson came by and said:

"Don't speak like that to those dumb animals."

Farmer—"You are just the man I want to see."

Parson—"And why?"

Farmer—"Tell me, how did Noah get these into the ark?"

[1584]

A mountaineer took his son to a school to enroll him.

"My boy's arter larnin', what dya have?" he asked the teacher.

"We offer English, trigonometry, spelling, etc.," she replied.

"Well, give him some of that thar trigernometry; he's the worst shot in the family."

[1585]

A hillbilly family was in desperate circumstances. The local religious zealot offered the following prayer at a nearby camp meeting:

"Oh, Lord," he prayed, "help us to act as Thy messengers here on earth to these poor people. Help us not only to pray for them but to supply their need of food, Oh Lord. Put it in our hearts to carry them a barrel of flour, a barrel of pork, a barrel of sugar, a barrel of pepper—oh hell, that's too much pepper!"

[1586]

A civil engineer stepped on to the broken-down porch of a dilapidated shack high in the hills. A mountaineer wife sat on the porch, resting comfortably.

The engineer tipped his hat.

"Howdy, madam," he began. "I just came here to tell you we're going to dynamite that wooden bridge down the road. So when you hear a loud explosion, don't worry about it."

The hill-billy woman nodded.

"Whut time ye gonna dynamite the bridge?"

"Tomorrow morning," replied the engineer. "At eight."

The hill-billy woman puffed on her pipe.

"Cain't ye make it six o'clock?" she drawled. "Then I won't have ter set the alarm clock fer my husband!"

[1587]

The following appeared in a rural weekly paper: "It is reported that one of the fastidious newly married ladies of this town kneads bread with her gloves on. This incident may be somewhat peculiar, but there are others. The editor of this paper needs bread with his shoes on, he needs bread with his pants on, and unless some of the delinquent subscribers to this "Old Rag of Freedom" pony up before long he will need bread without a damn thing on, and Wisconsin is no Garden of Eden in the winter time."

[1588]

A teacher in a country school-house was instructing her class in the use of antonyms. "Now, children," she said, "what is the opposite of sorrow?"

"Joy," shrieked the class in unison.

"What is the opposite of pleasure?"

"Pain."

"And what is the opposite of woe?"

"Giddap."

[1589]

Neighbor—"How is that incubator doing that you bought?"

Mrs. Newbride—"I suppose it's all right, but I'm a little worried about it. It hasn't laid a single egg yet."

[1590]

"Did you ever do any public speaking?" asked the man in the largest rocker.

"Well," replied the chap on the three-legged stool, "I proposed to a girl in the country over a party line."

[1591]

One railroad has a regular form for reporting accidents to animals on its right of way. Recently a track foreman had the killing of a cow to report. In answer to the question, "Disposition of carcass?" he wrote: "Kind and gentle."

[1592]

The wife of a small farmer sold her surplus butter to a grocer in a near-by town. On one occasion the grocer said, "Your butter was underweight last week."

"Now, fancy that," said Mrs. Farmer. "Baby mislaid my weight that day, so I used the pound of sugar you sold me."

[1593]

An inspector, visiting a country school, was extremely annoyed at the noise made by the scholars in an adjoining room.

At last, unable to stand it any longer, he opened the door and burst upon the class.

Seeing one boy taller than the others and talking a great deal, he seized him by the collar, removed him to the next room, and stood him firmly in the corner.

"Now you stand there and be quiet!" he commanded.

Ten minutes later a small head appeared round the door, and a meek voice asked: "Please, sir—may we have our teacher back?"

[1594]

A country housewife decided to try her hand at cake-making. The result was somewhat on the heavy side; after offering it to the various members of the household she threw it to the ducks, in disgust.

A short time afterward two boys tapped at her door.

"Say, missus," they shouted, "your ducks have sunk."

[1595]

Farmer (showing friend over the farm)—"How many sheep would you guess were in that flock?"

Visitor (considers a moment and ventures)—"About five hundred."

"Absolutely correct! How did you guess it?"

"Waal, I jest counted the legs, and divided the number by four."

[1596]

Veterinary Surgeon—"The cow must take a tablespoon of this medicine twice daily."

Farmer—"But our cow has no tablespoons. She drinks out of a pail."

[1597]

"So you run a duck farm. Business picking up?"

"No; picking down."

[1598]

"When are you goin' to fix that front fence, Hiram?" asked the farmer's wife.

"Oh, next week, when Silas comes home from college."

"But what will the boy know about fixing a fence, Hiram?"

"He ought to know a heap. He wrote me that he'd been takin' fencing lessons for a month."

[1599]

A country youth was driving to the county fair with his sweetheart when they passed a booth where fresh popcorn was for sale.

"My! Abner, ain't that nice?" said the girl.

"Ain't what nice?" asked Abner.

"Why, the popcorn; it smells so awfully good," replied the girl.

"It does smell kind o' fine," drawled the youth. "I'll jest drive a little closer so you can get a better smell."

[1600]

Coming upon a football which the farmer's son had brought back from school, the rooster promptly called the hens around him. "Now, ladies," he said diplomatically, "I don't want to appear ungrateful, or raise any unnecessary fuss, but I do want you to see what's being done in other yards."

[1601]

"How do you sell your eggs?"

"I have often wondered."

[1602]

No wonder a hen gets discouraged. She can never find things where she lays them.

[1603]

At a small country town, a young and conceited lawyer, made certain proposals at a town meeting, which were objected to by a farmer. Highly enraged, he said to the farmer:

"Sir, do you know that I have been at two universities, and at two colleges in each university?"

"Well, sir," said the farmer, "what of that? I had a calf that sucked two cows, and the observation I made was, the more he sucked the greater calf he grew."

[1604]

Milkman—"Johnny, did you put water in the milk this morning?"

New hand—"Yes, sir."

"Don't you know that is wicked, Johnny?"

"But you told me to mix water with the milk."

"Yes, but I told you to put the water in first and pour the milk into it. Then, you see, we can tell the people we never put water in our milk."

[1605]

A young lady, finding herself stranded in a small town, asked an old man at the station where she might spend the night.

"There ain't no hotel here," he said, "but you can sleep with the station agent."

"Sir!" she exclaimed, "I'll have you know I'm a lady."

"That's all right,' drawled the old man, "so's the station agent!" and nearly died laughing.

[1606]

"Well," said the farmer, "he broke two spade handles yesterday."

"Working so hard?"

"No, leanin' on 'em."

[1607]

"If there were three crows on a fence post and I shot one, how many would be left?"

"Two left."

"I'm afraid you don't get the point. Let me repeat the joke. There were three crows on the fence post; I shot one. How many would be left?"

"Two left."

"No. None would be left, be- if I shot one, then the other two would fly away."

"Isn't that what I've been say- ing? Two left."

[1608]

A shiftless character in a small town piled into bed one night after a coon hunt, with shoes, clothes and all. After a while his wife shook him: "Get up, you got your shoes on."

To which he mumbled: "That's all right, they ain't my good ones."

[1609]

"I understand they have a cur- few law in this village," said the visitor to the proprietor of the general store.

"No," he answered, "they did have one, but they've abandoned it."

"What was the matter?"

"Well, the bell rang at 9 o'clock, and almost everybody complained that it woke them up."

[1610]

Tom was back in his village home for his holidays from college. One day he said to his mother: "May I tell you a narrative, Mother?"

The mother, not being used to hearing such big words, said, "What is a narrative, my boy?"

"A narrative is a tale," said Tom.

That night when going to bed, Tom said, "May I extinguish the light, Mother?"

His mother asked, "What do you mean by saying extinguish?"

"Extinguish means put out," said Tom.

A few days later Tom's mother was giving a party at their home, and the dog walked in. Tom's mother raised her voice and said: "Tom, take that dog by the narra- tive and extinguish him."

[1611]

A would-be chicken fancier had some difficulty with her flock and wrote the following letter to the Department of Agriculture:

"Something is wrong with my chickens. Every morning when I come out I find two or three lying on the ground cold and stiff with their feet in the air. Can you tell me what is the matter?"

After a little while she received the following letter from the De- partment:

"Dear Madam. Your chickens are dead."

[1612]

"So your wife takes in washing?" the judge asked a man who was up for vagrancy. "What do you do?"

"Well, Judge," explained the ac- cused, "I takes in the washin', the old woman does the washin', I takes the washin' back, the old woman collects the money and I talks her out of most of it."

[1613]

They were looking at a sign in the country store window which read: "Ladies Ready to Wear Clothes."

"Well, it's darn near time."

[1614]

Bill Jones may well be called the champion optimist. He was sitting on the roof of his house during a flood, watching the water flow past, when the neighbor who owned a boat rowed across to him.

"Hello, Bill!" said the man.

"Hello, Sam!" replied Bill, pleasantly.

"All your fowls washed away this morning?"

"Yes, but the ducks can swim."

"Orange trees gone, too?"

"Yes, but everybody said the crop would be a failure anyhow."

"I see the river's reached above your windows, Bill."

"That's all right, Sam," was the reply. "Them windows needed washin'."

[1615]

As Jones and Brown were talking together in the street, a donkey began to bray and wheeze and cough in a most distressing manner.

"What a cold that donkey has," said Jones, "and, by the way, that reminds me—how is your cough?"

[1616]

An aged and very wrinkled old woman, arrayed in the calico costume of the mountains, was summoned as a witness in court to tell what she knew about a fight in her house. The Judge asked her in a kindly voice what took place. She insisted it did not amount to much, but the Judge by his persistency finally got her to tell the story of the bloody fracas.

"Now, I tell ye, Jedge, it didn't amount to nuthin'. The fust I knowed about it was when Bill Saunder called Tom Smith a liar, en Tom knocked him down with a stick o' wood. One o' Bill's friends then cut Tom with a knife, slicin' a big chunck out o' him. Then Sam Jones, who was a friend of Tom's, shot the other feller and two more shot him, en three or four others got cut right smart by somebody. That nachly caused some excitement, Jedge, en then they commenced fightin'."

[1617]

In the days when the western United States was a broad expanse of wilderness, the story was told that a traveler asked a lone pioneer:

"Where is your house?"

"House? I ain't got no house."

"Then where do you live?"

"Live? I live in the woods, sleep on government land, eat raw bear and wild turkey, and drink out o' the Mississippi! An' I want to say that there's gettin' to be too many people 'round here. You're the second feller I seen in the last month, an' I heard there's a whole *family* jus' settled fifty miles down the river. I'm goin' to move on west again!"

[1618]

An old citizen in a country village, on having a subscription list handed him toward purchasing a new hearse for the place, thus excused himself:

"I paid five dollars for a new hearse forty years ago, and me and my folks hain't had the benefit of it yet."

[1619]

While Mrs. Perkins was in town she saw a young lady and gentleman playing lawn tennis. "Wal, I declar'!" she said, turning to Ebenezer, "they keep 'em separated with a net nowadays, don't they?"

[1620]

An old farmer made his wife keep a cash account. Each week he would go over it, growling and grumbling. On one such occasion he delivered himself on the following:

"Look here, Sarah, mustard plasters, fifty cents; three teeth extracted, two dollars! There's two dollars and a half in one week spent for your own private pleasure. Do you think I'm made of money?"

[1621]

"Well, Bill," asked a neighbor, "I hear the boss has a fever. How's his temperature today?"

The hired man scratched his head and decided not to commit himself.

"'Tain't fer me to say," he replied. "The boss died last night."

[1622]

A man left a bony horse on Main Street one Saturday, and, coming back a short time afterward, discovered that someone had placed a placard against the fleshless ribs bearing the notice, "Oats wanted—inquire within."

[1623]

"What are you raising in your garden this year?"

"Johnson's Plymouth Rocks, Brown's Leghorns and Smith's Wyandottes."

[1624]

A young woman had just returned to her farm home after several years in the big city. She was exhibiting the contents of her trunk to the admiration and amazement of her mother, who had bought her clothes for forty years at the village general store.

"And these," said the daughter, holding up a delicate silken garment, "are teddies."

"Teddy's. You don't say. Young men are certainly different from what they used to be."

WESTERN

[1625]

The old trapper was chased by a grizzly. When he had thrown away everything he carried, and found, nevertheless, that the bear was gaining rapidly, he determined to make a stand. As he came into a small clearing, he faced about with his back to a stump, and got out and opened his clasp-knife. The bear halted a rod away, and sat on its haunches, surveying its victim gloatingly. The trapper, though not usually given to praying, now improved the interval to offer a petition.

"O God," he said aloud, with his eyes on the bear, "if you're on my side, let my knife git 'im quick in 'is vitals, an' if you're on 'is side, let 'im finish me fust off. But, O God, if you're nootral, you jist sit thar on that stump, an' you'll see the darndest bear fight you ever hearn tell on!"

[1626]

"I suppose winning money from that tenderfoot was like taking candy from a child."

"Just about," replied Arizona Pete, "assumin' you have noticed what a howlin' fuss any kid kin put up if you try to grab his confectionery."

[1627]

He was unaware of the eccentricities to be found in the wild west when he entered what seemed to be the only hotel in the place. After ushering him to a table and giving the stranger a glass of ice water, the waiter inquired: "Will you have sausages on toast?"

"No; I never eat 'em," the guest replied.

"In that case," said the waiter, "dinner is over."

[1628]

A regiment of soldiers was making a long, dusty march across the rolling prairie. It was a hot, blistering day and the men, longing for water and rest, were impatient to reach the next town.

A rancher rode past.

"Say, friend," called out one of the men, "how far is it to the next town?"

"Oh, a matter of two miles or so, I reckon," called back the rancher. Another long hour dragged by, and another rancher was encountered.

"How far to the next town?" the men asked him eagerly.

"Oh, a good two miles."

A weary half-hour longer of marching, and then a third rancher.

"Hey, how far's the next town?"

"Not far," was the encouraging answer. "Only about two miles."

"Well," sighed an optimistic sergeant, "thank God, we're holdin' our own, anyhow!"

[1629]

A party of tourists in Arizona came upon an Indian brave riding a pony. A heavily burdened squaw walked beside him.

"Why doesn't the squaw ride?" asked the tourist.

"She got no pony."

[1630]

Two old settlers out in the Far West, confirmed bachelors, got to talking about cooking.

"I got one o' them cookery books once, but I never could do nothing with it."

"Too much fancy work in it, eh?"

"You've said it! Every one o' them recipes began the same way: 'Take a clean dish . . .' and that settled me."

[1631]

Arizona Ike—"What happened to that tenderfoot who was out here last week?"

Badger Pete—"Oh, he was brushin' his teeth with some of that newfangled tooth paste and one of the boys thought he had hydrophoby and shot him!"

[1632]

A tourist traveling through the Texas Panhandle got into conversation with an old settler and his son at a filling-station. "Looks as though we might have rain," said the tourist. "Well, I hope so," replied the native, "not so much for myself as for my boy here. I've seen it rain."

[1633]

"Say, pard, the sheriff wants you for that murder at Tonapah. Hev yu an alibi?"

"Shore—thet wuz the day I bumped off 'Spud' Jackson, over Carson City way."

[1634]

"Doesn't it ever rain around here?" a motorist asked one of the natives in the Far West.

"Rain?" The native spat. "Rain? Why, say, pardner, there's bullfrogs in this yere town over five years old that hain't learned to swim yet."

[1635]

Becoming tired of salt pork and hardtack which comprised their camp fare, lumberjacks took up a collection and sent one of their number to town for something fresh. He returned with ten quart bottles of whisky and a loaf of bread. The men howled indignantly:

"What in hell are we going to do with all that bread?"

[1636]

The tenderfoot thought he could ride, so he mounted the pony. A moment later he painfully picked himself out of the dust in one corner of the corral.

"Man, oh, man," he said, "but she bucked something fierce."

"Bucked!" said a nearby cowboy. "Rats! She only coughed."

[1637]

A certain middle-aged spinster has a vivid memory of Texas courtesy.

She was struggling with a hot cup of coffee in a small-town railway-station, trying to gulp it before the train pulled out. A cowboy, seated a couple of stools away, noted her plight, and seeing the guard waving to the woman, came to the fore.

"Here, ma'am, you can take my cup o' coffee. It's already saucered and blowed."

[1638]

Tourist (getting off the train in Kansas and holding on desperately to his hat)—"Phew! Does the wind always blow this way out here?"

Native (solemnly)—"Naw, indeed. It blows this way for six months o' the year, and then it turns round and blows the other way."

[1639]

"What are you doing these days, Gladys?"

"Working on a ranch where they raise hornless goats."

"But—"

"There are no butts."

[1640]

A Yale player was teaching some cowboys how to play football. He explained the rules and ended as follows:

"Remember, fellows, if you can't kick the ball, kick a man on the other side. Now let's get busy. Where's the ball?"

One of the cowboys shouted: "T'hell with the ball! Let's start the game!"

[1641]

A cow-puncher ordered a steak at a restaurant. The waiter brought it in rare—very rare. The cow-puncher looked at it and demanded that it be returned to the kitchen and cooked.

"It is cooked," snapped the waiter.

"Cooked—nothing," replied the cow-puncher. "I've seen cows hurt worse than that and get well."

[1642]

Into a Western cattle town came riding an old mule.

"How much for the mule?" asked a bystander.

"Jist a hundred dollars," answered the rider.

"I'll give you five dollars," said the other.

The rider stopped short, as if in amazement, and then slowly dismounted.

"Stranger," said he, "I ain't goin' to let a little matter of ninety-five dollars stand between me and a mule trade. The mule's yourn."

[1643]

A Texas rancher's wife ran off with a cowboy, leaving behind her three-year-old son. The rancher became bitter toward all women, and decided to bring his boy up entirely ignorant of women and their deceitful ways.

He made the boy acquainted with all the duties of the ranch, which consisted of many thousands of acres, in a deserted part of the state. The boy learned everything about cattle and horses, but nothing at all about women. When the boy became twenty-one, it became necessary for the father to take him to the nearest county seat, thirty miles away, to sign some legal papers.

The father sneaked him into the town before sunup, when no women would be around; kept him in the back room of a saloon, where he signed the papers; and at dusk started him home in the wagon, congratulating himself that the boy had remained uncontaminated by the sight of a woman.

Just as they passed a school building, a belated young teacher tripped down the steps and across the road.

"Oh, father, what's that?" exclaimed the boy.

"My son, that's a woman. You don't want to have anything to do with them."

"Oh, but I do, father! I like her! You must get her for me."

The father sighed; it had to be. He called after the school teacher, explained that his son had fallen in love with her and wanted to marry her, and asked her consent. She agreed, and the two were married at once.

When they reached the ranch, he said gruffly to the young couple, "I've got to leave you, to ride around the ranch. I'll return in five days. Meanwhile, you young people can get to know each other better."

At the end of the fifth day, he arrived again at the ranch house.

There was his son but no sign about of the young wife.

"Hello, father."

"Hello, son. How's your wife?"

"Ssh, father, we won't talk of her."

"Why, what do you mean? Where is she?"

The boy sighed. "It was a pity, father. The day after you left, she went down to the spring, to get a pail of water for the kitchen. You know that slippery stone above the spring? Well, she slipped on that, and broke her leg."

"The poor thing! Where is she now?"

The son turned blue eyes of wonder on his father. "Why, I had to shoot her, of course!"

[1644]

A man and his brother opened a law office at Idaho Springs under the firm name of "Ed. Wolcott & Bro." Later the partnership was dissolved. One of the brothers packed his few assets, including the sign that had hung outside of his office, upon a burro and started for Georgetown, a mining town farther up in the hills. Upon his arrival he was greeted by a crowd of miners who critically surveyed him and his outfit. One of them, looking first at the sign that hung over the pack, then at Wolcott, and finally at the donkey, ventured:

"Say, stranger, which of you is Ed?"

[1645]

"I was reading in the paper this morning about a Texas man who was struck by lightning while he was swearing. Remarkable occurrence, wasn't it?"

"Oh, I don't know. If lightning was to strike a Texas man when he wasn't swearing, it would be much more remarkable."

[1646]

"See here," said the Indian inspector at a Western reservation, "it is a violation of the law now to have more than one wife, and the law must be obeyed. When you get back home you tell all of your wives except one that they can no longer look upon you as their husband."

"You tell 'em," suggested the Indian after a moment's reflection.

[1647]

Two Western men travelled together two days in a train without a word ever passing between them. On the third day one of them at length ventured to remark that it was a fine morning.

"And who said it wasn't?" was the reply.

[1648]

A Mexican and an American worked together in a Western mine. On several occasions the Mexican had rabbit for dinner, and shared it with his workmate.

One day the American asked: "Where do you get rabbits, José? I can't find any."

"My wife she get 'um," José replied. "Ever' night they come 'round the house and make noise. She shoot 'um."

"Noise? Rabbits don't make a noise."

"Sure," asserted José, positively. "Go, 'Meow, meow.' "

[1649]

Stranger—"Is your society here very select?"

Arizona Al—"See them graves over thar? They was all filled by fellers who came to our dances without invitashuns."

[1650]

"Has the depression made a difference in the Bad Lands?"

"It has mixed up our politics quite considerable," answered Texas Joe. "The Bad Lands have some bold men. But we can't find anybody with nerve enough to take the job of collector of taxes."

[1651]

"Don't throw banana peels on the edge of the Grand Canyon," said a ranger to a careless tourist. "Do you want somebody to slip and fall three miles?"

[1652]

"Where's old Four-Fingered Pete?" asked Alkali Ike. "I ain't seen him around here since I got back."

"Pete?" said the bartender. "Oh, he went up to Hyena Tongue and got jagged. Went up to a hotel winder, stuck his head in and hollered 'Fire!' and everybody did."

[1653]

"Is this a healthy place?" asked a stranger of a native of a certain region of the West.

"It sure is," replied the native. "When I came here I couldn't utter a word. I had scarcely a hair on my head. I hadn't the strength to walk across the room, and I had to be lifted from my bed."

"That is wonderful," exclaimed the stranger. "How long have you been here?"

"I was born here."

[1654]

An Englishman on a visit to the West decided to go horseback riding. The cowboy who was to attend him asked: "Do you prefer an English saddle or a Western?"

"What's the difference?" he asked.

"The Western saddle has a horn," replied the attendant.

"I don't think I'll need the horn," said the Englishman. "I don't intend to ride in heavy traffic."

[1655]

A Texas Sheriff, with papers in a civil suit, entered the house of an attractive widow and said:

"Madam, I have an attachment for you."

The widow blushed, but said something about reciprocation.

"You must proceed to court."

"I prefer that you do that——"

"Come, hurry, please, the Justice is waiting."

"Oh, well, then you have the license, I suppose?"

The Sheriff cleared himself in time.

[1656]

The scene was the interior of a saloon in the Far West, and round the table were gathered as tough a gang as could be found in the whole of California. The game was fast and furious, the stakes were high.

Suddenly the dealer flung his cards on the table, and threateningly pulled out his six-gun.

"Boys," he shouted, "the game ain't a straight one! Slippery Sam ain't playing the hand I dealt him."

[1657]

"Do you think you can keep that desperado in jail?"

"I don't know," answered Cactus Jack. "We're doin' our best. We have fired two cooks he didn't like, given him credit at the licker dispensary and subscribed for all the magazines. But somehow we don't seem able to keep him satisfied."

[1658]

"Father's trip abroad did him so much good," said the daughter of the Westerner who struck it rich when oil was found on his rocky land. "He looks better, feels better, and as for appetite—honestly, it would just do your heart good to hear him eat!"

[1659]

A versatile real estate salesman of west Texas had just finished describing the glorious opportunities of that part of the country to a prospect in the East. "All west Texas needs," he said, "to become the garden spot of the world is good people and water."

"Huh!" replied the prospect, "that's all Hell needs."

[1660]

An Indian in New Mexico returned to the village for the third time to buy half a dozen bottles of cough syrup.

Druggist—"Someone sick at your house?"

Indian—"No sick."

Druggist—"Then what on earth all this cough syrup for?"

Indian—"Mm—me likeum on pancakes."

[1661]

"Did you try the simple plan of counting sheep for your insomnia?"

"Yes, doctor, but I made a mess of it. I counted ten thousand sheep, put 'em on the train, and shipped 'em to market. And when I'd got through counting the money I got for them it was time to get up."

[1662]

That Texas is large is evident from a cursory examination of the map. But its effect on the people of that state is not generally known. It is about six hundred miles from Brownsville, at the bottom of the map, to Dallas, which is several hundred miles from the top of the map. Hence the following conversation in Brownsville recently between two of the old-time residents:

"Where have you been lately, Bob? I ain't seen much of you."

"Been on a trip north."

"Where'd you go?"

"Went to Dallas."

"Have a good time?"

"Naw; I never did like them damn Yankees anyway."

[1663]

A quiet stranger refused the cowpuncher's command to drink for two reasons.

"Name them!" roared the terror of Pecos.

"I promised my grandmother on her death-bed that I would handle not, touch not, taste not the accursed stuff."

"And the other reason," insisted the bully, somewhat softened.

"I've just had a drink!"

[1664]

Insurance Man (putting questions to cowboy)—"Ever had any accidents?"

"No," was the reply.

"Never had an accident in your life?"

"Nope. A rattler bit me once, though."

"Well, don't you call that an accident?"

"Naw—he bit me on purpose."

[1665]

"I believe in calling a spade a spade," said the emphatic person.

"That's right, friend," replied Bronco Bob. "There was a man who nearly lost his life here by gittin' into a game an' tryin' to call a spade a club."

[1666]

A "Big Indian" strayed away from his camp and got lost. Inquiring the way back, he was asked: "Indian lost?"

"No," said he, disdainfully, "Indian no lost—wigwam lost." Striking his breast, he exclaimed, "Indian here!"

[1667]

Tourist (to Indian in heart of reservation)—"White man glad to see red man. White man hope big chief feel tip-top this morning."

Indian (calling)—"Hey, Jake, come here and listen to this bozo. He's great."

[1668]

"There!" triumphantly exclaimed a Deadwood editor, as a bullet came through the window and shattered the inkstand, "I knew that that new 'Personal' column would be a success."

[1669]

In a Western town close to a reservation, an Indian paid a debt of fifty dollars to the local supply house. The proprietor thanked him for the money, but the Indian stood with arms folded, evidently waiting for something else. The proprietor naturally asked the red man what he wanted, and received the reply:

"Waiting for a receipt."

"What do you want a receipt for?" asked the proprietor, "are you afraid that I will ask you for the money a second time?"

The Indian shrugged his shoulders and said: "When I go to meet the great Father Saint Peter he will want me to show receipt for fifty dollars which I paid you before I can enter heaven. I want to show receipt when I come to gate. I don't want to hunt all over hell to find you."

The Indian got his receipt.

LOONY LAWS

[1670]

Penal Code 6260, California State Vehicle Act, Chapter XVIII, Paragraph 187, reads:

"It is a misdemeanour to shoot at any kind of game bird or mammal—*except a whale,* from an automobile or airplane."

[1671]

Ordinance No. 16 of Columbus, Mont., provides that "any person who shall not lift his hat to the Mayor as he passes him on the street, will be guilty of a misdemeanor."

[1672]

And this is the law in Alabama:

"The teeth of a horse offered for sale to the public shall not be stained, discolored or otherwise camouflaged so as to be misleading indication of the animal's age and health."

[1673]

Wichita, Kan., Ordinance No. 381, reads:

"That it shall be unlawful for any person to throw upon or against another person in the city of Wichita, any confetti or similar

preparation or to throw same about in any street or public building or place in said city. It is further made unlawful for any person to throw as aforesaid any flour, talcum powder, rice or other substance or preparations for the purpose of annoying or harassing others."

[1674]

Boys are prohibited from throwing snowballs at trees within the city limits of Mt. Pulaski, Ill., according to Section 37 of Revised Ordinances of that city.

[1675]

All Wisconsin boarding houses, clubs, hotels, restaurants, must serve with every meal sold at twenty-five cents or more, not less than two-thirds of an ounce of cheese, according to Bill 223-S, adopted by the Wisconsin Legislature.

[1676]

And here is Section 1 of the Tennessee Act which incorporates the town of Ripley, in Lauderdale County, Tenn.:

"Be it enacted by the General Assembly of the State of Tennessee, that . . . the boundaries of said town of Ripley shall be as follows: Beginning at a stake in the West boundary line of the present limits of the old corporation . . . thence north eighty-five degrees and East to a *blackgum marked with a cross and with* mistletoe in the top, and with a blue bird sitting on a limb which tree is a short distance East of Ed Johnson's horse lot; . . ."

[1677]

Connecticut General Statutes Volume 2, page 1900, Section 6138, is a law punishing by fine or imprisonment the "enticing of a neighbor's bees."

[1678]

Section 21–2426 of the Revised Statutes of Kansas, 1923, reads as follows:

"It shall be unlawful for any person to exhibit in a public way within the State of Kansas, any sort of an exhibition that consists of the eating or pretending to eat of snakes, lizards, scorpions, centipedes, tarantulas, or other reptiles."

[1679]

The law of Shawnee, Okla., defines a nuisance as follows:

"When three or more dogs congregate on any private property *without the consent of the owner or occupant* and annoy such owners or occupants. . . ."

[1680]

Section 74, State Housing Act, of California reads:

"No horse, cow, calf, swine, sheep, goat, rabbit, mule or other animal, chicken, pigeon, goose, duck or other poultry shall be kept *in any apartment house or hotel* or any part thereof."

[1681]

Section 1 of Ordinance No. 32928 of Portland, Oregon, reads as follows:

"*Bathing without Suitable Dress.* It shall be unlawful to bathe in the waters of the Willamette River, or in the waters of any lake, slough or creek within the corporate limits of the City of Portland between the hours of six o'clock A.M. and half-past eight P.M. without wearing a suitable dress, *which shall cover the body from the neck to the knees,* and no person while so attired in said bathing suit or otherwise, shall unnecessarily expose himself to the public view"; *etc.*

[1682]

Ohio General Code, Title II, Chapter 20, Page 1590, Section 6281, provides:

"A person assaulted and lynched by a mob may recover, from the county in which such assault is made, a sum not to exceed five hundred dollars."

[1683]

And Act 64 of 1914 of the State of Louisiana, provides:

"No woman may wear hatpins which protrude from the crown of the hat more than ½ inch. In case such a pin is worn longer than ½ inch from the crown of the hat, it is to be protected by a shield or sheath."

[1684]

A city ordinance of Alderson, W. Va., states:

"No lions shall be allowed to run wild on the streets of this city."

[1685]

Section 64, Page 31, of the Ordinances of Calhoun, Georgia, is as follows:

"Any person or persons tying a tin box or any other article calculated to frighten, to any dog or any other animal, within the corporate limits of Calhoun, Georgia, upon conviction thereof, shall pay a fine," etc.

[1686]

North Dakota Compiled Laws 1913; Section 9998 reads:

"Every person who offers to sell any beef and fails to exhibit to the purchaser on demand the hide of the animal to be sold or sold, and does not keep such hide for ten days after the sale, at his place of residence, or refuses to allow the same to be inspected by any person, is punishable, etc."

[1687]

Ordinance No. 75169, of the City of Los Angeles, Calif., consists of the following prohibitions:

"It shall be unlawful for any person to have, keep or maintain, or cause to permit to be had, kept or maintained or to have in possession or under control within the City of Los Angeles, any elephant, bear, hippopotamus, rhinoceros, lion, tiger, leopard, wolf, or any poisonous reptile of any kind, without first applying to and receiving from the Board of Police Commissioners a permit to do so."

[1688]

And this is good law today in good old Kansas:

"When two trains approach each other at a crossing, they shall both come to a full stop, and neither shall start up until the other has gone."

[1689]

The following is still law in Pennsylvania, according to its statute books:

"*Good entertainment to be furnished*—Every innkeeper shall keep good entertainment for man and horse under penalty of $5. for every case of neglect."

[1690]

Please note these official Rules and Regulations of Cedar Hill Cemetery, Newark, N. J.:

"Visitors are admitted to the cemetery at the discretion of the Cemetery or its superintendent; no person with firearms, dogs, refreshments, or liquors will be permitted to enter the grounds; monuments constructed to serve as sun-baths, bird-baths and other novel features are not permitted; visitors will not be permitted to sit or lie upon the grass nor in the shrubbery; no person will be permitted to enter the Cemetery except through a gate."

[1691]

Section 21, Article VII of the Constitution of Indiana, adopted 1851, reads:

"Every person of good moral character, being a voter, shall be entitled to practice law in all courts of justice."

[1692]

The Code of the City of Columbia, Tenn., Chapter 5, Section 45, provides:

"It shall be unlawful for three or more persons to assemble upon any of the sidewalks of this corporation, so as to impede the free passage of persons upon the sidewalk."

[1693]

The following ordinance was passed by the city government of Waterloo, Neb., in 1910:

"It shall be illegal for any barber in this town to eat onions between 7 A.M. and 7 P.M."

[1694]

Abilene, Texas, is reported to have passed the following ordinance:

"It shall be unlawful for any person to idle or loiter on any street or thoroughfare, sidewalk, or alley, or in any store, theater, motor car, motion picture show, business house, or in the entrance or doorway of any place within the corporate limits of the city of Abilene for the purpose of plying the avocation of a flirt or masher.

"It shall further be unlawful for any man to stare at or make googoo eyes at, or in any other manner look at or make remarks to or concerning, or cough or whistle at, or do any other act to attract the attention of any woman upon or traveling along any of the sidewalks, streets, public ways of the city of Abilene with an intent or in a manner calculated to annoy such woman."

[1695]

And this is Section 338 of the statutes of El Paso, Texas:

"Churches and Hotels and All Public Places of Resort. In and at all public places of resort or amusement, such as churches or hotels or halls of assembly, or stores or markets or banking-rooms or railroad depots or street depots or waiting stations or saloons, shall be required at the expense of the owners or persons in charge of same, or under whose control or care the same are, to be provided with spittoons of a kind and number to efficiently contain expectorations into them," etc.

[1696]

According to Section 5539, 1928 Code of Alabama, "any person who engages in domino playing on Sunday . . . must be fined."

[1697]

Act 239 of the Michigan Laws of 1907 reads:

"An act to provide for the lawful taking of suckers, mullet, dogfish, and lawyers from the waters of the Sturgeon River."

[1698]

Finally, the great metropolis of New York City has this law on its statute books—Sanitary Code, Section 9, Article 2:

"If you have a dead horse, place it in the street at once with tag giving name and address; if not removed at twilight, put lights around properly protected carcass till called for."

AMERICANS ABROAD

[1699]

An American tourist and his wife, after their return from abroad, were telling of the wonders seen by them at the Louvre in Paris. The husband mentioned with enthusiasm a picture which represented Adam and Eve and the serpent in the Garden of Eden, in connection with the eating of the forbidden fruit. The wife also waxed enthusiastic, and interjected a remark:

"Yes, we found the picture most interesting, most interesting indeed, because, you see, we know the anecdote."

[1700]

"Traveled all over the world, eh? Went up the Rhine, I suppose?"

"Climbed it to the top."

"Saw the Lion of St. Mark?"

"Fed it."

"And visited the Black Sea?"

"Filled my fountain pen there."

[1701]

"Oh, I'm so glad to get my feet on vice versa again," said the American woman as the ship landed in France.

"My dear, you don't mean vice versa, you mean terra cotta," corrected her Yankee husband.

[1702]

Tourist abroad (pointing to menu)—"Waiter, bring me some of this."

Waiter—"Sir, the orchestra is now playing it."

[1703]

She—"Tell me about Switzerland, romantic Switzerland."

He—"Well, there are a few bad places as you come down the mountains, but in the main the roads are pretty good."

[1704]

Mrs. Yankus—"I think this scenery is just heavenly."

Mr. Yankus—"Um, I don't know. Take away the mountains and the lake and it is just like anywhere else."

[1705]

An American had made an exhaustive tour of France, but a friend in Paris thought that as the crown of his whole experience he would take him to dine at Voisin's.

"Let's go to Voisin's," he said. "You'll get the most marvelous old Burgundy and Bordeaux wines."

"Well," the visitor answered, "I'll go to Voisin's, if you like, but don't talk to me about old Burgundy and Bordeaux. What I am looking for is a good reliable French bootlegger who can get me a drink of ice water."

[1706]

"So you had a chance to see the king's palace in England, eh? What did you think of it?"

"Well, after seeing our own movie houses, filling stations, and hot-dog stands, it isn't very impressive."

[1707]

"So you come from New York," said an English lady to a traveling American. "I supposed, of course, you came from Boston."

"Why did you think that?" inquired the New York lady.

"Because I supposed all cultivated, intelligent Americans came from Boston."

"But what in the world made you think that?" was the natural question.

"Oh, I don't know, exactly. I think it was a Boston lady who told me."

[1708]

An Englishman and an American were presented to the ruler of one of the eastern countries. On looking over the Englishman's passport, the monarch said, "I see that you are a British subject." The Englishman admitted with pride that he was. Then, looking at the American passport, he turned to its owner, and said: "And you are a subject of the United States?"

"Subject? Subject, hell! I own part of the United States!" exclaimed the American.

[1709]

As a steamer was leaving Athens, a well dressed passenger approached the captain and pointing to the distant hills, inquired:

"What is that white stuff on those distant hills, captain?"

"That is snow, madam," replied the captain.

"Well," remarked the lady, "I thought so myself. But a gentleman just told me it was Greece."

[1710]

A young lady who had returned from a tour through Italy with her father informed a friend that he liked all the Italian cities, but most of all he loved Venice.

"Ah, Venice, to be sure!" said the friend. "I can readily understand that your father would like Venice, with its gondolas, and St. Markses and Michelangelos."

"Oh, no," the young lady interrupted, "it wasn't that. He liked it because he could sit in the hotel and fish from the window."

[1711]

"Has Harry traveled much?"

"Has he! He's been to half the places on his suit-case labels."

[1712]

A number of tourists were recently looking down the crater of Vesuvius. An American gentleman said to his companion:

"That looks a good deal like the infernal regions."

An English lady, overhearing the remark, said to another:

"Good gracious! How these Americans do travel."

[1713]

A rich American in Paris was asked by an art enthusiast if he had picked up a Van Dyke or Rembrandt in his European travels.

"Nothin' doin'!" he replied. "I now have a big garage jammed with cars made in God's country!"

[1714]

"And did you enjoy your trip through Switzerland?"

"Yes, very much. They had such attractive postcards all through that country."

[1715]

"Just got back from a trip around the world."

"Great. Did you stop off in Egypt?"

"Oh, yes."

"Go up the Nile?"

"Sure. Swell view from the top."

[1716]

In Paris last summer a southern girl was heard to drawl between the acts of "Chantecler": "I think it's mo' fun when you don't understand French. It sounds mo' like chickens!"

[1717]

"Of course, you spent some time under the spell of Millet's 'The Angelus'?" the Bostonian asked the man from Kansas, when they were comparing notes on the steamship returning to the United States. "I call it easily the masterpiece of the Louvre."

"So that impostor Millet hornswoggled you, too? Well, I'll be switched!" cried the Kansan. "What would you think if I told you he has palmed off as his own work a chromo that has hung in our kitchen thirty years?"

[1718]

"Did you have any difficulty with your French in Paris?"

"No—but the French people did."

[1719]

An American was being urged to betake himself to Athens to see the old ruins.

"Nope," he decided definitely, "I'm going to Paris to see the young ruins!"

[1720]

A Yankee tourist was out sightseeing in London. They took him aboard the old battleship *Victory*, which was Lord Nelson's flagship in several of his famous naval triumphs. An English sailor escorted the Yank over the vessel, and coming to a raised brass tablet on the deck, he said, as he reverently removed his hat:

" 'Ere, sir, is the spot where Lord Nelson fell."

"Oh, is it?" replied the American blankly. "Well, that ain't nothin'. I nearly tripped on the durned thing myself."

[1721]

Returned Tourist (to his friend) —"Well, I like Paris and Rome, but the best part of the whole thing was the trip over. Don't miss that, whatever you do, if you go to Europe."

[1722]

An Englishman, it is said, having heard a great deal about the Yankee propensity of bragging, thought he would make an experiment in the art himself. He walked up to a market woman's stand, and, pointing to some large watermelons, said: "What, don't you raise any bigger apples than these in America?"

"Apples!" said the woman, disdainfully; "anybody might know you was an Englishman. Them's huckleberries."

[1723]

Guide—"This tower goes back to William the Conqueror."

Tourist—"Why, what's the matter with it, isn't it satisfactory?"

[1724]

A wealthy American girl was attending a social at a country house in England.

"You American girls haven't such healthy complexions as we English women have," said an English duchess to the girl. "I always wonder why our noblemen take a fancy to your white faces."

"It isn't our white faces that attracts them," responded the American girl; "it's our greenbacks."

[1725]

Two American tourists, while in England, were standing in a streetcar for the simple reason that all the seats were filled. Finally an elderly English lady and her daughter began gathering together their belongings, preparing to get off at the next street.

Suddenly the elder lady nudged her daughter and whispered in evident fear:

"Mary, mind what I tell you. When we get off, do just as I do,

and back down out of the car. I can't tell you why now."

Dutifully the daughter obeyed and they both backed their way out of the car down to the street. Safely arrived on the pavement, the daughter naturally asked the reason for her mother's strange request and action.

"Mary," said the mother, "you saw those two American tourists? Well, when we started to get out I overheard one of them say to the other: 'When those two dames get off we'll pinch their seats!'"

[1726]

Mrs. Newrich had just returned from a tour of Europe with her husband. Her friends, of course, were eager to hear all about her experiences.

"Did you include Rome in your itinerary?" she was asked.

"I really don't know," she answered, and explained, "you see, my husband always bought the tickets."

[1727]

Guide (at ancient castle)—"This is the moat. Are there any questions you would like to ask?"

American—"Yes. How in heck could a fellow get one of those in his eye?"

[1728]

British Guide (showing places of interest)—"It was in this room that Lord Wellington received his first commission."

American Tourist (suddenly interested)—"How much was it?"

[1729]

The American lady in the course of her tour of England took in the birthplace of William Shakespeare at Stratford-on-Avon. She was thrilled to tears, and then some. On the way back, as she was standing on the station platform, she remarked gushingly:

"And just think! It was from this very platform that the immortal bard would depart whenever he went to town."

[1730]

"How did you find the weather in London?" asked the friend of the returned traveler.

"You don't have to find the weather in London," replied the traveler. "It bumps into you at every corner."

PART II

LOVE, COURTSHIP AND MARRIAGE

THE DEAR LADIES

[1731]

Mr. Brown was always courteous to women. One day when he was airing his views on politeness he remarked that he had never seen an ugly woman. A woman standing near, who happened to have a flat nose, overheard him and said: "Sir, look at me, and confess that I am ugly!"

"Madam," replied Mr. Brown, "like the rest of your sex, you are an angel fallen from the skies, but it was not your fault that you happened to land on your nose."

[1732]

Helen—"What kind of husband would you advise me to get?"

Hazel—"You get a single man and let the husbands alone."

[1733]

Jessie—"Her husband didn't leave her much when he died, did he?"

Jennie—"No; but he left her very often when he was alive."

[1734]

Jane—"I didn't accept Henry the first time he proposed."

Joan—"No, dear, you weren't there."

[1735]

Della—"Haven't you heard? Evelyn has just married Roger!"

Bella—"Roger! Not really? Why that was the man she was engaged to!"

[1736]

May—"My fiancé is telling everybody in Canada that he is coming home to marry the most beautiful girl in the world."

Edna—"Too bad, darling, after being engaged to you for such a long time."

[1737]

Joan—"Yes, dear. I assure you that my husband is the only man who has ever kissed me."

Mary—"Really, darling? Tell me —are you bragging or complaining?"

[1738]

Wanda—"He wore my photograph over his heart and it stopped a bullet when that bank bandit fired at him."

Ethel—"I'm not surprised, dear. It would stop anything."

[1739]

May—"People say I grow younger every day."

Mary—"Yes, years ago you were 30 and now you are only 25."

[1740]

At an evening party, a self-made business man was chatting with a pretty young woman.

"You know, I sometimes feel ashamed of my failure to keep abreast of modern science," he said. "Take the electric light, for example. I must confess I haven't the least idea how it works."

The pretty young thing gave him a patronizing smile.

"Why, it's very simple, really," she replied. "You just turn a switch and the light comes on. That's all there is to it."

[1741]

Christine—"Why don't you marry Percy?"

Catherine—"I will only marry a man who knows life and has learned its sorrows."

Christine—"I see—a widower."

[1742]

"There's a woman who suffers for her beliefs."

"Why, what does she believe?"

"She believes she can wear a number five shoe on a number seven foot."

[1743]

Maude—"The ring of sincerity was in his voice when he told me of his love."

May—"It should have been in his hand. A ring in the hand is worth two in the voice."

[1744]

"Phyllis, this is my birthday."

"Congratulations, Mabel. How old aren't you?"

[1745]

Gerald—"Why do girls kiss each other, and men do not?"

Gertrude—"Because girls have nothing better to kiss and men have."

[1746]

"What was her name before she married?"

"Before she married whom?"

[1747]

Nell—"Oh, he's so romantic. When he addresses me he always calls me 'Fair Lady.' "

Belle—"Force of habit, my dear. He's a street-car conductor."

[1748]

Sue—"I refused to marry Harry two months ago and he has been hitting up the booze ever since."

Kate—"Well, I calls that carrying a celebration too far."

[1749]

May—"A certain young man sent me some flowers this morning."

Maud—"Don't say a 'certain young man,' my dear. There is none of them certain until you've got them."

[1750]

Miss Green—"I know he's rich, but he isn't too old to be considered eligible?"

Mrs. Brown—"My dear, he's too eligible to be considered old."

[1751]

Mrs. Hawkins—"I have such an indulgent husband."

Mrs. Perkins—"Sometimes indulges too much, doesn't he?"

[1752]

Eva—"Dear Jack is so forgetful."

Celia—"Isn't he! At the party last night I had to keep reminding him that it's you he's engaged to and not me."

[1753]

Mary—"George wanted to kiss me last night."

Jane—"What cheek!"

Mary—"Neither. Smack on the lips."

[1754]

Ione—"The man who married Ethel got a prize."

Irene—"What was it?"

[1755]

"Did you tell her that what you said was in strict confidence?"

"No; I don't want her to think it was important enough to repeat."

[1756]

"Can you keep a secret, Dora?"

"I can; but it's just my luck to tell things to other girls who can't."

[1757]

He—"When I proposed to Flossie she asked me for a little time to make up her mind."

She (the hated rival)—"Oh! So she makes that up too, does she?"

[1758]

Dorothy—"I hear you're going to divorce your husband."

Marjorie—"Don't be silly. Why, I hardly know him."

[1759]

"Was Phyllis a success at Palm Beach?"

"Oh, yes, she got along swimmingly. In fact she managed to outstrip all the other girls."

[1760]

Anne—"Doesn't Mrs. Green believe in co-education of the sexes?"

May — Co-education? I should say not! Why she believes that a girl ought to be raised so carefully that when she sees a man she will say, 'What is that, mamma?'"

[1761]

Miss Thin—"Don't you think my new dress is just exquisite? They all say so."

Miss Perfect—"O, lovely! I think that dressmaker of yours could make a clothes pole look quite graceful."

[1762]

She—"Then you'll take me for a drive on Thursday?"

He—"Yes, but suppose it rains."

She—"Come the day before, then."

[1763]

"Mrs. Smith, did you say, in the hearing of my little girl, that I was a great rusty cat?"

"No, my dear Mrs. Jones; I said you were a great aristocrat."

[1764]

"I'd hate to be in your shoes," said a woman yesterday, as she was quarreling with a neighbor.

"You couldn't get in them," sarcastically remarked the neighbor.

[1765]

If there is one time more than another when a woman should be entirely alone it is when a line full of clothes comes down in the mud.

[1766]

First Lady—"Dear me, I never saw Mrs. Potts look so pale."

Second Lady—"Nor I; she's probably been out in the rain without an umbrella."

[1767]

Mrs. Blank (visiting)—"Really, James and I meant to call long before this, but somehow we kept putting off the evil day."

[1768]

Girl—"What's your opinion of these women who imitate men?"

Boy—"They're idiots."

Girl—"Then the imitation is successful."

[1769]

Mary—"Look at that woman—she looks as if she'd been poured into her dress."

Maude—"Yes, and forgot to say 'when.'"

[1770]

Rose—"Do you ever allow a man to kiss you when you're out motoring with him?"

Violet—"Never. If a man can drive safely while kissing me, he's not giving the kiss the attention it deserves."

[1771]

Maud—"That story you told about Alice isn't worth repeating."

Kate—"It's young yet; give it time."

[1772]

The following correspondence explains itself: "Dear Mrs. Jones, Please let me have a dozen tomatoes if you can.—Sallie Smith."

"Dear Mrs. Smith, We are not going to can; we propose to pickle.—Jane Jones."

[1773]

Mistress—"Clara, give the goldfish a few more ants' eggs—it is my birthday and I want to see happy faces around me."

[1774]

Mrs. Smith—"Very bad form, I call it, to ring me up during church hours."

Mrs. Jones—"Probably she knows you don't go to church."

Mrs. Smith—"Very likely; but she might have had the decency to assume that I do."

[1775]

First Girl—"Dick says he came from a good family."

Second Girl—"Yeh, and I'll bet he's footsore."

[1776]

"Ah, my dear," said her homely relative, "you will find that Time is a great healer."

"True, auntie," the girl replied, "but he's certainly a mighty poor beauty doctor."

[1777]

"What do women talk about when they are together?"

"Just what men talk about."

"Aren't they terrible?"

[1778]

Eloise—"I had a quiet little evening alone with a book last night."

Vivienne—"I'm afraid that's going to happen to me some night too."

[1779]

First Girl—"I don't see how you could engage yourself to that old Mr. Wiggs. He hasn't a tooth in his head and is pretty near bald."

Second Girl—"Well, my dear, you shouldn't be too severe on him; he was born that way."

[1780]

"So your wife entertained her club yesterday afternoon, eh?"

"That was the supposition, but when I sneaked in the back door the women were all talking at once, so I imagine each was entertaining herself."

[1781]

"Do you save up money for a rainy day, dear?"

"Oh, no! I never shop when it rains."

[1782]

Jack—"What do you think Maud Oldby would like for her birthday?"

Helen—"Not to be reminded of it."

[1783]

She—"I know nothing but good of Alice."

Other She—"Then let us talk of someone else."

[1784]

"Mrs. Chatter is getting a double chin."

"Too much work for one, I suppose."

[1785]

"So your husband objects to cats."

"Yes, indeed. He says that I feed all the cats in the neighborhood. Won't you stay and have tea?"

[1786]

Plump One—"In the bus, this morning, three men jumped up and offered me their seats."

Slim One—"Did you take them, dear?"

[1787]

Madge (after friends' tiff)—"Of course you speak to Helen when you pass her on the street."

Mabel—"Indeed I do not. Why, I don't even notice what she has on."

[1788]

Spinster—"So the waiter says to me, 'How would you like your rice?'"

Friend—"Yes, dearie, go on."

Spinster—"So I says wistfully, 'Thrown at me, big boy.'"

[1789]

He—"I've a sort of feeling I've danced with you before somewhere."

She—"So have I. The pressure of your foot seems familiar!"

[1790]

She was making the usual female search for her purse when the conductor came to collect the fares.

Her companion meditated silently for a moment, then, addressing the other, said:

"Let us divide this, Mabel; you fumble and I'll pay."

[1791]

Jane Gossip—"Why did they separate?"

Joan Gossip—"Nobody knows."

Jane Gossip—"Oh, how terrible!"

[1792]

First Girl—"Where were you on your vacation?"

Second Girl (listlessly) — "No man's land."

[1793]

Mary—"I'm sorry—I quite forgot your party the other evening!"

May—"Oh, weren't you there?"

[1794]

"Your wife is pretty game to go on that reducing diet."

"Yes, but she's a poor loser."

[1795]

"I often think you can tell people's character by their gardens."

"I do, too. There's Miss Richlove, who is as mercenary as she can be, and the prominent plants in her gardens are moneywort and marigold."

[1796]

She was telling an acquaintance about her girl friends.

"Yes," she said, "my friend Maud is only twenty-five, but she's been married three times. And all her husbands have been named William."

"You don't say!" replied he. "Why, she must be a regular Bill collector!"

[1797]

Niece—"Oh! isn't the water cold?"

Auntie—"Well, you will wear those flimsy bathing-suits."

[1798]

"Does she have her own way?"

"Does she? Why she writes her diary a week ahead of time."

[1799]

Jane—"How old are you?"

Joan—"I've just turned twenty-three."

Jane—"Oh, I see—thirty-two."

[1800]

"My wife has been using a flesh-reducing roller for nearly two months."

"And can you see any result yet?"

"Yes—the roller is much thinner."

[1801]

Maid (to spring-cleaning mistress)—"There are half a dozen men down-stairs with vacuum-cleaners. They say they have appointments to give demonstrations."

Mistress—"Yes, I sent for them. Put them in different rooms and tell them to get busy."

[1802]

"Miss Green, do let me help you to some more pudding."

"Well, I will take some more, but only a mouthful."

"Bella," said the hostess to the maid, "fill Miss Green's plate."

[1803]

"Jack makes me tired."

"It's your own fault, dear. You should stop running after him."

[1804]

"Bothered with time-wasting callers, are you? Why don't you try my plan?"

"What is your plan, Mrs. Jones?"

"Why, when the bell rings, I put on my hat and gloves before I press the button. If it proves to be some one I don't want to see, I simply say, 'So sorry, but I'm just going out.'"

"But suppose it's some one you want to see?"

"Oh then I say, 'So fortunate, I've just come in.'"

[1805]

"You say you saw a lot of her this summer?"

"Yes, I met her a number of times down at the bathing beach."

[1806]

At the Bronx Zoological Garden the other day a very inquisitive lady was making a nuisance of herself with the attendants. After asking the attendant in front of the tank containing the hippopotamus several silly questions, she finally inquired as to whether the occupant of the tank was a male or a female.

This last question was too much. He let his exasperation get the best of him. "After all, Madam, what difference does it make—unless you are another hippopotamus?"

[1807]

"Is she very pretty?"

"Pretty! Say, when she gets on a street-car the advertising is a total loss."

[1808]

The professor was asked to give his definition of woman. After clearing his throat, he began in his leisurely way:

"Woman is, generally speaking—"

"Stop right there, professor," interrupted a lowbrow; "if you talked a thousand years you'd never get any nearer to it than that."

[1809]

"What's the cause of Janet's unpopularity?"

"She won a popularity contest."

[1810]

Explorer—"D'ye know, I once went about in South America for months with a price on my head!"

Hostess—"Dreadful! I know the feeling. I came home from a sale once with the price-ticket on my hat!"

[1811]

"Have you known Phyllis long?"

"Oh, yes. I've known her ever since we were the same age!"

[1812]

"My dear, you must go to my new beauty doctor—she's simply marvelous. She'll make you look like another person."

[1813]

The members were attending the annual picnic of the United Association of Lady Vegetarians. The ladies were comfortably seated, and waiting for the kettle to boil, when, horror of horrors! a savage bull appeared on the scene.

Immediately a wild rush was made for safety, while the raging creature pounded after one lady who, unfortunately, had a red parasol. By great good fortune she nipped over the stile before it could reach her. Then, regaining her breath, she turned around.

"Oh, you ungrateful creature!" she exclaimed. "Here have I been a vegetarian all my life. There's gratitude for you!"

[1814]

Nancy—"Did Ethel inherit her beauty?"

Sally—"Yes, her father left her a drug store."

[1815]

Joan—"It's too bad of you. You said you wouldn't give away that secret I told you."

Jean—"I didn't give it away. I exchanged it for another."

[1816]

Muriel—"I don't intend to be married until after I'm thirty."

Mabel—"And I don't intend to be thirty until after I'm married!"

[1817]

"Isn't it remarkable how Alice keeps her age?"

"Yes, she hasn't changed it for ten years."

[1818]

Mabel—"George is just crazy about me."

Minnie—"Don't take too much credit to yourself. He was crazy before you ever met him."

[1819]

"Have you seen Norah's new evening frock?"

"No; what does it look like?"

"Well, in many places it's very like Norah."

[1820]

"If you tell a man anything it goes in at one ear and out at the other," she remarked.

"And if you tell a woman anything," he countered, "it goes in at both ears and out of her mouth."

[1821]

Mary—"I thought you and Tessie weren't speaking."

Roberta—"Oh, yes, we are now. I wanted to find out what Elsie told her about me."

[1822]

She—"I have found out one thing about that Mrs. Newcome. Whoever she is, she has certainly never moved in good society."

He—"How do you know that?"

She—"She shakes hands as if she meant it."

[1823]

"I was sorry for your wife in church this morning when she had a terrific attack of coughing and every one turned to look at her."

"You needn't worry about that. She was wearing a new spring hat."

[1824]

"Aren't some of the hats women wear absurd?"

"Yes," replied Miss Catty, "and yet when some people put them on they do look so appropriate."

[1825]

A lady with a huge brown-paper parcel came out of a chiropodist's establishment. She was furiously angry and said to the friend awaiting her: "Calls himself a chiropodist and can't stuff a dog!"

[1826]

The young lady walked boldly up to a woman whom she took to be the superintendent of the hospital.

"May I see Captain Williams, please?" she asked.

"May I ask who you are?"

"Certainly. I am his sister."

"Well, well. I'm glad to meet you. I'm his mother."

[1827]

Gertrude—"Well, anyway, George dresses like a gentleman."

Katherine—"Indeed! I never saw him dressing."

[1828]

Violet—"What is your worst sin?"

Vera—"My vanity. I spend hours before the mirror admiring my beauty."

Violet—"That isn't vanity, dear—that's imagination."

[1829]

Jane—"What do you say to a tramp in the park?"

Joan—"I never speak to the horrid things."

[1830]

The daughter of the house was talking over the problem of what to serve her bridge-club, a group of girls with finicky appetites.

One girl disliked salads, one refused sweets, another never ate fruit and still another shunned meat.

"Well," her disgusted younger

brother put in, "about the only thing left for that bunch is a good chaw of tobacco."

[1831]

"Gladys ought not to go in alone," said the seaside girl to her companion. "She was nearly drowned yesterday and Jim had to use artificial respiration."

"You mean Gladys had to use artificial drowning."

[1832]

Mrs. S.—"Bridget, if that's Mrs. Gabber, I'm not in."

Bridget (returning)—"It was, ma'am, and she was very glad to hear it."

[1833]

When the agent for the life insurance company paid Mrs. Smith the amount of insurance her husband had carried, he asked her to take out a policy on her own life.

"I believe I will," she said, "my husband had such good luck with his."

[1834]

Lady (in theater)—"Pardon me, sir, does my hat bother you?"

Gentleman behind—"No, but it bothers my wife. She wants one like it."

[1835]

Mr. Slowwit—"I-er-er-am going to tell you something that er-er-will no doubt surprise you. I-er-er-think—"

Miss Kutting—"Well, that is a surprise. Funny I never noticed it before. How long have you been thinking?"

[1836]

Joan—"Did you hear Erica is marrying her X-ray specialist?"

Jane—"Well, she's lucky. Nobody else could ever see anything in her."

[1837]

It was the first time she had been to dinner with them, and they smiled indulgently as she refused a Scotch and soda.

"I've never touched it in my life," she explained.

"Why not try?" urged her host. "See if you like the taste."

She blushed and shyly consented, and he poured her out a mixture, which she delicately raised to her lips.

"Why," she cried, "you've given me Irish whiskey!"

[1838]

Father—"It's a good plan, my dear, always to think before you speak."

Daughter—"But, dad, when I do that the girls have changed the subject."

[1839]

She—"What do you mean by telling your boy friend that I was deaf and dumb?"

Other She—"I didn't say deaf."

[1840]

A lady approached a surgeon and asked him if he would perform an operation.

"What for?" he inquired.

"Oh, anything you like. You see, I attend a lot of women's bridge parties and, never having had an operation, I simply can't take part in the conversation."

[1841]

"I see she's let her hair go dark again."

"Yes—off the gold standard."

[1842]

"That romantic Miss Passeigh says there is a secret connected with her birth."

"That's true—it's the date."

[1843]

"Mrs. Brown," cried Mr. Smith to his neighbor, "have you spoken to your boy about mimicking me?"

"Yes, I have," replied Mrs. Brown. "I've told him not to act like a fool."

[1844]

"Ah, Mrs. Mudge, one half of the world is ignorant of how the other half lives."

"Not in this village, Miss."

[1845]

Janet—"What do you do when you see an unusually beautiful girl?"

Anna—"I look for a while, then I get tired and lay the mirror down."

[1846]

"Hasn't Elsie got on a spiritual evening dress?"

"What do you mean, spiritual?"

"Well, there isn't much material in it."

[1847]

"What caused the rumpus at their house?"

"She asked him to bring home something to give as bridge prizes at her ladies' club and save her a trip down-town, and he brought home a couple of cook-books."

[1848]

"Pay your taxes with a smile," advised Mrs. Wealthy.

"I should love to," said Miss Comely, "but they insist on cash."

[1849]

Pearl—"You really ought to come to Spring Valley with me next summer. I had a wonderful time there this year. I won a beauty competition."

Ruby—"No, I think I'd rather go to a more crowded place."

[1850]

Woman (in crowded street car, to her friend)—"I wish that good-looking man would give me his seat."

Five men stood up.

[1851]

Maud—"So Jack said that I had a skin one loves to touch."

Marie—"Not exactly, dear; he said you had a skin you love to re-touch."

[1852]

"Do make yourselves at home, ladies," said a lady one day to her visitors. "I'm at home myself, and I would like you all to be."

[1853]

"So Turner made a fortune?"

"Yes, he invented a chocolate bonbon with a lettuce center for women on a diet."

[1854]

As the kindly Mrs. Gotcash thrust her fare into the taxi-driver's hand, she saw that he was wet and apparently cold after half an hour of pouring rain. "Do you ever take anything when you get soaked through?" she asked.

"Yes, ma'am," answered the cabby eagerly. "I generally do."

"Wait here in the vestibule," commanded the philanthropist. She opened the door and vanished, to reappear in a moment.

"Here," she said, putting a small envelope in the man's outstretched hand. "These are two-grain quinine capsules; you take two of them now and two more in half an hour."

[1855]

"They tell me that woman is a gossip. Do you think she is reliable."

"I know that whatever she says goes."

[1856]

Maud—"I'm sorry I couldn't come to your party yesterday."

Mary—"Dear me! Weren't you there?"

Maud—"Oh, why, of course I was! How stupid of me—I must have forgotten."

[1857]

Ladies, skip this paragraph! It is really unfit for publication. It got into the manuscript by some mistake, and I asked the printer to destroy it, or set it wrong side up.

If there's anything worries a woman,
It's something she ought not to know;
You can bet that she'll find it out somehow,
If you give her the least kind of show.
Now, we'll wager a half to a jitney
This poem she's already read—
If she had to stand on her head,
We knew she'd get at it somehow.

[1858]

Mrs. Brown—"She told me that you told her the secret I told you not to tell her."

Mrs. Green—"The mean thing! I told her not to tell you I told her."

Mrs. Brown—"Well, don't tell her that I told you she told me."

[1859]

Mrs. Gadabout — "That Mrs. Hardhead next door doesn't seem to have many friends."

Hostess (wearily) — "N-no. I wonder how she manages it?"

[1860]

"I do hope that my visits aren't boring to your husband, Julia, dear?"

"Oh, no, indeed. However depressed he is when you come, he's always happy when you go."

[1861]

"Gee, that rouge sure looks natural. For a while I thought it was your skin."

"Well, it's the next thing to it."

[1862]

"She certainly is polished, don't you think so?"

"Yes. Everything she says casts a reflection on someone."

[1863]

Clara—"You may not believe it, but I said 'No' to seven different men during the summer."

Maude—"Oh, I don't doubt it. What were they selling?"

[1864]

"It looks like a storm, Shirley! You had better stay for dinner."

"Oh, thanks, but I don't think it's bad enough for that."

[1865]

Mrs. A (on street)—"Who is that you just bowed to?"

Mrs. B—"Oh, she's our next-door neighbor."

Mrs. A—"But she didn't return your bow."

Mrs. B—"No! She never returns anything."

[1866]

"That girl over there shows distinction in her clothes."

"You mean distinctly, don't you?"

[1867]

"Did you tell her when you proposed that you weren't worthy of her? That always makes a good impression."

"Well, I was going to. But she told me so first."

[1868]

"Do you girls really like conceited men better than the other kind?"

"What other kind?"

[1869]

"You know her to speak to?"

"Oh, no, dear! Only to talk about!"

LOVE AND COURTSHIP

[1870]

Angela shook her head with finality. "No, Tom, I can never be yours. Sorry."

He took the blow quite calmly. "All right," he replied. "What about all my presents?"

"I'll return them, of course," she said coldly.

"Yes, I know you will," he exclaimed, with some warmth; "but who's going to return all those cigars I gave your father and the dimes I gave your beastly little brother?"

[1871]

"Well, and how are you getting on with your courtship of the banker's daughter?"

The young suitor beamed happily. "Not so bad," he replied. "I'm getting some encouragement now."

"Really," put in his friend. "Is she beginning to smile sweetly on you, or something?"

"Not exactly," replied the young man, "but last night she told me she had said 'No!' for the last time."

[1872]

Young Man—"Mr. Smith, your daughter has promised to be my wife."

Mr. Smith—"It was your own fault—what else did you expect if you kept hanging round here every night?"

[1873]

"Daughter," said the father, "your young man, Ferdinand, stays until a very late hour. Has not your mother said something to you about this habit of his?"

"Yes, father," replied the daughter sweetly. "Mother says men haven't altered a bit."

[1874]

Suitor (sighing)—"Well, since you don't want to marry me after all, perhaps you'll return my ring."

Girl (acidly)—"If you must know, your jeweler has called for it already."

[1875]

She (tenderly)—"When did you first know you loved me?"

He—"When I began to get mad when people said you were brainless and unattractive."

[1876]

Floyd had taken his girl friend to lunch and she had spoken to a nice-looking man at the next table.

"Is that man a friend of yours?" asked Floyd.

"Yes," she replied.

"Then I think I'll ask him to join us."

"Oh, Floyd, this is so sudden."

"What's so sudden?"

"Why—why—he's our minister."

[1877]

Jim—"That Jones girl doesn't seem to be very intelligent."

Jack—"No, she didn't pay any attention to me, either."

[1878]

"Are you engaged to Harold?"

"Yes, I have promised to marry him as soon as he has made his fortune."

"That isn't an engagement, that's an option."

[1879]

Ralph—"If you loved me, why did you refuse me at first?"

Ruth—"Just to see what you would do."

Ralph—"But I might have rushed off without waiting for an explanation."

Ruth—"Hardly. I had the door locked."

[1880]

She—"All extremely bright men are conceited."

He—"Oh, I don't know; I'm not."

[1881]

He was a bit shy, and after she had thrown her arms around him and kissed him for bringing her a bouquet of flowers, he arose and started to leave.

"I am sorry I offended you," she said.

"Oh, I'm not offended," he replied, "I'm going for more flowers."

[1882]

He (smoking a cigarette)— "Shall I blow you a ring?"

She—"You can blow me to one."

[1883]

The young man approached his sweetheart, sad and sorrowful. She watched him with anxious eyes, and asked:

"How did father take it?"

"All right," he replied.

"I'm so glad!" she cried.

"Well, I can't say that I am. At first he wouldn't listen to me."

"Did you tell him you had five thousand dollars saved and in the bank?"

"Yes, after all else had failed."

"And what did father do then?"

"Do!" replied the young man. "He borrowed it!"

[1884]

"I shuddered when Tom proposed."

"Was he so awkward?"

"Oh, no; he did it so well."

[1885]

He (after long silence, looking at clock)—"Is that an eight day clock?"

She (very bored)—"Well, why not stay a little longer and find out!"

[1886]

He—"We're coming to a tunnel —are you afraid?"

She—"Not if you take that cigar out of your mouth."

[1887]

Gene—"It would really be quite simple for us to marry, you know. Father is a minister."

Jean—"Oh, really? Then let's try it—my dad's a lawyer."

[1888]

He had proposed. She tossed her head haughtily.

"You!" came her scornful reply. "You want to marry me?"

"Yes," murmured the lover.

"But, my dear boy," she went on, "you've only known me three days."

"Oh, much longer than that really!" he said. "I've been two years in the bank where your father has his account."

[1889]

"I hear you are going to marry that old Mr. Gayboy."

"Yes, I've decided to accept him."

"You're making a mistake, my dear. He'll lead a double life."

"Well, if I don't marry him I'll lead a single life, and that is worse."

[1890]

She—"Jack, I was wrong to treat you the way I did. You'll forgive me, won't you, for being so angry with you all last week?"

He—"Sure! That's all right. I saved $22 while we weren't on speaking terms."

[1891]

"My girl and I are on the outs."

"Only a lovers' quarrel."

"No, this is serious. We got into a political discussion."

[1892]

He—"When I get up in the morning, you are in my first thoughts, darling."

Darling—"Yes, but Bob says that, too."

He—"Well, what if he does? I get up before him."

[1893]

Mabel—"What's worrying you, David?"

David—"I was just wonderin' if Dad would see to the milkin' while we're on our honeymoon, supposin' you said 'yes' if I asked you."

[1894]

He (with hands over her eyes) —"If you can't guess who it is in three guesses, I'm going to kiss you."

She—"Jack Frost; Davy Jones; Santa Claus."

[1895]

"My father," said the young woman to an admirer, "is a very good business man. When he was quite young he managed to make a large fortune. Would you like to hear how he did it?"

"Certainly," said the young man, "but tell me first, has he still got it?"

[1896]

Edna—"Jack is so original. He says things to me that nobody else would dream of saying."

May—"What's he been up to now—asking you to marry him?"

[1897]

"I understand that she fairly threw herself at him."

"Yes! They met in an automobile collision."

[1898]

"I'm terribly worried. I wrote Jack in my last letter to forget that I had told him I didn't mean to reconsider my decision not to change my mind, and he seems to have misunderstood me."

[1899]

"What made you quarrel with Conrad?"

"Well, he proposed to me again last night."

"Where was the harm in that?"

"My dear, I had accepted him the night before."

[1900]

Father—"That young man of yours stays very late. Doesn't he know how to say good-night?"

Daughter—"Oh, yes, Dad; better than any other boy I ever knew."

[1901]

She (tenderly)—"And are mine the only lips you have kissed?"

He—"Yes, and they are the sweetest of all."

[1902]

Father (at 1 A.M.)—"Is that young man asleep, Marie?"

Daughter—"Hush, Father! He has just asked me to marry him and make him the happiest man in the world."

Father—"Just as I thought. Wake him up."

[1903]

"So Hilda's broken it off with Bobby. I wonder if she still keeps his lovely letters?"

"No. As a matter of fact, they're keeping her now."

[1904]

"Would you marry a man for his money?"

"Not exactly. But I'd want my husband to have a lovely disposition, and if he didn't have money he'd very likely be worried and ill-natured."

[1905]

She—"I can not marry you, as I do not love you, but I will be a sister to you."

He—"Fine. How much do you think our father is likely to leave us?"

[1906]

Papa—"Why, hang it, girl, that fellow only earns ten dollars a week!"

Pleading Daughter—"Yes; but, Daddy, dear, a week passes so quickly when you're fond of one another."

[1907]

She—"I'm sorry to disappoint you, but the fact is, last night I became engaged to Ernest."

He (knowing her)—"Well, how about next week?"

[1908]

He—"The first time you contradict me I'm going to kiss you."

She—"You are not!"

[1909]

"Why did you break your engagement to Tom?"

"He deceived me. He told me he was a liver and kidney specialist, and I found out that he only worked in a butcher's shop."

[1910]

"What shall I do?" wailed the sweet young thing. "I'm engaged to a man who just cannot bear children."

"Well," remarked a kindly old lady, "you mustn't expect too much of a husband!"

[1911]

"Why do you want your letters returned?" asked the girl who had broken the engagement. "Are you afraid that I'll take them to court?"

"No," sighed the young man, "but I paid to have those letters written by an expert, and I may use them again some day."

[1912]

"But darling, we can't live on love."

"Sure we can. Your father loves you doesn't he?"

[1913]

Two young men were discussing matrimony.

"You wouldn't marry a girl just for her money, would you?"

"No," said the other fellow, "but I wouldn't have the heart to let her die an old maid just because she had money, either."

[1914]

An enthusiastic reader of a certain popular newspaper serial sent a specimen of her sweetheart's writing to the calligraphy expert on the staff of the paper.

"Enclosed please find specimen of my beau's handwriting," she wrote. "Can you tell me if he is likely to make a good husband?"

Back came the reply: "No, I'm afraid not, my dear. He's been a pretty rotten one to me for three years. However, thanks for the evidence."

[1915]

"Darling," whispered the ardent suitor, "I lay my fortune at your feet."

"Your fortune?" she replied in surprise. "I didn't know you had one."

"Well, it isn't much of a fortune, but it will look large besides those tiny feet."

[1916]

A young fellow one offered to kiss a Quaker maid.

"Friend," said she, "thee must not do it."

"O, by Jove I must," said the youth."

"Well, friend, as thee hast sworn, thee may do it, but thee must not make a practice of it."

[1917]

He—"I'm thinking of asking some girl to marry me. What do you think of the idea?"

She—"It's a great idea, if you ask me."

[1918]

Bill—"So she is to marry that young Parker. He has been jilted by half a dozen girls."

Jim—"Case of being well shaken before taken, I suppose."

[1919]

He—"Why didn't you answer the letter I sent you?"

She—"Why I didn't get any letter from you. And besides, I didn't like the things you said in it!"

[1920]

Father—"You first met my daughter at the seaside, I believe. She told me how she had attracted you."

Suitor—"Did she really, sir? Why, she told me you'd be furious if you found out she'd winked!"

[1921]

"Jack was the goal of my ambition, but alas!"

"What happened, dear?"

"Father kicked the goal."

[1922]

"If you loved a rich man and a poor man—what would you do?"

"I'd marry the rich and be good to the poor!"

[1923]

"Madge is going to be married."

"Who's the lucky man?"

"I am. She rejected me."

[1924]

"I was quite upset when Jack kissed me."

"Oh, I say! You'd been kissed before."

"Yes, but never in a canoe."

[1925]

Joe—"How come you go steady with Eloise?"

Hal—"She's different from other girls."

"How is that?"

"She's the only girl who will go with me."

[1926]

"Diane, I could die for your sake."

"You are always saying that, but you never do it."

[1927]

"Darling, will you be my wife?"

"Will you always let me do just what I like?"

"Certainly."

"Can Mother live with us?"

"Of course, dear."

"Will you give up the club and always give me money when I ask for it?"

"Willingly, my pet."

"I'm sorry. I could never marry such a booby."

[1928]

"I know what's passing in your mind," said the maiden. "I know, too, why you are calling here night after night, appropriating my time to yourself and keeping other nice young men away. You want me to marry you, don't you?"

"I—I do!" gasped the astonished young man.

"I thought so. Very well, I will."

[1929]

She—"All my life I have been saving my kisses for a man like you."

He—"Prepare to lose the savings of a lifetime."

[1930]

"What about the diamond necklace you promised me?"

"Excuse me, darling, but when I'm with you I forget everything."

[1931]

"I suppose you've heard rumors that I'm engaged to Peggy?"

"Yes. If it's true I congratulate you; if not, I congratulate Peggy."

[1932]

Angela—"Don't you think you ought to see my people before we get married?"

Alvin—"Oh, I don't know. Couldn't you describe them to me?"

[1933]

She—"Oh, good! You've asked Father."

He—"No, dear. I've just been in a motor smash."

[1934]

"It is a funny thing, but every time I dance with you the dances seem very short."

"They are. My fiancé is leader of the orchestra."

[1935]

"Must we say good night, sweetheart?"

"No, dear!" came a voice from the stairs. "Wait a few minutes and say 'good morning.'"

[1936]

"Daughter," said Dad sternly, "I hope there was none of this petting while you were out with that young man."

"Of course not," retorted daughter, sarcastically. "We simply got our heads together and tried to figure some way to help the President bring prosperity back."

[1937]

"Why don't you marry her?"

"She has a slight impediment in her speech."

"How sad. What is it?"

"She can't say yes."

[1938]

They were settling a number of preliminary details as young people will before they take the decisive step.

"Do you believe in allowances for married women?" she asked.

"Certainly," he replied. "I think a husband should make allowances for a lot of things."

[1939]

Ruth was a sweet girl. She was reading a book that gave the meaning of names. Her mother was watching her, and thinking of all the young men who were attracted to her.

"Mother," said Ruth, "it says Philip means lover of horses, and James means beloved. What does George mean, I wonder?"

"I hope, my dear," said her mother, "that George means business."

[1940]

"I grovel here in the dust at your feet," exclaimed the impassioned young suitor, as he sank on his knees before his adored one in the parlor.

"Dust! Dust! Do you mean to insult me?" she gasped. "After I spent the whole morning cleaning this room!"

[1941]

"I don't know whether I ought to recognize him in the city or not. Our acquaintance at the seaside was very slight."

"You promised to marry him, did you not?"

"Yes, but that was all."

[1942]

"So he broke your heart," said the friend to the sobbing girl.

"Not only that, he played cards with Father and broke him, too."

[1943]

"So the engagement is off?"

"Yes. She was so indignant when she heard about what he'd done that she tore off her engagement ring and flung it on to her right hand."

[1944]

"Do you love me, dear?"

"Dearly, sweetheart."

"Would you die for me?"

"No, my pet. Mine is an undying love."

[1945]

He was relating his adventures to his *fiancée*.

"I had to hack my way through almost impenetrable jungle," he said. "Chopping, slashing at thick undergrowth and trees."

"Oh, George," said she, "you'll be an expert at weeding the garden!"

[1946]

"Give me a kiss, darling."

"No, no. My mother is against kissing."

"But, my dear, I don't want to kiss your mother."

[1947]

"But if you don't really like the girl why ask her to marry you?"

"Well, her family have been very nice to me, and it's the only way I can repay them."

[1948]

Impecunious Youth (receiving Leap Year proposal)—"Honestly, Jean, marriage is out of the question. Why, I couldn't keep a mouse."

Jean (quite determined)—"Of course you could, darling. I love them."

[1949]

She—"Daddy is so pleased to hear you are a poet."

He—"Fine. He likes poetry, then?"

She—"Not at all. But the last friend of mine he tried to throw out was an amateur boxer."

[1950]

A girl went to a palmist to have her hand read.

"I see you are in love with a tall man with a front tooth missing," the woman told her.

"That's right."

"I see he has asked you to marry him."

"Yes, that's right."

"And his name is Bill Jones."

"That's marvelous! How can you tell from the lines on my hand?"

"It's not the lines I'm telling by," the palmist said. "It's the ring you're wearing. I gave it back to Bill two weeks ago!"

[1951]

"Frances was afraid the girls wouldn't notice her engagement ring."

"Did they?"

"Did they? Six of them recognized it at once."

[1952]

Donald—"I dreamed last night that I proposed to you. What is that a sign of?"

Dorothy—"It's a sign that you've got more sense when you're asleep than when you're awake."

[1953]

Joan—"What do you think I should do if you tried to kiss me?"

John—"I have no idea."

Joan—"Aren't you inquisitive either?"

[1954]

Percy (after the proposal)— "Have you ever loved before?"

Edith—"No, Percy. I have often admired men for their strength, courage, beauty, intelligence or something like that, you know; but with you, Percy, it is love— nothing else."

[1955]

Alma—"I think Arthur is horrid. I asked him if he had to choose between me and a million which he would take, and he said the million."

Amelia—"That's all right. He knew if he had the million you'd be easy."

[1956]

Mrs. Climber (socially inclined) —"My dear, I've picked out a husband for you."

Daughter—"Very well, but I tell you emphatically that when it comes to buying the wedding dress I'll select the material myself."

[1957]

"Where can I get a license?"

"A hunting license?" asked the clerk.

"No, the hunting is over. I want a license to marry the girl I've caught."

[1958]

"So my daughter has consented to become your wife. Have you fixed the day of the wedding?"

"I will leave that to my fiancée."

"Will you have a church or a private wedding?"

"Her mother can decide that, sir."

"What have you to live on?"

"I will leave that entirely to you, sir."

[1959]

"Well, Dick, my boy," said his uncle, "my congratulations! I hear you're engaged to one of the pretty Noyes twins."

"Rather!" replied Dick, heartily.

"But," said his uncle, "how on earth do you manage to tell them apart?"

"Oh," said the young man. "I don't try!"

[1960]

Rich Suitor—"I—er—suppose you are aware that I've been making advances to your daughter."

Impecunious Father (extending hand)—"Yes, put it there, son. And now how about her poor old father?"

[1961]

Her Mother—"My daughter sings, plays the piano, paints, understands botany, zoology, French, Italian—in fact is accomplished in every way. And you, sir?"

Prospective Son-in-Law—"Well, in an emergency I suppose I could cook a little and mend the socks."

[1962]

Girl—"So you've seen Daddy, darling? Did he behave like a lamb?"

Suitor (grimly)—"Absolutely! Every time I spoke he said 'Bah!' "

[1963]

Suitor—"Sir, I'd like to speak to you about your daughter."

Parent—"Why, what's she been doing now?"

[1964]

The girl was very rich and the young man was poor but honest. She liked him, but that was all, and he knew it. One night he had been a little more tender than usual.

"You are very rich," he ventured.

"Yes," she replied frankly. "I am worth one million two hundred and fifty thousand dollars."

"And I am poor."

"Yes."

"Will you marry me?"

"No."

"I thought you wouldn't."

"Then why did you ask me?"

"Oh, just to see how a man feels when he loses one million two hundred and fifty thousand dollars."

[1965]

Suitor—"Er—I—er—am seeking your daughter's hand—er—have you any objection, sir?"

Father—"None at all. Take the one that's always in my pocket."

[1966]

Eskimo Lover—"What would you say if I told you I had come a hundred miles through ice and snow with my dog team, just to tell you I love you?"

Eskimo Sweetie—"I'd say that was a lot of mush."

[1967]

Irate Parent—"While you stood at the gate bidding my daughter good-night, did it ever dawn upon you—"

The Suitor—"Certainly not, sir! I never stayed as late as that."

[1968]

"Cheer up, old man! There's other fish in the sea."

Rejected Suitor—"Yes, but the last one took all my bait!"

[1969]

With deep anguish, he begged her to reconsider her answer. "If you don't marry me I'll blow my brains out," he vowed.

"Oh, would you, really?" she gurgled. "I wish you would do it. It would be a great joke on father, for he thinks you haven't any."

[1970]

Mary—"But you've known the man only two weeks. You're not thinking of marrying him?"

Jennie—"Well, it isn't as if he were a stranger. A girl I know was engaged to him for a long time."

[1971]

Her Father—"I do hope you appreciate that in marrying my daughter you are getting a very big-hearted and generous girl."

Young Man—"I do, sir. And I hope that she inherits those fine qualities from her father."

[1972]

Jones visited the Widow Brown every evening and had tea with her.

"Why don't you marry her?" asked a friend.

"I have often thought about it," said Seller, "but where should I spend my evenings then?"

[1973]

"Dorothy, your boy friend seems very bashful," said mamma to her daughter.

"Bashful!" echoed the daughter, "bashful is no name for it."

"Why don't you encourage him a little more? Some men have to be taught how to do their courting. He's a good catch."

"Encourage him!" said the daughter, "he cannot take the most palpable hint. Why, only last night when I sat all alone on the sofa, he perched up in a chair as far away as he could get, I asked him if he didn't think it strange that a man's arm and a woman's waist seemed always to be the same length, and what do you think he did?"

"Why, just what any sensible man would have done—tried it."

"He asked me if I could find piece of string so we could measure and see if it was so."

[1974]

"And you say you were in the town I was born in last week?" she murmured softly.

"Yes!"

"And you thought of me, Bob?" she cooed.

"I did," replied Bob. "I said to myself, 'Why, isn't this where what's-her-name was born?'"

[1975]

"What did her father say when you asked him for her hand?"

"He wanted to know if I could support him in the same style that she did."

[1976]

Dad—"If my daughter has accepted you, why come to me?"

Swain—"I'd like some advice on the advisability of marrying her."

[1977]

A Voice—"Mary, what are you doing out there?"

Mary—"I'm looking at the moon, mother."

Voice—"Well, tell the moon to go home, and come in off that porch. It's half-past eleven."

[1978]

"They tell me your engagement is broken."

"Yes; and Bill behaved abominably."

"But I thought you broke it yourself?"

"So I did, but he made absolutely no fuss about it."

[1979]

A young man entered a jewelry store and handed the jeweler a ring with the stammered statement that he wished it marked "with some names."

"What names do you wish?" inquired the jeweler in a sympathetic tone.

"From 'Oliver to Irma,' " the young man blushingly whispered.

The jeweler looked from the ring to the young man, and said in a fatherly manner: "Take my advice, young man, and have it engraved simply, 'From Oliver.' "

[1980]

The advertising man was proposing. "Remember," he said, "this is the last day for this astounding offer."

[1981]

"How come you look so worried?"

"I'm trying to make up my mind about going to a wedding tomorrow."

"Who's getting married?"

"I am."

[1982]

"I'm writing to tell Jack that I didn't mean what I said in my last letter."

"What did you say in your last letter?"

"That I didn't mean what I said in the one before."

[1983]

May—"So you told Charlie you loved him after all?"

Mary—"I didn't want to but he just squeezed it out of me."

[1984]

"Did her father encourage you?"

"He smoked both cigars I had in my pocket and borrowed $25. Is that encouragement?"

" 'Encouragement'? My boy, it looks to me as if you were already a member of the family."

[1985]

The lights were turned low in the cozy library. She sat in the big armchair, her heart a-flutter, and her brain in a whirl.

He was to visit her that night. And he would take her in his arms. Perhaps they would be married.

The bell!

He entered, his hair slicked back and his bow tie on an elastic band. He advanced toward the table and removed three cigars from his vest pocket. Then he turned with outstretched arms.

"Stop!" she sobbed. "You have loved before."

[1986]

"I have always maintained," declared Charles, "that no two people on earth think alike."

"You'll change your mind," said his fiancée, "when you look over our wedding presents."

[1987]
Swain (in late hours) — "How can I ever leave you?"
Tired Father (poking his head around the door) — "Bus No. 30, train No. 9 or any taxicab!"

[1988]
Engineer's Sweetie—"And do you always think of me during your long night trips?"
Driver — "Do I? I've wrecked two trains that way already."
Sweetie—"Oh, you darling!"

[1989]
"Would you believe it? He actually ran away as they were standing at the altar!"
"Lost his nerve, I suppose?"
"No—found it again."

[1990]
"Sweetheart, if I'd known that tunnel was so long, I'd have given you a kiss."
"Gracious! Wasn't that you?"

[1991]
A bashful young man was seated on a bench with a pretty girl.
"Kiss me, why don't you kiss me?" she said.
"I can't—got sand in my mouth," he replied.
"Swallow it—you need it!" she countered.

[1992]
"Well, Julia, how's the matrimonial race coming off?"
"Oh, I'm on my twelfth lap, Uncle Will."

[1993]
"So you loved and lost?"
"On the contrary, I came out a winner."
"How was that?"
"She returned my presents and accidentally put in some of another fellow's."

[1994]
John—"Yes, I had a little balance in the bank, but I got engaged two months ago, and now——"
Joan—"Ah, love makes the world go round."
John—"Yes, but I didn't think it would go round so fast as to make me lose my balance."

[1995]
She—"Would you put yourself out for me?"
He—"Certainly."
She—"Then close the door as you pass out."

[1996]
Fiancé—"I haven't the courage to tell your father of my debts."
Fiancée—"What cowards you men are! Father hasn't the courage to tell you of his."

[1997]
He—"There are an awful lot of girls who don't want to get married."
She—"How do you know?"
He—"I've asked them."

[1998]
Irate Parent—"When that young cub who's paying you attention comes here again I'll sit on him."
Daughter—"Oh, let me do it, father."

[1999]
"Helene is two-thirds married to Bob."
"Really?"
"Yes; she's willing and the preacher is willing."

[2000]
Dorothy — "And Jack, the darling, told me I was the only girl he ever loved."
Della—"Yes, and doesn't he say it beautifully."

[2001]

Dentist's Daughter—"Well, dear, have you asked father for my hand yet?"

Shy Suitor—"No. Every time I step into his office I lose courage. Today I allowed him to pull another tooth."

[2002]

She had received his gift of flowers with rapture.

"Oh, they are perfectly lovely!" she exclaimed. "And there's even a little dew on them still."

"E-r—y-e-s," he stammered, "there's a little, but I intend to pay it on Saturday night."

[2003]

He—"Weren't we engaged last year?"

She—"I expect so, if you were staying in the same hotel as I was."

[2004]

Father—"But you wouldn't marry a man just because he is a good dancer?"

Polly—"Oh, no, Jack is clever at bridge, too."

[2005]

Irate Parent—"Didn't I see you kiss my daughter, sir?"

Nervy Youth — "How should I know? Do you think I'd be gawking around when I was doing a thing like that?"

[2006]

She—"Oh, I wish the Lord had made me a man."

He—"He did. I'm the man."

[2007]

"So you want to marry my daughter, eh?"

"Yes."

"Do you think you can divorce her in the manner to which she has become accustomed?"

[2008]

"Young man, do you think you can support my daughter on forty dollars a week?"

"I'm willing to try, sir—if that's the best you can do."

[2009]

"Broken off your engagement to Mary?"

"She wouldn't have me."

"You told her about your rich uncle?"

"Yes. She's my aunt now."

[2010]

"What gives you the impression that Jack and Betty are engaged?"

"She has a ring and he's broke."

[2011]

Fortune Teller—"You are going to marry a tall, dark man."

The Girl—"Can't you be specific? All four of them are tall and dark."

[2012]

Sister—"He's so romantic! Every time he speaks to me he starts 'Fair Lady.'"

Brother — "Romantic, hell. He used to be a street-car conductor."

[2013]

Daughter — "I've just accepted Mr. Welloff, mother."

Mother—"Gracious, child! I refused him myself twenty-five years ago."

Daughter—"I know; we've just had a good laugh about it."

[2014]

Mabel—"Have you heard I'm engaged to an Irish boy?"

Violet—"Oh, really!"

Mabel—"No, O'Riley."

[2015]

"Their engagement is still a secret."

"So everybody is saying."

[2016]

"Do you believe in telepathy, Miss White?" asked the bashful caller across the space that intervened.

"Telepathy? Er—I'm not sure I know what you mean, Mr. Jones."

"Why, thought transference, you know."

"Oh. Good gracious, no! If there was anything in it, you wouldn't be sitting where you are."

[2017]

"Somehow I can't get Jack to propose."

"Can't you give him a hint in some way?"

"I do. Every time he lights my cigarette I blow smoke-rings toward him."

[2018]

Irate Father — "You impudent puppy! You want to marry my daughter! And tell me, do you think you could give her what she's been used to?"

Suitor—"Er—yes, I think so, sir. I've a very violent temper myself."

[2019]

He — "Your little brother just saw me kiss you. What can I give him to keep him from telling?"

She—"He generally gets a dollar."

[2020]

He—"Could you learn to care for a fellow like me?"

She—"If he wasn't too much like you."

[2021]

"So Ethel returned your engagement ring?"

"Yes, she mailed it to me and she had the nerve to paste a label on the outside of the package: 'Glass, handle with care.' "

[2022]

"What were you and Mr. Smith talking about in the parlor?" asked her mother. "Oh, we were discussing our kith and kin," replied the young lady.

The mother looked dubiously at her daughter, whereupon her little brother, wishing to help his sister, said:

"Yeth they wath, Mother. I heard 'em. Mr. Thmith asked her for a kith and she thaid, 'You kin.' "

[2023]

He—"What charming eyes you have!"

She—"I'm glad you like them. They were a birthday present."

[2024]

Girl (spurning suitor)—"I wouldn't leave my happy home for any man."

Youth (brightly) — "All right, we'll live here."

[2025]

The fatal word had just been spoken. The rejected suitor was standing before her, listening to her elaborate explanations of her decision.

"I trust that I have made myself sufficiently plain," she said.

"It's only fair to give nature the credit for that," he murmured, as he retired in good order.

[2026]

"Have your parents given their consent to our union?"

"Not yet. Father hasn't expressed his opinion yet, and mother is waiting to contradict him."

[2027]

"What are the young man's intentions, daughter?"

"Well, he's been keeping me pretty much in the dark."

[2028]

Suitor—"How does your sister like the engagement ring I gave her, Bobby?"

Bobby—"Well, it's a little too small;—she has an awful hard time getting it off when the other fellows call!"

[2029]

Fay—"Do you intend to accept him?"

May—"That depends upon circumstances."

"What circumstances?"

"His."

[2030]

Frank—"I don't see how you tell those Smith twins apart."

Hank—"That's easy. Mabel always blushes when we meet."

[2031]

He had proposed and the girl had turned him down.

"Ah, well," he sighed dejectedly, "I suppose I'll never marry now."

The girl couldn't help laughing a little, she was so flattered.

"You silly boy!" she said. "Because I've turned you down, that doesn't mean that other girls will do the same."

"Of course it does," he returned with a faint smile. "If you won't have me, who will?"

[2032]

Father — "I doubt very much whether you would be able to support my daughter. I can hardly do it myself."

Suitor (brightly) — "Let's pool our resources!"

[2033]

He—"What is this thing called Love?"

She—"The tenth word in a telegram."

[2034]

She—"How old do you think I am?"

He—"You don't look it."

[2035]

Her Sweetie — "How long will it be until your sister makes her appearance?"

Younger Sister—"She's upstairs making it now."

[2036]

She—"Now that we're engaged dear, you'll give me a ring, won't you?"

He—"Yes dear, certainly. What's your number, darling?"

[2037]

"Well, dearest, what did your father say when he found that I wanted to marry you?"

"At first he demurred because he didn't want to lose me, but I explained that he could have me, and that he would have you to boot."

"That sounds all right, except for the 'to boot' part."

[2038]

He—"I could go on loving you like this forever!"

She—"Oh, go on!"

[2039]

He (at 11 P. M.) — "Did you know I could imitate any bird you can name?"

She—"No, I didn't. Can you imitate a homing pigeon?"

[2040]

A young man met a rival who was somewhat advanced in years, at the home of a girl they both courted, and, wishing to annoy him, inquired how old he was. "I can't exactly tell," replied the other; "but I can inform you that an ass is older at twenty than a man at sixty!"

[2041]

Parent—"Now on the question of money—can you keep going?"

Suitor—"Well, sir, you see—er—I'm afraid—"

Parent—"Precisely. Well, if you can't keep going, don't keep coming."

[2042]

"Daughter," said the father sternly, "I don't like that young man you go out with."

"Yeah?" retorted daughter. "Well, don't worry, you're simply poison to him, too."

[2043]

"I am proud of my girls and would like to see them comfortably married," said the old man to the young stranger. "I have made a little money; they will not go penniless to their husbands. There is Beatrice, twenty-five years old, and a really good girl. I shall give her $1000 when she marries. Then comes Bernice who won't see thirty-five again. I shall give her $3000, and the man who takes Beulah, who is forty, will have $5000 with her."

The young man reflected a moment and then asked, "You haven't one about fifty, have you?"

[2044]

Mother—"If that young man asks for a kiss, refuse it."

Daughter—"And if he doesn't ask for it?"

[2045]

Rich Man—"Would you love my daughter just as much as if she had no money?"

Suitor—"Why, certainly!"

Rich Man—"That's sufficient. I don't want any idiots in this family."

[2046]

He—"My train goes in fifteen minutes. Can you not give me one ray of hope before I leave you forever?"

She—"Er—that clock is half an hour fast."

[2047]

"Why did you break your engagement with that schoolteacher?"

"I didn't show up, one night, and she wanted me to bring a written excuse signed by my mother."

[2048]

"Darling, may I kiss your hand?" asked the young man with old-fashioned ways.

"Sure, kid, hop to it," said the Modern Jane, "but be careful you don't burn your nose on my cigarette."

[2049]

She—"She gave us something on our wedding anniversary—that plush tea-cosy—and we ought to reciprocate."

He — "Reciprocate? You mean retaliate."

[2050]

Father—"My dear, if you want a good husband, marry Mr. Goodheart. He really and truly loves you."

Daughter—"How do you know that, dad?"

Father—"Because I've been borrowing money off him for six months, and still he keeps coming."

[2051]

Happiest Man—"She said I was interesting and brave."

His Best Friend — "You could never marry a woman who deceived you from the start."

[2052]

Anita—"You're really sure you love me?"

Andrew—"Love you? Why, darling, while I was bidding you goodby on the porch last night your dog bit a piece out of the calf of my leg and I never noticed it till I got home."

[2053]

"I'll never ask another woman to marry me as long as I live."

"Refused again?"

"No—accepted."

[2054]

Sister — "Captain Randall proposes in this letter. I wonder if he really loves me—he's only known me a week."

Brother—"Oh, then, perhaps he does!"

[2055]

Bess — "Tess, I'm the happiest girl alive! I'm marrying the man I want!"

Tess—"Pooh, you goose, that's nothing to the joy of marrying the man some one else wants!"

[2056]

"I shall never marry," Reginald declared, "until I meet a woman who is my direct opposite."

"Well, Reggie," said Mabel, "there are a number of intelligent girls in this neighborhood."

[2057]

"If you don't marry me I'll jump off a three hundred foot cliff."

"Sounds like a lot of bluff to me."

[2058]

"You know, dad, he always said he'd never marry until the right girl came along."

"Well, how does he know you are the right one?"

"Oh, I told him I was."

[2059]

Father—"So you want to marry my daughter, eh? Have you any business judgment?"

Suitor—"Well, sir, I'm trying to get into your family, am I not?"

[2060]

"How's Mabel's affair with Jack going on?" asked Mrs. Flatte.

"Their engagement has been broken off," said Mabel's mother stiffly.

"Well, I'm surprised to hear that," said Mrs. Flatte. "I was always given to understand that Mabel adored every hair in the young man's head."

Mabel's mother sniffed.

"But not every hair on his shoulder as well," she shot back.

[2061]

"I'm not the happiest person in the world, but I'm next to the happiest," murmured the supreme egotist as he took the sweet young thing into his arms.

[2062]

"What did papa say when you asked him for me?"

"He didn't say anything. He fell on my neck and wept."

[2063]

He took her hand in his and gazed proudly at the engagement ring he had placed on her finger only three days before.

"Did your friends admire it?" he inquired, tenderly.

"They did more than that," she replied. "Two of them recognized it!"

[2064]

He—"There are two men I really admire."

She (sarcastically)—"Who's the other?"

[2065]

He—"You should see the altar in our church."

She—"Lead me to it!"

[2066]

He—"I always kiss the stamps on your letters, because I know that your lips have touched them."

She—"Oh, dear! and to think that I dampen them on Fido's nose."

[2067]

Frances—"What do you mean by kissing me?"

Frank—"I just couldn't help myself."

Frances—"But you just did."

[2068]

He (at the masquerade)—"You don't know me but give me a kiss anyway."

She—"I don't recognize the voice but the phrase is familiar."

[2069]

Maude—"Jack is telling around that you are worth your weight in gold."

Ethel—"The foolish boy. Who is he telling it to?'

Maude—"His creditors."

[2070]

Old Gentleman (bewildered at an elaborate wedding)—"Are you the bridegroom?"

Young Man — "No, sir. I was eliminated in the semifinals."

[2071]

Father — "Remember, my boy, beauty is only skin deep.

Son—"Deep enough for me. I ain't no cannibal."

[2072]

Accepted Suitor—"I know I'm not much to look at."

The Girl — "Still, you'll be at work all day."

[2073]

It was the night after their engagement had been announced. He had been kissing her almost steadily for ten minutes. The moment he stopped she began to cry.

"Dearest, you have ceased to love me."

"No, I haven't," he replied, "but I must breathe."

[2074]

He — "What would I have to give you for just one little kiss?"

She—"Chloroform."

[2075]

He (having just kissed her) — "Ah! That was indeed a triumph of mind over matter!"

She — "Yes, I didn't mind, because you didn't matter."

[2076]

She—"The man I marry must be as brave as a lion, but not forward; handsome as Apollo, but not conceited; wise as Solomon, but meek as a lamb; a man who is kind to every woman, but loves only me."

He—"How lucky we met!"

[2077]

Dan—"I saw Mary out with Bob last night. Thought she had thrown him over."

Jim—"She did—but you know how a girl throws."

[2078]

Robert (seriously) — "Do you think your father would object to my marrying you?"

Eve—"I don't know; if he's anything like me he would."

[2079]

Suitor—"And where is your sister, Jimmy?"

Jimmy — "She just ran upstairs to change rings when she saw you coming."

[2080]

"You look as if you were all in. What's wrong?"

"Last night I called on that new girl I was telling you about. Her mother opened the door and let me in—and then and there she demanded to know what my intentions were."

"That must have been very embarrassing."

"Yes, but that wasn't the worst of it. Just as the mother had finished speaking, the girl shouted down the stairs: 'Mother, that isn't the one!'"

[2081]

In the dimly lit conservatory Frank had asked Irene to marry him. She had consented with fitting modesty.

"Frank, dear," she murmured, "am I the only girl—"

"Now, look here, dearest," he interrupted, "don't ask me if you are the only girl I ever loved. You know as well as I do that—"

"Oh, that wasn't the question at all, Frank," she answered. "I was just going to ask you if I was the only girl that would have you."

[2082]

"I'll be frank with you," said the young man when the embrace was over. "You're not the first girl I ever kissed."

"And I'll be frank with you," she answered. "You have a lot to learn."

[2083]

Bill—"I'm afraid to propose to her."

Tom—"Has she offered you no encouragement?"

Bill—"Oh, yes. She gives me a hot gin punch when I call, but one ain't enough."

[2084]

Her Wealthy Father—"How can you have the cheek to ask for my daughter when you are earning such a small salary?"

Suitor — "Well, you see, I didn't like to turn down my job until I was sure of your consent."

[2085]

She (gushingly)—"Will you love me when I am old?"

He—"Love you? I shall idolize you. I shall worship the ground under your little feet. I shall—um —er—You are not going to look like your mother, are you?"

[2086]

"Are they in love?"

"They must be. She listens to him describe a ball game and he listens to her telling how her cousin's new dress was made."

[2087]

"You look like a nice, sensible girl. Let's get married."

"No, I'm just as nice and sensible as I look."

[2088]

He had been calling on her twice a week for six months, but had not proposed.

"Ethel," he said, "I-er-am going to ask you an important question."

"Oh, George," she exclaimed, "this is so sudden! Why, I—"

"No, excuse me," he interrupted; "what I want to ask is this: What date have you and your mother decided upon for our wedding?"

[2089]

He — "That young brother of yours saw me kiss you just now. What should I give him to keep him quiet?"

She (absent-mindedly) — "He usually gets a quarter."

[2090]

Suitor—"I wish to marry your daughter, sir."

Dad — "Do you drink, young man?"

Suitor—"Thanks a lot, but let's settle this other thing first."

[2091]

Mother — "I can't help thinking that Mabel would be happier if she married a man with less money than Mr. Lee."

Father—"Don't you worry. He'll soon have less if I know Mabel."

[2092]

They had been sitting in the swing in the moonlight alone. No word broke the stillness for half an hour until—

"Suppose you had money," she said, "what would you do?"

He threw out his chest, in all the glory of young manhood. "I'd travel!"

He felt her warm, young hand slide into his. When he looked up, she was gone. In his hand was a nickel!

[2093]

Suitor—"I would like to marry your daughter."

Business Man — "Well, sir, you can leave your name and address, and if nothing better turns up, we can notify you."

[2094]

Him—"Say, do your eyes bother you?"

Her—"No—why?"

Him—"Well, they bother me!"

[2095]

Lover (eloping with his adored) —"How much is the fare?"

Taxi Driver—"That's all right, sir. The young lady's father settled all that!"

[2096]

"Why don't Peter and Polly make up?"

"They'd like to, but unfortunately they can't remember what they quarreled about."

[2097]

"Dora, darling, will you marry me?"

"No, but I will always admire your good taste."

[2098]

He — "Have you ever been in love?"

She—"That's my business."

He—"Well—How's business?"

[2099]

"You get prettier every day," he flattered.

"Yes," she told him. "I'm living on a diet of brown bread and water to improve my complexion."

"And how long can you keep that up?" he asked.

"Oh, indefinitely!"

"Then, darling, let's get married," he said quickly.

[2100]

"If you refuse me," he swore, "I shall die."

She refused him.

Sixty years later he died.

[2101]

Nervous Suitor—"Sir, er—that is, I would like to—er, that is, I mean I have been going with your daughter for five years—"

Father—"Well, waddye want—a pension?"

[2102]

She—"Let's talk about you for a while."

He—"Yes, dear."

She—"Well, then, what does a young man like you see in a girl like me?"

[2103]

Bashful Suitor—"I love the good, the true and beautiful."

Alice—"This is so sudden; but I'm sure Father will consent."

[2104]

"Did you ever get your diamond back from that peach you were stuck on?"

"No; she's the cling-stone variety, y'know."

[2105]

He (throwing stones into water)—"I am only a pebble in your life."

She—"Then why not be a little boulder?"

[2106]

George—"I proposed to that girl and would have married her if it hadn't been for something she said."

Fred—"What did she say?"

George—"No!"

[2107]

Prospective Father-in-Law—"If I give my daughter a large dowry, what have you to offer in exchange?"

Prospective Son-in-Law—"I can give you a receipt."

[2108]

Mabel—"Did you ask father for my hand?"

Jack (bitterly)—"Yes, I asked him over the 'phone, and he replied, 'I don't know who's speaking, but it's O.K. with me.' "

[2109]

"You've been out with worse-looking fellows than I am, haven't you?"

She did not reply.

"I said, you've been out with worse-looking fellows than I am, haven't you?"

"I heard you the first time. I was trying to think."

[2110]

"Gertie," said her father, "I don't mind your young man smoking my cigars, but I do object to him taking the morning papers when he says good night."

[2111]

Anita—"And if I refuse you, Alfred, will you kill yourself?"

Alfred—"That has been my usual custom."

[2112]

He—"Would you marry a sap just for his money?"

She—"Are you gathering statistics or proposing?"

[2113]

"So she proved untrue to you, eh?"

"Yes, she went back to her husband."

[2114]

"You didn't carry out your plans to elope?"

"No, I found father was planning to move and I didn't know where we'd find him when we got back."

[2115]

He took her in his arms.

"Oh, darling," he murmured: "I love you so. Please say you'll be mine. I'm not rich like Oscar Russell. I haven't a car, or a fine house, or a well-stocked cellar, but, darling, I love you, and I can not live without you!"

Two soft arms stole around his neck, and two ruby lips whispered in his ear:

"And I love you, too, darling; but where is this man Russell?"

[2116]

"Dearest," sighed the young man, "couldn't you learn to love me?"

"I might," said the girl. "I learned to eat spinach."

[2117]

The doctor answered the 'phone. Turning to his wife, he said: "Quick, get me my bag. The man says he cannot live without me."

"Just a minute," said his wife, who had picked up the receiver, "that call is for our daughter, Ethel."

[2118]

He—"If I do say it, you are the only girl I ever loved."

She—"If I do say it, you are the only fellow who ever made me believe that lie."

[2119]

Floyd—"Marry me and your smallest wishes will always be fulfilled."

Frieda—"I am able to do that myself. What I want is a man who will gratify my biggest wishes."

[2120]

"Would you—er—advise me to—er—marry a beautiful girl or a sensible girl?"

"I'm afraid you'll never be able to marry either, old man."

"Why not?"

"Well, a beautiful girl could do better, and a sensible girl would know better."

[2121]

Mother—"Louise, your hair is all mussed up. Did that young man kiss you against your will?"

Louise—"He thinks he did, mother."

[2122]

He—"I understand kisses speak the language of love."

She—"Yes?"

He—"Well, let's talk things over."

[2123]

"Fred, stop!"

"You don't mean it, Mabel?"

"You just kiss me again and see."

[2124]

"I seem to remember that girl Who is she?"

"She was my stenographer last year."

"She's charming! Why did she leave you?"

"She was too conscientious for me. One day I proposed marriage to her, and what do you think she did? She took all that I said down in shorthand and brought it, nicely typewritten, for me to sign!"

[2125]

Fair Young Thing (to friend)— "Not only has Jack broken my heart and wrecked my whole life, but he has spoiled my entire evening."

[2126]

"So you want to become my son-in-law?"

"Er—not exactly. I only wanted to marry your daughter."

[2127]

Father—"Daughter, isn't that young man rather fast?"

Daughter—"Yes, but I don't think he'll get away."

[2128]

"Daughter," said the father, "is that young man serious in his intentions?"

"Guess he must be, dad," she replied. "He's asked me how much I make, what kind of meals we have, and how you and mother are to live with."

[2129]

Bill—"Well, what did she say when you proposed to her?"

Jim—"I didn't propose. Before I got a chance she told me she loved Emerson, Longfellow and Poe, and what chance did I have with a girl who is in love with three other fellows?"

[2130]

"Is Madge still looking for her ideal man?"

"Good heavens, no! She's far too busy looking for a husband."

[2131]

She—"How dare you say my father is a wretch!"

He—"Well, I told him I could not live without you, and he said he would willingly pay the funeral expenses!"

[2132]

"Am I good enough for you?" sighed the young man.

"No," said the girl candidly, "you're not; but you're too good for any other girl."

[2133]

Eva—"Did you enjoy your ride last evening with that young doctor?"

Edith—"Indeed I did. He has a most charming roadside manner."

[2134]

The young man at the summer resort, who had become engaged to the pretty girl, received information that led him to question her:

"Is it true that since you came up here you've got engaged to Billy, Ed, George and Harry, as well as me?"

The young lady assumed an air of disdain.

"What is that to you?" she demanded.

"Just this," he replied gently. "If it's so, and you have no objection, we fellows will all chip in together to buy an engagement ring."

[2135]

He—"Do you believe in love at first sight?"

She—"Well, I think it saves a lot of time."

[2136]

He—"When I marry I shall lead a handsome girl and a wonderful cook to the altar."

She—"Heavens! That would be bigamy!"

[2137]

They had just become engaged.

"I shall love," she cooed, "to share all your troubles."

"But darling," he murmured, "I have none."

"No," she agreed, "but I mean when we are married."

[2138]

He—"Do you believe kissing is unhealthy?"

She—"I couldn't say—I've never . . ."

He—"You've never been kissed?"

She—"I've never been sick."

[2139]

Mr. Caution—"Would you say 'Yes' if I asked you to marry me?"

Miss Careful—"Would you ask me to marry you if I said I would say 'Yes' if you asked me to marry you?"

[2140]

She arrived home exhausted. "What on earth have you been doing?" queried her mother.

"Bill asked me to go for a walk with him and we've walked miles and miles," she replied. "When I was about worn out, I suggested we should take a bus, but he demurred at the expense."

"Do you mean to say that he was too stingy to pay the fare?" asked the mother.

"Well, that's the idea," she replied. "But I did have my way in the end and we took a bus home."

The mother straightened her lips, put on her hat and coat and grabbed her purse. Off she hurried down the street to where Bill lived. She rang the bell and he opened the door.

"I've brought seven cents to pay for the outing you had with my daughter," she said.

Bill took the coins. "Thanks very much, Mrs. Jones," he replied. "You shouldn't have bothered to come to-night. Anytime tomorrow morning would have been quite all right."

[2141]

It was approaching midnight and the young man still hovered around the door. The stillness was suddenly shattered by a loud crash upstairs.

"Gracious, dear," said the timid lover, "what could that be?" "Oh," replied the miss, "that's just papa dropping a hint."

[2142]

Gladys—"Listen, Mabel. This is what my boy friend says in his letter. 'Darling, I think of you all day—your naturally waved hair, your brownish-gray eyes, your slightly prominent cheekbones, your twenty-four-inch waist—'"

Mabel—"Well, that's a queer sort of love-letter!"

Gladys—"Oh, didn't you know? Bob writes those descriptions of missing people for the police."

[2143]

Friend—"You will soon forget her and be happy again."

Jilted Suitor—"Oh, no, I shan't! I've bought too much for her on the installment system!"

[2144]

"You say you are going to marry a woman with $50,000 a year income, and try to persuade me it is a love match?"

"It is—I love money."

[2145]

He was a sentimental youth, who had been suffering for some time from severe lovesickness.

"What's the matter?" asked his father.

"I can hardly tell you," he faltered. "I—I—I have at last proposed, and I have been turned down."

"Tut-tut," replied the father, cheerfully. "It will turn out all right in the end. A woman's 'No' often means 'Yes.'"

"Perhaps it does," was the sorrowful reply. "But this woman didn't say 'No.' She said 'Rats!'"

[2146]

Marie—"Did you give Bob any opportunities to propose?"

Mabel—"Yes, but goodness, I couldn't tell him they were opportunities, could I?"

[2147]

"And upon what income do you propose to support my daughter?"

"Five thousand a year."

"Oh, I see. Then with her private income of five thousand a—"

"I've counted that in."

[2148]

Blushing, she hid her face on her father's shoulder. "He loves me," she said.

"Then I suppose he wants to marry you?" the old man grunted.

"Yes, Dad."

"What's his income?"

She started. "I don't know," she murmured, "but the coincidence is very strange."

"What coincidence?" asked her father.

"Edward," she answered, "asked the very same question about your income."

[2149]

He had gone into the library to put the thing up to her father, and she was anxiously waiting on the front porch.

"Well," said the suitor when he returned, "he asked me how I was fixed, and I told him I had $3,000 in the bank."

"And what did he say to that?"

"He borrowed it."

[2150]

Percy—"How would you—aw—like to own—aw—a little puppy, Miss Dovely?"

Miss Dovely—"This is so sudden, Mr. Chappingham."

[2151]

"Could you learn to love me?" asked the young man.

"Well," sighed the young lady, "I learned shorthand in three weeks."

[2152]

"Jack, you didn't shave this evening."

"No, dear. I shaved this morning and it makes my face sore to shave twice a day."

"Well, it makes my face sore when you shave only once."

[2153]

Algernon—"There is something I should say to you before we become man and wife, Beatrice. It is something you should know. It may make a difference in your feeling toward me. Beatrice, I am a somnambulist."

Beatrice—"That's all right, Algernon. Don't let it worry you a bit. While my people are staunch Presbyerians and must always remain such, we can go to my church part of the time and to your church part of the time."

[2154]

She (pouting)—"I believe you would sooner play cards with papa than sit in the parlor with me."

He—"No, darling, I wouldn't; but we must have the money to get married on."

[2155]

"I must tell you that my daughter can bring her husband only her beauty and her intellect."

"I don't mind—many young couples have started in a very small way."

[2156]

"Darling, will you make me the happiest of men in three letters meaning eternal bliss?"

"My answer is two letters meaning eternal freedom."

[2157]

Helen—"He told me I was the prettiest and most interesting girl he had ever met."

Aunt Irma—"And you will trust yourself for life with a man who starts to deceive you at the beginning of your engagement?"

[2158]

Daughter—"He says he thinks I'm the nicest girl in town. Shall I ask him to call?"

Mother—"No, dear; let him keep on thinking so."

[2159]

Niece (to Uncle who has suggested a theater)—"Thanks awfully, Uncle, but one of my friends is picking me up here to go and dance somewhere."

Uncle—"Dear me—one of your friends! In my young days a young lady was only taken out by the man to whom she was affianced."

Niece—"That's all right, Uncle. He *is* one of my fiancés."

[2160]

"Bob and Anne are going to be married."

"Anne! I thought she was one of these modern girls who don't believe in marriage."

"So did Bob."

[2161]

"Mary is keeping her engagement a secret."

"How do you know?"

"She told me."

[2162]

"Why did Marjorie break off your engagement?"

"Because I stole a kiss."

"How ridiculous of a girl objecting to her fiancé stealing a kiss from her."

"Oh, but you see I didn't steal it from her."

[2163]

"I love you. You are the most wonderful girl in the world. You are the object of my dreams, the light of my life, the hope of my hope, my inspiration and my ambition. I would fight dragons, conquer the world for you. I would give my life for you. Will you be mine?"

"Do you like me, Freddie?"

[2164]

Father—"Say, it's two o'clock. Do you think you can stay all night?"

Suitor—"I'll have to telephone home first."

[2165]

"I am ending it all because of my fiancée. She returned my ring."

"You are lucky. Mine got so fat that she couldn't get the ring off."

[2166]

He—"Sweetheart, I love you terribly."

She—"You certainly do."

[2167]

She—"You say I'm the most beautiful, divine, and gorgeous creature in the whole world? Are you trying to kid me?"

He—"No, I'm trying to kiss you."

[2168]

"Dear Alice," wrote the young man, "pardon me, but I'm getting so forgetful. I proposed to you last night, but really forget whether you said yes or no."

"Dear Bob," she replied by note, "so glad to hear from you. I know I said 'no' to some one last night, but I had forgotten just who it was."

[2169]

He—"There is one word that will make me the happiest man in the world. Will you marry me?"

She—"No."

He—"That's the word."

[2170]

"Then, Adelgitha, you will be mine?"

"Yes, Ferdinand, if pa is willing. I always do what he wants me to."

"But will he give his consent?"

"He will. Pa always does what I want him to."

[2171]

A young man who was particular about his washing wrote a note to his washerwoman and one to his girl, and, by a strange fatality, put the wrong address on each envelope and sent them off.

The washerwoman was well pleased at an invitation to take a ride the next day, but when the young lady read, "If you muss my shirt bosom, and rub the buttons off my collar anymore, as you did the last time, I will go somewhere else," she cried all the evening, and vowed that she would never speak to him again.

[2172]

A young man who thought he had won the heart, and now asked the hand in marriage, of a certain young widow, was asked by her, "What is the difference between myself and Mr. Baxley's Durham cow?"

He naturally replied, "Well, I don't know."

"Then," said the widow, "you had better marry the cow."

[2173]

"But dad, Fred has character. You can read it in his eyes."

"Then, Elsie, I've just blackened his character."

[2174]

"Lips that touch liquor shall never touch mine."

"Your lips?"

"No, my liquor."

[2175]

Bill—"That was the unkindest cut of all, as the poet says."

Harry—"What was?

Bill—"I showed her one of my boyhood pictures with my father holding me on his knee, and she said, 'My, who is the ventriloquist?' "

[2176]

"I hope you don't think I'm conceited," he said, after he had finished telling her all about himself.

"Oh, no," she replied. "But I'm just wondering how you can keep from giving three hearty cheers whenever you look at yourself in the glass."

[2177]

"No, Henry, I don't think a manicurist should marry a dentist."

"And why not?"

"If we fought, it would be tooth and nail."

[2178]

Father—"Why won't you marry Bill?"

Daughter—"I will only marry a man who knows life and has learned its sorrows."

Father—"I see—a widower."

[2179]

"Yes, she rejected me, but she did it in a most encouraging way."

"How was that?"

"As I went away, she pointed to the footprints that I had made on the carpet, and said: 'The next time you come to propose to me, I want you to wipe your shoes clean!' "

[2180]

A young man refused the glass of wine set before him at dinner. The host, a venerable justice, was quite surprised.

"What, no wine?" he asked.

"No, thank you," the young man confirmed his refusal.

"Not one little glass of sweet harmless wine?" asked the justice's beautiful daughter, her own glass held daintily near her charming lips.

"No." The youth was stubborn, in spite of the urging of the pretty girl who endeavored to thrust the liquor upon him.

"That is really too bad," said the justice. "What beverage do you prefer?"

"I never drink wine," the young man explained, "but, if you insist, I'll have a snifter of some good old rye or scotch!"

[2181]

Mabel—"I have just learned that my fiancé had already promised to marry two other girls."

Madge—"What engaging ways he must have."

[2182]

Rural Parent—"Young man, I have noticed that you are paying attention to my daughter. Now, is it all on the square?"

Rural Lover—"No—it's mostly on the porch."

[2183]

"The girl you were speaking to, Jack, seemed rather cold to you."

"Yes; she's an old flame."

[2184]

"Julia, do you know what love is?"

The young man put the question in an intense voice.

"Yes," was the firm answer.

"But do you really know?" he asked again. "Have you ever been the object of an undying love as all pervading as the air, as wonderful and sparkling as the stars? Have you ever loved and been loved like that, Julia?"

In an agony of suspense, he waited for her answer.

"Have I?" she murmured. "In my bedroom I have a trunk of letters, a box full of photographs, and seven engagement rings!"

[2185]

"I'm telling you for the last time that you can't kiss me."

"Fine! I knew you would weaken sooner or later."

[2186]

He—"We had better organize a mutual admiration society. I admire your eyes. What do you admire about me?"

She—"Your good taste."

[2187]

Her Mother—"And so you are going to be my son-in-law?"

Her Fiancé—"By Jove! I hadn't thought of that."

[2188]

Young Woman (holding out hand)—"Will you please tell me how to pronounce the name of the stone in this ring? Is it turkoise or turkwoise?"

Jeweler (after inspecting it)—"The correct pronunciation is 'glass.'"

[2189]

Suitor—"I hope, sir, that you will consider me in the nature of an investment, even if I may not pay regular dividends."

Girl's Father—"My dear boy, don't talk of dividends. I shall be glad if you don't levy regular assessments on me."

[2190]

Mary—"Harry, you remind me of an hour glass."

Harry—"In what respect?"

Mary—"The more time given you, the less sand you seem to have."

[2191]

Nancy—"That big, good-looking lifeguard is going to call on me to-night."

Sally—"Well, if he tries to kiss you, for heaven's sake don't struggle—he might punch you on the jaw from force of habit."

[2192]

A Quaker's advice to his son on his wedding day:

"When thee went a courting I told thee to keep thy eyes open; now that thou art married, I tell thee to keep them half shut."

[2193]

"Lilian, did that young man smoke in the parlor last night? I found burned matches there."

"Oh, no, father; he just lit one or two to see what time it was."

[2194]

Father—"And you think you will be able to give my daughter all she wants?"

Suitor—"Yes, sir; she says she only wants me."

[2195]

"Papa and mamma both say I can select my own husband and marry anyone I please."

"They have a good opinion of you, haven't they?"

[2196]

"So you think Jack's a flirt."

"A flirt! Why, he can tell the owner of any lipstick in the tennis club by simply tasting it."

[2197]

"Did her father come between you?"

"No; merely behind me."

[2198]

She—"Two months ago I was mad about George. Now I can't see him at all. Strange how changeable men are."

[2199]

"But isn't he a nice young man, Mamma?"

"Not at all, my dear. He reminds me of your father at his age."

[2200]

"Are you sure he loves you?"

"Absolutely. He objects to my bathing suit."

[2201]

Woman Friend—"No wonder Edith won't look at you. It's your own fault. You act like a slave—fawning and cringing before her, as if you didn't dare to call your soul your own."

Mr. Wormley—"Don't women like that kind of thing?"

Woman Friend—"Um—not until after marriage."

[2202]

"Why are you going to marry that police captain?"

"It is against the law, you know, to resist an officer."

[2203]

"When we are married, dear, we must have a hyphenated name—it's so much smarter. What would go well with Eaton?"

Small Brother (from behind davenport)—"How about 'Moth'?"

[2204]

He—"Oh, Peggy, I shall be so miserable all the while I'm away from you."

She—"Oh, darling, if I could be sure of that it would make me so happy!"

[2205]

"Do not be so cast down," she said; "it grieves me greatly to give you so much pain."

He looked up and laughed.

"Don't worry," he said; "my proposal was just a freak election bet."

[2206]

"I love you! I love you!" he murmured for the nineteenth time. "Speak! Answer me!"

The maiden coyly hung her head.

"I—oh, Tom, this is so sudden!" she pleaded.

He drew her close to him.

"Don't be afraid, darling!" he said gently. "Would you like me to ask your mother first?"

With a sudden cry of alarm she threw her arms around his neck.

"No, no!" she gasped. "Mother is a widow. I want you myself!"

[2207]

He—"I've wanted to ask you a question for weeks."

She—"And I've had the answer ready for months."

[2208]
A bashful villager escorted an equally bashful young lady. As they approached the dwelling of the damsel, she said entreatingly, "Zekill, don't tell anybody you beau'd me home."

"Sary," said he, emphatically, "don't you mind, I am as much ashamed of it as you are."

[2209]
He—"I think of you with every breath I draw."

She—"Let's put a stop to that."

[2210]
"Young man, how dare you? What do you mean by embracing my daughter?"

"I—I was just carrying out the scriptural injunction "hold fast that which is good.""

[2211]
"You know, you're not a badlooking girl."

"Oh, you'd say so even if you didn't think so."

"We're even then. You'd think so even if I didn't say so."

[2212]
Visitor—"Where does this lane lead to?"

Native—"Well, it's led half of the young folks around these parts into trouble."

[2213]
She—"I've been asked to get married lots of times."

He—"Who asked you?"

She—"Mother and Father."

[2214]
Inquiring Schoolboy—"Daddy, what effect does the moon have on the tide?"

Dad. (from the depths of his newspaper)—"Not any, son. Only on the untied."

[2215]
"Engaged to four girls at once!" exclaimed the horrified uncle. "How do you account for such conduct?"

"I don't know," said the graceless nephew. "Cupid must have shot me with a machine gun."

[2216]
"I've half a mind to get married."

"Watch out! Reno's full of people who used only half their minds in getting married."

MARRIED LIFE

[2217]
Maid—"Mistress has a new husband."

Cook—"Do you think he'll stay?"

[2218]
Ruth—"I, too, had an ideal once."

Rose—"How did you come to lose it?"

Ruth—"I married it."

[2219]
"My husband has taken all the cash out of baby's money-box."

"My dear!"

"Yes, and just when there was nearly enough for the new hat I wanted."

[2220]
Government Officer—"Are you married or single?"

Applicant—"Married."

Officer—"Where were you married?"

Applicant—"I don't know."

Officer—"You don't know where you were married?"

Applicant—"Oh, I thought you said 'why.'"

[2221]

Bill—"Is it possible for a woman to keep a secret?"

Jim—"Oh, yes. My wife and I were engaged several weeks before she said anything to me about it."

[2222]

Mrs. Jones—"Does your husband remember your wedding anniversary?"

Mrs. Smith—"No; so I remind him of it in January and June, and get two presents."

[2223]

With a charming air of romance and pleasant sentimentality, the company were discussing how each married couple among them first met.

"And where did you first meet your wife?" the little man in the corner was asked.

"Gentlemen, I did not meet her," he replied, solemnly. "She overtook me."

[2224]

Wife (heatedly)—"You're lazy, you're worthless, you're bad-tempered, you're shiftless, you're a thorough liar."

Husband (reasonably) — "Well, my dear, no man is perfect."

[2225]

"My best friend dined with us last Sunday and was so impressed with my bride's cooking that he sent her a carving set."

"That was nice."

"Not so very. He sent her three chisels and a mallet."

[2226]

"Now, Jack dear, if I do all the cooking for a month, what will I get?"

"You get my life insurance and your freedom."

[2227]

A clergyman, while engaged in catechizing a number of boys in a class, asked one of them for a definition of matrimony. The reply was:

"A place of punishment where some souls suffer for a time before they can go to heaven."

"Good boy," said the clergyman, "take your seat."

[2228]

"And how many closets are there in the house you have just bought, dear?" asked the sweet young bride.

"There are sixteen," replied the husband.

"But that's hardly enough, Henry."

"What do you want with more than sixteen closets? That's enough to hang your clothes in, is it not?"

"Yes, dear. But you'll want part of one for your clothes, won't you, Henry?"

[2229]

"Jack's getting terribly absent-minded. Just the other day he kissed a woman by mistake."

"Thought it was his wife, eh?"

"No, it was his wife."

[2230]

A widow consulted a medium, who put her into communication with her late husband.

"Peter," said the woman, "are you happy now?"

"I am very happy," replied the spirit of Peter.

"Are you happier than you were on earth with me?"

"Yes, I am far happier than I was on earth with you."

"Tell me, Peter, what is it like in heaven?" asked the woman.

"Heaven!" exclaimed Peter. "I'm not in heaven!"

[2231]

"Does your husband ever pay you compliments?"

"Well, sometimes he says, 'You're a nice one!' "

[2232]

"I'll be good for a penny, mother," coaxed little William, hopefully.

"Oh, Willie," reproved his mother, "why can't you be like your father? He isn't good for a penny. He's good for nothing!"

[2233]

"What are you cutting out of the paper?"

"About a man securing a divorce because his wife went through his pockets."

"What are you going to do about it?"

"Put it in my pocket."

[2234]

"How can I get my husband to discuss his business affairs with me?" inquires a correspondent.

"Ask him when he intends to buy a new car."

[2235]

He—"I wonder why women pay more attention to beauty than they do to brains?"

She—"Because no matter how stupid a man is, he is seldom blind."

[2236]

Judge—"The police say that you and your wife had some words."

Prisoner—"I had some, but didn't get a chance to use them."

[2237]

Man—" 'The husband ought to have a voice in the furnishing of the home,' says a woman writer.' "

Brother—"Oh, but he does—the invoice."

[2238]

"Is your wife economical?"

"Sometimes. She had only twenty-six candles on her fortieth birthday cake last night."

[2239]

Wife—"I'm going to give you a piece of my mind."

Hubby—"Just a small helping, please."

[2240]

She was writing to their son, congratulating him on his engagement.

"My darling boy," wrote the mother, "what glorious news! Your father and I rejoice in your happiness. It has long been our greatest wish that you should marry some good woman. A good woman is Heaven's most precious gift to man. She brings out all the best in him and helps him to suppress all that is evil."

Then there was a postscript in a different handwriting:

"Your mother has gone for a stamp. Keep single, you young fool."

[2241]

Bride—"What do you give your husband when the dinner does not suit him?"

Mrs. Oldwed—"His coat and hat."

[2242]

Bachelor (dreamily) — "Sometimes I yearn for the peace and comfort of married life."

Married Friend—"Well, you have nothing on me."

[2243]

"A husband leads a dog's life," said Mr. Allen.

"That's right," agreed Mrs. Allen. "He growls all day and snores all night."

[2244]

Mrs. Jenkins (with magazine)— "It says here that a South Sea Island wife isn't supposed to talk until her husband speaks first."

Mr. Jenkins—"I'll bet some of those husbands are fools enough to do it."

[2245]

The twins had been brought to be christened.

"What names?" asked the clergyman.

"Steak and Kidney," the father answered.

"Bill, you fool," cried the mother, "it's Kate and Sydney."

[2246]

"Darling, I have to go to New York on business," said the young married man. "It will only take about three or four days and I hope you won't miss me too much while I'm gone, but—"

"I won't," answered his young wife, positively, "because I'm going with you."

"I wish you could, dear, but it won't be convenient this time. What would you want to go for, anyhow? I'm going to be too busy to be with you, and—"

"I have to go. I need clothes."

"But, darling—you can get all the clothes you want right here on Adams Street."

"Thank you. That's all I wanted."

[2247]

"Here's a wonderful thing," said Mrs. Jones. "I've just been reading of a man who reached the age of 40 without learning how to read or write. He met a woman and, for her sake, he made a scholar of himself in two years."

"That's nothing!" replied her husband. "I know a man who was a profound scholar at 40. He met a woman, and for her sake he made a fool of himself in two days."

[2248]

"You say you haven't anything to be thankful for?" said the clergyman. "Now, look at your neighbor Hanford, who has just lost his wife by pneumonia."

"Well, that don't do me any good; I ain't Hanford."

[2249]

They were standing before a large painting entitled "Echo" in an art museum.

"I suppose," said one man, "it is appropriate to depict Echo as a woman, because she always has the last word."

"On the other hand," returned the second man, "an echo speaks only when spoken to."

[2250]

A minister congratulated a lady on her silver wedding anniversary for living twenty-five years with the same man.

"But he is not the same man he was when I first got hold of him," she replied.

[2251]

The defendant acknowledged that he hadn't spoken to his wife in five years, and the judge put in a question.

"What explanation have you," he asked severely, "for not speaking to your wife in five years?"

"Your Honor," replied the husband, "I didn't like to interrupt the lady."

[2252]

Wife—"You've broken my heart. I am going back to my mother."

Hubby—"You can't. You haven't the heart to go."

[2253]

Mr. Jones—"My dear, this book is a remarkable work. Nature is marvelous! Stupendous! When I read a book like this, it makes me think how lowly, how insignificant is man."

Mrs. Jones—"A woman doesn't have to wade through four hundred pages to discover that!"

[2254]

"Hello, old man! How you've changed! What's making you look so old?"

"Trying to keep young," was the reply.

"Trying to keep young?"

"Yes—nine of them," was the gloomy response.

[2255]

Edna—"My husband just ran off with another woman. Oh, I just c-can't control myself!"

Madge—"You mustn't try, dearie. You'll feel better after a good laugh."

[2256]

Bride—"I made this pudding all by myself."

Hubby—"Splendid! But who helped you lift it out of the oven?"

[2257]

Wife—"Have a look at the cake I decorated for my birthday party. Don't you think my sense of design is wonderful?"

Husband (counting the candles) —"Yes, but your arithmetic is terrible."

[2258]

Wife—"It's about time to think about where we shall spend the summer."

Mr. Tightwad—"I wish you'd say 'pass' the summer, Helen; 'spend' is so confoundedly suggestive."

[2259]

He—"When I married you I thought you were an angel."

She—"It's quite plain you did. You thought I could manage without either clothes or hats."

[2260]

A man, accompanied by his wife, visited a tailor to order a suit. The couple disagreed over the material and style of making, and his wife lost her temper.

"Well," she said, turning away, "please yourself: I suppose you are the one who will wear the clothes."

"Well," observed the husband, meekly, "I didn't suppose you'd wear the coat and vest."

[2261]

Husband (tripping over loose carpet)—"I shall lose my temper with this confounded carpet in a minute!"

Wife—"That's right, dear, do. Then take a stick and give it a jolly good beating out on the lawn."

[2262]

Homely Wife (in hospital)—"My husband seems a lot brighter this morning. He says he's just longing to get home again."

Nurse—"Yes; I'm afraid the anesthetic hasn't worn off yet."

[2263]

"Henry," whispered his wife, "I'm convinced there's a burglar down-stairs."

"Well, my dear," replied her husband, drowsily, "I hope you don't expect me to have the courage of your convictions."

[2264]

Wife—"I haven't a single decent dress."

Husband—"You wouldn't wear it if you had one."

[2265]
"What birthday present are you going to give your husband?"
"Oh, a hundred cigars."
"What did you pay for them?"
"Nothing! For the past few months I have taken one or two from his box daily. He has not noticed it, and will be delighted with my tact in getting the kind he always smokes."

[2266]
"Before Albert was married he said he would be the boss or know the reason why."
"And now?"
"He knows the reason why."

[2267]
In the golden twilight, the newly married couple arrived at the hotel where they were to spend the honeymoon.
"At last, my darling," sighed the groom when they were alone; "at last we are really one!"
"Yes, dear," replied the bride, patting her curls into place; "but from a practical standpoint, it will be advisable to order dinner for two."

[2268]
"You say that Gaybird loves his wife more since she has sued another woman for alienation of affections?"
"Yes, he never suspected before that his wife considered his affections worth $100,000."

[2269]
The young bride was asked what she thought of married life.
"Oh, there's not much difference," she replied. "I used to wait up half the night for George to go, and now I wait up half the night for him to come home."

[2270]
Wife—"So you think my new ball gown looks like the deuce?"
Hubby—"In the card sense, my dear. The deuce, you know, is the lowest possible cut."

[2271]
"The doctor told my wife she should take exercise."
"And is she doing it?"
"If jumping at conclusions and running up bills can be called exercise."

[2272]
"Do you remember when we met in the revolving door?"
"Goodness, yes. That was when we started going around together, wasn't it?"

[2273]
His wife returned from the morning shopping expedition and called her husband into the room from the garden.
"Frederick," she said heavily, "when you came home last night you told me you had been to the Grand Hotel with Mr. Wilson. I've just met Mrs. Wilson, and she said you were both at the Trocadero. Why did you lie to me?"
Hubby groaned.
"When I came home last night I couldn't say 'Trocadero.'"

[2274]
"I never take my trouble home with me from the office."
"I don't have to either; mine's also usually there at home waiting for me."

[2275]
"Do you know that your wife is telling around that you can't keep her in clothes?"
"That's nothing. I bought her a home, and I can't keep her in that either."

[2276]

"So your wife has gone to Palm Beach for her health. What did she have?"

"Five hundred dollars her father gave her."

[2277]

"Just think, while I was out with some fellows the other night, a burglar broke into our house."

"Did he get anything?"

"I'll say he did—my wife thought it was me coming home."

[2278]

She—"Do you like my new gown?"

He—"Yes, but I would suggest that you get into it a little farther."

[2279]

He was deeply in love with his wife, but awfully careless about money matters. He started away on a long business trip, leaving her short of money, and promising to send her a check—which he forgot to do. The rent came due and she telegraphed:

"Dead broke. Landlord insistent. Wire me money."

Her husband answered:

"Am short myself. Will send check in a few days. A thousand kisses."

Exasperated, his wife replied:

"Never mind money. I gave landlord one of the kisses. He was more than satisfied."

[2280]

"Have you and your wife ever had any difference of opinion?"

"Yes, but she didn't know it."

[2281]

Husband (arriving home late)—"Can't you guess where I've been?"

Wife—"I can; but go on with your story."

[2282]

Husband—"No, dear, we can't go to Seabeach. We must think of all the bills we owe."

Wife—"But can't we think of them just as well down there?"

[2283]

She—"You think more of that old radio than you do of me."

He—"Well, I get less interference from it."

[2284]

Mrs. Gray—"I like to have a man about, don't you?"

Mrs. Green—"Provided I know what he is about."

[2285]

Mrs. Newlywed (giving first order to butcher over the 'phone) —"Please send me a pound of steak."

"And what else, please?"

Mrs. Newlywed — "And — and some gravy."

[2286]

"I understand your wife came from a fine old family."

" 'Came' is hardly the word—she brought it with her."

[2287]

"I think you're a wretch. My first husband said I was far and away the best wife in the world."

"So you are, when you're far and away!"

[2288]

"Hubby, do you love me?"

"Yes."

"How much do you love me?"

"How much do you need?"

[2289]

"Awfully sorry to hear that your wife has run away with your chauffeur."

"Oh, that's all right. I was going to discharge him anyway."

[2290]
Two friends met for the first time in several years. "Well, old man," one said, "I hear you finally got married. Congratulations, for I also hear you have an excellent and a most accomplished wife."
"Yes, indeed," was the reply. "My wife is accomplished. She is perfectly at home in literature, at home in art, at home in music, at home in science, in short—at home everywhere, except—"
"Except what?"
"Except at home."

[2291]
Husband (angrily)—"What! no supper ready? This is the limit! I'm going to a restaurant."
Wife—"Wait just five minutes."
Husband—"Will it be ready then?"
Wife—"No, but then I'll go with you."

[2292]
"This book of Universal Knowledge will tell you everything you ought to know," declared the agent at the door.
"Don't need it," growled Mr. Grouch, "my wife tells me all that —and a lot more besides."

[2293]
Husband—"I want to buy you something useful for your birthday. What can you suggest?"
Wife—"Oh! I think a really useful diamond ring would do as well as anything."

[2294]
Hubby—"I can't eat this stuff."
Young Bride—"Never mind, dear. I have some lovely recipes for making up left-overs."
Hubby—"In that case I'll eat it now."

[2295]
A fellow dialed his home telephone number.
"Hello," he said. "Is that Mrs. Brown?"
"Yes."
"This is Jack speaking. I say, dear, will it be all right if I bring home a couple of fellows to dinner?"
"Certainly, darling."
"Did you hear what I said?"
"Yes—you asked if you could bring home a couple of fellows to dinner. Of course you can, dear."
"Sorry, madam," said the fellow as he hung up. "I've got the wrong Mrs. Brown."

[2296]
Husband—"Going to church, eh! To show your new furs, I suppose."
Wife—"No, dear, to show everybody what a generous hubby I've got."

[2297]
Husband—"I have brought you this beautiful string of pearls for your birthday, darling."
Wife—"But you knew I wanted a motor-car."
Husband—"I know, dearest, but I have tried everywhere and can't get an imitation car."

[2298]
"Bill's wife always laughs at his jokes."
"They must be pretty clever."
"No—she is."

[2299]
"Do you think a man should tell all his thoughts and actions to his wife?"
"That would be a waste of time. She already knows all his thoughts, and the neighbors keep her informed of his actions."

[2300]

Bride—"These eggs are very small. I must ask the egg-dealer to let the hens sit on them a little longer."

[2301]

"My husband and I attend to our budget every evening. It is more economical."

"How so, dear?"

"By the time we get it balanced, it is too late to go anywhere."

[2302]

Young Wife—"Oh, I'm so miserable. My husband has been out all the evening, and I haven't the faintest idea where he is."

Experienced Friend—"My dear, you mustn't worry. You'd probably be twice as miserable if you did know."

[2303]

Walter—"Seems like common sense would prevent many divorces."

Bessie—"It would prevent just as many marriages."

[2304]

Young Husband—"Last night when I got home, my wife had my chair drawn up before the fire, my slippers ready for me to put on, my pipe filled, and—"

Cynic—"How did you like her new hat?"

[2305]

"Does your husband always lie to you?"

"No, some nights I'm too tired to ask questions."

[2306]

Hubby—"Don't bring me any more bills. I simply can't face them."

Wifey—"But, dear, I don't want you to face them. I want you to foot them."

[2307]

"What's this, honey?" said Mrs. Youngbride's husband as he speared a slab from the dish.

"Lucifer cake, dear."

"I thought you said you were going to make angel cake."

"I was, but it fell."

[2308]

Bridegroom—"I thee endow with all my worldly goods."

His Father—"There goes his bicycle!"

[2309]

A young married man in Boston met a friend of his bachelor days and insisted on his coming home with him to lunch. His wife was unprepared for visitors, and calling him aside told him she had only one dozen oysters, and that when his friend had eaten his quota of four he must not be asked to take any more. In spite of his promise to remember, when the guest had eaten his four the host pressed him to take more. The wife looked distressed and the friend declined. The husband insisted, the wife looked in agony, and the guest firmly refused to have the rest of the oysters brought from the kitchen.

Later, the wife said to her husband:

"How could you urge him to have more oysters when I had explained to you that there weren't any more?"

"I'm very sorry," said the penitent husband, "but I forgot all about it."

"Forgot about it! What do you suppose I was kicking you under the table for?" retorted his wife.

"But you didn't kick *me*," said the husband.

[2310]

"Who is really the boss in your house?" inquired the friend.

"Well, of course, Maggie assumes command of the children, the servants, the dog, the cat and the canary. But I can say pretty much what I please to the goldfish."

[2311]

Youth (to friend)—"Er—how much do I pay for a marriage license, old fellow?"

Friend (already married)—"Two dollars down, and your entire salary each week for the rest of your life."

[2312]

Bride—"I'd like a shoulder of smoked ham."

Butcher—"I am extremely sorry that we haven't any just now. How about a nice fresh leg of spare rib instead?"

[2313]

"Have you noticed how reluctant the young men of today are to marry and settle down?"

"Yes, I believe you're right."

"They seem to fear marriage. Why, before I was married I didn't know the meaning of fear."

[2314]

Young Husband—"This meat is not cooked; nor is the pie."

Young Wife—"I did it like the cookery book but as the recipe was for four people and we are only two I took half of everything and cooked it for half the time it said."

[2315]

Mother—"I really believe you'd be happier if you married a man who had less money."

Daughter—"Don't worry, mother —he will have less in a very short time!"

[2316]

"I can't imagine how you get money out of your husband."

"Oh, I simply say I'm going back to mother, and he immediately hands me the fare."

[2317]

A certain celebrated Arctic explorer had met an Eskimo native, who wore an expression of extreme worriment.

The explorer demanded the reason.

"My wife asked me to match a piece of goods for her," was the answer.

"And is that so much of a job?"

"It's liable to be. She wants me to match that polar bearskin gown she wears."

[2318]

Wife—"I think, you might talk to me while I sew."

Husband—"Why don't you sew to me while I read."

[2319]

"Is your husband fond of home cooking?"

"Oh, yes, we always dine at a restaurant that makes a specialty of it."

[2320]

Slimkins and his young wife had just completed their first quarrel.

"I wish I were dead," she sobbed.

"I wish I was, too," he blurted out.

"Then I *don't* wish I was," and the war continued.

[2321]

"So you let your husband carry a latchkey?"

"Oh, just to humor him. He likes to show it to his friends to let them see how independent he is—but it doesn't fit the door!"

[2322]

Small Boy—"Dad, how do they catch lunatics?"

Father—"With face powder, beautiful dresses, and pretty smiles, my son."

[2323]

Jean—"So Tom and you are to be married? Why, I thought it was a mere flirtation."

Joan—"So did Tom."

[2324]

Hubby—"You are affectionate only when you want money."

Wifey—"And isn't that often enough?"

[2325]

"Do you give your wife a personal allowance?" asked Brown.

"We tried it, but it didn't work," answered Smith.

"How was that?"

"She always spent it before I could borrow it back."

[2326]

A woman was reading the newspaper, and looked up to say to her husband:

"I don't believe it! This paper says that the average woman has a vocabulary of only 500 words."

"Seems like a small stock," said the man. "But think of the turnover!"

[2327]

She—"Married women wear wedding rings. Why don't married men wear something to distinguish them from single ones?"

He—"They do. Worried looks."

[2328]

Wife—"Dear, I've set my heart on a Rolls Royce."

Hubby—"Yes? Well, that's the only part of your anatomy that'll ever set on one."

[2329]

An old Quaker, not careful of the teachings of his faith, was discovered by his wife kissing the cook behind the door. But the Quaker was not disturbed. "Wife," said he gently, "if thee doesn't quit thy peeking thee will make trouble in the family."

[2330]

Two friends met in the street. One of them remarked on the dirty state of the other's hands.

"Why," he exclaimed, "your hands are covered with soot."

"That's because I was down at the station seeing my wife away," replied the friend.

"But how does that affect your hands?"

"I patted the engine."

[2331]

Wife—"I'm reading a mystery book."

Husband—"Why, that looks like our household budget."

Wife—"It is."

[2332]

Gardener—"Mr. Jones, I am going to leave, sir. I can't stand the Missus!"

Mr. Jones—"Too strict, is she?"

Gardener—"Yes, sir. Mrs. Jones keeps forgetting that I can leave any time, and bosses me about just as if I was you!"

[2333]

"You mean to say you were not at your own daughter's wedding? Where were you?"

"I was looking for a job for the groom."

[2334]

Pete—"My wife doesn't understand me, does yours?"

John—"I don't know, I've never heard her even mention your name."

[2335]

He (to wife in ultra gown)— "Do you like wearing this evening dress?"

She—"I feel that nothing is more becoming to me."

He—"I have no doubt of that; but wouldn't that be going a trifle too far?"

[2336]

Wifey—"There are times when I wish I were a man."

Hubby—"When?"

Wifey—"When I pass a milliner's shop and think how happy I could make my wife by giving her a present of a new hat."

[2337]

"What's wrong, Henry?" asked his wife.

"My razor," boomed the voice within the bathroom. "It doesn't cut at all."

"Don't be silly. Your beard can't be tougher than linoleum."

[2338]

"Did he take his misfortunes like a man?"

"Precisely. He laid the blame on his wife."

[2339]

"Did you give your wife that little lecture on economy you talked about?"

"Yes."

"Any results?"

"Yes—I've got to give up smoking."

[2340]

Newlywed Husband—"Do you mean to say there's only one course for dinner tonight? Just cheese?"

Wife—"Yes, dear. You see, when the chops caught fire and fell into the dessert I had to use the soup to put it out."

[2341]

The jealous husband spied his wife dancing with too much abandon. He glided up to her on the dance floor.

"Everybody's staring at you, Emily," he whispered. "You'd better tell your partner not to dance so close to you."

"You'd better tell him, honey," answered the wife. "I don't even know the guy."

[2342]

Wife (with newspaper)—"Just think of it! A couple got married a few days ago after a courtship which lasted fifty years."

Hubby—"I suppose the poor old man was too feeble to hold out any longer."

[2343]

Professor of Chemistry—"Which combination dissolves gold quickest?"

Student—"The marriage combination."

[2344]

Host—"When I was a young man I always said I'd never be satisfied till I'd smothered my wife in diamonds."

Guest—"Most laudable. But why in diamonds?"

[2345]

John had been invited to the funeral of a neighbor's third wife, and, as he had attended the funerals of the first two, his own wife was surprised when he informed her he was not going.

"But why are you not going to this one?" asked his wife.

"Well, Mary, it's like this. I feel a bit awkward to be always accepting Bill's invitations when I never have anything of the sort to ask him back to."

[2346]

"Henry, do you love me still?"

"Yes—better than any other way."

[2347]

"A bride wears white," said the speaker, "as a symbol of happiness, for her wedding day is the most joyful day in her life."

"And why do men wear black?" someone asked.

[2348]

"Brown says he is always ready to grant his wife's smallest wish. Do you believe it?"

"Oh, yes—if it's small enough."

[2349]

Wife (from above)—"Ready in a minute!"

Husband (a little later)—"No hurry now, dear! I've got to shave again!"

[2350]

A young couple got married and directly after the ceremony they left for a honeymoon trip through the southern states. When they arrived in a resort village in the mountains they decided to stay for a short while at the summer hotel. Immediately after their arrival they employed a colored man to look after their baggage, the bridegroom giving him explicit instructions about removing all the rice and labels from their trunks so that no one would know that they were newlyweds. He tipped the negro generously to insure against that worthy letting the news leak out that they were just recently married.

Two or three days later, whenever the bride left her room she noticed that everyone rushed to get a view of her. She informed her husband of the guests' strange actions and he, feeling sure that the negro baggageman had broken his word, called the latter to his room.

"What does this mean, Sam? I told you to be very particular about not letting any of the guests here discover that we were just recently married. We have told no one. You were the only other person who knew. Now how does it happen that everyone gapes at us when we pass, and that all those old girls out on the front porch are continually whispering when we appear?"

"Hones' to goodness, boss, I ain't tol' nobody a-tall dat you uns was jes' married. De fac' am, boss, dat I tol' 'em jes' de opposite. I tol' 'em you uns wa'n't married a-tall, but was jes' good friends."

[2351]

"And remember, my son," said the father of the groom, "the early husband gets his own breakfast."

[2352]

Amos—"In view of the fact that you said you always had the last word with your wife, how does it happen that she continually orders you about?"

Andrew—"I meant what I said. I always do have the last word. Whenever we have an argument, I always say, All right."

[2353]

"Papa, what makes a man always give a woman a diamond engagement ring?"

"The woman."

[2354]

Mrs. Newlywed (indignantly)—"I've told you to keep out of the kitchen, Dick. Now see what you've done—knocked down my cookery book and lost my page, and I haven't the faintest idea what I was cooking!"

[2355]

She insisted on taking innumerable frocks with her, and they arrived at the station loaded with luggage.

"I wish," said the husband, thoughtfully, "that we'd brought the piano."

"Don't try to be funny," came the frigid reply.

"I'm not trying to be funny," he explained sadly. "I left the tickets on it."

[2356]

She—"How did they ever come to marry?"

He—"Oh, it's the same old story. Started out to be good friends, you know, and later on changed their minds."

[2357]

Mrs. Smith—"The post offices are very careless sometimes, don't you think?"

Mrs. Jones—"Yes, dear, why?"

Mrs. Smith—"My husband sent me a postcard yesterday from Philadelphia, where he is staying on business, and the silly post office people put an Atlantic City mark on the envelope."

[2358]

"Pa, a man's wife is his better half, isn't she?"

"We are told so, my son."

"Then if a man marries twice there isn't anything left of him, is there?"

"Correct, my son."

[2359]

Friend (gazing aloft)—"Aren't you worried when you see your husband looping the loop?"

Aviator's Wife—"Oh, no. You see I remove all his loose change from his pockets before he goes up."

[2360]

Customer—"Have you a book called 'Man, the Master of Women?'"

Salesgirl—"The fiction department is on the other side, sir."

[2361]

"How did you stop your husband staying late at the club?"

"When he came in late I called out, 'Is that you, Jack,' and my husband's name is Robert."

[2362]

"My dear," said Mrs. Newlywed, her face flushed with the excitement of her afternoon in the kitchen, "I want you to be perfectly frank with me now. What would you suggest to improve these doughnuts I made today?"

"Well," replied Mr. Newlywed, lifting one with a slight effort, "I think it might be better if you made the hole bigger."

[2363]

Bill—"Have you a speaking acquaintance with that lady?"

Dan—"I have a listening acquaintance of long standing. She is my wife."

[2364]

"I'm worried—it's raining and my wife is down-town."

"Oh, she'll probably step inside some store."

"That's just it."

[2365]

Heck—"In England to 'take orders' means to enter the church."

Peck—"It's slightly different over here—you enter the church, get married and then take orders."

[2366]

"Are they a well mated couple?"

"Yes, indeed; he snores and she's deaf."

[2367]

She (tearfully)—"You said if I'd marry you you'd be humbly grateful."

He (sourly)—"Well, what of it?"

She—"You're not; you're grumbly hateful."

[2368]

Wife—"I'm afraid the mountain air would disagree with me."

Hubby—"My dear, it wouldn't dare!"

[2369]

"I think it's time we got our daughter married and settled down, Eugene. She will be twenty-eight next week, you know."

"Oh, don't hurry, my dear. Better wait till the right sort of man comes along."

"But why wait? I didn't!"

[2370]

"What's the matter with that guy?"

"He is complaining to his wife that his stenographer doesn't understand him."

[2371]

"By jove, I left my purse under the pillow!"

"Oh, well, your servant is honest, isn't she?"

"That's just it. She'll take it to my wife."

[2372]

Crystal Gazer—"I see—I see a buried treasure—"

Client—"Yes—never mind that. It's probably my husband's first wife. I know all about her."

[2373]

Solomon's 999th Wife—"Sol, are you really and truly in love with me?"

Solomon—"My dear, you are one in a thousand."

[2374]

Mrs. Green—"Caleb, didn't I hear the clock strike two as you came in?"

Mr. Green—"You did, my dear. It started to strike ten, but I stopped it to keep from waking you up."

[2375]

When Mr. Sycamore's wife died he had ordered that Mrs. Sycamore's hat should remain hanging on the hat-rack just as she had left it.

After a year had elapsed Mrs. Sycamore No. 2 was ushered in. As she passed by the hat-rack he requested that that hat might remain undisturbed.

A few years later Mr. Sycamore was bringing his third wife to his home. He paused before the hat-rack where the two hats hung. He repeated his request.

"I will not disturb those hats," said she, "but the next hat that hangs there will be a man's."

And it was.

[2376]

"Some women believe everything a man tells them."

"Yes," replied Mr. Smith. "Before I married Charlotte I told her I would be her slave for life, and her trusting nature refuses to accept any compromise."

[2377]

"What made you marry Daddy, Mummy?"

"So you're beginning to wonder, too!"

[2378]

Willie (glancing over stock market page)—"Pa, what is 'short covering'?"

Father—"Your mother's latest party dress, my son."

[2379]

"I wish you'd come down off your high horse," her husband growled. "Oh, Bill," retorted his ultra-modern wife, "why do you insist on using such old-fashioned expressions? Why don't you learn to motorize your thinking?"

[2380]

Bill—"Did your wife have you on the carpet for getting in so late last night?"

Jack—"Well, it may have been the carpet she had me on, but it seemed more like a red-hot stove to me!"

[2381]

Doctor—"Have you any idea how your wife caught this terrible cold?"

Husband—"I think it was on account of her coat."

"Too thin, eh?"

"No; it was last winter's one, and she didn't wear it."

[2382]

"I see," said the man who reads, "that over in Australia they have earthworms ten feet long."

"Yeah?" growled the old married grouch. "Well, over here there are plenty of them between five and six feet tall who are worn to a frazzle earning money for families who are trying to keep up with the Joneses."

[2383]

"I'm happy and all that, of course, still I wish my wife wouldn't talk so much about her last husband."

"Forget it! Mine's always talking about her next."

[2384]

Mr. Close (to wife)—"You remind me of an angel, darling; you are always harping on something and never seem to have anything to wear."

[2385]

The timid girl who before marriage blushes and hesitates about accepting even a bunch of flowers or a box of candy from "him" will after marriage grab his pay envelope before he gets in the front door.

[2386]

"Just look at old Phillips over there—thoroughly enjoying himself! And I've always understood he was a woman-hater."

"So he is; but she's not with him tonight."

[2387]

Smith—"My wife sure is thrifty. She made me a necktie out of an old dress of hers."

Jones—"That's nothing. My wife made her a dress out of one of my ties."

[2388]

"For goodness sake," scolded the angry wife, after having asked her husband for the fifth Sunday to accompany her to Church, "the neighbors will soon be talking about us as they did about poor Mr. and Mrs. Brown. The only time they went out together was when the gas stove exploded."

[2389]

Hubby—"We must think of the future. We ought to economize more. If I were to die where would you be?"

Wifey—"Why, I'd be right here. The question is, where would you be?"

[2390]

"Father, did Edison make the first talking-machine?"

"No, my son, God made the first talking-machine, but Edison made the first one that could be cut off."

[2391]

Thinking to restrain his wife's extravagance, the husband presented her with an account book and gave her fifty dollars.

"Write down what I give you on one page," he explained, "and on the opposite page write down what happens to it. That will enable you to know how much you have spent at the end of any given time."

When next her husband asked to see the book, his wife told him eagerly, "I did just as you told me. See."

On one page was written: "Received $50.00." On the opposite page was noted: "Spent it all."

[2392]

Mrs. De Style (at modiste's, as mannequins display gowns) — "Which do you like best, Robert?"

Husband—"I prefer the tall brunette—er—that is, I mean the pink chiffon, my dear."

[2393]

She—"Statistics prove that marriage is a preventive against suicide."

He—"Yes. And statistics also prove that suicide is a preventive against marriage."

[2394]

Canvasser—"Madam, I am taking data for the new political directory. What party does your husband belong to?"

Mrs. Peck—"Take a good look, Mister—I'm the party!"

[2395]

First Eskimo Wife—"Does your husband stay out late during the winter nights?"

Second Eskimo Wife — "Late! Why, last night he didn't get home till half-past January."

[2396]

He—"I wonder why it is we can't save anything."

She—"It's the neighbors, dear; they are always doing something we can't afford."

[2397]

A freshman took his father to the college football match.

"Father," he said as they took their seats, "you'll see more excitement for your two dollars than you ever saw before."

"Oh, I don't know," grunted the old man; "two dollars was all I paid for my marriage license."

[2398]

"Are you waiting for me, dear?" she said, coming downstairs at last, after spending half an hour fixing her hat.

"Waiting," exclaimed the impatient husband. "Oh no, not waiting —sojourning."

[2399]

"Your wife is a brilliant talker. I could listen to her all night."

"I have to."

[2400]

"Hubby, if I were to die would you marry again?"

"That question is hardly fair, my dear."

"Why not?"

"If I were to say yes you wouldn't like it, and to say never again wouldn't sound nice."

[2401]

She—"I wonder if you'll love me when my hair has turned to gray."

He—"Why not? I've loved you every time you've changed color so far."

[2402]

"What caused the explosion at your house?"

"Powder on my coat sleeve."

[2403]

She—"Why so thoughtful, dear?"

He—"I have one dollar over this week and can't remember which installment I forgot to pay."

[2404]

"Pa," said Johnnie, "what's a monologue?"

"It's a conversation being carried on by a man and his wife, son," growled his dad.

[2405]

Magistrate—"So you broke an umbrella over your husband's head. What have you to say?"

Defendant—"It was an accident, sir."

Magistrate—"How could it be an accident?"

Defendant—"Well, I had no intention of breaking the umbrella!"

[2406]

"Just as Hopkins and the widow Jones started up the aisle to the altar every light in the church went out."

"What did they do then?"

"Kept right on going, the widow knew the way."

[2407]

They had new neighbors and the wife was much interested in them. In a few days she reported:

"They seem a most devoted couple, John. He kisses her every time he goes out, and even waves kisses to her from the sidewalk. Why don't you do that?"

"Why don't I?" replied John. "Good heavens! I don't even know her yet."

[2408]

Wife (at bathroom door)—"Dinner's on the table, John. Hurry and finish your bath."

Husband—"Coming, dear! Just one more stanza and I'm through."

[2409]

A traveling salesman declared that he had the most perfect wife that ever lived.

"Isn't it monotonous to go through life with such a paragon?" his companion asked.

"Well, I may have put it a little strong—absence makes the heart grow fonder, you know!" said the home-going husband. "If she has any little fault at all, it's a tendency to profanity when intoxicated!"

[2410]

"Before we were married you called me an angel."

"I know it."

"And now you don't call me anything."

"Well, you ought to be glad that I possess such self-control."

[2411]

"Pa," said Clarence, looking up from his history lesson, "who was it that said we haven't started to fight yet?"

"A bride and groom who were still on their honeymoon, I guess," growled his dad.

[2412]

"Does your wife miss you much?"

"No. She throws remarkably straight for a woman."

[2413]

Mrs. Jones—"I'm so sorry, dear Mrs. Smith, to hear about your husband going off with the cook. It's awful."

Mrs. Smith—"Yes, it's awful. I shall never be able to get another cook as good as she was."

[2414]

ACT I: "Oh, boy!"

ACT II: "Obey!"

ACT III: "Oh, baby!"

[2415]

"How did you get to know your wife before you married?"

"I didn't know her before I married."

[2416]

Counsel—"Is it true that your wife was, at one time, thinking of taking up the law before she married you?"

Henpecked One—"Yes, but now she is satisfied to lay it down."

[2417]

"Were you annoyed because I sharpened a pencil with your razor?" asked the attractive wife.

"Twice," replied the patient husband. "After I had given up trying to shave, I tried to write with the pencil."

[2418]

"I can read my husband like a book."

"Then be careful to stick to your own library, my dear."

[2419]

"You seem to have the queerest nickname for your husband," said Mrs. Brown to her neighbor. "Imagine calling him theory. Why do you call him theory?"

Came the reply, "He so seldom works."

[2420]

The Child—"Mother, what is 'leisure'?"

The Mother—"It's the spare time a woman has in which she can do some other kind of work, dearie."

[2421]

"Last night I questioned my husband for hours about where he'd been."

"What did you finally get out of him?"

"A fur coat."

[2422]

Young Housewife—"Honey, since you've already eaten three helpings of my first batch of biscuits, I'm going to bake some more for you tomorrow morning. Won't that be lovely? Won't that be—Speak to me, darling, speak to me!"

[2423]

Wife—"How do you like the potato salad?"

Hubby—"It's delicious. Did you buy it yourself?"

[2424]

Hubby—"You didn't have a rag on your back when I married you."

Wife—"Anyway, I've plenty of them now."

[2425]

The returned reveler crept quietly into his bedchamber as the gray dawn was breaking. Sitting on the edge of the bed, he cautiously untied his shoes. But, with all his care, his wife stirred in bed, and he presently was all too well aware of a pair of sleepy eyes regarding him over the edge of the sheet.

"Why, Stanley," yawned the little woman, "how early you are this morning!"

"Yes, my dear," replied Stanley, stifling a groan, "I've got to go to Boston for the firm today."

And replacing his footgear the wretched man dragged his aching limbs out again into the cold and heartless streets.

[2426]

"If you had it to do over again would you marry me, dear?"

"Of course, if I *had* to do it over again."

[2427]

He—"What have you ever done to benefit your fellow man?"

She—"I married you, didn't I?"

[2428]

"I was shocked to hear that Peter had eloped with your wife. I thought he was your best friend."

"He is, but he doesn't know it yet."

[2429]

Wife—"You don't love me any more. When you see me crying now, you don't ask why."

Husband—"I'm awfully sorry, my dear, but these questions have already cost me such a lot of money."

[2430]

Wife—"John, I'm awfully disappointed. You haven't given me anything for my twenty-ninth birthday."

Husband—"Twenty-ninth? You have forgotten, darling. I gave it you *last* year."

[2431]

"The rapidly increasing divorce rate," remarked the wit, "indicates that America is indeed becoming the land of the free."

"Yes," replied the prosaic friend, "but the continued marriage rate suggests that it is still the home of the brave."

[2432]

"Dear Emily," he wrote. "Words cannot express how much I regret having broken off our engagement. Will you please come back to me? Your absence leaves a space no one can fill. Please forgive me and let us start all over again, I need you so much. Yours forever, Bob.

"P.S.—By the way, congratulations on winning the sweepstake."

[2433]

Reader—"Dear Editor: What's the best way to find out what a woman thinks of you?"

Editor—"Marry her."

[2434]

Wife (trying on hats)—"Do you like this turned down, dear?"

Husband—"How much is it?"

Wife—"Eleven dollars."

Husband—"Yes, turn it down."

[2435]

"Getting this fifty dollars from my husband was like taking candy from a baby."

"Honest?"

"Yes, he put up a terrific holler."

[2436]

"What did you buy your husband for his birthday?"

"Well, knowing he wanted a diary, I bought him one that locked; he's so particular about his notes."

"And surely you bought something for yourself?"

"Oh, yes; I bought myself a duplicate key for the diary."

[2437]

Mrs. Newlywed — "We hadn't been married a week when he hit me with a piece of sponge cake."

Judge—"Disorderly conduct. Five dollars and costs."

Mrs. Newlywed (sobbing)—"And I'd made the cake with my own hands."

Judge—"Assault with a deadly weapon—one year."

[2438]

"What's the matter, Roger—you look terrible."

"My wife's on a diet."

[2439]

Mr. Newlywed—"Is the steak ready now, dear?"

Mrs. Newlywed—"I'm sorry I'm so long, George, but it looked hopeless grilled, and it doesn't look much better fried, but if you'll be patient a little longer, I'll see what boiling does to it."

[2440]

"Does your wife really obey you?"

"Sometimes. When I say, 'Go ahead and never mind me,' she always does."

[2441]

"I never could understand why a fellow should not be allowed to have more than one wife."

"Well, after you are married you'll realize that the law protects those who are incapable of protecting themselves."

[2442]

"Why does a red-headed woman always marry a meek man?"

"She doesn't. He just gets that way."

[2443]

"And has she made him a good wife?"

"I don't know. But I do know she has made him a very good husband."

[2444]

Jones had occasion to reprimand his wife. "I think, dear," he said soothingly, "that you fib a little occasionally."

"Well, I think it's a wife's duty," was her response, "to speak well of her husband occasionally."

[2445]

It was close to 8:15, and the gallery was crowded.

"Two single seats," announced the genial usher, facing the standing crowd.

"But you wouldn't separate a daughter from her mother, would you?" politely asked the older of the two women who were close to the aisle.

"You're quite right, madam; I wouldn't," replied the usher. "I did that once, and I've been regretting it ever since!"

[2446]

"What, you and your wife don't speak when you are alone?"

"We always shout."

[2447]

Mrs. Newlywed had not come out very well in her first experience with the cook-book and gas range. She ran to the telephone and called up her mother.

"Mother," she sobbed, "I can't understand it. The receipt says clearly, 'Bring to boil on brisk fire, stirring for two minutes. Then bea' it for ten minutes' . . . and when I came back again it was burned to a crisp!"

[2448]

He (after long argument)—"I wonder what would happen if you and I ever agreed on anything."

She—"I'd be wrong."

[2449]

Wifey—"There's an old clothes man at the door."

Hubby—"Tell him I've got all I need."

[2450]

The haggard-looking man got into conversation with the happy, carefree bachelor on their train journey to the North.

"Yes," said the former, "I'm the father of six daughters."

"Then you and your wife have six mouths to feed," replied the bachelor.

Haggard-face shook his head.

"No; we have twelve," he returned. "They are all married."

[2451]

Wife (on a boating excursion)— "If the boat foundered, whom would you save first, the children or me?"

Husband—"Me."

[2452]

Her Husband—"But why should we move? You were perfectly delighted with this neighborhood when we came here a year ago."

Mrs. Chatterton—"I know I was, but I'm tired of talking about the same old neighbors for a whole year."

[2453]

Wife—"I've bought you a beautiful surprise for your birthday—it has just arrived."

Husband—"I am curious to see it."

Wife—"Wait a minute and I will put it on."

[2454]

A man went to his doctor and requested treatment for his ankle.

After a careful examination, the doctor inquired: "How long have you been going about like this?"

"Two weeks."

"Why, man, your ankle is broken! How you managed to get around is a marvel. Why didn't you come to me at first?"

"Well, doctor, every time I say something is wrong with me, my wife declares I'll have to stop smoking."

[2455]

Mrs. Newlywed—"I'm sorry, dear, but dinner is a little burnt to-night."

Mr. Newlywed—"What? Did they have a fire at the delicatessen to-day?"

[2456]

Wife—"John, is it true that money talks?"

Husband—"That's what they say, my dear."

Wife—"Well, I wish you'd leave a little here to talk to me during the day. I get so lonely."

[2457]

First Business Woman—"Well, I must hurry home to dinner. I love a good home-cooked meal, don't you?"

Second—"Yes, but I'm beginning to suspect my husband's spending his afternoons in the movies. I'm positive that pudding last night came from the delicatessen."

[2458]

Little Barbara—"Mother, are you the nearest relative I've got?"

Her Mother—"Yes, dear, and your father is the closest."

[2459]

"My husband certainly does enjoy smoking in his den. Does your husband have a den?"

"No, he growls all over the house."

[2460]

Musical Wife—"It's strange, but when I play the piano, I always feel extraordinarily melancholy."

Husband—"So do I, dearest."

[2461]

She (in poetical mood)—"What are the wild waves saying?"

He—"Sounds like 'splash.' "

[2462]

"We have been married a year and never quarrel. If a difference of opinion arises and I am right, Felix always gives in immediately."

"And if he is right?"

"That never occurs."

[2463]

"Do you believe that the moonlight makes people silly, George?" asked the sweet young bride after the honeymoon.

"Well, dear," remarked the husband from behind his evening paper, "you know I proposed marriage to you in the moonlight."

[2464]

Single Gent—"What's the best month to get married in?"

Married Person—"Octembruary."

Single Gent—"Why, there's no such month."

Married Person—"Just so."

[2465]

Customer—"I want a nice present for my husband. "What do you advise?"

Shopkeeper—"May I ask how long you have been married, madam?"

Customer—"Oh, about fifteen years."

Shopkeeper—"Bargain counter in the basement, madam."

[2466]

The two men hadn't met for years.

"And is your wife still as pretty as she used to be?" asked the first.

"Oh, yes," replied the second, "but it takes her much longer."

[2467]

"I've decided on a name for the baby," said the young mother. "I shall call her Euphrosyne."

Her husband did not care for the selection, but being a tactful fellow, he was far too wise to declare his objection.

"Splendid," he said cheerfully. "The first girl I ever loved was called Euphrosyne, and the name will revive pleasant memories."

There was a brief period of silence, then: "We'll call her Elizabeth, after my mother," said the young wife firmly.

[2468]

"Where did you go on your honeymoon?"

"Jack, darling, where *did* we go?"

[2469]

"Hey!" cried Satan to the new arrival, "you act as if you owned this dump."

"I do. My wife gave it to me."

[2470]

"I suppose you find your wife can live on your income all right?"

"Oh, yes, indeed; but it's up to me now to make another one for myself."

[2471]

Wife—"Oh, dear, I'm always forgetting."

Husband—"So I notice. Always for getting this or for getting that!"

[2472]

Posterity's way of complimenting a bride on her good old-fashioned domesticity will doubtless be to say cordially: "Why, you open cans just like your mother."

[2473]

He paused as he was about to enter the bathroom.

"Darling," he said to his wife, "I'm going to take a bath."

"Well, what about it?" she asked, puzzled.

"Well, I just want to warn you not to give my suit away while I'm out of it. It happens to be the only one I have left."

[2474]

There was a lady once, a member of a very high-hat literary society, who had a great admiration for the talents of her pastor.

"I consider that he pronounces his words almost perfectly," she said to her husband. "I cannot recall his ever having made a single mistake."

"Huh, I can," grunted the husband. "He did when he pronounced us man and wife."

[2475]

Man (to wife who has had twins) —"Will you never get over the habit of exaggerating?"

[2476]

He—"There are two periods in a man's life when a man doesn't understand woman."

She—"Indeed, and when are these periods?"

He—"Before marriage and after marriage."

[2477]

"Let all you husbands who have troubles on your minds stand up!" shouted the preacher at the revival.

Every man in the church rose to his feet except one.

"Ah!" exclaimed the preacher, "you are one in a million."

"It ain't that. I can't get up; I'm paralyzed!"

[2478]

"Excuse me, but I'm in a hurry! You've had that phone twenty minutes and not said a word!"

"Sir, I'm talking to my wife."

[2479]

The bride of a few weeks noticed that her husband was depressed.

"Gerald, dearest," she said, "I know something is troubling you, and I want you to tell me what it is; your worries are not your worries now, they are our worries."

"Oh, very well," he said. "We've just had a letter from a girl in New York, and she's suing us for breach of promise."

[2480]

"Who is that letter from?"

"What do you want to know for?"

"There you are! What do I want to know for? You're the most inquisitive person I ever met!"

[2481]

Jack—"Gladys married a self-made man, didn't she?"

Nancy—"Yes, but she was compelled to make extensive alterations."

[2482]

"My wife and I agree on everything."

"Have you no opinions of your own?"

[2483]

"Does your husband ever take advice?"

"Occasionally, when nobody is looking."

[2484]

"Are you sure it was a marriage license you gave me last month?"

"Certainly, sir; why?"

"Because I've led a dog's life ever since."

[2485]

Husband (during a quarrel)— "You talk like an idiot."

Wife—"I've got to talk so you can understand me."

[2486]

Husband (arriving home late)— "Can't you guess where I've been?"

Wife—"I can, but go on with your story."

[2487]

"To think," exclaimed the enthusiastic young husband, "that by the time we get all this furniture paid for we shall have genuine antiques!"

[2488]

"I suppose you carry a memento of some sort in that locket of yours?"

"Yes, it is a lock of my husband's hair."

"But your husband is still alive?"

"Yes, but his hair is gone."

[2489]

Wife—"This is our tenth anniversary. Let's have duck for dinner."

Husband—"Why kill the duck for what happened ten years ago?"

[2490]

"Mamma, what is a 'second-story man'?"

"Your father's one. If I don't believe his first story, he always has another one ready."

[2491]

Indignant Wife (to incoming husband)—"John, what does the clock say?"

Husband—"It shays 'tick-tock' and little doggies shay 'bow-wow' and cows shay 'moo-moo' and tiny kittens shay 'meow-meow' and big fat piggies shay 'oink-oink'."

[2492]

"Mother," she said, "I must have some money for a new dress. Will you ask daddy for it?"

"Ask him yourself, dear," was the mother's reply. "You are getting married in a month's time and you must have some practice."

[2493]

Sympathetic Neighbor—"I hear you lost your husband. It's a terrible thing."

Widow—"Yes, indeed. You know what you're losing but you don't know what you'll get the next time."

[2494]

"John," she said to her husband, "don't you think this talk about trial marriages is just horrid?"

"Oh, I dunno."

"Why, you don't believe in them yourself, do you?"

"Have to. If there's any marriage that ain't a trial, you just show me."

[2495]

"Does your wife like housework?"

"She likes to do nothing better."

[2496]

"I think long hair makes a man look so intelligent."

"I found one on my man's coat the other night and he looked darned foolish."

[2497]

"My wife ran away with my best friend."

"Was he good-looking?"

"I don't know. Never met the fellow!"

[2498]

"Well, how is your companionate marriage working out?"

"Terrible—I've lost my wife's address."

[2499]

Mrs. Newlywed had her first venture at cooking dinner in her own home, which passed successfully, and they sat in silence at opposite ends of the table, wondering at the novelty of it all and gazing at each other.

"Honestly, honestly—on your word of honor—did you like it, darling?" she asked finally.

"Never enjoyed anything so much in my life," he said, and swallowed a lump.

"Everything, everything — from soup to pudding?"

"Every mouthful, from soup to pudding," he said bravely.

"Oh, I am so relieved, then!" she said, as a huge sigh escaped her. "You see, I forgot to order the syrup for the sauce for the pudding, and I had to have something, so I took your cough syrup, and I was so afraid you'd taste it!"

[2500]

Meek voice over the telephone: "Doctor, this is Mr. Henpeck. My wife just dislocated her jaw. If you're out this way next week or the week after, you might drop in and see her."

[2501]

Wife—"Isn't it wonderful how the waves keep rolling in, darling?"

Husband—"Yes, they remind me of the household bills at home, dear."

[2502]

Mrs. Green—"You seem rather hoarse this morning, Mrs. Brown."

Mrs. Brown—"Yes, my husband came home very late last night."

[2503]

Bride—"You must not expect me to give up my girlhood ways all at once."

Husband—"That's all right, little girl; go on taking an allowance from your father just as if nothing had happened."

[2504]

Mrs. Henpecked (sarcastically)—"I suppose you've been to see a sick friend—holding his hand all evening!"

Mr. Henpecked (sadly)—"If I'd been holding his hand, I'd have made some money."

[2505]

"On the day on which my wedding occurred—"

"You'll pardon the correction, but affairs such as marriages, receptions, dinners, and things of that sort 'take place.' It is only calamities which 'occur.' You see the distinction?"

"Yes, I see. As I was saying, the day on which my wedding occurred—"

[2506]

Mrs. Brown—"Do you know, dear, I was reading the other day that an ostrich can see very little, and can digest anything."

Mrs. Smith—"What an ideal husband!"

[2507]

A man who disliked work was stretched out under the protecting shade of a tree when his wife went out and awakened him.

"Loafing, loafing, continually loafing!" she said.

"Well," he replied. "It beats doing nothing, don't it?"

[2508]

Wife—"My dear George, don't run away with the idea that I am ignorant. I know a great deal more than I care to tell."

Husband—"Well, my dear, I hope you will acquire a lot more of that kind of knowledge."

[2509]

The newlyweds had just got off their train.

"John, dear," said the bride, "let us try to make the people think we have been married a long time."

"All right, honey," was the answer, "you carry the suitcases."

[2510]

Caller—"Good morning, Mrs. Smith. I'm from the gas company. I understand there is something in the house that won't work?"

Mrs. Smith—"Yes, he's upstairs."

[2511]

"Talk about Napoleon! That fellow Simpson is something of a strategist himself."

"As to how?"

"Got his salary raised six months ago, and his wife hasn't found it out yet."

[2512]

Hubby—"You're three-quarters of an hour late. What do you mean keeping me standing around like a fool?"

Wifey—"I can't help the way you stand."

[2513]

"These spoons which Aunt Jane gave us as a wedding present are not real silver," announced the bride.

"How do you know? Are you a good judge of silver?" asked the groom.

"No," replied the bride, "but I know Aunt Jane."

[2514]

"Why do you consider Bill the world's luckiest man?"

"Because he has a wife and a cigarette lighter, and they both work."

[2515]

"A rich man must employ a valet, a laundress, a secretary, a cook, and a housekeeper."

"Yes—and the poor man just gets married."

[2516]

He—"You are always wishing for what you haven't got."

She—"Well, what else can one wish for?"

[2517]

Mrs. White—"I have just been reading that in the Saratoba Islands a wife can be bought for five dollars. Isn't it dreadful?"

Mr. White—"Well, I suppose there are profiteers there just as in any other country."

[2518]

"Allow me to present my wife to you."

"Many thanks, but I have one."

[2519]

"My husband thinks the world and all of a gift I gave him," Mrs. Hutchins said to a friend. I gave him a box of cigars last Christmas, and, although he's very fond of smoking, he hasn't touched them yet."

[2520]

"Does a rabbit's foot really bring good luck?"

"I should say so. My wife felt one in my money pocket once and thought it was a mouse."

[2521]

"I was outspoken at the meeting of the Woman's Club today," remarked Mrs. Smith.

"Hm-m!" hm-md her husband. "Who outspoke you?"

[2522]

"I was in an awkward predicament yesterday morning," said a married man to a friend.

"How was that?"

"Why, I came home late, and my wife heard me and said, 'John, what time is it?' and I said, 'Only twelve my dear,' and just then that cuckoo clock of ours sang out three times."

"What did you do?"

"Why, I just had to stand there and cuckoo nine times more."

[2523]

She (back from a honeymoon in Switzerland)—""Don't you remember that wonderful gorge in the Alps, dear?"

He—"Sure do; it was the squarest meal I got there."

[2524]

He—"And another thing. You never get me a hot meal when I come home."

She—"I like that. Why, you had a boiled egg only yesterday."

[2525]

Mrs. Clarke came running hurriedly into her husband's office one morning.

"Oh, Dick," she cried, as she gasped for breath. "I dropped my diamond ring off my finger, and I can't find it anywhere."

"It's all right, Bess," replied Mr. Clarke. "I came across it in my trousers pocket."

[2526]

"My wife kisses me evenings when I get home."

"Affection?"

"No; investigation."

[2527]

Young Husband—"I see that sugar has gone down two points."

Young Wife—"Has it? I'll get a couple of pounds today, then."

[2528]

"What! Another new dress? How ever do you think I can find the money to pay for it?"

"Darling, you know I'm not inquisitive."

[2529]

"I hear you've signed up as skipper on the good ship matrimony."

"No, my wife is the skipper. I married a widow. I'm her second mate."

[2530]

"Another bill," sighed her husband, "and we decided we were going to put a bit by for a rainy day."

"Yes, darling, but don't you see the bill is for my new raincoat?"

[2531]

"So your daughter's married, I hear. I expect you found it very hard to part with her."

"Hard! I should think so. Between you and me, my boy, I began to think it was impossible!"

[2532]

"My wife is always pleased with the latest wrinkle."

"So is mine—provided it isn't on her own face."

[2533]

"Why do you always call your wife 'Honey,' Mr. Brown?"

"Well, honey has always disagreed with me."

[2534]

He — "You were no spring chicken when I married you."

She—"No, I was a little goose."

[2535]

"Once upon a time a man got up early on Sunday morning to let the iceman in, and being unable to find his bathrobe, he slipped on his wife's kimono. When he opened the door he was greeted by a nice big kiss by the iceman. And the only way he can figure it out was that the iceman's wife had a kimono just like the one he had on."

[2536]

They were rather late in starting for the station and his wife said, "You run ahead, dear, and hold the train."

"Yeh!" he answered sarcastically. "And what particular hold would you like me to use—the head-lock, scissors or half-nelson?"

[2537]

"Mr. Smith, won't you buy a bouquet, to present to the lady you love?"

"That wouldn't be right; I'm a married man."

[2538]

She—"What are you, anyway, a man or a mouse?"

He—"A man. If I were a mouse I would have you on the table right now yelling for help."

[2539]

"Why isn't dinner ready?"

"Oh, I've been down-town bargain hunting all afternoon, and I just couldn't get home in time."

"Huh! Like all women—looking for something for nothing, I suppose?"

"Yes, indeed. Trying to get you a birthday present!"

[2540]

"I think your husband always dresses so nicely and quietly."

"You wouldn't think so if you were around some time when he finds a button or two missing."

[2541]

He—"One night when you were away I heard a burglar. You should have seen me going down-stairs three steps at a time."

Wife—"Where was he—on the roof?"

[2542]

"What did her father settle on them when they were married?"

"The rest of the family."

[2543]

"My husband is crazy about me. He says such nice things in his sleep, but he always calls me by the wrong name."

[2544]

The head of the house was reading a newspaper article very carefully. Presently he remarked to his wife:

"Do you know, dear, I think there is something in what this article says—that the cleverness of the father often proves a stumbling-block to the son."

His wife heaved a sigh of relief. "Well, thank goodness," she said, "our Bobby won't have anything to fall over."

[2545]

.. Wife—"I can't decide whether to go to a palmist or to a mind-reader."

Husband—"Go to a palmist. It's obvious that you have a palm."

[2546]

"Why did you tell Joe you married me because I'm such a wonderful cook? I can't boil a potato."

"But I had to give some excuse."

[2547]

She—"You used to say that I was all the world to you."

He—"Yes, but I've learned a lot about geography since then."

[2548]

Jones—"Don't you think long hair makes a man look awfully intellectual?"

Smith—"That depends. My wife found a long hair on my coat sleeve yesterday, and I looked a perfect ass."

[2549]

Hubby—"I don't believe in parading my virtues."

Wife—"You couldn't, anyway. It takes quite a number to make a parade."

[2550]

"Do you permit your wife to have her own way?"

"I should say not. She has it without my permission."

[2551]

"At eight o'clock, I said to my wife: 'Let's go out and have a sail.' At a quarter past eight we sallied forth. On the sea the boat capsized. We should have been drowned, but a passing dolphin let us get on his back and brought us safely to land. You smile; what do you find incredible in this?"

A Voice—"That about your wife being ready at a quarter past eight."

[2552]

Bridegroom—"I want a room, please, for my wife and myself."

Manager—"Suite, sir?"

Bridegroom—"Yes, rather, she's perfect."

[2553]

"Marriage," was the subject of the lecture, and the speaker got very poetic about it.

"Marriage should be one long harmony," he exclaimed, "like a piece of beautiful music played by a first-class orchestra—"

"Not an orchestra," interrupted a tired-looking man at the back of the hall, "but a band where 'brass' needs to predominate."

[2554]

"Strange Alice should invite that horrid grass-widow to her wedding; she has such a disagreeable past."

"Yes, my dear, but she's rich enough to furnish a very agreeable present."

[2555]

She was going through her husband's pockets, and came across a small visiting card, on which was neatly written: "Belle Brown, Gramercy 2012." When her husband came home, she confronted him with it. "And who is this hussy, whose card you're carrying around with you?" she demanded indignantly.

"Belle Brown is a racehorse, my dear, on whom I've made a couple of successful bets," he explained. "I was going to buy you a new hat from my last winning—"

She frowned. "And Gramercy 2012?"

"Oh, don't be silly. I book my bets through the Gramercy betting offices; 2012 stands for her odds in the next race, of course."

"Oh." The wife considered him thoughtfully. "I was mean to suspect you, John. Never mind the hat. I'll get it tomorrow."

So the matter passed off. Three days later, his wife met him, on his return from work, with a steely glitter in her eyes. He sensed at once that something was wrong.

"What's the matter, my dear?"

"Oh, nothing at all, of course. Your racehorse called you up this afternoon."

[2556]

"Did you have a good time at the Swankem resort?" asked the friend.

"First-rate," was the reply.

"Much to do there?"

"Not for me; but my wife and daughters were kept pretty busy."

"What doing? Driving?"

"Oh, no; dressing for meals."

[2557]

"I have told your wife that she must go to the mountains."

"That's all right, doctor; now tell me I must go to the seashore."

[2558]

"Darling, I'm sorry I've been so mean to you lately."

"Well, this is a fine time to be sorry. I'm dead broke."

[2559]

"I tried my best," sobbed the wife, "I got the very best Christmas cigars I could."

The husband again looked at the cigars in amazement.

"The clerk asked me what kind I wanted," she went on, "and I told him you were a middle-aged man and always dressed in black."

[2560]

Wifey—"Do you love me still?"

Hubby—"I might if you'd stay still long enough."

[2561]

"I thought the bride looked very tired."

"No wonder, the way she has been running after him."

[2562]

Mr. Newlywed—"Did you make that split-pea soup for dinner?"

Mrs. Newlywed—"I've started it, but we can't have it till tomorrow. It's taken me all day to split the peas."

[2563]

"Last week a grain of sand got into my wife's eye and she had to go to a doctor. It cost me three dollars."

"That's nothing. Last week a fur coat got in my wife's eye and it cost me three hundred."

[2564]

"I wish to goodness we could go home, mother, but dad wants to stop for three more dances."

"Yes, dear, your father is a trial, isn't he? But, after all, one can be old only once."

[2565]

"She calls her dog and her husband by the same pet name. It must cause frequent confusion."

"Not at all. She always speaks gently to the dog."

[2566]

"My wife is suffering untold agony."

"I am sorry. What is the matter with her?"

"She has an inflamed throat and can not talk about it."

[2567]

Wife—"Here is an interesting article on 'What a Woman Should Weigh.' "

Husband—"Does it, by any chance, mention her words?"

[2568]

"Is your husband a bookworm?"

"No, just an ordinary one."

[2569]

"I'm sorry I ever became your wife," she said bitterly.

"Oh," he flung back, "you were no young bird when I married you."

"No," she retorted, "but considering what I got I was an early bird."

[2570]

"Hello, here's your dressmaker's bill again. I thought I gave you the money for it."

"Oh, that went to pay my bridge losses. Debts of honor first, you know, dear."

[2571]

"Why do you feed every tramp who comes along? They never do any work for you."

"No," said his wife, "but it is quite a satisfaction to me to see a man eat a meal without finding fault with the cooking."

[2572]

A friend saw her mowing the lawn. She asked her whether her husband, Amos, was still taking life easy.

"Amos," she replied, "has only two regrets in life. One is that he has to wake up to eat, and the other that he has to quit eating to sleep."

[2573]

"Did you finish that sweater you were knitting?"

"No, I told my husband to bring me some yarn."

"And didn't he bring you the yarn?"

"Not the yarn I wanted. Only a yarn about not being able to match the shade."

[2574]

She—"You don't value my kisses as you used to."

He—"Value them? Why, before we were married I used to expect two or three dozen in payment for a box of candy, and now I consider only one of them sufficient payment for a new fur coat."

[2575]

About a year after her husband died, the widow herself died. When she arrived at the pearly gates she asked if she might see her former husband.

"What's his name?"

"Joe Smith."

"You'll have to give us a better identification. How about his last words? We classify new arrivals that way."

"Well," she replied, "just before he died Joe said, 'Katie, if you ever waste any of my hard-earned dollars, I'll turn over in my grave.'"

"Oh, sure we know him. We call him Whirling Joe up here."

[2576]

Husband (shouting upstairs to wife)—"For the last time, Mary, are you coming?"

Wife—"Haven't I been telling you for the last hour that I'll be down in a minute!"

[2577]

"Are you quite sure that it was a marriage license you gave me last month?"

"Of course! What's the matter?"

"Well, I thought there might be some mistake, seeing that I've lived a dog's life ever since."

[2578]

"Care to buy a nice letter-opener, sir?"

"Don't need one. I'm married."

[2579]

She—"What has kept you up so late?"

He—"I was fixing a new ribbon on my typewriter."

She—"You ought to be ashamed to own it. You get rid of her or there'll be trouble!"

[2580]

"You say you are your wife's third husband?" said one man to another during a talk.

"No, I am her fourth husband," was the reply.

"Heavens, man!" said the first man; "you are not a husband—you're a habit."

[2581]

Young Author—"The art in telling a story consists of knowing what to leave unsaid."

Married Rounder—"It doesn't make any difference, my boy. My experience is that she finds out, anyway."

[2582]

Mrs. Heck—"I wonder, Mrs. Peck, if I could borrow your rug-beater."

Mrs. Peck—"I'm sorry, Mrs. Heck, but he doesn't get home till five o'clock."

[2583]

Mr. Rounder (arriving home after midnight)—"I'm tired. I've had my nose to the grindstone since early morning."

Wife—"Then you'd better get a grindstone that doesn't get rouge, lipstick, and powder all over you."

[2584]

"You don't seem to think of anything but motoring. Why don't you put your wife before your car sometimes?"

"I'm scared of being found out."

[2585]

She—"Before we were married, you used to say you could listen to my sweet voice all night."

He—"Well, at that time I had no idea I'd ever have to do it."

[2586]

"My wife has the worst memory I ever heard of."

"Forgets everything, eh?"

"No; remembers everything."

[2587]

Poker Player — "You should worry if you come home late. You're king in your own home, aren't you?"

Henpeck—"Yes, but there's always a lady in waiting."

[2588]

She—"Why did you tell Mrs. Marshall her husband was dead when he had only lost all his money?"

He—"I thought I'd better break it to her gently."

[2589]

Mr. Peters—"At last we're out of debt."

Mrs. Peters—"Oh, thank goodness! Now I can get credit again."

[2590]

"Did the palmist tell you the truth about yourself?"

"Yes, but shucks! My wife has been doing that for years."

[2591]

Young Husband—"It seems to me, my dear, that these pancakes are rather heavy."

His Bride—"Then I'm afraid you're a poor judge, for the cookbook says they are light and feathery."

[2592]

Him—"My treasure!"

Her—"My treasury!"

[2593]

"When you quarreled to-day, you let your husband have the last word. That was not usual."

"No, but I wanted to give him a little pleasure; it's his birthday."

[2594]

Hubby—"You call that a hat? My dear, I shall never stop laughing."

Wifey—"Oh, yes you will. The bill will probably arrive to-morrow."

[2595]

A recent society bride had six bridesmaids in hyacinth blue silk and two pages in rich crimson velvet, with gold lace. A pale bridegroom completed the color scheme.

[2596]

"You do not speak as affectionately to me as you used to, Daniel, I fear you have ceased to love me."

"Ceased to love you," growled the husband. "There you go again. Ceased to love you! Why, I love you more than life itself. Now shut up and let me read the paper."

[2597]

Mother (telling fairy stories)— "Once upon a time—"

Little Boy—"Mummy, do fairy tales always begin like that?"

Mother—"No, darling; sometimes they begin, 'Awfully sorry, my dear, to have been detained at the office again tonight.'"

[2598]

The grateful woman wrote to the makers of the patent medicine:

"Four weeks ago I was so run down that I could not spank the baby. After taking three bottles of your wonderful compound I am now able to thrash my husband in addition to my other housework. God bless you!"

[2599]

He—"Adam would have been perfect, I suppose, if Eve had only been made first."

She—"How do you mean?"

He—"Well, she would have bossed the job of making Adam."

[2600]

Cynthia—"How is your husband?"

Dorothy—"I haven't seen him for five years. I think I must have said something to annoy him."

[2601]

"I see in the paper that a widower with nine children out in Iowa has married a widow with seven children."

"That wasn't a marriage, that was a merger."

[2602]

Tom—"I saw Brown the other day treating his wife the way I wouldn't treat a dog."

Jack—"Great Scott! What was he doing?"

Tom—"Kissing her."

[2603]

"Do you know what became of my evening gown? I can't find it anywhere."

"I just saw a moth fly out of your clothes closet."

[2604]

"Where am I?" the sick man exclaimed, waking from the long delirium of fever and feeling the comfort that loving hands had supplied. "Where am I—in heaven?"

"No, dear," cooed his wife; "I am still with you."

[2605]

"Did you hear about the awful fright George got on his wedding day?"

"Oh, yes; I was there. I saw her."

[2606]

"Stop, look, listen! Those three words illustrate the whole scheme of life," said he.

"How?"

"You see a pretty girl; you stop; you look; after you marry her, and for the rest of your life, you listen."

[2607]

Purchaser (who is selecting a wedding gift)—"Yes, I rather like that. What is the title?"

Picture Dealer—"'The Coming Storm'—would make a splendid wedding present."

[2608]

"What makes this meat taste so queer?" inquired Mr. Newlywed.

"I can't imagine," responded the fond bride, "I burned it a little but I put sunburn oil on it at once."

[2609]

"We have been married ten years, Jack, and not once in that time have I missed baking you a cake for your birthday. Have I?"

"No, pet, I can look back on those cakes as milestones in my life."

[2610]

Father—"But my dear Dorothy, your husband owes me a lot of money. I don't think he should expect me to lend him more."

Daughter—"Well, father, he has to get it somewhere and he has a certain sentiment about keeping his creditors in the family."

[2611]

He—"Now that we are married, perhaps I can point out a few of your defects."

She—"Don't bother dear, I know all about them. It's those defects that kept me from getting a better man than you."

[2612]

A poker player, whose wife constantly complained of his late hours, stayed out even later than usual one night. He told the following story of his attempt to get in unnoticed:

"I slipped off my shoes at the front steps, pulled off my clothes in the hall, slipped into the bedroom, and began to slip into bed with the ease of experience.

"My wife has a dog that on cold nights insists on jumping in the bed with us. So when I began to slide under the covers she stirred in her sleep and pushed me on the head.

" 'Get down, Fido, get down!' she said.

"And, gentlemen, I just did have presence of mind enough to lick her hand, and she dozed off again!"

[2613]

"You say you never have a quarrel with your wife?"

"Never. She goes her way and I go hers."

[2614]

Two men who had been bachelor cronies met for the first time in five years.

"Tell me, Tom," said one, "did you marry that girl, or do you still darn your own socks and do your cooking?"

"Yes," was Tom's reply.

[2615]

"But, my dear," bleated the poor little hen-pecked husband, "you've been talking for half an hour, and I haven't said a word."

"No," snapped his wife, "you haven't said anything, but you've been listening in a most aggravating manner, and I'm not going to stand for it."

[2616]

The teacher was having her trials, and finally wrote the mother: "Your son is the brightest boy in my class, but he is also the most mischievous. What shall I do?"

The reply came duly: "Do as you please, I am having my own troubles with his father."

[2617]

A youngster asked his father how wars began. "Well," said his father, "suppose America quarreled with England, and—" "But," interrupted the mother, "America must not quarrel with England." "I know," he answered, "but I am taking a hypothetical instance." "You are misleading the child," said mother. "No, I am not," he answered. "Yes, you are." "I tell you I am not! It's outrageous—" "All right, Dad," said the boy. "Don't get excited. I think I know how wars begin."

[2618]

"The doctor said that my wife and I need more exercise, so I've bought myself a set of golf clubs," said Gubb to his neighbor.

"And what have you bought for your wife?"

"A lawn-mower."

[2619]

Two friends, one married and the other a bachelor, were at the latest play, admiring the performance of a famous actor.

"By Jove," the married man murmured, "he's wonderful. The way he displays affection toward the leading lady, eh?"

"Yes—pretty good," the bachelor agreed, "but, you know he's been married to her for eighteen years."

"What? Really married! Gosh—what an actor!"

[2620]

"I say, Jane, isn't it time baby said 'Daddy'?"

"No, John; I've decided not to tell him who you are until he gets stronger."

[2621]

"I got big-hearted this morning and gave a bum five dollars."

"What did your husband say about it?"

"Thanks."

[2622]

A newly-married woman was showing off to a friend the treasures of her home, including a neat sports-car.

"I suppose your father got you that?" said the visitor.

"Not likely," was the indignant reply, "George wouldn't accept such a thing. All that father pays for is the rent and the housekeeping expenses."

[2623]

"When you have an argument at your house, does your wife take part?"

"No, she takes all of it."

[2624]

Mrs. Brown was displaying a large lampshade she had just bought.

"Isn't that perfectly lovely, my dear? And it cost only two dollars!"

Her husband looked anything but pleased.

"If you wear that to church tomorrow you'll go alone," he said. "There's a limit to everything, including hats!"

[2625]

Wife–"Dear, I saw the sweetest little hat downtown today."

Husband–"Put it on; let's see how you look in it."

[2626]

Husband–"Now what about it? You were always pointing out how smart our neighbour Mrs. Blazer was. Her husband has gone bankrupt."

Wife–"Did he owe you anything?"

Husband–"No."

Wife–"Then I can't see what his bankruptcy has to do with my dresses."

[2627]

Mrs. Nuwed to her husband–"Darling, will you lend me $20, and only give me ten of them? Then you'll owe me ten, and I'll owe you ten, and we'll be straight."

[2628]

Wifey–"John, what punishment should be meted out to a man who proposes to a woman and then refuses to marry her?"

Hubby–"He should be compelled to marry her."

[2629]

Mrs. Holdfast–"I dreamed last night that you generously gave me a hundred dollar bill to buy some new dresses today. Surely, you wouldn't do anything to spoil such a beautiful dream, would you?"

Mr. Holdfast–"Certainly not. To show you I am as generous as you dreamed, you may keep that hundred dollar bill I gave you."

[2630]

Two men, Smith and Jones, were discussing the merits and otherwise of their respective wives.

"You know," said Smith, "my wife tells me that almost every night she dreams that she is married to a millionaire."

"You're darn lucky," replied Jones. "Mine thinks that in the daytime."

[2631]

"No, thank you, I'll stay at home," said a man who had been invited to join a party visiting the Zoo. "My eldest daughter does the kangaroo walk, my second daughter talks like a parrot, my son laughs like a hyena, my wife watches me like a hawk, my cook's as cross as a bear, and my mother-in-law says I'm an old gorilla! When I go anywhere I want a change!"

[2632]

Hubby (critically)—"Why in the world did you choose lemon as the color of your new dress?"

Wifey—"I don't know, dear, unless it was because I had such a hard time squeezing the price out of you."

[2633]

George—"Do you play an instrument of any kind, John?"

John (sadly)—"Only second fiddle at home."

[2634]

"And you tell me several men proposed marriage to you?" he said savagely.

"Yes; several," the wife replied.

"Well, I wish you had married the first fool who proposed."

"I did."

[2635]

"You deceived me before I married you. You told me you were well off."

"So I was—but I didn't know it."

[2636]

"Before we were married you called me an angel."

"I know it."

"And now you don't call me anything."

"You ought to be glad I possess such self-control."

[2637]

"Hello, dear. How's the pain in the neck?"

"Oh! He's out golfing!"

[2638]

Husband—"I suppose you only married me because I had a little money."

Wife—"Paul, that's unfair. You know I'd have married you if you'd had twice as much."

[2639]

The lecturer was a faddist on food.

According to him, most of the stuff we eat ought to have killed us years ago. Meat was murderous, vegetables were vicious, and even water was full of germs.

As a final burst, he pointed an accusing finger at one bored man in the front row of the audience.

"You, sir!" he demanded. "Can you tell me what it is that most of us eat at one time or another, yet it is the worst thing in the world for us?"

The bored man knew the answer to that one.

"Wedding cake!" he retorted, without any hesitation.

[2640]

Wife—"But, my dear, you've forgotten again that today is my birthday."

Husband—"Er—listen, love. I know I forgot it, but there isn't a thing about you to remind me that you are a day older than you were a year ago."

[2641]

Smith—"I wear the trousers in my home."

Friend—"Yeah, but right after supper I notice you wear an apron over them."

[2642]

"What are all these blonde hairs doing on this vest you wore last winter?" asked Mrs. Gay, as she held up the article she was going to hang out to air.

"What are they doing there?" replied Mr. Gay. "Why, you were a blonde last winter, weren't you?"

[2643]

"Mamma, do all angels fly?"

"Yes, Willie, why do you ask?"

"Cause I heard dad call the hired girl an angel the other day. Will she fly, too?"

"Yes, Willie, tomorrow."

[2644]

She–"Don't the bride look stunning?"

He–"Yeah, and don't the groom look stunned?"

[2645]

Wife–"Oh, you needn't think you're so wonderful. The night you proposed to me you looked absolutely silly!"

Husband–"A coincidence. The fact is, I was absolutely silly!"

[2646]

"John, I'm sure I heard a mouse squeak!"

"Well, do you want me to get up and oil it?"

[2647]

Six-year-old Mary awoke about two in the morning.

"Tell me a story, mamma," she pleaded.

"Hush, darling," said mother, "daddy will be in soon and tell us both one."

[2648]

"Does your husband talk in his sleep?"

"No, and it's terribly exasperating. He just grins."

[2649]

"You often cook much more for dinner than we use, darling."

"Of course! If I didn't, how could I economize by making left-over dishes?"

[2650]

Mrs. Brown (ready to go shopping) –"Mrs. Green has a new hat, darling."

Mr. Brown (slyly)–"Well, dear, if Mrs. Green were as attractive as you are she wouldn't have to depend so much on new hats."

[2651]

Mrs. Smith was relating her grievances over the garden fence.

"My husband is such a flirt," she complained. "I just can't trust him anywhere."

"Never mind, my dear," her friend consoled her. "He's probably only reverting to type."

"That's where you're wrong," said Mrs. Smith grimly. "He's reverting to typists."

[2652]

He–"If a man steals, no matter what, he will live to regret it."

She–"How about those kisses you used to steal before we were married?"

He–"You heard what I said."

[2653]

Mrs. Jones–"Does your husband consider you a necessity or a luxury?"

Mrs. Smith–"It depends, my dear, on whether I am cooking his dinner or asking for a new dress."

[2654]

Mrs. Brown–"Do you think I'm going to wear this old squirrel coat all my life?"

Mr. Brown (brightly)–"Why not, dear? The squirrels do."

[2655]

Wife–"Let me see that letter you've just opened. I can see from the handwriting it's from a woman and you turned pale when you read it."

Husband–"You can have it. It's from your milliner."

[2656]

Pa–"I think I'll go down-stairs and send Nancy's young man home."

Ma–"Now, Elmer, remember the way we used to court."

Pa–"Gosh, I hadn't thought of that. Out he goes!"

[2657]

Little Diana–"Mother, they are going to teach us domestic silence at school now."

Mother–"Don't you mean domestic science?"

Father–"There is a bare hope our little girl means what she is saying."

[2658]

Wife (aboard train vacation bound) –"Horrors; I forgot to turn off the electric iron!"

Husband–"Don't worry. It's all right. Nothing can burn very long, for I forgot to turn off the water in the bathtub."

[2659]

"I am sorry that I am late for dinner. I got arrested for speeding on the way home," Mr. Newlywed explained rather sheepishly. "Have to appear tomorrow morning and get ten dollars or fifteen days."

"What a Providence!" exclaimed his bride. "You must take the fifteen days, Peter. The cook has just left!"

[2660]

"Does your wife spend her evenings at home, generally speaking?"

"She does, and is."

[2661]

"John," she said, "I've got a lot of things I want to talk to you about —"

"Good," said her husband, "I'm glad to hear it. Usually you want to talk to me about a lot of things you haven't got."

[2662]

The family quarrel had reached its height. "I wish to goodness I'd taken my mother's advice and never married you!" cried the wife to her spouse.

Hubby swung round. "Do you mean to tell me," he demanded, "that your mother tried to stop you marrying me?"

Wifey nodded.

"Good heavens!" cried hubby, his voice filled with remorse. "How I've wronged that woman!"

[2663]

Passenger–"Have I time to say good-bye to my wife?"

Porter–"I don't know, sir, how long have you been married?"

[2664]

"The Beatties are so quiet tonight. Is there anything wrong?"

"No; they're always that way. When he proposed he just held up a diamond ring and said 'Eh?' and she looked at it and said 'Uh-huh.' "

[2665]

"I notice the Joneses seem to get along much better these days."

"Yes, ever since he went home this summer and saw the girl he was in love with twenty years ago."

[2666]

His daughter: "Daddy Darling, Jack and I love each other, and we've come to ask your consent. We've been married for a month, so we're sure we will be happy."

[2667]
A young lady entered a book store and inquired of the gentlemanly clerk—a married man, by-the-way—if he had a book suitable for an old gentleman who had been married fifty years.

Without the least hesitation the clerk reached for a copy of Parkman's "A Half Century of Conflict."

[2668]
"My wife is prolonging her visit. I need her at home, but it seems useless to write suggesting that she return."

"Get one of the neighbors to suggest it, my boy."

[2669]
He—"Who spilled mustard on this waffle, dear?"
She—"Oh, John! How could you? This is lemon pie."

[2670]
Doctor—"I would advise you, madam, to take frequent baths, plenty of fresh air and dress in cool gowns."
Husband (an hour later)—"What did the doctor say?"
Wife—"He said I ought to go to Saratoga, and afterwards to the mountains and to get some new light gowns at once."

[2671]
"Which of those two men is the bridegroom?"
"The anxious-looking one—the cheerful one is the bride's father."

[2672]
Mr. Homebody—"I see you keep copies of all the letters you write to your wife. Do you do it to avoid repeating yourself?"
Mr. Faraway—"No. To avoid contradicting myself."

[2673]
"And how's your wife?"
"Not so good; she's just had quinsy."
"Gosh! And how many does that make you now?"

[2674]
The man who brags, "I run things in my house," usually refers to the lawn mower, washing machine, vacuum sweeper, baby carriage and the errands.

[2675]
She—"I never saw a married couple who got on so well together as Mr. and Mrs. Ross."
He—"Humph! I know! Each of them does exactly as *she* likes."

[2676]
"Were you excited when you first asked your husband for money?"
"Oh, no, I was calm—and collected."

[2677]
Deciding to give his wife a pleasant surprise, a man took home some flowers and a box of candy. "Florence, you look tired," he said to his wife. "Slip on your best gown and we will go to the theatre."

She burst into tears. "It was b-bad enough to have the baby f-fall down the back steps and to b-burn my hand in the k-kitchen," she sobbed, "b-but to h-have y-you come home intoxicated is t-too much!"

[2678]
Mrs. Gray—"You're looking very happy this morning. Have you had good news?"
Mrs. Green—"Wonderful! My husband has broken down and we're going to Palm Beach for the winter."

[2679]

"The man who gives in when he is wrong," said the street orator, "is a wise man; but he who gives in when he is right is—"

"Married!" said a meek voice in the crowd.

[2680]

"Yes," said the young wife, proudly, "father always gives something expensive when he makes presents."

"So I discovered when he gave you away," rejoined the young husband.

[2681]

"My wife is very irritable; the least thing sets her off."

"You're lucky at that, mine's a self-starter."

[2682]

A speaker before a woman's organization, talking on Persia, was telling about how careless the men over there are with their wives, and said it was no uncommon sight to see a woman and a donkey hitched up together. Then he laughed, and said when he made that statement in a speech at Buffalo one of the ladies in the audience piped up:

"That's not so unusual—you often see it over here too."

[2683]

"Some women make up their minds, but let me tell you what my wife said to me:

"'You can stay at home if you want to, but I've made up my face to go out.'"

[2684]

Boy–"Do you know, Dad, my Sunday school teacher says that in some parts of Africa a man doesn't know his wife until he marries her."

Dad–"Why single out Africa?"

[2685]

Wife (complainingly)–"You never praise me up to any one."

Hub–"I don't, eh! You should hear me describe you at the employment office when I'm trying to hire a cook."

[2686]

Hubby–"What became of that unpaid bill the Dunn Company sent to us?"

Wife–"Oh, that? I sent it back marked insufficient funds."

[2687]

"My wife always has the last word."

"You're lucky. Mine never gets to it."

[2688]

"That young wife certainly worships her husband."

"Yes, she places burnt offerings before him every day."

[2689]

Husband–"Let's have some fun this evening!"

Wife–"O. K., and please leave the light on in the hallway if you get home before I do."

[2690]

Bill—"My wife doesn't understand me; does yours?"

Jim–"I don't think so, I've never heard her mention your name."

[2691]

Wife–"Where have you been so late?"

Husband–"Stop me if you've heard this one."

[2692]

Mr. Wiseacre–"Haven't I always given you my salary check the first of every month?"

Mrs. Wiseacre–"Yes, but you never told me you got paid on the first and fifteenth, you embezzler!"

[2693]

"I hear that Mrs. Highbride is much disappointed in her husband."

"Dreadfully. She understood he was a home-loving man and now he wants to tag along with her everywhere she goes."

[2694]

Charged with wife-beating, a Los Angeles husband was ordered to kiss his wife every day for six months. The woman always pays.

[2695]

A parson with a sense of humor has put up a sign in his church: "No mistakes rectified after leaving the altar."

[2696]

"Your wife seems a garrulous woman."

"Garrulous? Why, if I suddenly went dumb it would take her a week to find it out."

[2697]

"Are you sure your wife knows I'm going to your home for dinner tonight?"

"Knows! Well, rather! Why, my dear fellow, I argued with her about it this morning for nearly half an hour."

[2698]

Wife (referring to guest)–"He's a most attractive man; is he married?'"

Husband–"I dunno. He's a reserved chap—keeps all his troubles to himself!"

[2699]

"And how do you get on with your missus?"

"I've a splendid working arrangement with her. In the forenoon she does what she wants and in the afternoon I do what she wants."

[2700]

Mr. Cutting–"Woman is nothing but a rag, a bone and a hank of hair."

Mrs. Cutting–"Man is nothing but a brag, a groan and a tank of air."

[2701]

"Men are too mean for anything," said the young bride.

"What's the trouble now?" asked her best friend.

"Why, I asked Jack for the car today, and he said that I must be content with the splendid carriage that nature gave me."

[2702]

"So you wish to open a joint account with your husband. What kind?"

"Oh, just a deposit account for him—checking for me."

[2703]

The young wife was heartbroken.

"What's the matter?" asked a friend.

"Oh, my husband is so absent-minded. After breakfast he left a tip on the table, and when I handed him his hat he handed me another tip."

"Well, that's nothing to worry about. It's just force of habit."

"That's what worries me. He kissed me when I gave him his coat."

[2704]

Daughter–"But Dad, don't you believe that two can live as cheaply as one?"

Father–"I certainly do. Right now your mother and I are living as cheaply as you."

[2705]

"What's the matter, Elmer—you look terrible."

"My wife's on a diet."

[2706]

"But, madam, you have no claim. Your husband did not insure his life; he took out a policy against fire."

"That's what I claim. He has been cremated."

[2707]

"I want to bring young Wooley home to dinner tonight," said the husband.

"Bring him tonight!" shrieked his wife. "You know that the maid left without notice and the baby's cutting teeth, and I've got a cold, and the butcher says we can't have any more meat until we pay the bill. . . ."

"Yes, I know all that," he interrupted. "That's why I want to bring him home. I like the young fathead and he's thinking of getting married."

[2708]

The henpecked plumber rang the bell. The master and the mistress of the house came to the door together. As they all three stood in the hall, the husband—a methodical man—announced: "I wish, before you go upstairs, to acquaint you with my trouble."

The plumber shyly dropped his eyes.

"Pleased to meet yer, ma'am," he mumbled as he held out his hand to the wife.

[2709]

"Still engaged to Julia?"

"No."

"Good!"

"What?"

"Good; how'd you get rid of her?"

"What?"

"How'd you drop the old hag?"

"I married her."

[2710]

"I woke up in the middle of the night and found a burglar going through my pockets."

"What did you do?"

"Just laughed at him. My wife had gone through them earlier in the evening."

[2711]

"Does your hubby expect you to obey him?"

"Oh, no, dear. You see, he's been married before."

[2712]

"Let's get our wives together tonight and have a big evening."

"O. K., but where shall we leave them?"

[2713]

Wife (as husband is leaving)—"Dear, will you remember to bring home something for the rats this evening?"

Hubby—"Something for the rats? Certainly not! If the rats can't eat what we have in the house, let them leave."

[2714]

Rent Collector's Wife—"What are you looking so worried about, Horace?"

Rent Collector—"The landlord's become a client of our firm and if I don't collect my rent I will get fired for inefficiency."

[2715]

Fortune-Teller—"You wish to know about your future husband?"

Customer—"No; I wish to know about the past of my present husband for future use."

[2716]

Hubby—"The bank has returned that check."

Wife—"Isn't that splendid! What can we buy with it this time?"

[2717]

Mr. Brown had just returned to the city and was introduced to the new nurse, who was unusually pretty.

"She is sensible and scientific, too," said Mrs. Brown, "and she says she will allow no one to kiss the baby while she is near."

"No one would want to," replied Mr. Brown.

"Indeed!" snapped the fond mother.

"I mean, not while she is near," faltered the father, endeavoring to make things better.

The nurse did not stay long.

[2718]

Wife–"The world is full of rascals. This morning, the milkman gave me a counterfeit half-dollar."

Hubby–"Where is it, my dear?"

Wife–"Oh, I've already got rid of it—luckily the butcher took it."

[2719]

Hubby (just returned home)–"Well, we had a grand meeting at the lodge tonight."

Wife–"Oh, did you dear? I'm so glad."

Hubby–"Ahem! Yes, I made three speeches."

[2720]

"I understand your wife is quite ill."

"Yes, she had a slight cold; tried to cure herself by reading a daily health hint and is suffering from a typographical error."

[2721]

"My husband won a thousand dollars at poker the other night and he split with me."

"He gave you half?"

"No, he took his thousand and left!"

[2722]

She came into the police station with a picture in her hand.

"My husband has disappeared," she sobbed. "Here is his picture. I want you to find him."

The inspector looked up from the photograph.

"Why?" he asked.

[2723]

They were discussing an elopement, and one lady turning to her friend said:

"Don't you believe it would kill you if your husband was to run away with another woman?"

"It might," was the cool reply. "Great joy sometimes kills."

[2724]

A lecturer on optics, in explaining the mechanism of the organ of vision, remarked:

"Let any man gaze closely into his wife's eye, and he will see himself looking so exceedingly small that——"

The lecturer's voice was drowned by the shouts of laughter and applause which greeted his scientific remark.

[2725]

"My wife is so very tender-hearted she won't even whip cream."

"That's nothing. My wife won't beat rugs, and tears come to her eyes every time she has to skin those helpless little onions."

[2726]

Brown–"Your wife is a very systematic woman, isn't she?"

Jones–"Yes, very. She works on the theory that you can find whatever you want when you don't want it by looking where it wouldn't be if you did want it."

[2727]
"My wife has been nursing a grouch all the week."
"Been laid up, have you?"

[2728]
Friend (to Jones putting up arch in garden)–"What on earth are you putting up that thing for?"
"Oh, just a whim of the wife's."
"Why didn't you talk her out of it?"
"You don't know my wife. She has a whim of iron."

[2729]
He was always losing his collar button while dressing. His wife suggested that he hold his collar button in his mouth. The next morning she was startled by an unusual commotion.
"What's the matter?" she asked anxiously.
"I've swallowed the collar button," said the husband.
"Well," responded his wife, "there's one comfort: for once in your life you know where it is."

[2730]
"Hello! This is Mrs. Jones. Will you send some nice cutlets right away?"
"I'm sorry, but we haven't any cutlets."
"Well, then, a couple of nice lean pork chops."
"We haven't any pork chops either, Mrs. Jones."
"Oh, how provoking! Then a small sirloin steak will have to do."
"We haven't any steak."
"For heaven's sake! Aren't you Smith the butcher?"
"No, I'm Smith the florist."
"Oh! Well, send me a dozen white lilies. My husband must be starved to death by now."

[2731]
"It says the man was shot by his wife at close range."
"Then there must have been powder marks on the body."
"Yes; that's why she shot him."

[2732]
"If it isn't the door-bell or telephone," mumbled the busy housewife, "it's the ring around Willie's wrists, neck, or the bathtub."

[2733]
Mr. Jones found some holes in his stockings and asked his wife: "Why haven't you mended these?"
"Did you buy that coat you promised me?"
"No-o," he replied.
"Well, then, if you don't give a wrap I don't give a darn."

[2734]
A widower, having taken another wife, was, nevertheless, always paying some panegyric to the memory of his late spouse, in the presence of his present one; who one day added, with great feeling, "Believe me, my dear, nobody regrets *her loss* more than I do."

[2735]
He had risked his life to rescue the girl from a watery grave and, of course, her father was grateful.
"Young man," he said, "I can never thank you sufficiently for your heroic act. You incurred an awful risk in saving my only daughter."
"None whatever, sir," replied the amateur life-saver, "I am already married."

[2736]
She–"I consider, John, that sheep are the stupidest creatures living."
He (absent-mindedly)–"Yes, my lamb."

[2737]
Wifey–"I'm going up-town this afternoon."
Hubby–"Shopping?"
Wifey–"No, I won't have time. I just want to get some things I need."

[2738]
"Come now, own up. Who is the head of your household?"
"Well, my wife used to be, but since my daughters have grown up, we have a commission form of government."

[2739]
He (not a brilliant conversationalist)–"Something came into my mind just now and went away again."
She (bored)–"Perhaps it was lonely."

[2740]
"John, dear, I'm to be in amateur theatricals. What will people say when I wear tights?"
"They'll probably say I married you for your money."

[2741]
"I bought that dress for a ridiculous price."
"Perhaps so, but certainly not for an absurd figure."

[2742]
A young matron was seated one spring morning on the porch of her pretty suburban cottage, busily engaged in plying her needle. A coat of her husband's was in her lap. Looking up from her work, when her husband appeared in the doorway, the young woman exclaimed, somewhat fretfully:
"Really, Eugene, it is too bad, the careless way your tailor put this button on. This is the sixth time I have had to sew it on for you."

[2743]
Mrs. Wilkens–"Oh, Harry, I'm just in love with that hat in the window!"
Wilkens–"Nonsense, dear. Love is an affair of the heart, not of the head."

[2744]
"Poor old Tomkins has two wives to support now," remarked the cash-order collector to Mrs. Brown the other morning.
"Good heavens!" Mrs. Brown replied. "You don't mean to say he's a bigamist?"
"Oh no. Nothing like that; but his son got married last week."

[2745]
He–"You are always wishing for what you haven't got."
She–"Well, what else can one wish for?"

[2746]
"Is your husband a member of any secret society?"
"He thinks so, but he talks in his sleep."

[2747]
She–"The Lord made us beautiful and dumb."
He–"How's that?"
She–"Beautiful so the men would love us—and dumb so we could love them."

[2748]
"Just fancy, my wife even takes my shoes off with her own hands."
"When you come in at night?"
"No, when I want to go out."

[2749]
Wife (at dance)—"This is the twelfth time you've been to the refreshment buffet."
Husband–"Oh, that's all right. I tell everybody I'm getting something for you."

[2750]

Indignant Bridegroom (bursting in upon editor of local paper)–"Look here, I distinctly told you I was going to live at the old manse! What the blazes do you mean by saying in your rotten little rag that 'the happy couple will make their home at the old man's'?"

[2751]

She–"I wonder who invented that superstition about Friday being an unlucky day."

He–"Oh, some poor fish."

[2752]

A man dashed into the fire station. He was tremendously excited, and burst out with: "I'm sorry to interrupt you all, but my wife has disappeared again."

One of the firemen looked up.

"That's too bad," he sympathized, "but why tell us firemen? Why not notify the police?"

The intruder shook his head.

"I don't dare tell the police," he exclaimed. "I told them the last time she disappeared—and they went out and found her!"

[2753]

"Don't you think Mrs. Strongmind's husband is naturally a gentle, patient man?"

"Sometimes I think he is and sometimes I think he's just plain scared."

[2754]

"Was your marriage one of those trial and error things?"

"Just the opposite. First came the error, then the trial."

[2755]

Visitor–"I can't understand why you have no telephone here?"

Club Manager–"The majority of our members are married."

[2756]

They were rehearsing for the wedding. The organ had ceased its roaring, and the bride and groom stood with clasped hands before the altar. There was a holy stillness throughout the sacred edifice and the solemnity of the sanctuary exalted almost all the hearts of the group gathered at the chancel.

The most notable exception was the heart of the professional master of ceremonies.

It was not exalted to any appreciable extent.

"Do you take this woman to be"—

The master of ceremonies critically contemplated the happy pair.

"—your wedded—don't squeeze hands—wife?"

The groom's lips moved.

"Don't open your mouth too wide."

The groom looked scared and whispered something.

"Look pleasant, please—do you take this man to be your wedded —the chin a little higher—husband —eyes not quite so much obscured —there."

The bride trembled and gasped unintelligibly.

"Will you cherish, protect—a little more on the right foot—and defend—look to the altar—until death doth—not quite so much bend in the knee—part?"

The groom nervously signified that he would.

"Will you love—don't be thinking how your dress hangs—honor and—don't get too close to the groom—obey?"

"Yes," ventured the bride.

"Don't make the responses too confidently — whom God hath

joined let no man—don't exchange glances—put asunder."

The organ roared again. The party wended its way from the church, but the exaltation was in a measure abated.

[2757]

"I told my wife I would shoot any man who had flirted with her at the seaside."

"What did she say?"

"She told me to bring a machine-gun."

[2758]

"Times certainly have changed," sighed Smith.

"How so?" asked Robinson.

"Why, at a little family party last night, the women talked politics while the men got off in a corner and exchanged recipes."

[2759]

Smith–"I wonder if that fat old girl over there is really trying to flirt with me?"

Jones–"I can easily find out by asking her; she is my wife."

[2760]

"Has the laundry made a mistake?" asked Brown. "This shirt is so tight I can hardly breathe."

"Yes, it's your shirt all right," replied his wife, "but you've got your head through a buttonhole."

[2761]

Eloping Bride–"Here's a telegram from papa!"

Bridegroom (eagerly)–"What does he say?"

Bride–"Do not come home and all will be forgiven."

[2762]

She–"I remember the time when you were just crazy to marry me."

He–"So do I, but I didn't realize it at the time."

[2763]

They'd been "having words" because he came home very late again.

"Well, at any rate, I'm a man of my word," he snapped angrily. "I do call a spade a spade."

"Maybe, Henry," his wife retorted; "but you don't call a club a club; you call it working late."

[2764]

"You are certainly kind to send your wife away for a rest."

"Yes, heaven knows I need it."

[2765]

She–"Well, dear, I've been acting on your advice. I put a hundred dollars in the bank this month."

He–"Fine! It isn't so hard, is it?"

She–"No; I simply tore up all the bills."

[2766]

"Now that you are married I suppose you will take out an insurance policy?"

"Oh, no! I don't think she's going to be dangerous."

[2767]

The bridegroom was in a poetic frenzy as he strolled along the seashore. "Roll on, thou deep and dark blue ocean, roll," he recited to his bride.

"Oh, Percy," she exclaimed, "how wonderful you are. It's doing it."

[2768]

He–"But, Alice, you don't want that!"

She–"How will I know until I get it?"

[2769]

Wife–"As the weather is still cold, I should like to look at some furs. Will you come with me?"

Husband–"Yes—let's go to the Zoo!"

[2770]

"Do you know what I think of married life?"

"Are you married?"

"Yes."

"Yes."

[2771]

Husband–"But you must admit that men have better judgment than women."

Wife–"Oh, yes—you married me, and I you."

[2772]

He–"Oh, you mustn't blame me for my ancestors."

She–"I don't. I blame them for you."

[2773]

Mr. Newlywed–"Did you sew the button on my coat, darling?"

Mrs. Newlywed–"No, love; I couldn't find the button, and so I just sewed up the buttonhole."

[2774]

Mr. Peck–"Would you mind compelling me to move on, officer? I've been waiting on this corner three hours for my wife!"

[2775]

He–"I thought that lamb was a little tough."

She–"Oh, let's not talk chop."

[2776]

Wife–"Can you see figures in the fire, Jack?"

Husband–"Yes, dear."

Wife–"What figures can you see?"

Husband–"Eight dollars a ton."

[2777]

"What power on earth made you return to your wife when everybody agreed she was wrong?"

"Water power."

"Aw, come, be serious!"

"I mean it—I couldn't bear her crying."

[2778]

"Do you know why we call our language the Mother Tongue?"

"Because Father never gets a chance to use it."

[2779]

Poetic Bridegroom– "I could sit here forever, gazing into your eyes, and listening to the wash of the ocean."

Practical Bride–"Oh! That reminds me, darling, we have not paid our laundry bill yet."

[2780]

"You have my sympathy, old man."

"Why?"

"My wife got a new hat, and she's calling on your wife tomorrow."

[2781]

He–"Isn't it wonderful, my dear? They've actually found in the tomb couches and chairs thirty centuries old and in good condition."

She–"I have always said, John, that it pays in the long run to buy the best."

[2782]

Maid–"Madam, master is lying unconscious in the hall with a piece of paper in his hand and a large box by his side."

Mrs. Green (joyously)–"Oh, my new hat has arrived?"

[2783]

"You see; marriage hasn't changed him at all. He's as big a drunkard as he ever was."

"Yes, but he used to drink for pleasure; now it's from sorrow."

[2784]

"Yes, I heard a noise and got up, and there, under the bed, I saw a man's leg."

"Good heavens! The burglar's?"

"No; my husband's. He'd heard the noise, too."

[2785]

"Your wife likes to go South every year, eh?"

"Yeah. She loves to spend the winter in the rotogravure sections."

[2786]

Mr.–"You want to be careful about packing away your Winter clothes, my dear. The moths are likely to get into them."

Mrs.–"You needn't be alarmed about the moths. They are not going to bother with plush when they can get genuine seal-skin at the woman's who lives next door."

[2787]

She–"Is my hat on straight, Henry?"

He–"Quite straight, my dear. Now do hurry—we're late already."

She–"Well, I shall have to go back then—this isn't the sort of hat that is worn straight!"

[2788]

Interviewer–"What made you a multimillionaire?"

Multimillionaire–"My wife."

Interviewer–"Ah, her loyal help—"

Multimillionaire–"No, no. I was simply curious to know if there was *any* income she couldn't live beyond."

[2789]

"Poor Lola! She got cruelly deceived when she married old Goldrox."

"Why, didn't he have any money?

"Oh, yes, plenty of money, but he was ten years younger than he said he was."

[2790]

"Mrs. Upton's pet dog has been run over; she'll be heartbroken."

"Don't tell her abruptly."

"No, I'll begin by saying it's her husband."

[2791]

Tombstone Dealer (after several futile suggestions)–"How would just a simple 'Gone Home' do for an inscription?"

The Widow–"I guess that will be all right. It was always the last place he ever thought of going."

[2792]

"John, dear, you simply must stop mumbling in your sleep."

"Don't be so curious. I absolutely refuse to talk out loud."

[2793]

She (with newspaper)–"It says here that the Eskimos use fish-hooks for money."

He–"Gee! It must be tough on their wives getting fish-hooks out of hubby's pocket while he's sleeping."

She–"Oh, well, the nights are six months long up there, dear."

[2794]

Telephone Operator – "It costs seventy-five cents to talk to Bloomfield."

Caller–"Can't you make a special rate for just listening? I want to call my wife."

[2795]

"What's the matter with your wife? She looks all broken up."

"She got a terrible shock."

"How was it?"

"She was assisting at a rummage sale at the church and she took off her new $2 hat and somebody sold it for 30 cents."

[2796]

"Do you pretend to have as good a judgment as I have?" exclaimed an enraged wife to her husband.

"Well, no," he replied slowly, "our choice of partners for life shows that my judgment is not to be compared with yours."

[2797]
"She treated me shamefully."
"Ah! but she treated me worse."
"Impossible! She jilted me."
"Yes; but she married me."

[2798]
John–"If I'd known you were so extravagant I would never have married you."
Jane–"If I hadn't been, father would never have let you."

[2799]
Bridegroom–"And now, dear, that we are married, let us have a clear understanding about our affairs. Do you wish to be president or vice-president?"
Bride (sweetly)–"Neither. You be both. I'll be just the treasurer."

[2800]
"Before Jim's marriage he always said marriages were made in heaven."
"Yes, he still says they're made there, but now he always adds that heaven can't be the place it's cracked up to be."

[2801]
"How did your wife get on with her slimming diet."
"Fine — she disappeared completely last week!"

[2802]
Two women were talking about their husbands in that indulgent manner they are accustomed to use when on that subject.
"John is perfectly helpless without me," said one.
"Harry is that way, too," said another. "I don't know what would become of him if I was away from him for a week."
"Isn't it a fact?" sighed a third. "Sometimes I think my husband is a child, the way I have to look after

him. Why, whenever he is sewing on buttons, mending his clothes, or even darning his socks, I always have to thread the needle for him."

[2803]
Hubbie had had a few drinks too many.
Wife–"If it were the first time, Archibald, I could forgive it, but you came home in just the same state in November, 1916."

[2804]
"Did any of your family ever make a brilliant marriage?"
"Only my wife."

[2805]
"Why don't you buy a bouquet?" asked the lady selling flowers.
"I don't need one," Mr. Smith answered, moving on.
"Why not buy one for the woman you love?" she called after him.
"I can't. That wouldn't be right. You see, I'm a married man," he paused long enough to answer.

[2806]
"I'll tell you what's the matter, Fred. You don't praise your wife enough. Even if things don't go right, there's no use growling. Praise her efforts to please, whether they are successful or not. Women like praise, and lots of it."
Fred–"All right. I'll remember it."
Fred (at dinner, same evening)–"My dear, this pie is just lovely! It's delicious. Ever so much better than those my mother used to make. She couldn't equal this pie if she tried a month."
Wifie–"Huh! You've made fun of every pie I ever made, and now—"
Fred–"But this is lovely."
Wifie–"Yes, and it came from the bakery. You never praised my cooking like that."

LOVE, COURTSHIP AND MARRIAGE

[2807]

He–"But you promised at the altar to obey me."
She–"Of course. I didn't want to make a scene."

[2808]

Tom–"Was it a big wedding?"
Tim–"Yes. I got in line twice to kiss the bride and nobody noticed it."

[2809]

"Is your wife fond of listening in?"
"Not half so much as she is of speaking out."

[2810]

"Nowadays many couples are omitting the word 'obey' from the marriage ceremony. Do you think that right?"
"Well, it never bothered my wife any."

[2811]

Doctor–"This is a very sad case, very sad indeed. I much regret to tell you that your wife's mind is gone—completely gone."
Mr. Peck–"I'm not at all surprised, doctor. She's been giving me a piece of it every day for fifteen years."

MOTHERS-IN-LAW

[2812]

Mother – "And now tell me what you meant by introducing me to Mr. Brown as your aunt?"
Daughter–"Forgive me, mother, but Mr. Brown appears to be on the point of proposing, and it would not do to run any risks. He has a strong prejudice against mothers-in-law."

[2813]

"Before we were married, you said mother could stay with us whenever she pleased."
"Yes, but she hasn't pleased yet."

[2814]

Mother-in-Law (angrily)–"It's about time the mothers-in-law disappeared from the comic papers."
Son-In-Law–"Yes. I think they ought to disappear altogether."

[2815]

Wifie–"I have a surprise for you, Harry."
Hubby–"Oh, have you? And how long is your mother going to stay?"

[2816]

"John dear," said Mabel, as her lord and master entered the house, "I've just had a letter from mother, and she is coming to visit us. It is a pretty expensive trip for little Muddy, and I wondered if we couldn't help her out a little."
"Of course we can," said John, giving his wife a generous kiss. "Just you write and tell her that I'll be only too glad to pay for her railroad ticket back home again as soon as she decides to go."

[2817]

Husband–"So I was talking in my sleep last night, eh? That's strange. I was dreaming of your mother."
Wife–"Why is it strange?"
Husband–"I don't see how I got a chance to say a word."

[2818]

Husband (to cook)–"My mother-in-law is coming on a long visit to-morrow. I've made out a list of her favorite dishes for you."
Cook–"Yes sir."
Husband–"Well, the first time you serve one of them, you're fired."

[2819]

"My husband got angry last night and told me to go to the devil."

"What are you going to do about that?"

"I'm going straight home to mother."

[2820]

"Do you know that your dog bit my mother-in-law yesterday?"

"No; is that so? Well, I suppose you will sue me for damages?"

"Not at all. What will you take for the dog?"

[2821]

She–"And when we're married, darling, we'll have a nice little house right near mother, so she can drop in any time."

He–"You bet. We'll get one right by the river."

[2822]

Husband–"Didn't I telegraph you not to bring your mother with you?"

Wife – "That's what she wants to see you about."

[2823]

Waiter–"Have another glass of beer sir?"

Husband (to his wife)–"Shall I have another glass, Henrietta?"

Wife (to her mother)–"Shall he have another, mother?"

[2824]

Bride–"Pierre is perfectly wonderful to me, mother. He gives me everything I ask for."

Mother – "That merely shows, my dear child, that you are not asking enough."

[2825]

"Darling," she said, "when we are married you'll have a woman in the house who really knows how to cook."

"Well," said darling, "that's pleas-ant news. I didn't know that you were expert in the cooking line."

"I'm not," she replied, "but when we are married mother is coming to live with us."

[2826]

"Jim," said Brown, "what did you call your mother-in-law after you got married?"

"Well, I'll tell you," replied Jones, "for the first year I addressed her as 'Say,' and after that we called her 'Grandma.' "

[2827]

The young wife was in tears when she opened the door for her husband. "I've been insulted," she sobbed. "Your mother insulted me."

"My mother," he exclaimed. "But she is a hundred miles away."

"I know, but a letter came for you this morning and I opened it."

He looked stern. "I see, but where does the insult come in?"

"In the postcript," she answered. "It said: 'Dear Alice, don't forget to give this letter to George.' "

[2828]

"Is your wife's mother enjoying her trip to the mountains?"

"I'm afraid not. She's found some-thing at last that she can't walk over."

[2829]

"Why did you break off your engagement, Jack?"

"Well, we were looking over an apartment when her mother remarked that it was rather small for three."

[2830]

Wife–"I wish you'd bring home a pineapple, John. Mother is coming today, and you know she'd give half her life for a good pineapple."

John–"Really! Then I'll bring two!"

[2831]

"Who will help a man to correct personality defects if not his wife?" asks a heart-throb editor.

Well, sister, there is his wife's mother.

[2832]

Wife's Mother (to gardening son-in-law)–"I hope you're being careful when you dig up a worm, Richard. Remember it can feel and think just as well as you can."

[2833]

"I must say these are fine biscuits!" exclaimed the young husband.

"How could you say those are fine biscuits?" inquired the young wife's mother, in a private interview.

"I didn't say they were fine. I merely said I must say so."

DIVORCE

[2834]

"So Mrs. Potter has got a divorce. What was the trouble, incompatibility?"

"No, merely the first two syllables."

[2835]

"On what grounds do you seek a divorce, Mr. Jones?"

"Incompatibility. I want a divorce, and my wife doesn't."

[2836]

Johnson–"What was the most expensive piece of jewelry you ever bought?"

Thompson–"My wedding ring. I'm paying fifty dollars a week alimony."

[2837]

She–"A man's speech has been restored by the kick of a mule."

He–"A divorce is less painful and gets the same results."

[2838]

"When a woman marries and then divorces her husband inside of a week what would you call it?"

"Taking his name in vain."

[2839]

"Make me the happiest man in the world!" he begged.

So she agreed on two hundred a month alimony, and gave him a divorce.

[2840]

"Maud has made some swell marriages, but divorced all her husbands."

"Yes, she moves in the best triangles, so to speak."

[2841]

"How is it I see Jones and his former wife together so much lately? I thought they were separated."

"Oh, theirs is a companionate divorce."

[2842]

Alice–"Are you married?"

Virginia–"Am I? Three judges have refused me a divorce!"

[2843]

Her legal adviser–"Madam, you have had three husbands, and every one of them either went crazy or turned out to be worthless. Yet you are thinking of marrying again!"

Fair Client–"Yes, sir. I want a safe and sane fourth."

[2844]

"What did you divorce your husband for?"

"Two hundred dollars a month."

[2845]

"When the Judge ruled that Caldwell had to pay alimony, how did he feel about it?"

"Chagrined."

"And how did his wife feel about it?"

"She grinned."

[2846]

Agitated Caller–"I want something to quiet my nerves."

Lawyer–"But I'm not a doctor, I'm a lawyer."

"Yes, I know. I want a divorce."

[2847]

The tired-looking man sat facing the lawyer. "So you want a divorce from your wife," said the latter. "Aren't your relations pleasant?"

"Mine are," came the answer, "but hers are simply terrible."

[2848]

Voice on phone–"Is that Mr. Roamer's second wife?"

"No, I'm his third; you've got the wrong number!"

[2849]

"Your husband has a new suit."

"No, he hasn't."

"Well, something's different."

"It's a new husband."

[2850]

Mrs. Ex-Smith-Jones-Brown-Robinson, etc. (to her secretary)–"Perkins, go over the list again carefully. I'm quite sure I'm shy one alimony check this month."

[2851]

"You have a charming wife."

"Sorry, old man, but she's spoken for two divorces ahead."

[2852]

"How long has your cook been with you?"

"Oh, about three husbands."

[2853]

In a Western divorce case a man accuses his wife of being "sullen, mean, irritable, morbid, disagreeable, nasty, bitter, jealous, heckling, loathsome, insulting, miserly, selfish, uncivil, and inconsiderate." But could she cook?

[2854]

"I'd like to know if I can get a divorce from my husband," said the dainty young thing.

"What has your husband done?" inquired the lawyer.

"Is it necessary to say that?" she asked.

"We must, of course, make some charge against him. State what he's done."

"Well, as a matter of fact, he hasn't done anything," she said. "I haven't got a husband, but I'm engaged to a man and I just wanted to see how easy I could get a divorce in case of need."

[2855]

The Bachelor–"How we change as we grow older!

The Divorcee–"Yes, d'you know, I used to marry men I wouldn't invite to dinner now!"

[2856]

"My husband is the kindest, most considerate husband in the world."

"Why the outburst, dear?"

"He's going to let me get a divorce on the grounds of extreme cruelty."

[2857]

Friend (to young wife contemplating divorce)–"Remember, dear, you took your husband for better or for worse."

Young Wife–"But I didn't take him for good, did I?"

[2858]

"You complain that you have had to support your wife's family?" the court questioned the man seeking a divorce.

"Yes, your honor."

"How much of a family has she?"

"Four children, your honor."

"Who is their father?"

"I am, your honor."

[2859]

"And are the divorce laws so very liberal in your section?"

"Liberal? Say! They are so liberal that nobody ever heard of a woman crying at a wedding out there."

BACHELORS AND SPINSTERS

[2860]

"You can get anything from a mail-order house," remarked the lady next door.

"Everything, alas, but a male," sighed the spinster.

[2861]

Friend–"Did you get any replies to your advertisement that a lonely maiden sought light and warmth in her life?"

Spinster–"Yes, two from electric-light companies and one from a gas company."

[2862]

"A bachelor has nobody to share his troubles."

"Why should a bachelor have any troubles?" asked the married man.

[2863]

A spinster was entertaining a number of little girls from a charitable institution. After the lunch-eon, the children were shown through the place, in order that they might enjoy the many beautiful things it contained.

"This," said the spinster, indicating a statue, "is Minerva."

"Was Minerva married?" asked one of the little girls.

"No, my child," said the spinster, with a smile; "Minerva was the Goddess of Wisdom."

[2864]

"Uncle Tom," said his young nephew to an old bachelor, "tell me about some of the narrow escapes you've had from the women."

"Boy," was the response, "if there was any narrow escapes, the women had 'em!"

[2865]

Abner Scott loved Sophie Simpkins, a spinster, but never had courage enough to propose, being invariably overwhelmed with shyness when he met her. At last he determined to put his fate to the test and phoned her.

"Miss Simpkins?"

"Miss Simpkins speaking."

"Er—will you marry me Miss Simpkins?"

"Yes! Who is speaking?"

[2866]

"Cats," my dear," said the spinster, "I hate the very sight of them. I had a sweet little canary and some cat got that. I had a perfect parrot, and some cat got that; I had an adorable *fiancé*, and—oh, don't mention cats to me!"

[2867]

"Laura could have married anybody she pleased."

"Then why is she still single?"

"She never pleased anybody."

[2868]

The spinster pooh-poohed anyone who suggested that it was too bad she did not have a husband.

"I have a dog that growls, a parrot that swears, a fireplace that smokes, and a cat that stays out all night. Why should I want a husband?"

[2869]

"Is it true, Miss Elderleigh, that you are going to be married soon?"

"Well, no, it isn't. But I am very grateful for the rumor."

[2870]

Helen—"How is your bachelor friend?"

Horace—"When I saw him last he was mending slowly."

Helen—"Why, I didn't know he'd been ill."

Horace—"He hasn't been. He was sewing buttons on his clothes."

[2871]

A girl asked an old bachelor whether he had been disappointed in love.

"No, I never was exactly disappointed in love," he replied. "I was more what you might call discouraged. You see, when I was very young I became very much enamored of a young lady of my acquaintance; I was mortally afraid to tell her of my feeling, but at last I screwed up my courage to the proposing point. I said, 'Let's get married.'

"And she said, 'Good Lord! Who'd have us!'"

[2872]

Mrs. Smith (with newspaper)—"It says here that a woman in Kansas City has just cremated her third husband."

Miss Willing—"Heigho! Isn't that just the way? Some of us can't get one and other women have husbands to burn."

[2873]

"Why have you never married?" a friend asked an old bachelor.

"Well, once upon a time, in a crowd," replied the bachelor, "I trod on a lady's gown. She turned furiously, beginning, 'You clumsy brute!' Then she smiled sweetly and said, 'Oh, I beg pardon! I thought you were my husband! No; it really doesn't matter in the least.'"

[2874]

Mrs. Neighbor—"I've been looking for my husband for two hours."

Spinster—"That's nothing. I've been looking for one for 20 years and haven't found him yet."

[2875]

It was on a sleighride. The Old Maid heaved a deep sigh, for the benefit of the eligible young man at her side.

"What's the matter, Miss Smithkins?"

She managed an artistic catch in her throat. "Nobody loves me; and my hands are cold."

"Oh, that's all right," he comforted her. "God loves you—and you can sit on your hands."

PART III

HOME AND SCHOOL HUMOR

BABIES

[2876]

Johnny–"What makes the new baby at your house cry so much, Tommy?"

Tommy–"It don't cry so very much —and, anyway, if all your teeth were out, your hair off, and your legs so weak you couldn't stand on them, I guess you'd feel like crying yourself."

[2877]

"I hear there's a new baby over at your house, William," said the teacher.

"I don't think he's new," replied William. "The way he cries shows he's had lots of experience."

[2878]

Jimmie carried the following excuse to the teacher the next morning: "Please excuse Jimmie from being absent. He had a new baby brother. It was not his fault."

[2879]

The Visitor–"Does your new baby brother cry much, Ethel?"

Little Ethel–"He cries when you stick pins in him or make faces at him or bounce him up and down. But what can you expect? He's too little to swear."

[2880]

Little Freddie's mother was in the hospital, and he was paying a visit to see his new brother. He wandered into an adjoining room which was occupied by a woman with a broken leg.

"Hello," he said. "How long have you been here?"

"Oh, about a month."

"Let me see your baby," he then asked.

"Why, I haven't a baby," the woman replied.

"Gee, you're slow," said Freddie. "My mama's been here just two days and she's got one."

[2881]

"I suppose your baby reigns as king in your family."

"No—Prince of Wails."

[2882]

While a young mother was bathing her baby, a neighbor's little girl came in and watched the process. The child was holding a doll minus an arm and leg and much knocked about generally.

"How long have you had your baby?" she asked the mother.

"Three months."

"My, but you've kept her nice!" exclaimed the little girl.

[2883]
Nurse–"Well, Bobby, you have a new baby brother for a Christmas present."
Bobby–"Oh, zowie! May I be the first to tell Mother?"

[2884]
Little Jimmie had watched his mother prepare food for the new baby in the home. On being asked what the new brother ate, he replied:
"Why, Aunt Ida, he eats the formula."

[2885]
Little Girl (to mother)–"Ma, I'm afraid baby will have seven years of hard luck. He swallowed a piece of mirror."

[2886]
The Pastor–"So God has sent you two more little brothers, Dolly?"
Dolly (brightly)–"Yes, and He knows where the money's coming from; I heard Daddy say so."

[2887]
Visitor–"Well, Joe, how do you like your new little sister?"
Joe–"Oh, she's all right, I guess; but there are lots of things we needed worse."

[2888]
A little girl arrived at kindergarten all out of breath with excitement.
"Why, what's the matter?" asked her teacher.
"We've got a new baby at our house," she replied. "Won't you come and see it?"
"Oh, thanks!" said the teacher. "But I think I had better wait until your mother is better."
"It's all right," said the girl. "You don't have to be afraid—it's not catching."

[2889]
Nurse–"Don't you like your new baby sister, Johnnie?"
Johnnie–"She's all right, but I wish she had been a boy. Willie Smith has got a new sister, and now he'll think I'm trying to copy him."

[2890]
Little Frank, who had removed with his family to a new house, was taken to visit the new tenants of the old house, with whom his mother was on friendly terms.
The chief object of interest was a recently arrived baby.
Frank was much taken with the infant, and on his way home remarked:
"Mother, it's a pity we moved from that house. If we'd stayed a bit longer we should have got that baby."

[2891]
Caller–"And what are the twins to be named, Johnny?"
Johnny–"Helen and Maria."
Caller–"Why, no, Johnny; it can't be that."
Johnny–"Well, anyhow, that's what pop said when the nurse brought 'em in."

[2892]
"I hear you have a little sister?"
"Yes," answered the small boy.
"Do you like her?"
"I wish it was a boy, 'cause then I could play marbles, baseball, and other games with her."
"Then why don't you exchange her for a brother?"
"Can't," was the answer. "It's too late now. We've used her four days."

[2893]
"I'm fed up on that," cried the baby, pointing to the high chair.

[2894]

Tiny Clara heard her mother say that a neighboring lady had a new baby. The tot puzzled over the matter, and at last sought additional information:

"Oh, mumsy, what is she going to do with her old one?"

[2895]

Johnnie was gazing at his one-day-old brother squealing in his cot.

"Has he come from Heaven?" inquired Johnnie.

"Yes, dear," said his mother.

"No wonder they put him out."

[2896]

Little Terence aged six, was being congratulated by his teacher. "I hear," smiled the teacher, "that you have a new baby brother."

"Not only one," grunted little Terence. "Two of them!"

"That's wonderful," beamed the teacher. "You must be very proud."

"Aw, what's so hot about it?" growled the six-year-old. "We didn't even make the newsreel!"

[2897]

A youngster was being shown a new baby who was very bald.

"Where did he come from?" he asked.

"From heaven."

Turning to his mother, the boy said:

"Gee, they cut hair close in heaven, don't they?"

[2898]

"Mother, how much do people pay a pound for babies?"

"Babies are not sold by the pound, darling."

"Then why do they always weigh them as soon as they are born?"

[2899]

Father–"Your new little brother has just arrived."

Modern Child–"Where did he come from?"

Father–"From a far-away country."

Child–"Another darned alien."

[2900]

Willie–"We have a new baby at our house."

Bobby–"Is it a girl or boy?"

Willie–"I don't know; they have not put its clothes on yet."

[2901]

Stranger–"How old is your little baby brother?"

Little Girl–"He's a this year's model."

[2902]

Proud Mother–"Yes, he's a year old now, and he's been walking since he was eight months old."

Bored Visitor–"Really? He must be awfully tired."

[2903]

Boston Child–"Mamma! Mamma! The baby has fell out of the window!"

Boston Mother–" 'Fallen,' you mean, dear. Quick! run for the doctor!"

[2904]

"Does the baby look like his father?"

"Oh, no. My husband would be furious."

[2905]

A little girl said there was a new baby at her house.

"Has the baby come to stay?" she was asked.

"I think so," she said, "he's taken all his things off."

[2906]

"Why are you writing to the Director of the Census?"

"We've got a new baby."

[2907]

"What is your new brother's name?"

Little Jane—"I don't know yet. We can't understand a word he says."

[2908]

Mother—"Baby is going to be an auctioneer when he grows up."

Husband—"How do you know?"

Mother—"He already has your watch under the hammer."

[2909]

"And has your baby learned to talk yet?"

"Oh my, yes. We're teaching him to keep quiet now."

[2910]

A newly created papa received the glad tidings in a telegram:

"Hazel gave birth to a little girl this morning; both doing well."

On the message was a sticker reading: "When you want a boy call Western Union."

[2911]

Father (awaiting the news)—"Well, nurse, will it use a razor or a lipstick?"

[2912]

"John's wife doesn't know where the baby gets his bad temper from."

"That's strange. Most young mothers can place that sort of responsibility in a jiffy."

[2913]

Fat Man (fondling baby)—"What do you think of my son, Jim?"

Jim (surveying father)—"Well, I'd say that he was a stave off the old barrel."

[2914]

"Believe me, my baby is the loveliest in the world."

"What a coincidence that we should meet—so is mine."

[2915]

"Did you tell Mr. Jones that he is father of triplets?"

"No, he is still shaving."

[2916]

Willie—"Ma, if the baby was to eat tadpoles, would it give him a big bass voice like a frog?"

Mother—"Good gracious, no! They'd kill him."

Willie—"Well, they didn't!"

[2917]

Willie—"I'll bet we have something at our house you don't have. We have a new baby."

Bobbie—"Aw, gee; we have more than that at our house. We have a new Daddy."

[2918]

"Lord, you are late, sir," said the nurse meeting the young husband at the door; "it's two o'clock, and sir, here's news for you! You're the father of two bouncing babies! Twins, sir, twins!"

"Strange coincidence," said the young father, "two o'clock and two babies. Thank heaven I did not come home at twelve."

[2919]

"What in the world shall I do with the baby, Harry? She's crying for the moon."

"That's nothing. Wait till she's eighteen, and she'll want the earth."

[2920]

Young father (looking at triplets the nurse has just brought out)—"Hmmm! We'll take the one in the middle."

[2921]

Caller—"So the angels have brought you a new baby sister."

Elsie (disgustedly)—"To see the fuss nurse makes over her you'd think she came from Paris."

[2922]

A man was discovered by his wife one night standing over his baby's crib. Silently she watched him. As he stood looking down at the sleeping infant, she saw in his face a mixture of emotions—rapture, doubt, admiration, despair, ecstasy, incredulity. Touched and wondering alike at this unusual parental attitude and the conflicting emotions the wife with eyes glistening arose and slipped her arms around him.

"A penny for your thoughts," she said, in a voice tremulous. He blurted them out:

"For the life of me, I can't see how anybody can make a crib like that for three forty-nine!"

[2923]

"So you have adopted a baby to raise? Well, it may turn out all right, but don't you think you are taking chances?"

"Not a chance. No matter how many bad habits the child may develop, my wife can't say he inherits any of them from my side of the house."

[2924]

Friend–"They say the baby looks like you."

Father–"The only likeness I can see is we're both bald-headed."

[2925]

The young father was wheeling a baby carriage around the block on a very hot afternoon.

"My dear!" came a voice from an upper window of his house.

"Now let me alone!" he called back. "We're all right."

An hour later the same voice pleaded: "Charles dear!"

"Well, what do you want?" he replied. "Anything wrong in the house?"

"No, Charles dear, but you have been wheeling Nancy's doll all the afternoon. Isn't it time for the baby to have a turn?"

[2926]

"Oh, when he's about three, Ethel. He's only a baby yet, Ethel. Babies can't talk."

"Oh, yes, they can, father," insisted Ethel, "for Job could talk when he was a baby."

"Job! What do you mean?"

"Yes," said Ethel. "Nurse was telling us today that it says in the Bible, 'Job cursed the day he was born.'"

[2927]

Momma (singing)–"By low, my baby."

Poppa–"That's right you tell him to buy low and I'll teach him to sell high."

[2928]

Young Husband (in early morning)–"It must be time to get up."

Wife–"Why?"

"Baby's fallen asleep."

[2929]

"What did you give baby for his first birthday?"

"We opened his money-box and bought the little darling a lovely electric iron."

[2930]

Excited Young Father–"Quick! Tell me! Is it a boy?"

Nurse–"Well, the one in the middle is."

[2931]

Wife–"That new maid of ours must be from New York. She speaks of the nursery as the 'noisery.'"

Hubby–"Well, I rather think that's the way it should be pronounced."

[2932]

Wifey–"Oh, Bill, baby can walk."
Hubby–"That's fine. Now he can walk up and down at night by himself."

[2933]

Young Wife–"Now, Bill, I want you to go around to the minister and arrange for having the baby christened."
Bill (shipyard worker)–"You mean to say you are going to let somebody hit that little thing over the head with a bottle?"

[2934]

The bachelor went to see his married sister's new baby. He watched the infant carefully through the regular routine of the day. When asked later to describe the new arrival, he thought a moment, and then said:
"Hmm. Very small features. Clean-shaven. Very red in the face, and a very hard drinker."

THE LITTLE DARLINGS—AND DEVILS

[2935]

"Mother," said Johnny, "is it correct to say you 'water a horse' when he's thirsty?"
"Yes, quite correct."
"Then [picking up a saucer], I'm going to milk the cat."

[2936]

At the Children's Hospital Johnny was the terror of the ward. He was always in trouble. One day a weekly visitor, who knew his character, said to him:
"Johnny, if you are good for a

week, I'll give you a dime when I come again."
A week later she stood before Johnny's bed again.
"Well," she said, "I'm not going to ask the nurses if you've behaved. You must tell me yourself. Do you deserve the dime?"
There was a moment's silence. Then from among the sheets a small voice said:
"Gimme a penny."

[2937]

Little Boy–"Was that policeman ever a little baby?"
Mother–"Why, yes, of course."
Boy–"Oh, mummy, I should love to see a baby policeman."

[2938]

"Mummy, do give me another piece of sugar," said little Helen.
"But you've had three already," her mother pointed out.
"Just one more, mummy."
"Well, this must be the last."
"Thank you, mummy—but I must say you've got no will-power."

[2939]

A small boy stood in the entrance to the cobbler's shop watching the man at work.
"What do you repair boots with, mister?" he suddenly asked.
"Hide," replied the cobbler sharply.
"E-r-r, eh?" asked the boy.
"I said hide," replied the cobbler impatiently.
"What for?" the boy insisted, somewhat surprised.
"Hide! The cow's outside," sighed the man.
"Don't care if it is. Who's afraid of a cow, anyway?" said the youngster defiantly.

[2940]

"Thomas, what is the matter with your brother?" asked the mother of the boys.

"He's crying," replied Thomas, "because I'm eating my cake and won't give him any."

"Is his own cake finished?" asked the mother.

"Yes, and he cried while I was eating that, too."

[2941]

Neighbor–"Where is your brother, Freddie?"

Freddie–"He's in the house playing a duet. I finished first."

[2942]

Willie–"Papa, if I was twins would you buy the other boy a banana, too?'"

Papa–"Certainly, my son."

Willie–"Well, papa, you surely ain't going to cheat me out of another banana just 'cause I'm all in one piece?"

[2943]

Dickey–"My Dad is an Elk, a Lion, and a Moose."

Mickey–"What does it cost to see him?"

[2944]

"What time does the next train come in?" asked Edward, aged six, of the old rural station agent.

"Why, you little rascal, I've told you five times before that it comes in at 4:44."

"I know it," replied Edward, "but I like to see your whiskers wobble when you say '4:44.'"

[2945]

The doctor of a country village had two children who were acknowledged by the inhabitants as being the prettiest little girls in the district.

While the two children were out walking one day, they happened to pass quite near two small boys; one lived in the village and the other was a visitor.

"I say," said the latter to his friend, "who are those little girls?"

"They are the doctor's children," replied the village boy. "He always keeps the best for himself."

[2946]

"Mayn't I be a preacher when I grow up?" asked the small boy.

"Of course you may, my pet, if you want to," his mother replied.

"Yes I do. I s'pose I've got to go to church all my life, anyway, and it's a good deal harder to sit still than to stand up and holler."

[2947]

A few years ago a gentleman who had lost his nose was invited out to tea. "My dear," said the old lady of the house to her little daughter, "I want you to be very particular and make no remarks about Mr. Jenkins' nose."

Gathered around the table, everything was going well; the child peeped about, looking rather puzzled, and at last startled the table:

"Ma, why did you tell me to say nothing about Mr. Jenkins' nose? He hasn't got any."

[2948]

"Peter, why do bells ring at Christmas?"

"Because someone is pulling the rope."

[2949]

Willie–"Teacher says we're here to help others."

Pa–"Of course we are."

Willie–"Well, what are the others here for?"

[2950]

Mother–"Tommy, the canary has disappeared."

Tommy–"That's funny. It was there just now when I tried to clean it with the vacuum-cleaner."

[2951]

"Mother, I just took a splinter out of my hand with a pin."

"A pin! Don't you know that's dangerous?"

"Oh, no, Mother, I used a safety pin."

[2952]

Mother–"Tommy, wouldn't you like to have a pretty cake with five candles on it for your party?"

Tommy–"I think I'd rather have five cakes and one candle, Mama."

[2953]

Father was sitting in the arm-chair one evening, when his little son came in and showed him a new penknife, which he said he had found in the street.

"Are you sure it was lost?" inquired the father.

"Of course, it was lost! I saw the man looking for it!" replied the youngster.

[2954]

Little Danny–"Mother, may I have a nickel for the old man who is outside crying?"

Mother–"Yes, dear, but what is the old man crying about?"

Danny–"He's crying, 'Salty peanuts, five cents a bag.'"

[2955]

For the third time she said to her little son, "Run quickly and wash your hands for dinner."

He looked over his hands and then returned the verdict:

"Mother, they aren't really dirty —just kinda blurred."

[2956]

An electrician returned home from work one night to find his small son waiting for him with his right hand swathed in a bandage.

"Hello, sonny!" he exclaimed. "Cut your hand?"

"No, Dad," was the reply. "I picked up a pretty little fly and one end wasn't insulated."

[2957]

A little miss of four came tearfully to her mother one morning with the complaint, "How can I button my dress when the button is in the back and I'm in the front?"

[2958]

Mother (to small daughter who wants the light left on)–"But you sleep in the dark at home, darling."

Small Daughter–"Yes, but it's my own dark at home, Mummie."

[2959]

"Ouch, Mummie, I hurt my toe!" cried small Janey, who was playing out in the garden.

"Which toe, dear?" I inquired, as I examined her foot.

"My youngest one," sobbed Janey.

[2960]

Tommy's Aunt–"Won't you have another piece of cake, Tommy?"

Tommy (on a visit)–"No, I thank you."

Tommy's Aunt–"You seem to be suffering from loss of appetite."

Tommy–"That ain't loss of appetie. What I'm sufferin' from is politeness."

[2961]

Mother (teaching alphabet)–"Now, dear, what comes after O?"

Child–"Yeah!"

[2962]

When supper was served Helen refused a second helping of ice-cream with a polite but wistful, "No, thank you!"

"Do have some more, dear!" her hostess urged.

"'Mother told me to say, 'No, thank you,'" Helen explained naively, "but I don't think she could have known how small the first helping was going to be!"

[2963]

"Mom," said the little daughter of the grass widow who was planning to marry a grass widower.

"What is it, dear?" asked her mother.

"Do you get this daddy cheaper because he is second hand?" she inquired.

[2964]

Elsie—"Willie and I have been down-stairs in the dining-room, Mr. Smith. We've been playing Husband and Wife!"

Mr. Smith—"How did you do that, my dear?"

Elsie—"Why, Willie sat at one end of the table, and I sat at the other; and Willie said, 'This food isn't fit to eat!' and I said, 'It's all you'll get!' and Willie said, 'Damn!' and I got up and left the room!"

[2965]

They were at dinner and the dainties were on the table.

"Will you take tart or pudding?" asked Papa of Tommy.

"Tart," said Tommy promptly.

His father sighed as he recalled the many lessons on manners he had given the boy.

"Tart, what?" he queried kindly.

But Tommy's eyes were glued on the pastry.

"Tart, what?" asked the father again, sharply this time.

"Tart, first," answered Tommy triumphantly.

[2966]

"Mummie, you're not nearly so pretty as Nurse."

"Don't you think so, dear?"

"No. We've been walking round the park for an hour and not a single policeman has kissed you!"

[2967]

Guest—"Your little daughter looks so good and quiet."

Hostess—"I hadn't noticed. Mary, come here—what naughtiness have you been up to now?"

[2968]

Little Joan—"What do the angels do in heaven, mummy?"

Mother—"They sing and play harps."

Little Joan—"Haven't they any radios?"

[2969]

Grandma—"Would you like to go to the fair and ride on the merry-go-round?"

Modern Child—"I don't mind if it will amuse you."

[2970]

"Uncle Jack took us to a picture gallery, and there was a picture of a lot of early Christians, poor dears, who'd been thrown to a lot of lions and tigers, who were devouring them!"

Ethel (with more sympathy)—"Yes, and mamma, dear, there was one poor tiger that *hadn't got* a Christian."

[2971]

Peter (saying his prayers)—"And please make Cyril give up throwing stones at me. By the way, I've mentioned this before."

[2972]
Visitor—"What was your mummie's name before she was married?"
Young Innocence—"I think it must have been 'Savoy.' That's the name on our towels."

[2973]
"Mummy, why does it rain?"
"To make things grow. To give us apples, pears, corn, flowers——"
"Then why does it rain on the pavement?"

[2974]
Mrs. Mannerly (to her little daughter, who has just returned from tea with friends)—"I hope you said 'No, thank you' oftener than 'Yes, thank you.' "
Mabel—"Yes, I did. I hadn't been eating more'n half an hour before they began saying, 'Don't you think you've eaten enough?' 'Aren't you afraid you'll make yourself ill?' And I said: 'No, thank you,' every time."

[2975]
"Did you share the three sticks of candy between your little brother and yourself?"
"Yes, but it was awkward to divide the three, so I ate one first."

[2976]
Mother—"Who ever taught you to use that dreadful word?"
Tommy—"Santa Claus, mama."
Mother—"Santa Claus?"
Tommy—"Yes, mama, when he fell over a chair in my bedroom on Christmas eve."

[2977]
Uncle Bob—"Well, Frankie, what are you going to do this vacation?"
Frankie—"Last year I had mumps and chicken-pox. This year I don't know what I'm going to do."

[2978]
"Is the doctor in?" inquired the caller.
"No, sir," answered his five-year-old boy.
"Have you any idea when he will be back?"
"I don't know, sir—he went out on an eternity case."

[2979]
A minister meeting a neighbor's boy who had just come out of a fight on New Year's Day with a fearful black eye, put his hand on the boy's head and said:
"My boy, I pray you may never fight again, and that you may never receive another black eye."
"That's all right," said the boy. "You go home and pray over your own kid. I gave him two of 'em."

[2980]
"How do you like your new daddy, Johnny?" the son of the grass widow who had recently tripped up the altar again, was asked.
"Oh, he's all right in some ways," replied the kid, "but he can't do my home work as good as the other one did."

[2981]
"Ma, is Mr. Jones an awfully old man?"
"No, dear, I don't believe so. What makes you ask?"
"Well, I think he must be, because I heard Pa say last night that Mr. Jones raised his ante."

[2982]
Butcher—"What are you running for, sonny?"
Boy—"I'm tryin' to keep two fellers from fightin'."
Butcher—"Who are the fellows?"
Boy—"Johnny Jones and me!"

[2983]

"So that cornet provides you with a weekly income? Do you play in a band?"

"Oh, no! Dad gives me 50 cents a week not to play it."

[2984]

Small Boy (to governess)–"Miss Smith, please excuse my speaking to you with my mouth full, but my little sister has just fallen into the pond."

[2985]

Little Bobby had got hold of the newspaper and was reading the headlines aloud.

" 'Man Imprisoned for Deserting His Wife,' " he read at length. Then, after a brief pause for thought, he added: "Oh, mum—now I know why dad doesn't leave you!"

[2986]

Tommy had been playing with his sister in the garden, and their screams had attracted mother.

"What are you doing, children?" she asked.

"We're playing Indians, mummy, and I'm scalping Betty," replied Tommy.

"You're doing what?"

"Oh, I'm not really scalping her properly—just taking her hair off with the shears!"

[2987]

Mother (proudly)–"This is my son, Freddie, Mrs. Higgins. Isn't he a bright little fellow?"

Freddie (accustomed to being shown off in public)–"What was that clever thing I said yesterday, Mother?"

[2988]

Elsie–"My mama got a nice present yesterday an' she frew her arms around papa's neck. What does your mama do when she gets a nice present?"

Eddie–"She tells daddy she'll forgive him, but he mustn't stay out late again."

[2989]

"Do your new spectacles help your eyes, Johnny?" asked the neighbor.

"Yes'm. I never have my eyes blacked now like I used to before I wore 'em."

[2990]

"Madam," shouted the angry neighbor, "your little Reginald has just thrown a brick through our window!"

"And would you bring me the brick?" beamed Reginald's mother. "We are keeping all the little mementoes of his pranks."

[2991]

"Was papa the first man who ever proposed to you, Mama?"

"Yes; but why do you ask?"

"I was just thinking that you might have done better if you had shopped around a little more."

[2992]

Father–"Fancy a big boy like you being afraid to sleep in the dark."

Five-Year-Old–"It's all very well for you, you've got mother to look after you."

[2993]

"Mother," asked the little one, on the occasion of a number of guests being present at dinner, "will the dessert hurt me, or is there enough to go round?"

[2994]

Governess–"Methusaleh was nine hundred years old."

Bobby–"What became of all his birthday and Christmas presents?"

[2995]

Aunt Ethel–"Well, Beatrice, were you very brave at the dentist's?"

Beatrice–"Yes, auntie, I was."

Aunt Ethel–"Then, there's the dollar I promised you. And now tell me what he did to you."

Beatrice – "He pulled out two of Willie's teeth!"

[2996]

Betty on a visit to her aunt, being offered some left-over fragments, politely declined them.

"Why, dear, don't you like turkey?" inquired her aunt.

"Only when it's new," said Betty.

[2997]

"Willie," said his mother. "I wish you would run across the street and see how old Mrs. Brown is this morning."

"Yes'm," replied Willie, and a few minutes later he returned and reported:

"Mrs. Brown says it's none of your business how old she is."

[2998]

A little girl refused some food at the table with an emphatic, "I don't like it."

"Oh, don't say that," chirped up her younger brother. "The more you don't like a thing the gooder it is for you."

[2999]

With a grinding of brakes the officer pulled up his motor car and shouted to a little boy playing in the field: "I say, sonny, have you seen an airplane come down anywhere near here?"

"No, sir!" replied the boy, trying to hide his sling-shot. "I've only been shooting at that bottle on the fence."

[3000]

"What are you children doing?"

"We're playing church," replied Jack.

"But worshipers shouldn't whisper in church," admonished nurse.

"Oh, we're the choir," said Mary.

[3001]

Four-year-old Doris was getting ready for bed. Suddenly she turned to her mother and asked: "Mother, are we going to move tomorrow?"

"Yes, dear, this is the last night you will sleep here."

"Then," said wee Doris, kneeling beside her bed, "I'd better say good-by to God now if we move to Boston in the morning."

[3002]

Little Boy (calling father at office) –"Hello, who is this?"

Father (recognizing son's voice)– "The smartest man in the world."

Little Boy–"Pardon me, I got the wrong number."

[3003]

"Mama, I'se got a stomach ache," said Nellie Bly, aged 6.

"That's because you've been without lunch. Your stomach is empty. You would feel better if you had something in it."

That afternoon the minister called, and in the course of conversation remarked that he had been suffering all day with a severe headache.

"That's because it's empty," said Nellie. "You'd feel better if you had something in it."

[3004]

Photographer–"Watch and see the dicky bird."

Child–"Just pay attention to your exposure so that you do not ruin the plate."

[3005]

"Papa, are you growing taller all the time?"

"No, my child. Why do you ask?"

" 'Cause the top of your head is poking up through your hair."

[3006]

Mother (who is teaching her child the alphabet)–"Now, dearie, what comes after 'g?'"

The Child–"Whiz!"

[3007]

A lad was being taunted by a playmate for being an adopted child:

"Huh! They came and picked me out of a hundred kids, but your folks had to take you!" was the retort.

[3008]

Father (teaching small daughter to tell the time)–"These are the hours—and these are the minutes—and these the seconds."

Little Girl (still puzzled) – "But where are the jiffies, Daddy?"

[3009]

Small Boy–"Why don't you come to my church?"

Other Small Boy–" 'Cause I belong to another abomination!"

[3010]

A boy with a pea shooter, ran out of ammunition, and discovering a box of compound cathartic pills, tried one. To his great joy, it fit.

There was a boarding-house near by, and every Tuesday noon a big pan of custard was placed upon the window sill to cool. From his vantage ground in the window of another house, the boy shot all the pills into the custard.

Never again did the custard appear on Tuesday or any other day.

[3011]

Little Edna (seeing mother's new evening dress, just arrived)–"Oh mamma, how lovely! Will you wear it tonight?"

Mother – "No, dear, not tonight. This is for when ladies and gentlemen come to dinner."

Edna – "Oh, mamma, let's pretend just for once that papa's a gentleman."

[3012]

Visitor–"And what are you going to do when you grow up dear?"

Bobbie–"I'm going to raise mint."

Visitor–"Mint?"

Bobbie–"Yes, that's where Daddy says all our money comes from."

[3013]

The piano teacher was expected any minute, and William was preparing to take his lesson.

"Did you wash your hands?" inquired mother.

"Yes."

"And your face?"

"Yes, mother."

"And did you wash behind your ears?"

"On her side I did, mother."

[3014]

Junior–"Say, mother, how much am I worth?"

Mother–"Why, you're worth a million to me, dear."

Junior–"Well, then, could you advance me a quarter?"

[3015]

The nurse had been giving the twins a bath. Later hearing the twins laughing in bed, she said. "What are you children laughing about?"

"Oh, nothing," replied Edna, "only you have given Edith two baths, and haven't given me any."

[3016]

Tom—"My pa is very religious. He always bows his head and says something before meals."

Dick—"Mine always says something when he sits down to eat, but he don't bow his head."

Tom—"What does he say?"

Dick—"Go easy on the butter, kids, it's fifty cents a pound."

[3017]

Little Willie (running home)—"Oh, mother, there's going to be trouble down at the grocer's."

Mother—"Why?"

Willie—"Mrs. Jones has a baby girl and Mr. Jones had a sign in his window for a week, 'Boy Wanted.'"

[3018]

Tommy — "Grandma, if I was invited out to dinner, should I eat pie with a fork?"

Grandma—"Yes, indeed, Tommy."

Tommy—"You haven't got a pie in the house that I could practise on, have you, Grandma?"

[3019]

A little boy was saying his go-to-bed prayers in a very low voice.

"I can't hear you, dear," his mother whispered.

"Wasn't talking to you," said the small one firmly.

[3020]

"Willie, I hear you've been fighting with one of those boys next door and have given him a black eye."

"Yes'm. You see, they's twins and I wanted some way to tell them apart."

[3021]

Jackie (to departing relative) — "There's no hurry, auntie, daddy has put the clock a whole hour ahead."

[3022]

"How is your little brother, Johnny?"

"Sick abed. He hurt himself."

"That's too bad. How did he do it?"

"We were playing who could lean furthest out of the window, and he won."

[3023]

A little four-year-old knelt beside the bed on retiring, and after repeating, "Now I lay me," added an extemporaneous prayer as follows:

"Please, God, take care of papa, take care of mamma, take care of auntie, and be sure to take care of yourself."

[3024]

Little Betty, watching the farm hands spreading out a stack of hay to dry, could contain her curiosity no longer, so she politely asked:

"Is it a needle you're looking for?"

[3025]

Little Brother—"What's etiquette?"

Little Bigger Brother—"It's saying 'No, thank you,' when you want to holler 'Gimme!'"

[3026]

The young daughter of a radio announcer called upon to say grace at a family dinner, bowed her head and said in loud clear tones,

"This food comes to us through the courtesy of Almighty God."

[3027]

Small City Boy — "Say, dad, how many kinds of milk are there?"

Father — "Well, there's evaporated milk, buttermilk, malted milk and —but why do you wish to know?"

"Oh, I'm drawing a picture of a cow and I want to know how many spigots to put on her."

[3028]
"Daddy, can you still do tricks?"
"What do you mean, my son, 'do tricks'?"
"Well, mamma says that when you were young you used to drink like a fish."

[3029]
It was Anthony's first ride in a railway train, and the succession of wonders reduced him to a state of hysterical astonishment. The train rounded a slight bend and, with a shriek of its whistle, plunged into a tunnel. There were gasps of surprise from the corner where Anthony was kneeling. Suddenly the train rushed into broad daylight again, and a small voice was lifted in wonder.
"It's tomorrow!" exclaimed the small boy.

[3030]
Mother—"Johnny, if you eat more cake, you'll burst."
Johnny—"Well, pass the cake and get outa the way."

[3031]
"Oh, you cruel boy!" exclaimed the prominent member of the Anti-Vivisection League. "However could you cut that poor little worm in two?"
Johnny met her gaze without flinching. "It—it seemed so lonely," he replied.

[3032]
"Mama," said her little six-year-old daughter, "please button my dress."
"You will have to do it yourself, dear," was the reply. "Mother's too busy."
"Oh, dear!" exclaimed the little girl. "I don't know what I'd do without myself."

[3033]
Jimmy (watching something tasty going into sick-room)—"Please, Ma, can I have the measles when Willie's done with them?"

[3034]
Little Lottie, aged four, who was spending a week with her aunt in the country, had developed a great fondness for milk. One day, having drunk as much as her aunt thought good for her, she was informed that she could not have any more.
"Pshaw!" exclaimed the indignant little miss, "I don't see why you want to be so stingy with your old milk. There's two whole cowfuls out in the barn."

[3035]
Father—"Now I want to put a little scientific question to you, my son. When the kettle boils, what does the steam come out of the spout for?"
Son—"So that mother can open your letters before you get them!"

[3036]
In this family there was a large number of small children. Little Willie, age six, was taken in one morning to see his father, who happened to be laid up with influenza. Little Willie was quiet, almost reverent, in the sickroom. When it was time for him to go, he went up to his father's bedside and said:
"I bin good, ain't I, pop?"
"Yes, son," the old man whispered.
"Well, then, kin I see the baby?"

[3037]
Little Bobbie (aged four, seeing a full-length picture of his grandmother for the first time)—"But, mother, didn't grandma have any legs?"

[3038]

"Two little boys were talking. One said to the other: "Aren't ants funny little things? They work and work, and never play."

"Oh, I don't know about that," replied the other. "Every time I go on a picnic they are there."

[3039]

A woman inquiring about a little girl's father, was told that he was very sick. The woman replied, "Oh, he only thinks he's sick." Meeting the little girl several days later, she again inquired about her father. The girl replied, "He thinks he's dead."

[3040]

A boy was selling lemonade from two bowls on the same stand. In front of one bowl was a sign "Five cents a glass." In front of a second bowl was a sign "Two cents a glass."

An old gentleman stopped, looked at the signs, and bought a glass of lemonade at two cents. He smacked his lips and ordered another.

When he had finished, he asked: "How do you expect to sell any lemonade at five cents when you offer such a good drink for two cents?"

"Well, mister, it's this way," said the boy. "The cat fell in that two-cent bowl about fifteen minutes ago, so I thought I'd better sell it out fast before the news spread too far."

[3041]

Mother (teaching her son arithmetic)—"Now take the Smith family—there's mummy, daddy, and the baby. How many does that make?" *Bright Son*—"Two and one to carry."

[3042]

Mother (to small son)—"Now, Johnnie, you can't have the hammer to play with. You'll hit your fingers." *Johnnie* — "No, I won't, Mummie. Doris is going to hold the nails."

[3043]

There was an earthquake recently which frightened inhabitants of a certain town. One couple sent their little boy to stay with an uncle in another district, explaining the reason for the nephew's sudden visit.

A day or two later the parents received this telegram:

"Am returning your boy. Send the earthquake."

[3044]

They had hash on Monday for dinner, after a roast of beef on Sunday, as happens in all well-regulated families. Father had said grace, when Bobbie said:

"I don't see why you asked another blessing this evening, father. You did it yesterday over this. It's the same old stuff."

[3045]

A mother was talking in a lofty way to her small daughter about worldly matters.

"There's one thing I want to know, Mamma," said the little girl. "When I grow to be a big lady will my husband be a man like Daddy?"

The mother nodded and said he would be.

"Oh, he will, will he?" replied the precocious miss. "And if I don't marry, do I grow up to be like Auntie?" she continued.

"Exactly," came the mother's response.

"Then, ma," said the little girl, "I'm in an awful mess."

[3046]

"Are your father and mother in?" asked the visitor of the small boy who opened the door.

"They was in," said the child, "but they is out."

"They was in. They is out. Where's your grammar?"

"She's gone upstairs," said the boy, "for a nap."

[3047]

A boy was about to purchase a seat for a movie in the afternoon. The box-office man asked, "Why aren't you in school?"

"Oh, it's all right, sir," said the youngster earnestly. "I've got measles."

[3048]

"If you are good, Willie, I'll give you this bright new penny."

"Haven't you got a dirty old nickel?"

[3049]

Sitting in a concert-hall waiting for the concert to begin, a man, seeing a little boy in front of him looking at his watch, bent forward and asked, "Does it tell the time?"

"No," answered the little boy. "You look at it."

[3050]

"Is ink so very expensive, father?"

"Why, no, what makes you think so?"

"Well, mother seems quite disturbed because I spilled some on the hall carpet."

[3051]

A small boy was asked to dine at the home of a distinguished professor. His mother questioned him on his return, "You are sure you didn't do anything that was not perfectly polite?"

"Why, no, nothing to speak of."

"Then something did happen."

"Well, while I was trying to cut the meat it slipped off to the floor. But I made it all right," said the boy.

"What did you do?"

"Oh, I just said carelessly, 'that's always the way with tough meat.'"

[3052]

A lady was entertaining her friend's small son.

"Are you sure you can cut your meat?" she asked, after watching his struggles.

"Oh, yes," he replied, without looking up from his plate. "We often have it as tough as this at home."

[3053]

"You're a pretty sharp boy, Tommy."

"Well, I ought to be. Pa takes me into his room and strops me three or four times a week."

[3054]

A little boy who slept with his big brother complained to his mother one morning about the discomforts he suffered.

"It's an awful hard bed, mother, and, what's more, Bob takes up quite half of it."

"Well," replied the mother, "why shouldn't Bob have a half?"

"But, mother," added the youngster, "he always takes the middle half."

[3055]

It was Frankie's first visit to the Zoo.

"What do you think of the animals?" inquired Uncle Horace.

After a critical inspection of the exhibit the boy replied, "I think the kangaroo and the elephant should change tails."

[3056]

Dick's mother made it a rule that if he came to the dinner table late he was not to speak a single word during the meal. Yesterday he arrived, as usual, after everybody had set down. As soon as he entered the room he began with, "I say, mother," but his mother quickly reminded him of the rule.

"But, mother—" he persisted.

"Not a word," said the stern parent who meant the rule to be enforced.

When dinner was over, his mother asked what he wanted to say.

"Oh, I only wanted to say, mother, that baby was filling father's socks with condensed milk."

[3057]

Old Gentleman(to little boy eating an apple)–"Look out for the worms, sonny."

Little Boy–"When I eat an apple the worms have to look out for themselves."

[3058]

Mother – "When that naughty boy threw stones at you, why did you not come and tell me, instead of throwing them back at him?"

Junior–"What good would it do to tell you? You couldn't hit the side of a garage."

[3059]

"I wouldn't cry like that if I were you," said a lady to little Betty.

"Well," said Betty, between her sobs, "you can cry any way you like, but this is my way."

[3060]

Mother–"Why are you making faces at that bulldog?"

Small Child (wailing)–"He started it."

[3061]

"What's the matter, Bobby? You look mournful."

"That's what's the matter—I'm more'n full."

[3062]

A lady who had boasted highly at a dinner party of the good manners of her little darling, addressed him thus:

"Charlie, my dear, won't you have some beans?"

"No," was the ill-mannered reply of the petulant cherub.

"No!" exclaimed the astonished mother. "No what!"

"No beans," said the child.

[3063]

The sweet little girl had a violent tussle with her particular chum. Her mother reprimanded her, and concluded by saying:

"It was Satan who suggested to you the pulling of Jenny's hair."

"I shouldn't be surprised," the child replied musingly. "But," she added proudly, "kicking her in the shins was entirely my own idea."

[3064]

Father–"Isn't it wonderful how little chicks get out of their shells?"

Son–"What gets me is how they get in."

[3065]

Johnny was very proud of his mangy mutt. He was playing with it, when a passing gentleman stopped and asked Johnny:

"What kind of a dog is that, sonny?"

"He's a police dog, sir!" the boy replied.

"What! A police dog? He doesn't look like one."

"Oh, I know it," was Johnny's answer, "but you see, sir, he's in the secret service!"

[3066]

Little Bobby was sitting with his mother in church during the wedding of her eldest daughter. Halfway through the service, he observed his mother crying.

"Why are you crying, mama?" he asked. "It's not your wedding."

[3067]

Little Steve, six, was a profanity addict, which caused his mother anguish no end.

One day Steve got an invitation to a playmate's birthday party. As he left the house, his mother's final caution was "Stephen, I've asked Mrs. Wilson to send you straight home the minute you use one bad word."

Twenty minutes later Steve was back home. His mother was angry. Steve was sent to bed. His attempts at explanation were ignored. A little later, however, his mother softened and went upstairs to see how Steve was taking it. Sitting at his bedside, she inquired:

"Tell me truthfully, Steve, just why Mrs. Wilson sent you home? What did you do?"

Little Steve, humiliated, but still wrathful, replied:

"Do? Do hell! I didn't do nothing. That damned party ain't til tomorrow."

[3068]

Mother (to beloved daughter) – "Now, darling, show everybody how nicely you can recite. A little ship was on the—"

The Darling–"Thea."

Mother–"It sailed along so pleasant—"

The Darling–"Lee."

Mother–"It was the peaceful time of—"

The Darling–"Night."

Mother–"And all was calm and—"

The Darling–"Bwight."

Mother–"Splendid! Now recite another one, darling!"

[3069]

A little girl four years old was alone in the nursery with the door closed and fastened when her little brother arrived and expressed a desire to come in. The following was the dialogue:

"I wants to tum in, Sissy."

"But you tan't tum in, Tom."

"But I wants to."

"Well, I'se in my nightie gown an' nurse says little boys mus'n't see little girls in their nightie gowns."

There was a period of silence during which the astonished little boy reflected on the mystery. It was ended by Sissy's calling out:

"You tan tum in now, Tom—I tooked it off."

[3070]

"You cannot get eggs without hens," said the speaker stressing the point.

"My dad can," piped a small voice from the rear.

"Please explain yourself, little boy," said the speaker.

"He keeps ducks," yelled the boyish voice from the rear.

[3071]

During a terrific thunderstorm the young parents thought their child might be awake and afraid, so they visited the nursery.

The boy was a bit restless, and presently opened his eyes and said: "What's daddy doing with the radio now?" and dropped off to sleep again.

[3072]

Little Ralph came to Montreal from his home in Labrador, where he had never seen a colored person. One day when he was out walking with his Uncle Tom they happened to pass a colored woman, and the little fellow asked:

"Say, uncle, why did that woman black her face?"

"Why, she hasn't blacked her face. That is her natural color," replied the uncle.

"Is she black like that all over?" asked Ralph.

"Why, yes."

"Gosh, uncle, you know everything, don't you?"

[3073]

"Are caterpillars good to eat?" asked little Tommy at the dinner table.

"No," said his father; "what makes you ask a question like that while we are eating?"

"You had one on your lettuce, but it's gone now," replied Tommy.

[3074]

"Up-ss-daisy," said the old lady upon seeing a little boy fall down.

"Up-ss-daisy, hell," said the little boy, "I'm hurt."

[3075]

"Oh, mamma!" Willie rushed breathlessly into the parlor. "A great big brown bear chased me all the way home from school!"

"Oh, Willie!" said his mother reproachfully. "You mustn't tell a story like that."

"But it isn't a story!" denied Willie vigorously. "If you don't believe it, you can look yourself—it's still right outside our yard. I was scared most to death, for fear it would eat me before I got in!"

The mother walked to the window. "Willie Jones," she said sternly, "go into the bedroom, and kneel down and ask God to forgive you for that story. I saw the big dog that chased you."

A few minutes later Willie came out of the bedroom, smiling amiably.

"Did you ask God to forgive you," inquired his mother.

"Yessum, I did; and God said, 'Never you mind about that, Willie; I thought that big dog was a bear myself, until I got another good look at him'!"

[3076]

Dorothy, the little daughter of a tire salesman, had seen triplets for the first time.

"Oh, mother," she cried on returning home, "what do you think I saw today?"

"I can't imagine, dear. What?"

"A lady that had twins—and a spare."

[3077]

Hostess (at party)—"Does your mother allow you to have two pieces of pie when you are at home, Willie?"

Willie (who has asked for a second piece)—"No, ma'am."

"Well, do you think she'd like you to have two pieces here?"

"Oh," confidentially, "she wouldn't care. This isn't her pie!"

[3078]

Father took his young daughter to the movies. He occupied a seat near the middle of the theater, while the young lady went down in the front row to join some other children. The news reel was showing a raging forest fire, which evidently frightened the little girl and she came back to take a seat beside her father.

"What's the matter?" he asked. "Did the fire frighten you?"

"Oh, no!" she replied. "The smoke got in my eyes."

[3079]

A very small boy was trying to lead a big St. Bernard up the road.

"Where are you going to take that dog, my little man?" inquired a passer-by.

"I — I'm going to see where — where he wants to go first," was the breathless reply.

[3080]

Small Boy–"Dad, the barometer has fallen."

Father–"Very much?"

Small Boy (with guilty look)– "About five feet—it's broken."

[3081]

Neighbor–"Does your dog love you, little boy?"

Teddy–"You bet he does. He knows if he didn't I'd kick the stuffin' out of him."

[3082]

Both the photographer and the mother had failed to make the restless little four-year-old sit still long enough to have her picture taken. Finally, the photographer suggested that "the little darling" might be quiet if her mother would leave the room for a few minutes. During her absence the picture was successfully taken. On the way home the mother asked:

"What did the nice man say to make mother's little darling sit still?"

"He thed, 'You thit thtill, you little newthuns, or I'll knock your block off,' tho I that thtill," she explained.

[3083]

The little girl had been visiting. When it was time for her to be going home, her hostess said: "Good-by, Gretchen; you must come again soon. We should like to see more of you."

"But there isn't any more of me," replied Gretchen.

[3084]

"Do you know why I am going to punish you, Arthur?"

"No, dad; why?"

"Because you hit a boy smaller than yourself."

"Oh, I thought perhaps it was because I'm smaller than you."

[3085]

"Papa, has Mr. Smith's eyes got feet?"

"Why do you ask such a question, my boy?"

"Because I heard mother say that at a party the other evening, Mr. Smith's eyes followed her all around the room."

[3086]

A little girl's brother set a trap to catch birds. The little girl thought it was wrong and cruel. She wept at first, then her mother noticed she became cheerful again, and she was asked the cause.

"I prayed for my brother to be a better boy."

"What else?" asked her mother.

"I prayed that the trap would not catch any birds."

"What else?"

"Then I went out and kicked the old trap all to pieces."

[3087]

Little Lucy–"Mother, I must be a very good child. You never keep a maid more than a week or two, but I've been with you ten years."

[3088]

Little Billy, aged 4, was being shown the shape of the earth on a globe atlas by his mother. After pointing to all countries with their peculiar shapes, she asked:

"Now, Billy, what shape is the world?"

Billy, looking very wise and happy, beamed on her with: "It's in a terrible shape, daddy says."

[3089]

A little girl, sitting in church watching a wedding, suddenly exclaimed:

"Mummy, has the lady changed her mind?"

"What do you mean?" the mother asked.

"Why," replied the child, "she went up the aisle with one man and came back with another."

[3090]

Grandmother had come to visit her son, the pastor, and Mary, her five-year-old granddaughter, was entertaining her with the story of a wonderful dog.

Mary–"And the dog flew and f-l-e-w and f-l-e-e-e-w away up into the sky."

Grandmother (reprovingly)–"Now, Mary, tell it right; you know a dog can't fly."

Mary (triumphantly) – "Oh, yes, grandmother, that dog could fly; it was a bird dog."

[3091]

A little boy who had been used to receiving his old brother's old toys and clothes recently remarked:

"Ma, will I have to marry his widow when he dies?"

[3092]

"Tommy, why are you scratching yourself?"

"No one else knows where I itch."

[3093]

"There, now," cried little Bessie the other day rummaging through a drawer in the bureau, "grandpa has gone to heaven without his spectacles."

[3094]

Fond Mother–"How much do you charge for taking children's photographs?"

Photographer–"Five dollars a dozen."

Fond Mother–"You'll have to give me more time, I have only ten now."

[3095]

"Ma," said an intelligent boy of nine, "I don't think Solomon was so rich as they say he was."

"Why, my dear, what could have put that into your head?" asked the astonished mother.

"Because the Bible says he slept with his fathers, and I think if he had been so rich he would have had a bed of his own."

[3096]

Mother wanted to spend Saturday afternoon shopping, and father —a statistician—reluctantly agreed to abandon his golf and spend the afternoon with the three small and energetic children.

When mother returned father handed her this:—

Dried tears—9 times.

Tied shoes—13 times.

Toy balloons purchased—3 per child.

Average life of balloon—12 seconds.

Cautioned children not to cross street—21 times.

Children insisted on crossing street—21 times.

Number of Saturdays father will do this again—0.

[3097]

Wife–"I'm afraid you'll think me rather extravagant, dear, but I spent twenty dollars today on a boat, and a train, and a fire-engine, and a box of soldiers, and some nine pins for Willie's birthday. By the way, what are *you* going to buy him?"

[3098]

When Willie's father came home to supper there was a vacant chair at the table.

"Well, where's the boy?"

"William is upstairs in bed." The answer came with painful precision from the sad-faced mother.

"Why, wh—what's up? Not sick, is he?"

"It grieves me to say, Robert, that our son—your son—has been heard swearing on the street! I heard him."

"Swearing? Scott! I'll teach him to swear!" And he started upstairs in the dark. Half-way up he stumbled and came down with his chin on the top step.

When the atmosphere cleared a little, Willie's mother was saying sweetly from the hallway, "That will do, dear. You have given him enough for one lesson."

[3099]

"It is extraordinary that Mrs. Jenks can never see any faults in her children," observed Mrs. Smith.

"Mothers never can," remarked her husband.

"What an absurd idea, James! So like a man, I'm sure I should see faults in our children at once — if they had any."

[3100]

Father–"Robert, I am supposed to punish you for defying your mother today. I admire your courage. Now, every time I whack this pillow, you holler."

[3101]

Uncle Ben was visiting little Betty who had been ill.

"Well, my dear," he said, "and how did you find yourself this morning?"

Betty opened her big, innocent blue eyes:

"Oh, Uncle, I just opened my eyes—and there I was!"

[3102]

An old gentleman, clad in a somewhat youthful suit of light gray flannel, sat on a bench in the park enjoying the spring day.

"What's the matter, sonny?" he asked a small urchin who lay on the grass and stared at him intently. "Why don't you go and play?"

"Don't want to," the boy replied.

"But it is not natural," the old gentleman insisted, "for a boy to be so quiet. Why don't you want to?"

"Oh, I'm just waitin'," the little fellow answered. "I'm just waitin' till you get up. A man painted that bench about fifteen minutes ago."

[3103]

Willie was invited to a party, where, of course, refreshments were bountifully served.

"Won't you have something more, Willie?" the hostess said.

"No, thank you," replied Willie, with an expression of great satisfaction. "I'm full."

"Well, then," smiled the hostess, "put some fruit and cakes in your pockets to eat on the way home."

"No, thank you," came the rather startling response of Willie, "they're full, too."

[3104]

Fond Mother–"Yes, Genevieve is taking French and Algebra. Say 'Good morning' to Mrs. Jones in Algebra, darling."

[3105]

"Mother," said a little boy after coming from a walk. "I've seen a man who makes horses."

"Are you sure?" asked his mother.

"Yes," he replied. "He had a horse nearly finished when I saw him. He was just nailing on his feet."

[3106]

A little girl in southern California was having her first glimpse of snow. "Oh, mother, what is it—what is it?" she shouted excitedly.

"Why, that is snow, Peggy. Whatever did you think it was?"

"Snow! Why, it looks like popped rain!"

[3107]

A youngster went into the parlor to see a visitor who was with his father.

"Well, my little man," said his father's friend, "what are you looking at me for?"

"Why," replied the boy, "daddy told me that you were a self-made man, and I want to see what you look like."

"Quite right," said the gratified guest, although ugly and fat. "I am a self-made man."

"But what did you make yourself like that for?" asked the boy.

[3108]

Sonny–"Mother, we're going to play elephants at the zoo and we want you to help us."

Mother–"What on earth can I do?"

Sonny–"You can be the lady who gives them peanuts and candy."

[3109]

Billie (who has eaten his apple)–"Let's play Adam and Eve."

Pattie–"How do we do that?"

Billie–"You tempt me to eat your apple and I'll give in."

[3110]

Bessie was just finishing her breakfast as her father stooped to kiss her before going down town. The little one gravely took up her napkin and wiped her cheek.

"What, Bessie?" said her father. "Wiping away father's kiss?"

"Oh, no!" said she, looking up with a smile. "I'se rubbing it in."

[3111]

Elsie–"Mummy; if I wuz a fairy I'd change everyfing into cake, an' eat it all up."

Mother–"I'm afraid such a lot of cake would make you sick."

Elsie–"Oh! But I'd change myself into a Nelephant first."

[3112]

In order to discourage the use of objectionable words the father had evolved a system of fines, somewhat after this fashion:

Hang it—One cent.

Darn it—Two cents.

Gosh—Three cents.

Gosh darn it—Five cents.

The boy who was to be reformed by this method studied the tariff with considerable interest, but it was some time before he spoke.

"Well," he said at last, "I guess I know some words that would cost a quarter."

[3113]

An elderly woman was escorting two little girls around the zoo. While they were looking at the stork, she told them the legend of the ungainly bird—how it was instrumental in bringing them to their mammas.

The children looked at each other with sly glances, and presently one whispered to the other:

"Don't you think we ought to tell the dear old thing the truth?"

[3114]

Mother–"I hope you didn't take a second piece of cake at the party?"

Bobby–"No. I took two pieces first time."

[3115]

Uncle John came to stay, and before he left he gave his nephew five dollars. "Now be careful with that money, Tommy," he said. "Remember the saying, 'A fool and his money are soon parted.' "

"Yes, Uncle," replied Tommy, "but I want to thank you for parting with it, just the same."

[3116]

Little Mary was left to fix lunch, and when the mother returned with a friend she noticed Mary had the tea strained. "Did you find the lost strainer?" Mother asked.

"No, Mother, I couldn't, so I used the fly swatter," Mary replied.

Mother nearly swooned, so Mary hastily added: "Don't get excited, Mother, I used the old one."

[3117]

Freddie was playing at Bobby's house. When it was time to go home, it started to rain. Mrs. Jones, however, gave Freddie Bobby's raincoat and galoshes.

"Don't take so much trouble, Mrs. Jones," said Freddie politely.

"I'm sure your mother would do as much for Bobby," she replied.

"My mother would do more," said Freddie. "She'd ask Bobby to stay to supper."

[3118]

As mother tucked little Tommy up in bed, he raised his puzzled eyes to hers.

"Are we going to take pussy with us when you and me go to visit granny next week?" he asked.

Mother shook her head.

"No, sonny; I'm sorry we can't. But what made you think so?"

"Well, I heard daddy telling Mr. Jones that the mouse wouldn't half have a fine time when the cat was away next week."

[3119]

A small boy had watched a telephone repair man climb a pole, connect the test set and try the connection with the test board. There was some trouble obtaining the connection. The youngster listened a few minutes and rushed into the house exclaiming, "Mamma, come out here quick. There is a man up a telephone pole talking to heaven."

"What makes you think he is talking to heaven?"

" 'Cause he hollered 'Hello! Hello! Hello! Good Lord, what's the matter up there, can't anyone hear?' "

[3120]

"Well, Peggy," said the neighbor, "and how do you like your new governess?"

Peggy thought a moment and then said: "I half like her and I half don't like her, but I think I half don't like her the most."

[3121]

Mamma–"Frankie, dear, come kiss your new governess."

Frankie–"No; I don't dare to, I'm afraid."

Mamma–"Why, dearie?"

Frankie–"Dad kissed her yesterday, an' she slapped his face."

[3122]

Little Bessie was sitting on her grandfather's knee one day, and after looking at him intently for a time, said:

"Grandpa, were you in the Ark?"

"Certainly not, my dear," answered the astonished old man.

"Then why weren't you drowned?"

[3123]

Mother was warning little Nancy about being careful crossing streets.

"Oh, don't worry," the child assured her mother. "I always wait for the empty space to come by."

[3124]

A six-year-old youngster had seen his first football game. The feature that caught his chief approval became evident when he concluded his prayers that night with:

God bless mama,
God bless papa,
God bless Freddie,
Rah! Rah! Rah!

[3125]

A young boy's parents had paid a visit to the home of a neighbor one evening, and the neighbor thought, naturally, when she answered the doorbell the next morning and found the boy at the door, that his parents had forgotten something.

"Please, Mrs. Brown," said the boy, "may I look at your dining room rug?"

The woman was astonished but said, "Why, of course, Bobby; come right in."

The lad gazed at the rug for several minutes. Then he turned to its owner:

"It doesn't make *me* sick," he said.

[3126]

Auntie—"When I was a child, I was told that if I made ugly faces, I would stay like it."

Little Pamela—"Well, you can't say you weren't warned, Auntie."

[3127]

Little Sally stood in the doorway, one hand on the door knob. For a moment she gazed at her mother, who was preparing to go out.

"Mother," she said, "do you know what I am going to give you for your birthday when it comes?"

"No, dear," answered the mother. "Please tell me."

"A nice hairpin tray with gold flowers on it all around," said the little girl.

"But, my dear," exclaimed the mother. "I have a nice one like that already."

"No, you haven't, mother," Sally answered. "I have just dropped it on the floor."

[3128]

Little Jane, whose grandmother was visiting her family, was going to bed when her mother called:

"Don't forget, dear, to include grandma in your prayers tonight, that God should bless her and let her live to be very, very old."

"Oh, she's old enough," replied Jane. "I'd rather pray that God would make her young."

[3129]

A little boy was begging his father to let him go to the movies. The father refused permission.

"I've told you no, and I mean it," he said. "Use your will-power a little and forget about the show."

"I ain't got no will-power, and I don't want no will-power," replied the boy. "I want to go to the show."

[3130]

The model husband arrived home one evening and found his three-year-old son lighting up a cigar. He raced into the kitchen, where his wife was preparing dinner.

"Margie," he announced, breathlessly, "this is terrible. I just caught our boy lighting a cigar!"

His wife was shocked, too.

"I'll put a stop to it right now," she cried. "That kid is altogether too young to be playing with matches!"

[3131]

Mother–"If you wanted to go fishing, why didn't you come and ask me first?"

Johnny–"Because I wanted to go fishing."

[3132]

The railway coach was crowded and a none too well dressed little boy had taken a seat alongside a very haughty and fashionably dressed woman. The boy was sniffling in a very annoying manner. Finally the woman turned to the boy and asked:

"Have you got a handkerchief?"

"Yes," replied the boy, "but I don't lend it to strangers."

[3133]

Two small boys were out hunting in the woods and one of them stopped and picked up a chestnut burr.

"Tommy!" he called excitedly. "Come here! I've found a porcupine egg!"

[3134]

Little Boy–"My sister can ride and play tennis and golf and can do everything a man can do."

Companion–"I'll bet she can't scratch a match like my daddy does."

[3135]

The boy hurried home to his father with an announcement:

"Me and Joe Peck had a fight today."

The father nodded gravely.

"Mr. Peck has already called to see me about it."

The little boy's face brightened.

"Gee, Pop! I hope you made out 's well 's I did!"

[3136]

Betty, aged four, was taken by her governess to have tea with an aunt. Presently she began to eat a piece of very rich cake.

"Oh, I just love this chocolate cake!" she exclaimed. "It's awfully nice."

"Betty, dear," corrected her governess, "it is wrong to say you 'love' cake, and I've frequently pointed out that 'just' is wrongly used in such a sentence. Again, 'awfully' is quite wrong, 'very' would be more correct, dear. Now repeat your remark, please."

Betty obediently repeated: "I like chocolate cake; it is very good."

"That's better, dear," said the governess, approvingly.

"But it sounds as if I was talking about bread," protested the little girl.

[3137]

The family was seated at the table with a guest, who was a business acquaintance of Dad's, all ready to enjoy the meal, when the five-year-old son blurted out: "Why, mother, this is roast beef!"

"Yes," answered the mother, "what of it?"

"Well, Pop said this morning that he was going to bring a big fish home for dinner tonight."

[3138]

Teacher–"How many fingers have you?"

Bobbie–"Ten."

Teacher–"Well, if four were missing, what would you have then?"

Bobbie–"No music-lessons."

[3139]

Johnny had been the guest of honor at a party the day before, and his friend was regarding him enviously.

"How was it? Have a good time?" he asked.

"Did I?" was the emphatic answer. "I ain't hungry yet!"

[3140]

"Jimmy, auntie will never kiss you with a dirty face."

"That's what I thought."

[3141]

Dear Old Lady–"Can your little brother talk yet?"

Small Boy—"Yes, mum; he can say 'thank you' for a penny."

[3142]

Bobby had been to a birthday party, and, knowing his weakness, his mother looked him straight in the eye and said, "I hope you didn't ask for a second piece of cake?"

"No," replied Bobby. "I only asked Mrs. Smith for the recipe so you could make some like it and she gave me two more pieces just of her own accord."

[3143]

"Grandpa, did you once have hair like snow?"

"Yes, my boy."

"Well, who shoveled it off?"

[3144]

Teacher asked a seven-year-old girl what a bridegroom was.

"Please, teacher," was the reply, "it's a thing they have at weddings."

[3145]

Little Boy–"Come quick, Mr. Policeman! There's a man been fightin' my father for half an hour."

Officer–"Why didn't you tell me before?"

Boy–" 'Cause father was gettin' the best of it until a minute ago."

[3146]

A little girl was describing her first experience in an elevator. "We got into a little room," she said, "and the upstairs came down."

[3147]

Small Child (who has repeatedly been knocked over by the sea)–"I don't fink these silly waves want me in their sea, Mummy."

[3148]

"But, darling, if your earache is better, why do you keep on crying?"

"I'm waiting for D-Daddy to c-come home. He's never s-seen me with an earache!"

[3149]

Mother–"Why did you strike your little sister?"

Young Bobby–"Well, we were playing Adam and Eve, and instead of tempting me with the apple, she ate it herself."

[3150]

Bobby–"Ma, what was the name of the last station?"

Mother–"Don't bother me, I don't know. Don't you see I'm reading?"

Bobby–"Gosh, that's too bad you don't know, cause Little Brudder got off there."

[3151]

"Oh, mother," exclaimed little Gerald when he saw a snake for the first time, "come here quick. Here's a tail wagging without any dog!"

[3152]

Passer-by – "What would your mother say, little boy, if she could hear you swear like that?"

Boy–"She'd be tickled to death if she could hear it."

Passer-by–"How can you lie like that?"

Boy–"That's no lie. She's stone deaf."

[3153]

Mother–"Why are you sitting there when you ought to be in bed?"

Peter–"There's a mosquito in my room."

Mother–"It hasn't bitten you, has it, darling?"

Peter–"No, but it came close enough for me to hear its propeller."

[3154]

"Jimmie," said his mother, severely, "there were two pieces of cake in the pantry this morning and now there is only one. How is that?"

"I don't know," replied Jimmie, regretfully. "It must have been so dark I didn't see the other piece."

[3155]

Little Billy–"My big sister's got two doctors."

Little Leroy–"Huh, mine's got two lawyers."

Little Billy–"My big sister's gonna have an operation."

Little Leroy–"Mine's gonna have a separation."

[3156]

Thoughtful Child (with memories of recent shopping expedition)– "Did you get me in a bargain basement, mummy?"

Mother–"Whatever do you mean, darling?"

Child–"Well—my fingers are all different sizes."

[3157]

Father (to Jimmie, coming home in a bedraggled condition)–"Great Scot! How you look!"

Jimmie–"Yes, pa, I fell in a mudhole."

Father–"What! And with your new pants on?"

Jimmie–"Yes. I didn't have time to take them off."

[3158]

"Grandpa," said a little girl, "I've just come from the kitchen, and I saw something running across the floor without any legs. What do you think it was?"

"I cannot guess, my dear," said the grandfather.

"Water, grandpa."

[3159]

Mother–"What did your father say when he saw his broken pipe?"

Innocent–"Shall I leave out the swear-words, mother?"

Mother–"Certainly, my dear."

Innocent–"Then I don't think he said anything."

[3160]

Marjorie–"Will I get everything I pray for, mama?"

Mother (cautiously) – "Everything that's good for you, dear."

Marjorie (disgustedly)–"Oh, what's the use, then; I get that anyway."

[3161]

"How did you like the party, Jackie?"

"Awful! You said I could eat as much as I liked, and I couldn't."

[3162]

"Does your face hurt much?" Johnny asked sister's suitor.

"No, Johnny. What made you think my face ached?"

"Sister said you were painfully homely."

[3163]
"Mummy, do you love me?"
"Of course."
"Then why not divorce daddy and marry the man at the candy store?"

[3164]
"Daddy," said five-year-old Elsie, "do you think mummy knows much about bringing up children?"
"What makes you ask that?" asked her father.
"Well," replied Elsie, "she makes me go to bed when I am wide awake and she makes me get up when I am awfully sleepy."

[3165]
A grocer leaned over the counter and yelled at a boy who stood close to an apple barrel:
"Are you tryin' to steal them apples, boy?"
"No—no, sir," the boy faltered. "I'm tryin' not to!"

[3166]
Mother—"Now, Bobby, was it you that picked all the white meat off this chicken?"
Bobby—"Well, mother, to make a clean breast of it, I did."

[3167]
An enterprising youngster had started a new business. His business card gives the following information:
Mr. Harvey Hector, Jr.
Personal Escorter
Tots and Kiddies took
to school and returned,
prompt in perfect cond-
dishin—if received that
way. Military dicipline.
Rates 25c a week. Refined
conversashin. No extra
charge for nose wipin.
All I ast is a trial.

[3168]
"Mummy, Tom has taken the largest piece of cake, and it is unfair, because he was eating cake three years before I was born."

[3169]
"My father and I know everything in the world," said a small boy to his companion.
"All right," said the latter, "Where's Asia?"
It was a stiff question, but the little fellow answered coolly, "That is one of the questions my father knows."

[3170]
Little Betty had been allowed to stay up to dinner one night on the strict understanding that she should behave very well and not ask for anything on the table.
When dessert came all the guests were attended to, but she was overlooked.
She sat despondently for a time, and then was struck by a bright idea. She exclaimed in a loud voice, "Who wants a clean plate?"

[3171]
Little Girl (to playmate)—"So long, Elsie, momma's giving a party and I gotta go home and make precocious remarks."

[3172]
Visitor—"Do you like reciting, dear?"
Child—"Oh, no, I hate it, really. But Mummy makes me do it when she wants people to go."

[3173]
"Run upstairs and wash your face, darling. I think Grandma wants to take you driving with her."
"Hadn't we better find out for certain, Mummie?"

[3174]

Joan, five, out to tea, was puzzled when she saw the family bow their heads for grace.

"What are you doing?" she asked. "Giving thanks for our daily bread," she was told. "Don't you give thanks at home, Joan?"

"No," said Joan, "we pay for our bread."

[3175]

Willie–"Mamma, do people that lie ever go to heaven?"

Mother–"Why, of course not, Willie."

Willie–"Gee! I bet it's lonesome up in heaven with only God and George Washington."

[3176]

Betty was taken to the museum by auntie. They went into the Egyptian room, and there saw a mummy. Betty asked what it was.

"That is some one's mummy, dear," answered auntie.

"Auntie," she confided, "I'm glad my mummy's not like that!"

[3177]

A little miss of four, looking out of the window one day, noticed a small spaniel dog whose tail had been cut off, leaving only a short stub.

Calling to her mother, she asked: "Say, mamma, did that dog's tail get broke off, or did they drive it in?"

[3178]

"Didn't you promise me to be a good boy?"

"Yes, father."

"And didn't I promise you a thrashing if you weren't?"

"Yes, father, but as I've broken my promise, you needn't keep yours."

[3179]

Tommy–"Mother, let me go to the zoo to see the monkeys?"

Mother–"Why, Tommy, what an idea! Imagine wanting to go to see the monkeys when your Aunt Betsey is here."

[3180]

"You must not fight. Haven't you been taught to love your enemies?"

"He's not my enemy—he's my brother."

[3181]

The parents of a bright little boy were having him "show off" to a visitor.

"I suppose he has learned his letters?" said the visitor.

"Oh, yes."

"What is the first letter of the alphabet, Bobby?" the visitor inquired.

"A," said Bobby.

"Very good; and what comes after A?"

"All the rest of them," was Bobby's reply.

[3182]

Jimmie–"Wot's de best way to teach a girl to swim?"

Johnny–"Well, yer want ter take her gently down to de water, put your arm 'round her waist, and—"

Jimmie–"Oh, cut it out. It's my sister."

Johnny–"Oh, push her off the dock."

[3183]

Betty–"How did mama find out you didn't really take a bath?"

Billy–"I forgot to wet the soap."

[3184]

"Pa!"

"What is it, Teddy?"

"How many legs would you have to pull off a centipede to make him limp?"

[3185]

Minister–"Do you say your prayers every night, Oswald?"

Oswald–"No. Some nights I don't want anything."

[3186]

Barbara (saying her prayers)–"And bless Daddy and Mummy and make them happy—if they're not too old for that sort of thing."

[3187]

Mother–"Now do you know where bad little girls go?"

Daughter–"Yes, they go most everywhere."

[3188]

A mother listening to the evening prayer of her sleepy little daughter was astonished and amused to hear the following:

"Now I lay me down to sleep
I pray the Lord my soul to keep.
When he hollers let him go,
Eenie, meenie, miny, mo."

[3189]

Little Daughter–"Why is father singing so much tonight?"

Mother–"He's trying to sing the baby to sleep."

Little Daughter–"Well, if I was baby I'd pretend I was asleep."

[3190]

"Look here, now, Archie," said a father to his little son, who was naughty, "if you don't say your prayers you won't go to Heaven."

"I don't want to go to Heaven," sobbed the boy; "I want to go with you and mother."

[3191]

A little four-year-old girl said the other day, "Muvver, how long is it to my birthday?"

"Not very long, dear."

"Well," she asked, "is it time for me to begin being a good girl?"

[3192]

"Ma, do I have to wash my face?"

"Certainly!"

"Aw, why can't I just powder it like you do yours?"

[3193]

"Now, then, what should a polite little boy say to a lady who has given him a penny for carrying her parcels?"

"I am too polite to say it, madam."

[3194]

"Good gracious, Junior, I forgot to shake the bottle before I gave you that medicine."

"Don't worry, mummy, I'll turn a few handsprings."

[3195]

Street-Car Conductor–"How old are you, my little girl?"

Little Boston Girl–"If the corporation doesn't object, I'd prefer to pay full fare and keep my own statistics."

[3196]

Stern Parent–"Willie, I'd like to go through one whole day without once scolding or punishing you."

Willie–"Well, mother, you have my consent."

[3197]

Little Willie had gone to bring the kittens in. His father, hearing a shrill meowing, called out:

"Don't hurt the kittens, Willie!"

"Oh, no," said Willie, "I'm carrying them very carefully by the stems!"

[3198]

Johnnie–"Why does the whistle blow for a fire?"

Billy–"It doesn't blow for the fire, it blows for water. They've got the fire."

[3199]

The lawyer was sitting at his desk, so absorbed in his work that he did not hear the door as it was pushed gently open, nor see the curly head that was thrust into his office. A little sob attracted his notice, and turning, he saw a face that was streaked with tears and told plainly that feelings had been hurt.

"Well, my little man, did you want to see me?"

"Are you a lawyer?"

"Yes. What do you want?"

"I want"—and there was a resolute ring in his voice—"I want a divorce from my papa and mamma."

[3200]

Little Alice was talking to her dolly, and said to her, looking lovingly into her face:

"You is bootiful, dolly, very bootiful; but you is dot no brains."

[3201]

News Photographer (lining up children for a picture at the Transit Valley Country Club) *to small boy*– "Smile nicely, at this little girl over here."

Small Boy–"Aw heck, that's my sister."

[3202]

A little girl, on seeing sawdust plentifully sprinkled on the floor of a meat store, remarked to her mother:

"Mummy, the man must have broken a lot of dolls!"

[3203]

Candid letter from a twelve-year-old, acknowledging a present:

"Dear Aunt Matilda:

"Thank you for your gift. I have always wanted a pincushion but not very much."

[3204]

Mother (as Margery concludes her prayer)–"You prayed God to bless mamma, papa and grandpa, why didn't you ask Him to bless Aunt Jane also?"

Margery–"I didn't think it would be polite to ask for so much all at once."

[3205]

"You must be pretty strong," said Willie, aged six, to the pretty young widow who had come to call on his mother.

"Strong? What makes you think so?"

"Daddy said you can wrap any man in town around your little finger."

[3206]

"Lenny, you're a pig," said a father to his little five-year-old boy. "Now, do you know what a pig is, Lenny?"

"Yes, sir; a pig's a hog's little boy."

[3207]

Caller–"I wonder if I can see your mother, little boy. Is she engaged?"

Willie–"Engaged! She's married."

[3208]

Mother–"Which apple do you want, Junior?"

Junior–"The biggest one."

Mother–"Why, Junior! You should be polite and take the little one."

Junior–"Well, mamma, should I lie just to be polite?"

[3209]

They were entertaining at dinner. Suddenly a child's voice was heard from the floor above, "Mother."

"What is it, Archie?" she asked.

"There's only clean towels in the bathroom. Shall I start one?"

[3210]

A young business man returned home after a tough day at the office and found his two daughters, both of about kindergarten age, acting up pretty boisterously. He gave them both a moderately severe scolding and sent them off to bed. The next morning he found a note pinned to his bedroom door:

"Be good to your children and they will be good to you. God."

[3211]

"Ronny, didn't your conscience tell you not to do that?"

"Yes, mummy, but you said I must not believe all I hear."

[3212]

"My boy, when you grow up I want you to be a gentleman."

"I don't want to be a gentleman, pop—I wanna be like you."

[3213]

A father, whose looks are not such as to warrant the breaking up of all existing statues of Apollo, tells this on himself:

"My little girl was sitting on my lap facing a mirror. After gazing intently at her reflection for some minutes, she said: 'Papa, did God make you?'

"'Certainly, my dear,' I told her.

"'And did He make me, too?'— taking another look in the mirror.

"'Certainly, dear. What makes you ask?'

"'Seems to me He's doing better work lately.'"

[3214]

Two small girls were playing together one afternoon in the park.

"I wonder what time it is," said one of them at last.

"Well, it can't be four o'clock yet," replied the other with mag-nificent logic, "because my mother said I was to be home at four—and I'm not."

[3215]

Mother (at dinner)–"Peggy, darling, you should not scratch your nose with your spoon."

Peggy–"Oh, mother—ought I have used a fork?"

[3216]

Mother–"Come here, Johnnie; I have some good news for you."

Johnnie (without enthusiasm)– "Yes, I know; father is home again."

Mother–"Yes, but how did you know?"

Johnnie–"My bank won't rattle any more."

[3217]

Rich Little Girl (seeing some poorly cared for children go by)–"Poor little things! They can have no nurses—only mothers."

[3218]

A visitor asked a little girl, "And what will you do, my dear, when you are as big as your mother?"

"Diet," said the child.

[3219]

"What's the matter, little boy?" said the kindhearted man. "Are you lost?"

"No," was the manful answer; "I ain't lost; I'm here. But I'd like to know where father and mother have wandered to."

[3220]

"Look, Daddy," said a little six-year-old, "I pulled this cornstalk right up all by myself."

"My, but you are strong!" said his father.

"I guess I am, Daddy. The whole world had hold of the other end of it."

[3221]

Freddie's mother was buying fruit and vegetables from a huckster. As Freddie was eyeing the cherries, the huckster told him to take a handful. But Freddie said no.

"What's the matter? Don't you like them?" asked the huckster.

"Yes," replied Freddie.

"Then go ahead and take some."

Freddie still hesitated, whereupon the huckster put a generous handful in the boy's cap. After the huckster had driven on the mother asked: "Why didn't you take the cherries when he told you to?"

Freddie winked as he said: " 'Cause his hand was biggr'n mine."

[3222]

"Have you lost another tooth, Emily?" asked auntie, who noticed an unusual lisp.

"Yes'm," replied the four-year-old, "and I limp now when I talk."

[3223]

Willie–"Won't your pa spank you for staying out so late?"

Tommy (whose father is a lawyer)–"Naw, I'll get an injunction from ma postponing the spanking, and then I'll appeal to grandma and she'll have it made permanent."

[3224]

Kind Gent–"Do you know what happens to little boys who smoke?"

Small Boy–"Yes, I do. Why every time they go anywhere to have a quiet smoke, they get bothered by rude old men."

[3225]

Mother–"I sent my little boy for two pounds of plums and you only sent a pound and a half."

Grocer–"My scales are all right, madam. Have you weighed your little boy?"

[3226]

The old lady stooped and looked into the little darling's face, and patted his wee head. "Say Mama for me, sweetness," she cooed softly. The baby didn't make a sound. The old lady became more urgent. "Come, little one, say Mama for poor me." Finally the baby looked at her and gurgled crossly: "How the hell do you expect me to talk when I'm only three months old?"

[3227]

Bobby–"Sister must be able to see in the dark."

Mother–"How so?"

Bobby–"Because last night when she was sitting with Mr. Staylate in the parlor, I heard her say, 'Why, Tom, you haven't shaved!' "

[3228]

"Why did you put that mud turtle in your sister's bed?"

"Because I couldn't find any frogs."

[3229]

"Melvin! MELVIN!"

"What, ma?"

"Are you spitting in the fish bowl?"

"No, ma, but I'm comin' pretty close."

[3230]

Mother (to small son who is going to a party)–"Now, dear, what are you going to do when you've had enough to eat?"

Little Tommy–"Come home."

[3231]

"What's the matter, little boy?"

"Ma's gone and drowned all the kittens."

"Dear me! That's too bad."

"Yep, she—hoo-hoo—promised me I could do it."

[3232]

"Now, Willie, do have a little courage. When I have medicine to take I don't like it any more than you do; but I make up my mind that I will take it, and I do."

"And when I have medicine to take," replied Willie, "I make up my mind that I won't take it, and I don't."

[3233]

Six-year-old Harry wanted to buy his sister a little Christmas present. His heart throbbed with joy at the thought, though he had in his pocket only ten cents. Nevertheless, he went around the shops and came back with a very satisfied look. His mother asked him what he had bought.

"I got her a cream puff," he said.

"Well, you know, Harry," said his mother, "that won't last until Christmas."

"That's what I thought after I bought it, Mother," replied Harry calmly, "and so I ate it."

[3234]

A little city boy was visiting his country cousin.

"What do you know about cows? You don't even know if that's a jersey cow."

"I don't know from here 'cause I can't see it's license."

[3235]

Johnny–"These pants that you bought for me are too tight."

Mother–"Oh, no, they aren't."

Johnny–"They are, too, mother. They're tighter'n my own skin."

Mother–"Now, Johnny, you know that isn't so."

Johnny–"It is, too. I can sit down in my skin, but I can't sit down in these pants."

[3236]

"Why are you crying, little girl?"

" 'Cause my brother has holidays and I don't."

"Well, why don't you have holidays?"

" 'Cause I don't go to school yet."

[3237]

"Jessie, I have told you again and again not to speak when older persons are talking, but wait until they stop."

"I've tried that already, mamma. They never do stop."

[3238]

Little Elaine surprised her mother with this postscript to her bedtime prayer:

"And, dear Lord, please send the beautiful snow to keep the little flowers warm through the winter."

Climbing into bed, she confided to her mother:

"That's the time I fooled Him. I want the snow so I can go sliding with my new sled!"

[3239]

Father–"When I was a little boy, I always ate the crusts."

Willie–"Did you like them?"

Father–"Of course, I did!"

Willie–"Then you can have mine."

[3240]

Dad–"Son, I'm spanking you because I love you."

Son–"I'd sure like to be big enough to return your love."

[3241]

"What a boy you are for asking questions," said the father. "I'd like to know what would have happened if I'd asked as many questions when I was a boy."

"Perhaps," suggested the young hopeful, "you'd have been able to answer some of mine."

[3242]

Tommie had always been much afraid of dogs.

One day, after a struggle to get him to pass a large dog which stood on the corner, his mother scolded him for his unnecessary fear.

"Well," was the reply, "you'd be afraid of dogs if you was as low down as I am."

[3243]

Visitor-"If your mother gave you a large apple and a small one and told you to divide with your brother, which apple would you give him?"

Johnny-"D'ye mean my big brother or my little one?"

[3244]

Bessie came running to her grandmother holding a dry, pressed leaf, obviously the relic of a day long gone by. "I found it in the big Bible, grandma," she said. "Do you s'pose it belonged to Eve?"

[3245]

Jean had been naughty and had been sent into the den to "think things over." After a while she came out all smiles and said, "I thought and I prayed."

"Fine!" said her mother. "That will help you to be good."

"Oh, I didn't ask God to help me to be good," said the child. "I just told Him to help you put up with me."

[3246]

"Emily," said the little girl's mamma, who was entertaining callers in the parlor, "you came downstairs so noisily that you could be heard all over the house. Now go back and come downstairs like a lady."

A little later Emily appeared quietly in the parlor.

"Did you hear me come downstairs this time, mamma?"

"No dear; I am glad you came down quietly. Now, don't ever let me have to tell you again not to come down noisily. Now tell these ladies how you managed to come down like a lady the second time, when the first time you made so much noise."

"The last time I slid down the banisters," explained Emily.

[3247]

Willie (doing his homework)-"What is the distance to the nearest star, Daddy?"

"I'm sure I don't know, Willie."

"Well, I hope, then, you'll feel sorry tomorrow when I'm getting punished for your ignorance."

[3248]

"Papa, when you see a cow ain't you afraid?"

"Of course not, Evelyn."

"When you see a great big worm ain't you afraid?"

"No, of course not."

"When you see a horrid, monstrous bumblebee ain't you afraid?"

"No, certainly not!"

"Ain't you afraid when it thunders and lightnings?"

"No, no, you silly child."

"Papa, ain't you afraid of nothing in this world 'ceptin' mamma?"

[3249]

"How old are you, sonny?" asked the inquisitive old man of the little boy on the beach.

"Six," came the brisk reply.

"Six," echoed the old man, "and yet you are not as tall as my umbrella."

The boy drew himself up to his full height. "How old is your umbrella?" he asked.

[3250]

Father–"I am obliged to punish you and it will pain me."

Johnny–"But, father, if you've done nothing wrong why pain yourself?"

[3251]

Johnny–"It's funny, ain't it, that everybody in our family's some kind of an animal?"

Father–"What do you mean?"

Johnny–"Why, mother's a dear, and baby is a little lamb, and I'm the kid, and you're the goat."

[3252]

When Bobby was told by his mother that she was born in Maryland, his father in Vermont, his sister in Indiana and he in Ohio, he said: "Gee, Ma, how'd we all get together?"

[3253]

"Herbert," said the mother of her six-year-old son, "is it possible that you are teaching the parrot to use slang?"

"No, mamma," replied Herbert. "I was just telling him what not to say."

[3254]

"Here, young man, you shouldn't hit that boy when he's down."

"G'way! What do you think I got him down for?"

[3255]

Eva–"Mother, Tillie gets a dime every time she takes cod liver oil."

Mother–"And what does she do with the money?"

Eva–"Well, she puts it in a box until she gets 50 cents; then her mother buys more cod liver oil."

[3256]

Little Ethel–"Don't you like to play with paper dolls any more?"

Little Willie–"No. I cut them out long ago."

[3257]

The ardent young suitor drew his girl's young brother aside.

"Jimmy," he said, "how would you like to earn some pocket money for yourself?"

"Love to," came from the youth. "What do you want me to do?"

"Well," said the lover, lowering his voice, "I'll give you a quarter if you can get me a lock of your sister's hair."

"Easy," replied Jimmy. "And if you gimme a dollar I'll get you the wig."

[3258]

"Say, pa, what do you call a person that reads heads?"

"A phrenologist, my boy."

"Gee. Then ma must be one of those things. She felt of my head this afternoon and said right away, 'you've been swimming.'"

[3259]

Visitor–"How old are you, sonny?"

Boston Boy–"That's hard to say, sir. According to my latest school tests, I have a psychological age of 11 and a moral age of 10. Anatomically, I'm 7; mentally, I'm 9. But I suppose you refer to my chronological age. That's 8—but nobody pays any attention to that these days!"

[3260]

"Mother, what does dee-dee stand for?"

"Doctor of Divinity, my dear. Don't they teach you such things in school?"

"Oh, yes; but it doesn't sound right here."

"Read it out loud, dear."

"The witness said he heard the defendant say 'I'll make you suffer for this, I'll be Doctor of Divinity if I don't.'"

[3261]

An elderly gentlemen was riding on a street car the other day. A boy began to laugh, and laughed so he couldn't stop. The old gentleman told his mother that the boy needed a spanking and she replied that she didn't believe in spanking on an empty stomach, whereupon the man said, "Neither do I; turn him over."

[3262]

"Pa, what are ancestors?"

"Well, my son, I'm one of yours. Your grandpa is another."

"Oh! Then why is it people brag about them?"

[3263]

A little fellow was learning from his aunt about Grant, Lee, and other famous leaders of the Civil War. "Is that the same Grant we pray to in church?" he inquired innocently.

"Pray to in church? You are mistaken, dear," said the aunt.

"No, I'm not," he insisted, "for during service we always say, 'Grant, we beseech Thee, to hear us.' "

[3264]

Visitor—"Well, and do you do a good deed every day, Tommy?"

Tommy—"Yes, sir. Yesterday, I visited my aunt in the country, and she was glad. To-day, I came back home again, and she was glad again!"

[3265]

Father (to son who has stolen sweetmeats from the table)—"Put back those sweets at once, you wretch!"

Son—"Hush, Father! Don't let all these people know how badly I have been brought up!"

[3266]

"Oh, mother, a truck went by as big as a house!"

"Bobbie, why do you exaggerate so terribly? I've told you 20 million times about that habit of yours, and it doesn't do a bit of good!"

[3267]

Little Cindy had not been observing the proper table manners, and as a punishment she was made to eat her dinner at a little table in the corner of the dining room. She was ignored by the rest of the family until they heard her saying grace:

"I thank thee, Lord, for preparing for me a table in the presence of mine enemies."

[3268]

Willie was doing penance in the corner. Presently he thought aloud pensively.

"I can't help it if I'm not perfect," he sighed. "I never heard of but one perfect boy, anyway."

"Who was that?" asked his mother, thinking to point a moral.

"Papa," came the silencing reply, "when he was little."

[3269]

Johnnie—"Let me see your shoes, won't you, Mr. Allrich."

Mr. Allrich—"Why, what do you want to see my shoes for?"

Johnnie—" 'Course I heard pop tellin' sis the other day that you was 'well heeled,' and I want to see what kind they are."

[3270]

"Tell me, Jimmie, do you ever peep through the keyhole when your sister and I are sitting here on the davenport alone?"

"Sometimes, when mother or sister Jane aren't looking."

[3271]

Mother–"Now, Willie, why don't you go and play with your little friends?"

Willie–"I have only one little friend, and I hate him."

[3272]

Mother–"I don't think the man upstairs likes Johnnie to play on his drum."

Father–"Why?"

Mother–"Well, this afternoon he gave Johnnie a knife and asked him if he knew what was inside the drum."

[3273]

Mother–"Willie, it is time you were up. The birds were all up long ago."

Willie (drowsily)–"Well, if I had to sleep in a nest of sticks and straws I'd get up early, too!"

[3274]

Into the crowded bus came a stout woman, dressed in many colors, who squeezed into the only vacant seat. Then a childish voice broke the silence.

"Mummy, it's a lady!"

"Hush, dear," said his mother; "I know it is!"

The small boy looked puzzled.

"But, mummy," he shrilled, "you just said to daddy, 'what ever's this object coming in?'"

[3275]

Mother–"But, Betty, why do you not want to come and visit Mrs. Brown with me?"

Betty–"My dolly hasn't a thing to wear."

[3276]

"Pa, may I ask you a question?"

"Certainly, my child."

"Well, where is the wind when it doesn't blow?"

[3277]

Mother (who has guest at dinner)–"Cindy, don't talk with your mouth full."

Cindy–"But, mummy, what am I to do? When I talk with my mouth empty, you always say, 'Cindy, go on with your dinner.'"

[3278]

One day little Flora was taken to have an aching tooth removed. That night, while she was saying her prayers, her mother was surprised to hear her say: "And forgive us our debts as we forgive our dentists."

[3279]

Little Willie was in a store with his mother when he was given candy by one of the clerks.

"What must you say, Willie?"

"Charge it," he replied.

[3280]

"Papa, is this a camel's hair brush?"

"Yes, my child, that's a camel's hair brush."

"Golly, papa, it must take him a terrible long time to brush himself."

[3281]

Mother (to Bobby who has been fibbing)–"Do you know what happens to little boys who tell lies?"

Bobby–"Yes. They ride for half fare."

[3282]

Ma–"Don't you think Emily sings with a good deal of feeling?"

Pa–"Yes but I hope she doesn't feel as bad as it sounds."

[3283]

Father (reprovingly) – "Do you know what happens to liars when they die?"

Johnny–"Yes, sir; they lie still."

[3284]

Willie, aged five, carries water for the chickens. At breakfast one day an egg was too soft for him. After looking at it a moment he cried out:

"Mamma, these chickens have been having too much water."

[3285]

Bobby–"I ain't goin' to say my prayers tonight, mother. I'm goin' to take a chance."

[3286]

Mrs. Robinson was an extremely careful mother and had repeatedly cautioned her six-year-old daughter against handling any object that might contain germs. One day the little girl came in and said:

"Mother, I am never going to play with my puppy any more, because he has germs on him."

"Oh, no!" replied her mother. "There are no germs on your puppy."

"Yes, there are," insisted the child. "I saw one hop."

[3287]

Sally (aged 3, to her older sister)– "I'm as tall as you."

Nancy–"No, you're not. Stand up and see. There, you only come to my mouth."

Sally–"Well, I don't care. I'm as tall the other way; my feet go down as far as yours."

[3288]

"Has Bobbie been eating between meals?"

"Bobbie has no between meals."

[3289]

"Have you ever heard the story of Algy and the bear?" asked a boy of his father. "It's very short. 'Algy met a bear; the bear was bulgy; the bulge was Algy.' "

[3290]

The camp counselor was explaining the rules of a new game.

"If the enemy calls your number from his side of the battlefield," she said, "you must be a 'dead man' immediately. Drop just where you are and lie still."

Ten minutes later, came an agonized whisper from the youngest camper:

"Please may I move now? I'm a dead man, but I'm on an ant-hill!"

[3291]

Visitor–"Why, no, Betty, I haven't been away. What made you think I had?"

Little Betty–"Why, my papa and mamma both said that you and your wife had been at Loggerheads for two or three weeks."

[3292]

"Whose little girl are you?"

"I'm papa's little girl."

"And why aren't you mamma's little girl?"

" 'Cause the decree gave me to papa."

[3293]

Mother–"Your face is clean, but how'd you get your hands so dirty?"

Small Son–"Washin' my face."

[3294]

Uncle–"And what are you going to be when you grow up, Freddy?"

Freddy–"I'm going to be a philanthropist; those people always seem to have such a lot of money."

[3295]

A kind old gentleman seeing a small boy who was carrying a lot of newspapers under his arm said: "Don't all those papers make you tired, my boy?"

"Naw, I don't read 'em," replied the lad.

[3296]

Little Willie came home in a sad state. He had a black eye and numerous scratches and contusions, and his clothes were a sight. His mother was horrified at the spectacle presented by her darling. There were tears in her eyes as she addressed him rebukingly:

"Oh, Willie, Willie! How often have I told you not to play with that naughty Peck boy!"

Little Willie regarded his mother with an expression of deepest disgust.

"Say, ma," he objected, "do I look as if I had been playing with anybody?"

[3297]

Visitor—"Your son is rather small for his age, isn't he?"

Proud Mother—"Oh, no; most boys of his age are overgrown, I think."

[3298]

"Gee, pop, there's a man at the circus who jumps on a horse's back, slips underneath, catches hold of its tail and finishes up on the horse's neck!"

Dad—"That's easy. I did all that the first time I ever rode a horse."

[3299]

"Does your son play on the piano?"

"No; he can't climb that high yet."

[3300]

"Are you an actress, auntie?"

"No, darling, why do you ask?"

"Because Daddy said when you came we'd have a scene."

[3301]

"Daddy, who was Hamlet?"

"Bring me the Bible, you ignoramus, and I'll show you who he was."

[3302]

Alice for the first time saw a cat carrying her kitten by the nape of its neck.

"You ain't fit to be a mother," she cried scathingly. "You ain't hardly fit to be a father!"

[3303]

Grandpa—"My little man, you shouldn't say, 'I ain't going.' You should say, 'I am not going,' 'He is not going,' 'They are not going,' 'We are not going,' 'You are not going.'"

Little Johnny—"Ain't nobody going?"

[3304]

"Teacher" was giving her class a little weekly talk on painting, illustrated by reproductions of famous pictures. "Sir Joshua Reynolds," she said, "was able to change a smiling face into a frowning one with a single stroke of the brush."

"Huh," little Johnnie was heard to mutter, "my maw kin do that!"

[3305]

"Mama, I want a dark breakfast."

"Dark breakfast? What do you mean, child?"

"Why, last night you told Mary to give me a light supper, and I didn't like it."

[3306]

A little boy with a terrible toothache went to the dentist to have the bad tooth pulled out. When the painful operation was over he asked the dentist to let him have the tooth.

"What do you want the tooth for?" asked the dentist.

"I am going to take it home, fill it with sugar and watch the darn thing ache."

[3307]

"Papa, what kind of a robber is a page?"

"A what?"

"It says here that two pages held up the bride's train."

[3308]

"Uncle Louis," said little Eleanor, "do you know that a baby that was fed on elephant's milk gained 20 pounds in a few weeks?"

"Nonsense! Impossible!" exclaimed Uncle Louis. "Whose baby was it?"

"The elephant's baby," remarked little Eleanor.

[3309]

Oliver was careless about his personal effects. When his mother saw clothing scattered about on the chair and floor, she inquired: "Who didn't hang up his clothes when he went to bed?"

A muffled voice from under the covers murmured: "Adam."

[3310]

"Mother, can I have those apples on the sideboard?"

"Yes, dear!"

"Oh, I'm so glad you said yes."

"Why, are you so hungry?"

"No—but I've eaten them already."

[3311]

Auntie–"What did little Margaret get at the birthday party?"

Mother–"Three books, four handkerchiefs, and the measles."

[3312]

"Did you give the penny to the monkey, dear?"

"Yes, mama."

"And what did the monkey do with it?"

"He gave it to his father, who played the organ."

[3313]

Mother took Willie to his first concert. The conductor was leading the orchestra and directing the soprano soloist as well. Willie was greatly interested.

"Mother, why is that man shaking his stick at the lady?" he asked.

"Hush; he is not shaking his stick at her."

"Then what is she screaming for?"

[3314]

"How many times must I tell you, Willie, that one must keep his eyes closed during prayer?"

"Yes, mamma, how do you know I don't?"

[3315]

Irate Mother (at dinner)– "Johnny, I wish you'd stop reaching for things. Haven't you a tongue?"

Johnny–"Yes, Mother, but my arm's longer."

[3316]

Father–"Aren't you ashamed to be at the bottom in a class of twenty-eight boys?"

Willie–"Oh, that's not so bad."

Father–"What do you mean, not so bad?"

Willie–"Suppose there were fifty boys."

[3317]

"My sister is awfully lucky," said one little boy to another.

"Why?"

"She went to a party last night where they played a game in which the men either had to kiss a girl or pay a forfeit of a box of chocolates."

"Well, how was your sister lucky?"

"She came home with thirteen boxes of chocolates."

[3318]

Small Girl—"Mummy, how do angels get their nighties on over their wings?"

[3319]

"So you're lost, little man? Why didn't you hang onto your mother's skirt?"

Youngster—"Couldn't reach it."

[3320]

A pretty little girl of seven entered a store in a small town and said:

"I want some cloth to make my dolly a dress."

The merchant selected a remnant and handed the child the package.

"How much is it?" she asked.

"Just one kiss," was the reply.

"All right," said the child, as she turned to go. "Grandma said to tell you she would pay you when she came in tomorrow."

[3321]

Little Bobbie, while at a neighbor's, was given a piece of bread and butter, and politely said, "Thank you."

"That's right, Bobbie," said the lady. "I like to hear little boys say 'thank you.'"

"Well," rejoined Bobbie. "If you want to hear me say it again, you might put some jam on it."

[3322]

Father criticized the sermon, mother disliked the blunders of the organist, and the eldest daughter thought the choir's singing atrocious.

The subject had to be dropped when the small boy of the family, with the schoolboy's love of fair play, chipped in with the remark:

"Dad, I think it was a good show for a penny."

[3323]

The mother thought her little girl ought to be examined for any possible abnormal tendencies, so she took the tot to a psychologist. Among other questions, the man of science asked:

"Are you a boy or a girl?"

"A boy," the little girl answered.

Somewhat taken aback, the psychologist tried again. "When you grow up, are you going to be a woman or a man?"

"A man," the little girl answered.

Afterwards, as they were returning home, the mother asked, "Why did you make such strange replies to what the man asked you?"

The little girl drew herself up with dignity. "The old silly," she said. "If he was going to ask me crazy questions, I was going to give him crazy answers. He couldn't kid me."

[3324]

"Do you go to school, my little man?" inquired the caller.

"Naw," replied the little man, "I'm sent."

[3325]

The old man sighed as he took the golden-haired, laughing boy upon his knees and stroking his shining tresses, said: "How I should like to feel like a child again."

Little Johnnie ceased his laughter, and looking soberly up into his grandfather's face, remarked: "Then why don't you get mamma to spank you?"

[3326]

Little Joy, seven years old, remarked as she helped herself to the last biscuit on the plate:

"This won't matter to me, for I've been an old maid about all my life, anyhow."

[3327]

The barber had used his electric clippers in cutting small Betty's hair.

"I guess my neck wasn't clean," she told her mother on coming home, " 'cause that man used his vacuum cleaner on it."

[3328]

The boy was very small and the load of sand he was pushing in the wheelbarrow was very, very big.

A benevolent old gentleman, putting down his bundles, lent him a helping hand.

"Really, my boy," he puffed, "I don't see how you manage to get that barrow up the gutters alone."

"I don't," replied the appreciative kid. "Dere's always some jay a-standin' round as takes it up for me."

[3329]

Betty (who has been served with a wing of chicken)–"Mother, can't I have another bit? This is nothing but hinges."

[3330]

Little Bobby ran to his mother, sobbing as though his heart would break.

"Why, what's the matter, Bobby?" asked his mother.

"Oh, Daddy was hanging a picture and he dropped it on his toes," answered Bobby between sobs.

"Why, that's nothing to cry about, you should laugh at that," said his mother.

"I did," Bobby replied.

[3331]

Mother (to little girl who had been sent to the hen house for eggs)– "Well, dear, were there no eggs?" *Little Girl*–"No, mummie, only the one the hen uses for a pattern."

[3332]

"Paw?"

"Now what?"

"Why didn't Noah swat both flies when he had such a good chance?"

[3333]

"You don't love me," Flossie wailed to her mother, after she had been severely scolded for her naughty behavior.

"Yes, I do love you," was the reply.

"Well, you don't talk like it."

"How do you wish me to talk, Flossie?"

"I want you to talk to me as you do when you have company."

[3334]

Voice from House – "Willie-ell What's your brother crying about? Didn't I tell you to give him anything he wanted?"

Willie–"Yes, ma; but now that I've dug him a hole, he wants me to bring it in the house."

[3335]

"Daddy, what's a 'feebly'?"

"A 'feebly'?"

"Yes, Daddy."

"How is it used?"

"Why, here in this book it says, 'The man had a feebly growing down on his chin.' "

[3336]

"Why, what are you crying so for, sonny?" asked Dad of his four-year-old heir.

"I heard you say you were going to get a new baby and I suppose that means you'll trade me in on it," he sobbed.

[3337]

Mother–"What do you want to take your cod liver oil with, today, Junior?"

Junior–"With a fork."

[3338]

"Mama," said little Elsie, "I do wish I had some money to give you for the poor children."

Her mother, wishing to teach her the lesson of self-sacrifice, said, "Very well, dear; if you would like to go without sugar for a week, I'll give you the money instead, and then you will have some."

The little one considered solemnly for a moment, and then said, "Must it be sugar, mama?"

"Why, no, darling; not necessarily. What would you like to do without?"

"Soap, mama," was Elsie's answer.

[3339]

"Oh, I feel so bad 'cause Major's dead—my nice old collie!" sobbed Bobby.

"Shucks!" said Billy, the neighbor's boy, "My grandmother's been dead a week, and you don't catch me crying."

Bobby gave his eyes and nose a swipe with his hand, and, looking up at Billy, sobbed:

"Yes, but you didn't raise your grandmother from a pup."

[3340]

Three-year-old Nancy was a radio fan. Nancy listened with rapt attention to everything—music, speeches, and station announcements.

One night she knelt to say her "Now I lay me." At the end she paused a moment, and then said:

"Tomorrow night at this time there will be another prayer."

[3341]

Pa to ma—"Bobbie wants to know why vitamins were put in spinach and cod liver oil instead of in cake and candy."

[3342]

"Mother," said little Nelly, looking up to the starry skies one bright evening, "what a delightful place heaven must be, when its wrong side is so beautiful."

[3343]

The little boy was gazing pensively at a gooseberry-bush.

"What's the matter, darling?" asked his mother.

"Have gooseberries any legs, mother?" asked the little chap.

"No, darling, of course they haven't," said his mother.

The boy's look became more pensive than ever.

"Then I guess I must have swallowed a caterpillar," he said.

[3344]

Betty (finishing her prayers)–"And please make me a good girl and help me to eat up my food—but never mind about the spinach."

[3345]

Jackie–"Oh, mother! Just look at that man! He hasn't a hair on his head."

Mother–"Hush, dear, he will hear you."

Jackie–"Oh, doesn't he know it?"

[3346]

Little Boy–"Please, I want the doctor to come and see mother."

Servant–"Doctor's out. Where do you come from?"

Little Boy–"What! Don't you know me? Why we deal with you. We had a baby from here last week!"

[3347]

Mother–"What in the world has happened to you? Your shirt is full of holes."

Tommy–"We've been playing grocery store and I was the Swiss cheese."

[3348]

"Won't you have some more cake, dear?" asked the hostess.

"How many times have you passed it?" questioned Sallie.

"Three times, I believe. Why do you ask?"

"Well, mother said I must not take any the second time; but she didn't say a thing about the third time."

[3349]

Lady–"Why, you naughty boy. I never heard such language since the day I was born."

Small Boy–"Yes, mum; I s'pose dere wuz a good deal of cussin' de day you wuz born."

[3350]

"The teacher is mad. Yesterday he told us that four and one makes five, but today he told us that it was three and two!"

[3351]

Mother–"Another bite like that and you will have to leave the table."

Hungry Boy–"Another bite like that and I'll be through."

[3352]

The conductor came to the mother and her little boy on the street car.

"How old is your little boy, madam?" the conductor asked, to determine whether the boy should pay a fare or not.

"Just four," the mother answered, truthfully.

"All right, madam," the conductor acknowledged.

The little boy looked quizzically at the conductor, and evidently felt that further information should be vouchsafed.

"And mother," he said solemnly, "is just thirty-one."

[3353]

"But, Betty dear," advised her mother, "you are not getting all the peelings off the potatoes!"

"Yes, I am, mother," replied Betty, "all except in the dimples."

[3354]

The father lectured his young son on the evils of fisticuffs as a way of settling disputes.

"Don't you know that when you grow up you can't use your fists to settle an argument?" the father began. "You must begin to use peaceful and amicable means of arriving at a decision. Try to reason things out. Try to discover by logic and evidence which is right, and abide by the right. Remember that might does not make right; though the strong may win over the weak, that still does not prove that the weak is wrong."

"I know, dad," said the boy kicking at the grass. "But this was different."

"Different? How different? What were you and Johnny arguing about that you had to fight over it?"

"Well, he said he could whip me and I said I could whip him, and there was only one way to find out which of us was right."

[3355]

Four-year-old Johnny came running into the house.

"Mumsy, do you know Jacky Brown's neck?"

His mother did not answer this apparently irrelevant question.

"Mumsy, I said—you know Jacky Brown's neck?"

"Well, yes," his mother capitulated. "I suppose I do know Jacky's neck. Why?"

"Well, just now he fell into the pond up to it."

[3356]

Two small boys were discussing the capabilities of their mothers, who were active club members.

"My mother can talk on just about any subject," one lad declared proudly.

"Aw, shucks," retorted the other, "my mother can talk without any subject at all."

[3357]

Little Girl (who has been allowed to stay up with stuffy grown-ups)– "May I go to bed, mummie? I'm tired of this night life."

[3358]

"Mother," said Peggy, who had just seen a large toadstool sprouting, "do babies grow or can you buy them?"

"They grow, dear," replied Mother.

"Well," said the four-year-old, "I think there's one coming up in the backyard now."

[3359]

Willie's younger sister called to her mother in sudden alarm. When the mother came to the window to learn the trouble, the little girl cried:

"Mama, quick! Willie's takin' off his clothes. He'll soon be barefoot all over."

[3360]

Mrs. Jones was getting dinner ready when in came little Fred with a happy smile on his face.

"What has mamma's darling been doing this morning?" asked his mother.

"I have been playing Postman," replied little Fred.

"Postman?" exclaimed his mother. "How could you do that when you had no letters?"

"Oh, but I had," replied Fred. "I was looking in your trunk up in your room and I found a packet of letters tied 'round with a ribbon, and I posted one under every door in the street."

[3361]

"Mamma, do pigs have babies?"

"Why of course, my dear."

"Some one told me they had little pigs."

[3362]

Father–"Troubled with dyspepsia in school to-day? Why, that's a strange thing for a boy to have."

Johnny–"I didn't have it; I had to spell it."

[3363]

"Pop, will I look like you when I grow up?"

"Everybody seems to think so, son."

"Well, I won't have to grow up for a long time, will I, Pop?"

[3364]

"Father."

"Well, what is it?"

"It says here, 'A man is known by the company he keeps.' Is that so, Father?"

"Yes, yes, yes."

"Well, Father, if a good man keeps company with a bad man, is the good man bad because he keeps company with the bad man, and is the bad man good because he keeps company with the good man?"

[3365]

Tommy–"That problem you helped me with last night was all wrong, Daddy."

Father–"All wrong, was it? Well, I'm sorry."

"Well, you needn't exactly worry about it, because none of the other daddies got it right, either."

[3366]

A mother teaching her little daughter, four years old, pointed to something in a book, and asked:

"What is that, my dear?"

"Why, don't you know?" inquired the child.

"Yes," said the mother; "but I wish to find out if you know."

"Well," responded the little one, "I do know."

"Tell me, then, if you please."

"Why no," insisted the little miss, "you know what it is, and I know what it is, and there is no need of saying anything more about it."

FAMILY HUMOR

[3367]

The Kid–"Pop, how soon will I be old enough to do as I please?"

The Old Man–"I don't know. Nobody has ever lived that long yet."

[3368]

"Mamma, when the fire goes out where does it go?"

"My dear boy, I don't know. You might just as well ask me where your father goes when he goes out."

[3369]

Jimmy–"If a boy is a lad and he has a step father, is the boy a stepladder?"

[3370]

"Dad, what is influence?"

"Influence, my son, is a thing you think you have until you try to use it."

[3371]

A father said, "Now, son, start saving the pennies and put them in this yellow box, and when you get five pennies give them to me and I'll give you a nickel and you can put that in this blue box; then, when you get five nickels give them to me and I'll give you a quarter and you can put it in this red box."

Seventeen years later the boy discovered that the red box was the gas-meter.

[3372]

A high school girl, seated next to a famous astronomer at a dinner party, struck up a conversation with him by asking, "What do you do in life?"

He replied, "I study astronomy."

"Dear me," said the girl. "I finished astronomy last year."

[3373]

Father (at son's twenty-first birthday party)–"You are of age now and you ought to help me a little."

Son–"Yes, dad, what can I do for you?"

Father–"You might pay the last three instalments on your baby perambulator."

[3374]

"Have you any children, Mr. Smith?"

"Yes—three daughters."

"Do they live at home with you?"

"Not one of them—they are not married yet."

[3375]

Mother–"I'm afraid Robert is burning the candle at both ends."

Father–"Huh! That boy has cut the candle in two and lit it up all four ends."

[3376]

Peggy–"I want to help you, dad. I shall get the dressmaker to teach me to cut out gowns."

Dad–"I don't want you to go that far, Peg, but you might cut out cigarettes and taxi bills."

[3377]

"I hear your son is getting on."

"Rather. Two years ago he wore my old suits—now I wear his."

[3378]

"Daddy, what is your birth stone?"

"A grindstone, my dear."

[3379]

"Pop!"

"Yes, my son."

"What is a gardener?"

"A gardener is a man who raises a few things, my boy."

"And what is a farmer?"

"A man who raises a lot of things."

"Well, what is a middleman, Pop?"

"Why, he's a fellow who raises everything, my son."

[3380]

Teacher—"Johnny, what's the difference between a battle and a massacre?"

Johnny—"A battle is where a whole lot of whites kill a few Indians, and a massacre is where a whole lot of Indians kill a few whites."

[3381]

"What do you mean by coming in so late?" demanded the angry parent.

A sudden thought came to the boy.

"Oh, dad," he said, "I forgot to tell you—I knew you wouldn't mind—I was sitting up with the sick son of the sick man you are always telling mother you sat up with."

[3382]

"What does a volcano do with lava?" asked Freddy.

"Give it up," replied his father.

"That's right," said Freddy.

[3383]

"Father," said the small boy, "what is psychology?"

"Psychology, my son, is a word of four syllables that you ring in to distract attention when the explaining gets difficult."

[3384]

"What are you reading, Charlie?"

"It's a book called 'Child Training,' that I borrowed from Mrs. Jones," returned the young son.

"Do you find it amusing?" laughed his mother.

"I'm not reading it for that. I merely wanted to see if I had been brought up properly."

[3385]

Father—"Ned, why are you always at the bottom of your class?"

Ned—"It doesn't really matter, dad. We get the same instruction at both ends of the class."

[3386]

Young Son—"What is luck, father?"

Father—"Luck, my son, is something that enables another fellow to succeed where we have failed."

[3387]

"Pa, what's dignity?"

"Dignity, my son, is what you think you possess until the boss says, 'What is the meaning of this?'"

[3388]

Willie—"Paw, does bigamy mean that a man has one wife too many?"

Paw—"Not necessarily, my son. A man can have one wife too many and still not be a bigamist."

[3389]

"Pa, what's phonetic spelling?"

"It's a way of spelling that I often got whipped for when I was your age."

[3390]

A father had been lecturing his young hopeful upon the evils of staying out late at night and getting up late in the morning.

"You will never amount to anything," he continued, "unless you turn over a new leaf. Remember that the early bird catches the worm."

"How about the worm, father?" inquired the young man. "Wasn't he rather foolish to get up so early?"

"My son," replied the father solemnly, "that worm hadn't been to bed all night; he was on his way home."

[3391]

"Sit down!" said a nervous old gentleman to his son, who was making too much noise.

"I won't do it," was the impudent answer.

"Well, then, stand up. I will be obeyed!"

[3392]

"Father, have you cut all four of your wisdom teeth?"

"Yes, son. I have purchased a used car, accepted a nomination, been chairman of a local reception committee, and married your mother."

[3393]

"Pop, what do we mean by a good listener?"

"A good listener, my son, is a man to whom it is possible to tell a funny story without reminding him of one of his own."

[3394]

"What does 'close quarters' mean, Ma?"

"It's a definition of my trying to get twenty-five cents from your father."

[3395]

"Pa, what branches did you take when you went to school?"

"I never went to high school, son, but when I attended the little log school-house they used mostly hickory and beech and willow."

[3396]

A very nice old lady had a few words to say to her granddaughter.

"My dear," said the old lady, "I wish you would do something for me. I wish you would promise me never to use two words. One is swell and the other is lousy. Would you promise me that?"

"Why sure, Granny," said the girl. "What are the words?"

[3397]

Willie—"I say, Pa, what is an empty title?"

Pa—"An empty title, my son, is your mother's way of referring to me as the head of the house when there are visitors present."

[3398]

Wife (reading)—"It says here they have found a sheep in the Himalaya Mountains that can run forty miles an hour."

Her Hubby—"Well, it would take a lamb like that to follow Mary nowadays."

[3399]

First Girl Hiker—"I inserted an advertisement in our local newspaper recently under a box-number for a male partner to accompany me on a fortnight's hiking-trip."

Second Girl—"How interesting. Did you have many replies?"

First Girl—"Yes, hundreds, but there was a terrible row in the house over it."

Second Girl—"Good gracious, why?"

First Girl—"Father was one of the applicants!"

[3400]

Father–"When I was a boy I thought nothing of a ten mile walk. "

Son–"Well, I don't think so much of it, myself."

[3401]

Daughter (having just received a beautiful set of mink skins from her father)–"What I don't see is how such wonderful furs can come from such a low, sneaking, little beast."

Father–"I don't ask for thanks, dear, but I really insist on respect."

[3402]

Mother–"I had a frank discussion with our daughter today about the facts of life."

Father–"Did you learn anything new?"

[3403]

"You ought to be ashamed," the father told his loafing son. "When George Washington was your age, he had become a surveyor, and was hard at work."

"And when he was your age," the boy replied, "he was President of the United States."

[3404]

Small Boy (to father)–"The world is round, isn't it?"

Father–"It is."

Boy–"Then if I wanted to go east I could get there by going west, couldn't I?"

Father–"Yes, and when you grow up you will be a taxicab driver."

SCHOOL CHILDREN AND TEACHERS

[3405]

The teacher was trying to impress upon her pupils the importance of doing right at all times, and to bring out the answer, "Bad habits," she inquired: "What is it that we find so easy to get into and so hard to get out of?"

There was silence for a moment and then one little fellow answered. "Bed."

[3406]

Teacher–"Tommy, where was the Declaration of Independence signed?"

Tommy–"At the bottom, I guess."

[3407]

Mother–"Well, Jimmy, do you think your teacher likes you?"

Jimmy–"I think so, mummy, because she puts a big kiss on all my sums."

[3408]

Teacher–"Willie, how do you define ignorance?"

Willie–"It's when you don't know something and somebody finds it out."

[3409]

Teacher–"Alfred, you may spell the word neighbor."

Alfred–"N-e-i-g-h-b-o-r."

Teacher–"That's right. Now, Tommy, can you tell me what a neighbor is?"

Tommy–"Yes, ma'am. It's a woman that borrows things."

[3410]

The lengthy recital had drawn to a close, ice-cream and cake had been served, and the teacher was bidding the students good-by. One of the little performers had brought her small brother with her. As he was about to leave, the teacher beamingly said, "Well, Bobby, did you enjoy the recital?"

"Yes," answered Bobby, "all but the music."

[3411]

Teacher—"If I take a potato and divide it into two parts, then into four parts, and each of the four parts into two parts, what would I have?"

Little Emily—"Potato salad!"

[3412]

Ethel was just home after her first day at school. "Well, darling," asked her mother, "what did they teach you?"

"Not much," replied the child. "I've got to go again."

[3413]

Teacher—"Tommy, how many wars was Spain engaged in during the 17th century?"

Tommy—"Seven."

Teacher—"Seven? Enumerate them."

Tommy—"One, two, three, four, five, six, seven."

[3414]

Teacher—"What have the various expeditions to the North Pole accomplished?"

Jimmy—"Nothin' 'cept to make the geography lessons harder."

[3415]

The teacher had been telling her pupils about the animals. "Now," she said, "name some things that are very dangerous to get near to, and have horns."

Tom—"Motor cars."

[3416]

The teacher asked his pupils to write an essay, telling what they would do if they had five million dollars.

Every pupil except little Sammy began writing immediately. Sammy sat idle, twiddling his fingers and watching the flies on the ceiling.

Teacher collected the papers, and Sammy handed in a blank sheet.

"How is this, Sammy?" asked teacher. "Is this your essay? Every other pupil has written two sheets or more, while you have done nothing!"

"Well," replied Sammy, "that's what I would do if I were a millionaire!"

[3417]

Schoolmaster—"This makes the fifth time I have punished you this week. What have you to say?"

Youth—"I am glad it's Friday, sir."

[3418]

Teacher—"Johnny, to what class of the animal kingdom do I belong?"

Johnny—"I don't know, teacher. Pa says you're an old hen and ma says you're an old cat."

[3419]

Teacher—"Johnny, can you tell me what a waffle is?"

Johnny—"Yes'm, it's a pancake with a non-skid tread."

[3420]

Teacher (who has found Tommy out before)—"Did your father write this essay on 'Why I love teacher'?"

Tommy—"No, he didn't; mother stopped him."

[3421]

"Father," said Jimmy, running into the drawing-room, "there's a big black cat in the dining-room."

"Never mind, Jimmy," said the father, drowsily; "black cats are lucky."

"This one is; he's had your dinner!"

[3422]

Father—"Why were you kept in at school?"

Son—"I didn't know where the Azores were."

Father—"Well, in the future just remember where you put things."

[3423]

Teacher was going to give an object lesson. "Tommy," she began, "why does your father put up storm windows every fall?"

"Well," said Tommy, "Mother keeps at him until he finally gives in."

[3424]

A corpulent teacher was giving a lesson to a class of small children on a canary.

Teacher–"Can any boy tell me what a canary can do and I can't?"

Sharp Boy–"Please, miss, have a bath in a saucer!"

[3425]

Teacher–"Now, Johnny, what did Caesar exclaim when Brutus stabbed him?"

Johnny–"Ouch!"

[3426]

"Johnny," said the teacher, "you may tell us how many are two and two."

"Two and two," Johnny promptly replied, "are four."

"That is very good, Johnny," commended the teacher.

"Good!" said Johnny. "Great guns, it's perfect!"

[3427]

Teacher–"Seven cows are walking along a path in a single file. Which one can turn around and say, 'I see six pairs of horns?'"

Bobby–"Why, the first cow."

Teacher–"Wrong, Bobby, cows cannot talk."

[3428]

"George," said the teacher, "is there any connecting link between the animal kingdom and the vegetable kingdom?"

"Yeth, ma'am," answered George promptly. "Hash."

[3429]

Teacher–"Did Longfellow have many fast friends?"

Elsie–"Longfellow had many fast friends, but Anna and Phœbe Cary were the fastest."

[3430]

Charles has just entered school.

"What is your name?" the teacher asked.

"Charles," was the reply.

"Charles what?" the teacher questioned.

"Oh, that's all right," the youngster said, "just call me Charles."

[3431]

Teacher–"Which is farther away, England or the moon?"

Johnny–"England."

Teacher–"England? What makes you think that?"

Johnny–" 'Cause we can see the moon and we can't see England."

[3432]

Teacher–"Yes, Johnny, Lapland is rather thinly populated."

Johnny–"How many Lapps to the mile, teacher?"

[3433]

The teacher had been giving a lecture to his class on modern inventions. "Can any of you boys," he said, "tell me of anything of importance which did not exist fifty years ago?"

"Me," exclaimed the brightest pupil.

[3434]

"Johnny," said the teacher, "who were the two strongest men of olden times?"

"Samson and Hercules."

"Can you tell me anything about them?"

"Oh, yes. Samson was a regular Hercules."

[3435]

"James, have you whispered to-day without permission?"

"Only wunst."

"Leroy, should James have said 'wunst'?"

"No'm, he should have said 'twict.' "

[3436]

Father–"I got a note from your teacher today."

Son–"That's all right, pa. I'll keep it quiet."

[3437]

Teacher–"Name the constituents of quartz?"

His Father's Son–"Pints."

[3438]

Teacher–"What ancient ruler was it who played on the fiddle while Rome was burning?"

Jimmie–"Hector, ma'am."

Teacher–"No, not Hector. Hector was no ruler, but a Trojan prince. Try again."

Jimmie–"Then it was Duke."

Teacher–"Duke? What do you mean, Jimmie?"

Jimmie–"Well, then it must have been Nero. I knew it was somebody with a dog's name."

[3439]

Teacher (to pupil) – "Spell 'Straight.' "

Pupil–"S-T-R-A-I-G-H-T."

Teacher–"Correct; what does it mean?"

Pupil–"Without ginger ale."

[3440]

Teacher–"Walter, spell FROG."

Walter (rather frightened)–"F—R——F—R——"

Then the boy sitting in back of him stuck him with a pin and he yelled, "Oh, gee!"

Teacher–"Correct!"

[3441]

Teacher–"Johnny, can you tell me how iron was discovered?"

Johnny–"I heard Dad say yesterday that they smelt it."

[3442]

The schoolmistress was giving her class of young pupils a test on a recent natural history lesson.

"Now, Bobby Jones," she said, "tell me where the elephant is found."

The boy hesitated for a moment; then his face lit up.

"The elephant, teacher," he said, "is such a large animal that it is scarcely ever lost."

[3443]

Teacher–"What was George Washington noted for?"

Johnny–"His memory."

Teacher–"What makes you think his memory was so great?"

Johnny–"They erected a monument to it."

[3444]

"Freddie, you mustn't laugh out loud in the schoolroom."

"I didn't mean to do it. I was smiling, and the smile busted."

[3445]

"Why are you late, Freddie?" asked the teacher angrily.

"Please, ma'am, it was late when I started from home."

"Then why didn't you start early?"

"Please, ma'am, it was too late to start early."

[3446]

Teacher–"In what battle did Gen. Wolfe, when hearing of victory, cry, 'I die happy'?"

Johnny–"I think it was his last battle."

[3447]

When teacher asked in what part of the world the most ignorant people were to be found, a small boy volunteered quickly, "In New York."

The teacher was amazed, and questioned the lad as to where he had obtained such information.

"Well," he replied, "the geography says that's where the population is most dense."

[3448]

Teacher–"Frank, what is a cannibal?"

Frank–"Don't know, mum."

Teacher–"Well, if you ate your father and mother, what would you be?"

Frank–"An orphan, mum."

[3449]

"What's the shape of the earth?" asked the teacher of Johnny.

Johnny said it was round.

"How do you know it is round, Johnny?"

Then Johnny replied: "All right, it's square, then. I don't want to start an argument about it."

[3450]

Teacher–"We are going to have a little talk on wading birds. Of course, the stork is one—what are you laughing at, Elsie?"

Little Elsie–"Oh, but, teacher—the idea of there being any storks!"

[3451]

Teacher–"Why, Willie, what are you drawing?"

Willie–"I'm drawing a picture of God."

Teacher–"But, Willie, you mustn't do that; nobody knows how God looks."

Willie–"Well, they will when I get this done."

[3452]

School Superintendent (cross-questioning the terrified class)–"And now I want you boys to tell me who wrote 'Hamlet.'"

Frightened Boy–"P-p-please, sir, it —it wasn't me."

That same evening the superintendent was talking to his host, the squire of the village. The superintendent said:

"Most amusing thing happened today. I was questioning the class over at the school, and I asked a boy who wrote 'Hamlet.' He answered tearfully, 'P-p-please, sir, it wasn't me.'"

After loud and prolonged laughter, the squire said:

"That's pretty good, and I suppose the little rascal had done it all the time!"

[3453]

The teacher had been reading the story of "Ali Baba and the Forty Thieves" to her class of small boys. When she reached the end she closed the book and proceeded to question them regarding the story.

"Now, can any one tell me," she said, "what Ali Baba said when he wanted to open the entrance to the cave?"

One child, an ardent film fan, promptly replied:

"Open, sez me!"

[3454]

"Now, then, Tommy Brown," said the teacher, "I want to set you a little problem. Suppose there were five children and their mother had only four potatoes to share between them. She wants to give each child an equal share. How would she do it?"

"Mash the potatoes," said the boy.

[3455]

Mother–"The teacher complains you have not had a correct lesson for a month; why is it?"

Son–"She always kisses me when I get them right."

[3456]

Teacher (in history class)–"Johnny, for what was Louis XIV chiefly responsible?"

Johnny (positively)–"Louis XV, ma'am."

[3457]

The teacher was testing the knowledge of the kindergarten class. Slapping a half dollar on the desk, she said sharply, "What is that?" Instantly, a voice from the back of the row said, "Tails."

[3458]

"Bobby," said the teacher sternly, "do you know that you have broken the eighth Commandment by stealing James's apple?"

"Well," explained Bobby, "I might just as well break the eighth and have the apple as to break the tenth and only covet it."

[3459]

Teacher–"Children, there will be only a half-day of school this morning."

Johnny (in back seat)–"Whoopee! Hurray!"

Teacher–"Silence. We'll have the other half this afternoon."

[3460]

Some pupils were asked at a school examination whether they knew the meaning of the word "Scandal."

One little girl held up her hand, and being told to answer the question she replied:

"Nobody does nothing, and everybody goes telling of it everywhere."

[3461]

"Dear Teacher," wrote an indignant mother, "You must not whack Tommy. He is a delicate child and isn't used to it. We never hit him at home except in self-defense."

[3462]

Junior came to school with the glad news that his father had work again.

"What is he doing?" asked the teacher.

"Oh, he's got a hard job," said the child. "He's got to watch six watchmen."

[3463]

A teacher was making a strenuous effort to get good attendance in her room. Looking over her class one morning, she saw that all except one were in their places.

"This is fine," she exclaimed, "all here except Jimmie Jones; and let us hope that it is something serious which keeps him away."

[3464]

The master, to impress on his pupils the need of thinking before speaking, told them to count fifty before saying anything important, and one hundred if it was very important.

Next day he was speaking, standing with his back to the fire, when he noticed several lips moving rapidly.

Suddenly the whole class shouted: "Ninety-eight, ninety-nine, a hundred. Your coat's on fire, sir!"

[3465]

Aunt–"And how did Jimmy do his history examination?"

Mother–"Oh, not at all well, but there, it wasn't his fault. Why, they asked him things that happened before the poor boy was born!"

[3466]

Teacher–"Johnny, can you tell me what a hypocrite is?"

Johnny–"Yes'm; it's a boy who comes to school these days with a smile on his face."

[3467]

Teacher–"Well, how stupid you are, to be sure! Can't multiply eighty-eight by twenty-five! I'll wager that Charles can do it in less than no time."

Abused Pupil–"I shouldn't be surprised. They say that fools multiply very rapidly these days."

[3468]

The pupil was asked to paraphrase the sentence: "He was bent on seeing her."

He wrote: "The sight of her doubled him up."

[3469]

Student–"Teacher, will you help me with this problem?"

Teacher–"I would, only I don't think it would be right."

[3470]

Teacher–"I have went. That's wrong, isn't it?"

Johnny–"Yes, ma'am."

Teacher–"Why is it wrong?"

Johnny–"Because you ain't went yet."

[3471]

Teacher–"Now, Johnny, tell me what kind of clothes pussy wears."

Johnny–"Clothes?"

Teacher – "Yes — does she wear wool? Does she wear feathers?"

Johnny–"You poor lady. Ain't you never seen a cat?"

[3472]

Teacher–"Johnny, if you had six apples and I asked you for three, how many would you have left?"

Johnny–"Six."

[3473]

Mother–"Why were you kept after school today, Johnny?"

Johnny–"Teacher told us to write an essay on 'The Result of Laziness,' and I turned in a blank sheet of paper."

[3474]

Teacher–"Now, boys, there is a wonderful example in the life of the ant. Every day the ant goes to work and works all day. Every day the ant is busy. And in the end what happens?"

Johnny–"Someone steps on him."

[3475]

An instructor was conducting a science course at a local high school. One of the requirements in the written quiz was "Define a bolt and nut and explain the difference, if any." A girl wrote:

"A bolt is a thing like a stick of hard metal such as iron with a square bunch on one end and a lot of scratching wound around the other end. A nut is similar to the bolt only just the opposite being a hole in a little chunk of iron sawed off short, with wrinkles around the inside of the hole."

The startled professor marked that one with a large "A."

[3476]

At a school-board examination the inspector asked a boy if he could forgive those who had wronged him. "Could you," said the inspector, "forgive a boy, for example, who had insulted or struck you?"

"Y-e-s, sir," replied the lad, very slowly, "I—think—I—could; but," he added, in a much more rapid manner, "I could if he was bigger than I am."

[3477]

The genius of a local man had carried him to big success in business without much aid of education.

He was asked to distribute the prizes at a school, and made the usual speech of good counsel.

"Now, boys," he said, "always remember that education is a great thing. There's nothing like education. Take arithmetic. Through education we learn that twice two makes four, that twice six makes twelve, that seven sevens make— and then there's geography."

[3478]

Teacher–"How old is your grandmother?"

Pupil–"I don't know, but we have had her quite a while."

[3479]

Teacher–"What animal is satisfied with the least nourishment?"

Robert–"The moth, teacher. It eats nothing but holes."

[3480]

It was the first day of school and a teacher was enrolling a group of six-year-olds when she came to one lad whose father had quite a reputation for swearing.

"And what's your name, my little man?" she asked.

"Freddie Smith."

"Do you know your a-b-c's?"

"Hell, no!" the boy replied. "I've only been here ten minutes."

[3481]

Teacher–"Tommy, name five things that contain milk."

Tommy–"Butter an' cheese, ice cream, an' two cows!"

[3482]

A boy wrote a composition on the subject of the Quakers, whom he described as a sect who never quarreled, never got into a fight, never clawed each other and never jawed back. The composition contained a postscript in these words: "Pa's a Quaker, but ma isn't."

[3483]

"What is the difference," asked the teacher in arithmetic, "between one yard and two yards?"

"A fence!" said Tommy.

Then Tommy sat on the ruler six times.

[3484]

"Now, I want Albert to have a thoroughly modern and up-to-date education," said his mother, "including Latin."

"Yes, of course," said the headmaster, "though Latin is, as you know, a dead language."

"Well, all the better. Albert's going to be an undertaker."

[3485]

Very stern parent indeed, "Come here, sir! What is this complaint the schoolmaster has made against you?"

Much injured youth, "It's just nothing at all. You see, Jimmy Hughes bent a pin, and I only just left it on the teacher's chair for him to look at, and he came in without his specs and sat right down on the pin and now he blames me for it!"

[3486]

An inspector, examining a class in religious knowledge, asked the following question of a little girl, intending it for a catch: "What was the difference between Noah's Ark and Joan of Arc?" He was not a little surprised when the child, answering, said: "Noah's Ark was made of wood and Joan of Arc was maid of Orleans."

[3487]

A teacher entered the classroom and noticed a girl student, sitting with her feet in the aisle and chewing gum.

"Ethel," exclaimed the teacher, "take that gum out of your mouth and put your feet in."

[3488]

Teacher–"Correct the sentence, 'Before any damage could be done the fire was put out by the volunteer fire brigade.'"

Boy–"The fire was put out before any damage could be done by the volunteer fire brigade."

[3489]

Teacher–"Johnny, how old is a person who was born in 1902?"

Johnny–"Man or woman?"

[3490]

Teacher–"Johnny, do you know who built the Ark?"

Johnny–"No."

Teacher–"Correct for once in your life."

[3491]

Teacher–"What happened to Lot's wife when she looked back?"

Pupil–"She was turned into a pillar of salt."

Teacher–"And what did Lot do?"

Pupil–"Looked around for a fresh wife."

[3492]

It was the first day of a new term, and the teacher asked a small girl in her class—a new pupil—what her father's name was.

"Daddy," replied the child.

"Yes, I know," said the teacher. "But what does your mother call him?"

"She doesn't call him anything," was the quick answer. "She likes him."

[3493]

The teacher was trying to get her class to understand something about the ether. "What is it that pervades all space," she asked— "something which no wall or door can shut out?"

"The smell of boiled cabbage," spoke up the class wit.

[3494]

Teacher–"Don't you know that punctuation means that you must pause?"

Willie–"'Course I do. An auto driver punctuated his tire in front of our house Sunday and he paused for half an hour."

[3495]

A Gloucester schoolma'am had been telling her pupils something about George Washington, and finally she asked:

"Can any one now tell me which Washington was—a great general or a great admiral?"

The small son of a fisherman raised his hand, and she signaled him to speak.

"He was a great general," said the boy. "I seen a picture of him crossing the Delaware, and no great admiral would put out from shore standing up in a skiff."

[3496]

The teacher was explaining to the class the meaning of the word "recuperate." "Now, Tommy," she said to a small boy, "when your father has worked hard all day, he is tired and worn out, isn't he?"

"Yes, ma'am."

"Then, when night comes, and his work is over for the day, what does he do?"

"That's what mother wants to know," Tommy explained.

[3497]

A teacher asked the class to name the States of the United States. One child responded so promptly and accurately as to bring forth this comment from the teacher: "You did very well—much better than I could have done at your age."

"Yes you could," said the child consolingly, "there were only thirteen then."

[3498]

The little boy came to his mother. "Ma," he said, "I have something to tell you. My teacher kissed me."

"Well, were you a good boy and did you kiss her back?"

"Of course not!" he denied indignantly. "I kissed her face!"

[3499]

A school teacher who had been telling a class of small pupils the story of the discovery of America by Columbus, ended with:

"And all this happened more than 400 years ago."

A little boy, his eyes wide open with wonder, said, after a moment's thought:

"Gee! What a memory you've got."

[3500]

The father was reading the school-report which had just been handed to him by his hopeful son. His brow was wrathful as he read: "English, poor; French, weak; mathematics, fair"; and he gave a glance of disgust at the quaking lad.

"Well, dad," said the son, "it is not as good as it might be, but have you seen that?" And he pointed to the next line, which read: "Health, excellent."

[3501]

Teacher—"Johnny, why does Missouri stand at the head in mule-raising in the United States?"

Johnny—"Because the other end is dangerous."

[3502]

Teacher—"Tommy, if your father could save a dollar a week for four weeks what would he have?"

Tommy—"A radio, a new suit, and a set of furniture."

[3503]

Teacher (during written English test)—"White a sentence with the word 'analysis' in it."

Pupil's Exam Paper—"The teacher told us to look up the word 'analysis' in the dictionary."

[3504]

Teacher—"Now, Tommy, suppose a man gave you $100 to keep for him and then died, what would you do? Would you pray for him?"

Tommy—"No, sir; I would pray for another like him."

[3505]

Teacher (in grammar class)—"Willie, please tell me what it is when I say 'I love, you love, he loves.'"

Willie—"That's one of them triangles where somebody gets shot."

[3506]

"If I cut a beefsteak in two," asked the teacher, "then cut the halves in two, what do I get?"

"Quarters," answered the boy.

"Good. And then again?"

"Eighths."

"Correct. Again?"

"Sixteenths."

"Exactly. And then?"

"Thirty-seconds."

"And once more?"

"Hamburger!" cried the little boy, impatiently.

[3507]

The inspector was paying a hurried visit to a slightly over-crowded school.

"Any abnormal children in your class?" he inquired of one harassed-looking teacher.

"Yes," she replied, with knitted brow, "two of them have good manners."

[3508]

Small Boy–"I say, dad, teacher said this morning that the law of gravity kept us on the earth. Is that right?"

Father–"Yes, my boy, that is correct."

Small Boy–"Well, how did we get on before that law passed?"

[3509]

Son–"Pop, I got into trouble at school today an' it's all your fault."

Pop–"How's that?"

Son–"Remember I asked you how much $500,000 was?"

Pop–"Yes, I remember."

Son–"Well, 'a helluva lot' ain't the right answer."

[3510]

Teacher–"Tell me something about oysters, Johnny."

Johnny–"They are very lazy. They are always found in beds."

[3511]

"I say, dad," said the enthusiastic schoolboy returning home, "we gave a wonderful show at school. Lots of parents came, and though some of them had seen it before, they all had a fine time."

"How do you know?" asked his father.

"Why, they laughed all through the play," the boy replied.

"And what was the play?" the parent asked.

" 'Hamlet,' " said his offspring.

[3512]

Teacher–"Johnny, can you define nonsense?"

Johnny–"Yes, teacher—an elephant hanging over a cliff with his tail tied to a daisy."

[3513]

The teacher was telling her class a long, highly embellished story of Santa Claus, and the mirth of Willie Jones eventually got entirely beyond his control.

"Willie," said the teacher sternly, "what did I whip you for yesterday?"

"Fer lyin'," promptly answered Willie; "an' I was jest wonderin' who was goin' to whip you."

[3514]

Teacher–"Let me hear how far you can count."

Eugene–"One, two, three, four, five, six, seven, eight, nine, ten, Jack, Queen, King."

[3515]

On the last day of school prizes were distributed. When one boy returned home his mother was entertaining callers. "Well, my boy," said one of the callers, "did you get a prize?"

"No," replied the boy, "but I got horrible mention."

[3516]

Teacher–"Robert, if you are always very kind and polite to all your playmates, what will they think of you?"

Robert–"Some of 'em would think they could lick me!"

[3517]

Teacher (brightly)–"As we walk out-of-doors on a cold winter's morning and look about us, what do we see on every hand?"

Class (as a man)–"Gloves!"

[3518]

Teacher–"Now, Robert, what are you doing—learning something?"
Robert–"No, sir; I'm listening to you."

[3519]

Teacher–"Who was the first man?"
Scholar–"Washington; he was first in war, first in—"
Teacher–"No, no; Adam was the first man."
Scholar–"Oh! if you're talking of foreigners, I s'pose he was."

[3520]

Teacher–"If you subtract fourteen from a hundred sixteen, what's the difference?"
Tommy–"Yeh, I think it's a lot of foolishness, too."

[3521]

Rollo's mother was greatly distressed because he had such poor marks in his school work. She scolded, coaxed, even promised him a dime if he would do better. The next day he came running home.

"Oh, mother," he shouted, "I got a hundred!"

"And what did you get a hundred in?"

"In two things," replied Rollo without hesitation. "I got forty in readin' and sixty in spellin'."

[3522]

"Yes," the teacher explained, "quite a number of plants and flowers have the prefix 'dog.' For instance, the dog rose and the dog-violet are well-known. Can you name another?"

There was silence, then a happy look illuminated the face of a boy at the end of the class.

"Please, Miss," he called out, proud of his knowledge, "collie-flowers."

[3523]

It was Timothy's first day at school. He walked up to the teacher's desk and announced: "I ain't got no pencil!"

Shocked at his expression, the teacher exclaimed: "Oh, Timothy, I have no pencil."

A sympathetic look crossed the small boy's face, and he replied: "You ain't, either? Well, we're both in the same fix."

[3524]

Johnny giggled when the teacher read the story of a man who swam a river three times before breakfast.

"You do not doubt that a trained swimmer could do that, do you?" asked the teacher.

"No, sir," replied Johnny, "but I wonder why he didn't make it four times and get back to the side where his clothes were."

[3525]

A teacher asked her class to draw a picture of that which they wished to be when they grew up. The pupils went diligently to work with paper and pencil, some drawing pictures of soldiers, policemen, fine ladies, etc. They all worked hard, except one little girl, who sat quietly holding her pad and pencil in hand.

The teacher, observing her, asked:

"Don't you know what you want to be when you grow up, Anna!"

"Yes, I know," replied the little girl, "but I don't know how to draw it. I want to be married."

[3526]

Teacher–"Johnny, would you like to go to heaven?"
Johnny–"Yes, but mother told me to come right home after school."

[3527]

Teacher–"Dream you are a lark flitting through the welkin."
Jimmy–"I'd rather be an elephant and squirt water through my nose."

[3528]

Johnny—"Papa, would you be glad if I saved a dollar for you?"
Papa–"Certainly, my son."
Johnny–"Well, I saved it for you, all right. You said if I brought a first-class report from my teacher this week you would give me a dollar, and I didn't bring it."

[3529]

Teacher – "What does *unaware* mean?"
Susie–"It's the last thing you take off at night."

[3530]

Teacher–"Willie, did your father whip you for what you did in school yesterday?"
Pupil–"No, ma'am; he said the licking would hurt him more than it would me."
Teacher–"What rot! Your father is too sympathetic."
Pupil–"No, ma'am; but he's got the rheumatism in both arms."

[3531]

Danny, along with many other little lads, went to school for the first time, and like many other little boys' fathers, Danny's father asked him how he liked his teacher.

"All right," was the reply.

"Is your teacher smart?" teasingly persisted the questioner.

"Well, she knows more than I do," admitted Danny.

[3532]

Teacher–"I hope I didn't see you looking at Fred's book, Tommy."
Tommy–"I hope you didn't, too, sir."

[3533]

"I wish," said an anxious mother to her careless son, "I wish you would pay a little attention to your arithmetic."

"Well, I do," was the reply; "I pay as little attention to it as possible."

[3534]

A boy was asked by his history teacher to tell the story of Queen Elizabeth and Sir Walter Raleigh.

"Well," said the movie-nurtured modern boy, "the queen was hopping out of her taxi, and Sir Walter Raleigh spread his coat in front of her and said, 'Step on it, baby.'"

[3535]

There is a precocious six-year-old boy in a Vermont school, who is wonderful on spelling and definition. The other day his teacher asked him to spell matrimony.

"M-a-t-r-i-m-o-n-y," said the youngster, promptly.

"Now define it," said the teacher.

"Well," replied the boy, "I don't exactly know what it means, but I know mother's got enough of it!"

[3536]

Teacher–"Jimmie, what's a peninsula?"
Jimmie–"A rubber neck."
Teacher–"No. It's a neck running out to sea."
Jimmie–"That's a rubber neck, isn't it?"

[3537]

On being asked to write down a definition of "capital punishment," a Glasgow schoolboy submitted this:

"Being locked in an ice-cream or chocolate factory for a week-end would, in my opinion, be capital punishment."

[3538]

A teacher called for sentences using the word "beans."

"My father grows beans," said the bright boy of the class.

"My mother cooks beans," said another pupil.

Then a third popped up: "We are all human beans."

[3539]

"I'm at the head of my class, pa," proudly said Teddy.

"Dear me, son, how did that happen?" cried his father.

"Why the teacher asked us this morning how to pronounce C-h-i-h-u-a-h-u-a, and nobody knew," said Teddy, "but when she got down to me I sneezed and she said that was right."

[3540]

Teacher–"Johnny, who was Anne Boleyn?"

Johnny–"Anne Boleyn was a flat iron."

Teacher–"What on earth do you mean?"

Johnny–"Well, it says here in the history book 'Henry, having disposed of Catherine, pressed his suit with Anne Boleyn.' "

[3541]

Teacher–"What is an octopus?"

Small Boy–"It's an eight-sided cat."

[3542]

A school girl was required to write an essay of two hundred and fifty words about an automobile. She submitted the following:

"My uncle bought an automobile. He was riding in the country when it busted up a hill. I guess this is about fifty words. The other two hundred are what my uncle said when he was walking back to town, but they are not fit for publication."

[3543]

A little girl presented herself for enrolment the first day of school. She looked very much like a true daughter of Italy.

"You are an Italian?" asked the teacher.

"No'm," was the reply.

"But wasn't your father born in Italy?"

"Yes'm."

"And wasn't your mother born in Italy?"

"Yes'm."

"Well, you must be Italian."

"No'm, I'm Irish," she insisted. "I was born in Boston."

[3544]

"Jimmie," said the teacher, "why don't you wash your face? I can see what you had for breakfast this morning."

"What was it?"

"Eggs."

"Wrong, teacher. That was yesterday."

[3545]

Junior came home from his first day of school. "Well, son," greeted the father, "how did you like it?"

"Aw, they asked me my name and I told them. Then they asked me your name, and I told them. Then they asked me where I was born. I didn't want to be a sissy and say a maternity ward, so I just told them Yankee Stadium."

[3546]

The teacher was proud of the results of her labors during the past few weeks. Day after day she trained her pupils in fire drill and at last they seemed perfect.

"Now," she said one day, "what would you do if I told you the building was on fire?"

Like one voice came the children's answer.

A few days later a lecturer visited the school. Said the teacher with a beaming smile: "Now, children, what would you do if I were to tell you that Dr. Wisehead was going to lecture here today?"

Everyone knew!

"We would rise promptly, put away our books, then quietly and without disorder file into the street!"

[3547]

"What is the plural of man, Willie?" asked the teacher.

"Men," answered Willie.

"And, the plural of child?"

"Twins," was the unexpected reply.

[3548]

Teacher–"Who can tell me what the former ruler of Russia was called?"

Class (in unison)–"Tsar."

Teacher–"Correct; and what was his wife called?"

Class–"Tsarina."

Teacher–"What were the Tsar's children called?"

There was a pause, and then a timid voice in the rear piped up: "Tsardines!"

[3549]

Teacher–"Didn't Jimmy Green help you do this sum?"

Willie–"No'm."

Teacher–"Are you sure he didn't help you?"

Willie–"No'm, he didn't help me; he did it all."

[3550]

Teacher–"Sonny, why are you late for school every morning?"

Sonny–"Every time I come to the corner a sign says, 'School—Go Slow.'"

[3551]

"Johnnie," said the teacher reprovingly, "you mis-spelled most of the words in your composition."

"Yes'm," explained Johnnie; "I'm going to be a dialect writer."

[3552]

Little Tommy had spent his first day at school.

"What happened?" he was asked on his return home.

"Nothin'. A woman wanted to know how to spell cat, and I told her."

[3553]

Contrary Mary–"It ain't the school I don't like; it's the principal of the thing."

[3554]

A little boy had been absent from school and the teacher sent him home to get an excuse from his mother. He came running back to school and handed the paper to his teacher. This is what his mother had written.

"Dear Teacher: Please excuse my Tommy from being absent. He got wet in the A. M. and had to be dried in the P. M."

[3555]

"Archimedes," read the schoolboy, aloud, "leaped from his bath shouting, 'Eureka! Eureka!'" "One moment," said the teacher. "What is the meaning of 'Eureka?'" "'Eureka' means I have found it," said the boy. "Very well. What had Archimedes found?" questioned the teacher. The boy hesitated, then ventured, hopefully. "The soap, sir!"

[3556]

Mother–"And did my little pet learn anything at school today?"

The Pet–"I learned two kids better'n to call me mamma's little pet!"

[3557]

A school-teacher asked the pupils to write a short essay and to choose their own subjects.

A little girl sent in the following paper:—

"My subjek is 'Ants.' Ants is of two kinds, insects and lady uncles.

"Sometimes they live in holes and sometimes they crawl into the sugar bole, and sometimes they live with their married sisters.

"That is all I know about ants."

[3558]

Teacher–"What is meant by Hobson's choice?"

Bright Pupil–"Mrs. Hobson, sir."

[3559]

Teacher was giving a lesson on the weather idiosyncrasies of March. "What is it," she asked, "that comes in like a lion and goes out like a lamb?"

And little Julia, in the back row, replied: "Father."

[3560]

"Now, boys," said the teacher, "tell me the signs of the zodiac. You first, Thomas."

"Taurus, the Bull."

"Right! Now, you, Harold, another one."

"Cancer, the Crab."

"Right again. And now it's your turn, Albert."

The boy looked puzzled, hesitated a moment and then blurted out: "Mickey, the Mouse."

[3561]

Pupil–"Do you think it's right to punish folks for things they haven't done?"

Teacher–"Why, of course not, Willie."

Pupil–"Well, I didn't do my home work."

[3562]

"What is cowhide chiefly used for?" a teacher asked his class one day.

A boy raised his hand.

"I know, sir. To keep the cow together, sir," was the reply.

[3563]

Teacher–"And what was Nelson's farewell address?"

Bright Boy–"Heaven, ma'am."

[3564]

After looking over his son's report card, father said:

"Bob, if you had a little more spunk, you'd stand better in your grades. And by the way, do you know what spunk is?"

"Sure, Dad. It's the past participle of spank."

[3565]

Teacher (to little girl learning to write)–"But where is the dot over the i?"

"It's in the pencil yet!"

[3566]

The teacher was telling the class about the discovery of the law of gravity. She said:

"Sir Isaac Newton was sitting on the ground looking at a tree. An apple fell on his head and from that he discovered gravitation. Just think, wasn't that wonderful?"

"Yes'm, an' if he had been settin' in school lookin' at his books, he wouldn't have discovered nothin'," piped a small boy in the last row.

[3567]

The visitor was examining the class.

"Can any little boy tell me what a fish-net is made of?" he inquired.

"A lot of little holes tied together with strings," smiled the never-failing bright boy.

[3568]

Teacher–"What do you call the last teeth we get?"
Pupil–"False teeth."

[3569]

Teacher (warning her pupils against catching cold)–"I had a little brother seven years old, and one day he took his new sled out in the snow. He caught pneumonia, and three days later he died."
Silence for ten minutes.
Voice from the Rear–"Where's his sled?"

[3570]

Grade one was having a lesson on birds.
After some discussion the fact was established that birds eat fruit.
One little girl, however, was unconvinced.
"But, teacher," she asked, raising her hand, "how can the birds open the cans?"

[3571]

Little Albert came home from school with a new book under his arm. "It's a prize, Mother," he said.
"A prize? What for, dear?"
"For natural history. Teacher asked me how many legs an ostrich had and I said three."
"But an ostrich has two legs."
"I know that now, Mother, but the rest of the class said four; so I was nearest."

[3572]

Robert returned from school with his report card for his mother's inspection. "But, dear," she said, "what's the trouble? Why have you such poor grades this month?"
"There's no trouble, mom," was the quick reply. "You know yourself things are always marked down after the holidays."

[3573]

"Now, then, Johnny," said his teacher, "if your father gave you seven cents and your mother gave you six and your uncle gave you four more, what would you have?"
Johnny wrinkled up his forehead and went into silence for the space of several minutes.
"Come, come," said the teacher impatiently. "Surely you can solve a simple little problem like that."
"It ain't a simple problem at all," replied the boy, "I can't make up my mind whether I'd have an ice-cream soda or go to the movies."

[3574]

The teacher was giving a written examination in European geography. One question was:
"Why does the sun never set on the British flag?"
Robert wrote for the answer:
"Because they take it in at night."

[3575]

A teacher had told her class of youngsters that Milton, the poet, was blind. The next day she asked if any of them could remember what Milton's great affliction was.
"Yes'm," replied one little fellow; "he was a poet."

[3576]

Teacher–"How was it your homework sums were all correct?"
Pupil–"Dad is away from home."

[3577]

Little Tommy was asked by his teacher to illustrate the difference between prose and poetry. He pondered awhile and then said, "There was a young man named Rees who went into the sea up to his ankles.
"That's prose," he said, "but if the water had been a few inches higher, it would have been poetry."

[3578]

A teacher examining a class in Natural History, said, "Speaking of sheep, can any of you tell me the names of the male, the female and the offspring?"

"Yes, teacher," replied one youngster, "Ram the Daddy, Dam the Mammy, and Lam' the Kid."

[3579]

Teacher–"Why did Joshua command the sun to stand still?"

Tommy–"I guess it didn't agree with his watch."

[3580]

Teacher (in geography lesson)–"Now can anybody tell me where we find mangoes?"

Knowing Little Boy–"Yes, miss, wherever woman goes."

[3581]

Stern Schoolmaster–"Now, then, young man; tell me how you can prove that the earth is round."

Timid Pupil–"Please, sir, I didn't say it was round."

[3582]

In school a boy was asked this question in physics: "What is the difference between lightning and electricity?"

And he answered: "Well, you don't have to pay for lightning."

[3583]

Teacher–"Tommy, what is one-half of one-tenth?"

Small Boy–"I don't know exactly, teacher, but it can't be very much."

[3584]

Teacher–"What are the products of the West Indies?"

Boy–"I don't know."

"Come, come! Where do you get sugar from?"

"We borrow it from the next-door neighbor."

[3585]

Teacher–"What is the surest way to keep milk from souring."

Dorothy–"Leave it in the cow."

[3586]

Teacher (to bring out the idea of size)–"Mention a difference between an elephant and a flea."

Tommy–"Well, an elephant can have fleas, but a flea can't have elephants."

[3587]

Teacher–"Did your father help you with this problem?"

Willie–"No, I got it wrong myself."

[3588]

During History class the teacher asked, "What happened in 1483?"

"Luther was born," answered a student promptly.

"Correct! What happened in 1487?"

After a long pause, "Luther was four years old."

[3589]

The class had been instructed to write an essay on winter. One child's attempt read as follows:

"In winter it is very cold. Many old people die in winter, and many birds also go to a warmer climate."

[3590]

"Now," said the teacher, impressively, "why should we endeavor to rise by our own efforts?"

"Because," replied Tommy, "there's no knowing when the alarm-clock will go wrong."

[3591]

"Robert," said the teacher, to drive home the lesson which was on charity and kindness, "if I saw a man beating a donkey and stopped him from doing so, what virtue would I be showing?"

"Brotherly love," said Bobby.

[3592]

Teacher–"Tommy, come up here and give me what you've got in your mouth."

Tommy–"I wish I could—it's the toothache."

[3593]

Father (meaningly)–"Who is the laziest member of your class, Tommy?"

Tommy–"I don't know, pa."

Father–"I should think you should know. When all the others are industriously studying or writing their lessons, who is it sits idly in his seat and watches the rest, instead of working himself?"

Tommy–"The teacher."

[3594]

School-teacher (to little boy)–"If a farmer raises 3,700 bushels of wheat and sells it for $1 per bushel, what will he get?"

Little Boy–"An automobile."

[3595]

The teacher was giving the youngsters a mental drill. "Now, Bobby, tell me which month has 28 days in it."

Bobby had forgotten. After a moment he had the answer: "They all have."

[3596]

"Dad, teacher does not know what a horse is."

"Impossible, my boy."

"Well, I drew a horse and showed it to her and she asked me what it was supposed to be."

[3597]

"How many ribs have you, Johnny?" asked the teacher.

"I don't know, ma'am," giggled Johnny, squirming around on one foot; "I'm so awful ticklish I never could count 'em."

[3598]

Teacher–"Every day we breathe oxygen. What do we breathe at night, Willie?"

Willie–"Nitrogen."

[3599]

The teacher, wishing to explain to a little girl the manner in which a lobster casts its shell when he has outgrown it, said: "What do you do when you have outgrown your clothes? You throw them aside, don't you?"

"Oh, no," replied the little one, "we let out the tucks!"

[3600]

Teacher (answering the telephone) –"You say Billy Smith has a bad cold and can't come to school? Who is this speaking?"

Voice (with assumed hoarseness)– "This is my father."

[3601]

Teacher (looking over Teddy's home work)–"I don't see how it's possible for a single person to make so many mistakes."

Teddy (proudly)–"It isn't a single person, teacher. Father helped me."

[3602]

"Now, my little boys and girls," said a teacher, "I want you to be very still—so still that you can hear a pin drop."

For a minute all was still, and a little boy shrieked out,

"Let her drop!"

[3603]

Teacher was telling her class little stories in natural history, and she asked if any one could tell her what a ground-hog was. Up went a little hand, waving frantically.

"Well, Carl, you may tell us what a ground-hog is."

"Please, ma'am, it's a sausage."

[3604]

Teacher–"Correct this sentence: 'It was me that spilt the ink.' "

Pupil–"It wasn't me that spilt the ink."

[3605]

Teacher–"Robert, explain what are the functions of the skin."

Bobby–"The chief function of the skin is to keep us from looking raw."

[3606]

Teacher–"When was Rome built?"

Percy–"At night."

Teacher–"Who told you that?"

Percy–"You did. You said Rome wasn't built in a day."

[3607]

A school inspector said to a pretty teacher:

"Do you teach observation?"

"Yes."

"Then I will test the class. Now, children, shut your eyes and sit still." The inspector made a slow, chirping sort of noise and followed with: "Now, children, what did I do?"

One little boy piped out: "Kissed teacher."

[3608]

A school-teacher had found her class of boys reluctant in their writing of English compositions. At last she conceived a great idea to stimulate their interest—to write an account of a ball game.

It seemed that she was successful. With one exception, the boys threw themselves at the task and evolved youthful masterpieces. The backward one chewed reluctantly at his pen and was then struck by a burst of genius. When the teacher opened his paper, it read:

"Rain, no game."

[3609]

Little Elsie had been naughty in school. By way of punishment, she was directed by the teacher to remain in her seat after the session until she had written an original composition containing not less than fifty words. In a surprisingly short space of time, she offered the following, and was duly excused:

"I lost my kitty, and I went out and called, Come, kitty."

[3610]

Teacher–"How many bones have you in your body."

Willie–"Nine hundred."

Teacher–"That's a good many more than I have."

Willie–"Yeah, but I had sardines for lunch."

SUNDAY SCHOOL

[3611]

The teacher of a Sunday school class explained the story of Elijah and the prophets of Baal—how Elijah built the altar, put wood upon it, and cut the bullock in pieces and laid them on the altar.

"And then," she said, "he commanded the people to fill four barrels with water and pour it over the altar, and they did this four times. Now, can anyone tell why this water was poured over the bullock on the altar?"

"To make the gravy!" came a prompt reply.

[3612]

Teacher, wishing to arouse the interest of her Sunday School class, asked them to write down the names of their favorite hymns.

All the scholars bent their heads over pencil and paper for a few minutes, and handed in their slips. All except Jane.

"Come, Jane," said the teacher, "write down the name of your favorite hymn and bring me the paper."

Jane wrote, and with downcast eyes and flaming cheeks, handed the teacher a slip of paper bearing the words "Willie Smith."

[3613]

"What is the rod of affliction?" the Sunday-school teacher asked.

"Goldenrod," shouted the little girl whose mother has hay-fever every fall.

[3614]

A Sunday-school class had been carefully drilled for the coming of the district superintendent. Johnnie was to answer "God" when the question "Who made you?" was propounded. Jimmie was to pipe up "Out of the dust of the earth" in answer to the second question.

"Who made you?" asked the district superintendent when the great day of the review arrived. Again the opening question. Still no answer.

"Please, sir," spoke up a freckled-faced youngster, "the little boy God made is home with the measles."

[3615]

Little girl, all excitement after Sunday-school, says to her mother:

"Oh, Mother, we've been learning the books of the Bible and there's an Amos in it but no Andy!"

[3616]

"Billy," asked a Sunday-school teacher, "what did the Israelites do after they crossed the Red Sea?"

"I dunno, but I guess they dried themselves."

[3617]

"This morning," said the teacher of an early Sunday school class, "the subject of the lesson is Ruth the gleaner. Who can tell me anything about Ruth?"

A small boy raised his hand.

"Well, Willie, what do you know about Ruth?" said the teacher encouragingly. And Willie piped out in a shrill little voice: "He cleaned up sixty home runs in one season."

[3618]

"I'm very much afraid I'll not meet you in heaven, Johnny," said a Sunday-school teacher to a mischievous pupil.

"Why," exclaimed the incorrigible youth, "what have you been doing now?"

[3619]

Asked at a scripture examination to describe the sufferings of Job, a little girl wrote:

"Job had one trouble after another. First he lost his cattle, then he lost his children, and then he had to go and live in the desert with his wife."

[3620]

The Sunday school class was reviewing the wonderful lesson of Jacob when he used a stone for a pillow and had the dream of the angels ascending and descending on the ladder above him. The young lady teacher asked if there were any questions.

"If the lovely angels had wings,"

asked a twelve-year-old, "whaddey have to climb up and down the old ladder for?"

"Ah-hem!" said the teacher, "are there any more questions?"

[3621]
Sunday School Teacher—"Johnny, what can you tell me about Aaron?"
Johnny—"His name was the first in the telephone book."

[3622]
"Freddie," said the Sunday school teacher, "can you tell me what we must do before we can expect forgiveness of sin?"

"Yes, sir," replied the boy. "We must sin."

[3623]
Minister—"And what does your mother do for you when you've been a good girl?"
Margery—"She lets me stay home from church."

[3624]
Bobbie—"Mother I don't mind going to Sunday school any other day, but it just spoils Sunday."

[3625]
Little six-year-old Harry was asked by his Sunday-school teacher:
"And, Harry, what are you going to give your darling little brother for Christmas this year?"

"I dunno," said Harry; "I gave him the measles last year."

[3626]
Sunday School Teacher—"Now, Johnny, what do you think a land flowing with milk and honey would be like?"
Johnny—"Sticky!"

[3627]
Clergyman (pinching a little boy's bare leg)—"Who's got nice, round chubby legs?"
Little Boy—"Mamma."

[3628]
A Sunday-School visitor asked the children what he should talk about, and got an immediate answer: "Talk about three minutes."

[3629]
A Sunday-school teacher had been telling her class of little boys about crowns of glory and heavenly rewards for good people.

"Now, tell me," she said at the close of the lesson, "who will get the biggest crown?"

There was silence for a minute or two, then a bright little chap piped out:

"Him wot's got t' biggest 'ead."

[3630]
Dora had returned from Sunday School where she had been for the first time.

"What did my little daughter learn this morning?" asked her father.

"That I am a child of Satan," was the beaming reply.

[3631]
"Johnny, where do you think God is this morning?" asked the Sunday School teacher.

"In our bathroom," was the reply.

"What on earth makes you say that?" asked the amazed teacher.

" 'Cause just before I left I heard pa say, 'My Lord! How long are you going to be in there?' "

[3632]
"What do you like most in the church, Willie?" asked his mother on their way home from the services.

"I like best where they pass around the money. I only got a dime this time though." Turning to his father, Willie asked, "How much did you get, dad?"

[3633]

Sunday School Teacher–"My word! Doesn't that little boy swear terribly?"

Backslider–"Yes'm, he sure do. He knows the words, but he don't put no expression in them."

[3634]

Sunday School Teacher–"Willie, do you know what becomes of boys who use bad language when they're playing marbles?"

Willie–"Yes, miss. They grow up and play golf."

[3635]

A clerical gentleman in examing the Sunday School, asked the class before him if any could tell him anything about the apostle Peter. A little girl raised her hand much to the gratification of her examiner.

"Come up here, my little girl," said he; "I am glad you remember your Bible lesson so well. Now tell the other boys and girls what you know about Peter."

The little girl was quite willing, and commenced: "Peter, Peter, punkin-eater, had a wife and couldn't keep her; so he put her in a—" but before she could get a punkin shell the school was in a roar.

[3636]

Sunday School Teacher–"Can you tell something about Good Friday, James?"

James–"Yes'm; he was the fellow that did the housework for Robinson Crusoe."

[3637]

Sunday School Teacher–"Why in your prayers do you only ask for your daily bread instead of asking enough for a week?"

Boy–"So we can get it fresh every day."

[3638]

The pastor was examining one of the younger classes, and asked the question: "What are the sins of omission?" After a little silence one young lady offered:

"Please, sir, they're sins we ought to have committed, and haven't."

[3639]

Preacher–"Do you say your prayers at night, little boy?"

Jimmy–"Yes, sir."

Preacher–"And do you always say them in the morning, too?"

Jimmy–"No, sir. I ain't scared in the daytime."

[3640]

A little girl attending an Episcopal Church for the first time, was amazed to see all kneel suddenly. She asked her mother what they were going to do. Her mother replied, "Hush, they're going to say their prayers."

"What with all their clothes on?"

[3641]

"Can any child give me a Commandment with only four words in it?" asked the Sunday School teacher.

A hand was raised immediately. "You may answer, Robert," said the teacher.

"Keep off the grass!"

[3642]

"Well, Bobby," said the minister to the small son of one of his deacons, "what is the news?"

"Popper's got a new set of false teeth."

"Indeed," said the minister restraining a desire to laugh, "and what will he do with the old set?"

"Oh, I suppose," replied Bobby, "they'll cut 'em down and make me wear 'em."

[3643]

Sunday School Teacher—"Now, Tommy, what happens to a man who never thinks of his soul, but only of his body?"

Tommy—"Please, teacher, he gets fat."

[3644]

Sunday-School Teacher—"Now, Charlie, what can you tell me about Goliath?"

Charlie—"Goliath was the man David rocked to sleep."

[3645]

"Sometimes there are rude boys in Sunday School who giggle and smile at little girls, and sometimes the little girls smile at them, but I hope my little girl does not behave like that."

Susie—"No, indeed, grandma. I always stick out my tongue at them."

[3646]

At the Sunday school party:

Johnny (to Willie opposite)—"Pass the cake."

Teacher—"If——if——"

Johnny—"If he don't, I'll kick his shins for him."

[3647]

Parson—"Do you know where bad little girls go?"

Nellie—"Of course I do!"

Parson—"Where do they go?"

Nellie—"They go down to the railroad station to see the traveling salesmen come in."

[3648]

Rodney (after being to Sunday School)—"Say, dad, our lesson told about the evil spirits entering the swine."

Father—"Yes, my son. What do you wish to know?"

Rodney—"Was that the way they got the first deviled ham?"

[3649]

"So you attend Sunday School regularly?" asked the minister of little Betty.

"Oh, yes, sir," said little Betty.

"And you know your Bible?"

"Oh, yes, sir."

"Could you, perhaps, tell me something that is in it?"

"I could tell you everything that's in it."

"Indeed." And the minister smiled. "Do tell me, then."

"Sister's steady's snapshots are in it," said little Betty promptly, "and ma's recipe for vanishin' cream is in it, and a lock of my hair, cut off when I was a baby is in it, and the pawn ticket for pa's watch is in it."

[3650]

Bessie had a new dime to invest in an ice cream soda.

"Why don't you give your dime to the missions?" said the minister, who was calling.

"I thought about that," said Bessie, "but I think I'll buy the ice cream and let the druggist give it to the missions."

[3651]

The little daughter of a newspaper editor came back from Sunday School with an illustrated card in her hand.

"What's that you have there, little one?" the editor asked.

"Oh," said the child, "just an ad about heaven."

[3652]

"Did you behave in church?" asked an interested relative when Junior returned from the service.

"Course I did," replied Junior. "I heard the lady back of us say she never saw a child behave so."

[3653]

The rector had invited the village boys to the rectory for a strawberry tea. After they had finished he, seeking to point the moral, said: "Now, boys, wasn't that nicer than breaking into my garden and helping yourselves?"

"Oh, yes," chorused the boys.

"And why was it nicer?" he asked a chubby-faced boy.

"Because, sir," was the reply, "we shouldn't have had any sugar and cream with them."

[3654]

"Well, my son, what did you learn in Sunday School today?"

"We learned all about a cross-eyed bear."

"About a what?"

"Yes, sir, named Gladly. We learned a song about him: all about 'Gladly, the cross I'd bear.' "

[3655]

Clergyman (concluding story)—"And now, children, would you like to ask any questions?"

Bobby – "Yes, sir. Please, how do you get into your collar?"

[3656]

"Teacher?"

"Well, Johnny?"

"Is there a Christian flea?"

"What on earth ever put that idea into your head?"

"The preacher read it today from the Bible: 'The wicked flee, when no man pursueth.' "

"Why, Johnny, that means that the wicked men flee."

"Oh. Then is there a wicked woman flea?"

"No, no. It means that the wicked flee, runs away."

"Why do they run?"

"Who?"

"The wicked fleas."

"No, no! Don't you see? The wicked man runs away when no man is after him."

"Oh. Is there a woman after him?"

"Johnny, we have no more time. Children, go home!"

[3657]

"Just think, children," said the missionary, "in Africa there are six million square miles where little boys and girls have no Sunday School. Now, what should we all strive to save money for?"

"To go to Africa!" cried a chorus of cheery voices.

[3658]

The title of the Sunday school lesson was, "The Rich Young Man," and the golden text was, "One thing thou lackest." The teacher asked a little tot to repeat the two, and looking earnestly into the young lady's face, the child said, "One thing thou lackest — a rich young man."

[3659]

"Thanks very much," said the minister, as little Tommy handed up his offering for the harvest festival; "I must call round this afternoon and thank your mother for these eight beautiful apples."

"P-please, sir," stammered Tommy, "would you m-mind thanking her for t-twelve apples?"

[3660]

Little Tommy came home from Sunday school with the distressing news that he had lost the penny given him for the collection.

"But that is three Sundays running you have lost your penny," his mother complained.

"Well," replied Tommy, "I must win sooner or later."

[3661]
Sunday School Teacher–"Now, Jimmy, I want you to memorize to-day's motto, 'It is more blessed to give than to receive.'"
Jimmy–"Yes'm, but I know it now. My father says he has always used that as his motto in his business."
Teacher – "Oh, how noble of him! And what is his business?"
Jimmy – "He's a prize-fighter, ma'am."

[3662]
In reply to the query, "Who brought gifts to the Infant Jesus?" which appeared on the Scripture examination paper of a Sunday school, one pupil appended: "Mr. Frankincense and Mr. Myrrh."

[3663]
Sunday School Teacher – "Robert, who were the Pharisees?"
Bobby–"The Pharisees were people who fasted in public and in secret devoured widows' houses."

[3664]
A Sunday school teacher was explaining the omnipresence of the Deity to his scholars, and ended by telling them that he was everywhere.
Whereupon a red-headed boy asked: "Is he in my pocket?"
The teacher replied that the question was rather profane but he would answer. "Yes, he is everywhere."
"I've got you there," said the boy, "I ain't got no pocket."

[3665]
Two little girls were comparing progress in catechism study. "I've got to original sin," said one. "How far have you got?"
"Me? Oh, I'm way beyond redemption," said the other.

[3666]
A little four-year-old suddenly lost interest in Sunday school. She had enjoyed so much learning about Moses that her mother could not understand the change of attitude.
"Why don't you want to go, daughter?" she asked.
"Oh," was the astonishing reply, "I don't 'ike to go to Sunday school since Moses died."

[3667]
Sunday School Teacher (to pupil)– "Now, my little man, can you explain the cause of Adam's fall?"
Little Man (emphatically)–"Yes, sir; 'cause he hadn't any ashes to throw on the sidewalk."

[3668]
"Moses had indigestion like you have, mother," announced small Elinor at the Sunday dinner table.
"Why, what makes you think so?" questioned her astonished mother.
"Because our Sunday School teacher said, 'God gave Moses two tablets.'"

[3669]
"When Lot's wife looked back," said the Sunday school teacher, "what happened to her?"
"She was transmuted into chloride of sodium," answered the boy with the goggles.

[3670]
Little Raymond returned home from Sunday school in a very joyous mood. "Oh, mother," he exclaimed, "the teacher said something awfully nice about me in his prayer this morning!"
"Isn't that lovely! What did he say, pet?" questioned the mother.
"He said, 'O Lord, we thank thee for our food and Raymond.'"

[3671]

A lady asked a pupil of a Sunday school, "what was the sin of the Pharisees?"

"Eating camels, ma'am," was the quick reply.

She had read that the Pharisees "strained at gnats and swallowed camels."

[3672]

A visiting speaker to a Sunday school was called upon to address the children. Thinking to be facetious, he asked this question:

"What would you do before so many bright boys and girls who expected a speech from you, if you had nothing to say?"

"I'd keep quiet," replied a small boy.

[3673]

The Sunday School Teacher asked: "When did Moses live?"

After the silence had become painful she ordered: "Open your Old Testaments. What does it say there?"

A boy answered: "Moses, 4000."

"Now," said the teacher, "why didn't you know when Moses lived?"

"Well," replied the boy, "I thought it was his telephone number."

[3674]

The Sunday school teacher addressed his class of small boys.

"Who led the children of Israel into Canaan?"

There was no reply volunteered.

"That little boy on the end seat," said the teacher. "You answer the question. Who led the children of Israel into Canaan?"

"It wasn't me, teacher, 'cause I just moved here last week."

[3675]

Tommy went to church, but, as a rule, he did not pay particularly close attention to the sermon. One Sunday, however, he must have been more attentive than usual— the Sunday that the minister preached on the creation and the origin of Eve after Adam had a pain in his side.

During the next week, after running hard in a game of tag, Tommy was seized with a spasm of pain and came running into the house with one hand clasped against his lower ribs.

"Oh, mama!" he called. "I got a pain! You don't suppose I'm going to have a wife, do you?"

[3676]

"How many of you boys," asked the Sunday school superintendent, "can bring two other boys next Sunday?"

There was no response until a new recruit raised his hand hesitatingly.

"Well, William?"

"I can't bring two, but there's one little feller I can lick, and I'll do my damnedest to bring him."

[3677]

"Now, children," said the Sunday school teacher, "I have told you the story of Jonah and the whale. Willie, you may tell me what this story teaches."

"Yes'm," said Willie, the bright-eyed son of the pastor; "it teaches that you can't keep a good man down."

[3678]

Parson—"Do you know where little boys go when they smoke?"

Boys—"Yep; up the alley."

SERVANTS

[3679]

"Did the children behave when you bathed them?" inquired the mistress of the new French nurse, when she returned home from the card party.

"All but ze biggest boy, and how he fight and kick before I get him in ze water," replied the nurse.

"Which biggest boy? We've only one boy, Freddy, and he's not two years old."

"Eet is not leetle Freddy, I mean. Eet is ze big boy with glasses and curly hair."

"Good gracious! That's not my boy, that's my husband."

[3680]

"I want a man to do odd jobs about the house, run on errands, one who never answers back and is always ready to do my bidding," explained a lady to an applicant for a post in the household.

"You're looking for a husband, ma'am, not a servant!" said the seeker for work.

[3681]

Mistress–"Bridget, I'm tired of your carelessness. Only look at that dust on the furniture. It's six weeks old at the very least."

Bridget–"Shure, it's no fault av moine. Oi've been here only t'ree weeks."

[3682]

Stern Mistress (to maid)–"You are discharged, Perkins, for allowing the master to kiss you. What sort of reference do you expect from me after that?"

Pretty Maid–"Well, you might at least say that I tried to please every one, madam."

[3683]

Maid (having dropped expensive vase)–"Those colored bits will look lovely in the rock garden, ma'am."

[3684]

"And you have had the same servant for two years?"

"Yes," replied Mr. Crosslots. "She says she doesn't believe in changing after she has gone to the trouble of teaching a family her ways."

[3685]

"Look here," said the worried householder to the new maid, "why did you tell your mistress what time I came home last night when I asked you not to?"

"I didn't," replied the maid. "She asked me what time you got in, and I told her I was too busy cooking the breakfast to look at the clock."

[3686]

Nurse–"I lost sight of the child, ma'am."

Ma'am–"Good gracious! Why didn't you speak to a policeman?"

"I was speaking to one at the time, ma'am."

[3687]

Mrs. A.–"Shall I ask the cook for references?"

Mr. A.–"References don't mean much. Get her to submit samples."

[3688]

Lady (engaging new maid)–"And what denomination are you?"

Maid–"Well, mum, mother goes to the Baptist church and father to the Methodist, but speaking for myself, I'm radio."

[3689]

"Only cheese for lunch?"

"Yes, the cutlets caught fire and it spread to the apple tart, so I had to take the soup to put it out."

[3690]

"So you think you would be a suitable valet for me," said the old man to the applicant. "I must remind you that I'm pretty much of a wreck. I have a glass eye, a cork leg, an artificial arm that needs looking after, not to mention a wig and false teeth."

"That would be all right, sir," responded the other. "I've had plenty of practise. You see, I once worked in the assembly-room of a big motor concern."

[3691]

Mistress (severely)–"If this occurs again, Jane, I shall be compelled to get another servant."

Jane–"I wish you would, mum, there's quite enough work for two of us."

[3692]

"How is it the biscuits were so hard this morning, Mandy?"

"I'se sorry, ma'am, but Ah ain't feeling right pert this mawnin'. My system's kinda run down, so I eat the only yeast cake there was in the house."

[3693]

Mistress (explaining routine to new cook)–"Now, my husband always goes to his club on Wednesday evenings."

Cook–"I understand, ma'am. So he won't want no breakfast on Thursdays."

[3694]

Mistress–"No mail this morning?"

Maid–"No, the postman and the housemaid have quarreled."

[3695]

New Maid–"How do I announce dinner? Do I say 'Dinner is ready' or 'Dinner is served'?"

Mistress–"If it is like it was yesterday, just say 'Dinner is burnt.'"

[3696]

"Now, Lena," the mistress asked her new Swedish servant, "are you a *good* cook?"

"Ya-as, 'm, I tank so," said the girl, with perfect naïveté, "if you vill not try to help me."

[3697]

Valet–"Sir, wake up, wake up."

Master–"What is the idea?"

Valet–"It's time for your sleeping tablets."

[3698]

The maid had been to the pictures, and on her return her employer asked, "Did you enjoy it?"

"Oh, yes," said she. "It was lovely, Mum!"

"And what was the picture?"

The maid thought for a moment, then said: "I don't know, Mum . . . I went with my young man!"

[3699]

Mistress–"Whose was that man's voice I heard in the kitchen?"

Maid–"Oh—'m—my brother—'m."

Mistress–"What is his name?"

Maid–"Er—I think it's Herbert, 'm."

[3700]

Mrs. Smithers was explaining the routine to the new cook.

"We lunch precisely at one on Wednesday," she said, "as on that day we always go for a spin in the car at two."

"Very good, mum," replied the cook, "but I shall have to leave the washin' up till we gets back again!"

[3701]

Mistress–"Do you think you will settle down here? You've left so many situations."

Maid–"Yes, m'm. But remember I didn't leave any of them voluntarily."

[3702]

The suburban husband was about to leave his home for the station when his wife detained him.

"John," she said, "I wish you'd go out to the kitchen and give Bridget a good talking to before you go to business."

"How's that?" he asked. "I thought you were very satisfied with her."

"So I am, dear," replied his wife; "but she's beating some carpets for me this morning, and she does it better when she's angry."

[3703]

"You have an admirable cook, yet you are always growling about her to your friends."

"Do you suppose I want her lured away?"

[3704]

Mistress (discovering butler helping himself from cellarette)—"Robert, I am surprised."

Butler—"So am I, ma'am. I thought you was out."

[3705]

Eliza," said a friend of the family to the old colored washerwoman, "have you seen Miss Edith's fiancé?"

"No, ma'am," she answered, "it ain't been in the wash yet."

[3706]

Two nursemaids were wheeling their infant charges in the park when one asked the other:

"Are you going to the dance to-morrow afternoon?"

"I am afraid not."

"What! And you so fond of dancing!"

"I'd love to go, but to tell you the truth, I am afraid to leave the baby with its mother."

[3707]

Mistress—"I can see a spider web in the corner, Ethel! To what do you attribute that?"

Maid—"To a spider, ma'am."

[3708]

It was the duty of Janet, the maid, to tie up Jeff, the house dog, every night before she retired. One night she failed in her duty, and next morning found Jeff loose.

He had played havoc with the contents of the larder. When the mistress heard the news, she inquired:

"Has he eaten much, Janet?"

"Every blessed thing," replied the maid, "except the dog biscuits!"

[3709]

A gentleman, talking with his gardener, expressed his admiration at the rapid growth of the trees.

"Why, yes, sir," says the man; "please remember that they have nothing else to do."

[3710]

"We are celebrating our maid's jubilee to-day."

"Has she been with you twenty-five years?"

"No, she is the twenty-fifth we have had this year."

[3711]

"Have you been touching the barometer, Jane?"

"Yes'm. It's my night out, so I set it for 'fine'."

[3712]

Mistress—"And how is your newly married daughter getting on, Mrs. Simpkins?"

Cook—"Oh, nicely, thank you, ma'am. She finds her husband a bit dull; but then, as I tells her, the good ones are dull."

[3713]

Teacher–"Leander swam the Hellespont every night to see Hero. That is the strongest proof of love we have."

Pupil–"I know a better."

"What is that?"

"Our maid loves the postman, so she writes a letter to herself every night to make sure he will come the next day."

[3714]

"Of course you, too, must often change cooks?"

"Oh, don't speak of it! We suffer from such a continual going and coming that we've decided this winter to equip our kitchen with revolving doors."

[3715]

Mistress (to departing maid who has asked for a reference)–"Of course, Norah, I shall have to tell Mrs. Smith of your uncontrollable temper."

Norah–"Thank you very much, Mum. It'll p'raps make 'er mind 'er P's and Q's."

[3716]

Mistress–"I shall be very lonely, Bridget, if you leave me."

Bridget–"Don't worry, mum. I'll not go until ye have a houseful of company."

[3717]

Husband–"From the glimpse I had of her this morning I rather like our new cook. There seems to be plenty of go about her."

Wife–"Yes, she's gone."

[3718]

"I hope you are habitually truthful, Norah."

"I am on me own account, mum. I only tells lies to the callers for the family."

[3719]

Husband (to wife)–"Who is that strange woman I just saw in our kitchen?"

Wife–"Sh-h-h! That's the cook-of-the-month."

[3720]

Visitor–"Why does your servant go about the house with her hat on?"

Mistress–"Oh, she's a new girl. She only came this morning, and hasn't yet made up her mind whether she'll stay."

[3721]

The hired girl had been sent down to the brook to fetch a pail of water, but stood gazing at the flowing stream apparently lost in thought.

"What's she waiting for?" asked her mistress, who was watching.

"Dunno," wearily replied her husband. "Perhaps she hasn't seen a pailful she likes yet."

[3722]

Mistress–"Have you finished cleaning the brass ornaments yet?"

Maid (sore about something)–"Yes, ma'am—all except your rings and bracelets."

[3723]

"You have got a new servant, I see, Mrs. Newlywed?"

"Yes; I got her about a week ago."

"How do you like her?"

"Very much indeed. She lets me do almost as I like about the house."

[3724]

Mrs. O'Brien–"And so yez wants to get a cook?"

Mrs. Gotcash–"Yes, that is what I came here for."

Mrs. O'Brien–"Well, have yez any riferinces."

[3725]

"Jane," said a lady to her servant, "you have broken more than your wages amount to. What can be done to prevent this?"

"I really don't know, mum," said Jane, "unless you raise my wages."

[3726]

Mistress (to new maid)–"Be careful when you dust these pictures, Mary; they are all Old Masters."

Maid–"Good gracious! Who'd ever think you'd been married all these times, mum!"

[3727]

Mary, in applying for a position, was asked if she had any references.

"Yes, ma'am. Here it is."

The letter read: "The bearer of this letter is leaving me after one month's work. I am perfectly satisfied."

[3728]

The energetic woman addressed her hired girl in a discouraged tone:

"Here it is Monday morning and tomorrow will be Tuesday, and the next day Wednesday—the whole week half gone, and nothing done yit!"

[3729]

Mistress–"You must exercise a little will power with him, nurse."

Nurse–"I do try to, mum, but you don't know his won't power."

[3730]

The new maid was talkative, and related some of her experiences in service.

"You seem to have had a good many situations," was the lady's comment as the girl paused. "How many different mistresses have you had, all told?"

"Fifteen, all told," the maid declared promptly; "yes, mum, all told eggzactly what I thought of them."

[3731]

Maid–"You know that old vase, mum, you said 'ad bin' handed down from generation to generation?"

Mistress (anxiously)–"Yes?"

"Well, this generation 'as dropped it!"

[3732]

Mistress (to new servant)–"Why, Bridget, this is the third time I've had to tell you about the finger-bowls. Didn't the lady you last worked for have them on the table?"

Bridget–"No, mum, her friends always washed their hands before they came."

[3733]

Mistress–"Bridget, where did you get that dreadful eye."

Bridget–"Me brother gave it to me, mum; and what'll the neighbors say? Me with an eye like that and no husband."

[3734]

Mistress (to butler)–"Why is it, John, every time I come home I find you sleeping?"

"Well, ma'am, it's this way: I don't like to be a-doing *nothing*."

[3735]

Mistress–"But aren't you rather short for a nursemaid?"

Nursemaid–"Quite the opposite, madame. Supposing I drop a baby, it doesn't have so far to fall."

[3736]

"Can you serve company?" asked the housewife when she was hiring the servant.

"Yes, mum; both ways."

"What do you mean?" asked the puzzled one.

"So's they'll come again, or stay away."

[3737]

A woman desperately seeking a good servant interviewed a husky girl in an employment office, who was a recent importation from Lapland. The dialogue was as follows:
"Can you do fancy cooking?"
"Naw."
"Can you do plain cooking?"
"Naw."
"Can you sew?"
"Naw."
"Can you do general housework?"
"Naw."
"Make the beds, wash the dishes?"
"Naw."
"Well," cried the woman in puzzled exasperation, "what can you do?"
"I milk reindeer."

[3738]

Mistress–"Why didn't you answer the telephone?"
New Maid–"I was afraid, Ma'am."
Mistress–"Then why didn't you call me, you simpleton?"
New Maid–"I wouldn't dare to call you anything like that, Ma'am."

[3739]

Neurich–"Be sure you get a good-looking nurse for baby."
Mrs. Neurich–"Why?"
Neurich–"I want him to have police protection."

[3740]

The lady wished her servant to be pleased with her new place. "You'll have a very easy time of it here," she said sweetly, "as we have no children to annoy you."

"Oh," said the colored girl generously, "I'se very fond of chilluns, so don't restrict yo'se'f on my account, miss."

[3741]

Mistress (to new maid)–"Regarding your evenings out, I'm willing to meet you halfway."
Maid–"Oh, that's all right. I don't mind coming home in the dark."

[3742]

The Mistress–"My last maid was too familiar with the policeman. I hope I can trust you?"
The Maid–"Oh, yes, madam, I can't bear them. I've been brought up to hate the very sight of them. Pa's a burglar."

[3743]

Mistress (to new maid)–"Now, Norah, I always take my bath at 9 every morning."
" 'Sall right, mam, it won't interfere with me a bit. I'm never ready fer mine b'fore 10."

[3744]

Mistress–"Mary, these balusters seem always dusty. I was at Mrs. Brown's to-day, and her stair rails are clean and as smooth as glass."
Servant–"Yes, ma'am, but she has three small boys."

[3745]

Two foreign-looking girls, evidently domestics, were discussing their employers. "The missus is fine," said one, "but her husband is very cross."
"He is?"
"Yeah. But I get even with him. Every time he scolds me, I put starch in his handkerchiefs."

[3746]

"I want a very careful chauffeur —one who doesn't take the slightest risks," warned the would-be employer.
"I'm your man, sir," answered the applicant. "Can I have my salary in advance?"

[3747]

Mistress—"If my husband should bring some friends home to dinner tonight, are you prepared?"

Cook—"Yes, ma'am. My bag is already packed."

[3748]

Wife (at desk)—"I've been asked for a reference for our last maid. I've said she's lazy, unpunctual and impertinent. Now can I add anything in her favor?"

Husband—"You might say that she's got a good appetite and sleeps well."

[3749]

Mrs. Brown's husband was a writer, and he pounded the typewriter at home, turning out manuscripts of one kind and another, which he sold for sufficient recompense to enable the Browns to afford a maid. The new girl had been working only a little over a week, however, when she came to her mistress, and said:

"You pay me four dollars a week, mum."

"Yes, Sally," Mrs. Brown acknowledged. "And I can't afford to pay you any more than that."

"I know, mum," Sally agreed, glancing back at the room where Mr. Brown was reading up on a subject about which he was preparing to write an article. "But I want to be fair, mum. I'm willin' to work for only three dollars till your husband gets a job."

[3750]

"I don't want to complain, cook," said her mistress, "but that friend who comes to see you stays much too late. I couldn't get to sleep last night because of her laughter."

"I'm sorry, ma'am," replied the cook. "I was telling her about that time you tried to make a cake."

[3751]

Mistress (to new maid)—"Now, when you wait on the guests at dinner, I want you to be very careful not to spill anything."

Maid—"Don't worry. I won't say a word."

[3752]

Woman—"Nora, did you sweep behind that door?"

The Maid—"Yes, mum. I sweeps everything behind the door."

[3753]

Mistress—"Can you explain why it is, Mary, that every time I come into this kitchen I find you reading?"

New Maid—"It must be those rubber heels of yours, mum."

[3754]

Mary—"Please, madam, I've knocked the marble clock off the side-board."

Madam—"Has it stopped?"

Mary—"No, madam, it's gone straight through to the basement."

[3755]

"Have you given the goldfish fresh water?"

"No ma'am, they ain't finished the water I gave them yesterday yet."

[3756]

Mistress—"You will cut and roll the lawn, weed the gravel path, pot some chrysanthemums, plant all those rose-bushes, clean out the greenhouse, and see to the heating apparatus, and—"

New Gardener—"Excuse me, madam, but is this a day's work or a five-year plan?"

[3757]

Maid—"I'm sorry, but she said to tell you that she is not at home."

Mr. Jones—"Oh, that's all right, just tell her that I'm glad I didn't come."

[3758]

Husband (at dinner)–"By George, this is a regular banquet. Finest spread I've sat down to in an age. What's up? Do you expect company?"

Wife–"No, but I think the cook does."

[3759]

"Really, Mary, you might at least see that the plates are clean."

"Well, mum, I owns to them thumb marks, but that dried mustard was there afore I come."

[3760]

Mistress (reading new maid's references)–"Six places in a year?"

Maid–"Yes, ma'am. The days of the good mistress are over."

[3761]

"Is Mrs. Amos a well informed woman?"

"Yes, indeed—her cook has lived with all the other families in the neighborhood!"

[3762]

A wealthy society lady had just engaged a new maid and was instructing her in the duties of waiting on the table.

"At dinner, Mary," she explained, "you must remember always to serve from the left and take the plates from the right. Is that clear?"

"Yes, ma'am," answered the girl condescendingly. "What's the matter, superstitious or something?"

[3763]

First Maid (bragging about a party given the day before by her mistress)–"And they all came in limousines, and had on the grandest clothes, and wore the biggest diamonds."

Neighbor's Maid–"And what did they talk about?"

First Maid–"Us."

[3764]

Butler (to new cook)–"Mind you, I'm not saying anything about your cooking—but there's been a terrible run on cheese and biscuits in the dining-room to-night!"

[3765]

A woman was interviewing the girl who was applying for a job as general housemaid. Afternoons off and wages had been fully discussed, when the girl asked:

"Do you do your own stretchin'?"

"Do we do our own what?" asked the woman.

"Stretchin'."

"I don't quite understand what you mean," replied the matron.

"Stretchin'," explained the girl. "Do you put the stuff on the table and stretch fer it, or do I have to shuffle it around?"

[3766]

Mistress–"Now, Matilda, I want you to show us what you can do to-night. We have a few very special friends coming for a musical evening."

Maid–"Well, ma'am, I ain't done no singin' to speak of for years, but if you-all insists upon it, you can put me down for 'The Holy City.' "

[3767]

"So that new girl of yours is lazy?"

"Lazy! Why, the other morning I caught her putting popcorn into the pancakes to make them turn over themselves."

[3768]

Mrs. Brown rebuked her maid: "I wrote your name with my finger in the dust on the dining-room mantelpiece this morning."

"I know you did, mum," replied the girl, "an' you spelled it wrong."

[3769]

Mistress (to new servant)–"Remember, Jane, we like to be served at table with alacrity."

Jane–"Yessum, and when will you have it—after the soup?"

[3770]

Maid (rushing into room)–"Brandy, quick!"

Mistress (giving brandy)–"What is the matter?"

Maid–"Brandy."

Mistress (after fourth brandy)–"What is the matter?"

Maid–"Ah, now I have recovered from the shock."

Mistress–"What shock?"

Maid–"I broke your best Chinese vase."

[3771]

Madame (to servant)–"Marie, go quickly and buy me the book, 'How to Remain Young and Beautiful'."

Servant–"Oui, Madame, I will tell them it is urgent."

[3772]

Mistress–"I notice that your policeman friend calls frequently. Do you think he means business?"

Cook–"I think he does. He's already beginning to complain about my cooking."

[3773]

Mistress–"Be careful not to drop those china dishes, Norah."

Maid–"Don't worry, mum. If they did fall they're too light to hurt my feet."

[3774]

Mistress–"Nora, I saw a policeman in the park today kiss a baby. I hope you will remember my objection to such things."

Nora–"Sure, ma'am, no policeman would ever think iv kissin' yer baby whin I'm around."

[3775]

Maid–"Mr. Brown called about his account this morning, sir!"

Master–"And you told him I'd just left for California?"

Maid–"Yes, and that you wouldn't be back till late this evening."

[3776]

Mrs. Jones–"I understand you've got your divorce, Sally. Did you get any alimony from your husband?"

Laundress–"No, Mrs. Jones, but he done give me a first-class reference."

[3777]

The mistress who engaged a new cook made a tour of investigation after she had kept her a week and found a policeman locked up in the pantry. "How did this man get here?" she asked severely.

"I'm sure I don't know," was the reply. "He must have been left over by the last cook."

[3778]

Mistress–"Did you enjoy your day at the seaside, Mary?"

Mary–"No, I didn't, mum, all the picture houses was full, so we had ter wander around the beach, and watch the ships all day."

[3779]

Country Cousin (in town)–"Out in the country we have to treat the maids and other help like members of the family."

City Cousin–"Goodness! Really? Here we have to treat them with great respect."

[3780]

Mistress–"Why don't you light the fire?"

Maid–"Because there ain't no coal."

Mistress–"Why didn't you let me know before?"

Maid–"Because we had some before."

[3781]

Mistress–"What is your name?"
Maid–"Miss Arlington."
Mistress–"Do you expect to be called Miss Arlington?"
Maid–"No, ma'am; not if you have an alarm clock in my room."

[3782]

Master–"Mary, has anybody telephoned while I've been out?"
Maid–"Yes, sir, but I could not make out the name. To be on the safe side, I said you would let him have something on account to-morrow."

[3783]

"My new housemaid is a treasure," declared Mrs. Johnson. "I had a bridge party the other evening, and one woman failed to turn up. You know how it is—she gave me no notice whatever."

"Very annoying."

"The housemaid, however, put on one of my gowns and fitted in beautifully."

"That was helpful."

"Yes, and I won her week's wages."

[3784]

"I knew an artist once who painted a cobweb on the ceiling so realistically that the maid spent hours trying to get it down."

"Sorry, dear, I just don't believe it."

"Why not? Artists have been known to do such things."

"Yes, but not maids!"

[3785]

Mistress (to new maid)–"Why, it seems to me you want very large wages for one who has had so little experience."
Maid–"Sure, mum, ain't it harder for me when I don't know how?"

[3786]

"What beautiful scallops you have made on the pies, Mandy! How do you do it?"

"Ah's glad you like dem, Mam. Ah just used mah false teeth to make de impresses."

[3787]

Old Maid–"Has the canary had its bath yet?"
Servant–"Yes, ma'am. You can come in now."

[3788]

"The dinner was delicious. You must have an old family cook."

"Yes, indeed; she's been with us ten or twelve meals."

[3789]

"Jane," cried the mistress, re-reproachfully, "you informed me a while ago that you were going to have a little sleep."

"Yes, Madam," replied the maid.

"Then," pursued her mistress, "what were you doing at the garden gate when the soldiers passed by?"

"Having forty winks," answered the maid, unabashed.

[3790]

Maid–"Please, Mrs. Whaite, will you come up to the bathroom at once? I can't make out whether Mr. Whaite is scalding to death or singing."

[3791]

Head Cook–"Didn't I tell you to notice when the soup boiled over?"
Assistant–"I did. It was half-past ten."

[3792]

"Nora, you were entertaining a man in the kitchen last night, were you not?"

"That's for him to say. I did my best."

[3793]

"I understand you are looking for a new maid."

"Yes, our last one handled china like Japan."

[3794]

Having need of three cents the mistress of the house went to the top of the back stairs. "Bessie," she called to the maid below, "have you any coppers down there?"

"Yes'm—two," faltered Bessie, "but they're both my cousins, please, m'm."

[3795]

Lady (at party)—"Where is that pretty maid who was passing out cocktails a while ago?"

Hostess—"Oh, are you looking for a drink?"

Lady—"No, I'm looking for my husband."

[3796]

"When we are married I must have three servants."

"You shall have twenty, dear, but not all at once."

[3797]

Mrs. Littletown—"This magazine looks rather the worse for wear."

Mrs. Neartown—"Yes, it's the one I sometimes lend to the servant on Sundays."

Mrs. Littletown—"Doesn't she get tired of always reading the same one?"

Mr. Neartown—"Oh, no. You see, it's the same book, but it's always a different servant."

[3798]

Maid—"I left my last place because I was asked to do something I did not like."

Prospective Mistress—"Really! What was that?"

Maid—"Look for another job."

[3799]

"Matilda, when you wait on the table tonight, don't display any jewelry before my guests, please."

"Oh, I'm not afraid, ma'am."

[3800]

"It seems to me, Bridget, that it is the worst mistresses who get the best cooks."

Bridget—"Oh, go on wid your blarney now."

[3801]

Mrs. Cobb—"Was the grocer's boy impudent to you again when you telephoned your order this morning?"

Maid—"Yes, Mrs. Cobb, he was that; but I fixed him this time. I sez, 'Who the hell do you think you're talkin' to? This is Mrs. Cobb at the phone talkin'.' "

[3802]

Guest—"What a pretty name your maid has!"

Hostess—"Oh, that isn't her real name. We just call her 'Dawn' because she's always breaking."

[3803]

"You say you have no references? What explanation have you for that?"

"Why, yer see, mum, I've always stayed in wan place until the payple doid, mum!"

[3804]

The new maid was complaining to her mistress. "It's about your husband, madam," she said shyly. "Every time he sees me he wants to kiss me. He asks me to sit on his lap, and——"

"That's enough, Mary," interrupted her mistress. "Just go right on with your work and don't pay any attention to him. He used to try the same thing with me!"

[3805]

Mistress–"Mary, Mary! Yesterday you broke two vases and to-day you have broken three plates and four cups. What will be broken to-morrow, at this rate?"

Maid–"Not so much, ma'am. It is my afternoon out."

[3806]

"What were those unusual greens we had to-night, Cook?"

"You remember, ma'am, you said those geraniums in the garden looked so lovely you could eat them?"

"Yes."

"Well, you have!"

[3807]

Mrs. A (with newspaper)–"It says here that cooks are often decorated in France."

Mr. A–"I sometimes feel like crowning the one we've got."

[3808]

"Tell me, my dear, how do you manage to get the maid up so early in the morning?"

"It was rather clever of me. I introduced her to the milkman."

[3809]

"Do you think the new cook is going to settle down with us?" asked Mr. Jorkins.

"I'm a bit doubtful," replied his wife. "A letter came for her this morning, and the envelope was re-addressed five times."

[3810]

The applicant for a job as housemaid was being interviewed by the agent and was asked if she had any preference in the kind of family she would like to work for.

"Any kind," she said, "except highbrows. I worked for a pair of them once, and never again. Him and her was fighting all the time, and it kept me running back and forward from the keyhole to the dictionary till I was worn to a frazzle."

[3811]

The small, nervous husband was having an unpleasant interview with the large, muscular cook, whom he was reprimanding on account of her numerous breakages.

"Look here," said she, "you can't frighten me—I'm a 'dreadnought,' that's what I am!"

"Well," replied the other, looking at the heap of broken china, "I would rather say—er—that you are a destroyer!"

[3812]

Cook–"Yes, ma'am, I'm leavin' in exactly three minutes."

Mrs. West–"Then put the eggs on to boil and we'll have them right for once!"

[3813]

Mistress–"Mary, I saw a man kissing you at the back door last night. Was it the postman or the policeman?"

Maid–"Was it before eight o'clock or after?"

[3814]

"Is your former cook happy since she inherited a fortune?"

"No, she's all dressed up and no place to leave."

PART IV

COLLEGE WIT AND HUMOR

IN THE CLASSROOM

[3815]
Prof.–"Name two pronouns."
Stude–"Who, me?"

[3816]
Prof.–"This exam will be conducted on the honor system. Please take seats three seats apart and in alternate rows."

[3817]
First Student–"Great Scott! I've forgotten who wrote 'Ivanhoe.' "
Second Ditto–"I'll tell you if you tell me who the dickens wrote 'The Tale of Two Cities.' "

[3818]
Frosh–"Professor, I can't go to class today."
Prof.–"Why?"
Frosh–"I don't feel well."
Prof.–"Where don't you feel well?"
Frosh–"In class."

[3819]
A professor reproved his students for coming late to class.

"This is a class in English composition," he remarked with sarcasm, "not an afternoon tea."

At the next meeting one girl was twenty minutes late. The professor waited until she had taken her seat. Then he remarked bitingly:

"How will you have your tea, Miss Jones?"

"Without the lemon, please," Miss Jones answered quite gently.

[3820]
First Freshman in Math Exam–"How far are you from the correct answer?"
Second Freshman in Math Exam–"Two seats."

[3821]
Prof.–"Nobody ever heard of a sentence without a predicate."
Stude–"I have, Professor."
Prof.–"What is it?"
Stude–"Thirty days."

[3822]
Prof (in geology)–"The geologist thinks nothing of a thousand years."
Soph–"Great guns! And I loaned a geologist ten dollars yesterday!"

[3823]
College Senior–"What would you advise me to read after graduating?"
English Professor–"The 'Help Wanted' column."

[3824]
Professor–"Time is money: how do you prove it?"
Student–"Well, if you give twenty-five cents to a couple of tramps, that is a quarter to two."

373

[3825]
Voice On Phone–"John Smith is sick and can't attend classes today. He requested me to notify you."
Professor–"All right. Who is this speaking?"
Voice–"This is my roommate."

[3826]
Dean–"Where are your parents?"
Co-ed–"I have none."
Dean–"Where are you guardians?"
Co-ed–"I have none."
Dean–"Where are your supporters?"
Co-ed–"Sir! You are forgetting yourself."

[3827]
First Co-ed–"Does that Prof like you?"
Second Co-ed–"Oh, he must. At least every paper he hands back to me is covered with kiss marks."

[3828]
Prof.–Mr. Twirp, what do you know about French syntax?"
Stude–"Gosh, I didn't know they had to pay for their fun."

[3829]
Hmmmm da da daaa, do da da
    Alma Mater thee,
Hmmmm doo do classic halls,
    Hmmmm la la doo doo ivied
        walls,
Alma Mater three!
Hmmmmmm da da do la
    Hopes and fears,
Hmmmmmmmm loo da loo loo
    da la years
Alma Mater threeeeee!

[3830]
Frosh One–"I hear you got thrown out of school for calling the dean a fish."
Frosh Two–"I didn't call him a fish. I just said, 'That's our dean,' real fast."

[3831]
"Did you pass your exam?"
"Well, it was like this—you see—"
"Shake! Neither did I."

[3832]
Geology Professor–"What kind of rock is this?"
Student–"Oh! I just take it for granite."

[3833]
English Prof.–"What was the occasion for the quotation, 'Why don't you speak for yourself, John?' "
Sophomore–"John Alden was trying to fix up a blind date for his roommate, Miles Standish."

[3834]
"Which was the greater of the two," asked the History Professor, "Caesar or Hannibal?"
The student replied: "If we consider who Caesar and Hannibal were, and ask ourselves which of them was the greater, we must decidedly answer in the affirmative."

[3835]
"Why did you come to college, anyway? You are not studying," said the Professor.
"Well," said Willie, "I don't know exactly myself. Mother says it is to fit me for the Presidency; Uncle Bill, to sow my wild oats; Sis, to get a chum for her to marry, and Pa, to bankrupt the family."

[3836]
Pro–"Can you tell me anything about the great chemists of the 17th century?"
Con–"They are all dead, sir."

[3837]
Chemistry Professor–"What can you tell me about nitrates?"
Student–"Well—er—they're a lot cheaper than day rates."

[3838]

Professor (in freshman science class)–"Who is the greatest inventor the world has ever known?"

Freshman–"An Irishman by the name of Pat Pending."

[3839]

Instructor–"What is the feminine of bachelor?"

Student–"Er-r—lady-in-waiting."

[3840]

Second Classman (on educational trip to museum)–"Say! Don't start looking at things or we'll never get around!"

[3841]

A professor was teaching a medical class. He explained the use of the tourniquet in stopping the flow of blood, and showed how the pressure should be applied between the cut and the heart.

"What would you do in case a man had a brain hemorrhage?" continued the professor.

"I'd put a tourniquet on his neck!" was the bright reply of one of the students.

[3842]

At a college examination a professor asked: "Does the question embarrass you?"

"Not at all, sir," replied the student; "not at all. It is quite clear. It is the answer that bothers me!"

[3843]

Said the professor:

"If there are any dumbbells in the room, please stand up."

A long pause and then a lone freshman stood up.

"What, do you consider yourself a dumbbell?"

"Well, not exactly that, sir, but I do hate to see you standing by yourself."

[3844]

The more we study, the more we know.

The more we know, the more we forget.

The more we forget, the less we know.

The less we know, the less we forget.

The less we forget, the more we know.

So why study?

[3845]

Professor–"Hawkins, what is a synonym?"

Student–"It's a word you use in place of another when you cannot spell the other one."

[3846]

During a Christmas exam, one of the questions was "What causes a depression?" One of the students on pro wrote: "God knows! I don't. Merry Christmas!"

The exam paper came back with the prof's notation: "God gets 100. You get zero. Happy New Year."

[3847]

Professor–"Now, if I were to be flogged, what would that be?"

Class (in unison)–"That would be corporal punishment."

Professor–"But if I were to be beheaded?"

Class (still in unison)–"Oh, that would be capital!"

[3848]

Dean–"And where have you been for the last week?"

Stude–"Stop me if you've heard this one!"

[3849]

The professor rapped on his desk and shouted:

"Gentlemen—order!"

The entire class yelled: "Beer!"

[3850]

"Sedentary work," said the college lecturer, "tends to lessen the endurance."

"In other words," butted in the smart student, "the more one sits, the less one can stand."

"Exactly," retorted the lecturer; "and if one lies a great deal, one's standing is lost completely."

[3851]

Soph–"But I don't think I deserve an absolute zero."

Prof.–"Neither do I, but it is the lowest mark that I am allowed to give."

[3852]

"You in the back of the room, what was the date of the signing of the Magna Carta?"

"I dunno."

"You don't, eh? Well let's try something else. Who was Bonny Prince Charley?"

"I dunno."

"Well, then, can you tell me what the Tennis Court Oath was?"

"I dunno."

"You don't! I assigned this stuff last Friday. What were you doing last night?"

"I was out drinking beer with some friends."

"You were! What audacity to stand there and tell me a thing like that! How do you ever expect to pass this course?"

"Wal, I don't know, mister. Ye see, I just come in to fix the radiator."

[3853]

"If the Dean doesn't take back what he said to me this morning, I am going to leave college."

"What did he say?"

"He told me to leave college."

[3854]

Mechanics Professor–"Name a great time-saver."

Sophomore–"Love at first sight."

[3855]

Professor–"I won't begin today's lecture until the room settles down."

Voice (from the rear)–"Go home and sleep it off, old man."

[3856]

Professor–"What kept you out of class yesterday—acute indigestion?"

Co-ed–"No, a cute engineer."

[3857]

"On a recent survey of the question it was found that the college that produced the most U. S. Presidents was—"

"Yes, go on" (breathlessly).

"—the electoral college."

[3858]

First Plebe–"I got in trouble with the prof. this morning."

Second Plebe–"How come?"

First Plebe–"He said that all questions could be answered by yes or no, and asked if any one could give him one that couldn't. I asked him if he had stopped swearing."

[3859]

"When rain falls, does it ever arise again?" asked the professor of chemistry.

"Yes, sir."

"When?"

"Why, in dew time—"

"That will do. You can sit down."

[3860]

The bright student looked long and thoughtfully at the second examination question, which read: "State the number of tons of coal shipped out of the United States in any given year." Then his brow cleared and he wrote:

"1492—none."

[3861]

"Professor," said Miss Dingley, "I want you to suggest a course in life for me. I have thought of journalism——"

"What are your own inclinations?"

"Oh, my soul yearns and throbs and pulsates with an ambition to give the world a life-work that shall be marvelous in its scope, and weirdly entrancing in the vastness of its structural beauty!"

"Woman, you're born to be a milliner."

[3862]

Chemistry Professor–"Jones, what does HNO_3 signify?"

Student–"Well, ah, er'r—I've got it right on the tip of my tongue, sir."

Chemistry Professor–"Well, you'd better spit it out. It's nitric acid."

[3863]

"I am delighted to meet you," said the father of the college student, shaking hands warmly with the professor. "My son took algebra from you last year, you know."

"Pardon me," said the professor, "he was exposed to it, but he did not take it."

[3864]

History Lecturer–"Can any of you tell me what makes the Tower of Pisa lean?"

Corpulent Lady–"I don't know, or I'd take some myself."

[3865]

Fullback (looking at semester grades)–"Well, I'm as famous as Washington now."

Halfback–"How do you figure that?"

Fullback–"Well, I went down in history."

[3866]

Professor–"What's the most common impediment in the speech of American people?"

Freshman–"Chewing-gum."

[3867]

The university president was delivering his baccalaureate speech. In the audience were an elderly man and woman, obviously foreigners, who were having some trouble understanding the president's address to the class, of which their son was a member.

"What he say?" finally demanded the mother, frowning.

"Who?" asked the father.

"The beega fella in black robes. What he say?"

"He say school is out."

[3868]

Prof.–"Gentlemen, I am dismissing you ten minutes early today. Please go out quietly so as not to wake the other classes."

[3869]

The college boys thought to play a prank on the "prexy," who was in the habit of reading from the Bible each morning. They pasted two leaves of the Bible together, being careful to choose two particular leaves. Next morning the president began to read:

"Now Johial took unto himself a wife of the daughter of Belial." Here he paused slightly to turn the page, and then continued: "She was eighteen cubits in height and ten cubits in breadth."

Here he paused again and scrutinized both pages carefully. Then he resumed: "Now Johial took unto himself a wife of the daughters of Belial," and turning the page went on with, "She was eighteen cubits in height and ten cubits in breadth, and was pitched within and without—"

In painful exasperation the president broke off, perhaps realizing that muted mirth was abroad in his audience.

"Young gentlemen," he said, removing his spectacles the better to peer at them all, "I can only add that 'man is fearfully and wonderfully made'—and—er—woman also."

[3870]

History Prof.–"Who was Talleyrand?"

Student–"A fan dancer, and cut the baby talk."

[3871]

Math Professor–"Now, Mr. Zilchguard, if I lay three eggs here and five eggs here, how many eggs will I have?"

Mr. Zilchguard (with a questioning glance)–"I don't believe you can do it, sir."

[3872]

"I was reading some good poetry today."

"I prefer prose."

"I'll take amateurs, but what's that got to do with poetry?"

[3873]

Prof.–"Before we begin the examinations, are there any questions?"

Frosh–"What's the name of this course?"

[3874]

It was a sleepy sort of day, the class was about half the usual size and the Prof. was calling the roll in a half-absent manner. To each name someone had answered "here" until the name Smith was called. Silence reigned supreme for a moment only to be broken by the Prof.'s voice.

"My word! Hasn't Mr. Smith any friends here?"

[3875]

Prof.–"Wake up that fellow next to you."

Stude–"You do it, Prof., you put him to sleep."

[3876]

"Did you make the debating team?"

"N-n-no. They s-s-said I w-w-wasn't t-t-tall enough."

[3877]

Professor–"Every man in this college could get a job with the city if he wanted it!"

Student–"Isn't that a rather sweeping statement?"

[3878]

"It's going to be a real battle of wits, I tell you," said the sophomore member of the debating-team.

"How brave of you," said his room-mate, "to go unarmed."

[3879]

The astronomy professor was lecturing. "I predict the end of the world in fifty million years."

"How many?" cried a frightened voice from the rear.

"Fifty million years."

"Oh," said the voice with a deep sigh of relief, "I thought you said fifteen million."

[3880]

Professor–"You can't sleep in my class."

Student–"If you didn't talk so loud I could."

[3881]

Math Teacher–"Now we find that X is equal to zero."

Student–"Gee! All that work for nothing."

[3882]

Policeman–"Where are you going in such a hurry?"

Student–"I just bought a new text-book and I am trying to get to class before it goes out of date."

[3883]

The professor, at a girls' college, wrote on the blackboard, "LXXX." Then, peering over his spectacles at a good-looking girl in the first row, he asked:

"Young lady, I'd like to have you tell me what that means."

"Love and kisses," the girl replied.

[3884]

A farmer visited his son's college. Watching students in a chemistry class, he was told they were looking for a universal solvent.

"What's that?" asked the farmer.

"A liquid that will dissolve anything."

"That's a great idea," agreed the farmer. "When you find it, what are you going to keep it in?"

[3885]

"What does John do with that loud red tie of his?"

"He wears it in history lecture. When his head falls down on his chest the tie wakes him up again."

[3886]

Several college presidents were discussing what they would like to do after they retired.

"Well," said one of them, "I know what I'd like to do. I'd like to be superintendent of an orphan asylum so I'd never get any letters from parents."

"I've a much better ambition," exclaimed another. "I want to be warden of a penitentiary. The alumni never come back to visit."

[3887]

"So that distinguished-looking gentleman in the tall hat is your leading citizen, eh? Has he received many degrees from colleges?"

"Has he? Why, he has received so many degrees we call him the 'Human Thermometer.'"

[3888]

The distinguished reception committee of Harvard University searched in vain for Sir Walter Raleigh, descendant of the famous personage in English and American history, due for a course of lectures at Harvard.

Missing him at the train, the delegation searched the waiting-rooms. They espied an impressive-looking stranger, and the chairman accosted him.

"Pardon me, are you Sir Walter Raleigh?" he asked.

"Thunder, no!" he answered with emphasis. "I'm Christopher Columbus. Sir Walter is in the next room playing cards with Queen Elizabeth!"

[3889]

Professor–"Tell me one or two things about John Milton."

Student–"Well, he got married and he wrote 'Paradise Lost.' Then his wife died, and he wrote 'Paradise Regained.'"

[3890]

Medical Professor–"What would you do in the case of a person eating poisonous mushrooms?"

Student–"Recommend a change of diet."

[3891]

Professor–"What did you find out about the salivary glands?"

Stude–"I couldn't find out a thing, Professor; they're too darn secretive."

[3892]

The Professor–"A diamond is the hardest known substance, inasmuch as it will cut glass."

Cynical Student–"Glass! My dear sir, a diamond will even make an impression on a woman's heart."

[3893]

"Our economics prof talks to himself. Does yours?"

"Yes, but he doesn't realize it—he thinks we're listening."

[3894]

The mathematics professor noticed that one of his pupils was day-dreaming, and not following his work on the blackboard. To recall his attention he said, sharply: "Brown, Brown, board!"

The boy, startled, looked up.

"Yes, sir, very," came the reply.

[3895]

English Exam. Question – "Give three collective nouns?"

Student's Answer–"Flypaper, wastebasket and vacuum cleaner."

[3896]

"I shall now illustrate what I have in mind," said the professor as he erased the board.

[3897]

Professor of Economics–"You boys of today want to make too much money. Why, do you know what I was getting when I got married?"

Voice from Last Row–"No, and I'll bet you didn't either."

[3898]

Her–"Have you been up before the Dean?"

Him–"Oh, I don't know. What time does he get up?"

[3899]

"How was the geology lecture?"

"Fine, I was rocked to sleep."

[3900]

Prof.–"How do you test the temperature of a baby's bath?"

Co-ed–"You fill the tub with water and put the baby in it. If the baby turns red, it's too hot; if the baby turns purple, it's too cold; and if the baby turns white, it needed a bath."

[3901]

Prof.–"Take this sentence. 'Let the cow be taken out of the lot.' What Mood?"

Frosh–"The cow."

[3902]

Stude–"I'm indebted to you for all I know."

Prof.–"Oh, don't mention such a mere trifle."

[3903]

Math. Prof.–"If there are 48 states in the Union, and superheated steam equals the distance from Bombay to Paris, what is my age?"

Frosh–"Forty-four, Sir."

Prof.–"Correct. How did you prove it?"

Frosh–"I have a brother who is twenty-two and he is only half nuts."

[3904]

First Student–"The dean says he is going to stop smoking in the college."

Second Student–"Huh! Next thing he'll be asking us to stop it too."

[3905]

A college freshman was being severely criticized by his professor.

"Your last paper was very difficult to read," said the professor. "Your work should be so written that even the most ignorant will be able to understand it."

"Yes, sir," said the student. "What part didn't you get?"

[3906]
Professor in Physiology – "This morning we will consider the heart, liver, kidney, and lungs."
Tired Student–"Just another organ recital."

[3907]
"See you're getting quite chummy with your Profs."
"Yep. Familiarity sometimes breeds exempts."

[3908]
Prof.–"Oxygen is essential to all animal existence. There could be no life without it. It was discovered only a century ago."
Stude–"What did they do before it was discovered?"

[3909]
Prof.–"A fool can ask more questions than a wise man can answer."
Stude–"No wonder so many of us flunk in our exams!"

[3910]
Eng. Prof.–"Mr. Brown, correct this sentence: 'Girls is naturally better looking than boys.'"
Brown–"Girls is artificially better looking than boys."

[3911]
Professor–"What is a monarchy?"
Freshman–"A people governed by a king."
Professor–"Who would reign if the king should die?"
Freshman–"The queen."
Professor–"And if the queen should die?"
Freshman–"The jack."

[3912]
'Now," said the professor cheerfully. "Please pass all your test papers to the side of the room and kindly insert a carbon sheet under paper so I can correct all the errors at once."

[3913]
First Ag Stude–"What part of a cow do the chops come from?"
Second Ag Stude–"Don't you know?"
First–"Do you?"
Second–"Haven't you ever heard of a cow licking its chops?"

[3914]
"There is direct and indirect taxation. Give me an example of indirect taxation."
"The dog tax, sir."
"How is that?"
"The dog does not have to pay it."

[3915]
The professor was delivering the final lecture of the term. He dwelt with much emphasis on the fact that each student should devote all the intervening time preparing for the final examinations.
"The examination papers are now in the hands of the printer. Are there any questions to be asked?"
Silence prevailed. Suddenly a voice from the rear inquired:
"Who is the printer?"

[3916]
Freshman–"Is he dumb? He can't even tell Galsworthy from gallstone."
Another Frosh–"And who was gallstone?"

[3917]
Prof.–"Young man, are you the teacher of this class?"
Stude–"No, sir."
Prof.–"Then don't talk like an idiot!"

[3918]
"When water becomes ice," said the professor, "what is the greatest change that takes place?"
"The price, sir."

[3919]

You'll probably agree that a professor who comes three minutes early to class is extremely unusual—in fact, he's in a class by himself.

[3920]

Professor—"What great law is Newton credited with discovering?"
The Class (in unison)—"The bigger they are the harder they fall."

[3921]

"I hear Bill was thrown out of college for cribbing."
"Yep!"
"What happened?"
"He sneezed while he was taking an exam in Russian and they threw him out for conjugating a verb."

[3922]

"He was kicked out of school for cheating!"
"How come?"
"He was caught counting his ribs in a hygiene exam."

[3923]

After considerable effort the freshman finally finished his examination paper, and then at the end wrote:
"Dear Professor, If you sell any of my answers to the funny papers I expect you to split fifty-fifty with me."

[3924]

Eng. Prof.—"What's the difference between an active verb and a passive verb?"
Co-ed—"An active verb shows action and a passive verb shows passion."

[3925]

Statistics show that Yale graduates have 1.3 children.
While Vassar graduates have 1.7 children.
Which proves that women have more children than men.

[3926]

Judge—"And you say you were attacked by a crowd of hoodlums?"
Latin Professor—"Hoodla, your honor."

[3927]

A visiting clergyman conducting exercises at Hobart College used the six letters forming the name of the institution for the headings of the subdivisions of his extended address—"H" for Holiness, "O" for Obedience, "B" for Beneficence, "A" for Adoration, "R" for Righteousness, "T" for Triumph. He gave fifteen or twenty minutes to every subject.
As they made their weary way for the exit, one student said to another: "Darned good thing we are not attending the Massachusetts Institute of Technology!"

[3928]

Professor—"You missed my class yesterday, didn't you?"
Unsubdued Student—"Not in the least, sir, not in the least."

[3929]

A professor, while tramping through a field, found himself confronted by an angry bull. Wishing only to pass and not to offend the beast, the professor said, "My friend, you are my superior in strength, and I am your superior in mind, and so, being so equally gifted, let us arbitrate the matter."
"Oh, no," replied the bull. "Let's toss for it."
The professor lost.

[3930]

Professor—"So, sir, you said that I was a learnéd jackass, did you?"
Freshie—"No, sir. I merely remarked that you were a burro of information."

[3931]

In one of our eastern college classes the professor was unable to stay for the class, so he placed a sign on the door which read as follows:

"Professor Blank will be unable to meet his classes today."

Some college lad, seeing his chance to display his sense of humor after reading the notice, walked up and erased the "c" in the word "classes." The professor, noticing the laughter, wheeled around, walked back, looked at the student, then at the sign with the "c" erased—calmly walked up and erased the "l" in "lasses," looked at the flabbergasted student and proceeded on his way.

[3932]

"Did you pass that refrigeration course exam?"

"Sure. I knew it cold."

[3933]

Professor–"And are you sure that this story is original?"

Student–"Certainly, it is."

Professor–"Great heavens! To think that I would live to see the day when I would meet Rudyard Kipling."

[3934]

Prof.–"What are you doing in college, anyway?"

Frosh–"I was about to ask you the same question."

[3935]

Temperance Lecturer–"Here's an argument drawn from nature. If I lead a donkey up to a pail of water and a pail of beer, which will he drink?"

Unconverted–"The water."

Lecturer–"Right. Why?"

Unconverted–"Because he's an ass."

[3936]

The dean of the Law Department was very busy and rather cross. The telephone rang.

"Well, what is it?" he snapped.

"Is that the city gas-works?" said a woman's soft voice.

"No, madam," roared the dean; "this is the University Law Department."

"Ah," she answered in the sweetest of tones, "I didn't miss it so far, after all, did I?"

[3937]

This is Professor Brown talking. No—not Bond—Brown. B as in Brontosaurus, R as in Rhizophoracæ, O as in Ophisthotelæ, W as in Willingbalya and N as in Nucifraga—Brown. Do you comprehend?

[3938]

Math. Instructor–"What do we mean when we say the whole is greater than any of its parts?"

Stude–"A restaurant doughnut."

[3939]

Plebe–"I've added those figures ten times, sir."

Prof.–"Good boy."

Plebe–"And here's the ten answers."

[3940]

A professor was one day nearing the close of a history lecture and was indulging in one of those rhetorical climaxes in which he delighted when the hour struck. The students immediately began to slam down the movable arms of their lecture chairs and to prepare to leave.

The professor, annoyed at the interruption of his flow of eloquence, held up his hand:

"Wait just one minute, gentlemen. I have a few more pearls to cast."

[3941]

Prof.–"What is Platonic love?"
Stude–"Warming chairs, burning lamps, playing victrolas, sitting around a sorority house, and leaving at 10:30."

[3942]

"Never state as a fact anything you are not certain about," the professor instructed his class in journalism, "or you will get into libel suits. In such cases use the words, 'alleged,' 'claimed,' 'reputed,' 'rumored,' and so on."

A month later one of the bright students of the class submitted the following society note to the college paper:

"It is rumored that a card party was given yesterday by a number of reputed ladies. Mrs. Smith, gossip says, was hostess. It is alleged that the guests with the exception of Mrs. Brown, who says she hails from Porterville, were all from here. Mrs. Smith claims to be the wife of Jonathan Smith, the so-called 'Honest Man' trading on Adams Street."

[3943]

Prof.–"Never mind the date. The examination is more important."
Student–"Well, sir, I wanted to have something right on my paper."

[3944]

Prof. of Political Economy–"Who's the Speaker of the House?"
Stude–"Mother."

[3945]

"Why is the history professor sore on you?"

"The prof. says to me, 'What German chieftain captured Rome?' So I says to him, 'It was Hannibal, wasn't it?' So he says, 'Don't ask me. I'm asking you.' So I says, 'I don't know either, prof.'"

[3946]

Prof.–"Didn't you have a brother in this course last year?"
Stude–"No sir, it was I. I'm taking it over again."
Prof.–"Extraordinary resemblance, though—extraordinary!"

[3947]

Prof.–"Will you men stop exchanging notes in the back of the room?"
Stude–"Them ain't notes, them's cards. We're playing bridge."
Prof.–"Oh, I beg your pardon."

[3948]

Professor at Agricultural School–"What kinds of farming are there?"
New Student–"Extensive, intensive, and pretensive."

ABSENT-MINDED PROFESSORS

[3949]

Absent-minded Prof.–"Lady, what are you doing in my bed?"
Lady–"Well, I like this bed, I like this neighborhood. I like this house, and I like this room. And, anyway, I'm your wife!"

[3950]

Absent-minded Prof.–"I forgot to take my umbrella this morning."
Wife–"When did you miss it?"
Prof.–"When I reached up to close it after the rain had stopped."

[3951]

The absent-minded professor was busy in his study. "Have you seen this?" said his wife, entering. "There's a report in the paper of your death."

"Is that so?" returned the professor without looking up. "We must remember to send a wreath."

[3952]

"Do you want gas?" asked the dentist as he placed the patient in the chair.

"Yes," said the absent-minded professor. "About five gallons—and take a look at the oil."

[3953]

The much preoccupied professor walked into the barber's shop and sat in a chair next to a woman who was having her hair bobbed.

"Haircut, please," ordered the professor.

"Certainly," said the barber. "But if you really want a haircut would you mind taking off your hat first?"

The customer hurriedly removed his hat. "I'm sorry," he apologized as he looked around. "I didn't know there was a lady present!"

[3954]

Absent-minded Professor's Wife– "Wait, John. Are you sure you've forgotten everything?"

[3955]

Doctor (breaking in on engrossed Dean)–"My dear sir, I am happy to report that a little boy has just arrived."

Dean (from force of habit)–"Tell him I won't be able to see him for a few days at least."

[3956]

The Bootblack–"Light or dark, sir?"

The Absent-minded Professor–"I'm not particular but please don't give me the neck."

[3957]

Friend–"Ah, professor, I hear your wife has had twins. Boys or girls?"

Prof. (absent-minded)–"Well, I believe one is a girl, and one a boy, but it may be the other way around."

[3958]

He was, in fact, the absent-minded professor, and he was strap-hanging in a street-car. The other arm clasped a half dozen bundles. He swayed to and fro. Slowly his face took on a look of apprehension.

"Can I help you, sir?" asked the conductor.

"Yes," said the professor with relief. "Hold on to this strap while I get my fare out."

[3959]

Reporter–"What is the professor's research work?"

Professor's Housekeeper–"It consists principally of hunting for his spectacles."

[3960]

When they pulled the professor, half drowned, from the water, he sputtered, "How exasperating! I've just recalled the fact that I can swim."

[3961]

While reading at home, a professor found he had need of a bookmark. Seeing nothing else handy, he used his wife's scissors, which lay on the sewing-table. A few minutes later the wife wanted the scissors, but a diligent search failed to reveal them.

The next day the professor appeared before his class and opened his book. There lay the scissors. He picked them up and, holding them above his head, shouted:

"Here they are, dear!"

Yes, the class got it.

[3962]

"So you use three pairs of glasses, professor?"

"Yes, one pair for long sight, one pair for short sight and the third to look for the other two."

[3963]

Absent-minded Professor (to servant)–"You say there is a collector at the door? Did you tell him I was out?"

Servant–"Yes, sir, but he didn't believe me."

Absent-minded Professor–"Well, I guess I will have to go and tell him myself."

[3964]

Yesterday we heard positively the last one on our friend, the absent-minded professor. He slammed his wife and kissed the door.

[3965]

Bewildered Prof. (on looking into hairbrush)–"Guess I need a shave."

[3966]

Professor–"I've been robbed of my gold snuff-box."

Wife–"Didn't you feel a hand in your pocket?"

Professor–"Yes, but I thought it was my own."

[3967]

The absent-minded professor perfected a parachute device. He was taken up in a balloon to make a test of the apparatus. When he had arrived at a height of a thousand feet, he climbed over the edge of the basket, and dropped out. He had fallen three hundred feet when he remarked to himself, in a tone of deep regret:

"Dear me! I've gone and forgotten my umbrella."

[3968]

"Where is the car?" demanded Mrs. Dingley.

"Dear me!" ejaculated Professor Dingley. "Did I take the car out?"

"You certainly did. You drove it to town."

"How odd! I remember now that after I got out I turned around to thank the gentleman who gave me the lift and wondered where he had gone."

[3969]

An absent-minded professor of drawing came down the steps of his home in the college town to take a cab for the train and seeing an old, knock-kneed and spavinned nag hitched to an ancient vehicle, cried: "Dear, dear! Rub it out and do it all over again!"

[3970]

Absent-minded Professor (to Pharmacist)–"Give me some prepared monacetic-acidester of salicyllic acid."

Pharmacist–"Do you mean aspirin?"

Absent-minded Professor – "That's right! I can never think of that name."

[3971]

The professor, who was famous for the wool-gathering of his wits, returned home, and had his ring at the door answered by a new maid. The girl looked at him inquiringly:

"Um—ah—is Professor Thompson at home?" he asked, naming himself.

"No, sir," the maid replied, "but he is expected any moment now."

The professor turned away, the girl closed the door. Then the poor man sat down on the steps to wait for himself.

[3972]

"Professor, why are you taking home such a large box of chocolates?"

"To be on the safe side. This morning my wife gave me a loving kiss—that means that it's either her birthday or our wedding anniversary."

[3973]

Hostess (at evening party)–"What, going already, Professor? And must you take your dear wife with you?"
Professor–"Indeed, I'm sorry to say I must!"

[3974]

Waiter – "Haven't you forgotten something, sir?"
Professor–"Why, I thought I gave you the customary tip."
Waiter–"You did, sir, but you forgot to eat."

[3975]

Wife–"Why don't you put the cat out as I told you?"
Absent-minded Professor–"I put something out. Ye gods! It must have been the baby!"

[3976]

Absent-minded Professor (going around in a revolving door)–"Bless me! I can't remember whether I was going in or coming out."

[3977]

Wife–"Do you realize, dear, that it was twenty-five years ago today that we became engaged?"
Absent-minded Professor–"Twenty-five years! Bless my soul! You should have reminded me before. It's certainly time we got married."

COLLEGE LIFE

[3978]

The boys were arriving back at the fraternity house after the summer vacation.
"What have you been doing this summer?" one asked another.
"Working in my dad's office. And you?"
"I've been loafing, too."

[3979]

"Why didn't you shave this morning?"
"I thought I did but there were twelve of us using the same mirror this morning and I must have shaved some other guy."

[3980]

"Who was that alumnus I seen you with last night?"
"That was no alumnus, that was just an ordinary drunk."

[3981]

"Is this dance formal, or can I wear my own clothes?"

[3982]

Overheard at a sorority:
"He's a good kid, isn't he?"
"Yes, if he had some brains he'd be a smart boy, if he knew how to use them."

[3983]

"What sort of toothbrush do you want?"
"Lemme have a big one—there's thirty fellows in our fraternity."

[3984]

A student, getting back to school late, had difficulty in obtaining a suitable place of lodging.
One landlady, showing him a dingy bedroom, remarked persuasively, "As a whole, this is quite a nice room, isn't it?"
"Yes, madam," he agreed, "but as a bedroom it's no good."

[3985]

Voice (over telephone) – "Hello. Hello. This is Judge Babington Peterson McFeatherson the Third. Will you please tell my son, Cravenwood Rutherford McFeatherson the Fourth, that I would like to speak to him."
Frosh–"Hey, Mac, your old man wants to speak to you."

[3986]

"I had a narrow escape last night!"

"What's that?"

"Well, I woke up in the middle of the night and saw something white in my room. So I grabbed my gun and shot it. When I put on the light, I discovered it was my shirt."

"I don't see what's so narrow in that."

"Well, suppose I had forgotten to take off my shirt last night."

[3987]

Freshman (finishing a letter)–"I'd send you that five I owe you, but I've already sealed the letter."

[3988]

"I see by the paper that nine professors and one student were killed in a wreck."

"Poor chap."

[3989]

Junior–"I bet you come from a burg where all the hicks congregate at the post office for their mail."

Freshie–"What's a post office?"

[3990]

"Give me a match, Bill."

"Here it is."

"Well, can you beat that? I've forgotten my cigarettes."

"S'too bad; give me back my match."

[3991]

First Burglar–"Where've you been?"

Second Burglar–"Robbing one of the fraternity houses."

First Burglar–"Lose anything?"

[3992]

On the hunt for excitement, the eager freshman asked: "Can you suggest something in the way of a good time?"

The disconsolate junior muttered: "The Dean."

[3993]

Applicant for Room–"What are your terms for students?"

Landlady (in college town)–"Bums, loafers, dead beats and wonderful promisers."

[3994]

At Hahved two sophomores assigned to room together started to get acquainted.

"My name's Alexander the Great," said the first.

"That's funny, I'm Charlemagne," was the reply.

Oddly enough, they were both lying.

[3995]

He–"Does John Jones, a student, live here?"

Landlady–"Well, Mr. Jones lives here, but I thought he was a night watchman."

[3996]

Frosh–"I woke up last night with the feeling that my watch was gone, so I got up and looked for it."

Soph–"Well, was it gone?"

Frosh–"No, it was going."

[3997]

Boarding House Lady–"Do you want a room?"

Stude–"No, I want to disguise myself as a banana and sleep in the fruit dish."

[3998]

Said the bell-hop to a noisy college drinking party in a hotel bedroom: "I've been sent to ask you to make less noise, gentlemen. The gentleman in the next room says he can't read."

"Tell him," was the reply of one of the collegiates, "that he ought to be ashamed of himself. Why, I could read when I was five years old."

[3999]

It was reported to the Dean that one of the students was in the habit of absorbing more liquor than was good for him. The Dean determied to do his duty and look into the matter.

Meeting the young man under suspicion in the yard shortly after breakfast one day the Dean marched up to him and demanded, "Young man, do you drink?"

"Why, why, why," stammered the young man, "why Dean, not so early in the morning, thank you."

[4000]

"So you say the water that you get here at the fraternity house is unsafe?"

"Yeah."

"Well, tell me, what precautions do you take against it?"

"First we filter it."

"Yes."

"Then we boil it."

"Yes."

"Then we add chemicals to it."

"Yes."

"And then we drink beer."

[4001]

In a college town a student called at a boarding house to inquire about rooms.

"And what do you charge for your rooms?" he asked.

"Five dollars up," was the reply.

"Yes, but I'm a student," he said, thinking the price a little high.

"That being the case, the price is $5 down."

[4002]

First Beta–"This butter is so strong it walks over to the cup of coffee and says, 'How do you do?' "

Second Loafer–"Yes, but the coffee is too weak to answer."

[4003]

Proctor (exceedingly angry)–"So you confess that this unfortunate Freshman was carried to this frog pond and drenched? Now what part did you take in this disgraceful affair?"

Sophomore (meekly)–"The right leg, sir."

[4004]

The dean was investigating a charge made by the sorority girls that the men who lived in the fraternity house next door never lowered their shades.

The dean looked out of the sorority window and said:

"Why, I can't see into any of the fraternity house windows."

"Oh, yes, you can!" said the girls. "All you have to do is to get up on a chair."

[4005]

Roommate (during intermission)–"How do you like the date I dug up for you?"

Ditto–"Rotten! Throw her back, and start digging some place else!"

[4006]

Rupert–"What did you do with the cuffs I left on the table last night?"

Roland–"They were so soiled I sent them to the laundry."

Rupert–"Ye gods, the entire history of England was on them."

[4007]

Freshman–"Say, what's the idea of wearing my raincoat?"

Roommate–"Well, you wouldn't want our new suit to get wet, would you?"

[4008]

Beggar–"Have you got enough money for a cup of coffee?"

Student–"Oh, I'll manage somehow, thank you."

[4009]

Student–"Where are we going to get that check of yours cashed, pal?"
Roommate–"I couldn't say. I can't think of a single place where I'm unknown."

[4010]

"Tell me the story of the police raiding your fraternity."
"Oh, that's a closed chapter now."

[4011]

"I think this talk about a college man's life being all wine, women, and song is exaggerated."
"It certainly is—you never hear singing in a dormitory."

[4012]

"Are you a college man?"
"No, a horse just stepped on my hat."

[4013]

"What kinda guy is your roommate?"
"Well, last night he barked his shins on a chair, and said, 'Oh, the perversity of inanimate objects.' "

[4014]

Landlady–"I'll give you just three days in which to pay your board."
Student–"All right. I'll pick the Fourth of July, Christmas and Easter."

[4015]

First Stude–"Being broke makes me writhe!"
Second Stude–"Don't writhe, telegraph!"

[4016]

First Fraternity Man–"Say, Jim, I wonder if I could borrow that blue necktie of yours?"
Second Fraternity Man–"What's the matter? Couldn't you find it?"

[4017]

Judge (to amateur yegg)–"So they caught you with this bundle of silverware. Whom did you plunder?"
Yegg–"Two fraternity-houses, Your Honor."
Judge (to Sergeant)–"Call up the downtown hotels and distribute this stuff."

[4018]

"You college men seem to take life pretty easy."
"Yes; even when we graduate we do it by degrees."

[4019]

George (sitting down to the piano) –"Well, boys, what do you want me to play?"
Chorus (lustily)–"Dead."

[4020]

Collegiate–"Open this door."
Roommate–"Can't. Key's lost."
Collegiate – "Good gosh! What would you do if there is a fire?"
Roommate–"I won't go."

[4021]

Freshman–"Well, me lad, I underwent a thorough physical examination today and the doc says that I'm as sound as a nut."
Soph–"Oh! He's also an alienist?"

[4022]

"I wish some college clothes."
"Athletic, humorous, or studious?"

[4023]

Maid–"Shall I take this little rug out and beat it?"
Man–"That's no rug, that's my roommate's towel."

[4024]

Freshman–"I feel like a two-year-old!"
Sophomore–"Horse or egg?"

FLAMING YOUTH

[4025]

"Pearl swears she has never been kissed by a man."

"Well, isn't that enough to make any girl swear?"

[4026]

"I hate people who are vague and non-committal, don't you?"

"Mmmmm!"

[4027]

She–"I'm not myself tonight."

Brute–"Then we ought to have a good time."

[4028]

"Darling, am I the first man you ever loved?"

"Yes, Reginald. All the others were fraternity boys."

[4029]

The girl student was trying to freeze out the young man who wanted to marry her. Said she: "Circumstances compel me to decline a marital arrangement with a man of no pecuniary resources."

"Er," he stammered. "I don't get you."

"That's what I'm telling you!" was the icy reply.

[4030]

Police Sergeant–"A college student, eh?"

Prisoner–"Yes, sir."

Patrolman–"It's a stall. I frisked him twice and there ain't a single magazine blank on him."

[4031]

"Dorothy, don't you speak to him any more?"

"No! Whenever I pass him I give him the geological survey."

"Geological survey?"

"Yes, that's what is commonly known as the stony stare."

[4032]

She–"That moon fills me with hunger for something."

He (hastily)–"Let's dance."

[4033]

Sally–"I don't like some of these modern dances. They're nothing but hugging set to music."

Nancy–"Well, what is there about that to which you object?"

Sally–"The music."

[4034]

The following conversation took place in physical examination of freshmen:

Examiner–"Calf?"

Frosh–"Fourteen inches."

Examiner–"Thigh?"

Frosh–"Twenty-six inches."

Examiner–"Neck?"

Frosh–"Yes."

[4035]

"My, but Frank is getting round-shouldered!"

"Too much study I guess."

"Study nothing! The trouble with him is that he's been kissing too many short girls."

[4036]

"Don't you think George dresses nattily?"

"Natalie who?"

[4037]

"I never wear gloves when I call on my girl."

"Why not?"

"Oh, I feel better without them."

[4038]

Editor–"That coed draws well, doesn't she?"

Asst. Ed. (absently)–"Yep; there were ten of us there last night."

[4039]

"She was only the optician's daughter—two glasses and she made a spectacle of herself."

[4040]

He–"He's just bashful. Why don't you give him a little encouragement."
She–"Encouragement? He needs a cheering section!"

[4041]

"Did you take Dot for a joy ride last night?"
"No, just for a ride."

[4042]

"The more I look at you, dear, the more beautiful you seem."
"Yes?"
"I ought to look at you oftener."

[4043]

"I was kissed so often last night that I lost count."
"By the same man?"
"No; he was a changed man after the first kiss."

[4044]

He (to girl in ultra gown)–"Do you like wearing evening dress?"
She–"I feel that nothing is more becoming to me."
He–"I have no doubt of that; but wouldn't that be going a trifle too far?"

[4045]

When the very, very fat young woman walked into the room, four fellows over by the punch bowl started laughing and pointing.
"There they go," she muttered angrily, "having fun at my expanse again."

[4046]

An old lady who had been introduced to a doctor who was also a professor in a university, felt somewhat puzzled as to how she would address the great man.
"Shall I call you 'doctor' or 'professor'?" she asked.
"Oh! just as you wish," was the reply; "as a mater of fact, some people call me an old idiot."
"Indeed," she said, sweetly, "but then, they are people that know you."

[4047]

"Hasn't Gayboy been mixed up in several divorce suits?"
"Yes; he's a graduate of a co-respondents' school."

[4048]

A collegiate moustache must have inspired the installment plan. You know, a little down and then a little more each week.

[4049]

"Why do you always address the letter-carrier as professor?"
"It's a sort of honorary title. I'm taking a course by mail."

[4050]

"Hello, little girl! Want a ride?"
"No thanks. I'm walking back from one now."

[4051]

"I won't have Mr. Jones kissing you like that, Mabel."
"But, Dad, give him a chance. He's only just beginning."

[4052]

Elsie–"I'm forgetting men."
Ethel–"So am I. I'm for getting a couple of them as quick as possible."

[4053]

"Was it very crowded at the cabaret last night?"
"Not under my table."

[4054]

"Remember that co-ed who was always flirting with the professors so she'd get good grades?"
"Yeah, what's she doing now?"
"Petting the milk man so she'll be sure to get Grade A."

[4055]

Joe College (in court for speeding) –"But, Judge, it's simply in me to do everything fast."
Judge–"All right, see how fast you can do thirty days."

[4056]

"What did you say when Jack threatened to kiss you?"
"I told him I'd just like to see him."
"And then?"
"Well, Jack always tries to do what I like."

[4057]

He–"Want me to call you a taxi?"
She–"Yes."
He–"You're a taxi."

[4058]

He dropped around to a girl's house, and as he ran up the steps he was confronted by her little brother.
"Hi, Billy."
"Hi," said the brat.
"Is your sister expecting me?"
"Yeah."
"How do you know?"
"She's gone out."

[4059]

"Lips that touch wine shall never touch mine," declared the fair co-ed. And after she graduated she taught school for years and years and years and years.

[4060]

The English language is a funny thing. Tell her that time stands still when you look into her eyes, and she'll adore you, but just try telling her that her face would stop a clock!

[4061]

"Do you really approve of the nude in art?"
"Yes, I was born that way."

[4062]

Her–"For goodness' sake, use two hands."
Him–"Can't; I gotta drive with one."

[4063]

"I told you you might kiss my hand, but you kissed my lips, too! How dare you?"
"Oh, a hand-to-mouth existence is good enough for me!"

[4064]

"Girls make me tired," said the fresh young man. "They are always going to palmists to have their hands read."
"Indeed!" said she sweetly; "is that any worse than men going into saloons to get their noses red?"

[4065]

Charlotte–"What kind of a car has Tom?"
Dorothy–"A pray-as-you-enter!"

[4066]

He–"That's a flimsy dress you're wearing."
She–"That's a flimsy excuse for staring."

[4067]

"So you think Dora's face is her fortune."
"I'm sure of it. It runs into a nice little figure."

[4068]

Two students were passing a residence where one of the occupants has forgotten to lower the shade.
"That girl's not a bit shy, is she?"
"Well—not exactly—but she's certainly retiring."

[4069]

"Do you think a woman believes you when you tell her she is the first girl you ever loved?"
"Yes, if you're the first liar she has ever met."

[4070]

Percy–"I'm going to kiss you like you've never been kissed before."

Mabel–"Oh, yes, I have."

[4071]

Joan–"He's worth in the neighborhood of a million dollars, I've heard."

Jane–"Good! That's my favorite neighborhood."

[4072]

"Who's the girl with the Spanish heels?"

"Those aren't heels—they're darn nice fellows."

[4073]

"You look sweet enough to eat."

Sophie–"I do eat. Where shall we go?"

[4074]

He (as they drove along a lonely road)–"You look lovelier to me every minute. Do you know what that's a sign of?"

She–"Sure. You're about to run out of gas."

[4075]

"How is it that you can kiss so divinely?"

"Oh, I used to blow the bugle in the Boy Scouts."

[4076]

Stude–"I would rather be tight than be President."

[4077]

"You had no business to kiss me," she said.

"But it wasn't business; it was pleasure," he responded.

[4078]

She–"Did anyone ever tell you how wonderful you are?"

He–"Don't believe they ever did."

She–"Then where'd you get the idea?"

[4079]

"Do you have a faculty for making love?"

"No; we have a student body."

[4080]

She–"I don't neck."

He–"May I press you for particulars?"

[4081]

"I've a friend I'd like you girls to meet."

Athletic Girl–"What can he do?"

Chorus Girl–"How much has he?"

Literary Girl–"What does he read?"

Society Girl–"Who are his family?"

Religious Girl–"What church does he belong to?"

College Girl–"Where is he?"

[4082]

Mother–"Did I see you kissing that young Allen last night?"

Beryl–"Well, Mother, he told me he had just lost an uncle and I felt so sorry for him."

"If I know anything about that young man he won't have a relative left in a week's time!"

[4083]

"Would you consider it improper if I kissed your hand?"

"No, but I think it would be decidedly out of place."

[4084]

It doesn't matter how watchful and vigilant a girl is; if a fellow kisses her, it is ten to one he will do it right under her nose.

[4085]

"That bashful boyfriend of mine is a G-man."

"A government man?"

"Naw. All he can say is 'gee!'"

[4086]

"How did she get along at the seashore?"

"Oh, in fine shape."

[4087]

"So you're getting married? To whom?"

"To Mary. She's a lovely girl and I think she's very economical."

"What makes you think so?"

"Well, she's always trying to reduce expenses. When I go to see her, every evening, she puts out the light, and she insists that we both sit on the same chair."

[4088]

Pam–"Hasn't Harvey ever married?"

Beryl–"No, and I don't think he intends to, because he's studying for a bachelor's degree."

[4089]

"I hate women, and I'm glad I hate 'em, 'cause if I didn't hate 'em, I'd like 'em, and I hate 'em."

[4090]

A sophisticated girl is one who knows how to refuse a kiss without being deprived of it.

[4091]

She (at concert)–"What's that book the conductor keeps looking at?"

He–"That's the score of the overture."

She–"Oh, really, who's winning?"

[4092]

Mother (to house-mother)–"And are you sure that all of the parties at the university will be well chaperoned?"

House-mother – "Absolutely. Very well chaperoned."

Mother–"Well, then, I don't want her to go to the university. I want her to have a good time."

[4093]

Co-eds are divided into two species: those who shut their eyes when kissing, and those who look to see if you do.

[4094]

"Say you love me. Say it! Say it! For heaven's sake, say it!"

"It!"

[4095]

Maisie–"Do you know, I wouldn't trust Tony too far."

Daisy–"I wouldn't trust him too near."

[4096]

Rosie–"Aren't you getting Johnnie and Bill confused?"

Mary–"Yes, I get Johnnie confused one night and Bill the next."

[4097]

She–"How old do you think I am?"

He–"Oh, about twenty-one."

She–"How did you guess?"

He–"I didn't; I just counted the rings under your eyes."

[4098]

Frosh–"I was out with a nurse last night."

Co-ed–"Cheer up. Maybe your mother will let you go out without one sometime."

[4099]

Stude–"Le's give a cheer for college comics."

Stewed–"Raw! Raw! Raw!"

[4100]

"I wore more clothes than any other girl at the Artists' and Models' Masquerade."

"Is that so? How did you go?"

"Unnoticed."

[4101]

He (awkward dancer)–"It was nice of you to give me this dance."

She (sweetly)–"Not at all—this is a charity ball."

[4102]

He–"I'm one fellow who believes in long engagements."

She–"Oh, a cynical lover, eh?"

He–"No, I'm an actor."

[4103]

Jane–"Would you be insulted if that good looking stranger offered you some champagne?"
Joan–"Yes, but I'd probably swallow the insult."

[4104]

"Daughter, is that young man down there yet?"
"Damn right, I am. What's it to you?"

[4105]

At a formal dance a sophomore discovered that he was standing on his lady friend's train. He had the presence of mind to remark: "Though I may not have the power to draw an angel from the skies, I have pinned one to the earth."
She excused him.

[4106]

Harry–"She sure gave you a dirty look."
Pete–"Who?"
Harry–"Mother Nature."

[4107]

He–"You know, I'm funny—always throw myself into anything I undertake."
Pretty Girl–"How splendid! Why don't you dig a well?"

[4108]

"And after he kissed you three times, then what?"
"Well—then he began to get sentimental."

[4109]

"Would you call for help if I tried to kiss you?"
"Do you need help?"

[4110]

Co-ed–"I'd like to see the captain of this ship."
Sailor–"He's forward, Miss."
Co-ed–"That's all right. This is a pleasure trip."

[4111]

He–"I long ago made up my mind to kiss every girl who made that silly remark, 'How interesting.' "
She–"How interesting!"

[4112]

"Hey! Sit down in front!"
"Quit yer kidding. I don't bend that way."

[4113]

She–"Your kisses are like a popular drink."
He–"Powerful?"
She–"No, old fashioned."

[4114]

"Well, how was the burlesque dance?"
"Abdominal!"

[4115]

She–"Darling, your kisses thrill me to the very bottom of my feet."
He–"Well, they should. They're soul kisses."

[4116]

Teacher–"What was the Tower of Babel?"
Student–"Wasn't that where Solomon kept his 500 wives?"

[4117]

She–"How do you like my new coat?"
He (looking at her face)–"Fine, only you got it on too thick!"

[4118]

Most fellows after fooling around a while, find out that their pet lamb is just a little bossie.

[4119]

He–"What would you say if I kissed you?"
She–"I wouldn't be in a position to speak."

[4120]

She–"Thanks for the hug."
He–"Oh the pressure was all mine."

[4121]
"Oh Marie, je t'adore."
"Shut it yourself. You opened it."

[4122]
College Lad (arrested for speeding)
–"But, Your Honor, I am a college boy."
Judge–"Ignorance doesn't excuse anybody!"

[4123]
She–"I just saw Dot walking down the street with her new evening gown under her arm."
He–"Don't tell me the styles have come to that!"

[4124]
"So yer finnaly hurd from dat collitch boy who took yer out?"
"Yah. And he's a real gent, he is. He asked me if I got home from the dance awl right."

[4125]
And then there was the Alpha Phi who was so dumb she thought a buttress was a female goat.

[4126]
"Darling, you would be a marvelous dancer but for two things."
"What are they, sweetheart?"
"Your feet."

[4127]
"Gee, you're a swell dancer. Did you take dancing lessons?"
"No, but I took wrestling lessons."

[4128]
She (after a quarrel)–"Leave this house. I never want to see you again. Go this instant."
He–"I have one last request to make before I go."
She (sweetly, oh very sweetly)–"Well, what is it?"
He (brutally)–"Before I leave forever, would you mind getting off my lap?"

[4129]
"Did Clarice enjoy her date with Joe last night?"
"She was never so humiliated in her life. When he started to eat his soup, five couples got up and began dancing."

[4130]
It has been our experience with women scholars that the Ph.D. must stand for "Petticoat Hangs Down."

[4131]
He–"Let's sit this one out; no one will be the wiser."
She–"Oh, yes; you will."

[4132]
"She was only a photographer's daughter."
"Yes, she sits in a dark room and awaits developments."

[4133]
Wife (to late returning husband)–
"Is that you, John?"
John–"It better be."

[4134]
He–"I like your form."
She–"Must we go all over that again?"

[4135]
Mother–"Son, I don't want to see you going around with that wild girl any more."
Son–"Aw, heck, maw, she ain't wild. Anybody can pet her."

[4136]
And then one day she turned and saw that he was smiling at her! She smiled back at him! No, he didn't turn away, he didn't disappear—he looked at her more intently than before!
"Smile like that again," he said.
She blushed and dimpled. And he laughed and laughed.
"Just as I thought," he said. "You look like a chipmunk."

[4137]

"Mary turned me down when I asked her for another dance."

"Well, she knows her bunions."

[4138]

"I'm going to marry a patrolman."

"How thrilling! What's his name?"

"I don't know his name, but I've got his number."

[4139]

Old–"What's a college censor?"

Line–"A censor is a person that can see three meanings to a college joke that has only two meanings."

[4140]

We know one co-ed who was cured of that cute little habit of coyly injecting an "r" sound into each word.

Male (over phone)–"Hello, cutie."

Co-ed–"Why, Phillurp, when did you get back?"

Male–"Just a while ago. Say, how about a date tonight, kid. What are you doing?"

Co-ed (coyly)–"Nurthin'."

Male–"Gosh, excuse me. I didn't know."

[4141]

Baby Stork–"Mama, where did I come from?"

[4142]

He–"I don't know what's the matter. I never danced so poorly before."

She–"Oh, then you have danced before?"

[4143]

Mother–"Ethel, Robert brought you home very late last night."

Ethel–"Yes, it was late, Mother. Did the noise disturb you?"

Mother–"No, dear, it wasn't the noise. It was the silence."

[4144]

"What is your idea of heaven?"

"Methuselah's age and Solomon's wives."

[4145]

"I believe they were intended for each other."

"Yes, he's a pie face, and she's such a piece of cheese."

[4146]

"I'm a bird imitator, gal."

"I'll say you are! Why not give me a good kiss and quit pecking at me?"

[4147]

Little Willie is so distressed, he got a pair of pink pajamas and a military hair brush for Christmas and now he doesn't know whether to go to West Point or Harvard.

[4148]

He–"Darling, I have been thinking of something for a long, long time. Something is trembling on my lips . . ."

She–"Why don't you shave it off?"

[4149]

"I've finished with that girl."

"Why?"

"She asked me if I danced."

"What's so insulting about that?"

"I was dancing with her when she asked me."

[4150]

"What? You were out with Betty last night? But I thought she threw you over."

"Well, you know how a girl throws!"

[4151]

Gigolo–"Tomorrow evening I'm going out to the suburbs to see a model home."

Gigolette–"Listen here, son, if there's any model to see home you let somebody else do it."

[4152]

"Darling, as I kissed you then, love was born."

"That's fine, dear, but wipe that birthmark off your lips."

[4153]

Every year college deans pop the routine question to their undergraduates: "Why did you come to college?" Traditionally the answers match the question in triteness. But one co-ed unexpectedly confided:

"I came to be went with—but I ain't yet!"

[4154]

"Sire, Lady Godiva rides without."

Sire (after glancing without)–"Very tactfully put, my man."

[4155]

She–"John, dear, I wouldn't let anyone else kiss me like this."

He–"My name isn't John."

[4156]

"Ha, ha, that's a yolk on me," said the Swedish lady as she dropped an egg on the front of her dress.

[4157]

The Gay Nineties–A gig and a gal.

The Roarin' Twenties–A flivver and a flapper.

The Dipsy Forties–A plane and a Jane.

[4158]

They sat on the beach. Her hair caressed his face. Her head rested on his shoulders. Her lips looked down on his. Finally she murmured, "Why don't you kiss me?"

"I can't," he said, "some sand got in my mouth."

"Swallow it, boy, swallow it," she said, "If any one ever had need of sand, you certainly are the guy."

[4159]

He–"Ah, you have a lovely mouth."

She–"You've been all over that before."

[4160]

She–"Say, you're too rough."

He–"But mine's true love, and it never did run smooth."

[4161]

"You look sweet enough to eat," He whispered soft and low

"I am," said she quite hungrily, "Where do you want to go?"

[4162]

"So you took that pippin home from the movie last night."

"Yeh."

"How far does she live from the theater?"

"Oh, three soda-fountains and a candy-store."

[4163]

Voice on phone–"Is Hugh there?"

Sweet Thing (answering)–"Hugh who?"

Voice–"Yoo-hoo yourself!"

[4164]

He–"How about a little ride, Cutie?"

She–"Are you going north?"

He–"Yes, I am."

She–"Give my regards to the Eskimos."

[4165]

Bill–"I'll marry a girl that can cook and make a home, and not one of those who can only play bridge."

Bob–"Fine. Come over and meet our housemaid."

[4166]

Betty–"Oh, Archibald, you're too slow."

Archie–"I'm afraid I don't grasp you."

Betty–"Yes, that's just it."

[4167]

A date with a modern girl is an open and shut proposition; she's always eating.

[4168]

Frosh–"Am I the only man you have ever kissed?"

Deb–"Yes, and by far the best looking."

[4169]

The roadster skidded around the corner, jumped in the air, knocked down a lamp-post, smacked three cars, ran against a stone fence, and stopped. A girl climbed out of the wreck.

"Darling," she exclaimed, "that's what I call a kiss!"

[4170]

"What did you do when he disapproved of your bathing-suit?"

"Oh, I just laughed it off."

[4171]

"Why do girls roll their stockings?"

"They're afraid the teddy bears will chew the tops off them."

[4172]

Archibald–"I don't remember very clearly, but did I shock the hostess last night?"

Algernon–"Did you shock her—her eyebrows haven't come down yet!"

[4173]

"Honey, I'd go through fire and water for you."

"Okay, make it fire. I'd rather have you hot than all wet."

[4174]

Cutie–"Darling, sometimes you're masculine and at other times so effeminate. How is that?"

Cootie–"I suppose it's hereditary. Half my ancestors were males and the other half were females."

[4175]

"Astounding cheek, hasn't he?"

"Don't know, darling. Didn't dance with him."

[4176]

"Are you fond of nuts?"

"Is this a proposal?"

[4177]

He–"Do you indulge greatly in terpsichorean art?"

She–"Oh, why bother about such things, let's dance!"

[4178]

He had rather liked the look of her, and suggested a run in his car. When they had gone a few miles, the girl said:

"Now, before we drive any farther, I want you to understand that I don't flirt, so don't try to hold my hand or kiss me. Is that quite clear?"

The young man gulped and said, "Yes."

"Now," said the girl, brightly, "since that is settled and done with, where shall we go?"

He murmured: "Home."

[4179]

And then there's the shoemaker's daughter who gave the boys her awl.

[4180]

"Why the toothbrush in your coat lapel?"

"It's my class pin—I go to Colgate."

[4181]

"Why do you think he's from the North?"

"He dances as if he had snow-shoes on."

[4182]

"Here's where I cut a good figure," said the college girl, as she sat on a broken bottle.

[4183]

She–"Am I your father?"
He–"No, why?"
She–"Then quit pawin' me."

[4184]

"Who is that fellow with the long hair?"
"He's the sophomore from Yale."
"Oh, I've often heard of those Yale locks."

[4185]

"They say you can tell a girl's character by her clothes."
"Nonsense! Girls must have more character than that!"

[4186]

Clara–"They say that one evening's dance is equivalent to walking ten miles."
Maud–"That was in the old style. Now it's equivalent to climbing one hundred trees."

[4187]

The sun trickled lightly through cypress leaves into the crystal pool. Odysseus awoke, wiped the salt water from his eyes, and peered cautiously around the bush. There, in the speckled light, stooped Nausicaa, her lithe body bending to and fro as she dipped her linens into the limpid waters. Her rosy figure was like a nude Aphrodite, chiseled in pink marble. For some minutes The Wanderer sat spellbound, his eyes riveted to the swaying body. Then he loosed his tongue, for he could no longer hold his peace.
"Gad!" he hissed, "double-jointed."

[4188]

A Boston girl being asked if she was once engaged to a Harvard student named Jackson, languidly replied, "I am not certain about the name."

[4189]

Country road. Youth and Maiden in car. Car falters, then stops.
Calloused Youth–"Outta gas, by cracky!"
Poor-but-Honest-Girl–"Oh yeah?" (Produces flask from somewhere.)
C.Y. (in a highly receptive tone)– "Aaah! what's in that flask?"
P.B.H.G.–"Gasoline."

[4190]

"Does your son burn the midnight oil?"
"Yes, and a lot of gasoline with it."

[4191]

Once upon a time a girl went riding with a man and when they reached a dark lonely road he stopped the car and said: "Girl, there's something wrong with the engine." So—he gets out and opens his tool kit and proceeds to repair the engine; gets back in the car and drives the girl home.

[4192]

Mother–"After all, he's only a boy and boys will sow their wild oats."
Father–"Yes, but I wouldn't mind if he didn't mix in so much rye."

[4193]

A lovely girl with red hair entered the car and sat down beside a youth.
Youth (edging away)–"I must not get too close or I shall catch fire."
Girl–"Don't be alarmed; green wood never catches fire."

[4194]

"Can you drive with one arm?"
"Sure."
"Okay, have an apple."

[4195]

"Shall we sit here and talk?"
"No, thanks, I am so tired. Let us dance instead."

[4196]
"Statistics show that the eyesight of boys is superior to that of girls."
"Yeh! I know. I fell for a girl last summer who can't see me at all."

[4197]
She—"I want a lipstick."
Clerk—"What size, please?"
She—"Three rides and a house party."

[4198]
She clung to him. He could feel the subtle warmth of her burning into his soul. Something within him stirred. He touched her bare shoulders with the tips of his fingers, her hot breath in his face.
"My Gosh," he said, trembling. "What would you have me do?"
She lifted her eyes to his—eyes in which burned an inscrutable fire.
"Pick up your feet, you poor fish, and don't step on my gown again until this dance is over," she murmured.

[4199]
"I got a real kick out of kissing Jane, last night."
"Any more than usual?"
"Yea, the old man caught me."

[4200]
She—"Now tell me the truth—do you men like the talkative women as well as you do the other kind?"
He—"What other kind?"

[4201]
"Will you be true to me?" asked the debutante daughter of a broker to her college boy friend.
"As true as steel," quoth he.
"Common or preferred?" she snapped back.

[4202]
He—"May I kiss you?"
She—"Heavens! Another amateur!"

[4203]
"Did you know, dear, that that tunnel we just passed through was two miles long and cost $12,000,-000?" asked the young man of his sweetheart.
"Oh, really?" she replied, as she started to rearrange her disheveled hair. "Well, it was worth it, wasn't it?"

[4204]
She—"You remind me of the ocean."
He—"Wild, romantic and restless?"
She—"No, you just make me sick."

[4205]
"I was out over the speedway today, and in thirty seconds I did a mile in four laps."
"That's nothing. I know a young lady who did thirty miles in one lap, and she would have done more if I hadn't got a cramp in my knees."

[4206]
Irate father—"I'll teach you to kiss my daughter."
Cornelius—"You're too late. I've already learned."

[4207]
He—"Do you believe in platonic love?"
She—"Well, I wouldn't mind trying it as a starter."

[4208]
Mother (severely)—"Dora, did I see that young man stroking your hair on the porch last night?"
Daughter—"It's a mere habit with him, Mother. He used to stroke on the varsity eight."

[4209]
Poetic Lover—"Just one kiss. Love makes the world go round."
Campus Amazon—"So does a smash on the jaw."

[4210]

The young man straightened his tie and with brave determination entered the living room.

"Er, could I see you for a moment, sir?"

"Absolutely, my boy. What can I do for you?"

"Well, sir, you see it's like this-er. Phyllis thought we'd better ask you first."

"Yes, go right ahead. Young people nowadays usually don't ask."

"Er—well—we've been going together for quite some time now and Phyllis thought it'd be all right if I'd ask you."

"Why certainly, Bob, you're a fine boy and I've always been fond of you."

"Then can I take your car tonight?"

[4211]

A bashful student who had been keeping steady company with a fair co-ed for nearly three years. Times were bad, and the continual reduction in his spending allowance was much too well reflected in the economies he had to practice when dating. One evening he said to the girl friend:

"Peggy, you know I've always relied on you, and may I—that is—would you—er—r—can you—ah—Peggy, will you marry me?"

"Oh-h-h," Peggy sighed with apparent relief. "You certainly gave me a fright. I thought you wanted to borrow some money."

[4212]

She (driving her new car)—"Would you like to see where I was vaccinated?"

He (expectantly)—"Yes, indeed."

She—"Well, keep your eyes open; we'll drive by there pretty soon."

[4213]

"Good heavens! Who gave you that black eye?"

"A bridegroom—for kissing the bride after the ceremony."

"But surely he didn't object to that ancient custom?"

"No—but it was two years after the ceremony."

[4214]

"I took that pretty girl from the store home the other night, and stole a kiss."

"What did she say?"

"Will that be all?"

[4215]

Him—"I hope you'll dance with me tonight."

Her—"Oh, certainly. I hope you don't think I came down here merely for pleasure."

[4216]

He drew her close to him, kissed her with all the first fires of passion. No one would have guessed they were married.

They were not.

[4217]

Soph.—"How does it happen you came to Harvard? I thought your father was a Yale man."

Fresh.—"He was. He wanted me to go to Yale; I wanted to go to Princeton. We had an argument and he finally told me to go to H—."

[4218]

He—"Say, Mabel, may I come over tonight?"

She—"Sure, John, come on over."

He—"Why, this is not John."

She—"This is not Mabel, either."

[4219]

"What do you do when in doubt about kissing a girl?"

"Give her the benefit of the doubt."

ATHLETICS

[4220]

"Let's sit this one out," remarked the coach as he pulled the thick headed quarterback out of the game.

[4221]

Dumb Dora—"I don't see how football players ever get clean!"

Ditto—"Silly, what do you suppose the scrub teams are for?"

[4222]

Coach (to quarterback)—"Get in the game there and *run that team!* An' don't forget to watch the bench for signals!"

[4223]

Mrs. Greene (at her first football game)—"Oh, isn't it awful? Why, they will kill that poor boy underneath."

Daughter—"Don't be silly, mother! He doesn't mind it; he's unconscious by this time."

[4224]

Girl at Game (watching huddle on the field)—"There they're at it again! I do hope Bill won't repeat that story I told him last night."

[4225]

She—"Did you get hurt when you were on the eleven?"

Jack—"No; it was while the eleven were on me."

[4226]

She—"Tell me about the track meet."

Freshman—"Dear me, no. I never tell racy stories."

[4227]

Reporter—"What shall I say about the peroxide blondes who made such a fuss at the ball game?"

Editor—"Say, the bleachers went wild."

[4228]

He (at football game)—"That fellow out there playing center will be our best man before the season is over."

She—"Oh, Jack, this is so sudden."

[4229]

The co-ed's football team was losing and the tears streamed down her cheeks.

"I'll kiss those tears away," said her escort.

He did the best he knew how, but the tears still flowed on. Finally he asked, "Will nothing stop them?"

"No," she murmured. "It's asthma, but go on with the treatment."

[4230]

"At the football game hundreds of girls were turned down for seats."

"That's a new idea in seating."

[4231]

Captain—"Whoever he is, there is a dirty sneak crook on this squad. In the past week I have lost a set of Stanford shoulder pads, a Yale sweater shirt, a pair of Harvard pants, a Northwestern blanket, and a couple of Y. M. C. A. towels."

[4232]

"There's a fine fellow in the college crew."

"Yes, he's a gentleman and a sculler."

[4233]

There are two kinds of colleges in America—those that wish they had fired the coach last fall, and those that wish they hadn't.

[4234]

"Was your father a college man?"

"Yes, but we never mention it. The college he went to had a rotten football team."

[4235]

"What is your brother in college?"

"A half back."

"I mean in studies."

"Oh, in studies he's away back."

[4236]

"That's a swell rooting section they have at that college. What makes it so good?"

"Oh, they give all the rooters a cheering drink."

"Of what?"

"Don't be dumb. Root beer, of course."

[4237]

He–"Look! Our captain is going to kick a goal."

She–"What did the goal do?"

[4238]

Fan–"How about your team? Are they good losers?"

Coach (after a disastrous season)– "Good? Hell, they're perfect."

BACK HOME

[4239]

Son in college was applying pressure for more money from home.

"I can not understand why you call yourself a kind father," he wrote his dad, "when you haven't sent me a check for three weeks. What kind of kindness do you call that?"

"That's unremitting kindness," wrote the father in his next letter.

[4240]

Proud Father–"Well, son, now that you're a grad what are you going to do?"

Offspring–"I'm going to talk to you about the good old days."

[4241]

Father – "What was the hardest thing you learned at college?"

Son – "How to open beer bottles with a half-dollar."

[4242]

Two college girls were having lunch together.

"My dear," said one, "why do you always call your mother 'the mater'?"

"Because," answered the other girl, "she managed to find husbands for all my seven sisters."

[4243]

"They tell me your son in college is quite an author. Does he write for money?"

"Yes, in every letter."

[4244]

A son at college wrote his father: "No mon, no fun, your son."

The father answered:

"How sad, too bad, your dad."

[4245]

"Say, dad, remember that story you told me about when you were expelled from college?"

"Yes."

"Well, I was just thinking, dad, how true it is that history repeats itself."

[4246]

Dear Pop and Mom–"Don't be surprised if my grades aren't so good this spring, as I have Astronomy labs at night, Union classes on coking during the day, and a Campusology course that requires lots of attention."

Love,
Leonora

[4247]

"The waiter laughed when I spoke to him in French. No wonder, it was my old prof."

[4248]

Thompson–"So your son is in college? How is he making it?"
Johnson – "To be exact, he isn't making it. I'm making it and he's spending it."

[4249]

"Goodness, Sarah, what a kitchen!" exclaimed Mrs. Smith. "Every pot, pan, and dish is dirty. The table is a perfect litter and—why, it will take you all night to clear things up. What have you been doing?"

"Nothing, ma'am," explained Sarah. "Your daughter has just been showing me how they boil a potato at her cooking class in college."

[4250]

"Has your son's college education proved of any real value?"

"Yes, indeed, it's entirely cured his mother of bragging about him."

[4251]

They were home for Christmas, and coming from different colleges, they had quite a lot to talk over. Finally the conversation swung into the inevitable discussion of the relative merits of the girls they had met. Waxing eloquent, the first stated that his girl was not only refined, but very well educated. As proof, he exhibited her last letter.

The second read the letter and then pondered for a few moments. "Well," he said, "there's no doubt that she's refined, but I don't think she's so well educated. Why over here on the last page she spells *spit* with two *t's.*"

[4252]

Yes – "What can take the place of a college education? Nothing! Look at the man who only finished high school. Where is he now?

He's the motorman on the street car. But where is the man who has gone through college and has his diploma?"
Weak voice–"He's the conductor."

[4253]

Pa–"Well, s o n, h o w a r e your marks?"
Son–"They're under water."
Pa – "What do you mean under water?"
Son–"Below 'C' level."

[4254]

Communist Father–"What do you mean by staying away from college? What do you mean by playing truant?"
Son–"Class hatred, father."

[4255]

Father – "Did you give Rita that copy of 'What Every Girl Should Know'?"
Mother of Co-ed – "Yes, and she's writing a letter to the author suggesting the addition of three new chapters."

[4256]

Two men were discussing the vexed question of the education of their children. Said one:

"What's your boy going to be when he finishes his education?"

"An octogenarian, I think," replied the other.

[4257]

The father was a Princeton man and quite a grouch. His son had just finished his first term and exultingly reported that he had stood next to the head of his class.

"*Next* to the head!" the father exclaimed. "What do you mean? I'd like to know what you think I'm sending you to college for? *Next* to the head! Why aren't you at the head, where you ought to be?"

The son was much crestfallen. Upon his return to Princeton he studied harder than ever and at the end of the term he won the coveted place. When he went home that year he felt very proud. It would be great news for the old man.

When the announcement was made, the father contemplated his son for a few minutes in silence. Then, with a shrug, he remarked: "At the head of the class, eh? Well, that's a fine commentary on Princeton University!"

[4258]

Extract from a letter received by a mother from her daughter at college:

"I realize, mother, that daddy is paying a lot to keep me at school and that I must try and learn something. I am taking up contract bridge."

[4259]

"Where have you been for the last four years?"

"At college taking medicine."

"And did you finally get well?"

[4260]

Friend—"And what is your son going to be when he's passed his final exam?"

Father—"An old man."

[4261]

"What is your daughter working for at college—an M. A.?"

"No, an M-R-S."

[4262]

Dad (sternly) – "Where were you last night?"

Son—"Oh, just riding around with some of the boys."

Dad – "Well, tell 'em not to leave their hairpins in the car."

[4263]

Three boys from Yale, Princeton and Harvard were in a room when a lady entered. The Yale boy asked languidly if some fellow ought not to give a chair to the lady; the Princeton boy slowly brought one, and the Harvard boy deliberately sat down in it.

[4264]

Bob, now in his freshman year at college, wrote home to Dad:

"Dad, I've decided to cut school and get married. I'm engaged to a regular peach."

Dad replied: "Better take my advice, my son, and leave the peach on the parent stem until you are able to preserve it."

[4265]

Doctor—"Now say 'Ah'."

Patient—"None of that. I'm a Yale man."

[4266]

She was home from college for the holidays, and the old folks were having a reception in her honor. During the event she brought out some of her new gowns to show to the guests. Picking up a beautiful silk creation, she held it up before the admiring crowd.

"Isn't this perfectly gorgeous!" she exclaimed. "Just think, it came from a poor little insignificant worm!"

Her hard-working father looked a moment, then he turned and said: "Yes, darn it, an' I'm that worm!"

[4267]

Small Boy – "What is college bred, pop?"

Pop (with son in college) – "They make college bread, my boy, from the flour of youth and the dough of old age."

[4268]

Fond Mother–"Now that Harold is through college, are you going to take him into the business with you?"

Frank Father – "I dunno. Couldn't you use him for a bridge prize?"

[4269]

"Is that man rich?"

"Is he! He's so rich he doesn't know his son's in college."

[4270]

"There's a college graduate at the door. He wants a job."

"What can he do?" asked the self-made man.

"He says he's pretty good in Greek."

"Umph! Tell him I haven't sold $2 worth of goods to Greece since I've been in the export business."

[4271]

A college boy's definition of a male parent is, "The KIN you love to touch."

[4272]

We've heard that college-bred means a four-year loaf made with dad's dough. Some crust, eh?

[4273]

"A telegram from George, dear."

"Well, did he pass the examination this time?"

"No, but he is almost at the top of the list of those who failed."

[4274]

By the time the present-day college boy succeeds in accumulating the horse-hide, the pigskin, the coonskin and finally the sheepskin, poor father hasn't much hide left.

[4275]

"My son's home from college."

"How do you know?"

"I haven't had a letter from him for three weeks."

[4276]

Ezra–"How is that son of yours getting along in college?"

Eben–"Just fine! He's a professor now."

Ezra–"Do tell!"

Eben–"Yep. He writes that he is teaching English in Billiard Academy."

[4277]

The old couple were eating their first meal with their son after his return from college.

"Tell us, John," said the father, "what have you learned at college?"

"Oh, lots of things," said the son, as he recited off his course of studies. "Then," he concluded, "I also studied logic."

"Logic," said the old man; "what is that?"

"It's the art of reasoning," said the son.

"The art of reasoning?" said the father. "What is that, my boy."

"Well," replied the son, "let me give you a demonstration. How many chickens are on that dish, father?"

"Two," said the old man.

"Well," said John, "I can prove there are three." Then he stuck his fork in one and said: "That is one, isn't it?"

"Yes," said the father.

"And this is two?" sticking the fork in the second.

"Yes," replied the father again.

"Well, don't one and two make three?" replied John triumphantly.

"Well, I declare," said the father, "you have learned things at college. Well, mother," continued the old man to his wife, "I will give you one of the chickens to eat and I'll take the other, and John can have the third. How is that, John?"

[4278]

When his daughter returned from the girl's college, the farmer regarded her critically, and then demanded:

"Ain't you a lot fatter than you was?"

"Yes, faw-ther," the girl admitted. "I weigh one hundred and forty pounds stripped for 'gym.'"

The father stared for a moment in horrified amazement, then shouted:

"Who in thunder is Jim?"

[4279]

Two father of sons in college were comparing notes.

"My son's letters always send me to the dictionary," said one father.

"You're lucky," said the other. "My son's letters always send me to the bank."

[4280]

"I suppose you will miss your boy while he is at college?"

"Yep," replied Farmer Perkins. "I dunno what I'll do without him. He got the live stock so they won't move unless he gives 'em the college yell, an' I can't remember it."

[4281]

A young man who had received his diploma from a leading university had been looking around successively for a position, for employment, and for a job. Entering an office, he asked to see the manager, and while waiting he said to the office-boy:

"Do you suppose there is any opening here for a college graduate?"

"Well, dere will be," was the reply, "if de boss don't raise me salary to t'ree dollars a week by termorrer night."

[4282]

Alumnus—"Why, I'm sorry to hear that. How did Brother Jones die?"

Active—"He fell through some scaffolding."

Alumnus—"What on earth was he doing up there?"

Active—"Being hanged!"

[4283]

"Hard work never killed anybody," said the father.

"That's just the trouble, Dad," returned the son, just out of college. "I want to engage in something that has the spice of danger in it."

[4284]

Papa—"Son, are you pursuing your studies faithfully?"

Son—"Yes indeed, father. I'm always behind."

PART V

THE BUSINESS WORLD

OFFICES

[4285]
"You've already had leave, Ferguson, to see your wife off on a journey — for your mother-in-law's funeral—for your little girl's measles—your boy's christening—what is it now?"
"I'm going to get married, sir."

[4286]
Son (entering office)–"Well, dad, I just ran up to say hullo."
Dad–"Too late, my boy. Your mother ran up to say hullo, and got all my change."

[4287]
The owner of a large business concern bought a number of signs reading, "Do it Now," and had them hung around the office, hoping to inspire his people with promptness and energy in their work. In his private office one day soon afterward a friend asked him how the scheme affected the staff. "Well, not just the way I thought it would," answered the proprietor. "The cashier skipped with thirty thousand dollars, the head bookkeeper eloped with the private secretary, three clerks asked for an increase of salary, and the office boy lit out to become a bandit."

[4288]
A young man just out of college sought the advice of a hard-headed and successful business man. "Tell me, please, how I should go about getting a start in the great game of business."
"Sell your wrist watch and buy an alarm clock," was the laconic reply.

[4289]
Jones (over the phone) – "Are you going to pay us that account?"
Smith–"Not just yet."
Jones–"If you don't, I'll tell all your other creditors that you paid us."

[4290]
A fiery tempered Southern business man wrote the following letter:
"Sir, my stenographer, being a lady, cannot type what I think of you. I, being a gentleman, cannot think it. You, being neither, will understand what I mean."

[4291]
Employee–"Sir, can you let me off tomorrow afternoon to go Christmas shopping with my wife?"
Employer – "Certainly not! We are too busy!"
Empoyee (much relieved)–"Thank you, sir, you are very kind!"

411

[4292]
Father (intense with excitement)–
"Well, boy, what happened when you asked the boss for a raise?"
Son–"Why, he was like a lamb."
Father–"What did he say?"
Son–"Baa."

[4293]
Boss–"Simpkins, you've been drinking again. Now once and for all let me tell you that I'll do all the drinking that's done around here."
Simpkins–"You can't, sir. It would kill you in a week."

[4294]
A certain firm had the following legend printed on its salary receipt forms:
"Your salary is your personal business, and should not be disclosed to any one."
The new employee, in signing the receipt added: "I won't mention it to anybody. I'm just as much ashamed of it as you are."

[4295]
"Hello, Bill, I hear you have a new youngster at your house," said his employer.
The new father glanced around the office apprehensively. "For Heaven's sake, you can't hear him 'way up here, can you?"

[4296]
Boss–"You are twenty minutes late again. Don't you know what time we start work at this office?"
New Employee–"No, sir, they're always at it when I get here."

[4297]
"The man who is always punctual in keeping an appointment never loses anything by it."
"No; only about half an hour waiting for the other fellow to show up."

[4298]
"No, I didn't take the job. There was no future to it. The owner's daughter was already married."

[4299]
"What do you think of the head of the firm?"
"Swell!"

[4300]
"Sir, I want to tender my resignation."
"Never mind making it tender— make it brief."

[4301]
Agent–"Don't you wish your office furnishings insured against theft?"
Boss–"Yes, all except the clock. Everybody watches that."

[4302]
"Just why do you want a married man to work for you, rather than a bachelor?" asked the curious chap.
"Well," sighed the boss, "the married men don't get so upset if I yell at them."

[4303]
A traveling salesman visiting a large business office, boasted to the manager that he could pick out all the married men among the employees. Accordingly, he stationed himself at the door, as they returned from dinner, and mentioned all those he believed to be married. In almost every case he was right.
"How do you do it?" asked the manager.
"The married men wipe their feet on the mat; the single ones don't."

[4304]
Boss–"What do you want?"
Clerk–"May I use your 'phone? My wife told me to ask you for a salary increase, but she forgot to tell me how much."

[4305]

"How is it that you are late this morning?" the clerk was asked by his manager.

"I overslept," was the reply.

"What? Do you sleep at home as well?" inquired the manager.

[4306]

A young boy, undergoing an examination for a position, came across the question: "What is the distance of the earth from the sun?" He wrote his answer as follows:

"I am unable to state accurately, but I don't believe the sun is near enough to interfere with a proper performance of my duties if I get this clerkship."

He got the job.

[4307]

Here is a letter that very effectively speaks for itself:

The Idxal Typxwritxr Company
Gxntlxmxn:

Wx hxrxby wish to acknowlxdgx rxcxipt of your shipmxnt of onx of your xxtra-spxcially quixt typxwritxrs.

Howxvxr, upon opxning thx shipmxnt wx found that for thx timx bxing wx shall bx sorxly handicappxd. In gxnxral, thx typxwritxr is in pxrfxct mxchanical condition xxcxpt for onx dxtail. Through somx xrror of assxmbly thxrx sxxms to bx rathxr xmbarrassing omission —thxrx is no lxttxr on thx machinx for "x," thx fifth lxttxr of thx alphabxt.

Will you plxasx bx so kind xithxr to sxnd us anothxr machinx or havx this onx sxrvicxd as soon as possiblx.

Sincxrxly,
Xric Wxlls, Prxsidxnt,
Thx Xxcxlsior Xxprxss Co.

[4308]

The question of the c o r r e c t plural of the word "mongoose" was solved by a gentleman who wanted a pair of these interesting and affectionate creatures.

He wrote to a dealer: "Sir, please send me two mongeese."

He did not like the look of this, tore up the paper, and began again: "Sir, please send me two mongooses."

This version did not satisfy him any better than the first, so he wrote: "Sir, please send me a mongoose, and, by the way, send me another."

[4309]

Arthur – "So your new job makes you independent?"

Albert–"Absolutely. I get here any time I want before eight, and leave just when I please after five."

[4310]

"Why does this manager seem so partial to young Saunders?"

"Because he's the only fellow on the staff who isn't taking correspondence lessons to become manager himself!"

[4311]

"Who's calling?" was the answer to the telephone.

"Watt."

"What is your name, please?"

"Watt's my name."

"That's what I asked you. What's your name?"

"That's what I told you. Watt's my name."

A long pause, and then, from Watt, "Is this James Brown?"

"No, this is Knott."

"Please tell me your name."

"Will Knott."

Whereupon they both hung up.

[4312]
*(As Outlined by the secretary
over the telephone)*
A. M.
"He hasn't come in yet."
"I expect him in any minute.
"He just sent word in he'd be a little late."
"He's been in, but he went out again."
"He's gone to lunch."
P. M.
"I expect him in any minute."
"He hasn't come back yet. Can I take a message?"
"He's somewhere in the building. His hat is here."
"Yes, he was in, but he went out again."
"I don't know whether he'll be back or not."
"No, he's gone for the day."

[4313]
"How is Simpson getting along in business?"
"Wonderfully; but he's terribly discouraged."
"How's that?"
"Well, they're so busy filling and shipping orders they haven't any time to hold a conference."

[4314]
"Sir, my wife said I was to ask for a raise."
"Good. I'll ask my wife if I may give you one."

[4315]
"Did you ever run for office?"
"Yes. I did yesterday morning when the alarm clock failed to go off."

[4316]
Boss – "Look here, you've entered this debit item under credit."
New Clerk–"Sorry, sir; you see I'm left-handed."

[4317]
First business man–"Was the conference a success? What did you decide?"
Second business man–"It was great! We've decided to have another conference next week."

[4318]
Employe – "I have been here 10 years doing three men's work for one man's pay. Now I want a raise."
Employer (slightly Scotch)–"I can't give you a raise but if you'll tell me who the other two men are I'll discharge them."

[4319]
Clerk – "Sir, I'd like my salary raised."
Boss–"Well, don't worry. I've raised it somehow every week so far, haven't I?"

[4320]
"That new office manager speaks very highly of us, Ella. I heard him say we were perfect nonentities!"

[4321]
"I feel like I'd like to punch the boss in the jaw again."
"Gosh! Did you say *again?*"
"Yeah. I felt like doing it once before today."

[4322]
"What's your name," said the clerk. "Spell it, please."
"O double T I double U E double L double—"
"Just a minute. Begin again, please."
The man dutifully began again. "O double T I double U—"
"I give up. What *is* your name?"
"My name is Ottiwell Wood, spelled O, double T, I, double-U, E, double L, double-U, double O, D."

[4323]

A certain business man was in a Pullman smoker when the general pest approached him and attempted to start a conversation with this question, "How many people work in your office?"

"Oh," replied the quiet gentleman, getting up and throwing his cigar away, "I should say, at a rough guess, about two-thirds of them."

[4324]

"Get my broker, Miss Jones."
"Yes, sir, stock or pawn?"

[4325]

The president of a large corporation had occasion one day to reprimand an employee for his inefficiency, whereupon the inefficient young man began finding fault with the way in which the president was managing affairs. The head of the corporation turned angrily toward the speaker.

"Are you the president of this corporation?" he demanded.

"No, sir; of course not," answered the employee.

"Well, then," thundered the president, "don't talk like a fool."

[4326]

A young clerk was called to the front office.

"Of all my clerks," began the boss, "I notice you seem to be most interested in your work. No hours seem too long for you and you never let the slightest detail escape you."

"Yes, sir?" said the clerk with glowing and expectant satisfaction.

"Yes," continued the boss, "and so I am forced to fire you. It is such young men as you who learn here and then go out and start a rival business."

[4327]

Secretary – "A man has just called. He wishes you to tell him the secret of your success in life."
Financier – "Is he a journalist—or—or a detective?"

[4328]

A certain sales manager has a very loud voice. One morning, when he was shouting in his office, the managing director asked his secretary, "What's all this noise about?"

"Mr. Blank is talking to San Francisco, sir," was the reply.

"Then why on earth doesn't he use the telephone?" asked the managing director.

[4329]

"How long have you been working for the National Company?"
"Ever since the office manager threatened to discharge me."

[4330]

Here is a letter taken down exactly as dictated by a dreamy stenographer:

Dear Mr. Umpstead:

Let's see. What'll I tell the old jackass. In reply to yours of the sixteenth we are surprised to learn the super-power two-ton used truck you purchased from us is not giving perfect satisfaction. We had to sell it quick before it fell to pieces.

As you know, Mr. Umpstead, we inspect all used cars thoroughly before turning them over to the purchaser. Your truck was in excellent condition when it left our garage. That's a swell dress you have on. New, isn't it?

It is possible your driver is at fault. Four miles to the gallon is very poor mileage for a truck in such good condition as yours. Four gallons to the mile would be about right. I never noticed before you had a dimple in your chin. Bring it around and we will have our expert mechanic make the proper adjustments.

Sincerely yours,
Just sign it yourself.

STENOGRAPHERS

[4331]

Typewriter Salesman (entering a city office)–"I have come about an attachment I have for your typewriter."
Clerk – "Well, I'm sorry she is out, and, what's more, she and I are engaged."

[4332]

"Don't stop me; I'm going into this shop and buy a new cover for my typewriter."
"But that's a fur shop."
"Well?"

[4333]

The boss came in early and found his bookkeeper kissing the stenographer.
"Is this what I pay you for?" he asked.
"No, I do this free of charge," replied the bookkeeper.

[4334]

"I thought your secretary was blonde?"
"She was, but she's gone off the Gold Standard."

[4335]

New Typist (following rapid-fire dictation)–"Now, Mr. Jones—what did you say between – 'Dear sir' and 'Sincerely Yours?'"

[4336]

"What is the difference between a beautiful and a dumb stenographer?"
"You can fire the dumb one."

[4337]

"It's a bottle of hair-tonic, dear."
"Oh, that's very nice of you, darling."
"Yes, I want you to give it to your stenographer at the office. Her hair is coming out rather badly on your coat."

[4338]

Employer (to newly-hired typist)–"Now I hope you thoroughly understand the importance of punctuation?"
Stenographer – "Oh, yes, indeed. I always get to work on time."

[4339]

Senior Partner–"That new stenographer spells ridiculously."
Junior Partner – "Does she? Well, if she does, it's about the only word she can spell, so far as my observation goes."

[4340]

Employer–"When you called up my wife and told her I would be detained at the office, and would not be home until very late, what did she say?"
Stenographer–"She said: 'Can I depend on that?'"

[4341]

Discovering yet another mistake in his letters, the enraged employer summoned his new typist.
"You came here with good testimonials, Miss Brown," he barked, "and do you mean to tell me you don't know the King's English?"
"Of course I know it," she replied, indignantly "Otherwise he wouldn't be King, would he?"

[4342]

"I say, George," said the young business man to his friend, "where do you buy your typewriter ribbons?"

"I don't," replied the other. "I usually buy her flowers."

[4343]

First Steno – "George's mustache makes me laugh."

Second Steno – "Tickled me, too."

[4344]

"Yessir, as soon as we married, my wife fired my secretary."

"Why, I thought she used to be a secretary, herself."

"Yes, that's why she fired her."

[4345]

"Miss Jones," said the employer, "I may say that you're a very attractive girl."

"Really!" said the typist, blushing.

"You dress well and your voice is well modulated. Your deportment is also beyond reproach."

"You really mustn't pay me so many compliments," she protested.

"Oh, that's all right! I only wanted to put you in a cheerful frame of mind before taking up the matter of punctuation and spelling."

[4346]

"My word, Dick, you've got the latest thing in stenographers."

"She is certainly that. She never gets here till ten."

[4347]

Pretty Caller – "Do you think the manager will see me now?"

Clerk – "Certainly, madam, the manager always has time to see pretty girls."

Pretty Caller – "Well, tell him that his wife is here."

[4348]

"Wonder why the boss keeps that stenographer, she can't spell."

"No; casting a spell is her strong point."

[4349]

What a stenog can't understand is why, when she is such a treat for the boss's eyes, he should get so nasty about a few misspelled words and balled-up letters.

[4350]

The boss frowned.

Calling for his office manager, he said, "That secretary—you certainly didn't engage her on account of her grammar."

"Grammar?" said the office manager. "When you were emphasizing the importance of grammar—well, I thought you said 'glamour'!"

[4351]

Stenographer (applying for position) – "I may say that I'm regarded as quite smart. I've won several prizes in crossword and jigsaw puzzles, and word picture competition lately."

Employer – "Yes, but I want some one who can be smart during office hours."

Stenographer – "Oh, this was during office hours!"

[4352]

"How do you like that new stenographer you hired?"

"She does splendidly with her nails, but she has no apparent interest in my letters."

[4353]

"Every time I want you, you're engaged on the 'phone, Miss Blank!"

"They were business calls, sir."

"Well, don't address my clients as darling in future."

[4354]
Stenographer–"Your little girl wants to kiss you over the phone."
Busy Manager–"Take the message. I'll get it from you later."

[4355]
The absent-minded professor has nothing on the absent-minded business man who kissed his wife and then started to dictate a letter.

[4356]
Stenog–"Boss, will you advance me my next week's salary?"
Boss–"Certainly not. I never make advances to my stenographers."

OFFICE BOYS

[4357]
An office boy was telling his friend about his new job.
"W h e n d o y o u hafter get to work?"
"Any time I want to."
"Aw, go-wan! Watcha tryin' to do, kid me?"
"Nope. I c'n go to work any time I feel like it, just so I ain't no later than eight o'clock."

[4358]
"Why, look here," said the business man who was in need of a boy, "aren't you the same boy who was in here a week ago?"
"Yes, sir," said the applicant.
"I thought so. And didn't I tell you then that I wanted an older boy?"
"Yes, sir. That's why I'm back. I'm older now."

[4359]
The head of the business discovered that he had left his pocket knife at home and, as he needed one urgently, he asked the different clerks, but none of them happened to have one. Finally the office boy hustled in and the business man called him, asking if he was able to produce the desired a r t i c l e. Jimmy handed over his "pigsticker."
"How is it, Jimmy, that you alone out of my entire staff seem to have a pocketknife with you?" smiled the proprietor, eyeing Jimmy with undisguised admiration.
"Dunno, sir," replied the youth, "unless it's because my wages are so low that I can't afford more'n one pair of pants."

[4360]
Employer–"What's become of the cigarettes in the box on the desk?"
Office Boy–"Haven't touched them, sir."
E m p l o y e r–"Haven't you? Why, there are only half a dozen there!"
Office Boy–"Yes, sir. Them's them I haven't touched!"

[4361]
A business man had in his employ an office-boy who was addicted to the bad habit of telling in other offices what happened in that of his employer. The boss finally decided to discharge him. In doing so, he gave him this advice:
"Johnny, you must never hear anything that is said in the office. Do what you are told, but turn a deaf ear to conversation that does not include you."
The boss thought that his stenographer might learn the same worthy lesson. He turned to her and said:
"Miss Smith, did you hear what I said to Johnny?"
"No, sir," she replied promptly.

[4362]

The Boss (smiling) – "On the way to Smith & Sons you will pass a baseball field and—"
Office Boy (hopefully)–"Yes, sir?"
The Boss (still smiling) – "Well, pass it."

[4363]

Employer – "Can't you get here earlier mornings?"
Office Boy – "Yes, sir; when the wind is at my back."

[4364]

Employer–"Do you think you know enough to be useful to this office?"
Office Boy–"Know enough? Why, I left my last place because the boss said I knew too much."

[4365]

Thinking to please the lad, the manager of the office offered to promote the office-boy to junior clerk.
"And, of course, it will mean a small raise," he added, and waited for the outburst of thanks, which didn't come.
The boy thought hard for a moment, and then said:
"If it's all the same to you, sir, I'd rather go on looking after the postage book and the petty cash on my present salary."

[4366]

"Is the new office boy any good?"
"Not much, sir. He spent most of the morning trying to get 'Established 1891' on the 'phone."

[4367]

Boss–"There's $10 gone from my cash drawer, Johnny; you and I were the only people who had keys to that drawer."
Office Boy–"Well, s'pose we each pay $5 and say no more about it."

[4368]

Boss–"Can't you find something to do?"
Office Boy–"Gee whiz: Am I expected to do the work and find it, too?"

[4369]

Office Boy (nervously)–"Please, sir, I think you're wanted on the 'phone."
Employer–"You think! What's the good of thinking?"
"Well, sir, the voice at the other end said, 'Hello, is that you, you old idiot?'"

[4370]

"Tell your boss I've come to see him," growled the tall, broadshouldered man to the slim little office-boy. "My name is Williams."
The boy looked at the visitor with awe. "So you're Mr. Williams," he said. "How very awkward."
Williams–"What do you mean—awkward?"
Office Boy–"I've got orders to throw you out."

[4371]

Possible Employer–"H'm! so you want a job, eh? Do you ever tell lies?"
Office Boy–"No, sir, but I kin learn."

[4372]

Boss (to office boy, who is half an hour late)–"You should have been in here at nine o'clock."
Office Boy–"Why, what happened?"

[4373]

Office Boy–"Sorry, madam, but Mr. Brown has gone to lunch with his wife."
The Wife–"O! Well . . . tell Mr. Brown his stenographer called."

[4374]

A firm advertised for a stenographer and next morning was overwhelmed with applicants. The office boy was told to admit no more.

Shortly after this an aggressive lady arrived, and pushing her way past the others, demanded to see the boss. By this time the office boy had grown deaf to all protestations, and had but one answer.

"Not today, madam," he said.

"But I'm his wife."

"Not today, madam," was the inexorable answer.

[4375]

Employer–"Yes, I advertised for a good strong boy. Think you can fill the bill?"

Applicant–"Well, I just finished whipping nineteen other applicants outside the door."

[4376]

Boss–"I'm surprised at you! Do you know what they do with boys who tell lies?"

Office Boy–"Yes, sir. When they get old enough the firm sends them out as salesmen."

[4377]

Boss–"Leary, did you make that round blot in the ledger?"

Office Boy–"Yes, sir; isn't it a beauty?—without a compass, too!"

[4378]

Caller–"Is the boss in?"

New Office Boy–"Are you a salesman, a bill collecter or a friend of his?"

Caller–"I'm all three."

Office Boy–"The boss is in conference. He is out of town. Step in and see him."

[4379]

Willie–"Hello! Why are you standin' here in front of the office you got fired from last week? Waitin' to get taken back?"

Jimmie–"Not much! I just wanted to see if they was still in business."

[4380]

"Have you had any experience as an office-boy?"

"I should say I had, mister; why, I'm a dummy director in three mining-companies now."

[4381]

"I've had a hard day," said the tired business man aboard the evening train for home. "One of my office boys asked the afternoon off to attend his aunt's funeral. So, being onto his scheme, as I thought, I said I'd go along too."

His friend chuckled. "Great idea! Was it a good game?"

"That's where I lost out," sadly admitted the man of business. "It was his aunt's funeral."

[4382]

Chief Clerk (to office boy)–"Why on earth don't you laugh when the boss tells a joke?"

Office Boy–"I don't have to; I quit on Saturday."

[4383]

Caller–"Who's the responsible man here?"

Office Boy–"If you mean the fellow that always gets the blame, it's me."

[4384]

Office Boy–"Sorry, but you can't see Mr. Brown."

Caller–"Is he in conference?"

Office Boy–"No, he's busy."

[4385]

Two financiers who were partners discovered that an office boy in their employ had been tampering with the petty cash.

One of them was so much enraged that he desired to send for the police, but the other was a calm and just man. He took a more moderate and humane view of the situation.

"No, no," he said; "let us always remember that we began in a small way ourselves."

EFFICIENCY EXPERTS

[4386]

"My husband is an efficiency expert in a large office."

"What does an efficiency expert do?"

"Well, if we women did it, they'd call it nagging."

[4387]

"Better consider my course in efficiency training. I can show you how to earn more money than you are getting."

"I do that now."

[4388]

Solicitor (to business man absorbed in detail)–"I have here a most marvelous system of efficiency, condensed into one small volume. It will save you fully 50 per cent of your time, and so—"
Business Man (interrupting irritably)–"I already have a system by which I can save 100 per cent of my time and yours. I'll demonstrate it now— Good-day!"

[4389]

"Mr. Wampus, I fear you are ignoring our efficiency system."

"Maybe so, Mr. Gump," responded the clerk addressed, "but somebody has to get the work done."

[4390]

Efficiency Expert–"I am very gratified to see how many new men you have taken on since I installed my system."

"Yes, I hired 'em to take care of the system."

[4391]

"I suppose at the efficiency expert's wedding you didn't do anything so wasteful as throwing rice."

"Oh, yes we did; but as a concession to his teaching we had the rice done up in cotton bags, each missile weighing two pounds."

[4392]

There's a story about an efficiency expert who only says his prayers once a year, New Year's Day. The rest of the time he just jumps into bed, and says "ditto."

[4393]

"You didn't seem to be very hot about the efficiency expert," remarked the secretary.

"No," replied the boss, "his explanation of how I could cut the overhead was over my head."

DRUG STORES

[4394]

"How about two of them?" asked the druggist of the man who was buying a toothbrush. "One for your wife?"

"No, thanks. When I buy a new one, I always give her the old one."

He paused while several other customers in the store gasped, and then he added: "She uses it to clean her shoes."

[4395]

"I understand Jones has been given a medal by the Society for Pharmaceutical Research."

"Yes, he has invented three new types of sandwiches."

[4396]

A man entered a drug-store and asked for a dozen two-grain quinine pills.

"Do you want them put in a box, sir?" asked the clerk, as he was counting them out.

"Oh, no, certainly not," replied the customer. "I was thinking of rolling them home."

[4397]

Customer (to druggist)–"Gimme a tablet."

Druggist–"What kind of tablet?"

Customer–"A yellow one."

Druggist–"But what's the matter with you?"

Customer–"I want to write a letter."

[4398]

Customer–"You're sure one bottle will cure a cold?"

Druggist–"It must, sir—nobody's ever come back for a second."

[4399]

Customer – "Good heavens, Mr. Druggist, I'm poisoned! It must have been the sandwiches my wife gave me."

Pharmacist–"Yes, that's it. I tell you, you're taking a chance every time you eat a sandwich that isn't prepared by a registered pharmacist."

[4400]

Prospective Customer – "Do you keep fountain pens here?"

Drugstore Clerk (brightly)–"No, we sell them."

Prospective Customer–"Okay, but keep the one you might have sold me if you hadn't been so smart."

[4401]

Customer in Drugstore (on Sunday morning)–"Please give me change for a dime."

Druggist–"Here it is. I hope you'll enjoy the sermon."

[4402]

A young lady came into a drug store and asked if it were possible to disguise castor oil. "It's horrid stuff to take, you know. Ugh!" And she shuddered.

"Why, certainly," said the druggist. Another young lady sat down and ordered a chocolate ice-cream soda. The druggist asked the first patron if she would not have one too. With a smile she accepted the invitation, and drank it down with much gusto.

"Now tell me, Doctor, how would you disguise castor oil?"

The druggist beamed all over. "Aha, my dear young lady, I just gave you some—in that soda—"

"But, good heavens, Doctor! Why, I wanted it for my sister!"

[4403]

"A fortnight ago you sold me a plaster to get rid of my rheumatism."

"Yes."

"Now I want something to get rid of the plaster."

[4404]

Customer (in drug store)–"A mustard plaster."

Drug Clerk (force of habit)–"We're out of mustard; how about mayonnaise?"

[4405]

Customer–"So you've got rid of that pretty clerk you had?"

Druggist–"Yes, all my gentlemen customers kept saying that a smile from her was as good as a tonic!"

[4406]

An invitation to dinner had been sent to the new doctor. In reply the hostess received an absolutely illegible letter.

"I must know if he accepts or declines," she declared.

"If I were you," suggested her husband, "I should take it to the druggist. A pharmacist can always read doctor's letters, however badly written."

The pharmacist looked at the sheet of notepaper which she had handed him, and without waiting for her explanation went into his dispensary and returned a few minutes later with a bottle which he handed over the counter.

"There you are, madam," he said. "That will be 50 cents."

[4407]

Old Lady (to druggist)–"I want a box of canine pills."

Druggist–"What's the matter with the dog?"

Old Lady (indignantly)–"I want you to know, sir, that my husband is a gentleman."

The druggist put up some quinine pills in profound silence.

[4408]

"Has putting in that lunch counter helped your business?" asked Jones of the druggist.

"Well, it has about tripled the sale of indigestion tablets," he replied.

[4409]

Two druggists were talking about one of their confrères who had just died.

"He was a great druggist," said one.

"He was," admitted the other. "But don't you think he made his chicken-salad a little too salty?"

[4410]

Thweet Young Thing–"I want thome adhethive plasther."

Druggist–"What thickness?"

Thweet Young Thing–"Don't mock me, thir!"

[4411]

Druggist (to his stout wife)–"Don't come into the shop for a minute. I am trying to sell six bottles of my fat-reducing mixture."

[4412]

Heard at the soda fountain:

Youth (after lamenting that he wasn't married so he could have his breakfast at home, instead of in a drug store)–"Gimme a cup of coffee and—"

"Cream doughnuts?" ventured the attendant.

"No."

"Jelly doughnuts?"

"No, I'm sick of cream doughnuts and jelly doughnuts."

Feminine Customer (at far end of counter)–"Fry him a hard-boiled egg."

[4413]

Customer–"I can not sleep at night —the least little sound disturbs me. I'm a victim of insomnia. Even a cat on our back fence distresses me beyond words."

Druggist–"This powder will be effective."

Customer–"When do I take it?"

Druggist–"You don't. Give it to the cat in milk."

GROCERS AND BUTCHERS

[4414]

Butcher–"Round steak, madam."

Bride–"The shape doesn't interest me, so long as it's tender."

[4415]

A boy entered a grocery store and said to the storekeeper:

"Gimme a dime's worth of asafetida."

The storekeeper tied up the package and the boy said: "Dad wants you to charge it."

"All right; what's your name?"

"Shermerhorn."

"Take it for nothin'," he said, "I ain't goin' to spell 'asafetida' and 'Shermerhorn' for no dime."

[4416]

One of the fruit-stall men in the city market was striving hard to add a few cents to the total of his sales.

"We've got some fine alligator pears," he suggested.

"Silly," laughed the very, very young housewife. "We don't even keep a goldfish."

[4417]

"It's tough to pay forty cents a pound for meat."

"Mmm. But it's tougher when you pay only twenty."

[4418]

"How much are your peaches?"

"Penny each, lady."

"I'll have one, please."

"Givin' a party?"

[4419]

Williams was always a bad payer, but one day he walked into the shop of the local grocer, and paid the whole of his account without a murmur.

"That letter you sent me did it," he explained to the man behind the counter. "I've never seen one like it. Why, it would get money out of a stone. How did you put it together?"

The grocer smiled sadly.

"I took the best bits out of the letter my wife sent me when she was vacationing at an expensive resort," he explained.

[4420]

"Do you keep animal crackers?"

"No, but we have some very nice dog biscuits."

[4421]

A man went into a butcher's shop, and finding the owner's wife in attendance, in the absence of her husband, thought he would have a joke at her expense, and said, "Madam, can you supply me with a yard of pork?"

"Yes, sir," said she. And then turning to a boy, she added, "James, give that gentleman three pigs' feet!"

[4422]

Mrs. Newlywed—"Aren't these eggs rather small today?"

Grocer—"Yes'm, but the farmer who sells me my eggs had to start to town early this morning and took them out of the nest too soon."

[4423]

A grocer recently had a pound of sugar returned, with a note stating that it contained too much sand for table use, and not enough for building purposes.

[4424]

When the grocer informed her that the price of eggs was sixty cents a dozen she exclaimed: "Why, that's five cents for each egg."

"Yes, mum," said the man, "but you must remember that one egg is a whole day's work for a hen."

[4425]

Fish Dealer—"Lobsters, madam; nice lobsters? Look, they're all alive."

Lady—"Yes, but are they fresh?"

[4426]

The deceased groceryman knocked at the gates of Hell and asked entrance.

"Why do you come here?" demanded Satan.

"I want to collect some old accounts from a couple of my former customers who died before me."

"How do you know they are here?"

"Well, every time I tried to collect, this is the place they recommended me to."

[4427]

A woman went into a butcher shop one evening to buy some meat. A strange man followed her into the store and stood about while she was at the counter. Suddenly she screamed, and the man turned and ran out of the store, and right into the arms of a passing patrolman. On searching him he was found to be armed. Later he was identified as a notorious hold-up man.

"Mrs. Jones, if you hadn't screamed I would certainly have been robbed," declared the butcher gratefully. "But how did you know he was a bandit?"

"I *didn't* know," protested Mrs. Jones. "I screamed when you told me what the roast was going to cost me."

[4428]

Customer (to rural storekeeper playing cards)–"Do you know there are two customers in the store?"

Rural Storekeeper (keeping on playing)–"That's all right. Keep quiet and they'll go away again."

[4429]

"Gimme an all-day sucker," the youngster demanded of the candy man.

He was handed one.

"Looks kind of small," remarked the youth looking at it doubtfully.

"Yeah, the days are getting shorter."

[4430]

Butcher–"I can't give you any more credit, sir. Your bill is bigger now than it should be."

Customer–"I know that. Just make it out as it should be and I'll pay it."

[4431]

Customer–"Three of those apples you sent me were rotten. I am bringing them back."

Storekeeper – "That's all right, madam. You needn't bring them back. Your word is just as good as the apples."

[4432]

The grocer had just put a new boy to work, and among the other instructions was this:

"If you don't happen to have what a customer wants, suggest something else as nearly like it as possible."

Soon a woman came into the store and asked the boy, "Have you any fresh green stuff today?"

"No, ma'am," answered the boy, "but we have some nice bluing."

[4433]

Housewife–"I don't like the looks of that codfish."

Storekeeper–"Well, if you want looks, why don't you buy a goldfish?"

[4434]

Customer–"Are those eggs strictly fresh?"

Grocer (to his clerk)–"Feel of those eggs, George, and see if they're cool enough to sell yet."

[4435]

A Western store ran the following advertisement:

"Apples, oranges, imported nuts. Come early and avoid the rush. The early bird gets the worm."

[4436]

Fish Dealer–"Fresh, lady? Why this fish breathed its last just as you came in the door."

Customer (sniffing)–"And what a breath it had!"

[4437]

A red-haired boy applied for a job in a butcher shop. "How much will you give me?"

"Three dollars a week; but what can you do to make yourself useful around a butcher shop?"

"Anything."

"Well, be specific. Can you dress a chicken?"

"Not on $3 a week," said the boy.

[4438]

A little girl knocked at the front door of the grocery store one Sunday morning. Her chum, the daughter of the grocer, stuck her head out of the second story window, and said: "Nancy, we've all been to camp meeting, and got converted. If you want milk on the Sabbath you'll have to come around to the back door of the store."

[4439]

Grocery Keeper (to his sons)–"Jonathan, did you charge that rum?"

"Yes."

"Timothy, did you charge that rum?"

"Yes, sir."

"Joseph, did you charge that rum?"

"Yes, sir-ee."

"All right—so have I."

[4440]

A new clerk, right fresh from the country, was helping out in a local general store during the holiday rush. One of the town's matrons approached the clerk and asked for some anchovy paste. The clerk hesitated for a moment and then walked over to the tablet-and-pencil counter and said:

"No, we don't have anchovy paste, but here is some excellent mucilage."

MISCELLANEOUS STORES

[4441]

A young man approached the counter at which Christmas cards were being sold.

"Have you anything sentimental?" he asked.

"Here's a lovely one," replied the salesgirl. "To The Only Girl I Ever Loved."

"That's fine, I'll take four—no—six of those, please."

[4442]

Lady–"Where can I change this dress?"

Floorwalker–"Ladies' room is on the second floor."

[4443]

A salesman was dismissed because of a lack of courtesy to customers. A month later the sales manager spotted him walking about in a police uniform.

"I see you've joined the force, Jones," said the sales manager.

"Yes," replied Jones. "This is the job I've been looking for all my life. On this job the customer is always wrong."

[4444]

Complainant—"I've been getting threatening letters through the mail. Isn't there a law against that?"
Post-Office Inspector—"Of course there is. It's a very serious offense to send threatening letters. Have you any idea who's doing it?"
Complainant—"Sure. The Bumpus Furniture Company."

[4445]

The pretty girl entered a store. It was crowded, but presently one of the salesmen approached.
"Anybody waiting on you?" he asked, politely.
The girl blushed and replied: "Yes, but he won't come in!"

[4446]

Customer—"Take a look at what you did to this!"
Laundryman—"I can't see anything wrong with that piece of lace."
Customer—"Lace, hell, that was a sheet!"

[4447]

"Hear the latest about Newrich?"
"No. What now?"
"He bought a Louis XIV bed, but it was too small for him, so he sent it back and asked for a Louis XVI."

[4448]

Pretty Sales Girl—"Could I interest you in a bathing costume, sir?"
Mr. Gay—"You certainly could, baby, but my wife is over there at the glove counter."

[4449]

Woman—"I was to have met my husband here three hours ago. Have you seen him?"
Floorwalker – "Possibly, madam. Anything distinctive about your husband?"
Woman—"Yes, I imagine he's purple by this time."

[4450]

Two clothing merchants were bragging to each other about their salesmen.
"One of my men," said one of them, "is the smartest salesman in this city. Why, the other day a man came in for a pair of shoelaces, and before he left my man had sold him a suit of clothing and an overcoat."
"That's nothing," said the other merchant. "Last week we had a woman come in to buy a suit of black clothing to bury her husband in. And before she left my store my salesman had sold her a suit with an extra pair of trousers."

[4451]

Instalment Collector – "See here, you're seven payments behind on your piano."
Purchaser—"Well, the company advertises 'Pay As You Play.'"
Instalment Collector—"What's that got to do with it?"
Purchaser—"I play very poorly."

[4452]

"What is your occupation?"
"It isn't an occupation, it's a pursuit. I'm a bill collector."

[4453]

Young Lady (at counter)—"I want to see some gloves."
Clerk—"What kind, kid?"
Young Lady—"Sir, how dare you!"

[4454]

"I want some collars for my husband," said Mrs. Jones, "but I am afraid I have forgotten the size."
"Thirteen and a half, ma'am?" suggested the shop assistant.
"That's it. How did you know?"
"Men who let their wives buy their collars for them are always about that size, ma'am," explained the observant salesman.

[4455]

Lady (at almond counter)–"Who attends to the nuts?"
Wise Guy–"Be patient, I'll wait on you in a minute."

[4456]

Customer–"I want to try on that suit in the window."
Salesman–"Sorry, sir, but you'll have to use the dressing-room."

[4457]

A man once applied for a job in a dry-goods house. His appearance wasn't prepossessing, and references were demanded. After some hesitation, he gave the name of a driver in the firm's employ. This driver, he thought, would vouch for him. A clerk sought out the driver, and asked him if the applicant was honest. "Honest?" the driver said. "Why, his honesty's been proved again and again. To my certain knowledge he's been arrested nine times for stealing and every time he was acquitted."

[4458]

Jones–"Why do you have such misspelled words and bad grammar on the signs in your windows?"
Storekeeper–"So people will think I'm a fool and come in expecting to get the best of me. Thanks to those signs, business is the best I've had in years."

[4459]

Merchant (to applicant for job)–"Sorry, but I only employ married men."
Applicant–"Do you happen to have a daughter, sir?"

[4460]

Manager (pointing to cigarette-end on floor)–"Smith, is this yours?"
Smith (pleasantly)–"Not at all, sir. You saw it first."

[4461]

A man walked into a hat shop.
"I've just lost a bet," he said, "and I want a soft hat."
The salesman, selecting a hat from the shelf behind him, handed it to the prospective customer with the remark:—
"This is the softest hat we've got."
The customer gazed at it speculatively. "What I want," he said, reluctantly, "is something a little more tender. I've got to eat it."

[4462]

Proprietor–"What is the dispute about, Miss Green? Remember in this store the customer is always right. What did that man say?"
Clerk–"Oh, he only said you were the toughest old shark in this town."

[4463]

Fair Customer (to salesman displaying modern bathing suit)–"And you're sure this bathing suit won't shrink?"
Salesman–"No, miss; it has nowhere to shrink to."

[4464]

Smith entered a big store and made his way to the gardening department. "I want three lawn-mowers," he said.
The assistant stared hard at him. "Three, sir?" he echoed. "You must have a very big estate."
"Nothing of the kind," snapped Smith, grimly. "I have two neighbors."

[4465]

"Yes," said the storekeeper, "I want a good, bright boy to be partly indoors and partly outdoors."
"That's all right," said the applicant, "but what becomes of me when the door slams shut?"

[4466]

A gentleman had completed his purchases and the clerk, in filling out the sales slip, asked: "What is the name, please?"

"Jepson," replied our hero.

"Chipson?"

"No. Jepson. Sixteen twenty-one West—."

"Your first initial, please."

"Oh, K."

"O.K. Jepson."

"Excuse me, it isn't O.K. You didn't understand; I said 'Oh.'"

"O. Jepson."

"No. Rub out the O. and let the K. stand."

The clerk began to look haggard. "Will you please give me your initials again?"

"I said K."

"Pardon, you said O.K."

"I said 'Oh'——."

"Just now you said K."

"Allow me to finish. I said 'Oh' because I didn't understand what you were asking me. I didn't mean it was my initial. My name is Kirby Jepson.

"No! Not O. but K. Here, give me the pencil and I'll write it myself. There, I guess it's O.K. now."

[4467]

Fair Customer–"I'd like to try on that one over there."

Salesman–"I'm sorry, madam, but that is the lampshade."

[4468]

The owner of a cheap watch brought it into the jeweler's shop to see what could be done for it. "The mistake I made, of course," he admitted, "was in dropping it."

"Well, I don't suppose you could help that," the jeweler remarked. "The mistake you made was picking it up."

[4469]

Mrs. Smith–"Can you alter this dress to fit me?"

Salesman–"Certainly not. That isn't done any more. You will have to be altered to fit the dress."

[4470]

Tailor–"What! You want four pairs of trousers with this suit?"

Patron–"That's right. You see, I've just received a playful St. Bernard as a present."

[4471]

Lady (in a pet store)–"I like this dog, but his legs are too short."

Salesman–"Too short! Why, madam, they all four reach the floor."

[4472]

Stranger–"I noticed your advertisement in the paper this morning for a man to retail imported canaries."

Proprietor of Bird Store–"Yes, sir. Are you looking for a job?"

Stranger–"Oh, no; I merely had a curiosity to know how the canaries lost their tails."

[4473]

Manager–"Why didn't that man buy anything? What did he want to see?"

Pretty Salesgirl–"Me, tomorrow night."

[4474]

"Now, now, Thompson, what's this customer's complaint?"

"It's not a complaint, sir. He wants two shoes that squeak in the same key."

[4475]

Customer–"What! Five hundred dollars for that antique? Why, I priced it last week and you said three hundred and fifty."

Dealer–"Yes, I know; but the cost of labor and materials has gone up so!"

[4476]

A bewildered man entered a ladies' specialty shop. "I want a corset for my wife," he said.

"What bust?" asked the clerk.

"Nothin'. It just wore out."

[4477]

Caller—"These flowers are for the phone girls."

Boss—"Thank you, sir. You compliment our service."

Caller – "Compliment nothing! I thought they were all dead."

[4478]

"These are especially strong shirts, madam. They simply laugh at the laundry."

"I know that kind; I had some which came back with their sides split."

[4479]

Manager—"From your references I see you've had four places in the last month."

Applicant—"Yes, sir, but that shows how much in demand I am."

[4480]

"What's the idea of that cross-eyed man for a store detective?"

"Well, look at him. Can you tell who he is watching?"

[4481]

Maiden Aunt (in department store) –"Now I—er—want a nice toy, please, suitable for a small boy whose father is very corpulent and unable to do any kneeling."

[4482]

"I want to buy a toy train for my little boy."

"Next floor, please, sir. Men's Hobbies!"

[4483]

A boy looking for something to do saw the sign "Boy Wanted" hanging outside of a store. He picked up the sign and entered the store.

The proprietor met him. "What did you bring that sign in here for?" asked the storekeeper.

"You won't need it any more," said the boy cheerfully. "I'm going to take the job."

[4484]

"Glad to see you getting in on time these mornings, Mr. Latterly," said the store manager.

"Yes, sir, I've got a parrot now."

"A parrot. What for? I advised you to get an alarm clock."

"I did, sir, but after a few mornings I got used to it, and it failed to wake me. So I got a parrot and now when I retire I hang the alarm clock over his cage. It wakes the parrot, and what the bird says would arouse anybody."

[4485]

"Does your firm allow you to take tips?"

"No, lady, but if they asked if you gave me one, I'd lie like anything to save you."

[4486]

"I'd like to see something cheap in a straw hat."

"Certainly sir. Try this one on, sir, and the mirror's on your left."

[4487]

A man bought a canary from a pet store.

"You're sure this bird can sing?" he said, suspiciously.

"He's a grand singer."

The customer left. A week later he reappeared.

"Say! This bird you sold me is lame!"

"Well, what did you want—a singer or a dancer?"

[4488]

"I want a pair of stockings."

"For your wife, or shall I show you something better?"

[4489]

Collector–"Say, I want to collect some back payments on your antique furniture."

Head of the House–"You're crazy. I never bought any antique furniture on the installment plan."

"Well, maybe it wasn't antique when you bought it."

[4490]

The Bright Young Thing entered the men's shop and approached the counter.

"I want a present for an old gentleman for Christmas," she said.

"Yes, m'am," replied the clerk. "Something nice in ties?"

"No; he has a beard," the girl explained.

"H'm," the clerk murmured thoughtfully. "Perhaps a fancy vest might be suitable?"

"No; it's a long beard," came back the answer.

The clerk sighed wearily.

"Well, how about carpet slippers?"

[4491]

"I want to buy a petticoat."

"Yes, miss; period costumes on the third floor."

[4492]

A clerk in a miscellaneous store was serving a caller. The manager was at a desk some distance away, but he overheard the clerk say: "No, madam, we haven't had any for a long time."

"Oh, yes, we have," interrupted the manager; "I will send to the warehouse immediately and have some brought for you."

The lady went out laughing. The manager turned to the clerk: "Never refuse anything; always send out for it."

"Well, you see," replied the clerk, "she said to me, 'We haven't had any rain lately.'"

[4493]

"And you say you guarantee these canaries?"

"Guarantee them? Why, madam, I raised them from canary seed!"

[4494]

A young fellow, a clerk in a store, troubled by the cost of living, went in to ask his testy old employer for a raise. The employer listened impatiently. Finally, he exclaimed:

"Why, when I was your age I supported a family on what you're getting now."

"Yes," retorted the young man, "but they didn't have cash registers in those days."

[4495]

The shoe dealer was hiring a clerk. "Suppose," he said, "a lady customer were to remark while you were trying to fit her, 'Don't you think one of my feet is bigger than the other?' what would you say?"

"I should say, 'On the contrary, madam, one is smaller than the other.'"

"The job is yours."

[4496]

The hard-to-please customer shook her head. "I don't like these shoes," she told the salesman. "The soles are too thick."

"Is that the only objection, madam?" asked the salesman. She nodded. "Then, madam," he added, "if you take the shoes I can assure you that the objection will gradually wear away."

[4497]

"No," said the old man, sternly. "I will not do it. Never have I sold anything by false representation, and I will not begin now."

For a moment he was silent, and the clerk who stood before him could see that the better nature of his employer was fighting strongly for the right.

"No," said the old man, again. "I will not do it. It is an inferior grade of shoe, and I will never pass it off as anything better. Mark it, 'A Shoe Fit for a Queen,' and put it in the window. A queen does not have to do much walking."

[4498]

A bookseller had an "account rendered" returned to him with the following reply scrawled across the billhead:

"Dear Sir—I never ordered this beastly book. If I did, you didn't send it. If you sent it, I never got it. If I got it, I paid for it. If I didn't, I won't. Now go and hang yourself, you fathead.—Yours very respectfully, John Jones."

[4499]

Salesman–"Madam, this fire extinguisher is guaranteed to give you service for fifty years."

Elderly Lady–"But I shan't be here all that time."

Salesman (misunderstanding her meaning)–"Oh, but you can take it with you when you go!"

[4500]

Antique Dealer–"Here I have a very rare old revolver from the time of the Romans."

Customer–"But surely they didn't use revolvers?"

Antique Dealer–"Ah—that is why it's so rare."

[4501]

"What would you say about a man who hasn't even paid you for the hat he wears?"

"I'd say he's in debt over his ears."

[4502]

"Can you beat it?"

"What now?"

"They sold me this stuff on the 'pay-as-you-can' plan, and now they insist I pay when I can't."

[4503]

First Floorwalker–"Poor old Perkins has completely lost his hearing. I'm afraid he'll lose his job."

Second Floorwalker – "Nonsense. He's to be transferred to the Complaint Department."

[4504]

An order—and an acknowledgement:

"Send radio—if good, will send check."

"Send check—if good, will send radio."

[4505]

A clerk in a shoe store was trying to persuade his customer that a certain pair of uncomfortable shoes fitted him.

"Those shoes are too narrow and too pointed," said the customer.

"Oh," said the salesman, "but they are wearing narrow, pointed shoes this season."

"That may be," answered the suffering gentleman, "but unfortunately, I am still wearing my last season's feet."

[4506]

"Where's the cashier?"

"Gone to the races."

"Gone to the races in business hours?"

"Yes, sir, it's his last chance of making the books balance."

[4507]
Customer–"The price of these shoes seems high. Wasn't there something said about a movement to have it reduced?"
Clerk–"Yes—but it's not on foot yet."

[4508]
"What can we play up at this time of year?" asked the manager of the department store drug shop.
"Well," said his assistant, "it is the football season, so how about hot-water bottles for boy friends to take along for their sweeties to sit on in those cold concrete stadiums?"

[4509]
Salesman–"Ladies and gentlemen, I have here the famous flexible comb that will stand any kind of treatment. You can bend it double —you can hit it with a hammer— you can twist it—you can—"
Interested Listener–"Say, mister, can you comb your hair with it?"

[4510]
"I came in here to get something for my wife."
"What are you asking for her?"

[4511]
Customer–"How much are your bibles?"
Salesgirl–"Fifty cents each."
Customer–"Oh, for goodness sakes!"
Salesgirl–"Yes ma'm."

[4512]
A woman who had visited every department of one of the big New York stores and worried the majority of the salesmen without spending a penny, so exasperated one of them that he ventured to make a mild protest. "Madam," he asked, "are you shopping here?"
The lady looked surprised, but not by any means annoyed. "Certainly!" she replied. "What else should I be doing?"
For a moment the salesman hesitated; then he blurted out, "Well, madam, I thought perhaps you were taking an inventory!"

[4513]
An elderly lady entered a shop and asked to be shown some tablecloths. The salesman brought a pile and showed them to her, but she said she had seen those elsewhere —nothing suited her.
"Haven't you something new?" she asked.
The man brought another pile and showed them to her.
"These are the newest pattern," he said. "You will notice the edge runs right round the border and the center is in the middle."
"Dear me, yes. I will take half a dozen of those," said the lady.

[4514]
The man entered a cigar-store, bought a cigar, and then left. Five minutes later he dashed back.
"That cigar," he shouted, "is simply awful."
"It's all very well for you to complain," said the storekeeper, "you've only got one; I've got hundreds of the darn things."

[4515]
Salesman–"These stockings are the very latest pattern, fast colors, holeproof, won't shrink, priced far lower than elsewhere and a very good yarn."
Customer–"Yes, and you tell it well."

[4516]
"Your opening sale has closed. What now?"
"Our closing sale opens."

[4517]

"Say," said the man as he entered the clothing-store. "I bought this suit here less than two weeks ago, and it is rusty-looking already."

"Well," replied the clothing-dealer, "I guaranteed it to wear like iron, didn't I?"

[4518]

"Why did you engage that man as cashier? He squints, has a crooked nose and outstanding ears."

"Of course. He will be so easy to identify if he ever absconds."

[4519]

A western bookseller wrote to a house in Chicago asking that a dozen copies of Canon Farrar's *Seekers After God* be shipped to him at once. Within two days he received this reply by telegraph: "No seekers after God in Chicago or New York. Try Philadelphia."

[4520]

The customer announced that she wanted to select three ensembles, suitable for European travel. The alert saleswoman fitted her out with three complete wardrobes that included such accessories as hats, gloves, shoes, and purses.

The woman was delighted. After putting in the entire morning at this pleasant task, she thanked the girl politely and said:

"Well, those are just the sort of clothes I'll buy if my husband ever lets me go to Europe."

[4521]

A certain young man wrote the following letter to a prominent business firm, ordering a razor:

"Dear Sirs—Please find enclosed 50c for one of your razors as advertised and oblige—John Jones.

"P. S.—I forgot to enclose the 50c,

but no doubt a firm of your high standing will send the razor anyway."

The firm addressed received the letter and replied as follows:

"Dear Sir—Your most valued order received the other day and will say in reply that we are sending the razor as per request, and hope that it will prove satisfactory.

"P. S.—We forgot to enclose the razor, but no doubt a man with your cheek will have no need of it."

[4522]

The old lady was mad as she approached the clerk in the pet shop. "That parrot I bought yesterday uses violent language."

"That's right, lady," said the clerk. "He does swear a bit, but you ought to be thankful he doesn't drink or gamble."

[4523]

A man looking at some neckties tossed one or two aside contemptuously. Lingering after having made his purchase, he noticed that the clerk put those he had so positively rejected in a separate box.

"What becomes of those?" he inquired.

"We sell them to the women who come in here to buy ties for men."

[4524]

The sweet young thing had been unable to buy the article she wanted, but in each case the clerk had assured her that "next time" it would assuredly be in stock. One day she called at the store to find a new clerk on the job.

"Do you have spats yet?" she inquired.

The clerk blushed. "No, ma'am," he stammered; "I'm not living with my wife now."

[4525]

"I can't do a thing with Jones," said the manager. "I've had him in three departments, and he dozes all day."

"Put him at the pajama counter," suggested the proprietor, "and fasten a card on him with these words: 'Our pajamas are of such superior quality that even the man who sells them can not keep awake.'"

[4526]

"Pa," asked little Willie, "what's a counter-irritant?"

"A counter-irritant?" said Pa, who worked in a department store, "I guess that must be a woman who shops all day and doesn't buy anything."

[4527]

Customer—"Satisfied? Certainly I'm satisfied. I've nothing but praise for you."

Tailor—"Then I suppose it's not much good my sending the bill in again, sir?"

[4528]

Joking Customer—"How much are your four-dollar shoes?"

Smart Salesman—"Two dollars a foot."

[4529]

A man bought a store. In six months it had failed. Later on, meeting the original owner, he halted him and said:

"You know that business you sold me as a going concern?"

"Yes, what of it?"

"Nothing, only it's gone."

[4530]

"This seal coat is fine. But will it stand rain?"

"Madam, did you ever see a seal with an umbrella?"

[4531]

A rather stout woman was making herself a nuisance in the big store which was holding its annual sale. Nothing, it seemed, would suit her, and the unfortunate sales girl was beginning to get a little weary.

"Haven't you anything ready-made that will fit me?" asked the customer at last."

"Yes; the umbrellas and the hand-kerchiefs are downstairs, madam," the girl replied.

[4532]

"I'm sorry I can't suit you in dress goods."

"Well, the fact is," said the lady, "that what I really want to buy is a refrigerator."

[4533]

In a certain store they have a book in which a record is kept of the exact reason why any customer leaves without making a purchase.

The other day a woman customer took up a good deal of time looking at black dresses, finally leaving without buying.

The clerk—a temporary hand—solemnly approached the book and entered up: "Customer only looking at black dresses—not buying. Husband not dead yet."

[4534]

"Mr. Jones," a man asked his tailor, "how is it you have not called on me for my account?"

"Oh, I never ask a gentleman for money."

"Indeed! How, then, do you get on if he doesn't pay?"

"Why," replied the tailor, hesitating, "after a certain time I conclude he is not a gentleman and then I ask him."

[4535]

Customer (in furniture store)–
"What is that piece called?"
Salesgirl (behind counter)–"High-
boy."
Customer–"Uh-er. How do you
do?"

[4536]

A family moved from the city to
the suburbs, and were told they
ought to get a watchdog to guard
the premises at night. So they
bought the largest dog that was for
sale in the kennels of a near-by
dealer.

Shortly afterwards the house was
entered by burglars, who made a
good haul while the dog slept. The
householder went to the dealer and
told him about it.

"Well, what you need now," said
the dealer, "is a little dog to wake
up the big dog!"

[4537]

Customer–"I hear my son has owed
you for a suit for three years."
Tailor–"Yes, sir; have you called to
settle the account?"
Customer–"No, I'd like a suit myself on the same terms."

[4538]

The head of the store was passing through the packing room and
saw a boy lounging against a box
whistling cheerfully.

"How much do you get a week?"
he asked.

"Ten dollars, sir."

"Here's a week's pay—get out."

When he next saw the foreman,
he asked, "When did we hire that
boy?"

"We never hired him; he just
brought in a package from another
firm."

[4539]

Friend–"I suppose you have your
share of doubtful bills on your
books?"
Merchant–"I only wish they were.
There's no question about most of
them."

[4540]

"My husband is away so much of
the time I want a parrot for company. Does this one use rough
language?"

"Lady, with this bird in the house
you'd never miss your husband."

[4541]

Dealer–"Did I understand you to
say that the parrot I sold you uses
improper language?"
Cultured Customer–"Perfectly awful. Why, yesterday I heard him
split an infinitive."

[4542]

Shopper–"But this talking doll
won't talk."
Bright Clerk–"No, I'm sorry. You
see, it's supposed to belong to the
diplomatic service."

[4543]

"I fear that young man I gave a
job to last week is dishonest."

"Oh, you shouldn't judge by appearances!"

"I'm not; I'm judging by disap-
pearances in this case."

[4544]

A stammerer went into a bird
shop and asked:

"D-d-do y-y-y-you have all k-k-
k-kinds of b-b-b-birds?"

"Yes, sir. All kinds."

"I w-w-w-want a p-p-p-parrot."

"Yes, sir. Here's a beauty."

"Is h-h-h-he a g-g-g-good t-t-t-
talker?"

"Well, if he can't talk better than
you I'll not charge you for him,"
was the answer.

THE BUSINESS WORLD

437

REAL ESTATE

[4545]

"Yes, she's married to a real-estate agent and a good, honest fellow, too."

"My gracious! Bigamy?"

[4546]

"Look here, you swindler!" roared the owner of the suburban property to the real-estate man. "When you sold me this house, didn't you say that in three months I wouldn't part with it for $20,000."

"Certainly," said the real-estate dealer calmly, "and you haven't, have you?"

[4547]

"That fellow is too slick for me. Sold me a lot that was two feet under water. I went around and demanded my money back."

"Did you get it?"

"Get nothing. He sold me a motor-boat."

[4548]

Renting Agent—"This house has one or two drawbacks which I feel I must mention. It is bounded on the north by the gasworks, on the south by a rubber factory, on the east by a vinegar distillery, and on the west there is a glue factory."

Prospect—"Good heavens! Imagine showing us such a place! What a neighborhood!"

Renting Agent—"Quite so. But there are advantages. The rent is cheap, and you can always tell which way the wind is blowing."

[4549]

Real-Estate Agent—"Well, what do you think of our little city?"

Prospect—"I'll tell you, brother. This is the first cemetery I ever saw with lights."

[4550]

"Bill used to call his house over there 'The Nutshell.' Wonder why he changed the name?"

"He got tired having funny people calling to ask whether the kernel was in."

[4551]

Landlord (to prospective tenant)—"You know we keep it very quiet and orderly here. Do you have any children?"

"No."

"A piano, radio, or victrola?"

"No."

"Do you play any musical instruments? Do you have a dog, cat, or parrot?"

"No, but my fountain pen scratches like hell sometimes."

[4552]

A builder took a prospect to see some inexpensive houses he had just erected. The prospect stood in one room, the builder in the next one, and the latter asked, "Can you hear me?" in a very low voice.

"Very faintly!" answered the prospect.

"Can you see me?"

"No."

"Them's walls for you, ain't they?" replied the builder.

[4553]

"Have you any abandoned farms for sale?"

Real-Estate Agent—"I will have one in about two weeks that I just sold to Jones!"

[4554]

Architect—"Have you any suggestions for the study, Mr. Quickrich?"

Quickrich—"Only that it must be brown. Great thinkers, I understand, are generally found in a brown study."

[4555]

"Well, old man, get through the hard times all right?"

"Oh, so so."

"Still occupying that penthouse?"

"Yes, I've managed somehow to keep a roof under my feet."

[4556]

"How *can* you stand these small rooms?"

"Oh, everything is in proportion. We even use condensed milk."

[4557]

A man called up a bird store the other day and said:

"Send me 30,000 cockroaches at once."

"What in heaven's name do you want with 30,000 cockroaches?"

"Well," replied the householder, "I am moving today and my lease says I must leave the premises here in exactly the same condition in which I found them."

[4558]

One day an inspector of a New York tenement house found four families living in one room, chalk lines having been drawn in such a manner as to mark out a quarter for each family.

"How do you get along here?" inquired the inspector.

"Very well," was the reply, "only the man in the farthest corner keeps boarders."

[4559]

Mrs. Newrich (looking over house plan)–"What's this thing here going to be?"

Architect–"That is an Italian staircase."

Mrs. Newrich–"Just a waste of money. We probably won't ever have any Italians coming to see us."

[4560]

Fair Young Real Estate Agent–"Could I interest you in New City?"

Susceptible Gentleman–"Lady, you could interest me anywhere."

[4561]

"Why don't you give your new bungalow a name? Something appropriate. Other people do. There's 'Seldom Inn,' 'Walk Inn,' 'Cozy Inn,' and a lot of others."

"That's an idea. As I've just finished paying for it, I'll name it 'All Inn.' "

[4562]

Two second-story men picked out a place for an after-midnight job. One stood guard below while his pal went up the eave-trough. He was gone a ticklishly long time. Finally he came down and the pair beat it through an alley.

"Well, does I git half de swag or doesn't I?" muttered the housebreaker who had stood guard.

"Sure Moike," said the other, "you'se kin have four of 'em."

"Four of 'em, whaddya mean?"

"Why, dat place we busted into was a real estate guy's palace, an' before I could fade away he sold me eight suburban lots."

[4563]

Landlord–"What is the complaint?"

Tenant – "The bathroom faucet won't run; would you mind having the hole in the roof shifted over the tub?"

[4564]

"It is very strange that no one has ever been able to find Captain Kidd's treasure."

"Oh, well, Captain Kidd isn't the only man who has put his money into real estate and couldn't get it out."

[4565]

Visitor–"I suppose they ask a lot for the rent of this sumptuous apartment."

Hostess–"Yes, they asked Harold seven times last month."

[4566]

"Have you any children?" demanded a house-renter.

"Yes," replied the other solemnly, "six—all in the cemetery."

"Better there than here," said the landlord, consolingly; and proceeded to execute the desired lease.

In due time the children returned from the cemetery, where they had been sent to play, but it was too late to annul the contract.

[4567]

"People who live in these apartment buildings don't know anything about each other I hear," said the man from the country.

"No," replied the apartment dweller, "but you can't have cabbage for dinner without everybody else in the building finding it out."

[4568]

"I like our new apartment, but the neighbors can hear everything we say."

"Well, why don't you hang a heavy tapestry on the walls?"

"But then we couldn't hear what the neighbors say."

[4569]

"How do the Joneses seem to like their little two-room kitchenette apartment?"

"Oh, they have no room for complaint!"

[4570]

Enthusiastic Agent–"Now, there is a house without a flaw!"

Harvard Man–"My gosh, what do you walk on?"

[4571]

"So you are building a new house, eh? How are you getting along with it?"

"Fine. I've got the roof and the mortgage on it, and I expect to have the furnace and the sheriff in before fall."

[4572]

Real Estate Agent–"I tell you, sir, the death rate in this suburb is lower than in any other part of the country."

Near Victim–"I believe you. I wouldn't be found dead here myself."

[4573]

"Sell your house yet?"

"We've decided not to after reading the agent's description. It seemed to be just the place we were looking for!"

INSURANCE

[4574]

The insurance adjuster who had been investigating the fire turned to go.

"I came down here to find out the cause of this fire and I have done so," he remarked.

"That's what I want to know. What caused it?" remarked the house owner.

"It's a plain case of friction."

"What-ya-mean—friction?"

"The fire was undoubtedly caused by rubbing a three thousand dollar insurance policy on a two thousand dollar house."

[4575]

An insurance company wrote out a $1,000 life policy in the name of one Samuel Johnson. Premiums were paid promptly for a few years, but suddenly stopped. After sending a few delinquent notices, the company received this reply:

"Dear Sirs: Please excuse us as we can't pay any more premiums on Sam. He died last May. Yours truly, Mrs. S. Johnson."

[4576]

"My friend," began the man with the bagful of religious tracts, persuasively, "have you ever reflected on the shortness of life and the fact that death is inevitable?"

"Have I?" replied the business man. "Well, I should say so. I am an insurance agent."

[4577]

"What would I get," inquired the man who had just insured his property against fire, "if this building should burn down tonight?"

"I would say," replied the insurance-agent, "about ten years."

[4578]

"Why in the world did you ever write a policy on a man ninety-eight years old?" asked the indignant insurance-inspector.

"Well," explained the new agent, "I looked in the census-report and found there were only a few people of that age who die each year."

[4579]

Two insurance agents—an American and an Englishman—were talking about their rival methods. The Britisher was holding forth on the system of prompt payment carried out by his people—no trouble, no fuss, no attempt to wriggle out of payment.

"If a man died tonight," he continued, "his widow would receive her money by the first post tomorrow."

"You don't say?" said the American. "See here, now, you talk of prompt payment! Well, our office is on the sixth floor of a building sixty-nine stories high. One of our clients had his offices in the forty-ninth story, and he fell out of his window. We handed him his check as he passed our floor."

[4580]

"Did you have a good time at the dance last night?"

"Kinda."

"Who was that fellow I saw you with just after the dance?"

"He is a stranger in town."

"Handsome, isn't he?"

"Nerviest guy I ever seen."

"I noticed he had his arm rather tightly about you."

"I didn't mind that so much."

"What then?"

"Do you know why he had me clutched that way?"

"No."

"Well, would you believe it, he had me that way so I couldn't escape, and all the time we were dancing he was trying to sell me some life insurance."

[4581]

A colored agent was summoned before the Insurance Commissioner.

"Don't you know," said the commissioner, "that you can't sell life insurance without a state license?"

"Boss," said the darkey, "you shuah said a moufful. I knowed I couldn't sell it, but I didn't know the reason."

[4582]

The man was being examined and cross-examined for life insurance. He had been put through a severe physical inspection, and had had to answer numerous questions about himself, his past, his ancestors, and so on. Finally, the examiner asked:

"You don't dissipate, do you? Not living fast, or doing anything in excess?"

The prospective risk, a little man with an apologetic air, seemed very frightened by this prolonged procedure. He thought a moment, and then hesitantly replied:

"I—er—I sometimes chew a piece of gum."

[4583]
Overheard on the beach at a coast resort. Small boy to his mother:

"Mummy, may I go in to swim?"

"Certainly not, my dear, it's far too deep."

"But daddy is swimming."

"Yes, dear, but he's insured."

BANKS

[4584]
"Father," said Dorothy, "that bank in which you told me to put my money is in a bad way."

"In a bad way?" returned her father, "Why, my child, that's one of the strongest banks in the country. What in the world gives you that idea?"

"Well," said Dorothy, "it returned one of my checks today for $25 marked 'No funds.' "

[4585]
A young man was asked what his father did.

He replied: "He cleans out the bank."

"Janitor or president?" asked the questioner.

[4586]
A Cleveland man stopped a newsboy in New York saying: "See here, son, I want to go to the Fifth National Bank. I'll give you a dollar if you direct me to it."

With a grin, the boy replied: "All right, come along," and he led the man to a building a half-block away.

The man paid the promised fee, remarking, however, "That was a dollar easily earned."

"Sure!" responded the lad. "But you mustn't fergit that bank-directors is paid high in Noo Yawk."

[4587]
"Did anybody drop a roll of bills with a rubber band around them?"

"Yes, I did," said several voices in the bank lobby.

"Well, I just picked up the rubber band," said the old gentleman calmly.

[4588]
"This check is doubtless all right," said the paying teller politely, "but have you anything about you by which you could be identified?"

The pretty young thing faltered, "I have a mole just above my left knee."

[4589]
A certain banker was being called upon by a delegation from a charitable institution. He instructed his secretary to make up some excuse for not seeing them.

"I'm sorry," she informed the delegate, "but Mr. Smith can't see you. He has a sprained back."

"Well," said the delegate, "go back and tell Mr. Smith that I didn't come here to wrestle with him, but to speak with him."

[4590]

"Our bank has just gone through a reorganization."

"What was the matter?"

"We found we had more vice-presidents than depositors."

[4591]

A letter came into the Chase National Bank recently, from a customer of the bank who happens to be a prominent furrier in Australia. Two years ago, this customer was complaining bitterly about the depression, but now:

"Dear Sirs:

"Am sending draft for a thousand pounds, with which please credit my account. Last year I crossed a kangaroo with a raccoon, and now I'm raising fur coats with pockets."

[4592]

The cashier of the small town bank had once been the local judge.

"Your check is all right, sir," he said one day to a stranger, "but you haven't offered sufficient proof of your identity, so that I don't see my way clear to cashing it for you."

Evidently the stranger knew who the cashier was, for he retorted, "I've known you to hang a man on less evidence, judge."

"That's possible," was the answer, "but when it comes to letting go of hard cash, we have to be very careful."

[4593]

"I used to know Mr. Smithers, who was with your firm. I understand he is a tried and trusted employee—"

The banker looked at his questioner coldly.

"He was trusted, yes; and he will be tried, if we're fortunate enough to catch him."

[4594]

Proud Father (to bank manager)—"I want to see you about opening an account for the new arrival at our house. How shall we distinguish it from mine?"

Manager—"Suppose we call it the Fresh Heir Fund?"

[4595]

A blithe young lady walked into a bank the other day and addressed the paying teller: "I want to have this check cashed."

"Yes, madam," replied the teller; "please indorse it."

"Why, my husband sent it to me. He is away on business."

"Yes, madam, but just indorse it. Sign it on the back, please, and your husband will know we paid it to you."

She went to the desk and in a few minutes returned to the window with the check indorsed: "Your loving wife, Edith."

[4596]

"I hope you are not afraid of microbes," apologized the paying teller as he cashed the school-teacher's check with soiled currency.

"Don't worry," said the young lady, "a microbe couldn't live on my salary."

[4597]

Banker—"What do you mean by telling me that you had had seven years' experience in a bank when you never had a job before?"

Youth—"Well, you advertised for a man with imagination."

[4598]

Jan. 2—Wanted—Teller, First National Bank.

Jan. 3—W. Smith has been appointed teller at the First National Bank.

Jan. 4—Wanted—W. Smith.

[4599]

"I want to know," said the grim-faced woman, "how much money my husband drew out of the bank last week."

"I cannot give you that information, madam," answered the man in the cage.

"You're the paying teller, aren't you?"

"Yes, but I'm not the telling payer."

[4600]

"What size bank is the one you work in?"

"Well, it takes a good story two weeks to get from the president back to the president."

[4601]

On his deathbed a manufacturer named six bankers as his pallbearers and explained that as they had carried him for so long that they might as well finish the job!

[4602]

An acquaintance of a man who ran a newsstand in front of a bank tried to borrow five dollars from him.

"It would give me the greatest pleasure to help you out," said the newsstand man, "if it were not for an agreement with the bank."

"I don't follow you," said the hard-up person.

"Well, it's this way. I agree not to make any loans if the bank will not sell any newspapers. Too bad—but I'm bound!"

[4603]

Perkinson—"Did you hear about Willard Elkins, the bank cashier, stealing fifty thousand and running away with his best friend's wife?"
Simpson—"Good heavens! Who'll teach his Sunday-school class to-morrow?"

STOCK BROKERS

[4604]

"Who was that fellow who jumped out the twenty-fourth story window?"

"Oh, he was a guy who was always getting in on the ground floor."

[4605]

"I hear that you dropped some money in Wall Street. Were you a bull or a bear?"

"Neither, just a plain, simple ass."

[4606]

"I am very optimistic about the future of business."

"Then why do you look so worried?"

"I'm not certain my optimism is justified."

[4607]

"Do you know that Noah was the greatest financier that ever lived?"

"How do you make that out?"

"Well, he was able to float a company when the whole world was in liquidation."

[4608]

"Dad," said the financier's son, running into his father's office, "lend me five hundred."

"What for, my boy?"

"I've got a sure tip on the market."

"How much shall we make out of it?" asked the old man cautiously.

"A couple of hundred sure," replied the boy eagerly. "That's a hundred each."

"Here's your hundred," said his father. "Let's consider that we have made this deal and that it has succeeded. You make a hundred and I save four hundred."

[4609]

"Good morning, sir. I'm a bond salesman."

"That's all right, my good fellow. Here's a half dollar—go buy yourself a square meal."

[4610]

A stock broker was forced by illness to take a vacation from his business of buying and selling stocks, and was in the hospital. The nurse was taking his temperature.

"What is it now, nurse?" he asked.

She answered, "102."

"When it gets to 102½, sell," said the broker.

[4611]

"How did Richleigh make all his money?"

"By judicious speculation and investment."

"And how did Poorman lose all his money?"

"Gambling on the stock market."

[4612]

"I had a mighty queer surprise this morning," remarked the stock broker. "I put on my last summer's thin suit on account of this extraordinary hot weather, and in one of the trousers pockets I found a big roll of bills which I had entirely forgotten."

"Were any of them receipted?" asked a pessimist.

[4613]

A broker sought admission at the pearly gates.

"Who are you?" said St. Peter.

"I am a Wall Street broker."

"What do you want?"

"I want to get in."

"What have you done that entitles you to admission?"

"Well, I saw a decrepit woman on Broadway the other day and gave her two cents."

"Gabriel, is that on the records?"

"Yes, St. Peter; it's marked down to his credit."

"What else have you done?"

"Well, I crossed the Brooklyn Bridge the other night and met a newsboy half frozen to death and gave him one cent."

"Gabriel, is that on the records?"

"Yes, St. Peter."

"What else have you done?"

"Well, I can't recollect anything else just now."

"Gabriel, what do you think we ought to do with this fellow?"

"Oh, give him back his three cents and tell him to go to hell."

[4614]

First Wall Street Broker–"Anything to do today?"

Second Wall Street Broker–"Certainly not."

"Come to a funeral with me. It will cheer you up a bit."

[4615]

"Say, Joe, you're a broker; can't you give me a tip?"

"I know something that is now about twenty, and within six months I can guarantee it to be over ninety."

"Sounds fine! What is it?"

"The temperature."

SALESMEN

[4616]

Customer–"To what do you owe your extraordinary success as a house-to-house salesman?"

Salesman–"To the first five words I utter when a woman opens the door: 'Miss, is your mother in?'"

[4617]

Several traveling salesmen were seated in the smoking compartment of the train. They were bemoaning the generally demoralized conditions of business, as they found it. Finally they turned to the quiet little man in the corner.

"And how do you find things, brother?"

"Never better since I've been on the road."

"For the love of Pete, and what's your line, may we ask?"

"Selling red ink."

[4618]

Merchant (to book salesman)– "'Salesmanship'! Huh! I've no use for your book. I've forgotten more about Salesmanship than you ever knew!"

Salesman– "Ah! Then may I show you this work on 'Memory Training'—complete in twenty-four volumes?"

[4619]

Book Salesman– "This book will do half your work."

Business Man– "Good; I'll take two."

[4620]

The strong man at the circus took a lemon and cut it in half. He took one half in his hands and squeezed out the juice, using all his strength. Then he said:

"Anyone in the audience who can squeeze another drop of juice out of this half-lemon gets $25."

Several huskies walked up to the platform. They squeezed with all their power, but not a drop came out. Then a scrawny, little man walked up. He took the lemon-rind in one hand. About a pailful of juice came out.

The strong man was astounded.

"Who the hell are you?" he asked.

The little man looked up at him disdainfully. "I'm a buyer for a chain store corporation."

[4621]

The live-wire salesman walked into the factory and demanded an interview with the manager.

"Look here, sir," he began, energetically, "I'd like to talk to your men and sell them my correspondence course on how to put fire and sparkle into their work."

The manager turned pale.

"Get out of here," he roared. "Get out, you idiot—this is a dynamite factory!"

[4622]

First Salesman– "Any business?"

Second Salesman– "Well—yes. The wife gave me some orders this morning."

[4623]

A traveling salesman sent in his card by the office-boy to the manager of a large concern, whose inner office was separated from the waiting-room by a glass partition. When the boy handed his card to the manager the salesman saw him impatiently tear it in half and throw it in the waste-basket; the boy came out and told the caller that he could not see the boss. The salesman told the boy to go back and get him his card; the boy brought out five cents, with the message that his card was torn up. Then the salesman took out another card and sent the boy back, saying: "Tell your boss I sell two cards for five cents."

He got his interview.

[4624]

"I made some very valuable contacts to-day."

"I didn't make any sales, either."

[4625]

An advertising salesman who, upon arriving at the hotel, was met by the porter who wanted to know how many trunks he carried.

"I use no trunks," the salesman replied.

"Oh, I thought you wuz one of these traveling salesmen gentlemen," said the porter.

"I am, but I sell brains, understand? I sell brains."

"Well, excuse me, boss, but youse the furst travelin' fella that's been here this season who ain't carryin' no samples."

[4626]

Business Man—"I can't see you now, you'll have to arrange with my secretary for an appointment."
Salesman—"I tried to, but she's booked for two weeks ahead."

[4627]

A sales manager had one of his salesmen on the carpet. The young salesman resented the call-down and becoming quite huffy, said:

"Don't talk to me that way. I take orders from no man!"

"Now we're getting somewhere," said the sales manager. "That's just what I'm raising hell about."

[4628]

Sales Manager—"I think it's a good time to sell the Joneses a car."
Salesman—"What makes you think so?"
Sales Manager—"Their neighbors have a new one."

[4629]

Success Expert – "What's your name?"
Greek Client—"Gus Poppapopupopulos."
Success Expert—"Get a job selling motorcycles."

[4630]

"Mr. Smith," said the head of the firm, "I notice there's a considerable item for meals in your expense account."

"Er—I was entertaining customers and prospective buyers, sir."

"All right. I'm not complaining, but I hope you will bear in mind that we are selling tractors, and no lady of the chorus ever buys a tractor."

[4631]

A salesman, seeing his prospect sitting disconsolately looking out of the window, asked him:

"What's the matter to-day?"

"I promised my wife a Pomeranian, and the best price I can get on one is $150, and it's too much," was the reply.

"You're right, it's too much," quickly responded the salesman, "I can sell you one for $75."

"Fine," said the prospect, beaming. "When can you make delivery?"

"Just a minute. I'll find out," said the salesman, who rushed out and down to a public telephone booth. Getting his partner on the 'phone, he said:

"Say, listen; I've sold a guy here a Pomeranian for $75. What in hell is a Pomeranian?"

[4632]

A new salesman set forth on his first trip for the house with instructions to report from day to day. From his first stop the firm got this message:

"Putting up at swell hotel here. Dandy room with bath and southern exposure. Feeling fine."

The house wired him at once:

"So glad; love and kisses; goodbye!"

[4633]

"Yes, me and Bill are in partnership in this selling game, but we don't carry the same goods."

"Explain yourself."

"Well, Bill goes around selling a stove polish that leaves a stain on your fingers, and two days later I go around with the only soap that will take it off."

[4634]

"Chief, we'll have to have this establishment reëquipped electrically, one of these days. Who'll we get to do the job?"

"Bring in young Smith, of our sales force. He hasn't done anything but wire the house since he's been on the road."

[4635]

Business Man—"Well, if it isn't John Corcoran, the man I met up in Maine one rainy night six years ago at the Moose River Junction railway station.

Salesman—"Good-by, sir."

Business Man—"Aren't you going to try and sell me something?"

Salesman—"No. I sell memory-training courses."

[4636]

Trade was bad. At the end of another blank day the discouraged salesman called on another prospective customer and asked to show his samples.

"No, there is nothing I want to-day," said the customer.

"But will you just examine my line of goods?" the salesman persisted.

The customer would not.

"Then," said the salesman meekly, "will you let me use a part of your counter to look at them myself, as I have not had the opportunity for some time?"

[4637]

Said one traveling salesman to another in a restaurant:

"What's the matter, Bill? You are only eating crackers and milk. Are you on a diet?"

"No, on commission."

[4638]

Sales Manager—"What's this big item on your expense-account?"

Traveling Salesman—"Oh, that's my hotel bill."

Sales Manager—"Well, don't buy any more hotels."

WORKING-MEN

[4639]

"What's happened? Have you had an accident?"

"No. I just bet Jim he couldn't carry me up a ladder on his neck, and I won."

[4640]

A group of laborers were eating their midday meal and skylarking around, when one of them let out a yell.

"Hey, what's the matter, Jim?"

"Got a damned splinter in my finger."

"Well, why don't you pull it out?"

"What, on my own time? Not much!"

[4641]

"Here's your pay for loafing seven hours."

"Excuse me—eight hours."

[4642]

Foreman—"Do you think you're fit for really hard labor?"

Applicant—"Well, some of the best judges in the country have thought so."

[4643]

After six months at a new factory, the superintendent developed a feeling that he wasn't popular, so he called aside an old worker.

"Bill," said the superintendent, "how is it the men don't seem to like me? Why, at my last place they gave me a silver teapot when I left."

"Only a silver teapot?" said the candid worker. "Gosh, if you'd only leave here we'd make it a gold tea service!"

[4644]

"Are you looking for work, my man?"

"Not necessarily—but I'd like a job."

[4645]

"Where have you been?" inquired the employer.

"Having my hair cut," replied the workman.

"Well, you can't have your hair cut on my time," protested the exasperated employer.

"Why not?" demanded the wage-earner sturdily. "It grew on your time."

[4646]

Country Cousin (after prolonged inspection of building operations)—"I don't see the sense of putting statues on the top of your buildings."

Friend—"Statues? Those a r e n ' t statues. They're *bricklayers*."

[4647]

"I've just been reading about a machine which does the work of ten men. It almost has brains."

"Not if it does all that work."

[4648]

Carpenter—"Didn't I tell you to notice when the glue boiled over?"

Assistant—"I did. It was a quarter past ten."

[4649]

Foreman—"Say Thompson, that man is doing twice as much as you are."

Thompson—"Sure! I keep tellin' the poor sap, but you can't learn him nothin'."

[4650]

"I hear the men are striking."

"What for?"

"Shorter hours."

"Luck to 'em. I always did think sixty minutes was too long for an hour."

[4651]

A man named Dodgin was recently appointed foreman at a factory, but his name was not known to all the employees. One day while on his rounds he came across two men sitting in a corner, smoking, and stopped near them.

"Who are you?" said one of the men.

"I'm Dodgin, the new foreman," he replied.

"So are we," replied the other workers, "sit down and have a smoke."

[4652]

The plumber was a mild sort of man, but he could not get away from the fact that his assistant was terribly lazy.

For a long time he said nothing, but at last he could contain his exasperation no longer.

"Bill, you get on my nerves standing there with both hands in your pockets," he said. "For Heaven's sake, take one of them out."

[4653]

Would-be Employer—"Have you any references?"

Would-be Employee—"Sure, here's the letter: 'To whom it may concern. John Jones worked for us one week, and we're satisfied.'"

[4654]
Employer–"For this job you've got
to know French and Spanish, and
the pay is eighteen dollars a week."
"Lord, Mister! I ain't got no edi-
cation; I'm after a job in the yards."
"See the yard-boss. We'll start you
in at forty."

[4655]
Plumber–"Well, have you brought
all the tools?"
New Boy–"Yes, Sir."
Plumber–"You would!"

[4656]
"Are you a clock watcher?" asked
the employer of the candidate for a
job.
"No, I don't like inside work,"
replied the applicant, without heat,
"I'm a whistle listener."

[4657]
"Got any references?" asked the
plumber.
"Yes," replied the applicant for
the assistant's position, "but I've
left 'em at home—I'll go and get
them."
"Never mind, you'll do."

[4658]
Plumber–"Well, here we are! And
we haven't forgotten a single tool."
Householder–"But you've come to
the wrong address."

[4659]
"What will you charge me to
paint my boat," asked a man of a
painter.
"Twelve dollars a day," was the
reply.
"Good Lord! I wouldn't pay
Michelangelo that price," exclaimed
the boat owner.
"Well, I tell you one thing," declared the painter; "if that wop is
taking the job for less, he ain't no
member of the union!"

[4660]
Foreman–"What's the big idea of
quitting?"
Riveter–"Oh, I don't mind hammering rivets all day long, but the man
who works with me hums incessantly."

[4661]
Foreman–"Ya know ya ain't sup-
posed to smoke while yer workin'."
Laborer–"Who says I'm workin'?"

[4662]
Plumber (arriving late)–"Well, how
is it?"
Happy Husband–"Not so bad, while
we were waiting for you I taught
my wife how to swim."

[4663]
Foreman–"How is it that you're
only carrying one plank when the
others are carrying two?"
Worker–"Well, I suppose they're
too lazy to make a double journey
like I do!"

[4664]
"Tell me, why has your brother
gone crazy?"
"You see, he worked in a round-
house and he went crazy trying to
find a corner to spit his chew into."

MISCELLANEOUS BUSINESS

[4665]
A merchant in a Wisconsin town
who had a Swedish clerk sent him
out to do some collecting. When he
returned from an unsuccessful trip
he reported:
"Yim Yonson say he vill pay ven
he sells his hogs. Yim Olson he vill
pay ven he sells his wheat and Bill
Pack say he vill pay in Yanuary."
"Well," said the boss, "that's the

first time Bill ever set a date to pay. Did he really say he would pay in January?"

"Vell, aye tank so," said the clerk, "he said it bane a dam cold day ven you get that money. Aye tank that bane in Yanuary."

[4666]

The young man who answered the classified advertisement, "Opportunity of a Lifetime," found himself in the presence of a nervous individual.

"What I am looking for is somebody to do all my worrying," he explained. "Your job will be to shoulder all my cares."

"That's some job, how much do I get?" asked the applicant.

"You get $20,000 to make every worry of mine your own," replied the overwrought individual.

"Where is the $20,000 coming from?"

"Ah, that's your first worry!"

[4667]

"How can I pay when I haven't any money?" said the debtor. "You can't get blood out of a turnip."

But the collector was ready for him: "You're not a turnip—you're a *beat*."

[4668]

In a small town where two brothers are engaged in the retail coal business a religious revival was held and one of the brothers got converted. For weeks he tried to persuade his partner in business to join the church. One day he asked:

"Why can't you get religion and join the church like I did?"

"It's a fine thing for you to belong to the church," replied the other, "but if I join the church who'll weigh the coal?"

[4669]

Lady (to peddler)—"No, thank you, we never buy anything at the door."
Peddler—"Then I've just the thing for you, Madam. You will, I am sure, appreciate these tasteful little 'No Peddlers' notices."

[4670]

"I have been in this business since 1908.

"I have been pleasing and displeasing the people ever since.

"I have been cussed and discussed, boycotted, talked about, lied about, lied to, hung up, held up, stood up, robbed, etc.

"The only reason I am staying in business now is to see:

"What the hell is going to happen next!"

[4671]

A smart buyer telephoned for price on a carload of canary bird seed. Later he asked if the same price would hold good on half a car. Having been assured of this, he later called up and wanted to know if the price would be the same on five hundred pounds. The seller finally agreed to make the same price. Later he called up and wanted to know if the same price would hold good on one hundred pounds. The dealer, very much out of patience, replied, "If you will send your darn old canary over to our store we will feed him for nothing."

[4672]

"How did you make your fortune?"

"I became the partner of a rich man; he had the money and I had the experience."

"How did that help?"

"Now he has the experience and I the money."

[4673]
"Everybody puts their nose into my business."

"Cheer up."

"I'm not growling. I manufacture handkerchiefs."

[4674]
A manufacturer said they were running about fifty-fifty—an order in the morning, a cancellation in the afternoon.

[4675]
"My wife and myself are trying to get up a list of club magazines. By taking three you get a discount."

"How are you making out?"

"Well, we can get one that I don't want and one that she doesn't want, and one that neither wants for $2.25."

[4676]
A traveling salesman visited a small town and sold the proprietor of its general store some merchandise. When the goods arrived they were not as represented and the merchant consequently returned them. The wholesale house attempted to collect the bill and drew a sight draft on the merchant through the local bank, which returned the check unhonored. The house wrote the postmaster about the financial standing of the merchant and the postmaster laconically replied with an O. K. By return mail the house requested the postmaster to secure a lawyer to collect the amount and received the following reply:

"The undersigned is the merchant on whom you attempted to palm off your worthless goods. The undersigned is the president and owner of the bank to which you sent your sight draft. The undersigned is the postmaster to whom you wrote and the undersigned is the lawyer whose services you sought to obtain for your nefarious business. If the undersigned were not also the preacher of the church of this place he would tell you to go to hell."

[4677]
This is from a circular of the Zanesville (Ohio) Chamber of Commerce:

"Zanesville is an exceptionally rich city; so rich, in fact, that every blade of grass has a green back, every bird has a bill, the chimneys have their drafts, and the maids wash our front doors with gold dust; every horse has a check, and every ditch has two banks; even our streets are flushed and the lawns get a rake off; every cloud has a silver lining and every flower in the city has a scent; when you put a five dollar bill in your pocket you double it, and when you take it out you find it in creases. Now do you want to leave here or not?"

[4678]
A firm that wired withdrawal of a recent order got this answer: "You'll have to be patient and take your turn. There are 5,000 cancellations ahead of you."

[4679]
"Was his bankruptcy due to a lack of brains?"

"Yes, a lack and a lass."

[4680]
Newsboy—"Great mystery! Fifty victims! Paper, mister?"

Passer-by—"Here, boy, I'll take one." (After reading a moment.) "Say, boy, there's nothing of the kind in this paper. Where is it?"

Newsboy—"That's the mystery, guvnor. You're the fifty-first victim."

[4681]
Somebody asked a college professor how science helped business, and he replied, "What would the suspender business amount to without the law of gravitation?"

[4682]
"I don't know whether I like these photos or not," said the young woman. "They seem rather indistinct."
"But, you must remember, madam," said the wily photographer, "that your face is not at all plain."

[4683]
"And you wouldn't begin a journey on Friday?"
"Most certainly not."
"That's a silly superstition."
"It's no superstition in my case. My pay day is Saturday."

[4684]
Friend—"Did you ever run up against a mathematical problem that stumped you?"
Famous Mathematician—"Yes, indeed. I could never figure out how, according to the magazine ads, eighty-five percent of the dentists recommend one brand of toothpaste, ninety-two percent recommend another brand, and ninety-five percent recommend still another brand."

[4685]
Official—"No, I can't find you a job. I have so many people here after jobs that I can't even remember their names."
Applicant—"Couldn't you give me the job of keeping a record of them?"

[4686]
"You made a mistake in your paper," said an indignant man, entering the editorial sanctum of a daily journal. "I was one of the competitors at an athletic entertainment last night, and you referred to me as the well-known lightweight champion."
"Well, are you not?" inquired the sporting editor.
"No, I'm nothing of the kind!" was the angry response; "and it's confoundedly awkward, because I'm a coal dealer."

[4687]
Customer—"Why do you charge extra for each of my cuffs?"
Manager of Laundry—"Because you make pencil notes on them."
Customer—"Why should that make such a difference?"
Manager—"The girls waste so much time trying to make them out."

[4688]
"I'm a very busy man, sir. What is your proposition?"
"I want to make you rich."
"Just so. Leave your recipe with me and I'll look it over later. Just now I'm engaged in closing up a little deal by which I expect to make $7.50 in real money."

[4689]
A wholesale dealer who had a lot of trouble in getting a certain retailer to pay his bills finally lost patience and wrote the merchant a threatening letter. He received the following reply:
"Dear Sir: What do you mean by writing me a letter like that?
"Every month I place all my bills in a hat and then figure out how much money I have to pay on my accounts. Then I have my bookkeeper draw as many bills out of the hat as I have money to pay.
"If you don't like my way of doing business, I won't even put your bills in the hat."

[4690]

First Manufacturer – "How's business?"

Second Manufacturer – "Picking up a little. One of our men got a $50,000 order yesterday."

"Go away. I don't believe that."

"Honest he did—I'll show you the cancellation."

[4691]

"John's in the fireworks manufacturing business now."

"How's he getting on?"

"So far, all the reports are favorable."

[4692]

"Here's a letter from Dunleigh asking that we send him a part of what's due him, and enclosing a stamp for a reply. What shall I do about it?" asked one of the two impecunious partners.

"Send him back the stamp on account," replied the resourceful partner.

[4693]

"We are dunning him, but without much effect."

"Are you unremitting?"

"Yes, and so is he."

[4694]

Editor of a Missouri weekly paper carried this notice:

"Attention subscribers. W h e n your subscription expires come in and renew promptly if you want me to give you a good boost toward the golden gate when you expire."

[4695]

Head of Business College – "In teaching shorthand and typewriting, we are strong for accuracy."

Inquirer – "How are you on speed?"

Head of Business College – "Well, of last year's class, six married their employers within six months."

[4696]

Tourist – "Was that one of your prominent citizens? I noticed you were very respectful and attentive to him."

Garage Man – "Yes, he's one of our early settlers."

"Early settler? Why he's quite a young man yet."

"True enough. I mean he pays his bills the first of every month."

[4697]

An advertising agency was having a long and tedious consultation with its latest customers, a distillery combine. At last the agency men were cheered by one of the clients saying, "Have you sampled our products? This one's our best Scotch. Has anyone a corkscrew?"

Fourteen pairs of eyes sparkled. Six corkscrews were produced.

The distillery man selected one, expertly removed the cork from the bottle and said authoritatively: "The proper way to sample liquor is to wet your finger with a couple of drops, then place the finger on the underside of the tongue."

[4698]

Radio Announcer – "The 10 minutes' silence on your radio, ladies and gentlemen, was not due to a technical breakdown, but was sent to you by courtesy of Blanko Noiseless Typewriters."

[4699]

Just as an auctioneer was saying "Gone?" his audience went through the floor into the cellar, but happily without hurting any of them. The auctioneer, as soon as he found his legs, remarked that the accident would enable him to sell lower than before, and called for a bid, and they bid him "Good-night."

[4700]

"How's business with you, old man?"

"Oh, lookin' up."

"What do you mean, lookin' up?"

"Well, it's flat on its back, isn't it?"

[4701]

The president of the local gas-company was making a stirring address.

"Think of the good the gas-company has done," he cried. "If I were permitted a pun I should say, 'Honor the Light Brigade.'"

And a customer immediately shouted, "Oh, what a charge they made!"

[4702]

A captain of industry was noted for showing up on various work projects in his organization, and inquiring about the number of men employed. Invariably he would instruct the foreman to lay off several. In time he went the way of all flesh. As his body was being carried from the funeral parlor, he raised up in his coffin and asked:

"How many pall bearers are carrying me?"

"Six, sir," someone replied.

"Um-m-m, six. Better lay off two."

[4703]

"My boy," said the magnate to his son, "there are two things that are vitally necessary if you are to succeed in business."

"What are they, dad?"

"Honesty and sagacity."

"What is honesty?"

"Always—no matter what happens or how adversely it may affect you—always keep your word once you have given it."

"And sagacity?"

"Never give it."

[4704]

"Say, Jim," said the friend of the taxicab-driver, standing in front of the vehicle, "there's a purse lying on the floor of your car."

The driver looked carefully around and then whispered: "Sometimes when business is bad I put it there and leave the door open. It's empty, but you've no idea how many people'll jump in for a short drive when they see it."

[4705]

A young man dashed into the electrician's shop, his face flushed with anger. "Didn't I ask you yesterday morning to send a man to mend our doorbell?" he roared, "and didn't you promise to send him round at once?"

"But we did, sir," broke in the manager. "I'm quite sure of it! Hi, Bill!" he called to one of his workmen at the back of the office. "Didn't you go round to Park Lodge yesterday to do that job?"

"Yessir," replied Bill. "I went round all right, and I rang the bell for over ten minutes, but I couldn't get no answer, so I guessed they must all be out."

[4706]

"Don't you think I stand a good chance of making a fortune out of that mine?"

"Out of it, yes. In it, no."

[4707]

Mr. Dealer—"What kind of coal do you wish, mum?"

Mrs. Newlywed—"Dear me, I am so inexperienced in these things. Are there various kinds?"

Mr. Dealer—"Oh, yes. We have egg coal, chestnut—"

Mrs. Newlywed—"I think I'll take egg coal. We have eggs oftener than we have chestnuts."

[4708]

"What is your gross income?"

"I have no gross income."

"No income at all?"

"No gross income. I have a net income. I'm in the fish business."

[4709]

A business man, asked to say grace, and being unaccustomed to the ceremony: "Dear Lord, we are in receipt of your kind favors of recent date and beg to thank you. We hope to merit your continued courtesy."

[4710]

Customer–"I want a ton of coal."

Dealer–"Yes, sir. What size?"

Customer–"Well, if it's not asking too much, I would like a 2000-pound ton."

[4711]

"I'm so sorry to hear that your factory was burnt down. What do you manufacture?"

"Fire extinguishers."

[4712]

"I expect a lot of dirty work when I start my new business."

"Treachery, eh?"

"No, I'm opening a laundry."

[4713]

A bright little newsie entered a business office and, approaching a glum-looking man at one of the desks, began with an ingratiating smile.

"I'm selling thimbles to raise enough money to——"

"Out with you!" interrupted the man.

"Wouldn't you like to look at some nice thimbles?"

"I should say not!"

"They're fine, and I'd like to make a sale," he continued.

Turning in his chair to fully face the lad, the grouch caustically inquired:

"What'n seven kinds o' blue blazes do you think I want with a thimble?"

Edging towards the door to make a safe getaway, the boy answered: "Use it for a hat."

[4714]

"You say this fellow is crooked?"

"Is he crooked? Say, he's so crooked even the wool he pulls over your eyes is half cotton."

[4715]

Businessman (who had got on in life)–"Yes, when I first came to New York I had only a dollar in my pocket with which to make a start."

Interviewer–"How did you invest that dollar?"

Businessman–"Used it to pay for a telegram home for more money."

[4716]

Mrs. Williams demanded the removal of the telephone from her house. Said the language of the lineman at work on the wires in front of her residence was so loud and blasphemous she wanted no further dealings with a corporation that employed such ruffians.

The company acknowledged receipt of her complaint, but begged the suspension of cancellation until it could make its usual thorough investigation. Mrs. Williams agreed to wait.

At the end of a week the aggrieved patron received the following report:

"Dear Madam: We have gone into the alleged rowdyism of our employes with great care, and have found the facts to be as follows: Richard Smith and Jeremiah Jones were repairing broken wires in front of your home. In receiving a bucket of hot metal which Smith was hauling up to the crosstrees, Jones (on duty aloft) accidentally tipped the receptacle and let a quantity of the molten lead fall on the shoulders and down the back of Smith. Whereupon Smith looked up at Jones and said: 'Be a little more careful with that stuff hereafter, Jeremiah.' Respectfully submitted."

[4717]

"My business is looking up," said the astronomer.

"Mine is going up in smoke," complained the cigar-maker.

"Mine is all write," chuckled the author.

"Mine is just sew, sew," remarked the tailor.

"Mine is growing," the farmer boasted.

"Ours is pretty light," snapped the electric light man.

"Mine is picking up," smiled the cheerful rag picker.

"Mine is looking better," opined the optician.

[4718]

"I understand that the boss's son started at the foot of the ladder and worked up."

"Oh, yeh! But the ladder was stepped on an upper floor."

[4719]

The sweet young thing entered the office of the fashionable dog kennels and tripped up to the handsome young man at the desk.

"I want a pet," she cooed.

"I'd love to," he answered sadly, "but the boss is awfully strict."

[4720]

A retail dealer in refrigerators doing business in one of the large cities wrote to a manufacturer ordering a carload of refrigerators. The manufacturer wired him:

"Cannot ship refrigerators until you pay for your last consignment."

"Unable to wait so long," wired back the refrigerator dealer, "cancel order."

[4721]

"There goes that Mr. Sharp. I wonder how he made all his money?"

"Heaven knows!"

"Ah, that must be why he always looks so worried."

[4722]

"Oh, Mr. Jones," said Miss Dash, "I saw an advertisement saying that you could furnish your home by soap premiums. Every time you buy a piece of soap you get a furniture certificate. I am going to be married: do you think I could furnish my house that way?"

"Why, yes, Miss Dash," replied Mr. Jones, "I had a friend who got all the furniture for a six-room house that way. The company only had to send him furniture for one room; the other five were full of soap."

[4723]

A prominent business man fell in love with an actress and decided to marry her, but for the sake of prudence he employed a private detective to report on her life. When he received the report it read as follows:

"The lady has an excellent reputation. Her past is without blemish. She has an excellent circle of pleasant friends—the only breath of scandal is that lately she has been seen a great deal in the company of a business man of doubtful repute."

[4724]

"Johnny," said his teacher, "if coal is selling at $6 a ton and you pay your dealer $24 how many tons will he bring you?"

"A little over three tons, ma'am," said Johnny promptly.

"Why, Johnny, that isn't right," said the teacher.

"No, ma'am, I know it ain't," said Johnny, "but they all do it."

[4725]

"Hello, is this the Better Business Bureau?"

"Yes."

"Well, how'd you like to come down and make ours a little better?"

[4726]

A firm of shipowners wired one of their captains: "Move heaven and earth; get here on Friday."

Just as they were becoming very anxious, they got the reply: "Raised hell and arriving Thursday."

[4727]

Undertaker–"Depression? I'll say so! Why, I haven't buried a living soul for a month!"

[4728]

"You are suffering from brain fag and ennui," announced the specialist. "You should take more interest in your business."

"I would like to," replied the patient.

"Then why don't you?" demanded the specialist.

"The law won't let me," replied the patient. "I'm a pawnbroker."

[4729]

In a New York street a small truck loaded with glassware collided with a large truck laden with bricks, and practically all of the glassware was smashed. Considera-ble sympathy was felt for the driver as he gazed ruefully at the shattered fragments. A benevolent-looking old gentleman eyed him compassionately.

"My poor man," he said, "I suppose you will have to make good this loss out of your own pocket?"

"Yep," was the melancholy reply.

"Well, well," said the philanthropic old gentleman, "hold out your hat—here's fifty cents for you; and I dare say some of these other people will give you a helping hand too."

The driver held out his hat and over a hundred persons hastened to drop coins in it. At last, when the contributions had ceased, he emptied the contents of his hat into his pocket. Then, pointing to the retreating figure of the philanthropist who had started the collection, he observed: "Say, maybe he ain't the wise guy! That's me boss!"

[4730]

A lusty-lunged auctioneer was addressing a crowd in a small town. Taking up a box of cigars, he shouted, "You can't get better, gentlemen. I don't care where you go."

"No," replied a cynical voice from the crowd, "you can't. I smoked one last week, and I'm not better yet."

[4731]

"Everything I plan goes up in smoke."

"Why, I thought you were a successful business man."

"I am—I manufacture fireworks."

[4732]

"What is a debtor, pa?"

"A man who owes money."

"And what is a creditor?"

"The man who thinks he's going to get it."

PART VI

THE PROFESSIONS

LAWYERS

[4733]

Client (just acquitted on burglary charge)–"Well, good-by. I'll drop in on you some time."
Counsel–"All right, but make it in the daytime, please."

[4734]

Judge–"The two men were fighting with chairs. Didn't you try to establish peace?"
Witness–"No, there was not a third chair."

[4735]

"Why is it that a judge has so little time left for himself?"
"I suppose it's because he is so busy."
"Wrong. It's because he hands out so much time to other people."

[4736]

Judge–"Have you ever been up before me?"
Accused–"I don't know. What time do you get up?"

[4737]

"Repeat the words the defendant used," said the lawyer.
"I'd rather not. They were not fit words to tell a gentleman."
"Then," said the attorney, "whisper them to the judge."

[4738]

A district attorney objected to a lawyer calling the State's evidence "tainted testimony." His objection was sustained by the judge, before whom the case is being being tried. "The testimony isn't tainted," he declared.
" 'Tis," replied the lawyer.
"Tain't," voiced the judge.

[4739]

Judge–"Do you understand the nature of an oath, Madam?"
Witness–"I should say I do. I was in the car that bumped into your car against signals this morning."

[4740]

The magistrate looked severely at the small, red-faced man who had been summoned before him, and who returned his gaze without flinching.
"So you kicked your landlord downstairs?" queried the magistrate. "Did you imagine that was within the right of a tenant?"
"I'll bring my lease in and show it to you," said the little man, growing redder, "and I'll wager you'll agree with me that anything they've forgotten to prohibit in that lease I had a right to do the very first chance I got."

THE PROFESSIONS

[4741]

A lawyer was defending a man accused of housebreaking, and said to the court:

"Your Honor, I submit that my client did not break into the house at all. He found the parlor window open and merely inserted his right arm and removed a few trifling articles. Now, my client's arm is not himself, and I fail to see how you can punish the whole individual for an offense committed by only one of his limbs."

The judge considered this argument for several moments, and then replied:

"That argument is very well put. Following it logically, I sentence the defendant's arm to one year's imprisonment. He can accompany it or not, as he chooses."

The defendant smiled, and with his lawyer's assistance unscrewed his cork arm, and, leaving it in the dock, walked out.

[4742]

Two friends met on the street after not having seen each other for some time. One of them was using crutches.

"Hello!" said the other man. "What's the matter with you?"

"Street-car accident," said the man on crutches.

"When did that happen?"

"Oh, about six weeks ago."

"And you still have to use crutches?"

"Well, my doctor says I could get along without them, but my lawyer says I can't."

[4743]

An old Negro was charged with chicken stealing, and the judge said:

"Where's your lawyer, uncle?"

"Ain't got none, Jedge."

"But you ought to have one," returned the court. "I'll assign one to defend you."

"No, sah, no sah, please don't do dat," begged the defendant.

"Why not?" persisted the judge. "It won't cost you anything. Why don't you want a lawyer?"

"Well, Ah'll tell yo', Jedge," said the old man confidentially. "Ah wants ter enj'y dem chickens mah-self."

[4744]

"You are lying so clumsily," said the judge to the defendant, "that I would advise you to get a lawyer."

[4745]

Judge—"You are fined ten dollars."
Mrs. Bargains (absent-mindedly) —"Sorry, but that's a little more than I care to pay."

[4746]

A sailor was called into the witness-box to give evidence.

"Well, sir," said the lawyer, "do you know the plaintiff and defendant?"

"I don't know the drift of them words," answered the sailor.

"What! Not know the meaning of 'plaintiff' and 'defendant'?" continued the lawyer. "A pretty fellow you to come here as a witness! Can you tell me where on board the ship it was the man struck the other?"

"Abaft the binnacle," said the sailor.

"Abaft the binnacle," said the lawyer. "What do you mean by that?"

"A pretty fellow you," responded the sailor, "to come here as a lawyer, and don't know what 'abaft the binnacle' means!"

[4747]

"And now, Mrs. Sullivan," said Lawyer Thomson, "will you be kind enough to tell the jury whether your husband was in the habit of striking you with impunity?"

"Wid what, sir?"

"With impunity."

"He wuz, sir, now and thin; but he sthruck me ofthener wid his fisht."

[4748]

A lawyer was arguing a complicated case, and looked up authorities back to Julius Caesar. At the end of an hour and a half, in the most intricate part of his plea, he was pained to see what looked like inattention. It was as he had feared. The judge was unable to appreciate the nice points of his argument.

"Your Honor," he said, "I beg your pardon; but do you follow me?"

"I have so far," answered the judge, shifting wearily about in his chair, "but I'll say frankly that if I thought I could find my way back, I'd quit right here."

[4749]

By way of reward of faithful political service an ambitious bartender was appointed police magistrate.

"What's the charge against this man?" he asked when the first case was called before him.

"Drunk, your honor."

"Guilty or not guilty?"

"Sure, sir," said the accused, "I never drink a drop."

"Have a cigar, then," urged his honor as he absent mindedly polished the top of the desk with his handkerchief.

[4750]

The lawyer was endeavoring to pump some free medical advice out of the doctor.

"Which side is it best to lie on, Doc?"

"The side that pays you the retainer."

[4751]

"I shall have to give you ten days or $20," said the judge.

"I'll take the $20, Judge," said the prisoner.

[4752]

A lawyer was cross-examining a witness. He asked:

"And you say you called on Mrs. Jones, May second. Now will you tell the jury just what she said?"

"I object to the question," interrupted the lawyer on the other side.

There was nearly an hour's argument between counsel, and finally the judge allowed the question.

"And as I was saying," the first lawyer began again, "on May second you called on Mrs. Jones. Now what did she say?"

"Nothing," replied the witness. "She was not at home."

[4753]

A diminutive lawyer, appearing as a witness in one of the courts, was asked by a gigantic counsellor what profession he was of, and having replied that he was an attorney:

"You a lawyer," said the giant counsellor, "why I could put you in my pocket."

"Very likely you could," rejoined the other, "but if you did, you would have more law in your pocket than you ever had in your head."

[4754]

"Did you know anything about this case?" the juror was asked.

"No."

"Have you heard anything about it?"

"No."

"Have you read anything about it?"

"No. I can't read."

"Have you formed any opinion about the case?"

"What case?"

"Accepted."

[4755]

"Silence in the court!" thundered a Kentucky judge. "Half a dozen men have been convicted already without the court's having been able to hear a word of the testimony."

[4756]

"Speak to the jury, sir—the men sitting behind you on the benches."

The witness at once turned round, and, making an awkward bow, said, with great gravity of manner:

"Good morning, gentlemen!"

[4757]

Prisoner-"It is difficult to see how I can be a forger. Why, I can't sign my own name."

Judge-"You are not charged with signing your own name."

[4758]

"Your honor," said the foreman of the jury, "this attractive lady is suing this gentleman for ten thousand dollars for a stolen kiss."

"Correct," responded the judge. "You are to decide if it is worth it."

"That's the point, your honor. How can we decide its value without a sample?"

[4759]

Prisoner-"Judge, I don't know what to do."

Judge-"Why, how's that?"

Prisoner-"I swore to tell the truth but every time I try some lawyer objects."

[4760]

Lawyer-"Now that we have won, will you tell me confidentially if you stole the money?"

Client-"Well, after hearing you talk in court yesterday, I am beginning to think I didn't."

[4761]

A burlesque comedian was once a witness in a suit for slander, and the opposing counsel in the courtroom said: "You are a burlesque comedian, I believe?"

"Yes."

"Is not that a low calling?"

"I don't know; but it's so much better than my father's that I am rather proud of it."

"What was your father's calling, may I ask?"

"He was a lawyer," said the burlesque comedian.

[4762]

"I couldn't serve as a juror, Judge. One look at that fellow convinces me he's guilty."

"Sh-h! That's the district attorney!"

[4763]

The judge decided that certain evidence was inadmissible. The attorney took strong exceptions to the ruling, and insisted that it was admissible.

"I know, your Honor," said he, warmly, "that it is proper evidence. Here I have been practicing at the bar for forty years, and now I want to know if I am a fool?"

"That," quietly replied the court, "is a question of fact, and not of law, and so I won't pass upon it, but will let the jury decide."

[4764]

It happened in the court-room during the trial of a husky young man who was charged with assault and battery. Throughout an especially severe cross-examination the defendant stoutly maintained that he had merely pushed the plaintiff "a little bit."

"Well, about how hard?" queried the prosecutor.

"Oh, just a little bit," responded the defendant.

"Now," said the attorney, "for the benefit of the judge and the jury, you will please step down here and, with me for the subject, illustrate just how hard you mean."

Owing to the unmerciful badgering which the witness had just been through, the prosecutor thought that the young man would perhaps overdo the matter to get back at him, and thus incriminate himself.

The defendant descended as per schedule, and approached the waiting attorney. When he reached him the spectators were astonished to see him slap the lawyer in the face, kick him in the shins, seize him bodily, and, finally, with a supreme effort, lift him from the floor and hurl him prostrate across a table.

Turning from the bewildered prosecutor, he faced the court and explained mildly:

"Your honor and gentlemen, about one-tenth that hard!"

[4765]

They had reached a juncture in the trial when the court advised the attorney to withdraw with his client and give him the benefit of the best advice he could think of.

After fifteen minutes he returned to the court-room without his client.

"Where's the prisoner at the bar?" asked the judge.

"He's skipped," replied the lawyer. "That was the best advice I could give him."

[4766]

A celebrated lawyer once said that the three most troublesome clients he ever had were a young lady who wanted to be married, a married woman who wanted a divorce, and an old maid who didn't know what she wanted.

[4767]

Attorney Blank was examining a witness in court the other day.

"Have you ever been arrested before?" he asked the man.

"No, sir!" the witness answered emphatically.

"Have you ever been in this court before?"

"No, sir!"

"Are you sure of that?"

"Yes, sir!"

"Your face looks very familiar—very familiar. Where have I seen you before?"

"Well, sir," the witness calmly answered, "I am a bartender in the saloon across the street from here."

[4768]

A woman of mixed breeding was up before a western justice of the peace, charged with unmercifully beating her small child.

"I don't understand how you can have the heart to treat your own child so cruelly."

"Jedge, you evuh been a parent

to a wuthless French-Spanish-Chickataw boy like this here cub of mahn?"

"Never—no, never!" ejaculated the judge, with great vehemence, getting red in the face.

"Then don't talk; you don't know nuthin' about it."

[4769]

As a judge was leaving the bench one day he slipped, bumped down several steps and landed with some violence on the floor. An alarmed court attache ran to help him up, inquiring solicitously: "I hope Your Honor is not hurt?"

"No, no," replied the judge, rubbing himself tenderly, "my honor is safe enough, but the seat is bruised confoundedly."

[4770]

An elderly man of convivial habits, but also bookish, was haled before the bar of justice in a small country town.

"Ye're charged with bein' drunk and disorderly," snapped the magistrate. "Have ye anything to say why sentence should not be pronounced?"

"Man's inhumanity to man makes countless thousands mourn," began the prisoner, in a flight of oratory. "I am not so debased as Poe, so profligate as Byron, as ungrateful as Keats, so intemperate as Burns, so timid as Tennyson, so vulgar as Shakespeare, so—"

"That'll do, that'll do," interrupted the magistrate. "Seven days. And, Officer, take down that list of names he mentioned and round 'em up. I think they're as bad as he is."

[4771]

A man walking along a city street fell through an open sewer hole and broke his leg. He engaged a famous attorney, brought suit against the city for two thousand dollars and won the case. The city appealed the case to the Supreme Court, but again the lawyer won the decision.

After the claim was settled the lawyer sent for his client and handed him a dollar bill.

"What's this?" asked the man, looking at the dollar.

"That's your damages, after deducting my fee, the cost of appeal and other expenses," replied the attorney.

The man looked at the dollar again, turned it over and carefully scanned the other side. He then looked up at the lawyer and said: "What's the matter with this dollar? Is it counterfeit?"

[4772]

"Are all the news-cameramen here?"

"Yes, your honor."

"Lights O.K.?"

"Yes, your honor."

"Sound O.K.?"

"Yes, your honor."

"Good! Then let justice takes its course."

[4773]

Judge—"How could you swindle people who trusted in you?"

Prisoner—"But, Judge, people who don't trust you can not be swindled."

[4774]

"Are you positive," demanded counsel, "that the prisoner is the man who stole your car?"

"Well," answered the witness, "I was until you cross-examined me. Now I'm not sure whether I ever had a car at all."

[4775]
For the fourth time, the corporation lawyer conducting the cross-examination led the witness to the accident.

"You say that after the car passed, the man was seen lying on the ground with his scalp bleeding? Did the car hit him?"

"Naw," replied the exasperated witness, "The conductor leaned out and bit him as he went by."

[4776]
A young lawyer was once making his first effort, and had thrown himself on the wings of imagination into the seventh heaven, and was preparing for a higher ascent when the judge struck his rule on the desk once or twice, and exclaimed to the astonished orator: "Hold on, my dear sir, don't go any higher, you are already out of the jurisdiction of this court."

[4777]
Bursting open the door marked "Private," the butcher confronted the local lawyer.

"If a dog steals a piece of meat from my shop, is the owner liable?" he asked the man behind the desk.

"Certainly," replied the lawyer.

"Very well, your dog took a piece of steak worth half a dollar about five minutes ago."

"Indeed," he returned smoothly. "Then if you give me the other half, that will cover my fee."

[4778]
"And what is a contingent fee?" asked a clerk of a lawyer.

"A contingent fee to a lawyer means if I don't win your suit I get nothing. If I do win it you get nothing. See?"

[4779]
"What did you have at the first saloon you stopped?" asked a lawyer of a witness in an assault and battery case.

"What did we have? Four glasses of beer, sir."

"What next?"

"Two glasses of whisky."

"Next?"

"One glass of brandy."

"Next?"

"A fight."

[4780]
Two attorneys, one decidedly glum of countenance, met on the street.

"Well, how's business?" the first asked of the dismal one.

"Rotten!" the pessimist replied. "I just chased an ambulance twelve miles, and found a lawyer in it."

[4781]
The judge pointed with his cane at the prisoner before him. "There's a great rogue at the end of this stick."

The prisoner smirked, "At which end, Your Honor?"

[4782]
"Your office is as hot as an oven," said a client to his lawyer.

"So it ought to be. I make my bread here."

[4783]
Judge (during an inquiry into a case of alleged bribery)—"You say you received £25 to vote Conservative and also received the same amount to vote Liberal?"

Witness—"Yes, my lord."

Judge—"And for whom did you vote at the finish?"

Witness (indignantly)—"I voted, my lord, according to my conscience."

[4784]

First Lawyer–"I've just taken the case of that woman who says she shot her husband because she loved him."

Second Lawyer–"I suppose your plea will be that spring is the time for tender shoots."

[4785]

Farmer–"An' how's Lawyer Jones doing, Doctor?"

Doctor–"Poor fellow, he's lying at death's door."

Farmer–"That's grit for ye; at death's door, an' still lying."

[4786]

A man being subpoenaed as a witness on a trial for an assault, one of the counsel, who was notorious for brow-beating witnesses, asked him what distance he was from the parties when the assault happened; he answered:

"Just thirteen feet eleven inches and a half."

"How come you to be so exact?" said the counsel.

"Because I expected some fool or other would ask me," said the witness, "and I just measured it."

[4787]

Justice Brown was presiding over an action for damages when the following dialogue between lawyer and witness took place:

"Did you see the witness knocked down?"

"Who, me?"

"Yes, you."

"No, not me."

"Did you see the defendant at all?"

"Who, me?"

"Yes, you."

"No."

"Then why are you here?"

"Who, me?"

"Yes, you."

"To see justice done."

"Who, me?" demanded Justice Brown.

[4788]

A judge was pointing out to his Court that a witness was not necessarily to be regarded as untruthful because he altered a statement he had previously made. "For instance," he said, "when I entered this Court today I could have sworn that I had my watch in my pocket. But then I remembered I had left it in the bathroom at home."

When the judge got home that night his wife said: "Why all this bother about your watch—sending four or five men for it?"

"Good heavens!" said the judge; "I never sent anyone! What did you do?"

"I gave it to the first one who came; he knew just where it was."

[4789]

The Judge–"So you claim you robbed that delicatessen store because you were starving? Why didn't you take something to eat instead of stealing all the cash out of the register?"

The Accused–" 'Cause I'm a proud man, Judge, an' I make it a rule to pay for everything I eat."

[4790]

"You have been convicted on nineteen counts, and you are hereby committed to the state prison upon a cumulative sentence of ninety-nine years. Have you anything to offer?"

"Nothin', Judge, except that you're pretty free with another man's time."

[4791]

"What have you to charge against the defendant?" a lawyer asked a Kentucky colonel.

"Suh," replied the colonel, "that man is a bigoted Republican."

"He's what?"

"Bigoted, suh. Don't you know what it means to be bigoted?"

"Why, no," replied the lawyer, who was something of a wag. "Will you define the term, sir?"

"Suhtainly," said the colonel. "A bigoted Republican is a man who knows too much to be what he ain't and too little to be what he is."

[4792]

A lawyer acquaintance just out of college was pleading his first case. The nasty railroad company had killed twenty-four of his farmer client's hogs. The young lawyer was trying to impress the jury with the magnitude of the injury.

"Imagine twenty-four hogs, gentlemen! Twenty-four! Twice the number there are in the jury box."

[4793]

A prominent local attorney had subpoenaed a certain youngster as an important witness. No sooner had the little lad climbed the witness chair than the lawyer started to fire questions at him.

"Have you an occupation?" asked the legal one.

"Nope."

"What occupation does your father follow?"

"None."

"Does he ever do anything to help support the family?"

"Odd jobs once in a great while."

"Then tell me, isn't your father a worthless fellow, loafer, deadbeat, and a cad?"

"I don't know," answered the witness, "you better ask him; he's sittin' over there in the jury."

[4794]

"I can't bear a fool," said a lawyer to a farmer.

"Your mother could," said the farmer.

[4795]

"You have a pretty tough looking lot of customers to dispose of this morning, haven't you?" remarked the friend of the magistrate who had dropped in at the police court.

"Huh!" rejoined the dispenser of justice, "you are looking at the wrong bunch. Those are the lawyers."

[4796]

"May it please your honor," said a lawyer, addressing one of the city judges, "I brought the prisoner from jail on a habeas corpus."

"Well," said a fellow in an undertone, who stood in the rear of the court, "these lawyers will say anything. I saw the man get out of a cab at the court door."

[4797]

"Judge," said the punny prisoner, "give me a sentence with the word freedom in it."

[4798]

Lawyer–"Now, sir, did you, or did you not, on the date in question or at any time, say to the defendant or anyone else that the statement imputed to you and denied by the plaintiff was a matter of no moment or otherwise? Answer me, yes or no."

Bewildered Witness–"Yes or no, what?"

[4799]

"What was the most confusing case you ever had?" asked the doctor of the lawyer.

"Case o' champagne," returned the lawyer. "I hadn't got half through it before I was all muddled up."

[4800]

"Gentlemen of the jury, you have heard the facts of both sides. Mr. Brown had a public fight with Mr. Smith. Mr. Brown had in his possession at the time one butcher knife, two razors, one set of brass knuckles, and a blackjack. Mr. Smith had on his person, one sickle, one hatchet, two meat saws, a cleaver, and an icepick. Both men plead 'Not Guilty,' each asserting a plea of self-defense. I judge you have reached a verdict."

"We have, your honor."

"And that verdict—"

"We, the jury, would have cheerfully paid one dollar per man to have seen the fight."

[4801]

"Gents," a fat man said in a hotel smoking room, "I hate to hear you lambasting lawyers the way you've been doing. A lawyer last year made me a present of one hundred and fifty dollars."

"Yes, he did!"

"Come off!"

"What are you giving us?"

But these gibes and jeers didn't move the fat man.

"It's the solemn truth, gents," he said. "You see, I was injured in a railroad accident last year, and this lawyer sued the railroad company, and got five thousand dollars damages. His bill was five thousand one hundred and fifty dollars, but he didn't say a word about the one hundred and fifty dollars balance. He made me a present of it."

[4802]

"Where did the car hit him?" asked the coroner.

"At the junction of the dorsal and cervical vertebrae," replied the medical witness.

The burly foreman rose from his seat.

"Man and boy, I've lived in these parts for fifty years," he protested ponderously, "and I have never heard of the place."

[4803]

A lawyer engaged in a case tormented a witness so much with questions, that the poor fellow at last cried out for water.

"There," said the judge, "I thought you would pump him dry."

[4804]

A judge set aside the unjust verdict of a jury against an unpopular man, with the remark, "Enter the verdict, Mr. Clerk. Enter, also, set aside, by the court. I want it to be understood that it takes thirteen men to steal a man's farm in this court."

[4805]

Lawyer—(to defendant)—"Who was your wife before you were married?"

Defendant—"I don't recall having a wife then."

[4806]

"Did you present your account to the defendant?" inquired a lawyer of his client.

"I did, sir."

"And what did he say?"

"He told me to go to the devil."

"And what did you do then?"

"Why, then, I came to you."

[4807]

"What were you doing about that livery stable last night?" a judge asked the suspect, a cowpoke.

"Circulatin' roun', judge; jes' circulatin' roun'."

"Clerk, make a notation: 'Withdrawn from circulation for 60 days.' "

[4808]

An impecunious young lawyer once received the following letter from a tailor to whom he was indebted:

"Dear Sir: Kindly advise me by return mail when I may expect a remittance from you in settlement of my account."

Yours truly,

J. Snippen."

The lawyer immediately replied:

"Dear Sir: I have your request for advice of a recent date, and beg leave to say that not having received any retainer from you I cannot act in the premises. Upon receipt of your check for $250 I shall be very glad to look the matter up for you and to acquaint you with the results of my investigations.

"I am, sir, with great respect, your most obedient servant,

Barclay B. Coke."

[4809]

"I want to be excused," said a worried-looking juryman addressing the judge. "I owe a man ten dollars, and as he is leaving for a post abroad to be gone some years I want to catch him before he gets on board, and pay the ten dollars. It may be my last chance."

"You are excused," returned His Honor in icy tones. "I don't want anybody on the jury who can lie like that."

[4810]

A woman was testifying in behalf of her son, "that he had worked on a farm ever since he was born." The lawyer, who cross-examined her, said:

"You assert that your son worked on a farm ever since he was born?"

"I do."

"What did he do the first year?"

"He milked!"

[4811]

Witness (in an English Court)–"The shock caused my wife to go off into asterisks."

[4812]

Judge–"It seems to me that I have seen you before."

Prisoner–"You have, your Honor; I gave your daughter singing lessons."

Judge–"Thirty years."

[4813]

Aggrieved One–"She's been throwing things at me ever since we was married."

Magistrate–"Then why have you not complained before?"

Aggrieved One–"This is the first time she's hit me."

[4814]

A little man was ushered into the witness-box. After the usual preliminaries, the magistrate told him to tell the court what happened.

The man began in rambling narrative and finally ended up with:

"And then my wife hit me on the head with an oak leaf."

"Well, that couldn't have hurt you, surely," said the magistrate.

"Oh, couldn't it?" replied the little man, with feeling. "It was the oak leaf from the center of the dining-room table."

[4815]

Magistrate–"You've committed six burglaries in a week."

Prisoner–"That's right. If every one worked as hard as I do we'd be on the road to prosperity."

[4816]

Lawyer–"When I was a boy my highest ambition was to be a pirate."

Client–"You're in luck. It isn't every man who can realize the dreams of his youth."

[4817]

An Irish lawyer having lost his client's cause, which had been tried before three judges, one of whom was esteemed a very able lawyer, and the other two but indifferent ones, some of the other barristers indulged in a good deal of merriment on the occasion.

"Well, now," said the vanquished counsellor, "who the devil could help it, when there were a hundred judges on the bench?"

"A hundred," said a bystander, "why, man, there were but three."

"By St. Patrick," replied the defeated lawyer, "and how do you make out there's only three. There were one and two ciphers."

[4818]

A witness was asked to tell what he found on the premises.

"Naught but barren nothingness, as Shakespeare says," testified the witness.

"Never mind what Shakespeare says!" commanded the court. "If he knows anything about this case he can be summoned!"

[4819]

"As a matter of fact," said the lawyer of the defendant, trying to be sarcastic, "you were scared half to death, and don't know whether it was a motor car or something resembling a motor car that hit you."

"It resembled one all right," the plaintiff made answer. "In fact, I was forcibly struck by the resemblance."

[4820]

The lawyer called his clerk and said to him: "Smith, you have been employed by me for five years. To mark my appreciation of this you will henceforth be addressed as Mr. Smith."

[4821]

Examining Lawyer–"Are you acquainted with any of the attorneys in this case?"

Prospective Juror (excitedly turning to judge)–"Not guilty, Your Honor!"

[4822]

Judge–"And for the levity you have shown during your trial I shall give you an additional fine of $10. How does that suit you?"

Prisoner–"That's what I would call extra fine."

[4823]

"Is that Peabody, Finchley, Longworth, and Fitzgerald?"

"Yes, this is Peabody, Finchley, Longworth, and Fitzgerald."

"I want to speak to Mr. Smith."

[4824]

A young barrister paused in the midst of a boring harangue and said to Lord Ellenborough: "Is it the pleasure of the court that I should proceed with my statement?"

Lord Ellenborough replied: "Pleasure, Mr. ——, has been out of the question for a long time; but you may proceed."

[4825]

After a young lawyer had talked nearly five hours to a jury, who felt like lynching him, his opponent, a grizzled old veteran, arose, looked sweetly at the judge, and said:

"Your honor, I will follow the example of my young friend who has just finished, and submit the case without argument."

[4826]

An Irish lawyer once addressed the court as "gentlemen," instead of "your honors." After he had concluded, a brother of the bar reminded him of his error. He immediately arose to apologize thus:

"May it please the court, in the heat of debate I called yer honors gentlemen. I made a mistake, yer honors."

[4827]

The witness was undergoing a cross-examination. The lawyer had badgered him unmercifully, and finally said with a mixture of solemnity and fierceness, "Can you look me in the eye and repeat that?"

The witness looked at him a moment and asked quietly, "Which eye?"

[4828]

A man in North Carolina, accused of horse-stealing, was saved from conviction by the powerful plea of his lawyer. After his acquittal by the jury, the lawyer took him aside, and asked smilingly, "Honor bright, now, Bill, you did steal that horse, didn't you?"

"Now, look a-here, Judge," was the reply, "I allers did think I stole that horse. But since I hearn yore speech to the jury, I'll be doggoned if I ain't got my doubts about it."

[4829]

Client–"I know the evidence is strongly against my innocence, but I have $50,000 to fight the case."

Lawyer–"As your attorney, I assure you that you'll never go to prison with that amount of money."

And he didn't, he went there broke.

[4830]

In a certain court case one of the lawyers caused much amusement by referring to opposing counsel as "Mr.—er—shall we say Necessity."

This went on for some time until the judge interrupted.

"Might I ask, Mr. Robinson," he said, "why you continually refer to learned counsel as 'Mr. Necessity'?"

"Because he knows no law," was the biting answer.

[4831]

The lawyer for the defense was cross-examining a witness in a robbery case.

"When did the robbery take place?" demanded the counsel in a bullying tone.

"I think——" began the witness, but the lawyer interrupted him.

"We don't care what you think, sir. We want to know what you know."

"Then if you don't want to know what I think," said the witness quietly, "I may as well leave the box. I can't talk without thinking—I'm not a lawyer."

[4832]

Judge Gruff–"Aren't you ashamed to be seen here in court so often?"

Prisoner–"Why, no your honor; I always thought it was a very respectable place."

[4833]

An Irishman stopped before a grave in a cemetery, containing the tombstone declaring: "Here lies a lawyer and an honest man."

"An' who'd ever think," he murmured, "there'd be room for two men in that one little grave!"

[4834]

Judge–"The jury having acquitted you of the charge of bigamy, you are freed to leave the court and go home."

Prisoner–"Thank you, your honor, but I want to be on the safe side —which home?"

[4835]

Judge–"You stole eggs from this man's store. Have you any excuse?"

Accused–"Yes, I took them by mistake."

Judge–"How is that?"

Accused–"I thought they were fresh."

[4836]

The District Attorney, questioning a witness, asked: "You are a barber, aren't you?"

The witness replied, pompously, "I am a tonsorial artist."

"Well, now," put in the judge, "isn't that splitting hairs?"

[4837]

A railroad shopman had been drawn on a Federal grand jury and didn't want to serve. When his name was called he asked the judge to excuse him. "We are very busy at the shops," said he, "and I ought to be there."

"So you are one of those men who think the railroad couldn't get along without you," remarked the judge.

"No, your honor," said the shop-man. "I know it could get along without me, but I don't want it to find it out."

"Excused," said the judge.

[4838]

They were hearing the evidence in Mrs. Biff McGee's suit for divorce. Mrs. Biff was telling tales of cruelty, almost beyond belief, when good old Biff stepped up to the bench and said:

"Judge, you can't believe a word that woman says. She's punch-drunk!"

[4839]

"Pa, what is a retainer?"

"What you pay a lawyer before he does any work for you, my son."

"Oh, I see. It's like the quarter you put in the gas-meter before you get any gas."

[4840]

As a minister and a lawyer were riding together, says the minister to the lawyer:

"Sir, do you ever make mistakes in pleading?"

"I do," says the lawyer.

"And what do you do with mistakes?" inquired the minister.

"Why, if large ones I mend them; if small ones I let them go," said the lawyer. "And I pray, sir," continued he, "do you ever make mistakes in preaching?"

"Yes, sir, I have."

"And what do you do with mistakes?" said the lawyer.

"Why, sir, I dispose of them in the same manner as you do. Not long since," continued he, "as I was preaching, I meant to observe that the devil was the father of liars, but made a mistake and said the father of lawyers. The mistake was so small that I let it go."

[4841]

A man on trial for his life was being examined by a group of alienists. Suddenly one doctor shouted at him: "Quick, how many feet has a centipede?"

The man came back in a dry, dry voice:

"Gad, is that all you have to worry about?"

[4842]

Lawyer–"Well, if you want my honest opinion—"

Client–"No, no. I want your professional advice."

[4843]

Magistrate (to witness)–"Why didn't you go to the aid of the defendant during the fight?"

Witness–"I didn't know which was going to be the defendant."

[4844]

Judge–"Have you anything to say, prisoner, before sentence is passed upon you?"

Prisoner–"No, your lordship, except that it takes very little to please me."

[4845]

"Just what good have you done to humanity?" asked the judge before passing sentence on the pickpocket.

"Well," replied the confirmed criminal, "I've kept three or four detectives working regularly."

[4846]

Magistrate–"What is the man charged with?"

Constable–"He is a camera fiend of the worst kind, sir."

Magistrate–"But he shouldn't have been arrested just because he has a mania for taking pictures."

Constable–"It isn't that, sir—he takes the cameras."

[4847]

Judge (to prisoner, aged sixty)–"The sentence is thirty years' penal servitude."

Prisoner (in tears)–"Your honor, I shall not live long enough to serve the sentence."

Judge (in kindly tone)–"Don't worry, do what you can."

[4848]

A man was charged with shooting a number of pigeons, the property of a farmer. Counsel for the defense tried to frighten the farmer.

"Now," he remarked, "are you prepared to swear that this man shot your pigeons?"

"I didn't say he shot 'em," was the reply. "I said I suspected him of doing it."

"Ah! Now we're coming to it. What made you suspect the man?"

"Well, first, I caught him on my land with a gun. Secondly, I heard a gun go off and saw some pigeons fall. Thirdly, I found four of my pigeons in his pocket, and I don't think the birds flew there and committed suicide."

[4849]

After serving a week on a jury, a man was asked:

"You must have listened to so much law in the past week that you are almost a lawyer yourself now."

"Yes," said the juryman, "I am so full of law that I'm going to find it hard to keep from cheating people after I get back to business."

[4850]

"Have you ever appeared as a witness before?"

"Yes, your honor."

"In what suit?"

"My blue serge."

[4851]

A judges little daughter, who had attended her father's court for the first time, told her mother:

"Papa made a speech, and several other men made speeches to twelve men who sat all together, and then these twelve men were put in a dark room to be developed."

[4852]

"You're a dirty shyster," snarled one of the lawyers to the other, "and before this case is through I'll show you up for the crooked ape that you are."

"Sez you," snapped the other. "You are a cheat and a liar."

"Come, come," broke in the judge. "Let the case proceed now that the learned counsel have identified each other."

[4853]

"Your honor," said the prosecuting attorney, "your bull pup has went and chawed up the court Bible."

"Well," grumbled t h e C o u r t, "make the witness kiss the pup; we can't adjourn court to get a new Bible."

[4854]

An English lawyer being sick, made his last will, and gave all his estate to fools and madmen: being a s k e d t h e reason for so doing; "From such," said he, "I *had* it, and to such I *give it* again."

[4855]

In western Georgia a jury convened to inquire into a case of suicide. After sitting through the evidence, the twelve men retired, and, after deliberating, r e t u r n e d with the following verdict:

"The jury are all of one mind— temporarily insane."

[4856]

A judge asked a woman her age. "Thirty," she replied.

"You've given that age in this court for the last three years."

"Yes. I'm not one of those who says one thing today and another thing tomorrow."

[4857]

Judge – "What were you doing in that place when it was raided?"

Locksmith – "I was making a bolt for the door."

[4858]

Judge (in traffic court)–"I'll let you off with a fine this time, but another day I'll send you to jail."

Driver–"Sort of a weather-forecast, eh, Judge?"

"What do you mean?"

"Fine today—Cooler tomorrow."

[4859]

It seems the gate broke down between Heaven and Hell. St. Peter appeared at the broken part of the gate and called out to the devil, "Hey Satan. It's your chance to fix it this time."

"Sorry," replied the boss of the land beyond the Styx. "My men are too busy to worry about fixing a mere gate."

"Well, then," scowled St. Peter, "I'll have to sue you for breaking our agreement."

"Oh, yeah," yeah'd the devil, "where are you going to get a lawyer?"

[4860]

Lawyer (for shoplifter)–"Medical witnesses would testify in this court that my unfortunate client is suffering from kleptomania. Your Honor, you know what that is."

Judge–"Yes, it's a disease the people pay me to cure."

[4861]

The difference between an ordinary suit and a lawsuit, is that the former gets cleaned and pressed, while the latter is pressed and it is the litigant that gets cleaned.

[4862]

A man caught a boy in his garden stealing apples, and handed him to the police.

As it was the boy's first offense, the judge let him off, but told him never to yield to such temptation again, adding: "You have flown from the evil one."

"So I did, sir," replied the boy, "but he caught me before I got over the fence!"

[4863]

A rich farmer applied to an attorney about a lawsuit, but was told he could not undertake it, being already engaged on the other side; at the same time he gave him a letter of recommendation to a professional friend. The farmer, out of curiosity, opened it, and read as follows:

"Here are two fat wethers fallen out together.

"If you'll fleece one, I'll fleece the other.

"And make 'em agree like brother and brother."

This letter cured both parties, who promptly settled their difference without recourse to courts.

[4864]

"Now, John," said the judge, "tell us why you insulted this lady."

"Well, y'r Honor, I picked this lady up in me cab and took her to where she wanted to go an' when she got out she gave me the exact c h a n g e, a n d no more, an' I sez

under my breath, 'You stingy ol' hen,' an' she heard me."

"Perhaps, John, you can tell us just what is your idea of a lady."

"Well, y'r Honor, I picked up a lady the other day an' took her to her destination an' she gave me a five dollar bill an' me, bein' an honest man, I reaches fur me change, but sez she, 'Aw, t'hell with the change, go buy yourself a shot o' gin.' Now, that's what I consider a lady."

[4865]

J u d g e—"Y o u are charged with throwing your mother-in-law out of the window."

Jones—"I done it without thinking, sir."

Judge—"Yes, but don't you see how dangerous it might have been for anyone passing at the time?"

[4866]

While a judge was trying a case he was disturbed by a young man in the rear of the room lifting chairs and looking under things.

"Young man," said the j u d g e, "what's all the noise about?"

"Your Honor," replied the young man, "I've lost my overcoat, and I'm trying to find it."

"Well," said the judge, "people often lose whole suits in here without making all that disturbance."

[4867]

A well-known lawyer was always lecturing his office boy, whether he needed it or not. One day he chanced to hear the following conversation between the boy and the one employed next door:

"How much does he pay you?" asked the latter.

"I get $5000 a year," replied the lawyer's boy, "ten dollars a week in cash and the rest in legal advice."

[4868]

Judge—"Why did you steal the pearl necklace from the jeweller's shop window?"

Prisoner—"Because it had on it 'Avail yourself of this splendid opportunity,' and I couldn't resist it!"

[4869]

A policeman rose in a Western court to testify against a prisoner.

"Wot's this here feller charged with?" the magistrate demanded.

"Bigotry, judge," the police answered. "He's got three wives."

"Three!" cried the magistrate. "Why, you ignoramus, that ain't bigotry. That's trigonometry!"

[4870]

A man had been convicted on circumstantial evidence. The conviction made him a violator of the habitual criminal statute, which carries a sentence of life imprisonment. In proving the prisoner's previous convictions, his record was placed before the court by the prosecutor and its examination revealed the man had been in prison at the time of the commission of the crime for which he had last been convicted.

"Good heavens, man!" exclaimed his attorney. "Why didn't you tell us this?"

"I thought it might prejudice the jury against me," he replied.

[4871]

Judge—"Have you anything to offer the court before sentence is passed on you?"

Prisoner—"No, your honor, my lawyer took my last dollar."

[4872]

Lawyer (to rattled witness) – "Did you, or did you not, on the aforementioned day, Tuesday, January nineteen, feloniously and with malicious afore-thought listen at the keyhole of the third floor rear apartment then occupied as a residence by the defendant in this action on Seventieth Street near Park Avenue, and did you not also on the Friday following the Tuesday in January before referred to communicate to your wife the information acquired and repeat the conversation overhead on that occasion with the result that the gossip of your wife gave wide and far currency to the overheard conversation before mentioned? Did you or did you not? Answer Yes or No."

Witness—"Huh?"

[4873]

Judge—"What induced you to strike your wife?"

Defendant—"Well, she had her back to me. The frying-pan was handy, and the back door was open, so I thought I'd take a chance."

[4874]

A shilling subscription having been set on foot to bury an attorney who had died very poor, Lord Chief Justice Norbury exclaimed, "Only a shilling to bury an attorney! Here's a guinea; go and bury one-and-twenty of them."

[4875]

The magistrate was a very keen golfer. He was trying the case of a man who was summoned for cruelty to his wife.

"My client," said the defending counsel, "is a much maligned man. His wife is constantly nagging him and, in the end, driven to desperation, he beat her into silence with a golf club."

The magistrate leaned forward with a sudden show of interest.

[4876]

Lawyer – "Then you say this man was drunk?"

Witness – "I do not. I simply said he sat in his car for three hours in front of an excavation waiting for the light to turn green."

[4877]

A physician of an acrimonious disposition, and having a thorough hatred of lawyers, reproached a lawyer with the use of phrases utterly unintelligible.

"For example," said he, "I never could understand what you lawyers mean by docking an entail."

"That is very likely," answered the lawyer, "but I will explain it to you: it is doing what you doctors never consent to — *suffering a recovery.*"

[4878]

A lawyer became somewhat acrimonious in his cross-examination, but the little woman who was in the witness-box remained calm.

Eventually the lawyer said: "You say you had no education, but you answered my questions s m a r t l y enough."

The defendant meekly replied: "You don't have to be a scholar to answer silly questions."

[4879]

A famous lawyer was called in to see a man in the county jail accused of murder.

When he returned to his office, his secretary said, "Well, did you take the case, Mr. Blank?"

"No, I didn't take it."

"Why, didn't you think the man was justified in his act?"

"My son," said the lawyer, "he certainly was not financially justified in committing murder."

[4880]

"Sam, do you solemnly swear to tell the truth, the whole truth and nothing but the truth?"

"Ah does, sah."

"Well, Sam, what have you got to say for yourself?"

"Jedge, wif all dem limitations you jes' put on me, Ah don't believe Ah has anything at all to say."

[4881]

Lawyer (whose client is under arrest) – "You say you've a perfect answer to this wife murder charge. What is it?"

Client – "She wasn't my wife."

[4882]

"Smith certainly is a foxy fellow. He's drawn up his will in such a way that the lawyers can't get more out of it than his own heirs."

"How's that?"

"Why, he left half his fortune to one of the best lawyers in the country, provided he saw to it that the other half went to Smith's children intact."

[4883]

"Haven't I seen you before?" asked the judge.

"Maybe," replied the tailor. "So many men owe me money I can't remember their faces."

[4884]

An intelligent-looking farmer had been examined by both defense and prosecution and was about to be accepted, when t h e p r o s e c u t o r chanced to ask:

"Do you believe in capital punishment?"

The farmer hemmed and hawed and after a moment's reflection replied:

"Yes, sir, I do, if it ain't too severe."

[4885]

Lawyer–"You say you saw the man stabbed in the hay-field with a fork. What kind of a fork?"

Witness–"Well, did you ever see a tuning-fork or an oyster-fork in a hay-field?"

[4886]

Debt-Collector–"Shall I call tomorrow?"

Young Lawyer–"Twice, if convenient! I have an idea that folks think you are a client."

[4887]

"You've been convicted fourteen times of this offense — aren't you ashamed to own to that?"

"No, your honor. I don't think one ought to be ashamed of his convictions."

[4888]

"Hurrah! Hurrah!" cried a young lawyer, who had succeeded to his father's practice, "I've settled that old Chancery suit at last."

"Settled it!" cried the astonished parent, "why I gave you that as *an annuity* for your life."

[4889]

"You have heard what the last witness said," persisted the counsel, "and yet your evidence is to the contrary. Am I to infer that you wish to throw doubt on her veracity?"

The polite young man waved a deprecating hand.

"Not at all," he replied. "I merely wish to make it clear what a liar I am if she's speaking the truth."

[4890]

A successful old lawyer tells the following story anent the beginning of his professional life:

"I had just installed myself in my office," he said, "had put in a phone and had preened myself for my first client who might come along when, through the glass of my door I saw a shadow. Yes, it was doubtless some one to see me. Picture me, then, grabbing the nice, shiny receiver of my new phone and plunging into an imaginary conversation. It ran something like this:

" 'Yes, Mr. S.,' I was saying as the stranger entered the office, 'I'll attend to that corporation matter for you. Mr. J. had me on the phone this morning and wanted me to settle a damage suit, but I had to put him off, as I was too busy with o t h e r c a s e s. But I'll manage to sandwich your case in between the others somehow. Y e s. Y e s. A ll right. Goodby.'

"Being sure, then, that I had duly impressed my prospective client, I hung up the receiver and turned to him.

" 'Excuse me, sir,' the man said, 'but I'm from the telephone company. I've come to connect your instrument.' "

[4891]

"Are you the judge of reprobates?" the lady inquired.

"I am judge of probate," was the answer.

"Well, t h a t's what I want, I guess. You see, my husband died untested and left several little infidels, and I want to be their executioner!"

[4892]

"Are you the defendant?" asked the prosecuting attorney of the old Negro who had taken the stand.

"Naw, sah, boss, not me."

"Then who are you?"

"I'se the gen'l'man what stole the chickens."

[4893]

Knowing that it was unethical but feeling that it was justified, the attorney hired a stubborn-looking, stolid, unsophisticated juryman to hold out for life imprisonment. It seemed that this was the only way to save his client from the death penalty.

The jury finally went out and was out for hours. Finally late on the second day, the jury filed in, and rendered a verdict of guilty with a recommendation that the prisoner be sentenced to life imprisonment.

As the lawyer was paying his man, he asked, "You had a difficult time of it, didn't you? I'm certainly glad you succeeded in swinging the jury your way."

"Yeah," was the answer. "It was pretty tough. They were all for acquittal, at first, but I finally convinced 'em."

[4894]

"No, your honor," said the prisoner, "I was certainly not drunk, though I may have been intoxicated."

"Well," said the magistrate, "I intended to fine you five dollars, but in view of your explanation I make it a v-spot."

[4895]

"You seem to have plenty of intelligence for a man in your position," sneered a barrister, cross-examining a witness.

"If I wasn't on oath I'd return the compliment," replied the witness.

[4896]

"Pardon me," said the stranger, "are you a resident here?"

"Yes," was the answer. "I've been here goin' on fifty years. What kin I do for you?"

"I am looking for a criminal lawyer," said the stranger. "Have you any here?"

"Well," said the other, "we're pretty sure we have, but we can't prove it."

[4897]

A browbeating lawyer was demanding that a witness answer a certain question either in the negative or affirmative.

"I cannot do it," said the witness. "There are some questions that cannot be answered by a 'yes' or a 'no,' as any one knows."

"I defy you to give an example to the court," thundered the lawyer.

The retort came like a flash: "Are you still beating your wife?"

[4898]

The judge who was about to deliver a severe sentence looked at the defendant in the dock and began: "This robbery was consummated in an adroit and skilful manner."

The prisoner blushed and interrupted: "Come now, your honor. No flattery, please."

[4899]

A farmer who was a witness in a hog-stealing case seemed to be stretching a point or two in favor of the accused.

"Do you know the nature of an oath?" the prosecuting attorney roared.

"Sure."

"Do you know you are not to bear false witness against your neighbor?"

"I'm not bearin' false witness against him. I'm bearin' false witness for him."

[4900]

A Federal judge at Fort Smith was questioning an Indian witness. "Now then, what is your occupation?"

"Me carpenter."

"What sort of carpenter?"

"Jack-leg carpenter."

"What in the world is a jack-leg carpenter?"

"Carpenter not first class."

"Please explain more fully just what you mean by a jack-leg carpenter."

"Me not sure, but think same difference 'tween first class carpenter and jack-leg, as 'tween first class judge and you."

[4901]

Judge–"What possible excuse could you have for acquitting the prisoner?"

Foreman–"Insanity, sir."

Judge–"What, all twelve of you?"

[4902]

After a difference of opinion with the judge, the lawyer turned on his heel and showed his back.

"Are you trying to show your contempt for the court?" the judge demanded.

"No, indeed," was the attorney's reply. "I'm trying to conceal it."

[4903]

Western Lawyer—"Well, Zeb, so you want me to defend you? Have you got any money?"

Zeb—"No suh, I got no money but I got me a new palomino pony."

Western Lawyer—"Well, you can certainly raise money on a palomino pony. Now let's see—just what do they accuse you of stealing?"

Zeb—"A palomino pony."

[4904]

The cripple thumped his crutch on the ground as he confronted his lawyer. "Heavens, man, your bill is outrageous!" he exclaimed. "You are taking four-fifths of my damages. I never heard of such extortion."

"I furnished the skill, the eloquence and the necessary legal learning for your case," said the lawyer coolly.

"Yes," said the client, "but I furnished the case itself."

"Bosh!" sneered the lawyer. "Anybody could fall down a coal hole."

[4905]

The judge wished to make sure that the witness understood the solemnity of the occasion.

"Do you know what that oath means?" the judge asked.

"Sure I do," the witness answered. "That oath means if I swear to a lie I gotta stick to it."

[4906]

The pompous judge glared sternly over his spectacles at the tattered prisoner who had been dragged before the bar of justice on a charge of vagrancy.

"Have you ever earned a dollar in your life?" he asked in scorn.

"Yes, your honor," was the response. "I voted for you at the last election."

[4907]

First Lawyer–"As soon as I realized it was crooked business I got out of it."

Second Lawyer–"How much?"

[4908]

"You are accused of stealing a chicken. Have you anything to say about it?"

"I took it for a lark."

"No resemblance whatsoever. Ten days."

[4909]

Magistrate–"Have you anything to say before I pass sentence?"

Burglar–"Yes, m'lud. It's a bit thick bein' identified by a bloke wot kept 'is head under the bedclothes the whole time."

[4910]

"You are a nuisance," said the judge. "I must commit you."

"You have no right to commit a nuisance even if you are a judge," was the quick retort.

[4911]

"I want you to understand," said Young Spender, "that I got my money by hard work."

"Why, I thought it was left to you by your rich uncle!"

"So it was; but I had to work to get it away from the lawyers."

[4912]

"Yes," said the lawyer to his client, the grocer, "you've got the best case I've ever heard."

"Thanks," said his client, grabbing up his hat and making for the door.

"Where are you going?" asked the astonished lawyer.

"I'm going to settle this case out of court," the other informed him.

"But I've told you it's the best case I've ever heard."

"Maybe," said his client, "but not for me. I've told you the other fellow's story."

[4913]

A long-winded attorney was arguing a technical case before one of the judges of the superior court in a western state. He had rambled on in such a desultory way that it became very difficult to follow his line of thought, and the judge had just yawned very suggestively.

With just a trace of sarcasm in his voice, the tiresome attorney ventured to observe: "I sincerely trust that I am not unduly trespassing on the time of this court."

"My friend," returned his honor, "there is a considerable difference between trespassing on time and encroaching upon eternity."

[4914]

A man was arraigned for assault and battery and brought before the judge.

Judge–"What is your name, occupation, and what are you charged with?"

Prisoner–"My name is Sparks; I am an electrician, and I'm charged with battery."

Judge (after recovering his equilibrium)–"Officer, put this guy in a dry cell."

[4915]

"Here's my bill," said the lawyer. "Please pay down $100, and $25 a week thereafter for ten weeks."

"Sounds like buying an automobile," said the client.

"I am," returned the attorney.

[4916]

Magistrate–"This man's watch was fastened in his pocket by a safety-pin. How did you manage to get it?"

Prisoner–"Well, Judge, I usually gets $10 fer six lessons."

[4917]

After considering all aspects of a difficult case in the domestic relations court, the judge said to the prisoner,

"The best thing for you to do is to become reconciled to your wife."

"What's the next best thing?" asked the man hastily.

[4918]

The defense attorney was cross-examining the witness, who was a fetching blonde with two lovely big blue eyes. The lawyer leaned forward.

"Where were you," he thundered, "on Monday night?"

The blonde smiled sweetly.

"Automobile riding," she replied.

"And where were you," bellowed the lawyer, "on Tuesday night?"

"Automobile riding," repeated the beautiful blonde.

The lawyer leaned still closer.

"And what," he murmured, "are you doing tomorrow night?"

The prosecuting attorney leaped from his chair.

"Your Honor," he protested, "I object to that question!"

The judge, a tolerant gentleman, shrugged his shoulders.

"And why do you object?" he inquired mildly.

The prosecuting attorney drew himself up in righteous indignation.

"Because," he snapped, "I asked her first!"

[4919]

A firm of lawyers rang up a stock broker, and the following conversation took place:

"Good morning, are you Mr. Denman?"

"Yes, who is this?"

"This is Hullet, Crafrig, Studge, Minardy, Gowle, and Scarrow."

"Oh, good morning, good morning, good morning, good morning, good morning, good morning."

[4920]

There was a clash between the lawyer and the magistrate. The latter ordered the lawyer to sit down, and as the lawyer, being deaf, didn't hear him and went on talking, the magistrate fined him $10.

The lawyer leaned toward the clerk of the court and cupped his hand behind his ear.

"What did he say?" he inquired.

"He fined you $10," explained the clerk.

"What for?"

"For contempt of court."

The lawyer shot a poisonous look toward the bench and thrust a hand into his pocket.

"I'll pay it now," he said. "It's a just debt."

[4921]

"You say you met the defendant on a street car, and that he had been drinking and gambling?" said the attorney for the defense during the cross-examination.

"Yes," replied the witness.

"Did you see him take a drink?"

"No."

"Did you see him gambling?"

"No."

"Then how do you know," demanded the attorney, "that the defendant had been drinking and gambling?"

"Well," explained the witness, "he gave the conductor a blue chip for his carfare and told him to keep the change."

[4922]

"Have you anything to say before I pass sentence on you?"

"Yes, your honor, I should like you to have your lunch first."

[4923]

Pickpocket (visiting friend in jail)—"I hired a lawyer for you this morning, Slim, but I had to hand him my watch as a retainer."

Pal—"And did he keep it?"

Pickpocket—"He thinks he did."

[4924]

The attorneys for the prosecution and defense had been allowed fifteen minutes each to argue the case. The attorney for the defense had commenced his argument with an allusion to the old swimming-hole of his boyhood days. He told in flowery oratory of the balmy air, the singing birds, the joy of youth, the delights of the cool water—

And in the midst of it he was interrupted by the drawling voice of the judge:

"Come out, Chauncey," he said, "and put on your clothes. Your fifteen minutes are up."

[4925]

The witness was on the stand during an important trial.

"You say," thundered the defense attorney, "that you saw the two trains crash head-on while doing sixty miles an hour. What did you say when this happened?"

The witness shrugged.

"I said to myself," he replied, "'this is a helluva railroad!'"

[4926]

The lawyer surveyed the tattered client as he listened, and decided that he would be lucky to obtain a ten-dollar fee. He named that amount as necessary to secure the prisoner's release. Thereupon, the client drew forth a large roll of bills, and peeled off a ten. The lawyer's greedy eyes popped.

"What jail is your son in?" he inquired craftily.

"In the county jail."

"In the county jail, not the city jail!" was the exclamation in a tone of dismay. "That's bad—very bad. It will cost you at least fifty dollars."

[4927]

An old rodeo rider was crossing-tender at a spot where an express train made quick work of a buggy and its occupants. Naturally he was the chief witness, and the entire case hinged upon the energy with which he had displayed his warning signal.

A grueling cross-examination left him unshaken in this story:

The night was dark and he had waved his lantern frantically, but the driver of the carriage paid no attention to it.

Later, the division superintendent called the flagman to his office to compliment him on the steadfastness with which he had stuck to his story.

"You did wonderfully, Curly," he said. "I was afraid at first that you might waver in your testimony."

"Nosir, nosir," Curly exclaimed, "but I done feared ev'ry minute that 'ere durn lawyer was gwine ter ask me if mah lantern was lit."

[4928]

"Why did you throw the pot of geraniums at the plaintiff?"

"Because of an advertisement, your honor."

"What advertisement?"

"'Say it with flowers.'"

[4929]

Lawyer—"Are you acquainted with any of the men on the jury?"

Witness—"Yes, sir, more than half of them."

Lawyer—"Are you willing to swear that you know more than half of them?"

Witness—"Oh, if it comes to that, I'm willing to swear that I know more than all of them put together!"

THE PROFESSIONS

[4930]

Here is a story about a young lawyer in his early days at the Bar when he represented a railway company, one of whose vehicles had run down a boy. The boy's case was that his arm was so badly injured that he could no longer lift it above his head. The clever young lawyer's cross-examination of the boy was carried out very, very quietly—and very, very effectively:

"Now, my boy," he said, "your arm was hurt in the accident?"

"Yes, sir," said the boy.

"And you cannot lift your arm high now?"

"No, sir."

"Would you mind," said the lawyer very gently, "just showing the jury once more how high you can raise your arm since the accident?"

The boy lifted it with an apparent effort just to the shoulder level.

"And how high could you lift it before the accident?" asked the lawyer, in his most innocent manner, and up went the arm straight over the boy's head.

[4931]

Judge—"What is this man charged with?"

Officer—"Intoxication, your honor."

Prisoner – "Judge, I'm as sober as you are this minute."

Judge – "Pleads guilty — 10 days! Next case!"

[4932]

A tough mug who was being sworn as a witness in court.

"Do you promise to tell the truth, the whole truth, and nothing but the truth, so help you God!" said the clerk.

"Why not?" said the tough guy. "I'll try anything once."

[4933]

Little Willie – "What is a lawyer, paw?"

Paw—"A lawyer, my son, is a man who induces two other men to strip for a fight, and then runs off with their clothes."

[4934]

A couple of old codgers got into a quarrel and landed before the local magistrate. The loser, turning to his opponent in a combative frame of mind, cried: "I'll law you to the Circuit Court."

"I'm willin'," said the other.

"An' I'll law you to the Supreme Court."

"I'll be thar."

"An' I'll law to hell!"

"My attorney'll be there," was the calm reply.

[4935]

"And how much would you say this colt was worth?" asked the railroad claim-agent of the farmer.

"Not a cent less than $500!" emphatically declared that sturdy son of the soil.

"Pedigreed stock, I suppose?"

"Well, no," the bereaved admitted reluctantly. "But you could never judge a colt like that by its parents."

"No," the attorney agreed dryly. "I've often noticed how crossing it with a locomotive will improve a breed!"

DOCTORS

[4936]

Doctor—"Deep breathing, you understand, destroys microbes."

Patient – "But, doctor, how can I force them to breathe deeply?"

[4937]

The two doctors found their new patient in a strong perspiration, and both put their hands under the bed-clothes in order to feel his pulse, but, by accident, got hold of each other's hand.

"Nothing serious," said one doctor.

"He's probably drunk," said the other doctor.

[4938]

A young man consulted a doctor about "tobacco heart" which he believed he had contracted from excessive smoking.

"Doctor," said he, "do you believe that the use of tobacco tends to shorten a man's days?"

"Do I?" exclaimed the doctor, "I know it does. I tried to stop once, and the days were about ninety hours long."

[4939]

Medical Professor – "What would you do in the case of a person eating poisonous mushrooms?"

Student–"Recommend a change of diet."

[4940]

A doctor told his patient that there was nothing really the matter with him. "All you require is more outdoor life; walk two or three miles regularly every day; what's your business?"

"I'm a letter-carrier, doc."

[4941]

Doctor–"Well, Mr. Jones, how are you feeling this morning?"

Jones – "Much better, thank you. The only thing that troubles me is my breathing."

Doctor–"Um—yes. We must see if we can't get something to stop that."

[4942]

Patient–"Can this operation be performed safely, doctor?"

Doctor–"That, my dear sir, is just what we are about to discover."

[4943]

Patient – "What shall I do? I have water on the knee."

Doctor–"Wear pumps."

[4944]

"Well, what is the matter with your husband?"

"I think, doctor, he is worrying about money."

"Ah! I think I can relieve him of that!"

[4945]

"I saw the doctor today about my loss of memory."

"What did he do?"

"Made me pay him in advance."

[4946]

Professor–"Now, Mr. Jones, assuming you were called to attend a patient who had swallowed a coin, what would be your method of procedure?"

Young Medico–"I'd send for a preacher, sir. They'll get money out of anyone."

[4947]

The doctor was questioning the new nurse about her latest patient. "Have you kept a chart of his progress?"

The nurse blushingly replied, "No, but I can show you my diary."

[4948]

"I don't like your heart action," the doctor said, applying the stethoscope again. "You have had some trouble with angina pectoris, haven't you?"

"You're right in a way, Doctor," said the young man sheepishly, "only that isn't her name."

[4949]
Doctor No. 1 – "Did you hold the mirror to her face to see if she was still breathing?"
Doctor No. 2 – "Yes, and she opened one eye, gasped and reached for her powder puff."

[4950]
Miss Jones (after an appendectomy) – "Oh, Doctor, will the scar show?"
Doctor – "Not if you're careful."

[4951]
The man was suffering from a bronchial attack, and as a result of it he was unable to speak above a whisper. The illness was slight, but painful, and he decided to call at the residence of the doctor who had just moved to town.

The patient appeared one evening at the doctor's front door, rang the bell, and after a short wait stood facing the doctor's young and pretty wife.

"Is the doctor at home?" he asked in his bronchial whisper.

"No," the young wife whispered in reply. "Come right on in."

[4952]
"Who is your family doctor?"
"I can't tell you."
"Why not? Don't you know his name?"
"Yes. Dr. Smith used to be our family doctor but nowadays mother goes to an eye specialist; father to a stomach specialist; my sister goes to a throat specialist; my brother is in the care of a lung specialist and I'm taking treatments from an osteopath."

[4953]
"Doc," said he, "if there is anything the matter with me, don't frighten me half to death by giving it a scientific name. Just tell what it is in plain English."

"Well," said the doctor, "to be frank with you, you are just plain lazy."

"Thank you, doctor," sighed the patient with relief. "Now give me a scientific name for it, so I can go home and tell the missus."

[4954]
"Do you believe in dieting for beauty?"
"Absolutely. A woman cannot eat her cake and have it, too."

[4955]
"Old Brown won't live long; he has one leg in the grate."
"You mean one leg in the grave."
"No; he's going to be cremated."

[4956]
"You followed my prescriptions, of course?"
"Indeed I did not, doctor, for I should have broken my neck."
"Broken your neck!"
"Yes, for I threw your prescriptions out of a third floor window."

[4957]
"I'm worried. My girl is running around with that new doctor in town."
"Feed her an apple a day."

[4958]
"Farmer Brown, I can't come out to see you any more."
"Why, what's the matter, doctor?"
"Why, every single time I come out, your ducks insult me."

[4959]
"What is your greatest wish, Doctor, now that you have successfully passed for your degree?"
Young Doctor – "To put 'Dr.' before my own name, and 'Dr.' after the name of other people."

[4960]

Doctor – "Tell your wife not to worry about that slight deafness. It's merely an indication of advancing years."
Husband – "Er—doc, w o u l d y o u mind telling her yourself?"

[4961]

"Don't you think, doctor, you've rather overcharged for attending Jimmy when he had the measles?"
"You must r e m e m b e r, M r s. Browne, that includes twenty-two visits."
"Yes, but you forget he infected the whole school!"

[4962]

"Do you think I shall live until I'm ninety, doctor?"
"How old are you now?"
"Forty."
"Do you drink, gamble, smoke, or have you any vices of any kind?"
"No. I don't drink, I never gamble, I loathe smoking; in fact, I haven't any vices."
"Well, wottinell do you want to live another fifty years for?"

[4963]

"What's that you're goin' to give Bill?"
"An anesthetic. After he takes it he won't know anything."
"Lor', Bill don't need that, he don't know anything now."

[4964]

An epileptic dropped in a fit on the streets, and was taken to a hospital. Upon removing his coat there was found pinned to his waistcoat a slip of paper on which was written:
"This is to inform the house-surgeon that this is just a case of plain fits: not appendicitis. My appendix has already been removed twice."

[4965]

Young Doctor – "Why do you always ask your patients what they have for dinner?"
Old Doctor – "It's a most important question, for according to their ménus I make out my bills."

[4966]

A man called upon a physician for advice. The physician diagnosed the case as one of nerves, and prescribed accordingly. The fee was five dollars and the prescription two dollars. The man had only five dollars. He said to the physician:
"Doc, five dollars is all I have. Lend me two dollars and I'll have the prescription filled."
The physician gazed at the man for a moment, then said: "I have made a mistake in my diagnosis. Your nerve is all right. You are afflicted with an enlarged gall. There is no remedy for that."

[4967]

A patient complained to the doctor that his hair was coming out.
"Won't you give me something to keep it in?" he begged.
"T a k e t h i s," the doctor said kindly, and he handed the patient a pill box.

[4968]

The doctor smiled as he entered the room.
"You look much better today."
"Yes. I followed the directions on your medicine bottle."
"What were they?"
"Keep the bottle tightly corked."

[4969]

Fair Patient – "They tell me, doctor, you are a perfect lady killer."
Doctor – "Oh, no—no! I assure you, my dear madam, I make no distinction between the sexes."

[4970]

A doctor was called upon to attend a man who was giving signs of mental disturbance, and diagnosed the case as being one of brain fag.

"This man is in a serious state," the physician said to the wife of the patient; "you should have called me sooner."

"But, d o c t o r," protested the woman, "when he was in his right mind he wouldn't have a doctor."

[4971]

A d o c t o r w a s diagnosing the complaint of a pretty young girl.

"You've got acute appendicitis," he said at last. The girl sat up indignantly.

"Say, don't get fresh," she said. "I want to be examined, not admired."

[4972]

The doctor had an inveterate punster and wit among his patients. One day he was late in making his rounds, and explained to the incorrigible humorist that he had stopped to attend a man who had fallen down a well.

With a groan of agony, the wit mustered up strength enough to murmur: "Did he kick the bucket, doctor?"

[4973]

Doctor – "Did you tell that young man of yours what I thought of him?"

Daughter–"Yes, Papa, and he said that you were wrong in your diagnosis, as usual."

[4974]

A lady sent her little girl to see the doctor. When she returned, the fond mother said, "Mary, did the doctor treat you?"

"No," said Mary, "he charged me two dollars."

[4975]

A member of the faculty in a London medical college was appointed an honorary physician to the king. He proudly wrote a notice on the blackboard in his classroom:

"Professor Jennings informs his students that he has been appointed honorary physician to His Majesty, King George."

When the professor returned to his classroom in the afternoon he found written below his notice this line: "God save the King."

[4976]

Girl – "Doctor, is there anything wrong with me?"

Doctor–"Yes, but it's trifling."

Girl–"Oh, but I don't think that's so very wrong, do you?"

[4977]

"I see you gave that little chorine a private room," observed the first surgeon.

Second Doc–"Yes, she was too cute for wards."

[4978]

"I can't sleep," wailed a voice in his ear, as the doctor got out of bed to answer the telephone at three in the morning.

"Hold the wire," said the doctor crustily. "I'll sing you a lullaby."

[4979]

Patient – "Do you think my face will get all red if I eat too many sweets, doctor?"

Doctor – "I don't know. I won't make any rash promises!"

[4980]

"Doctor," asked a patient, "I am feeling much better now, and I want you to let me have your bill."

"Nonsense, sir," said the physician, "do be calm; you are not strong enough for that yet!"

[4981]

A doctor was called in to see a rather testy aristocrat.

"Well, sir, what's the matter?" he asked cheerily.

"That, sir," growled the patient, "is for you to find out."

"I see," said the doctor thoughtfully. "Well, if you'll excuse me for an hour or so I'll go along and fetch a friend of mine — a veterinarian. He is the only chap I know who can make a diagnosis without asking questions."

[4982]

"Did you go to the doctor the other day, John?"

"Yes, I did."

"And did he find out what you had?"

"Very nearly."

"What do you mean, very nearly?"

"Well, I had $3.40 — and he charged me $3.00!"

[4983]

"How's your husband?"

"He's worse."

"But I thought the doctor said yesterday he was getting better?"

"So he did, so he did. But today he says poor Sam'l has gone an' got the convalescence."

[4984]

Physician's Wife – "Now, my dear, you must positively forget shop if you are going into society with me."

Her Hubby – "What have I done?"

Physician's Wife – "Why, you feel the pulse of every one who extends a hand."

[4985]

Lady (who has brought her son to the hospital for treatment) – "It's his head, doctor. He's had it on and off ever since he was born."

[4986]

A doctor who had taken up as his specialty the treatment of skin diseases, was asked by a friend how he happened to select that branch of medicine.

"There were three perfectly good reasons," replied the physician. "My patients never get me out of bed at night; they never die; and they never get well."

[4987]

The doctor was examining a naval hospital orderly for advancement in rating. "What would you do if the captain fainted on the bridge?"

"Bring him to," warbled the aspiring orderly.

"Then what?" asked the doctor.

"Bring him two more," returned the man promptly.

[4988]

"Doctor, I am sorry to drag you so far out in the country on such a bad night."

"Oh, it's all right because I have another patient near here so I can kill two birds with one stone."

[4989]

In a medical school, a student was having a hard time with his examination. It contained many questions that were too difficult for him.

He was asked, "How would you induce a copious perspiration?"

He wrote, "I would have the patient take the medical examination in this college."

[4990]

Fussy Lady Patient – "I was suffering so much, doctor, that I wanted to die."

Doctor – "You did right to call me in, dear lady."

[4991]

"Isn't Doctor Blank your throat doctor?"

"I thought he was until he sent me his bill. He's a skin specialist."

[4992]

A preacher had a brother, a medical doctor, whom he very much resembled. A gentleman met the latter one day and said:

"You preached a fine sermon on Sunday, Doctor"; to which he replied:

"I am not the brother that preaches; I am the one that practises."

[4993]

A man in a hospital was quite ill, and the doctor ordered a diet of sherry and egg.

He was asked how he liked it, and said:

"I wouldn't mind it if only the sherry was as old as the egg, and the egg as new as the sherry."

[4994]

"Did you say the man was shot in the woods, doctor?"

"No, I said he was shot in the lumbar region."

[4995]

Patient—"Great Scott, doctor! What an awful bill for one week's treatment."

Doctor—"My dear fellow, if you knew what an interesting case yours was, and how strongly I was tempted to let it go to a post mortem you wouldn't grumble at a bill three times as big as this."

[4996]

"I am taking a rest cure."

"Oh, what do you do?"

"I sit every day for three hours in the waiting-room of a very busy doctor."

[4997]

"Your husband is too fond of strong coffee," said the doctor. "You must not let him have it. He gets too excited."

"But, doctor, you should see how excited he gets when I give him weak coffee."

[4998]

Even the best of specialists often fall down in their diagnoses.

"Ah," said the doctor, looking into one eye, "it is easy for me to see what is the matter with you! This is not merely eye trouble; it is an affection of the nervous system. There are all the signs of liver trouble, of fatty degeneration of the heart, of a bad blood supply. The only thing I can recommend is—"

"Here, here!" cried the patient. "Isn't it about time you looked into the other eye? That's my glass one, you know."

[4999]

First Doctor—"Well, doctor, I had a peculiar case today."

Second Doctor—"What was it, please?"

First Doctor—"I attended a grass widow who is afflicted with hay fever."

[5000]

A sweet young thing in distress came in and said: "I've broken my glasses. Do I have to be examined all over again?"

"No," sighed the optician, "just your eyes."

[5001]

The patient was convalescing after an operation for appendicitis. His friend asked him how he was getting along.

"Pretty well," was the answer. "After my first operation, they had to cut me open again. It seems the surgeon had left a sponge in me and they had to get that out."

"But you got over it all right?"

"Oh, yes, only I had another operation yesterday. They found a scalpel which had been sewed up in me by mistake."

"Surely you're all right now, though," the friend said encouragingly.

But the patient suffered a severe relapse, for just then the doctor hurried through the ward saying:

"Has anyone seen my hat around here? I left it somewhere yesterday."

[5002]

"How is your doctor son getting on in his practise?"

"Excellently—he is now occasionally able to tell a patient there is nothing wrong with him."

[5003]

A very fat man asked the doctor to prescribe for a complaint, which he declared was sleeping with his mouth open.

"Sir," said the doctor, "your disease is incurable. Your skin is too short, so that when you shut your eyes your mouth opens."

[5004]

"Why did you tear the back part out of that new book?" asked the long-suffering wife of the absent-minded doctor.

"Excuse me, dear," said the famouse surgeon, "the part you speak of was labelled 'Appendix' and I took it out without thinking."

[5005]

"Do you think raw oysters are healthy?" asked a lady of her physician.

"Yes," he replied, "I never knew one to complain."

[5006]

"This tonic is no good."

"What's the matter?"

"All the directions it gives are for adults, and I never had them."

[5007]

Doctor (ecstatically)–"Sir, yours is a case which will enrich medical science!"

Patient–"Oh, dear, and I thought I wouldn't have to pay more than five or ten dollars."

[5008]

"When I was a boy," said a gray-haired physician, who was in a reminiscent mood, "I wanted to be a soldier, but my parents persuaded me to study medicine."

"Oh, well," consoled his sympathetic neighbor, "such is life. Many a man with wholesale ambitions has to content himself with a retail business."

[5009]

Patient–"Doctor, I'm bothered with a queer pain. When I bend forward, stretch out my arms and make a semicircular movement with them, a sharp sting comes in my left shoulder."

Doctor–"But why make such motions?"

Patient – "Well, if you know any other way for a man to get on his overcoat, I wish you'd let me know."

[5010]

"Doctor, I want you to look after my office, while I'm on my vacation."

"But I've just graduated, doctor. I've had no experience."

"That's all right, my boy. My practice is strictly fashionable. Tell the men to play golf and ship the lady patients off to Europe."

[5011]

"Troubled with your throat, eh! Ever gargled with salt water?"

"Yes. I was nearly drowned while swimming last summer."

[5012]

"As I understand it, Doctor, if I believe I'm well, I'll be well. Is that the idea?"

"It is."

"Then, if you believe you are paid, I suppose you'll be paid."

"Not necessarily."

"But why shouldn't faith work as well in one case as in the other?"

"Why, you see, there is considerable difference between having faith in Providence and having faith in you."

[5013]

First Doctor—"You have cured your patient. What is there to worry about now?"

Younger Ditto – "I don't know which of the medicines cured him."

[5014]

Doctor (complacently)–"You cough more easily this morning."

Patient (querulously)–"I should. I've been practicing all night."

[5015]

Patient–"My wife tells me I talk in my sleep, doctor. What should I do?"

Doctor – "Nothing that you shouldn't."

[5016]

"Doctor, what should a woman take when she is run down?"

"The license number, madame, the license number."

[5017]

A Dublin doctor sent in a bill to a lady as follows: "To curing your husband till he died."

[5018]

Doctor–"I can do nothing for your complaint. It is hereditary."

Patient–"Then send the bill to my father."

[5019]

"The thing for you to do," said the doctor to the man with the frazzled nerves, "is to stop thinking about yourself—to bury yourself in your work."

"Gosh!" returned the patient, "and me a concrete mixer."

[5020]

"My treatment is doing you good. You are looking much better today."

"Oh, I always look much better in this hat."

[5021]

"The doctor said he'd have me on my feet in a fortnight."

"And did he?"

"Sure. I've had to sell my automobile."

[5022]

A writer says that it was formerly the practice of surgeons to bleed their patients for the slightest ailment. Why formerly?

[5023]

"On the whole, you are getting along famously," said the doctor. "Your left leg is swollen, but that does not bother me."

"By thunder!" ripped out the patient, "if yours were swollen that wouldn't trouble me either!"

[5024]

Young M. D.–"Well, Dad, now that I'm hanging out my shingle, can't you give me some rules for success?"

Father M. D.–"Always write your prescriptions illegibly and your bills very plainly."

[5025]
The other day a dignified husky gentleman called at a doctor's office. He said that his throat was troubling him and asked for an examination.

The doctor probed around with various instruments. Then the following dialogue took place:

Doctor–"I am afraid you have what is called 'clergyman's sore throat.' "

Patient (startled) – "The hell you say!"

Doctor (hastily)–"Of course I may be wrong. The examination was not thorough. I will look again."

[5026]
"My little daughter has swallowed a gold piece and has got to be operated on. I wonder if Dr. Robinson is to be trusted?"

"Without a doubt. He's absolutely honest."

[5027]
A doctor went out West to practice his profession. An old friend met him on the street one day and asked him how he was succeeding in his business.

"First-rate," he replied. "I've had one case."

"Well—and what was that?"

"It was a birth," said the doctor.

"How did you succeed with that?"

"Well, the old woman died, and the child died, but I think I'll save the old man yet!"

[5028]
A young doctor who had set up practice in a rural district, and whose business was not flourishing, was sitting in his office reading one afternoon when his hired girl appeared at the door.

"Them boys is a-swipin' of the green apples off that tree in the back yard again, sir. Should I drive 'em away?"

The young doctor walked over to the window, considered a moment, and then, leveling his eyes at the servant, replied:

"No."

[5029]
The ten-year-old son of a physician, together with a friend, was playing in his father's office, during the absence of the doctor, when suddenly the first lad threw open a closet door and disclosed to the terrified gaze of his little friend an articulated skeleton.

When the visitor had sufficiently recovered from his shock to stand the announcement the doctor's son explained that his father was extremely proud of that skeleton.

"Is he?" asked the other. "Why?"

"I don't know," was the answer; "maybe it was his first patient."

[5030]
Doctor–"How often does the pain come on?"

Patient–"Every five minutes."

Doctor–"And lasts?"

Patient–"Well, a quarter of an hour, at least."

[5031]
The octogenarian, during the middle of an operation for the rejuvenation of youth, became very impatient.

"Don't be so restless," growled the doctor.

The poor man went on moaning and sobbing.

"Don't cry, the pain will soon vanish."

"I'm not crying because of pain," explained the old man, "I'm afraid I'll be late for school."

[5032]

"What happens to people who allow themselves to become run down?" asked a patient.

"They wind up in hospital," replied the doctor.

[5033]

A patient in the infirmary awoke after an operation and found the blinds of the room drawn.

"Why are those blinds down, doctor?" he asked.

"Well," said the physician, "there's a fire burning across the alley and I didn't want you to wake up and think the operation had been a failure."

[5034]

"Some time ago," said the pompous doctor, "when I started the practice of medicine, I was very poor. I used to sit in my office day after day, waiting for patients. I sat, indeed, like Patience on a monument."

"And now," suggested the young doctor deferentially, "you have monuments on all your patients."

[5035]

"Is the doctor treating her for nervousness?"

"Oh, dear, no. She's rich enough to have psychoneurosis."

[5036]

Specialist—"You are suffering from nervous exhaustion. I can cure you for the small sum of $2000."

Patient—"And will my nerve be as good as yours then?"

[5037]

Rural Doctor (meeting patient)—"I've — er — taken the liberty of sending in my little account again."

Patient—"Is that so? Well, acting on your advice, I'm avoiding business worries for the present."

[5038]

"My girl has varicose veins, doctor. What do you advise?"

"Rubber stocking."

"But, doctor! How do I know she'll let me?"

[5039]

Doctor—"What? Troubled with sleeplessness? Eat something before going to bed."

Patient—"Why doctor, you once told me never to eat anything before going to bed."

Doctor (with dignity)—"Pooh, pooh! That was last January. Science has made enormous strides since then."

[5040]

Doctor (to patient)—"You've had a pretty close call. It's only your strong constitution that pulled you through."

Patient—"Well, doctor, remember that when you make out your bill."

[5041]

Fair Maid—"Oh, sir, what kind of an officer are you?"

Officer—"I'm a naval surgeon."

Fair Maid—"My goodness! How you doctors do specialize."

[5042]

Mrs. Jones—"Good morning, Doctor. I'm so terribly upset to hear of the death of Mrs. Spinks. It was so sad, and to think you were treating her for asthma and then for her to go and die of heart disease!"

Doctor (with determination)—"Mrs. Jones, when I treat a patient for asthma, that patient dies of asthma."

[5043]

Patient—"How can I ever repay you for your kindness to me?"

Doctor—"By cheque, postal order, or cash."

[5044]
Tell us this–"Does a doctor doctor a doctor according to the doctored doctor's doctrine or doctoring, or does the doctor doing the doctoring doctor the other doctor according to his own doctoring doctrine."

[5045]
"It's a little hard for young doctors to get a start."
"I know. I'm raising whiskers."
"They will help. And I'll loan you some of my magazines for 1922 to put in your anteroom."

[5046]
Doctor – "There goes the only woman I ever loved."
Nurse – "Why don't you marry her?"
Doctor–"I can't afford to. She's my best patient."

[5047]
Doctor (after removing his barber's appendix)–"And now, my dear sir, how about a little liver or thyroid operation? And your tonsils need trimming terribly."

[5048]
Patient–"Will the anesthetic make me sick?"
Doctor–"No, I think not."
Patient–"How long will it be before I know anything?"
Doctor–"Aren't you expecting too much of an anesthetic?"

[5049]
In a confidential little talk to a group of medical students an eminent physician took up the extremely important matter of correct diagnosis of the maximum fee.
"The best rewards," he said, "come, of course, to the established specialist. For instance, I charge twenty-five dollars a call at the residence, ten dollars for an office consultation, and five dollars for a telephone consultation."
There was an appreciative and envious silence, and then a voice from the back of the theater, slightly thickened, spoke:
"Doc," it asked, "how much do you charge a fellow for passing you on the street?"

[5050]
"Do you guarantee results in your nerve treatment?" asked the prospective patient.
Specialist–"I do. Why, a man came to me for nerve treatment, and when I had finished with him he tried to borrow $50."

[5051]
"Oh, doctor," cried a wild-eyed man, "I'm dreadfully afflicted. The ghosts of my departed relatives come and perch on the tops of the fence posts all around my garden when dusk is falling. I can look out any evening and see a couple of dozen spooks sitting on the fence, waiting, waiting, waiting. What shall I do?"
"Sharpen the tops of the posts," advised the doctor.

[5052]
Doctor–"What was the most you ever weighed?"
Patient–"154 pounds."
Doctor–"And what was the least you ever weighed?"
Patient–"8¼ pounds."

[5053]
"You must give up coffee and—"
"I never drink it, Doctor."
"And stop smoking."
"I don't smoke."
"Humph! that's bad. If you haven't anything to give up, I'm afraid I can't do much for you."

[5054]

"What are the chances of my recovering?" asked the bed-ridden man.

"One hundred percent," the physician reassured him. "Medical records show that nine out of every ten die of the disease you have. Yours is the tenth case I've treated. Others all died. Statistics are statistics. You're bound to get well."

[5055]

The instructor in the Medical College exhibited a diagram.

"The subject here limps," he explained, "because one leg is shorter than the other."

He then turned to one of the students, and addressed him:

"Now, Mr. Sneed, what would you do in such a case?"

Young Sneed pondered earnestly and replied with conviction:

"I have an idea, sir, that I should limp, too."

[5056]

"Good morning, Mrs. Kelly," said the doctor, "did you take your husband's temperature, as I told you?"

"Yes, Doctor, I borrowed a barometer and placed it on his chest; it said 'very dry,' so I bought him a pint o' beer an' he's gone back to work."

[5057]

An absent-minded grocer called on his old friend, the family doctor, one evening. They chatted for a couple of hours, and as the grocer rose to go, the doctor asked: "Family all well, I suppose?"

"Good heavens!" exclaimed his visitor, "that reminds me. My wife's having a fit."

[5058]

"Doctor," said the sick man, "the other doctors seem to differ from you in their diagnosis of the case."

"I know," replied the physician cheerfully, "but the post-mortem will show that I am right."

[5059]

"Thanks for the lift," said the woman, as she climbed from the plastic surgeon's chair.

[5060]

"Oh, Doctor, I have sent for you, certainly; still, I must confess that I have not the slightest faith in modern medical science."

"Well," said the doctor, "that doesn't matter in the least. You see, a mule has no faith in the veterinary surgeon, and yet he cures him all the same."

[5061]

A specialist is one who has his patients trained to become ill only in his office hours. A general practitioner is likely to be called off the golf course at any time.

[5062]

Pretty Nurse–"Every time I take the patient's pulse it gets faster. What shall I do?"

Doctor–"Blindfold him."

[5063]

"Jim will be in the hospital a long time."

"Why, have you seen the doctor?"

"No, the nurse."

[5064]

"I saw the doctor you told me to see."

"Did you tell him I sent you?"

"Yes, I did."

"What did he say?"

"He asked me to pay in advance."

[5065]
Young Woman (to her neighbor at dinner)–"Guess whom I met today, Doctor?"
Doctor–"I'm afraid I'm not a good guesser."
"You're too modest. Aren't you at the top of your profession?"

[5066]
Patient–"Doctor, what I need is something to stir me up—something to put me in fighting-trim. Did you put anything like that in this prescription?"
Doctor–"No. You will find that in the bill."

[5067]
"That was a pretty hard doctor's bill I had to pay."
"How was that?"
"You see it was for injuries I received by being thrown from a horse I was riding by the doctor's advice."

[5068]
Lady–"Are you fond of lobster salad, Doctor?"
Doctor–"No, I'm not fond of it, but I'm grateful to it."

[5069]
Doctor–"Would you have the price if I said you needed an operation?"
Patient–"Would you say I needed an operation if you thought I didn't have the price?"

[5070]
Doctor–"My dear sir, it's a good thing you came to me when you did."
Patient–"Why, Doc? Are you broke?"

[5071]
He–"At which joint did your friend have his arm amputated?"
She–"That's a mighty disrespectful way to speak of a hospital."

[5072]
Young Doctor–"I took my new car to have it repaired and the garage man charged me $500."
Old Medico–"You could get a new car for that."
Young Doctor–"Well, you see, he didn't know what was the matter with it so he called a consultation."

[5073]
"Madam, your husband must have absolute rest."
"Well, Doctor, he won't listen to me—"
"A very good beginning, madam; a very good beginning."

[5074]
The conceited young man had been in the hospital for some time and had been extremely well looked after by the pretty young nurse.
"Nurse," said the patient, one morning. "I'm in love with you. I don't want to get well."
"Don't worry," replied the nurse, cheerfully, "you won't. The doctor's in love with me, too, and he saw you kissing me this morning."

[5075]
A physician, on presenting his bill to the executor of the estate of a deceased patient, asked, "Do you wish to have my bill sworn to?"
"No," replied the executor, "the death of the deceased is sufficient evidence that you attended him professionally."

[5076]
Routine in the offices of the eminent bone and muscle specialist went on with almost machine-like regularity. The famous doctor had

a highly trained corps of attendants who directed the stream of patients through his inner offices.

One morning, a young, neatly-dressed chap appeared in the doctor's reception rooms. In answer to the query of the nurse in charge, the youth said he wished to see the famous surgeon privately.

"Have you an appointment?" asked the nurse.

"No."

"Then this is your first visit here?"

"Yes."

"Then go into that dressing room there, remove all your clothing, even to your shoes and sox. When you have finished, or shortly after, a bell will ring twice. That will be your signal. Enter Dr. Blank's office through the door in the dressing room marked 'Office.'"

"But——" the boy blushingly began to protest.

The nurse in charge stopped him with a gesture.

"If you really want to see the doctor, you must conform to the rules which he has set down. He does not modify them for anyone."

Still murmuring protests, the boy allowed himself to be hustled into the dressing room where he began to disrobe. After a short while his signal came and he opened a door and tripped across the sill into the famous doctor's office, clad in nothing but a few beads of perspiration.

The eminent specialist was seated at his desk.

"Well," he barked, as the youth came into the room, "what's the matter with you?"

"They ain't nothin' the matter with me, Doc," answered the new arrival.

"Well what in blazes are you doing in my office?"

"I came," said the boy, "to see if you'd care about renewing your subscription to *Collier's Magazine.*"

[5077]

"Doctor, I want to thank you for your great medicine."

"It helped you, did it?" asked the doctor very much pleased.

"It helped me wonderfully."

"How many bottles did you find it necessary to take?"

"Oh, I didn't take any of it. My uncle took one bottle, and I am his sole heir."

[5078]

A gravedigger, walking in the streets of a small town chanced to turn and noticed two doctors walking behind him. He stopped till they passed and then followed on behind them.

"And why this?" asked they.

"I know my place in this procession," said he.

[5079]

Hospital Nurse–"You say financial difficulties brought you here?"

Patient–"Yes. I saw my tailor coming, crossed the road to avoid him, and halfway across I saw another creditor on the other side. I did not know what to do, hesitated and went under a car."

[5080]

"Isn't it remarkable that Brown's luck should stay with him to the very last?"

"How was that?" queried the other.

"He was operated on for the removal of a pearl he had accidentally swallowed while eating oysters, and when the pearl was examined it was found to be valuable enough to pay for both the operation and funeral."

DENTISTS

[5081]

Dentist – "Open wider please — wider."
Patient– "A-A-A-Ah."
Dentist (inserting rubber gag, towel and sponge)–"How's your family?"

[5082]

"I am sorry, madam, but I shall have to charge you ten dollars for pulling your boy's tooth."

"Ten dollars! Why, I understood you to say that you charged only two dollars for such work!"

"Yes," replied the dentist, "but this youngster yelled so terribly that he scared four other patients out of the office."

[5083]

A boy and his mother stood looking at a dentist's showcase.

"If I had to have false teeth, mother, I'd take that pair," said the small boy, pointing.

"Hush, Willie," interposed the mother quickly, shaking his arm, "Haven't I told you it's bad manners to pick your teeth in public?"

[5084]

Dentist– "I'm sorry, but I'm all out of gas."
Girl in Chair– "Ye Gods! Do dentists pull that old stuff, too?"

[5085]

Dentist– "Have you seen any small boys ring my bell and run away?"
Policeman – "They weren't small boys—they were grown-ups!"

[5086]

Patient– "Do you extract teeth painlessly?"
Dentist– "Not always—the other day I nearly dislocated my wrist."

[5087]

Dentist– "You needn't open your mouth any wider. When I pull your tooth I expect to stand outside."

[5088]

Willie– "I have an awful toothache."
Tommie– "I'd have it taken out if it was mine."
Willie– "Yes, if it was yours, I would, too."

[5089]

"Papa, why is it that dentists call their offices dental parlors?"

"Because they are drawing-rooms, my son."

[5090]

First Cannibal– "Have you seen the dentist?"
Second Cannibal– "Yes, he filled my teeth at dinner time."

[5091]

Gerald– "Have you ever come across a man who, at the slightest touch, caused you to thrill and tremble in every fiber of your being?"
Mabel– "Yes, the dentist."

[5092]

Judge (in dentist chair)–"Do you swear that you will pull the tooth, the whole tooth, and nothing but the tooth?"

[5093]

Judge– "Why did you strike this dentist?"
Prisoner– "Because he got on my nerves."

[5094]

Dentist– "Which tooth do you want extracted?"
Pullman Porter– "Lower seven."

[5095]

"Mummy, that dentist wasn't painless like he advertised."

"Why, did he hurt you?"

"No! but he yelled just like any other dentist when I bit his finger."

[5096]

"I've just been having a tussle with the dentist."

"Which beat?"

"It ended in a draw."

[5097]

"Pardon me for a moment, please," said the dentist to the victim, "but before beginning this work I must have my drill."

"Good heavens, man!" exclaimed the patient irritably. "Can't you pull a tooth without a rehearsal?"

[5098]

One hears a great deal about the absent-minded professors, but none more absent-minded than the dentist who said soothingly as he applied the pliers to his automobile:

"Now, this is going to hurt just a little."

[5099]

Dentist (to talkative patient)–"Open your mouth and shut up."

[5100]

"I had a most enjoyable time at the dentist's this afternoon."

"I don't see how that could be."

"It's true. When I went in another dentist was working on my dentist's teeth."

[5101]

"Did you get your money?" asked the wife of the dentist who had just returned from the delinquent patient's home.

"Not a cent," growled the dentist, "and worse than that, he insulted me, and gnashed my teeth at me!"

[5102]

"Have you been a dentist very long?"

"No, I was a riveter till I got too nervous to work up high."

[5103]

Maybe the magazines one finds in the dentist's waiting-room are put there to indicate how long the dentist has been practising.

[5104]

Victim–"Hey, that wasn't the tooth I wanted pulled."

Dentist–"Calm yourself, I'm coming to it."

[5105]

Dentist (speaking to the world war veteran about to have a tooth extracted)–"Do you remember the great war song hit?"

Patient–"No. What was the title of it?"

Dentist–"The Yanks Are Coming."

[5106]

Jones (meeting friend)–"Why the broad grin?"

Brown–"I've just come from my dentist's."

Jones–"Is that anything to laugh about?"

Brown–"Yes—he wasn't in and won't be for two days."

[5107]

I believe that the members of the dental profession are the only men who can tell a woman to open or close her mouth and get away with it.

[5108]

Dentist–"Thought you said this tooth hadn't been filled before?"

Patient (feebly)–"No, it hasn't."

Dentist–"Well, there are traces of gold on my instrument."

Patient (more feebly)–"Perhaps you've struck my back collar-stud!"

[5109]

Dinah had been having trouble with an ulcerated tooth for some time before she got up enough courage to go to a dentist. The moment he touched her tooth she screamed bloody murder.

"What are you making such noise for?" demanded the doctor. "Don't you know that I'm a 'painless dentist'?"

"Well, sah," retorted Dinah, "mebbe yo' is painless, but Ah isn't."

PREACHERS

[5110]

A missionary in a slum once laid his hand on a man's shoulder and said:

"Friend, do you hear the solemn ticking of that clock? Tick-tack; tick-tack. And oh, friend, do you know what day it inexorably and relentlessly brings nearer?"

"Yes—pay day," the workingman, replied.

[5111]

A woman was sitting in a café when a clergyman and his wife entered and sat down at the next table.

After a while the clergyman went out and bought a paper. He came back so deeply engrossed in it that he didn't notice he had taken his seat at the wrong table, where the lone woman sat.

Still not realizing his error and still enthralled in the paper, he said, "Well, my dear, what are we going to have?"

The woman was so astonished that she could not reply, and the clergyman, receiving no answer, peeped above his paper. Seeing his error, he said, "Oh, I'm sorry. . . . Wrong wife!"

[5112]

A certain minister, who was noted for his long sermons, with many divisions, that one day when he was advancing among the teens he reached at length a kind of resting-place in his discourse, when, pausing to take breath, he asked the question, "And what shall I say next?"

A voice from the congregation responded, "Amen."

[5113]

A young lady sat next to a distinguished bishop at a church dinner. She was somewhat modest and diffident, and was rather awed by the bishop's presence. For some time she hesitated to speak to him, waiting for what she considered a favorable opportunity. Finally, seeing some bananas passed, she turned to him and said:

"I beg your pardon, but are you fond of bananas?"

The bishop was slightly deaf, and leaning forward, asked:

"What did you say?"

"I said," repeated the young lady, blushing, "are you fond of bananas?"

The bishop thought a moment, and then said:

"If you want my honest opinion, I have always preferred the old-fashioned nightshirt."

[5114]

A clergyman and a barber quarreling, the former said:

"You have lived like a knave, and you will die like a knave."

"Then," said the barber, "you will bury me like a knave."

[5115]

The preacher's evening discourse was dry and long, and the congregation gradually melted away. The sexton tiptoed up to the pulpit and slipped a note under one corner of the Bible. It read:

"When you are through, will you please turn off the lights, lock the door, and put the key under the mat?"

[5116]

A clergyman was telling his congregation of the effects of intemperance, and said: "I hope the time soon will come when all liquor will be poured into the river. Now let us sing hymn No. 94."

Some members of the congregation smiled when they opened the hymn books and read the title, "Shall We Gather at the River?"

[5117]

Deacon Jones was deaf; but he was energetic as they make 'em. His particular function in the Log City Presbyterian church was selling the new hymnal to the members at seventy-five cents a copy.

One day, after the preacher finished his sermon, he arose and said: "All you who have children to baptize will please present them next Sabbath."

Deaf Deacon Jones, anxious to be of assistance, and supposing the announcement concerned the hymnals, rose and cried out: "All you who haven't, can get as many as you want by calling on me, at seventy-five cents apiece."

[5118]

"Did you hear Robinson snoring in church this morning? It was simply awful."

"Yes, I did—he woke me up."

[5119]

A preacher walked into a saloon, ordered milk and by mistake was served a milk punch.

After drinking it, the holy man lifted his eyes to heaven and was heard to say: "O Lord, what a cow!"

[5120]

A clergyman, lecturing on Palestine, remarked concerning one very rugged locality:

"The roads up these mountains are too steep and rocky for even a donkey to climb, therefore I did not attempt the ascent."

[5121]

"Six days of the week he's invisible, and on the seventh he's incomprehensible," was the account which a dissatisfied old lady gave of her pastor and his ministrations.

[5122]

A preacher amazed his congregation one Sunday morning with this announcement:

"You don't love me, because you don't pay my salary. You don't love one another, for there are no weddings. And God doesn't seem to want you, because nobody dies.

"Now, since I have the honor to have been appointed chaplain for the penitentiary, this will be my last Sunday among you, and I will ask the choir to stand and sing, 'Meet Me There.'"

[5123]

"What a delightful baby!" said the nervous young minister, visiting a parishioner. "And how old is—er —he, she, or it, as the case may be?"

"Just five weeks, sir," replied the proud mother.

"Well, well!" said the minister, helpfully. "Your youngest, I suppose?"

[5124]
Said a Baptist to a Methodist brother:
"I don't like your church government—it has too much machinery about it."
"Yes, but then you see," said the Methodist, "it don't take near so much water to run it."

[5125]
A local celebrity's presence as chairman at a church entertainment was desired, and two of the committee waited upon him with a deferential request. The required promise was duly obtained.
"You may rely on me," said the big man. "Friday, the 21st, in the parish hall. It's quite a non-sectarian affair, I suppose?"
"Bless your heart, sir," came the reply, "the place was only whitewashed last week. You won't find nothing of the kind on the premises."

[5126]
A vain clergyman asked an old man how he had enjoyed his sermon.
"I like one passage at the end very much," said the old man.
"Which was that?" asked the clergyman.
"The one from the pulpit to the vestry," said the old man.

[5127]
A church was raising funds for a new church and the minister was calling on members for subscriptions. One of the pillars of the church rose and said: "I subscribe five dollars." Just at that instant a piece of plaster fell on his head. Half stunned, he mumbled "f-f-five hundred dollars," and the minister prayed "Oh Lord, hit him again."

[5128]
New Curate–"What did you think of the sermon on Sunday, Mrs. Jones?"
Parishioner–"Very good indeed, sir. So instructive. We really didn't know what sin was till you came here."

[5129]
The Rector–"It's terrible for a man like you to make every other word an oath."
The Man–"Oh, well, I swear a good deal and you pray a good deal, but we don't neither of us mean nuthin' by it."

[5130]
Clergyman (to Mrs. Jones, whose little son has just been christened)–"Oh, Mrs. Jones, I have never seen a child that has behaved so well at a christening!"
Mrs. Jones–"Well, you see, it's because my husband and I have been practicing on him with a watering can for a whole week!"

[5131]
It was Sunday morning in a men's class in a famous Presbyterian church school.
"Will you please tell me," said a member to the teacher, "how far in actual miles Dan is from Beersheba? All my life I have heard the familiar phrase 'from Dan to Beersheba,' but I have never known the distance."
Before the answer could be given, another member arose in the back of the room, and inquired:
"Do I understand that Dan and Beersheba are the names of places?"
"Yes."
"That is one on me. I always thought they were husband and wife, like Sodom and Gomorrah."

[5132]

"I expect six clergymen to dine with me on such a day," said a gentleman to his butler.

"Very good, sir," said the butler. "Are they High Church or Low Church, sir?"

"What on earth can that signify to you?" asked the astonished master.

"Everything, sir," was the reply. "If they are High Church, they'll drink; if they are Low Church, they'll eat!"

[5133]

Willie got very tired of the long sermon at church.

"If we give him the money now, ma, will he let us go out?" he asked in a loud whisper.

[5134]

A minister, substituting for a friend in a remote country parish, was greatly surprised on observing the old verger, who had been collecting the offertory, quietly abstract a fifty-cent piece before presenting the plate at the altar rail. After service he called the old man into the vestry and told him with some emotion that his crime had been discovered. The old verger looked puzzled for a moment. Then a sudden light dawned on him. "Why, sir, you don't mean that old half-dollar of mine? I've led off with that for the last fifteen years!"

[5135]

Bishop Doane of Albany was at one time rector of an Episcopal church in Hartford, and Mark Twain, who occasionally attended his services, played a joke on him one Sunday.

"Dr. Doane," he said at the end of the service, "I enjoyed your service this morning. I welcomed it like an old friend. I have, you know, a book at home containing every word of it."

"You have not," said Dr. Doane.

"I have so."

"Well, send that book to me. I'd like to see it."

"I'll send it," the humorist replied.

Next morning he sent an unabridged dictionary to the rector.

[5136]

A Bishop had been speaking with some feeling about the use of cosmetics by girls.

"The more experience I have of lipstick," he declared, warmly, "the more distasteful I find it."

[5137]

The minister answered the doorbell. "Excuse me for interrupting you, sir," said the caller, "but I am collecting for the poor. Do you happen to have any old clothes?"

"Yes," answered the minister.

"Would you be willing to give them to me? I can assure you that they will be put to a worthy use."

"No, I cannot give them to you."

"What do you do with them?"

"Each night I brush them carefully, fold them, and hang them over a chair. Each morning I put them on again."

[5138]

The preacher was reading the Scripture when an old lady broke in: "What kind of a Bible are you using, parson?"

"I'm reading from the revised version," he answered.

"Hm!" she said. "The King James version was good enough for St. Paul and it's good enough for me."

[5139]

A local citizen burst into the office of a railroad official and demanded:

"I want you to give orders that the engineer of the express that passes through Elm Grove at 11:15 be forbidden to blow the whistle on Sunday mornings."

The railroad official retorted: "Why, that's impossible. What leads you to make such an unreasonable request?"

"Well, our preacher preaches until he hears the train whistle blow —and that confounded express was 35 minutes late last Sunday."

[5140]

A fundamentalist deacon who was the leader in a congregation down South, wrote to the bishop to explain the need of a minister for the church. He concluded his appeal as follows:

"Send us a Bishop to preach. If you can't send us a Bishop, send us a Sliding Elder. If you can't send a Sliding Elder, send us a Stationary Preacher. If you can't spare him, send us a Circus Rider. If you can't spare him, send us a Locust Preacher. And if you can't send a Locust Preacher, send us an Exhauster."

[5141]

The minister advertised for a man-servant and next morning a nicely dressed young man rang the bell.

"Can you start the fire and get breakfast by seven o'clock," asked the minister.

"I guess so," answered the young man.

"Well, can you polish all the silver, wash the dishes and keep the house neat and tidy?"

"Say, parson," said the young fellow, "I came here to see about getting married—but if it's going to be as much work as all that you can count me out right now."

[5142]

The impatient clergyman had been at the ticket window many times with inquiries about the belated train. At last he showed up with the solemn interrogation:

"Are there any tidings from the overdue accommodation?"

"Not a damned tiding!" the ticket agent replied.

[5143]

Once, while Bishop Talbot, the giant "cowboy bishop," was attending a meeting of church dignitaries in St. Paul, a tramp accosted a group of churchmen in the hotel porch and asked for aid.

"No," one of them told him, "I'm afraid we can't help you. But you see that big man over there?" pointing to Bishop Talbot. "Well, he's the youngest bishop of us all, and he's a very generous man. You might try him."

The tramp approached Bishop Talbot confidently. The others watched with interest. They saw a look of surprise come over the tramp's face. The bishop was talking eagerly. The tramp looked troubled. And then, finally, they saw something pass from one hand to the other. The tramp tried to slink past the group without speaking, but one of them called to him:

"Well, did you get something from our young brother?"

"No," he admitted, "I gave him a dollar for his damned new cathedral at Laramie!"

[5144]

Two ministers were driving in a cab to the station, and were in some anxiety lest they should miss their train. One of them pulled out his watch and discovered it had stopped.

"How annoying!" he exclaimed. "And I always put such faith in that watch!"

"In a case like this," answered the other, "good works would evidently have answered the purpose better."

[5145]

A curate having been criticized by his bishop for attending a ball, the former replied:

"My lord, I wore a mask."

"Oh, well," returned the bishop, "that puts a new face on the affair."

[5146]

The Vicar (appealing from the pulpit on behalf of the Christmas dinner fund)–"What we want, my friends, is not abstract sympathy, but concrete plum puddings."

[5147]

She–"Poor cousin Jack! And to be eaten by those wretched cannibals!" *He*–"Yes, my dear child; but he gave them their first taste in religion!"

[5148]

Church service was over, and three members walked home together, discussing the message they had heard.

"I tell you," said the first, enthusiastically, "Doctor Blank can certainly dive deeper into the truth than any minister I ever heard!"

"Yes," said the second man, "and he can stay under longer."

"Yes," echoed the third, "and come up drier!"

[5149]

Rector (going his rounds)–"Fine pig that, Mr. Dibbles; uncommonly fine!"

Contemplative Villager–"Ah, yes, sir, if we was only all of us as fit to die as him, sir!"

[5150]

"This is the gate of Heaven," read the sign over the churchyard gate in front of a church which was being restored, while below was a notice in large letters: "Go round the other way."

[5151]

Rev. Henry Ward Beecher sent the following note to the New York Ledger:

"I have just received a curious letter from Michigan, and I give it to you *verbatim:*

" 'Owasso City, Mich., 1870.

" 'April Fool.'

"I have hear of men who wrote letters and forgot to sign their names, but never before met a case in which a man signed his name and forgot to write the letter."

[5152]

An Indiana minister says he doesn't mind members of the congregation pulling out their watches on him, but it gets his goat to have them put the darn things up to their ears to see if they are going.

[5153]

The minister met Tom, the village ne'er-do-well, and, much to the latter's surprise, shook him heartily by the hand.

"I'm so glad you have turned over a new leaf, Thomas," said the good man. "I was delighted to see you at the prayer-meeting last night."

"Oh," said Tom after a moment of doubt. "So that's where I was."

[5154]

There is a preacher in Ohio who should have his salary raised for making the following announcement from his pulpit: "Brethren, the janitor and I will hold our regular prayer-meeting next Wednesday evening as usual."

[5155]

Minister (at baptism of baby)–"His name, please."

Mother–"Randolph Morgan Montgomery Alfred Van Christopher McGoof."

Minister (to assistant)–"A little more water."

[5156]

The minister called on Mrs. Mac-Shoddie.

"By the way," he remarked after a while, "I was sorry to see your husband leave the church last Sunday right in the middle of my sermon. I trust nothing was seriously the matter with him?"

"Oh, no, sir," replied Mrs. Mac-Shoddie. "It was nothing very serious; but, you see, the poor man does have a terrible habit of walkin' in his sleep."

[5157]

The vicar had received a couple of tickets for the opera from one of his parishioners. Finding that he was unable to go, he rang up some friends and said: "An unfortunate dinner engagement keeps me from attending the opera tonight; could you use the tickets?"

"We should be glad to do so," was the reply, "but we are your unfortunate hosts."

[5158]

A Methodist minister in the West, living on a small salary, was greatly troubled to get his monthly instalment. He at last told the non-paying trustees that he must have his money, as his family were suffering for the necessaries of life.

"Money," replied the steward, "you preach for money! I thought you preached for the good of souls."

The minister replied: "Souls! I can't eat souls; and if I could, it would take a thousand such as yours to make a meal."

[5159]

A dear old Methodist, obliged to remain in a certain town over Sunday, started out to attend service in one of the churches of his own faith; but losing his way, and seeing an open church door just across the street, he entered, not knowing to what creed the congregation held. As the service progressed, his religious emotions waxed warmer and warmer, until finally he gave vent to them by shouting out, "Praise God!" Immediately one of the ushers tapped him on the shoulder and said: "You can't do that in this church, sir."

[5160]

"There ought to be a special place in Heaven for ministers' wives."

"Perhaps you're right," responded the minister's wife, "but I would much rather go with my husband."

[5161]

The evening lesson was from the Book of Job and the minister had just read, "Yea, the light of the wicked shall be put out," when immediately the church was in total darkness.

"Brethren," said the minister with scarcely a moment's pause, "in view of the sudden and startling fulfilment of this prophecy, we will spend a few minutes in silent prayer for the electric lighting company."

[5162]

A burglar, who had entered a poor minister's house at midnight, was disturbed by the awakening of the occupant of the room he was in. Drawing his weapon, he said:

"If you stir, you are a dead man. I'm hunting for your money?"

"Let me get up and strike a light," said the minister, "and I'll hunt with you."

[5163]

"I have a feeling that the devil is present in this meeting today!" said the minister.

"Amen!" cried an old brother, from a far corner. "You've got him in close quarters! Lock the doors, and give him where he comes from!"

[5164]

Once upon a time there was an Indian named Big Smoke, employed as a missionary to his fellow Smokes.

A white man encountering Big Smoke, asked him what he did for a living.

"Umph!" said Big Smoke, "me preach."

"That so? What you get for preaching?"

"Me get ten dollars a year."

"Well," said the white man, "that's damn poor pay."

"Umph!" said Big Smoke, "me damn poor preacher."

[5165]

A clergyman was quite ill as a result of eating many pieces of mince pie.

A brother minister visited him and asked him if he was afraid to die.

"No," the sick man replied, "but I should be ashamed to die from eating too much."

[5166]

Wife–"Did you notice the chinchilla coat on the woman sitting in front of us at church this morning?"

Husband–"Er—no. Afraid I was dozing most of the time."

Wife–"Um! A lot of good the service did you."

[5167]

A bashful curate found the young ladies in the parish too helpful. At last it became so embarrassing that he left.

Not long afterwards he met the curate who had succeeded him.

"Well," he asked, "how do you get on with the ladies?"

"Oh, very well indeed," said the other. "There is safety in numbers, you know."

"Ah!" was the instant reply. "I only found it in Exodus."

[5168]

In the congregation of a church during Sunday morning service was a young bride, whose husband was an usher. Becoming terribly worried about having left the roast in the oven, she wrote a note to her husband, sending it to him by another usher.

The latter, thinking it was a note for the pastor, hurried down the aisle and laid it on the pulpit. Stopping abruptly in the middle of his sermon to read the note, the astonished pastor was met with this written injunction:

"Please go home and turn off the gas."

[5169]

The clergyman's eloquence may have been at fault, still he felt annoyed to find that an old gentleman fell asleep during the sermon on two consecutive Sundays. So, after service on the second week, he told the boy who accompanied the sleeper that he wished to speak to him in the vestry.

"My boy," said the minister, when they were closeted together, "who is that elderly gentleman you attend church with?"

"Grandpa," was the reply.

"Well," said the clergyman, "if you will only keep him awake during my sermon, I'll give you a nickel each week."

The boy fell in with the arrangement, and for the next two weeks the old gentleman listened attentively to the sermon. The third week, however, found him soundly asleep.

The vexed clergyman sent for the boy and said: "I am very angry with you. Your grandpa was asleep again today. Didn't I promise you a nickel a week to keep him awake?"

"Yes," replied the boy, "but grandpa now gives me a dime not to disturb him."

[5170]

An itinerant musician was stranded in a village one Sunday morning, and as he was playing his cornet in the street, he was approached by the clergyman of the parish, who said, "Do you know the Fourth Commandment, my good man?"

"No," he replied, "but if you will just whistle it over, I'll do my best."

[5171]

"I have an announcement to make this morning," said the minister. "If any of you are contemplating matrimony, you will please present yourselves to me immediately after the singing of the hymn, 'Mistaken Souls That Dream of Heaven.'"

[5172]

Doctor (to patient being examined for nervous disorder)–"Do you talk in your sleep?"

Parson–"No, doctor, I talk in other people's."

[5173]

"How late do you usually sleep on Sunday morning?"

"It all depends."

"Depends on what?"

"The length of the sermon."

[5174]

An English bishop received the following note from the vicar of a village in his diocese:

"My Lord: I regret to inform you of the death of my wife. Can you possibly send me a substitute for the week-end?"

[5175]

An Episcopal pastor and a Roman Catholic priest had neighboring churches and didn't get along very well. After some time, however, they met and decided to forget past grievances.

"For, after all," said the man of the Episcopal faith, "we are both doing the Lord's work."

"That is true," said the priest. "Let us therefore do His work to the best of our ability: you in your way," concluded the Roman, and then added with a twinkle, "and I in His!"

[5176]

The bridegroom, who was in a horribly nervous condition, appealed to the clergyman in a loud whisper, at the close of the ceremony:

"Is it kisstomary to cuss the bride?"

The clergyman replied:

"Not yet, but soon."

[5177]

A clergyman and one of his elderly parishioners were walking home from church one frosty day when the old gentleman slipped and fell flat on his back. The minister looked at him a moment, and, being assured that he was not much hurt, said to him:

"Friend, sinners stand on slippery places."

The old gentleman looked up as if to assure himself of the fact, and said:

"I see they do; but I can't."

[5178]

Charles Lamb was in the habit of wearing a white cravat, and in consequence was sometimes taken for a clergyman. Once at a dinner table, among a large number of guests, his white cravat caused such a mistake to be made, and he was called on to "say grace." Looking up and down the table, he asked, in his inimitable lisping manner:

"Is there no cl-cl-clergyman present?"

"No, sir," answered a guest.

"Then," said Lamb, bowing his head, "let us thank God."

[5179]

A certain lady induced her husband, who was not a regular churchgoer, to accompany her to evening service. During the sermon he fell asleep, snoring at first softly and at length so noisily that the good lady was constrained to give him a sharp nudge in the hope of rousing him.

To her consternation, however, as he slowly awakened, he exclaimed in a loud tone: "Let me alone! Get up and light the fire yourself—it's your turn!"

[5180]

On one occasion the minister delivered a sermon of but ten minutes' duration—a most unusual thing for him.

Upon the conclusion of his remarks he added: "I regret to inform you, brethren, that my dog, who appears to be peculiarly fond of paper, this morning ate that portion of my sermon that I have not delivered. Let us pray."

After the service the clergyman was met at the door by a man who, as a rule, attended divine service in another parish. Shaking the good man by the hand he said:

"Doctor, I should like to know whether that dog of yours has any pups. If so I want to get one to give to my minister."

[5181]

The sermon had lasted an hour and a half already—an hour and a quarter to the major prophets, and the preacher had not got a third of the way through the minor ones yet. At last, he paused impressively, and exclaimed: "And Habbakuk—where shall we put him?"

A man rose in the back row. "He can have my seat, Mister."

[5182]

An Episcopal clergyman, on his first visit to Fort Smith, was being shaved by a Cherokee barber, who was addicted to occasional sprees. There was an unmistakable odor of whisky around the barber's face; and the razor suddenly cut the parson's face decidedly.

"You see, Light Horse, that comes from taking too much drink," said the man of God.

"You right," agreed the barber. "Drink make skin tender, for a fack."

[5183]

A clergyman who had accepted an invitation to officiate at Sunday services in a neighboring town entrusted his new curate with the performance of his own duties. On returning home he asked his wife what she thought of the curate's sermon.

"It was the poorest one I ever heard," she replied, promptly— "nothing in it at all."

Later in the day the clergyman, meeting his curate, asked him how he had got on.

"Oh, very well," was the reply. "I didn't have time to prepare anything, so I preached one of your unused sermons."

[5184]

Two men of God came to an inn late one bitter cold night.

Very sensibly the venerable prelate was on his knees but a short time. The younger ecclesiast prolonged his devotions nothwithstanding the chill. As he got under the covers he remarked to his companion:

"You didn't pray very long, Bishop?"

"No," said the Bishop, "I keep prayed up."

[5185]

Late one night a jolly looking sailor and a buxom lass called on a minister in a small seaport town and informed him that they wanted to be married right away.

Everything seemed satisfactory, and the ceremony was about to begin when the clergyman thought to make sure of his fee.

"How much is it?" asked the sailor.

"Five dollars," said the clergyman.

"And I have but two," exclaimed Jack. Then an inspiration coming to him he said with the best of good nature, "Well, sir, never mind, marry us as far as it will go."

[5186]

"Boys," said the good old clergyman to the boys in the Bible class, "you should never lost your tempers. You should never swear, or get excited or angry. I never do. Now to illustrate. You see that big fly on my nose. A good many wicked men would get angry at that fly, but I don't. I never lose my temper. I simply say—'Go away, fly—go away—' Good God! It's a bee, damn it all!"

[5187]

"Good evening, my young friend," the clergyman said solemnly, "do you ever attend a place of worship?"

"Yes, indeed, sir, every Sunday night," replied the young fellow with a smile. "I'm on my way to see her now."

[5188]

The clergyman on his vacation wrote a long letter concerning his traveling experiences to be circulated among the members of the congregation. The letter opened in this form:

"Dear Friends:

"I will not address you as ladies and gentlemen, because I know you so well."

[5189]

"I understand," said a young woman to another, "that at your church you are having such small congregations. Is that so?"

"Yes," answered the other girl, "so small that every time our rector says 'Dearly Beloved' you feel as if you had received a proposal!"

[5190]

A golfing clergyman had been beaten badly on the links by a parishioner thirty years his senior and had returned to the clubhouse rather disgruntled.

"Cheer up," his opponent said. "Remember, you win at the finish. You'll probably be burying me some day, I expect."

"Even then," said the preacher, "it will be your hole."

[5191]

The hat was passed around a certain congregation for the purpose of taking up a collection. After it had made the circuit of the church, it was handed to the minister—who, by the way, had exchanged pulpits with the regular preacher—and he found not a penny in it. He inverted the hat over the pulpit cushion and shook it, that its emptiness might be known; then, raising his eyes to the ceiling, he exclaimed with great fervor:

"I thank God that I got back my hat from this congregation."

[5192]

"I thought your minister was to have a call to Minneapolis."

"He did expect it, but he went up there to preach a trial sermon and took his text from St. Paul, so it's all off."

[5193]

The worthy shepherd of the Mission Methodist church in a burst of passionate eloquence in denunciation of the world's wickedness declared:

"Hell is full of cocktails, high-balls, short skirts and one-piece bathing suits!"

Voice from the gallery:

"Oh, Death, where is thy sting?"

[5194]

A minister came to the Episcopal church of a nearby city to speak.

"Do you wish to wear a surplice?" asked the rector.

"Surplice!" cried the visitor. "Surplice! I am a Methodist. What do I know about surplices? All I know about is a deficit!"

[5195]

"Why don't you go to church?" asked the minister of the non-church goer.

"Well, I'll tell you. The first time I went to church they threw water in my face, and the second time they tied me to a woman I've had to keep ever since."

"Yes," said the minister. "And the next time you go they'll throw dirt on you."

[5196]

The exactness of a Boston minister, a great precisionist in the use of words, sometimes destroyed the force of what he was saying. On one occasion, in the course of an eloquent prayer, he pleaded:

"O Lord! waken thy cause in the hearts of this congregation and give them new eyes to see and new impulse to do. Send down Thy lev- or lee-ver, according to Webster's or Worcester's dictionary, whichever Thou usest, and pry them into activity."

[5197]

During the Sunday morning sermon a baby began to cry at the top of its voice, and its mother carried it toward the door.

"Stop!" said the minister. "Your baby is not disturbing me."

The mother turned toward the pulpit and addressed the preacher:

"Oh, he ain't, ain't he? Well, you're a-disturbin' of him."

[5198]

At a religious meeting a lady persevered in standing on a bench, and thus intercepting the view of others, though she was repeatedly requested to sit down.

A reverend old gentleman at last rose and said gravely, "I think if the lady knew she had a large hole in each of her stockings she would not exhibit them in this way."

This had the desired effect—she immediately sank down on her seat. A young minister standing by blushed to the temples, and said, "Oh, brother, how could you say that was not the fact?"

"Not the fact!" replied the old gentleman; "if she had not a large hole in each of her stockings, I would like to know how she gets them on."

[5199]

A visitor in a certain town which had four churches and adequately supported none, asked a pillar of one poor dying church, "How's your church getting on?"

"Not very well," was the reply, "but, thank the Lord, the others are not doing any better."

[5200]

A minister requested his congregation to read the first ten verses of Hebrews xiv before hearkening to the sermon on "Liars" the following Sunday morning.

"How many have read the verses in Hebrews xiv, as requested last Lord's day?" asked the pastor as he arose for the sermon. "Please raise the hands."

There was quite a showing of hands.

"That will do," said the minister sadly. "It happens there is no fourteenth chapter of Hebrews. I there-fore dedicate my remarks on 'Liars' this morning to the brethren and sisters who have just held up their hands!"

[5201]

A Scotch minister in a strange parish, wishing to know what his people thought of his preaching, questioned the beadle:

"What do they say of Mr. ——?" (his predecessor).

"Oh," said the beadle, "they say he's not sound."

"What do they say of the new minister?" (himself).

"Oh, they say he's all sound!"

[5202]

A deacon was lifting one of those detailed petitions to the Throne of Grace that the congregation are expected to overhear.

"Lord, send the unfortunate people of this community such sustenance as they sorely need. Send them a wagon-load of bread, and a barrel of salt, Lord, and a barrel of pepper—no, thunder, Lord that's too much pepper!"

[5203]

Nurse—"What church do you belong to?"

Patient—"None."

Nurse—"Well, what church do you go to when you do go?"

Patient—"If you must know, the church which I stay away from most of the time when I don't go is the Baptist."

[5204]

A M. E. bishop's description of the kind of preaching addressed to rich sinners in some of the aristocratic congregations:

"Brethren, you must repent, as it were, and be converted in a measure, or you will be damned to some extent."

[5205]

A noted eastern judge while visiting in the West went to church on Sunday; which isn't so remarkable as the fact that he knew beforehand that the preacher was exceedingly tedious and long-winded to the last degree. After the service the preacher met the judge in the vestibule and said:

"Well, your Honor, how did you like the sermon?"

"Oh, it was wonderful," replied the judge. "It was like the peace and mercy of God."

"Oh, I scarcely hoped to achieve that," said the preacher much flattered, "How can you make such a comparison?"

"Why, very easily," replied the magistrate. "It was like the peace of God, because it passed all understanding, and, like His mercy, I thought it would have endured forever."

[5206]

A well-known Bishop, while visiting at a bride's new home for the first time, was awakened quite early by the soft tones of a soprano voice singing "Nearer, My God, to Thee." As the Bishop lay in bed he meditated upon the piety which his young hostess must possess to enable her to begin her day's work in such a beautiful frame of mind.

At breakfast he spoke to her about it, and told her how pleased he was.

"Oh," she replied, "that's the hymn I boil the eggs by; three verses for soft and five for hard."

[5207]

A village congregation raised the salary of their minister from $300 to $400. The good man objected, for three reasons:—"First," said he, "you cannot afford to give more than three hundred; secondly, because my preaching is not worth more than three hundred; thirdly, because I have to collect the salary myself, which heretofore has been the hardest part of my labors among you, and had I to collect an additional hundred, it would kill me."

[5208]

A truly eloquent parson in the South had been preaching for an hour or so on the immortality of the soul.

"I looked at the mountains," he declaimed, "and could not help thinking 'Beautiful as you are, you will be destroyed, while my soul will not.' I gazed upon the ocean and cried 'Mighty as you are, you will eventually dry up, but not I!'"

[5209]

The following notice was tacked to the door of a village church:

"There will be preaching in this church a week from next Wednesday, Providence permitting, and there will be preaching here whether or no on Monday following, upon the same subject, He that believeth and is baptized shall be saved, and he that believeth not shall be damned at 3:30 in the afternoon."

[5210]

The minister arose to address his congregation. "There is a certain man among us today who is flirting with another man's wife. Unless he puts five dollars in the collection box, his name will be read from the pulpit."

When the collection plate came in, there were nineteen five dollar bills and a two dollar one with this note attached: "Other three pay day."

[5211]
A clergyman was once accosted on the street by a man who thought he knew the churchman's face, but could not quite place it.

"Now, where in hell have I seen you?" he asked perplexedly.

"From where in hell do you come, sir?" said the clergyman.

[5212]
A Kentucky home-spun preacher made an earnest effort to convert a particularly vicious old mountaineer named Jim, who was locally notorious for his godlessness. But the old man was hard-headed and stubborn, firmly rooted in his evil courses, so that he resisted the pious efforts in his behalf.

"Jim," the preacher questioned sadly at last, "ain't you teched by the story of the Lord what died to save your soul?"

"Humph!" Jim retorted contemptuously. "Air ye aimin' to tell me the Lord died to save me, when He ain't never seed me, ner knowed me?"

"Jim," the missionary explained with fervor, "it was a darn sight easier for the Lord to die for ye jest because He never seed ye than if He knowed ye as well as we-alls do!"

[5213]
A clergyman was recently telling a marvelous story, when his little girl said, "Now, pa, is that really true, or is it just preaching?"

[5214]
This is one of Mark Twain's stories:

"Some years ago in Hartford, we all went to church one hot, sweltering night to hear the annual report of Mr. Hawley, a city missionary who went around finding people who needed help and didn't want to ask for it. He told of the life in cellars, where poverty resided; he gave instances of heroism and devotion of the poor. When a man with millions gives, he said, we make a great deal of noise. It's a noise in the wrong place, for it's the widow's mite that counts.

"Well, Hawley worked me up to a great pitch. I could hardly wait for him to get through. I had $400 in my pocket. I wanted to give that and borrow more to give. You could see the greenbacks in every eye. But instead of passing the plate to the crowd then, he kept on talking and talking and talking, and as he talked it grew hotter and hotter and hotter, and we grew sleepier and sleepier and sleepier. My enthusiasm went down, down, down, down—$100 at a clip—until finally, when the plate did come around, I stole ten cents out of it. It all goes to show how a little thing like this can lead to crime."

[5215]
Prison Chaplain (to prisoner about to be discharged)–"Now, my man, try to remember what I said in my sermon last Sunday and make up your mind never to return to this place."

Prisoner (deeply moved)–"No man who ever heard you preach would want to come back here."

[5216]
A clergyman had occasion to preach to the inmates of an insane hospital. During his sermon he noticed that one of the patients paid the closest attention, his eyes riveted upon the preacher's face, his body bent eagerly forward. Such

interest was most flattering. After the service, the speaker noticed that the man spoke to the superintendent, so as soon as possible the preacher inquired.

"Didn't that man speak to you about my sermon?"

"Yes."

"Would you mind telling me what he said?"

The superintendent tried to side-step, but the preacher insisted.

"Well," he said at last, "what the man said was, 'Just think, he's out and I'm in.'"

[5217]

Tearful Parishioner (saying farewell to a departing minister)–"I don't know what we will do when you are gone, Dr. Blank."

Departing Minister – "Oh, the church will soon get a better man than I am."

Tearful Parishioner–"That's what they all say, but they keep getting worse and worse."

[5218]

Minister's Wife–"Wake up! There are burglars in the house."

Minister–"Well, what of it? Let them find out their mistake themselves."

[5219]

A stranger entered the church in the middle of the sermon and seated himself in the back pew. After a while he began to fidget. Leaning over to the white-haired man at his side, evidently an old member of the congregation, he whispered:

"How long has he been preaching?"

"Thirty or forty years, I think," the old man answered.

"I'll stay then," decided the stranger. "He must be nearly done."

[5220]

Dorothy was light-hearted and merry over everything. Nothing appealed to her seriously. So, one day, her mother decided to invite a very serious young parson to dinner, and he was placed next the light-hearted girl. Everything went well until she asked him:

"You speak of everybody having a mission. What is yours?"

"My mission," said the parson, "is to save young men."

"Good," replied the girl, "I'm glad to meet you. I wish you'd save one for me."

[5221]

An evangelist was exhorting his hearers to flee the wrath to come.

"I warn you," he thundered, "that there will be weeping, and wailing and gnashing of teeth!"

At this point an old lady in the gallery stood up.

"Sir," she shouted, "I have no teeth."

"Madam," roared the evangelist, "teeth will be provided."

[5222]

When one oyster met another in the stew at the church supper, the first asked the second:

"What are you doing here?"

"As this is a church supper, it is my business to be here," answered the second oyster.

"Well, if this is a church supper," rejoined the first, "why are both of us here?"

[5223]

A young clergyman, after his first sermon, wished to invite the mourners to view the remains, became confused and said:

"We will now pass around the bier."

[5224]

The new minister in a Tulsa church was delivering his first sermon. The Indian caretaker was a critical listener from a back corner of the church. The minister's sermon was eloquent, and his prayers seemed to cover the whole category of human wants. The Indian listened carefully but completely without expression.

After the services one of the deacons asked the caretaker what he thought of the new minister. "Don't you think he offers up a good prayer?"

"Him sure do. Him ask Lord for things other preacher don't know He have."

[5225]

The sexton had been laying the new carpet on the pulpit floor, and had left a number of tacks scattered about.

"See here, James," said the parson, "what do you suppose would happen if I stepped on one of those tacks right in the middle of my sermon."

"Well, sir," replied the sexton, "I reckon there'd be one point you wouldn't linger on."

[5226]

A clergyman was preaching on the subject of future punishment. "Yes, my brethren," said he, "there is a hell; but—" (drawing out his watch and looking at it) "we shall not go into that just now."

[5227]

A Southern preacher called on a minister in New England.

He found him at his desk, writing.

"What are you-all doin' there?" he asked.

"I'm preparing notes for my sermon next Sunday. I always write my message in advance."

The Southern preacher shook his head in dismay.

"Don' never do that," he said. "The devil's a-lookin' over your shoulder and knows everything you gwan to say, and he's preparin' for you. Now I don't make no notes, and when I gets up to talk neither the devil nor me knows what ahm gonna say."

[5228]

A Boston minister once noticed a crowd of urchins clustered around a dog of doubtful pedigree.

"What are you doing, my little men?" he asked, with fatherly interest.

"Swappin' lies," volunteered one of the boys. "The feller that tells the biggest one gets the purp."

"Shocking!" exclaimed the minister. "Why, when I was your age I never thought of telling an untruth."

"Youse win," chorused the urchins. "The dog's yours, mister."

[5229]

A pompous Bishop of Oxford was once stopped on a London street by a ragged urchin.

"Well, my little man, and what can I do for you?" inquired the churchman.

"The time o' day, please, your lordship."

With considerable difficulty the portly bishop extracted his timepiece.

"It is exactly half past five, my lad."

"Well," said the boy, setting his feet for a good start, "at 'alf past six you go to 'ell!"—and he was off like a flash and around the corner. The bishop, flushed and furious, his watch dangling from its chain, floundered wildly after him. But as he rounded the corner he ran plump into the outstretched arms of the venerable Bishop of London.

"Oxford, Oxford," remonstrated that surprised dignitary, "why this unseemly haste?"

Puffing, blowing, spluttering, the outraged Bishop gasped out:

"That young ragamuffin—I told him it was half past five—he—er—told me to go to hell at half past six."

"Yes, yes," said the Bishop of London with the suspicion of a twinkle in his kindly old eyes, "but why such haste? You've got almost an hour."

[5230]

An old lady in church was seen to bow whenever the name of Satan was mentioned. One day the minister met her and asked her the reason. "Well," she replied, "politeness costs nothing, and you never can tell."

[5231]

Mr. Jones had recently become a father of triplets. The minister stopped him on the street to congratulate him.

"Well, Jones," he said, in his best felicitatory bass, "I hear that the Stork has smiled on you."

"Smiled on me!" repeated Jones. "He laughed out loud at me!"

[5232]

An old preacher dropped his pocketbook. A tough character picked it up and returned it to the preacher, who thanked him, adding: "Yet some people say you are not honest."

"Well, parson," said the tough character, "I'm honest to goodness."

POLITICIANS

[5233]

Said a man who was digging on a government job to the foreman: "I dug this hole where I was told to and began to put the dirt back like I was supposed to. But all the dirt won't go back in. What'll I do?"

For a long while the foreman pondered the problem. Then: "I have it. There's only one thing to do. You'll have to dig the hole deeper."

[5234]

"Some of our Congressmen drink more than they can stand."

"How do you know?"

"Why, I read the other day in the paper about one member who made a speech from the floor of the House."

[5235]

Colonel Boodle had prepared an oration to be given at the dedication of the new courthouse. He took his bosom friend, Colonel Swag, into his confidence and said to him:

"I want you to be present when I deliver this speech. You must start the laughter and applause. Every time I take a drink of water you are to applaud and every time I wipe my forehead you are to laugh."

"Better switch signals, Kunnel," said his friend. "It's sure to start me off laughing if I see you up there taking a drink of water."

[5236]

Citizen–"These ignorant foreigners should not be allowed to vote."

Politician–"That's just what I was thinkin'. Half of 'em look so much alike I can't tell which ones I've given two dollar bills to, an' which ones I haven't."

[5237]

Street Orator—"We must get rid of radicalism, Socialism, Bolshevism, Communism and Anarchism."

Voice from the Crowd—"And while we're about it, why not throw in rheumatism?"

[5238]

Harris—"And your brother, who was trying so hard to get a Government job, what is he doing now?"

Brown—"Nothing. He got the job."

[5239]

They were looking down into the depths of the Grand Canyon.

"Do you know," asked the guide, "that it took millions and millions of years for this great abyss to be carved out?"

"Well, well!" ejaculated the traveler. "I never knew this was a government job."

[5240]

A large Republican meeting was held in a county seat in Ohio, which was attended by a small boy who had four young puppy dogs which he offered for sale. Finally, one of the crowd, approaching the boy, asked: "Are these Republican pups, my son?"

"Yes, sir."

"Well, then," said he, "I'll take these two."

About a week afterward the Democrats held a meeting at the same place, and among the crowd was to be seen the same boy and his two remaining pups. He tried for hours to obtain a purchaser, and finally was approached by a Democrat and asked: "My little lad, what kind of pups are these you have?"

"They're Democratic pups, sir."

The Republican who had purchased the first two happened to be in hearing, and broke out at the boy:

"See here, you young rascal, didn't you tell me that those pups that I bought of you last week were Republican pups?"

"Y-e-s, sir," said the young dog-merchant; "but these ain't—they've got their eyes open."

[5241]

"Father," said the small boy, "what is a demagogue?"

"A demagogue, my son, is a man who can rock the boat himself and persuade everybody that there's a terrible storm at sea."

[5242]

"Why don't you take a holiday and go fishing?"

"Why should I?" rejoined the Senator. "I can send a secretary fishing, and let him announce the catch publicly, while I remain at home and take some much-needed rest."

[5243]

Willie—"Pa, what is a politician?"

Father—"Son, a politician is a human machine with a wagging tongue."

"Then, what is a statesman?"

"It is an ex-politician who has mastered the art of holding his tongue."

[5244]

A Kentuckian had seventeen children, all boys. When they came of age they voted uniformly the Democratic ticket—all except one boy. The father was asked to explain this evident fall from grace.

"Waal," he said, "I've always tried to bring them boys up right, in the fear of the Lord and Democrats to the bone, but John, the onery cuss, got to readin'."

[5245]

A lank, disconsolate-looking farmer stood on the steps of the town hall during the progress of a political meeting.

"Do you know who's talking in there now?" demanded a stranger briskly, pausing for a moment beside the farmer. "Or are you just going in?"

"No, sir; I've just come out," said the farmer decidedly. "Congressman Smiffkins is talking in there."

"What about?" asked the stranger.

"Well," continued the countryman, passing a knotted hand across his forehead, "he didn't say."

[5246]

The chairman of the central committee was receiving reports from the county committees.

"Things never looked better for a clean sweep for the Republican ticket than they do this fall," reported one county Warwick. "It's dollars to doughnuts that we'll even elect the candidate for judge of probate."

"What makes that so important?" the chairman asked.

"Well, you see the Democrats put up a man who had only one arm several years ago and we've never been able to overcome the appeal of that empty sleeve. But he's our meat this time, boys. We Republicans have nominated a man who is paralyzed from his neck up!"

[5247]

"What would be a good way to raise revenue and still benefit the people?"

"Tax every political speech made in this country."

[5248]

Citizen–"Is it too late for me to register to vote?"
Registrar–"What party?"

[5249]

Disappointed Candidate–"And I thought sure I heard the voice of the people calling me."
Friend–"It must have been yourself thinking out loud."

[5250]

Candidate–"We must grow more wheat and—"
Heckler in Crowd–"Yes, but what about hay?"
Candidate–"I'm discussing human food now, but I'll come to your specialty in a moment."

[5251]

I suppose it is not irreverent to say that practically all candidates receive some help in preparing their public documents. In the case of a certain Mayor of New York of several years ago it was necessary not only to write the speech but to spell the longer words phonetically so that he could pronounce them. He was so dependent upon these prepared scrips that on one occasion at a patriotic banquet he astonished all listeners by declaiming "What we need is more of the spirit of one-seven-seven-six."

[5252]

The political speaker was warming up to his subject.

"As Daniel Webster says in his great dictionary—" he began by way of illustration.

"Hey!" came a voice from the audience. "It was Noah who wrote the dictionary."

"You are mistaken, my friend," said the speaker unabashed. "Noah built the ark."

[5253]

"I'm taking political economy at college."

"That's a useless course. Why learn to economize in politics? It's not being done."

[5254]

Candidate–"I suppose in this campaign the proper thing for me to do is to stand on my record."

Political Boss–"No, to jump on the other fellow's."

[5255]

"All these delegates for me?"

"Those are candidates, friend."

[5256]

Full of enthusiasm, she had gone in for politics, and was out of the house most of the day. The other night she returned at ten o'clock and sank into an armchair.

"Everything's grand," she said. "We're going to sweep the country."

Her husband looked round wearily and said:

"Why not start with the dining-room?"

[5257]

Foreman–"And what are you two fellows doing?"

Political Job Holders–"We're carrying these boards over to that lumber pile."

Foreman – "But where are the boards?"

Political Job Holders–"For gosh sakes, Sam, we've forgot the boards."

[5258]

A politician was once speaking before a small assembly in a village. In the course of his speech he introduced some expression which disgusted his hearers, who thereupon started moving away. The ora-tor, seeing this, put up his hands and said:

"Pause, friends!" But the answer he got was from a local wag, who cried amid laughter:

"Aye, an' real dirty ones they are too!"

[5259]

Six political job holders were carrying the body of a man who had been killed into an undertaker's establishment. The undertaker was very much annoyed. "Why," he asked, "didn't you bring this man's body here at three o'clock, as you promised? It's now after six."

"Sorry," replied the leader, "but we had to wait until the five o'clock whistle blew to find out which one of the men was dead."

[5260]

A Chicago newspaper points out that the Government prints and distributes the speeches made by Congressmen without the slightest profit. It might also be added they are read the same way.

[5261]

Thomas B. Reed was one of the Legislative Committee sent to inspect an insane asylum. There was a dance on the night the committee spent in the investigation, and Mr. Reed took for a partner one of the fair unfortunates to whom he was introduced. "I don't remember having seen you here before," said she; "how long have you been in the asylum?" "Oh, I only came down yesterday," said the gentleman, "as one of the Legislative Committee."

"Of course," returned the lady, "how stupid I am! However, I knew you were an inmate or a member of the Legislature the moment I looked at you. But how was I to know? It is so difficult to know which."

[5262]

A western politician running for office was very much incensed at certain remarks which had been made about him by the leading paper of the town. He burst into the editorial room like a dynamite bomb, and exclaimed, "You are telling lies about me in your paper, and you know it!"

"You have no cause for complaint," said the editor coolly. "What in the world would you do if we told the truth about you?"

[5263]

"Can't the Democrats of this town get together?" inquired the political exhorter in Kentucky.

"Get together!" answered the man with court-plaster on his ear; "why, it takes eleven deputy sheriffs to keep 'em apart!"

[5264]

A Republican candidate, in a house-to-house canvass, was trying to persuade a voter to ballot for that ticket.

"No," said the voter, "my father was a Democrat, and so was my grandfather, and I won't vote anything but the Democratic ticket."

"That's no argument," said the candidate, "suppose your father and your grandmother had been horse thieves; would that make you a horse thief?"

"No," came the answer, "I suppose in that case I'd be a Republican."

[5265]

Politician–"My boy says he would like a job in your department."
Official–"What can he do?"
Politician–"Nothing."
Official–"That simplifies it. Then we won't have to break him in."

[5266]

Candidate (in impassioned speech) –"I am willing to trust the people."

"I wish you'd open a grocer's shop, then!" said a little man in the audience.

[5267]

Colonel Watson, a well-known politician of Virginia, enjoyed great personal popularity on account of his affable manners, and whenever he was a candidate for office ran ahead of the ticket. He generally spoke to everybody he met, professing to know them. On one occasion, during a presidential campaign, he met a countryman, whom he shook by the hand, and commenced:

"Why, how do you do, thir? I am very glad to thee you; a fine day, thir. I thee you thill ride your fine old gray, thir."

"No, sir; this horse is one I borrowed this morning."

"Oh! ah! well, thir, how are the old gentleman and lady?"

"My parents have been dead about three years, sir."

"But how ith your wife, thir, and the children?"

"I am an unmarried man, sir."

"Thure enough. Do you thill live on the old farm?"

"No, sir; I have just arrived from Ohio, where I was born."

"Well, thir, I gueth I don't know you afther all. Good morning, thir."

[5268]

He was earnestly but prosily orating at the audience. "I want land reform," he wound up, "I want housing reform, I want educational reform, I want—"

And said a bored voice in the audience: "Chloroform."

[5269]

"I am out of politics for good," announced the Political Boss.

"Whose?" questioned the green reporter.

[5270]

"So your wife is going in for politics, eh?" said the neighbor.

"Yes," sighed the meek one, "she's gone down-town now to get a new hat to throw into the ring."

[5271]

A West Side politician got his first dinner coat, recently, in time for a dressy function to which he was invited. He had a little trouble tying his tie, so he dropped in at the corner saloon and asked the bar-keep which of the customers was good at tying a bow tie.

"That fellow at the end of the bar there," said the bar-keep with a laconic gesture.

The politician approached the somber-looking gentleman designated.

"Would you mind tying this for me?" he asked, pulling his tie out of his pocket and slipping it under his collar.

"Sure," said the man, "but not that way. You'll have to lie down."

An explanatory comment came from another bar patron.

"You see, he's an undertaker," he said.

[5272]

The political orator was taking an unconsciously long time for his speech. He bellowed forth over his hearers' weary heads:

"I am speaking for the benefit of posterity."

A heckler promptly shouted: "Yes, and if you don't be quick about it, they'll be along to hear you!"

[5273]

"My father was just itching for an office."

"Did he get over it?"

"Yes. They scratched him at the polls."

[5274]

Chairman (of political banquet)– "Gentlemen, before I introduce the next speaker, there will be a short recess, giving you all a chance to go out and stretch your legs."

Guest–"Who is the next speaker?"

Chairman–"Before telling you who he is, I would rather wait until you come back."

[5275]

Bill Smathers has two sons. One is in politics and the other isn't much good either.

[5276]

"When I arose to speak," related a martyred statesman, "some one hurled a base, cowardly egg at me and it struck me in the chest."

"And what kind of an egg might that be?" asked a fresh young man.

"A base, cowardly egg," explained the statesman, "is one that hits you and then runs."

[5277]

Mrs. Deleigh (meeting politician at party)–"I've heard a great deal about you."

Politician (absently)–"Possibly, but you can't prove it."

[5278]

Teacher–"Johnny, spell gravy."

Politician's Son–"G-r-a-f-t."

[5279]

"The office should seek the man, you know."

"Yes, that's all right," replied the candidate, "but I gave it plenty of time, and it seemed bashful."

[5280]

A candidate for Congress found himself in the course of touring the constituency in front of a house near which a number of children were playing. Intent on his own business, the politician stopped for a moment to chat with the comely woman leaning upon the gate. Politely doffing his hat, the candidate inquired:

"Madam, I may kiss these beautiful children, may I not?"

"Certainly," replied the lady.

When he had finished his wholesale contract the candidate turned to the attractive woman at the gate and said:

"Seldom have I seen lovelier children. Yours, madam?"

The woman blushed deeply.

"Ah, of course they are," gallantly suggested the politician. "The little treasures, from whom else could they have inherited those eyes and rosy cheeks, those comely figures, and those musical voices."

But still the lady blushed.

"By the way, madam," said he, "may I impose upon your good nature to the extent of asking that you tell your husband that Mr. Cockrell called upon him this afternoon?"

"I fear there's some mistake, sir. I have no husband. This is an orphan asylum."

[5281]

Woman (about to attend political meeting)—"I'm not prejudiced at all. I'm going with a perfectly open and unbiased mind to listen to what I'm convinced is pure rubbish!"

[5282]

"Who, father, is that gentleman?" said the small boy, pointing to a man standing on the dais of the National House of Representatives.

"That, my son," said the father, "is the chaplain of the House."

"Does he pray for the members?" asked the small boy.

The father thought a minute and then said: "No, my son; when he goes into the House he looks around and sees the members sitting there and then he prays for the country."

[5283]

A colored voter had tried his best to follow the reasoning of the political spokesman.

As he came out of the assembly hall, a fellow Texan asked him, "Who war de speaker?"

"Aw didn't jes' git de gemmen's name," was the reply, "but he suhtainly did 'preciate hisself powerful highly."

[5284]

Mayor Mitchel of New York was talking at a dinner about office-seekers.

"A good man had just died," he said, "and with unseemly haste an office-seeker came after his job.

"Yes, sir, though the dead man hadn't been buried, yet this office-seeker came to me and said, breathlessly:

" 'Mr. Mayor, do you see any objection to my being put in poor Tom Smith's place?'

" 'Why, no,' said I. 'Why, no, I see no objection, if the undertaker doesn't.' "

[5285]

"What makes you think the baby is going to be a great politician?" asked the young mother, anxiously.

"I'll tell you," answered the young father, condently; "he can say more things that sound well and mean nothing at all than any kid I ever saw."

[5286]

A politician was invited to give a talk on Americanism to the pupils of the grammar school he had attended as a boy.

"When I see your smiling faces before me," he began in the accepted oratorical style, "it takes me back to my childhood. Why is it, my dear girls and boys, you are all so happy?"

He paused for the rhetorical effect, and instantly up went a grimy hand from the front row.

"Well, my lad, what is it?"

"The reason we're so happy," replied the boy, "is if you talk long enough we won't have a geography lesson this morning."

[5287]

Political Speaker—"What we need is a working majority and then—"
A Voice—"Better reverse it, mister. What we really need is a majority working."

[5288]

A member of the House of Representatives asserted pompously his convinction that he could not be wrong.

"I know I'm right," he thundered. "And I'd rather be right than be president!"

"Don't worry," retorted an honorable opponent, "you'll never be either."

[5289]

"Oh yes, my father was a great politician in his day."

"Yes, what did he run for?"

"The border!"

[5290]

"Have you noticed her hat? Looks as if it had been stepped on."

"Well, she had it in the ring, but now she's out of politics."

[5291]

A Southern politician, when candidate for office on the Republican ticket, related the following story of his campaign.

"Once I told three sharecroppers that I'd give a big turkey to the one who'd give the best reason for his being a Republican.

"The first one said: 'Ahm a 'publican 'cause the 'publicans is fer bigga crop sharin'—'

"'Very good, Pete,' said I. 'Now, Bill, let me hear from you.'

"'Well, ahm a 'publican 'cause of the pertective tariff.'

"'Fine!' I exclaimed. 'Now, Clete, what have you to say?'

"'Well now,' said Clete, scratching his head and shifting from one foot to the other, 'Ah'd say ahm a 'publican 'cause ah wants that turkey.'

"And he got it."

[5292]

A group of congressmen was conferring. Said one: "We've got a one hundred and twenty million dollar appropriation to spend which will get us each thousands of votes."

"I've got an idea," said one, "on how to spend it. How about building a bridge over the Mississippi River, lengthwise?"

[5293]

"I hold in my hand here a bright and shining silver dollar," announced the candidate to a group of young Americans. "That dollar goes to the lad who is level-headed enough to belong to the same party as I do.

Then turning to a bright-eyed urchin at his left, he asked:

"What's your politics, son?"

"What's yours?" piped the young opportunist.

[5294]

A Senator once disposed of a minor politician who challenged him to a debate by simply giving the following fable to the press:

A skunk once challenged a lion to a single combat. The lion promptly declined the honor of such a meeting.

"How," said the skunk, "are you afraid?"

"Very much so," quoth the lion, "for you would only gain fame by having the honor to fight a lion, while every one who met me for a month to come would know that I had been in company with a skunk."

[5295]

"There were some things in your speech that I didn't quite understand."

"Probably," replied Senator Blank, "those were the topics I referred to in a confident, offhand way, so as to avoid disclosing that I don't understand 'em either."

[5296]

"I rise for information," said a member of a political meeting.

"I am very glad to hear it," said a bystander, "for no one needs it more."

[5297]

"Papa, what's a 'liberal Republican'?"

"Wait, son, I'll look it up."

"But papa, that book you are consulting is Bullfinch's Mythology."

"I know, son, I know."

[5298]

"A statesman is supposed to be familiar with all public questions."

"Yes," replied Senator Blank, "but not necessarily with all the answers."

[5299]

On a government road job one of the political job holders was assigned to go up the road and warn the motorists that the way was partially blocked and to drive carefully. The worker assigned to that duty was afflicted with laryngitis. A motorist drove up and the worker stopped him.

"What's the matter?" asked the motorist.

The worker with laryngitis whispered huskily, "There's a government road job up the road."

"That's all right," whispered the driver. "I'll go by quietly so we won't wake 'em."

[5300]

Political Speaker—"I'm pleased to see such a dense crowd here to-night."
Voice—"Don't be too pleased. We ain't all dense."

[5301]

"Have you heard my last speech?" asked a political haranguer of a wit.

"I sincerely hope so," was the reply.

[5302]

During a municipal campaign in Chicago a politician dropped in one morning to see a certain grocer. During the conversation that took place, the politician asked, "And I may count upon your support, may I not?"

"Why, no, I am sorry to say," replied the grocer. "The fact is, I have promised my support to the other candidate."

The politician laughed. "Ah," said he, "in politics, promising and performing are two different things."

"In that case," said the grocer cordially, "I shall be glad to give you my promise, sir."

[5303]

Senator Mark Hanna was walking through his mill one day when he heard a boy say:

"I wish I had Hanna's money and he was in the poorhouse."

When he returned to the office the senator sent for the lad, who was plainly mystified by the summons.

"So you wish you had my money and I was in the poorhouse," said the Senator grimly. "Now supposing you had your wish, what would you do?"

"Well," said the boy quickly, his droll grin showing his appreciation of the situation, "I guess I'd get you out of the poorhouse the first thing."

Mr. Hanna roared with laughter. "You might as well push that boy along," he said to one of his assistants; "he's too good a politician to be kept down."

[5304]

A candidate for Congress from a certain New England state was never shy about telling the voters why they should send him to Washington.

"I am a practical farmer," he said boastfully, in the course of an address to an agricultural group. "I can plow, reap, milk cows, shoe a horse—in fact, I should like for someone to tell me one thing about a farm which I cannot do."

Then, in the impressive silence, a voice asked from the back of the hall:

"Can you lay an egg?"

[5305]

A young lawyer from the North sought to locate in the South. He wrote to a friend in Alabama, asking him what the prospect seemed to be in the city for "an honest young lawyer and Republican."

In reply the friend wrote: "If you are an honest lawyer, you will have absolutely no competition. If you are a Republican, the game laws will protect you."

[5306]

The Ward Boss was in the chair as usual, master of all he surveyed. The meeting got tied into a knot over a point of order, raised by a newcomer into the Ward.

"Mr. Chairman, I move we leave it to Cushing's Manual!" he cried.

The Ward Boss was on his feet ablaze with wrath. "Th' minute Cushings Manual stips into this m'ating," he said, "Timothy Moriarty stips out!"

[5307]

The foreman on a political job ran short of shovels and wired Washington, asking for more. The next day he received this reply:

"Have no more shovels, tell the men to lean on each other."

[5308]

The congressman's wife sat up in bed, a startled look on her face. "Jim," she whispered, "there's a robber in the house."

"Impossible," was her husband's sleepy reply. "In the Senate, yes, but in the House, never."

[5309]

"Don't cheer, boys. No one party is large enough to hold all the crooks."

[5310]

"Sure, an' I ain't no party-man Dennis. I vote iv'ry time for the best man."

"An' how can ye be tellin' who's the best man, till the votes is counted?"

[5311]

"What's the election today for? Anybody happen to know?"

"It is to determine whether we shall have a convention to nominate delegates who will be voted on as to whether they will attend a caucus which will decide whether we shall have a primary to determine whether the people want to vote on this same question again next year."

[5312]

"What we want is a candidate who isn't too radical nor yet too conservative; in short, a middle-of-the-road man."

"Then Smathers is the man to nominate. He's been a bus driver for years."

[5313]

"Are you going abroad next summer?"

"No," answered Senator Blank, "What's the use of traveling around among people who don't speak my language, and who couldn't vote for me even if they did?"

[5314]

Doctor–"I have to report, sir, that you are the father of triplets."
Politician–"Impossible! I'll demand a recount."

[5315]

A prominent business man who had been invited to speak at a political meeting was placed last on the list of speakers. Moreover, the chairman introduced several speakers whose names were not on the program, and the audience was tired out when he eventually introduced the last speaker: "Mr. Jenkins will now give us his address."

"My address," said Mr. Jenkins, rising, "is 155 Lane Park, and I wish you all good-night."

[5316]

"Mr. Chairman," complained the speaker, stopping in his address, "I have been on my feet nearly ten minutes, but there is so much ribaldry and interruption, I can hardly hear myself speak."

"Cheer up, guv'nor," came a voice from the rear, "you ain't missin' much."

[5317]

"My dear," said the politician's young wife to her husband, "the baby was trying to talk again."

"What was he talking about?"

"I think it must have been politics. He started very calmly, but in a few minutes he was as angry and red in the face as he could be. It is perfectly wonderful how he takes after you."

[5318]

"Yes, I used to be in politics myself. I was dog catcher in my town for two years, but finally lost the job."

"What was the matter? Change of mayors?"

"Nope. I finally caught the dog."

[5319]

A candidate addressing his constituency was surprised by a voice which, calling from the back of the hall, said: "Well, I don't care what you say, I wouldn't vote for you if you were the angel Gabriel."

Came the reply: "If I were the angel Gabriel, you wouldn't be in my constituency."

[5320]

Percival–"Daddy, do they raise political plums from seeds?"
Daddy (who never had one)–"No, young man. Political plums are more often the result of a bit of clever grafting."

[5321]

A political speaker, warning the public against the imposition of heavier tariffs on imports said, "If you don't stop shearing the wool off the sheep that lays the golden egg, you'll pump it dry."

[5322]

Scene in the counting room of the election committee in a small town in Georgia.

Time—Two hours before the closing of the polls.

Official counter—"Say, what do ah do with this heah Republican ballot?"

[5323]

"Mother," dad said, "I'm going to find out what Jackie wants to be when he grows up. Watch."

He put a ten-dollar bill on the table; it represented the banker. Next to it he placed a brand new Bible, representing the clergyman. And beside the Bible he placed a bottle of whiskey, representing the bum.

Mother and Dad hid where they could see the articles on the table. Jackie, whistling happily, entered the room and spied the arrangement on the table. He looked around to see that he was alone. Satisfied, he picked up the bill and held it to the light, and replaced it. He fingered the pages of the new Bible. He looked around once more. Then he quickly uncorked the bottle and smelled the contents. And, in a motion, he stuffed the bill in his pocket, lodged the Bible under his arm, grabbed the bottle by the neck, and slid out of the room, still whistling.

"My goodness, Mother," dad exclaimed, "he's going to be a politician."

[5324]

A surgeon, an architect, and a politician were arguing as to whose profession was the oldest.

Said the surgeon: "Eve was made from Adam's rib, and that surely was a surgical operation."

"Maybe," said the architect, "but prior to that, order was created out of chaos, and that was an architectural job."

"But," interrupted the politician, "somebody created the chaos first!"

[5325]

"I have decided," remarked Senator Blank, "to train my memory."

"What system will you use?"

"I don't know. I'm looking for one that will enable me, when I am interviewed, to remember what to forget."

[5326]

The foreman on a political job was bawling out one of his slowest workers. "I know the sort of fellow you are," said the foreman. "You're the sort of fellow who'd like to stay in bed all day and get things done, just by pushing buttons."

"Not me," was the reply. "Who'd push the buttons?"

[5327]

Two politicians chatting: "What do you consider the object of legislation?"

"The greatest good to the greatest number."

"What do you consider the greatest number?"

"Number one."

[5328]

"What do you think of our two candidates for mayor?"

"Well, I'm glad only one can be elected."

[5329]

"There's no use denying it," observed Farmer Perkins, "Smoothy is the man to send to Congress!"

"I don't know much about that," persisted Farmer Homespun.

"Well, I do. He's for the farmer every time. Why, he says if he's elected he'll introduce a bill to stop the importation of French fried potatoes!"

[5330]

A Congressman, who is recognized as an authority in matters of state, had been to Baltimore one afternoon with his family. When they left the train at Washington, on their return, his wife discovered that her umbrella, which had been intrusted to the care of her husband, was missing.

"Where's my umbrella?" she demanded.

"I'm afraid I've forgotten it, my dear," meekly answered the Congressman. "It must still be in the train."

"In the train!" snorted the lady. "And to think that the affairs of the nation are intrusted to a man who doesn't know enough to take care of a woman's umbrella!"

[5331]

"Some of your constituents are disagreeing with you," said the trusted lieutenant.

"Well, keep tab on them," replied Senator Blank, "when enough disagree with me to constitute a reliable majority, I'm going to turn around and agree with them."

[5332]

Who was the first Democrat in the world?

A.—Christopher Columbus.

Q.—How come?

A.—When he left Spain his trip was government financed, was it not?

Q.—When he left Spain, he didn't know where he was going, did he?

A.—No, he didn't.

Q.—When he got to America, he didn't know where he was going, did he?

A.—That's right.

Q.—When he got home, he couldn't tell where he had been, could he?

[5333]

A politician was seeking re-election.

"Fellow citizens," he said, "I stand before you on my record. If you had a hired man who had worked for you for a long time, would you not think it right for you to keep on employing him?"

A voice from the audience broke in with:

"Not if he got to thinkin' that he owned the whole darned farm."

[5334]

Candidate—"Say, Jim, will you vote for me to-day?"

Jim—"No, I can't, but I will say you are my second choice."

Candidate—"Well, that's good, Jim. Who is your first choice?"

Jim—"Why, any other darned man in the town would come before you."

[5335]

"That's the home of our representative in the legislature," the host pointed out to the guest as they rode by.

"An ornate pile," the visitor exclaimed. "What is it made of?"

"Can't give you all the materials," the citizen answered, "but it is common report that a great many 'ayes' and 'noes' went into its construction."

[5336]

"Haven't your opinions on this subject undergone a change?"

"No," replied Senator Blank.

"But your views, as you expressed them some time ago?"

"Those were not my views. Those were my interviews."

[5337]

First Senator-"What did the crowd do when you told them you had never paid a cent for a vote and never would?"

Second Senator-"Well, a half-dozen or so applauded, but most of them got up and went out."

[5338]

The foreman on a political job started bawling out one of his men. "We've had slow men on this job," he said, "but you are the slowest person I have ever seen. Aren't you quick at anything?"

"Well," yawned the workman, "Nobody can get tired as quick as I can."

[5339]

Father (admiring his recently born heir)-"That fellow will be a great statesman one of these days."

Mother-"Oh, Charles, dear, do you really think he will?"

"Sure of it. Look how easily he wriggles out of everything."

[5340]

"What is political pie?"

"It is a lot of crust with apple-sauce and plums."

[5341]

Politician-"Congratulate me, my dear, I've won the nomination."

His Wife (in surprise)-"Honestly?"

Politician-"Now what in thunder did you want to bring up that point for?"

[5342]

"Why did they provide the Capitol with a rotunda?"

"It's a good place for statesmen who like to run around in circles."

[5343]

Young Hopeful-"Father, what is a traitor in politics?"

Veteran Politician-"A traitor is a man who leaves our party and goes over to the other one."

Young Hopeful-"Well, then, what is a man who leaves his party and comes over to yours?"

Veteran Politician-"A convert, my son."

[5344]

Just before the breaking up of Congress, as several of the members were making themselves merry in the lobby, one of them jollied another on the very religious strain in which he had indulged in the last speech he had inflicted upon the house.

"I'll bet you five dollars," said Macarty, "you can't repeat the Lord's Prayer now, if you try."

"I'll take you up," said Kolloch, and, assuming an appropriate religious air, recited:

Now I lay me down to sleep,
I pray the Lord my soul to keep;
If I should die before I wake,
I pray the Lord my soul to take.

"There! I told you I could."

"Well, I give up," said Macarty, paying over the money. "I wouldn't have thought you could do it."

[5345]

The reporter came idly into the office. "Well," said the editor, "what did our eminent statesman have to say?"

"Nothing."

"Well, keep it down to a column."

[5346]

Reporter–"I've got a perfect news story."

City Editor–"The man bite the dog?"

Reporter "Naw, a bull threw a Congressman."

[5347]

Two political job holders were off on a binge. "I'm going to leave this job soon and I want you to come with me," said one of the boys after his eighth drink. "I know a place in Africa where there's a lot of gold just lying around waiting for someone to pick it up."

"I knew there was a catch in it," replied his friend.

"What's the catch?"

"You've got to bend over."

[5348]

A politician rushing to address a meeting at an election was accosted by a henchman.

"What do you think about the political situation now?" the henchman asked.

"Don't bother me now!" replied the politician. "I've got to talk. This is no time to think."

FAMOUS MEN

[5349]

Mark Twain was a guest of honor at an opera box-party given by a prominent member of New York society. The hostess had been particularly talkative all during the performance—to Clemens's increasing irritation.

Toward the end of the opera, she turned to him and said gushingly:

"Oh, my dear Mr. Clemens, I do so want you to be with us next Friday evening. I'm certain you will like it—the opera will be 'Tosca.' "

"Charmed, I'm sure," replied Clemens. "I've never heard you in that."

[5350]

An accused criminal once smirked up at Lord Bacon, trying him as Chancellor, "Your Highness ought to let me free. We're really kin. For my name's Hogg—and Hogg's kin to Bacon!"

"Not until it's hung," said Bacon drily.

[5351]

Lloyd George was addressing a meeting in South Wales when the chairman, thinking to be witty at the chancellor's expense, remarked to the audience that he was a little disappointed in Lloyd George's appearance.

"I had heard so much about Mr. Lloyd George," he said, "that I naturally expected to meet a big man in every sense; but, as you can see for yourselves, he is very small in stature."

Many an orator would have been grievously upset by such an unfortunate beginning to the proceedings, but not so Lloyd George.

"I am grieved to find," he said, with mock seriousness, "that your chairman is disappointed in my size, but this is owing to the way you have here of measuring a man. In North Wales we measure a man from his chin up, but you evidently measure him from his chin down!"

[5352]

A socialist once called upon Baron Rothchild, the wealthy banker, and argued with him as to the unfairness of one man having so much money and so many million of people with practically none. He asked for a more equitable distribution of wealth.

At this point Rothchild called in his secretary and asked him how much money his total wealth consisted of. Then he referred to an almanac and figured out the total population of the world. He then made a simple calculation and calling his secretary, said, "Will you give this gentleman sixteen cents. That is his share of my wealth."

[5353]
Champ Clark loved to tell of how in the heat of a debate Congressman Johnson of Indiana called an Illinois representative a jackass. The expression was unparliamentary, and in retraction Johnson said:

"While I withdraw the unfortunate word, Mr. Speaker, I must insist that the gentleman from Illinois is out of order."

"How am I out of order?" yelled the man from Illinois.

"Probably a veterinary surgeon could tell you," answered Johnson, and that was parliamentary enough to stay on the record.

[5354]
A certain grandson of Queen Victoria, when a freshman at Oxford, had spent all of his allowance and, what is worse, gone ten pounds in debt.

He appealed to his royal grandmother, asking her for an advance on future remittances. He didn't get it. Instead, he received a lengthy letter from that austere lady containing some reproof and much, much advice.

In due course the young man replied to this. He had, he said, decided to heed everything his grandmother had to say about conserva-

tism and thrift and had, in fact, already begun by selling the original of her letter to a collector for twenty-five pounds.

[5355]
It being reported that Lady Caroline Lamb had, in a moment of passion, knocked down one of her pages with a stool, the poet Moore, to whom this was told by Lord Strangford, observed:

"Oh! nothing is more natural for a literary lady than to double down a page."

"I would rather," replied his lordship, "advise Lady Caroline to *turn over a new leaf*."

[5356]
When Whistler had finished a portrait of a well-known celebrity, he asked him whether he liked it.

"No, I can't say I do, Mr. Whistler, and you must really admit it's a bad work of art."

"Yes," replied the artist, looking at his sitter through his monocle, "but then you must admit that you are a bad work of nature."

[5357]
When Jenny Lind, the Swedish Nightingale, gave a concert to the Consumption Hospital in London the proceeds of which concert amounted to 1,776*l*. 15*s.*, and were to be devoted to the completion of the building, Jerrold suggested that the new part of the hospital should be called "The Nightingale's Wing."

[5358]
Macready's handwriting was cruelly illegible, and especially when writing orders of admission to the theatre. One day, at New Orleans, Mr. Brougham obtained one of these from him for a friend. On handing it to the gentleman, the latter ob-

served, that if he had not known what it purported to be, he would never have suspected what it was. "It looks more like a prescription than anything else," he added.

"So it does," said Mr. Brougham; "let us go and have it made up."

Turning into the nearest drug store, the paper was given to the clerk, who gave it a careless glance, and then proceeded to get a phial ready, and to pull out divers boxes. With another look at the order, down came a tincture bottle, then the phial was half filled. Then there was a pause. The gentleman attendant was evidently puzzled. At last he broke down completely, and rang for his principal, an elderly and severe-looking individual, who presently emerged from the inner sanctum. The two whispered together an instant, when the old dispenser looked at the document, and with an expression of pity for the ignorance of his subordinate, boldly filled the phial with some apocryphal fluid, and coolly corked and labeled it. Then handing it to the gentlemen who were waiting, he said, with a bland smile:

"A cough mixture, and a very good one. Fifty cents, if you please."

[5359]

Oscar Wilde, upon hearing one of Whistler's *bon mots* exclaimed: "Oh, Jimmy; I wish I had said that!"

"Never mind, dear Oscar," was the rejoinder, "you will!"

[5360]

Oscar Wilde reached his climax: "And so you Philistines have invaded the sacred sanctum of art!"

A spectator: "I suppose that's why we are being assaulted with the jawbone of an ass."

[5361]

"How is it," said a gentleman to Sheridan, "that your name has not O attached to it? Your family is Irish, and no doubt illustrious."

"No family has a better right to O than our family," said Sheridan; "for we owe everybody."

[5362]

Edgar Wallace once was telling a scribbler friend what a great business the film industry was. "Why," said Wallace, "it's marvelous. I write a scenario in a couple of days and they pay me a fortune for it. You ought to get into it," he advised.

"Yes, I know," returned his friend, "but it's too strange for me. I once was asked by a film company to submit something. I sent them four scenarios and blamed if they didn't return me nine!"

[5363]

The late Justice Oliver Wendell Holmes and an associate went strolling one afternoon. The nonagenarian and his companion passed an intriguing young damsel. Wistfully the Justice turned for a lingering glance. "Ah," he said, "Ah, to be seventy again!"

[5364]

James Gordon Bennett hated drinkers and the boys who worked with him were all aware of it. One of the pressmen returned from a bender with a beautiful black eye.

As luck would have it, James Gordon popped into the pressroom that day. The fellow spotted him before Bennett saw him, and rather than explain the "shiner" and run the risk of being fired chose to rub printer's ink all over his face. On his tour of inspection around the pressroom Bennett came upon the besmudged pressman busily burying his nose in his work.

"Who's the fellow?" he asked the foreman. Upon being told, Bennett asked, "What do you pay him?" The foreman quoted the figure.

"Double it!" snapped Bennett. "He's the only one in the place who seems to be doing any work."

[5365]

Somebody lightheartedly told the late Lord Salisbury that a bishop was greater than a judge, for a judge could only say, "You be hanged," whereas the prelate could say, "You be damned." "Yes," commented the Marquis, "but when a judge says 'You be hanged,' you are hanged."

[5366]

Jerrold had a favorite dog that followed him everywhere. One day in the country, a lady who was passing turned round and said, audibly, "What an ugly little brute!"

Whereupon Jerrold, addressing the lady, replied, "Oh, madam! I wonder what he thinks *about us* at this moment!"

[5367]

Returning from hunting one day, George III. entered affably into conversation with his wine merchant, Mr. Carbonel, and rode with him side by side a considerable way. Lord Walsingham was in attendance; and watching an opportunity, took Mr. Carbonel aside, and whispered something to him.

"What's that? what's that Walsingham has been saying to you?" inquired the good-humored monarch.

"I find, sir, I have been unintentionally guilty of disrespect; my lord informed me that I ought to have taken off my hat whenever I addressed your Majesty; but your Majesty will please to observe, that whenever I hunt, my hat is fastened to my wig, and my wig is fastened to my head, and I am on the back of a very high-spirited horse, so that if anything *goes off* we must *all go off together!*"

The king laughed heartily at this apology.

[5368]

Daniel O'Connell, the great Irish patriot, once met a conceited literary friend, and exclaimed: "I saw a capital thing in your last pamphlet."

"Did you?" eagerly replied his delighted listener. "What was it?"

"A pound of butter."

[5369]

President Taft, wearing the largest bathing suit known to modern times, threw his substantial form into the cooling waves of Beverly Bay. Shortly afterward one neighbor said to another: "Let's go bathing."

"How can we?" was the response. "The President is using the ocean."

[5370]

King Henry VIII., designing to send an embassy to Francis I. at a very dangerous juncture, the nobleman selected begged to be excused, saying, "Such a threatening message to so hot a prince as Francis I. might go near to cost him his life."

"Fear not," said old Harry, "if the French king should take away your life, I will take off the heads of a dozen Frenchmen now in my power."

"But of all these heads," replied the nobleman, "there may not be *one to fit* my shoulders."

[5371]

W. S. Gilbert of light-opera fame was always full of whimsies. At the Garrick Club one evening he made the astounding statement that Shakespeare was a very obscure writer. His statement was immediately protested by most of those present, and he was asked to prove it.

"Well," said Gilbert, "what do you make of this passage?"

" 'I would as lief be thrust through a quickset hedge as cry "plosh to a callow throstle." ' "

"There's nothing obscure in that," said one member. "It's perfectly clear. Here's a man, a great lover of the feathered songsters, who rather than disturb the caroling of the little warbler prefers to go through the intense pain of thrusting himself through a thorny hedge. But I don't know that passage. In what play does it occur?"

"In no play," said Gilbert. "I've just invented it. And jolly good Shakespeare, too!"

[5372]

A French taxicab driver once played a joke on Sir Arthur Conan Doyle. The man had driven Sir Arthur from the station to a hotel and, when he received his fare, he said: "Merci, M. Conan Doyle."

"Why, how do you know my name?" asked Sir Arthur.

"Well, sir, I have seen in the papers that you were coming from the south of France to Paris; your general appearance told me that you were English; your hair had been clearly last cut by a barber of the south of France. I put these indications together and guessed at once that it was you."

"That is very remarkable. You have no other evidence to go upon?"

"Well," said the man, "there was also the fact that your name was on your luggage."

[5373]

Longfellow, the poet, was introduced to one Longworth, and some one noticed the similarity of the first syllable of the names.

"Yes," said the poet, "but in this case I fear Pope's line will apply— 'Worth makes the man, the want of it the fellow.' "

[5374]

In the course of one of his lecture trips, Mark Twain arrived at a small town. Before dinner he went to a barber shop to be shaved.

"You are a stranger?" asked the barber.

"Yes," Mark Twain replied. "This is the first time I've been here."

"You chose a good time to come," the barber continued. "Mark Twain is going to read and lecture tonight. You'll go, I suppose?"

"Oh I guess so."

"Have you bought your ticket?"

"Not yet."

"But everything is sold out. You'll have to stand."

"How very annoying!" Mark Twain said with a sigh. "I never saw such luck! I always have to stand when that fellow lectures."

[5375]

The great American advocate Joseph Choate, was once trying a case in New York against a lawyer from Westchester county. This man sneered at the polished address of the Manhattan celebrity, and warned the jury not to be misled by his Chesterfieldian urbanity.

Choate rose smilingly to reply. "Don't bother about my Chesterfieldian urbanity," he wooed the jury. "You'd better be sure that you're not misled by my opponent's Westchesterfieldian suburbanity."

[5376]

A lady consulting St. Francis of Sales on the lawfulness of using rouge: "Why," said he, "some pious men object to it; others see no harm in it; I will hold a middle course, and allow you to use it on one cheek."

[5377]

Dr. Johnson was observed by a musical friend of his to be extremely inattentive at a concert, whilst a celebrated solo player was running up the divisions and sub-divisions of notes upon his violin. His friend, to induce him to take greater notice of what was going on, told him how extremely difficult it was. "Difficult, do you call it, sir?" replied the doctor; "I wish it were *impossible.*"

[5378]

Through the good offices of an influential American residing in Paris, an ambitious young girl from New York obtained an audience with Sacha Guitry, the famous actor, who graciously consented to hear her recite.

After listening to a classical or two, the great actor went up to the young aspirant for histrionic honors and placed his hand on her head, as in benediction.

"My dear child," said he, "marry soon. Good-by!"

[5379]

During a newspaper men's convention a number of journalists were one afternoon talking of the tricks of "the faithless types," when "Marse" Henry Watterson said:

"While I've heard of a great many funny typographical breaks in my time, about the oddest and most humorous transposition of the types that ever came within my observation was that in a New York paper some years ago. That sheet used to print its shipping news on the same page with the obituaries. Imagine the glee with which its readers found the captions exchanged one morning, whereby a long list of respectable names were set forth under the marine head, 'Passed Through Hell Gate Yesterday.' "

[5380]

When P. T. Barnum, later of circus fame, was running his famous museum in New York, he discovered that persons were paying admission and staying for hours. The place soon became so crowded each day that others could not get in. Barnum wondered how he could empty the museum without offending his patrons, so that the turnover would be greater. Finally, he hit upon a plan. He had a sign made which he placed over a door leading to an exit into a rear street. It worked, for people soon began to follow the sign to see what new curiosity awaited them. The sign read: TO THE EGRESS.

[5381]

A person who dined in company with Dr. Johnson endeavored to make his court to him by laughing immoderately at everything he said.

The doctor bore it for some time with philosophical indifference; but the impertinent *ha, ha, ha!* becoming intolerable, "Pray, sir," said the doctor, "what is the matter? I hope I have not said anything that *you* can comprehend."

[5382]

A certain dramatic translator, introducing a well-known comedian to Madame Vestris, said:

"Madame, this is Mr. B——, who is not such a fool as he looks."

"True, madame," said the comedian; "and that is the great *difference* between me and my friend."

[5383]

In a parliamentary speech, an admirer of Lloyd George, then Prime Minister, referred to him as the "Wizard of Britain."

"I beg pardon, you mean the Blizzard of Wales," broke in Jack Jones of the Laborite opposition.

The House roared.

[5384]

Dr. Johnson, the lexicographer, was once assailed by a fishwoman with foul epithets. Whereupon he turned upon her, and berated her terribly. He called her a noun, an adverb, an interjection, an adjective, and thus like, until she waxed as mad as a hornet.

[5385]

"Billy" Van, in telling about his experiences on a street car, says that one day he was on a car, hanging on to a strap when, with a jerk, the car swung around a curve, taking him off his feet and landing him squarely in the lap of a very fat lady near the front of the car. Becoming highly indignant, she yelled. "Get out of my lap, you heathen!"

"Madam," said "Billy," turning to her with a polite bow, "it must be evident that I am no heathen—I am a Laplander."

[5386]

Mark Twain once sat in the smoking room of a steamer and listened for an hour to some remarkable stories. Then he drawled, "Boys, these feats of yours that you've been telling about recall an adventure of my own in Hannibal. There was a fire in Hannibal one night, and Old Man Hankinson got caught in the fourth story of the burning house. It looked as if he was a goner. None of the ladders was long enough to reach him. The crowd stared at one another with awed eyes. Nobody could think of anything to do.

"Then all of a sudden, boys, an idea occurred to me. 'Fetch a rope!' I yelled.

"Somebody fetched a rope, and with great presence of mind I flung the end of it up to the old man. 'Tie her round your waist!' I yelled. Old Man Hankinson did so, and I pulled him down."

[5387]

Dwight Moody, the revivalist, once entered a Chicago drug store distributing tracts. At the back of the store sat an elderly and distinguished citizen reading a morning newspaper. Moody approached this gentleman and threw one of the temperance tracts upon the paper before him. The old gentleman glanced at the tract, and then looking up benignantly at Moody, asked: "Are you a reformed drunkard?"

"No, sir, I am not!" cried Moody, drawing back indignantly.

"Then why don't you reform?" quietly asked the old gentleman.

[5388]

Sir Andrew Clark was Gladstone's physician, and was known to the great statesman as a "temperance doctor," who very rarely prescribed alcohol for his patients. On one occasion he surprised Gladstone by recommending him to take some wine. In answer to his illustrious patient's surprise he said:

"Oh, wine does sometimes help you get through work! For instance, I have often twenty letters to answer after dinner, and a pint of champagne is a great help."

"Indeed!" remarked Gladstone; "does a pint of champagne really help you to answer the twenty letters?"

"No," Sir Andrew explained; "but when I've had a pint of champagne I don't care a rap whether I answer them or not."

[5389]
When Gladstone had finished a long speech in which he attacked the policies of Prime Minister Disraeli, the latter rose and said, "The man needs no reply. He is inebriated by the exuberance of his own verbosity."

[5390]
Johnson defined oats:

"A grain, which in England is generally given to horses, but in Scotland supports the people."

"Yes," retorted Lord Ellibank, "and where in the world will you find such horses and such men?"

[5391]
When Dr. Johnson courted Mrs. Porter, whom he afterwards married, he told her that he was of mean extraction; that he had no money; and that he had had an uncle hanged!

The lady, by way of reducing herself to an equality with the Doctor, replied, that she had no more money than himself; and that, though she had not had a relation hanged, she had fifty who *deserved hanging*.

[5392]
The father of Mrs. Siddons had always forbidden her to marry an actor, and of course she chose a member of the old gentleman's company, whom she secretly wedded. When Roger Kemble heard of it, he was furious. "Have I not," he exclaimed, "dared you to marry a player?"

The lady replied, with downcast eyes, that she had not disobeyed.

"What, madam! have you not allied yourself to about the worst performer in my company?"

"Exactly so," murmured the timid bride; "nobody can call *him* an actor."

[5393]
An old Harvard instructor used to tell the story of the time Theodore Roosevelt was a student in his class. One day young Roosevelt was rehearsing a poem to be recited for public declaration. He got as far as a line that read: "When Greece, her knees in suppliance bent."

Then he stuck and couldn't go any further. Again he repeated: "When Greece, her knees——" and still he stuck.

Once more he repeated the four words, when finally the instructor said: "Roosevelt, suppose you grease her knees again, and then perhaps she'll go."

[5394]
If a person isn't going to drink, we like to see him handle his nondrinking like George Russell, the great Irish mystic, who likes the dipthong Æ. When Æ was in Hanover, he was asked if he cared for a drink. The Irish poet refused as gracefully, "Thank you, no. You see, I was born intoxicated."

[5395]

When William Dean Howells, the author, was consul at Venice, he was quite stout, but he was good-natured about it, like most other fat men.

He was visited one day by a friend, who was very tall and lanky. "Howells," said this man, "if I were as fat as you are, I would hang myself."

"Well," said Howells, "if I ever decide to take your advice I'll use you for the rope."

[5396]

At one time President Wilson was riding along a country road near Washington accompanied only by the secret service man who was detailed to guard him. They passed a small boy by the roadside. Presently the President turned to his companion and said:

"Did you see what that boy did?"

"No, sir; what did he do?"

"He made a face at me," said the President, shaking his head gravely.

The secret service man was shocked. The President waited a moment and then asked:

"Did you see what I did?"

"No, sir."

"Well," said the President with a twinkle in his eye, "I made a face right back at him."

[5397]

Speaker Reed, who was noted for his wit, was once making a tour of his state, Maine, during a presidential campaign. He spoke in many cities. In one town a Democrat sat in the front row of seats, and "heckled" the speaker, as they call it in England.

He kept on asking questions, to which Reed answered courteously, although it was the obvious inten-

tion of the Democrat to make him lose his temper. Finally, finding that he could do nothing with the Speaker, the Democrat said:

"Aw, go to hell!"

Reed answered:

"I have traveled in many parts of the State, and have spoken at many meetings, but this is the first time I have received an invitation to the Democratic headquarters."

[5398]

The birth centenary of Eiffel, builder of the famous Paris tower, recalled to a Liverpool *Post* writer this story concerning William Morris.

During the English poet-artist's last visit to Paris he spent much of his time in the Eiffel Tower Restaurant, having all his meals and doing all his writing there.

"You must be very much impressed by the tower," a friend remarked to him.

"Impressed!" cried Morris. "I stay here because it is the only place in Paris where I can avoid seeing the damned thing."

[5399]

The story is told of James Smithson, founder of the Smithsonian Institution, that when five doctors had failed to discover what ailed him, he observed:

"I desire that you perform an autopsy to discover what is the matter with me, for I am dying to know what my ailment is myself."

[5400]

A Princton alumnus recalls how President Francis Landy Patton once dealt with a class who got on his nerves by shelling peanuts while he was lecturing. He said:

"Young gentlemen, I had hoped

before I reached this point in the lecture that the visible supply of peanuts would be exhausted. I realize that these lectures to which you are compelled to listen put a great strain upon you, and I have no desire to interfere with your natural right to seek that refreshment which will enable you to bear up under that strain. But I am a somewhat nervous man, and I must admit that the constant popping of peanuts is somewhat disturbing to me. I wish that in the future you would be willing to substitute some less audible means of refreshment, say spongecake."

[5401]

In his autobiography, "Days of Our Years," M. Pierre van Paassen tells of an Italian officer who, at a luncheon at the opening of the Italian Pavilion at the Paris Exhibition, started to tell of Fascist successes.

"Our Duce," he said, "ordered us to take Ethiopia, and we took it in the face of fifty-one nations determined to destroy us. He told us to take the Iron Ring around Bilbao; the next morning it was ours.

"We have eight million bayonets —nothing can stop us. Let us be frank about it: if the Duce ordered his army to march into France tomorrow, what really could stop us?"

There was an embarrassed silence. A French guest broke in.

"Monsieur seems to forget the French Customs service," he remarked.

[5402]

Jack London was late in delivering a story which he promised a New York magazine.

The editor, after repeated efforts to get the story, at last called at London's hotel and sent up the following note:

"Dear Jack London: If I don't receive the story within twenty-four hours, I'll come up to your room and kick you downstairs, and I always keep my promises."

London replied: "Dear Dick—if I did all my work with my feet, I'd keep my promises, too."

[5403]

Scott the explorer applied to Lloyd George for assistance for his last polar expedition. The Chancellor, as he then was, advised Scott to see a certain rich landowner who was interested in polar research. The explorer did so, and again called on Lloyd George.

"Were you successful?" asked the Chancellor.

"He's giving me a thousand," was the reply, "but he has undertaken to raise £50,000 if I can persuade you to come with me, and I'm to have a million if I manage to leave you there."

[5404]

Henry Ward Beecher said, that if any college should put two D's after his name he should feel inclined to put a dash between them and send them back.

[5405]

One day Luther Burbank was walking in his garden when he was accosted by an officious acquaintance who said:

"Well, what are you working on now?"

"Trying to cross an eggplant and milk-weed," said Burbank.

"And what under heaven do you expect from that?"

Burbank calmly resumed his walk. "Custard pie," he said.

[5406]

"Call that a kind man," said an actor, speaking of an absent acquaintance; "a man who is away from his family, and never sends them a farthing! Call that kindness!"

"Yes, *unremitting* kindness," Jerrold replied.

[5407]

"How could you have had brain fever?" sneered Huey Long, at a Republican Senator. "It takes strong brains to have brain fever."

"How did you find that out?" was the reply.

[5408]

Henry Ward Beecher asked Park Benjamin, the poet and humorist, why he never came to hear him preach. Benjamin replied, "Why, Beecher, the fact is, I have conscientious scruples against going to places of amusement on Sunday."

[5409]

Alfred Utley, the famous fiddler of pioneer days, was writing a letter one day when he asked a friend how to spell a certain word.

"Why don't you buy a dictionary?" asked the friend.

"What would I do with a dictionary? If I can't spell the words I couldn't find 'em, and if I can spell 'em I don't need a dictionary."

[5410]

Elwes, the noted miser, used to say, "If you keep one servant, your work is done; if you keep two, it is half done; and if you keep three, you may *do it yourself.*"

[5411]

Wendell Phillips was traveling through Ohio once when he fell in with a car full of ministers returning from a convention. One of the ministers, a southerner from Kentucky, was naturally not very cordial to the opinions of the great abolitionist and set out to embarrass Phillips. So, before the group of ministers, he said:

"You are Wendell Phillips, are you not?"

"Yes," answered the great abolitionist.

"And you are trying to free the niggers, aren't you?"

"Yes, sir; I am."

"Well, why do you preach your doctrines up here? Why don't you go over into Kentucky?"

"Excuse me, are you a preacher?"

"I am, sir."

"Are you trying to save souls from hell?"

"Yes, sir; that is my business."

"Well, why don't you go there then?" asked Phillips.

[5412]

Charles Lamb, the famous English essayist, stammered slightly when excited. A fond mother irritated him one day by dandling her infant in front of his face and gushing:

"Oh, Mr. Lamb, do tell me how you like babies."

"I like 'em b-b-boiled, ma'am. *B-boiled!*" he replied.

[5413]

Dwight W. Morrow caught a train from his home for New York. Arriving there, he forgot what he was supposed to do. So he wired his secretary.

"Why am I in New York? What am I supposed to do?"

His secretary replied that he was on his way to Princeton to deliver an address.

And he proceeded on his way.

[5414]

Judge Ben B. Lindsey was lunching one day—it was a very hot day—when a politician paused beside his table. "Judge," said he, "I see you're drinking coffee. That's a heating drink. In this weather you want to drink iced drinks, Judge—sharp iced drinks. Did you ever try gin and ginger ale?"

"No," said the Judge, smiling, "but I have tried several fellows who have."

[5415]

A boorish fellow took the liberty of questioning Alexandre Dumas rather too closely about his genealogical tree. "You are a quadroon, Mr. Dumas," he began.

"I am, sir," quietly replied Dumas.

"And your father?"

"Was a mulatto."

"And your grandfather?"

"A negro," hastily answered the dramatist, whose patience was waning.

"And may I inquire what your great grandfather was?"

"An ape, sir!" thundered Dumas. "An ape, sir; my pedigree commences where yours terminates."

[5416]

Franklin, when ambassador to France, being at a meeting of a literary society, and not well understanding the French when declaimed, determined to applaud when he saw a lady of his acquaintance express satisfaction.

When they had ceased, a little child, who understood the French, said to him, "But, grandpapa, you always applauded the loudest when they were *praising you!*"

Franklin laughed heartily and explained the matter.

[5417]

Mark Twain was visiting H. H. Rogers and the host led the humorist into his library.

"There," he said, as he pointed to a bust of white marble, "what do you think of that?" It was a bust of a young woman, coiling her hair—a graceful example of Italian sculpture. Mr. Clemens looked at it for a moment—then said:

"It isn't true to nature."

"Why not?" asked Mr. Rogers.

"She ought to have her mouth full of hairpins."

[5418]

Prof. Albert Einstein gave what he considered the best formula for success in life. "If a is success in life, I should say the formula is a equals x plus y plus z, x being *work* and y being play."

"And what is z?" inquired the interviewer.

"That," he answered, "is keeping your mouth shut."

[5419]

Boswell, dining one day with Dr. Johnson, asked him if he did not think that a good cook was more essential to the community than a good poet.

"I don't suppose," said the doctor, "that there's a *dog* in the town but what thinks so."

[5420]

Napoleon was one day searching for a book in his library, and at last discovered it on a shelf somewhat above his reach. Marshal Moncey, one of the tallest men in the army, stepped forward, saying: "Permit me, sire; I am higher than your majesty."

"You are longer, marshal," said the emperor, with a frown.

[5421]

George Ade, in his quality of cynical bachelor, said at the Chicago Athletic Club:

"I was sitting with a little girl of eight one afternoon. She looked up from her Hans Andersen and said:

" 'Does m-i-r-a-g-e spell marriage, Mr. Ade?'

" 'Yes, my child,' said I."

[5422]

Dean Briggs of Harvard, in an article in *The Atlantic Monthly* on President Eliot, tells how a clergyman who had attended the opening service in the college chapel, went straight to the rectory of Phillips Brooks to tell him how fine it was to see President Eliot singing:

"Am I a soldier of the Cross,
A follower of the Lamb?"

"Asking questions, as usual," said Dr. Brooks.

[5423]

One day some time ago a burglar was arrested in the home of a Washington matron, and the next evening at dinner she told Supreme Court Justice Oliver Wendell Holmes all about it. "I went right down to the jail and talked to that burglar," she said earnestly. "I told him how evil his way of life was, and how much happier he would be if he reformed. I talked to him for two hours."

"Poor man," murmured Holmes. "Poor man!"

[5424]

A lady who had forgotten that Whistler hated Turner said to him: "Oh, Mr. Whistler, my husband has discovered in a second-hand shop what he thinks are two real Turners. Will you come and tell us whether they are real Turners or imitation Turners?"

"Well, ma'am," replied Whistler, adjusting his monocle, "that is a fine distinction."

[5425]

When Maurice Margarot was tried at Edinburgh for sedition, the Lord Justice asked him, "Hae you ony counsel, mon?"

"No."

"Do you want to hae any appointed?"

"I only want an interpreter to make me *understand* what your lordships say."

[5426]

Among Sir William Rothenstein's famous sitters was Professor Einstein, whose portrait he did in Berlin.

"During one of the sittings," says Rothenstein, "a solemn stranger, looking, I thought, like an old tortoise, sat listening to Einstein, who, so far as I could understand, was putting forward tentative theories, his expressive face radiant, as he expounded his ideas.

"From time to time the stranger shook his heavy head, whereupon Einstein paused, reflected, and then started another strain of thought. When I was leaving, the presence of a third party was explained.

" 'He is my mathematician,' said Einstein, 'who examines problems which I put before him, and checks their validity. You see I am not myself a good mathematician!' "

[5427]

John L. Sullivan was asked why he had never taken to giving boxing lessons.

"Well, son, I tried it once," replied Mr. Sullivan. "A husky young man took one lesson from me and went home a little the worse for wear. When he came around for his second lesson he said: 'Mr. Sullivan, it was my idea to learn enough about boxing from you to be able to lick a certain young gentleman what I've got it in for. But I've changed my mind,' says he. 'If it's all the same to you Mr. Sullivan, I'll send this young gentleman down here to take the rest of my lessons for me.'"

[5428]

John Godfrey Saxe was walking up Broadway, when he was accosted by a friend, who asked where he was bound.

The poet replied, "To Boston this afternoon, *Deo volente.*"

"What route is that?" asked the inquirer.

"By way of Providence, of course," said Saxe.

[5429]

Upon a reception of the Marquis Lafayette in Philadelphia, during his last visit to this country, Colonel Forrest, one of the Revolutionary officers, upon being presented, burst into tears, upon which Judge Peters, who was standing at the side of the marquis, dryly observed:

"Why, Tom, I took you for a Forrest tree, but you turn out to be a weeping willow."

[5430]

Daniel Webster once good-naturedly wrote a letter for an ignorant servant, and when he had asked him, "Is there anything else you wish to say, Mike?"

The man scratched his head and finally said, "Yes, if you please. Just say they must excuse the poor scholarship and want of sense the letter shows."

[5431]

A composer once brought a manuscript to Rossini, who, on listening, every minute took off his hat and put it on again. The composer asked whether he was so warm.

"No," said Rossini: "but I am in the habit of taking off my hat whenever I meet an old acquaintance, and there are so many I remember in your composition, that I have continually to bow."

[5432]

Henry Clay, finding himself in need of money, went to the Riggs Bank and asked for the loan of $250 on his personal note. He was told that while his credit was perfectly good, it was the inflexible rule of the bank to require an indorser. The great statesman hunted up Daniel Webster and asked him to indorse the note.

"With pleasure," said Webster. "But I need some money myself. Why not make your note for five hundred, and you and I will split it?"

This they did. And today the note is in the Riggs Bank—unpaid.

[5433]

A friend once wrote Mark Twain a letter stating that he was in very bad health, and concluding: "Is there anything worse than having toothache and earache at the same time?"

The humorist wrote back. "Yes, rheumatism and Saint Vitus's dance."

[5434]

Mark Twain, in making an after-dinner speech, once said:

"Speaking o' fresh eggs, I am reminded of the town of Squash. In my early lecturing days I went to Squash to lecture in Temperance

Hall, arriving in the afternoon. The town seemed very poorly billed. I thought I'd find out if the people knew anything at all about what was in store for them. So I turned in at the general store.

" 'Good afternoon, friend,' I said to the general storekeeper. 'Any entertainment here tonight to help a stranger while away his evening?'

"The storekeeper, who was sorting mackerel, straightened up, wiped his briny hands on his apron, and said:

" 'I expect there's goin' to be a lecture. I been sellin' eggs all day.' "

[5435]

Horace Greeley's illegible handwriting is amusingly illustrated in the following letters:

Tribune Office, New York City.
May 12, 1869.
Mr. M. B. Castle,
Sandwich, Ill.
Dear Sir:

I am overworked and growing old. I shall be 60 next Feb. 3. On the whole, it seems I must decline to lecture henceforth except in this immediate vicinity, if I do at all. I cannot promise to visit Illinois on that errand, certainly not now.

Yours truly,
Horace Greeley.

The reply to this letter was:

Sandwich, Ill.
May 16, 1869.
Hon. Horace Greeley,
New York Tribune.
Dear Sir:

Your acceptance to lecture before our association next winter came to hand this morning. Your penmanship not being the plainest, it took some time to translate it; but we succeeded and would say your time, Feb. 3, and the terms, $60, are entirely satisfactory. As you suggest, we may be able to get you other engagements.

Respectfully,
M. B. Castle.

[5436]

A lady, after performing, with the most brilliant execution, a sonata on the pianoforte, in the presence of Dr. Johnson, turning to the philosopher, took the liberty of asking him if he was fond of music.

"No, madam," replied the doctor; "but of all *noises,* I think music is the least disagreeable."

[5437]

Paderewski once visited a small town in upstate New York. While strolling along one afternoon, he heard a piano, and, following the sound, came to a house on which was a sign reading:

"Miss Smith. Piano lessons 25 cents an hour."

Pausing to listen he heard the young women trying to play one of Chopin's nocturnes, and not succeeding very well. Paderewski walked up to the house and knocked. Miss Smith came to the door and recognized him at once. Delighted, she invited him in and he sat down and played the nocturne as he only could, afterward spending an hour in correcting her mistakes. Miss Smith thanked him and he departed.

Some months later he returned to the town, and again he took the same walk. He soon came to the home of Miss Smith, and, looking at the sign, he read:

"Miss Smith (Pupil of Paderewski). Piano lessons $1.00 an hour."

[5438]

"My rubber," said Nat Goodwin, the famous actor, describing a Turkish bath that he once had in Mexico, "was a very strong man. He laid me on a slab and kneaded me and punched me and banged me in a most emphatic way. When it was over and I had gotten up, he came up behind me, before my sheet was adjusted, and gave me three resounding slaps on the back with the palm of his enormous hand.

" 'What the blazes are you doing?' I gasped, staggering.

" 'No offense, sir,' said the man, 'it was only to let the office know that I was ready for the next bather. You see, sir, the bell's out of order in this room.' "

[5439]

Paderewski, the famous pianist, once praised a young society man who was distinguished as a polo player for his clever playing.

The young man said it was different indeed from Paderewski's performance!

"Oh," answered Paderewski, "the difference between us is perfectly clear. You are a dear soul who plays polo, while I am a poor Pole who plays solo."

[5440]

A gentleman was describing to Douglas Jerrold the story of his courtship and marriage—how his wife had been brought up in a convent, and was on the point of taking the veil, when his presence burst upon her enraptured sight, and she accepted him as her husband. Jerrold listened to the end of the story, and then quietly remarked, "Ah! she evidently thought you better than *nun*."

[5441]

One of the Kembles made his first appearance on the stage as an opera singer. His voice was, however, so bad, that at a rehearsal the conductor of the orchestra called out, "Mr. Kemble! Mr. Kemble! you are murdering the music!"

"My dear sir," was the quiet rejoinder, "it is far better to murder it outright, than to keep on *beating it as you do.*"

[5442]

Booth, the tragedian, had a broken nose. A lady once remarked to him, "I like your acting, Mr. Booth; but, to be frank with you—*I can't get over your nose!*"

"No wonder, madam," replied he, "the bridge is gone!"

[5443]

Sheridan was once staying at the house of an elderly maiden lady in the country, who wanted more of his company than he was willing to give.

Proposing one day to take a stroll with him, he excused himself on account of the badness of the weather. Shortly afterwards she met him sneaking out alone. "So, Mr. Sheridan," said she, "it has cleared up."

"Just a *little,* ma'am—enough for one, but not enough for two."

[5444]

Sheridan was one day much annoyed by a fellow-member of the House of Commons, who kept crying out every few minutes, "Hear! hear!" During the debate he took occasion to describe a political contemporary that wished to play rogue, but had only sense enough to act fool. "Where," exclaimed he, with great emphasis—"Where shall we find a more foolish knave or a more *knavish fool* than he?"

"*Hear! hear!*" was shouted by the troublesome member.

Sheridan turned round, and, thanking him for the prompt information, sat down amid a general roar of laughter.

[5445]

The regular routine of clerkly business ill suited the literary tastes and the wayward habits of Charles Lamb.

Once, at the India House, a superior said to him, "I have remarked, Mr. Lamb, that you come very *late* to the office."

"Yes, sir," replied the wit, "but you must remember that I go away *early*."

The oddness of the excuse silenced the reprover.

[5446]

George Ade had finished his after-dinner speech at a gathering of notables, and when he had seated himself a well-known lawyer who was also an amateur wit, rose, shoved his hands deep into his trousers' pockets, as was his habit and laughingly inquired of those present:

"Doesn't it strike the company as a little unusual that a professional humorist should be funny?"

When the laugh had subsided, Ade drawled out:

"Doesn't it strike the company as a little unusual that a lawyer should have his hands in his own pockets?"

[5447]

Quiller-Couch in a lecture at Cambridge condemned first the fancy phrases so common in the magazines and popular novels,—

and then he said that these phrases were as absurd to cultivated ears as the telegram that the babu sent from Bombay to announce the death of his mother.

"The babu's telegram ran:

"'Regret to announce that hand which rocked the cradle has kicked the bucket.'"

[5448]

Chesterfield was at a rout in France where Voltaire was one of the guests. Chesterfield seemed to be gazing about the brilliant circle of ladies. Voltaire accosted him: "My lord, I know you are a judge, which are the more beautiful, the English or the French ladies?"

"Upon my word," replied Chesterfield, with his usual presence of mind, "I am no judge of paintings."

Some time afterward Voltaire, being in London, happened to be at a nobleman's party with Chesterfield; a lady in the company, prodigiously rouged, directed her whole discourse to Voltaire, and engrossed his whole conversation. Chesterfield came up, tapped him on the shoulder, and said: "Sir, take care that you are not captivated."

"My lord," replied the French wit, "I scorn to be taken by an English craft under French colors."

[5449]

When Charles Darwin was visiting the country house of a friend, the two boys of the family thought they would play a joke on the scientist. So they caught a butterfly, a grasshopper, a beetle, and a centipede, and out of these creatures they made a strange composite insect. They took the centipede's body, the butterfly's wings, the grasshopper's legs, and the beetle's head, and they glued them together

THE PROFESSIONS

549

carefully. Then, with their new bug in a box, they knocked at Darwin's door.

"We caught this bug in a field," they said. "Can you tell us what kind of a bug it is, Mr. Darwin?"

Darwin looked at the bug and then looked at the boys. He smiled slightly.

"Did you notice whether it hummed when you caught it, boys?" he asked.

"Yes," they answered, nudging one another.

"Then," said Darwin, "it is a hum-bug."

[5450]

A line in one of Moore's songs reads thus: "Our couch shall be roses bespangled with dew." To which a sensible girl, according to Landor, replied: " 'Twould give me the rheumatiz, and so it would you!"

[5451]

At one time J. M. Barrie attended a rehearsal accompanied by a friend, at which a lively discussion arose between two of the actresses as to the possession of the center of the stage during a certain scene. While the manager poured oil upon the troubled waters, Barrie sat carelessly swinging his feet from the rail of an adjoining box. Finally the friend, who was an exceedingly temperamental fellow, could stand it no longer.

"Good Lord, Barrie!" he exclaimed earnestly, "this will ruin your play! Why don't you settle matters yourself? You could if you only would."

Barrie shook his head gravely, but with a merry twinkle in his eye. "No," he replied, "the Lord made only one man who could ever manage the sun and the moon, and you remember even he let the stars alone."

[5452]

When Paderewski was on his last visit to America he was in a Boston suburb, when he was approached by a bootblack who called:

"Shine?"

The great pianist looked down at the youth whose face was streaked with grime and said:

"No, my lad, but if you will wash your face I will give you a quarter."

"All right!" exclaimed the youth, who forthwith ran to a neighboring trough and made his ablutions. When he returned Paderewski held out the quarter, which the boy took but immediately handed back, saying:

"Here, Mister, you take it yourself and get your hair cut."

[5453]

Booth Tarkington told this story concerning himself:

"I was strolling around an artists' Red Cross fair when two pretty girls of sixteen or so came up and one asked me for my autograph. 'I haven't got a fountain pen,' I said, much flattered. 'Will a pencil do?'

" 'Yes,' said the girl, and so I took out my pencil and signed my name in the morocco-bound book that she had given me.

"The young lady studied the signature with a frown. Then she looked up and said: 'Aren't you Robert W. Chambers?'

" 'No,' said I, 'I'm Booth Tarkington.'

"The disgusted young girl turned to her friend with a shrug of the shoulders, and said, 'Lend me your eraser, May.' "

[5454]

Here are three Samuel Goldwyn stories:

Goldwyn in a talk to his employees started off with: "Gentlemen, I want you to know that I am not always right—but I am never wrong."

And the one about some visitor admiring his wife's hands. "Yes," said Goldwyn, "she has got beautiful hands—I am thinking of having a bust made of them."

And when he decided not to join a certain undertaking by several Hollywood producers, Goldwyn said: "Gentlemen, include me out!"

[5455]

John Randolph and Henry Clay once had a quarrel in the Senate at Washington. For several weeks they did not speak, when one day they met on Pennsylvania Avenue. Each saw the other coming up the side walk which was very narrow at that particular point, and each was meditating as to how far he would turn out for the other to pass. As Randolph came up he looked the grand old Kentuckian straight in the eye and, keeping the sidewalk, hissed:

"I never turn out for scoundrels!"

"I always do," said Mr. Clay as he stepped politely out into the mud and let Randolph have the walk.

[5456]

Alphonsus, King of Naples, had a court fool whose custom it was to enter all the stupidities committed by his superiors in a large notebook. One day the King entrusted a huge sum of money to a Moor in his employ with which to travel in Arabia and buy horses. The fool

jotted this incident down in his book. Idly thumbing its pages shortly after, the King discovered the entry and called the jester to his presence to explain. "Well, sire," began the fool, "it was monstrously silly of you to give a man so much cold cash—you'll never see it again!"

"And if he does come back?" asked the monarch.

"Then I'll cross out your name in my record and put his there instead."

[5457]

Sir Lewis Morris was complaining to Oscar Wilde about the neglect of his poems by the press. "It is a complete conspiracy of silence against me, a conspiracy of silence. What ought I to do, Oscar?"

"Join it," replied Wilde.

[5458]

Benjamin Franklin, having been touched by an impecunious relative to the extent of $50, was asked for a sheet of paper so that the borrower could give him a note for the amount. "What!" exclaimed Franklin, "do you want to waste my stationery as well as my money?"

[5459]

One is not even safe in bed, for as Mark Twain inquired: "Do not more people die there than anywhere else?"

[5460]

"I am no hand at public speaking," said Wilbur Wright at a banquet in Paris in honor of the Wright Brothers' first demonstration of a successful airplane flight in France, "and on this occasion I must content myself with a few words. As I sat here listening to the speaker who preceded me, I have heard comparisons made to the eagle, to the swallow and to the hawk, as typifying skill and speed in the mastery of the air; but somehow or other I could not keep from thinking of another bird, which, of all the ornithological kingdom is the poorest flier and the best talker. I refer to the parrot."

[5461]

An American once wrote to Kipling, saying: "I hear that you are retailing literature at one dollar a word. I enclose one dollar for which please send me a sample."

Kipling kept the dollar and wrote, "Thanks."

Two weeks later the American wrote, "Sold the 'Thanks' anecdote for two dollars. Enclosed please find forty-five cents in stamps, that being half the profits on the transaction, less the postage."

[5462]

Rachmaninoff told in New York the other day a story about his boyhood.

"When I was a very little fellow," he said, "I played at a reception at a Russian count's, and, for an urchin of seven, I flatter myself that I swung through Beethoven's 'Kreutzer Sonata' pretty successfully.

"The 'Kreutzer,' you know, has in it several long and impressive rests. Well, in one of these rests the count's wife, a motherly old lady, leaned forward, patted me on the shoulder, and said: 'Play us something you know, dear.'"

[5463]

Professor Albert Einstein's favorite story concerns himself.

In a certain debating society, the subject of relativity came up. One member took it upon himself to elucidate the all-absorbing scientific theory. He explained, propounded and twisted the subject for an hour. When he had finished from sheer exhaustion, a listener spoke up.

"You know, after listening to you, I think you are really greater than Einstein himself on his own topic. According to statistics, only twelve men in the whole world understand Einstein—but *nobody* understands you."

[5464]

Mark Twain and Chauncey M. Depew once went abroad on the same ship. When the ship was a few days out they were both invited to a dinner, and when speech-making time came, Mark Twain had the first chance. He spoke twenty minutes and made a great hit. Then it was Mr. Depew's turn.

"Mr. Toastmaster and Ladies and Gentlemen," said the famous raconteur as he rose, "Before this dinner Mark Twain and myself made an agreement to trade speeches. He has just delivered my speech, and I thank you for the pleasant manner in which you received it. I regret to say that I have lost the notes of his speech and cannot remember anything he was to say."

Then he sat down, and there was much laughter.

[5465]

Eugene Field was at a dinner in London when the conversation turned to the subject of lynching in the United States.

It was the general opinion that a large percentage of Yankees met death at the end of a rope. Finally the hostess turned to Field and asked:

"You, sir, must have often seen these affairs?"

"Oh, yes," replied Field, "hundreds of them."

"Then do tell us about a lynching you have seen yourself," broke in half a dozen voices at once.

"Well, the night before I sailed for England," said Field, "I was giving a dinner party at a hotel to a party of intimate friends when a colored waiter spilled a plate of soup over the gown of a lady at an adjoining table. The gown was utterly ruined, and the gentlemen of her party at once seized the waiter, tied a rope around his neck, and at a signal from the injured lady swung him into the air."

"Horrible!" said the hostess with a shudder. "And did you see all this yourself?"

"Well, no," admitted Field apologetically. "Just at that moment I happened to be downstairs killing the Negro chef for putting mustard in the blanc mange."

[5466]

Talleyrand, the great diplomatist, one day found himself between Madame de Stael and Madame Recamier, both intimate friends, both celebrated. "You say charming things to us both, but which do you prefer?" said Madame de Stael suddenly.

"Madame, such a question is a veritable ambush. Take care the penal code."

"Prince, no subterfuge here! Which do you prefer, my friend, or myself? Come, speak; is it the brunette or the blonde?"

"It will be her who will honor me with a look."

"What, still diplomatic? Well, I will put the question in another form. Suppose while sailing on the Seine this evening, the boat should upset, and we should be in danger of drowning, which one would you help?"

"Both at once, or the one which was in the greatest danger."

"But, monseigneur, be frank for once in your life. Suppose the peril to be equally imminent."

"Well, I would give my right hand to the baroness and the left to Madame Recamier."

"But if you could save only one —one of us—do you understand?"

"Well, madame, you who know so many things, I suppose you can swim," replied Talleyrand.

[5467]

President Taft told this story on himself. "There is a lad of my acquaintance in New Haven," he said, "who used to bite his nails. 'See here,' said his nurse to him one day, 'if you keep biting your nails like that, do you know what will happen to you?'

" 'No,' said the youngster. What?'

" 'You'll swell up like a balloon and burst.'

"The boy believed his nurse. He stopped biting his nails at once. About a month after the discontinuance of his habit he encountered me at luncheon. He surveyed me with stern disapproval. Then he walked over and said to me accusingly:

" 'You bite your nails!' "

[5468]

Will Rogers pulled this one on an unsuspecting waiter:

"I say, waiter, there's a roach in my soup that is drowning."

The head-waiter was called over at this calamity, especially to so distinguished a guest. Very much flabbergasted and upset he asked of his guest, "Is there anything I can do to make this horrible occurrence all right with you, sir?"

"Yes," smiled Mr. Rogers, shifting his gum, "next time you put a roach in my soup either teach him how to swim or strap a life preserver on his back!"

[5469]

While driving through the East Side one day Otto Kahn, the banker, saw a big sign painted on the front of a little clothing store, which read:

A. COHEN
Cousin of
OTTO KAHN

Mr. Kahn was naturally indignant and called in his attorney and demanded that he take steps immediately to have the honored name of Kahn removed from the sign, even if it cost $5,000 to do it. A few days later Mr. Kahn drove by the same store again, to see what had been done about the offending sign. He found it had been changed to

A. COHEN
Formerly Cousin of
OTTO KAHN

[5470]

Leonard Bacon, the theologian, was attending a conference and some assertions he made in his address were vehemently objected to by a member of the opposition. "Why," he expostulated, "I never heard of such a thing in all my life!"

"Mr. Moderator," rejoined Bacon calmly, "I cannot allow my opponent's ignorance, however vast, to offset my knowledge, however small."

[5471]

Benjamin Franklin, when a child, found the long graces said by his father irksome. One day, after the winter's provisions had been salted, he said, "I think, father, if you said grace over the whole cask, once for all, it would be a vast saving of time."

[5472]

When Mark Twain went to borrow a book from a neighbor's library the owner said he would be happy to accommodate him again, but he had adopted a rule that any volume taken from his library must be used on the premises.

The next week the neighbor dropped over for the loan of Mark's lawn mower. "Take it and welcome!" chirruped Mark, "only under a recently-adopted policy it is not to be used away from my own lawn!"

[5473]

Balzac was once lying awake in bed, when he saw a man enter his room cautiously, and attempt to pick the lock of his writing desk. The rogue was not a little disconcerted at hearing a loud laugh from the occupant of the apartment, whom he supposed asleep.

"Why do you laugh?" asked the thief.

"I am laughing, my good fellow," said Balzac, "to think what pains you are taking, and what risk you run, in hope of finding money by night in a desk where the lawful owner can never find any by day."

The thief "evacuated Flanders" at once.

[5474]

A wag, reading in one of Brigham Young's manifestoes, "that the great resources of Utah are her women," exclaimed, "It is very evident that the prophet is disposed to *husband his resources*."

[5475]

Ambassador Walter Hines Page was at one time editor of The World's Work and, like all editors, was obliged to refuse a great many stories. A lady once wrote him:

"Sir: You sent back last week a story of mine. I know that you did not read the story, for as a test I had pasted together pages 18, 19, and 20, and the story came back with these pages still pasted; and so I know you are a fraud and turn down stories without reading same."

Mr. Page wrote back:

"Madame: At breakfast when I open an egg I don't have to eat the whole egg to discover it is bad."

[5476]

Senator Reed Smoot once spoke before a large crowd of Swedes. There was but little applause. He was followed by a man who spoke to them in their native tongue. The applause was deafening, and Smoot cheered as loudly as the best of them. Then, still clapping his hands, he leaned over to the chairman of the meeting. "What did he say?" he asked.

"He was interpreting your speech to them," replied the chairman gravely.

[5477]

Doctor Hill, a noted wit, physician, and man of letters, having quarreled with the members of the Royal Society, who had refused to admit him as an associate, resolved to avenge himself.

At the time that Bishop Berkeley had issued his work on the marvelous virtues of tar-water, Hill addressed to their secretary a letter purporting to be from a country-surgeon, and reciting the particulars of a cure which he had effected. "A sailor," he wrote, "*broke* his leg, and applied to me for help. I bound together the broken portions, and washed them with the celebrated *tar-water*. Almost immediately the sailor felt the beneficial effects of this remedy, and it was not long before his leg was completely *healed!*"

The letter was read, and discussed at the meetings of the Royal Society, and caused considerable difference of opinion. Papers were written for and against the tar-water and the restored leg, when a second letter arrived from the (pretended) country practitioner:

"In my last I omitted to mention that the broken limb of the sailor was a *wooden leg!*"

[5478]

On a visit to New York City M. Mumm dined with friends at a Park Avenue restaurant. The proprietor was obsequious. Would M. Mumm, he wondered, care for champagne? He had a special treat. Some of M. Mumm's own 1915, in fact.

"An excellent wine," observed M. Mumm, after making the connoisseur's tests. "Truly an excellent champagne—but 1915 was the year when I didn't make any."

[5479]

Champ Clark once told the story of an old southern colonel who, returning home after a considerable absence, asked a friend, "What's the news?"

"Well, the legislature has passed a law makin' it a crime to shoot a Republican," the friend answered.

"You don't say!" exclaimed the colonel, in some amazement. "In what month?"

[5480]

Bernard Shaw is a past-master at the ready retort. A young woman sitting next to him at dinner remarked: "What a wonderful thing is youth!"

"Yes—And what a crime to waste it on children," G. B. S. replied sagely.

[5481]

When Mark Twain edited a newspaper in Missouri, one of his subscribers wrote him that he had found a spider in his paper and wished to know whether it meant good luck or bad.

Twain replied: "Finding a spider in your paper is neither good luck nor bad. The spider was merely looking over our paper to see which merchant was not advertising, so that he could go to that store, spin his web across the door and lead a life of undisturbed peace ever afterward!"

[5482]

Somebody once asked Professor Charles Townsend Copeland (Copey to his friends at Harvard) why he lived on the top floor of Hollis Hall, in his small, dusty old rooms, and suggested that he move.

"No," said Copey, "no, I shall always live on the top floor. It is the only place in Cambridge where God alone is above me." Then after a pause, "He's busy—but He's quiet."

[5483]

Gibbon, the historian, was one day attending the trial of Warren Hastings in Westminster Hall, and Sheridan, having perceived him there, took occasion to mention "the luminous author of 'The Decline and Fall of the Roman Empire.' " After he had finished, one of his friends reproached him with flattering Gibbon.

"Why, what did I say of him?" asked Sheridan.

"You called him the luminous author."

"Luminous. Oh, I meant voluminous!"

[5484]

In pre-Hitler days, in Berlin, Herr Remarque, the author of "All Quiet on the Western Front," was talking to an American girl.

The American, speaking in German, asked Remarque why he had never visited the United States. His answer was that he knew only a few sentences in English.

"What are the sentences?" inquired the girl.

Whereupon Remarque, speaking slowly in somewhat guttural English, said: "How do you do? I love you. Forgive me. Forget me. Ham and eggs, please."

"Sakes alive!" ejaculated the American girl. "Why, with that vocabulary you could tour my country from Maine to California."

[5485]

The story is told of an extra man who once worked in a motion-picture with John Barrymore. It seems that the extra crashed the gates of a party where Barrymore was a guest. Slapping him on the back he said: "Hello, Barrymore, old boy! How are you?"

Barrymore coolly replied: "Don't be formal. Call me kid."

[5486]

When in England, Governor Foss, of Massachusetts, had luncheon with a prominent Englishman noted for boasting of his ancestry. Taking a coin from his pocket, the Englishman said: "My great-great-grandfather was made a lord by the king whose picture you see on this shilling."

"Indeed!" replied the governor, smiling, as he produced another coin. "What a coincidence! My great-great-grandfather was made an angel by the Indian whose picture you see on this cent."

[5487]
A nobleman wished Garrick to be candidate for the representation of a borough in Parliament. "No, my lord," said the actor. "I would rather play the part of a great man on the stage than the part of a fool in Parliament."

[5488]
Mark Twain told this story to prove that he was a success right from the start. At the time this incident occurred he was a compositor on a small country newspaper. A few hours before the afternoon edition went to press, a man came in to place a classified ad in regard to his lost dog. "Do you think I put that ad in our paper?" said Twain. "Why man, I went right out, found that dog before the afternoon edition was on the street and claimed the reward."

[5489]
Daniel Webster was the guest at dinner of a solicitous hostess who insisted rather annoyingly that he was eating nothing at all, that he had no appetite, that he was not making out a meal. Finally, Webster wearied of her hospitable chatter, and addressed her in his most ponderous senatorial manner:

"Madam, permit me to assure you that I sometimes eat more than at other times, but never less."

[5490]
"No man is so well known as he thinks he is," once said Enrico Caruso, the world-famed tenor. "While motoring in New York State," continued the great singer, "the automobile broke down and I sought refuge in a farmhouse while the car was being repaired. I became friendly with the farmer, who asked me my name and I told him it was Caruso.

"The farmer leaped to his feet and seized me by the hand. 'Little did I think I would see a man like you in this here humble kitchen, sir!' he exclaimed. 'Caruso. The great traveler, Robinson Caruso!'"

[5491]
Leslie Howard insists that it once happened in a London theater where he was getting experience in repertory. The company put on different shows every night and sometimes two different shows a day. This was most confusing to the cast.

One afternoon Howard forgot his lines and rushed backstage to the company director. "Quick," the star asked, "what's my line?"

"Quick," the director returned, "what's the play?"

[5492]
When John Quincy Adams was eighty years of age, he met in the streets of Boston an old friend, who shook his trembling hand and said, "Good morning, and how is John Quincy Adams today?"

"Thank you," replied the ex-President, "John Quincy Adams himself is well, quite well, I thank you. But the house in which he lives at present is becoming quite dilapidated. It is tottering upon its foundation. Time and the seasons have nearly destroyed it. Its roof is pretty well worn out. Its walls are much shattered, and it trembles with every wind. The old tenement is becoming almost uninhabitable, and I think John Quincy Adams will have to move out of it soon. But he himself is quite well, quite well!"

[5493]

A story of Winston Churchill— told by Gertrude Atherton:

"Shortly after he left the Conservative side of the House (of Commons) for the Liberal, he was taking a certain young woman down to dinner, when she looked up at him coquettishly, and remarked with the audacity of her kind:

" 'There are two things I don't like about you, Mr. Churchill.'

" 'And what are they?'

" 'Your new politics and mustache.'

" 'My dear madam,' he replied suavely, 'pray do not disturb yourself. You are not likely to come in contact with either.' "

[5494]

On the way to the office of his publishers one crisp fall morning, James Whitcomb Riley met an unusually large number of acquaintances who commented conventionally upon the fine weather. This unremitting applause amused him. When greeted at the office with "Nice day, Mr. Riley," he smiled broadly.

"Yes," he agreed. "Yes, I've heard it very highly spoken of."

[5495]

An editor met the late Sir James Barrie, the famous author of *Peter Pan,* at a dinner.

"Sir James," he said, "I suppose some of your plays do better than others. They are not all successes, I imagine."

Barrie leaned toward him confidentially. "No," he said, his eyes twinkling, "some Peter out and some Pan out."

[5496]

William Dean Howell is credited with telling this Shakespeare story:

"In Stratford," he says, "during one of the Shakespeare jubilees, an American tourist approached an aged villager in a smock, and said: 'Who is this chap Shakespeare, anyway?'

" 'He were a writer, sir.'

" 'Oh, but there are lots of writers. Why do you make such an infernal fuss over this one? Wherever I turn I see Shakespeare hotels, Shakespeare cakes, Shakespeare chocolates, Shakespeare shoes. What the deuce did he write—magazine stories, attacks on the government, shady novels?'

" 'No, sir; oh, no, sir,' said the aged villager. 'I understand he writ for the Bible, sir.' "

[5497]

Joseph Chamberlain was the guest of honor at a dinner in an important city. The Mayor presided, and when coffee was being served the Mayor leaned over and touched Mr. Chamberlain, saying, "Shall we let the people enjoy themselves a little longer, or had we better have your speech now?"

[5498]

Soon after Al Smith was elected governor of New York for the first time, he went to Sing Sing to visit the state's prison. After being shown the buildings by the warden, the governor was asked to speak to the inmates. He was embarrassed, having never spoken to the inmates of a prison before, and did not know quite how to begin. Finally, he said: "My fellow citizens." Then he remembered that when one goes to state's prison, he is no longer a citizen. So, the governor was even more embarrassed, and said: "My fellow convicts." That did not sound just right, so Al said, "Well, anyhow, I'm glad to see so many of you here."

[5499]
There is a story of a visit John Barrymore paid to a haberdasher in Hollywood. After ordering this and that, he turned to leave.

"And your name?" the clerk asked innocently.

"Barrymore," was the chill reply.

"Which Barrymore, please?"

John surveyed him coldly. "Ethel."

[5500]
Lord Kelvin, the great Scotch scientist, once paid a visit with a friend to some well-known electrical works. They were escorted over the workshops by the senior foreman, a man of much intelligence and an enthusiastic electrician. Entirely unaware of his visitor's identity, he minutely explained the details of the plant and machinery, and lectured him in his *rôle* of layman quite professionally. Lord Kelvin's friend was on the point of interrupting several times, but an amused signal from the great master of electricity kept him silent. When the tour of inspection was complete, Lord Kelvin quitely turned to the foreman, and asked: "What, then is electricity?" This was a poser for the man, who, somewhat shamefaced, confessed that he could not say. "Well, well," said Lord Kelvin gently, "that is the only thing about electricity which you and I don't know."

[5501]
Robert Louis Stevenson, while in San Francisco was explaining to a friend at a restaurant a peculiarity of the local waiters which was that under no circumstances would they admit that they did not have anything that might be called for on the bill-of-fare.

"They will take your order for a slice of the moon," said he, "and go away as if they meant to fetch it, and then come back and say that they are just out of it."

To prove it he called the waiter and said:

"A double order of broiled behemoth."

"Yes, sir," said the waiter, "will you have it rare or well done?"

"Well done," said Stevenson.

Pretty soon the waiter returned. "I am very sorry, but we are just out of behemoth."

"What, no more behemoth?" asked the novelist in feigned astonment.

The waiter lowered his voice.

"We have some more, sir," he whispered confidentially, "but the truth is, I would not bring it to you as it was not quite fresh."

[5502]
To Oscar Hammerstein, famous impresario, came a disheveled looking person and unfolded this plan:

"I will do an act on your stage that will be the talk of the world. You can advertise it in advance and you can charge a hundred dollars a ticket. Now here is my proposition: If you'll put fifty thousand dollars in escrow for my wife, I'll go on your stage, and in full view of your audience, commit suicide."

"Marvelous," answered Hammerstein, "But what will you do for an encore?"

[5503]
Somebody in Brattleboro came down to New York to ask Fisk for a donation to help them build a new fence around the graveyard where he is now buried.

"What in thunder do you want a new fence for?" exclaimed the Colonel. "Why, that old fence will keep the dead people in, and live people will keep out as long as they can, any way!"

[5504]
When Bishop Phillips Brooks sailed from America on his last trip to Europe, a friend jokingly remarked that while abroad he might discover some new religion to bring home with him. "But be careful of it, Bishop Brooks," remarked a listening friend; "it may be difficult to get your new religion through the Custom House."

"I guess not," replied the Bishop, laughingly, "for we may take it for granted that any new religion popular enough to import will have no duties attached to it."

[5505]
Chauncey M. Depew once told this story:

"Last time I was traveling in the South I had to put up overnight at a second-rate hotel in western Georgia. I said to the clerk when I entered, 'Where shall I autograph?'

" 'Autograph?' said the clerk.

" 'Yes; sign my name, you know.'

" 'Oh, right here.' As I was signing my name in the register, in came three roughly-clothed, unshorn fellows immediately recog-

nizable as Georgia crackers. One of the men advanced to the desk.

" 'Will you autograph?' asked the clerk, his face aglow with the pleasure that comes from the consciousness of intellectual superiority.

" 'Certainly,' said the Georgia cracker, his face no less radiant than that of the clerk: 'mine's rye.'

"There was no escape for the clerk and he treated with as good grace as he could command under the circumstances. Next morning I said to him: 'That was too bad, the way you got caught last night.'

" 'Well, I suppose I shouldn't complain,' he replied; 'but the next time I speak a foreign language in my own country, I'll know what I'm talking about.' "

[5506]
Eugene Field, sad of countenance and ready of tongue, once strayed into a New York restaurant and seated himself for luncheon. A voluble waiter came to Field and said, "Coffee, tea-chocolate, ham-an' 'ggs-beefsteak-mutton-chop fish-balls-hash'n'-beans," and much more to the same purpose.

Field looked at him long and solemnly, and at last replied:

"Oh, friend, I want none of these things. All I want is an orange and a few kind words."

[5507]
"How do you grow old so gracefully?" an admirer asked Alexandre Dumas.

"Madam, I give all my time to it."

[5508]
Ed Wynn, the comedian, is to blame for the story about the American hero who won a Croix de Guerre but he was so ugly they couldn't find a French general to kiss him.

[5509]

Mark Twain constantly received letters and photographs from men who had been told that they looked like him. One was from Florida, and the likeness, as shown by the man's picture, was really remarkable—so remarkable, indeed, that Mr. Clemens sent the following acknowledgment:

"My Dear Sir: I thank you very much for your letter and the photograph. In my opinion you are certainly more like me than other of my doubles. In fact, I am sure that if you stood before me in a mirrorless frame I could shave by you."

[5510]

A drunken Congressman said to Horace Greeley one day: "I am a self-made man."

"Then, sir," replied Greeley, "the fact relieves the Almighty of a great responsibility."

[5511]

The story is told of Isadora Duncan, famous dancer, and George Bernard Shaw, famous Irish wit and dramatist, that the dancer once wrote to him with the proposal that, according to eugenics, it was to be regretted that they could not together be the parents of a child. "Think," she said, "what a child it would be, with my body and your brain."

Shaw was equal to the occasion, for he retorted, as the story goes: "I know, but suppose the child was so unlucky as to have my body and your brain?"

[5512]

Once when Henry Ward Beecher was in the midst of an eloquent political speech some wag in the audience crowed lie a cock. It was done to perfection and the audience was convulsed with laughter. The great orator's friends felt uneasy as to his reception of the interruption. But Mr. Beecher stood perfectly calm. He stopped speaking, listened till the crowing ceased, and while the audience was laughing he pulled out his watch. Then he said: "That's strange. My watch says it is only ten o'clock. But there can't be any mistake about it. It must be morning for the instincts of the lower animals are absolutely infallible."

[5513]

George Ade, with a fellow American, was traveling in the Orient, and his companion one day fell into a heated argument with an old Arab. Ade's friend complained to him afterward that although he had spent years in studying Arabic in preparation for this trip he could not understand a word that the native said.

"Never mind," replied Ade consolingly. "You see, the old duffer hasn't a tooth in his head, and he was only talking gum-Arabic."

[5514]

General Lee one day found Dr. Cutting, the army surgeon, who was a handsome and dressy man, arranging his cravat complacently before a glass. "Cutting," said Lee, "you must be the happiest man in creation, because you are in love with yourself, and you have not a rival upon earth."

[5515]

Robert Ingersoll was famous for the library of infidel books which he possesses. One day a reporter called on Ingersoll for an interview, and among other questions, asked: "Would you mind telling me how much your library cost you, Mr.

Ingersoll?" Looking over at the shelves, he answered: "Well, my boy, these books cost me, anyhow, the governorship of Illinois, and perhaps the Presidency of the United States!"

[5516]

A woman once took Dr. Johnson to task for putting improper words in his dictionary.

"Madam," said the distinguished lexicographer, "you have been looking for them."

[5517]

When Carter Glass first began to make himself heard, in 1913, in caucuses of his party in the Senate, he talked rather ponderously and frigidly. On one such occasion, the subject seemed to warm him up and soon he was not emphatic but pugnacious. At this point one of his partisans in the causus shouted:

"Give 'em hell, Carter!"

Mr. Glass' reply has become historic. It was:

"Hell? Why use dynamite when insect powder will do?"

[5518]

At a social tea at which Dr. Oliver Wendell Holmes was present, the hostess, who had put the cream of her acquaintance on parade and quite expected and looked for effusive admiration from the great man, said to him as he was about to leave:

"Well, doctor, what do you think of afternoon tea?"

He replied in these four strikingly graphic words:

"It is giggle—gabble—gobble—git!"

[5519]

Newell Dwight Hillis, famous New York preacher and author, some years ago took charge of the First Presbyterian Church of Evanston, Illinois. Shortly after going there he required the services of a physician, and on the advice of one of his parishioners called in a doctor noted for his ability properly to emphasize a good story, but who attended church very rarely. He proved very satisfactory to the young preacher, but for some reason could not be induced to render a bill. Finally Dr. Hillis, becoming alarmed at the inroads the bill might make in his modest stipend, went to the physician and said, "See here, Doctor, I must know how much I owe you."

After some urging, the physician replied: "Well, I'll tell you what I'll do with you, Hillis. They say you're a pretty good preacher, and you seem to think I am a fair doctor, so I'll make this bargain with you. I'll do all I can to keep you out of heaven if you do all you can to keep me out of hell, and it won't cost either of us a cent. Is it a go?"

[5520]

William Penn, the great Pennsylvania Quaker, was once advising a drunkard to leave off his habit of drinking intoxicating liquors.

"Can you tell me how to do it?"

"Yes," answered Penn, "it is just as easy as to open thy hand, friend."

"Convince me of that, and I will promise upon my honor to do as you tell me," replied the drunkard.

"Well, my friend, when thou findest any vessel of intoxicating liquor in thy hand, open the hand that contains it before it reaches thy mouth and thou wilt never be drunk again."

And the drunkard kept his promise.

[5521]

During one of Senator Vest's campaign tours in the early nineties, it was necessary for him to sojourn overnight in the town of St. Charles, Missouri. The best hostelry the place afforded was poor enough, and at breakfast Vest was especially put out by the stuff that was placed before him for coffee.

After having sampled the beverage, Vest with a frown called for the proprietor. When that individual had appeared, the senator asked, with a wave of his hand toward the offending liquid smoking innocently before him:

"Sir, what is this stuff?"

"Coffee," meekly replied the proprietor, somewhat taken aback.

"Coffee!" repeated Vest, in fine scorn; "my friend, I could insert a coffee bean in my mouth, dive into the Missouri river, swim to the town of Alton, Illinois, and I'll guarantee that one could bail up much better coffee than this, sir, over the entire route!"

[5522]

George Bernard Shaw has confessed that the only time he has been at a loss and taken aback was an evening years ago, when a messenger arrived at his home to take some Shaw copy to a newspaper. The great man was at dinner. The lad came in, looked at the vegetarian plate before Shaw and said: "Have you just finished or are you just starting?"

[5523]

Whistler, the painter, was at a dinner one night, and an awful bore came up to him and said, "Do you know, Mr. Whistler, I passed your house last night."

"Thanks," said Whistler.

[5524]

Hitler went to a fortuneteller and asked her, "On what day will I die?" The seeress assured him that he would die on a Jewish holiday. "Why are you so sure of that?" demanded Hitler.

"Any day," she replied, "on which you die will be a Jewish holiday."

[5525]

Mozart, who was a pupil of Haydn's, once made a bet with the master that he could compose a piece that Haydn could not play.

Within five minutes Mozart dashed off a script and handed it to Haydn.

"What's this?" he exclaimed after he had played a few bars. "Why here is a note to be played in the middle of the keyboard, when the hands are stretched out to both ends of the piano. Nobody can play such music."

Smilingly, Mozart took Haydn's place at the instrument and when he came to that note, he leaned forward and struck it with his nose—a member with which Mozart was amply supplied.

[5526]

It was once remarked to Lord Chesterfield that man is the only creature endowed with the power of laughter. "True," said the peer, "and you may add, perhaps, that he is the only creature that deserves to be laughed at."

[5527]

A visitor to Mark Twain's home commented upon the abundance of books, and the rather limited accommodations for them.

"Yes," agreed Mark, a bit wistfully, "yes, but it's so difficult to get friends to loan you *shelves*."

[5528]

Alexander H. Stevens, Senator from Georgia and later Vice-President of the Confederacy, was the smallest man in the Senate, weighing less than eighty pounds, and standing less than five feet high. A huge Western Congressman once frothed at the mouth, seeking to answer him. "You! You! Why, I could *swallow* you, and never know I'd et a thing!"

"In that case, you'd have more brains in your belly than you ever had in your head," replied Stevens.

[5529]

Will Rogers, acting as toastmaster at a dinner one evening, was annoyed by the lengthy talk of the man he had just introduced. The long-winded bore finally ended his oratory and Rogers arose and said, "You have just listened to that famous Chinese statesman, On Too Long."

[5530]

Calvin Coolidge had humor and sense enough to escape that exaggeration of the ego which afflicts a good many of our Presidents. Awakening from a nap in the middle of a presidential executive day, he opened his eyes, he grinned and asked a friend, "Is the country still here?"

[5531]

A Washington matron once boasted she could make President Coolidge talk. Cornering him at a dinner, she sought to make good her boast.

"Oh, Mr. President," she said, trying to disarm him with frankness, "I have made a bet that I can make you say at least three words."

"You lose," Coolidge replied.

[5532]

A young skeptic in the congregation once interrupted Billy Sunday with the question:

"Who was Cain's wife?"

The Evangelist answered in all seriousness:

"I honor every seeker after knowledge of the truth. But I have a word of warning for this questioner. Don't risk losing salvation by too much inquiring after other men's wives."

[5533]

Nat Goodwin had an unenviable reputation among his fellow actors for—well, shall we call it extreme parsimony? One day he approached a table in the Lambs Club, New York, at which two other historians were seated, and remarked that he was thinking of writing his autobiography.

"With the accent on the 'buy?'" asked one of the actors meaningly.

"No," put in the other quickly, "with the accent on the 'ought to.'"

[5534]

Stepping out between the acts at the first production of one of his plays, Bernard Shaw said to the audience:

"What do you think of it?"

This startled everybody for the time being, but presently a man in the pit assembled his scattered wits and cried:

"Rotten!"

Shaw made a curtsey and melted the house with one of his Irish smiles.

"My friend," he said, shrugging his shoulders and indicating the crowd in front, "I quite agree with you, but what are we two against so many?"

[5535]

Bill Nye, the famous humorist, said in his naive manner: "There should be a book in every home. To the ignorant, the pictures will be pleasing. The wise will revel in its wisdom, and the housekeeper will find that with it she may easily emphasize a statement or kill a cockroach."

[5536]

It is related of the great Dr. Clarke, that when in one of his leisure hours he was enjoying himself with a few friends, he observed Beau Nash approaching; upon which he suddenly stopped:

"My boys," said he, "let us be *grave:* here comes a *fool.*"

[5537]

An anecdote about Dr. Randall Davidson, bishop of Winchester, is that after an ecclesiastical function, as the clergy were trooping in to luncheon, an unctuous archdeacon observed: "This is the time to put a bridle on our appetites."

"Yes," replied the bishop, "this is the time to put a bit in our mouths!"

[5538]

Samuel F. B. Morse was an eminent painter before he invented telegraphy. He painted a scene showing a man in death-agony once, and asked a physician friend to examine it: "Well?" Morse inquired after the doctor had scrutinized the picture. "What's your opinion?"

The physician removed his spectacles, turned to Morse and commented: "Malaria!"

[5539]

Mark Twain once said: "When I was a boy of 14, my father was so ignorant I could hardly stand to have the old man around. But when I got to be 21, I was astonished at how much the old man had learned in seven years."

[5540]

On the first night of a new production, Oscar Hammerstein was heard to observe that a play is like a cigar.

"How's that?" asked a friend.

"Well," was the ex-cigarmaker's explanation, "if it's good, everybody wants a box, if it's bad, no amount of puffing will make it draw."

[5541]

One Sunday after President Coolidge had returned to the White House from church, where he had gone alone, Mrs. Coolidge inquired:

"Was the sermon good?"

"Yes," he answered.

"What was it about?"

"Sin."

"What did the minister say?"

"He was against it."

[5542]

An absurd blunder is related in Tom Moore's Diary about John Kemble. He was performing one of his favorite parts at some country theatre, and was interrupted from time to time by the squalling of a child in the gallery, until at length, angered by this rival performance, Kemble walked with solemn steps to the front of the stage, and addressing the audience in his most tragic tones, said: "Ladies and gentlemen, unless the play is stopped, the child cannot possibly go on."

[5543]

Charles Dickens told an American story of a young lady, who, being intensely loved by five young men, was advised to "jump overboard, and marry the man who jumped in after her."

Accordingly, next morning, the five lovers being on deck, and looking very devotedly at the young lady, she plunged into the sea head-foremost. Four of the lovers immediately jumped in after her. When the young lady and four lovers were out again, she says to the captain, "What am I to do with them now, they are so wet?"

"Take the *dry one.*" And the young lady did, and married him.

PART VII

ENTERTAINMENT AND SPORTS

BROADWAY

[5544]
Willie Collier, the comedian, was an irrepressible member of a barnstorming combination, which some twenty years ago did the "tank" towns of the Middle West.

The company had been doing a poor business for several weeks when a certain town in Illinois was reached. Just before the curtain went up that night, Collier was standing at the curtain "peephole," sizing up the audience.

"How's the house, Willie?" asked another player.

"Well," answered Collier, "there are some out there. But," he added impressively, "we're still in the majority, old boy, still in the majority!"

[5545]
A chorus man out of a job was given a small part in a play. He merely had to walk on, seat himself and say, "Well, here I am." At rehearsal he did not give satisfaction.

"No," bellowed the director. "Try it again. Now come on like a man."

"My goodness," simpered the chorus man, "for $15 a week he wants me to do character parts."

[5546]
The manager of a touring theatrical company wired to the proprietor of the theater in a small town where his company was due to appear.

"Would like to hold rehearsal next Monday afternoon at three. Have your stage manager, carpenter, property man, electrician, and all stage hands present at that hour."

Four hours later he received the following reply: "All right. He'll be there."

[5547]
"Have you noticed the utter absence of comment upon my last play?" asked the author, of a bosom friend. "It is plain that I am the victim of a conspiracy of silence. What would you do about it?"

"I'd join it if I were you!" the bosom friend replied.

[5548]
"We had quite a prominent actor as a guest at our house the other evening."

"Gracious! didn't you find it hard to entertain him?"

"Oh, no, we just handed him a bunch of photographs and a number of his own was among them. He amused himself for hours."

[5549]

"How's the acoustics in the new theater?"

"Splendid. The actors can hear every cough."

[5550]

"After tonight I am going to have you killed in Act I instead of Act III," the stage manager said to his leading man.

"Wherefore the change?" asked the heavy villain.

"I don't want to take the chance of having the audience do it!" replied the manager.

[5551]

A dramatic critic arrived at the opening of a play after the first act had been acted. The producer was hurt.

"You are an influential writer," he said. "Is it fair that you should come to my play at this time? How can you write a fair review of this production when you haven't seen the first act?"

"Don't worry," came from the critic. "I'm in a poker game up at the Newspaper Club and am $18 ahead. You'll get a good notice. I just came in for a program."

And away he went.

[5552]

Celebrity (after a lengthy monopoly of the conversation)–"But enough about me; let us talk about yourself. Tell me—what do you think of my part in the new play?"

[5553]

Blonde Chorine–"What's the matter with the leading lady?"

Brunette Chorine–"She's only got nine bouquets tonight."

"Good heavens, isn't that enough?"

"Nope; she paid for ten."

[5554]

Lawyer (to actress bride)–"But surely you don't want to arrange for a divorce on your honeymoon. When did you quarrel?"

Bride–"At the church—he signed his name in the register in bigger letters than mine."

[5555]

"Would you mind telling me what you think of my abilities as shown by my impersonations of you?" asked the mimic of the distinguished actor.

"Well," said the other cheerfully, "one of us is awful."

[5556]

"Do you remember the actor who played the part of Lincoln for so long that he actually thought he was Lincoln?" He walked, talked and dressed like Lincoln all the time. One day he was walking down Broadway, clothed in the cape and high hat of Lincoln's period. Someone pointed him out and remarked 'that fellow will never be satisfied until he's assassinated!' "

[5557]

Cannibal–"We've just captured an actor."

Chief–"Hurray! I was hoping for a good ham sandwich."

[5558]

Producer–"If I make you a star you must lead a life of strict decorum."

Actress–"But can't my understudy do that?"

[5559]

He–"But what reason have you for refusing to marry me?"

She–"Papa objects. He says you are an actor."

He–"Give my regards to the old boy and tell him I'm sorry he isn't a newspaper critic."

[5560]
Actor (modestly)–"As a matter of fact, I have received letters from ladies in almost every place in which I have appeared."
Rival–"Landladies, I presume."

[5561]
It was a deathbed scene, but the director was not satisfied with the hero's acting.
"Come on!" he cried. "Put more life in your dying."

[5562)]
"This is ridiculous," said the infuriated producer. "Do you realize that in the last scene you actually laughed when you were supposed to be dying?"
"At my salary," answered the actor, not without dignity, "death is greeted with laughter and cheers."

[5563]
"There is nothing an actor hates more than the sound of people coming in while the play is in progress."
"Unless it's the sound of people going out."

[5564]
"In this scene you make love to a caveman. Can you do it?"
"Well, I'll give the beast that's in me."

[5565]
A chorus girl introduced her young man to another chorus girl, with the result that he transferred his affections. The aggrieved girl gave her rival a piece of her mind in a letter, which read:
"You Heartless Creature: You know very well we had been going about together for six months. Wait till I lay my hands on you, you good-for-nothing, bleached blonde. I'll scratch out your eyes, pull out your hair, your teeth, and throw acid on you. Yours truly, C—— N——.
"P. S.—Please excuse pencil."

[5566]
"His last play had the audience in the aisles."
"Applauding?"
"No, stretching and yawning."

[5567]
"O, Mother, why are the men in the front baldheaded?"
"They bought their tickets from scalpers, my child."

[5568]
Wife–"I think I've seen this play 'Asbestos' before.
Hubby–"Don't show your ignorance, that is a Latin word meaning 'Welcome.' "

[5569]
The new play was a failure. After the first act, many left the theater; at the end of the second, most of the others started out. A cynical critic as he rose from his aisle seat raised a restraining hand.
"Wait!" he commanded loudly. "Women and children first!"

[5570]
"Did you know," said one ham actor to another, "that some of these radio singers get $75,000 a year?"
"Is that so? Why that's what the President of the United States gets."
"Yeah, and can you imagine— the President can't sing a lick!"

[5571]
He (in telephone booth)–"I want a box for two."
Voice (at the other end)–"Sorry, but we don't have boxes for two."
He–"But aren't you the box office of the theater?"
Voice–"No, we are the undertakers."

[5572]

An old Shakespearian actor was engaged at a London music-hall to give tragic readings from Shakespeare. His reception was anything but complimentary.

When he came off the stage, he was approached by a kindly Cockney comedian who had been watching his performance from the wings.

"Don't take any notice of 'em," he said sympathetically. "I've been watching your turn, and I think you're darned funny!"

[5573]

"I don't know what to give Lizzie for a Christmas present," one chorus girl is reported to have said to her mate while discussing the gift to be made to a third.

"Give her a book," suggested the other.

And the first one replied meditatively, "No, she's got a book."

[5574]

Two Broadway actors sat in a restaurant. At the end of the meal, one requested a loan.

"Can I borrow ten dollars for a week?" he asked.

"Sure," replied the other, counting out the money.

As they arose, the latter man spoke again.

"Remember," he reminded, "that's only for a week."

"You'll get your money," he screamed. "Stop hounding me!"

[5575]

The tragedian had just signed a contract to tour South Africa. He told a friend of it at the club. The friend shook his head dismally.

"The ostrich," he explained in a pitying tone, "lays an egg weighing anywhere from two to four pounds."

[5576]

A famous critic was asked his opinion of a new four-act play which had been, in the language of Broadway, a "flop." He replied:

"After the first act, the audience sat quiet and I applauded. After the second act, the audience hissed, and I sat quiet. And after the third act I went out to the box office, and bought a ticket, and joined the rest of the audience in hissing."

[5577]

"Did that new play have a happy ending?"

"Sure, everybody was glad it was over."

[5578]

A Broadway stage director was rebuking an English actor.

"Go on," he said, "drop your aitches, can't you?"

"I'm supposed to be acting the part of a British peer," argued the Englishman.

"I know that," said the director, "but all you English drop your aitches, don't you?"

"Good gracious, no!" the Englishman responded.

The director pondered a moment and then said, "Well, drop 'em anyhow. The guys on this side expect it!"

[5579]

"Do you remember what Juliet said to Romeo on the balcony?"

"No."

"Why in hell didn't you get orchestra seats?"

[5580]

Then there was the sad case of the actor who fell off a ship passing a lighthouse. He drowned swimming circles to keep in the spotlight.

[5581]

"Is Minerva Muddle making a name for herself on the stage?"

"I should say she is. She has changed it three times already, and still she doesn't seem to be satisfied with it."

[5582]

Director–"Have you ever had any stage experience?"

Applicant–"Well, I had my leg in a cast once."

[5583]

Friend–"So your great Russian actor was a total failure?"

Manager–"Yes. It took all our profits to pay for running the electric light sign with his name on it."

[5584]

Actor–"Yes, my friends, usually my audiences are glued to their seats."

Friend–"What a quaint way of keeping them there!"

[5585]

First Actor–"I can't get into my shoes."

Second Actor–"What! Feet swelled, too?"

[5586]

Stage Hand–"You received a tremendous ovation; they're still clapping. What did you say?"

Actor–"I told them I would not go on with my act until they quieted down."

[5587]

Son–"Daddy dear, what is an actor?"

Daddy–"An actor? My son, an actor is a man who can walk to the side of a stage, peer into the wings filled with theatrical props, dirt and dust, other actors, stage-hands, old clothes and other claptrap, and say: 'What a lovely view there is from this window.'"

[5588]

The ambitious young actor had set out to conquer the world with "Hamlet," but the tour soon ended and he was compelled to walk home.

"Didn't they like you?" asked a sympathetic friend.

"They didn't seem to," replied the actor, sadly.

"But didn't they ask you to come before the curtain?"

"Ask me!" repeated the would-be Hamlet, with tears in his eyes. "Ask me! They dared me!"

[5589]

It seems that when the Crown Prince of the Royal Family of Barrymores was appearing on Broadway in the stage production of "Hamlet," J—— C—— occupied a stage box at one of the matinee performances.

It is quite a well-known fact that Miss C—— on all her excursions into the public limelight is not only seen but heard—and this particular afternoon proved no exception to the rule.

John Barrymore hadn't been on the stage five minutes when he knew that J—— C—— was in the audience. But he didn't acknowledge her presence until the end of the performance when, in making his customary curtain speech, he bowed in the direction of Miss C——'s box and said:

"And, in conclusion, may I take this opportunity to thank Miss J—— C—— for the privilege of co-starring with her this afternoon?"

[5590]

Manager–"Is this play of yours clean?"

Author–"Clean! I should say so. Why, there's a bathroom scene in the first act."

[5591]

A man walked into the grocery store. "I want all the rotten eggs you have," he demanded.

"What do you want with stale eggs?" asked the clerk. "Are you going to see the new comedian at the theater tonight?"

"Sh-sh-sh," hissed the buyer nervously, "I am the new comedian."

[5592]

A ham actor complained long and loud to the producer about the size of his name in the lights.

"Oh," groaned the actor, "I know I'm not a star, but I do think that my name should be featured. Why don't you mention the name of the show plus the principals, and then before my name put: 'And—?' "

" 'AND!' " screamed the fed-up producer. "Why not 'BUT?' "

[5593]

An actor, long unemployed, became desperate and advertised in a Broadway journal as follows:

"Engagements wanted. — Small part, such as dead body or outside shouts."

[5594]

"How was the attendance at your new musical comedy?"

"Well, on the opening night nobody came, but next day at the matinee the attendance fell off a bit."

[5595]

Otis Skinner, the famous actor, told of a performance of one of his plays at which there was present a delegation of young women from a fashionable school. Throughout the play they giggled and chattered so much that it was difficult for Mr. Skinner and the members of his cast to get through their lines.

After the performance the girls were taken back of the stage to meet Mr. Skinner. They gushed over him, and one of them said:

"Oh, Mr. Skinner, we enjoyed the play so much! But do you know, there must be something wrong with the acoustics of this theater. There were times when we could hardly hear you."

"That is strange," replied the actor. "I found not the least difficulty in hearing you."

[5596]

She (at comedy)–"Are they putting that poor man out for laughing?"

He–"No. The manager has sent for him to find out what he was laughing at."

[5597]

The critic in the theater lobby was an old gentleman. His criticism, which was for his wife's ears alone, consisted of these words:

"Well, you would come!"

[5598]

First Actress (behind the scenes)– "Did you hear the way the public wept during my death scene?"

Second Actress–"Yes, it must have been because they realized that it was only acted!"

[5599]

The critic started to leave in the middle of the second act of the play.

"Don't go now," said the manager. "I promise there's a terrific kick in the next act."

"Fine," was the retort; "give it to the author."

[5600]

The actor was visibly downcast.

Wife–"Did you get any applause?"

Actor–"Yes, it sounded like a caterpillar crawling over a Persian carpet whilst wearing rubber shoes."

[5601]
Beerbohm Tree liked to make a dramatic entrance in his plays, and in one he had to enter by flinging open a pair of double doors and standing a moment on the threshold in an impressive attitude. On the opening night he had got thus far when a voice shouted from the gallery:
"Next station Marble Arch!"

[5602]
"What have you in this town in the way of a good show?"
"Only the censors."

[5603]
Affable Fellow Passenger–"So you are an actor? I am a banker, and I think it must be at least fifteen years since I was at the theater."
Actor–"And I'm quite certain it's at least fifteen years since I was at a bank."

[5604]
Theatrical Manager–"Your last act was magnificent, Miss De Fleur! Your suffering was almost real."
Leading Lady–"It was. I've got a large nail in my shoe."
Theatrical Manager – "Well, for heaven's sake leave it in until the end of the run!"

[5605]
Dramatist–"I wish I could think of a big strong situation that would fill the audience with tears."
Theater Manager–"I'm looking for one that will fill the tiers with audience."

[5606]
Actor (to colleague)–"What delightfully cold weather, Laddie. We're sure to get some good applause today from the unreserved parts of the house, while they're getting their hands and feet warm!"

[5607]
First Chorine–"Did you tell anybody of your secret marriage?"
Second Ditto–"No, I'm waiting for my husband to sober up—I want him to be the first to know."

[5608]
Girl (applying for chorus job)–"Mother says I sing beautifully."
Manager–"Bring me a recommendation from the neighbors and I'll give you a tryout."

[5609]
John Barrymore was in San Francisco on the morning of the earthquake. He was thrown out of bed by one of the shocks, spun around on the floor and left gasping in a corner. Finally, he got to his feet and rushed for a bathtub, where he stayed all that day. Next day he ventured out. A soldier, with a bayonet on his gun, captured Barrymore and compelled him to pile bricks for two days.
Barrymore was telling his terrible experience in the Lambs' Club in New York.
"Extraordinary," commented Augustus Thomas, the playwright. "It took a convulsion of nature to make Jack take a bath, and the United States Army to make him go to work."

[5610]
The dramatist mistook the noise in front and was distressed to find that although they wanted to see him, what they wanted to see him for was something very different from his expectations.
But he dodged behind the curtain just in time, and dodged back again to reproach the gallery.
"It's true," he said, "that I haven't made a hit. But neither have any of you!"

[5611]
"Not very amusing, is he?"
"No, he couldn't even entertain a doubt."

[5612]
A friend visited a theatrical manager in his office, and asked, "Busy?"
"Very busy this morning," said the manager. "I've just hired ten chorus girls in five minutes."
"Gosh!" said the friend. "You surely are quick at figures!"

[5613]
Stage Manager (discussing chorusgirl who has been given a small singing part)–"Well, what do you think of her?"
Producer – "A peach — but no Melba."

[5614]
A group of men, of which a celebrated comedian was the center, were discussing actors, their qualities, and what some conceived to be their weaknesses.
"No matter what is said," remarked a non-professional, "no matter what foibles they may have, actors are always charitable."
"Charitable," exclaimed the comedian. "You are right. I never saw one yet who wouldn't take the other's part if he got a chance."

[5615]
Stepping from a taxi in front of the Lambs Club, a hurrying author presented the driver with a twenty-dollar bill to pay a meter charge of $1.10. The driver snorted, and remarked that it was the first twenty he had seen since shortly before the depression, and to expect him to change it amounted to mockery. The passenger turned to an actor shading himself on the Lambs stoop, and asked for a dollar and a quarter.
"If I had a dollar and a quarter," returned the actor, "do you think I'd imperil it hanging around here?"

[5616]
The man at the theater was annoyed by the conversation in the row behind.
"Excuse me," he said, "but we can't hear a word."
"Oh," replied the talkative one: "and is it any business of yours what I'm telling my wife?"

[5617]
"Your play needs to be more realistic."
"What do you mean?"
"Well, here you have a scene in the home of a young married couple—and in the second scene, occurring six months later, the furniture is in exactly the same place."

[5618]
Stage Hand–"Did you say you wanted a window or a widow?"
Stage Manager–"I said window, but they're both much alike. When I get near either of them I always look out."

[5619]
Stage Manager (almost curtain time)–"Good God, man, you can't go on like this! Never in my life have I seen any one as drunk as you are."
Leading Man–"Hav'n'y'—hic! Jush wait'l y' she my understudy!"

[5620]
"These love scenes are rotten. Can't the leading man act as if he were in love with the star?"
"Can't act at all," said the director. "Trouble is, he is in love with her."

[5621]

Rev. Dr. Puff–"My dear sir, I am a minister of the Gospel, and, as I intend preaching a sermon against the stage, I thought I would ask you for a ticket of admission to your show, in order that I might see for myself the extent of this great immorality."

Manager (to ticket-seller)–"Charlie, give the doctor a seat in the orchestra, and charge it to advertising."

[5622]

A road show was making a tour of one night stands, and had arrived in a little town billed to play "Romeo and Juliet" at the local opera house. Shortly after the troupe got in town the leading man approached the manager with a look of great distress. "I must have ten cents," he implored.

"Ten cents!" shouted the manager. "I never saw such a fellow—always howling for money. What do you need money for in this town?"

"I must have a shave," the actor explained. "You can't expect a fellow to play Romeo with a three-days' growth of beard."

The manager thought for a moment, and put his hand in his pocket. Then a happy smile broke over his face, and his hand came out of his pocket empty. "That's all right," he declared. "We'll just change the bill to 'Othello.' "

[5623]

A man received the following note from his actor son, who had joined a touring company:

"I have made a great success. Will you send me $25 to pay the landlady?—Your devoted son, Algy.

"P.S.—Since writing this letter,

I am ashamed to ask you, so I ran after the postman and tried to get it back. I pray it does not reach you."

The son was surprised when he received this reply: "Dear Algy, your prayer was answered. The letter did not reach me."

[5624]

Manager (of revue)–"Is there a doctor in the audience?"

Wise Guy–"I am not a doctor, but I am studying anatomy."

[5625]

Patron–"The love scene in your play isn't half so natural as it used to be last season. The same people do it, too."

Manager–"Yes; but the lovers were married a few months ago."

[5626]

"Poor Hamming is dead, but in his time he was a leading actor in many moving scenes."

"Yes; he was the best scene shifter I ever met."

[5627]

"I'm studying to be a musical comedy actress."

"How are you getting along?"

"Great! I can now sleep until noon without any difficulty."

HOLLYWOOD

[5628]

The boys who drive for the motion-picture studios resent being called chauffeurs. They want to be called drivers. Most of the actors call their drivers by name and chat with them. Recently a woman star, to whom a special car and driver were assigned, let a week go by without bothering to learn his name, and always addressed him as "Chauffeur." He thought that was long enough, so he swung around in his seat, grinning yet determined.

"Miss," he said, "I'm no chauffeur. I'm a driver."

"Why," she asked, "what's the difference?'

The answer was instantaneous and positive: "One hundred dollars a month and no dogs to wash!"

[5629]
The new "find" was about to be starred in a picture.

One scene was where the girl was to jump from a high cliff into the water.

Upon examining the jumping point and the landing place, the girl ran to the director and said:

"I won't make that jump, I absolutely refuse to do it. There's only a foot of water at the bottom of that cliff."

"That's all right," answered the director, "do you think we want you to drown?"

[5630]
During the making of the moving picture, "The Penguin Pool Murder," the director was showing a visitor around. As they gazed at the penguin, the director said:

"The bird is hired, of course, and we pay $150 a week for him."

A little extra standing near by remarked quietly:

"And I had to be born a human!"

[5631]
A recent movie comedy showed on the screen a bevy of shapely girls disrobing for a plunge in the "old swimming-pool." They had

just taken off shoes, hats, coats and were beginning on— a passing freight-train dashed across the screen and obscured the view. When it had passed, the girls were frolicking in the water.

An old railroader sat through the show again and again. At length an usher tapped him on the shoulder.

"Aren't you ever going home?" he asked.

"Oh, I'll wait a while," was the answer. "One of these times that train's going to be late."

[5632]
"Did you hear the joke about the film star?"

"No, what is it?"

"Her secretary didn't keep the records straight and now she finds she has had two more divorces than she's had weddings."

[5633]
A script was submitted to a producer. The movie boss took one quick look at the title and handed it back to the author with a sorrowful smile.

The author of the story was puzzled. He hadn't been in pictures very long.

"But you didn't read it!"

The big boss was patient. "The title. 'The Optimist!' Me and you knows what it means but how many of them thick skulls out in front is gonna know it's a eye doctor?"

[5634]
The movie manager was furious. "What's the matter?" asked his assistant. "Is anything wrong?"

"Anything wrong!" he snorted. "Why, you've advertised for next week: 'Smiling Eyes—with a strong cast!'"

[5635]

"Where do you suppose those scenario writers get their ideas?"

"Well, judging from the product, I should say they get them from each other."

[5636]

A cinema actor, suing for a breach of contract, described himself as the greatest actor in the world.

One of his friends took him to task for so loudly singing his own praises.

"I know," replied the actor, "it must have sounded somewhat conceited, but, remember, I was on oath."

[5637]

The Censor–"About this picture, *Beaches and Peaches,* you call it an educational film. What does it teach?"

The Movie Producer–"Anatomy."

[5638]

Solicitor–"Would you indorse our cigarette for two thousand dollars?"

Movie Actor–"For two thousand dollars I'd smoke the darn things."

[5639]

Director–"That Indian wants two hundred dollars to act the part."

Producer–"Offer him a hundred, tell him it's only a half-breed part."

[5640]

The movie actor who had been divorced four time proposed again.

"Why, I rather like you, John," said the young woman, "but, you see, I've heard so many things about you—"

"My dear," interrupted the much-married actor, "you really must not believe these old wives' tales."

[5641]

A prominent Hollywood movie star demanded a big increase of salary in her new contract.

"But, good heavens!" protested the head of the concern, "that is more than we pay the presidents of our big oil and insurance companies."

"All right," said the star, "then let your big oil and insurance presidents come out here and vamp for you."

[5642]

Ardent Male–"I'd love to be married to you some day."

Screen Star–"All right, I'll put you on my wedding list."

[5643]

Film Magnate (entering studio)–"Who's that?"

Director–"Why, that's Napoleon."

Film Magnate–"Why did you get such a little man to play such an important part?"

[5644]

Two men had just made their exit out of the theater, and evidently it had been a very poor picture by the expression on their faces, when one turned toward the other and said, "You know, it certainly is wonderful how pictures have advanced these last few years."

"How so?"

"Well, first there were the silent pictures, then there were talkies, and now this one smells!"

[5645]

Friend–"Say, there's a bunch of people outside waiting to see you. Among them is a bishop who says he married you some time ago."

Film Actress–"Gee! I'm practically certain I never married a bishop."

[5646]

Cinema Star (introducing latest husband to her little girl)–"Now, darling, this is your new daddy." *Darling*–"Oh, will you put something in my visitors' book, please?"

[5647]

"Well, I finally got into the movies."

"How did you do it?"

"Paid them a quarter."

[5648]

A neighborhood movie theater treasurer is picking up big-time ways.

As a patron walked away, leaving change on the counter, she was asked what she did in a case like that.

"I always rap on the window with a sponge," she replied.

[5649]

And then there are cynics who claim that movies would be better if they shot less films and more actors.

[5650]

Philip Merivale was making his first movie for Hollywood. The studio executives did their best to make him feel at home, but his director was a little apprehensive on the first day of shooting. "I know it must be hard for you, Mr. Merivale," he said, "working without an audience."

"Not at all," answered Mr. Merivale. "I've just been acting Shakespeare in New York."

[5651]

A young couple were seated in the balcony of a magnificent movie palace, which also presents elaborate stage productions of singers and dancers. During the stage show the young man asked an usher where he could get a drink of water. He was given complicated directions: "Go downstairs, turn to your right until you see the crimson rugs, straight ahead until you pass two trees, turn to your left, etc."

He tried to remember the instructions, got lost and wandered vainly about. Finally he came to a stream of fresh water, quenched his thirst and returned to his seat.

"Gee, I missed most of the show," he told his companion. "What happened in the finale?"

"You should know," the lady informed, "you were in it."

[5652]

A man went into a pet shop to buy a parrot.

"Here is a fine talking bird," said the assistant. "For years he was the companion of a big movie producer—weren't you, Polly?"

"Yes, sir!" shrilled the parrot. "Yes, yes, yes, yes. Yes, indeed! You're absolutely right. Yes, sir!"

[5653]

The lawyer was rehearsing the beautiful actress as to her appearance in the divorce court. She listened with mild interest and finally asked a question.

"Who plays the part of the judge?"

[5654]

"How do the writers of film scenarios get new ideas?" asks a writer.

"They don't."

[5655]

Movie Star–"Let me introduce you to my husband."

Director–"Delighted. I am always glad to meet any husbands of yours."

[5656]

"But I've signed your book before," said the much publicized film-actor.

"Yes, sir, but when I get ten of yours I can swap them for one of George Arliss."

[5657]

Another, who may be said to have his ups and downs is the unfortunate chap who happens to get an aisle seat at a movie.

[5658]

Film Star—"Yes, I said I wanted a home with at least twelve children."

Friend—"My dear, what makes you say such foolish things?"

"The publicity department."

[5659]

The Hollywood magnate told an assistant that in his opinion a certain writer was the only man for a film they had under consideration. The assistant was tactfully doubtful.

"Don't you think, perhaps he's a little too caustic?" he suggested.

"Do I care how much he costs?" demanded the producer. "Get him!"

[5660]

A stylish Hollywood hostess recently sent out elaborate invitations for "Bearer and One Wife" to an elaborate Hollywood party.

[5661]

An agent was trying to sell Sam Goldwyn a prominent actor. Goldwyn told the agent that he wasn't interested in established stars, that he wanted to build his own actors.

"Look how I developed Jon Hall," said Goldwyn. "He's a better leading man than Robert Taylor will ever be—some day."

[5662]

He (at the movies)—"Can you see all right?"

She—"Yes."

He—"Is there a draft on you?"

She—"No."

He—"Is your seat comfortable?"

She—"Yes."

He—"Will you change places with me?"

[5663]

A moving-picture actress has had her legs insured for a million dollars. To the film star, of course, this is mere pin money.

[5664]

"Didn't anybody criticise you for filming an automobile in ancient Babylon?"

"No. But I had a dozen letters calling my attention to the fact that the car showed a California license tag."

[5665]

A producer recently imported an alien star.

"She's a nize goil," he announced, "and I'm gonna loin her English."

[5666]

Movie Director—"Unmarried?"

Applicant—"Twice."

[5667]

Film Star (newly married)—"And is this your new home?"

Bridegroom—"It is, precious."

Film Star—"Say, it looks mighty familiar. Are you sure I haven't been married to you before?"

[5668]

There is one advantage in reading the novel before seeing the film version; it makes it more difficult to guess the plot of the picture.

[5669]

"How do you like your new publicity agent?" asked the film star's friend.

"Oh, he's wonderful," she cried, beaming with enthusiasm. "We've been robbed twice, our house has been burned, our car has been wrecked, and I have had my life threatened by an anonymous enemy since we employed him."

[5670]

Admirer–"What a charming necklace?"

Film Star–"Yes, isn't it adorable? Made entirely of my wedding rings."

[5671]

A Los Angeles car owner was having his eyes tested for a driver's license. Pointing to chart on the wall, the examining officer asked the man to identify the things he saw.

"What is in the large circle in the center?" he asked.

"That is the figure 18," the man replied.

"Wrong," said the officer, "That is a picture of Mae West talking to Katharine Hepburn."

[5672]

A Friend–"So sorry I couldn't be present at your wedding."

Movie Actress–"Never mind, I'll have another one soon."

[5673]

The film actress was suing for breach of promise and the case filled columns in the newspapers.

On the fourth day of the case the judge received a note from the plaintiff.

"Please stop the case," it read. "I've just discovered the defendant is my husband!"

[5674]

A prominent New Yorker was getting a special trip around one of the studios. He was even taken into the dressing room of one of the stars. On the wall was a large photograph of Tennyson. The visitor remarked:

"I see you are an admirer of Tennyson."

"Who is Tennyson?" asked the actor.

"That's his picture," said the New Yorker. "That's Tennyson, the poet."

"Why, is that old file a poet!" exclaimed the movie star. "I got him for a study in wrinkles."

[5675]

"So the marriage of those two movie-stars has been called off, eh!"

"Yes; they couldn't agree as to whose name should be first on the wedding invitations."

[5676]

Registrar–"Have you been married before, madam? And if so, to whom?"

Film Star–"What's the big idea? Memory test?"

[5677]

Movie Director–"Now, here is where you jump off the cliff."

Nervous Actor–"Yeah, but suppose I get injured or killed?"

Movie Director–"Oh, that's all right. It's the last scene in the picture."

[5678]

Daughter of First Film Star–"How do you like your new father?"

Daughter of Second Film Star–"Oh he's very nice."

"Yes, isn't he? We had him last year."

[5679]
Then there was the novelist who got the idea for his second novel from the screen version of his first one.

[5680]
Film Star–"What the public expects from a film star. First I had to learn to talk for the talkies, now I have to blush for the color films."

[5681]
Author–"Can I sell you a scenario?"
Movie Producer–"G'wan, we've had a scenario for years."

[5682]
Mrs. Williams could only find two aisle seats, one behind the other. Wishing to sit with her sister, she cautiously surveyed the man in the next seat. Finally she leaned over and whispered: "I beg your pardon, sir, but are you alone?"
Without even turning his head in the slightest, but twisting his mouth and shielding it with his hand, he muttered: "Cut it out, sister, cut it out; the wife's with me."

[5683]
Guest–"Do you know the lady over there?"
Hotel Manager–"Certainly. She is a film star, but just now I do not know her name."
"Does she come to this hotel often?"
"Yes, every honeymoon."

[5684]
Fat Man (in a movie to little boy sitting behind him)–"Can't you see, little fellow?"
Little Fellow–"Not a thing."
Fat Man–"Then keep your eye on me and laugh when I do."

[5685]
First Girl Usher–"What's up? You look tickled."
Second Girl Usher–"A boy friend of mine came in with his latest girl, and I've separated them."

[5686]
Producer–"Our last picture was a super production."
Critic–"I thought it looked as if a super had produced it."

[5687]
A joyous event had taken place in the home of the film-producer.
"Here is the son and heir, sir," said the nurse, smiling coyly.
The producer gave it a perfunctory glance. "Sorry," he said absently, "not quite the type!"

CIRCUSES AND SHOW BUSINESS

[5688]
The circus was doing badly and funds sank lower and lower. At last the cashier pinned up a notice announcing that in future salaries would be paid as funds permitted, and that artists would be paid in the alphabetical order of names.
Next day Zero, the strong man, called on the cashier.
"I have come," he said, "to tell you that I have changed my name."
"Oh!" replied the cashier. "And what are you going to call yourself now?"
"Achilles."

[5689]
"Are you the celebrated lion tamer?"
"No, I only comb the lions and clean their teeth."

[5690]

A circus side-show advertised a dwarf who was five feet in height. When a citizen expressed surprise to the proprietor, he replied, "That's the wonderful thing about him. He's the tallest dwarf in the world."

[5691]

The portly man was trying to get to his seat at the circus. "Pardon me," he said to a woman, "did I step on your foot?"

"Possibly so," she said, after glancing at the ring. "All the elephants are still out there. You must have."

[5692]

The circus proprietor looked more than usually worried as he faced the troupe on Friday.

"Gentlemen," he began, "as you all know business is very bad just now. Last week I could only manage to pay you all half wages. This week things have been even worse."

He stopped for a moment and looked with growing anxiety at the angry faces round him. Then, wiping his damp forehead, he went on:

"I've gone carefully into the matter and find there is enough cash in hand to pay—er—three of you this week. The lucky three are Hercules, the strong man; Dave Dauntless, the lion tamer; and Strangler Sam, the all-in wrestler!"

[5693]

Circus Manager–"Well, what's wrong now?"
India Rubber Man–"Every time the strong man writes a letter he uses me to rub out the mistakes."

[5694]

"What are you doing now?"

"I have found a new circus turn—the friendship of a lion and a goat."

"But aren't there quarrels between them?"

"Oh, yes, they have their little quarrels, but then we buy a new goat."

[5695]

The usual crowd of small boys was gathered about the entrance of a circus tent in a small town one day, pushing each other and trying to get a glimpse of the interior. A man standing near watched them for a few minutes, then walking up to the ticket-taker he said with an air of authority:

"Let these boys in, and count them as they pass."

The gateman did as requested, and when the last one had gone in he turned and said: "Twenty-eight, sir."

"Good," said the man, smiling, as he walked away, "I thought I guessed right."

[5696]

"Yes," said the old man. "I have had some terrible disappointments, but none stands out over the years like the one that came to me when I was a boy."

"And what was it?"

"When I was a boy I crawled under a tent to see a circus and discovered it was a revival meeting."

[5697]

A certain night club advertises a chorus of fifty, but we are positive some of them aren't a day over forty-five.

[5698]

"Lurino was fired from the circus when he got the swelled head."

"Was he an acrobat?"

"No, he used to put his head in the lion's mouth."

[5699]

"The female giant married the india-rubber man yesterday."

"Is that so? I thought she'd do something like that."

"Why?"

"She always wanted somebody she could twist around her fingers."

[5700]

Magician (to youngster he has called up on the stage)–"Now, my boy, you've never seen me before, have you?"

Boy–"No, Daddy."

[5701]

The sleight-of-hand performance was not going very well.

"Can any lady or gentleman lend me an egg?" asked the conjuror, coming down to the footlights.

"If we'd had one," shouted a man in the audience, "you'd have it before this."

[5702]

A theatrical agent persuaded the conductor of a variety-broadcast to use Joe Frisco in a five-minute bit. "I got you a five-minute bit on the air," the agent then told Joe. "What can you do in that time?"

"J-j-just," the stuttering comic informed, "c-c-clear m-m-my th-th-throat!"

[5703]

"I hear that Romer's Flea Circus got stranded in Allentown."

"Yes—the leading lady ran off with a poodle."

[5704]

A lanky, mustached individual upped to the manager of a Forty-second Street dime museum last week and asked for employment.

"Who are you?" asked the manager.

"I'm Egbert, the Egg King," drawled the fellow.

"What's your specialty?"

"I eat three dozen hen eggs, two dozen duck eggs, and one dozen goose eggs at a single sitting."

"Sounds pretty good. I suppose you know our policy."

"What's that?"

"Four shows a day."

"O. K.!"

"And do you think you can go through them with your act?"

"I know I can."

"On Saturdays we often have as many as six shows and on some holidays we give a performance every hour."

Egbert, the Egg King hesitated. "In that case, I must have one thing understood before I join your show."

"What's that?"

"No matter how rushing business is at this museum," replied Egbert, "you gotta gimme time enough to eat my regular meals at my hotel!"

[5705]

Theatrical Agent–"Good news! I've booked your performing pigeons for a six weeks' tour."

"Too late—I've eaten the act!"

[5706]

Night-Club Habitué (staggering out of dive at 4 A.M.)–"Good Lord, what is that strange odor around here?"

Doorman–"That, sir, is fresh air."

STAGE AND RADIO GAGS

[5707]

"Do you know, Marty, that they don't hang men with wooden legs in China?"

"Zat so, why?"

"They use rope."

[5708]

"Are mosquitoes religious?"

"Yes. They first sing over you and then prey on you."

[5709]

"What's the difference between the mumps and the measles?"

"Why, in the mumps you shut up and in the measles you break out."

[5710]

"Did you hear about the wooden wedding?"

"I'll bite."

"Two Poles were married."

[5711]

Mike–"I got one of those suits with two pairs of pants."

Gus–"How do you like it?"

Mike–"Not so well. It's too hot wearing two pairs of pants."

[5712]

Ernie–"My uncle can play the piano by ear."

Gurney–"That's nothing. My uncle fiddles with his whiskers."

[5713]

Burns and Allen said their greatest laugh came from a gag they used to do in vaudeville.

Gracie set it up by saying, "My sister put in a new swimming pool last night, and we had more fun diving."

George–"Yeah, that's great sport."

Gracie–"We'll have even more fun tomorrow when they put in the water."

[5714]

"I wouldn't want to be a widow's second husband."

"Well, I'd rather be a widow's second husband than her first, doncher-know."

[5715]

"Say, Captain, I'm sick; how far are we from land?"

"About three miles."

"Which way?"

"Straight down."

[5716]

"If it wasn't for one thing I'd call your brother a bald-faced liar."

"What's that?"

"His mustache."

[5717]

"Do you want to get wise to making money fast?"

"Sure I do."

"Well, glue it to the floor."

[5718]

"I saw a girl on the lawn today with her stocking on wrong side."

"What did you do?"

"Turned the hose on her."

[5719]

"We will proceed to read from the Book of Numbers," said the preacher as he opened the telephone directory.

[5720]

"I have no luck with women."

"Lucky fellow!"

[5721]

He–"There are several things I can always count on."

She–"What are they?"

He–"My fingers."

[5722]

"Which travels faster—heat or cold?"

"Heat, because you can catch cold easily."

[5723]

"Say, Sam; did you hear the latest news?"

"No, I did not."

"They are going to make every police officer wear rubber boots."

"What for?'"

"To keep them from waking each other up."

[5724]

"He was a failure as an architect, so he went on the stage."

"Is he drawing better houses?"

[5725]

"My wife thinks I'm perfect."

"Yes, I heard her say so."

"Did you? When?"

"The time she called you an idiot."

[5726]

"A woman fell overboard from a ship yesterday, and a shark came up and looked her over and went away."

"He never touched her?"

"No. He was a man-eating shark."

[5727]

Brown—"Do you know, I'm losing my memory. It's worrying me to death."

Jones (sympathetically) – "Never mind, old man. Forget all about it!"

[5728]

"Could one refer to the Venus de Milo as the girl who got the breaks?"

"Why not? It's an 'armless joke."

[5729]

"Waiter, I find that I have just enough money to pay for the dinner, but I have nothing in the way of a tip for yourself."

"Let me add up that bill again, sir."

[5730]

"What did the young lady do after you proposed?"

"Oh, she sighed, and then I sighed."

"Well, you must have had a circus."

"No; only a sighed-show."

[5731]

"What kind of a hen lays the longest?"

"What kind?"

"A dead hen."

[5732]

"My face is my fortune."

"A panhandler, eh?"

[5733]

"Does electricity have any meaning to you?"

"Only in a dim way."

[5734]

"I see you are mentioned in one of the books just published."

"Indeed! What book?"

"The directory."

[5735]

"Have you seen the new noiseless baby carriages?"

"I don't think much of them. Noiseless babies would be more to the point."

[5736]

"Why do you call him 'Mr. Gimlet'? That isn't his name."

"I know. But he's such a bore!"

[5737]

"There's a man outside with a wooden leg named Smith."

"What's the name of his other leg?"

[5738]

"Do you know Art?"

"Art who?"

"Artesian."

"Sure. I know Artesian well."

[5739]

"I started out on the theory that the world has an opening for me."

"And you found it?"

"Well, rather. I'm in the hole now."

[5740]

"What's the best cure for sea-sickness?"

"Give it up."

[5741]

"She's always looking for a man who'll give her the shirt off his back."

"She's a golddigger?"

"No, a laundress!"

[5742]

"Do you believe that dark-haired men marry first?"

"No, it's the light-headed ones."

[5743]

"Can you tell me why they call all the bad actors 'hams'?"

"I suppose it's because of their constant association with eggs."

[5744]

"I take a cold shower every morning."

"Why brag about it?"

"Gosh, that's why I take it!"

[5745]

She–"What are you thinking of?"

He–"Nothing."

She–"Oh, do take your mind off yourself."

[5746]

"Joe has a glass eye."

"Did he tell you that?"

"No; it just came out in the conversation."

[5747]

Freddy–"What is an iceberg, Daddy?"

Daddy–"Why, it's a kind of a permanent wave, son."

[5748]

"I quarreled with Meyer. I should have beaten him black and blue if I hadn't been prevented."

"Who prevented you?"

"Meyer."

[5749]

First Slapsticker–"By der vay, didt you knowed dot id iss now der fashion to dress accorting to der color of der hair?"

Second Slapsticker–"I am amazement!"

First Slapsticker–"Sure iss id! A man vich has brown hairs shouldt ought to vear a brown suit. Synonymous, a man vich has gray hairs shouldt ought a gray suit to vear."

Second Slapsticker–"Say, tell me, how shouldt id a baldt-headted man dress?"

[5750]

"Why do you suppose Hotstuff passes by here every day eating an apple?"

"I guess he's on his way to see that old girl of his, the doctor's wife."

[5751]

"You see that old boy over there? He thinks in terms of millions."

"He doesn't look to me like a financier."

"He isn't. He's a bacteriologist."

[5752]

"Ever buy anything at a rummage sale?"

"Yes, I bought back my Sunday pants the last time our church gave one."

[5753]

"I saw you at the theater last night with a lady I didn't recognize, but I think it was your wife."

"Certainly it was my wife—but don't tell her about it."

[5754]
"I got a bright idea out of a corner of my brain today."
"Ah, a stowaway."

[5755]
"How did you find the weather while you were away?"
"Just went outside and there it was."

[5756]
"I suppose the hired girl does all the heavy work in your house?"
"Not all; my wife makes the biscuit, pies and puddings."

[5757]
"You say your sister makes up jokes; then she's a humorist?"
"No; she works in a beauty parlor."

[5758]
"They tell me that whiskey has been the death of more men than bullets."
"Well, I'd rather be full of whiskey than bullets, wouldn't you?"

[5759]
"They tell me in Mexico you can get three pounds of sugar, a pound of coffee, a quart of whiskey and a wife for three dollars.
"I'll bet it's rotten whiskey."

[5760]
"Do you know what is the very best skin food."
"No, I do not."
"Why, sausages."

[5761]
A reader doesn't understand why goods sent by ship constitute a cargo, while goods sent in a car are a shipment.

[5762]
"Who invented the hole in the doughnut?"
"Oh, some fresh air fiend, I suppose."

[5763]
"What's a 'country club' Pa?"
"Knickers, neckers, and knockers."

[5764]
"Have you noticed the latest thing in men's clothes?"
"Yes. Women."

[5765]
"Has that florist any children?"
"Two: a girl who is a budding genius and a son who is a blooming idiot."

[5766]
"How's your insomnia?"
"Worse and worse. I can't even sleep when it's time to get up."

[5767]
"Didn't you feel a strange sensation the first time you kissed a girl?"
"No, she was no stranger and she was no sensation."

[5768]
"When I bought this dog you said he was splendid for rats. Why, he won't touch them."
"Well, ain't that splendid for rats?"

[5769]
"What a horrible noise comes from that radio set!"
"Well, I guess you would make just as bad a noise if you were coming out of ether."

[5770]
"Do you know why an acrobat's life is like a girl's underwear?"
"No, why?"
"Because one slip is enough."

[5771]
"What do the three balls in front of a pawnshop mean?"
"Two to one you don't get it back."

[5772]

"I heard a new one the other day; I wonder if I've told it to you?"

"Is it funny?"

"Yes."

"Then you haven't."

[5773]

"My youngest boy is troubled with halitosis."

"Too bad. How did he get it?"

"He hasn't got it. He just can't spell it."

[5774]

"I've changed my mind."

"Thank Heaven! Does it work any better now?"

[5775]

"What was the subject of your debate this evening?"

"Whiskey."

"Was it well discussed."

"Yes; most of the members were full of the subject."

[5776]

"What's the difference between vision and sight?"

"Do you see those two girls sitting in the centre, there?"

"Yes."

"Well, the pretty one I should call a vision of loveliness, but the other one—she's a sight."

[5777]

"The radio will never take the place of newspapers."

"Why?"

"You can't start a fire with a radio set."

[5778]

"I'm suffering dreadfully from insomnia. I've tried all sorts of remedies, but I can find nothing that will send me to sleep."

"Why don't you try talking to yourself?"

[5779]

"Say, that's a bad gash you have on your forehead, how did you get it?"

"I bit myself."

"Come, come, now, how could you bite yourself on the forehead?"

"I stood on a chair."

[5780]

"Do you know that when I go to heaven I'm going to tell Bill Shakespeare that I don't believe he wrote all those plays."

"Ah, but suppose he doesn't happen to be in heaven?"

"In that case you can tell him."

[5781]

"That horse knows as much as I do."

"Well, don't tell anybody. You may want to sell him some day."

[5782]

"What's the matter here?"

"Man broke his neck."

"What story did he fall from?"

"Didn't fall—tried to see the top of the building."

[5783]

"What's the matter with your feet?"

"I've got corns."

"Why don't you do something for them?"

"Why should I? They've never done anything for me."

[5784]

"What did that telephone girl say to you when she broke the engagement?"

"Ring off."

[5785]

"My wooden leg pained me terribly last night."

"How's that?"

"A friend hit me over the head with it."

[5786]

"I'll have you know I'm a self-made man."

"Yes, so I have assumed. But who interrupted you?"

[5787]

"Some men thirst after fame, some after love, and some after money."

"I know something that all thirst after."

"What's that?"

"Salted almonds."

[5788]

"I used to snore so loud I'd wake up; but I cured myself. I sleep in the next room now."

[5789]

"He's a tight one, you say?"

"Tight? He wouldn't give a beggar a bite if he owned the Sandwich Islands."

[5790]

"Where is the population of this country the most dense."

"That's an easy one — from the neck up, brother."

[5791]

"Hey, look—the barometer's falling!"

"Tsk, tsk—probably wasn't nailed up right."

[5792]

"I have made a will leaving my brains to the hospital and just got an acknowledgement from the authorities."

"Were they pleased?"

"They wrote that every little thing helps."

[5793]

"If you are going to borrow money, borrow it from a pessimist."

"Why a pessimist?"

"He never expects to get it back."

[5794]

"What is your chief worry?"

"Money."

"Oh, I didn't know you had any!"

"I haven't."

[5795]

"How old should you say she is?"

"Oh, somewhere in the middle flirties!"

[5796]

"What makes you so uneasy? Is your conscience troubling you?"

"No; it's my winter underwear."

[5797]

"So your uncle is dead. Did he leave much?"

"Only his old clock."

"Well, there won't be much bother winding up his estate."

[5798]

"Well, Sam, I'll tell you how it is. You see, I married a widow, and this widow had a daughter. Then my father, being a widower, married our daughter, so you see my father is my own son-in-law."

"Yes, I see."

"Then again my step-daughter is my step-mother, ain't she? Well, then, her mother is my grandmother, ain't she? I am married to her, ain't I? So that makes me my own grandfather, doesn't it?"

[5799]

"I have a terrible toothache and want something to cure it."

"Now, you don't need any medicine. I had a toothache yesterday and I went home and my loving wife kissed me and so consoled me that the pain soon passed away. Why don't you try the same?"

"I think I will. Is your wife at home now?"

[5800]

"What's that piece of cord tied around your finger for?"

"My wife put it there to remind me to post a letter."

"And did you post it?"

"No; she forgot to give it to me."

[5801]

"Have a cigar?"

"No, thanks—sworn off smoking."

"Well, put one in your pocket for tomorrow."

[5802]

"Why should a straw hat never be raised to a lady?"

"Well, that's a very hard question."

"Because no matter how much you shake it, or how much she appreciates it, it is never felt."

[5803]

"Did you get the check I sent you?"

"I got it twice—once from you and once from the bank."

[5804]

"This government report states that the life of a paper dollar is only seven or eight month."

"Well, I have never had one die on my hands."

[5805]

"That little dancer isn't a gold digger any longer."

"Oh, has she changed her ways?"

"No, she's heard about platinum."

[5806]

"I saw in a paper the other day that in some of the out-of-way places of the world they still use fish for money."

"What a sloppy job they must have trying to get chewing gum out of a slot machine."

[5807]

I have a great memory. I can recite all the names on three pages of the New York telephone directory. Wanna hear me? All right then, Cohen, Cohen, Cohen, Cohen, Cohen.

[5808]

"It takes Bill a day and a night to tell a story."

"He'd make a good bookkeeper, I should think."

"Why?"

"Never short in his account."

[5809]

"Are you looking for me, old man?"

"I don't even know your old man!"

[5810]

"What's the date today?"

"Let me look in the newspaper you have in your pocket."

"No use, it's yesterday's paper."

[5811]

"But you said she sang beautifully."

"No, I didn't."

"What did you say?"

"I said she was a beautiful singer."

[5812]

"Don't you think I sing with feeling?"

"No, if you had any you wouldn't sing."

[5813]

"They say that an apple a day will keep the doctor away."

"Why stop there? An onion a day will keep everybody away."

[5814]

"Why does an ostrich have such a long neck?"

"Because its head's so far from its body, I guess!"

[5815]

"Taking anything for your hay fever?"

"Yes, I'm taking boxing lessons to wallop the first man who gives me free advice."

[5816]

"Always remember that one swallow does not make a spring."

"No, but the swallows the size that you take would make one fall all right."

[5817]

"I drink about fifty cups of coffee a day."

"My Gawd. Doesn't that keep you awake?"

"It helps."

[5818]

"What, your son is an undertaker? I thought you said he was a doctor?"

"No, I said he followed the medical profession."

[5819]

"Do you smoke?"
"No."
"Do you drink?"
"No."
"Do you eat hay, then?"
"No."
"Gad! You're not a fit companion for man or beast."

[5820]

"What raw materials are imported from France?"

"Books and plays."

[5821]

"I gave a foot-ball player one dollar today."

"Did you get it back?"
"No; I got it half-back."

[5822]

"Have you a poor memory for faces?"

"Yes, for poor faces."

[5823]

"You would be a good dancer, but for two things."

"And they are?"
"Your feet!"

[5824]

I wish they would invent a new expression; it's "always the blushing bride."

Well, when you consider the sort of husbands the girls have to marry, it's enough to make them blush.

[5825]

"Mary has a wonderful husband."
"Yes? Houzat?"

"Why, he helps her do all the work. Monday he washed the dishes with her. Tuesday he dusted with her. And tomorrow he is going to mop the floor with her."

[5826]

"When I arrived at my girl's house last night, I found someone else had beaten me to the sofa."

"Your hated rival?"
"No, the installment collector."

[5827]

"Never saw such a crowd at our church before."

"New minister?"

"No; it was burned down last night."

[5828]

"My wife is a very hard woman to please."

"But she wasn't always that way."
"How do you know?"

"Why, she married you, didn't she?"

[5829]

"Why is Miss Jones wearing black?"

"She is in mourning for her husband."

"Why, she never had a husband!"
"No, that is why she mourns.

[5830]

"What do you think of that cigar?"

"It's so good I'm sure you must have given me the wrong one."

[5831]

"A certain girl is growing on me."

"What's so awful about that?"

"I'm her reducing specialist!"

[5832]

"Wise men are always in doubt. Only idiots are sure of their case."

"Are you sure of that?"

"Yes, absolutely."

[5833]

"I wonder why old man Smith puts all his savings under his pillow every night?"

"Reckon he wants people to know that he has money enough to retire on."

[5834]

"Why is it that a red headed woman always marries a meek man?"

"She doesn't. He just gets that way."

[5835]

"What is puppy love?"

"It's the beginning of a dog's life."

[5836]

"Believe it or not, but when I see red I'm happy."

"How's that?"

"I sell sunburn remedy."

[5837]

"They always said that old man Jones was good to his folks."

"Yes, he was, he was hardly ever home."

[5838]

"See if you can laugh that off," said the fat man's wife, wiring a button onto his vest.

[5839]

"And what makes you think there is a woman in the moon?"

"No man would stay up there that long alone, and be out every night."

[5840]

"Did you hear the story about the peacock?"

"No."

"It's a beautiful tale."

[5841]

"This liniment makes my arm smart."

"Why not rub some on your head?"

[5842]

"Did you see that charming girl smile at me?"

"Yes, the first time I saw you, I, too, had to smile."

[5843]

"I suppose you think I'm a perfect idiot?"

"Oh, none of us is perfect."

[5844]

"You should meet my husband. He makes a living with his pen."

"Oh, so he's a writer?"

"No, he raises pigs."

[5845]

"Do you believe marriage is a lottery?"

"No; in a lottery a man is supposed to have a chance."

[5846]

"He seems to be very clever."

"Yes, indeed. He can even do the problems that his children have to work out at school."

[5847]

"Bill's nowhere near the fool he was."

"Has he reformed?"

"No, he's dieting."

[5848]

"Can you stand on your head?"

"Nope. It's too high."

[5849]

"Why does Dingley wear his hair so long?"

"So he can create the impression that his mind is fertile."

[5850]

"Why was Solomon the wisest man in the world?"

"Because he had so many wives to advise him."

[5851]

"I am chilled to the bone."

"Why don't you put on your hat?"

[5852]

"What's worse than eating hash at a restaurant where you don't know what's in it?"

"Eating it at home where you do know."

[5853]

"I see your wife's back from Florida."

"I always knew she wore a low-neck gown, but never thought you could see her back from that distance."

[5854]

"My doctor told me how I could live to be a hundred and fifty years old, said I must not chew, smoke, drink or play cards. Stay in nights, abstain from all sweets and starches. He said: you may not live to be a hundred and fifty, but it will seem like it.

[5855]

"My husband had a funny dream last night and chewed the insides out of the pillow."

"Did he feel sick today?"

"No, just a little down in the mouth."

[5856]

"The violinist's execution was simply marvelous."

"Wasn't it, though? You could see the audience hanging on every note."

[5857]

"How big is a battleship?"

"What kind of battleship?"

"A big one!"

"How big?"

[5858]

"I always tell my wife everything that happens."

"That's nothing. I tell my wife lots of things that never happen."

[5859]

"My Uncle William has a new cedar chest."

"So! Last time I saw him he just had a wooden leg."

[5860]

"What do you think of these new French shorts they're showing?"

"O. K., I guess, but I still like the newsreels better."

[5861]

"I see there is a plan to tax the barbers $1 each annually, won't it work a hardship on them?"

"They can easily scrape up the money."

[5862]

Then there was the bow legged floor walker who said, "Walk this way, please."

[5863]

"I want to do something big and something clean."

"Then wash an elephant."

[5864]

"Does your wife support you?"

"No, but she holds me up every pay-day."

[5865]

"So you're down to the seaside now?"

"Yes, and it's great. By the way, speaking of seaside, if a man gets a biff in the eye and it swells up like a mountain, doesn't it follow that the other side of his face is the see-side?"

[5866]

"I wonder who this telegram is from."

"Western Union: I recognize the handwriting."

[5867]

"Where is the best place to hold the world's fair?"

"Around the waist."

[5868]

"Guess my pen will have to go on itching."

"Why?"

"I'm out of scratch paper."

[5869]

"I had a fall last night which rendered me unconscious for several hours."

"You don't mean it? Where did you fall?"

"I fell asleep."

[5870]

"He called me an ass!"

"Don't stand for it."

"What'll I do?"

"Make him prove it."

[5871]

"What an awful gash you have on your forehead!"

"Oh, next to nothing — next to nothing."

[5872]

"What was the first thing the grasshopper said after it was created?"

"Oh, Lord! How you make me jump!"

[5873]

"They laughed when I started to make a new kind of dynamite, but when I dropped it, they exploded."

[5874]

"Say did you ever see a mermaid?"

"Well not exactly, but I did see a fish-woman."

[5875]

"What kind of a fellow is Blinks?"

"Well, he is one of those fellows who always grab the stool when there is a piano to be moved."

[5876]

"I married a widow with six children. I had five myself by my late wife. We have been married four years and our union had been blessed with three more, and the other day my wife came in hurriedly and said, come into the yard, quick! for goodness sake, hurry! there is a terrible row going on, and I said, 'what is it?' 'Well,' she said 'your children and my children are whipping *our* children.'"

[5877]

"How can I avoid falling hair?"

"Jump out of the way."

[5878]

"Say, why do they call our language the mother-tongue?"

"Because the father so seldom gets a chance to use it."

[5879]

"They laughed at me when I sat down at the piano—I had forgotten to bring the stool."

[5880]

"Do you like codfish balls, Mr. Fox?"

"I don't know, Mrs. Stubbins; I never attended any."

[5881]

"I didn't raise my daughter to be fiddled with," said the pussycat as she rescued her offspring from the violin factory.

[5882]

"Does the giraffe get a sore throat if he gets wet feet?"

"Yes, but not until the next week."

[5883]

"Why is a clock like a vain, pretty young lady?"

"I fail to see any resemblance. Why?"

"Because it's all face and figure, has no head to speak of, is very hard to stop after it is wound up, and has a striking way of calling attention to itself every hour of the day."

[5884]

"Have you any close relatives?"

"All of 'em are."

[5885]

"Do you want to get next to something there's a lot of money in?"

"Sure."

"Well, go down town and lean up against a bank."

[5886]

"I got sick last night eating eggs."

"Too bad."

"No, only one."

[5887]

Girl—"Every time I look at you I think of a great man."

Boy Friend—"You flatter me. Who is it?"

Girl—"Darwin."

[5888]

"There's one bet I think is always good."

"What's that?"

"The alphabet."

[5889]

"I have forgotten more than you'll ever know."

"I would rather know what you have forgotten than what you remember."

[5890]

"Shipwrecked for a whole week."

"My, my, do tell."

"Lived the week on a can of sardines."

"Tsk, tsk, how could you move around?"

[5891]

"Why are men's eyes like the sparrows?"

"Because they flit from limb to limb."

[5892]

"It must be nice to own a chain of stores."

"Yes; you can spend all your time on the links."

[5893]

"Who were the first gamblers?"

"Adam and Eve."

"How so?"

"Didn't they shake a paradise?"

[5894]

"Why do they have most all radio broadcasting stations on top of tall buildings?"

"So nobody can throw bricks at the performers."

[5895]

"Pa, why do they joke so much about wives roasting their husbands?"

"Because the old fools pull off so much raw stuff."

[5896]

"Yes, he's a year old now, and he's been walking since he was eight months."

"Really? He must be awfully tired!"

[5897]

"Brown was a mighty smart fellow."

"Smart nothing; he just married a millionaire's daughter, that's all."

"That's all? Did you ever try to marry a millionaire's daughter?"

[5898]

"I got a hunch."

"Really, I thought you were just roundshouldered."

[5899]

"I aim to tell the truth."

"Yes, and you are probably the worst shot in America."

[5900]

"Aren't people funny?"

"Yes. If you tell a man that there are 270,678,934,341 stars in the universe he'll believe you — but if a sign says 'Fresh Paint,' that same man has to make a personal investigation."

[5901]

"I hear Brown fell down on his pharmacy examination."

"Yes—he got mixed on the difference between a club and a Western sandwich."

[5902]

"Why is a lady's belt like an ash cart?"

"Give it up."

"Because it goes round and gathers the waist."

[5903]

"My brother was fired from his job for not watching his step."

"What's his job?"

"He's a tap dancer."

[5904]

"My dog took first prize at the cat show."

"How was that?"

"He took the cat."

[5905]

"What would be the proper thing to say if, in carving the duck, it should skid off the platter and into your neighbor's lap?"

"Be very courteous. Say, 'May I trouble you for that duck?'"

[5906]

"Smith has left his umbrella again. I do believe he would leave his head if it were not fastened to him."

"Yes, I gues you're right. I heard him say only yesterday that he was going to Colorado for his lungs."

[5907]

"Pop, what is a layman?"

"A layman, my son, is a pedestrian who jumped too late."

[5908]

"How did you get that bump?"

"My wife threw a vase at me."

"Why on earth didn't you duck?"

"I did, but she allowed for it."

[5909]

"What's the difference between a lemon and a head of cabbage?"

"I don't know."

"You would be a nice one to send after lemons."

[5910]

"As your friend, I ought to tell you, that Jim Johnson is going around telling all kinds of lies about you."

"Oh, that's O.K. But if he ever starts telling the truth, let me know. I'll break his neck."

[5911]

"Can you tell me why the hand of the Statue of Liberty is just eleven inches long?"

"Why, certainly; if they had made it an inch longer, it would have been a foot."

[5912]

"What is worse than a giraffe with a sore throat?"

"I can't imagine anything worse. What is worse?"

"A centipede with chilblains."

[5913]

"What's the best exercise for reducing?"

"Just move the head slowly from right to left when asked to have a second helping."

[5914]

"That girl looks like Helen Black, doesn't she?"

"Why, that dress ain't black."

[5915]

"Your dog howled all night."

"That's a sign of death. Whose, I wonder?"

"Your dog's, if he howls again tonight."

[5916]

"Who was the blonde you were out with Wednesday and Thursday?"

"She was the brunette I was out with Monday and Tuesday."

[5917]

"My hair has been giving me a great deal of trouble lately; can you suggest anything?"

"Don't let that worry you, old man; it'll come out, all right."

[5918]

"I'm in an awful predicament."

"What's the trouble?"

"I've lost my glasses and I can't look for them until I've found them again!"

[5919]

"I thought you were dead."

"What gave you that impression?"

"I heard a man speak well of you this morning."

[5920]

"It was while traveling in Switzerland on the verge of a mountain gorge, that I proposed to Miss Smith."

"Horrors! Suppose she had thrown you over."

[5921]

"I hear that Jim had an accident."

"Yes, some one gave him a tiger cub, and told him it would eat off his hand."

"Well?"

"It did."

[5922]

"How do you get down off an elephant?"

"You climb down."

"Wrong!"

"You grease his sides and slide down."

"Wrong!"

"You take a ladder and get down."

"Wrong!"

"Well, you take the trunk line down."

"No, not quite. You don't get down off an elephant; you get it off a goose."

[5923]

"How do you like bathing beauties?"

"Can't tell. I never bathed any."

[5924]

"I heard something this morning that opened my eyes."

"So did I—an alarm clock."

[5925]

"He calls himself a dynamo."

"No wonder; everything he has on is charged."

[5926]

"Some men are born great, some achieve greatness—"

"And some just grate upon you."

[5927]

"What is this kleptomania that I read so much about in the papers. Is it catching?"

"No, it is taking."

[5928]

"So you're not going to Paris, this year?"

"No—it's London we're not going to this year; it was Paris we didn't go to last year!"

[5929]

"Have you planted anything in your garden yet?"

"Only my watch, fountain pen, lodge pin and seven lead pencils."

[5930]

"What is the right way of pronouncing this word 'Fascist'?"

"Oh, it's quite easy. Just as if you were slightly tight!"

[5931]

"Say, what became of that girl you made love to in the hammock?"

"We fell out."

[5932]

"Have you any poor relations?"

"Not one that I know."

"Have you rich relations?"

"Not one that knows me."

[5933]

"I am always ill the night before a journey."

"Then why don't you go a day earlier?"

[5934]

"What kind of a plant is the Virginia creeper?"

"It isn't a plant; it's a railroad."

[5935]

"Didn't I meet you in Toledo?"

"No, I never was in Toledo."

"Neither was I. It must have been two other fellows."

[5936]

"Do you know, I started in life as a barefooted boy?"

"Well, I wasn't born with shoes on."

[5937]

"What's the best way to tell a bad egg?"

"I don't know, but I would suggest that if you have anything really important to tell a bad egg, why—break it gently."

[5938]

"I know how to solve the unemployment problem."

"Many great men have tried and failed. How would you do it?"

"If we could place all the men on one continent and all the women on another continent, everybody would be busy in no time."

"And what would everybody be so busy doing?"

"Why boat-building, of course."

[5939]

"Well, back from visiting the great musician? How did you find him?"

"Brushed the hair aside and there he was."

[5940]

"What the deuce do you mean by telling Mary that I am a fool?"

"Heavens! I'm sorry—was it a secret?"

[5941]

"The more lawyers the longer the case."

"The more doctors the shorter the case."

[5942]

"I know a fellow who got into trouble being frank and earnest."

"Yeah!"

"Yeah! Frank in New York and Ernest in Brooklyn."

[5943]

"Jones isn't too pleased he's got twins. He only wanted one child."

"Well, what do you expect? He married a telephone girl, and they always give the wrong number."

[5944]

"Have you heard the story about the ear of corn?"

"No. I never did."

"Then ask the Kernel."

[5945]

"Lucy sure does ring the bell for one with so few advantages."

"How do you figure it?"

"Every day she punches a time clock at the factory."

[5946]

"I suppose Thompson is the most pious fellow I know."

"Why, he never struck me that way. In fact I always thought him rather wordly."

"Well, I happen to know for a fact that he never kisses his girl without saying grace."

"Why, what in the world does he do that for?"

"That's her name."

[5947]

"The Lincoln Highway has signs all along warning the petters."

"What do the signs say?"

"Beware of soft shoulders."

[5948]

"I love the Swiss Alps. They've given me some of my happiest moments."

"Why, you've never been in Switzerland!"

"No, but my wife has."

[5949]

"I've eaten beef all my life, and now I'm as strong as an ox!"

"That's funny, I've eaten fish all my life and I can't swim a stroke."

[5950]

"What time do you get up in summer?"

"As soon as the first ray of the sun comes in my window."

"Isn't that rather early?"

"No. My room faces west."

[5951]

"I notice that you smoke your cigarettes shorter."

"Yeh. That's because I smoke 'em longer."

[5952]

"What is Swiss cheese, really?"

"It's a sort of round animal with a thick yellow skin, and has to be shot twenty-five or thirty times before it is dead. You'll find lots of defunct Swiss cheese in delicatessen stores full of bullet holes."

[5953]

"Why is a young couple making love on the beach like a bull-dog on a cake of ice?"

"Give it up."

"Because it's dog-on-nice."

[5954]

"Say, did you know that Massachusetts is noted for boots and shoes."

"Yes, and Kentucky is noted for shoots and booze."

[5955]

"Why do people have candles on their birthday cakes for?"

"Oh, just to make light of their age."

[5956]

"Have you ever seen anything faster than an airplane?"

"Yes, once I was shipwrecked on a desert island with a dozen chorus girls."

"And what traveled so fast under those circumstances?"

"A rescue ship!"

[5957]

"My brother is working with 5000 men under him."

"Where?"

"Mowing lawns in a cemetery."

[5958]

"Does the animal trainer in a circus get much money?"

"He sure does. He gets the lion's share of the money."

[5959]

"Were you at the races yesterday?"

"No."

"Then I guess you've got it."

"Got what?"

"Five dollars. I need it."

[5960]

"My wife's a fine shot. She can hit a dollar every time."

"That's nothing. My wife goes through my trousers and never misses a dime."

[5961]

"What is that bird?"

"That is a magpie."

"It's not my idea of a magpie."

"Perhaps not, but it's God's idea of a magpie."

[5962]

"Gosh, I need five bucks and I don't know where to get it."

"I'm glad of that. I was afraid you thought you could get it from me."

[5963]

"There's a man outside who says he has a dual personality."

"Tell him to go chase himself."

[5964]

"Do you know some things are getting very cheap now?"

"What, for instance?"

"Well, you can get all the cologne that you want for a scent."

[5965]

"Did your watch stop when it hit the floor?"

"Sure, did you think it would go on through?"

[5966]

"Do you ever pause and reflect on the opportunities you have missed?"

"No. It would be just my luck to miss some more while I was reflecting."

[5967]

"A moth leads an awful life."

"How come?"

"He spends the summer in a fur coat and the winter in a bathing suit."

[5968]

"What happened to that fellow who was accused of forging your signature to a check?"

"He was remanded for a medical examination."

[5969]

"Poor old Johnson bends over backwards to give his wife every luxury."

"Business man?"

"No, contortionist."

[5970]

"Did you ever notice how easy barbers get acquainted?"

"How do you account for it?"

"Because they never hesitate to scrape an acquaintance."

[5971]

"Is it possible to confide a secret to you?"

"Certainly. I will be as silent as the grave."

"Well, then, I have a pressing need for two bucks."

"Do not worry. It is as if I had heard nothing."

[5972]

"I think that fellow is a bad egg."

"No, he's too fresh for that."

[5973]

"How did Freddie lose all his money? Preferred stock?"

"No, preferred blondes."

[5974]

"I suppose your home-town is one of those places where everyone goes down to meet the train."

"What train?"

[5975]

"When I get a cold I buy a bottle of whiskey for it, and within a few hours it's gone."

"My, that's a short time to get rid of a cold."

"Rid of the cold, hell. It's the whiskey that goes."

[5976]

"So she turned you down, eh?"

"Yes. I made the mistake of confessing that my heart was in my mouth when I proposed."

"What had that to do with it?"

"Oh, she said she couldn't think of marrying a man whose heart wasn't in the right place."

[5977]

"What is the outstanding contribution that chemistry has given to the world?"

"Blondes!"

[5978]

"Isn't this beastly weather we're having?"

"I don't understand?"

"Isn't it raining cats and dogs?"

[5979]

"When it comes to eating, you'll have to hand it to Venus de Milo."

"Why?"

"How else could she eat?"

[5980]

"How do you find yourself these cold mornings?"

"Oh, I throw back the covers and there I am."

[5981]

"You hammer nails like lightning."

"I'm fast, you mean?"

"No, you never strike twice in the same place."

[5982]

"I have a rare old victrola. It was once in the possession of George Washington."

"But there was no such thing as victrolas in Washington's time."

"That's what makes it so rare."

[5983]

"How much did old Moneybags leave?"

"Oh, he left it all. He didn't take any with him."

[5984]

"I went to see a spiritualist last night."

"Was he good?"

"No, just medium."

[5985]

"So you worked your way up from the bottom."

"Yes, I started out as a bootblack, and now I'm a hairdresser."

[5986]

"This certainly is a unique town."

"Yeah, from the French 'une' for one and the Latin 'equis' for horse."

[5987]

"You remember that nice iceman we used to have?"

"Yes."

"He's gone on the stage."

"Was he a success?"

"No; very much of a frost."

[5988]

"Are you any good at palmistry?"

"Well, not exactly, though the other night I did look at a lady's hand, and one glance told me she was going to be lucky."

"Why, how did you tell?"

"Because she had the four aces in it."

[5989]

"Did you hear about the accident my brother had? He fell against the piano and hit his head."

"That's too bad. Did he hurt himself?"

"Oh, no; not much. You see he only hit the soft pedal."

[5990]

"Yes, I came face to face with a lion once. To make matters worse, I was alone and weaponless . . ."

"Goodness! What did you do?"

"What could I do? First I tried looking straight into his eye-balls, but he kept crawling up on me. Then I thought of plunging my arm down his throat, grabbing him by the tail and turning him inside out, but I decided it would be too dangerous. Yet, he kept creeping up on me; I had to think fast . . ."

"How did you get away?"

"I just left him and passed on to the other cages."

[5991]

"If I could only marry some rich girl, I'd have no more trouble about money."

"Why don't you do it, then?"

"My wife might raise a row if I did."

[5992]

"I can't find a single pin. Where do they all go to, anyway?"

"It's hard to tell, because they're pointed in one direction and they're headed in another."

[5993]

"You can catch more flies with sugar than you can with vinegar."

"That may be so, but what do I want with a lot of flies?"

[5994]

"I've never heard an ill word spoken regarding this town."

"I suppose that's because it's bad form to speak ill of the dead."

[5995]

"You know Fatty Johnson, the butcher. What do you suppose he weighs?"

"I don't know, what does he weigh?"

"Meat."

[5996]

"Do you exercise after the morning bath?"

"Yes, I generally step on the soap as I get out."

[5997]

"Why don't you like girls?"

"They're too biased."

"Biased?"

"Yes, bias this and bias that—until I'm busted."

[5998]

"I'm gonna sneeze."

"At who?"

"Atchoo!"

[5999]

"There was a story afloat down town today that Jones was embarrassed on account of the fall of May wheat."

"You don't say; who is she?"

[6000]

"Mr. Loring is quite a linguist, isn't he?"

"I never knew it."

"Oh, yes, he talks three languages."

"What are they?"

"Horse, baseball, and golf."

[6001]

"There seems to be a strange affinity between a darky and a chicken. I wonder why?"

"Naturally enough. One is descended from Ham and the other from eggs."

[6002]

"Do you think a woman should tell everything she knows?"

"Yes, but that's all."

[6003]

"Why is it impossible for a woman ever to be president of the United States?"

"Because to be president a person must be at least thirty-five years of age."

[6004]

"Have you a cigarette?"

"Lots of them, thanks."

[6005]

"New suit?"

"Yep, isn't it a swell fit?"

"Fit, hell—it's a convulsion!"

[6006]

"You say that he is real sure of himself?"

"I'll say he is. He even does crossword puzzles with a pen."

GOLF

[6007]

"My wife says if I don't chuck golf, she'll leave me."

"I say—hard luck!"

"Yes-es. I'll miss her."

[6008]

"This caddy of mine is a thief. I'm afraid he'll swipe this new golf ball of mine."

"I wouldn't putt it past him."

[6009]

Golf Widow-"You think so much of your old golf game that you don't even remember when we were married."

Bug-"Of course I do, my dear; it was the day I sank that thirty-foot putt."

[6010]

Yvonne-"Whatever induced Dora to take up golf so suddenly?"

Yvette-"Oh, she read a newspaper article about somebody finding a diamond in the rough."

[6011]

Two golfers, slicing their drives into the rough, went in search of the balls. They searched for a long time without success, a dear old lady watching them with kind and sympathetic eyes.

At last, after the search had proceeded for half an hour, she spoke to them.

"I hope I'm not interrupting, gentlemen," she said sweetly, "but would it be cheating if I told you where they are?"

[6012]

Friendly Golfer (to player searching for lost ball)-"What sort of a ball was it?"

Caddy (butting in)-"A brand new one—never been properly hit yet!"

[6013]

"If you spend so much time at golf you won't have anything laid aside for a rainy day."

"Won't I? My desk is loaded up with work that I've put aside for a rainy day."

[6014]

Golfer-"Terrible links, caddy, terrible!"

Caddy-"Sorry, sir, these ain't links —you got off them an hour ago."

[6015]

He had joined a golf club, and on his first round he hit the ball a mighty swipe which by some miracle landed it in the hole in one.

At the second tee came another miracle. Again he did the hole in one, and as the ball disappeared into the hole he turned round, white and trembling.

"Gosh!" he breathed. "I thought I'd missed it that time."

[6016]

Poor Golfer—"Well, how do you like my game?"

Caddy—"I suppose it's all right, but I still prefer golf."

[6017]

No matter how you slice it, it's still a golf ball.

[6018]

He was so proud of his play as a golfer that he wanted to show off. So he invited his mother-in-law along to watch him.

As he started off for the first tee, he said to his opponent:

"I'm particularly anxious to make a terrific drive. That's my wife's mother standing over there."

"Sorry, old man," said the other; "but you can't expect to hit her at two hundred yards."

[6019]

Wife—"John, you play golf altogether too much, you are neglecting your business."

Golf Nut—"The doctor says I must take my iron every day."

[6020]

I hear that "Pete" was hiring a caddy at the Country Club one day last week. The following conversation took place:

"Can you count?" asked Pete.

"Yes, sir," said the boy.

"Can you add up?"

"Yes, sir," was the answer.

"Then, how many are four and five and three?" from Pete.

"Nine, sir."

"Come on," said Pete. "You'll do."

[6021]

In Washington they tell the story of a clergyman who had been badly beaten in the links by a parishioner thirty years his senior and had returned to the clubhouse rather disgruntled.

"Cheer up," his opponent said, "Remember, you win at the finish. You'll probably be burying me some day."

"Even then," replied the preacher, "it will be your hole."

[6022]

An Irishman crossing the golf links got hit by a ball. The player hurried up and finding that Pat was not seriously hurt, he said sharply, "Why didn't you get out of the way?"

"An' why should I get out of the way?" said the Irishman angrily. "I didn't know there was any murderers around here."

"But I called 'fore,'" said the player, "and when I say 'fore' that's a sign you are to get out of the way."

"Oh, it is, is it?" said Pat. "Well, when I say 'foive,' it's a sign that you are goin' to get hit in the jaw. Foive!"

[6023]

Irate Golfer—"You must take your children away from here, madam. This is no place for them."

Mother—"Don't you worry—they can't hear nothing new. Their father was a sergeant-major, he was."

[6024]

Two casual golf acquaintances were walking toward the green when they sighted two women coming over a hill.

"I say," remarked one of the men, "here comes my wife with some old hag she's picked up somewhere."

"And here comes mine with another," retorted the other, icily.

[6025]

Plant Supt.—"Why did you persuade Uncle Tom to take up golf? Now he'll live forever."

Plant Supt.'s Brother—"Don't you believe it—he'll swear himself into apoplexy."

[6026]

Physician (to rich patient)—"You're all run down. I suggest that you lay off golf for a while and get a good rest at your office."

[6027]

An inventor has produced a golf ball which squeaks when it is lost. At present the golfer does that.

[6028]

A certain sportsman was playing over a golf course in Scotland, and playing very badly.

"Dear, dear!" he remarked at last, "there canna be worse players than myself!"

"Weel, weel, maybe there are worse players," commented the caddy consolingly, "but they dinna play."

[6029]

First Newsboy—"Chimmie's got a job as caddy for a golf club. Is dere much money in dat?"

Second Ditto—"De salary ain't much, but dey makes a lot extra backin' up fellers when dey lies about de scores dey made."

[6030]

The two beginners were playing golf. The next green was 300 yards away and over numerous hazards.

One shut his eyes and took a lusty swing. By a freak of chance he connected with the ball and sent it sailing for the green. It bounded directly into the cup for a hole in one.

"You've made a hole in one," exclaimed the other in an awed voice.

"I'll wager two to one I could do it again," bragged the first.

"Okay," grunted his friend, "It's a wager—but on one condition."

"Sure," agreed the confident one. "What's the condition?"

"This time," said the other, "you've got to make the shot with your eyes open!"

[6031]

The millionaire, whose daughter the young man had just saved, was insistent that he accept a cash reward. Finally, to save an embarrassing situation, our hero said casually:

"Well, if you insist, just give me a golf club."

A week later he received a telegram from the father:

"Have bought for you the Westend Golfer's Club, and am now negotiating for the Sunnyside Links."

[6032]

And then there was the condemned golfer who asked the hangman, "Mind if I take a couple of practice swings?"

[6033]

"I suppose you play golf?"

"No," replied Mr. Newrich. "I can't say that I play it. But I am still working at it."

[6034]

A tramp was sleeping behind the bunker of a golf course when the club secretary, prowling around, kicked him none too gently and ordered him to clear out.

"And who are you?" demanded the tramp.

"I'm secretary of the club," said the official.

"Well," replied the tramp, "that's no way to get new members."

[6035]

Visitor–"I hear you've lost your parrot that used to swear so terribly."

Hostess–"Yes, poor dear, we found him dead on the golf links."

[6036]

Dear Old Lady–"No, I'm afraid I know very little about golf. I couldn't even tell one end of a caddie from the other."

[6037]

The great difference between learning to drive a car and to play golf is that in one case you hit everything, and in the other you hit nothing.

[6038]

Some railroad laborers who worked near a golf course were vastly intrigued by the game. They saw a golfer knock the ball into a rut and have a hard time extricating it. Then he got into a sand trap and well-nigh failed to get out.

At length he got a good shot and the ball trickled directly into the cup. Whereupon an Irish laborer who had watched the previous difficulties said sympathetically:

"Now, mister, yez *arre* in a helluva fix!"

[6039]

Smith–"You seldom see such beautiful golf as that man plays. His drives were corking, his approaches superb and he never missed a putt."

Jones–"How much were you beaten by?"

Smith–"Why, I won!"

[6040]

An enthusiastic golfer came home to dinner. During the meal his wife said: "Willie tells me he caddied for you this afternoon."

"Well, do you know," said Willie's father, "I thought I'd seen that boy before."

[6041]

Rich Man–"There's no sense in teaching the boy to count over 100. He can hire accountants to do his bookkeeping."

Tutor–"Yes, sir, but he'll want to play his own game of golf, won't he?"

[6042]

First Caddie–"What's your man like, Skeeter?"

Second Caddie–"Left-handed, and keeps his change in his right-hand pocket."

[6043]

Another shower of pebbles and stones is reported to have fallen in Central Mexico. The latest theory regarding this phenomena is that some place near the American border a determined golfer is trying to get out of a sand trap.

[6044]

"Did you read recently how a golfer got 828 holes out of a single golf ball?"

"Yes, I only got 36 holes out of the same brand of ball."

"Well, considering your game yours is the stronger testimonial!"

[6045]

With half a hundred people looking on, he stepped up to his ball, took a mighty swing, and missed. Again he addressed the pellet, swung and whiffed. A third time he tried, but to no avail. The crowd became highly embarrassed. But not so our hero. With a nonchalant smile he turned to the assembled multitude and remarked. "Tough course, isn't it?"

[6046]

"How's your daughter's golf?" asked one grande dame of another.

"She says she is going around in less and less every week."

"I don't doubt that. I asked about her golf."

[6047]

"What do you think would go well with my purple and green golf socks?"

"Hip boots."

[6048]

"I am sorry," said the dentist, "but you can not have an appointment with me this afternoon. I have eighteen cavities to fill." And he picked up his golf-bag and went out.

[6049]

Club Expert—"Your trouble is that you don't address the ball properly."

Novice—"Well, I was polite to the darn thing as long as possible."

[6050]

An enthusiastic golfer died and found himself before the Pearly Gates. Being of cautious disposition, he thought he would do some investigating before entering the Celestial City. He approached St. Peter, and inquired, "Do you have any links in heaven?"

St. Peter shook his head. He seemed never to have heard of them.

"No links," exclaimed the golfer. "You must surely have a golf course. Why, you're not up-to-date at all."

And he turned sadly away to try his luck in hell.

Coming to the domains ruled over by Sathanus, he was welcomed by an imp.

"Do you have a golf course here?" he inquired.

"Certainly," the imp replied. "We have all the modern improvements."

The golfer's face lit up. Here was evidently the abode for him. "Lead me to it," he urged.

"Yes, sir, right this way, sir," and the imp led him to a distant part of hell. Before the golfer, stretched a course more wonderful than any of which he had ever dreamed.

"Fine," he exclaimed. "Now, son, get me some sticks and balls, and I'll have the game of my life."

"We haven't any," the imp replied.

"What," exclaimed the golfer. "Not any clubs and balls with a fine course like this?"

"No, sir," replied the imp, grinning fiendishly, "that's the hell of it."

[6051]

Earth flew in all directions as the crimson-faced would-be golfer attempted to strike the ball. "My word," he blurted out to his caddie, "the worms will think there's an earthquake."

"I don't know," replied the caddie, "the worms 'round here are crafty. I'll bet most of them are hiding underneath the ball for safety."

[6052]

A professional golfer in his advice to beginners says that lifting the elbow is the cause of erratic drives and wild swings. This is particularly true when the elbow lifting starts in the clubhouse.

[6053]

"My husband is very frank and plain-spoken. He always calls a spade a spade."

"So does mine. But I can't tell you what he sometimes calls his golf-clubs."

[6054]

"Murphy got rich quick, didn't he?"

"He got rich so quick that he can't swing a golf club without spitting on his hands."

[6055]

A dictionary of golfing terms is to be published. If it's complete it will be banned from the mails.

[6056]

Golfer–"Hi, caddie! Isn't Major Pepper out of that bunker yet? How many strokes has he had?"

Caddie–"Seventeen ordinary, sir, and one apoplectic!"

[6057]

Golf Pro–"Tee the ball."

Fellow–"Sure, I see it, but why the baby talk?"

[6058]

A sign on a Scottish golf course reads as follows:

"Members will refrain from picking up lost balls until they have stopped rolling."

[6059]

Statistician says there are more than 300 kinds of games played with balls. We, personally, have seen more than 300 kinds of games played with golf balls.

[6060]

Don Marquis, author and playwright, once offered to play an expert golfer at five dollars a hole and give the expert two strokes in the bargain.

"I'll take that bet!" was the immediate reply. "Now where do I get my two strokes?"

"I don't care where you take the second," said Don Marquis, "but the first has to be a stroke of apoplexy."

[6061]

Golfer (far off in the rough)–"Say, caddy, why do you keep looking at your watch?"

Caddy–"It isn't a watch, sir; it's a compass."

[6062]

A British society is promoting a Home of Aged Golfers. How aged does a golfer have to be before he becomes interested in a home?

[6063]

"When I put the ball where I can reach it," said the stout golfer, when asked how he liked the game, "I can't see it, and when I put it where I can see it, I can't reach it."

[6064]

"Does he play much golf a day?"

"Oh, thirty-six holes, roughly speaking."

"And how many without cursing?"

[6065]

Golf liars have one advantage over the fishing kind—they don't have to show anything to prove it.

[6066]

A Liverpool man claims to have invented a game which in some respect resembles golf. We have been playing a game like that for years.

[6067]

After the first hole, the Englishman turned to his Scotch opponent. "How many did you take?" he asked.

"Eight," replied the Scotsman.

"I took seven, so that's my hole," said the Englishman.

After the second hole, the Englishman asked the same question. This time the Scotsman shook his head.

"Na, na, laddie," he replied, "it's mae turn to ask first now."

[6068]

It's no sin to play golf on Sunday, but the way some play is a crime.

[6069]

Golfer–"If you laugh at me again, I'll knock your block off."

Caddie–"Haw, haw, you wouldn't even know what club to use."

[6070]

At a golf club one Sunday morning a member turned up late. Asked why, he said it was really a toss-up whether he should come there that morning or go to church.

"And I had to toss up fifteen times," he added.

[6071]

Golfer (to members ahead)–"Pardon, but would you mind if I played through? I've just heard that my wife has been taken seriously ill."

[6072]

Golfer–"Notice any improvement since last year?"

Caddy–"Had your clubs shined up, haven't you, sir?"

[6073]

"What do you think is the most difficult thing for a beginner to learn about golf?"

"To keep from talking about it all the time."

[6074]

A golfer, no matter how badly he played, was never heard to swear. One day one of his opponents remarked upon this fact.

"Yeh, it's true, I don't cuss," admitted the fozzler, "but let me tell you this. Every time I miss I spit. And whenever I spit, the grass don't grow again no more."

[6075]

"Why do you play golf so much?"
"It keeps me fit."
"What for?"
"Golf."

[6076]

Lady Golf Novice (after tenth swipe at ball)–"Thank goodness it's gone at last."

Caddie–"It isn't the ball that's gone miss—it's your wrist watch."

[6077]

Golfer (peevishly)–"I'll report you to the caddie master as soon as we get back."

Caddie–"Huh! I needn't start worryin' for ages yet!"

[6078]

Golfer Brown–"Confound it, you almost hit my wife."

Golfer Green–"Did I? Well have a shot at mine."

[6079]

A keen golfer had a charming girl on his right at dinner, and gave her graphic descriptions of his achievements with the clubs, hardly allowing her time to say more than "Really!"

During the dessert he remarked: "I'm afraid I've been monopolizing the conversation and talking nothing but golf."

"Oh never mind," said the girl. "But you might tell me: What is golf?"

[6080]

The golfer had lost his ball, and, not unnaturally, was inclined to be annoyed with his caddie.

"Why the deuce didn't you watch where it went?" he asked angrily.

"Well, sir," said the boy, "it don't usually go anywhere, and so it took me unprepared like."

[6081]

A golf-professional, hired by a big department store to give golf-lessons, was approached by two women.

"Do you wish to learn to play golf, madam?" he asked one.

"Oh, no," she said, "it's my friend who wants to learn. I learned yesterday."

[6082]

Mrs. Brown—"While you were abroad did you visit the Holy Land?"

Mrs. Golfer—"I didn't, but my husband did. He wouldn't go home until he'd played St. Andrews."

[6083]

Four men were playing golf on a course where the hazard on the ninth hole was a deep ravine.

They drove off. Three went into the ravine and one managed to get his ball over. The three who dropped into the ravine walked up to have a look. Two of them decided not to try to play their balls out and gave up the hole. The third said he would go down and play out his ball. He disappeared into the deep crevasse. Presently his ball came bobbing out and after a time he climbed up.

"How many strokes?" asked one.

"Three."

"But I heard six."

"Three of them were echoes!"

[6084]

"My doctor tells me I can't play golf."

"So he's played with you, too."

[6085]

"What was your score?" asked a golfer.

"Seventy-two," replied the novice.

"Seventy-two? That's good!"

"It's not so bad," agreed the novice, "but I'm hoping to do better at the second hole."

[6086]

Golfer—"Absolutely shocking! I've never played so badly before."

Caddie—"Oh! You have played before, then!"

BRIDGE

[6087]

A New York four has beaten a London four at bridge. London Bridge is falling down.

[6088]

"What did you bid no trump on? I had three aces and four kings."

"Well, if you really want to know—one jack, two queens and four drinks."

[6089]

The old quarrel between North and South has spread out to include East and West, and is now called contract bridge.

[6090]

Two men were getting ready for a dip in a swimming pool.

"Your shins are in pretty bad shape," remarked one. "Hockey player?"

"Oh, no," was the reply. "I just led back my wife's weak suit."

[6091]

"Shall we have a friendly game of cards?"

"No, let's play bridge."

[6092]

Wife (reading from paper)–"Here's an old hen they've found with two hearts."

Husband–"Yeah? Well, I played bridge with her the other night."

[6093]

Old Bridger–"Come on—we're only playing for one-tenth of a cent."

New Bridger–"You can't kid me— they don't make coins as small as that."

[6094]

"How about the sermon?"

"The minister preached on the sinfulness of cheating at bridge."

"You don't say! Did he mention any names?"

[6095]

The newest ailment is "Bridge Wrist," due to constantly inhibited desires to strangle one's partner.

[6096]

"Hello! Is this the city bridge department?"

"Yes! What can we do for you?"

"How many points do you get for a little slam?"

[6097]

Bill–"There are two things Bridge has taught women, concentration and self-control."

Jim–"Not to mention the art of opening cans and how to pick up a meal at the delicatessen."

[6098]

The ardent bridge player made a death-bed request that he be buried with simple honors.

[6099]

"Does your wife play bridge for money?"

"Maybe she plays for it, but she never gets any."

[6100]

"Have you ever seen a prize-fight?"

"No, I've never seen a prize-fight, but I have looked in on a women's afternoon bridge party."

[6101]

"Fourth for bridge!"

"Okay!"

"That's great! Now all we need's a third."

[6102]

Husband (testily, after losing badly at Bridge) – "You might have guessed I had no heart, partner."

Wife (sweetly)–"Quite; but I thought you had a brain, darling."

[6103]

Dr. Parr had a high opinion of his own skill at whist (ancestor of Bridge) and could not even tolerate the want of it in his partner. Being engaged with a party in which he was unequally matched, he was asked by a lady how the fortune of the game turned, when he replied, "Pretty well, madam, considering that I have *three* adversaries."

[6104]

Mrs. Fozzle (to Bridge expert)– "In the same circumstance, how would you have played the hand?"

Bridge Expert–"Under an assumed name, ma'am."

[6105]

Mother–"It takes two to make a quarrel."

Daughter–"No, mother, you need four to play bridge."

HUNTING

[6106]

"Gus," said Bill, as he caught up with Gus on the way back to camp, "are all the rest of the boys out of the woods yet?"

"Yes," said Gus.

"All six of them?"

"Yes, all six of them."

"And they're all safe?"

"Yep," answered Gus, "they're all safe."

"Then," said Bill, his chest swelling, "I've shot a deer."

[6107]

Major Sneaksnifter was telling the guests of his remarkable ability as an explorer and hunter.

"On one occasion," he rumbled, "I suddenly came face to face with an enormous lion. I never have seen such a huge beast. He stood only a few feet from me and was the perfect picture of ferocity.

"He roared: I fired, I hit him right between the yours."

One of the guests asked, "Yours? What's yours?"

Said the major, "I'll have a whiskey-soda." And the guest treated.

[6108]

Doris Duck was paddling happily about the lake one day when she spied a good-looking, shiny stranger duck that she had never seen before. Doris swam up to the stranger and said coyly, "Hello, there." The other duck answered not a word. "Hello, there," said Doris a little more sharply. Still no reply. "Aw go to hell, then," grated Doris, playing ducks and drakes with duck etiquette. Just then she spied a hunter aiming a gun at them from the wooded shore. Being essentially very kind-hearted, Doris took time to shout a warning to the surly one before she dove.

When she came cautiously to the surface Doris could see the hunter nowhere, but right where she had been floated, the strange duck all shot to pieces, to splinters in fact.

"Aha! wooden duck, eh!" said Doris.

[6109]

"Did you have any luck hunting tigers in India?"

"Marvelous luck. Didn't come across a single tiger."

[6110]

Hunter–"Just met a great big bear in the woods!"

Second Hunter–"Good! Did you give him both barrels?"

First–"Both barrels be blowed. I gave him the whole blooming gun."

[6111]

Big game hunters in Saskatchewan will continue to wear white instead of changing to a red uniform. This means that more hunters will continue to be shot in mistake for swans instead of for redheaded woodpeckers.

[6112]

"Have you the firmness of character that enables a person to go on and do his duty in the face of ingratitude, criticism, and heartless ridicule?"

"I ought to have. I cooked for a camping party last summer."

[6113]

Sportsman (having emptied both barrels at a rabbit)—"There, Jack, I'm sure I hit that one."

Gillie–"Well, 'e certainly did zeem to go faster after you shot at him, zur."

[6114]

Native—"Sahib, I saw a lot of tiger tracks about a mile north of here."
Hunter—"Good! Which way is south?"

[6115]

Angry Guide—"Why didn't you shoot that tiger?"
The Timid Hunter—"He didn't have the right kind of expression on his face for a rug."

[6116]

A few guides who survived the deer season stand a chance of being mistaken for rabbits.

[6117]

While a shooting party was out for a day's sport a raw young sportsman was observed taking aim at a pheasant running along the ground.

As it is unsportsmanlike to shoot a bird while it is on the ground, a companion shouted: "Hi, there, never shoot a running bird!"

"What do you take me for, you idiot?" came the reply. "Can't you see I'm waiting till it stops?"

[6118]

Free suggestion to amateur deer hunters: If it doesn't wear a vest, a necktie, a mustache or a hat, and doesn't smoke a pipe, it is probably a cow.

[6119]

There was once a man who was out gunning in the Alps. Sighting an eagle, he took aim and brought the bird down. As he was retrieving his game, a second man rode up on a horse.

"My good man," said the man on the horse to the hunter, "you should have saved your shot. The fall alone would have killed the eagle."

[6120]

She—"Didn't you tell me you hunt bear?"
He—"Madam, you wrong me. I always wear a hunting outfit."

[6121]

Big-Game Hunter—"Once while I was having a meal in the jungle a lion came so close to me that I could feel his breath on the back of my neck. What did I do?"
Bored Listener—"Turned your collar up?"

[6122]

A party of high-powered and over-dressed hunters from the city were pushing through swamp country when they came upon a small bare-foot boy with a sling shot.

"And what are you hunting for?" one of the party asked.

"I don't know," replied the boy. "I ain't seen it yet."

[6123]

"I shall miss you while you are on your hunting trip, dear," said the young wife affectionately, "and I shall pray that the hunters you are going with will do the same."

[6124]

Two hunters had been out several hours and one of them had been growing uneasy. Finally panic overtook him. "We're lost!" he cried to his companion. "What on earth shall we do?"

"Keep your shirt on!" said his phlegmatic companion. "Shoot an extra deer and the game warden will be here in a minute and a half."

[6125]

"In many States a hunting license entitles you to one deer and no more."

"Just like a marriage license."

[6126]

Sportsman–"Is there much good hunting in these parts, my good man?"

Native–"Sure, there's plenty hunting, but damned little finding."

[6127]

A hard-up sportsman bought a hunter and put off payment for a time. Later he met the man who sold him the horse.

"I am not satisfied with that animal," he said.

"Why, what's the trouble?" asked the dealer.

"Well, it won't hold its head up," said the sportsman.

"Oh, that's all right, sir; it's his pride. Just you wait till he's paid for!"

[6128]

"What sort of a chap is Jim to camp out with?"

"He's one of those fellows who always takes down a mandolin about the time it's up to somebody to get busy with the frying pan."

[6129]

First Sportsman–"It's getting awfully late and we haven't hit a thing yet."

Second Sportsman–"Let's miss two more and then go home."

[6130]

Judge–"You are accused of shooting squirrels out of season. Have you any plea?"

Hunter–"Yes, your honor. Self-defense."

[6131]

After a long, weary quest an amateur hunter cried exultingly:

"Ha! a partridge at last!"

"Serves him right," growled the bag-carrier, "for flying in front of your gun!"

[6132]

A tourist traveling in the Rocky Mountains was introduced to an old hunter who claimed to have killed no fewer than a hundred bears.

"Bill," said the introducer, "this feller wants to hear some narrer escapes you had from bears."

"Young man," said Bill, "if thar's been any narrer escapes, the bears had 'em."

[6133]

First Simple Nimrod–"Hey, don't shoot. Your gun isn't loaded."

His Partner–"Can't help that; the bird won't wait."

[6134]

"Hello, old man, had any luck shooting?"

"I should say I did! I shot 13 ducks in one day."

"Were they wild?"

"Well—no—not exactly; but the farmer, who owned them, was."

[6135]

First Hunter–"Killed anything?"

Second Hunter–"Not a thing! Wish I'd gone motoring now."

[6136]

"Be careful with that gun. You just missed shooting me."

"Did I? I'm very sorry."

[6137]

Tragedy in a nutshell: Lion and two lion-hunters; lion and one lion-hunter; lion.

FISHING

[6138]

Two old cronies were fishing together at about the same place in the stream. One man had been having excellent luck, landing some real beauties. But the other man was doing no good at all.

"What's the matter?" asked the lucky fisherman, "why do you suppose you haven't caught any? We're both at the same place in the stream and, by George, we're even using the same kind of bait."

"Search me," answered the second man. "Maybe my worm isn't trying."

[6139]

"I notice that in telling about that fish you caught you vary the size of it for different listeners."

"Yes, I never tell a man more than I think he will believe."

[6140]

"How many fish have you caught, uncle?" asked someone, observing an old colored man fishing on the banks of a stream. "Well, suh," answered the aged angler thoughtfully, "ef I ketch dis heah one I'm after, and two mo', I'll have three."

[6141]

A returned vacationist tells us that he was fishing in a pond one day when a country boy who had been watching him from a distance approached him and asked, "How many fish yer got, mister?"

"None yet," he was told.

"Wel, yer ain't doin' so bad," said the youngster. "I know a feller what fished here for two weeks an' he didn't get any more than you got in a half an hour."

[6142]

The drunk halted in front of an enormous stuffed tarpon in a glass case. He stared at it for a minute or two in silence. Then he said: "The fella who caught—hic—that fish is a—hic—liar!"

[6143]

He had had hard luck fishing, and on his way home he entered the fish market and said to the dealer, "Just stand over there and throw me five of the biggest of those trout!"

"Throw 'em? What for?" asked the dealer in amazement.

"So I can tell the family I caught 'em. I may be a poor fisherman, but I'm no liar."

[6144]

An angler, who had been trying to hook something for the last six hours, was sitting gloomily at his task, when a mother and her small son came along.

"Oh!" cried out the youngster, "do let me see you catch a fish!"

Addressing the angler, the mother said, severely: "Now, don't you catch a fish for him until he says 'Please!'"

[6145]

While a small boy was fishing one Sunday morning he accidentally lost his foothold and tumbled into the creek. As an old man on the bank was helping him out he said: "How did you come to fall in the river, my little man?"

"I didn't come to fall in the river. I came to fish," replied the boy.

[6146]

There was once a remarkably kind boy who was a great angler. There was a trout stream in his neighborhood that ran through a rich man's estate. Permits to fish the stream could now and then be obtained, and the boy was lucky enough to have a permit.

One day he was fishing with another boy when a gamekeeper suddenly darted forth from a thicket. The lad with the permit uttered a cry of fright, dropped his rod, and ran off at top speed. The gamekeeper pursued.

For about half a mile the gamekeeper was led a swift and difficult chase. Then, worn out, the boy halted. The man seized him by the arm and said between pants:

"Have you a permit to fish on this estate?"

"Yes to be sure," said the boy, quietly.

"You have? Then show it to me."

The boy drew the permit from his pocket. The man examined it and frowned in perplexity and anger.

"Why did you run when you had this permit?" he asked.

"To let the other boy get away," was the reply. "He didn't have none!"

[6147]

"By the way, wife, did you put my cooking outfit in the bag? I'll want to fry some of the fish we catch."

"Yes, dear, and you will also find a can of sardines there, too, and some crackers and cheese."

[6148]

Belleville – "Is Glenshaw getting ready for the fishing season?"

Butler – "Well, I saw him buying an enlarging device for his camera."

[6149]

"Lo, Jim! Fishin'?"

"Naw; drowning worms."

[6150]

"While fishing one day," said the old-timer, "I ran short of bait and was temporarily at loss as to what to do. Upon looking down near my feet, I noticed a small snake which held a frog in its mouth. I removed the frog and cut it up for bait, feeling very fortunate that my eyes had lighted on the snake at that moment.

"I did, however, feel a bit guilty at relieving the poor reptile of his meal, and in order to give him a slight recompense for my supply of bait, I poured a few drops of whisky into its mouth. Fortunately for my conscience, the snake seemed to leave in a contented mood, and I turned and went on fishing.

"Some time had passed when I felt something hitting against the leg of my boot. Looking down, I saw the identical snake, laden with three more frogs!"

[6151]

The local minister, off on a vacational fishing trip, was horrified to hear a youthful angler using words that were dyed a dark, deep electric blue.

"My boy," he remonstrated, "don't you know that the fish will never bite if you swear like that?"

"I know I ain't very good at it," replied the youngster apologetically, "but I thought maybe I could get some little ones on the few words I know. Here, you take my pole and see what *you* can do."

[6152]

Jones came back from his fortnight's holiday proud of his bulging muscles.

"Look at these arms," he said.

They were certainly in good condition. His colleagues put it down to rowing, but Jones withered them with scorn.

"Rowing be blowed," he snorted. "I got them pulling fish up."

[6153]

"Speaking about showers of fish," said the solemn looking man from his seat on a cracker box in the general store, "reminds me of the time we were marooned on an island in the blue Pacific. For two hours there was a shower of fresh mackerel and, strange to say, they all dropped into a salt lake on the mountainside. That brined them."

"Whew!" the old codgers chorused in unison.

"But that's not the strangest part of the story. Ten days later a cyclone came along, picked up the brined mackerel and dropped them into a hot spring. That boiled them; and, gentlemen, they were the finest boiled mackerel you ever tasted. I thought about sending some home to the folks, but——"

There was a sudden interruption and six strong men took the story teller outside and ducked him in the horse trough.

[6154]

He had been fishing patiently for several hours without a bite when a small urchin strolled up.

"Any luck, mister?" he called out.

"Run away, boy," growled the angler, in gruff tones.

"No offense, sir," said the boy, as he walked away, "only I just wanted to say that my father keeps a fish shop down to the right, sir."

[6155]

The tyro fisherman, in the excitement of his first catch, kept on reeling the poor little fish until his jaws were pressing against the rod.

"All you got to do now, neighbor," exclaimed an old-timer, "is to climb the pole and choke him to death."

[6156]

A Florida fisherman had to be taken to the hospital after a three hour struggle with a six foot tarpon. It is believed that he severely strained himself in his efforts to illustrate the size of his catch.

[6157]

"Why does a woman say she's been shopping when she hasn't bought a thing?"

"Why does a man say he's been fishing when he hasn't caught anything?"

[6158]

The man on the bridge addressed the solitary fisherman.

"Any luck?" he asked.

"Any luck!" was the answer. "Why, I got forty pike out of here yesterday."

"Do you know who I am?"

"No," said the fisherman.

"I'm the chief magistrate here, and all this estate is mine."

"And do you know who I am?" asked the fisherman, quickly.

"No."

"I'm the biggest liar in Virginia."

[6159]

A fisherman got such a reputation for stretching the truth that he bought a pair of scales and insisted on weighing every fish he caught, in the presence of a witness.

One day a doctor borrowed the fisherman's scales to weigh a new-born-baby. The baby weighed forty-seven pounds.

[6160]

Stranger–"In what direction does the village lie, my friend?"

Native–"Wal, it's liable to lie in any old direction that comes handy, but at this time of the year it's mostly about fish."

[6161]

Parson—"Do you know the parables, my child?"

Johnny—"Yes, sir."

Parson—"And which of the parables do you like best?"

Johnny—"I like the one where somebody loafs and fishes."

[6162]

Lady (to small boy who is fishing) —"I wonder what your father would say if he caught you fishing on Sunday?"

Boy—"I don't know. You'd better ask him. That's him a little farther up the stream."

[6163]

"Oh, I've forgotten the bait!" exclaimed the first fisherman.

"What?" yelled the other. "Why, you puddin' headed, blank idiot, how in thunder did you—"

"What's the matter with you?" retorted the other. "You had as much right to remember the can as I had. When I put the worms in it—"

"Oh, the can," interrupted the other with a look of relief, "I thought you meant the bottle."

[6164]

"I disapprove of all brutal sports, prize-fighting, angling—"

"Good heavens! How can you name those two sports in the same breath?"

"Why not? Isn't it the object of both pugilist and angler to land a hook in the jaw?"

[6165]

Talkative Lady—"A big man like you might be better occupied than in cruelly catching little fish."

Angler—"Perhaps you're right. But if this fish had kept his mouth shut he wouldn't be here."

[6166]

"My goodness!" remarked the old gentleman as he stopped the young lad with the fine catch of trout. "You've had a very successful day, young man. Where did you catch all these fish?"

"Just walk down that path marked 'Private' and keep right on till you come to a notice, 'Trespassers will be prosecuted.' A few yards farther on there's a fine pool in the river marked 'No fishing allowed,' and there you are, sir!"

[6167]

Scene: Psycho peeping over Asylum wall. Man fishing nearby.

Psycho—"Caught anything?"

Man—"No."

Psycho—"How long you waiting?"

Man—"Three hours."

Psycho—"Come inside."

[6168]

"I say, Gadsby," said Mr. Smith, as he entered a fishmonger's with a lot of tackle in his hand, "I want you to give me some fish to take home with me. Put them up to look as if they'd been caught today, will you?"

"Certainly, sir. How many?"

"Oh, you'd better give me three or four—mackerel. Make it look decent in quantity without appearing to exaggerate, you know."

"Yes, sir. You'd better take salmon, tho."

"Why? What makes you think so?"

"Oh, nothing, except that your wife was here early this morning and said if you dropped in with your fishing-tackle I was to persuade you to take salmon, if possible, as she liked that kind better than any other."

[6169]

Fisherman–"I tell you it was that long. I never saw such a fish!"
Friend–"I believe you."

[6170]

Friend–"Did you fish with flies?"
Returning Camper–"Fish with them? We fished with them, camped with them, ate with them and slept with them."

[6171]

Son–"Father, what is the biggest fish you ever caught?"
Father–"You had better go and ask your mother, I have forgotten what I told her."

[6172]

Two Cape Cod fishermen had an argument one day as to which was the better mathematician. Finally the captain of the fishing smack proposed the following problem for them as a test:

If a fishing crew caught 500 pounds of cod and brought their catch to port and sold it for six cents a pound, how much would they receive for the fish?

The two old fellows got to work, but neither seemed able to master the intricacies of the deal in fish, and they were unable to arrive at an answer.

At last old Bill turned to the captain and asked him to repeat the problem. The captain started off: "If a fishing crew caught 500 pounds of cod and——"

"Wait a minute, there, wait a minute," said Bill. "Is it codfish they caught?"

"Yep," answered the captain.

"Durn it all," said Bill. "It ain't no wonder I couldn't get an answer. Here I been figuring on salmon all the time."

[6173]

Justice Brewer was with a party of New York friends on a fishing trip in the Adirondacks, and around the camp fire one evening the talk naturally ran on big fish. When it came his turn the jurist began, uncertain as to how he was going to come out:

"We were fishing one time on the Grand Banks for—er—for—"

"Whales," somebody suggested.

"No," said the Justice, "we were baiting with whales."

[6174]

Smith–"Hope is really a wonderful thing."
Jones–"True. One little nibble keeps a man fishing all day."

[6175]

One Guy–"Did you mark that place where fishing was so good?"
Another Guy–"Yes, I put an X on the side of the boat."
First Guy–"That's silly. What if we should get another boat?"

[6176]

Angler–"You've been watching me for three hours. Why don't you try fishing yourself?"
Onlooker–"I ain't got the patience."

[6177]

"Any fishing around here?"
"Some," answered the barefoot boy.
"What do you catch?"
"You said 'fishin', not 'ketchin'."

[6178]

Jeanne, aged four, was fishing with her father, who was wearing his fishing license on the back of his hat. Not having a great deal of luck, Jeanne offered the following suggestion: "Daddy, turn your hat around so the fish can see your license."

[6179]

Curtis goes to a state, noted for fishing, once a year on a fishing trip. The last time he was up there the fish were biting so good that he couldn't stop when he had caught the limit.

A deputy game warden caught him with the goods and brought him into court.

"You are charged with having caught 18 more black bass than the law allows. Are you guilty or not guilty?" the judge asked.

"Well, I'm guilty," Curtis had to admit.

"Ten dollars and costs."

Curtis paid the fine and then asked the judge: "And now, Your Honor, may I have several type-written copies of the court record made to take back and show to my friends?"

[6180]

Judge–"What is the defendant's reputation for veracity?"

Witness–"Excellent, your honor, I've known him to admit that he'd been fishing all day and hadn't got a single bite."

[6181]

An enterprising burglar is in the habit of going about with a rod and line and fishing clothes through windows while the owners sleep. The last time he got only a shirt, and he has been talking ever since about the trousers that got away.

[6182]

"Say!" yelled the farmer, who owned the pond, "don't you see that sign: No Fishing Here?"

"I sure do," said the disgusted fisherman. "The fellah that printed that sign knew what he was talkin' about!"

[6183]

An enthusiastic angler was telling some friends about a proposed fishing trip to a lake in Colorado which he had in contemplation.

"Are there any trout out there?" asked one friend.

"Thousands of 'em," replied the angler.

"Will they bite easily?" asked another friend.

"Will they? Why, they're absolutely vicious. A man has to hide behind a tree to bait his hook."

[6184]

An old boatsman who rowed a skiff for Phillips Brooks when the beloved churchman went in quest of the denizens of the deep, was performing a similar service for another clerical angler who recalled what a noble soul the bishop was.

"Right ye are," the oarsman assented, " 'cept his swearing."

"Bishop Brooks swear? Impossible!" the preacher fisherman exclaimed.

"Oh, but he did, leastwise he swore onct. He hooked a beautiful bass and got the wriggling fellow up to the boat, an' just as I went to get him with the hand-net, he flopped clean off the hook. 'I say that's too damned bad, Bishop!' I said. And he said, 'Yes, it is.' But that's the only time I ever heard him use such language."

[6185]

"You'll be a man like one of us some day," said the patronizing sportsman to a lad who was throwing his line into the same stream.

"Yes, sir," he answered, "I s'pose I will some day, but I b'lieve I'd rather stay small and ketch a few fish."

[6186]
"How are they biting to-day, old man?"

"On the neck and legs mostly."

[6187]
A school teacher had drawn on the blackboard a picture of a boy fishing. "See the boy fishing," she admonished the class. "Even pleasure requires *patience*. He must sit quietly and wait. He must be very *patient*. Now, children, if you were going fishing, what would you most need?"

Back came the answer in a rousing chorus: "BAIT."

[6188]
Coming home one Sunday afternoon with a string of trout, Robbie was suddenly confronted by the local minister. There was no way of escape, but the boy rose to the occasion. Going up to the minister, he said: "Minister, d'ye see what thae troots got for nabbin' worms on Sunday?"

[6189]
A minister walking along a brook one Sunday observed a boy fishing. After seeing him catch several fish, he approached the boy and said:

"My boy, don't you know it is not right to be fishing on Sunday; and, besides, it is very cruel to insert that sharp hook into that poor beetle."

The Boy–"Oh, say, mister, dat ain't no beetle; dat's only an imitation bug."

Minister–"Oh, I thought it was a real bug."

Boy (lifting a string of fish out of the brook)–"So did these suckers."

[6190]
A wag went out a fishing one day, and not meeting with the best luck, determined on having some fun. He went home and deposited what he had caught, and a neighbor passing by, soon after, asked:

"What luck to-day?"

"O," answered the wag, "not much—I caught a hundred or two."

"A hundred or two," replied the neighbor, with great surprise; "I'll bet you a dollar you didn't."

"Accepted," said the wag; whereupon he uncovered a pile near him and a couple of fish lay there, scarcely through with their death struggles, remarking: "There they are—I have won the wager."

"How so?" returned his neighbor, "here are only two."

"Well," replied the wag, "that is just as I told you—a hundred or two."

[6191]
You can't tell. Maybe a fish goes home and lies about the size of the bait he stole.

[6192]
"There's Jones; he's so fond of fishing he seems to have fishing on the brain."

"Fishing tackle, you mean; I've often seen him when his brain was reeling."

[6193]
A small boy was late for Sunday school. His teacher asked the cause.

"I was going fishing, but my daddy wouldn't let me," said the boy.

"You're lucky to have a fine father like that," said the teacher. "And I suppose he explained to you why you shouldn't go on Sunday."

"Yes, ma'am," replied the boy. "He said there wasn't enough bait for both of us."

[6194]

Teacher–"Explain the line of 'least resistance'?"

Bright Pupil–"A fishing line without any bait on it."

BASEBALL

[6195]

Coach–"What this team needs is life!"

Manager–"Oh, no, thirty days is enough."

[6196]

Wife–"John, why are you so delighted at his sliding second base—do you know him personally?"

[6197]

Wife (second inning of second game)–"Let's go, John. This is where we came in!"

[6198]

"We'll have to get the whole force to handle the crowds to-day."

"Parade? Convention?"

"Neither. The president of the ball club has advertised for an office boy."

[6199]

The schoolboy who wonders why he has to study decimal fractions gets his answer when figuring baseball percentages.

[6200]

"Was I fast! Lissen, guy, when I played for the Giants, every time I hit one of the many home runs I reached first base before the spectators could hear the crack of the bat. Then when I rounded second, the second baseman usually said something that made me sore, so I slapped the third baseman in the catcher's mouth. Not bad, eh?"

[6201]

Ball Fan–"How do you account for the slump in Thirston's fielding average?"

Sporting Editor–"He goes after too many high balls."

[6202]

An Englishman was seeing his first game of baseball, and the "fan" was explaining the different plays as they were being made.

"Don't you think it's great?" enthusiastically asked the "fan."

"Well," replied the Englishman, "I think it's very exciting, but also a very dangerous game."

"Dangerous nothing," replied the fan.

Just then a runner was put out at second base.

"What has happened now?" asked the Englishman.

"Chick Smith has died at second," laconically replied the fan.

"Died at second?" replied the astonished Briton. "I knew it was a dangerous game."

[6203]

Bride–"Who is the man in the blue coat, darling?"

Groom–"That's the umpire, dear."

Bride–"Why does he wear that funny wire thing over his face?"

Groom–"To keep from biting the ball players, precious."

[6204]

Co-ed (at baseball game)–"Oh, look, we have a man on every base!"

Another Co-ed–"That's nothing, so has the other side."

[6205]

At the base ball game.

She–"What's the man running for?"

He–"He hit the ball."

She–"I know. But is he required to chase it, too?"

[6206]
They arrived at the fifth inning.
"What's the score, Jim?" he asked
a fan.
"Nothing to nothing," was the
reply.
"Oh, goody!" she exclaimed. "We
haven't missed a thing!"

[6207]
An irate enthusiast, who had
watched his home team go down
in defeat, stopped the umpire as he
was leaving the field.
"Where's your dog?" he commanded.
"Dog?" ejaculated the umpire. "I
have no dog."
"Well," said the grouchy one,
"you're the first blind man I ever
saw who didn't have a dog."

[6208]
They were getting up a ball game
in a small town and lacked one
player. They finally persuaded an
old fellow to fill in, although he
said he had never played before.
He went to the bat and the first
ball pitched he knocked over the
fence. Every one stood and watched
the ball, even the batter. Excitedly
they told him to run. "Shucks!" he
said, "what's the use of running, I'll
buy you another ball."

[6209]
"I can tell you the score of the
game before it starts."
"What is it?"
"Nothing to nothing."

[6210]
"It is awful, Mrs. Smith, the way
sports are degenerating. My boy was
dismissed from the ball team because he was too honest."
"What was the matter?"
"He wouldn't steal bases."

[6211]
An Englishman was in the United
States for the first time. Some of his
friends in New York took him to
see the Yankees play baseball. After
the Yanks had been hitting the opposing pitcher all over the lot the
Englishman was heard to remark:
"Jolly good pitcher, eh, what? Hits
the bloomin' bat every time."

[6212]
First Baseball Player–"You didn't
get on so well with that millionaire's daughter, eh?"
Second Baseball Player–"Terrible—
no hits, no runs, no heiress."

BOXING

[6213]
Boxing Instructor–"That was what
they call a half hook."
Pupil (nursing his jaw)–"Well, you
can keep the other half."

[6214]
Boxer–"Isn't it a long distance from
the dressing-room to the ring?"
Opponent–"Yes, but you won't have
to walk back."

[6215]
Boxer–"Have I done him any damage?"
Disgusted Second–"No, but keep
swinging. The draft might give him
a cold."

[6216]
Boxing Instructor (after first lesson)–"Now, have you any questions to ask?"
Beginner (dazed)–"Yes; how much
is your correspondence course?"

[6217]

The second hammered on the resined boards. "Hit 'im; hit 'im," he vainly entreated his principal, but the heavy-weight aspirant, hopelessly outclassed, failed to comply. He recoiled dazedly from a serious attack, and clutched despairingly at the ring-post.

"Not with that, you fool," shouted his second, "you'll be disqualified."

[6218]

Two men were to take part in a boxing match, and surreptitiously each backed himself heavily to lose the fight. During the progress of the bout one accidentally hit his opponent a light tap on the face, whereupon the recipient of the blow lay down and the referee proceeded to count him out. The other was in a quandary, but just with the call of "nine" a magnificent idea came to him. He rushed to the prostrate man and kicked him, and was instantly disqualified.

[6219]

A negro boxer was to fight a heavyweight champion. When he reached the ring it was noticed that he hung back.

"It's all right, Sam," said his trainer. "Just say to yourself, 'I'm going to beat him,' and you'll win."

"That's no good, boss," replied Sam. "I know what a liar I am."

[6220]

The boxer returned to his dressing-room looking drawn and haggard, for he had just had a terrific beating in the ring. He felt absolutely done, and looked it. He opened his eyes when the promoter approached.

"Hard lines, Jack," said the promoter, as he gazed down at his battered charge, "but I've good news for you!"

"Well, what's the good news?"

"I've been lucky enough to fix a return match for you!"

[6221]

"What did you think of the big fight last night, Bill?" asked the navvy of his pal.

"Fight!" replied Bill, scornfully. "If the missus and me 'ad put up a show like that on Saturday night, the kids would 'ave booed us!"

[6222]

"Now you got to keep away from this guy," the second whispered into the cauliflowered ear of his principal. "Jab him an' get away or he'll use his right. You got to keep that left hand out there an' don't let him get set to use his right. He's a cinch to try to get you to slug with him, but don't do it, or he'll get his right over sure."

"I got you," the fighter nodded, "I'll do just like you say, but suppose he does get his right over anyway? What'll I do?"

"Nothin'," the second instructed. "Just relax and me an' the referee will carry you to your corner."

[6223]

Reporter—"Could I speak to Mr. Brown, the boxer?"

Boxer's Wife (acidly)—"Well, he is not up yet. Since he became a professional pugilist he hasn't ever got up before the stroke of ten."

[6224]

President of Boxing Club—"Now there is the question of colors. Any suggestions?"

Member—"I suggest black and blue."

[6225]

"So you want to be a champion boxer, huh? Let's hear you yell, 'foul'!"

[6226]

Heavyweight Boxer–"The trouble is, doctor, that I can't sleep a wink."

Doctor–"You must practise autosuggestion a little. Why not lie on your back, relax, and count slowly up to ten?"

HORSE RACING

[6227]

Hyde–"Were you lucky at the races yesterday?"

Wyde–"I should just think I was! I found a quarter after the last race, so I didn't have to walk home."

[6228]

Sam Riddle's pet topic of conversation is the remarkable success of Man o' War's sons and daughters. His dinner partner one evening was a young woman whose racing knowledge had been limited to a day or two at the course on some fashionable occasion. She listened attentively most of the evening to a recounting of the glories and performances of Man o' War's offspring. There was a lull and some one across the table asked her: "What do you think of disarmament?"

"Why, I don't know—is it by Man o' War, too?"

[6229]

The jockeys and horses had lined up for the start of the steeplechase, but a delay occurred because a tall, raw-boned beast obstinately refused to yield to the importunities of the starter. The patience of that worthy was nearly exhausted. "Bring up that horse!" he shouted; "bring him up! You'll get into trouble pretty soon if you don't!"

The rider of the stupid animal, a youthful Irishman, yelled back: "I can't help it! This 'ere's been a cab 'orse, and 'e won't start till the door shuts, an' I ain't got no door!"

[6230]

"Is horse racing a clean sport?"

"Well, it cleans quite a few every day."

[6231]

"What happens to the horses you follow, Albert?"

"Oh, they usually follow the other horses."

[6232]

A poorly dressed man was standing in front of a vacant store building, and from her window above the store a woman noticed that several people stopped, in passing, and gave him some money. It was a scene that touched her deeply. She wrote on a piece of paper, "Take Courage," placed the paper in an envelope with a two-dollar bill and tossed it to the man.

Several days later, when she was returning from an out of town visit, she was accosted by the man, who said:

"Here's your $52, lady. 'Take Courage' won at twenty-six to one."

[6233]

"Isn't it dreadful? The minister's son has decided to become a jockey. He was to have been a minister, you know."

"Well, he'll bring a lot more people to repentance than he would as a minister."

SPORTS IN GENERAL

[6234]

She–"Does skating require any particular application?"
He–"No; arnica or horse liniment —one's as good as the other."

[6235]

"How's Smith in the high jump? Any good?"
"Naw, he can hardly clear his throat."

[6236]

The runner was as safe as a quart of grape-juice at a college prom.
The second-baseman couldn't catch a cold in Siberia.
Whoosis lifted a fly that was higher than a diamond necklace at Tiffany's.
The umpire was blinder than an earthworm in a London fog.
The home team got more runs than a pair of silk stockings in a bramble patch.
The game was tighter than a Pullman car window.
The twirler had as many curves as a Broadway chorus.
The stands were as crowded as a sophomore's roadster.

[6237]

Lady (to instructor)–"Don't you think that horseback riding gives one a headache?"
Instructor–"Oh, no; quite the reverse!"

[6238]

As the cup was handed over into the youth's hands, there went up cries of "Speech! Speech!" and the hubbub broke out anew. Meanwhile the lad was able to collect his thoughts and, of course, to catch his breath. Then he stepped up on a bench. There came an abrupt and eager hush!
"Gentlemen," he said, "I have won this cup by the use of my legs. I trust I may never lose the use of my legs by the use of this cup."

[6239]

A minister told his flock that he had a "call" to go to another church. One of the deacons asked how much more he was offered.
"Three hundred dollars," was the reply.
"Well I don't blame you for going," remarked the deacon, "but you should be more exact in your language, Parson. That isn't a 'call,' that's a 'raise.'"

[6240]

Our captain of polo was dancing with a haughty and statuesque young woman, and not making a very good job of it.
Presently he said: "I'm afraid I'm not dancing well this evening. As a matter of fact, I'm a little stiff from polo."
And the young woman answered icily: "It's a matter of indifference to me where you are from."

[6241]

"How would you like to learn to ski?"
"Oh, I'd jump at the chance."

[6242]

"How long have you been learning to skate?"
"Oh, about a dozen sittings."

[6243]

Heard on the tennis-court:
"Poor fellow, he lost his amateur standing, and now he can't make a cent."

[6244]

Green, who was the local athletic champion, had been holding forth at great length. None of the club regulars could do anything about it. But presently one of the visitors looked up.

"I'll bet," he said cheerfully, "ten dollars that I can wheel something in a wheelbarrow from one street lamp to the next, and you can't wheel it back!"

Green looked him over—not a very hefty sort of bloke. He thought of bags of cement, bricks, and old iron, and concluded that whatever the stranger could do he could better.

"Taken," he said.

The stranger smiled, and with a couple of witnesses they set out. A wheelbarrow was borrowed and taken to the nearest street lamp.

The stranger rubbed his hands, picked up the handles. "Get in, Green old man," he said.

[6245]

"Our fencing team lost again last night."

"Ah, foiled again!"

[6246]

She—"It looks as though you had raised Ned at your club last night."
He—"I did; and, what is worse, he raised me back."

[6247]

A traveling salesman, detained in a certain village overnight, was introduced in the town's hotel to a crazy little billiard-table and a set of balls of a uniform, dirty-gray color.

"But how do you tell the red from the white?" he asked.

"Oh," replied the landlord, "you soon get to know them by their shape."

[6248]

"What's the matter, John? You look kind o' weather-beaten this morning."

"That's exactly what I am. I bet five dollars it would rain yesterday, and it didn't!"

[6249]

"Is he really as fast a runner as they say?"

"Is he fast? Say, he can run so fast that all the men he races with have to run twice as fast as he does to keep up with him."

[6250]

Old Lady (witnessing tug-of-war for the first time)—"Wouldn't it be simpler, dear, for them to get a knife and cut it?"

[6251]

A man wandered into a tennis tournament the other day and sat down on the bench.

"Whose game?" he asked.

A shy young thing sitting next to him looked up hopefully.

"I am," she replied.

[6252]

"Are you going to learn to ski this winter?"

"No, I'm going to let it slide."

[6253]

Beginner—"Now, my man, I want to hire a horse. How long can I have it out?'"

Groom—"Well, sir, we usually leave that to the horse."

[6254]

"He is the recording secretary of a chess club."

"But what does he do?"

"Oh, he reads the hours of the last meeting."

[6255]

"What did you think of the Horse Show?"

"I didn't see a single frock I liked."

[6256]

Grandmother was bitterly opposed to gambling games—especially poker—but gave her sanction to the playing of authors. So the grandchildren engaged her interests in the game of her choice. Her enthusiasm increased as the game progressed, and while she knew that the cards used were a deck of authors, she didn't know that the game she was playing was poker, and that grandmother was enthusiastically playing Whittiers wild.

[6257]

The champion athlete in bed with a cold was told that he had a temperature.

"How high is it, Doctor?" he wanted to know.

"A hundred and one."

"What's the world's record?"

[6258]

A young lady entered a crowded car with a pair of skates slung over her arm. An elderly gentleman arose to give her his seat.

"Thank you very much, sir," she said, "but I've been skating all afternoon, and I'm tired of sitting down."

[6259]

"This means a good deal to me," said the poker player as he stacked the cards.

[6260]

"Do you play cards?"

"Yes, we burn the midnight Hoyle."

[6261]

"That's very sporting of you to cheer the team that gave you such a handsome beating," said the stranger to a burly member of the village football team.

"Oh, aye," said the burly one with a smirk. "We can tak a whackin' wi' t' best."

"So I see. By the way, where's the referee?"

"Referee? Oh, he's int' canal!"

[6262]

"Yes, my husband's laid up, a victim of football."

"But I didn't know he even played the game."

"He doesn't. He sprained 'is larynx at the match last Saturday."

[6263]

A very thin fullback was annoyed by the attentions of a small dog during a Rugby match.

At last, when play had moved to the other end, the back turned and shouted to the spectators: "Whoever owns this dog might call him off."

A voice responded: "Come here, Spot. Them ain't bones, boy—them's legs."

[6264]

A certain old lady was so concerned about one of the villagers who was unable to write, that she persuaded the village schoolmaster to give him some lessons. Some time later she met the villager and said to him:

"Well, George, I suppose you are now able to read the Bible fairly easily?"

"Lor' bless you, mum," he replied, "I was out of the Bible and into the football news over a week ago!"

TALL STORIES

[6265]

Dr. Walter Adams, astronomer at Mount Wilson Observatory told a story of gratitude:

"A hunter in the jungle came across an elephant limping. The hunter followed it. Finally it toppled over. The hunter examined its feet. In one there was a large thorn. This he removed.

"Years passed and the hunter was in a cheap seat at a circus. A turn was given by a troupe of performing elephants. One of these elephants reached in its trunk, encircled his waist, and lifted him from his cheap seat and set him down in a seat in a private box."

[6266]

They were discussing dogs, and the tales were getting "pretty tall" when one of the group took the lead.

"Smith," he said, "had a most intelligent dog. One night Smith's house caught fire. All was instant confusion. Old Smith and his wife flew for the children and bundled them out in quick order. Everyone was saved, but old Rover dashed back through the flames. Soon the animal reappeared, scorched, and burned with—what do you think?"

"Give up," cried the eager listeners.

"With the fire insurance policy wrapped in a damp towel, gentlemen."

[6267]

The old timers in the club insisted that the new member should relate a tale. He refused at first, but under pressure yielded, and gave a vivid account of a shipwreck at sea during one of his voyages. He described the stress of the terrible situation with such power that his hearers were deeply impressed. He reached the point in his account where only the captain and himself and half a dozen others were left aboard the doomed vessel, after the last of the boats had been lowered.

"And then," he concluded, "a vast wave came hurtling down on us. It was so huge that it shut out all the sky. It crashed over the already sinking ship in a torrent of irresistible force. Under that dreadful blow the laboring vessel sank, and all those left on board of her were drowned."

The narrator paused and there was a period of tense silence. But presently someone asked:

"And you—what became of you?"

"Oh, I," was the reply, "why I was drowned with the rest of them."

[6268]

The guide in Yellowstone Park, when asked why he was lacking the first finger of his right hand, answered:

"I've been a guide, man and boy, for twenty-five years, and I just naturally wore that finger off pointing out places of interest to inquisitive tourists."

[6269]

"Last summer," said the tall story teller, "I was off the coast on a fishing trip, and while we were out on deck early in the evening, smoking and chatting, a great cloud of mosquitoes, all of them monstrous birds, came out from shore and settled on the boat. And do you know, in fifteen minutes they had stripped it of every inch of canvas, and left the masts bare as beanpoles!"

The listeners were inclined to scoff at this revelation, but one of the party interposed, "Well, don't be astonished. I can vouch for that. It was only a week after that I was on a trip along the coast, and the same swarm of mosquitoes came out after us."

The first speaker didn't seem to appreciate this unexpected support, for he said, "Humph! They did, eh? Well, how did you know they were the same mosquitoes?"

"How did I know?" repeated the other with a chuckle. "How did I know? Why, confound it, they all had on canvas overalls."

[6270]

A Yankee passenger in an English train was beguiling his fellow passengers with tall stories and remarked, "We can start with a twenty-story apartment house this month, and have it finished by next."

This was too much for the burly Yorkshireman, who sat next to him. "Man, that's nowt," he said. "I've seen 'em in Yorkshire when I've been going to work just laying the foundation stone and when I've been coming home at neet they've been putting the folk out for back rent."

[6271]

"Yes," said the yarn-spinning old mariner, in the corner of the railway carriage, "for three days and nights we worked at the pumps, and still the water gained on us. At last we gave up the hopeless struggle. There we was—sinkin', sinkin', expecting to perish every 'arf a minute. It was horful time, believe me. Sudden-like we

feels the wessel a-rising up through the water. She riz till her keel was a'most out o' water, and we rides into port right on top o' the waves. We was saved! 'Ow it happened was, we had a cargo of yeast on board, and when the water reached it, it rose and rose, till it fairly lifted up the ship!"

[6272]

The Californian described his native state's big trees as follows:

"Big trees? Why out our way they felled a hollow tree over a ravine that was too deep and would cost too much to build a bridge across. One day when I was comin' through this tree-bridge with a load of hay I met another man with a load of hay coming through the other end. I couldn't go back or go ahead, so I just backed into a hollow branch and let the other fellow go past me."

[6273]

"Crop failures?" asked the old timer.

"Yes, I've seen a few in my day. In 1898 the corn crop was almost nothing. We cooked some for dinner, and my father ate fourteen acres of corn at one meal!"

[6274]

Three turtles—two large ones and a little one—went to a bar to quench their thirst. Each ordered a mug of sarsaparilla. When it had been placed on the bar, one of the large turtles commented that it was raining. Whereupon there was a lively discussion and it was decided they ought to have their umbrella, and that the little turtle should go home for it. The little turtle demurred to the idea, expressing the fear that if he went for the umbrella, the two big turtles would drink the sarsaparilla while he was gone. After much discussion the big turtles convinced the little one that they would not drink his sarsaparilla, and he started after the umbrella.

Three weeks passed, and finally one of the big turtles said:

"Let's drink the little guy's sarsaparilla."

"I've been thinking the same thing," said the other, "so that's just what we'll do."

From down at the end of the bar near the door, a shrill voice cried:

"If you do, I won't go after that umbrella!"

[6275]

He was an American in London, and he had hired a Cockney guide to show him about the city.

"How long did it take to put that up?" he asked his guide as they passed a large hotel building.

"Why, about six months, I should say."

"Six months!" exclaimed the American. "Why it wouldn't take us more than six weeks to put up a building like that in New York."

They passed an office building which was apparently quite new.

"And how long were they building that?" asked the Yankee.

"About four weeks," answered the Cockney.

"Four weeks!" said the American. "Now back in New York we'd build a place like that in six days."

Nothing more was said until they approached the houses of Parliament.

"Say, that's not a bad looking place. How long did they take building that?"

"Well, you may not believe me," answered the guide, "but that building wasn't there when I crossed the bridge last night."

[6276]

Lyin' Jack's best story was of an elk he once killed that had a spread of antlers 15 feet wide. He always kept these, as he said, in the loft of his cabin. One time after a long absence Lyin' Jack showed up in Benton. The boys were all glad to see him and, after a round or two of drinks, asked for a story.

"No, boys," said Jack, "I'm through. For years, I've been telling these lies—told 'em so often I got to believing 'em myself. That story of mine about the elk with the 15 foot horns is what cured me. I told about that elk so often that I knowed the place I killed it. One night I lit a candle and crawled up in the loft to view the horns—an' I'm damned if they weren't there!"

[6277]

A patriotic Yankee went to Switzerland, and when asked how he liked the Alps, remarked, "Wal, now that you speak of it, I do remember seein' a bit of risin' ground round there."

[6278]

"I hear you are in a new business now."

"Yes."

"What are you doing?"

"I'm farming."

"What do you raise?"

"All kinds of vegetables. Would you believe it, we raised a head of cabbage there so large that one day it was raining and a regiment of soldiers was passing, and they all got under one leaf of the head of the cabbage. By the way, what are you doing now?"

"I'm running a boiler factory. Would you believe it, we made a boiler there the other day two miles long and a mile and a half wide."

"My goodness! what are you making such a big boiler for?"

"To cook that head of cabbage in you were talking about."

[6279]

A traveler was boasting that in his country they generally raised ninety or one hundred bushels of corn to the acre, and each stock had nine ears and was twelve feet high. "That is nothing to the corn down here; we have nine ears to the stock too, but we also have a peck of shelled corn hanging to each tassel, and we never could raise beans with it."

"Why?" said the other.

"Because the corn grew so fast it always pulled up the beans."

[6280]

Two farmers, sitting by the stove in the village store, were engaging in a little exaggeration fest.

"Naow, I oncet had a nephew," said one, "who was as fast a critter as ever I see. Why he use tew hev people shoot at him, and then outrun the bullet for five miles and get clean away."

"Wal, yew won't think that's so fast when yew hear about my cousin. Why that man could blow out the light and then be undressed by the time the room got dark."

[6281]

A Georgian in New York City was telling about the prowess of 'mosquitoes in his native state. One night a number of the insects got into his room in Georgia. He took a candle and went around burning them. He got them all except one big ferocious fellow that seemed to be the leader. He cornered that one and held the candle under it, but the skeeter just turned around and blew the candle out.

[6282]

An Irishman who had been in Alaska told the following story:

"I landed me boat on an island. I went ashore and when I got up to about the middle of the island I met the biggest bear I ever see in me life.

"There was one tree on the island and I made for that tree. The nearest limb was a big one which was about twenty feet from the ground, and I jumped for it."

Somebody listening to the story said: "Did you manage it?"

The Irishman replied:

"I didn't grab it going up, but I caught it coming down."

[6283]

The High Diver was advertised to give his performance as a crowning feature on the last day of the annual fair and races in a small county seat.

The High Diver, clad in silken tights, ascended to the top of a slender ladder, spindling ninety feet aloft, and, after poising himself there for a moment, plunged headlong, describing a graceful curve in his downward flight. Then, with a great splash he landed in the tank below, immediately emerging from it, in his glittering spangles, amid the plaudits of the admiring multitude.

Naturally enough that night,

when the community loafers assembled at their favorite general store, the achievement of the afternoon was the main topic of the evening.

The official liar held in as long as he could; and when he no longer could contain himself, he spoke up and said:

"Wal, I hain't denyin' but what that feller is consid'able of a diver —but I had a cousin oncet that could a-beat him."

The village skeptic gave a scornful grunt.

"Yeah," he drawled, "I thought you'd be sayin' somethin' of thet gen'rul nature before the evenin' was over. Who, fer th' sake o' argument, was this yere cousin o' yourn?"

"Wal," replied the liar, modestly, "he wan't no one in especial and perticular, exceptin' the champeen diver of the world—that's all."

"And whut did he ever do to justify that there title?" demanded the skeptic.

"Wal," said the liar, "he done consid'able things in the divin' line, which was his specialty. I recollect oncet he made a bet of a hundred dollars that he could dive from Liverpool, England, to Noo York City."

The skeptic gave a groan of resignation.

"I suppose," he said, "that you're going' to ask us to believe he won that there bet."

"No, I hain't," stated the liar. "I hain't a-goin' to lie to you. That was the one bet in his hull life my cousin ever lost. He miscalculated and come up in Denver, Colorado!"

[6284]

An American in London, who was badgered by the English on almost every topic, at last determined to go on the Mississippi steamboat style, and brag about everything. His first chance occurred at an exhibition of paintings, where a picture of a snowstorm attracted general admiration. "Is not that fine?" asked a Britisher. "Could you show anything as natural as that in America?"

"Pooh!" answered the American, "That is no comparison to a snowstorm picture painted by a cousin of mine a few years since. That painting was so natural, sir, that a mother, who uncautiously left her babe sleeping in a cradle near it, on returning to the room found her child frozen to death!"

[6285]

"When I was in India," said the club bore, "I saw a tiger come down to the water where some women were washing clothes. It was a very fierce tiger, but one woman, with great presence of mind splashed some water in its face—and it slunk away."

"Gentlemen," said a man in an armchair, "I can vouch for the truth of this story. Some minutes after this incident I was coming down to the water, I met this tiger, and, as is my habit, stroked its whiskers. Gentlemen, those whiskers were wet."

[6286]

"Speaking of rain," said Colonel Austin, "I've seen it rain so danged hard it rained into the muzzle of my gun and busted the durned thing at the breech! The water began to rise on us—I've seen it rise so rapidly in my house that it flowed up the chimney and streamed 300 feet up into the air! Why, we put out a barrel without any heads in it, and it rained into the bunghole of that barrel faster than it could run out at both ends!

"And—wind! One day it blew a new row of post holes I'd just had dug clear into the next county. Deacon Smivvers told me it blew his cook stove seventeen miles, and came back next morning and got the griddles. It blew a convention of Elks up against the courthouse, and the next morning they went around with shovels and scraped them off, to use 'em as circus posters!"

[6287]

They were speaking of the wheat crops in Kansas, before they were cut down to counteract overproduction. A Kansas farmer remarked:

"I don't know just how many bushels we raised, but my men stacked all they could out of doors and then stored the rest of the crop in the barn."

[6288]

"It was so cold where we were," boasted the Arctic explorer, "that the candle froze and we couldn't blow it out."

"That's nothing," said his rival. "Where we were the words came out of our mouths in pieces of ice, and we had fry them to see what we were talking about."

[6289]

Boasting of the farms in the Dakotas, a native said:

"We have some farms out our way that are pretty good size. I've seen a man on one of our big farms start out in the spring and plow a straight furrow till fall. Then he harvested back. And that's not all. It is the usual thing to send young married couples out to milk the cows, and their children come back with the milk."

[6290]

"Talking of ants," said the American story teller, "we've got 'em as big as crabs out West. I've seen 'em fight with long horns, which they use as lances, charging each other like savages."

"They don't compare with the ants I saw in the Far East," said an inoffensive individual nearby. "The natives have trained them as beasts of burden. One of 'em could trail a ton load for miles with ease. They worked willingly, but occasionally they turned on their attendants and killed them."

But this was drawing the long bow a little too far.

"I say, old chap," said a shocked voice from the corner, "what sort of ants were they?"

"Eleph-ants," replied the inoffensive individual.

[6291]

Believe this story or not, as you wish.

A man had a farm near a river. At one time the river began to rise, and he saw that his land would be submerged.

He transferred his family and also his stock and movable property to higher ground. There was on his farm exactly two miles of barbed-wire fence. It was five-wire fence, and there were thirty-two barbs to the rod, or a grand total of 102,400 barbs. The farmer and his hired man, baited every one of these barbs with a small bit of meat. They finished and managed to escape to the high land just as the water came up.

For twenty-six hours the water remained five feet above the top of the fence. Then the river receded, and the man went down and examined his fences. He found a fish hanging from every barb except three, or 102,397 in all. There were pike, perch, tench, roach, barbel, bream, and many other varieties.

They averaged 10 pounds each in weight, giving him the astonishing total of 1,046,893 pounds of fresh fish. He discharged his hired man because he had not properly baited the three barbs which failed to catch any fish.

[6292]
"Horses!" said the Yankee to the Canadian. "Guess you can't talk to me about horses. I once had an old mare that licked the fastest express train on a forty-mile-run."

"That's nothing!" said the Canuck. "I was out about fifty miles from my house on my farm one day when a frightful storm came up. I turned the pony's head for home and, do you know, he raced the storm so close for the last ten miles that I didn't feel a drop, while my dog, only ten yards behind, had to swim the whole distance."

[6293]
An American traveling in Scotland got into a conversation with a local farmer, and, in the course of the talk he remarked:

"I guess you haven't heard about the cattle salve we have in the United States. You simply cut off a cow's tail, rub the salve on the

stump, and you'll have a new tail on the cow in a week's time."

"Hoot, mon, that's naething. Ye ocht tae see the embrocation we ha'e at the place I coom frame. Ye simply cut a coo's tail aff, rub the salve on the tail, an' in a week's time a new coo grows on the auld tail."

[6294]
"I remember when I was a lad," said the old salt to Bobby. "I had to fight for my life with sixteen cannibals, and only one got away —"

"But," objected Bobby, "last year you told me it was eight cannibals."

"Yes," he said easily, "but you was too young then to know the whole horrible truth."

[6295]
A native of Virginia was once asked if he had ever seen the famous Natural Bridge. "See it?" he ejaculated. "I should say so. My father helped to build it."

[6296]
An American just returning to the United States was dining with an Englishman, and the latter complained of the mud in the United States.

"Yes," said the American, "but it's nothing to the mud in England."

"Nonsense!" said the Englishman.

"Fact," the Yankee replied. "Why this afternoon I had a remarkable adventure—came near to getting into trouble with an old gentleman—all through your confounded mud."

"Some of the streets are a little greasy at this season, I admit," said the Englishman. "What was your adventure, though?"

"Well," said the American, "as I was walking along I noticed that the mud was very thick, and presently I saw a high hat afloat on a large puddle of very rich ooze. Thinking to do some one a kindness, I gave the hat a poke with my stick, when an old gentleman looked up from beneath, surprised and frowning.

" 'Hello!' I said. 'You're in pretty deep!'

" 'Deeper than you think,' he said. 'I'm on the top of a bus!' "

[6297]

An American and a Scot were walking one day near the foot of one of the Scotch mountains. The Scot, wishing to impress the visitor, produced a famous echo to be heard in that place. When the echo returned clearly after nearly four minutes, the proud Scotsman, turning to the Yankee, exclaimed:

"There, mon, ye canna show anything like that in your country."

"Oh, I don't know," said the American, "I guess we can better that. Why, in my camp in the Rockies, when I go to bed I just lean out the window and call out, 'Time to get up; wake up!' and eight hours afterward the echo comes back and wakes me."

[6298]

A man who was boasting of the unusual height of a relative of his was annoyed by one of the company, who said he had a brother twelve feet high.

"Impossible!" snarled the boaster.

"Well, two halves make a whole, don't they?" asked the other.

"Yes," was the reply.

"Well then, I've got two half-brothers, each of whom is six feet high, and twice two makes twelve feet. Isn't that right?"

[6299]

An American who saw Vesuvius in eruption, when twitted on the fact that the United States had nothing to compare with that, said simply, "I should say not. What's more, Niagara Falls would put that thing out in less than two minutes."

[6300]

"Yes, ma'am," the old salt confided to the inquisitive lady, "I fell over the side of the ship, and a shark he came along and grabbed me by the leg."

"Merciful providence!" his hearer gasped, "And what did you do?"

"Let him have the leg, o' course, ma'am. I never argues with sharks."

[6301]

A Missourian is responsible for this:

"There are trees so tall in Missouri that it takes two men and a boy to look to the top of them. One looks till he gets tired, then another commences where he left off."

[6302]

"Talking of hens," remarked the American visitor, "reminds me of an old hen my dad once had. She would hatch out anything from a tennis ball to a lemon. Why, one day she sat on a piece of ice and hatched out two quarts of hot water."

"That doesn't come up to a club-footed hen my mother once had," remarked the Irishman. "They had been feeding her by mistake on sawdust instead of oatmeal. Well, sor, she laid twelve eggs and sat on them, and when they hatched eleven of the chickens had wooden legs and the twelfth was a wood-pecker!"

[6303]
A kind-hearted clergyman asked a convict how he came to be in jail. The fellow said, with tears in his eyes, that he was coming home from prayer-meeting, and sat down to rest, fell asleep, and while he was asleep there the county built a jail around him, and when he awoke the jailer wouldn't let him out.

[6304]
Speaking of high buildings, there is one in New York City that is so high that they put hinges on it halfway up so they can let it down at night so the moon can pass over it. You can stand on top of it and twist the tail of the dog star, and eat ice cream out of the milky way. You can reach up and tickle the feet of the angels as they fly by.

[6305]
A traveling man on his regular route stopped overnight frequently at a certain small town and, as there was nothing to do in the evening, fell into the habit of attending the usual gathering round the grocery-store stove.

There was one old man who had quite a reputation as a gunner and the salesman got to know him well. After an absence of some time, the salesman finally made his town again and as usual went to the store for the evening. The old man was there and this question, naturally, was asked:

"How is the gunning this fall, uncle?"

The old man shook his head in a dismal sort of way and answered:

"Not very good, but I did have a little luck the other day. I took the old gun out, and saw a fox lying beside a rock. I pulled up the gun to fire and I'll be blamed if another fox didn't come out and lie down on the other side of the rock. I fired at the sharp edge of the rock, the bullet split and killed both foxes.

"The gun kicked so that it knocked me over into a brook that was behind me, and my right hand landed on a muskrat and my left on a beaver.

"When I got up out of the water my trousers were so full of brook trout that they burst a suspender button and it flew and killed a partridge."

[6306]
Said the loose-tongued West-erner:

"It was so hot in the Yakima Valley last week that the heat affected the animals. I saw a hound dog chasing a jack rabbit, and they were both walking."

[6307]
In the early days in the lead mines of Wisconsin, pioneers told and heard strange stories about hoop-snakes. In one particular they all agreed—the snakes, in pairs, about the 15th of May would come rolling up from Illinois. Then they would disappear, and not be seen again until August. During that month strange sights might be seen on lonely stretches of prairie—hundreds of them playfully chasing one another.

They were a green snake—the males about six and the females five feet long. About four inches from the ends of their tails grew a hard, curved horn, from two to four inches in length.

They were considered the most dangerous snakes in the Northwest.

[6308]

A boy in Kansas climbed a cornstalk to see how the sky and clouds looked and that stalk grew so fast that the boy couldn't climb down. The boy was clear out of sight. Three men took the contract for cutting down the stalk with axes to save the boy from a horrible death by starvation, but the stalk grew so rapidly that they couldn't hit twice in the same place. The boy lived on green corn alone and threw down over four bushels of cobs. The boy might have been pushed up so high that he would have frozen to death if he hadn't been rescued by an airplane.

[6309]

A New Yorker was handing it out to a country man.

"Look at that sky-scraper going up! The workmen who are putting the finishing touches on the upper 20 stories have gone down to the 50th floor for lunch while the tenants on the first 40 floors are moving out because the building is old-fashioned!"

[6310]

An Easterner met a California miner at a touring camp. "You have a healthy climate in California, I understand," said the Easterner.

"Healthy? It ain't anything else. Why, stranger, there you can choose any climate you like, hot or cold, and that, too, without

travelin' more than fifteen minutes. Jest think o' that the next cold mornin' when you get out o' bed. There is a mountain there—the Sary Nevady they call it—with a valley on each side of it, one hot and one cold. Well, get on the top of that mountain with a double-barrelled gun, and you can, without movin', kill either summer or winter game, jest as you wish."

"What! have you ever tried it?"

"Tried it? Often, and should have done very well, but for one thing. I wanted a dog that would stand both climates. The last dog I had froze his tail off while pintin' on the summer side. He didn't get entirely out of the winter side, you see; true as you live."

[6311]

A couple of tramps were having a little boasting fest over the jungle fire.

Said Tramp Number One: "Why once't I wuz on a rattler down in Texas that went so fast the telegraph poles looked like a picket fence."

Said Tramp Number Two: "Huh! Dat ain't nothin'. Once't I was ridin' de blinds on a fast train between Chi and N'Yawk, and we wuz goin' so fast dat de milestones got so close tergether I t'ought we wuz goin' t'rough a graveyard."

[6312]

An American and a Scotsman were discussing the cold experienced in winter in the North of Scotland.

"Why, it's nothing at all compared to the cold we have in the United States," said the American. "I can recollect one winter when a sheep, jumping from a hillock into a field, became suddenly frozen on the way, and stuck in the air like a mass of ice."

"But, man," exclaimed the Scotsman, "the law of gravity wouldn't allow that."

"I know that," replied the American. "But the law of gravity was frozen, too!"

[6313]

"Speaking of animals remembering," said the elderly man, "when I was a boy I once gave a circus elephant a stick of striped candy."

"Well?"

"After that, whenever that circus was to parade in the town, the barbers had to take in their striped poles."

PART VIII

QUOTATION DICTIONARY

[6314]
Ability:
They are able because they think they are able.
—*Vergil.*

Ability is nothing without opportunity.
—*Napoleon.*

Ability is found to consist mainly in a high degree of solemnity.
—*Ambrose Bierce,*
"Devil's Dictionary."

We judge ourselves by what we feel capable of doing, while others judge us by what we have already done.
—*Longfellow.*

[6315]
Absence:
Absence makes the heart grow fonder.
—*Thomas Haynes Bayle,*
"Isle of Beauty."

Absence makes the heart go wander.
—*Gerald Barzan, "Letters."*

Achilles absent, was Achilles still.
—*Homer.*

How like a winter hath my absence been
From thee, the pleasure of the fleeting year!
What freezings have I felt, what dark days seen!
What old December's bareness everywhere.
—*Shakespeare.*

A short absence is safest.
—*Ovid.*

[6316]
Abstinence:
I can't drink a little, therefore I never touch it. Abstinence is as easy to me as temperance would be difficult.
—*Samuel Johnson.*

The more a man denies himself, the more shall he obtain from God.
—*Horace.*

[6317]
Absurdity:
Every absurdity has a champion to defend it.
—*Goldsmith.*

[6318]
Actor:
Let the actor beware!
—*Latin maxim.*

641

When an actor has money, he doesn't send letters but telegrams.
—*Chekhov.*

Players, sir! I look upon them as no better than creatures set upon tables and joint-stools to make faces and produce laughter, like dancing dogs.—But, sir, you will allow that some players are better than others? —Yes, sir; as some dogs dance better than others.
—*Samuel Johnson.*

[6319]

Adversity:
Adversity makes men remember God.
—*Livy.*

In time of prosperity friends will be plenty;
In time of adversity not one in twenty.
—*English proverb, attr. to John Clarke.*

Adversity is the trial of principle. Without it a man hardly knows whether he is honest or not.
—*Henry Fielding.*

Adversity has the effect of eliciting talents, which, in prosperous circumstances, would have lain dormant.
—*Horace.*

[6320]

Advice:
One can give advice comfortably from a safe port.
—*Schiller.*

Tis good to go on foot when one hath a horse.
—*French proverb.*

In giving advice I advise you, be short.
—*Horace.*

To attempt to advise conceited people is like whistling against the wind.
—*Thomas Hood.*

[6321]

Affectation:
Almost every man wastes part of his life in attempts to display qualities which he does not possess.
—*Samuel Johnson.*

All affectation is the vain and ridiculous attempt of poverty to appear rich.
—*Johann Kaspar Lavater.*

[6322]

Age:
Man fools himself. He prays for a long life, and he fears an old age.
—*Chinese proverb.*

Nothing is more dishonourable than an old man, heavy with years, who has no other evidence of his having lived long except his age.
—*Seneca.*

[6323]

Alimony:
You never realize how short a month is until you pay alimony.
—*John Barrymore.*

Alimony is like buying oats for a dead horse.
—*20th century Americana.*

[6324]

Ancestry:
Beware of men who flourish with hereditary honors.
—*Latin proverb.*

Good wine needs no bush.
—*Shakespeare.*

Birth and ancestry, and that which we have not ourselves achieved, we can scarcely call our own.
—*Ovid.*

[6325]
Animal:
Animals are such agreeable friends. They ask no questions, they pass no criticisms.
—*George Eliot.*

A mule has neither pride of ancestry nor hope of posterity.
—*Robert G. Ingersoll.*

[6326]
Appearance:
An ape is an ape, a varlet's a varlet, Though clothed in silk, or clothed in scarlet.
—*Spanish proverb.*

We are never so ridiculous from the habits we have as from those we affect to have.
—*La Rochefoucauld.*

[6327]
Apprenticeship:
By trimming fools about the gill, a barber's 'prentice learns his skill.
—*French proverb.*

[6328]
Art:
Good work rarely sells. I believe this of any art.
—*Arthur Wing Pinero.*

Art hath an enemy called ignorance.
—*Ben Jonson.*

Every artist was first an amateur.
—*Emerson.*

[6329]
Author:
Abuse is often of service. There is nothing so dangerous to an author as silence.
—*Samuel Johnson.*

Those authors are to be read at schools that supply most axioms of prudence.
—*Samuel Johnson.*

When I want to read a book, I write one.
—*Disraeli.*

[6330]
Avarice:
The darkest day in a man's career is that wherein he fancies there is some easier way of getting a dollar than by squarely earning it.
—*Horace Greeley.*

Great abundance of riches cannot be gathered and kept by any man without sin.
—*Erasmus.*

If money be not thy servant, it will be thy master. The covetous man cannot so properly be said to possess wealth, as that it may be said to possess him.
—*Bacon.*

[6331]
Bachelor:
Bachelors know more about women than married men; if they didn't they'd be married too.
—*H. L. Mencken.*

By persistently remaining single a man converts himself into a permanent public temptation.
—*Oscar Wilde.*

[6332]
Beauty:
Money is the best cosmetic.
—*Gregory Nunn.*

The loveliest faces are to be seen by moonlight, when one sees half with the eye and half with the fancy.
—*Persian proverb.*

Remember that the most beautiful things in the world are the most useless; peacocks and lilies, for instance.
—*John Ruskin.*

[6333]

Biography:

Biography is the only true history.

—*Thomas Carlyle.*

[6334]

Blessing:

In blindman's land those who are blessed with one eye are kings.

—*French proverb.*

No blessing lasts forever.

—*Plautus.*

We mistake the gratuitous blessings of heaven for the fruits of our industry.

—*Roger L'Estrange.*

[6335]

Blind:

A good marriage would be between a blind wife and a deaf husband.

—*Montaigne.*

If the blind lead the blind, both shall fall into a ditch.

—*The Bible.*

Blessed are the blind, for they know not enough to ask why.

—*Ernest Renan.*

There's none so blind as they that won't see.

—*Swift.*

[6336]

Books:

Books have led some to learning and others to madness.

—*Petrarch.*

A room without books is a body without a soul.

—*Cicero.*

Make your books your companions.

—*The Talmud.*

The drift of literary fiction is largely shown by the department store. The reader has gone slumming.

—*Opie P. Read.*

[6337]

Bootlegging:

Prohibition may be a disputed theory, but none can complain that it doesn't hold water.

—*Tom Masson.*

Uncle Sam is to erect a barbed wire fence at El Paso to keep out bootleg. If they ever spill any of the stuff on the fence, good-bye fence.

—*Los Angeles Express.*

Prohibition helped to beautify American home life. It got rid of the rings around the bath tubs.

—*Gerald F. Lieberman.*

[6338]

Business:

Honesty is the soul of business.

—*Dutch proverb.*

The business of America is business.

—*Calvin Coolidge.*

Let the buyer beware.

—*Latin maxim.*

[6339]

Candidate:

I never vote for the best candidate, I vote for the one who will do the least harm.

—*Franklin K. Dane.*

The world is weary of statesmen whom democracy has degraded into politicians.

—*Disraeli.*

[6340]

Cannibalism:

I have spoken of love. It is hard to go from people who kiss one another to people who eat one another.

—*Voltaire.*

Whenever cannibals are on the brink of starvation, Heaven, in its infinite mercy, sends them a nice plump missionary.

—*Oscar Wilde.*

[6341]

Celibacy:

As to marriage or celibacy, let a man choose which he will, he is sure to repent.

—Socrates.

[6342]

Ceremony:

Nothing is more ridiculous or troublesome than mere ceremony.

—French proverb.

[6343]

Children:

To the ass, or the sow, their own offspring appears the fairest in creation.

—Latin proverb.

Teach your child to hold his tongue, He'll learn fast enough to speak.

—Franklin, "Poor Richard."

It is a wise child that knows his own father.

—Homer.

[6344]

Christians:

If Christian nations were nations of Christians there would be no wars.

—Soame Jenyns.

Christianity, with its doctrine of humility, of forgiveness, of love, is incompatible with the state, with its haughtiness, its violence, its punishment, its wars.

—Tolstoy.

Christianity is completed Judaism, or it is nothing.

—Disraeli.

[6345]

Civilization:

We veneer civilization by doing unkind things in a kind way.

—George Bernard Shaw.

Civilization, or that which is so called, has operated two ways to make one part of society more affluent and the other part more wretched than would have been the lot of either in a natural state.

—Thomas Paine.

[6346]

Conceit:

Conceit is incompatible with understanding.

—Tolstoy.

A man who is always well satisfied with himself is seldom so with others, and others as little pleased with him.

—La Rochefoucauld.

[6347]

Conformity:

To rebel in season is not to rebel.

—Greek proverb.

[6348]

Conservative:

A conservative is someone who believes nothing should be done for the first time.

—Franklin K. Dane.

A conservative is a man who will not look at the new moon, out of respect for that "ancient institution," the old one.

—Douglas Jerrold.

A statesman who is enamored of existing evils, as distinguished from the Liberal, who wishes to replace them with others.

—Ambrose Bierce, "Devil's Dictionary."

[6349]

Conversation:

Conversation is a serious matter. There are men with whom an hour's talk would weaken one more than a week's fasting.

—19th century, English, uncredited.

[6350]

Cooking:
Do not overdo what has already been overdone.

—*Terence.*

We may live without friends; we may live without books;
But civilized man cannot live without cooks.

—*Owen Meredith.*

[6351]

Courage:
Fortune favors the bold.

—*Juvenal.*

Muster your wits: stand in your own defence;
Or hide your heads like cowards, and fly hence.

—*Shakespeare.*

[6352]

Court:
A court is an assembly of noble and distinguished beggars.

—*Talleyrand.*

[6353]

Courtship:
The days just prior to marriage are like a snappy introduction to a tedious book.

—*Wilson Mizner.*

[6354]

Coward:
To know what is right and not to do it is the worst cowardice.

—*Confucius.*

Courage leads to heaven; fear to death.

—*Seneca.*

[6355]

Crime:
It is to their crimes that most great men are indebted for their gardens, their palaces, their tables, their fine old plate—their love.

—*Latin proverb.*

Most people fancy themselves innocent of those crimes of which they cannot be convicted.

—*Seneca.*

[6356]

Critic:
It is easier to pull down than to build up.

—*Latin proverb.*

Critics! . . . those cut-throat bandits in the path of fame.

—*Robert Burns.*

Blame where you must, be candid where you can, and be each critic the good-natured man.

—*Robert Burns.*

What a blessed thing it is that nature, when she invented, manufactured and patented her authors, contrived to make critics out of the chips that were left!

—*Oliver Wendell Holmes.*

[6357]

Death:
A man who does not benefit the world by his life does it by his death.

—*19th century, uncredited.*

The last limit of all things.

—*Horace.*

Whom the gods love die young.

—*Menander.*

If death did not exist it would be necessary to invent it.

—*J. B. Milhaud.*

Strange, is it not? that of the myriads who
Before us pass'd the door of Darkness through,
Not one returns to tell us of the Road
Which to discover we must travel too.

—*Omar Khayyam.*

For he who lives more lives than
one
More deaths than one must die.
—*Oscar Wilde,*
"Ballad of Reading Gaol."

[6358]
Demagoguery:
A good trumpeter has the power
to rouse fools into making slaughter.
—*Vergil.*

[6359]
Democracy:
For if the people be governors
who shall be governed?
—*John Cotton.*

Democracy becomes a government of bullies tempered by editors.
—*Emerson.*

The motive power of democracy
is love.
—*Bergson.*

If there were a people consisting
of gods, they would be governed
democratically. So perfect a government is not suitable to men.
—*Rousseau.*

[6360]
Destiny:
Destiny is a Paris driver pushing
a taxicab with my name on it.
—*Franklin K. Dane.*

Thy fate is the common fate of
all;
Into each life some rain must
fall,—
—*Longfellow.*

We are all sure of two things, at
least; we shall suffer and we shall
all die.
—*Goldsmith.*

[6361]
Devil:
Why should the devil have all the
good times?
—*18th century English question.*

Speak of the devil and he appears.
—*Italian proverb.*

One sees more devils than vast
hell can hold.
—*Shakespeare.*

The devil can cite Scripture for
his purpose.
—*Shakespeare.*

[6362]
Diet:
The best way to lose weight is to
develop an orthodox belief in some
religion that doesn't allow any fun.
—*Gregory Nunn.*

My soul is dark with stormy riot:
Directly traced over to diet.
—*Samuel Hoffenstein.*

Bachelor's fare: Bread, cheese,
and kisses.
—*Swift.*

[6363]
Diplomat:
To deceive a diplomat speak the
truth, He has no experience with
it.
—*Greek proverb.*

[6364]
Disease:
Fate favors the physician by inventing lingering disease for which
there is no cure—and the sani-
tariums by inventing lingering cures
for which there is no disease.
—*Franklin K. Dane.*

Fear the doctor more than the
disease.
—*Latin proverb.*

[6365]
Divorce:
Divorce is born of perverted
morals and leads to vicious habits.
—*Pope Leo XIII.*

The height of ingratitude is the failure of Reno to erect a monument to Henry VIII.

—*Gerald F. Lieberman.*

[6366]
Doctor:
God heals and the doctor takes the fee.

—*Franklin.*

A young doctor makes a humpy graveyard.

—*Old English proverb.*

[6367]
Dogs:
The dog in the kennel barks at his fleas, but the dog that is hunting does not feel them.

—*19th century Americana.*

I am his Highness' dog at Kew;
Pray tell me, sir, whose dog are you?

—*Alexander Pope.*

[6368]
Drink:
Leave off all thin potations and addict thyself to sack.

—*Shakespeare.*

Drink! for you know not whence you came, nor why:
Drink! for you know not why you go, nor where.

—*Omar Khayyam.*

[6369]
Economics:
Among the propensities of human nature which almost exceed understanding come the parsimony of the rich and the extravagance of the poor.

—*19th century Americana.*

[6370]
Editors:
Don't be dismayed by the opinions of editors, or critics. They are only the traffic cops of the arts.

—*Gene Fowler.*

[6371]
Education:
Natural ability without education has more often raised man to glory, than education without natural ability.

—*Cicero.*

Man can acquire knowledge but not wisdom. Some of the greatest fools ever known were learned men.

—*Spanish proverb.*

[6372]
Efficiency:
If all efficiency experts were laid end to end—I'd be in favor of it.

—*Al Diamond.*

[6373]
Ego:
The fallacy whereby a goose thinks he's a swan.

—*19th century Americana.*

When all is summed up, a man never speaks of himself without loss; his accusations of himself are always believed, his praises never.

—*Montaigne.*

[6374]
Election:
The only thing we learn from a new election is we learned nothing from the old.

—*Gerald Barzan.*

Did you too, O friend, suppose democracy was only for elections, for politics, and for a party name?

—*Walt Whitman.*

[6375]

Epigrams:

The value of short sayings of wise and excellent men is beyond estimate. Like rays of sunshine and the sparks of diamonds.

—*J. Tillotson.*

Epigrams succeed where epics fail.

—*Persian proverb.*

[6376]

Epitaph:

The most touching epitaph I ever encountered was on the tombstone of the printer of Edinburgh. It said simply: "He kept down the cost and set the type right."

—*Gregory Nunn.*

If men could see the epitaphs their friends write they would believe they had got into the wrong grave.

—*19th century Americana.*

[6377]

Ethics:

The legal profession, like the medical profession, has a Canon of Ethics. And, as in the latter instance, it is generally ignored.

—*Gerald F. Lieberman.*

A set of rules laid out by professionals to show the way they would like to act if they could afford it.

—*Gerald F. Lieberman.*

[6378]

Evil:

The evil that men do survives them. They murder after their death by the sentiments they have propagated and by the laws they have made.

—*Latin proverb.*

The evil that men do lives after them;
The good is oft interred with their bones.

—*Shakespeare.*

[6379]

Expedience:

Men resort to expedience when honor gets a little risky.

—*Franklin K. Dane.*

[6380]

Facts:

Facts do not cease to exist because they are ignored.

—*Aldous Huxley.*

I grow daily to honor facts more and more, and theory less and less.

—*Thomas Carlyle.*

Get your facts first, and then you can distort 'em as much as you please.

—*Mark Twain.*

[6381]

Faith:

Belief without evidence in what is told by one without knowledge, of things without parallel.

—*Ambrose Bierce,*
"Devil's Dictionary."

There lives more faith in honest doubt,
Believe me, than in half the creeds.

—*Tennyson.*

If you have any faith, give me, for heaven's sake, a share of it! Your doubts you may keep to yourself, for I have a plenty of my own.

—*Goethe.*

[6382]

Fame:

The fame of great men ought always to be estimated by the means used to acquire it.

—*La Rochefoucauld.*

If you would not be forgotten as soon as you are dead, either write things worth reading or do things worth writing.

—*Franklin.*

[6383]

Family:

The rich never have to seek out their relatives.

—*Italian proverb.*

The hatred of relatives is the most violent.

—*Tacitus.*

[6384]

Fashion:

Fashion is the most powerful force in creation. It rules the women, who rule the men, who rule the world.

—*19th century Americana.*

Fashion is a form of ugliness so intolerable that we have to alter it every six months.

—*Oscar Wilde.*

I see that the fashion wears out more apparel than the man.

—*Shakespeare.*

[6385]

Fate:

Thou seest two bricks baked together, from the same clay and furnace. One shall be laid on top of a minaret, and the other at the bottom of an outhouse.

—*Moasi, king of the poets of Persia, 11th century.*

The Moving Finger writes; and, having writ,
Moves on: nor all your Piety nor Wit
Shall lure it back to cancel half a Line,
Nor all your Tears wash out a Word of it.

—*Omar Khayyam.*

[6386]

Food:

The most dangerous food a man can eat is wedding cake.

—*20th century Americana.*

Master, I marvel how the fishes live in the sea.
Why, as men do a-land: the great ones eat up the little ones.

—*Pericles.*

[6387]

Fools:

Get the fools on your side and you can be elected anything.

—*Franklin K. Dane.*

A fool must now and then be right, by chance.

—*William Cowper.*

A learned fool is more foolish than an ignorant fool.

—*Moliere.*

A fool and his money can go places.

—*Gene Fowler.*

This fellow is wise enough to pay the fool;
And to do that well craves a kind of wit.

—*Shakespeare.*

[6388]

Fortune:

Good fortune and evil fortune come to all things alike in this world of time.

—*Moasi, king of the poets of Persia, 11th century.*

Luck affects everything; let your hook always be cast; in the stream where you least expect it, there will be a fish.

—*Ovid.*

[6389]

Freedom:

Farewell my good master, homeward I fly:

One day thou shalt gain the same freedom as I.

—*Jelaleddin of Persia.*

Many politicians are in the habit of laying it down as a self-evident proposition that no people ought to be free till they are fit to use their freedom. The maxim is worthy of the fool in the old story who resolved not to go into the water till he had learned to swim.

—*T. B. Macaulay.*

[6390]

Friendship:

If all persons knew what they said of each other there would not be four friends in the world.

—*Pascal.*

There are three faithful friends: an old wife, an old dog, and ready money.

—*Franklin.*

In all distresses of our friends We first consult our private ends.

—*Swift.*

Those friends thou hast, and their adoption tried,

Grapple them to thy soul with hoops of steel;

But do not dull thy palm with entertainment

Of each new-hatch'd, unfledg'd comrade.

—*Shakespeare.*

[6391]

Funeral:

A pageant whereby we attest our respect for the dead by enriching the undertaker.

—*Ambrose Bierce, "Devil's Dictionary."*

[6392]

Future:

The future is no more uncertain than the present.

—*Walt Whitman.*

I never think of the future. It comes soon enough.

—*Albert Einstein.*

There was the Door to which I found no key;

There was the Veil through which I might not see.

—*Omar Khayyam.*

[6393]

Gambling:

The only man who makes money following the races is the one who does it with a broom and shovel.

—*Elbert Hubbard.*

Man is a gaming animal.

—*Charles Lamb.*

A mode of transferring property without producing any intermediate good.

—*Samuel Johnson.*

[6394]

Genius:

Genius borrows nobly.

—*Emerson.*

Genius is one per cent inspiration and ninety-nine per cent perspiration.

—*Edison.*

There is no great genius without a mixture of madness.

—*Aristotle.*

[6395]

Gift:

Those gifts are ever more precious which the giver has made precious.

—*Ovid.*

[6396]

God:

Every man for himself, and God for us all.

—*Spanish proverb.*

How gracious are the gods in bestowing high positions; and how reluctant are they to insure them when given.

—*Lucian.*

Man is certainly stark mad; he cannot make a flea, and yet he will be making gods by dozens.

—*Montaigne.*

[6397]

Golden Rule:

All things whatsoever ye would that men should do to you, do ye even so to them: For that is the law of the prophets.

—*Matthew.*

The purification of politics is an iridescent dream . . . the Golden Rule has no place in a political campaign.

—*John James Ingalls.*

Every creature alive lives by the Golden Rule, which they take to mean get all the gold you can.

—*Noah Goldstein.*

Do not do unto others as you would that they should do unto you. Their taste may not be the same.

—*George Bernard Shaw, 1903.*

[6398]

Gossip:

A malignant sore throat is a danger, a malignant throat not sore is worse.

—*19th century Americana.*

There is only one thing in the world worse than being talked about, and that is not being talked about.

—*Oscar Wilde.*

[6399]

Government:

The best form of government for a nation is that under which it lives. To desire otherwise is folly.

—*Montaigne.*

No man undertakes a trade he has not learned, even the meanest; yet every one thinks himself sufficiently qualified for the hardest of all trades—that of government.

—*Socrates.*

Themistocles said, "The Athenians govern the Greeks; I govern the Athenians; you, my wife, govern me; your son governs you."

—*Plutarch.*

[6400]

Grammar:

As for the adjective, when in doubt leave it out.

—*Mark Twain.*

I am the King of Rome, and above grammar.

—*Sigismund.*

[6401]

Gratitude:

Gratitude is a useless word. You will find it in a dictionary but not in life.

—*Balzac.*

The gratitude of most men is but a secret desire of receiving greater benefits.

—*La Rochefoucauld.*

[6402]

Happiness:

An agreeable sensation, arising from contemplating the misery of others.

—*Ambrose Bierce,*
"Devil's Dictionary."

[6403]

Hate:
The hatred of those who are near to us is the most violent.
—*Tacitus.*

How hatred is by far the longest pleasure;
Men love in haste, but they detest at leisure.
—*Byron.*

[6404]

Heaven:
What they do in heaven we are ignorant of; what they do not we are told expressly.
—*Swift.*

Help thyself and Heaven will help thee.
—*La Fontaine.*

Heaven without good society cannot be heaven.
—*Thomas Fuller.*

[6405]

Helpmate:
The wife, or bitter half.
—*Ambrose Bierce, "Devil's Dictionary."*

[6406]

History:
History belongs to the winner.
—*Gerald F. Lieberman.*

An account, mostly false, of events mostly unimportant, which are brought about by rulers mostly knaves, and soldiers mostly fools.
—*Ambrose Bierce, "Devil's Dictionary."*

History is indeed little more than the register of the crimes, follies, and misfortunes of mankind.
—*Edward Gibbon.*

[6407]

Hollywood:
In Hollywood blood is thicker than talent.
—*Joe Laurie, Jr.*

[6408]

Home:
Home is home, though it be homely.
—*English proverb.*

My notions on life are much the same as they are about travelling. There is a good deal of amusement on the road, but after all, one wants to rest.
—*Robert Southey.*

There's no place like home—after the other places close.
—*Joe Laurie, Jr.*

[6409]

Honesty:
There are no such things as honest people, there are only people less crooked.
—*Gerald F. Lieberman.*

Occasionally, when honesty was the best policy, he was honest.
—*Gregory Nunn.*

[6410]

Honor:
What is Honor? A word! What is that word Honor? Air!
—*Shakespeare.*

Honor before profit; where practical.
—*Gerald Barzan.*

An honest man is one who's never been caught.
—*19th century Americana.*

But without money honor is nothing but a malady.
—*Racine.*

[6411]

Hope:

Hope is the thing that ends with lilies on it.

—*Gerald F. Lieberman.*

Hope is a very thin diet.

—*Thomas Shadwell.*

To hope is to enjoy.

—*Jacques de Lille.*

He that waits for a dead man's shoes may long enough go barefoot.

—*French proverb.*

[6412]

Humor:

Fear not a jest. If one throws salt at thee thou wilt receive no harm unless thou hast sore places.

—*Latin proverb.*

Even the gods love jokes.

—*Plato.*

[6413]

Husband:

Married men make the best husbands.

—*James Huneker.*

Husbands love your wives, and be not bitter against them.

—*Colossians.*

God give me a rich husband, though he be an ass.

—*Thomas Fuller, "Gnomologia."*

[6414]

Hypocrisy:

It is not what they profess but what they practice that makes them good.

—*Greek proverb.*

With people of limited ability modesty is merely honesty. But with those who possess great talent it is hypocrisy.

—*Schopenhauer.*

[6415]

Ignorance:

Ignorance is not privileged by titular degrees.

—*Latin proverb.*

Oh, the ignorance of us upon whom Providence did not sufficiently smile to permit us to be born in New England.

—*Horace Porter.*

Where ignorance is bliss,
'Tis folly to be wise.

—*Thomas Gray.*

[6416]

Illusion:

It is respectable to have no illusions—and safe—and profitable—and dull.

—*Joseph Conrad.*

Imagination is more important than knowledge.

—*Albert Einstein.*

[6417]

Income:

There are few sorrows however poignant in which a good income is of no avail.

—*Robert Frost.*

[6418]

Individualism:

An individualist is one who pays his taxes with a smile.

—*Al Diamond.*

[6419]

Infidelity:

When love becomes labored we welcome an act of infidelity towards ourselves to free us from fidelity.

—*La Rochefoucauld.*

[6420]

Inflation:
The nation is prosperous on the whole, but how much prosperity is there in a hole?
—*Will Rogers.*

[6421]

Inspiration:
Inspiration in matters of taste will not come twice.
—*Balzac.*

A writer is rarely so well inspired as when he talks about himself.
—*France.*

[6422]

Invective:
If ever I utter an oath again may my soul be blasted to eternal damnation.
—*George Bernard Shaw.*

[6423]

Investment:
Hard work is the soundest investment. It provides a neat security for your widow's next husband.
—*Gregory Nunn.*

[6424]

Jealousy:
Plain women are always jealous of their husbands. Beautiful women never are. They are always so occupied with being jealous of other people's husbands.
—*Oscar Wilde.*

Yet he was jealous, though he did not show it,
For jealousy dislikes the world to know it.
—*Byron.*

[6425]

Journalism:
Journalism is unreadable and literature is unread. —*Oscar Wilde.*

[6426]

Judge:
Judges, like the criminal classes, have their lighter moments.
—*Oscar Wilde.*

The hungry judges soon the sentence sign,
And wretches hang that jury-men may dine.
—*Alexander Pope.*

[6427]

Judgment:
My salad days, when I was green in judgment.
—*Shakespeare.*

[6428]

Jury:
A jury consists of twelve persons chosen to decide who has the better lawyer.
—*Robert Frost.*

The nature of all men is so formed that they see and discriminate in the affairs of others, much better than in their own.
—*Terence.*

[6429]

Justice:
There is no such thing as justice, in or out of court.
—*Clarence Darrow.*

Thrice is he arm'd that hath his quarrel just,
And he but naked, though lock'd up in steel,
Whose conscience with injustice is corrupted.
—*Shakespeare.*

Thrice is he armed that hath his quarrel just;
And four times he who gets his fist in fust. —*Josh Billings.*

[6430]

Kisses:
An alms which enriches him who receives without impoverishing her who gives.

—*19th century Americana.*

This done, he took the bride about the neck
And kiss'd her lips with such a clamorous smack
That at the parting, all the church did echo.

—*Shakespeare.*

[6431]

Knowledge:
Knowledge is of two kinds. We know a subject ourselves, or we know where we can find information upon it.

—*Samuel Johnson.*

For knowledge too is itself a power.

—*Bacon.*

Knowledge is power—if you know it about the right people.

—*Franklin K. Dane.*

[6432]

Lady:
Men, some to quiet, some to public strife;
But every lad would be queen for life.

—*Alexander Pope.*

A lady, if undrest at Church looks silly,
One cannot be devout in dishabilly.

—*George Farquhar.*

[6433]

Landlord:
Give a landlord an inch and he'll build an apartment house.

—*Saul Antin.*

[6434]

Language:
It was Greek to me.

—*Shakespeare.*

No man fully capable of his own language ever masters another.

—*George Bernard Shaw.*

I have been speaking prose without knowing it for more than forty years.

—*Moliere.*

[6435]

Law:
There is no departing from the words of the law.

—*Latin maxim.*

The English laws punish vice; the Chinese laws do more, they reward virtue.

—*Goldsmith.*

[6436]

Lawyer:
It is with lawyers as it is with doctors; the less we have to do with either, the better.

—*19th century Americana.*

A good lawyer is a bad neighbor.

—*French proverb.*

It has been said that the course to be pursued by a lawyer was first to get on, second to get honor, and third to get honest.

—*George M. Palmer.*

[6437]

Legislature:
It could probably be shown by facts and figures that there is no distinctly native American criminal class except Congress.

—*Mark Twain.*

[6438]

Liberal:

A liberal is a conservative whose conscience is on display.

—*Jerome Gioia.*

He that defers his charity until he is dead is, if a man weighs it rightly, rather liberal of another man's goods than his own.

—*Bacon.*

A man who has both feet planted firmly in the air can be safely called a liberal.

—*20th century Americana.*

Liberalism is trust of the people tempered by prudence; conservatism, distrust of the people tempered by fear.

—*Gladstone.*

[6439]

Liberty:

Proclaim liberty throughout all the land unto all the inhabitants thereof.

—*Leviticus.*

In America we believe in Life, Liberty—and the pursuit.

—*Al Diamond.*

Those who would give up essential liberty to purchase a little temporary safety deserve neither liberty nor safety.

—*Franklin.*

[6440]

Liars:

He who comes from afar may lie without fear of contradiction as he is sure to be listened to with the utmost attention.

—*French proverb.*

[6441]

Life:

If a man would live in peace he should be blind, deaf, and dumb.

—*Turkish proverb.*

One life;—a little gleam of Time between two Eternities.

—*Carlyle.*

For life in general, there is but one decree: youth is a blunder, manhood a struggle, old age a regret.

—*Disraeli.*

Ah Love! could you and I with him conspire
To grasp this sorry Scheme of Things entire
Would we not shatter it to bits
—and then
Re-mould it nearer to the Heart's Desire?

—*Omar Khayyam.*

[6442]

Literature:

People do not deserve to have good writings; they are so pleased with bad.

—*Emerson.*

Literature always anticipates life. It does not copy it, but molds it to its purpose.

—*Oscar Wilde.*

[6443]

Logic:

Logic is the technique by which we add conviction to truth.

—*Jean De La Bruyere.*

Men are apt to mistake the strength of their feeling for the strength of their argument. The heated mind resents the chill touch and relentless scrutiny of logic.

—*Gladstone.*

[6444]

Loneliness:
Be good and you will be lonely.
—*Mark Twain.*

[6445]

Love:
If, as the poets say, love has moved mountains and forests, and so deeply touched the hearts of men that all of the oceans, and the rivers, and the lakes, are made up of tears love has shed; if this poetic lyricism be true, then the love of which they sing is the love of money.
—*Gerald F. Lieberman.*

A truce to your volumes, your studies give o'er: for books cannot teach you love's marvelous lore.
—*Hafiz of Persia.*

When a scholar goes to seek out a bride he should take along an ignoramus as an expert.
—*The Talmud.*

[6446]

Lovers:
The quarrels of lovers are the re-suscitation of love.
—*Terence.*

[6447]

Luck:
He dances well to whom fortune pipes.
—*Italian proverb.*

Yes, there's a luck in most things; and in none more than being born at the right time.
—*Edmund Clarence Stedman.*

[6448]

Maiden:
There was a maiden speech, so inaudible that it was doubted whether, after, the young orator really did lose his virginity.
—*Disraeli.*

[6449]

Majority:
The majority is always wrong. The minority is rarely right.
—*Henrik Ibsen.*

[6450]

Man:
Man is to man either a god or a wolf.
—*Erasmus.*

How great in number are the little minded men.
—*Plautus.*

There are times when one would like to hang the whole human race, and finish the farce.
—*Mark Twain.*

I wonder men dare trust themselves with men.
—*Shakespeare.*

[6451]

Manners:
The best mannered people make the most absurd lovers.
—*Diderot.*

Good manners is the art of making those people easy with whom we converse. Whoever makes the fewest persons uneasy, is the best bred in the company.
—*Swift.*

[6452]

Marriage:
Second marriage is the triumph of hope over experience.
—*Samuel Johnson.*

A husband and wife who have separate bedrooms have either drifted apart or found happiness.
—*Balzac.*

Matrimony,—the high sea for which no compass has yet been invented.
—*Heine.*

It happens, as with cages: the birds without despair to get in, and those within despair of getting out.
—*Montaigne.*

What God hath joined together no man shall ever put asunder: God will take care of that.
—*Bernard Shaw.*

Men marry because they are tired, women because they are curious: both are disappointed.
—*Oscar Wilde.*

[6453]
Medicine:
Medicine can only cure curable disease, and then not always.
—*Chinese proverb.*

Doctors are men who prescribe medicines of which they know little, to cure diseases of which they know less, in human beings of whom they know nothing.
—*Voltaire.*

[6454]
Memory:
The best memory is that which forgets nothing but injuries. Write kindness in marble and write injuries in the dust.
—*Persian proverb.*

[6455]
Mercy:
The court is most merciful when the accused is most rich.
—*Hebrew proverb.*

We hand folks over to God's mercy, and show none ourselves.
—*George Eliot.*

[6456]
Minority:
A minority is always compelled to think; that is the blessing of being in the minority.
—*Leo Baeck.*

[6457]
Miracle:
Many a man who is willing to be shot for his belief in a miracle would have doubted, had be been present at the miracle itself.
—*G. C. Lichtenberg.*

[6458]
Miser:
Misers part with nothing until they die. Then they give up the ghost.
—*Latin proverb.*

'Tis strange the miser should his cares employ
To gain those riches he can ne'er enjoy;
Is it less strange the prodigal should waste
His wealth to purchase what he ne'er can taste?
—*Alexander Pope.*

[6459]
Mob:
It is an easy and vulgar thing to please the mob, and no very arduous task to astonish them.
—*C. C. Colton.*

It is the proof of a bad cause when it is applauded by the mob.
—*Seneca.*

[6460]

Moderation:
  Be moderate in everything, including moderation.
                        —Horace Porter.

  Moderation in temper is always a virtue; but moderation in principle is always a vice.
                        —Thomas Paine.

[6461]

Modesty:
  No modest man ever did or ever will make a fortune.
                —Mary Wortley Montagu.

  Modesty died when false modesty was born.
                        —Mark Twain.

[6462]

Monarchy:
  Kings have long hands.
                        —Ovid.

  The type of government they have in England is called a limited mockery.
                        —College exam.

[6463]

Money:
  Every man now worships gold; all other reverence being done away.
                        —Propertius.

  He catches the best fish who angles with a golden hook.
                        —Latin proverb.

[6464]

Monotony:
  The custom of allowing a man to have only one wife.
                —20th century Americana.

[6465]

Monument:
  A reminder of one who has been forgotten.
                —19th century Americana.

  Deeds, not stones, are the true monuments of the great.
                        —J. L. Motley.

[6466]

Morality:
  Morality is simply the attitude we adopt towards people whom we dislike.
                        —Oscar Wilde.

  Do not be too moral. You may cheat yourself out of much life so.
                        —Thoreau.

  We know no spectacle so ridiculous as the British public in one of its periodical fits of morality.
                        —Macaulay.

[6467]

Mortgage:
  An empty purse and a new house make a man wise, but too late.
                        —Portuguese proverb.

  The meek may inherit the earth, but the other kind inherits the mortgage.
                        —Noah Goldstein.

[6468]

Mother:
  God could not be everywhere, therefore he made mothers.
                        —The Talmud.

[6469]

Mule:
  Asses speak only of horses.
                        —Heine.

[6470]

Murder:

If you murder an innocent man you are responsible for the blood of his unborn descendants, and the weight of this responsibility is yours to carry to the end of time.

—*The Mishna.*

For murder, though it have no tongue, will speak
With most miraculous organ.

—*Shakespeare.*

[6471]

Music:

O Music! Miraculous art! A blast of thy trumpet and millions rush forward to die; a peal of thy organ and uncounted nations sink down to pray.

—*Disraeli.*

The history of a people is found in its songs.

—*Jellinek.*

[6472]

Name:

Fool's names, like fool's faces
Are often seen in public places.

—*Thomas Fuller.*

I would rather make my name than inherit it.

—*W. M. Thackeray.*

Good name in man and woman,
    dear my lord,
Is the immediate jewel of their
    souls:
Who steals my purse steals trash;
    'tis something, nothing;
'Twas mine, 'tis his, and has been
    slave to thousands;
But he that filches from me my
    good name
Robs me of that which not enriches
    him,
And makes me poor indeed.

—*Shakespeare.*

[6473]

Nature:

It is too late to go back to the order of nature or the truth in history.

—*John R. Paxton.*

History teaches virtue, nature preaches vice.

—*Ludwig Boerne.*

[6474]

Necessity:

Necessity makes the best soldiers.

—*Josephus.*

I hold that to need nothing is divine, and the less a man needs the nearer does he approach divinity.

—*Socrates.*

[6475]

Neighbor:

Love your neighbor as yourself; but don't take down the fence.

—*Sandburg.*

Your own safety is at stake when your neighbor's house is in flames.

—*Horace.*

[6476]

Neutrality:

When in doubt who will win, be neutral.

—*Swiss proverb.*

[6477]

News:

No news is good news.

—*Ludovic Halevy.*

When we hear news we should always wait for the sacrament of confirmation.

—*Voltaire.*

None loves the messenger who brings bad news.

—*Sophocles.*

[6478]

New Year:

God send you happy, God send you happy

We pray God send you a happy New Year.

—*Song of the Old English Caroliers.*

Ring out the old, ring in the new,
Ring happy bells, across the snow;
The year is going, let me go;
Ring out the false, ring in the true.

—*Tennyson.*

I can no longer bring myself to wish anyone a Happy New Year. Not when I think of what would make them happy.

—*Gerald F. Lieberman.*

[6479]

Oath:

A liar freely gives his oath.

—*Cornielle.*

I'll take thy word for faith, not ask thine oath;

Who shuns not to break one will sure crack both.

—*Shakespeare.*

[6480]

Obscenity:

It is the grossness of the spectator that discovers nothing but grossness in the subject.

—*Hazlitt.*

[6481]

Omens:

The leaves fall before the tree dies.

—*French proverb.*

Without a sign, his sword the brave man draws,

And asks no omen but his country's cause.

—*Homer.*

[6482]

Opinion:

A mass of men equals a mass of opinions.

—*Latin proverb.*

Error of opinion may be tolerated where reason is left free to combat it.

—*Thomas Jefferson.*

Truth is one forever absolute, but opinion is truth filtered through the moods, the blood, the disposition of the spectator.

—*Wendell Phillips.*

[6483]

Opportunity:

Men never moan over the opportunities lost to do good, only the opportunities to be bad.

—*Greek proverb.*

Do when ye may, or suffer ye the nay, in love 'tis the way.

—*Old English proverb.*

There is a tide in the affairs of men,

Which, taken at the flood, leads on to fortune;

Omitted, all the voyage of their life

Is bound in shallows and in miseries.

—*Shakespeare.*

[6484]

Orator:

What orators want in depth they give you in length.

—*Montesquieu.*

It is a thing of no great difficulty to raise objections against another man's oration,—nay, it is a very easy matter; but to produce a better in its place is a work extremely troublesome.

—*Plutarch.*

[6485]

Originality:
Originality is plagiarism unde-
tected.

—*Uncredited. Many sources.*

If they haven't heard it before it's
original.

—*Gene Fowler.*

[6486]

Pain:
Pain is life.

—*Charles Lamb.*

Time heals old pain, while it cre-
ates new ones.

—*Hebrew proverb.*

One pain is lessen'd by another's
anguish.

—*Shakespeare.*

[6487]

Parenthood:
Maternity is a matter of fact, pa-
ternity a matter of opinion.

—*Franklin K. Dane.*

Some of the dirtiest dogs, past
and present, had mothers.

—*Gregory Nunn.*

The first half of our lives is
ruined by our parents and the second half by our children.

—*Clarence Darrow.*

[6488]

Partnership:
Forty for you, sixty for me
And equal partners we will be.

—*Gerald Barzan,*
"Business Was Business."

In business partnerships and marriage partnerships, O' the cheating
that goes on.

—*Saul Antin.*

[6489]

Passion:
Subdue your passion or it will
subdue you.

—*Horace.*

The ruling passion, be it what it
will,
The ruling passion conquers reason still.

—*Alexander Pope.*

[6490]

Past:
What's past is prologue.

—*Shakespeare.*

The good of other times let people state;
I think it lucky I was born so
late.

—*Ovid.*

[6491]

Patience:
O' the mass of arms, the brilliant
leadership, the courage and magnitude of the ancient armies of
Greece, combined to conquer the
city of Troy—all that, and ten years
of perseverance.

—*Hipponax the Satirist.*

Patience is a necessary ingredient
of genius.

—*Disraeli.*

[6492]

Patriotism:
It is the patriotic duty of every
man to lie for his country.

—*Alfred Adler.*

Our country! In her intercourse
with foreign nations, may she always be in the right; but our country, right or wrong.

—*Stephen Decatur.*

[6493]

Peace:
When monarchs through their bloodthirsty commanders lay waste a country, they dignify their atrocity by calling it "Making Peace."
—*Tacitus.*

If they want peace, nations should avoid the pin-pricks that precede cannon-shots.
—*Napoleon.*

[6494]

Pedigree:
Do well and you will have no need of ancestors.
—*Voltaire.*

Birth and ancestry, and that which we have not ourselves achieved, we can scarcely call our own.
—*Ovid.*

She descended from a long line her mother listened to.
—*Gypsy Rose Lee.*

[6495]

Pedantry:
The boastful blockhead ignorantly read,
With loads of learned lumber in his head.
—*Alexander Pope.*

[6496]

People:
It is the nature of all people to believe every calamity happening to them a trial, and every one happening to others a judgment.
—*19th century. Many Sources.*

You can fool some of the people all of the time, and all of the people some of the time, but you cannot fool all of the people all the time.
—*Abraham Lincoln.*

[6497]

Perseverance:
No man drowns if he perseveres in praying to God; and can swim.
—*Russian proverb.*

Great works are performed not by strength but by perseverance.
—*Samuel Johnson.*

[6498]

Philanthropy:
The worst of charity is that the lives you are asked to preserve are not worth preserving.
—*Emerson.*

Steal the hog, and give the feet for alms.
—*George Herberg.*

[6499]

Philosophy:
The origins of disputes between philosophers is, that one class of them have undertaken to raise man by displaying his greatness, and the other to debase him by showing his miseries.
—*Pascal.*

Philosophy: A route of many roads leading from nowhere to nothing.
—*Ambrose Bierce,*
"Devil's Dictionary."

[6500]

Physician:
Though physician to others, yet himself full of sores.
—*Latin proverb.*

No matter what conditions
Dyspeptic come to feaze,
The best of all physicians
Is Apple-pie and cheese!
—*Eugene Field.*

[6501]

Piety:

Those who have loved God most have loved Man least.

—*Robert Green Ingersoll.*

I'm religiously opposed to religion.

—*Victor Hugo.*

Thou villain, thou art full of piety.

—*Shakespeare.*

[6502]

Pilgrims:

The Pilgrim fathers landed on the shores of America and fell upon their knees, then they fell upon the aborigines.

—*Horace Porter.*

How much better might it have been if Plymouth Rock landed upon the Pilgrims.

—*19th century Americana.*

[6503]

Plagiarism:

The only good copies are those which make us see the absurdity of bad originals.

—*La Rochefoucauld.*

Instead of forming new words I recommend to you any kind of artful management by which you may be able to give cost to old ones.

—*Horace.*

Perish those who said our good things before we did.

—*Donatus.*

Take the whole range of imaginative literature, and we all are wholesale borrowers. In every matter that relates to invention, to use, or beauty or form, we are borrowers.

—*Wendell Phillips.*

When 'Omer smote 'is bloomin' lyre,

He'd 'eard men sing by land an' sea;

An' what he thought 'e might require,

'E went an' took—the same as me!

—*Kipling.*

[6504]

Platitude:

Rectitude, platitude, high-hatitude.

—*Margot Asquith.*

[6505]

Pleasure:

When pleasure interferes with business, give up business.

—*20th century proverb.*

Rich the treasure; sweet the pleasure.

—*Dryden.*

But pleasures are like poppies spread;

You seize the flower, its bloom is shed.

Or like the snow falls in the river,

A moment white—then melts forever.

—*Robert Burns.*

The rule of my life is to make business a pleasure, and pleasure my business.

—*Aaron Burr.*

In everything satiety closely follows the greatest pleasures.

—*Cicero.*

[6506]

Poet:

Good poets are like angels of Heaven.

—*Persian proverb.*

A poet can survive everything but a misprint.

—*Oscar Wilde.*

A man is either mad or he is making verses.

—*Horace.*

[6507]

Politician:

An honest politician is one who when he's bought stays bought.
—*Simon Cameron.*

I don't know why politicians are called servants, unless it's because a good one is hard to find.
—*Gerald F. Lieberman.*

[6508]

Politics:

A strife of interests masquerading as a contest of principles.
—*Ambrose Bierce,*
"Devil's Dictionary."

Politics: The highest calling to the lowest falling.
—*Gregory Nunn.*

In politics nothing is contemptible.
—*Disraeli.*

O, that estates, degrees, and offices
Were not deriv'd corruptly, and that clear honour
Were purchased by the merit of the wearer!
—*Shakespeare.*

[6509]

Polygamy:

An endeavor to get more out of life than there is in it.
—*Elbert Hubbard.*

The greatest testimony to man's willingness to take chances.
—*Joe Laurie, Jr.*

[6510]

Population:

Man tends to increase at a greater rate than his means of subsistence.
—*Charles Darwin.*

[6511]

Posterity:

Posterity is that which is denied an author until he is in the public domain.
—*Franklin K. Dane.*

He hungered for posterity; and he died from hunger.
Gregory Nunn.

[6512]

Poverty:

Poverty is no sin, and that is the best thing you can say about poverty.
—*19th century Americana.*

I've never been poor—but I've been broke.
—*Mike Todd.*

Poverty sits by the cradle of all our great men, and rocks them up to manhood; and this meager foster-mother remains their faithful companion throughout life.
—*Heine.*

[6513]

Power:

The secret of power is the knowledge that others are more cowardly than you are.
—*Ludwig Boerne.*

Power, after love, is the first source of happiness.
—*Stendhal.*

[6514]

Prayer:

Pray to God for what men can give you and your prayers may be answered.
—*Arab proverb.*

Father of Light! great God of Heaven!

Hear'st thou the accents of despair?
Can guilt like man's be e'er forgiven?
Can vice atone for crimes by prayer?
—*Byron.*

[6515]
Preaching:
The worse scoundrels make the best preachers.
—*German proverb.*

Hear how he clears the points o' Faith
Wi' rattlin' an' thumpin'!
Now meekly calm, now wild in wrath.
He's stampin', an' he's jumpin'!
—*Robert Burns.*

[6516]
Preface:
If he (Dryden) had written nothing but his prefaces . . . each of them would have entitled him to the preference and distinction of excelling in his kind.
—*William Cosgreve.*

Read all the prefaces of Dryden
For these our critics much confide-in,
(Tho' merely writ at first for filling to raise the volume's price a shilling.)
—*Swift.*

[6517]
Prejudice:
Inequality is as dear to the American heart as liberty itself.
—*William Dean Howells.*

Opinions founded on prejudice are always sustained with the greatest violence.
—*Hebrew proverb.*

[6518]
President:
I would rather be right than President.
—*Henry Clay.*

[6519]
Press:
Freedom of the press is useless when people do not understand what they read.
—*Gerald F. Lieberman.*

A would-be satirist, a hired buffoon,
A monthly scribbler of some low lampoon,
Condemn'd to drudge, the meanest of the mean,
And furbish falsehoods for a magazine.
—*Byron.*

[6520]
Pride:
Pride goeth before destruction; and an haughty spirit before a fall.
—*The Bible.*

Pride is at the bottom of all mistakes.
—*Ruskin.*

[6521]
Principle:
Success is the ability to rise above principle.
—*Gerald F. Lieberman.*

A precedent embalms a principle.
—*Disraeli.*

[6522]
Privacy:
The privacy of public office, the publicity of private life.
—*Latin proverb.*

[6523]

Prodigy:
Full many a pupil has gained more wealth than his master.
—*Greek proverb.*

[6524]

Profession:
All professions are conspiracies against the laity.
—*George Bernard Shaw.*

[6525]

Profit:
Nobody ever lost money taking a profit.
—*Traditional.*

[6526]

Prohibition:
There is a crying for wine in the streets. All joy is darkened. The mirth of the land is gone.
—*The Bible.*

Prohibition may be a disputed theory, but none can complain it doesn't hold water.
—*Tom Masson.*

[6527]

Prologue:
Courtship is to marriage as a very witty prologue to a very dull play.
—*Congreve.*

[6528]

Property:
Property is robbery.
—*Latin proverb.*

By right or wrong
Lands and goods go to the strong.
—*Emerson.*

[6529]

Prosperity:
The very bond of love.
—*Shakespeare.*

Prosperity discovers vice, adversity discovers virtue.
—*Bacon.*

[6530]

Protestation:
The lady doth protest too much, me thinks.
—*Shakespeare.*

[6531]

Prudery:
A prude is one who virtuously flies from the temptation of her desires.
—*Ambrose Bierce,*
"Devil's Dictionary."

[6532]

Psychiatry:
A form of horizontal confession subscribed to by those who would like to know why they do things that have always been done.
—*Gerald F. Lieberman.*

A diversion for the rich, a palliative for the poor, and a boon to the furniture industry. To the sex connotation of the common couch it has added the luster of a college diploma.
—*Gerald F. Lieberman.*

[6533]

Puritan:
The Puritan hated bear-baiting, not because it gave pain to the bear, but because it gave pleasure to the spectators.
—*Thomas Babington Macaulay.*

[6534]

Quarrel:

The fiercest quarrels do not always argue the greatest offenses.
—*Terence.*

Those who in quarrels interpose,
Must often wipe a bloody nose.
—*John Gay, "Fables."*

[6535]

Quotation:

A quotation at the right moment is life bread to the famished.
—*The Talmud.*

Classical quotation is the parole of literary men all over the world.
—*Samuel Johnson.*

The wisdom of the wise and the experience of ages may be preserved by quotation.
—*Isaac D'Israeli.*

[6536]

Railroads:

A road on rails, faster'n the eye can flicker
So east and west kin swap their lies quicker.
—*19th century song.*

[6537]

Rascal:

The world belongs to the rascals,
Heaven belongs to the good.
—*Arabian proverb.*

Make yourself a good man, then you can be certain there is at least one less skunk in the world.
—*19th century Western American prayer.*

[6538]

Real Estate:

The meek shall inherit the earth, and delight in the peaceful abundance.
—*The Bible.*

The meek may inherit the earth, but the earth inherits all of us.
—*Gregory Nunn.*

[6539]

Reason:

We live not according to reason, but according to fashion.
—*Seneca.*

Reason is the enemy of faith.
—*Martin Luther.*

Among civilized nations reason has always been an occupational hazard.
—*Gerald F. Lieberman.*

Many are destined to reason wrongly; others, not to reason at all; and others, to persecute those who do reason.
—*Voltaire.*

[6540]

Rebellion:

Rebellions of the belly are the worst.
—*Bacon.*

Men seldom, or rather never for a length of time and deliberately, rebel against anything that does not deserve rebelling against.
—*Carlyle.*

[6541]

Relatives:

An advantage of poverty, your relatives gain nothing by your death.
—*Hebrew proverb.*

[6542]

Religion:

When it is a question of money all men are of the same religion.
—*Voltaire.*

God made man on the last day. When He saw what he had done He took off. The effort to bring Him back is what men call religion.
—*Anonymous.*

In religion we believe only what we do not understand, except in the instance of an intelligible doctrine that contradicts an incomprehensible one. In that case we believe the former as a part of the latter.

—*Ambrose Bierce,*
"Devil's Dictionary."

Redemption is the fundamental mystery of our holy religion, and who believeth in it shall not perish, but have everlasting life in which to try to understand it.

—*Ambrose Bierce.*

A great perhaps.

—*Rabelais.*

[6543]
Republican:
Republicans are for both the man and the dollar, but in case of conflict the man before the dollar.

—*Abraham Lincoln.*

[6544]
Reputation:
How many people live on the reputation of the reputation they might have made.

—*Oliver Wendell Holmes.*

Judge a man by the reputation of his enemies.

—*Arabian proverb.*

How many worthy men have we seen survive their own reputation!

—*Montaigne.*

[6545]
Retribution:
Retribution breeds retribution. Shun it, and you will live beyond your tormentors.

—*Hebrew proverb.*

The divine wrath is slow indeed in vengeance, but it makes up for its tardiness by the severity of the punishment. —*Valerius Maximus.*

[6546]
Revenge:
Revenge is sweet, sweeter than life itself—so say fools.

—*Juvenal.*

The best revenge is to be unlike him who performed the injury.

—*Marcus Antoninus.*

[6547]
Revenue:
The wisest of men have not stopped their enemies from gathering revenue, they have prevented them from spending it.

—*Latin proverb.*

[6548]
Revolution:
Let the ruling classes tremble at the Communist revolution. Workers of the world unite. You have nothing to lose but your chains.

—*Karl Marx.*

The Communist revolution took the chains from the legs of the people and wound them around their necks. If there were no chains there would have been no revolution.

—*Samuel Bonom.*

[6549]
Reward:
Those who give hoping to be rewarded with honor are not giving, they are bargaining.

—*Philo.*

Truth is its own reward.

—*Philo.*

[6550]
Rich:
Ah, if the rich were rich as the poor fancy riches.

—*Emerson.*

A rich man is either a scoundrel or the heir of a scoundrel.

—*Spanish proverb.*

[6551]
Right:
Might was the measure of right.
—Lucan.

[6552]
Rumor:
Rumor is a pipe, blown by surmises, jealousies, conjectures.
—Shakespeare.

I cannot tell how the truth may be;
I say the tale as 'twas said to me.
—Scottish lay.

What some invent the rest enlarge.
—Swift.

[6553]
Sabbath:
The Sabbath was made for man, and not man for the Sabbath.
—The Bible.

I can't believe the Bible meant God's message to read only one day of rest in seven. Some off-days were lost in translation.
—Gerald F. Lieberman.

[6554]
Saint:
Some reputed saints that have been canonized ought to have been cannonaded.
—Charles Caleb Colton.

Satan trembles when he sees
The weakest saint upon his knees.
—Old English hymnal.

The worst of madmen is a saint run mad.
—Alexander Pope.

[6555]
Salad:
I wrote them in my salad days, when the world seemed rose-colored and I was green.
—Gerald F. Lieberman.

My salad days; when I was green in judgment.
—Shakespeare.

[6556]
Satire:
Bitter the jest when satire comes too near truth and leaves a sharp sting behind it.
—Tacitus.

[6557]
Scholar:
A mere scholar, who knows nothing but books, must be ignorant even of them.
—Hazlitt,
"The Ignorance of the Learned."

When a woman turns to scholarship there is usually something wrong with her sexual opportunities.
—Nietzsche,
"Beyond Good and Evil."

[6558]
School:
After a fellow gets famous it doesn't take long for someone to bob up that used to sit by him in school.
—Kim Hubbard.

At boarding schools, the relaxation of the junior boys is mischief, and of the seniors vice.
—Mary Wollstonecraft.

[6559]
Science:
Steam is no stronger now than it was a hundred years ago but it is put to better use.   —Emerson.

Science is always wrong. It never solves a problem without creating ten more.
—George Bernard Shaw.

[6560]

Secrets:
Keep no secrets of thyself from thyself.
—*Greek proverb.*

Women keep no secrets, and I know many men who are women in this regard.
—*La Fontaine.*

[6561]

Servant:
The tongue is the worst part of a bad servant.
—*Juvenal.*

The difference between a man and his valet: they both smoke the same cigars, but only one pays for them.
—*Robert Frost.*

[6562]

Sex:
The thing that takes up the least amount of time and causes the most amount of trouble is sex.
—*John Barrymore.*

Much of our most highly valued cultural heritage has been acquired at the cost of sexuality.   —*Freud.*

[6563]

Shakespeare:
I don't know whether Lord Bacon wrote Shakespeare's works or not, but if he didn't he missed the greatest opportunity of his life.
—*Horace Russell.*

If we wish to know the force of human genius we should read Shakespeare. If we wish to see the insignificance of human learning we may study his commentators.
—*Hazlitt.*

[6564]

Sin:
Some rise by sin, and by virtue fall.
—*Shakespeare.*

More sinners are cursed at not because we despise their sins but because we envy their success at sinning.
—*Macaulay.*

O Thou, who didst with pitfall and with gin
Beset the Road I was to wander in,
Thou wilt not with Predestined Evil round
Enmesh, and then impute my Fall to Sin!
—*Omar Khayyam.*

[6565]

Sincerity:
It is dangerous to be sincere unless you are also stupid.
—*George Bernard Shaw.*

A wit should be no more sincere than a woman constant.
—*Congreve.*

[6566]

Slander:
Throw plenty of mud and some of it is bound to stick.
—*Hipponax the Satirist.*

Calumnies are injurious even after they are refuted. Like Spanish flies, they sting when alive and blister when dead.
—*19th Century, uncredited.*

[6567]

Snobbery:
That which we call a snob by any other name would still be snobbish.
—*Thackeray.*

It's the high class people you have to give passes to.   —*Ziegfeld.*

[6568]

Sobriety:
Water, taken in moderation, cannot hurt anybody.
—*Mark Twain.*

[6569]

Socialism:
I don't look for much to come out of government ownership as long as we have Democrats and Republicans.
—*Kin Hubbard.*

[6570]

Society:
In our society a man is known by the company he owns.
—*Gerald F. Lieberman.*

I suppose Society is wonderfully delightful.
To be in it is merely a bore.
But to be out of it is simply a tragedy.
—*Oscar Wilde.*

A system in which the two great commandments were, to hate your neighbour and to love your neighbour's wife.
—*Macaulay.*

[6571]

Soldiers:
The worse the man the better the soldier. If soldiers be not corrupt they ought to be made so.
—*Napoleon.*

When the military man approaches, the world locks up its spoons and packs off its womankind.
—*George Bernard Shaw.*

[6572]

Soul:
God, if there is a God, take my soul, if I have a soul.
—*Ernest Renan.*

Alas my soul, thou pleasing companion of this body, thou fleeting thing, art thou now deserting it? Wither are thou flying?
—*Hadrian.*

[6573]

Speech:
When at a loss how to go on, cough.
—*Ancient Greek proverb.*

A closed mouth catches no flies.
—*French proverb.*

Speech is the vestibule to the palace of love.
—*Jami of Persia.*

You taught me language; and my profit on't
Is, I know how to curse.
—*Shakespeare.*

[6574]

Spinster:
When there is an old maid in the house a watchdog is unnecessary.
—*Balzac.*

[6575]

Specialist:
No man can be a pure specialist without being in the strict sense an idiot.
—*George Bernard Shaw.*

[6576]

Stage:
There is that smaller world which is the stage, and that larger stage which is the world.
—*Issac Goldberg.*

[6577]

State:
Some laws of state aimed at curbing crime are even more criminal.
—*Friedrich Engels.*

[6578]

Statesman:

A statesman is one who lies in state.

—*Uncredited.*

Honest statesmanship is the wise employment of individual manners for the public good.

—*Abraham Lincoln.*

[6579]

Status:

A mighty pomp, but made of little things.

—*Vergil.*

At a round table there is no dispute about place.

—*Italian proverb.*

Away with these trappings to the vulgar; I know them in and out.

—*Persius.*

[6580]

Stocks:

Everytime my broker advises me to buy stocks to go up they go down, every time he tells me to buy to go down they go up; it's lucky for him they can't go sideways.

—*Gerald F. Lieberman.*

[6581]

Stockmarket:

My family wasn't affected by the crash of '29. They went broke in '28.

—*Gerald Barzan.*

[6582]

Stupidity:

Some men, though patrician, are also stupid. —*Cicero.*

Against stupidity the gods are helpless. —*Schiller.*

[6583]

Style:

Ignorance is never out of style. It was in fashion yesterday, it is the rage today, and it will set the pace tomorrow.

—*Franklin K. Dane.*

Style is the dress of thoughts.

—*Chesterfield.*

[6584]

Success:

There is no more fatal blunder than he who consumes the greater part of his life getting his living.

—*Thoreau.*

Success is the necessary misfortune of life, but it is only to the very unfortunate that it comes early.

—*Trollope.*

The one unpardonable sin against one's fellows.

—*Ambrose Bierce,*
"Devil's Dictionary."

All you need in this life is ignorance and confidence, and then success is sure.

—*Mark Twain.*

[6585]

Suicide:

I hate all the bleeders, the bleeding, the bled,
The sucking, the kissing of getting ahead;
No wonder so many have killed themselves dead.

—*Gerald F. Lieberman.*

Suicide is confession.

—*Daniel Webster.*

[6586]

Superstition:

Superstition is the religion of feeble minds.

—Edmund Burke.

Modern religion is the fermented hope of all superstitions, brewed into cocktails of love without kisses.

—Gerald F. Lieberman.

[6587]

Tact:

It is bad judgment to speak of halters in the house of a man who was hanged.

—Cervantes.

To have the reputation of possessing the most perfect social tact, talk to every woman as if you loved her, and to every man as if he bored you.

—Oscar Wilde.

[6588]

Talent:

Talent is a loan from God for the relief of man's estate.

—Jelalladin of Persia.

A great deal of talent is lost to the world for want of a little courage.

—Sidney Smith.

[6589]

Taste:

A different man, a different taste.

—Ancient Greek proverb.

[6590]

Taxes:

It is the duty of a good shepherd to shear his flock, not flay them.

—Tiberius.

Every dish of fish brought to the table is paid for once to the fisherman and six times to the state.

—J. R. McCulloch.

Taxation without representation is tyranny.

—James Otis.

Taxation with representation ain't so hot either.

—Gerald F. Lieberman.

[6591]

Temperance:

Temperance is simply a disposition of the mind which binds the passions.

—Thomas Aquinas.

Pitted against hard drinking Christians the abstemious Mahometans go down like grass before the scythe.

—Ambrose Bierce,
"Devil's Dictionary."

[6592]

Television:

Television is called a medium because anything good on it is rare.

—Fred Allen.

Television made a great contribution to the elimination of harmful drug addiction. It broke millions of the sleeping pill habit.

—Gerald F. Lieberman.

[6593]

Temptation:

Even the just may sin with an open chest of gold before them.

—Latin proverb.

Familiarity breeds attempt.

—Franklin K. Dane.

I can resist everything except temptation.

—Oscar Wilde.

[6594]

Testimony:

There are three things a man must do alone. Be born, die, and testify.

—*James J. Walker.*

[6595]

Theatre:

Theatres are like brothels; one never knows what he will find inside—or whom.

—*Uncredited.*

One of my chief regrets during my years in the theatre is that I couldn't sit in the audience and watch me.

—*John Barrymore.*

[6596]

Thief:

We hang the petty thieves and appoint the great ones to public office.

—*Aesop.*

The robb'd that smiles steals something from the thief:
He robs himself that spends a bootless grief.

—*Shakespeare.*

[6597]

Think:

Think twice before you speak to a friend in need.

—*Ambrose Bierce,*
"Devil's Dictionary."

There are lots of people who can't think seriously without injuring their minds.

—*John Jay Chapman.*

Don't think!!—Just be Right.
—*Richard Kane.*

[6598]

Thrift:

A penny saved is a penny wasted.
—*Al Diamond.*

[6599]

Time:

Time on time revolving we descry,
So moments flit, so moments fly.
—*Ovid.*

Know we how many tomorrows the gods intend for our todays?
—*Euripides.*

The present will not long endure.
—*Pindar.*

Leave the dead moments to bury the dead.

—*Owen Meredith.*

[6600]

Togetherness:

We must indeed all hang together or we shall hang separately.
—*Franklin.*

[6601]

Tomorrow:

Tomorrow do thy worst, I have lived today.   —*Dryden.*

Tomorrow is nothing, today is too late; the good lived yesterday.
—*Martial.*

Tomorrow, and tomorrow, and tomorrow,
Creeps in this petty pace from day to day,
To the last syllable of recorded time;
And all our yesterdays have lighted fools
The way to dusty death.
—*Shakespeare.*

[6602]

Tongue:
Many have fallen by the edge of the sword, but more have fallen by the tongue.

—*The Bible.*

[6603]

Trade:
Free trade is not a principle; it is an expedient.

—*Disraeli.*

[6604]

Tragedy:
In the theatre there is comedy and tragedy. If the house is packed it's a comedy, otherwise it's a tragedy.

—*Sol Hurok.*

[6605]

Travel:
See one mountain see them all.

—*Socrates.*

The well travelled may lie with impunity.

—*French proverb.*

[6606]

Treason:
Marriage is the treasonous betrayal of love.

—*The Troubadors.*

[6607]

Trial:
A fox should not be of the jury at a goose's trial.

—*Thomas Fuller.*

[6608]

Truth:
Truth has never been fashionable.

—*Opie P. Read.*

Discovery of truth is the sole purpose of philosophy . . . and has a fair prospect of existing to the end of time.

—*Ambrose Bierce, "Devil's Dictionary."*

Truth is always strange.

—*Byron.*

[6609]

Tyranny:
Smart tyrants retire rich.

—*Voltaire.*

Slaves would be tyrants were the chance theirs.

—*Victor Hugo.*

[6610]

Ugliness:
God's gift to virtue.

—*Ambrose Bierce, "Devil's Dictionary."*

[6611]

Understanding:
A brainy matter that enables one having it to know a house from a horse. Its nature and laws have been exhaustively expounded by Locke, who rode a house, and Kant, who lived in a horse.

—*Ambrose Bierce, "Devil's Dictionary."*

There are those who understand everything till one puts it into words.

—*Francis Bradley.*

[6612]

Undertaker:
The houses he makes lasts till doomsday.

—*Shakespeare.*

Honor the undertaker. He always carries out what he undertakes.
—*19th century Americana.*

[6613]
Unemployment:
When more and more people are thrown out of work unemployment results.
—*Calvin Coolidge.*

[6614]
Union:
In union there is strength.
—*Laberius.*

In union suits there is length.
—*Gregory Nunn.*

In unions there are strikes.
—*Franklin K. Dane.*

[6615]
Universe:
Man's God has nothing to do with the universe.
—*Mussolini.*

The solar system has no anxiety about its reputation.
—*Emerson.*

[6616]
Utopia:
This is Utopia, right now. Anything is possible in this world, and nothing is possible anywhere else.
—*Gerald F. Lieberman.*

To a warden Utopia is an escape-proof jail.
—*Gregory Nunn.*

[6617]
Valor:
Brave deeds are wasted when hidden.
—*Pascal.*

Said the commander of the delinquent brigade, "I am persuaded that any further display of valor by my troops will bring them into collision with the enemy."
—*Horace Porter.*

[6618]
Vanity:
In outward show so splendid and so vain; 'tis but a gilded block without a brain.
—*Phaedrus.*

Vanity, all is vanity.
—*The Bible.*

Vanity plays lurid tricks with our memory.
—*Joseph Conrad.*

[6619]
Vegetable:
One who is proud of ancestry is like a turnip; there is nothing good of him but that which is underground.
—*Samuel Butler.*

[6620]
Vice:
Welcome Vice, if it comest alone.
—*Spanish proverb.*

Be good and you will be lonely.
—*Mark Twain.*

If he does really think that there is no distinction between virtue and vice, why sir, when he leaves our house, let us count our spoons.
—*Johnson.*

There is no vice so simple but assumes
Some mark of virtue on his outward parts.
—*Shakespeare.*

[6621]

Victory:

To the victor belongs the spoils.
—*William Learned Marcy.*

To whom God will, there be the victory.
—*Shakespeare.*

But if we have such another victory, we are undone.
—*Pyrrhus.*

He got the better of himself, and that's the best kind of victory one can wish for.
—*Cervantes.*

[6622]

Vintner:

I often wonder what the vintners buy one half so precious as the stuff they sell.
—*Omar Khayyam.*

These traitorous thieves, accursed and unfair,
The vintners that put water in our wine.
—*Villon.*

[6623]

Virgin:

The modest fan was lifted up no more,
And virgins smiled at what they blushed before.
—*Alexander Pope.*

Virginity for some women is the only virtue.
—*Gerald Barzan.*

[6624]

Virtue:

I always admired virtue—but I could never imitate it.
—*Charles II.*

I prefer an accommodating vice to an obstinate virtue. —*Moliere.*

Virtue may be assailed, but never hurt,
Surprised by unjust force, but not enthralled;
Yea, even that which mischief meant most harm
Shall in the happy trial prove most glory.
—*Milton.*

Most men admire
Virtue who follow not her lore.
—*Milton.*

[6625]

Vote:

I have learned to hold popular opinion of no value.
—*Alexander Hamilton.*

The symbol of a freeman's power to make a fool of himself and a wreck of his country.
—*Ambrose Bierce,
"Devil's Dictionary."*

Sink or swim, live or die, survive or perish, I give my hand and my heart to this vote.
—*Daniel Webster.*

[6626]

Wages:

A fair day's wages for a fair day's work.
—*Carlyle.*

The wages of sin are high—but you get your money's worth.
—*Franklin K. Dane.*

If you do your fair day's work, you are certain to get your fair day's wage—in praise or pudding, whichever happens to suit your taste.
—*Alexander Smith.*

[6627]

War:

He belonged to that army known as invincible in peace, invisible in war.

—*William Tecumseh Sherman.*

Love is like war; easy to begin but very hard to stop.

—*H. L. Mencken.*

God is always on the side of the strongest battalion.

—*Voltaire.*

As long as there are sovereign nations possessing great power, war is inevitable.

—*Albert Einstein.*

War is not "inevitable" but proceeds from definite and removable causes.

—*Goldsworthy Lowes Dickinson.*

[6628]

Water:

It may be readily believed that many are quite ignorant of the taste of water.

—*Westminster Review.*

Water, water, everywhere,
And all the boards did shrink;
Water, water, everywhere,
Nor any drop to drink.

—*Coleridge,*
"Ancient Mariner."

Somewhere, behind space and time,
Is wetter water, slimier slime.

—*Rupert Brooke.*

His answer trickled through my head
Like water through a sieve.

—*Lewis Carroll.*

[6629]

Weakness:

There is a physical weakness which stems from mental ability, and a mental weakness which comes from physical ability.

—*Joseph Juberg.*

Credulity is the man's weakness, but the child's strength.

—*Lamb.*

You cannot run away from a weakness, you must some time fight it out or perish; and if that be so, why not now, and where you stand.

—*Robert Louis Stevenson.*

[6630]

Wealth:

He does not own his money whose money owns him.

—*St. Cyprian.*

He that's rich is wise.

—*Defoe.*

Get place and wealth, if possible, with grace;
If not, by any means get wealth and place.

—*Alexander Pope.*

Wealth maketh many friends.

—*The Bible: Proverbs.*

[6631]

Weather:

Its warmth was not heat, and its cool was not cold.

—*Ferdusi of Persia.*

Everybody talks about the weather but nobody does anything about it.

—*Mark Twain.*

Probably nor'-east to sou'-west winds, varying to the southard and westard and eastard and points between; high and low barometer, sweeping round from place to place; probably areas of rain, snow, heat and drought, succeeded or preceded by earth quakes with thunder and lightning.

—*Mark Twain.*

For it's always fair weather
When good fellows get together
With a stein on the table and a good song ringing clear.

—*Richard Hovey.*

[6632]

Wedding:

The time approached; to church
the parties went:
At once with carnal and devout
intent.

—*Alexander Pope.*

It destroys one's nerves to be
amiable every day to the same human being.

—*Disraeli.*

[6633]

Wedlock:

The land of marriage has this
peculiarity: that strangers are desir-
ous of inhabiting it, while its natural inhabitants would willingly be
banished from thence.

—*Montaigne.*

Socrates was killed by an over-
dose of wedlock.

—*School exam.*

It is a woman's business to get
married as soon as possible, and a
man's to keep unmarried as long as
he can.

—*George Bernard Shaw.*

[6634]

West:

Go West, young man, and grow
up with the country.

—*Horace Greeley.*

The farther west he went the
more he was convinced that the
wise men came from the east.

—*Horace Russell.*

Out where the handclasp's a little
    stronger,
Out where the smile dwells a little
    longer,
That's where the West begins.

—*Arthur Chapman.*

[6635]

Wicked:

Give me the wicked over the foolish. The wicked occasionally are not
wicked.

—*Alexandre Dumas.*

All wickedness is but little to the
wickedness of a woman.

—*The Bible.*

[6636]

Widow:

The tragedy of Mormonism is, a
single death makes a dozen widows.

—*19th century Americana.*

Rich widows are the only second-
hand goods that sell at first-class
prices.

—*Franklin.*

[6637]

Wife:

All wives are unjustly slighted
for the faults of a few.

—*Terence.*

Seek a wife in your own sphere.

—*Latin proverb.*

Here lies my wife; here let her lie!
Now she's at rest, and so am I.

—*Dryden.*

He who findeth a wife, findeth a
good thing.

—*The Bible: Proverbs.*

[6638]

Wind:

I came like Water, and like Wind
I go.

—*Omar Khayyam.*

Blow, blow, thou winter wind;
thou art not so unkind as man's ingratitude.

—*Shakespeare.*

[6639]

Wine:
And if the Wine you drink, the Lip you press,
End in what All begins and ends in—Yes.

—*Omar Khayyam.*

So heed me fellow peasants, for that is what we are
It's best to die the winer's death, than fiddle for the Czar.

—*Traditional.*

Let schoolmasters puzzle their brain,
With grammar, and nonsense, and learning;
Good liquor, I stoutly maintain,
Gives genius a better discerning.

—*Goldsmith.*

[6640]

Wisdom:
The first step to wisdom is to avoid the common fallacy which considers everything profound that is obscure.

—*Gregory Nunn.*

Wisdom is not wisdom when it is derived from books alone.

—*Horace.*

The ant is knowing and wise, but he doesn't know enough to take a vacation.

—*Clarence Day.*

[6641]

Wise:
The wits of the wise the brew can beguile; and make the sage frolic, and make the sad smile.

—*Homer.*

A wise man sees as much as he ought, not as much as he can.

—*Montaigne.*

[6642]

Wit:
Wit is the fetching of congruity out of incongruity.

—*Addison.*

There is not less wit nor less invention in applying rightly a thought one finds in a book, than in being the first author of that thought.

—*Thomas Haynes Bayly.*

The salt with which the American humorist spoils his intellectual cookery by leaving it out.

—*Ambrose Bierce,*
"Devil's Dictionary."

[6643]

Witness:
One witness one liar; more witnesses, all liars.

—*Greek proverb.*

As to the juror or the witness, bribe both.

—*Latin proverb.*

[6644]

Woman:
When a woman is openly bad she is then at her best.

—*Latin proverb.*

Tongue in the mouth of woman is one of God's less agreeable blunders.

—*The Talmud.*

Woman has this in common with angels, that suffering beings belong especially to her.   —*Balzac.*

There is a tide in the affairs of women
Which, taken at the flood, leads —God knows where.   —*Byron.*

[6645]

Words:

Words, as is well known, are the great foes of reality.

—*Joseph Conrad.*

[6646]

World:

I have not loved the world, nor the world me.

—*Byron.*

All the world's a stage, and all the clergymen critics.

—*Gregory Nunn.*

[6647]

Worship:

Wives worship the grounds their husbands have coming to them.

—*20th century Americana.*

[6648]

Writing:

It took me fifteen years to discover I had no talent for writing, but I couldn't give it up because by that time I was too famous.

—*Robert Benchley.*

[6649]

Wrong:

The best way to convince a fool he is wrong is to let him have his own way.

—*Josh Billings.*

It is better to suffer wrong than to do it, and happier to be sometimes cheated than not to trust.

—*Johnson.*

[6650]

Yesterday:

Think then you are To-day what Yesterday you were—To-morrow you shall not be less.

—*Omar Khayyam.*

I do today from memory what yesterday I did in passion.

—*Gerald Barzan.*

[6651]

Youth:

Youth is the best time to be rich; and the best time to be poor.

—*Euripides.*

Youth is a wonderful thing; what a crime to waste it on children.

—*George Bernard Shaw.*

[6652]

Zeal:

It is false zeal to keep truth while wounding charity.

—*Pascal.*

[6653]

Zoo:

A zoo is a place of refuge where ferocious animals are protected from people.

—*Franklin K. Dane.*

PART IX

RACES AND NATIONS

ENGLISH

[6654]
She–"You can take me to the dance on the pier to-night if you like—unless (coyly)—you meet somebody more attractive in the meantime."
He–"I say! That's jolly sporting of you—we'll leave it like that then, shall we?"

[6655]
An American was explaining to a British visitor the construction of an electrical sign his concern was about to place on Broadway, New York. "It will contain," he said, "20,000 red lights, 17,000 blue lights, 10,000 white lights, and a central sunburst of orange and purple." The Englishman was impressed. "Most extraordinary," he said. "But don't you think, old chap, that it will be just a bit conspicuous?"

[6656]
"Did you cancel all my engagements, as I told you, Smithers?"
"Yes, sir, but Lady Millicent didn't take it very well. She said you were to marry her next Monday!"

[6657]
A young officer at the front wrote home to his father:
"Dear Father: Kindly send me £50 at once; I lost another leg in a stiff engagement and am in the hospital without means."
The answer was:
"My Dear Son: As this is the fourth leg you have lost (according to your letters), you ought to be accustomed to it by this time. Try and wobble along on any other you may have left."

[6658]
An Englishman was once persuaded to see a game of baseball, and during the play, when he happened to look away for a moment, a foul tip caught him on the ear and knocked him senseless. On coming to himself, he asked faintly, "What was it?"
"A foul—only a foul!"
"Good heavens!" he exclaimed. "A fowl? I thought it was a mule."

[6659]
Visitor–"And wot was you thinkin' of doing wiv your boy, Mrs. Smith?"

Mrs. Smith–"Well 'e's that fond of animals 'is father was thinkin' of making a butcher of 'im."

[6660]

Client–"Can I have the photo of the lady with £50,000 dowry?"
Matrimonial Agent–"No photographs issued of ladies with dowries over £10,000."

[6661]

One of the crew of a big liner chanced to pick up a first-cabin menu card, and, seeing at the top "Table d'hote," turned to his pal and inquired:

"What does this 'ere mean, Joe?"

"Well," said Joe, "it's like this 'ere. Them swells in the saloon have some soup, a bit of fish, a bit of this, a bit of that, and a bit of summat else, and call it 'table dottie.' We have 'table dottie,' only we mixes it all together and calls it stew."

[6662]

"Look 'ere—I asks yer for the last time for that 'arf-dollar yer owes me."

"Thank 'evins!—that's the end of a silly question."

[6663]

"Say, doctor," said the brawny scrubwoman, "yer gettin' a perty good thing out of tendin' that rich Smith boy, ain't yer?"

"Well," said the doctor amused, "I get a pretty good fee, yes. Why?"

"Well, Doc. I 'opes yer won't forget that my Willie threw the brick that 'it 'im."

[6664]

The Duke of Marlborough had an emu given to him. It was sent to Blenheim, and great interest was taken in the chances of its capacity for procreation in that country.

Eventually it laid an egg. The Duke and Duchess were away from home, so a telegram was sent to the latter by the agent to apprise her of the event. It was in these terms:

"Emu has laid an egg; in the absence of your grace have put goose to sit on it."

[6665]

"Do you wish the court to understand that you refuse to renew your dog license?"

"Yes, your worship, but—"

"We want no 'buts.' You will be fined. You know the license has expired."

"Yes, and so has the dog."

[6666]

Careful Husband (with newspaper) –"I see that butter has gone up to one and sixpence."
Wife–"Don't worry, dear, I've been paying one and tenpence for some time."

[6667]

Mrs. Maggs–"Wot excuse does he make fer not lookin' fer a job?"
Mrs. Daggs–"All of 'em."

[6668]

Peddler–"Any teapot spouts, pencils, pens, plates, or baskets to-day, mum?"
Lady of the House–"If you don't go away I'll call the police."
Peddler–"'Ere you are mum— whistles, sixpence each."

[6669]

Doctor, to Cockney patient–"Now, my man, what about this ear?"
Patient–"This 'ere wot?"

[6670]

Regular Customer–"I shall want a large quantity of flowers from you next week for my daughter's coming out."

Flower Woman–"Yes, mum. You shall 'ave the very best for 'er, pore dear. Wot were she put in for?"

[6671]

Two young Englishmen were in a row boat in the middle of the ocean. One handled the oars, rowing away for all he was worth. The other sat in the stern, steering the boat by means of a makeshift rudder.

Suddenly, a liner came into view. The man at the oars kept rowing frantically, pausing only when the liner crossed the path of the small boat. Then he cupped his hands.

"Hey, there!" he shouted. "Is this the Atlantic or the Pacific?"

A sailor aboard the big vessel gazed down at the row boat.

"This is the Pacific," he shouted back.

The rudder-man waved his fist at the oarsman.

"You hear that, you fool!" he howled. "I told you not to row so fast!"

[6672]

A snobbish old major was asked by a firm if he'd recommend a certain man for the job. The major wrote back:

"Mr. Blank is an excellent young man. He is the son of Major Blank, the grandson of General Blank, the cousin of Sir Henry Blank, the nephew of Lord Blank, and he is otherwise well related."

The firm wrote back:

"Thank you very much for your letter of recommendation concerning Mr. Blank. But we must point out that we require him for clerical work—not for breeding purposes."

[6673]

The Englishman and his valet had been speeding westward across the United States for four days and three nights. The English, of course, are used to traveling about on a comparatively small island. Finally, wondering what his servant might be thinking about, the Englishman asked him point-blank what were his thoughts.

"I was just thinking, sir, about the discovery of Hamerica," the valet answered. "Columbus didn't do such a wonderful thing, hafter all, when he found this country, did he, now, sir? Hafter hall's said and done, 'ow could 'e 'ave 'elped it?"

[6674]

"Poor Old Jim! 'E's so near-sighted 'e's working 'imself to death."

"Wot's 'is near-sight got to do with it?"

"Well, 'e can't see when the boss ain't looking, so 'e 'as to keep on shoveling all the time!"

[6675]

A British tar was asked by a French sailor why the British Navy always was victorious.

"That's easy to answer," replied the Briton. "We always pray before we start fighting."

"But so do we," retorted the Frenchman.

"Yes," came the rejoinder, "but we pray in English."

[6676]

An English bishop had no sense of music. One day in an East-end church, when he was standing unrecognized at the back, he joined in the hearty singing.

At last a man at his side could stand it no longer, and, giving him a dig in the ribs, whispered, "I say, guv'nor, do dry up. You're spoiling the whole blinking show."

[6677]

Sailor's Wife—"So you'll be back in four years, will you?"

Sailor—"Aye, but I may be a bit late on this trip."

Sailor's Wife—"Well, if you are, don't let's 'ave any of your old excuses about the ship going down an' 'aving to walk 'ome."

[6678]

Guide—"Quick! There's a full-grown leopard. Shoot him on the spot!"

Lord Dumbleigh—"Which spot? I say, be specific, my man."

[6679]

Magistrate—"I cannot understand you. . . . You admit murdering this poor old woman for a paltry half-a-crown!"

Prisoner—"Well, Guv'nor, half-a-crown here and half-a-crown there . . . it soon mounts up, yer know!"

[6680]

"What are you studying in college now?" asked the fond mother of her son, who was a freshman.

"We have just taken up molecules."

"That's fine. I hope you will like them. I always tried to get your father to wear one, but he could not keep it in his eye."

[6681]

Englishman—"Odd names your towns have. Hoboken, Weehawken, Oshkosh, Poughkeepsie."

American—"I suppose they do sound queer to English ears. Do you live in London all of the time?"

Englishman—"No indeed. I spend part of my time at Chipping Norton, and divide the rest between Bigglewade and Leighton Buzzard."

[6682]

Lord Dormer and Mr. Monckton, the member of parliament for Stafford, both stuttered dreadfully. Once, upon the occasion of their meeting in London, Mr. Monckton seeing Lord Dormer making a vain attempt to give utterance to his words, said to him:—"My Dear Lo-or-or-ord, wh-wh-y do-on't you go to the m-a-a-n that cu-u-u-cured me?"

[6683]

"Yes, sir, our household represents the United Kingdom of Great Britain," said the proud father of number one to the rector. "I am English, my wife's Irish, the nurse is Scotch and the baby wails."

[6684]

A visitor from London startled at dead of night by a terrifying hoot asked: "What cawn that terrifying sound mean?"

"It's an owl," his host explained.

"H'I know, but who's 'owling?"

[6685]

Three slightly deaf men were motoring from the north to London in an old, noisy car, and hearing was difficult. As they were nearing the city, one asked:

"Is this Wembly?"

"No," replied the second, "this is Thursday."

"So am I," put in the third. "Let's stop and have one."

[6686]

A gentleman, with the same Christian and surname, took lodgings in the same house with James Smith. The consequence was, eternal confusion of calls and letters. Indeed, the postman had no alternative but to share the letters equally between the two.

"This is intolerable, sir," said our friend, "and you must quit."

"Why am I to quit more than you?"

"Because you are James the Second—and must abdicate."

[6687]

A townsman was waiting at a country railway station. At last a train was signaled and the stationmaster and his staff of three lined up on the platform. The train, however, passed straight through, and the townsman noticed a man leaning out of the carriage window with a notebook in his hand.

"Was that an official looking to see if you are on duty?" he asked.

"No," explained the stationmaster; "that was the company's tailor measuring us for new uniforms."

[6688]

The English are a phlegmatic race. I was once week-ending with an Englishman and his wife. Entirely by accident, I happened one day on the Englishman's wife in her bath. Making a hurried retreat I immediately sought out my host, who was reading in his room, and proffered an apology. He brought his head up out of his book and regarded me for a moment.

"Skinny old thing, isn't she?" he remarked.

[6689]

An American was touring Wales, and on entering a hotel in one town noticed the words "Tam Htab" written on the mat.

"Ah!" he said, "I suppose that's Welsh for Welcome."

"No, sir," replied the doorman. "That's the bath mat upside down."

[6690]

An American attended a rowing regatta on the Thames, honored by the presence of the royal family and retinue.

Between events the little diving lads entertained the crowds by going to the bottom for the coppers tossed into the river. The American commenced to flip silver dollars into the stream. A Londoner laid a restraining hand on his arm.

"My word," he warned, "you'll 'ave the king diving!"

[6691]

A Frenchman learning English said to his tutor: "English is a queer language. What does this sentence mean: 'Should Mr. Noble, who sits for this constituency, consent to stand again, he will in all probability have a walkover'?"

[6692]

He liked showing off, and seized the occasion of dining with some friends at a restaurant.

"Waitah," he called in a swaggering voice, "bring me some verulam and ova."

About fifteen minutes later the waiter returned with a plate of bacon and eggs.

"Bacon and eggs, sir," he exclaimed. "In ordinary English it would be a shilling, but in classical language it costs half a crown. 'Let the punishment fit the crime,' as we used to say at Oxford. Anything else, sir?"

[6693]

Sam had been carpenter at a provincial theater for half a century and the proprietors thought it was time he was retired on a pension. But Sam chose to consider himself insulted by the well-meant offer.

"I wouldn't 'ave took the job at all," he grumbled, "if I 'adn't thought it was goin' to be permanent."

[6694]

"With all due reverence, my boy, I really think our English custom at the telephone is better than saying 'Hello' as you do in the United States."

"What do you say in England?"

"We say, 'Are you there?' Then, of course, if you are not there, there is no use in going on with the conversation."

[6695]

A party at the Zoological Gardens stood puzzled before a bird.

"It's a heagle," said one.

"It's not," said another, "it's a howl."

They appealed to a by-stander.

"Both wrong," he said shortly, "it's a nawk!"

[6696]

The copiousness of the English language perhaps was never more apparent than in the following character, by a lady, of her own husband:

"He is," says she, "an abhorred, barbarous, capricious, detestable, envious, fastidious, hard-hearted, illiberal, ill-natured, jealous, keen, loathsome, malevolent, nauseous, obstinate, passionate, quarrelsome, raging, saucy, tantalising, uncomfortable, vexatious, abominable, bitter, captious, disagreeable, execrable, fierce, grating, gross, hasty, malicious, nefarious, obstreperous, peevish, restless, savage, tart, unpleasant, violent, waspish, worrying, acrimonious, blustering, careless, discontented, fretful, growling, hateful, inattentive, malignant, noisy, odious, perverse, rigid, severe, teasing, unsuitable, angry, boisterous, choleric, disgusting, gruff, hectoring, incorrigible, mischievous, negligent, offensive, pettish, roaring, sharp, sluggish, snapping, snarling, sneaking, sour, testy, tiresome, tormenting, touchy, arrogant, austere, awkward, boorish, brawling, brutal, bullying, churlish, clamorous, crabbed, cross, currish, dismal, dull, dry, drowsy, grumbling, horrid, huffish, insolent, intractable, irascible, ireful, morose, murmuring, opinionated, oppressive, outrageous, overbearing, petulant, plaguy, rough, rude, rugged, spiteful, splenetic, stern, stubborn, stupid, sulky, sullen, surly, suspicious, treacherous, troublesome, turbulent, tyrannical, virulent, wrangling, yelping dog-in-a-manger."

[6697]

Mrs. Gubbins—"I'm glad to 'ear your 'usband's up and about again, Mrs. Miggs."

Mrs. Miggs—"Yes, the doctor says 'e 'as marvelous powers of vituperation."

[6698]

A young subaltern joined a guards depot, his upper lip as yet unadorned with even the suspicion of down. The adjutant sent for him.

"You must grow a mustache."

"Yes, sir."

"And not one of those Chaplin affairs—a proper mustache."

"Yes, sir."

The interview was finished, but the subaltern did not move, so the adjutant asked: "Well, what more do you want?"

"Any particular color, sir?"

[6699]

He had got a job as collector for a gas company.

"Take this master key and go round and empty all the coin-boxes;

get all the pennies and shillings," said the manager.

Three weeks later he walked into the office. "Can I have another key? I've lost t'other one."

"Certainly," replied the manager. "But where have you been all this time? The cashier has stopped late every Friday night, expecting you to come for your wages."

"Great guns!" exclaimed the collector, beaming broadly. "Do I get wages as well?"

[6700]

Schoolmaster–"Where was Nelson killed?"

"Trafalgar Square," was the reply.

"Indeed!" said the teacher, "then I suppose Wellington was killed at Waterloo Station?"

"No, sir," responded William, "that was Napoleon."

[6701]

An American touring in the country with an English friend stopped to point out to him a signpost on which some wag had printed this sign:

"This way to Squedunk. Those who cannot read apply at the blacksmith's opposite."

The American roared with laughter, but the Englishman looked puzzled. After they had returned home that night, the Englishman came into his host's room roaring with laughter.

"Ah," he said, "I see the joke now —suppose the blacksmith were out?"

[6702]

A recent visitor to an English prison discovered among the inmates a man whom he knew. This particular prisoner had been finally laid by the heels for swindling, though for quite a time he had cut a large figure in English public life. But there he was making sacks.

The visitor went up to him and said, "Why how do you do, Mr. Bottomley? What are you doing—sewing?"

"No—reaping."

[6703]

"Are you quite sure this bus is going to Shepherd's Bush?"

"If it isn't, lady," said the conductor, "I'm in a worse mess than you are!"

[6704]

Just after the war an Englishman visited New York. Sugar was scarce, and in attempting to cross Fifth Avenue at Forty-second Street, he dropped a bag of it. Scrambling to get it he held up the traffic.

"What the hell are you trying to do?" said the traffic cop.

"My deah fellow," replied the Englishman, "I must have my sugar, don't you know!"

"Well," replied the cop, raising his club, "here's a couple of lumps for your coco."

When the Englishman woke up the next morning in the hospital he said: "The joke's on the Bobby. I never take cocoa, don't you know."

When this story was related to another Englishman, he mused a bit and then said:

"Even if he did, they never use lump sugar in cocoa, don't you know!"

[6705]

Customer (severely)–"I came here yesterday for a sixpenny packet of quinin, and you gave me morphin!"

Chemist's Assistant–"Oh, did I?

That will be another tenpence-ha'-penny."

[6706]

"See here, my man, you must not burst in here without knocking, don't you know?" said an English bathing beauty to the old fellow whose business it was to gather up wet suits and towels at the beach. "Some of these days you will be coming in here before we are good and ready for you, can't you understand?"

"Nary a bit of danger, lady. I allus peeps in through the keyhole 'fore I makes bold to enter."

[6707]

Mrs. 'Opkins–"You're not lookin' too 'appy, Mrs. 'Iggs?"

Mrs. 'Iggs–"No, it's this 'ere uncertain weather. One day it's 'ot and the next it's cold; yer never know wot to pawn."

[6708]

"Are they fresh?" asked a woman buying fish from a costermonger. The coster looked at his long-dead stock.

"Fresh, mum? Why just look at 'em." And turning to his wares he shouted, "Lie still, can't yer? Lie still!"

[6709]

It was a London bus and two "smart" young things were talking at the top of their voices in an affected jargon.

At last the conductor could stand it no longer. As the bus neared a stopping-place, he called out in a high-pitched voice: "Darlings, here's too, too sweet Smith Street!"

After that silence reigned.

[6710]

Wife (to boxer returning from fight)–"'Ow did you git on, Bill?"

Bill–"Fine—put 'im to sleep in the third round."

Wife–"Good. Well, now you can try your 'and on the baby."

[6711]

Overheard at a street corner in the British election: "What's this here election aboot, onyway?"

"It's as the Government canna carry oot the thingamajig withoot a clear whatdyecall it. And unless the thingamybob is put richt the hale thing will bust up. Have ye no heard aboot it?"

"A'd heard aboot it, but A didna ken ony details till the noo."

[6712]

At a party in England, the headmaster of a local school felt that he had partaken rather freely of champagne; he determined to be careful and avoid showing any of the usual signs of tipsyness.

When they rose from the table someone suggested that the hostess exhibit "the latest addition to her family." She agreed and presently the nurse appeared with a dainty pink basket containing twins.

The headmaster was nearest and, mindful of his determination, he steadied himself and said as he gazed into the basket:

"What a beautiful baby!"

[6713]

Tourist (having looked over historic castle, to butler)–"We've made a stupid mistake. I tipped his lordship instead of you."

Butler–"That's awkward. I'll never get it now."

[6714]

"Uncle," said a young man who thought that his guardian supplied him rather sparingly with pocketmoney, "is the Queen's head *still* on the sovereign?"

"Of course it is, you stupid lad! Why do you ask that?"

"Because it is now such a length of time since *I saw one.*"

[6715]

"How did you get that black eye, Mrs. Higgins?"

"Well, sir, me 'usband came out of prison on 'is birthday."

"Yes."

"And I wished 'im many 'appy returns."

[6716]

In the elevator of a big store she noticed a very attractive poster advertising beauty treatment. Out of curiosity she asked the elevator attendant (a funny little Cockney) where the beauty parlor was.

He turned and gave her a good look, noticed presumably that she did not use make-up at all, and then said, "You don't want ter go there mucking your face about. Why not stay as y'are—plain but 'olesome?"

[6717]

The fog was very thick, and the Chief Officer of the tramp steamer was peering over the side of the bridge. Suddenly, to his intense surprise, he saw a man leaning over a rail, only a few yards away.

"You confounded fool!" he roared. "Where the devil do you think your ship's going? Don't you know I've the right of way?"

Out of the gloom came a sardonic voice:

"This ain't no blinkin' ship, guv'nor. This 'ere's a light'ouse!"

[6718]

Diner–"I see that tips are forbidden here."

Waitress–"Lor' bless yer, mum, so was the apples in the Garden of Eden."

[6719]

First Englishman–"Charley, did you hear that joke about the Egyptian guide who showed some tourists two skulls of Cleopatra—one as a girl and one as a woman?"

Second Ditto–"No, let's hear it."

[6720]

"I'll give you thirty shillings for that pup."

"Can't be done, sir. That pup belongs to my wife, an' she'd sob 'er 'art out, but I tell yer what—spring another ten bob an' we'll let 'er sob!"

[6721]

It was a sultry day, and the two sailors had just been released from a hot spell of duty aboard.

Immediately they reached shore, they made a bee-line for the first public house they saw, and ordered two quarts of ale.

The men emptied their tankards in one draught, whilst the barmaid looked on in undisguised admiration.

The man who had paid stood a second or two wetting his lips meditatively, and then turned to his comrade with a grin. "'Tain't so bad, Bill?" he remarked. "Shall we have some?"

[6722]

A kind-hearted English Vicar one day observed an old woman laboriously pushing a perambulator up a steep hill. He volunteered his assistance and when they reached the top of the hill, said, in answer to her thanks:

"Oh, it's nothing at all. I'm delighted to do it. But as a little reward, may I kiss the baby?"

"Baby? Lor' bless you, sir, it ain't no baby, it's the old man's beer."

[6723]

When the pipe-band of a certain regiment of Scots played for the first time on Church Square, Pretoria, a Kaffir listening to the band was asked what he thought of it.

After a few seconds' consideration he replied: "Plenty no good, boss. No beginning, no middle, no finish, all one like."

[6724]

Charlady (observing artist's small son drawing pictures)–"I do think Lionel's clever, mum. He must have inhaled it from his father."

[6725]

The new maid was full of her own importance. She had worked on the Continent and felt superior to the other servants.

One day she was telling "below stairs" some of her experiences.

"How do the foreign dishes compare to English ones?" asked one of her audience.

"Oh," replied the maid, airily, "they break just the same."

[6726]

A London householder reported to the police that a tall, thin burglar whom he had encountered in the garden, struck him a violent blow on the head. A constable solved the mystery and captured the assailant by treading on the rake, too.

[6727]

Soulful Lady (rhapsodizing over the view)–"Exquisite. This is exactly like heaven."

Driver of the Charabanc Party–"Lumme. Alf! She's been about a bit!"

[6728]

The Christmas guest was being shown to his bed in the haunted room by his host's faithful, but rather sinister-looking, retainer.

At the door of the room, they paused.

"B-b-by the way," said the guest, "has anything—er—unusual ever happened in connection with this room?"

"Not for over fifty years, sir," said the servant hollowly.

"And what happened then?" asked the guest, with a sigh of relief.

"A gentleman who spent the night here appeared at breakfast the next morning," came the reply.

[6729]

"Young Rose 'Awkins is goin' abaht sayin' you're in love with 'er, 'Arry. Is that right?"

"Garn! Don't tike no notice of 'er. I might 'ave give 'er a clip or two over the ear, but that's all there is in it."

[6730]

Doctor–"Your master is decidedly better, Thompson, but very irritable. He must not be thwarted."

Butler–"He expressed a desire to wring my neck, sir."

Doctor–"Well—er—humor him."

[6731]

A London doctor touring in the provinces had difficulty in obtaining suitable lodgings in a small town.

One lady, showing him a dingy bedroom, remarked persuasively, "As a whole, this is quite a nice room, isn't it?"

"Yes, madam," he agreed, "but as a bedroom it's no good."

[6732]

A patriotic candidate applied to a yeoman for his vote, promising to exert his influence to turn out the

Ministry and procure a new one.
"Then I won't vote for you," said the farmer.

"Why not?" asked the candidate.

"I thought you was a friend of your country," said the farmer.

"So I am," replied the patriot.

"So am I," said the yeoman; "and for that reason I don't want to change the Ministry. I know well enough when I buy hogs lean they eat like gluttons, but when they've once got a little fat they don't want half so much to keep 'em; so for that reason I'm for sticking to the present set, as they *won't devour* half as much as *a new one.*"

[6733]

Two young ladies on the promenade of a seaside resort had been watching the vessels pass through a telescope loaned them by an "ancient mariner." On handing the glass back one of them remarked that it was a very good one.

"Yes, miss," said the old tar; "that 'ere telescope was given me by Lord Nelson."

"Good gracious! Why, Nelson has been dead nearly a hundred years."

"Well, I'm blowed," remarked the salty one, quite abashed, "'ow the time do fly."

[6734]

Lady–"And what sort of person is Mrs. Robinson, Colonel?"

Colonel–"Oh, the sort of person who calls a table napkin a serviette."

Lady–"But I always call it a serviette."

Colonel (undefeated)–"Then you know exactly what kind of person she is."

[6735]

A British officer on the Gold Coast was renowned for the excellent coffee which was served at his parties. On one occasion when the brew was especially good, the visitors sent for the black cook, and asked him for his recipe.

"Me take plenty boil water and milk and stir in coffee," he explained.

"But how do you strain it so cleverly?" he was asked.

"Me take master's silk socks."

"What?" roared the astonished host, "you take my best silk socks to strain coffee?"

"No, no, master," whined the terrified native, "me never use his clean socks!"

[6736]

Mrs. Profiteer–"Is this a pedigree dog?"

Dealer–"Pedigree? I should just think 'e is, Mum. Why, if the animal could only talk 'e wouldn't speak to either of us."

[6737]

Binks bought a new shirt, and on a piece of paper pinned to the inside found the name and address of a girl, with the words, "Please write and send photo." Scenting a romance, he wrote to the girl and sent his photo.

In due course he received a reply. It was only a note. "My chum and I had a bet on," it read, "as to what sort of a fellow would wear a shirt like that. My chum said a dude, I said a shrimp, and I'm glad to say I won."

[6738]

Seated around a table in a London grill-room were some Americans and one Englishman. A breezy American remarked, "I stayed out so late last night at a drinking-club that when I started home I met myself going to the office."

There was a general laugh. The Englishman smiled doubtfully.

Another American ventured: "You see the point, don't you? Just good-natured exaggeration."

"Yes," said the Englishman, a trifle more doubtfully; "I see. He would never recognize himself in that condition."

[6739]

Householder (facing burglar with revolver)–"Put all that stuff back on the sideboard at once, do you hear?"

Burglar–"Lumme, gov'nor, not all of it; be fair! 'Arf of it belongs next door."

[6740]

Mrs. Binks–"Well, this is good news, any'ow. Me daughter's written to say she's got a reg'lar job at last, as bridesmaid to a film-actress at 'Ollywood."

[6741]

The Girl (as they dance)–"Isn't it a topping floor and a topping band?"

Algy Pinhead–"I was just going to say that. You really must leave me something to talk about."

[6742]

Sherlock Holmes–"Ah, Watson, I see you have on your winter underwear."

Watson–"Marvelous, Holmes, marvelous! How did you ever deduce that?"

Holmes–"Well you have merely forgotten to put on your trousers."

[6743]

"Madam," said the ticket examiner, "you cannot travel first-class with a third-class ticket."

"But I'm one of the directors' wives," she protested.

"You couldn't do it, madam," he rejoined, "if you were the director's only wife."

[6744]

An American told an Englishman of the saying, "We feed the baby garlic so we can find her in the dark."

He said, "That's very effective, but rather indirect, don't you think?"

[6745]

The late King George in his younger days visited Canada in company with the Duke of Clarence. One night at a ball in Quebec, given in honor of the two royalties, the younger Prince devoted his time exclusively to the young ladies, paying little or no attention to the elderly ones and chaperons.

His brother reprimanded him, pointing out to him his social position and his duty as well.

"That's all right," said the young Prince. "There are two of us. You go and sing God save your Grandmother, while I dance with the girls."

[6746]

A family was getting into a new house. All the effects were moved by truck except a grandfather's clock which the husband, who was a lover of antiques, decided to tote himself. As he staggered around the corner with it, he bumped into an Englishman.

"Aw, h'I say, old fellow, wouldn't it be more convenient to carry a watch, now?" asked the visitor from overseas.

[6747]

The vicar was paying a visit to the houses of his poorer parishioners, and in one of the houses he asked a good many questions about the family. A very grubby but very cheerful little boy attracted the kindly cleric's attention, and he asked him his name.

"Reginald d'Arcy Smif, sir," replied the boy, with a grin.

The vicar turned to the boy's father.

"What made you give the boy a name like that?" he asked.

"'Cause I want 'im ter be a professional boxer," returned the parent, "an' wiv a name like that he'll get plenty o' practise at school."

[6748]

The Bishop of London, speaking at a meeting recently, said that when he was in America he had learned to say to his chauffeur, "Step on the gas, George"; but so far he had not summoned sufficient courage to say to the Archbishop of Canterbury, "O.K., Chief."

[6749]

A British visitor was admiring the mechanism of an American canning factory. The superintendent, who was showing him about, said smilingly, "You see, we're very economical here in America. We eat all we can, and all we can't we can."

The Englishman looked puzzled; and, after half an hour, when he had gotten half a dozen blocks from the factory, he saw the point, and burst into a roar of laughter.

The street car conductor stared at him in amazement. Feeling that an explanation was needed, the Englishman said blandly, "I'm just laughing at the wit of you Americans, you know. The superintendent of the canning factory just told me a whizzer. He said, 'We eat all we're able to, and all we're not, we tin!' "

[6750]

Wife—" 'Ere you are, just 'ome after doin' two years for arson, and now you can't even make the kitchen fire draw!"

[6751]

The prison visitor was going round the cells, and was asking rather fatuous questions. "Was it your love of drink that brought you here?" she asked a prisoner.

"Lor', no, miss," replied the man, "you can't get nothin' here!"

[6752]

In one of the lesser Indian hill wars an English detachment took an Afghan prisoner. The Afghan was very dirty. Accordingly two privates were deputed to strip and wash him.

The privates dragged the man to a stream of running water, undressed him, plunged him in, and set upon him lustily with stiff brushes and large cakes of white soap.

After a long time one of the privates came back to make a report. He saluted his officer and said disconsolately:

"It's no use, sir. It's no use."

"No use?" said the officer. "What do you mean? Haven't you washed that Afghan yet?"

"It's no use, sir," the private repeated. "We've washed him for two hours, but it's no use."

"How do you mean it's no use?" said the officer angrily.

"Why, sir," said the private, "after

rubbin' him and scrubbin' him till our arms ached I'll be hanged if we didn't come to another suit of clothes."

[6753]
"Why do you pull that wheelbarrow instead of push it, like you ought to?" a man asked a workman.

"Well, guv'nor," was the answer, "h'I 'ates the sight of the bloomin' thing."

[6754]
A weary telegraph-agent, stationed many miles from anywhere in the Sudan, in the hottest part of summer wired his superior officer: "Please relieve me; can't stay here; am surrounded by lions, elephants and wolves."

The officer wired back: "There are no wolves in the Sudan."

Whereupon the weary one replied: "Referring to my wire of yesterday, cancel wolves."

[6755]
An English tourist was on his first visit to Niagara Falls, and the guide was trying to impress him with its magnificence.

"Grand," suggested the guide.

The visitor did not seem much impressed.

"Millions of gallons a minute," explained the guide.

"How many in a day?" asked the tourist.

"Oh, billions and billions," answered the guide.

The visitor looked across, and down and up, as if gaging the flow. Then he turned away with a shrug, apparently unaffected.

"Runs all night, too, I suppose," he remarked.

[6756]
In the good old days of romance and adventure a king's jester one day found His Majesty bending over a basin and washing his face.

In a spirit of fun the jester gave the king a resounding kick on that part of his sacred person situated directly behind his stomach.

Deeply enraged, the king ordered the immediate execution of his audacious jester, but finally consented to pardon him if he would make an apology more outrageous than the original insult.

The condemned jester reflected for a moment and then remarked: "Will Your Majesty please forgive me. I did not know it was you. I thought it was the queen."

[6757]
Butler—"The post, m'lady."

Old Lady—"Ah, Christmas cards, I suppose, Jenkins. Well, just examine them, will you? and if you consider any of them too familiar, just destroy them, Jenkins."

[6758]
Vicar (to gardener digging up neglected garden) – "It's wonderful what the hand of man can do with a piece of earth, with the aid of Divine Providence."

Gardener—"You should 'ave seen this place, sir, when Divine Providence 'ad it all to itself."

[6759]
"Tom," said a colonel to one of his men, "how can so good and brave a soldier as you get drunk so often?"

"Colonel," replied he, "how can you expect all the virtues that adorn the human character for sixpence a-day?"

[6760]

"Yes," said Mrs Bloggs, who was discussing her next-door neighbor, "I got one 'ome on 'er properly yesterday. She was 'anging 'er washin' out on the line, and when I sees her old man's shirt, I says, 'Wot, 'as your 'usband joined the Fascists?' Prides 'erself on 'er washing, she does!'"

[6761]

After an immense amount of trouble, the vicar of a country parish succeeded in reconciling two old women who had been quarreling for years. He even induced them to meet under the vicarage roof.

In his drawing-room they shook hands. After an embarrassed silence one of them said:

"Well, Mrs. Tyler, I wish you all you wishes me."

"An' who's saying nasty things now?" snapped Mrs. Tyler.

[6762]

"What's the matter up at Tom's house?"

"They're taking 'im away in the ambulance for beatin' 'is missus."

[6763]

Charles Francis Adams was escorting a British friend to view the different objects of attraction in the vicinity of Boston, brought him to Bunker Hill. They stood looking at the splendid monument, when Mr. Adams remarked:

"This is the place, sir, where Warren fell."

"Ah!" replied the Englishman, evidently not posted up in local historical matters, "did it hurt him much?"

Mr. Adams looked at his friend. "Hurt him," said he, "he was killed, sir."

"Ah! he was, eh?" said the Eng-

lishman, still eyeing the monument, and commencing to compute its height in his own mind, layer by layer. "Well, I should think he would have been, to fall so far."

[6764]

An Englishman was deeply moved by the ballad: "You Can't Drive a Nail with a Sponge No Matter How Much You Soak It."

"By Jove, that's clevah, deucedly clever. 'You Cawn't Drive a Nail with a Sponge 'Owsoever Wet h'It h'Is!' I must remember that one, surely!"

[6765]

An old lady who could not see eye to eye with the taxi-driver on the question of fare, finally remarked: "Don't you try to tell me anything, my good man. I haven't been riding in taxis for five years for nothing."

"No," replied the driver, "but I bet you had a blarsted good try!"

[6766]

A London 'bus driver had shouted, "'Igh 'Oborn!" till the passenger on the seat behind him could no longer resist the temptation to make a joke.

"Excuse me," said the passenger, "but haven't you dropped something?"

"I see wot you're driving at," returned the driver, keenly, "but never mind. I shall pick it up when we get to Hoxford Street."

[6767]

New Butler—"At what time, Sir, would you wish to dine as a rule?"
Profiteer—"What time do the best people dine?"
New Butler—"At different times, Sir."
Profiteer—"Very well. Then I, too, will dine at different times."

[6768]

Professor (at table)–"James the First introduced the turkey into this country."
Host (trying to carve)–"And this must be the beggar he introduced."

[6769]

"Cup o' tea, weak," said a customer at a London coffee stall. When the decoction was brought to him he eyed it critically.

"Well, what's wrong with it? You said weak, didn't you?"

"Weak, yes," was the reply, "but not 'elpless."

[6770]

"Yes," prattled the elderly lady, "that is the Duke and Duchess; the couple behind them are the Mayor and the Mayoress, and those on the right are the Vicar and the—er—Vixen."

[6771]

The club bore was telling for the twentieth time about his trip to India and what he saw there.

"You can believe what you like," he said, "but I can tell you some of those fakirs can throw a rope into the air, then climb up it themselves and completely disappear."

After a short silence a member inquired with a yawn, "Can you by any chance do the trick yourself?"

[6772]

Rustic (discussing merit of savings bank with vicar)–"Well, sir, I allus do as my father did—keep my money in t'owd stockin' at 'ome."
Vicar–"But you lose the interest that way."
Rustic–"No, I doan't, sir; I puts a bit extra away for that."

[6773]

Week-end Guest (on Wednesday) –"Really, old chap, I haven't the nerve to impose upon your hospitality longer. Could I ask you for a bottle of nerve tonic?"

[6774]

White–"Do you know, I'm losing my memory—it's worrying me to death."
Heather–"Never mind, old chap. Just forget all about it."

[6775]

A celebrated comedian arranged with his greengrocer, one Berry, to pay him quarterly; but the greengrocer sent in his account long before the quarter was due. The comedian, in great wrath, called upon the greengrocer, and, laboring under the impression that his credit was doubted, said: "I say, here's a *mull*, Berry; you have sent in your *bill*, Berry; before it is *due*, Berry. Your father, the *elder*, Berry, would not have been such a *goose*, Berry; but you need not look *black*, Berry; for I don't care a *straw*, Berry; and I shan't pay you till *Christmas*, Berry."

[6776]

"And when Mrs. Gubbins sez you wasn't no lidy, wot did yer say?"

"I sez, 'Two negatives means an infirmary,' and I knocks 'er down. She is now in the 'orspital."

[6777]

A newly-formed club in England meets semi-weekly. On Tuesday the members listen to American jokes and on Saturday they meet to enjoy a hearty laugh.

[6778]

A social worker with more enthusiasm than sense called upon Terry Shea, night watchman, at his home.

"I hope, Mr. Shea," she said, "that you do not squander your money in liquor and riotous living. I'm trying to interest the people of the neighborhood in the new savings bank which has just been started. May I ask where you deposit your wages?"

"I'd just as soon tell ye as not," replied Mr. Shea. " 'Tis £3 a week I make. When I've paid the rent, the grocery bill, and the milkman, and bought what's needed for Maggie an' my five children, I deposit the rest of my money in barrels. Mostly, ma'am, I use sugar barrels. They're bigger an' hold more. But when I can't get them, I make shift with plain flour barrels."

[6779]

The poor fellow had fallen forty feet on to concrete outside a seaside hotel. He lay bruised, battered, and semi-conscious.

The hotel-keeper rushed out and, raising his reeling head, held a glass of sherry to his lips.

"Lumme!" he gasped, "how far have I got to fall to get a whiskey?"

[6780]

Getting wrong numbers over the telephone is not always the fault of the operator. Faulty enunciation is more often to blame. This incident illustrates one of the difficulties an operator has to overcome in answering calls:

An Englishman speaks over the telephone:

"Yes, this is Mr. 'Arrison. What, you can't 'ear? This is Mr. 'Arrison —haitch, hay, two hars, a hi, a hess, a ho and an hen—'Arrison."

[6781]

When the Earl of Bradford was brought before the lord chancellor to be examined on the application for a statute of lunacy against him, the question was asked him from the woolsack.

"How many feet has a sheep?"

"Does your lordship," answered Lord Bradford, "mean a live sheep, or a dead sheep?"

"Is it not the same thing?" said the chancellor.

"No, my lord," returned Lord Bradford. "There is much difference; a live sheep may have four legs, a dead sheep has only two; the two forelegs are shoulders, but there are only two legs of mutton!"

[6782]

"What a big family you have, Mrs. Jones," said the visitor.

"Yes'm. And the funny thing is that all the names begin with a haitch. There's 'Orace, 'Erbert, 'Enry, 'Ugh, 'Ubert, 'Arold, 'Arriet and 'Etty—all except the last one, and we 'ad 'er named Halice."

[6783]

"My dorter is goin' to play Beethoven tonight."

"I 'ope she wins."

[6784]

Guide—"This castle has stood for 600 years. Not a stone has been touched, nothing altered, nothing replaced."

Visitor—"Um, they must have the same landlord we have."

[6785]

A British soldier was sentenced to be flogged. During the flogging he laughed continually. The harder the lash was laid on, the harder the soldier laughed.

"Wot's so funny about bein'

flogged?" demanded the sergeant. "Why," the soldier chuckled, "I'm the wrong man."

[6786]

They were boasting about radio sets.

"You know," said the American, "in America we have radios so powerful that is possible to hear the announcer's heart beating."

"That's nothing," the Englishman replied. "I tuned in on Egypt last night, and in less than ten minutes the sand was up to my knees."

[6787]

An Australian barrister tells of a black fellow charged in a country town with stealing. His solicitor decided to put him in the box to give evidence in his own behalf. The magistrate, being doubtful if he understood the nature of an oath, undertook to examine him on the point.

"Jacky," he said, "you know what will happen to you if you tell a lie?"

"My oath, boss," replied Jacky, "me go down below—burn long time."

"Quite right," replied the magistrate. "And do you know what will happen if you tell the truth?"

"Yes, boss. We lose 'em case."

[6788]

Once a year the newsboys of a certain district of London are taken for an outing up the Thames by a gentleman of the neighborhood, where they can bathe to their heart's content.

As one little boy was getting into the water a friend observed: "I say, Bill, ain't you dirty!"

"Yes," replied Bill. "I missed the train last year."

[6789]

Magistrate – "What started the trouble between you and the plaintiff?"

Defendant–"Well, yer honor, it was like this. 'E threw 'is beer over me —I 'its 'im across the face wiv my bag of tools—then 'e cuts my 'ead open wiv a bottle—an' the next thing we knows we find ourselves quarrelin'!"

[6790]

Mrs. Horty (engaging new cook)– "I suppose you know that my husband is extremely particular about his food?"

Cook–"Yes, I know, mum. They're all alike. My ole man was jest the same. I never cooked anything to please 'im in me life."

[6791]

Enterprising Vendor–"I say, mum, 'ave you got such a thing as a match you could give me?"

Kind Lady–"I haven't one in the place."

Enterprising Vendor–"Well, will you buy a few boxes? I sells 'em, mum."

[6792]

Young Knut–"I say, waitah, nevah bring me a steak like that again."

Waiter–"Why not sir?"

Young Knut–"It simply isn't done, old thing!"

[6793]

In the course of an argument, a Canadian informed an Englishman that the inhabitants of the Old Country were too reserved. "Oh, nonsense," replied the Englishman. "Why, years ago, when I was in the Cambridge 'eight,' I knew all the other fellows quite well . . . that is, all excepting one, and he was away up in the bow."

[6794]

Harry said to Archibald that he should pull down his curtains; that he saw him holding his wife on his lap the night before.

"The joke is on you, 'Arry," chortled Archibald. "H'I was not 'ome last night."

[6795]

"Who was Perkin Warbeck?" a schoolboy was asked by his teacher.

"Perkin Warbeck," replied the boy, "was a pretender. He pretended to be the son of a king, but he wasn't. He was the son of respectable parents."

[6796]

Burglar (to belated assistant)–"You're late. I told you 'arf past one."

Young Burglar–"I forgot the number of the 'ouse. I've had to break into every 'ouse in the street."

[6797]

A traffic expert in New York, in speaking of traffic jams abroad, says that the London drivers and chauffeurs enliven many an occasion by their wit and sarcasm. One London driver drew up, when he saw a pedestrian directly in his way, and leaned over and very politely inquired:

"I say, sir, may I awsk what are your plans?"

[6798]

Facetious One–"Why so gloomy, old chap?"

Gloomy One–"Just heard my uncle has cut me out of his will. He's altered it five times in the last two years."

Facetious One–"Ha! Evidently a fresh heir fiend, what?"

[6799]

The successful man was lecturing to an admiring audience.

"I must say," he concluded, "that I owe everything I have to my wife."

"Hey," shouted a tradesman at the back of the hall, "you're not forgetting my bill, are yer?"

[6800]

Mrs. Brown–"I hear the vicar thinks your daughter has a real genius for reciting, Mrs. Smith."

Mrs. Smith–"Yes. All she wants, he says, is a course of electrocution, just to finish 'er off, like."

[6801]

Green–"You must be keen on the talkies, old boy, to go twice a week."

Howarth–"It's not that exactly. You see, if I don't go regularly I can't understand what my children are saying."

[6802]

Charwoman (to neighbor with whom she is having a spat)–"What I say is, there is ladies an' ladies—an' you ain't neither."

[6803]

Unseen by the referee, the all-in wrestler bit his opponent severely.

"You're biting," hissed the sufferer.

"Well," gasped his adversary, "do yer expect me to swaller yer in a lump?"

[6804]

Two London cabmen were glaring at each other. "Aw, what's the matter with you?" demanded one.

"Nothing's the matter with me."

"You gave me a narsty look," persisted the first.

"Well," responded the other, "now you mention it, you certainly have a narsty look; but I didn't give it to you."

[6805]

"My poor fellow, where did you learn to use such terrible oaths?" a Bishop asked a Coster.

"Y' cawn't learn h'it, y'reverince —h'its a bloomin' gift!"

[6806]

Lady–"Yes, they are very nice gooseberries, but aren't they dirty?"

Street Vendor–"Dirty? Think I can wash 'em and part their 'air in the middle for tuppence a pound in these times?"

[6807]

The chief constable of a small English town was also an expert veterinary surgeon. One night his telephone bell rang.

"Is Mr. Blank there?" said an agitated voice.

Mrs. Blank answered yes, and inquired:

"Do you want my husband in his capacity of veterinary surgeon or as chief constable?"

"Both, madam," came the reply. "We can't get our new bulldog to open his mouth, and—there's a burglar in it."

[6808]

Constable (to speeding foreigner)– " 'Ere, you mustn't go rushing abaht like that. What's yer name?"

Speeding Foreigner–"*Je ne comprends pas.*"

Constable—" 'Ow d'yer spell it?"

[6809]

A Southerner was trying to make an English visitor believe the negroes speak the aboriginal language. Calling up a husky idler at the railway station, he asked:

"Wah he?"

To which the black man made instant reply:

"Wah who?"

"Incredible!" cried the Englishman, as he made a note of the survival of the Indian language in the Southland.

[6810]

The Prince of Wales heartened the Tommies by visiting them in their camps at the front, during the First World War.

Upon one occasion he got a hearty laugh from a print of the reigning sovereigns displayed upon the wall of a soldier's hut.

Underneath the King's portrait appeared "George the Fifth," to which had been added this inscription below Queen Mary's portrait: "The Other Four-Fifths."

[6811]

'Arry (holding communication with the departed spirit of his wife)–"Is that you 'Arriet?"

"Yes."

"Are you 'appy, 'Arriet?"

"Very 'appy."

" 'Appier than you was with me?"

"Much 'appier."

"Where are you, 'Arriet?"

"In 'ell."

[6812]

"Remember, darling, you won't always be a junior clerk in a moldy old solicitor's office."

"That's a fact! I've already got a week's notice."

[6813]

" 'Allo, Bill! I 'avn't seen you for weeks—." Bill's pal stopped suddenly. "But wot's wrong, man? You're looking mighty seedy. Been ill, eh?" he asked.

Bill passed a horny hand across his brow.

"No," Bill sighed, "I ain't been ill. It's work wot's doing for me—work from seven in the morning till six at night, and only one hour off. Think of it, mate!"

"Well, well!" replied the other. "And 'ow long 'ave you been there?"

"I ain't been there yet," retorted Bill. "I begin tomorrer," he added gloomily.

[6814]

Skeptic–"If you have such an infallible remedy for baldness, why don't *you* use it?"

Subtle Barber (very bald)–"Ah, sir, I sacrifice my appearance to bring 'ome to clients the 'orror of 'airlessness."

[6815]

Steeplejack–"'Ullo, Bert! Where's that mate you took on—the chap that used to be an artist?"

Second Ditto–"'Aven't you 'eard? Soon as he laid a couple of bricks, he stepped back off the scaffolding to admire 'is work."

[6816]

The vicar, awarding prizes at the local dog show, was scandalized at the costumes worn by some members of the younger fair sex.

"Look at that youngster," said he; "the one with cropped hair, the cigarette and breeches, holding two pups. Is it a boy or a girl?"

"A girl," said his companion. "She's my daughter."

"My dear sir!" The vicar was flustered. "Do forgive me. I would never have been so outspoken had I known you were her father."

"I'm not," said the other. "I'm her mother."

[6817]

Mrs. Maggs had invited her neighbor to see the new decorations. The house had been repainted, and after examining the living-rooms they went into the bedroom.

"My!" said Mrs. Diggs admiringly. "Isn't it pretty? But what are the lovely pictures painted on the ceiling for?"

"For my 'usband," explained Mrs. Maggs. " 'E likes to 'ave something to look at on Sundays."

[6818]

Visitor–"What nice buttons you are sewing on your little boy's suit. My husband once had some like that on his suit."

Vicar's Wife–"Yes, I get all my buttons out of the collection plate."

[6819]

A British tar, home on leave and celebrating the occasion, had got himself into a dilemma. He had hired a taxi, only to discover when approaching his destination that he was penniless. He had dined and wined, not wisely, but too well. But the British navy is a training-school of resourcefulness. He caught up the speaking tube, shouted "Stop!" and jumped out. "I just want to pop into this tobacconist's and get some matches," he explained to the driver. "I've dropped a pound note somewhere in the cab and can't find it in the dark." He entered the tobacconist's, and as he did so the cab and its driver vanished into the night, as he had anticipated.

[6820]

Rich Uncle (a strict Sabbatarian)–"I am extremely sorry to learn that Eustace is in the habit of visiting a golf club on the Sabbath!"

Loyal Wife (brightly)–"Oh, but he doesn't play. He only pops over there for a few drinks and a game of bridge!"

[6821]

A new system of memory training was being taught in a village school, and the teacher was becoming enthusiastic.

"For instance," he said, "supposing you want to remember the name of a poet—Bobby Burns. Fix in your mind's eye a picture of a policeman in flames. See—Bobby Burns?"

"Yes, I see," said a bright pupil. "But how is any one to know it does not represent Robert Browning?"

[6822]

Soulful Lady–"There are times, Mr. Simpkins, when I feel convinced I was on earth in ancient Egypt."
Youth–"I say, you know, it's jolly rare for a girl to joke about her age like that."

[6823]

"I think it's a disgusting state of affairs when one reads of comedians earning more than cabinet ministers!"

"Oh, I dunno. On the whole they're funnier!"

[6824]

A woman in an English court, charged with shoplifting, was asked by the magistrate if she had anything to say on her own behalf.

"Yes, sir, I have," she replied hopefully. "I take only British goods."

[6825]

Butler–"I have to inform your lordship that there's a burglar downstairs."
His Ludship–"Very well, Parkinson; bring my gun and sports suit —the heather mixture."

[6826]

Passenger–"Porter, two of my trunks are missing.'
Porter–"Yes, lady, but don't worry your 'ead about 'em—this ain't a dressy place."

[6827]

Mrs. Higgins and Mrs. Brown after a quarrel were making up at the ladies' bar.

"Well, Mrs. 'Iggins," said Mrs. Brown, "I bears yer no malice." She raised her glass. "So 'ere's lookin' at yer, an' 'eaven knows that's a heffort!"

[6828]

Manager–"The lady 'olds the lump of sugar between 'er lips, and the lion will take it between 'is teeth. Now, I offer a thousand pounds to any member of the audience who will perform this trick!"
Voice (from the crowd)–"Righto, 'guv'nor. I'm on. Just take that there lion away!"

[6829]

Booking Clerk (at small village station)–"You'll have to change twice before you get to York."
Villager (unused to traveling)– "Goodness me! And I've only brought the clothes I be standing up in!"

[6830]

Teacher–"What are the races that have dominated England since the invasion of the Romans?"
Small Boy–"The Grand National and the Derby, miss."

[6831]

An English schoolboy wrote an essay on "The Stormy Petrol." When the master, a gentleman with a refreshing humor, saw it he wrote on the margin, "Hail to thee, blithe spirit! Bird thou never wert."

[6832]

A "doggy" lady met an English friend who propounded this riddle. "What do you see when you look down a dog's throat?" The lady could not guess, and was amused by the answer, which is "The seat of his pants."

So on her return home she asked her husband, "What do you see when you look down a dog's throat?"

Her husband confessed bafflement.

"Why," said the lady between gusts of laughter, "the seat of his trousers, you silly."

[6833]

Soap-Box Orator (winding up his speech)–"An' that, lidies and gentlemen, is the 'ole kettle o' fish in a nutshell."

[6834]

An American took an Englishman to a theater. An actor in the farce, about to die, exclaimed: "Please, dear wife, don't bury me in Yonkers!"

The Englishman turned to his friend and said: "I say, old chap, what *are* yonkers?"

[6835]

Lodger – "Madam, this morning when I bathed I found only a nailbrush in the bathroom. I can't wash my back with a nail-brush."

Landlady–"Well, you've a tongue in your 'ead, 'aven't you?"

Lodger–"Yes, but I'm no swan."

[6836]

"Here's a ticket for the conjurin' show, Maggie."

"Thank ye, Donald," said his wife.

"And hark ye, Maggie, when he comes to that trick where he takes a teaspoon o' flour and one egg and mak's 20 oam'lettes, watch vera close."

[6837]

The Magistrate–"The prisoner says he had two glasses of 'double brown.' What is this 'double brown,' sergeant?"

The Sergeant (sadly)–"Not wot it was, your worship!"

[6838]

Conductor (helping stout lady on car) – "Yer should take yeast, mother, ter 'elp yer to rise better."

Stout Lady–"Take some yerself, lad, and then yer'd be better bred."

[6839]

Policeman–"Excuse me, sir, but if you're the 'pale-faced gentleman who looks like a lop-eared rabbit,' I was to tell you that your wife's gone home on the 33 bus."

[6840]

"Think o' poor old 'Arry bein' sent to jail! One o' the fastest working burglars in the game.'

"Ah, well, he's takin' his time now."

[6841]

An American in England was giving some illustrations of the size of his country.

"You can board a train in the State of Texas at dawn," he said, impressively, "and twenty-four hours later you'll still be in Texas!"

"Yes," said one of his English listeners, with feeling, "We've got trains like that here too."

[6842]

" 'E's so keen on gardening that 'e bought a 'cyclopedia about it, an' I caught 'im lookin' all through the o's to see 'ow to grow 'ops."

[6843]

"An' what's more, I ain't 'ad a day's illness in me life!"

"Lor lumme, what on earth d'yer find to talk about?"

[6844]

Wife—"But I enclosed a small file in that last pie I sent you, Bert."
Convict—"That's your blinkin' pastry again, Liz. I didn't notice it!"

[6845]

The cannibal king of the Mambas assures Britain that he has given up the habit of eating small boys. Youth, it appears, will no longer be served.

SCOTCH

[6846]

An Aberdonian went into a shop and bought an attaché case. "Shall I wrap it up for you?" asked the clerk.

"Oh, no, thank you," replied Sandy, "just put the paper and string inside."

[6847]

"Did ye hear about Sandy McCulloch findin' a box of corn plasters?"

"No, did he?"

"Yes—so he went and bought a pair of tight shoes."

[6848]

"McTavish is an excellent judge of whiskey, isn't he?"

"Ay, a grand judge—an' a merciless executioner."

[6849]

Three Scotchmen were in church one Sunday morning when the minister made a strong appeal for some very worthy cause, hoping that everyone in the congregation would give at least one dollar or more. The three Scots became very nervous as the collection plate neared them, when one of them fainted and the other two carried him out.

[6850]

Sandy was learning to play the bagpipes. One night, while he was strutting about the room, kirling for all he was worth, his wife attempted a mild protest.

"That's an awfu' noise ye're making," she said.

Sandy sat down and took off his boots; then got up and resumed his piping in his stockinged feet.

[6851]

In a small Scottish town, a local taxi-driver was ordered to pick up an elderly lady after a bridge party. Arriving at the house, he had waited some time when a friend of his passed and asked:

"Whit are ye daeing here, Jock?"

"I'm waitin' for an auld gambling besom in there!" was the biting reply.

His fare, who overheard the remark, complained next day to the man's employer, who was very annoyed.

"Did he say that? I'll talk to him! It's nae business of his whit ye are!"

[6852]

Minister—"I am sorry I didn't see you at church yesterday, Tummas."
Tummas—"Weel, ye see, it was siccan a wet day it wisna fit tae turn oot a dog in. But I sent the wife, sir."

[6853]

A Scotchman was playing golf one bitter cold day. At the end of the round he slipped something into the caddie's hand and said kindly "That's for a glass of hot whiskey, my man."

The caddie opened his hand and discovered a lump of sugar!

[6854]

Minister–"Mackintosh, why don't you come to church now?"

Mackintosh–"For three reasons, sir. Firstly, I dinna like yer theology; secondly, I dinna like yer singin'; and thirdly, it was in your kirk I first met my wife."

[6855]

"What was all the fuss about in front of the movie theater?"

"Two Scotchmen were trying to get in on the same ticket on the ground that they were half-brothers."

[6856]

McTavish was homeward bound one night when he was waylaid by three thieves. He defended himself with great courage and obstinacy, and the struggle that followed was long and bloody. At length, however, he was overpowered. The thugs, anticipating a rich booty after the extraordinary resistance they had experienced, began to go through his pockets. They were baffled to find that the whole treasure which the Scot had been defending at the hazard of his life was a bent sixpence.

"Only a sixpence," exclaimed one of the disgusted rogues, nursing his bruises.

"Weel, we're lucky at that," said another, "if he had had eighteen-pence he would ha' killed all o' us."

[6857]

The following conversation was overheard by some mean spy at a Glasgow "close mouth."

"Jean, tell me wha's bonnie wee doo (turtle dove) are ye?"

"Uch awa'! Ye ken fine yersel', Jock."

"Then ye love me, Jean?"

"Ay, indeed! Twa pies last nicht and twa the nicht—wha wadna, Jock?"

[6858]

In an English political meeting one of the candidates patriotically orated: "I was born an Englishman, I have lived an Englishman, I hope I shall die an Englishman." From the back of the hall, in an unmistakable accent, came the question, "Mon, hae ye no ambeetion?"

[6859]

Scotchmen laugh at jokes about themselves in the papers. One of them laughed at some Scotch jokes over a fellow passenger's shoulder this morning.

[6860]

A newly appointed Scotch minister on his first Sunday of office had reason to complain about the scanty collection.

"Mon," replied one of the elders, "they are close—vera close. But," confidentially, "the auld meenister he put three or four saxpence into the plate hissel', just to gi'e them a start. Of course he took the saxpence out later."

The new minister tried the same plan, but the next Sunday he again reported a dismal failure. The total collection was not only small, but he was grieved to find that his own sixpences were missing.

"Ye may be a better preacher than the auld meenister," exclaimed the elder, "but if ye had half the knowledge o' the world, an' o' yer ain flock in perticular, ye'd ha' done what he did an' glued the saxpences to the plate."

[6861]

A Scotchman in planning his new home left the roof off one room.

A friend asked the reason for this.

"Oh, that's the shower," replied the Scotchman.

[6862]

Two Scotchmen were out hunting deer. One of them was new at the game, and as they had gotten into rather a tight place, the tension was high. All of a sudden, a fine big moose stepped into the clearing.

Sandy was terribly startled as he had never seen such a fine, big animal before, and he cried, "Oh, Jock, look, what'd you call that?"

Jock replied, "Why, mon, that's a moose."

"Well," said Sandy with a sickly laugh. "If that's a moose I don't keer to see a rat."

[6863]

This incident is related of a Scotch doctor, new to the gun, who adventured upon a day's rabbit shooting.

Chased by the ferrets, bunny was a rather quick-moving target, and the medico was not meeting with the success he had anticipated.

"Hang it all, man!" he exclaimed, impatiently, to the keeper that accompanied him, "these beasts are too quick for me."

"Aye, doctor," replied the pawky keeper, "but ye surely didna expect them tae lie still like yer patients till ye kill them!"

[6864]

Maggie had her full share of Scottish prudence and economy. She had worn her old bonnet so long that neighbors offered to get a new one for her. They asked if she would prefer straw or silk as material.

"Weel," replied Maggie, "since ye insist on giein' me a bonnet, I think I'll take a straw one; it will, maybe, just be a mouthful for the coo when I'm through with it."

[6865]

Clerk–"And you get an extra pair of pants with this suit."

Scotchman–"Throw in an extra coat and I'll take it."

[6866]

The oldest tinker in Scotland died recently, having tramped the country till he was nearly ninety.

A Highland minister once tried to influence him.

"Have you ever been inside a kirk, Donald?" he asked.

"Naw! But I've seen the ootsides o' mony a braw kirk."

"Can you say the Lord's Prayer?"

"Naw! Every man to his trade. Can you sodder (solder) a tin can?"

[6867]

The easterly wind had dried the land, and the crops were suffering from the drought, so the agriculturists of the parish waited on the minister with a request to "put up a word or twa for rain."

The minister, who had a reputation for the efficacy of his supplications on previous occasions, heard the deputation gravely, and, after a silence, during which he carefully scanned the horizon, replied: "A wull, but A'll bide a wee till the win's mair off the west!"

[6868]

A lawyer, examining a Scotch farmer, said: "You'll affirm that when this happened you were going home to a meal. Let us be quite certain on this point, because it is a very important one, and be good enough to tell me, sir, with as little prevarication as possible, what meal it was that you were going home to."

"You would like to know what meal it was?" said the Scotchman.

"Yes, sir; I should like to know," replied the counsel, sternly and impressively; "and be sure you tell the truth."

"Well, then," said the Scotchman, "it was just oatmeal!"

[6869]

A magician performing in a Northern town put a woman into a box from which there was no apparent outlet, and shut the lid. When he opened it again there was nothing inside but a couple of rabbits.

After the performance a Scotsman went to the magician and asked him if he could perform the same trick if his (the Scotsman's) wife were to get into the box.

"Why yes," answered the magician. "But are you anxious to get rid of your wive?"

"Weel," answered the Scot, "it's no sae much that, but wee Wullie got me tae promise him twa rabbits for his birthday!"

[6870]

Young Angus had been out for the evening with his best girl. When he arrived home he found his father still sitting up. The old man looked up and shook his head.

"Hae ye been oot wi' yon lassie again?" he asked.

"Aye, dad," replied young Angus. "Why do ye look sae worried?"

"I was just wonderin' how much the evening cost."

"No more than half a croon, dad."

"Aye? That was no sae much."

"It was a' she had," said Angus.

[6871]

A taxicab passenger, arriving at his destination, paid the fare but did not tip the driver.

"You forgot something," said the driver.

"What?" asked the passenger in honest bewilderment, slapping his pockets and peering back into the cab.

"Your bagpipes," retorted the driver.

[6872]

Then there is the story of the Scot's wife whose doctor told her she needed salt air. She woke up next morning, and her husband was fanning her with a herring.

[6873]

A good story is told about a Scotchman that went to a horse race for the first time in his life. This Scotchman was a feeble-minded old man, and the companion that took him to the race meeting presently persuaded him to wager a sixpence in the third race on a forty-to-one shot.

By some amazing miracle this outsider won, and when the bookmaker gave old Sandy a golden sovereign and his sixpence the winner could not believe his eyes.

"Do you mean to tell me," he said, "that I get all this for my saxpence?"

"I do," said the bookmaker.

"Ma conscience!" muttered Sandy. "Tell me, mon, hoo long has this thing been going on?"

[6874]

A Scotch gentleman asked a friend of his to pay a visit to his house to hear his daughter sing.

After she had finished singing, the proud father said to his friend: "Well, hoo dae ye like it? Wha' dae ye think o' her execution?"

"Mon, I'm in favor o' it!"

[6875]

A Scotchman had heart disease. So he never bought a railway ticket for any farther than from one station to the next.

[6876]

An American tourist sat beside a working man on top of a Glasgow tramway car. Crossing the river by the Jamaica bridge the American asked:

"What do you call this trickle of water?"

"Oh, that's the River Clyde," said the worker.

"Gee-whiz! You call that a river? You should see our Mississippi."

"Did you Yankees make the Mississippi?" asked the Glasgow man.

"Wall, n—o!"

"Weel, we made this yin."

[6877]

Two Scotsmen were involved in a court case. McTavish related how the defendant, McLeish, came up and struck him. He proceeded: "So I just up and gives him a wipe. Just then his dog came along an' I hit him again."

"Hit the dog?" asked the magistrate.

"No. Hit McLeish. An' then I upped wi' a stoon and throed it at him and it rolled over and over."

"Threw a stone at McLeish?"

"No, the dog. An' he got up and hit me again."

"The dog?"

"No; McLeish. An' wi' that he stuck his tail between his legs an' went off."

"McLeish?"

"No; the dog. An' then he came back and pounded me."

"The dog came back and pounded you?"

"No; McLeish. An' he isn't hurt a little bit."

"Who isn't hurt?"

"The dog."

[6878]

Cuttem, the barber, was talking of a man who had joined his shave and haircut club at so much a week. "That chap McMean has a marvelous growth—comes in twice a day for a shave, and every few days for a haircut."

Cuttem went up in the air when the other informed him, "Why, there are two McMeans—Angus and Donald—and they are twins."

[6879]

A Scotchman strolled into a smart "gentlemen's outfitter's" and said to the salesman, "I want a necktie."

The salesman then produced a box of eye-twisters, which he introduced with the remark:

"Here are some that are very much worn, sir."

"Oh, away, mon!" retorted the son of Scotland, offended. "I didna want yin that's verra much worr-rn! I hae plenty o' them at home."

[6880]

Sandy—"I want a cheap coathanger."

Assistant—"Yes, sir, twopence."

Sandy—"Twopence! Is there nothing cheaper?"

Assistant—"Yes, sir, a nail."

[6881]

An Aberdeen town councillor was asked the reason why the Aberdonians do not resent the canny stories that are told about them.

"Resent them! Na! Na! The prosperity o' this city is bein' built up by haddies and jokes. Cannie stories have made this the best kenned place on earth. Aberdeen's a tourist center now. Americans are drovin' in in their hunners. And it's a dune withoot a farthin' on the rates. Man, it's grand cheep publeecity!"

[6882]

Mac arrived at the office half an hour late. "What does this mean?" inquired his boss.

"Well, it was like this," replied Mac. "I squeezed the tube of toothpaste too much, and it took me a good half hour to get the stuff back into the tube."

[6883]

"Do you know the only place where Scotchmen are ever seen giving their fiancées rings?"

"In Aberdeen?"

"No, in telephone booths."

[6884]

A certain canny Scotsman had carried on a courtship of long duration without definitely committing himself. The girl, if she worried herself at the long probation, gave no sign until one morning her tardy lover, thumbing a small notebook, said:

"Maggie, I hae been weighing up your guid points, and I hae already got to ten. When I get a dozen I'm goin' tae ask ye the fatal question."

"Weel, I wish ye luck, Jock," answered the maiden. "I hae also gotten a wee book, and I've been puttin' doon your bad points. There are

nineteen in it already, and when it reaches the score I'm goin' tae accept the blacksmith!"

[6885]

Donald and Jeanie were putting down a carpet, when Donald slammed the end of his thumb with the hammer and began to pour forth his soul in language befitting the occasion.

"Donald, Donald!" shrieked Jeanie, horrified. "Dinna swear that way!"

"Wummun!" vociferated Donald, "gin ye know ony better way, now is the time to let me know it."

[6886]

The Scotchwoman called on her minister with a solemn countenance. She explained that she and her brother John were probably the only ones in his flock who would go to heaven, for they were the only ones who did not have any false doctrines in their creed.

"I'm glad to hear," said the minister, with a light irony, "that there are two of you who are absolutely right."

"Aweel, I'm no sayin'," the woman went on. "Times I hae ma doots o' John."

[6887]

A Scottish farmer of a miserly disposition bought a horse at a fair, and on the way home he thought a drink of water would refresh it, so he got a pail of water; but the animal would not take it. When he got home he offered it a feed of corn; but much to his surprise it would not touch that, either.

"Weel," he muttered to himself, "if only I was sure ye were a guid worker, ye're the verra horse for me."

[6888]

Have you heard the one about the Scotchman who was given a pair of spats and then went out and had them half-soled?

[6889]

A commercial traveler, held up in the Orkneys by a storm, telegraphed to his firm in Aberdeen: "Marooned here by storm. Wire instructions."

The reply came: "Start summer holidays as from yesterday."

[6890]

Scot–"This London's a fine toon. There's free parks with free music, free museums, free picture galleries, and in the grand restaurants where I get my dinner I'm always coming across a threepenny bittie hidden under the plate as a surprise."

[6891]

A Scotsman lost his wife, and a friend was condoling with him on his bereavement. "Eh, Sandy, 'tis a sair loss ye hae had!" he said.

"Mon, 'tis that," answered Sandy. "And tae think! 'Twas a week ago that the doctor ordered a box of pills for her, and she hadna time tae take but half of them!"

[6892]

Englishwoman (in Scotland)–"I want a sheep's head, and it must be English."

Butcher (flinging a head to his assistant)–"Here, Jock, tak' the brains oot o' this."

[6893]

A Scottish lady invited a gentleman to dinner on a particular day and he had accepted with the reservation, "If I am spared."

"Weel, weel," replied she, "if ye're deid I'll no' expect ye."

[6894]

The town-clerk of a small town in Scotland had the misfortune to lose his leg in a railway accident. As a mark of appreciation of his long services, the council provided him with an artificial limb. A few months afterwards the same official was unlucky enough to have his other leg fractured in a trap-accident.

The mishap was naturally the topic of much discussion in the little town, and one old man was heard to remark: "It's a gey bad business for the puir man, but is it his ain leg or the leg that belongs to the toon that's broken?"

[6895]

"Is old Angus a typical Scotsman?"

"Is he? He's saved all his toys for his second childhood!"

[6896]

And there was the Scotchman who bought only one spur. He figured that if one side of the horse went the other was sure to follow.

[6897]

Sandy was an elder in the church, and a truly pious man. He had an eye for beauty and a love for it, but he married Tina because he knew she would make him an excellent wife.

"I suppose Tina is a handsome lass?" said Sandy's cousin, who met him in Glasgow not long after the marriage, and had never seen the bride. "I ken ye've gude taste, Sandy."

"Aweel," said the bridegroom cautiously, "she's the Lord's handiwork, Tammas, but I'm no' prepared to say she is His masterpiece."

[6898]
"What started the Grand Canyon?"
"A Scotchman lost a penny in a ditch."

[6899]
Angus—"Sandy, ye ken I'm a thrifty man. What would ye advise me to tak to the golden wedding?"
Sandy (after a little thought)—"Mon, I'd tak a goldfish."

[6900]
Dr. Abernathy, the famous Scottish surgeon, was a man of few words, but he once met his match in a woman. She called at his office in Edinburgh one day and showed a hand, badly inflamed and swollen. The following dialogue, opened by the doctor, took place:
"Burn?"
"Bruise."
"Poultice."
The next day the woman called again, and the dialogue was as follows:
"Better?"
"Worse."
"More poultice."
Two days later the woman made another call, and this conversation ensued:
"Better?"
"Well. Fee?"
"Nothing," exclaimed the doctor. "Most sensible woman I ever met!"

[6901]
A Scotchman was going on the excursion to New York by way of the Reading Railroad. He handed the agent a ten-dollar bill as the agent called, "Change at Jersey City."
"No jokes, now," said the Scotchman, "I want my change right away."

[6902]
A Scotchman woke up one morning to find that in the night his wife had passed away. He leaped from his bed and ran, horror-stricken, into the hall.
"Mary," he called downstairs to the general servant in the kitchen, "come to the foot of the stairs, quick."
"Yes, yes," she cried. "What is it? What is it?"
"Boil only one egg for breakfast this morning!" he said.

[6903]
"Now, McTavish," said the doctor, "it's like this: You've either to stop the whiskey or lose your eyesight, and you must choose."
"Ay, weel, doctor," said McTavish, "I'm an old man noo, an' I was thinkin' I ha'e seen about everything worth seein'."

[6904]
The roof of a certain kirk was in need of repairing, but the leading elder could not be convinced that such was the case. At a meeting convened to consider the matter a lump of plaster descended on this elder's head. When he had recovered from the shock he rose and said:
"I am now convinced that the roof must be redone immediately. In fact I'll give five pounds mysel!"
Upon which the minister closed his eyes and prayed fervently:
"Oh, Lord, hit him again!"

[6905]
A lady was the owner of a small shop, and her lover acquired the habit of seeing her home and of carrying the cash bag that contained the day's takings, which was generally heavy. "You must be doin'

weel," remarked her ardent suitor, frequently.

"Oh, ay," the lady would reply, "it's a guid bit business." But she did not disclose the fact that the bag contained the counter weights besides the moderate drawings. The canny lover only discovered that fact after his marriage to her.

[6906]

"How much whiskey can a Scotchman drink?"

"Any given quantity."

[6907]

"Do you Scotchmen mind all the stories that are told about you?" asked an American of a Scotsman.

"Of course we do!" answered the Scot.

"Why?" the American asked.

"Because they are all told at our expense," replied the other man.

[6908]

The Scotch patient was fumbling in his pocket.

"You don't need to pay me in advance," said the dentist.

"I'm no going to," was the reply. "I'm only counting ma money before you give me the gas."

[6909]

Sandy arrived at Euston when noon was striking. He called a taxi, asked the driver to take him to Waterloo, mentioned that he had a train to catch at three o'clock.

Scenting a greenhorn, the taxi-driver made a long detour, and for nearly three hours Sandy sat back enjoying the sights of London.

At two-thirty the taxi drew up at Waterloo, the driver all smiles. Sandy hopped out and darted up to a policeman.

"What is the taxi fare from Euston to Waterloo?" he asked.

The policeman told him. Sandy handed him the money.

"Would you mind paying my fare, officer?" he said. "I've a train to catch." Then he dived into the station.

[6910]

Sandy joined a golf club and was told by the professional that if his name was on his golf-balls and they were lost, they would be returned to him when found.

"Good," said the Scot, "put my name on this ball."

The pro did so.

"Would you also put M.D. after it?" said the new member. "I'm a doctor." The pro obeyed.

"There's just one more thing," went on the Scot. "Can ye squeeze 'Hours 10 to 3' on as well?"

[6911]

An old Scotch farmer, who had been henpecked all his life, was about to die. His wife felt it was her duty to offer him such consolation as she might, and said:

"Sandy, you are about to go, but I will follow you."

"I suppose so, Jean," said the man, meekly, "but as far as I am concerned, you needna be in any extraordinary hurry about it."

[6912]

The captain of a steamer took on two hands—one a Kircaldy man without a written character, and the other from Dundee possessed of abundant documentary evidence as to his honesty. They had not been long at sea when they encountered rough weather, and the Dundee man, when crossing the deck with a bucket in his hand, was swept overboard.

The Kircaldy man saw what had happened and sought out the captain. "Dae ye mind yon mon from Dundee," he said, "that ye engaged wi' the fine character?"

"Yes," said the captain. "What of it?"

"He's awa' wi' yer bucket," was the reply.

[6913]
In a Scottish village one neighbor called at another's house. He was met at the door by his friend's wife, and the conversation which ensued went thus:

"Cauld?"

"Ay."

"Guan to be weety (rainy) I'm thinkin'."

"Ay."

"Is John in?"

"Ou, ay! He's in."

"Can I see him?"

"Na."

"But a winted tae see him."

"Ay, but ye canna see him. John's deid."

"Deid?"

"Ay."

"Sudden?"

"Ay."

"Verra sudden?"

"Ay, verra sudden."

"Did he say onything about a pot o' green pent afore he deid?"

[6914]
One of the clerks at the employment agency was a bit of a wit, and he was preparing to gain a laugh at the expense of the next in the line.

"Where were you born?" he asked the man, a Scotchman.

"Glasca'," was the reply.

"Glasgow! Whatever for?" continued the funny one.

"I wanted to be near mother," said the other with devastating meekness.

[6915]
He was a Scot, with the usual thrifty characteristics of his race. Wishing to know his fate, he telegraphed a proposal of marriage to his sweetheart back in the country. After waiting all day at the telegraph office for his reply, he received an affirmative answer late at night.

"Well, if I were you," said the operator who delivered the message, "I'd think twice before I'd marry a girl who kept me waiting so long for an answer."

"Na, na," replied the Scot. "The lass for me is the lass wha waits for the night rates."

[6916]
A tourist in Scotland came to a wide ferry. It was stormy and the wind was constantly increasing. The Scotch ferryman agreed to take the tourist across, but told him to wait until he had first taken a cow across.

When he had returned and started across with the traveler, the latter became curious.

"Will you tell me why you took the cow over and made me wait?" he asked.

"Weel, now," explained the ferryman, "you see, the coo wur valuable, and I feared th' wind wud increase so th' boat might upset on the second trip."

[6917]
A Scotchman, not feeling as well as usual, called on his family doctor. The doctor, after looking him over, prescribed a bottle of pills, to be taken, one before each meal; also a bottle of whisky, to be taken as a tonic—a small glass after each meal. The patient was to call again in a few days.

The fourth day later, the Scotchman called on the doctor again, stating he was feeling no better. The doctor, after looking him over again, asked him if he had been taking the pills regularly. The Scotchman said: "Weel, doctor, I may be a wee bit behint wi' the peels but I'm six weeks aheed wi' tha whusky."

[6918]
A Scotsman wishing to join the police force in Birmingham, was asked by the Inspector: "What would you do to disperse a crowd?"
"Weel," replied the Scot, "I dinna ken what ye wad dae in Birmingham, but if I were in Aberdeen, I'd pass round the hat."

[6919]
"I hear yer frien' Tamson's marriet again."
"Aye, so he is. He's been a dear frien' tae me. He's cost me three wedding presents an' twa wreaths."

[6920]
A certain old worthy had earned the reputation of being "sair on wives." At the funeral of his third spouse a friend condoled with him thus:
"It must be a vera great consolation to ye, John, that ye got a bit o' money wi' every ane o' yer late wives. Ye must be pretty weel aff noo?"
"Na, na!" replied the bereaved husband: "Man, to tell ye the honest truth, what wi' gettin' them *into* the hoose and *oot* o' the hoose there's been very little profit."

[6921]
A Scotchman complained to a friend that he had a ringing in his head.
"Do ye ken th' reason o' that?"
"I dinna ken."
"I'll tell ye. It's 'cause it's empty."

"And ha'e ye never a ringin' in your head?" asked the other.
"No, never."
"Do ye ken th' reason o' that?" asked the one who had been told his head was empty because of the ringing in it.
"I dinna ken."
"'Cause it's cracked."

[6922]
Two acquaintances, who had not seen Macpherson for some years, called at his house on Saturday evening. Mrs. Macpherson answered the door.
"Does Macpherson live here?" they asked.
"Ay," was the woman's reply, "jist carry 'im in!"

[6923]
"What makes you so gloomy today, Angus?" asked a sportsman of his ghillie.
"Weel, ye see, sir," replied Angus, "Lord A—— went off to England without payin' me, and yesterday he sent me ane o' thae cheque things. It was for six pounds. I took it to the bank and they only gi'ed me five pounds nineteen and sixpence."

[6924]
McTavish (to commercial traveler) —"No, Ah'm tellin' ye, mon, for the last time, an' Ah dinna ken why Ah'm pestered all day by travelers."
Commercial Traveler—"Well, sir, I can tell you that. You see, the commercial travelers' college down the road uses you as Lesson 6, called 'approaching the hopeless client.'"

[6925]
Two Scotchmen were watching a fooball game; one had a bottle; the other had only a thirst. The bottleman was talking very largely about

his knowledge of the game and what a fine player he was himself.

During the conversation he helped himself very liberally to the contents of his bottle, whereupon the thirsty one said: "Weel, I notice ye're a fine dribbler, but ye're nae guid at passing."

[6926]

A Scotch laddie was showing a woman tourist an old abbey, and on leaving him at the churchyard gate she rewarded him with only barren thanks, whereupon the canny Scotchman remarked:

"Weel, my leddy, when ye gang hame, if ye fin' oot that ye have lost your purse, ye maun recollect that ye havna had it oot here."

[6927]

An Englishman was invited to his Scots friend's home for Christmas dinner.

As the guests were seated round the table the host entered with a steaming plum pudding.

The Englishman turned to the host's daughter.

"They do say," he said smilingly, "that the one who finds the three-penny-piece in their portion of pudding will be lucky."

"Ay, and clever, too," put the host from the top of the table.

[6928]

Father–"Git yer jacket aff, young mon, an' come wi' me."

Jock–"Yer no' goin' ter lick me, are ya, father?"

Father–"I am that: didna I tell ye this mornin' that I'd settle wi' ye fer yer bad behavior?"

Jock–"Ay, but I thought it was only a joke, like whin ye telt the grocer ye'd settle wi' him."

[6929]

A Scotsman had to send an urgent telegram, and not wishing to spend more money than necessary wrote like this:

"Bruises hurt erased afford erected analysis hurt too infectious dead." (Ten words.)

The Scotsman who received it immediately decided it was: "Bruce is hurt. He raced a Ford. He wrecked it, and Alice is hurt, too. In fact she's dead." (Nineteen words.)

[6930]

"Good gracious! What have I done now?" gasped the young man, collapsing heavily on the car-seat.

"What's the matter, mon?" asked a startled Scotsman in the corner.

"Why, I've accidentally pulled the communication-cord while searching in my luggage," the other explained. "What shall I do? I'll be fined five pounds."

The Scot looked thoughtful.

"Don't worry, laddie, don't worry," he said calmly. "Just wi'e me three pound and I'll throw a fit."

[6931]

"Is the bride pretty?" she asked of a Scotchman.

"Aw think she's a reyt bonny wench to tawk to, as weel as bein' rich and cliver, but, if beauty's a sin, she wain't ha' that to onswer fur!"

[6932]

Three blood transfusions were necessary to save an American lady's life at a hospital. A brawny young Scotchman offered his blood. The patient gave him $50 for the first pint, $25 for the second pint—but the third time she only thanked him.

[6933]

Four separate wrecks had cast up four men on a lonely island of the South Seas. There were two Scotchmen and two Englishmen. After several years a passing steamer hove to and took the four aboard. Sandy and Donald found their way to the skipper's cabin, and in telling their experiences Sandy said:

"It would grieve you, mon, to see the Englishmen. Never a word did they speak all the time they were there; they were not introduced."

"And hoo did ye lads muck oot?" inquired the skipper.

"Aye, mon, the dee I found Donald on the beach we organized a Caledonian society, a golf club, and a Preesbyteerian church."

[6934]

"I hear that you and Maggie have been reconciled and are to be married after all," said McPherson.

"Quite right," replied McIntosh. "You see, Maggie has put on weight and we couldn't get the engagement ring off her finger."

[6935]

Seeing two men bathing on the Aberdeen beach a wealthy Englishman offered five pounds to the one who could stay longest under water. They are still searching for the bodies.

[6936]

A Scotsman was strolling along the quay one day, when his dog stopped beside a basketful of live lobsters. Instantly one of the lobsters snapped its claws on the dog's tail, and the surprised collie dashed off down the street, yelping.

The fishmonger for a moment was speechless with indignation, then, turning to his prospective customer, he bawled: "Mon, mon, whustel to yer dog; Whustel to yer dog."

"Hoot, mon," returned the other complacently, "whustel to your lobster!"

[6937]

A Scottish minister was on his usual rounds when he came across one of his old friends. "And how has the world been treating you, Jock?" asked the minister.

"Very seldom!" replied Jock sadly.

[6938]

"Is there any truth in the report that MacTavish has bought the gasoline station?"

"Well I don't know for sure, but the 'Free Air' signs have been taken down."

[6939]

Sandy (entering nursery garden)– "Have ye a nice cucumber?"

Gardener–"Aye, here's one. That will be five pence."

Sandy–"Too much. Have ye no' one for tuppence?"

Gardener–"Ye can hae this for tuppence."

Sandy–"All richt, here's the tuppence. But don't cut it off; I'll be calling for it in about a fortnight."

[6940]

A Scot was engaged in an argument with a conductor as to whether the fare was five or ten cents. Finally the disgusted conductor picked up the Scotsman's suit-case and tossed it off the train, just as they passed over a bridge. It landed with a splash.

"Mon," screamed Sandy, "isn't it enough to try and overcharge me, but now you try to drown my little boy?"

[6941]

"Are we going dutch on this," asked the sarcastic diner of a friend whose hand appeared to be caught in his pocket, "or are you going scotch?"

[6942]

Minister–"Now, Macpherson, why don't you fight against your longing for drink? When you are tempted, think of your wife at home."

Macpherson (thoughtfully)–"When the thirst is upon me, I am absolutely devoid of fear."

[6943]

Housekeeper–"Losh me Laird, ye'll no' have asket all thae folks to stop the nicht? There isna beds for the half o' them."

Laird—"Hoots, woman! dinna fash yersel'. Gie them plenty whiskey an' they'll find beds for themsels."

[6944]

A Scotchman had been presented with a pint flask of rare old Scotch whisky. He was walking briskly along the road toward home, when along came a car which he did not side-step quite in time. It threw him down and hurt his leg quite badly. He got up and limped down the road. Suddenly he noticed that something warm and wet was trickling down his leg.

"Oh, God," he groaned, "I hope that's blood!"

[6945]

"I canna get over it," said Sandy to his wife, who was also Scotch. "I put twa' shillin' in the plate at kirk this mornin' instead o' ma usual penny."

The beadle had noticed the mistake. He therefore said nothing when Sandy ignored the plate for twenty-three consecutive Sundays, knowing quite well that there are twenty-four pence in two shillings.

On the twenty-fourth Sunday, when Sandy would be dropping his twenty-fourth penny in the plate if he had maintained his regular rate of contribution, the beadle watched Sandy closely. Sure enough, Sandy ignored the plate. But the beadle instantly spoke up:

"Your time's up noo, Sandy."

[6946]

Macpherson called at the laundry for his parcel of linen.

"That will be three shillings," the laundress told him.

"But there are only two pairs of pyjamas," Macpherson complained, "and you charge one shilling a pair, don't you?"

"That's right, sir," the laundress replied. "The extra shilling is for the collars and socks you had in the pockets."

[6947]

A man dropped into a café one afternoon and seeing his Scotch friend Sandy standing at the bar indulging in a "lone one," walked up to the bar and greeted him thus:

"Will you have another one with me?"

"No, thank you," said Sandy, "but you can pay for this one if you will."

[6948]

"We never sell strong drink on the Sabbath," remarked the law-evading beer-seller, "you may have a glass free, and we will sell you this tasty pretzel for twenty-five cents."

After drinking two glasses, Sandy turned from the saloon-keeper with pain upon his face. "No?" he said, "I shall not buy your pretzels, they are too expensive."

[6949]

"It's twenty-five years since ye first cam tae work in my firm," said a Scotch manufacturer to one of his foremen, "—twenty-five years, an' ye've been a gude, honest an' faithful servant."

"Weel, I've always tried to dae my duty," replied the foreman.

"A' the time ye've been wi' me, the firm has grown and prospered," continued the manufacturer; "an' I'm gie'in ye something here that'll please ye and yer wife and the bairns," (placing a small parcel into the hands of his foreman.)

"Tak' it hame, Donald; tak' it hame. Nae thanks, noo, noo, ye deserve it."

The overwhelmed foreman hastened home with visions of rolls of banknotes in the little parcel.

When he reached home, he opened it in the presence of his wife and children. To his amazement out fell a portrait of his employer.

Next morning he was accosted by "the master" with:

"Weel, Donald, hoo did ye like the present I gave ye?"

"Oh," said Donald, "it's jist like ye!"

[6950]

Mr. McNab (to urchin)–"What's the matter, laddie?"

Urchin–"I've lost my 'apenny!"

Mr. McNab–"Aye, dinna grieve. Here's a match to find it."

[6951]

A modest Scotchman, in speaking of his family, said:

"The Douglas family is a verra, verra auld Scotch family. The line rins awa' back into antiquity. We dinna ken hoo far back it rins, but it's a lang, lang way back, and the history of the Douglas family is re-

corded in five volumes. In aboot the middle of the third volume, in a marginal note, we read, 'Aboot this time the warld was created.' "

[6952]

An Aberdonian sat at the bedside of his friend who was a patient in a nursing home.

"Ye seem to be a bit cheerier the day, John," said the visitor.

"Ay, man, I thocht I was gaun to dee, but the doctor tells me he can save my life. It's to cost a hunner pounds."

"Eh! that's terrible extravagance! Do ye think it's worth it?"

[6953]

"How much d'ye charge to press a pair of trousers?" Sandy asked the proprietor of the dry-cleaner's shop.

"A shilling is our charge," was the reply.

"All right," he said, after a while, "just press one leg for sixpence, and I'll have my photy taken side view instead of front."

[6954]

Englishman–"My ancestors have had the right to bear arms for more than two hundred years."

Scotchman–"Hoot man, ma ancestors ha had tae right tae bear legs for more than two thousand years."

[6955]

"You love the whisky too much, Donald, and you ought to know that the whisky is your enemy," said a Scottish clergyman to one of his parishioners who was too much addicted to the bottle.

"Eh, but, Meenister," slyly answered Donald, "don't ye aften tell us that we ocht tae love oor enemies?"

"Yes, Donald; but I never told you that you should swallow them."

[6956]

A Scotchman came upon an automobile overturned at a railway crossing. Beside it lay a man all smashed up.

"Get a doctor," he moaned.

"Did the train hit you? asked the Scotchman.

"Yes, yes; get a doctor."

"Has the claim agent been here yet?"

"No, no; please get a doctor."

"Move over, you," said the Scot, "till I lie down beside you."

[6957]

They say a Scotchman opened his pocket-book recently, and three moths flew out.

[6958]

Tom—"There's been a smash-and-grab raid at the jeweler's."

Dick—"Did they get away with it?"

Tom—"No! They were Scotch, and they were arrested when they came back for the brick."

[6959]

"Two pennyworth of bicarbonate of soda for indigestion at this time of night," cried the infuriated druggist, who had been aroused at 2 A.M., "when a glass of hot water would have done just as well!"

"Weel, weel," returned Mac-Dougal, "I thank ye for the advice, and I'll no bother ye after all. Good night!"

[6960]

Sandy Drummond met MacDonald, an old friend, after the passage of some years, and the following conversation took place:

"I've been married since I saw you last, Mac."

"Married, eh? That's fine!"

"Oh, no so fine, Mac. She was a scold."

"Married to a scold, you say? That's bad!"

"Oh, no so bad, Mac. She had money."

"A wife wi' money! That's fine."

"No so fine, Mac. She was close wi' it."

"A wife wi' money and close wi' it. That's bad."

"Oh, no so bad, Mac. She built us a house wi' it."

"A house o' ye're own, ye say? That's fine."

"No so fine, Mac. The house burned down."

"The new house built wi' the wife's money burned down, Sandy? That's bad for sure!"

"Oh, no so bad, Mac. She was in it!"

[6961]

A Scotsman visiting America stood gazing at a fine statue of George Washington, when an American approached.

"That was a great and good man, Sandy," said the American; "a lie never passed his lips."

"Weel," said the Scot, "I praysume he talked through his nose like the rest of ye."

[6962]

There's the Scotchman who signs all telegrams he sends his girl Xerxes. In that way he gets in two kisses without paying for them.

[6963]

Vicar—"You know, Thomas, you set the younger men of the parish a bad example by going into public houses on Sunday. Why don't you take your gallon of beer home on Saturday night?"

Thomas—"Ah, sir; I couldna gang t' sleep wi' a gallon o' beer in the hoose."

[6964]

A hunter was returning home from the field without a thing in his bag and feeling quite dejected, when suddenly he spied a flock of ducks swimming in a little pond, with an old Scotch farmer watching them.

"How much do you want to let me take a pot shot at those ducks?" the hunter asked the Scotchman.

"Half a dollar," was the immediate reply. The hunter let fly with both barrels, killing fourteen ducks.

"Well," the hunter said, smiling, as he paid the farmer, "I guess I got the best of that bargain."

"Ah, I dinna ken," replied the Scotchman. "They're no my ducks."

[6965]

Sandy, thrown off his guard by the unusual kindness of London kin, said he would show his appreciation of their hospitality by sending them a choice chicken when he reached home.

Weeks passed, but no fowl put in an appearance. Having occasion to go to Dunfermline, a relative reminded Sandy of his promise.

"Ay, it was my intention to remember ye wi' a fine hen," said Sandy, "but when I got hame I found the bird was better!"

[6966]

"My son writes that he's in a tight place."

"What's the trouble?"

"He's a waiter in Edinburgh."

[6967]

A Scotchman accosted by a military picket:

"Who are you?" challenged the soldier.

"I'm fine," answered Sandy. "Hoo's yersel."

[6968]

"Why have Scotsmen a sense of humour?"

"Because it's a gift."

[6969]

Sandy–"Hoo is it, Jock, that ye mak sic an enairmous profit off yer potatoes when ye gie a special price to each freend?"

Jock–"Well, I tak a half-crown off the price because he's a freend o' mine; then I tak ten pounds off the hundred weight because I'm a freend o' his."

[6970]

The "Millennium Dawn" evangelists were about to start a campaign in a Scottish town. One of their missionaries approached an elderly native who was standing in front of a hoarding studying one of their startling posters.

"My friend," said the evangelist, "I assure you it is perfectly true what you read there: 'Thousands living to-day will never die.' There may be some in this very town."

"Some?" replied the other. "It's my opinion they're nearly a' here. I've suspeckit something o' the kind sin' ever I was appointed gravedigger. The folk in this toon'll no' dee —they'll be to fell! They live but they'll no' let live."

[6971]

Friend–"There's your friend, Miss MacGregor, over there. Why don't you go over and speak to her?"

Scot–"Wheest, mon; she has na paid her fare yet."

[6972]

Mabel–"Doesn't that Scottish boy ever take you to the cinema, now?"

Phyllis (bitterly–"No, I think he must have found a girl who can see pictures in the fire!"

[6973]

"Verily, Hector did you hear the latest Scotch joke?"

"Proceed, Alcibiades."

"A Scotchman just offered $25,-000 for the first person to swim the Atlantic."

[6974]

A Scotchman was leaving on a fortnight's business trip and called back as he left home: "Good-bye, all, and Katherine, dinna forget to mak' leetle Donald tak' his glasses off when he's na looking at naething."

[6975]

A Scotchman gave a waiter a tip. The horse lost.

[6976]

Sandy came home after an absence of several years and looked up his former sweetheart. He found that she had not yet married, and sweet memories began to surge through his romantic Scotch brain.

"Ah, Mary," Sandy murmured softly, "ye're just as beautiful as ye ever were, an' I ha'e never forgotten ye, my bonnie lassie."

"And ye, Sandy," Mary cried, with moisture brightening her pretty blue eyes, "and ye, Sandy, ye're just as big a liar as ever ye were, an' I believe ye just the same as ever I did."

[6977]

An Irishman was being tried for intoxication.

"Pat, where did you buy the liquor?" asked the judge.

"Your Honor, I did not buy it. A Scotchman gave it to me."

"Thirty days for perjury."

[6978]

An Aberdonian approached a London bus and asked the conductor: "Fat's the fare frae here to the Strand?"

"Tuppence!" was the reply.

The cannie Scot ran to the next stopping-place and asked his question again:

"Still tuppence!" It was the same bus.

Determined to save his penny the Aberdonian ran on yet another stage.

"Fat's the fare to the Strand?"

"Thrippence! You're going the wrong way!"

[6979]

A visitor from Aberdeen lost a shilling in London. He immediately notified the police. A little later he came up a street all torn up preparatory to the laying of new water mains.

"Mon alive," he cried, "but they're most thorough in this city."

[6980]

"Is McPherson in?"

"Aye, but he's very busy; he's sharpening the phonograph needle for the party tonight."

[6981]

Scotchmen are proverbial for their caution.

Mr. MacTavish attended a christening where the hospitality of the host knew no bounds except the several capacities of the guests. In the midst of the celebration Mr. Mac-Tavish rose up and made rounds of the company, bidding each a profound farewell.

"But, Sandy, man," objected the host, "ye're not going yet, with the evenin' just started?"

"Nay," said the prudent Mac-Tavish. "I'm no' goin' yet. But I'm tellin' ye good-night while I know ye all."

[6982]

In order to eke out their scanty income a worthy couple in Innerleithen turned their parlor into a café.

Some weeks afterwards the male partner was asked how the new venture was succeeding.

"Oh, we're gettin' on grand—

grand! A wee traveler body cam' in the ither day—but the wife hadna the kettle boilin'."

[6983]
The canny Scot wandered into the pharmacy.

"I'm wanting threepenn'orth o' laudanum," he announced.

"What for?" asked the chemist suspiciously.

"For twopence," responded the Scot at once.

[6984]
"Well," said the Englishman to the Scot, as they alighted from the London-Glasgow express, "it's been a long and tiring journey."

"Ay," said the Scot, "an' so it ought tae be, for the money."

[6985]
"Do you mean to say that Sandy is famous for his after-dinner speaking?"

"I'll say! He always manages to be speaking on the telephone when the waiter brings the check."

[6986]
"So you're Scotch. Do you know there's a little Scotch in me, too?"

"Yes, I can smell it."

[6987]
Clerk–"Oh, sir, there's a Scotchman out there who wants to buy ten cents worth of poison to commit suicide. How can I save him?"
The Boss–"Tell him it'll cost twenty cents."

[6988]
Rab McNabb was warned to wear his cap over his ears lest he freeze them.

"Nae, I've had nae use for the tabs since the accident," said Nab.

"What accident?"

"Wee Willie Thompson asked me would I hae a drink, and I did nae hear him."

[6989]
Harry Lauder said at one of the innumerable banquets given him by the Caledonians of America: "I am a Scot. The other day I met a man who asked me what a Scot was and I up and says: 'A Scot, my dear boy, is a man who keeps the Sabbath and everythin' else he can lay his hands on.'"

[6990]
A Scotsman bought a shilling ticket for a lottery, the first prize being a Pony and Trap. One night a knock came to the door and a voice called: "Are ye in, Tam?"

Tam went to the door and saw a village cronie standing there with a pony and trap.

"Weel, Tam, ye'll be pleased to hear that you've won the first prize."

Tam scratched his head, walked round and had a good look. "Aye," he said, "that's the pony and trap richt enough, but where's the whip?"

[6991]
A Scotsman, having inquired of a taxi-cab driver the fare to a certain place, offered to toss for double or quits, to which the driver agreed. "Heads!" called the Scotsman. "It's tails," said the driver. "Just ma luck!" said the Scotsman. "Noo I shall hae tae walk."

[6992]
It had always been MacLaughlin's ambition to own a fur coat. After years of skimping, he achieved his wish. As he was striding down the street a friend approached him.

"Morning, MacLaughlin," remarked the friend, his teeth chattering from the wintry blasts. "'Tis a cold day!"

MacLaughlin lifted his chin regally from the depths of his fur coat.

"Hm-m, I didna ken that," he replied carelessly. "I havena' looked at the newspaper to-day."

[6993]

A supercilious Englishman was talking to a Scotchman. "You know, in Scotland, the men eat oatmeal; and, in England, we feed it to our horses."

"An' that's the very reason that English horses an' Scotch men are the finest in the world!"

[6994]

Wedding Guest – "This is your fourth daughter to get married, isn't it?"

MacTight–"Ay; and our confetti's gettin' awfu' gritty."

[6995]

A Londoner was telling funny stories to a party of commercial men.

An old Scotsman, sitting in a corner seat, apparently took not the smallest notice, and no matter how loud the laughter, went on quietly reading his paper. This exasperated the story-teller, until at last he said: "I think it would take an inch auger to put a joke into a Scotsman's head."

A voice from behind the paper replied: "Ay, man, but it wid need tae hae a finer point than ony o' yer stories, a'm thinking!"

[6996]

An Aberdonian sat on his bed one Sunday morning solemnly contemplating some money which he had taken from the pocket of his week-day trousers. "Let me see," he said to himself, "fan I went oot on the spree wi' thae Englishers I had one and four-pence—a shillin', a

thripenny bit and a penny. Noo I've only got the shillin' and the thripenny bit. What on earth did I do with the ither penny?"

[6997]

Taximan–"I'll have a job findin' the other sixpence change for yer."

Caledonian–"Ah, weel, the nicht's young."

[6998]

A canny couple from the North when on a visit to London took a journey in "The Underground." While descending in the elevator the old man was looking at a notice which read "Spitting strictly prohibited—penalty forty shillings." When his wife whispered to him:

"Eh, John! I think I'm gaen to be sick."

"No' here, woman! no' here!" cried John: "look at the notice! It costs twa pounds just to spit!"

[6999]

"If you print any more jokes about Scotsmen I shall cease borrowing your paper," writes a man from Aberdeen.

[7000]

Jock–"And how do you like your radio, Mac?"

Mac–"Mon, it's grand, but the wee light's hard to read by."

[7001]

A Scotchman entered a hotel and inquired what the rates were. He was told that the charges were $5 a day for rooms on the first floor, $4 for rooms on the second, $3 on the third, and $2 on the top floor. The Scot after a moment's reflection started for the door, when the clerk asked him if he considered the charges too high. "No," replied Sandy, "it's the building that's no' high enough."

[7002]

The Scotsman had lost a pound note. Sadly he entered the advertisement office of the local newspaper and handed in the notice he wanted inserted in the "Lost and Found" column.

The clerk read: "Lost, a £ note. Sentimental value."

[7003]

A Scotchman wrote to a friend "Why don't you write? You can fill your pen at the bank."

[7004]

A Scotsman was stripping wallpaper from the walls of his house when a friend called to see him.

"Well, Sandy," said the visitor, "are ye goin' to have new paper?"

"Na, na," replied Sandy, "Ah'm just movin' to another house."

[7005]

MacGregor and MacPherson decided to become teetotalers, but MacGregor thought it would be best if they had one bottle of whisky to put in the cupboard in case of illness.

After three days MacPherson could bear it no longer and said: "MacGregor, ah'm not verra weel."

"Too late, MacPherson, ah was verra sick m'sel' all day yesterday."

[7006]

A Scotchman returned to his native land after a thirty-year absence. Preparatory to his leaving America he wrote and asked his brothers to meet him at the station, and upon his arrival at the home town was met by two bearded men whom he had difficulty in recognizing.

"Why the beards?" he asked. "Dinna ye remember, Donald?" replied they. "You took the razor with you."

[7007]

The man who invented slow motion movies got his idea while watching a Scotchman reach for a restaurant check.

[7008]

The minister of a certain parish in Scotland was walking one misty night through a street in the village, when he fell into a deep hole. There was no ladder by which he could make his escape, and he began to shout for help. A laborer passing heard his cries, and, looking down, asked who he was. The minister told him, whereabouts the laborer remarked:

"Weel, weel, ye needna kick up sic a noise. You'll no be needed afore Sawbath, an' this is only Wednesday necht."

[7009]

Little Sandy arrived home from school completely out of breath. His mother asked him what was the matter.

"I ran all the way home behind a tramcar and saved a penny," Sandy replied.

"Not bad, my boy," said his father, looking up from his paper. "But why didn't you run home behind a taxi and save a shilling?"

[7010]

Sandy McPherson was dying and for three days his devoted wife had never left his bedside. Her neglected household duties began preying on her mind, and she decided to leave her post for a short time.

"Ye'll nae dee while I'm gane, will ye, Sandy? But if ye should dee, dinna forget tae blaw oot the candle afore ye gae."

[7011]

"What's the shape of the earth?" asked the teacher, calling suddenly on Wee Wullie.

"Round," said Wee Wullie.

"How do you know it's round?" asked the teacher.

"Well," says Wullie, "it's square then; I dinna want ony argument aboot it."

[7012]

A Scotsman and a Jew were brought up before a magistrate charged with being drunk and incapable. Both pleaded "Not Guilty."

"What reason have you, constable, for thinking that the accused were drunk?" asked the magistrate.

"Well, sir," replied the policeman, "Macdonald was throwing his money about."

"Um! yes—I see! But what about the other prisoner?"

"Isaacs was throwing it back at him."

[7013]

Scots Gangster–"Na, then, Laddie, ye'd better pay up, or I'll be taking ye for a—a walk."

[7014]

Anxious Mother (whose son has just been saved from drowning)– "Are ye the mon who rescued our Angus? Where's his bonnet?"

[7015]

A Scotchman went to the races and bet 25 cents on a ten to one shot and won. The bookmaker paid him in quarters, and the Scotchman picked them up, one at a time and bit them.

"Why are you doing that?" asked the bookmaker. "Do you think we are counterfeiters?"

"Nay, mon," the Scotchman replied; "I'm only makin' sure I'm not getting the one I gave ye."

IRISH

[7016]

Mike–"That's a queer pair of stockings you have on, Pat—one red and the other green."

Pat–"Yes, and I've another pair like it at home."

[7017]

"Well, Denis, I hear as how ye were the best man at Mike's wedding."

"Well, no, mum, not exactly that. I wuzn't in the weddin'—I were jist there; so I wuzn't the best man. But I wuz as good as any man there, an' thot's no lie!"

[7018]

Pat–"What be yer charge fer a funeral notice in yer paper?"

Editor–"Fifty cents an inch."

Pat–"Good heaven! An' me poor brother was six feet high."

[7019]

"Pat, here's a dollar I borrowed of ye last wake."

"Bedad, Mike, I'd forgot all about it."

"Och, why didn't ye say so?"

[7020]

"What is the difference between a sigh, an auto, and a donkey, Pat?" asked Mike.

"I don't know," replied Pat.

"Well," said Mike, "a sigh is oh, dear! An auto is too dear."

"Well," said Pat, "and what's a donkey?"

"You dear!" exclaimed Mike, as he bounced off.

[7021]

He was a good natured Irishman and was one of a number of men employed in erecting a new building. The owner of the building, who knew him, said to him one day:

"Pat, didn't you tell me once that a brother of yours is a bishop?"

"Yes, sor," replied Pat.

"And you a hodcarrier! The good things of this life are not equally divided are they?"

"No, sor," said Pat, as he shouldered his hod. "Poor fellow! My brother couldn't do this to save his loife!"

[7022]

"Mike, did ye put out the cat, before ye crept into bed?"

"Sure I did."

"I don't belave it!"

"Well, if yez think I'm a liar, g'wan an' put her out yerself!"

[7023]

An Irishman got a job at an observatory. During his first night's duty he paused to watch a learned professor who was peering through a large telescope. Just then a star fell.

"Man alive!" exclaimed the astonished Irishman. "You're a foine shot."

[7024]

Among the conditions of sale by an Irish auctioneer was the following: "The highest bidder to be the purchaser, unless some gentleman bids more."

[7025]

In certain parts of the West Indies the Negroes speak English with a broad brogue. They are said to be descended from Irish adventurers shipwrecked at the time of the Spanish settlers.

A gentleman from Dublin, upon arriving at a West Indian port, was accosted by a burly negro fruit vendor with, "Th' top uv th' mornin' to ye, an' would ye be after wantin' to buy a bit o' fruit, sor?"

The Irishman stared at him in amazement.

"An' how long have ye been here?" he finally asked.

"Goin' on three months, yer Honor," said the vendor, thinking of the time he had left his inland home.

"Three months, is it? Only three months an' as black as thot? Faith, I'll not land!"

[7026]

"Well, Pat, do the twins make much noise nights?"

"Noise! Shure, each wan cries so loud yez can't hear the other."

[7027]

O'Donnel who kept the corner saloon was in the back room playing pinochle with the boys. Hennessey, his barkeeper, interrupted him with this question: "Is Mahoney good for a drink?" Without looking up from his cards O'Donnel answered: "Has he had it?" "He has," replied the barkeeper. "He is," said the boss.

[7028]

Passing a cemetery one day, the Irishman paused at a startling inscription on a tombstone. He read the words: "I still live." After scratching his head in bepuzzlement for a moment, the Irishman ejaculated:

"Bejabbers, if I was dead I'd be honest enough to own up to it!"

[7029]

The Parson—"I intend to pray that you may forgive Casey for having thrown that brick at you."

O'Grady—"Mebbe yer Riv'rence 'ud be saving toime if ye'd just wait till oi get well, an' thin pray fer Casey."

[7030]

Mrs. Flynn–"This neighborhood seems pretty noisy, Mrs. O'Brien."

Mrs. O'Brien–"Yis, the only time there's any peace here is whin the trucks drown the noise."

[7031]

Casey–"Finnegan has been married foive years, but sorra the chick or child has he got."

Cassidy–"Thrue for ye. I wonder is that hereditary in his family or hers."

[7032]

An Irishman, out of work, went on board a vessel, and asked the captain if he could give him a job.

"Well," grinned the captain, handing the Irishman a bit of rope, "if you can find four ends to that rope, I'll engage you."

"Four ends, yer Honor! Well, now," showing one end of the rope, "there's one end."

"That's right."

He took hold of the other end, and held it out. "An' there's two ends—right?"

"Exactly."

"An' one end an' two ends make three ends, Capting?'"

The captain laughed. "But I said four."

With a wide sweep of his arm, Pat threw the rope into the harbor water. "There's an end to the whole rope, sir—an' three ends an' one more end makes four ends!"

[7033]

Englishman–"I'll never forget my feelings the first time I had breakfast in America, when the waitress leaned over my shoulder, and whispered in my ear: 'Are you through with the cereal?' It was some time before I discovered that she meant: 'Have you finished your porridge?'"

American–"Wal, shortly after I landed in England a waiter came up to me at luncheon and said: 'How did you find your chop, sir?' I replied: 'Oh, I looked behind the potato and there it was,' before I understood that he was asking me how I liked it."

Scotsman–"That's nothing to what happened to me once. I was in lodgings in a small town in the West of Ireland. Half an hour after I had finished my supper an exceedingly pretty girl came into my room and said: "Will I strip, now sir?' I fled into my bedroom and locked the door, but I found out afterwards that Irish girls always talk about 'stripping the table,' when they meant 'clearing away the dishes.' "

[7034]

"I say, Mike, how would you like to be buried in a Jewish cimmitery?"

"Faith, an' I'd rather die first!" Mike replied.

[7035]

"Well, Pat, my good fellow," said a victorious general to a brave son of Erin after a battle; "and what did you do to help us gain this victory?"

"Du?" replied Pat, "may it please yer honor, I walked up bouldly to wun of the inimy, and cut off his fut."

"Cut off his foot! and why did you not cut off his head?" asked the general.

"Ah, an' faith, that was off already," says Pat.

[7036]

The Irish beggar shambled over, holding out his hand. "Please give a poor old blind man a dime, sor."

"But you can see out of one eye."

"Thin make it a nickel."

[7037]

Casey hurried down to where poor Riley's body lay, after Riley had fallen three stories from the building on which they were both working.

"Are ye dead, Pat?"

"That Oi am."

"Faith, an' ye're such a liar Oi don't know whether to belave yez or not."

Riley did his best to lift up his head. "That proves Oi'm dead, ye dirthy doubter; if Oi wuz alive, ye wouldn't dare to call me a liar!"

[7038]

The priest was writing the certificate at a christening, and paused in an endeavor to recall the date. He appealed to the mother. "Let me see, this is the nineteenth, isn't it?"

"The nineteenth, bejabers! Yer riv'rence must be losin' yer mind. This is only the elivinth I've had."

[7039]

"You're undoubtedly the biggest numbskull I've ever had the misfortune to employ in my coal yard. I can't teach you a thing."

"Well," said Mike, "I larnt wan thing since I've been wid ye!"

"Yes? And what's that?" asked his employer.

"That sivinteen hundred makes a ton!"

Mike did not lose his job.

[7040]

Two Irishmen arranged to fight a duel with pistols. One of them was distinctly stout, and when he saw his lean adversary facing him he raised an objection.

"Bedad!" he said, "I'm twice as big a target as he is, so I ought to stand twice as far away from him as he is from me."

"Be aisy now," replied his second. "I'll soon put that right."

Taking a piece of chalk from his pocket he drew two lines down the stout man's coat, leaving a space between them.

"Now," he said, turning to the other man, "fire away, ye spalpeen, and remember that any hits outside that chalk line don't count."

[7041]

"Pat, if Mr. Jones comes back before I return, tell him that I will meet him at two o'clock."

"Ay, ay, sir; but what shall I tell him if he doesn't come?"

[7042]

Rafferty bored ten feet into a mining claim, and then abandoned it. Another took it up, and at eleven feet struck gold. When Rafferty heard the news, he exclaimed:

"I'll never leave another claim until I've gone a foot further!"

[7043]

"Pat," said the manager of the factory, "I want you to report to me at 6 o'clock tomorrow morning. Here's an alarm clock."

The next morning arrived. Pat was met by a frowning manager.

"Well, what was the matter? Didn't the alarm clock go off?"

"Oh, yes, sorr, it went off all right, but the trouble was that it went off while I was asleep."

[7044]

Monaghan's friend appeared the day after the wake, looking as if he had been in a football game or had been hit by a pile driver.

"And did you enjoy yourself at the wake?" Monaghan asked.

"We sure had the divil's own time," replied Pat. "There was only one sound nose left in the party after it was over, and that one belonged to the tay kittle."

[7045]
An old Irishwoman sent a parcel to her son, in which she inclosed the following note:
"Pat, I am sending your waistcoat; to save weight I have cut all the buttons off. Your loving mother.
"P. S.—You will find them in the top pocket."

[7046]
"Why are yez decoratin', Mrs. Murphy?"
"Me b'y Denny is comin' home the day."
"I t'ought it wuz for foive years he was sint up?"
"He wuz; but he got a year off for good behayvure."
"An' sure, it must be a great comfort for ye to have a good b'y like that."

[7047]
The Irish drill sergeant was putting a squad of green recruits through the different movements. He gave them "right dress." Try as he would, he couldn't get a straight line. Finally in exasperation, he shouted: "What's the matter wid yez? Can't ye line up? That line is as crooked as a corkscrew. All of yez fall out and take a look at it."

[7048]
"I was sorry to hear ye were in a free-for-all fight, Patrick."
"Free for all, ye're sayin'? Maybe free for some, but not for me. Faith, an' it's ten dollars an' costs it cost me at coort."

[7049]
The concert hall was crowded. The Irish attendant unable to find a seat for the pretty young miss, explained the situation to her in the following words:
"Indade, miss, I should like to give you a sate, but the empty ones is all full."

[7050]
A man came up, in his curiosity, to the bell-ringer of an Irish church in a rundown neighborhood. "Can you tell me, my man, why the bell is ringing?"
"Yis, Oi kin that," returned the Irishman promptly. "It's because I'm a-pullin' of the rope, sor."

[7051]
Saloonkeeper–"Here, you haven't paid for that whisky you ordered."
Irishman–"What's that you say?"
Saloonkeeper–"I said you haven't paid for that whisky you ordered."
Irishman–"Did you pay for it?"
Saloonkeeper–"Of course I did."
Irishman–"Well, thin, what's the good of both of us paying for it?"

[7052]
"Phwat did you get for your birthday, Pat?"
"A pair of opera glasses."
"And are they any good?"
"Foine! Ye see that church about a mile from here? Well, these glasses bring it so close that ye can hear the organ playing."

[7053]
Mike tripped and fell into a deep drain. His companions rushed to his assistance and found him lying motionless at the bottom. Pat got down beside him and giving him a shake, asked: "Are ye dead, Mike?"
"No," replied Mike, "but I'm spaichless."

[7054]
An Irishman was planting shade trees when a passing lady said:
"You're digging out the holes, are you, Mr. Haggerty?"
"No, mum. Oi'm diggin' out the dirt an' lavin' the holes."

[7055]

Two Irishmen driving through the country noticed that many of the barns had weather-vanes in the shape of huge roosters.

"Pat," said one man to the other, "can you tell me why they always have a rooster and niver a hin on the top av thim barns?"

"Shure," replied Mike, "an' it must be because av the difficulty they'd have in collicting the eggs."

[7056]

"Ah, good mornin', Mrs. Murphy, and how is everythin'?"

"Sure, an' I'm havin' a great time uv it between me husband and the fire. If I keep me eye on the wan, the other is sure to go out."

[7057]

Mrs. O'Reilly went shopping for a new suit to lay her late husband out in, for Mr. O'Reilly had departed this vale of tears only the day before. Mrs. O'Reilly had a reputation for always getting her money's worth.

"Well, an' did you get him a nice suit o' clothes?" asked a neighbor, when Mrs. O'Reilly returned home.

"I sure did," was the answer. "An' a bargain it was, too, with an extra pair o' pants, an' all."

[7058]

"Drink," said the Irish preacher, "is the greatest curse of the country. It makes yer quarrel with yer neighbors. It makes yer shoot at yer landlord, and it makes yer miss him."

[7059]

"Pat, do you understand French?"

"Yis, if it's shpoke in Irish."

[7060]

Wealthy Citizen–"But I said distinctly in my advertisement that I wanted 'a reliable colored coachman,' and you are a red-faced Irishman."

Applicant–"But shure, sor, isn't red as reliable a color as black?"

[7061]

"Come on in, Mike," the genial owner of the estate beckoned to the workman hesitating at the gate.

"That's a fierce dog ye've got," said Mike dubiously, pointing to an airedale barking furiously just within the place.

"Don't you know a barking dog never bites?"

"Sure, an' I know it," said Mike. "What I'm wonderin' is, does thot dog know it?"

[7062]

An Irishman got a job in a railway station. When the first train came in, however, he forgot the name of the station, so he called out:

"Here ye are for where ye are going. All in there for here, come out."

[7063]

Pat–"Moike, do yez know why an Irishman hits the pepper-box on the bottom an' a Dutchman hits it on the side?"

Mike–"Begorra, Pat, Oi don't. Why is it?"

Pat–"Shure, an' it's to get the pepper out, Moike."

[7064]

An Irish judge charged a jury, "A man who'd maliciously set fire to a barn, and burn up a stable full of horses and mules, ought to be kicked to death by a jackass, and I'd like to be the one to do it!"

[7065]

A stranger accosted an Irishman walking along a roadway in New

Jersey. "Say, Pat, how far is it to Newark?"

"How did ye know my name?"

"I guessed it."

"Thin guess how far it is to Newark."

[7066]

"My lord," said the foreman of an Irish jury seriously, as he gave the verdict, "we find that the man who stole the mare is not guilty."

[7067]

An Irishman was painting a house and working with great rapidity. Some one asked him why he was in such a rush. "I'm trying to get through," the Irishman replied, "before the paint gives out."

[7068]

Rooney—"Which would ye sooner be in, Casey—an explosion or a collision?"

Casey—"In a collision."

Rooney—"Why?"

Casey—"Because in a collision, there ye are; but in an explosion, where are ye?"

[7069]

"Mrs. Flanagan," said the landlord, "I've decided to raise your rent."

"Ah, now," beamed Mrs. Flanagan. "It's the darlint ye certinly are. I wor wonderin' how I cud raise it meself, sur."

[7070]

One cold wet night a Dublin jarvey had to take a long journey.

"Wait a minute, Tim," said the friendly passenger, when he had paid his fare, "and I'll send you out a drink."

In a short time a maid appeared with a tumbler of whisky and water. The jarvey took a sip, then he looked at the maid suspiciously.

"Tell me now," he said, "which did you put in first, the whisky or the water?"

"The whisky, of course," said the maid indignantly.

"Ah well, maybe I'll come to it yet, at the bottom of the glass," replied the jarvey.

[7071]

The midday whistle had blown when Murphy shouted, "Has anyone seen me vest?"

"Sure, Murphy," said Pat, "and ye've got it on."

"Right and I have," replied Murphy, gazing solemnly at his bosom, "and it's a good thing ye seen it or I'd have gone home without it."

[7072]

An Irishman spent his last cent to come to this country. After hunting for work for a couple of weeks, he became discouraged, and walked to the Battery. Here he sat on the dock, looking out to sea.

He began thinking what a fool he had been to spend all his money to come from Ireland, when he might have stayed on the old sod and still had his money in his pocket.

Just then he noticed a diver, who had been working under the dock, come to the surface, clamber ashore, and begin unscrewing his helmet. When he had the headpiece off, he heaved a long breath.

"Well!" marveled the Irishman aloud. "If I'd 'a' known as much as thot man, I'd have walked over from Ireland myself, an' saved all thot money!"

[7073]

Pat bet Mike that he could carry a hod of bricks to the top of a fifty-foot building, with Mike sitting on top of the hod. When near the top, Pat made a misstep, and nearly dropped Mike to the stone walk below.

Arriving at the top, Pat said, "Begorra, I've won the bet."

"Yer have," said Mike sadly. "But whin ye shlipped, I was sure I had yez."

[7074]

Pat was dawdling along on his way to work, looking half-asleep. Mike overtook him and slapped him heartily on the back.

"What's wrong wid ye this fine morning?" he cried. "It's half-asleep that ye're looking."

Pat turned a bleary eye on his friend. "And it's tired I am after feeling," he said. "Wasn't I up half the night?"

"What was the trouble?" Mike asked, anxiously.

"It was the cat," replied Pat. "Wasn't I sitting there till gone two waiting for her to come in so I could put her out for the night?"

[7075]

"I can tell you," said Pat, "how much water runs over Niagara Falls to a quart."

"How much?" asked Mike.

"Two pints."

[7076]

"Me father and a man named Dooley have been fighting for twenty years, but now they've stopped."

"Why? Did they bury the hatchet?"

"No; they buried Dooley."

[7077]

An Irish saloon-keeper in New York's East Side found his cash was always short, so he said to his bartender one day: "Bill, did you take any money out of the cash drawer last night?"

"Yes, I took my carfare home."

The Irishman regarded him unfavorably. "An' whin did ye move out to Los Angeles?"

[7078]

The foreman looked the applicant for work up and down.

"Are you a mechanic?" he asked.

"No, sorr," was the answer, "Oi'm a McCarthy."

[7079]

Patrick was interviewing St. Peter at the Gates of Paradise.

"Sure, it's a phoine snap ye have here, Saint Payter, holding down this soft job cintury after cintury, niver being turned out by change of administration or civil sarvice rules. It's a phoine snap!"

"Ah, but you must bear in mind, Patrick," rejoined the guardian of the gates, "that in Paradise a million years are but a moment, and a million dollars are but a cent."

"Thin will ye be loaning me a cint?" asked Patrick.

"Certainly," assented St. Peter, "in a minute!"

[7080]

Parish Priest–"Well, Pat, I'm glad to see you out again after your long illness. You have had a bad time of it."

Pat–"Indeed then I have, your reverence."

Parish Priest–"And when you were so near Death's door did you feel afraid to meet God?"

Pat–"No, your reverence. It was the other Gentleman."

[7081]

Governor of Prison (to recaptured convict)–"Out with it, man. How did you effect your escape?"

Distressed Convict–"Well, sir, me young wife sent me a file concealed in a cake, and I'm not sure now whether I ate the cake and sawed me way out with the file or ate the file and sawed me way out with the cake."

[7082]

An Irishman, after reaching America, was full of homesick brag, in which nothing in America even approached things of a similar variety in Ireland. In speaking of the bees of the ould sod he grew especially roseate and said:

"Why, the baze in that counthry is twice as big as in this. Indade, they're bigger than that. They're as big as th' shape ye have in this counthry!"

"Bees as big as sheep!" said his incredulous listener. "Why, what kind of hives do you have to keep them in?"

"No bigger than the ones in this counthry," was the reply.

"Then how do the bees get into the hives?" he was asked.

"Well," replied the Irishman, "that's their own dom lookout."

[7083]

Pat–"Say, what caused the explosion at the plant the other day?"
Mike–"Oh, Casey was carrying a load of dynamite when the noon whistle blew."

[7084]

Milligan–"If I be afther lavin' security equal to what I take away, will yez trust me till nixt week?"
Sands (the grocer)–"Certainly."
Milligan–"Well, thin, sell me two av thim hams an' kape wan av thim till I come agin."

[7085]

Pat–"Oi wouldn't throw ye a rope if ye was drownin'."
Mike–"Oi wouldn't touch it if ye did."

[7086]

An Irish soldier was given leave of absence the morning after pay day. When his leave expired he didn't appear. He was brought at last before the commandant for sentence, and the following dialogue is recorded:

"Well, Murphy, you look as if you have been celebrating."

"Yes, sur."

"Have you any money left?"

"No, sur."

"You had $35 when you left the fort, didn't you?"

"Yes, sur."

"What did you do with it?"

"Well, sur, I was walking along and I met a friend and we went into a saloon and spint $8. Thin we came out and I met another friend and we spint $8 more, and thin I come out and we met another friend and we spint $8 more, and thin we come out and we met another bunch of friends, and I spint $8 more—and thin I come home."

"But, Murphy, that makes only $32. What did you do with the other $3?" Murphy thought. Then he shook his head slowly and said:

"I dunno, Colonel, I reckon I must have squandered that money foolishly."

[7087]

Two Irishmen met once, and referred to the illness of a third.

"Poor Michael Hogan! Faith, I'm afraid he's going to die," said one.

"And why would he die?" asked the other.

"Oh, he's got so thin! You're thin enough, and I'm thin—but, by my sowl, Michael Hogan is thinner than both of us put together."

[7088]

"I say, Pat, isn't one man as good as another?"

"Of course he is, and a great deal better."

[7089]

An English clergyman turned to a Scotchman and asked him: "What would you be were you not a Scot?"

The Scotchman said: "Why, an Englishman, of course!"

Then the clergyman turned to a gentleman from Ireland and asked him: "And what would you be were you not an Irishman?"

The man thought a moment and said: "I'd be ashamed of meself!"

[7090]

"You say you're a lover of peace, but then you go and throw a brick at Casey?"

"Yes, sir—an' he was wery peaceful, too, after I throwed it!"

[7091]

An Irishman who was a steadfast teetotaler unfortunately had a very red nose. One day he had to go into a saloon on business. A cigar salesman from out-of-town invited all in the place to drink, to which invitation all readily responded save the Irishman.

The salesman went to him, and slapping him on the shoulder, said: "I say, old man, what are you going to have?"

"I thank you, sir-r, but I niver dhrink," was the quiet reply.

"What, you never drink?" said the salesman with a sarcastic laugh. "Now, if you never drink, will you please tell me what makes that nose of yours so red?"

The impertinence of the questioner at once aroused the irascibility of the Irishman, and he replied: "Sir-r, it is glowing with

proid because it is kept out of other people's business."

[7092]

"Do ye know O'Ryan?"

"I know him well."

"Can a person believe what he says?"

"Yis an' no. I've found out that, if he tells ye the truth, ye can believe iv'ry word of it; but whin he lies, ye'd better have no confidence in him at all."

[7093]

An Irishman was sitting in a station smoking, when a woman came in, and sitting beside him, remarked:

"Sir, if you were a gentleman, you would not smoke here!"

"Mum," he said, "if ye was a lady ye'd sit farther away."

Pretty soon the woman burst out again:

"If you were my husband, I'd give you poison!"

"Well, mum," returned the Irishman, as he puffed away at his pipe, "If you wuz me wife, I'd take it."

[7094]

When the priest asked Pat why he did not see him in church the day before, the communicant answered: "Dunno, your riverince, unless it was because I wasn't there."

[7095]

"Sure, Oi'll write me name on the back o' your note, guaranteein' ye'll pay ut," said Pat, smiling pleasantly as he indorsed Billup's note, "but Oi know doomed well ye won't pay ut. We'll have a laugh at th' ixpinse of the bank."

[7096]

An Irish crier at Ballinasloe was ordered to clear the Court. He did so with the following words:

"Now then, all ye blackguards that isn't lawyers must leave the Court."

[7097]

Pat had opened his first bank account and had taken to paying most of his debts by check. One day the bank sent him a statement, together with a packet of canceled checks. Of the statement Pat made neither head nor tail, but the returned checks greatly pleased him. "Mike," he said to a friend, "sure an' it's a smart bank I'm doin' business wid now."

"How's that?"

"Why, Oi paid all me bills wid checks, an' be jabbers if the bank wasn't slick enough to get ivery check back for me."

[7098]

"Your money or your life!" growled the footpad.

"Take me life," responded the Irishman. "I'm savin' me money for me old age."

[7099]

"Rah for Ireland!" yelled Pat.

"Rah for hell!" roared a disgusted Tory.

"Iverywan for his own country!" came back Pat.

[7100]

An English M.P. was once accosted by a distinctly drunk Irishman in the lobby of the House of Commons.

"Sir," said the Irishman: "you're a fool." "Sir," retorted the Englishman, "You're drunk." "I may be," replied the Irishman, "but I'll be sober tomorrow, and you'll still be a fool."

[7101]

"Come and have a dhrink, boys."

Pat came up and took a drink of whisky.

"How is this, Pat?" asked a bystander. "How can you drink whisky? Sure it was only yesterday ye towld me ye was a taytotler."

"Well," said Pat, evidently somewhat disconcerted, "you're right, Mister Kelly—it's quite right ye are —I am a taytotler, it's thrue, but I —I—I'm not a bigoted one!"

[7102]

Mike–"The trouble with Casey is he has no backbone."

Pat–"Faith, he has backbone enough if he'd only bring it to the front."

[7103]

"Well, Pat," the doctor greeted him breezily, "what can I do for you?"

"Faith, sure an' if I knowed thot, I wouldn't have to be payin' you two dollars fer tellin' me."

[7104]

The Irishman had been having a great argument and meant to finish off his opponent once and for all.

"The sooner I never see your face again," he said, "the better it will be for both of us when we meet."

[7105]

Doctor–"Your husband's not so well today, Mrs. Maloney. Is he sticking to the simple diet I prescribed?"

Mrs. Maloney–"He is not, sorr. He says he'll not be after starvin' himself to death just for the sake of livin' a few years longer!"

[7106]

Pat–"If wan af us gets there late, and the other isn't there, how will he know if the other wan has been there and gone, or if he didn't come yet?"

Mike–"We'll aisily fix thot. If Oi get there furrst I'll make a chalkmark on the sidewalk, and if you get there furrst you'll rub it out."

[7107]

"And it is upon the oaths of them two witnesses yer Honor is going to condimn me for theft?" asked Pat.

"Certainly," said the judge, "their testimony was ample to convince the jury of your guilt. Two witnesses saw you take the things."

"Oh, murther?" exclaimed Pat, "to condimn me on the oaths of two spalpeens who swear they saw me take the goods, whin I can bring forth a hundred who will swear they didn't see me do it."

[7108]

"Pat, why in the world do you drink so much?"

"Well, it's this way, yer Honor. Oi eat onions to kill the smell of the whisky, an' thin Oi have to drink more whisky to kill the smell of the onions."

[7109]

"The sun is all very well," said an Irishman, "but the moon is worth two of it; for the moon affords us light in the night-time, when we *want* it, whereas the sun's with us in the day-time, when we have *no occasion for it.*"

[7110]

American Traveler (to Hall-Porter of an Irish country hotel)–"How many mails a day are there in this hotel?"

Hall-Porter–"Three, sir; breakfast, dinner, and tay."

[7111]

Magistrate (to old offender)– "You here again?"

Old Offender–"Yes, your Honor."

Magistrate–"What's brought you here?"

Old Offender–"Two policemen, your Honor."

Magistrate–"Come, come, I know that. Drunk again, I suppose?"

Old Offender–"Yes, your Honor, both of them."

[7112]

The Irishman, hearing a rumor in the town that the bank in which he kept his savings had suspended payment, rushed round to see the cashier.

"Sure an' begorrah," he demanded, "Oi wish to draw out my money."

"Certainly, sir," replied the clerk. "How would you like it?"

"Oh, indade," said Pat. "Oi don't want it at all if you've got it. But if you haven't, Oi must have it!"

[7113]

An Irishman, who was an eligible bachelor, visited a widow in his district every evening and had tea with her. A friend suggested that he should marry the lady.

"I have often thought about it," he said, "but where should I spend my evenings then?"

[7114]

Four good fellows, old friends, met after long years in an Irish provincial town. They visited an inn and had several drinks. Then all four left for the railway station. On arrival at the train, three of the four got in and the train pulled out, leaving the fourth fellow standing on the platform, laughing until he was weak.

Station Master–"What the devil are you laughing at?"

Fourth Fellow–"Shure, they were supposed to be seeing ME off."

[7115]

The man finished writing his letter with the words: "I'd tell you more, but there's a snooping Irishman looking over my shoulder and reading every word I write."

"You're a liar!" the Irishman exclaimed.

[7116]

An Irishman, newly appointed crier in the county court in California, where there were many Chinese, was ordered by the judge to summon a witness to the stand.

"Call for Ah Song!" was the command.

Pat was puzzled for a moment. He glanced slyly at the judge, and found him as grave as an undertaker. Then, turning to the spectators, he blandly simpered:

"Gentlemen, would any of you favor his Honor with a song?"

[7117]

An Irishman who was rather too fond of strong drink was asked by the parish priest:

"My son, how do you expect to get into Heaven?"

The Irishman replied:

"Shure, and that's aisy! When I get to the gates of Heaven I'll open the door and shut the door, and open the door and shut the door, an' keep on doing that till St. Peter gets impatient and says, 'For goodness' sake, Mike, either come in or stay out!'"

[7118]

"I say, Pat, what are you about —sweeping out the room?"

"No," answered Pat, "I am sweeping out the dirt, and leaving the room."

[7119]

A gentleman riding with an old Irishman came in sight of an old gallows and to display his wit said: "Pat, do you see that?"

"To be sure I do," replied Pat.

"And where would you be today if the gallows had its due?"

"I'd be riding alone," replied Pat.

[7120]

Percy–"What do you think of Brown?"

Patrick–"He is one of these people that pat you on your back before your face and hit you in the eye behind your back."

[7121]

Sullivan and Foley got O'Connor into a card game. After a few minutes of play, Sullivan said, "Listen, Foley, I was passing Tiffany's jewelry store yesterday and—" He got no further. O'Connor cut him short with, "If you lead a diamond after that, I'll wreck the both of ye."

[7122]

O'Leary's wife awoke in the small hours to hear him stealthily moving things about in the kitchen.

"What might ye be lookin' for, darlin'?" she asked.

"Nothing," said O'Leary, "just nothing."

"Oh!" said his wife, helpfully. "Then ye'll find it in the bottle where the whisky used to be."

[7123]

Pat–"After all, it's a great pleasure to be missed by someone."

Mike–"Shure it is, Pat; if yez can be there t' enjy it."

[7124]

" 'Tis easy to see," said the tourist to Paddy, who was driving him around, "that your parents came from Ireland."

"No, sir, they did not," replied Paddy.

"What! Do you mean to say your parents did not come from Ireland?"

"No, sir; you are mistaken," replied Paddy; "they're there yit."

[7125]

Mrs. Casey—"An' phwat are yez doin' wid thot incoom-tax paper, Casey?"

Casey—"Oi'm thryin' to figger out how much money Oi save by not havin' anny."

[7126]

"An' poor O'Sull got sixteen years in Sing Sing."

"For phwhat?"

"For hommycide, I belave."

"Oh, shure that's nothing; I thought it might be for killin' somebody."

[7127]

A very beautiful lady, who was also rather vain, once wished to praise Ireland, and said to an assembled group of sons of Erin:

"I really think I was meant for an Irishwoman."

A gallant and witty old Irishman immediately responded with:

"Faith, madam, thousands would stand behind me in sayin' you was meant fer an Irishman!"

[7128]

Mike—"This is a great country, Pat."

Pat—"And how's that?"

Mike—"Sure, th' paper sez yez can buy a foive-dollar money order for eight cints."

[7129]

Pat—"Have yez an almanac, Moike?"

Mike—"I have not."

Pat—"Thin we will have to take the weather as it comes."

[7130]

"Hullo, Pat, I hear yer workin' part time. How's that?"

"Yer roight. I'm workin' on half toime down to the coal yards. Half a loaf is better 'n none."

[7131]

Mrs. Murphy—"How's yer husband arfer the accident?"

Mrs. O'Brien—"Faith, sumtoimes he's better an' sumtoimes he's worse, but from the way he swears and yills an' takes on whin he's betther, Oi think he's betther whin he's worse."

[7132]

In a Pacific Coast town there had been a slight earthquake shock, and Messrs. Clancy and Callahan had both felt it.

"Patrick," said Mr. Callahan solemnly, "what did ye think whin first the ground began to trimble?"

"Think?" ejaculated Mr. Clancy with scorn. "What man that has the use of his legs to run wit' and his lungs to roar wit' would be after thinkin' at a toime like thot?"

[7133]

It was a college town, and he was a freshman calling on a young lady he had known as a boy. The servant who admitted him asked for his name.

"Say an old friend"—very airily—"Amicus."

Bridget said, "Yis, sor," and retired; but in a moment returned to ask:

"If you plaze, sor, fwhat sort of a cuss did yez say it that yez wuz?"

[7134]

Mistress—"Well, Bridget, and how is your husband?"

Laundress—"Shure, an' he's all used up, mum."

Mistress—"Why, what ails him?"

Laundress—"Indade, thin, mum, last night he had sich bad dreams that he couldn't slape a wink all night, mum."

[7135]

Patrick had a big laugh. He saw a bull attack a man, and had to hold on to his sides with both hands, the scene was so funny. After a while the animal turned his attention in another direction, and poor Patrick, after exploring the heights, came down with a thump on the other side of the fence. He rubbed his wounds, and as he trudged along the worse for wear, he said to himself, "Faith, I'm glad I had my laugh when I did, or I wouldn't have had it at all."

[7136]

A bishop was traveling along and encountered an Irishman turning a windlass which hauled up ore out of a shaft. It was his job to do this all day long. His hat was off and the sun was pouring down on his unprotected head.

"Don't you know the sun will injure your brain if you expose it in that manner?" said the good man.

The Irishman wiped the sweat off his forehead and looked at the clergyman. "Do ye think I'd be doin' this all day if I had any brains?" he said, and gave the handle another turn.

[7137]

"Here I've been roasting over a hot stove," cried Bridget to Mike upon his return from work, "while you've been passing the day in that nice cool sewer!"

[7138]

At a meeting of a society composed of men from the Emerald Isle, a member made the following motion: "Mr. President, I move yee's that we whitewash the ceiling green in honor of the old flag."

[7139]

An Irishman was once brought up before a magistrate, charged with marrying six wives. The magistrate asked him how he could be so hardened a villain.

"Please, your Worship," said Pat, "I was just trying to get a good one."

[7140]

"Good morning, ma'am," began the temperance worker. "I'm collecting for the Inebriates' Home and——"

"Why, me husband's out," replied Mrs. McGuire, "but if ye can find him anywhere's ye're welcome to him."

[7141]

Since one foot was somewhat larger than the other, Pat had to have his shoes specially made for him. When he came to try on a new pair one day, he inadvertently tried to put the small shoe on the larger foot.

"Drat it!" he exclaimed, "I told the feller to make one shoe larger than the other an' here he's gone an' made one smaller than the other!"

[7142]

Standing by the entrance of a large estate in the suburbs of Dublin are two huge dogs carved out of granite.

An Englishman going by in a motor thought he would have some fun with the Irish driver.

"How often, Pat, do you feed those two big dogs?"

"Whenever they bark, sir," was the straightforward reply.

[7143]

An Irish clergyman was once lecturing a married couple about the disgraceful way they quarreled.

"Your cat and dog get on better together than you two," he said.

"Faith, then, your Reverence," was the reply, "if you'll tie them together you'll soon change your mind."

[7144]

An Irishman was carried to the hospital in an unconscious condition after a terrible fall. The surgeon made a brief examination, but shook his head significantly, and turned sympathetically to the anxious wife.

"Madam," he said, "I am sorry to tell you that your husband is dead."

"No I ain't," said the supposed corpse, opening one eye.

"Hush up, Terence," said the wife, "don't the doctor know better than you?"

[7145]

An Englishman and an Irishman lived in a coast town, and both owned boats. One day the Englishman decided to christen his, and on the stern painted: "Henry the Eighth."

"An' wot the divvle will I name mine?" mused the Irishman. Rejecting the suggestion of the others that he call his "George the Fifth," he became suddenly inspired, got out brush and paint and inscribed the legend:

"March th' Seventeenth."

[7146]

Pat determined to pass his favorite tavern on his way home. As he approached it he became somewhat shaky, but, after plucking up courage, he passed it. Then after going about fifty yards, he turned, saying to himself: "Well done, Pat, me bye. Come back and I'll treat you."

[7147]

The following notice was posted in a pleasure boat belonging to a steamship company on the Suir, Ireland. "The chairs in the cabin are for the ladies. Gentlemen are requested not to make use of them till the ladies are seated."

[7148]

They were trying an Irishman, charged with a petty offense, in an Oklahoma town, when the judge asked: "Have you any one in court who will vouch for your good character?"

"Yis, your Honor," quickly responded the Celt, "there's the sheriff there."

Whereupon the sheriff evinced signs of great amazement.

"Why, your Honor," declared he, "I don't even know the man."

"Observe, your Honor," said the Irishman, triumphantly, "observe that I've lived in the country for over twelve years an' the sheriff doesn't know me yit! Aint' that a character for ye?"

[7149]

Counsel to Irish Witness—"You're a nice sort of fellow you are."

Irish Witness—"I'd say the same about you, Sir, only I'm on my oath."

[7150]

Two Irishmen were among a class that was being drilled in marching tactics. One was new at the business, and, turning to his companion, asked him the meaning of the command "Halt!"

"Why," said Mike, "when he says 'Halt,' you just bring the foot that's on the ground to the saide av the foot that's in the air, an' remain motionless."

[7151]

"As I was going over the bridge the other day," said an Irishman, "I met Pat Hewins. 'Hewins,' says I, 'how are you?'

"'Pretty well, thank you, Donnelly,' says he.

"'Donnelly,' says I, 'that's not my name.'

"'Faith, then, no more is mine Hewins.'

"So with that we looked at each other agin, an' sure enough it was nayther of us."

[7152]

McGinniss was dying. The lawyer came to make his will; and his wife, Bridget McGinniss, saw to it that she sat in on this important ceremonial.

"State your debts as quickly as possible," said the man of law.

"Tim Reilly owes me forty dollars," moaned the sick man.

"Good," said the prospective widow.

"Jawn O'Neill owes me thirty-sivin dollars."

"Sensible to the last," beamed the wife.

"To Michael Callahan I owe two hundred dollars."

"Blessed mither of God! Hear the man rave!"

[7153]

A lady who owned and was very proud of a marble bust of Diana, and who had cautioned her Irish servant never to touch it, as she would do the dusting herself, unfortunately had an accident one day and the piece fell to the floor and was broken.

Bridget found her mistress wringing her hands and bewailing the catastrophe.

"Oh!" cried the lady, "I always knew that something dreadful would happen to it! It is Kismet! It is Kismet!"

"And phwat is Kismet, mam?" asked the servant.

"Fate, Bridget, fate."

The following Sunday while Bridget was walking in the park with her young man, he noticed that she seemed lame, and asked what was the matter.

"Arrah, Moike, I've corns on me Kismet!"

"What's your Kismet?" he asked.

"Me 'fate,' shure."

[7154]

Pat—"Have you christened your new baby yet?"

Mike—"We have."

Pat—"An' phwat did you call it?"

Mike—"Hazel."

Pat—"Sure, and with 223 Saints to name the kid after, ye had to go and name it after a nut."

[7155]

Doctor—"Did that cure for deafness really help your brother?"

Pat—"Sure enough; he hadn't heard a sound for years and the day after he took that medicine, he heard from a friend in America."

[7156]

Pat and Mike slept together when Pat went to visit his friend. The next morning they were checking up on how each had slept.

"Well, Pat, did y' hear the thunder last night?"

"No, Mike. Did it railly thunder?"

"Sure it did, as if hiven an' airth would come together."

"Why didn't y' wake me, Mike? Y' know I can't never slape when it thunders."

[7157]
Druggist—"What a bad cold you have, Mr. Casey. Can I offer you anything for it?"
Casey—"You may have it for nothing if you want it."

[7158]
Said an Irish justice to a blustering prisoner on trial: "We want nothing from you, sir, but silence, and very little of that."

[7159]
Mike—"So you believe in socialism, now, Pat?"
Pat—"Sure I do, it's the only way; divide up everything equal."
Mike—"You mean that if you had two horses you would give me one?"
Pat—"Sure I would."
Mike—"And if you had two cows, would you give me one?"
Pat—"Of course I would."
Mike—"And if you had two pigs, would you give me one?"
Pat—"You go to hell. You know I *got* two pigs."

[7160]
An Irishman got on a surface car the other day, with a pipe in his mouth. The conductor said, "Don't you see that sign up there, 'No smoking allowed?'"
"I'm not smokin' aloud."

[7161]
A hungry Irishman went into a restaurant on Friday and said to the waiter:
"Have yez any stewed whale?"
"No."
"Have yez any fried sharks?"
"No."
"All right," said the Irishman, "then, be gobbs, bring me a beefsteak smothered wid onions. The Lord knows I asked for fish."

[7162]
"I wish, Reverend Father," said Pat Curran to Father O'Leary, "that you were St. Peter, and had the keys to heaven, because then you could let me in."
"By my honor and conscience," replied Father O'Leary, "it would be better for you that I had the keys of the other place, for then I could let you out."

[7163]
Mrs. Casey (with fashion paper)—"What are aigrettes, Mike?"
Casey—"Weren't yes ever in sassiety, woman? Shure, it's what ye send when ye can't go."

[7164]
While Colonel Gilman, with the Middle Tennessee Regiment, was occupying Nashville during the Civil War, he stationed sentries and patrols in all the principal streets of the city.
One day an Irishman who had not been long enlisted was put on duty at a prominent crossing, and he kept a sharp and faithful watch. Presently a citizen came along.
"Halt! Who goes there?"
"A citizen," was the response.
"Advance and give the countersign."
"I have not the countersign," replied the indignant citizen, "and the demand for it at this time and place is unusual."
"Well, begorrah! ye don't pass this way until ye say Bunker Hill."
The citizen, appreciating the situation, smiled and advanced to the sentry, and cautiously whispered the magic words.
"Right! Pass on!" and the wide-awake sentinel resumed his beat.

[7165]

One of the bosses at Bethlehem Steel Corporation had to lay off an argumentative Irishman named Pat, so he saved discussion by putting the discharge in writing. The next day Pat was missing, but a week later the boss was passing through the shops and he saw him again at work. Then, the following colloquy occurred:

"Didn't you get my letter?"

"Yis, sur, Oi did," said Pat.

"Did you read it?"

"Sure, sur, Oi read it inside and Oi read it outside," said Pat, "and on the inside yez said I was fired and on the outside yez said: 'Return to Bethlehem Steel Corporation in five days.'"

[7166]

"Pwhut's a pessimist, Mike?"

"He's a feller phwat burns his bridges behind him an' thin crosses thim before he comes to thim."

[7167]

An Englishman went to some Irish races and bet on a race in which seven horses were running. Getting excited as the horses appeared, he said to his Irish friend who was watching the race through glasses:

"Where is my horse?"

"I don't know," replied the friend, "I'm only watching the first six."

[7168]

Englishman—"Well, Tim, supposing the Devil were to come here now, which do you think he'd take, you or me?"

Tim—"He'd take me, sir."

Englishman—"What makes you think that?"

Tim—"Because he'd be sure of your honor any time."

[7169]

A good Irish mother stepped into the telegraph office to send a message to her son, who was away on a trip. She seemed in some hesitation as she looked at the telegraph blank, so that the clerk, thinking perhaps she did not know how to write, obligingly offered to write the message at her dictation.

"Faith, an' I couldn't do that at all," was the answer. "Me boy wouldn't know yer writing."

[7170]

Pat, the new gardener, gazed wonderingly at the shallow basin containing water on the lawn.

"What's that for?" he asked the housewife.

"That's a bird bath," he was informed.

"Now, don't ye be a-foolin' me. What is it really?"

"A bird bath. Don't you believe me?"

"No," declared Pat with a shake of his head. "I don't believe there's a bird alive what can tell Saturday from any other night."

[7171]

It is sometimes difficult to fill a jury panel with persons wholly unprejudiced regarding the case to be heard.

During a certain trial the judge asked McGinnis if he had formed any opinion as to the guilt or innocence of the prisoner.

"Oi have not," replied the juryman.

"Have you any conscientious scruples against capital punishment?" was the next question.

Said McGinnis emphatically: "Not in this case, yer Honor."

[7172]

The main difference between an Irishman and a Dutchman is, when a Dutchman dies, he's dead; but when an Irishman dies, they have to watch him for three days and three nights.

[7173]

Michael Dugan, a journeyman plumber, was sent by his employer to the Hightower mansion to repair a gas-leak in the drawing-room. When the butler admitted him he said to Dugan:

"You are requested to be careful of the floors. They have just been polished."

"They's no danger iv me slippin' on thim," replied Dugan. "I hov spikes in me shoes."

[7174]

The Irish foreman of a gang of railway men was walking along his section of the line when he found one of his men sound asleep. With a smile, he said: "Slape on, ye idle spalpeen, slape on. So long as ye slape ye've got a job, but when ye wake up ye're out of work."

[7175]

An Englishman traveling in Kilkenny, arriving at a ford, hired a boat to take him across. In crossing he asked the boatman if any one had ever been lost in the passage. "Never," replied Pat; "my brother was drowned here last week, but we found him the next day."

[7176]

A priest bumped into Pat at the swinging doors of a barroom and said: "Sorry to see you coming out of such a place, my man!"

"Ver' well, we'll go right back in, Father. Anyshing t'blige."

[7177]

Pat wanted to borrow some money from Michael, who happened to have a small boy with him at the moment. "'Tis a fine kid you have there, Mike," said Pat. "A magnificent head and noble features. Could you loan me ten?"

"I could not," replied Mike. "'Tis me wife's child by her first husband."

[7178]

The Irish at home, in their little Emerald Isle are great sticklers for form, display and ceremony at wedding feasts. At one, where the groom was close-fisted and the preparations did not come up to the expectations of the invited guests a woman exclaimed with indignation, "I'd sell every stitch to me back, in order to get married dacently!"

[7179]

An Irish clergyman once horrified his congregation by assuring them, in a voice hoarse with emotion, that in a few years they would all be "smoldering in their graves."

[7180]

Pat, one day, walking down the street, noticed a green bird in a cage. Thinking to pet it he stroked its head. The bird turned quickly, screaming, "Hello! What do you want?" Pat shied off like a frightened horse, lifting his hat and bowing politely as he stuttered out: "Ex-excuse me s-sir, I thought you was a burrd!"

[7181]

An Irish country gentleman taking a walk over his estate, before breakfast, on turning a sharp corner, came face to face with a notorious poacher. The man walked straight up to him and said, "Good morning, Sir, and what brought you out so early?"

"I came out to see if I could

get an appetite for my breakfast. But what are you doing here, Paddy?" said the gentleman suspiciously.

"Sure, Sir," replied Paddy, "I just strolled out to see if I could get a breakfast for my appetite."

[7182]

An Irish evangelist always addressed his hearers as "dear souls," but he came to grief, when, addressing an audience in Ireland, he called them "dear Cork souls."

[7183]

The two Irishmen, newly arrived in America, had put up in a small room in Hoboken. One night, pestered with mosquitoes, they kept slapping at their faces and arms, trying to keep the pests off until they could get to sleep. Finally, about two o'clock in the morning, when they were both more than weary from their efforts, a firefly happened to sail through the open window.

"It's no use, Pat, me lad," said one. "Here comes one o' the critters a-searchin' fer us wid a lantern!"

[7184]

The penitent Pat revealed in the confessional the clandestine kiss imprinted upon the lips of Sullivan's consort.

"So you committed this sin, did you, Pat?" said the priest. "Did you kiss Mrs. Sullivan more than once?"

"Father," said Pat. "I am here to confess, not to brag!"

[7185]

A Scotchman and an Irishman were arguing as to the merits of their families. The Scotchman had the floor first. "I tell ye laddie, I'm sprung from the best stock in the world—from the stock of the kings of Scotland. I've got royal blood in my veins. An' what stock are you sprung from?"

"I come from the Caseys," said the Irishman simply. "They niver sprung from nobody—they sprung at 'em!"

[7186]

An Irishman who had accidentally broken a pane of glass was hurrying away as fast as he could, when, unfortunately for him, the proprietor appeared unexpectedly and seized him by the collar.

"Aha, my lad," exclaimed the outraged owner, "I've caught you breaking my window, now haven't I?"

"True for you, sir," replied the Irishman. "But sure did you not see me making off home as hard as I could for the money to pay for it?"

[7187]

"Can you tell me what steam is?" asked the examiner.

"Why, sure, sir," replied Patrick confidently. "Steam is—why—er—it's wather thos's gone crazy wid the heat."

[7188]

A motorist, on holiday in Ireland, was driving through Galway when he found himself lost. He stopped the car and called to a villager farther down the road.

"Can you tell me the way to Ballinasloe?" he asked.

The Irishman scratched his head.

"Sure, yer honor, you go down the road about ten miles, and then turn to the right——" Here he stopped and thought again. "No, you go back the way you've come and turn to the left——" Again he stopped. Then with a sudden burst of confidence, he added:

"Begorrah, if Oi was going to Ballinasloe Oi wouldn't start from here."

[7189]

"How about carrying more bricks in a hod than that, O'Shaughnessey?" said the Irish foreman.

"I can't—I feel sick—I'm trembling all over."

"Get busy with the sieve, then."

[7190]

"Biddy," says Pat, timidly, "did ye iver think o' marryin'?"

"Shure, now," says Biddy, looking demurely at her shoe, "shure, now, the subject has niver entered me mind at all, at all."

"It's sorry Oi am," says Pat, and he turned away.

"Wan minute, Pat," said Biddy, softly. "Ye've set me thinkin'."

[7191]

"Mike, I wish I knew where I was goin' to die. I'd give a thousand dollars to know the place where I'm going to die."

"Well, Pat, what good would it do if yez knew?'

"Lots," said Pat. "Shure I'd never go near that place."

[7192]

A Jew and an Irishman had argued hotly every day about the eternal life. The Jew fell mortally ill and was buried at sea, coal being used to weight the body according to age-long custom.

"Egorra, Oi knew where he was bound for all the toime," was Pat's comment, "but Oi niver dr'amed the h'athen would have to tote his own fuel!"

[7193]

"This bed is not long enough for me," said a tall Englishman, upon being ushered into a bedroom by an Irish attendant at a cheap hotel.

"Why, ye ain't taller than six feet, an' this bed is all of that," comforted the Hibernian.

"Yes, but I don't want my head and feet to be bumping the top and bottom of the bed all night, old thing."

"Ah, sir," said Pat shrewdly, "ye needn't worry. For the bed'll have two feet added to it, whin ye get in."

[7194]

A lady having her home remodeled called in a carpenter of Irish extraction and inquired if he was a carpenter.

"I am," said Pat.

"Can you do all kinds of work?"

"Sure I can," was the answer.

"Can you make a Venetian blind?"

"I can."

"How would you go about it?"

"I'd stick me thumb in his eye," said Pat.

[7195]

Casey–"I was much moved by a speech I heard yestiddy."

"Wot was it?"

"A park cop said 'gettinblazes-outofhere!'"

[7196]

Stopping with a friend near a military reservation, an Irishman was startled the first evening to hear the loud report of the sunset gun as the colors were hauled down.

"What was that?" he asked.

"That's sunset," was the laconic answer.

"Bejabbers, but the sun never goes down in ould Ireland with a bang loik that!"

[7197]

The good Father came upon Pat, the town disgrace, in a highly inebriated condition, tacking skillfully from telephone post to gate, and back again. "Pat, Pat, drunk again?"

"Are ye? So'm I, Father."

"Tut, tut, this is no time for levity. You in this beastly condition, Pat, after faithfully promisin' me two weeks ago, that you would nevermore get drunk—an' after takin' the pledge. It's a burnin' shame to you, an' a sin against God an' the Church, and sorry I am to be obliged to say so."

"Father Daly," said Pat, in a tone half tipsy, half laughing, "do ye say ye are sorry to see me so?"

"Yes, indade I am."

"Are you sure ye're very sorry?"

"Yis, very, very sorry."

"Well, thin, Father Daly, if you're very, very, very sorry—I'll forgive you!"

[7198]

Two Irishmen, meeting one day, were discussing local news.

"Do you know Jim Skelly?" asked Pat.

"Faith," said Mike, "an' I do."

"Well," said Pat, "he has had his appendix taken away from him."

"Ye don't say so!" said Mike. "Well, it serves him right. He should have had it in his wife's name."

[7199]

An artist who occupied a studio on the top floor of a large building was disposed to be very pleasant to the janitress.

"How many children have you, Mrs. O'Flarity?" he asked her one morning as she was polishing the doorknob.

"It's siven I have, sir," she replied, "and lucky I am, too. Bless 'em. Four by the third wife of me second husband, three by the second wife of me furst."

[7200]

The opera "Faust" was being presented in Dublin, and the scene had been reached in which Satan is seen conducting Faust through the gate of Hell. This was represented by a trap-door.

Satan got down all right, but Faust, who was represented by a rather stout singer, got stuck when about half way through. An Irishman in the gallery was heard exclaiming:

"Thank God, Hell is full!"

[7201]

"Faith," said he, "I know yez, I think. What's yer name?"

"Jones," was the answer.

"Jones, hey? Why, I knew three old maids by that name in Dublin. Was aither of them yer mother?"

[7202]

In New England when the circus comes into a country place there are always several natives on hand early in the day to help pitch the tents or feed the animals for a ticket into the show.

An Irishman named Pat presented himself one morning. The manager said, "I'm very sorry, Pat; we've got all the help we need. But I'll tell you—the lion died last night, and what's a circus without a lion. But we've kept his pelt with the head on it. Now if you'll simply crawl into that skin and lie down in the corner of the cage, so it will look as if the lion was sleeping, I'll give you two dollars."

Pat was glad to earn two dollars so easily and took the job. They put the skin on him and opened the door of the cage. But Pat drew back with a gasp, for there, glowering at him, was a great Bengal tiger in the further corner of the cage. The manager prodded him from behind, but Pat shouted, "I'll not go into the cage with that *baste* yonder."

Whereupon, to Pat's amazement, the Bengal tiger suddenly stood up and said, "Come right in, Pat; I'm an Irishman, too."

[7203]

Cop—"What's your name?"
Truck Driver—" 'Tis on the side o' me wagon."
Cop (trying to read name)—"It's obliterated."
Truck Driver—"Yer wrong. 'Tis O'Brien."

[7204]

"It's no use to feel my wrist," said Pat when the physician began feeling his pulse. "The pain is not there, sorr, it's in my head entoirely."

FRENCH

[7205]

A Paris shopkeeper wrote to one of his customers as follows:

"I am able to offer you cloth like the enclosed sample at nine francs the meter. In case I do not hear from you I shall conclude that you wish to pay only eight francs. In order to lose no time, I accept the last mentioned price."

[7206]

"The other day I met a French gentleman in New York City who thought he had mastered the English language.

" 'How do you do?' I said, on accosting him.

" 'Do vat?' he asked, in a puzzled manner.

" 'I mean, how do you find yourself?'

" 'Saire, I never lose myself?'

" 'You don't understand me; I mean, how do you feel?'

" 'How I feels? Oh, I feels smooth; you shust feel me.' "

[7207]

She—"So you're going to France. Do you know how to speak the language? Suppose you want to say 'egg,' what do you say?"
He—"You just say 'oof.' "
She—"But suppose you want two eggs?"
He—"You say 'twa oof' and the silly old maid gives you three, and you give her one back. Man, it's an awfully easy language."

[7208]

When a French visitor was bowled over by a speeding automobile, he said to the traffic officer who put him on his feet and helped to dust him off:

"Parlez vous Francaise?"

"Nix—Chevrolet coupe!" replied the policeman.

[7209]

An American Legionnaire on the 1937 pilgrimage to France who, upon reading the comprehensive claim on a restaurant window, "Ici on parle toutes les langues," said to the waiter:

"You must have a whole battalion of interpreters here."

"Not one," was the reply.

"Well, who speaks all the languages?"

"The customers, monsieur."

[7210]

A daily newspaper in Nice recently contained the following advertisement:

"Millionaire, young, good-looking, wishes to meet, with a view to marriage, a girl like the heroine in M—'s novel."

Within 24 hours the novel in question was sold out.

[7211]

Proprietor of French mountain hotel (to newly arrived guest)—"This is your room, sir. If you want a fine view over the mountains, put a franc in the slot and the shutters open for five minutes."

[7212]

A Frenchman was relating his experience in studying the English language. He said:

"When I first discovered that if I was quick, I was fast; that if I was tied, I was fast; if I spent too freely, I was fast; and that not to eat was to fast, I was discouraged. But when I came across the sentence, 'The first one won one-dollar prize' I gave up trying."

[7213]

Frenchman—"Ah, you climb the Matterhorn. That is a foot to be proud of."

Englishman—"Pardon me, sir, you mean 'feat.' "

Frenchman—"So you climb it more than once, eh?"

[7214]

A young Frenchman in the Sophomore class of an American college was invited to a musical entertainment given by his classmates, where there were sung, in honor of the foreigner, a number of French songs, and they were given in the best American-French.

"I say, old man," observed one of the sophomores, after the entertainment, "I suppose those French songs made you feel a little homesick, eh?"

"No," responded the Frenchman, "only sick."

[7215]

The celebrated French poet, Saint-Foix, who, in spite of his large income, was always in debt, sat one day in a barber's shop waiting to be shaved. He was lathered, when the door opened and a tradesman entered who happened to be one of the poet's largest creditors. No sooner did this man see Saint-Foix than he angrily demanded his money. The poet composedly begged him not to make a scene.

"Won't you wait for the money until I am shaved?"

"Certainly," said the other, pleased at the prospect.

Saint-Foix then made the barber a witness of the agreement, and immediately took a towel, wiped the lather from his face, and left the shop. He wore a beard to the end of his days.

[7216]

A Frenchman who recently came to New York was invited to a Golden Wedding Anniversary.

He could not get the purpose of it all and quietly inquired of a friend, "For why is this celebration?"

The Yankee answered, "You see those old people—they have been living together for 50 years and now they are celebrating their golden wedding."

"Ah!" exclaimed the Frenchman —"I see. He live with the lady 50 years and now he marry her. How noble."

[7217]

A Paris theater has found a means of making ladies remove their hats. Before the performance a strip appears on the screen curtain. "The management wishes to spare elderly ladies inconvenience. They are permitted to retain their hats." There follows a general stampede to remove hats.

[7218]

An Englishman in Paris had to visit the dentist.

"And, m'sieur," asked the servant in a tender tone, "whom shall I have the misery to announce?"

[7219]

A Frenchman stopped a newsboy in New York City to make some inquiries of his whereabouts. "Mon fren, what is ze name of zis street?"

"Well, who said 'twant?"

"What you call him, zis street?"

"Of course we do!"

"Pardonnez! I have not the name vat you call him."

"Yes, Watts we call it."

"How you call ze name of zis street?"

"Watts street, I told yer."

"Zis street."

"Watts street, old feller, and don't you go to make game o' me."

"Sacré! I ask you one, two, tree several times oftin, vill you tell me ze name of ze street—eh?"

"Watts street, I tole yer. Yer drunk, ain't yer?"

[7220]

The French Canadian endeavored to explain his bronchitis, but the confusion of the English language were almost too much for him. At last he said:

"I don't feel ver' good. I half a horse on t' t'roat; in fac', I half a colt."

[7221]

"Where is the American section in Paris?"

"The first ten rows of the Folies Bergère."

GERMAN

[7222]

A family moved from the city to a suburban locality and were told that they should get a watchdog to guard the premises at night. So they bought the largest dog that was for sale in the kennels of a neighboring dog fancier, who was a German. Shortly afterward the house was entered by burglars who made a good haul, while the big dog slept. The man went to the dog fancier and told him about it.

"Vell, vat you need now," said the dog merchant, "is a leedle dog to vake up the big dog."

[7223]

The meditative German delivered a monologue to his dog:

"You vas only a dog, but I vish I vas you. Ven you go your bed in, you shust turn round dree times and lie down; ven I go de bed in, I haf to lock up de blace, and vind up de clock, and put out de cat, and undress myself, and my vife vakes up and scolds, and den de baby vakes and cries and I haf to valk him de house around, and den maybe I get myself to bed in time to get up again.

"Ven you get up you shust stretch yourself, dig your neck a little, and you vas up. I haf to light de fire, put on de kiddle, scrap some vit my vife, and get myself breakfast. You be lays round all day and haf blenty of fun. I haf to vork all day and have blenty of drubble. Ven you die, you vas dead; ven I die, I haf to go somewhere again."

[7224]

"May it please the court," said an American lawyer to a German justice of the peace before whom he was trying a case, "this is a case of great importance. While the American eagle, whose sleepless eye watches over the welfare of this mighty republic, and whose wings extend from the Alleghenies to the Rocky Chain of the West, was rejoicing in his pride of place——"

"Shtop dare! I say vat hass dis suit to do mit de eagles? Dis suit hass nutin' to do mit de vild bird. It vas vun sheep," exclaimed the judge.

"True, your honor, but my client has rights and——"

"Your gliant hass no right to de eagle."

"Of course not, but the laws of language——"

"Vat I care for de laws of language, eh? I oondershtand de laws of de states und dot is enough for me. Talk aboudt de case alretty."

"Well, then, your honor, my client is charged with stealing a sheep and——"

"Dat vill do! Dat vill do! Ten dollars fine, und der court vill adjourn."

[7225]

Senator Spooner of Wisconsin said the best speech of introduction he ever heard was delivered by the German mayor of a small town in Wisconsin, where Spooner had been engaged to speak.

The mayor said:

"Ladies und shentlemen, I haf been asked to indrotoose you to the Honorable Senator Spooner, who vill make to you a speech, yes. I haf now done so; he vill now do so."

[7226]

A German who visited this country with a number of his colleagues was dining at an American house and telling how much he had enjoyed various phases of his visit.

"How did you like our railroad trains?" his host asked him.

"Ach, dhey are woonderful," the German replied; "so swift, so safe chenerally—und such luxury in all dhe furnishings und opp'indments. All is excellent excebt one thing— our wives do not like dhe upper berths."

[7227]

A German farmer was in search of a horse.

"I've got just the horse for you," said the liveryman. "He's five years old, sound as a dollar and goes ten miles without stopping."

The German threw his hands skyward.

"Not for me," he said, "not for me. I live eight miles from town, und mit dot horse I haf to valk back two miles."

[7228]

A German shoemaker left the gas turned on in his shop one night and upon arriving in the morning struck a match to light it.

There was a terrific explosion, and the shoemaker was blown out through the door almost to the middle of the street.

A passer-by rushed to his assistance, and, after helping him to rise, inquired if he was injured.

The little German gazed at his place of business, which was now burning quite briskly, and said:

"No, I ain't hurt. But I got out shust in time, eh?"

[7229]

"Dose Irish make me sick, alvays talking about vat gread fighders dey are," said a Teutonic resident of Hoboken, with great contempt. "Vhy, at Minna's vedding der odder night dot drunken Mike O'Hooligan butted in, und me und mein bruder, und mein cousin Fritz und mein frient Louie—vhy, ve pretty near kicked him oudt of der house!"

[7230]

Hans, the German butcher, was told he would lose his phone if he did not retract what he had said to a prominent citizen in the course of a conversation over the wire.

"Very vell, Hans vill apoloshize," he said. He called Main 7777.

"Ish dat you, Mister Doolittle?"

"It is."

"Dis is Hans, der putcher."

"Well?"

"Dis morning in der heat of disbleasure I tol' you to go to hell!"

"Yes?"

"Vell, don't go!"

[7231]

A steward on a river steamer was addressed by an uneasy and excited German, who wanted to put somebody off the boat. The candidate for a forcible disembarkation was pointed out, but the steward could see nothing out of the way. The German exclaimed:

"You don'd see nodings? Don'd you see dot man sidding dhere hugging dot vomans?"

"Well, yes," replied the steward; "but what of that? Hasn't a fellow a right to embrace his wife?"

"Got in Himmel," replied the German, dancing around; "dat's vot I vant him rundt oud for; dot's mine vife, und I haf shtood id so long as never vas, und I haf got madt."

[7232]

A German had in his employ a boy who was always about ten minutes late for business in the morning. After being called down on a number of occasions, the youngster turned over a new leaf, and eventually the German congratulated him, saying, "Hans, you are early of late; you used to be behind before and now you are first at last."

[7233]

Somebody asked a German to take venison. "No," said the German, "I never eatsh venshon, I don't think it ish so coot ash mutton."

"O!" said the German's friend, "I wonder at you saying so; if mutton were better than venison, why does venison cost so much more?"

"Vy?" replied the German, "I will tell vy—in dish world the peeples alwaysh prefer vat ish deer to vat ish sheep."

[7234]

A German who had been severely and painfully stepped on by a burly man who plowed his way through the crowded street car said: "Mine frent, I know that mine feet vas meant to be valked on, but dot brivilege belongs to me."

[7235]

A would-be grand opera singer asked a German music professor to hear her. He played her accompaniment and listened to her for a few minutes, but she sang so far off the key that he finally slammed down the piano and refused to continue.

"What's the matter?" inquired the lady in amazement. "Don't you like my singing?"

"Der trouble mit your singing, Madam," asserted Herr Professor, "is dot vedder I play on der vite keys or vedder I play on der black keys, you sing in der cracks."

[7236]

A young matron in whom the shopping instinct was strong asked a German butcher the price of a Hamburger steak.

"Twenty-five cents a pound," he replied.

"But," she said, "the price at the corner store is only twelve cents."

"Vel," asked Otto, "vy don't you buy it down there?"

"They haven't any," she explained.

"Oh, I see," replied the butcher. "Ven I don't have it I sell it for ten cents."

[7237]

An elderly German couple decided to buy the farm adjoining their property. The price agreed upon was $16,000, and they went to town to conclude the deal.

They entered the bank carrying an old battered milk pail with a tin cover, which they set on the floor between their chairs.

When the time came to pay, the old farmer pulled the pail up on his lap and started to count out an assortment of money, much of which had been out of circulation for some time.

Finally he reached the bottom, and stopped, obviously very upset.

"Why, there's only $14,000 here," he exclaimed.

His wife looked equally concerned for a moment; then her face brightened.

"Ach, papa, you brought the wrong pail!" she exclaimed.

[7238]

A German farmer who had had a pig stolen from him ascended the witness stand to identify the stolen property.

"Did that hog of yours have any ear-marks?" asked the attorney for the defence.

The German thought a while and then replied:

"Vell, de only ear-marks dat I remember vas his tail vas cut off."

[7239]

The wife of a German workman employed in a perambulator factory tried to induce him to steal a perambulator for their baby.

He refused to do this, but agreed to purloin sufficient parts to make a complete machine.

The great day for the assembly of the parts arrived. After five hours the wife went out to their backyard and found her husband in a state of exhaustion.

"It's no good," he said. "It always comes out a machine-gun."

[7240]

An old German farmer visited the county seat the first time in fifty years and saw his first electric fan in the general store.

"Py golly!" he said, smilingly, "dat's a dam'd lifely squirrel vot you got in dar, ain't it?"

[7241]

"What has become of Schmidt?"

"He went to America and has made a name for himself there."

"How?"

"He calls himself Smith now!"

[7242]

"Describe to the jury just how the stairs run in that house," the lawyer asked an old German who had witnessed a crime.

The old man looked dazed and scratched his head for a minute before attempting a reply. "You vant to know how der stairs run?" he repeated.

"Yes, if you please, how the stairs run."

"Vell," ventured the witness, slowly, "ven I am oopstairs dey run down, and ven I am downstairs dey run oop."

[7243]

The Germans upraised above their trenches the exultant boast, "Gott Mit Uns"—God with us.

The Americans, who understood the enemy's pretensions better than they did their language, met this claim with a slogan of their own: "We Got Mittens, Too!"

SWEDISH

[7244]

A tourist going through the Northwest, suffered a slight accident. Unable to find his monkey-wrench he went to a farm house and inquired of the Swede owner: "Have you a monkey-wrench here?"

"Naw," replied the Swede. "My brother bane got a cattle rench over there; my cousin got a sheep rench down there; but too cold for a monkey rench here."

[7245]

A very conscientious man met a friend and said, "Say, I'm awfully sorry, but you know I told you the other day that Oleson was a Swedenborgian?"

"Well, isn't he?" asked the other.

"No, I find he's a Norwegian."

[7246]

A Swedish farmer who wanted to make his permanent home in this country appeared for his naturalization papers.

"Are you satisfied with the general conditions of this country?" he was asked.

"Yah, sure," answered the hopeful one.

"And does this government of ours suit you?"

"Well, yah, mostly," stammered the man, "only I lak see more rain."

[7247]

A young Swede appeared at the county judge's office and asked for a license.

"What kind of a license?" asked the judge. "A hunting license?"

"No," was the answer. "Aye tank aye bane hunting long enough. Aye want marriage license."

[7248]

Up in Minnesota Mr. Olsen had a cow killed by a railroad train. In due season the claim agent for the railroad called.

"We understand, of course, that the deceased was a very docile and valuable animal," said the claim agent in his most persuasive claim-agentlemanly manner, "and we sympathize with you and your family in your loss. But, Mr. Olsen, you must remember this: Your cow had no business being upon our tracks. Those tracks are our private property and when she invaded them, she became a trespasser. Technically speaking, you, as her owner, became a trespasser also. But we have no desire to carry the issue into court and possibly give you trouble. Now then, what would you regard as a fair settlement between you and the railroad company?"

"Vall," said Mr. Olsen slowly. "Ay bane poor Swede farmer, but Ay shall give you two dollars."

[7249]

Evangelist—"Don't you want to come and labor in the Lord's vineyard?"

Ole—"No. Ay got fine job with Yon Yonson alreddy."

[7250]

A party of young people were amusing themselves by guessing the answers to conundrums. One of them asked, "Why is the pancake like the sun?"

"Because it rises in der yeast and sets behind der vest," was the answer given by a brilliant young Swede.

[7251]

It was a beautiful evening and Ole, who had screwed up courage to take Lena for a ride, was carried away by the magic of the night.

"Lena," he asked, "will you marry me?"

"Yes, Ole," she answered softly.

Ole lapsed into a silence that at last became painful to his fiancée.

"Ole," she said desperately, "why don't you say something?"

"Ay tank," Ole replied, "they bane too much said already."

[7252]

A small Swedish lad presented himself before a Minnesota schoolteacher, who asked him his name.

"Pete Peterson," he replied.

"And how old are you?" was the next question.

"I not know how old I bane," said the lad.

"Well, when were you born?" persisted the teacher.

"I not born at all; I got stepmutter."

[7253]

The new cook, who had come into the household during the holidays, asked her mistress:

"Where ban your son? I not seeing him round no more."

"My son," replied the mistress pridefully. "Oh, he has gone back to Yale. He could only get away long enough to stay until New Year's Day, you see. I miss him dreadfully, though."

"Yas, I knowing yoost how you feel. My broder, he ban in yail sax times since Thanksgiving."

[7254]

Little Greta came into the kitchen whilst mother was talking to the milkman. She just stood and stared.

Mother—"Well, Greta what do you say to the gentleman who brings you your nice milk every day?"

Greta (shaking hands)—"I am very glad to meet you. And how is your cow?"

CHINESE

[7255]

A New York importer received the following circular from a Chinese company in Shanghai:

"As an auspice of beatitude to the community, as an omnipotent daily utilized novelty, as a pioneer of the scientifical element, as a security to metal, as a short cut to the way of prosperity in the commercial world, as an agent to economy of both time and money, is the newly discovered wonderful Polishing Powder that to be heartily welcomed wheresoever.

"Despite the heavy sacrifice of capital and the consumption of brains, we have thereby succeeded in researching out the usage of this Polishing Powder.

"We lose no promptitude in taking this opportunity to recommend to the attention of the community. This Polishing Powder is the conqueror."

[7256]

The following letter was received by a New Jersey landlord from his Chinese tenant:

"Yes indeed, I arrears three months rent. If you were I should you pay and keep mouth shut, who is like damn fool to pay the thing unsatisfactory.

"Unless you patch the roof and put new paper on wall then I clear out. Later if you do not do I shall sue you damage for working hours. Many time the worked had done how-ever midnight rain, next morning all clothers wet I have start all over and waste my time for nothing."

[7257]

Chinese Patient (on telephone)— "Doctor, what time you fixee teeth fo' me?"

Doc—"Two-thirty—all right?"

Chinese—"Yes, tooth hurry me all right, but wha' time you fixee?"

[7258]

A firm advertising for a male stenographer received this reply:

"Sir: I am Chinese Bung Ho, but can drive a typewriter with good noise, and my English is it. My last job left itself from me for simple reason that big man has dead. It was on account of not my fault. So, honorable sirs, what of it? If I can be of big use to you I will arrive on same date as you can guess."

[7259]

"Name?" queried the immigration official.

"Sneeze," replied the Chinese proudly.

The official looked hard at him.

"Is that your Chinese name?" he asked.

"No, Melican name," said the Oriental blandly.

"Then let's have your native name."

"Ah Choo."

[7260]

The mistress of the house heard the bell ring and saw standing at the open front door a Chinese hawker. Quickly retreating, she called out to the maid:

"There's a Chinaman at the door. You go, Ella."

This was too much for the Chinese, who stuck his head well into the hall and shouted indignantly:

"You go 'ella yourself!"

[7261]

The Chinese are not given to flattery. A gentleman called at a Chinese laundry for his clothes. On receiving the package he noticed some Chinese characters marked upon it. He asked, pointing to the lettering:

"That's my name, I suppose?"

"No; 'scliption." was the Chinaman's bland reply. "'Lil ol' man, closs-eyed, no teeth.'"

[7262]

"Lighthouse no glood fol flog," says Chinaman. "Lighthouse he shine, whistle he blow, flog bell he ling, and flog he come just the same. No glood.

[7263]

In China when the subscriber rings up exchange the operator may be expected to ask:

"What number does the honorable son of the moon and stars desire?"

"Hohi, two-three."

Silence. Then the exchange resumes.

"Will the honorable person graciously forgive the inadequacy of the insignificant service and permit this humbled slave of the wire to inform him that the never-to-be-sufficiently-censured line is busy?"

[7264]

At a conference of Baptists, Methodists, and English Friends, in the city of Chengtu, China, two Chinamen were heard discussing the three denominations. One of them said to the other:

"They say these denominations have different beliefs. Just what is the difference between them?"

"Oh," said the other, "Not much! Big washee, little washee, no washee, that is all."

[7265]

Chinaman—"You tellee me where railroad depot?"

Citizen—"What's the matter, John? Lost?"

Chinaman—"No! me here. Depot lost."

[7266]

In a Hongkong shop-window two American tourists noticed some Chinese housecoats of particularly striking designs and stepped in to purchase one. One American undertook to do the bargaining.

"Wantum coatee," said he to the sleepy-eyed Oriental who shuffled up with a grunt. He placed several of the coats before them.

"How muchee Melican monee?" inquired the American.

"It would aid me in transacting this sale," said the Chinaman, "if you would confine your language to your mother tongue. The coat is seven dollars."

The American took it.

[7267]

One day a Chinese poor man met the head of his family in the street.

"Come and dine with us tonight," the mandarin said graciously.

"Thank you," said the poor relation. "But wouldn't tomorrow night do just as well?"

"Yes, certainly. But where are you dining tonight?" asked the mandarin curiously.

"At your house. You see, your estimable wife was good enough to give me tonight's invitation."

[7268]

A Chinese cook was walking through the woods. He turned around to see a grizzly bear following him, smelling of his tracks.

"Hm," said the Chinaman, "you like my tracks? Velly good, I make some more."

[7269]

It seems that a group of Chinese amateur actors were putting on a production. All went well until the middle of the second act, when one of the younger masculine players forgot his lines. He stammered around for what seemed an eternity, not knowing what to do. Finally another actor pulled his hair, and at the same time stage-whispered, "Hey, Wong, that's *your* cue."

"Yeah, I know it," replied Wong, "but you don't have to pull it off me, do you?"

[7270]

A middle-aged woman lost her balance and fell out of a window into a garbage can. Chinaman passing remarked: "Americans velly wasteful. That woman good for ten years yet."

[7271]

A guest at a New York banquet took pains to make himself agreeable to a Chinaman sitting next to him.

Somewhat at a loss for small talk he ventured, after the first course, to inquire, "Likee soupee?"

There was no reply except a genial beam. After the next course he followed up his first opening with "Likee fishee?" This evoked a still more genial beam.

Later in the evening the visitor from the Far East responded to a toast in perfect English.

On resuming his seat he asked his discomfited neighbor, "Likee speechee?"

[7272]

Hostess (who is trying to conceal from her party guests the fact that the Chinaman at the door is presenting a laundry bill)—"Well, John, is this a billet-doux?"

Hop Toy—"Yessum. Bill he due six months ago."

[7273]

A lady gave a reception to a group of college students. Among those present was a Chinese student who had studied a book of etiquette. Handed a cup of tea, he said:

"Thank you, sir or madam, as the case may be."

[7274]

Two Americans had just laid a wreath of flowers on a comrade's grave, and while crossing another section of the cemetery they saw a Chinaman lay some rice on the grave of a countryman.

One of the Americans asked, "When do you expect your friend to come and eat the rice?"

"When your friend comes to smell the flowers," was the reply.

OTHER NATIONS

[7275]

This is from "English for the Mass," a booklet published at Para:

"The American Sellsman is typically of an energy which is to admire in the warmth of the tropics. Of a youthfulness generally he breathes lively and walks springly, searching his customer loyally for the firm his. Yet under the breast of the American sellsman beats the heart warmness, therefore let us give greeting smiles with two hands open to him, crying 'welcome to Brazil, Mister.'"

[7276]

A missionary in India was having an earnest talk with a Hindu whom he hoped to convert to Christianity.

"Come, now," said the missionary, "wouldn't you like to go to Heaven when you die?"

The Hindu shook his head in polite regret.

"I do not think," he said, "that Heaven can be very good, or the British would have grabbed it years ago."

[7277]

An American teacher undertook the task of convincing an indolent native son of the Philippines that it was his duty to get out and hustle.

"But why should I work?" inquired the guileless Filipino.

"In order to make money," declared the thrifty teacher.

"But what do I want with money?" persisted the brown brother.

"Why, when you get plenty of money you will be independent and will not have to work any more," replied the teacher.

"I don't have to work now," said the native—and the teacher gave it up in disgust.

[7278]

A Spaniard, an American, and a Scotsman were discussing what they would do if they awoke one morning to discover that they were millionaires.

The Spaniard said he would build a bull ring.

The American said he would go to Paris to have a time.

The Scotsman said he would go to sleep again to see if he could make another million.

[7279]

Russian—"Our government aims at justice."

American—"Yes. It is fatally successful."

[7280]

A Mexican gazed through the bars at County Jailer H. E. Cox.

"Can you read and write?" demanded Cox during the booking process.

"Can write, not read," replied the prisoner.

"Write your name, then," said Cox. The Mexican scrawled huge letters across the page.

"What is that you wrote?" inquired the puzzled jailer.

"I don't know," said the Mexican, "I told you I can't read."

[7281]

Officer—"Flag of truce, Excellency."

His Excellency—"What do the revolutionists want?"

Officer—"They would like to exchange a couple of generals for a can of condensed milk."

[7282]

"There's a moose loose!"

"Are you English or Scotch?"

[7283]

"What is the smallest volume in the world?"

"Who's Who In Italy."

[7284]

Father of European Bride—"My daughter will have a dowry of $50,000, but of course I must make inquiries of your antecedents and prospects."

European Suitor—"Don't make any inquiries and I will take her for $25,000."

[7285]

Traveler (on European train)—"Shall I have time to get a drink?"

Guard—"Yes, sir."

Traveler—"Can you give me a guarantee that the train won't start?"

Guard—"Yes, I'll take one with you!"

[7286]

A ticket inspector entered a train at Chomutov, in Bohemia. He examined several tickets, and told each of the holders that he was in the wrong train. They must, he said, change at once. As his progress along the carriage continued, he found still more passengers who had made a mistake about the train. Then one of them had a bright idea, and asked the ticket inspector whether *he* was not in the wrong train. He was!

[7287]

By way of research, a gentleman decided to ask representative nationalities all the same question to compare their answers. The question propounded to each in turn was the following:

"What would you take to stand all night in the pouring rain?"

The Englishman answered: "I

should not like to do it for less than a guinea."

The Scotchman answered: "What would you be willing to pay?"

The Frenchman bowed politely and answered: "I should be happy to oblige you, but at the moment I have another engagement."

The Yankee replied: "I'll take a dollar."

The Irishman came back with: "An' sure, I think I'd take a cowld."

[7288]

"Dear Mr. Sir: Today I study in *Chronicle* distressful letter from Japan *Times* about ladies bad moral in short skirt.

"I opinionate letter serious and not joke.

"I am the police station and ever learned English at Sunday School from my dear lady teacher who very much love and affection our countrymen. Every day I strive to serve Country in control traffics but when windy day brow short skirt porice officer easy can misfocus eye and cause serious traffic corrision. So I pray Government shortly introduce new raw to compel ladies to obriterate rimbs. Many porice are very much agree."

[7289]

One Japanese bragged to another that he made a fan last twenty years by opening only a fourth section, and using this for five years, then the next section, and so on.

The other Japanese registered scorn.

"Wasteful!" he ejaculated. "I was better taught. I make a fan last a lifetime. I open it wide, and hold it under my nose quite motionless. Then I wave my head."

[7290]

An essay by a Japanese schoolboy:

"The banana are a great remarkable fruit. He are constructed in the same architectural style as the honorable sausage. Difference being, skin of sausage are habitually consumed, while it are not advisable to eat rapping of banana.

"Perhaps are also intrissing the following differences between the two objects. Banana are held aloft while consuming, sausage are usually left in reclining position. Banana are first green in culler, then gradual turn yellowish. Sausage start out with indefinite culler (resemble terrier cotta) and retain same hue indefinitely. Sausage depend for creation upon human being or stuffing mochine, while banana are pristine product of honorable mother nature. Both article resemble the other in that neither have pit or colonel of any kind.

"In case of sausage both conclusions are attached to other sausages, honorable banana on opposite hand are joined on one end to the stem, other termination are entirely loose.

"Finally, banana are strictly member of the vagitable kingdom, while afiliation of sausage is often undecided."

[7291]

An Italian was being examined for naturalization as a United States citizen.

"Who is the president of the United States?"

The foreigner answered correctly.

"And the vice-president?"

Again he answered correctly.

"Could you be president?"

"No, no."

"Why not?"

"Mister, you 'scuse me, please. I

vera busy—worka da mine all day now."

[7292]

A clergyman from northeastern Pennsylvania tells the story of an Italian who brought his baby to him to be baptized.

"Now," he said, "you see you baptize heem right. Last time I tell you I want my boy call 'Tom,' you call heem Thomas. Thees time I want heem call 'Jack,' I no want you call him Jackass!"

[7293]

An Italian was being examined for citizenship. The first question which the judge asked was: "How many states are there in the Union?"

"Donno, judge," replied the Italian. "I ask you how many banan' in a bunch. You donno. You know your biz, I know mine."

[7294]

The bald banker in a small town was in the habit of wearing his hat during business hours, for in summer the flies used his pate for a parade ground and in winter the cold air was uncomfortable as it swept the polished surface. Each week an Italian workman would come to the bank to get his paycheck cashed.

"Why don't you open an account with us?" the banker asked one day.

The Italian looked at the banker's hat, and then whispered confidentially:

"Me afraid, Mistah Boss, you alla time looka like you gonna maybe take da trip somewhere."

[7295]

"I speak four languages," proudly boasted the door man of a hotel in Rome to an American guest. "Yes, four—Italian, French, English, and American."

"But English and American are the same," protested the guest.

"Not at all," replied the man. "If an Englishman should come up now, I should talk like this: 'Oh, I say, what extraordinarily shocking weather we're having! I dare say there'll be a bit of it ahead.' But when you came up I was just getting ready to say: 'For the love o' Mike! *Some* day, ain't it? Guess this is the second flood, all right.'"

[7296]

An American traveling in Europe engaged a courier. Arriving at an inn in Italy, the man asked his servant to enter his name in accordance with the police regulations of that country. Some time after, the man asked the servant if he had complied with his orders.

"Yes, sir," was the reply.

"How did you write my name?" asked the master.

"Well, sir, I can't pronounce it," answered the servant, "but I copied it from your portmanteau, sir."

"Why, my name isn't there. Bring me the book." The register was brought, and, instead of the plain American name of two syllables, the following entry was revealed:

"Monsieur Warranted Solid
　　　　　Leather."

PART X

MISCELLANEOUS HUMOR

COMIC DICTIONARY

[7297]
Acquaintance—1. A person whom we know well enough to borrow from, but not well enough to lend to. 2. A degree of friendship called slight when its object is poor or obscure, and intimate when he is rich or famous.

[7298]
Actor—A man who tries to be everything but himself.

[7299]
Admiration—Our polite recognition of another's resemblance to ourselves.

[7300]
Adult—A person who has stopped growing at both ends and started growing in the middle.

[7301]
Advertising—Makes you think you've longed all your life for something you never even heard of before.

[7302]
Advice—The one thing which it is "More blessed to give than receive."

[7303]
After-Dinner Speaking—An occupation monopolized by men—women can't wait that long.

[7304]
Age—Something to brag about in your wine-cellar and forget in a birthday book.

[7305]
Alcohol—A liquid good for preserving almost everything except secrets.

[7306]
Alimony—1. When two people make a mistake and one of them continues to pay for it. 2. Man's cash surrender value.

[7307]
Alliance—In international politics, the union of two thieves who have their hands so deeply inserted in each other's pocket that they cannot separately plunder a third.

[7308]
America—A country where they lock up juries and let the defendants out.

[7309]
American—A person who yells for the government to balance the budget and borrows five dollars 'til payday.

[7310]
Americans—Those who think they are as good as anybody, and those who think they are better.

[7311]
Antique Furniture Collectors–Favorite song: "Oh, you take the highboy and I'll take the lowboy."

[7312]
Apartment–A place so small you can't swing a cat or throw a party.

[7313]
Appendicitis–A modern pain, costing about $200 more than the old-fashioned stomach-ache.

[7314]
Artistic Temperament–Seldom recognized until it's too old to spank.

[7315]
Athlete–A dignified bunch of muscles, unable to split the wood or sift the ashes.

[7316]
Average Man–One who thinks he isn't.

[7317]
Bachelor–1. A selfish, callous, undeserving man who has cheated some worthy woman out of a divorce. 2. A man who never makes the same mistake once.

[7318]
Bachelors–Married men may have better halves but bachelors have better quarters.

[7319]
Bank–An institution where you can borrow money if you can present sufficient evidence to show that you don't need it.

[7320]
Barber–A brilliant conversationalist, who occasionally shaves and cuts hair.

[7321]
Bargain–A disease common to women, caught in the Sunday papers and developed in department stores on Mondays.

[7322]
Bargain Sale–Where a woman can ruin one dress while she buys another.

[7323]
Baseball–A game in which the young man who bravely strikes out for himself receives no praise for it.

[7324]
Bigamist–One who makes the same mistake twice.

[7325]
Bigot–One who is obstinately and zealously attached to an opinion that you do not entertain.

[7326]
Birthday–Observed only by men and children.

[7327]
Bore–One who insists upon talking about himself when you want to talk about yourself.

[7328]
Bostonian–An American, broadly speaking.

[7329]
Brick–What your friends call you before you go to the wall—but never afterward.

[7330]
Bridge–A card game in which a good deal depends on a good deal.

[7331]
Broadway–A place where people spend money they haven't earned to buy things they don't need to impress people they don't like.

[7332]
Budget–A method of worrying before you spend instead of afterward.

[7333]
Business Man–One who talks golf all morning at the office and business all afternoon on the links.

[7334]
Caddie–A small boy, employed at a liberal stipend to lose balls for others and find them for himself.

[7335]
Cauliflower–A cabbage with a college education.

[7336]
Chauffeur–A man who is smart enough to operate an automobile, but clever enough not to own one.

[7337]
Childish Game–One at which your wife beats you.

[7338]
Chorus Girl–One who never worries about getting ahead because she doesn't need one.

[7339]
Christmas–A widely observed holiday on which the past nor the future is of so much interest as the present.

[7340]
Civilization–A process of creating more needs than means to supply.

[7341]
Civilized Nation–One that is horrified by other civilized nations.

[7342]
Co-ed–A girl who also goes to college.

[7343]
Collector–A man whom few care to see but many ask to call again.

[7344]
College Lad–A boy who likes to be treated with kindness by his parents, but not with unremitting kindness.

[7345]
Committee–A body that keeps minutes and wastes hours.

[7346]
Committee-of-five–Consists of a man who does the work, three others to pat him on the back, and one to bring in a minority report.

[7347]
Commuter–A traveling man who pays short visits to his home and office.

[7348]
Conscience–The voice that tells you not to do something after you have done it.

[7349]
Conservative–A man who is too cowardly to fight and too fat to run.

[7350]
Courtship–The period during which the girl decides whether or not she can do any better.

[7351]
Creditor–A man who has a better memory than a debtor.

[7352]
Criminal–One who gets caught.

[7353]
Critic–A wet blanket that soaks everything it touches.

[7354]
Cynic–A man who knows the price of everything and the value of nothing.

[7355]
Dachshund–Half a dog high by a dog and a half long.

[7356]
Debt–The only thing that doesn't become smaller when its contracted.

[7357]
Dentist–A person who finds work for his own teeth by taking out those of others.

[7358]

Detour–The roughest distance between two points.

[7359]

Diamond–A woman's idea of a stepping stone to success.

[7360]

Diplomacy–The patriotic art of lying for one's country.

[7361]

Diplomat–A man who convinces his wife that a woman looks stout in a fur coat.

[7362]

Double Jeopardy–When your doctor calls in a consulting physician.

[7363]

Drunk–Proved when he feels sophisticated and can't pronounce it.

[7364]

Earth–A solid substance, much desired by the seasick.

[7365]

Echo–The only thing that can cheat a woman out of the last word.

[7366]

Economy–Denying ourselves a necessary today in order to buy a luxury tomorrow.

[7367]

Ego–The only thing that can keep on growing without nourishment.

[7368]

Egotist–A man who tells you those things about himself which you intended to tell him about yourself.

[7369]

Encore–A greedy theater-goer's desire to get more than his money's worth.

[7370]

Engagement–In war, a battle. In love, the salubrious calm that precedes the real hostilities.

[7371]

English–The universal language, spoken almost everywhere now except in England and Boston.

[7372]

Enthusiast–One who preaches four times as much as he believes and believes four times as much as a sane man ought to.

[7373]

Epitaph–A statement that usually lies above about the one who lies below.

[7374]

Etiquette–A convenient code of conduct which makes lying a virtue and snobbishness a righteous deed.

[7375]

Experience–The name men give to their mistakes.

[7376]

Faith–Belief without evidence in what is told by one who speaks without knowledge, of things without parallel.

[7377]

Fame–Chiefly a matter of dying at the right moment.

[7378]

Fiction–It can't hold a scandal to biography.

[7379]

Firmness–That admirable quality in ourselves that is detestable stubbornness in others.

[7380]

Flattery–Cologne water, to be smelled of but not swallowed.

[7381]

Football–A game in which one side of the stadium wants to see eleven men killed and the other side of the stadium wants to see eleven men killed.

[7382]
Football Fan–One who knows the nationality of every man on the All-American team.

[7383]
Forty–The age when a woman stops patting herself on the back and begins under the chin.

[7384]
Friend–One who has the same enemies you have.

[7385]
Genius–One who can do almost anything except make a living.

[7386]
Gentility–Eating meat with a silver fork, neither being paid for.

[7387]
Girl–Always one of three things: hungry, thirsty, or both.

[7388]
Goat–A lamb who has kidded himself into believing that he knows Wall Street.

[7389]
Golf Ball–A small indented object which remains on the tee while a perspiring citizen fans it vigorously with a large club.

[7390]
Golfer–A man who hits and tells.

[7391]
Good Sport–One who will always let you have your own way.

[7392]
Helpmate–A wife, or bitter half.

[7393]
Hick–A person who looks both ways before crossing a one-way street.

[7394]
Highbrow–A person who can discuss sex and make you think he meant it all in a purely intellectual way.

[7395]
History–An account mostly false of events mostly unimportant.

[7396]
Honest Politician–One who when he is bought will stay bought.

[7397]
Honesty–Fear of being caught.

[7398]
Hope–A sentiment in the wag of a dog's tail when he is waiting for a bone.

[7399]
Horse-Sense–A degree of wisdom that keeps one from betting on the races.

[7400]
Hospitals–Places where people who are run down wind up.

[7401]
Hotel–A place where a guest often gives up good dollars for poor quarters.

[7402]
Hug–A roundabout way of expressing affection.

[7403]
Hypocrite–A man who sets good examples when he has an audience.

[7404]
Illegibility–A doctor's prescription written with a postoffice pen in the rumble seat of a second-hand car.

[7405]
Installment Paying – A condition which makes the months shorter and the years longer.

[7406]
Intuition–A fictitious quality in women—really suspicion.

[7407]
Irony–Giving father a bill-fold for Christmas.

[7408]

Janitor–The only man who makes a quick clean-up in Wall Street and gets away with it.

[7409]

Jimmy–An implement employed by men of acquisitive natures who cannot afford seats in the Stock Exchange.

[7410]

Joint Account–An account where one person does the depositing and the other the withdrawing.

[7411]

Joke–A form of humor enjoyed by some and misunderstood by most.

[7412]

June–The month of brides. The other eleven are devoted to divorcées.

[7413]

Jury–Twelve men chosen to decide who has the better lawyer.

[7414]

Keepsake–Something given us by someone we've forgotten.

[7415]

Kibitzer–A guy with an interferiority complex.

[7416]

Kiss–1. An indescribable something that is of no value to any one but is much prized by the right two. 2. A noun, though often used as a conjunction; it is never declined—it is more common than proper and is used in the plural and agrees with all genders.

[7417]

Laundry–A place where clothes are mangled.

[7418]

Lawsuit–Generally a matter of expense and suspense.

[7419]

Lawyer–One who defends your estate against an enemy, in order to appropriate it to himself.

[7420]

Lecture–An entertainment at which it costs but little to look intelligent.

[7421]

Lecturer–One with his hand in your pocket, his tongue in your ear and his faith in your patience.

[7422]

Liberty–Consists in giving every one full right to mind every one else's business.

[7423]

Life–First half ruined by our parents and second half by our children.

[7424]

Limb–The branch of a tree or the leg of an American woman.

[7425]

Lobster-Newburg–A dish ordered at hotels by those who usually get beans at home.

[7426]

Love–The feeling that makes a woman make a man make a fool of himself.

[7427]

Luck–Example. A guy once stooped to pick up a horse-shoe on the road and a car came along and knocked him over the fence into a field of four-leaf clovers.

[7428]

Luxury–Something that costs $7.63 to make and $20 to sell.

[7429]

Man–One who wishes he were as wise as he thinks his wife thinks he is.

[7430]
Man-About-Town–One who is on speaking terms with the head waiter.

[7431]
Marriage–1. The only life sentence that is suspended by bad behavior. 2. A delusion and a snore. 3. A rest period between romances.

[7432]
Married Man–One who has two hands with which to steer a car.

[7433]
Matrimony–Consists of Romance, Rice, Rocks.

[7434]
Middle Age–When a man says he is going to begin saving next month.

[7435]
Modern Age–When girls wear less on the street than their grandmothers did in bed.

[7436]
Modern Girl–Would make a wonderful cook if she could find a kitchen that was run by a steering wheel.

[7437]
Modern Literature–Neurotic, exotic, tommy-rotic.

[7438]
Modern Woman–Has been tried and found wanting—everything under the sun.

[7439]
Money–The mint makes it first and it's up to us to make it last.

[7440]
Money-grabber–Anybody who grabs more money than you can grab.

[7441]
Monologue–A conversation between a realtor and a prospect.

[7442]
Monopolist–A man who keeps an elbow on each arm of his theater chair.

[7443]
Mosquito–A small insect designed by God to make us think better of flies.

[7444]
Mother–A boy's best friend, and if he comes home late enough he may find her there.

[7445]
Neighbor–One who knows more about your affairs than you do.

[7446]
Nickel–Good to get the wrong number on the telephone.

[7447]
Nudist–A person who goes coatless and vestless, and wears trousers to match.

[7448]
Obesity–A surplus gone to waist.

[7449]
Opportunist–One who meets the wolf at the door, and appears the next day in a fur coat.

[7450]
Opportunity–A favorable occasion for grasping a disappointment.

[7451]
Optimism–A cheerful frame of mind that enables a tea kettle to sing though in hot water up to its nose.

[7452]
Optimist–One who thinks humorists will some day run out of definitions of an optimist.

[7453]
Orator–The fellow who's always ready to lay down your life for his country.

[7454]

Pacifist–One who cannot argue in favor of peace without using his fists.

[7455]

Pants–Trousers' country cousins.

[7456]

Paragon–The model man a woman regrets she gave up for the one she mistakenly married.

[7457]

Parents–One of the hardships of a minor's life.

[7458]

Patriot–A man who loves his country, and wants to make as much out of it as possible.

[7459]

Peace–In international affairs, a period of cheating between two periods of fighting.

[7460]

Pedestrian–The most approachable chap in the world.

[7461]

Pessimist–1. An optimist who endeavored to practice what he preached. 2. One who, of two evils, chooses them both.

[7462]

Philanthropist–One who returns to the people publicly a small percentage of the wealth he steals from them privately.

[7463]

Philosopher–One who instead of crying over spilt milk consoles himself with the thought that it was over four-fifths water.

[7464]

Philosophy–A route of many roads leading from nowhere to nothing.

[7465]

Photographer–One who can make an ugly girl as pretty as a picture.

[7466]

Pocket-book–The book whose contents rule the world.

[7467]

Poet–One who either puts fire into his verses or puts his verses into the fire.

[7468]

Poker–It's darkest just before you've drawn.

[7469]

Poker Face–The face that launched a thousand chips.

[7470]

Politician–A man who divides his time between running for office and running for cover.

[7471]

Politics–A matter of passing the buck or passing the doe.

[7472]

Polls–Places where you stand in line for a chance to decide who will spend your money.

[7473]

Polygamy–Now operated on the installment plan in America.

[7474]

Popular–To be gifted with the virtue of knowing a whole lot of uninteresting people.

[7475]

Popular Song Composer–A young man whose host of imitators died before he was born.

[7476]

Postscript–The only thing interesting in a woman's letter.

[7477]

Praise–What you receive when you are no longer alive.

[7478]

Promoter–A man who will furnish the ocean if you will furnish the ships.

[7479]
Prosperity–1. Being able to pay a little more for things we shouldn't buy anyway. 2. Something the business men create for the politicians to take credit for.

[7480]
Prune–A plum that has seen better days.

[7481]
Public Speaking–The art of diluting a two-minute idea with a two-hour vocabulary.

[7482]
Punctuality–The art of guessing how late the other fellow is going to be.

[7483]
Radical–Any one whose opinion differs from ours.

[7484]
Raise–The increase in pay you get just before going into debt a little further.

[7485]
Repartee–An insult with its dress-suit on.

[7486]
Reputation–A personal possession, frequently not discovered until lost.

[7487]
Respectability–The offspring of a liaison between a bald head and a bank account.

[7488]
Resort–A place where the tired grow more tired.

[7489]
Restaurant–An eating place that does not sell drugs.

[7490]
Rumor–A monster with more tales than an octopus.

[7491]
Sailor–A man who makes his living on water but never touches it on shore.

[7492]
Sandwich–An unsuccessful attempt to make both ends meat.

[7493]
Scotchman–One who wears kilts because they haven't any pockets.

[7494]
Sculptor–A poor unfortunate who makes faces and busts.

[7495]
Self-made Man–A horrible example of unskilled labor.

[7496]
Sinner–A stupid person who gets found out.

[7497]
Smokers–People who claim the more they fume, the less they fret.

[7498]
Spring–1. When a young man's fancy lightly turns to what the girl has been thinking about all winter. 2. The season of balls—golf, tennis, base and moth.

[7499]
Strength of Mind–A person who can eat one salted peanut.

[7500]
Subway–A place so crowded that even the men can't all get seats.

[7501]
Success–The one unpardonable sin against one's fellows.

[7502]
Swell-head–Nature's frantic effort to fill a vacuum.

[7503]
Synonym–A word you use when you can't spell the other one.

[7504]
Tabloid–A newspaper with a permanent crime wave.

[7505]
Telephone–An invention of the devil which abrogates some of the advantages of making a disagreeable person keep his distance.

[7506]
Temptation–Something which when resisted gives happiness and which when yielded to gives greater happiness.

[7507]
Theater–Holding a mirror up to a keyhole.

[7508]
Thermometer–A short glass tube that regulates the weather, and usually does a poor job.

[7509]
Tips–Wages we pay other people's hired help.

[7510]
Titian–The color a poor red-headed girl's hair becomes as soon as her father strikes oil.

[7511]
Tobacco–Found in many Southern States and in some cigarettes.

[7512]
True Love–Something many talk about but few have seen.

[7513]
Used Car–Not what it's jacked up to be.

[7514]
Usher–One who takes a leading part in a theater.

[7515]
Vulgarity–The conduct of others.

[7516]
War–Daft, draft, graft.

[7517]
Wedding–A funeral where you smell your own flowers.

[7518]
Wickedness–A myth invented by good people to account for the singular attractiveness of others.

[7519]
Window-screen – An arrangement for keeping flies in the house.

[7520]
Woman–1. Generally speaking, is generally speaking. 2. A side-issue at Creation, but the whole works now.

[7521]
Woman Motorist–When she holds out her hand you can be certain that she is either going to turn to the right, turn to the left, or stop.

[7522]
Women's Clothes–Go to extremes, but seldom to extremities.

[7523]
Worry–A state of mind that leads some persons to fear every time the tide goes out that it won't come in again.

[7524]
Yawn–The only time some married men ever get to open their mouths.

[7525]
Year–A period of three hundred and sixty-five disappointments.

[7526]
Yesmen–Fellows who hang around the man that nobody noes.

[7527]
Zeal–A certain nervous disorder afflicting the young and inexperienced.

WITTY SAYINGS

[7528]
Women give themselves to God
when the Devil wants nothing
more to do with them.—*Sophie
Arnould.*

[7529]
Wives are young men's mistresses, companions for middle age,
and old men's nurses.—*Francis
Bacon*

[7530]
Believe everything you hear said
of the world; nothing is too im-
possibly bad.—*Balzac*

[7531]
A husband should always know
what is the matter with his wife,
for she always knows what is not.
—*Balzac*

[7532]
The man who enters his wife's
dressing-room is either a philosopher or a fool.—*Balzac*

[7533]
Eat, drink, and be merry, for to-
morrow ye diet.—*William Gilmore
Beymer*

[7534]
Love in France is a comedy; in
England a tragedy; in Italy an
opera seria; and in Germany a
melodrama.—*Marguerite Blessing-
ton*

[7535]
When an actor has money, he
doesn't send letters but telegrams.
—*Anton Chekov*

[7536]
Polished brass will pass upon
more people than rough gold.
—*Chesterfield*

[7537]
Love is an ocean of emotions,
entirely surrounded by expenses.
—*Lord Dewar*

[7538]
The best doctor is the one you
run for and can't find.—*Diderot*

[7539]
I respect the institution of marriage—I have always thought that
every woman should marry, and no
man.—*Disraeli*

[7540]
We blame in others only the
faults by which we do not profit.
—*Alexander Dumas*

[7541]
Every hero becomes a bore at
last.—*Ralph Waldo Emerson*

[7542]
How many men would be mute
if they were forbidden to speak
well of themselves and evil of
others.—*Mme. de Fontaine*

[7543]
Only the men who do not care
about women are interested in
women's dresses. And the men who
like them never notice what they
wear.—*Anatole France*

[7544]
A writer is rarely so well inspired as when he talks about himself.—*Anatole France*

[7545]
The people who have no weaknesses are terrible; there is no way
of taking advantage of them.
—*Anatole France*

[7546]
He that falls in love with himself
will have no rivals.—*Franklin*

[7547]
There are three faithful friends: an old wife, an old dog, and ready money.—*Franklin*

[7548]
Keep your eyes wide open before marriage—half shut afterwards.—*Franklin*

[7549]
There is one thing more exasperating than a wife who can cook and won't, and that is the wife who can't cook and will.—*Frost*

[7550]
Time and tide wait for no man—but time always stands still for a woman of thirty.—*Frost.*

[7551]
A mother takes twenty years to make a man of her boy, and another woman makes a fool of him in twenty minutes.—*Frost*

[7552]
The world is full of willing people: some willing to work, the rest willing to let them.—*Frost*

[7553]
A receiver is appointed by the court to take what's left.—*Frost*

[7554]
A diplomatist is a man who always remembers a woman's birthday, but never remembers her age.
—*Frost*

[7555]
Most men who run down women are running down one woman only.—*Remy de Gourmont*

[7556]
Woman would be more charming if one could fall into her arms without falling into her hands.
—*Remy de Gourmont*

[7557]
Women still remember the first kiss after men have forgotten the last.—*Remy de Gourmont*

[7558]
Man begins by loving love and ends by loving a woman. Woman begins by loving a man and ends by loving love.—*Remy de Gourmont*

[7559]
Modesty is the delicate form of hypocrisy.—*Remy de Gourmont*

[7560]
The terrible thing about the quest for truth is that you find it.
—*Remy de Gourmont*

[7561]
The path of civilization is paved with tin cans.—*Elbert Hubbard*

[7562]
It is God who makes woman beautiful, it is the devil who makes her pretty.—*Victor Hugo*

[7563]
Second marriage: the triumph of hope over experience.—*Dr. Johnson*

[7564]
What is mind? No matter. What is matter? Never mind.
—*Thomas Hewitt Key*

[7565]
There are no ugly women; there are only women who do not know how to look pretty.—*La Bruyere*

[7566]
Life is a tragedy for those who feel, and a comedy for those who think.—*La Bruyere*

[7567]
It is a great misfortune neither to have enough wit to talk well nor enough judgment to be silent.—*La Bruyere*

[7568]
It is valueless to a woman to be young unless pretty, or to be pretty unless young.—*La Rochefoucauld*

[7569]
The same pride which makes us blame faults from which we believe ourselves free causes us to despise the good qualities we have not.—*La Rochefoucauld*

[7570]
We do not usually reckon a woman's first flirtation until she has had a second.—*La Rochefoucauld*

[7571]
The reason which often prevents us abandoning a single vice is having so many.—*La Rochefoucauld*

[7572]
One kind of happiness is to know exactly at what point to be miserable.—*La Rochefoucauld*

[7573]
Men often proceed from love to ambition, but they seldom return from ambition to love.—*La Rochefoucauld*

[7574]
Old men are fond of giving good advice, to console themselves for being no longer in a position to give bad examples.—*La Rochefoucauld*

[7575]
In their first passions women love the lover, in the others they love love.—*La Rochefoucauld*

[7576]
Most women do not weep for the loss of a lover to show that they had been loved so much as to show that they are worth being loved.—*La Rochefoucauld*

[7577]
Blessed are they who have nothing to say, and who cannot be persuaded to say it.—*James Russell Lowell*

[7578]
When you become used to never being alone you may consider yourself Americanized.—*André Maurois.*

[7579]
Man is always looking for someone to boast to; woman is always looking for a shoulder to put her head on.—*Henry Louis Mencken*

[7580]
Everybody sets out to do something, and everybody does something, but no one does what he sets out to do.—*George Moore*

[7581]
The great man learns only what he wants to learn; the mediocre man can learn what others think he should learn.—*George Moore*

[7582]
The picture of a woman one knows is never so agreeable a companion as the picture of a woman one has never seen.—*George Moore*

[7583]
People say you mustn't love your friend's wife, but how are you to love your enemy's wife?
—*George Moore*

[7584]
Insanity in individuals is something rare—but in groups, parties, nations, and epochs it is the rule.
—*Nietzsche*

[7585]
Marriage is a lottery in which men stake their liberty, and women their happiness.—*Mme. de Rieux*

[7586]
It is easier for a woman to defend her virtue against men than her reputation against women.
—*Rochebrune*

[7587]
Men *say* of women what pleases them; women *do* with men what pleases them.—*De Segur*

[7588]
Take care to get what you like, or you will end by liking what you get.—*George Bernard Shaw*

[7589]
The liar's punishment is not in the least that he is not believed, but that he cannot believe any one else.—*George Bernard Shaw*

[7590]
Do not love your neighbor as yourself. If you are on good terms with yourself it is an impertinence; if on bad, an injury.—*George Bernard Shaw*

[7591]
Titles distinguish the mediocre, embarrass the superior, and are disgraced by the inferior.—*George Bernard Shaw*

[7592]
In Heaven an angel is nobody in particular.—*George Bernard Shaw*

[7593]
Beware of the man who does not return your blow; he neither forgives you nor allows you to forgive yourself.—*George Bernard Shaw*

[7594]
A pessimist? A man who thinks everybody as nasty as himself, and hates them for it.—*George Bernard Shaw*

[7595]
First love is only a little foolishness and a lot of curiosity.—*George Bernard Shaw*

[7596]
Do not do unto others as you would that they should do unto you. Their tastes may not be the same.—*George Bernard Shaw*

[7597]
An Englishman thinks he is moral when he is only uncomfortable.—*George Bernard Shaw*

[7598]
Don't you know, as the French say, there are three sexes—men, women and clergymen.—*Sydney Smith*

[7599]
Blessed be he who expects nothing, for he shall never be disappointed.—*Swift*

[7600]
There are two times in a man's life when he should not speculate: when he can't afford it, and when he can.—*Mark Twain*

[7601]
Training is everything. The peach was once a bitter almond; cauliflower is nothing but cabbage with a college education.—*Mark Twain.*

[7602]
Noise proves nothing. Often a hen who has merely laid an egg cackles as if she had laid an asteroid.—*Mark Twain.*

[7603]
Doctors are men who prescribe medicines of which they know little, to cure diseases of which they know less, in human beings of whom they know nothing.—*Voltaire.*

[7604]
Fashion is a form of ugliness so intolerable that we have to alter it every six months.—*Oscar Wilde.*

[7605]
Men marry because they are tired, women because they are curious: both are disappointed.—*Oscar Wilde.*

[7606]
Women treat us just as humanity treats its gods. They worship us and are always bothering us to do something for them.—*Oscar Wilde.*

[7607]
Crying is the refuge of plain women, but the ruin of pretty ones. —*Oscar Wilde.*

[7608]
There is only one thing in the world worse than being talked about, and that is not being talked about.—*Oscar Wilde.*

[7609]
As soon as people are old enough to know better, they don't know anything at all.—*Oscar Wilde.*

[7610]
Marriage is the one subject on which all women agree and all men disagree.—*Oscar Wilde.*

[7611]
The old believe everything: the middle-aged suspect everything: the young know everything.—*Oscar Wilde.*

[7612]
A man who desires to get married should know either everything or nothing.—*Oscar Wilde.*

[7613]
As long as a woman can look ten years younger than her own daughter she is perfectly satisfied.—*Oscar Wilde.*

[7614]
Women are made to be loved, not to be understood.—*Oscar Wilde.*

[7615]
All the things I really like to do are either immoral, illegal or fattening.—*Alexander Woollcott.*

[7616]
The goodness of gold is tried by fire, the goodness of women by gold, and the goodness of men by the ordeal of women.—*Ancient proverb.*

[7617]
A deaf husband and a blind wife are always a happy couple.—*Danish proverb.*

[7618]
There are only two good women in the world; one of them is dead, and the other is not to be found.— *German proverb.*

[7619]
He who goes to law for a sheep loses his cow.—*Spanish proverb.*

[7620]
It ain't the things you don't know what gets you into trouble; it's the things you know for sure what ain't so.—*Negro saying.*

WISECRACKS

[7621]
It was Mark Twain who wrote that while everyone *talks* about the weather, no one ever *does* anything about it.

[7622]
The wife who drives from the back seat isn't any worse than the husband who cooks from the dining-room table.

[7623]
A Scotchman can drink any given amount.

[7624]
The first coeducational institution was Eden.

[7625]
If evolution works, Nature will produce a pedestrian who can jump three ways at once.

[7626]
Why have Scotchmen a sense of humor? Because it's a gift.

[7627]
We like a man that comes right out and says what he thinks, when he agrees with us.

[7628]
Many of the girls of the younger set aren't as black as they are painted, or even as pink.

[7629]
One great advantage of really being old is that one is beyond being told he is getting old.

[7630]
Religion is insurance in this world against fire in the next, for which honesty is the best policy.

[7631]
If a man still has his appendix and his tonsils, the chances are that he is a doctor.

[7632]
The cemeteries are filled with people who thought the world couldn't get along without them.

[7633]
A flying rumor never has any trouble in making a landing.

[7634]
For every woman who makes a fool out of a man there is another woman who makes a man out of a fool.

[7635]
Golf is about the only thing that depreciates above par.

[7636]
"Hear no evil, see no evil, speak no evil," and you'll never be a success at a tea party.

[7637]
The ideal man is as numerous as there are women to describe him.

[7638]
Modern fiction, says critic, runs too much to love. Yes, and modern love runs too much to fiction.

[7639]
Then, too, the world will make a beaten path to your door if you produce better clap-trap.

[7640]
Financial circumstances often alter legal cases.

[7641]
Pity the man who marries for love and then finds that his wife has no money.

[7642]
Some laws may seem to have no teeth, but they show unmistakable evidence of ivory.

[7643]
Stealing a kiss may be petty larceny, but sometimes it's grand.

[7644]
There's no justice. If you make out your income tax correctly you go to the poorhouse. If you don't you go to jail.

[7645]
Mirrors reflect without speaking and women speak without reflecting.

[7646]
The best thing about a popular song is that it is not popular very long.

[7647]
Many a man stays home nights because he has the house to himself.

[7648]
You cannot keep the home circle square with a triangle.

[7649]
People who live in glass houses shouldn't.

[7650]
Never give the boy all the allowance you can afford. Keep back some to bail him out.

[7651]
There are few persons with courage enough to admit that they haven't got it.

[7652]
Some people have tact, and others tell the truth.

[7653]
The deal the little nations get from the big ones is from the bottom of the pact.

[7654]
When a woman really loves a man, he can make her do anything she wants to do.

[7655]
The two chief causes of divorce, however, are matrimony and alimony.

[7656]
A widow and her money are soon married.

[7657]
Men are born with two eyes, but with one tongue, in order that they should see twice as much as they say.

[7658]
When two women suddenly become friendly, it is a sign that some third woman has lost two friends.

[7659]
When two egoists meet, it is a case of an I for an I.

[7660]
A good husband is one who feels in his pockets every time he passes a mail box.

[7661]
All is well that ends.

[7662]
Christmas comes, but once a year's enough.

[7663]
If matches were made in heaven, where did the cigar-lighters come from?

[7664]
The real college cheer is the check from home.

[7665]
All is fair in love and golf.

[7666]
A real executive is a man who can hand back a letter for a third retyping to a red-headed stenographer.

[7667]
The woman who concealed her instep now has a daughter who shows her step-ins.

[7668]
To speed is but human; to get caught, a fine.

[7669]
Give a convict enough rope and he'll skip.

[7670]
Spain has her matadors. The United States has her senators.

[7671]
Alas! Screening a picture doesn't take the trash out.

[7672]
The person who can withstand the high-pressure salesman illustrates the power of mind over patter.

[7673]
Many a checkered career ends in
a striped suit.

[7674]
A conservative politician is one
in office.

[7675]
Only Americans have mastered
the art of being prosperous though
broke.

[7676]
Where singleness is bliss 'tis folly
to be married.

[7677]
Opportunity knocks once, and
the neighbors the rest of the time.

[7678]
The difference between learning
to drive a motor and learning to
play golf is that when you learn to
play golf you don't hit anything.

[7679]
The beauty about rearing a large
family is that at least one of them
may not turn out like the others.

[7680]
There are two kinds of fishermen; those who fish for sport and
those who catch something.

[7681]
Physician says one million women are overweight. These, of
course, are round figures.

[7682]
Immigrants often weep when they
first see the Statue of Liberty; native Americans sometimes go into
hysterics.

[7683]
There are two reasons why some
people don't mind their own business. One is that they haven't any
mind, the other that they haven't
any business.

[7684]
A pathetic figure—the fellow who
went to Scotland to get a liberal
education.

[7685]
Modern version: Marry in haste,
repeat at pleasure.

[7686]
If all the people in the United
States stayed home on Sunday we'd
go automobile riding.

[7687]
A medical paper advances the
theory that "man is slightly taller
in the morning than he is in the
evening." We have never tested this,
but we have certainly noticed a tendency to become "short" toward
the end of the month.

[7688]
There are a million or more reasons why modern women dress as
they do, and every one is a man.

[7689]
The glass that cheers—milady's
mirror.

[7690]
Ignorance of the law does not
prevent the losing lawyer from collecting his bill.

[7691]
Some physicians direct their patients to lie always on the right side,
declaring that it is injurious to the
health to lie on both sides. Yet,
lawyers as a class enjoy good health.

[7692]
Grandmother says that one reason
why girls are naughty is because
they get the shingle in the wrong
place.

[7693]
The poet's scientific son might
say, "She was a television of delight. . . ."

[7694]
A rolling football gathers no score.

[7695]
The average straphanger's complaint is one of long standing.

[7696]
Two million years from now the scientists can start a row by claiming that the creatures of that period descended from Man.

[7697]
Nowadays, a couple marries and the first thing you know they have a little divorce.

[7698]
One small jack can lift a car, but it takes a lot of jack to keep it up.

[7699]
If all the college boys who slept in class were placed end to end they would be much more comfortable.

[7700]
Always borrow from a pessimist —he never expects it back anyhow.

[7701]
Youth must be served—and then carried out.

[7702]
"The play ended, happily," recently wrote a local critic. What a difference a comma can make!

[7703]
A professor once spent some time figuring out why professors are absent-minded. He forgot the answer.

[7704]
Then there's the absent-minded business man who took his wife to dinner instead of his stenographer.

[7705]
The difference between an amateur and a professional athlete is that the latter is paid by check.

[7706]
For most of us, life is what we make it, but for the pedestrian, it's *if* he makes it.

[7707]
Nothing irks a genuine college boy any more than shaking out the envelope from home and finding nothing in it but news and love.

[7708]
Many a man who in his time has cast sheep's eyes at a pretty girl, has afterwards had the wool pulled over them.

[7709]
If you let a cat out of the bag never try to cram it back again; it only makes matters worse.

[7710]
When you go to drown yourself, always pull off your clothes; they may fit your wife's second husband.

[7711]
Blessed are they that are ignorant; for they are happy in thinking that they know everything.

[7712]
How much happier we should be summer evenings if Noah had stepped on the male tumble bug before he left the ark.

[7713]
It is sad to see people squandering money and know you cannot help them.

[7714]
Slogan for revue producers: This is the dawn of a nude day.

[7715]
The stage is reported to be in a critical condition. Foul play is suspected.

[7716]
A tax cut is the kindest cut of all.

[7717]

Executive ability is the art of convincing your wife that you hired your pretty stenographer on account of her experience.

[7718]

Statisticians have figured the time lost in every other business operation. Now they might figure the time wasted in figuring statistics.

[7719]

There would be more incentive to success if successful men seemed to enjoy life more.

[7720]

A visiting English actor calls our critics the pan-Americans.

[7721]

Every man has his price, but some hold bargain sales.

[7722]

One reason so many poets are poor is that there are so many poor poets.

[7723]

A pessimist is a fellow who lives with an optimist.

[7724]

The apparel off proclaims the woman.

[7725]

A movie actress has just remarried her first husband. It must have been his turn again.

[7726]

The modern dance has developed in leaps and bounds.

[7727]

What this country needs is fewer people telling us what this country needs.

[7728]

It sometimes takes a girl a long time to learn that a flirtation is attention without intention.

[7729]

There is a Scotch doctor who had a patient who ran up a temperature of 108. The doctor put him in the cellar to heat the building.

[7730]

Who ever expected to see the day when a man would scold his wife for dropping ashes on his office floor?

[7731]

The bigger the summer vacation the harder the fall.

[7732]

The latest wedding-ring is very thin and narrow. The old-fashioned, cumbersome affair, of course, was made to last a life-time.

[7733]

Married couples have fewer arguments in winter than in summer. This is because a lot of husbands wear earmuffs in the winter.

[7734]

When a man's wife doesn't come home he begins to wonder what has happened to her. When a woman's husband doesn't come home, she begins to wonder who the hussy is.

[7735]

At twenty he thinks he can save the world; at thirty he begins to wish he could save part of his own salary.

[7736]

A man doesn't look for a happy ending to a love affair—merely one without hysterics.

[7737]

A Berlin faster claims to have gone forty-four days without food. It is our opinion that he should have either given his order to another waiter, or tried a different restaurant.

[7738]
New York restaurant men want to abolish the word "waiter." Right enough, it is usually the diners who do the waiting.

[7739]
It's what the guests say as they swing out of the driveway that really counts.

[7740]
First the bride selects the bridesmaid. Then the church. Then the trousseau. Then her lawyer. Then her detective.

[7741]
"An 'aye' for an I," muttered the candidate as he voted for himself.

[7742]
As a rule when a man is generous to a fault, it's his own fault he's generous to.

[7743]
Many a girl with a negative personality may be developed in a dark room.

[7744]
The summer hotel may be crowded but there's always room for one bore.

[7745]
A new process found in London will make cardboard as strong as iron. This answers a complaint from Scotland that Christmas cards wear out after a few seasons.

[7746]
If a woman is an hour late in returning home, and her husband is worried, she is flattered. If a man is three hours late he is angry if anyone is worried.

[7747]
Did you hear about the Scotchman who stood and snapped his fingers on the Fourth of July?

[7748]
Then there's the playboy who kept calling his girl friend a little sugar and wound up by paying her a lump sum.

[7749]
It's a sure sign of summer when a Scotchman throws his Christmas tree away.

[7750]
Mr. and Mrs. Jock MacGregor saved money on their honeymoon by staying at home and hearing the roar of Niagara Falls broadcast over the radio.

[7751]
The world's best after dinner speech: "Waiter, give me both checks."

[7752]
Artist's Model: "I don't feel in the nude for work, somehow."

[7753]
If you can't find it in the dictionary, the atlas or the Encyclopaedia Britannica, don't be discouraged. Ask for it at the drug store.

[7754]
Man and woman can get along nicely as life partners, if they can avoid being bridge partners.

[7755]
A man is that large irrational creature who is always looking for home atmosphere in a hotel and hotel service around the house.

[7756]
One of the big Christmas problems in this era is the question of what to get for the girl who doesn't smoke.

[7757]
A girl with cotton stockings never sees a mouse.

[7758]

"I visit my friends occasionally," remarked the book lover, "merely for the purpose of looking over my library."

[7759]

At a bankers' dinner the other evening a banker read a bad poem that he wrote, and nothing was done about it. But just let a poet write a bad check!

[7760]

The average man's life is now divided between worry over two tubes, radio and inner.

[7761]

A complicated traffic tangle was caused recently by a lady motorist who signaled that she was about to turn to the right, and did so.

[7762]

The director can't fire any of his chorus because he hasn't anything on any of them.

[7763]

Members of the younger generation are alike in many disrespects.

[7764]

One thing the discovery of the North Pole proved is that there's no one sitting on top of the world.

[7765]

All men are patriotic when they're called to serve on a jury in a bathing beauty contest.

[7766]

When better books are suppressed more people will read them.

[7767]

Among the makers of one-piece bathing suits, the thigh's the limit.

[7768]

If all the serial stories were placed end to end in this world they would have to be continued in the next.

[7769]

When Daniel got into the lions' den and looked around he thought to himself, "Whoever's got to do the after-dinner speaking, it won't be me."

[7770]

An eminent scientist announces that man does his best work at fifty, and we'll bet he's the same one that announced about ten years ago that he does it at forty.

[7771]

Why preach against modern dress when there's not enough left to talk about.

[7772]

A farmer is a man who makes his money on the farm and spends it in town. An agriculturist is a man who makes his money in town and spends it on the farm.

[7773]

Women are like money; keep 'em busy or they lose interest.

[7774]

Every woman has a secret desire to write—checks.

[7775]

Many a man lives by the sweat of his frau!

[7776]

Parents spend half their time worrying how a child will turn out and the rest of the time wondering when a child will turn in.

[7777]

A poet must use his imagination. He must imagine people are going to read his poems.

[7778]

You can't fool all the people all of the time, but the average politician is contented with a sizable majority.

[7779]
Nowadays, whatever is not worth saying is sung.

[7780]
Alas! Rich relatives are usually distant relatives or close relatives.

[7781]
The Scotch are a very inventive race. They have found a new use for wornout razor blades—they shave with them.

[7782]
Man is but a worm. He comes along, wiggles a bit, then some chicken gets him.

[7783]
A Scotchman recently sued a baseball company because he was hurt while watching a ball game. He fell out of a tree.

[7784]
The mother-in-law should be careful not to go too far, unless she stays there.

[7785]
The only thing at mother's knees these days is her skirt.

[7786]
What this country needs is a good five-cent nickel.

[7787]
Strange that men call money "dough." Dough sticks to your fingers.

[7788]
There's only one person who can speak louder than a senator and that's another senator.

[7789]
Pity the poor movie queen—she never knows where her next husband is coming from.

[7790]
A Hollywood wedding is, as a rule, a retake.

[7791]
What makes the happy ending of some movies is the mere fact that they have ended.

[7792]
About the only thing left in this world that can be shocked is grain.

[7793]
None of the anthropoid apes can emit musical sounds. But, on the other hand, none of them try to.

[7794]
Smoke and the world smokes with you; swear off and you smoke alone.

[7795]
A shining example of old-fashioned simplicity is an unpowdered nose.

[7796]
It's an ill wind that shows no pretty knees.

[7797]
A bride of eighteen faces the task of cooking 50,000 meals. Not if she can find a can-opener.

[7798]
When company stays too long, just treat them like members of the family and they'll soon leave.

[7799]
A man who sits in a swamp all day waiting to shoot a duck will kick if his wife has dinner ten minutes late.

[7800]
Every woman should have at least one husband to share her joys and her sorrows and her friends' secrets.

[7801]
When a man has a birthday he takes a day off, but when a woman has a birthday she takes a year off.

[7802]
Italy likes her duces wild.

[7803]
Why is a Scot called close. You can touch anybody who is close.

[7804]
Guests will happen in, in the best regulated families.

[7805]
It has been asked why more Americans do not own hippopotamuses. It probably is because none of the instalment stores have thought about selling hippopotamuses at a dollar down and a dollar a week thereafter.

[7806]
Whom the juries would acquit they first make mad.

[7807]
A member of a jazz orchestra recently went back to his job in a boiler factory. Possibly the poor fellow couldn't stand the noise.

[7808]
Yesterday we heard positively the last one on our friend, the absent-minded professor. He slammed his wife and kissed the door.

[7809]
If you wish to have a short winter, have your note come due in the spring.

[7810]
The disheartening thing about the average diet regime is it does so much for the will power and so little for the waistline.

[7811]
About all that is necessary for a divorce nowadays is a wedding.

[7812]
The time is approaching when the number of divorces will equal the number of marriages. Love is evidently finding a way—out.

[7813]
A thing of beauty is a joy until it goes in bathing.

[7814]
It usually takes five years for a tree to produce nuts, but this isn't true of a family tree.

[7815]
What every wife wants to know: how the other half lives.

[7816]
Every cosmetic dealer knows that woman's face is his fortune.

[7817]
A telephone pole never hits an automobile except in self-defense.

[7818]
Still, if nobody dropped out at the eighth grade, who would be ready to hire the college graduates?

[7819]
Children have become so expensive that only the poor can afford them.

[7820]
Every woman believes there are two sides to every question—her side and the wrong side.

[7821]
Our unfortunate experience is that a day off is generally followed by an off day.

[7822]
In some respects the idea of finger-printing children seems to be a good one. At least it will settle the question as to who used the guest towel in the bathroom.

[7823]
A French author says: "When I lost my wife, every family in town offered me another; but when I lost my horse, no one offered to make him good."

[7824]
When better predictions are made sport writers won't make them.

[7825]
The proverb, "Where there's a will there's a way" is now revised to "When there's a bill we're away."

[7826]
It is a known fact that a man with a college diploma and ten cents can get a cup of coffee anywhere.

[7827]
It's easy to pick out the best people. They'll help you do it.

[7828]
A bird in the hand is bad table manners.

[7829]
Some of the congressional investigators would look for bones in animal crackers.

[7830]
The man who is always asking for a loan is always left alone.

[7831]
The old songs are best because nobody sings them any more.

[7832]
The secret of success in writing is in hitting the right keys on the typewriter.

[7833]
When a bunch of girls get together, the Lord pity the first one who leaves.

[7834]
A man has less courage than a woman. Try to imagine one with twelve cents in his pocket trying on seven suits of clothes.

[7835]
There are two kinds of women: The fashionable ones and those who are comfortable.

[7836]
What man wants—all he can get. What woman wants—all she can't get.

[7837]
Polygamy would never work in this country. Think of six wives in a kitchenette!

[7838]
Most husbands are generous to a fault—if the fault's their own.

[7839]
One swallow doesn't make a summer, but it breaks a New Year's resolution.

[7840]
Some men are born great, some achieve greatness, and others thrust greatness upon themselves.

[7841]
In telling her age a woman is often shy—in more ways than one.

[7842]
One can get about everything on credit nowadays excepting money.

[7843]
People wouldn't get divorced for such trivial reasons if they didn't get married for such trivial reasons.

[7844]
Most holiday dinner repartee comes under the head of chestnut dressing.

[7845]
The modern woman doesn't want a man who can satisfy her smallest wish; what she wants is one who can attend to the larger ones.

[7846]
The oyster is not the only one who has a crab for a mate.

[7847]
Artists' models make only a bare living.

[7848]

The question is not where civilization began, but when will it.

[7849]

Never run after a street-car or a woman; another will be along presently.

[7850]

"My only regret is that I have but one wife to send to the country."

[7851]

The course of two loves never does run smooth.

[7852]

Five secrets of happiness: Money. Money. Money. Money. Money.

[7853]

A crusty old bachelor says he thinks it is a woman, and not her wrongs, that ought to be redressed.

[7854]

The old-time woman who saved her wedding dress for her daughter now has a daughter who saves her own wedding dress for her next wedding!

[7855]

A word to the wife is never sufficient.

[7856]

A word of advice: Don't give it.

[7857]

She's such a gold-digger she even purses her lips when she kisses you.

[7858]

The man who doesn't believe that women are hard losers never knew one who was trying to reduce.

[7859]

Some men are known by their deeds, others by their mortgages.

[7860]

If somebody would only discover a cough medicine for radios.

[7861]

God made women without a sense of humor so they could love men instead of laughing at them.

[7862]

A long-legged sheep in the Himalayas is able to run forty miles an hour. That's the kind of little lamb to follow Mary nowadays.

[7863]

Clothes often fake the man.

[7864]

A man always chases a woman until she catches him.

[7865]

The girl who thinks no man is good enough for her may be right but she is more often left.

[7866]

If men had no faith in one another, all of us would have to live within our incomes.

[7867]

An itch for office does not always lead to a niche in the temple of fame.

[7868]

A man who is always in a stew generally goes to pot.

[7869]

The law says girls are minors until they're twenty-one; but a lot of them are gold-diggers all of their lives.

[7870]

A little woman is a dangerous thing.

[7871]

Twenty years ago the girls never thought of doing the things they do nowadays. That's why they didn't do them.

[7872]

When a woman says, "You flatter me"—do so!

[7873]

When Grandma was a girl she didn't do the things the girls do today. But then the Grandmas didn't do the things the Grandmas do today.

[7874]

An Englishman walks into a restaurant as if he owned it. An American walks in as if he didn't care a damn who owned it.

[7875]

June is the month of weddings and cooing. The billing follows.

[7876]

The little boy who hides behind his mother's skirt has to get in his high-chair to do it.

[7877]

Many men who refuse to believe in Santa Claus are convinced they can beat Wall Street.

[7878]

Whiskey is about the only enemy man has succeeded in really loving.

[7879]

Dollars and sense do not necessarily travel together.

[7880]

A woman is never thoroughly interested in a newspaper article until she reaches the place where the balance is torn off.

[7881]

What the girls say—A thing of beauty is a boy forever.

[7882]

If you are in doubt whether to kiss a pretty girl, give her the benefit of the doubt.

[7883]

Don't take too much interest in the affairs of your neighbors. Six per cent will do.

[7884]

If thine enemy wrong thee, buy each of his children a drum.

[7885]

One marriage in every six ends in divorce, but the other five couples fight it out to the bitter end.

[7886]

A lawyer says that a dangerous year in married life is the first. Then follows the second, third, fourth, fifth and so on.

[7887]

The chemical constituents of a man are said to be worth 98 cents. Possibly it is that price which causes some women to run after them.

[7888]

Before marriage a man yearns for a woman. After marriage the "y" is silent.

[7889]

Life is just one fool thing after another; love is just two fool things after each other.

[7890]

A kiss is a peculiar proposition. Of no use to one, yet absolute bliss to two. The small boy gets it for nothing, the young man has to lie for it, and the old man has to buy it; the baby's right, the lover's privilege, and the hypocrite's mask. To a young girl, faith; to a married woman, hope, and to an old maid, charity.

[7891]

Women take to good hearted men. Also from.

[7892]

The chief difference between the movies and real life is that in the movies they are married at the end of all their difficulties.

[7893]
When writing love-letters to your girl, it's always an act of precaution to begin: "My dear sweetheart and gentlemen of the jury."

[7894]
A young woman called a policeman because a man tried to flirt with her. Lucky chap! She might have called a clergyman.

[7895]
If a husband talks in his sleep, and still gives no secrets away, it's a triumph of mind over mutter.

[7896]
Love makes a man think almost as much of a girl as he thinks of himself.

[7897]
Dramatic critics' motto: The flay's the thing!

[7898]
An actor believes that a small role is better than a long loaf.

[7899]
The tragedy of the flea is that he knows for a certainty that all of his children will go to the dogs.

[7900]
You can't keep a good golfer downtown.

[7901]
Father: A kin you love to touch.

[7902]
Beyond the Alps lies Italy and, lest we forget, behind the billboards lies America.

[7903]
Men are not good or bad; they are good and bad.

[7904]
It takes two to make a quarrel, and the same number to get married.

[7905]
Nobody loves a flat man.

[7906]
The reason there were fewer wrecks in the old horse-and-buggy days was because the driver didn't depend wholly on his own intelligence.

[7907]
It's funny how a woman will trust her body and soul in the hands of a man whose own mother wouldn't trust him with a nickel.

[7908]
The man who boasts only of his ancestors belongs to a family that is better dead than alive.

[7909]
If you lend a friend five dollars and you never see him again, it's worth it.

[7910]
I have discovered that the flu is both affirmative and negative. Sometimes the Eyes have it and sometimes the Nose.—*Willian Lyon Phelps.*

[7911]
What the five cent cigar needs is a good country.—*Ed Wynn.*

[7912]
The funniest thing about a girl is her sense of humor.

[7913]
If the devil ever laughs it must be at hypocrites, they serve him well and receive no wages.

[7914]
Most men flirt with the women they would not marry, and marry the women who would not flirt with them.

[7915]
Love makes time pass, and time makes love pass.

[7916]
Love consists of a little sighing, a little crying, a little dying—and a deal of lying.

[7917]
Some fellows believe in dreams until they marry one.

[7918]
An experienced husband is one who remembers his wife's birthday, but forgets which one it is.

[7919]
The first time a man kisses a girl she is rather surprised, the second time angry; the third time she almost likes it, and the fourth time she is waiting.

[7920]
If the folks who dictate women's fashions aren't careful, they'll work themselves out of a job some day.

[7921]
The secret of success is a secret to many people.

[7922]
In another hundred years civilization will have reached all peoples except those that have no resources worth stealing.

[7923]
The student today accumulates the horsehide, the pigskin, the coonskin, and by the time he has the sheepskin, father hasn't very much hide left either.

[7924]
Love is like getting drunk, marriage is like the headache the next morning, and divorce is the aspirin tablet.

[7925]
On an island in the South Pacific there are no taxes, unemployment, crime, beggars, jazz bands, radios or inhabitants.

[7926]
Consider the mosquito as an example. He rarely gets a slap on the back until he goes to work.

[7927]
Modern girls are fond of nice clothes, but they are not entirely wrapped up in them.

[7928]
Some girls keep their love letters; others let their love letters keep them!

[7929]
Kissing a girl is just like opening a bottle of olives—the first may come hard, but it's a cinch to get the rest.

[7930]
What this country needs is a man who can be right and President at the same time.

[7931]
A girl may love you from the bottom of her heart, but there's always room for some other guy at the top.

[7932]
The class yell of the School of Experience is "Ouch!"

[7933]
You can't choose your ancestors, but that's fair enough. They probably wouldn't have chosen you.

[7934]
Everything you say to a woman, will be used against you.

[7935]
Some day a magazine editor is going to achieve lasting fame by publishing stories as interesting as the advertisements.

[7936]
If all the people that eat at boarding houses were put at one long table, they would reach.

[7937]
Every man is a born collector!
First, he collects beetles, toads, and
marbles; then girls, kisses, and
fancy ties; then dollars, troubles,
and a family; then golf cups, after-
dinner stories, and old pieces of
string; and lastly, aches, symptoms,
and memories.

[7938]
Success in life depends on two
things—luck and pluck . . . luck
in finding somebody to pluck.

[7939]
A girl no longer marries a man
for better or worse. She marries him
for more or less.

[7940]
God first created the universe
and rested; God then created man
and rested; he finally created woman, and since then neither God
nor man has rested.

[7941]
A pedestrian is a case of survival
of the flittest.

[7942]
A lady novelist thinks that thirty
is a nice age for a woman. It is,
especially if she happens to be
forty.

[7943]
Nature is wonderful! A million
years ago she didn't know we were
going to wear spectacles, yet look
at the way she placed our ears.

[7944]
What this world needs is less permanent waves and more permanent
wives.

[7945]
Marriage vows might be a trifle
more accurate if the phrase were
changed to read, "Until debt do
us part."

[7946]
Did you hear of the Scotchman
who took the corners on two wheels
to save his tires?

[7947]
Frankness is the modern girl's
long suit, says a preacher. Apparently the only long suit she has.

[7948]
No man is a hero to his wallet.

[7949]
The old-fashioned man who had
a good head for figures now has a
grandson who has a great eye for
them.

[7950]
A penny saved is a pocket
burned.

[7951]
Almost any time now we may expect to see the restaurants retaliate
by putting in a line of drugs and
toilet articles.

[7952]
Reducing experts live on the fat
of the land.

[7953]
Some husbands can pay their
debts promptly, but most of us are
good to our wives.

[7954]
Love is the delusion that one girl
differs from another.

[7955]
A college education never hurt
anyone willing to learn something
afterwards.

[7956]
Life started from a cell, and if
justice is done a lot of it is going
to end there.

[7957]
The only people nowadays who
wake up and find themselves rich
are professional boxers.

[7958]

If women ever take to cigars as they have to cigarettes the men can get even on Christmas.

[7959]

Blessed are the pure, for they shall inhibit the earth.

[7960]

Neighbors are people who wonder when that damned party will end.

[7961]

A quartet is where all four think the other three can't sing.

[7962]

Our idea of a convincing talker is one who can show little Willie just wherein algebra is essential to his future success.

[7963]

Two halves make a hole, and the fullback goes through.

[7964]

Trouble with self-made men is that they quit the job too early.

[7965]

Those Wall Street men who are going back to the farm ought to be efficient when it comes to watering the stock and shearing the sheep.

LINCOLN STORIES

[7966]

The Southern commissioners had dined with President Lincoln and General Grant. When the commissioners left, Alexander H. Stephens (a little man, whose top weight was ninety pounds) enveloped his short, slender form in an English ulster, its tails falling to the ground and its collar sticking above Stephens' head. As Stephens made his exit, Lincoln exclaimed: "Grant, look at Stephens. Did you ever see such a little nubbin with as much shuck?"

[7967]

Once during the war, Barnum was at Washington exhibiting General Tom Thumb and Admiral Nutt. Mr. Lincoln said: "You have some pretty small generals, but I think I can beat you."

[7968]

"In early days," said Lincoln, "a party of men went out hunting for a wild boar. But the game came upon them unawares, and they, scampering away, climbed trees, all save one, who, seizing the animal by the ears, undertook to hold him. After holding him for some time and finding his strength giving way, he cried out to his companions in the trees:

" 'Boys, come down and help me let go!' "

[7969]

To a group of citizens who had called to urge him to emancipate the slaves, the President said it was impossible at that stage of the war, and that proclaiming the Negroes free would not make them free. By way of analogy, he asked his callers: "How many legs will a sheep have if you call the tail a leg?" "Five," was the reply. "You are mistaken," said Lincoln, "for calling a tail a leg don't make it so."

[7970]

As commander-in-chief of the army, Lincoln was disposed to treat his absent without leave cases with leniency.

"If the good Lord has given a

man a cowardly pair of legs," he
reasoned, "it is hard to keep them
from running away with him."

[7971]

The artist, Frank B. Carpenter,
who painted a picture of the Cabinet assembled to hear the Emanci-
pation Proclamation and witness
the signature of President Lincoln
to this historic document, told the
following story:

"One evening the President
brought a couple of friends into the
'state dining room' to see my picture. Something was said in the
conversation that ensued that 'reminded' him of the following circumstance: 'Judge ——,' he said,
'held the strongest ideas of rigid
government and close construction
that I ever met. It was said of him
on one occasion that he would hang
a man for blowing his nose in the
street, but he would quash the
indictment if it failed to specify
which hand he blew it with!' "

[7972]

After the battle of Antietam,
when McClellan's army lay unac-
countably idle, Lincoln,. with his
friend, O. M. Hatch of Illinois,
went to the front. They stood on
a hill from which they could view
the vast camp, and Lincoln said:

"Hatch, Hatch, what is all this?"

"Why," said Hatch, "that is the
Army of the Potomac."

"No, Hatch, no," said Lincoln,
"that is General McClellan's body-
guard."

[7973]

When Noah Brooks had carefully explained to President Lincoln how a California politician
had unwittingly been led into
speaking the truth, the President

recalled a similar circumstance
about a Negro barber in Illinois,
who was a great liar. A crowd in
front of the barber shop stood one
evening gazing with admiration at
the planet Jupiter. "Sho," said the
barber, "I've seen that star before.
I seen him 'way down in Georgy."
Said Lincoln: "Like your California
friend, he told the truth, but
thought he was lying."

[7974]

In the early part of the year 1865,
when Joe Johnson had reached
Raleigh with his army, fears were
entertained lest he might suddenly
join Lee, and the two crush Grant.
The congressman then representing
the Springfield (Ill.) district called
upon President Lincoln, when the
following conversation ensued:

Congressman–"They are becoming
anxious, some of them in the House,
about the situation. Have you received anything later? Aren't you
afraid Grant is making a mistake
in not moving?"

The President–"Do you remember
that Baptist revival in Springfield,
in such a year?"

Congressman–"I do not recall it."

The President–"Well, Bill, a hardened sinner, was converted. Upon
an appointed day the minister baptized the converts in a small stream.
After Bill had been plunged under
once, he asked the preacher to
baptize him again; the latter replied it was unnecessary. Bill, however, urged the matter, and he was
accordingly put under for the second time. As he came up, he again
asked, as a particular favor, that he
might be baptized just once more.
The minister, a little angered, answered that he had already been
under once more than the other

converts. Still Bill pleaded, and the preacher put him under for the third time. As Bill came up puffing and blowing, he shook the water from his hair and exclaimed: 'There! I'll be blowed if the devil can get hold of me now.' " The President continued, "General Grant is very much like Bill. He is determined on making sure of the thing, and will not move until he has."

[7975]
To a delegation who begged the commissionship of the Sandwich Islands for a certain man, urging that besides being a qualified man he was in bad health, President Lincoln said:

"Gentlemen, I am sorry to say that there are eight other applicants for the place and they are all sicker than your man."

[7976]
A friend thought Lincoln took much counsel with David Davis, Judge of the Circuit Court, but Lincoln enlightened him with the following story: "They had side judges down in New Hampshire, and to show the folly of the system, one who had been a side judge for twenty years said the only time the chief judge ever consulted him was at the close of a long day's session, when he turned to the side judge and whispered, 'Don't your back ache?' "

[7977]
A member of the church, being at a Presidential reception, closed some remarks with the pious hope that the Lord would be "on our side."

"I am not at all concerned about that," commented President Lincoln, "for we know that the Lord is always on the side of the right. But it is my constant anxiety and prayer that I and this nation should be on the Lord's side."

[7978]
Lincoln told the story of how he became possessed of a jack-knife.

"In the days when I used to be on the circuit (traveling on horseback from one county court to another) I was once accosted by a stranger, who said:

" 'Excuse me, sir, but I have an article which belongs to you.'

" 'How is that?' I asked, considerably astonished.

"The stranger took a jack-knife from his pocket.

" 'This knife,' said he, 'was placed in my hands some years ago, with the injunction that I was to keep it until I found a man homelier-looking than I am myself. I have carried it from that time till this; allow me to say, sir, that you are fairly entitled to the property.' "

[7979]
Douglas once thought to score off Lincoln by relating how, when he first knew him, Lincoln was a "grocery-keeper," selling among other things whiskey and cigars. "Mr. L.," said Douglas, "was a very good bartender!" But the laugh was on the other side when Lincoln made the following reply:

"What Mr. Douglas has said, gentlemen, is true enough; I did keep a grocery, and I did sell cotton, candles and cigars, and sometimes whiskey; but I remember in those days that Mr. Douglas was one of my best customers. Many a time have I stood on one side of the counter and sold whiskey to Mr. Douglas on the other side, but the difference between us now is this: I have left my side of the counter, but Mr. Douglas still sticks to his as tenaciously as ever."

[7980]

When complaints were made to Lincoln of the strenuous dictatorial methods of Secretary of War Stanton, Lincoln made this comparison:

"We may have to treat Stanton as they are sometimes obliged to treat a Methodist minister I know out West. He gets wrought up to so high a pitch of excitement in his prayers and exhortations that they put bricks in his pockets to keep him down. But I guess we'll let him jump awhile first."

[7981]

Lincoln and a judge were having a friendly contest of wits on the subject of horses, when Lincoln said:

"Well, look here, Judge! I'll tell you what I'll do. I'll make a horse trade with you, only it must be upon these stipulations: Neither party shall see the other's horse until it is produced here in the courtyard of the hotel and both parties must trade horses. If either party backs out of the agreement, he does so under a forfeiture of twenty-five dollars."

It was agreed, and Lincoln and the judge each left to find a horse for the joking trade, while a crowd collected to watch the fun. When the judge reappeared there was a great laugh at the incredibly skinny, dejected-looking animal, blind in both eyes, that he led. But the uproar came when Lincoln strode upon the scene with a carpenter's saw-horse on his shoulder. Relieving himself of his burden, Lincoln

with a disgusted air scrutinized the judge's animal.

"Well, Judge," he said, "this is the first time I ever got the worst of it in a horse trade."

[7982]

When practicing law in Illinois, Lincoln wrote upon a subscription paper passed to him in behalf of the worn-out trouser-seat of his opponent:

"I refuse to subscribe to the end in view."

[7983]

The Northern armies had been inactive for some time, when a telegram came to Lincoln from Cumberland Gap saying that firing had been heard toward Knoxville, where General Burnside was in much peril. Lincoln calmly remarked that he was glad of it. Some one expressing surprise at his remark, Lincoln said:

"You see, it reminds me of Mistress Sallie Ward, a neighbor of mine, who had a very large family. Occasionally one of her numerous progeny would be heard crying in some out-of-the-way place, upon which Mrs. Ward would exclaim, 'There's one of my children not dead yet.' "

[7984]

Lincoln once dreamed that he was in a great assembly where the people made a lane for him to pass through. "He is a common-looking fellow," said one of them. "Friend," replied Lincoln in his dream, "the Lord prefers common-looking people—that is why He made so many of them."

[7985]

Lincoln's innate democracy was humorously expressed in this remark about his ancestry: "I don't know who my grandfather was, and I am much more concerned to know what his grandson will be."

[7986]

From discussing the physical peculiarities of Douglas, who was a very small man, a group of Lincoln's friends turned to the question of how long a man's legs should be. Upon Lincoln's joining the group, he was asked the question.

"Well," he said, "I should think a man's legs ought to be long enough to reach from his body to the ground."

[7987]

John Bach McMaster, the historian, told that, as a boy, his first sight of Lincoln was at a reception where the guests were marshaled past the President by watchful ushers, and not allowed to come too close. One old chap, much disappointed at not having shaken hands with him, waved his hat and blurted out, "Mr. President, I'm from up in York State where we believe that God Almighty and Abraham Lincoln are going to save this country."

"My friend, you're half right," replied Lincoln.

[7988]

At the outset of the war, when the campaign was conducted coincidently by the chief newspapers, a correspondent of a New York journal called to propose still another plan to the plan-ridden President, who listened patiently, then said:

"Your New York papers remind me of a little story.

"Some years ago, there was a gentleman traveling through Kansas on horseback. There were few settlements and no roads, and he lost his way. To make matters worse, as night came on, a terrific thunderstorm arose, and peal on peal of thunder, following flashes of lightning, shook the earth or momentarily illuminated the scene. The terrified traveler then got off and led his horse, seeking to guide it as best he might by the flickering light of the quick flashes of lightning. All of a sudden, a tremendous crash of thunder brought the man to his knees in terror, and he cried out:

"'O Lord! if it's all the same to you, give us a little more light and a little less noise!'"

[7989]

A Congressman from New Jersey brought two citizens of that state to see President Lincoln out of idle curiosity, remarking as he introduced them: "Mr. President, this is Mr. X. and Mr. Y., and they are among the weightiest men in Southern New Jersey." Upon their departure, Lincoln observed: "I wonder that end of the state didn't tip up when they got off it."

[7990]

Receiving news that a brigadier-general and twelve army mules had been captured by the Confederates, Lincoln's comment was: "How unfortunate! Those *mules* cost us two hundred dollars apiece!"

[7991]

At one time in 1863, when all the prominent personages were called upon to make speeches, Lincoln at his turn said:

"I appear before you, fellow-citizens, merely to thank you for this compliment. The inference is a very fair one that you would hear me for a little while at least, were I to commence to make a speech. I do not appear before you for the purpose of doing so, and for several substantial reasons. The most substantial of these is that I have no speech to make. In my position it is somewhat important that I should not say any foolish things. (A voice, 'If you can help it.') It very often happens that the only way to help it is to say nothing at all. Believing that is my present condition this evening, I must beg of you to excuse me from addressing you further."

[7992]
Lincoln shrewdly triumphed over Judge Davis on one occasion, which is related by Whitney:

"I remember once that while several of us lawyers were together, including Judge Davis, Lincoln suddenly asked a novel question regarding court practice, addressed to no one particularly, to which the Judge, who was in the habit certainly of appropriating his full share of any conversation, replied, stating what he understood the practice should be. Lincoln thereat laughed and said, 'I asked that question, hoping that you would answer. I have that very question to present to the court in the morning, and I am very glad to find out that the court is on my side.' "

[7993]
When an opposing lawyer in a case argued that precedent was greater than law and that custom legalized all things, Lincoln demolished this position with one of his delightfully opposite stories that is also humorously descriptive of a

type of rural character in those days. The story is:

"Old Squire Bagley, from Menard, came into my office one day and said:

" 'Lincoln, I want your advice as a lawyer. Has a man what's been elected justice of the peace a right to issue a marriage license?'

"I told him no; whereupon the old squire threw himself back in his chair very indignantly and said:

" 'Lincoln, I thought you was a lawyer. Now, Bob Thomas and me had a bet on this thing, and we agreed to let you decide; but if this is your opinion I don't want it, for I know a thunderin' sight better. I've been a squire eight years, and I've issued marriage licenses all the time.' "

[7994]
Lincoln, while a member of Congress, took his stand against the Mexican War; and he declared those who argued the war was not a war of aggression made him think of the Illinois farmer who said: "I ain't greedy 'bout land. I only want what jines mine."

[7995]
When Lincoln heard that Fred Douglass was in Washington he sent for him to come to the White House and take tea. Douglass speaking of the occasion said, "Lincoln is the first white man I ever spent an hour with who did not remind me that I am a Negro."

[7996]
At one time during the American Civil War, Gen. George B. McClellan, then in command of the Union forces, was conducting a waiting campaign; and so careful was he to avoid mistakes that little

headway was evident. President Lincoln thereupon wrote him a letter:

"My dear McClellan: If you don't want to use the Army I should like to borrow it for a while. Yours respectfully, A. Lincoln."

[7997]

A woman with a commanding air told Lincoln: "Mr. President, you must give me a colonel's commission for my son. Sir, I demand it, not as a favor, but as a right. Sir, my grandfather fought at Lexington. Sir, my uncle was the only man that did not run away at Bladensburg. Sir, my father fought at New Orleans, and my husband was killed at Monterey."

"I guess, madam," said Lincoln, "your family has done enough for the country. It is time to give somebody else a chance."

[7998]

A fanatical temperance advocate called on Lincoln to protest against the reported whisky-drinking of General Grant. After listening to his harangue, Lincoln said:

"Find out the brand of whisky General Grant uses. I would like to furnish the same brand to my other generals."

[7999]

Abraham Lincoln loved jokes on himself.

One day a congressman called at the White House and found the President was suffering from a cold. He expressed his sympathy, to which Lincoln replied, "Well," and he looked down at his feet regretfully, for they were uncommonly large, "I expect colds. There's so much of me on the ground, you know."

[8000]

General Grant had a record that is rare in military annals. When he once took a place, he never surrendered it. Speaking of this to General Butler, Lincoln said: "When General Grant once gets possessed of a place he seems to hang on to it as if he inherited it."

[8001]

After Abraham Lincoln had sent the name of the Rev. Mr. Shrigley to the senate for confirmation as hospital chaplain in the army, a self-constituted committee of the Young Men's Christian Association called on him to protest against the appointment. After Mr. Shrigley's name had been mentioned the President said:

"O yes, I have sent it to the senate. His testimonials are highly satisfactory, and the appointment will no doubt be confirmed at an early day."

The committee spokesman replied: "But, sir, we have come not to ask for the appointment, but to solicit you to withdraw the nomination, on the ground that Mr. Shrigley is not evangelical in his sentiments."

"Ah!" said the President, "that alters the case. On what point of doctrine is the gentleman unsound?"

"He does not believe in endless punishment," was the reply.

"Yes," added another of the committee, "he believes that even the rebels themselves will finally be saved; and it will never do to have a man with such views hospital chaplain."

President Lincoln hesitated to reply for a moment, and then responded with emphasis: "If that be so, gentlemen, and there be any way under heaven whereby the rebels can be saved, then let the man be appointed!"

He was appointed.

[8002]

The only pun Abe Lincoln ever made was when he was splitting rails and his boss criticized his work severely.

"How do you feel now?" asked a fellow-workman.

Lincoln thought a minute and replied, "I feel I maul right."

[8003]

Secretary of War Stanton was both naturally and, by virtue of his office, bellicose, and when pestered by a swarm of annoyances his temper was often carried to a high point. One day, he complained to President Lincoln of a major-general, who had accused him of favoritism in grossly abusive terms. His auditor advised him to write a sharp rejoinder.

"Prick him hard!" were the words.

Mr. Stanton, encouraged by this backing, wrote feverishly, and read his letter aloud while the hearer kept favorably commenting:

"Right! Just it! Score him deeply! That's first rate, Stanton!"

But when the gratified author began folding up the paper to fit into an envelope the counsellor interrupted with:

"What are you going to do with it now?"

The Secretary was about to dispatch it, of course.

"Nonsense," said the President, "you don't want to send that letter. *Put it in the stove!* That's the way

I do when I have written a letter while I am mad. It is a good letter, and you've had a good time writing it, and feel better. Now, burn it, and write again."

[8004]

To Dubois and Hatch, who wanted an appointment which was filled, Lincoln telegraphed humorously:

"What nation do you desire General Allen to be made quartermaster-general of? This nation already has a quarter-master-general. —A. Lincoln."

[8005]

Major Whitney related this amusing court scene: "The first term of Davis's court that I attended the Judge was calling through the docket for the first time, in order to dispose of such cases as could be handled summarily, and likewise to sort the chaff from the wheat, when he came across a long bill in chancery, drawn by an excellent but somewhat indolent lawyer. On glancing at it he exclaimed: 'Why, Brother Snap, how did you rake up energy enough to get up such a long bill?'"

" 'Dunno, Jedge,' replied the party addressed, squirming in his seat and uneasily scratching his head. The Judge unfolded and held up the bill. 'Astonishing, ain't it? Brother Snap did it. Wonderful— eh, Lincoln?'

"This amounted to an order on Lincoln for a joke at this point, and he was ready, of course—he had to be; he never failed. 'It's like the lazy preacher,' drawled he, 'that used to write long sermons, and the explanation was, he got to writin' and was too lazy to stop.' "

[8006]

A Philadelphia man, an unmitigated bore, had repeatedly encroached upon the President's time, until the latter at last got rid of him by a simple and amusing expedient. The story was told by Justice Carter of the Supreme Court of the District of Columbia. On this day many delegations were waiting to see the President, but this man stayed and talked. Finally Lincoln walked over to a wardrobe in the corner of the Cabinet chamber, and, taking a bottle from the shelf, remarked to the man, who was bald-headed:

"Did you ever try this stuff for your hair?"

"No, sir, I never did."

"Well, I advise you to try it and I will give you this bottle. If at first you don't succeed, try, try again. Keep it up. They say it will make hair grow on a pumpkin. Now take it and come back in eight or ten months and tell me how it works."

The man, nonplussed, took the bottle and left without further speech. Judge Carter, coming in with a delegation, found the President in a fit of laughter.

[8007]

A would-be client detailed to Lincoln, at Springfield, Ill., a case in which he had a legal claim to a value of some hundreds of dollars. But his winning it would ruin a widow and afflict her six children.

"We shall not take your case, though we can doubtless gain it for you," responded Lincoln. "Some things that are right legally are not right morally. But we will give you some advice for which we will charge nothing. (The "we" included his partner, Mr. Herndon.) We advise a sprightly, energetic man like you to try your hand at making six hundred dollars in some other way."

[8008]

A picture of Lincoln, the irrepressible story teller, is found in the reminiscence of a court clerk:

"I was never fined but once for contempt of court. Davis fined me five dollars. Mr. Lincoln had just come in, and leaning over my desk had told me a story so irresistibly funny that I broke out into a loud laugh. The Judge called me to order, saying, 'This must be stopped. Mr. Lincoln, you are constantly disturbing this court with your stories.' Then to me: 'You may fine yourself five dollars.' I apologized, but told the Judge the story was worth the money. In a few minutes the Judge called me to him. 'What was that story Lincoln told you,' he asked. I told him, and he laughed aloud in spite of himself. 'Remit your fine,' he ordered."

[8009]

Upon one occasion Lincoln contested a case with Judge Logan, under whom he had studied law. The Judge was a man of great dignity, but was often very careless of his appearance, a trait which Lincoln knew and cleverly made use of in the trial.

"Gentlemen," said Lincoln to the jury, "you must be careful and not permit yourselves to be overborne by the eloquence of the counsel for defense. Judge Logan, I know, is an effective lawyer; I have met him too often to doubt that. But shrewd and careful though he be, still he is sometimes wrong. Since this trial began I have discovered that, with all his caution and fastidiousness, he hasn't knowledge enough to put his shirt on right."

A glance revealed that the Judge had his shirt—the stiff, pleated variety—put on backwards. The dignified Judge, thus made the object of laughter, was of course utterly disconcerted.

[8010]

In 1846, during a canvass for Congress, Lincoln attended a preaching service of Peter Cartwright's. Cartwright called on all desiring to go to heaven to stand up. All arose but Lincoln. Then he asked all to rise who did not want to go to hell. Lincoln remained still seated. "I am surprised," said Cartright, "to see Abe Lincoln sitting back there unmoved by these appeals. If Mr. Lincoln does not want to go to heaven and does not want to escape hell, perhaps he will tell us where he does want to go."

Lincoln slowly arose and replied, "I am going to Congress."

[8011]

To a man who asked how many men the Confederates had in the field, Lincoln replied: *"Twelve hundred thousand, according to the best authority."* "Good heavens," cried the man. "Yes, sir," repeated Lincoln, "twelve hundred thousand—no doubt of it. You see, all of our generals, when they get whipped, say the enemy outnumbers them from three or five to one, and I must believe them. We have four hundred thousand men in the field, and three times four make twelve. Don't you see it?"

[8012]

A foreign diplomat came in upon Lincoln while he was blacking his shoes.

"What, Mr. President, you black your own shoes?"

"Yes," Lincoln answered, "whose do you black?"

[8013]

A lawyer who studied in Mr. Lincoln's office tells a story illustrative of his love of justice. After listening one day for some time to a client's statement of his case, Lincoln, who had been staring at the ceiling, suddenly swung around in his chair, and said:

"Well, you have a pretty good case in technical law, but a pretty bad one in equity and justice. You'll have to get some other fellow to win this case for you. I couldn't do it. All the time, while talking to that jury, I'd be thinking: 'Lincoln, you're a liar,' and I believe I should forget myself and say it out loud."

[8014]

Someone asked Lincoln once whether he did not find the ceremonies of the Presidency irksome. "Yes, sometimes," said Lincoln. "In fact, I feel sometimes like a man who was ridden out of town on a rail, and said: 'If it wasn't for the honor of the thing, I'd rather walk!'"

[8015]

When government officials, who wished to secure the transfer of control over certain funds from other hands into their own, approached President Lincoln with this request, he met them with this story:

"You are very much like a man in Illinois whose cabin was burned down, and, according to the kindly custom of early days in the West, his neighbors all contributed something to start him again. In his case they had been so liberal that he soon found himself better off than before the fire, and got proud. One day a neighbor brought him a bag of oats, but the fellow refused it with scorn, and said, 'I am not taking oats now; I take nothing but money.' "

EPITAPHS

AMERICAN EPITAPHS

[8016]
Stowe, Vt.:
My wife from me departed
  And robbed me like a knave;
Which caused me broken hearted
  To sink into this grave.
My children took an active part,
  To doom me did contrive;
Which stuck a dagger in my heart
  That I could not survive.

[8017]
Boston (Granary Burying-ground):
Here I lie bereft of breath
Because a cough carried me off;
Then a coffin they carried me off in.

[8018]
Bayfield, Miss.:
Here lies my wife in earthly mould,
Who when she lived did naught but scold.
Peace! wake her not, for now she's still,
She had; but now I have my will.

[8019]
In a cemetery at Middlebury, Vt., is a stone, erected by a widow to her loving husband, bearing this inscription:

"Rest in peace—until we meet again."
IN MEMORY OF MRS. ALPHA
WHITE
WEIGHT *309 LBS.*
Open wide ye heavenly gates
That lead to the heavenly shore;
Our father suffered in passing through
And mother weighs much more.
                    —*Lee, Mass.*

[8021]
THOMAS MULVANEY
1724–1795
Old Thomas Mulvaney lies here
His mouth ran from ear to ear.
Reader, tread lightly on this wonder,
For if he yawns you're gone to thunder.
                    —*Middlefield, Mass.*

[8022]
Here lies the bones of Richard Lawton,
Whose death, alas! was strangely brought on.
Trying his corns one day to mow off,
His razor slipped and cut his toe off.
His toe, or, rather, what it grew to,
An inflimation quickly flew to.
Which took, alas! to mortifying,
And was the cause of Richard's dying.
                    —*Plymouth, Mass.*

[8023]
In Burlington Churchyard, Mass.:
Sacred to the memory of Anthony Drake,
Who died for peace and quietness sake;
His wife was constantly scolding and scoffin',
So he sought for repose in a twelve-dollar coffin.

[8024]

Neuralgia worked on Mrs. Smith
Till neath the sod it laid her.
She was a worthy Methodist
And served as a crusader.

—*Skaneatles, N. Y.*

[8025]

IN MEMORY
BETSY FITZHUGH
1796–1831
My wife
lies here.
I am glad
of it.

—*Brookfield, Conn.*

[8026]

Sacred to the Memory of
HENRY HARRIS,
*Born June 27, 1821, of Henry Harris
and Jane, His Wife, Died on the
4th of May, 1837, by the Kick of a
Colt in His Bowels*

Peaceable and quiet, a friend to his
father and mother, and respected
by all who knew him, and went to
the world where horses do not
kick, where sorrow and weeping
is no more.

—*Williamsport, Pa.*

[8027]

A tombstone in the graveyard at
Saratoga, N. Y., once bore the following somewhat carelessly worded
epitaph:

"Erected to the memory of John
Phillips accidentally shot at a mark
of affection by his brother."

[8028]

*IN MEMORY OF
ANNA HOPEWELL*

Here Lies the body of our Anna
Done to death by a banana.
It wasn't the fruit that laid her low
But the skin of the thing that made
her go.

—*Enosburg, Vt.*

[8029]

Bayfield, Miss.:

Stranger pause, my tale attend,
And learn the cause of Hannah's
end.
Across the world the wind did
blow,
She ketched a cold that laid her
low.
We shed a lot of tears 'tis true,
But life is short—aged 82.

[8030]

*SACRED TO THE MEMORY
OF
JARED BATES
WHO DIED AUG. THE 6TH, 1800*

His Widow, aged 24, lives at 7 Elm
Street, has every qualification for a
good wife, and yearns to be comforted.

—*Lincoln, Maine*

[8031]

*HERE LYES
SIDNEY SNYDER
1803–1823*

The wedding day decided was,
The wedding wine provided,
But ere the day did come along
He'd drunk it and died, did.
    Ah, Sidney! Sidney!
        —*Providence, R. I.*

[8032]

*TO THE FOUR HUSBANDS
OF MISS IVY SAUNDERS
1790, 1794, 1808, 18??*

Here lies my husbands, One, Two,
Three
Dumb as men could ever be.
As for my Fourth, well, praise be
God,
He bides for a little above the sod.
Alex, Ben, Sandy were the first
three's names,
And to make things tidy I'll add
his—James.

—*Shutesbury, Mass.*

[8033]

From Lost Creek, Colorado:

Here lies the clay of Mitchell Coots,
Whose feet yet occupy his boots.
His soul has gone—we know not where
It landed, neither do we care.
He slipped the joker up his sleeve
With vile intention to deceive,
And when detected, tried to jerk
His gun, but didn't get his work
In with sufficient swiftness, which
Explains the presence here of Mitch.
At Gabriel's trump, if he should wake,
He'll mighty likely try to take
The trump with that same joker he
Had sleeved so surreptitiously,
And which we placed upon his bier
When we concealed his body here.

[8034]

In Calvary cemetery, Chicago:

In memory of
John S——
who
departed this life
Jan. 13, 1859. Aged 28 years.
Cold is my bed, but oh, I love it,
For colder are my friends above it.

[8035]

Alexandria, Va.:

(Mr. James Danner, late of Louisville, having been laid by the side of his four wives received this touching epitaph.)

An excellent husband was this Mr. Danner,
He lived in a thoroughly honorable manner,
He may have had troubles,
But they burst like bubbles,
He's at peace now, with Mary, Jane, Susan and Hannah.

[8037]

CYNTHIA STEVENS
1742–1776

Here lies Cynthia, Stevens' wife,
She lived six years in calm and strife.
Death came at last and set her free,
I was glad and so was she.
—*Hollis, N. H.*

[8036]

Beneath this stone our baby lays,
He neither cries nor hollers,
He lived just one and twenty days,
And cost us forty dollars.
—*Burlington, Vt.*

[8038]

Here Betsy Brown her body lies,
Her soul is flying to the skies.
While here on earth she ofttimes spun
Six hundred skeins from sun to sun,
And wove one day, her daughter brags,
Two hundred pounds of carpet rags.

—*Winslow, Maine*

[8039]

AMOS SHUTE
1789–1842

He heard the angels calling him
From the Celestial Shore,
He flapped his wings and away he went
To make one angel more.
—*Canaan, New Hampshire*

[8040]

From Germantown, Pa.:

Here lies the bones of my boy Fritz,
The Lord killed him with ague fits.
He was too good to live with me,
So He took him home to live with He.

[8041]

Here, beneath this stone, there lies,
Waiting a summons to the skies,
  The body of Samuel Jinking;
He was an honest Christian man,
His fault was, that he took and ran
  Suddenly to drinking.
Whoever reads this tablet o'er,
Take warning now, and drink no
  more.

—*Augusta, Maine*

[8042]
SARAH SHUTE
1803–1840

Here lies, cut down like unripe
  fruit,
The wife of Deacon Amos Shute.
She died of drinking too much
  coffee,
Anno Dominy eighteen forty.

—*Canaan, New Hampshire*

[8043]

Underneath this pile of stones
Lies all that's left of Sally Jones.
Her name was Briggs, it was not
  Jones,
But Jones was used to rhyme with
  stones.

—*Skaneatles, N. Y.*

[8044]

Time magazine reports the following:
  Dr. William Rothwell, 71, well-
loved town character, who always
paid the check at parties; of heart
disease; in Pawtucket, R. I. His
tombstone: a boulder inscribed
". . . *This is on me.*"

[8045]
Huntington, West Va.:

"Here lies the body of J. Wesley
Webb, a firm believer in the Lord
Jesus Christ, Jeffersonian Democ-
racy and the M. E. Church."

[8046]
Baton Rouge, La.:

Here lies the body of David Jones.
    His last words were:
I die a Christian and a Democrat.

[8047]
IN MEMORY OF MR. PETER
DANIELS
1688–1746

Beneath this stone, a lump of clay,
  Lies Uncle Peter Daniels,
Who too early in the month of May
  Took off his winter flannels.

—*Medway, Mass.*

[8048]
Sacred to the Memory of Elisha
Philbrook and His Wife Sarah

Beneath these stones do lie,
Back to back, my wife and I!
When the last trumpet the air shall
  fill,
If she gets up, I'll just lie still.

—*Sargentville, Maine*

[8049]

Ledyard, Conn., on a man who
died of natural causes after several
attempts at suicide:
    He died an honest death.

[8050]

Beneath this stone, a lump of clay
  Lies Arabella Young
Who on the 21st of May
  Began to hold her tongue.

—*Hatfield, Mass., 1771*

[8051]
South Dennis, Mass.:

Of seven sons the Lord his father
  gave,
He was the fourth who found a
  watery grave.
Fifteen days had passed since the
  circumstance occurred,
When his body was found and
  decently interred.

British Epitaphs

[8052]
At Church Stretton, Salop:
On a Thursday she was born,
On a Thursday made a bride,
On a Thursday put to bed,
On a Thursday broke her leg,
and
On a Thursday died.

[8053]
In Grantham churchyard, Lincolnshire, England—on a sexton:
I, that have carried a hundred bodies brave,
Am by a fever carried to my grave;
I carried, and am carried, so that's even;
May I be porter to the gates of heaven.

[8054]
In the Minster churchyard, Ripon, Yorkshire, England:
    "Here lies poor
    but honest Bryan Tunstal;
    He was a most expert angler
        Until
    Death, envious of his merit,
        Threw out his line,
        Hooked him,
    And landed him here,
    The 21st day of April, 1790."

[8055]
In Cheltenham churchyard:
Here lies the body of Molly Dickie,
    the wife of Hall Dickie, tailor.
    Two great physicians first
        My loving husband tried
            To cure my pain—
                In vain;
        At last he got a third,
        And then I died.

[8056]
Epitaph for Sir John Yanbrugh:
Lie heavy on him, Earth! for he
Laid many heavy loads on thee!

[8057]
On Judge Boat, England, 1723:
Here lies Judge Boat within a coffin;
Pray, gentlefolks, forbear your scoffing.
A Boat a judge; yes; where's the blunder;
A wooden judge is no such wonder.
And in his robes, you must agree,
No boat was better decked than he.
'Tis needless to describe him fuller;
In short, he was an able sculler.

[8058]
On a profligate mathematician at Manchester:
    Here lies John Hill,
    A man of skill,
His age was five times ten;
    He ne'er did good,
    Nor never would,
Had he lived—as long again.

[8059]
From Bath Abbey:
    Here lies Ann Mann;
    She lived an old Maid and
    she died an old *Mann.*

[8060]
On Merideth, an organist at St. Mary Winton College, Oxford:
Here lies one blown out of breath,
Who lived a merry life, and died a Merideth.

[8061]
Over the grave of a Shropshire blacksmith:
My sledge and anvil lie declined,
My bellows too have lost their wind;
My fire's extinct, my forge decay'd,
And in the dust my body's laid:
My coal is out, my iron's gone,
My nails are drove, my work is done.

[8062]
Here Lies
Dame Mary Page,
Relict of Sir Gregory Page, Bart.
She Departed This Life
March 4th, 1728,
In the 56th Year of Her Age.
In 67 months she was tapped 66
times. Had taken away 240 gallons
of water, without ever repining at
her case, or even feating the opera-
tion.—*Bunhill Fields Burying
Ground, England*

[8063]
*The following quaint and sig-
nificant epitaph was inscribed upon
the tomb of a famous beer drinker
in one of the rural districts of
England:*
Beneath these stones repose the
    bones
Of Theodosius Grim;
He took his beer from year to year,
And then the bier took him.

[8064]
There is a peculiar class of epi-
taphs which, while commemorat-
ing the dead, serve also as an ad-
vertisement for the living. One of
these two-sided inscriptions may
still be seen in the churchyard of
Upton-on-Severn:
Beneath this stone, in hopes of
    Zion,
Doth lie the landlord of the Lion;
His son keeps on his business still,
Resigned unto the heavenly will.

[8065]
*From West Grinstead churchyard,
Sussex:*
Vast strong was I, but yet did dye,
And in my grave asleep I lye
My grave is stean'd round about.
Yet I hope the Lord will find me
out.

[8066]
*On Robert Trollop, Architect, in
Gateshead churchyard, Durham:*
Here lies Robert Trollop
Who made yon stones roll up;
When Death took his soul up,
His body fill'd this hole up.

[8067]
Falkirk, England:
Here under this sod and under
    these trees
Is buried the body of Solomon
    Pease.
But here in his hole lies only his
    pod
His soul is shelled out and gone up
    to God.

[8068]
*The following may be seen on a
tombstone in the churchyard of
Bridgford-on-the-Hill, Nottingham-
shire:*
Sacred to the memory of John
    walker, the only son of Benja-
    min and Ann Walker, engineer
    and palisade maker, died Sep-
    tember 23, 1832, aged 36 years.
Farewell, my wife and father dear,
    No engine powers now do I fear;
My glass is run, my work is done,
    And now my head lies quiet here.
Tho' many an engine I've set up,
    And got great praise from men;
I made them work on British
    ground,
    And on the roaring main.
My engine's stopped, my valves are
    bad,
    And lies so deep within;
No engineer could here be found
    To put me new ones in.
But Jesus Christ converted me,
    And took me up above;
I hope once more to meet once
    more,
    And sing redeeming love.

[8069]
The celebrated Daniel Lambert's epitaph, St. Martin's, Stamford Baron, England:

Altus in animo, in corpore maximus.

In remembrance of that prodigy in Nature,

DANIEL LAMBERT.

A native of Leicester, who was possessed of an exalted, convivial mind;
and in personal greatness had no competitor;
He measured 3 ft. 1 in. round the legs, 9 ft. 4 in. round the body, and weighed 52 st. 11 lb.
He departed this life on the 21st June, 1809,
Aged 39 years.
As a testimony of respect, this stone is erected by his friends in Leicester.

[8070]
Some years ago, the following epitaph was to be seen on a gravestone in a churchyard near *Shef-field, England:*

Beneath these stones
Lies William Jones,
The bailiff and the Bum;
When he died,
The devil cried,
Come, Billy, come.

[8071]
On Richard Groombridge, in Horsham churchyard:

He was.

[8072]
The famous epitaph on Sir John Strange compliments him at the expense of the whole legal profession:

Here lies an honest lawyer,
And that is Strange.

[8073]
On Oliver Goldsmith:

Here lies Nolly Goldsmith, for shortness called Noll,
Who wrote like an angel, but talked like poor Poll.

DAVID GARRICK, 1716–1779

[8074]
On a tomb in St. Pancras:

GODFREY HILL, æt. 46.

—Thus far am I got on my journey;

READER:
Canst thou inform me
What follows next?

[8075]
From Hyden churchyard, Yorks:

Here lies the body of
WILLIAM STRATTON, of Paddington,
buried 18th day of May, 1734, aged 97 years;
who had by his first wife
28 children;
by his second 17; was own father to 45;
grandfather to 86; greatgrandfather to 23.
In all 154 children.

[8076]
In Poole churchyard, on a tall man named DAY:

As long as long can be,
So long so long was he;
How long, how long, dost say?
As long as the longest DAY.

[8077]
In Kensington churchyard:

Here are deposited the remains of
MRS. ANNE FLOYER,
the beloved wife of Mr. Richard Floyer,
of Thistle Grove, in this parish.
Died on Thursday, the 8th of May, 1823.
God hath chosen her as a pattern for the other Angels.

[8078]

In Seven Oaks churchyard, Kent:
Grim Death took me without any
    warning
I was well at night, and died in the
    morning.

[8079]

The following from Westminster
Abbey, on John Gay, the Poet, is
said to have been written by him-
self:
Life is a jest, and all things show it;
I thought so once and now I know
    it.

              1688–1732.

[8080]

In Bedlington churchyard, Durham:
Poems and epitaphs are but stuff:
Here lies ROBERT BURROWS, that's
    enough.

[8081]

*On an old woman who kept a
pottery-shop in Chester, England:*
Beneath these stones lies old Kath-
    ering Gray,
Changed from a busy life to lifeless
    clay;
By earth and clay she got her pelf,
But now is turned to earth herself.
Ye weeping friends, let me advise,
Abate your grief and dry your eyes,
For what avails a flood of tears?
Who knows but in a run of years,
In some tall pitcher or bread pan,
She in her shop may be again?

[8082]

*The following quaint epitaph is
to be found in St. Giles's Cemetery
collection:*
    The mortal remains of
        JOHN BRINDELL,
  after an evil life of 64 years,
    Died June 18th, 1822,
and lies at rest beneath this stone.
    Pause, reader; reflect;
  "Eternity, how surely thine."

[8083]

*From Taibach Churchyard, South
Wales:*
Hurrah! my boys, at the Parson's
    fall,
For if he'd lived he'd a' buried us
    all.

[8084]

Epitaph of Susan Blake:
(Written by Sir Thomas More at
her urgent entreaty.)
Good Susan Blake in royal state
Arrived at last at Heaven's gate.
(After an absence of years and
having fallen out with her he
added these two lines):
But Peter met her with a club
And knocked her back to Beelze-
    bub.

[8085]

On THOMAS KEMP, *who was
hanged for sheepstealing:*
Here lies the body of THOMAS
    KEMP,
Who lived by wool and died by
    hemp;
There nothing would suffice the
    glutton
But with the fleece to steal the mut-
    ton;
Had he but worked and lived up-
    righter,
He'd ne'er been hung for a sheep-
    biter.

[8086]

*On a pugilist, in Hanslope church-
yard, near Wolverton:*
Strong and athletic was my frame
Far away from home I came,
And manly fought with Simon
    Byrnne
Alas! but lived not to return.
Reader, take warning by my fate,
Unless you rue your case too late;
And if you've ever fought before,
Determine now to fight no more.

[8087]
Another, from Falkirk, England:
At rest beneath this slab of stone,
Lies stingy Jimmy Wyett.
He died one morning just at ten
And saved a dinner by it.

[8088]
*A monument in Streatham
church, Surrey, bears testimony to
the virtues of*
ELIZABETH, wife of Major Gen.
  Hamilton,
who was married near forty-seven
  years,
            and
Never did one thing to disoblige
  her husband.
        She died in 1746.

[8089]
At Witchingham, on the tomb of
THOMAS ALLEYN *and his* TWO
WIVES, *ob., 1650:*
Death here advantage hath of life I
  spye,
One husband with two wives at
  once may lye.

[8090]
*From Painswick churchyard, near
Stroud, Gloucestershire:*
My wife is dead, and here she lies,
Nobody laughs and nobody cries:
Where she is gone to and how she
  fares,
Nobody knows, and nobody cares.

[8091]
From St. Agnes, Cornwall:
Here lies the body of Joan Car-
  thew,
Born at St. Columb, died at St.
  Cue;
Children she had five,
Three are dead, and two alive;
Those that are dead choosing rather
To die with their mother than live
  with their father.

[8092]
At Selby, Yorkshire:
Here lies my wife, a sad slattern and
  shrew,
If I said I regretted her, I should
  lie too!

[8093]
In a Devonshire churchyard:
Charity, wife of Gideon Bligh,
Underneath this stone doth lie.
Nought was she e'er known to do
That her husband told her to.

[8094]
*From a Suffolk County churchyard,
England:*
Here lies the body of Mary Ann,
Who rests in the bosom of Abra-
  ham.

[8095]
In Oxfordshire—A trifle previous:
Here lies the body of John Eldred,
At least, he will be here when he's
  dead;
But now at this time he is alive,
The 14th of August, Sixty-five.

[8096]
In a churchyard near Canterbury:
Of children in all she bore twenty-
  four:
Thank the Lord there will be no
  more.

[8097]
In Selby Churchyard, York:
This tombstone is a Milestone; ha,
  how so,
Because, beneath lies *Miles,* who's
  Miles below.

[8098]
St. Giles churchyard, Northampton:
Here lies a most dutiful daughter,
  Honest and just,
Awaiting the resurrection in hopes,
  To be one of the first.

[8099]

Lord Brougham (for an orator):
Here, reader, turn your weeping
  eyes,
  My fate a useful moral teaches;
The hole in which my body lies
  Would not contain one-half my
  speeches.

[8100]

In Cheltenham churchyard:
Here lies I and my two daughters,
Killed by drinking Cheltenham wa-
  ters;
If we had stuck to Epson salts,
We shouldn't be lying in these here
vaults.

[8101]

*From a churchyard near Salisbury
on a man named Button:*
Oh! Sun, Moon, Stars, and ye celestial Poles
Are graves then dwindled into but-
  ton-holes?

[8102]

*From Llangerrig churchyard,
Montgomeryshire:*
  From earth my body first arose
  But here to earth again it goes
  I never desire to have it more
  To plague me as it did before.

[8103]

*From St. Philip's churchyard, Birm-
ingham:*
  To the memory of James Baker,
who died January 27th, 1781.
  O cruel Death, how cou'd you be
so unkind
  To take him before and leave me
behind?
  You should have taken both of
us, if either,
  Which would have been more
pleasing to the survivor.

[8104]

*In West churchyard, Tranent, Eng-
land:*
Trumpets shall sound,
And archangels cry,
"Come forth, Isabel Mitchell,
And meet Wm. Matheson in the
sky."

[8105]

From St. Nicholas', Yarmouth:
  Here lyeth ye body of
    SARAH BLOOMFIELD,
      Aged 74
Cut off in blooming yuthe we can
but pity.

[8106]

*The following, in Harrow Church-
yard, is ascribed to Lord Byron:*
Beneath these green trees rising to
  the skies,
The planter of them, Isaac Green-
  tree, lies;
A time shall come when these
  green trees shall fall,
And Isaac Green tree rise above
  them all.

[8107]

*From Nettlebed churchyard, Ox-
fordshire:*
Here lies father, and mother, and
  sister, and I:
    We all died within the space
    of one short year:
They were all buried at Wimble except I,
    And I be buried here.

[8108]

Eastwell cemetery, Kent:
    Fear God,
  Keep the commandments,
      and
  Don't attempt to climb a tree,
For that's what caused the death of
me.

[8109]

On the tombstone of Dr. Walker, who wrote a work on "English Particles," is inscribed:
    Here lies Walker's Particles.

[8110]

From a churchyard in Pembroke-shire:
Here lie I, and no wonder I'm dead,
For the wheel of the waggon went over my head.

[8111]

This stone was raised by Sarah's lord,
Not Sarah's virtues to record—
For they're well known to all the town—
But it was *raised* to keep *her down.*
    —*Kilmurry Churchyard, Ireland*

[8112]

At Fosbrooke, in Northumberland:
Here lieth Matthew Hollingshead,
Who died from cold caught in his head.
It brought on fever and rheumatiz,
Which ended me—for here I is.

[8113]

The following was copied literally from an old tombstone in Scotland:
Here lies the body of Alexander Macpherson,
Who was a very extraordinary person;
He was two yards high in his stocking feet,
And kept his accoutrements clean and neat.
    He was slew
    At the battle of Waterloo,
    Plump through
The gullet; it went in at his throat
And came out at the back of his coat.

[8114]

Aberdeen, Scotland:
Here lies Martin Elmerod.
Have mercy on my soul, good God
As I would do were I Lord God
And you were Martin Elmerod.

[8115]

In a Scotch graveyard:
Here — lies my guid and gracious auntie,
Wham death has packed in his portmanty,
Three score years and ten did God gift her,
And here she lies, wha deil daurs lift her?

[8116]

Broom churchyard, Bedfordshire:
    God be praised
Here is Mr. Dudley senior, and Jane his wife also;
Who while living was his superior, but see what death can do.
Two of his sons also lie here, One Walter, t'other Joe;
They all of them went—in the year 1510—below.

[8117]

From Belturbet churchyard, Ireland:
    Here lies JOHN HIGLEY,
whose mother and father were drowned in their passage from America.
Had they both lived they would have been buried here.

[8118]

On a missionary in India:
Here lies the body of the Rev. T. Henry, M. A., who long laboured as a Christian missionary amongst the Rajputs.
He was shot by his chokedar.
"Well done, good and faithful servant."

SUGGESTED EPITAPHS

[8119]
Gone, oh, quite
Is X. L. Scott;
He was tight,
His brakes were not.
    —H. I. Phillips
    in the New York Sun.
Weep a bit
For Z. B. Lott;
He was lit—
His lights were not.
    —J. D. S.
    in the Macon Telegraph.
Shed some tears
For Y. K. Mott;
He had air—
His tires had not.
    —Carey Williams
in the Greensboro Herald-Journal.
Left on the road
Was Major Bott;
He was full—
His tank was not.
    —James Wells
    in the Dalton Citizen.

[8120]
For Oscar Barr
Please shed a tear;
He cranked his car—
'Twas still in gear.
    —Henry Wrenn
    in Jacksonville Journal.
And heave a sigh
For Oswald Doak:
He didn't know
His brakes were broke.
    —Macon Telegraph.

[8121]
Here lies till Gabriel's trumpet peal
The bones of Shelby Sharp.
He dozed while holding a steering
    wheel
And woke up holding a harp.

[8122]
Here lies the body of William Jay,
Who died maintaining his right of
    way;
He was right, dead right, as he sped
    along,
But he's just as dead as if he'd been
    wrong.

[8123]
Here lies the body of old Jim
    Lake—
    Tread softly, all who pass.
He thought his foot was on the
    brake,
    But gosh, it was on the gas.

[8124]
Here rests poor Mrs. Bill Mummers,
    Her weary heart sprung a bad
    leak
When her daughter of seventeen
    summers
    Stayed home every night for a
    week.

[8125]
A Tired Woman's Epitaph
Here lies a poor woman,
    Who always was tired;
She lived in a house,
    Where help was not hired;
Her last words on earth were,
    "Dear friends I am going;
Where washing ain't done,
    Nor sweeping nor sewing;
But everything there is exact to my
    wishes,
    For where they don't eat,
There's no washing of dishes;
    I'll be where loud anthems will
    always be ringing;
But having no voice, I'll be clear of
    the singing;
    Don't mourn for me now, don't
    mourn for me never,
I'm going to do nothing, forever
    and ever."

HUMOROUS ERRORS
Headlines

[8126]
JURY GETS DRUNK
DRIVING CASE HERE
—*Headline in Austin (Texas) paper.*

[8127]
MAN IS FATALLY SLAIN
—*Los Cruces (N. M.) paper.*

[8128]
NIGHT SCHOOL TO
HEAR PEST TALK
—*Oakland (Cal.) Tribune.*

[8129]
PRISONERS ESCAPE
FROM PRISON FARM
AFTER EXECUTION
—*Headline in Rochester & Beaver
(Pa.) paper.*

[8130]
DRIVER OF DEATH CAR HELD
ON SUSPICION OF NEGLI-
GIBLE HOMICIDE
—*Alhambra (Calif.) paper.*

[8131]
SUES BRIDE OF 4 MOUTHS
—*Scranton (Pa.) paper.*

[8132]
HOTEL BURNS. TWO HUN-
DRED GUESTS ESCAPE HALF
GLAD.
—*Headline in Boston Transcript.*

[8133]
INFANT MORALITY
SHOWS DROP HERE
—*Bridgeport (Conn.) paper.*

[8134]
BARE FEET AND
TINTED TONSILS
LATEST WITH SANDALS
—*Holyoke (Mass.) paper.*

[8235]
HAMM FAILS TO
IDENTIFY YEGGS
Oakland (Cal.) paper.

[8136]
SANTA ROSA MAN DENIES
HE COMMITTED SUICIDE
IN SOUTH SAN FRANCISCO
—*Headline in Burlingame (Calif.)
paper.*

[8137]
Bride Replaced on Highway 82.
—*Headline in El Paso (Tex.) pa-
per.*

[8138]
Enraged Cow Injures Farmer With
Ax—*Wichita Falls (Tex.) Record
News.*

[8139]
ONION PROSPECTS
REPORTED STRONG
—*Walla Walla (Wash.) paper.*

[8140]
CAROL'S CABINET QUILTS
—*Galveston (Tex.) paper*

[8141]
SENATE PASSES
DEATH PENALTY
Measure Provides for Electrocution
for All Persons Over 17.
—*Lansing State Journal.*

[8142]
NEBRASKA OFFICERS
BEST BANK BANDITS
—*Texas paper.*

[8143]
MISS KATHRYN K—— AND
MR. LEO S—— WILL EX-
CHANGE MARRIAGE COWS
—*Cambridge (Ohio) Jeffersonian.*

[8144]
MORE MEN FOUND WEDDED
THAN WOMEN
—*Washington Star.*

[8145]
LEWIS WINS AND
LOSES UNION SUIT
—*San Antonio Express.*

[8146]
"Prosecution Bases Case on Post-
Mortem Statements of Woman He
Killed."—*Scranton Republican.*

[8147]
TAXI DRIVER IS RETURNED
HERE; INDIANAPOLIS MAN
CHARGED WITH WRECKLESS
DRIVING.—*Headline in Rushville
(Ind.) paper.*

[8148]
THUGS EAT THEN
ROB PROPRIETOR
—*Dallas (Tex.) paper.*

[8149]
DEAD OFFICER
ON S. F. FORCE
FOR 18 YEARS
—*San Francisco paper.*

[8150]
SCENT FOUL PLAY IN DEATH OF
MAN FOUND BOUND AND HANGED.
—*Toledo Times.*

[8151]
COLOMA BRIDE
STANDS 46 TONS
TEST FRIDAY
—*Placerville (Calif.) paper.*

[8152]
SEND-A-DAME CHAIN LET-
TERS DELUGE CITY; INTER-
EST KEEN
*Headline in Kingsport (Tenn.)
paper.*

[8153]
DOG IN BED, ASKS DIVORCE
—*Galveston (Tex.) paper.*

[8154]
CAR LEAVES ROAD,
SUFFERS BROKEN NOSE
—*Healdsburg (Calif.) paper.*

[8155]
PEACE OR WAR
DEEMED NEAR
—*Oshkosh (Wis.) paper.*

[8156]
WILD WIFE LEAGUE
WILL MEET TO-NIGHT
—*Wheeling (W. Va.) Intelligencer.*

[8157]
BOY COOKS MUST
EAT OWN VITALS
—*Daytona Beach (Fla.) Sun
Record.*

[8158]
"LEONORE" ONLY OPERA
BEETHOVEN WROTE ON
MONDAY EVENING
—*San Antonio (Tex.) Express.*

[8159]
Former Prominent New Yorker
Had Liver in Paris for Eight Years
—*New York Evening Post.*

[8160]
BACHELORS PREFER BEAUTY
TO BRAINS IN THEIR WIVES
—*Denver Post.*

[8161]
LYING WEATHER FORECAST
—*Washington Herald.*

[8162]
"TANNHAEUSER" SUNK
BY METROPOLITAN
—*Philadelphia Inquirer.*

[8163]
Sam M—, 80, Held for Shooting
Grandmother's Husband.
—*Greensboro (N. C.) News.*

[8164]
2 CONVICTS
EVADE NOOSE;
JURY HUNG
—*Oakland Tribune.*

[8165]

40 Men Escape Watery Graves
    When Vessel Flounders in ale
        —*Springfield Republican.*

[8166]

WOMEN ARE BECOMING
    MORE BEAUTIFUL MEN;
    ALSO LOOKING BETTER
        —*Headline in Scranton (Pa.)
                            paper.*

[8167]

San Leon Man Quits Raising
Hogs for. Fruit.—*Headline in
Houston (Tex.) paper.*

[8168]

FOUR MISSOURIANS MADE
    ENSIGNS IN THE ARMY
—*Headline in Joplin (Mo.) paper.*

[8169]

Wife Gives Birth to a Boy;
    He Asks Old Age Pension
        —*Chicago Tribune.*

[8170]

PRESCRIPTION DEPARTMENT
    ADDED TO KENNEDY'S
    CUT RATE DRUG STORE
        —*Washington (Pa.) paper.*

[8171]

LOCAL MAN HAS
    LONGEST HORNS
            IN ALL TEXAS
        —*North Fort Worth News.*

[8172]

OFFICER CONVICTED
    OF ACCEPTING BRIDE
—*Raleigh News and Observer.*

[8173]

Huntington Cemetery
Reports Good Year;
    No Depression
        —*Patchogue (L. I.) paper.*

Text of Stories

[8174]

Women teachers must also stipulate that they "will not go out with any young man except insofar as it may be necessary to stimulate Sunday school work." This restriction is said to allow a great deal of lassitude.—*Charlotte (N. C.) paper.*

[8175]

Mrs. K—— continues under the doctor's car. However, at this writing, her condition is somewhat improved.—*Ambler (Pa.) paper.*

[8176]

Rev. A. J. and Mrs. Prosser say they had a dandy time out at their place last Thursday when 35 Baptist clergymen each with 35 wives broke in on them for a picnic.
            Nova Scotia paper.

[8177]

The Sunbeam Band of Central Baptist Church, meeting at ten o'clock at the church where transportation will be provided to a picnic which will be hell in the county.
        —*Winchester (Ky.) paper.*

[8178]

At the hospital, Mrs. —— explained that she stepped on a piece of soap and skidded right out the window. Her only injury was a wrecked etaoin etaoin.—*Beckley (W. Va.) paper.*

[8179]

Chicago has had the largest conflagration in its history since the famous cow of Betsy Ross kicked over the lamp in the gay 90's.
            —*Quebec paper.*

[8180]

"Physician Heel Thyself" is an injunction that the church can not escape.—*Cincinnati paper.*

[8181]

Miss —— ——, instructor of vice, sang, "Christian, Dost Thou See Them?"—*Staunton (Va.) paper.*

[8182]

After the wedding ceremony the Church of God orchestra struck up the old hymn, "The Fight Is On," and the audience came through with a big cheer.
Knoxville (Tenn.) paper.

[8183]

"Contributions of Youth to World Nudiness," was the subject discussed at a meeting held by the Women's Missionary Society.
—*Joplin (Mo.) paper.*

[8184]

Mrs. —— occasioned a lot of interest by wearing her back suspended from her waist at the back.
—*Los Angeles paper.*

[8185]

The accident occurred at Hillcrest drive and Santa Barbara Avenue as the dead man was crossing the intersection.—*Daly City (Calif.) paper.*

[8186]

Will the American working man be better or worse off with a maximum of 30 hours per week? The American Federation of Labor says "yes."—*Huntington (W. Va.) paper.*

[8187]

According to the complaint, Mr. O'D—— says her husband started amusing her three days before the marriage.—*Hebscher (Tex.) paper.*

[8188]

C—— H—— has bought a cow and he is now supplying his neighbors with milk, butter and eggs.
—*Vermont paper.*

[8189]

Some of the boy's methods are quite ingenious, the professors at the Institute have found. For instance, when asked to multiply 20 by 24 mentally, he gave the answer —600—in a few seconds.—*Pittsburgh paper.*

[8190]

Cheddar cheese is often called Hoop cheese because the curd is put into tinned-iron hoops which are lined with cheesecloth bandages and pressed with great pleasure.—*Ridgeway (Pa.) paper.*

[8191]

The annual Christmas party at the Ashley-street school was hell yesterday afternoon. — *Springfield (Mass.) paper.*

[8192]

Forty-tight members attended the luncheon which was prepared by Mrs. ——. —*Danbury (Conn.) paper.*

[8193]

F. W. C—— who has been ill with arithmetic was able to go out of the house Sunday.—*Warren (Ohio) paper.*

[8194]

After the games the guests were served a delicious salad course on trays which were centered with sugar plum trees. Those who had the pleasure of this sappy occasion were reluctant to leave so pleasant a fireside.—*Bastrop (La.) paper.*

[8195]

Alf —— and wife, have been living with his wife's people, have had to leave town on account of her parents having gone to live with the grand-parents.
—*Regina Leader-Post*

[8196]
If you happen to sit on the floor to put on shoes and stockings, do a flop, lift eggs in air, wriggle the toes.—*San Francisco Call Bulletin.*

[8197]
Out of those fifty guests more than thirty had been married to the same man for more than twenty years.—*Los Angeles Times.*

[8198]
In the mêlée Fine was struck over the head with some blunt object and knocked unconscious. Disengaging himself from the two men he drew his gun and fired three times.—*Cleburne (Tex.) Times-Review.*

[8199]
The beautiful deb was attired in an imported creation of jade-green crêpe trimmed with écrue lace around the punchbowl.—*Beacon (N. Y.) paper.*

[8200]
The Wee Playhouse has commenced rehearsing "Ladies of the Jury," a three cat play.—*Alfred (New York) paper.*

[8201]
It is against the law for a woman to be a hell-hop in Ohio.
—*Salamanca (N. Y.) paper.*

[8202]
Your name, signed to a note, a deed, a charge account, is your word that you will lie up to the agreements in the document.—*Ava (Mo.) paper.*

[8203]
The ladies of the Cherry Street Church have discarded clothing of all kinds. Call at 44 North Cherry Street for inspection.—*Louisiana newspaper.*

[8204]
R—— V——, crooner and orchestra leader, was shaken and bruised to-day, when his car left the road and overturned during a storm. It was feared his vocal cords were not injured.—*Bridgeville (Del.) dispatch in a San Luis Obispo paper.*

[8205]
Dr. D—— C——, noted health authority, who was to speak on "How to Keep Well," could not appear because of illness.—*Alameda (Calif.) Times-Star.*

[8206]
Senator —— —— is tight on the job at Washington.—*Havre (Mont.) paper.*

[8207]
Goethe said: "Against stupidity the gobs themselves fight in vain."
—*San Diego Union.*

[8208]
You can get an answer to any answerable question of fact or information by writing to the Question Editor.

Q. In what book of the Bible is the proverb: "God tempers the wind to the shorn lamb"?

A. It is on both sides of the river; Buda on one side and Pest on the other.

Q. How much monetary gold and silver is there in the world?

A. Approximately 1,200.

Q. When and where was King Edward VII of Great Britain born?

A. Chicago, New York, Philadelphia, Washington, D. C., and Baltimore, in the order named.

Q. Is the claims commission of the United States and Mexico still functioning?

A. Mixed with melted tar or pitch it is.—*Houston Press.*

[8209]

The feature of the day's program was a paper by Jim Corcoran, on "Banking, Its Origin and Development Through from the Time of the Roman Empire to the Present Day." Two minutes were given Jim to handle this task and he handled it splendidly.—*From a Rotary report in a Michigan weekly.*

[8210]

Mrs. G——, guild president, announces that the final meeting of the year will be hell, as usual, at her home, Tuesday, at 3 P. M. This meeting is always anticipated by members.—*Florida paper.*

[8211]

It is only a snake in the grass who will attempt to knife a man in the back with such lying insinuations.—*From a politician's statement in the Sacramento Bee.*

[8212]

A Jolly cab-driver was convicted Saturday of putting oil of mustard on the seat of a Yellow Cab in City Court.—*Memphis Press-Scimitar.*

[8213]

LAST MINUTE NEWS

Mrs. Jones let a can-opener slip last week and cut herself severely in the pantry.—*Pittsburgh suburban paper.*

[8214]

The big Sunday School Picnic held Tuesday at the Park was a hug success.—*Overbrook (Kan.) paper.*

[8215]

Grant Dalton lay back in his chair, apparently at ease; Philip standing with one foot on the fender and other on the mantel looked anything but happy.—*Charlotte (N. C.) Observer.*

[8216]

Which planet is larger, Juniper or Saturn?

Juniper.—*Questionnaire in the Clarksburg (W. Va.) Telegram.*

[8217]

The petty thieving that has been gradually accumulating lately in our beauteous village is a disgrace. It is also an enormous atrocity, leaving our village in a stigma.

The unanswerable michery of this year alone is nefandous. These inveterate, incongruous persons with a malignant disposition, whoever they are, should immediately be dealt with by the law.—*Wawansa (Manitoba) paper.*

[8218]

At four o'clock Prof. S—— P—— will give a lecture recital for the entertainment of the members, his subject being "Chromatic Fantasie and Fugue and Bach." The ladies who attend and hear Mr. P—— will consider themselves fortunate when he shall have finished.—*Oneonta (N. Y.) Star.*

[8219]

The wedding of Miss —— and Frederick —— will take place next Monday, the mother of the bride to be announced late to-day.—*Manhattan (Kan.) paper.*

[8220]

The opening number of the Minneapolis Symphony Orchestra under the direction of Henri Verbrugghen is "The Battered Bride."
—*Minneapolis Journal.*

[8221]

The murder of the man and the finding of the body was followed by a series of tragedies, including the suicide of the murdered man.
—*Idaho Falls Times-Register.*

[8222]

After a wedding reception at Sherry's, the bridegroom left on a honeymoon.—*Boston Post.*

[8223]

He was taken to St. Luke's hospital for treatment, but left there this morning with no bones broken. —*Tryon (N. C.) paper.*

[8224]

Any one not able to pay and stating so, will be buried Free of charge. —*Sherbrooke (Can.) Daily Record.*

[8225]

He lost his balance and was thrown to the street. The horse continued its mad dash down Tiogue Street for several hundred years, then stopped of its own accord. —*Providence Journal.*

[8226]

What with the expense of ribbon, postage, mailing tube, commission blank and others, it cost the State of Kentucky an average of 20¼ cents to crate a colonel.—*Kansas City paper.*

[8227]

F— P. C.——, of Lake City, 66 years old, candidate for Governor, was born on a farm in Columbia County 58 years ago.—*Orlando (Fla.) paper.*

[8228]

Mr. and Mrs. W. C. D— have willed their $0,000 ranch on the Pecos river to the Baptist General Conference of Texas.—*Santa Barbara (Calif.) paper.*

[8229]

"Hundreds of masks of the kind worn by the 'devil dancers' of old Ceylon, when they were engaged in exercising the devil."—*Birmingham Mail (England).*

[8230]

The Reynoldsburg Band will assist as usual in the Memorial Day program and will add snap to the occasion. Nothing adds dignity to a Memorial band.—*Reynoldsburg (Ohio) paper.*

[8231]

Three children died in a cloudburst near Memphis, Texas, as floods swept that section of the Southwest. Beneficial rains also fell in the San Angelo area.—*San Angelo (Calif.) paper.*

[8232]

Z— P— came home June 4th after completing a year's work at the University of Tennessee, Knoxville. She is taking a home economics course along with some education.—*Crossville (Tenn.) paper.*

[8233]

. . . and now it seems that our legislature is going to fail to utilize the greatest opportunity in Arkansas history to attract people from the entire nation to visit and admire our beautiful scenery and inimical hospitality.—*Arkansas paper.*

[8234]

"The spacious home of Judge and Mrs. Woodbury was the scene of a beautiful wedding last evening when their youngest daughter, Dorothy, was joined in holy deadlock to Mr. Wilkie."—*Nebraska newspaper.*

[8235]

What agonies must that author have endured who, writing of love, asserted in his manuscript that he kissed her under the silent stars, and found the compositor had made him declare that he kicked her under the cellar stairs.

[8236]

The Garden Club will meet Wednesday at 2:30 o'clock. The study subject will be: "Conservation of Native Pants."—*Tiptonville (Tenn.) paper.*

[8237]

Never throw away bones left from a roast or shoulder. Put them on in cold water, and if cooked several hours a very good soap may be obtained with the addition of diced vegetables.—*Louisville (Ky.) paper.*

[8238]

Desirability of marital law to give the United States Army full sway in relieving Louisville's flood victims was discussed to-day.—*Birmingham (Ala.) paper.*

[8239]

Columbia, Tenn., which calls itself the largest outdoor mule market in the world, recently held a mule parade, headed by the governor.—*New York magazine.*

[8240]

Through blinding fog and raging storm alert salesmen guard against unseen perils of the sea.—*Midland (Tex.) paper.*

[8241]

Not long ago a judge, famous for the reconciliations he has brought about between warring husbands and wives, exacted from certain husbands a promise that they would kill their wives every morning before leaving for business, and every evening when returning home.
—*Roanoke (Va.) paper.*

[8242]

Miss A— R— has returned from St. Louis where she went in the interest of her military business.
—*Owensboro (Ky.) paper.*

[8243]

Mrs. H. M. sued her husband for a divorce and separate maintenance, alleging that on the morning of May 4, he subjected her to the ignominy of being continued at the top of column 8.—*Petersburg (Va.) paper.*

[8244]

Sportsmen of his country are sharing with others in this state and with conservation leaders in many parts of the country the privilege of helping to save the noted Anderson Hill Wild Wife refuge.
—*Hutchinson (Minn.) paper.*

[8245]

Felt as though I had had a trip through the Blue Ridges and got a sentimental hankering to read some bore books with such a sweet and homely philosophy of family loyalty.—*Oklahoma City (Okla.) paper.*

[8246]

Miss S—— D—— of New Salem complained thieves killed a calf in a pasture and dragged it to her father's barn where they butchered it, for the second time within the last few weeks.—*Brownsville (Pa.) paper.*

[8247]

Many students and local fans are planning to follow the team to the scene of bottle.—*Athens (Ga.) paper.*

[8248]

The following correction appeared in a small town paper: "Our paper carried the notice last week that Mr. John Doe is a defective in the police force. This was a typographical error. Mr. Doe is really a detective in the police farce."—*Annapolis Log.*

[8249]
For cockroaches don't use sodium fluoride because children or cherished pets may eat the sodium fluoride instead of the cockroaches.
—*Houston (Tex.) paper.*

[8250]
Appointment of a master of chicanery probably will be made today by Judge K. in the suit of E. K. A. against R. K. K.—*Corpus Christi (Tex.) paper.*

[8251]
Looking very smart in a long mink coat and very fit after their trek around the world, the Charles G. Norisses came back home yesterday.—*San Francisco paper.*

[8252]
Unsettled to-night and Thursday, snow probable, not much change in temptation.—*Lead (S. D.) paper.*

[8253]
W. M. McG—— lost a finger when a poisoned dog to which he was administering an anecdote bit him.—*El Paso paper.*

[8254]
Charlie and Mary, who have been featured together in three previous pictures, are tarred together for the first time.—*Ocean City paper.*

[8255]
No Governor in many years has been able to love on the salary paid him, even though he is supplied with a furnished home rent-free.
—*Petersburg (Va.) paper.*

[8256]
The choir will offer an anthem during the worship period. Mr. and Mrs. J—— K—— will sing a duet "Bless the Lord" during the lifting of the offering.—*Aurora (Ill.) paper.*

[8257]
A—— went to work for the I—— M—— M—— Co., ten months ago, expressing a determination to learn the sipping business.—*Philadelphia paper.*

[8258]
n a county which has a population of approximately 40,000 there are only twenty-three paid officers, of whom eighteen are assigned to day duty, leaving only five on the night shirt.—*Washington (D. C.) paper.*

[8259]
After rushing to the hospital, he was examined by Dr. —— —— who put him on a diet that involved no foods and no liquids.—*Los Angeles (Calif.) paper.*

[8260]
A screaming crowd of 200 men and women to-night attempted to lynch S. S. . . . .
Two policemen defended the prisoner until refreshments arrived.
—*Honolulu paper.*

[8261]
Gone with the coal oil lamp, the boot jack and the tin cup are the threshing dinners of yore, in Madison county, with exhausted farm wives piling food on tables until the boards groaned, and threshing hands eating their way through three plate-loads of fried chicken, beef, and various other solid combustibles.—*Columbus (Ohio) paper.*

[8262]
Before the girls left the White House, Mrs. Roosevelt presented each of them with a little engraved picture of the Execution Mansion to keep as a souvenir.—*Jacksonville (Fla.) paper.*

[8263]

He told police that one of the men menaced him with a wench while the other covered him with a revolver.—*McConnelsville (Ohio) paper.*

[8264]

Bathing in the Easter dew, these people believe, will make them beautiful and guard them against all ham for the rest of the year.
—*Wilmington (N. C.) paper.*

[8265]

Mrs. H—— wore pale pink satin. Both the bride and Mr. H—— wore white trousers with dark coats.
—*Clay Center (Kan.) paper.*

[8266]

A Thanksgiving dinner was served at the home of Mr. and Mrs. —— ——, after the wedding of their daughter.—*Poughkeepsie paper.*

[8267]

Mrs. —— —— and —— —— were in —— last Monday shoplifting for Christmas.—*Newport (Wash.) paper.*

[8268]

All during the testimony he hardly moved in his chair. For the most of the time he rested his head on his chin.—*From a news item in the Ft. Worth Star-Telegram.*

[8269]

The farmers of Bloomington township, north of Lamoni, have called a meeting for March 16 to organize a protective chicken-stealing association.—*News item in the Des Moines Register.*

[8270]

Rev. Horace G—— returned from his Twin Cities yesterday and will take up his cuties at the church.
—*Newport (N. D.) paper.*

[8271]

Charles R—— suffered several broken and bruised legs last night when a sled on which he was riding, struck a tree.—*Troy paper.*

[8272]

"We are going to get that man if I have to put eight officers on his tail," declared Detective Captain Bruce Poole, Monday.—*Raleigh (N. C.) paper.*

[8273]

Nudism would be bared in Michigan under a bill introduced in the house Wednesday.—*Kalamazoo paper.*

[8274]

SOME ODDITIES

Here are some geographical oddities compiled by the National Geographic Society:

The city of Reno, Nevada, is 100 miles farther west than Los Angeles.

Jacksonville, Florida, is farther west than Cleveland, Ohio.

One travels south from Detroit to reach the nearest part of Canada.

At Panama the sun rises in the Pacific and sets in the Atlantic—due to a gigantic bend in the isthmus.

The city of New York lies west of the Pacific—at least that part of the Pacific that touches Africa, in Chile.—*Atlanta Chamber of Commerce periodical.*

[8275]

The Rotary Club held a white elephant party yesterday in connection with the noonday meeting in Hotel Chief. Many amusing girls were distributed, some of the most useful going to Harold A——, John L—— and Joseph R——.—*Adrian (Mich.) paper.*

[8276]

"I love you, too," she cried, and swaying toward him threw herself into his arms. His lips found and clung to her sweet, tremendous mouth.—*Story in the Minneapolis Sunday Journal.*

[8277]

This great event will be duly observed by the following program:
Innovation by Prof. John Kelly.
Music, "Hell to the Chief," by the Hokah Hornet Band.
Base Solo, "Oh, How They Lied!" by Past Grand Patriarch Del Stewart.—*Hakoah (Minn.) paper.*

[8278]

The district game warden filed four complaints, charging illegal fishing in Judge J. J. Padgett's court.
—*Waco News-Tribune.*

[8279]

The polls to-night will close at 7 o'clock, and voting should start soon after that.—*Manhattan (Kan.) Mercury.*

[8280]

Mother and babe are getting along nicely and the father is expected to recover within a few weeks.—*Eureka (Utah) paper.*

[8281]

On the grounds that a fall prevented her from dancing, skating and bedsledding, Mrs. Isabella H——, 72, of White Plains, is suing the New York Central railroad for $35,000.—*Halifax (Va.) paper.*

[8282]

A rural poet indited a sonnet to his sweetheart, entitled "I kissed her *sub rosa.*" The compositor knew better than that, and set it up in printer's Latin, "I kissed her snub nosa."

[8283]

Here a massacre of 450,000 Christians took place, 126 B.C.—*Caption in a Hollywood magazine.*

[8284]

You have to take a chance on everything in life, marriage included. There are no sure things, so marry your man and try to make marriage so pleasant for him he won't go wandering off in forbide pathsdnshrdluetaoiwshrdluetao.—*Nashville Banner.*

[8285]

Yale beat Princeton in the closest kind of a track meet the other day, 67, 2-3 to 67 1-3, and did it by taking a first and third in the final event. . . . The year before, Yale beat Princeton, 67 to 67, probably a runaway!—*Cumberland (Md.) paper.*

[8286]

Miss Harriett E—— will entertain a small party of friends at a buffet supper. Tight guests have been invited for the occasion.
—*Charlotte Observer.*

[8287]

Everybody knows now where Mr. Barbour will stand when he takes his seat.—*The Nation.*

[8288]

The bride was gowned in white lace. The bridesmaids' gowns were punk. The whole color scheme of the decorations was punk.—*New York paper, according to the West Virginia Mountaineer.*

[8289]

Mr. and Mrs. R—— left Wednesday for Rochester, Minnesota, where Mrs. R—— expects to have a garter removed by the Mayo Brothers.—*Fairmont Sentinel.*

[8290]

The couple stood before an improvised altar banked with summer blossoms while the Rev. M—— performed the wedding ceremony, using the ring service.

The bridegroom wore a gown of white georgette with matching accessories and carried an arm bouquet of pink carnations.—*Douglas (Ariz.) paper.*

[8291]

Minot retail merchants Friday had heartily indorsed the campaign waged by the local shoplifters and solicitors of advertising of dubious worth.—*Fargo (N. Dak.) paper.*

[8292]

Detached here last summer, —— specialized in the teaching of curses for naval science juniors.—*Seattle paper.*

[8293]

The famous "golden horseshoe" was filled, as usual, with gorgeously gowned and bejeweled women, immaculately togged men, with their ermine wraps, diamond brooches, necklaces, tiaras.—*Toronto Daily Star.*

[8294]

The ladies of the Helping Hand Society enjoyed a swap social on Friday evening. Everybody brought something they didn't need. Many of the ladies were accompanied by their husbands.—*Middlesex (Mass.) paper.*

[8295]

If these export credits can be arranged, and Carl Williams of the Board said that satisfactory progress was being made, the sales would be on a cash basis, with the banks doing the purchasers.
—*Detroit Free Press.*

[8296]

Did Mrs. —— plan the murder of the two women whose bodies were found in trunks a week before the crime was committed?
—*Bradenton (Fla.) paper.*

[8297]

They are taking a tent and cooking utensils and will vamp by the side of the road.—*Haverhill Herald.*

[8298]

On Tuesday afternoon, eight ladies of the neighborhood were guests of Mrs. L——. Catting over needlework and refreshments were enjoyed.—*Brookings (S. D.) paper.*

[8299]

Out of 31 days, 155 were clear, 11 partly cloudy, and 55 cloudy.
—*Morristown (N. J.) Daily Record.*

[8300]

After Governor B a l d r i d g e watched the lion perform, he was taken to Main Street and fed twenty-five pounds of raw meat in front of the Fox Theater.—*Idaho Statesman.*

[8301]

Several deer hunters in the northwoods area in the past week have been shot at by mistake for wild animals lighting cigars.—*Lincoln (Neb.) State Journal.*

[8302]

Mr. and Mrs. M—— R—— of Denver announce the birth of a small 7-year-old child, who didn't give his name.—*Rifle (Colo.) paper.*

[8303]

He was charged with violation of section 68 of the penal code making it a felony on the part of a public official to ask and receive a bride.
—*New York paper.*

[8304]
Mrs. I. W. G—— sang, "O Rest in the Lard," accompanied by Mrs. L——.—*Kingsport (Tenn.) paper.*

[8305]
Breaking the glass with a chair he climbed through and clung to the sill by his fingerprints until three detectives called on him to jump.—*New York Times.*

[8306]
Mrs. M. broke her arm recently. She is recovering nicely under the car of Dr. Downs.—*Riverside (N. J.) paper.*

[8307]
The regular meeting of the Women's Relief corps was held in Union Hall last evening. Due to sickness and other attractions there was only a small attendance.—*Winsted (Conn.) paper.*

[8308]
Adjacent the library is another completely equipped lovatory.—*Washington Post.*

[8309]
Sprinkle on the shelves a mixture of half borax and half sugar. This will poison every aunt that finds it. —*Norwich (Conn.) Bulletin.*

[8310]
There were five indictments against each of the accused, charging fraud, and twenty-two against H——, charging him with soliciting and accepting brides.—*Springfield (Ohio) Sun.*

[8311]
Simon Shields lost a horse the first of the week that he valued very highly. It was the one he went to housekeeping with.—*South Bend correspondence in a Council Grove (Kans.) paper.*

[8312]
The next meeting of the Legion will take place on February 10. Every man who died for his country is cordially invited to attend.—*Killdeer (N. Dak.) Herald.*

[8313]
Many friends will be pleased to learn of the continued improvement of Henry A. T—— at the Franklin Memorial Hospital. One of the nurses was discharged last week and he gains each day.—*Farmington (Me.) paper.*

[8314]
Q. Which States produce the most peanuts?
A. North Carolina, Georgia, Virginia, Alabama, and Texas. North Carolina has the largest yield per ache.—*New Britain Herald.*

[8315]
We note with regret that Mrs. J. H. A—— is recuperating from an automobile accident.—*Florida Baptist-Witness.*

[8316]
The bride is to be resurfaced with brick, laid herringbone style on a bed of sand with concrete mixture in the joints.—*Wilmington Evening Journal.*

[8317]
An hysterical mother today asked police to search for her 141-year-old daughter who disappeared last night. She is five feet, three inches tall, and weighs eleven pounds.—*Buffalo Evening Times.*

[8318]
On July 11, 1934, he suffered a stroke but with the loving care of his family and his kind and efficient nurse, he never fully recovered.—*Platteville (Wis.) paper.*

[8319]

Ortonville, Minn.—Special: The world's champion eater of sweet corn is Edwdard Kottwitz, of Ortonville, who ate 37 years at one sitting. Those who witnessed him set the "record" say that he ate without napkin and did not once get his ears or hair mussy.—*Iowa paper.*

[8320]

——, of Brewster, who has been in a New York hospital for two months with puss on the knee, will spend a month with his sister, Mrs. ——.—*Somers-Salem (N. Y.) paper.*

[8321]

"The P. O. Dep't is never questioned. Every person who presents a letter for mailing is fully confident that it will be safely carried to its destruction."—*Mountain Lake (Minn.) paper.*

[8322]

England is suffering from a plague of aunts. In many houses these have visited rooms on the second floor.—*Montpelier. (Vt.) paper.*

[8323]

Q. How can I prevent catching cold after shampooing the hair?
A. Rub the bread board or kitchen table (if wood) with these pieces, allow the wood to dry, then scour with soap and water. The acid makes the wood beautifully white.—*Atlantic City (N. J.) paper.*

[8324]

A congregation of about 200 people heard Rev. Mr. S—— preach on "Transfigured Hours." Vocal selections were murdered by the Misses Carolyn E—— and Rita B—— and the male quartet. — *Stoneham (Mass.) paper.*

[8325]

The choice is proper, and the act of presenting the plague to Mrs. —— is a nice courtesy.—*Henryetta (Okla.) paper.*

[8326]

Alfred —— of Harrisburg had the misfortune of getting hurt on his back and chest while milking this morning when a cow kicked. We wish her a speedy recovery.—*Prairie Du Sac (Wis.) paper.*

[8327]

Seven children of this community took advantage of the clinic in Rogers and were examined for tuberculosis and other diseases which the clinic offered free of charge.—*Fayetteville (Ark.) paper.*

[8328]

Mrs. Simpson, whose husband is a railroad conductor, has two other children. Leroy, 3½, and Dorothy, 12, but they are not twins.—*San Francisco Chronicle.*

[8329]

What is the "Catnip Club"???? Yes, that is the paramount topic in the smart circles of local society today, many having received swank invitations to the opening party Friday evening in the beautiful bathroom of the Thomas Jefferson Hotel. — *Birmingham News-Age Herald.*

[8330]

Coroner Ed Kraft said W—— had become demented and died of natural causes after an autopsy was performed. — *Evansville (Ind.) Courier.*

[8331]

After the striking of the bell at six o'clock, Frank B—— sank two of the bride's favorite old-time love-songs.—*Reedsburg (Wis.) paper.*

[8332]
This country should remember especially the last words that Goethe uttered: "More light."

His eyes were closing. But ours are open, light is abundant, there is no reason why we should scmfwy, shrdlu shrdlu shrdlu mfwet.—*Erie (Pa.) Dispatch-Herald.*

[8333]
The estate was valued in the will at "more than $20,000." One-third goes to the widow and two-thirds to each of the children."—*Washington Evening Star.*

[8334]
Fort Dodge, Ia.—Triplets born to the Rev. and Mrs. Frank Selby last week are the first in Fort Dodge in a decade. They have been named Donald James, Darrold Franklin, and Deloris Martha, and have twin aunts, twin great-uncles, and twin great-grand-uncles. The Rev. Mr. Selby, an evangelist, is a salesman for duplicating machines.—*Des Moines Tribune.*

[8335]
The bride is approximately eighteen feet wide from buttress to buttress.—*Kansas City paper.*

[8336]
Due to the fact that the publisher of *The News* was out of town Sunday, we failed to see Doctor Strong, who is a personal friend much to our regret.—*Crawford (Neb.) paper.*

[8337]
There is no unemployment in this district now. Every industry seems to be flourishing.

A daughter was born at the Hazelton Hospital, last week, to Mr. and Mrs. Allan B——.—*Prince Rupert (B. C.) paper.*

[8338]
Hardly had this episode occurred when Shaukart's son appeared with a knife and made his alleged threat to cut off the priest's head if the latter performed the ceremony. This would have been the greatest insult possible to any Mohammedan.—*New York World-Telegram.*

[8339]
No other trains run so far for so long a distance as the "Florida Special."—*Boston News Bureau.*

[8340]
My house was swept away clean and so was my barn, I had some mules in the barn, but they tell me they didn't get hurt.—*Memphis Commercial Appeal.*

[8341]
Blend sugar, flour and salt. Add egg and milk, cook until creamy in double boiler. Stir frequently. Add rest of ingredients. Mix well, serve chilled.

Funeral services will be held Thursday afternoon at 2 o'clock.—*Gettysburg (Pa.) paper.*

[8342]
Mr. and Mrs. David Wine of 2440 Lakeview Avenue, announce the approaching marriage of their daughter Laura to Juel Edward Soboroff.—*Chicago Tribune.*

[8343]
"Ike" Pritchard is home Tuesday with sinus trouble, something like Kenneth Yost had. He fell on the floor at Gothenburg when in a basket-ball game and gave his head an awful bump. It causes some worry to the folks at home. We are hoping that it does not prove only a temporary injury. — *Sumner (Neb.) paper.*

[8344]

At St. Louis, over a loud-speaker system, she told the throng with a smile:

"I am only here for a little while. I can only say a brief word. I am very pleased to have a chance to say hell, good-by and good luck."
—*Houston Post.*

[8345]

Cloys Potts, 23, and Serepta Coffee, 22, both of Peebles, secured a marriage license in Maysville, Kentucky, Monday, and were married in that city.—*Cincinnati Enquirer.*

[8346]

A son was born to Mr. and Mrs. E. A. Bruce at the Wyoming General Hospital April 21.

Rocket Want Ads Bring Results!
Rocky Springs (Wyo.) paper.

[8347]

Bradenton, Fla.—Mrs. Vernon O. Capo of Cortez, near here, today became the mother of twin boys.

Mrs. Capo has a twin sister.

Her husband has twin brothers.

The nurse who attended her has twin boys.

The doctor in the case has a twin brother.

And the man who reported the story has twin sons.—*Seattle Post-Intelligencer.*

[8348]

The Earl of Antrim at Glenarm, England, has given birth to healthy twin calves twice in eleven months.
—*Walla Walla (Wash.) Union.*

[8349]

Recovering from a head injury and shock caused by coming in contact with a live wife, Arthur E—— left Mercy Hospital Wednesday.—*Columbus Dispatch.*

[8350]

Dr. McW—— has been quite ill, caused by his death. He is away at present to have a little vacation.—*Presque Isle (Me.) Star-Herald.*

CHURCH ANNOUNCEMENTS

[8351]

"There is joy in the presence of the angels of God over one singer that repenteth."
Solo—Miss M—— A—— L—— ("Jesus Wants Me for a Sunbeam").
—*Washington (D.C.) church program.*

[8352]

A covered-dish supper will be served by the Truth Seekers Bible Class on Wednesday evening at 6:30. Husbands of members are also invited. Don't forget the "cats"!—*Bethlehem (Pa.) Church Bulletin.*

[8353]

10:30 A. M., Service with the sermon by the minister on the theme "Evil member in the Church." The vested choir will sing the hymn-anthem "Who Could It Be?"—*Beverley (Mass.) paper.*

[8354]
DINNER
M. E. CHURCH, WHEELING, MO.
Turkey .35c. Chicken or Beef .25c
Children .15c. and .20c.
—*Advertisement in Chillicothe (Missouri) paper.*

[8355]
ETHICAL
SPIRITUALIST TEMPLE
902 S. W. Fourth Avenue
Immorality Demonstrated
Sunday at 2:45 P. M.
—*Miami Herald.*

[8356]

The Junior Ladies Aid will serve an oyster at the church Saturday evening.—*Indianola (Iowa) Church Bulletin.*

[8357]
ARMAGEDDON

Earth's last war. How and where will it be fought? At Adventist church, Sunday night.—*Clearwater (Fla.) paper.*

[8358]
Sermon
"I Want More Than Bread"
Church Supper
To-Night
Sourbraten and
Roast Pork
—*Syracuse Church Bulletin.*

[8359]

Morning, "Intimations of Immorality"; night, "Enduring Enthusiasm."—*Church ad in an Oklahoma paper.*

[8360]
Hymn . . . . . No. 336
(Congregation standing)
Sermon, "What Are You Standing For?"
Dr. Fosdick,
—*Riverside Baptist Church, New York City*

[8361]

Englewood W.C.T.U. will hold Institute in Eng. Y.M.C.A. tomorrow, 10:30. Mrs. Bracer, Mrs. Booze, and others will speak. Cafeteria luncheon. Good attendance desired.
—*New Jersey church program.*

[8362]

Rodney Johnson, tenor, will sing "The Ford Is My Light."—*San Francisco News.*

VARIED ANNOUNCEMENTS

[8363]

Hear this truth-telling message. You may say I am a liar, but I'll prove it.—*Marshall (Mo.) paper.*

[8364]

The gentleman who kicked the lady at the show last evening seeks forgiveness. He was too dumfounded to offer an apology at the time. Be assured Madame that he is not in the habit of kicking women — especially when his wife is present.—*Ad in the Sioux Falls Argus-Leader.*

[8365]
NOTICE

My wife Anna P—— having refused to live with me and under my bed and board, I hereby notify all persons that I will not be responsible for any debts contracted by her. —*Roscoe (Va.) paper.*

[8366]

The Psychology Club will meet in regular session on Wednesday afternoon at three o'clock. The subject for discussion will be "The Use and Application of Powder."—*Corsicana (Tex.) paper.*

[8367]

Mr. S. B. F——, having left my bed and board, I will pay no debts contracted by him. Mrs. Lillian F——.

To Whom It May Concern — I wish to state that I have always paid all bills contracted by myself in the past, and will continue to do so in the future. I left the home of Mrs. Lillian F—— by her order, taking my bed with me. S. B. F——.
—*Personals in successive issues of the Meadville (Pa.) Evening Republican.*

[8368]

On and after this date I shall be responsible for no debts unless contracted by any other than myself.—*Cincinnati Enquirer.*

[8369]

Voters of Kline Township. On behalf of the Republican party I desire to express sincere appreciation for the loyalty of its voters and workers, regardless of adversities. I shall continue as in the past to serve unscrupulously in the execution of my public duty.—J. J. B——, Chairman Republican party.—*Hazelton (Pa.) paper.*

[8370]

8:45 P. M.

WMCA—Dr. Charles Fleischer, Thdownhb'tcR zsldBl'dls- oYT11.f "More Than News" —*Mount Vernon (N.Y.) paper.*

[8371]

In referring to Mr. Floyd M——'s notice in *Courier* Friday, I wish to state that I did not leave my bed, I took it with me, and there wasn't any board there to leave. Mrs. Floyd M——.

—*Dubois (Oreg.) paper.*

[8372]

ESTRAY NOTICE —Any one having a wife or husband, son or daughter, son-in-law or daughter-in-law, or father-in-law or mother-in-law or any other dear relative estray in the autumn evenings, will if they are anxious about these wanderers probably find them parked on my lot, in Clear Lake Villas. Those financially or otherwise responsible for these strays must either pay for stray space, furnish bail, or pay fine for trespass.

Will be glad to furnish inquirers with number of car or other information that will lead to recovery of these wandering ones.—*Ad in a Lakeport (Calif.) paper.*

[8373]

"The Man Who Married a Dumb Wife." Any one having the above mentioned and would care to loan them out may communicate with Mrs. C—— A——.—*Santa Rosa (Calif.) paper.*

[8374]

An ad in an Alabama weekly reads: "Anybody found prowling around my chicken house in the night will be found still there the next morning.—*Lee Richards.*"

[8375]

I will still act in the capacity of Peace Officer, and will be glad to serve any civil papers, and anyone wishing to be arrested for violating any of the State Laws, their patronage will be appreciated also.

SAM H——.

—*Clovis (N. Mex.) paper.*

[8376]

PERSONAL: Lawyer will read will tomorrow at residence of—— ——, who died June 19 to accommodate his relatives.—*Teaneck (N. J.) paper.*

ADVERTISEMENTS

[8377]

BUFFALO CAFE

for

GOOD THINGS TO EAT *and* DRINK

FISH MARKET

People's Funeral Home

for

NICE JOBS AND GOOD COACH

Service With a Smile

—*Advertisement in Pittsburg (Texas) paper.*

[8378]
BUY YOUR
FANCY NECKLACES
directly from the manufacturer
100 per cent. cheaper
—*Ad in the Paris Herald.*

[8379]
WE WANT YOUR
EGGS
AND WANT THEM BAD
PORTER & YOUNG
—*Display Ad in The Le Roy
(Minn.) Independent.*

[8380]
Why go elsewhere to be
cheated when you can
come here?
—*Advertisement in Burns (Ore.)
paper.*

[8381]
Saturday Morning 10:30 A.M.
EASTER MATINEE
Every child laying an egg in the
door man's hand will be admitted
free.—*Parsons (Pa.) paper.*

[8382]
CREAM PUFFS
6 for 29c.
The flakiest, puffiest of puffs cram-
med full of creamy mustard.
Treat the family.
—*Adv. in Pittsburgh paper.*

[8383]
CALL WIESER'S
for
HOME MADE
FRUIT CAKE
Solid Mahogany
—*Fredericksburg Free Lance-Star.*

[8384]
BIG CATTLE SHOW AT
TOLCHESTER BEACH
Go Over, See the Show and Meet
Your Friends.
—*Baltimore paper.*

[8385]
Well, you can tramp through the
markets daily—looking, pricing and
comparing. But there's an easier
way—a more accurate way—a more
up-to-the-minute way—READ THE
FOOL ADVERTISEMENTS IN
THIS NEWSPAPER. — *Winter
Haven (Fla.) paper.*

[8386]
Unexcelled Loveliness! Superb
Quality! Incredible Savings! While
Quantities Last! GREATER THAN
EVER! OUR THREE-DAY BABY
SALE!
—*Ad in a Chicago paper.*

[8387]
LUNCH WITH US
A complete lunch SERVICE
Try our PLATE Lunch—
Vaccine virus
Tetanus and Diphtheria
Antitoxins
PROPERLY REFRIGERATED
Prescription Druggist
—*Arizona college magazine*

[8388]
There is not a store in the Car-
olinas with so many imported and
exclusive fools as you find at. . . .
—*Advertisement in Charlotte
(N. C.) paper.*

[8389]
LET'S ALL MAKE THIS A
BIGGER AND BETTER
STATE FAIR
Leave Your Garments at Our Main
Plant Right on Your Way
to the Fair
—*Ad in the Shreveport (La.)
Journal.*

[8390]
HONEST VALUES
$28 Roadster $150
—*Memphis Commercial Appeal.*

[8391]
SPECIAL
FOUL
DINNER
45C
—*Ad in a Chatham (Ont.) paper.*

[8392]
GET RID OF AUNTS—
T—— does job in 24 hours. 25c. per
bottle.
—*Jamesville (Iowa) paper.*

[8393]
Electric Percolator Set
$9.95
50c Down—$50 Weekly
—*Schenectady (N.Y.) paper.*

[8394]
WHISKEY — You'll like this
bourbon, it's straight.
Ambulance Service 2-1700
HINES FUNERAL HOME
—*Peoria paper.*

[8395]
George M——, son of Prof. and
Mrs. E. S. M——, is now connected
permanently with the —— funeral
home, where he will be pleased to
see his friends.—*Shreveport paper.*

[8396]
DROP-LEAF TABLE
The leaves when opened will seat
6 people comfortably and there's an
automatic hinge that holds them
firmly in place.—*Ad in a Washington paper.*

[8397]
Sheer stockings — designed for
dressy wear, but so serviceable that
lots of women wear nothing else.—
*Advertisement in New York City
paper.*

[8398]
10 Years Same Spot—
Hines the Cleaner, 107½ South
Comstock.—*Whittier (Calif.) News.*

[8399]
15 MEN'S WOOL SUITS
$3.00
They won't last an hour!
—*Tacoma News Tribune.*

[8400]
QUALITY MEATS
Poultry Dressed to Order at Any
Time. Special Attention
Paid to Children.
—*Ad on the back of a blotter.*

[8401]
The factory stands back of each
mixer and fruit juice extractor
against all defects, for one year.
Truly it is a germ.—*Advertisement
in Los Angeles paper.*

[8402]
Frozen Egg Nogg and Mustachio
Ice Cream, and all the other choice
flavors. Oh, my can almost taste it!
Bath (Pa.) paper.

[8403]
Real Imported Kid Gloves. Fashioned of soft sins. Choice of black
or brown.—*Connellsville (Pa.) paper.*

[8404]
Widows made to order. Send
us your specifications.—*Ad in an
El Paso paper.*

[8405]
TOASTER $3.50
A gift that every member of the
family will appreciate. Auto-
matically burns toast.
—*Ad in the Riverside (Calif.)
Enterprise.*

[8406]
"I believe Holstein Milk best
adapted to feeding infants of any
of the breeds of cattle, and advise
mothers accordingly."—N. H.——
M. D., N. Y.—*Ad in a Douglas
(Ariz.) paper.*

[8407]
It makes a bath that refreshes, relaxes and stimulates. You step out of your tub ready to meet all comers.—*Soap ad in a New York paper.*

[8408]
HADES—Made to Order, 50c, and up; cleaned, 25c and up.—*St. Louis Post-Dispatch.*

[8409]
Swim at the new pool — With suits, 35c.; without suits, 50c.—*Newport newspaper.*

[8410]
Ladies Silk Rayon Bloomers 19c pr. Table Covers to Match 39c ea.
Mineola (L. I.) paper.

[8411]
Of All the Gifts—In the world what is greater than mother's love, and what expresses love better than flowers? We have plenty for every one. We have celery, cauliflower, cabbage, tomato and pepper plants. —*Ad in a Chehalis (Wash.) paper.*

[8412]
The fact that those we have served once return again, and recommend us to their friends, is a high indorsement of the service we render.
PELTON FUNERAL HOME
—*Ad in the Oshkosh Northwestern.*

[8413]
Our caskets are made in Holly. We invite you to become familiar with our plant and show room. Then you will know why you want a D—— M—— Casket every time.—*Holly (Mich.) Advertiser.*

[8414]
Fried spring children with French fried potatoes and cream slaw, 35c. —*Ad in an Altoona paper.*

[8415]
We are offering a special on goldfish for the holidays. Six goldfish and large owl, $1.00.—*Jasper (Ind.) Herald.*

WANT ADS

[8416]
WANTED—To trade saxophone in fancy case for fresh cow.—*Boone (Ia.) paper.*

[8417]
A young woman wants washing or cleaning daily.—*Ad in the Toronto Daily Star.*

[8418]
Bloodhound For Sale—What am I offered for one-year-old? Beautifull animal, gentle, good watch-dog. Will eat anything and especially fond of children. — *Port Angeles (Wash.) News.*

[8419]
One chaste longe and other furniture.—*Ad in a Mobile paper.*

[8420]
GIRLS
To sew on men's pants.
—*Ad in the Baltimore Sun.*

[8421]
Front room, suitable for two ladies, use of kitchen or two gentlemen.—*Hartford Times.*

[8422]
WANTED — Partner with some capital interested in bulldog raising for market. Opportunity make big money. Already have considerable acreage, breeding and hatching pens developed and stocked with fine breeders, now laying.—*Tampa Daily Times.*

[8423]
TOMBSTONE SLIGHTLY
USED. Sell cheap. Weil's Curiosity
Shop.—*Philadelphia Inquirer.*

[8424]
Wanted—One wealthy wife, by
young unemployed man of Talla-
hassee, not bad looking, and has
had experience in Madison.—*Talla-
hassee (Fla.) paper.*

[8425]
Experienced German girl or
woman, cooing and housework.—
Lawndale (Pa.) paper.

[8426]
Wanted—Man to lay about 600
sq. ft. concrete driveway, labor
only, will swap baby or started
chicks.—*Tampa Morning Tribune.*

[8427]
Will trade fire, life, automobile
insurance for anything can use.
Want lady with automobile.—
Riverside (Calif.) Enterprise.

[8428]
Man, honest, will take anything.
—*Ad in a Jacksonville paper.*

[8249]
For Sale: To a kind master, full
grown, domesticated tigress, goes
daily walk untied, and eats flesh
from the hand.—*Ad in a Calcutta
paper.*

[8430]
Colored Girl with wonderful
personality wants work as maid in
good family. Can cook and admire
children.—*Fort Wayne (Ind.)
Journal-Gazette.*

[8431]
A few boarders wanted at $25.00
per month. Nice rooms and males
as good as can be found in Hartsville are guaranteed.—*Hartsville
(S.C.) Messenger.*

[8432]
Wanted—Laundry driver, wet
and flat; married man preferred.
—*Boston Globe.*

[8433]
Wanted—to trade guitar for
shotgun.—*Sumner (Ia.) Gazette.*

[8434]
Swap—Drink mixer, glasses,
tray, etc., for good baby carriage.
—*Ossining paper.*

[8435]
To Let—Furnished room for
lady. Semi-private bath. Phone evenings.—*Crofton (Pa.) paper.*

[8436]
ARE YOU GOING EAST?
If you are going to Chicago or
Milwaukee, I can save you one-
third your face. Act quick. Phone
1133-J.—*Classified Ad in .the
Pueblo Chieftain.*

[8437]
Chauffeur, white, nice quarters,
beautiful country home exchanged
for services; kind treatment; could
use wife.—*New York Times.*

[8438]
Room with twins available at
Three Palms.—*Tampa Tribune.*

[8439]
Lost—Will person who took
glasses and fancy work from car
Friday morning please call 4503-W.
Invaluable to anyone but owner.
Reward—*Baton Rouge Morning
Advocate.*

[8440]
Wanted—A homeless woman to
keep house in a motherless home
for one man of thirty and one
little boy yrs old for board and
room and clothes, must be between
twenty-five and thirty-five, the year
around.—*Yakima (Wash.) paper.*

[8441]
Wanted—White girl for general sousework and care of children.—*Hartford Daily Times.*

[8442]
Attractive local officer for refined manicurist with good following.—*Florida Times-Union.*

[8443]
Educated, pure young Japanese poet seeks position as journalistic worker, window cleaner, tutor, housekeeper or schoolboy.—*Japan Advertiser (Tokyo).*

[8444]
Wanted—A mahogany living-room table, by a lady with Heppel-white legs.—*Atlanta Journal.*

[8445]
WANTED TO BUY
Wanted—Car for a cow, also radio for a steer.—*Bluefield (W. Va.) Daily Telegraph.*

[8446]
Lost or Stolen—Dog with long body and short legs. Long wavy medium brown to light hair. Large bushy tail. Hair on back near tail curly. Long hair on tail light color as well as hair on rear of hind legs.—*Bunker Hill (Ill.) paper.*

[8447]
Have you lost track of your creditors? Let us locate them.—*Advertisement in Indianapolis paper.*

[8448]
To Let—Violin by an old gentleman who has been in family 100 years and still has excellent tone and guaranteed to play.—*Atlanta Journal.*

[8449]
FOR TRADE—One good deer rifle for a woman.—*Advertisement in Cloverland (Mich.) paper.*

[8450]
MANICURIST—Must be good and fast.—*Advertisement in Detroit paper.*

[8451]
FILBERT, nr. Octavia—4 rooms, comfortably furn; $17.50, water, garbage free.—*San Francisco paper.*

[8452]
LOST—FOUND—STRAYED
Lost—Pink satin slip on State Street between Broadway and Douglas.—*Alton (Ill.) paper.*

[8453]
Model A, classy sport roadster. Humorous accessories.—*Pasadena paper.*

[8454]
Sale or trade—1933 Plymouth De Luxe coupe with heater and radio; also 2 fresh cows with valves.—*Youngstown (Ohio) paper.*

[8455]
Hodge, 113—Near Delaware, attractive warm, single, gentleman; reasonable.—*Buffalo paper.*

[8456]
Unusual opportunity for biscuit salesman with new modern institution; must have at least 2 years' experience within last 6 months or do not apply.—*Kansas City (Mo.) paper.*

[8457]
300 ACRES — PARTLY CUT over part old farm. No buildings. Side road. Hunting. Absolutely worthless. Price $600.—*Advertisement in Bangor (Me.) paper.*

[8458]
VANITY DRESSES
Large and roomy with beautiful mirrors at half their real value. Other odd pieces at low prices.—*Danville (Va.) paper.*

[8459]
WANTED—Don't cheat yourself
—Let us do it. P——'s Café. Plate
lunch 20c. Dinner 40c.—*Crawfords-
ville (Ind.) paper.*

[8460]
People who suffer from various
conditions like Neuritis, Arthritis,
Neuralgia, Rheumatic Trouble,
Colds and many other ailments,
can be destroyed without discom-
fort or loss of time to the patron.
—*Watertown (S. Dak.) paper.*

[8461]
Found—Young male cow. Owner
may have same by calling 2020
North Hayne.—*Pensacola (Florida) Journal.*

[8462]
Puppy—Boston Terrier, male, 6
months old. Has 36 license, also
player piano attachment and rolls.
C. B. W., West Monroe, N. Y.—
Syracuse (N.Y.) paper.

[8463]
Lost—Gentleman's small nurse,
$26 cash and diamond ring.—*Phil-
adelphia Evening Bulletin.*

[8464]
Large, lovely tapestry love seat;
will sell or exchange for two occasional chairs.—*Portland Telegram.*

[8465]
Wanted—Farm mule. Must be
reasonable.—*Ad in the Birmingham
Age-Herald.*

[8466]
Grocery and meat market with
loving rooms; no competition, a
bargain quick sale; leaving town.
—*San Antonio Light.*

[8467]
LOST
Large Red Woman's Purse
—*Albuquerque paper.*

[8468]
For Sale—Sideway Reversible
Baby.—*West Vancouver News.*

[8469]
CLOSING OUT SALE—Suits,
topcoats, o'coats, odd cats, $3 up.
—*Syracuse (N.Y.) paper.*

[8470]
LEAVING May 1 for Des
Moines, old, completely weaned
and fat and healthy. M—— E——,
1 mile north of Stuart Place Road.
—*Harlingen (Tex.) paper.*

[8471]
WANTED: A boy to take care
of horses who can speak German.
—*Parade of Youth.*

[8472]
Wanted.—A live barber. Quality
Barber Shop, 10 S. Vermillion St.
—*Danville (Va.) paper.*

[8473]
1934 CHEVROLET SEDAN. A
good running car, completely re-
finished. This one won't last long.
Only $145.—*Seattle (Wash.) paper.*

[8474]
For Sale—Large crystal vase by
lady slightly cracked.—*Long Island
paper.*

[8475]
What have you to offer in exchange for beautiful wire-haired
female?—*Advertisement in Dallas
paper.*

[8476]
For Sale.—A full blooded cow,
giving three gallons milk, 2 tons
of hay, a lot of chickens and a
cookstove.—*Montesan (Wash.) paper.*

[8477]
Wanted: A strong horse to do
the work of a country minister.—
Adv.—*Willimantic (Conn.) paper.*

[8478]
LOST AND FOUND
POLICE DOG, answers to name "Junior," male; $50 reward if returned to Washington Meat Market.—*Advertisement in Washington (D. C.) paper.*

[8479]
LOST—White Beagle dog with brown head on north end.—*Manitowac (Wis.) paper.*

[8480]
For Sale—Strictly fresh eggs 35c doz., call at Hall's Antique & Gift Shop.—*Winsted (Conn.) paper.*

[8481]
Before going on vacation have home exterminated; $1.50 up.—*Houston (Tex.) paper.*

[8482]
WANT MAN to do paperhanging in exchange for permanent wave. 223 North Byers.—*Advertisement in Joplin (Mo.) paper.*

[8483]
Young Lady—18 years as beginner in respectable office, or otherwise.—*Ad in Havana American.*

[8484]
86th West—Lady, pleasant, sunny (3 exposures).—*Apartment ad in the New York Times.*

SIGNS

[8485]
Sign in roadside eating place on a Maryland highway:
SOME PAY BEFORE DUE
SOME PAY WHEN DUE
SOME PAY WHEN PAST DUE
SOME NEVER DO
HOW DO YOU DO?

[8486]
This sign is displayed above the coffee percolator of a roadside dining car east of Lancaster, Pa.:
USE LESS SUGAR AND STIR
LIKE THE DEVIL.
WE DON'T MIND THE NOISE

[8487]
A sign that hangs in front of a Pennsylvania road house reads:
WE DON'T SELL BEER ON SUNDAY,
AND DAMN LITTLE ANY OTHER
TIME.

[8488]
This sign is posted over a Kentucky farmer's acres:
NOTIS
Trespassers will be percecuted to the full extent of two mongrel dogs which aint never been too sociable with strangers and one dubble br'l shotgun which aint loaded with sofa pillows. DAM if I ain't gittin tired of this hell raisin' round my place.

[8489]
In a cemetery at South Bethlehem, Pennsylvania, this sign appears: "Persons are prohibited from picking flowers from any but their own graves."

[8490]
A Kentucky electrical dealer who sells washing machines has the following sign in his window: "Don't kill your wife. Let our washing machines do the dirty work."

[8491]
A New York City employer has ordered the following notice to be posted in his business premises:
"Any workman desiring to attend the funeral of a near relative must notify the foreman before ten A. M., on the day of the game."

[8492]

The following sign is posted in a repair shop on the Pacific Coast:

NO CREDIT

(Sad stories of 3 delinquents)

One said, "I'll pay you if I live." He died.

One said, "I'll see you tomorrow." He went blind.

One said, "I'll pay you or go to hell." He must have gone.

[8493]

Sign seen in Oslo store window: "English Spoken, American Understood."

[8494]

Sign on a farm-gate in Ohio: "Peddlers beware! We shoot every tenth peddler. The ninth one just left."

[8495]

In a garage at Albuquerque, New Mexico, the following sign is posted:

"Don't smoke round the tank! If your life isn't worth anything, gasoline is!"

[8496]

In a large park in one of the Eastern Ohio cities there are seats about the bandstand with this notice posted on them:

"The seats in the vicinity of the bandstand are for the use of ladies. Gentlemen should make use of them only after the former are seated."

[8497]

Sign on a New York loft building: "Wanted—Woman to sew buttons on the fourth floor."

[8498]

A New York restaurant advertises: "Pies like mother used to make before she took to bridge and cigarettes."

[8499]

RESTAURANT

Oil, Gasoline, and Strawberries

—*Sign on a Quebec highway*

[8500]

There is a sign in Harlem in a window of West 134th Street, which is bad medicine for music: "Piano lessons. Special pains given to beginners."

[8501]

PORK SAUSAGES
FROM PIGS THAT
DIED HAPPY.

—*Sign in Seattle.*

[8502]

Sign on window of sporting goods store in Los Angeles:

WE SELL EVERYTHING A
GOLFER USES EXCEPT
PROFANITY,
AND IF YOU USE OUR
GOODS YOU WON'T NEED
THAT

[8503]

Sign seen over local dairy: "You can't beat our milk, but you can whip our cream."

BONERS

Here are humorous errors supposedly made by school children in oral and written examinations:

[8504]

Lady Godiva swam the English Channel.

[8505]

Garibaldi designed the Statue of Liberty.

[8506]

Captain John Smith was governor of New York.

[8507]
Furbelow means a vacation for soldiers.

[8508]
Bisquit Tortoni was the man who discovered radio.

[8509]
Robinson Crusoe was a great operatic tenor.

[8510]
Captain Jinks of the Horse Marines conquered San Juan Hill in the Spanish-American War.

[8511]
Iran is the bible of the Mohammedans.

[8512]
Electric volts are named after Voltaire, who invented electricity.

[8513]
In many states murderers are put to death by electrolysis.

[8514]
Pot-pourri is a French dish served in hot little pots.

[8515]
Persiflage is a green vegetable belonging to the spinach family.

[8516]
Telepathy is a code invented by Morse.

[8517]
Rio de Janeiro is the river dividing the United States and Mexico.

[8518]
Romain Rolland is a famous moving picture actor.

[8519]
Karl Marx is one of the Marx brothers.

[8520]
Florence Nightingale was a famous Swedish soprano.

[8521]
Flora and Fauna were the names of the Siamese twins.

[8522]
Marseillaise is a French salad dressing.

[8523]
Davy Jones was a famous train engineer.

[8524]
Thin silk material used for ladies underwear is called Crepe Suzette.

[8525]
"After me, the deluge" was said by Noah when he raised the gangplank of the ark.

[8526]
Alma Mater was a famous opera singer.

[8527]
A priori means first come first served.

[8528]
A cynosure is a judge or collector of art.

[8529]
A fjord is a Swedish automobile.

[8530]
A poetic license is a license you get so you can sell poetry.

[8531]
Daniel Boone was born in a log cabin he built himself.

[8532]
Madison gave his life for his country. He then married Dolly Madison.

[8533]
A midget is a little wharf whose native home is in Africa.

[8534]
A Scotland Yard measures two feet and ten inches.

[8535]
The Germans love to sail on junkers.

[8536]
Gretna Green is a poison used to kill rats.

[8537]
The Merchant of Venice was a famous Italian who bought and sold canal boats.

[8538]
Napoleon had three children, not one of whom lived to maternity.

[8539]
Pate de foi gras is an outdoor circus held in New Orleans every year.

[8540]
Augean Stables was named after the gangster "Little Augie."

[8541]
The natives of the Midi, France, were the first to wear middy blouses.

[8542]
Bambi is a book about Babe Ruth.

[8543]
Oedipus Complex was a famous queen of Ethiopia.

[8544]
Mata Hari means suicide in Japanese.

[8545]
Plenipotentiary is a place where foreign prisoners are kept.

[8546]
A diva is a swimming champion.

[8547]
Flotsam and Jetsam were a famous team of colored comedians.

[8548]
Philatelists were a race of people who lived in Biblical times.

[8549]
Moll Flanders is the story of a Belgian gun-girl.

[8550]
People who study or draw maps are called typographers.

[8551]
Phantasma is a disease of the lungs.

[8552]
Asperity is the drug from which aspirin is made.

[8553]
Naval Stores are places where the wives of naval men buy their supplies.

[8554]
When several businesses merge it is called a concubine.

[8555]
Pasteur found a cure for Rabbis.

[8556]
A psalmist is one who tells fortune by reading hands.

[8557]
Cosmic rays are electric treatments to make a woman beautiful.

[8558]
A doggerel is a little dog.

[8559]
Belvedere is the name given to the male deer.

[8560]
When a woman has many husbands it is called Pollyanna.

[8561]
A journeyman is a traveling man.

[8562]
The Metropolitan district of New York City is the district near the Metropolitan Opera House.

[8563]
A commonplace is a busy corner of a city or village.

[8564]
A troubador is a Spanish bull-fighter.

[8565]
An executive is the man who puts murderers to death.

[8566]
Tin Pan Alley is a street in the New York slums.

[8567]
St. Helena is famous as the island where the mutineers of the Bounty settled.

[8568]
A pemmican is a large bird with a large bill.

[8569]
People living on the equator are called equestrians.

[8570]
Open shop is a factory with windows and a closed shop is one that has air conditioning.

[8571]
The Diet of Worms was discovered by Izaac Walton.

[8572]
Columbine was the wife of the man who discovered America.

[8573]
Peter Minuit invented a very popular dance in the Colonial times.

[8574]
Bismarck, the father of the Kaiser, was very fond of herring.

[8575]
Pegasus is a hobby horse used by carpenters.

[8576]
An aviary is the place where aviators sleep.

[8577]
Autobiography is a history of motor cars.

[8578]
A Sabbatical year is a year with 53 Sundays.

[8579]
The eastern part of Asia is called Euthenasia.

[8580]
A Pomegranate is a lap dog.

[8581]
Ten Knights in a Bar Room was sung by the followers of King Arthur.

[8582]
A gulf is a piece broken off a peninsula.

[8583]
Mongoose is a Scotch male goose.

[8584]
Pidgin-English were pigeons used by the British to carry messages during the war.

[8585]
Armadillo is the Spanish navy which defeated the Duke of Wellington.

[8586]
Monsoon is French for Mister.

[8587]
Doctors who treat your eyes are called optimists.

[8588]
A polygon is another name for a Mormon.

[8589]
All people were petrified during the Stone Age.

[8590]
An Indian baby is called a caboose.

[8591]
Equinox is a country near the Panama Canal.

[8592]
An Agnostic is a plant from which bitters are made.

[8593]
Ponce de Leon never grew old.

[8594]
The mother of Abraham Lincoln died in infancy.

[8595]
A pedigree is a teacher in college.

[8596]
The American people have the right to partition Congress without going to jail.

[8597]
The Crusaders were little children sent on a cruise to Jerusalem during Shakespeare's time.

[8598]
Antimony is money inherited from your mother's sister.

[8599]
The Angelus is the home of the angels up in the sky.

[8600]
A geyser is slang for a hick.

[8601]
A mummy is the dead mother of a Gipsy.

[8602]
Cleopatra wore beautiful open-toed scandals.

[8603]
Nicotine is the man who invented cigarettes.

[8604]
Laissez-faire are lazy French women.

[8605]
History calls people Romans because they never stayed long in one place.

[8606]
A tambourine is a curved club which can be hurled so that it will come back near the place from which it was thrown.

[8607]
All strong men have good physics.

[8608]
A stowaway is the man with the biggest appetite on the boat.

[8609]
Seniors are Spanish men who make love to Spanish Senioritas.

[8610]
Conservation means table talk.

[8611]
When a man is married to one woman it is called monotony.

[8612]
The Golden Rule is that the man who first finds gold keeps it.

[8613]
When a man has more than one wife he is a pigamist.

[8614]
The Eighteenth Amendment to the Constitution destroyed whiskey.

[8615]
The earth resolves around the sun once every year.

[8616]
A flying buttress is a lady butler on airplanes.

[8617]
Boxing the compass means two prize fighters boxing in opposite directions in the same ring.

[8618]
A pulmotor is the kind of automobile engine that pulls instead of pushes the car.

[8619]
Kosher is Jewish pork.

[8620]
Latin Quarter is a French 25-cent piece.

[8621]
Kubla Khan is a colored secret society wearing white night shirts.

[8622]
Opium is a Chinese medicine discovered by Dr. Fu Manchu.

HOWLERS

When teacher asks Willie to construct a sentence using the word "Amazon", and he responds with, "You can pay for the eggs but the amazon (ham is on) me," Willie's answer is called a "howler." Following is an alphabetical collection of such howlers:

[8623]
Amazon–"You can pay for the eggs but the amazon me."

[8624]
Ammonia–"The shoes are beautiful, but have you tried ammonia to see if they will fit?"

[8625]
Amphibian–"So you think I amphibian, do you?"

[8626]
Antidotes–"My uncle likes me very much and my antidotes on me."

[8627]
Archaic–"We can't have archaic and eat it too."

[8628]
Arrears–"Brother and I both hate to wash in back of arrears."

[8629]
Asparagus–"Until the baby birds are old enough to fly, asparagus and gets food for them."

[8630]
Avenue–"I avenue baby sister."

[8631]
Balsam–"The balsam pitched hit Abie in the head."

[8632]
Bellicose–"Don't hit me in the bellicose it hurts."

[8633]
Boisterous–"Mary and I like playing with girls, what are you boisterous."

[8634]
Bulletin–"Pa got in a fight and now he has a bulletin his leg."

[8635]
Burden–"Dad went hunting but he didn't get a burden he came home mad."

[8636]
Butter–"She wanted to go butter mother wouldn't let her."

[8637]
Caddie–"He isn't the caddie used to be."

[8638]
Canada–"You bring the weiners and I'll bring a canada best sauerkraut."

[8639]
Catgut–"Our dog got fleas but our catgut kittens."

[8640]
Cigarette–"Cigarette life if you don't weaken."

[8641]
Collapse–"When fat women sit down what becomes of the thing they collapse."

[8642]
Commonplace–"Take that pencil out of your mouth, Willie, and commonplace it on my desk."

[8643]
Contrite–"Algernon writes beautiful poetry but I contrite a thing."

[8644]
Criminal–"Mamma's broke all the time because Papa's got to have rich criminal his food."

[8645]
Cuckoo–"We have a new cuckoo makes nice tarts."

[8646]
Curious–"Dad is getting better with the curious taking now."

[8647]
Daisies–"Ma's always glad when school starts because Johnnie's such a nuisance the daisies at home."

[8648]
Deceit–"Ma makes me wear pants with patches on deceit."

[8649]
Demure–"When people start to get rich demure they get demure they want."

[8650]
Denial–"Cleopatra lived and loved on denial."

[8651]
Diabetes–"That baseball team has sworn they'll either diabetes."

[8652]
Evanescent–"Well, evanescent my old pal Oscar."

[8653]
Examine–"I had fruit for breakfast in addition to examine bacon."

[8654]
Extradition–"Eat all you want, there's an extradition the pantry."

[8655]
Falsify–"When I put a book on my head it falsify move."

[8656]
Fanatic–"We like to dress up in the old things we get out of fanatic."

[8657]
Festival–"I can go to the movies, but festival I have to do my home work."

[8658]
Folder–"Children should always show proper respect folder people."

[8659]
Forfeit–"A dog seems to find forfeit better than two."

[8660]
Fundamental–"Sister went horseback riding yesterday, and now she has to eat fundamental."

[8661]
Gladiator–"That old hen wasn't laying any eggs, so I'm gladiator."

[8662]
Gruesome–"Father did not shave for a week, and gruesome whiskers."

[8663]
Hence–"The roosters do the strutting while the hence do the laying."

[8664]
Heresy–"Is that a crack in my soup plate or is it a heresy?"

[8665]
Himalaya–"Yesterday was Pa's birthday and Ma made himalaya cake."

[8666]
Historian–"That's historian he's stuck with it."

[8667]
Impolite–"He didn't offer Pa a cigarette so I won't give that impolite."

[8668]
Income–"I opened the door and income a cat."

[8669]
Insulate–"How come you got insulate?"

[8670]
Judicious–"Ham is not one of the judicious."

[8671]
Juicy–"When we came through the alley juicy what I saw?"

[8672]
Junior–"If you don't have showers in April, in junior flowers won't come up."

[8673]
Laziness–"It's no wonder baby doesn't get tired, he laziness crib all day."

[8674]
Lilac–"He's a nice kid but he can lilac anything."

[8675]
Malicious–"There was a big fight in our neighborhood and the malicious been called out."

[8676]
Mutilate–"I could get more sleep if our cat didn't mutilate every night."

[8677]
Muzzle–"If you're a good girl muzzle let you go to the movies."

[8678]
Nuisance–"I haven't had anything nuisance I was married."

[8679]
Partisan–"Ma got cheated on this spinach because the greater partisan."

[8680]
Porcupine–"Why is it that all through Lent it's for porcupine?"

[8681]
Propagate–"I don't like to ride that horse because he hasn't the propagate."

[8682]
Reverend–"Teacher says if I don't study I'll be in this grade for reverend ever."

[8683]
Safety Razor–"They are leaving the ship where she sank because it isn't safety razor."

[8684]
Screen–"I like my new dress because its screen."

[8685]
Shiver–I lost Mamma's watch and she'll be awful mad if shiver finds out."

[8686]
Stagnation–"If all the women left the country this would be a stagnation."

[8687]
Surgeon–"Willie likes his gray suit but he looks nicer with his blue surgeon."

[8688]
Swearing–"Ma bought this suit cheap and swearing better than she thought it would."

[8689]
Tattoo–"My Ma is very smart, she can sew and knit and crochet and tattoo."

[8690]
Toronto–"When you hit the ball you have toronto first base."

[8691]
Terrorize–"If Katie doesn't stop pulling my hair I'll terrorize out of her head."

[8692]
Tortuous–"I tortuous going to ask me to recite today."

[8693]
Tour–"The twins are always cutting up; the tour riding the same horse now."

[8694]

Vicious—"Best vicious for a Merry Christmas and a Happy New Year."

[8695]

Wiggle—"She wears her hat all the time because she's afraid her wiggle come off."

PUNS

[8696]

A man by the name of Day married a woman by the name of Knight and has three children. The oldest he called Dawn, because it was the first of Day; the second, Moon, because it was a reflection of Day at Knight; the third, Twilight, because it was the last of Day.

[8697]

Fox—"Say, Beavy, they tell me you can cut down any size tree."
Beaver—"Well, I've never been stumped yet."

[8698]

"So you are going to start a bakery?"
"If I can raise the dough."

[8699]

"Are you reading yourself to sleep with that story?"
"Yes, it's a great 'yawn.'"

[8700]

"When it comes to making a lining for a nest," softly quacked the eider duck, "I've got it down fine."

[8701]

John—"Don't you think I'm rather good looking?"
Jane—"In a way."
John—"What kind of a way?"
Jane—"Away off."

[8702]

A man, whose daughter had married a man by the name of Price, was congratulated by one of his friends, who remarked: "I am glad to see you have got a good price for your daughter."

[8703]

"How would you classify a telephone girl? Is hers a business or a profession?"
"Neither. It's a calling."

[8704]

"There's one strange thing about our soprano."
"No; you don't say so! What is it?"
"Merely that her solo is always sohigh."

[8705]

"O, Uncle John, Miss Green and Mr. Smith are in the parlor, and she has her head on his shoulder."
"That's all right, Willie. She has a lien on him."

[8706]

"Water! Water!" he cried weakly. "Will no one bring me a drink of water?" All around him for miles and miles stretched the white burning sand of the great desert. Once more he called out, and once more there was silence. But suddenly an inspiration struck his thirst-tortured brain. He wrung his hands, and held them above his mouth.

[8707]

Little Marvin found a button in his salad.
He remarked: "I suppose it fell off while the salad was dressing."

[8708]

The crow is not so bad a bird after all. It never shows the white feather and never complains without caws.

[8709]
"Have you much fish in your basket?" asked a person of a fisherman, who was returning.

"Yes, a good eel," was the rather slippery reply.

[8710]
"Your pants look rather sad to-day."

"What do you mean?"

"Sort of depressed."

[8711]
"When did Caesar reign?"

"I didn't know he rained."

"Didn't they hail him?"

[8712]
"Did you enjoy your chess game?"

"Oh, it was chess mediocre."

"What a pawn! What a pawn!"

[8713]
I hope I see you well, as the bucket said when it touched the water.

[8714]
"Can't you help a poor man, sir? I need bread."

"You will have to be a little more explicit. Do you need bread or knead bread? Are you a beggar that loafs or a loafer that begs."

[8715]
"See that dog chasing his tail?"

"Poor little cuss. He is trying to make both ends meet."

[8716]
"How did you happen to become a chiropodist?" he was asked.

"Oh," he replied, "I always was at the foot of my class at school, so just naturally drifted into this profession."

[8717]
St. Peter–"How did you get here?"

Latest Arrival–"Flu!"

[8718]
"Give an example of period furniture."

"Well, I should say an electric chair, because it ends a sentence."

[8719]
"Are you fond of tongue, sir?"

"I was always fond of tongue, madam, and I like it still."

[8720]
The irate customer shook his portrait in the photographer's face.

"Do I look like this picture? The thing's an outrage. Why you've given me an awful squint and the look of a prize fighter. Now, answer me, and no nonsense about it. Do you call that a good likeness?"

The tactful photographer scanned the print, then looked at the customer.

"The answer," he said, "is in the negative."

[8721]
"It's been a coal day when you're left," said the kindling-wood to the cinder.

"You're too chip-per," replied the cinder to the kindling wood.

"Go to blazes," said the match, as it dropped in and fired both up.

[8722]
Miss Joy was present at a party, and in the course of the evening some one used the quotation: "A thing of beauty is a joy forever," when she exclaimed: "Oh, I'm glad I'm not a beauty, for I shouldn't want to be a joy forever."

[8723]
Female Castaway–"Good heavens! Cannibals."

Male Ditto–"Now, now, don't get in a stew."

[8724]

A gentleman who had been arguing with an ignoramus until his patience was exhausted, said he didn't wish him dead, but he would be glad to see him—know more.

[8725]

"What is the secret of success?" asked the Sphinx.

"Push," said the Button.

"Never be led," said the Pencil.

"Take pains," said the Window.

"Always keep cool," said the Ice.

"Be up to date," said the Calendar.

"Never lose your head," said the Barrel.

"Make light of everything," said the Fire.

"Do a driving business," said the Hammer.

"Aspire to greater things," said the Nutmeg.

"Be sharp in all your dealings," said the Knife.

"Find a good thing and stick to it," said the Glue.

[8726]

"There!" she said, standing on her tiptoes, "I am about your size."

"On the contrary," said the disconsolate lover, "my sighs are about you."

[8727]

"Are you a doctor?" asked a young lady, stepping into a drug store.

"Naw," replied the youth behind the white counter. "I'm just the fizzician."

[8728]

She—"You got fooled on this diamond ring."

He—"I guess not. I know my onions."

She—"Maybe—but not your carats."

[8729]

"Why do they call money jack?"

"It lifts such a load off a fellow."

[8730]

"What is this here 'witching hour?' "

"You are ignorant—why that's the hour when your wife greets you with 'Which story is it this time?' "

[8731]

"We have no room for all this," said our night editor, glancing despairingly at a two-column obituary, "it must be cut down to proper diemention."

[8732]

"I hear the sea captain is in hard luck. He married a girl and she ran away from him."

"Yes; he took her for a mate, but she was a skipper."

[8733]

"Pray, Mrs. Smith, why do you whip your children so often?"

"Mrs. Worthy, I do it for their enlightenment. I never whipped one of them in my life, that he didn't acknowledge that it made him smart."

[8734]

"This job of bringing home the bacon is no joke," sighed one married man.

"No," growled the other one, "and on top of that I always have to stop at the bakery and bring home the bakin', too."

[8735]

Jeweler's Son—"Papa, how do you just a watch?"

Jeweler—"Adjust, my boy, not just just."

Jeweler's Son—"Well, papa, if you add just to just, it's just just, isn't it?"

[8736]
An observing man claims to have discovered the color of the wind. He says he went out and found it blew.

[8737]
"I spent last summer in a very pretty city in Switzerland."
"Berne?"
"No, I almost froze."

[8738]
Don't carry your handkerchief in your breast pocket. If you do you take a wiper to your bosom.

[8739]
Old maid's laughter—He! he! he!

[8740]
"Did you ever see the Catskill Mountains?"
"No, sir; but I've seen them kill mice!"

[8741]
Ma–"You've been drinking. I smell it in your breath."
Pa–"Not a drop. I've been eating frog's legs. What you smell is the hops."

[8742]
A woman in paroxysms of grief was said to have shed torrents of tears.
"Poor thing!" remarked an unfeeling punster; "she must have had a cataract in each eye."

[8743]
A henpecked husband, who had married his wife because she was handsome declared that a thing of beauty is a jaw forever.

[8744]
It is said that a human being has seven millions of pores through which perspiration and exhausted particles of the system escape. We are all pore creatures.

[8745]
"I hear that in the slugging match Sullivan was worsted."
"Oh, that's a yarn."

[8746]
"Mrs. Smith is simply mad on the subject of germs, and sterilizes or filters everything in the house!"
"How does she get along with her husband?"
"Oh, even their relations are strained!"

[8747]
Sydney Smith, passing through a by-street behind St. Paul's London, heard two women abusing each other from opposite houses. "They will never agree," said the wit; "they argue from different premises."

[8748]
Edwin told his girl that if she didn't marry him, he'd get a rope and hang himself right in front of her home.
"Oh, please don't do it, Edwin," she said. "You know father doesn't want you hanging around here."

[8749]
"What becomes of all those love triangles?"
"Most of them turn into wreck-tangles."

[8750]
A man by the name of Dunlop once defied a famous punster to perpetrate a pun on his name.
"Easy enough!" cried the wit. "Just lop off the last syllable and it's Dun!"

[8751]
"Is that marble?" said a man pointing to the bust of Kentucky's great statesman.
"No, sir, that's Clay," quietly replied the dealer.

[8752]

Man (in drug store)–"I want some consecrated lye."

Druggist–"You mean concentrated lye."

Man–"It does nutmeg any difference. That's what I camphor. What does it sulphur?"

Druggist–"Fifteen scents. I never cinnamon with so much wit."

Man–"Well, I should myrrh, myrrh! Yet I ammonia novice at it."

[8753]

"Will you marry me in spite of my trouble?"

"What is it?"

"Falling hair."

"You darling boy! To how much?"

[8754]

Suitor–"May I marry your daughter?"

Stern Father–"What is your vocation?"

Suitor–"I'm an actor."

Stern Father (angrily)–"Then get out before the foot lights."

[8755]

He met her at Friendship, Missouri, followed her to Love, Virginia, and asked her to name the day at Ring, Arkansas. They were married at Church, Iowa, and settled down at Home, Oregon, but the twins were born at Boise, Idaho.

[8756]

"Dr. Jekyll, tell me more about your alter ego."

"Scram son, you're getting under my Hyde."

[8757]

"Who's your cook now?"

"Della."

"Della who?"

"Della Katessen."

[8758]

He–"Look, darling, here is a diamond engagement ring for you."

She–"Oh, it is be-utiful, but honey, the diamond has a flaw in it."

He–"You shouldn't notice that— why, you're in love and love is blind."

She–"Yeah, but not stone blind."

[8759]

It is said that a pig ran away from the butcher, because he had heard that prevention is better than cure.

[8760]

"Captain Columbus," said a scared seaman on the *Santa Maria,* "if the world is really flat, like everybody says—"

"Stop fretting," interrupted Columbus impatiently, "I'm telling you the world isn't flat."

"But what makes you so sure?" persisted the seaman.

"If the world was flat," returned Columbus, "where would I have gotten the money to make this trip?"

[8761]

"I want to know how long girls should be courted."

"The same as short ones."

[8762]

"Do you like cycling with a party?"

"No; I prefer to cyclone."

[8763]

Henry–"So you liked me because I ignored you?"

Henrietta–"Yes, it was love at first slight."

[8764]

"But, Joe, I can't marry you, you're almost penniless."

"That's nothing, the Czar of Russia was Nicholas."

[8765]
The magician's wife knew he was up to his old tricks because she discovered a hare on his shoulder.

[8766]
When Mr. Alexander Gun was dismissed from the customs of Edinburgh, the entry made against his name in the books was: "A Gun discharged for making a false report."

[8767]
"Here, boy," said the man to the boy who was helping him drive a bunch of cattle, "hold this bull a minute, will you?"
"No," answered the boy, "I don't mind bein' a director in this company, but I'm darned if I want to be a stockholder."

[8768]
"I say, Tom-ass, how are things?" asked one smart aleck of his acquaintance named Thomas.
Unfortunately, the smart aleck had forgotten that his own name was Samuel, for Thomas retorted: "I'm fine, Sam-mule; and you?"

[8769]
"There was a terrible murder in the hotel to-day."
"Was there."
"Yes; a paper-hanger hung a border."
"It must have been a put-up job!"

[8770]
An awful curious bore, learning that a young lady was going to another city, asked: "What motive is taking you there, my dear?"
"I believe they call it a locomotive."

[8771]
A man's idea about marriage:
Before—Spooning around.
After—Forking over.

[8772]
"You know Archie? He beats his wife up every morning."
"You don't say!"
"Yes. He gets up at eight, and she gets up at nine."

[8773]
Nurse—"Oh, ma'am, what shall I do? The twins have fallen down the well!"
Parent—"Dear me! how annoying! Just go into the library and get the last number of *The Modern Mother's Magazine;* it contains an article on 'How to Bring Up Children.'"

[8774]
"Why do people always apply the name of 'she' to a city?"
"I don't know. Why is it?"
"Because every city has outskirts."

[8775]
"Who is he?" said a passer-by to a policeman, who was endeavoring to raise an intoxicated individual who had fallen into the gutter.
"Can't say, sir," replied the policeman, "he can't give an account of himself."
"Of course not," said the other, "how can you expect an account from a man who has lost his balance."

[8776]
George Washington—"Yes, father, I cannot tell a lie. I cut your sherry."

[8777]
"Will you marry me?"
"No, I'm afraid not."
"Oh, come on, be a support."

[8778]
Boogy—"Why do you say that scar on your forehead is a birthmark? It looks more like an old wound."
Woogy—"It is. You see, I accidentally got into the wrong berth."

[8779]

She–"Tell me the story of the girl who bleached her hair."

He–"I never tell girls off-color stories."

[8780]

"Did you ever see the 'reading pig' in the circus?"

"No; but I've seen a 'spelling bee' in the country."

[8781]

"Upon what does a pawnbroker live?"

"On the flat of the land."

[8782]

The wife of a well-known literary man, while reading one of his articles in the press, corrected it as she went along, and the errors were somewhat numerous. "Why, dear," she exclaimed, "you don't know the first rules in grammar, or else you are very negligent."

"Well, well, my love," he exclaimed, looking up from his work, "what is the matter now?"

"Why, in three cases you speak of our sex in the plural, and write it in the singular number."

"I can't help it," was the retort. "Woman is a singular being."

[8783]

"What's that you have there?"

"A clamp."

"Oh, so you're a vise guy."

[8784]

"Do you think there's music in the stars?"

"I don't know about that, but I know of the sun causing a belle to peel."

[8785]

"Her father married her mother for the bread she made."

"Her suitor wants to marry her for the dough she's got."

[8786]

A doctor and a military officer became enamored of the same lady. A friend asked her which of the two suitors she intended to favor. She replied that "it was difficult for her to determine, as they were such killing creatures."

[8787]

The street car conductor opened the door to the front platform to collect his fares. He encountered five policemen riding home from work.

"Five coppers," remarked the conductor, slamming the door, "and not a nickel in the bunch."

[8788]

Parting advice—Put a little water on the comb.

[8789]

"The butcher is an awkward fellow."

"Yes, I notice his hands are always in his weigh."

[8790]

Every dog has his day. Yes, and those with broken tails have their week ends.

[8791]

A scientific item says that there is a war on between the electron and the atom.

Up, Electrons, and Atom!

[8792]

A Frenchwoman whose mate threw her off a cliff 100 feet high has refused to prosecute. Maybe he convinced her it was a bluff.

[8793]

A cockney soldier was stationed at Plymouth. One evening he met a young man who was a native of Plymouth. The two got to yarning, and the Londoner thought to take a rise out of his provincial acquaintance.

"If you stand on London Bridge and shout," he told the Plymouth man, "you can walk across to the other side and buy the *Echo.*"

Of course, he meant the old *Echo* newspaper.

But the man from Plymouth was not so easily beaten. He had met Londoners before.

"That's nothing," he bluffed. "Why here in Plymouth you can stand on Plymouth Bridge and shout, and then go across to the other side and see the Sound."

[8794]

"How can I make anti-freeze?"
"Hide her woolen pajamas."

[8795]

"Could I see General Blank?"
"I'm sorry, but General Blank is ill today."
"What made him ill?"
"Oh, things in general."

[8796]

"Where do jellyfish get their jelly?"
"From ocean currents, I guess."

[8797]

It was the morning for freer mental exercise and teacher was putting her little class through a bit of abstract training.

"Now, Willie," asked she, turning to a freckled youth in the end row, "if a policeman found a watch on a tramp, what would you naturally infer about the watch?"

"That it was on the bum!" came the prompt answer.

[8798]

"Know anything about Latin syntax?"
"Don't tell me they had to pay for their fun, too?"

[8799]

Beth—"So Herbie hides under the sofa and reports every time you're hugged?"
Mildred—"Yes, he's a regular little press agent."

[1800]

"I saw a big rat in my cookstove and when I went for my revolver he ran out."
"Did you shoot him?"
"No. He was out of my range."

[8800]

Nothing more clearly expresses the sentiments of Harvard men in seasons of athletic rivalry than the time-honored "To hell with Yale!"

Once when Dean Briggs, of Harvard, and Edward Everett Hale were on their way to a game at Soldiers' Field a friend asked:

"Where are you going, Dean?"
"To yell with Hale," answered Briggs with a meaning smile.

[8802]

"Why, Tom, how are you, my good fellow? Where have you been for a week back?"

"Why, I'm better. I've been to Dr. Stickem's for a strengthening plaster, but how did you know I had a weak back?"

[8803]

The following correspondence is said to have taken place between a merchant and one of his customers:

"Sir, your account has been standing for two years. I must have it settled immediately."

Answer:

"Sir, things usually do settle by standing. I regret that my account is an exception. If it has been standing too long, suppose you let it run a little."

[8804]
"Are you the mate?" said a man to the Irish cook of a vessel.
"No," said he, "but I'm the man that boils the mate."

[8805]
Mrs. Jenkins complained in the evening, that the turkey she had eaten at Thanksgiving did not sit well.
"Probably," said Jenkins, "it was not a hen turkey."

[8806]
A young lady, who prided herself upon her geography, setting a candle aslant, remarked that it reminded her of the leaning tower of Pisa.
"Yes," responded her young man, "with this difference—that is a tower in Italy, while this is a tower in Grease."

[8807]
A comedian, by way of a puff for his approaching show, published these lines:

Dear public, you and I, of late,
    Have dealt so much in fun,
I'll crack you now a monstrous, great
Quadruplicated pun!

Like a grate full of coals I'll glow,
    A great full house to see:
And if I am not grateful, too,
    A great fool I must be.

[8808]
"It must be kind of difficult to eat soup with a mustache."
"Yes, it's quite a strain."

[8809]
"I have just got a new siren for my car."
"And what have you done with the little blonde you had last week?"

[8810]
"Why did you pick the grocer to play the bass drum in your band?"
"Because he's an honest fellow and gives full weight to every pound."

[8811]
Mrs. Brown (with newspaper)—"John, it refers here to some gunmen taking a man for a ride. What kind of a ride?"
Brown—"A slay ride, my dear."

[8812]
"I have a fresh cold," said a man to his acquaintance.
"Why do you have a fresh one, why don't you have it cured?"

[8813]
Aviator—"Wanna fly?"
Innocent—"Oo-o-ah!"
Aviator—"Wait, I'll catch one for you."

[8814]
"Is your house a warm one, landlord?" asked a gentleman in search of a house.
"It ought to be," was the reply, "the painter gave it two coats recently."

[8815]
"He's cleaned up a fortune in crooked dough."
"What was he anyhow, a counterfeiter?"
"No, a pretzel manufacturer."

[8816]
It is easy to breakfast in bed if you will be satisfied with a few rolls and a turnover.

[8817]
"Why so gloomy, old chap?"
"Just heard that my uncle has cut me out of his will. He's altered it five times in the last two years."
"Ha, evidently a fresh heir fiend."

[8818]

"Aren't you afraid your husband will neglect the cat while you are away?"

Gambler's Wife–"Oh, no. Bill always likes to see plenty in the kitty."

[8819]

They were walking by the seaside, and he sighed and she sighed.

[8820]

"If a man smashed a clock, could he be accused of killing time?"

"Not if he could prove that the clock struck first."

[8821]

"Bill, you young scamp, if you had your due, you'd get a good whipping."

"I know it, Daddy; but bills are not always paid when due."

[8822]

"What's a Greek Urn?"

"About fifteen a week unless he owns his own hash house."

[8823]

Why they call a sensational report a canard is because one canardly believe it.

[8824]

"What did you do when the ship sank in mid-ocean?"

"Oh, just grabbed a cake of soap and washed myself ashore."

[8825]

A bachelor says he dislikes young married couples, "because they are apt to give themselves heirs."

[8826]

"Waiter, this coffee is sheer mud —take it away."

"Sorry, sir; but it was only ground this morning."

[8827]

"Tough luck," said the egg in the monastery. "Out of the frying pan into the friar."

[8828]

"Why do you call this the Fiddle Hotel?"

"Because it's such a vile inn."

[8829]

You can get along at Christmas time without holly, but you must have the berries.

[8830]

In one of the towns of the Pacific coast a distinct earthquake shock was felt, and when the municipal building rocked perceptibly the city fathers left without bothering about formalities.

The clerk, a man of rules and regulations, was hard put to it to give his minutes the proper official tone. Finally he evolved this masterpiece:

"On motion of the city hall, the council adjourned."

[8831]

Anna Maria Story was married to Robert Short. A very pleasant way of making a story short.

[8832]

If a man has but one eye, let him get a wife, and she will be his other *I*.

[8833]

A young lady remarked to a male friend, that she feared she would make a poor sailor.

The gentleman promptly answered: "Probably; but I'm sure you would make an excellent mate."

[8834]

"Why do the ducks dive?"

"Guess they must want to liquidate their bills."

[8835]

"I can see, darling, that I am only a little pebble on the beach of your life."

"Well, go on. Be a little boulder."

[8836]

Shopper – "Have you anything snappy in rubber bands?"

Assistant–"No; but we have something catchy in fly-paper."

[8837]

"What was the use of the eclipse?" asked a young lady.

"Oh, it gave the sun time for reflection."

[8838]

"Do you think he'll make a good match?"

"I can prophesy he'll always be lit."

[8839]

"Why do poets always speak of the moon as silver?"

"It's because of the quarters and halves, I suppose."

[8840]

First Congressman–"I sowed ten pounds of grass seed and nothing came up. It's a shame!"

Second Congressman–"Yes, there ought to be a lawn!"

[8841]

Friend–"Going to hunt lions as usual this season."

Hunter–"No, I'm going to look for gnu game."

[8842]

"What makes petrified trees?"

" 'Tis said the wind makes them rock."

[8843]

Abdul–"Hurry up, Scherazzadi."

Abdul's Wife–"All right, Dear, I'll be there in a minare_."

[8844]

"Have you any complaints to make?" asked the prison governor.

"Yes," replied the prisoner, schooled in architecture; "the prison walls are not built to scale."

[8845]

Teacher–"Can any one tell me what happened after Napoleon mustered his army?"

Pupil–"Yes, sir, he peppered the enemy and took the citadel by assault."

Teacher–"Sit down, my lad. I'll have no sauce from you."

[8846]

Free verse: the triumph of mind over meter.

[8847]

It is the opinion of the doctor that the lawyer gets his living by plunder, while the lawyer thinks the doctor gets his by "pillage."

[8848]

"Have you a little fairy in your home?"

"No, but I have a little miss in my engine."

[8849]

"Whenever my wife needs money she calls me handsome."

"Handsome?'"

"Yes, hand some over!"

[8850]

"John, I bought some sheets, pillow cases and blankets today. Shall I put them down in my budget as cover charge or overhead?"

[8851]

"Can you define matrimony?"

"Yes! You go to adore, you ring a belle, and you give your name to a maid—and then you're taken in!"

[8852]

A Philadelphia judge and punster having observed to another judge on the bench that one of the witnesses had a vegetable head.

"How so?" was the inquiry.

"He has carroty hair, reddish cheeks, turnip nose, and sage look."

[8853]

She (very highhat)–"Sir! I'd have you know that my father is an English peer."

He–"Oh, thass all right. My old man is an American doc."

[8854]

He was an old and not very handsome widower.

"You are the sixth girl to whom I have proposed without avail."

"Well," said the girl, kindly, "maybe if you wear one when making your seventh proposal you'll have better luck."

[8855]

A garrulous fop, who had annoyed, by his frivolous remarks, his partner in the ballroom, among other empty things, asked whether "she had ever had her ears pierced?"

"No," was the reply, "but I have often had them bored."

[8856]

The Chinese Consul at San Francisco, at a recent dinner, discussed his country's customs.

"There is one custom," said a young girl, "that I cannot understand—and that is the Chinese custom of committing suicide by eating gold-leaf. I can't understand how gold-leaf can kill."

"The partaker, no doubt," smiled the Consul, "succumbs from a consciousness of inward gilt."

[8857]

Many public men consider themselves the pillars of the State who are more properly the caterpillars, reaching their high positions only by crawling.

[8858]

He–"Does the moon affect the tide?"

She–"No, only the untied."

[8859]

"What," the gentleman asked, "would you be, dearest, if I should press the stamp of love upon those sealing-wax lips of yours?"

She was equal to the occasion, for she promptly answered, "Why, I should be *stationery*, I guess."

[8860]

"This is so sodden!" said the recently married husband as he graciously accepted another product of his wife's baking.

[8861]

"There is an awful rumbling in my stomach—like a cart going over a cobblestone street."

"It's probably that truck you ate for dinner."

[8862]

"While I was in Europe I saw a bed twenty feet long and ten feet wide."

"Sounds like a lot of bunk."

[8863]

"How did you get on with Jeanette?" asked Dick.

The ardent young lover sighed. "I started off well," he replied. "I said I was knee deep in love with her."

"Sounds all right," said Dick. "What was her reaction to that?"

The young suitor grimaced. "She promised to put me on her wading list," he replied.

[8864]

"Did you hear the story about the peacock?'"

"No."

"It's a beautiful tale."

[8865]

"Tell me, Billy, why do they use knots instead of miles on the ocean?'"

"Because, darling, they've got to have the ocean tide."

[8866]

First Turk–"I think we've met somewhere before, don't you?"

Second Turk–"I can't remember your name, but your fez seems familiar."

[8867]

Strange, Moore, and Wright, three notorious punsters, were on a certain occasion, dining together, when Moore observed, "There is but one knave among us, and that's Strange."

"Oh, no!" said Wright; "there is one Moore."

"Ah!" said Strange; "that's Wright."

[8868]

"Only a silver watch," said the pawnbroker. "The last time I advanced you money on your watch it had a solid gold case."

"Yes," replied Hard-up, "but—er—circumstances alter cases, you know."

[8869]

A famous punster boasted that he could make a pun on any subject. When asked to do so at a banquet, he queried:

"Will someone name a subject?"

"The king!" someone called out.

Without a moment's hesitation, the punster punned: "The king is not a subject!"

[8870]

Fussy Old Lady–"I want two good seats for this afternoon, in the coolest part of the house."

"All right, madam, here are two in Z row."

[8871]

"Who was the smallest man in history?"

"The Roman soldier who went to sleep on his watch."

[8872]

First Egyptian–"Who was that lady I saw you eating with last night?"

Second ditto–"That was no lady. That was my mummy."

[8873]

"What now?"

"The radio marriage."

"A National hook-up, eh?'"

[8874]

The next time you make up a pun,
A father once said to his son,
   Go out in the yard
   And kick yourself hard,
And I will begin when you've done.

[8875]

Perplexed Oriental–"Our children velly white. Is velly strange."

"Well . . . occidents will happen."

[8876]

The pun is reputed to be the lowest form of wit. In this connection a good story is told, probably invented to suit the exigency of a moment, of the king's jester who punned incessantly until the king, in desperation, condemned the jester to be hanged. However, when the executioners had taken the jester to the gallows, the king, thinking that after all a good jester was not easy to find, relented, and sent a messenger post haste with a royal pardon.

Arriving at the gallows just in time, where the jester stood with the rope already about his neck, the messenger read the king's decree, to the effect that the jester would be pardoned if he would promise never to make another pun. The jester could not resist the temptation of the opportunity, however, for he cackled out:

"No noose is good news."

And they hanged him.

[8877]

"Plump bodies is a new phase in style's anatomy," says an exchange. The phase that launched a thousand hips.

[8878]

"What's worse than raining cats and dogs?"

"I don't know, unless it's hailing a street car."

[8879]

Boston Lady–"How much are these string beans?"

Boston Huckster – "Seventy-five cents a quart."

Lady–"Isn't that rather altitudinous?"

Huckster–"Yes, madam; but these are very high-strung beans."

[8880]

"If you want your parrot to talk you should begin by teaching it short words."

"That's strange. I supposed it would take quicker to polly-syllables."

[8881]

Baron Applegate – "They tell me that Lord Cheapside is a social failure."

Baron Slushbottom–"Yes, he hath no manors."

[8882]

Baby Ear of Corn–"Mama, where did I come from?"

Mama Ear of Corn–"Hush, dear; the stalk brought you."

[8883]

Inspecting a pair of trousers in his shop in Athens, a tailor queried: "Euripides?"

Customer–"Yah; Eumenides."

[8884]

Teacher–"Why don't you like our school, Willie?"

Willie–"Oh, it's not so much the school — it's the principal of the thing."

[8885]

Priest–"Do you take this woman for butter or for wurst?"

Groom – "Oh, liver alone, I never sausage nerve."

[8886]

A lady reproving a man during a hard frost for swearing, advised him to leave it off, saying it was a very bad habit.

"Very true, madam," answered he, "but at present it is too cold to think of parting with any *habit,* be it ever so bad."

[8887]

"What does the bride think when she walks into the church?"

"Aisle, Altar, Hymn."

[8888]

Teacher–"And you, Willie, can you tell the nationality of Napoleon?"

Willie–"Course I can."

Teacher–"That's right."

[8889]

"They caught the burglars that robbed the hotel last night."

"How?"

"They jumped on the scales and gave themselves a weigh."

[8890]

One of the best puns in the English language is found in the last lines of Thomas Hood's *Faithless Sally Brown:*

His death, which happened in his berth,
   At forty-odd befell;
They went and told the sexton,
   And the sexton tolled the bell.

[8891]

"Which weeds are the easiest weeds to kill?" asked the city chap of the farmer.

"Widow's weeds," replied the farmer, "you have only to say 'wilt thou' and they wilt."

[8892]

Mr. Pushup—"Samson had the right idea about advertising. He took two columns and brought down the house."

[8893]

A youth's mustache was the pioneer of the instalment plan—a little down and then a little more each week.

[8894]

"How did that play they put on in the jail turn out?"

"Marvelous, it was a cell out."

[8895]

One man's Mede is another man's Persian.

[8896]

First Roman (at a Christian massacre) – "We've got a capacity crowd, but still we're losing money. The upkeep on the lions must be pretty heavy."

Second Roman – "Yes, sir; these lions sure do eat the prophets."

[8897]

Always remember, no matter how bad prose may be, that it might be verse.

[8898]

Did it ever occur to you that you might call your sweetheart Revenge, because she is sweet? Or that a poor lawyer might be dubbed Necessity, because he knows no law? Or that a highway robber taking your watch might be named Procrastination, the thief of time? Or devoted pupils might nickname their monitor Experience, a dear teacher?

[8899]

"You slay me," said the condemned man to the hangman.

"That's noose to me," replied the hangman.

[8900]

There was a Turk, who was so polite he even salaamed the door.

[8901]

"I see in the papers that a guy ate six dozen pancakes."

"Oh, how waffle!"

[8902]

A rural editor, wishing to be severe upon a competitive publication, wrote: "The subscriber of the —— in this place tried a few days ago, to carry home some lard in a copy of that paper; but on reaching home, found that the concentrated lie had changed it to soap."

[8903]

"There's surely one great advantage in these short skirts."

"Yes?"

"They make it so much easier for the dear girls to get up stares."

[8904]

One of the best puns ever made by the Phœbe Cary was this: Why was Robinson Crusoe's man Friday like a rooster? Because he scratched for himself and Crusoe.

[8905]

A young woman once married a man by the name of Dust against the wish of her parents. After a short time they began to quarrel, and she attempted to return to her father's house, but he refused to receive her, saying, "Dust thou art, and unto Dust thou shall return."

[8906]

"I'm a pauper."

"Congratulations. Boy or girl?"

[8907]

King Arthur – "How much'll you take for this armor, Lance?"

Sir Lancelot – "Three cents an ounce, that's first class mail."

[8908]

"It's raining cats and dogs outside."

"Yeh, I know, I just stepped into a poodle."

[8909]

The Girl – "We'd love to go sleighing."

The Hero – "My, you're bloodthirsty!"

[8910]

The doctor's work fills six feet of ground, but the dentist's work fills an acher.

[8911]

"At what age were you married?" asked she inquisitively. But the other lady was equal to the emergency, and quietly responded, "At the parson age."

[8912]

Are the Michiganders any relation to the Portuguese, and if so, how much, and what?

[8913]

"What did you do last summer?"

"I worked in Des Moines."

"Coal or iron?"

[8914]

There he was, swimming in the cold water, battling heroically against the waves. "Just a half-mile more," he thought, "and I'll make the shore." His strokes were getting weaker. He could hardly lift an arm any more. The beach was only a few yards away. His last efforts were too much. He began to grow dizzy. Then his head began to swim and carried him to the shore.

[8915]

While witnessing a game of baseball, a boy was struck on the head, the bawl coming out of his mouth.

[8916]

"Has he ever tried to tell you about his forbears?"

"Gracious! Don't tell me he is an animal trainer!"

[8917]

Wife (looking over travel folders) – "Why not take an ocean cruise, dear?"

Husband – "Hm-m, beggars can't be cruisers."

[8918]

A man who detected a piece of bark in the sausage visited a butcher's shop to know what had come of the rest of the dog. The butcher was so affected that he could give him only a part of the tale.

[8919]

It is a queer woman who asks no questions, but the woman who does is the querist.

[8920]

A lively girl had a bashful lover named Locke. Getting out of patience with him, in her anger, she said that Shakespeare had not written half as many things as he ought about Shy Locke.

[8921]

"Fred," said a young man to his friend, after listening to his wonderful story, "do you know why you are like a harp struck by lightning?"

"No," says Fred; "I give it up."

"Because a harp struck by lightning is a blasted lyre."

[8922]

The grasshopper is something of a singer, but the potato bug is the most indefatigable musician. He plays on the tuber.

[8923]

Enthusiastic youth to friend, "That star over there is Mars."

Unsympathetic friend, "Is it? Then the other one, I suppose, is pa's."

[8924]

"Is she Hungary?" Jimmy asked.

"Alaska," said Johnny.

"Yes, Siam," she replied.

"All right. I'll Fiji," Jimmy offered.

"Oh, don't Russia," Johnny admonished.

"What if she Wales?" Jimmy demanded.

"Give her a Canada Chile," Johnny suggested.

"I'd rather have Turkey," she said. "Except that I can't have any Greece."

When the waiter brought the check, Johnny asked Jimmy, "I say, look and see how much has Egypt you."

[8925]

"Are you psychic?"

"Yes, seer."

[8926]

The tune the old cow died on must have been written in beef-flat.

[8927]

"Call me pet names—something typical of sweet sounds," he murmured.

She said he was a gay lute.

[8928]

She (belligerently) – "Why weren't you at the station with the car to meet me as usual?"

He (meekly)—"My dear, you ought to get into this habit of meetless days."

[8929]

Said he–"Matilda, you are my dearest duck."

Said she – "Augustus, you are trying to stuff me."

She was too sage for him.

[8930]

It is foolish for a man to try to make game of a boarding-house chicken by looking at it, under the impression that a steady gaze of the human eye will make any animal quail.

[8931]

A young lady while out walking heard, for the first time, of her mother's intention to marry again, and she was obliged to sit right down and cry about it. She could not go a step-farther.

[8932]

Suburban Resident – "It's grand to wake up in the morning and hear the leaves whispering outside your window."

City Man—"It's all right to hear the leaves whisper, but I never could stand hearing the grass moan."

[8933]

Pleasant-faced people are generally the most welcome, but the auctioneer is always pleased to see a man whose countenance is for bidding.

[8934]
Better to have loved a short girl than never to have loved a tall.

[8935]
Knott and Shott fought a duel. The result was that they changed conditions, Knott was shot and Shott was not. It was better to be Shott than Knott.

[8936]
A wag says: "A printer who set in type $10,000 to read $1,000, might have prevented his mistake by a little fourth-aught."

[8937]
A song heard by a hive: "Bee it ever so humble, there's no place like comb."

[8938]
Old Hornblower was talking very big about being entirely a self-educated man.
Sneerwell, who heard him, said, "Ah, I understand! You were at the school where every man was his own toot-er."

[8939]
Mr. Somerset is a bachelor. He could not persuade any of his female acquaintances to turn a Somerset.

[8940]
What is slosh?—It's snow matter.

[8941]
"We know a girl," says some one, "so industrious, that when she has nothing else to do she sits and knits her brows."

[8942]
At a dinner, this question was put to the guests: "Which is the stronger, lie or truth?"
After a moment's consideration, a wit spoke up: "Truth, for you may re-ly on it."

[8943]
Sign seen at a County Fair: Sensational! Daring! Thrilling! Breath-Taking! A Human Being Diving from a Height of Fifty Feet into a Pail of Water!
Cynic – "What's so daring about that? It's only a drop in the bucket."

[8944]
"Will you tell me," asked an old gentleman of a lady, "what Mrs. Jones maiden name was?"
"Why her maiden aim was to get married, of course," exclaimed the lady.

[8945]
As spring approaches, boys begin to feel gallant, and girls buoyant.

"YOU TELL 'EM" PUNS

[8946]
You tell 'em Aviator,
    You're a high flyer.

[8947]
You tell 'em, Bald Head,
    You're smooth.

[8948]
You tell 'em, Banana,
    You've been skinned.

[8949]
You tell 'em, Bank,
    You're safe.

[8950]
You tell 'em, Bean,
    He's stringing you.

[8951]
You tell 'em, Brake,
    You've got the drag.

[8952]
You tell 'em, Butcher,
    You've got lots of tongue.

[8953]
You tell 'em, Cabbage,
You've got the head.

[8954]
You tell 'em, Calendar,
You've got lots of dates.

[8955]
You tell 'em, Cashier,
I'm a poor teller.

[8956]
You tell 'em, Cat,
That's what you're fur.

[8957]
You tell 'em, Cemetery,
You are so grave.

[8958]
You tell 'em, Chloroform,
You can put them to sleep.

[8959]
You tell 'em, Church Bell,
I told you.

[8960]
You tell 'em, Cigarette,
You're lit up.

[8961]
You tell 'em, Clock,
You've got the time.

[8962]
You tell 'em, Crystal,
You're on the watch.

[8963]
You tell 'em, Cucumber,
I've been pickled.

[8964]
You tell 'em, Custard Pie,
You have a crust.

[8965]
You tell 'em, Dentist,
You've got the pull.

[8966]
You tell 'em, Dictionary,
You're full of information.

[8967]
You tell 'em, Doctor,
You've got the patience.

[8968]
You tell 'em, Dough,
You're well bred.

[8969]
You tell 'em, Electricity,
You can shock 'em.

[8970]
You tell 'em, Envelope,
You're well posted.

[8971]
You tell 'em, Gambler,
You've got winning ways.

[8972]
You tell 'em, Goldfish,
You've been around the globe.

[8973]
You tell 'em, Hard Boiled Egg,
You're hard to beat.

[8974]
You tell 'em, Horse,
You carry a tale.

[8975]
You tell 'em, Hunter,
I'm game.

[8976]
You tell 'em, June,
And don't July.

[8977]
You tell 'em, Manicurist,
I've been trimmed.

[8978]
You tell 'em, Moon,
You're out all night.

[8979]
You tell 'em, Mountain,
I'm only a bluff.

[8980]
You tell 'em, Operator,
You've got their number.

[8981]
You tell 'em, Owl,
    You're wise.

[8982]
You tell 'em, Piano,
    You're upright and square.

[8983]
You tell 'em, Playing Cards,
    You know the joker.

[8984]
You tell 'em, Printer,
    I'm not your type.

[8985]
You tell 'em, Railroad,
    It's not along my line.

[8986]
You tell 'em, September Morn,
    No one has anything on you.

[8987]
You tell 'em, Shoemaker,
    You know awl.

[8988]
You tell 'em, Simon,
    I'll Legree.

[8989]
You tell 'em, Skyscraper,
    You have more than one story.

[8990]
You tell 'em, Submarine,
    I can't seaplane.

[8991]
You tell 'em, Teacher,
    You've got the class.

CONUNDRUMS

[8992]
Which is the easier to spell—fiddle-de-dee or fiddle-dedum?
    The former, because it is spelled with more e's (ease).

[8993]
Why is a man who has nothing to boast of but his ancestors, like a potato?
    The best thing belonging to him is under ground.

[8994]
When rain falls, does it ever get up again?
    In dew time.

[8995]
Why is a student of theology like a merchant?
    He studies the prophets (profits).

[8996]
For what reasons does a duck go under the water?
    For divers reasons.
    For what reasons does she come out?
    For sun-dry reasons.

[8997]
Why is a pair of skates similar to an apple?
    Both are responsible for the fall of man.

[8998]
Why are all duels very short affairs?
    Because it only requires two seconds to arrange them.

[8999]
On which side of a pitcher is the handle?
    On the outside.

[9000]
What is that which we all can eat, and often drink, though it sometimes is a woman and often a man?
    We eat toast and drink a toast.

[9001]
Why is a person with his eyes closed like an inefficient schoolmaster?
    He keeps his *pupils* in darkness.

[9002]

Why is a vote in Congress like a cold?

Because sometimes the ayes (eyes) have it, and sometimes the noes (nose).

[9003]

What is the way to make a coat last?

Make the vest and trousers first.

[9004]

Why is it easier to be a clergyman than a physician?

Because it is easier to preach than to practise.

[9005]

A train operated by a Norwegian engineer starts to New York from Albany just as a train with a drunken engineer leaves New York for Albany. There's only one track, no switches or sidings, yet the trains do not collide. Why?

Because Norse is Norse and Souse is Souse and never the twain shall meet.

[9006]

Why are architects like famous movie stars?

Both draw good houses.

[9007]

Why had Eve no fear of the measles?

Because she'd Adam (had 'em).

[9008]

If the freezing point is 32 degrees, what is the squeezing point?

Two in the shade.

[9009]

Why does a chicken cross the road?

To get on the other side.

[9010]

When is coffee like the soil?

When it is ground.

[9011]

How were Adam and Eve kept from gambling?

Their pair o' dice was taken away from them.

[9012]

What connection is *b-e-e-r* to *b-i-e-r*?

Beer fills many a bottle and the bottle fills many a *bier*.

[9013]

Why is life the riddle of all riddles?

Because we must all give it up.

[9014]

Why is an old bachelor always right?

Because he is never miss-taken.

[9015]

Why doesn't it make any difference if a tramp wears a short coat?

Because it will be long enough before he gets another.

[9016]

If your uncle's sister is not your aunt, what relationship does she bear to you?

She is my mother.

[9017]

What is that which you cannot hold ten minutes, although it is as light as a feather?

Your breath.

[9018]

Why is a proud woman like a music book?

She is full of airs.

[9019]

What things increase the more you contract them?

Debts.

[9020]

What is that which makes everybody sick but those who swallow it?

Flattery.

[9021]
Why should no man starve on the deserts of Arabia?
Because of the *sand which* is there.

[9022]
What proves sailors to be very careless?
They are in a "mess" every day at sea.

[9023]
Why should a man named Ben marry a girl called Anne?
Because he would be Benny-fitted, and she Annie-mated.

[9024]
If a father gave one of his sons 19 cents and the other 6 cents, what time would it be?
Quarter to two.

[9025]
What is the difference between man and butter?
The older the man is the weaker he gets, but the older the butter is the stronger it is.

[9026]
What time is that which spelled backward and forward is the same?
Noon.

[9027]
Which has most legs, a horse or no horse?
A horse has four legs, no horse has five.

[9028]
Who are the most obedient and obliging class of men in the world?
Auctioneers. Why? Because they attend to everyone's bidding.

[9029]
What is the difference between a watchmaker and a jailer?
The one sells watches and the other watches cells.

[9030]
Why was Job always cold in bed?
Because he had such miserable comforters.

[9031]
How do bees dispose of their honey?
They cell it.

[9032]
What part of a fish weighs the most?
The scales.

[9033]
Of all things possessed of a long tongue and an empty head, why is a bell the most discreet?
Because it never speaks till it is tolled.

[9034]
Why are old bachelors bad grammarians?
Because when asked to conjugate they invariably decline.

[9035]
Why are pianos noble characters?
Because they are grand, upright, and square.

[9036]
What is the longest word in the English language?
Smiles, because there is a mile between the first and last letter.

[9037]
When is a spanking like a hat?
When it is felt.

[9038]
What is the difference between a secretary using a typewriter and sixteen ounces of sugar?
One pounds away and the other weighs a pound.

[9039]
How can a man be assured of keeping a woman's love?
By not returning it.

[9040]

Why are rainbows similar to policemen?

Both appear after the storm is over.

[9041]

Why was Adam a famous runner?

Because in the human race he was first.

[9042]

Why aren't short people as lazy as tall people?

Because they aren't as long in bed.

[9043]

When Adam and Eve left the Garden of Eden what did they do?

They raised Cain.

[9044]

What musical instrument should we never believe?

A lyre.

[9045]

Why is a candy sucker like a horse?

Because the more you lick it the faster it goes.

[9046]

When does a farmer act with great rudeness to his grain?

When he pulls its ears and threshes it.

[9047]

Why is a large coat like a banana skin?

Both are easy to slip on.

[9048]

What is the difference between a featherbed and a poor man?

One is soft down and the other is hard-up.

[9049]

When a lady faints, what figure does she need?

You must bring her 2.

[9050]

Why is a looking-glass unlike a giddy girl?

The one reflects without speaking, the other speaks without reflecting.

[9051]

Why should not a person lose his temper?

Because no one else wants it.

[9052]

Why is a dog biting his own tail like a good manager?

Because he makes both ends meet.

[9053]

Why is an interesting book like a toper's nose?

It is *read* (red) to the very end.

[9054]

Why is a watch dog larger by night than by day?

Because at night he is let out, and in the day he is taken in.

[9055]

What two "beaux" is it impossible for a girl to get rid of?

Her elbows.

[9056]

Why do Gypsies never become insane?

Because they lead no-mad lives.

[9057]

What is the difference between a pretty girl and a soldier?

The girl powders her face and the soldier faces powder.

[9058]

When is a doctor most annoyed?

When he is out of patients.

[9059]

Why are the stars the best astronomers?

Because they have studded (studied) the heavens since the Creation.

[9060]
Why is using tobacco like a ragged riding dress?
It is a bad habit.

[9061]
"Why do they call a Pullman porter doctor?"
"Because he has attended so many berths."

[9062]
What word do women favor most?
The last one.

[9063]
What three acts comprise the chief business of a woman's life?
Attract, contract, detract.

[9064]
What is the difference between a flea and an elephant?
An elephant can have fleas, but a flea can't have elephants.

[9065]
Why is a dentist similar to a farmer?
Both yank our roots.

[9066]
How long did Cain hate his brother?
As long as he was Abel.

[9067]
Why do hens always lay in the daytime?
Because at night they become roosters.

[9068]
Why does a stork stand on one foot?
If he'd lift the other foot, he'd fall down.

[9069]
What is the difference between a husband and a jilted suitor?
One kisses the missus and the other misses the kisses.

[9070]
Why is a nail fast in the wall like an old man?
Because it is in firm.

[9071]
Why is a railroad track a particularly sentimental object?
Because it is bound by close ties.

[9072]
Which is the best land for young children?
Lapland.

[9073]
Why is a kiss like scandal?
Because it goes from mouth to mouth.

[9074]
What is the proper place for proof-readers?
The house of correction.

[9075]
What is the difference between a cloud and a beaten child?
One pours with rain and the other roars with pain.

[9076]
Why are books your best friends?
Because, when they bore you, you can shut them up without giving offence.

[9077]
"What is the difference between a bird with one wing and a bird with two wings?"
"I give it up."
"A difference of a pinion."

[9078]
Why is Tom Bigger's four-year-old boy larger than his father?
Because he is a little Bigger.

[9079]
Why is a person approaching a lamp like a person about to get off a horse?
He is going to a light (alight).

[9080]

Why does a woman who gives her husband "a piece of her mind" usually take as much as she gives?

Because she generally manages to take away the peace of his.

[9081]

Why is a newly-born baby like a gale of wind?

Because it begins with a squall.

[9082]

What is the most popular cure among politicians?

Sinecure.

[9083]

Why is a hen sitting on a fence like a cent?

Because she has a head on one side and a tail on the other.

[9084]

When is a blow from a lady welcome?

When she strikes you agreeably.

[9085]

Why is a room full of married people empty?

Because there is not a single person in it.

[9086]

Where was Adam going when he was in his thirty-ninth year?

Into his fortieth.

[9087]

What is the difference between a blind man and a sailor in prison?

One can't see to go and the other can't go to sea.

[9088]

Why is a poor singer like a counterfeiter?

Because he is an utterer of bad notes.

[9089]

When does a chair dislike you?

When it can't bear you.

[9090]

Why are sardines such silly fish?

It's because they crawl into an opening in a can, lock themselves up and then leave the key outside.

[9091]

Why should a man never tell his secrets in a corn-field?

Because it has so many ears.

[9092]

What keeps the moon from falling?

It must be the beams.

[9093]

Of what trade are all the Presidents of the United States?

Cabinetmakers.

[9094]

Why didn't they play cards on Noah's Ark?

Because Noah sat on the deck.

[9095]

Why is the figure nine like a peacock?

It is *nothing* without its tail.

[9096]

What is the pain we make light of?

A window pane.

[9097]

What is the difference between a Christian and a cannibal?

The one enjoys himself, and the other enjoys other people.

[9098]

What is the difference between a sewing machine and a kiss?

One sews nice seams and the other seems nice.

[9099]

What is the difference between a man who has been to Niagara Falls and a man who has not?

One has seen a mist and the other missed a scene.

[9100]
What word of only three syllables combines in it twenty-six letters?
Alphabet.

[9101]
When is the only time that a ship is not on water?
When it is on fire.

[9102]
To what man do men always take their hats off?
The barber.

[9103]
Why is the horse the most humane of all animals?
Because he gladly gives the bit out of his mouth, and listens to every woe.

[9104]
What is the difference between a bucket of milk in a rain storm and a conversation between two confidence men?
One is a thinning scheme and the other is a skinning theme.

[9105]
Why is a man without whiskers impudent?
He is bare faced.

[9106]
Why does a minister always say "dearly beloved brethren" and not refer to the sisters?
Because the brethren embrace the sisters.

[9107]
Why a young lady dependent upon the letter Y?
Because without it she would be a "young lad."

[9108]
Why should soldiers be rather tired on the first of April.
Because they have just had a march of thirty-one days.

[9109]
What is the difference between the Prince of Wales, a bald-headed man, an orphan, and a gorilla?
The prince is an heir apparent, the bald man has no hair apparent, the orphan has nary parent, and the gorilla has a hairy parent.

[9110]
Why is an egg like a colt?
Because it can't be used until it is broken.

[9111]
Where are happiness and contentment always to be found?
In the dictionary.

[9112]
What is the difference between an auction and sea sickness?
One is the sale of effects, the other the effects of a sail.

[9113]
Why is a lovely young lady like a hinge?
She is something to adore.

[9114]
Which animal travels with the most, and which with the least, luggage?
The elephant the most, because he never travels without his trunk. The fox and the cock the least, because they have only one brush and comb between them.

[9115]
Why is a crow a brave bird?
He never shows a white feather.

[9116]
What must one do to have beautiful hands?
Nothing.

[9117]
Why is a cat's tail like the end of the world?
'Cause it's so fur to the end.

[9118]

What is the difference between a timid child and a shipwrecked sailor?

One clings to his ma and the other to his spar.

[9119]

Why can you never expect a fisherman to be generous?

Because his business makes him sell fish.

[9120]

What is that which Adam never saw, never possessed, yet left two to each of his children?

Parents.

[9121]

Why is a short negro like a white man?

Because he is not a tall black.

[9122]

Why is it impossible for a pretty girl to be candid?

Because she can't be plain.

[9123]

Why are potatoes and corn like certain sinners of old?

Because, having eyes, they see not, and having ears, they hear not.

[9124]

How many peas are there in a pint?

One (p).

[9125]

Why are our laws like the ocean?

Because the most trouble is caused by the breakers.

[9126]

Why is a gun like a jury?

It goes off when discharged.

[9127]

Why is a lawyer like a restless sleeper?

He lies first on one side and then on the other.

[9128]

To what age do most girls wish to attain?

Marri-age.

[9129]

Why are country girls' cheeks like a good cotton dress?

Because they are warranted to wash and keep their color.

[9130]

Which is the strongest day of the seven?

Sunday, because the others are week days.

[9131]

What is that which has neither flesh nor bone, and has four fingers and a thumb?

A glove.

[9132]

What's the difference between a hill and a pill?

A hill is hard to get up and a pill is hard to get down.

[9133]

Why is a horse a curious feeder?

Because he eats best when he has not a bit in his mouth.

[9134]

Why may carpenters believe there is no such thing as stone?

They never saw it.

[9135]

Why is the school yard always larger at recess?

Because there are more feet in it.

[9136]

Why is an ill-fed dog like a philosopher?

He is a thin cur (thinker).

[9137]

What would a pig do who wished to build himself a habitation?

Tie a knot in his tail and call it a pig's tie.

[9138]
What's the difference between an old maid and a girl fond of red-haired Irishmen?
One loves a cat and parrots, the other a Pat and carrots.

[9139]
What house pet is it that is so generally admired, sought after, and valued yet more abused, trampled upon, kicked about, looked down upon and whipped more than any other?
A carpet.

[9140]
Why is a pig the most extraordinary animal in creation?
Because you first kill him and then cure him.

[9141]
What is the difference between a bottle of medicine and a troublesome boy?
One is to be well shaken before taken, the other to be taken and then shaken.

[9142]
Why cannot a deaf man be legally convicted?
Because it is unlawful to condemn a man without a hearing.

[9143]
What animal would be likely to devour a near relation?
The ant-eater.

[9144]
Why is an old chair that has a new bottom put to it like a paid bill?
Because it has been re-seated (receipted).

[9145]
What is the best way to keep fish from smelling?
Cut off their noses.

[9146]
Why is a baker like a beggar?
He kneads bread.

[9147]
Why are birds melancholy in the morning?
Because their little bills are all over dew.

[9148]
At what season did Eve eat the apple?
Early in the fall.

[9149]
Why are some women like facts?
They are stubborn things.

[9150]
What is the difference between an old dime and a new penny?
Nine cents.

[9151]
There were three men in a boat with four cigarettes but no matches. What did they do?
They threw out one cigarette, and made the boat a cigarette lighter.

[9152]
How can it be proved that a horse has six legs.
He has fore legs in front and two behind.

[9153]
Why is a man who never bets as bad as a gambler?
Because he is no better.

[9154]
Why is coal the most contradictory article known to commerce?
Because, when purchased it goes to the cellar.

[9155]
What is the difference between the admission to a dime museum and the admission to Sing Sing?
One is ten cents and the other is sentence.

[9156]
In what does a lawyer resemble a woodcock?
In the length of his bill.

[9157]
What is the difference between a cat and a comma?
A cat has its claws at the end of its paws, a comma its pause at the end of a clause.

[9158]
What most frequently becomes a woman?
A little girl.

[9159]
Which is the most popular money of the United States?
Matrimony.

[9160]
Why is a dog's tail a great novelty?
Because no one ever saw it before.

[9161]
Why is a clock the most modest piece of furniture?
Because it covers its face with its hands, and runs down its own works.

[9162]
If you were going through the woods, which had you rather have, a lion eat you or a bear?
The lion eat a bear.

[9163]
What is that which occurs once in a minute, twice in a moment, and not once in a thousand years?
The letter M.

[9164]
Why was Noah the greatest financier on record?
Because he kept his Company (Limited) afloat when the rest of the world was in liquidation.

[9165]
Why does a donkey like thistles better than corn?
Because he is an ass.

[9166]
What shape is a kiss?
Elliptical. (A-lip-tickle.)

[9167]
Which is the largest room in the world?
The room for improvement.

[9168]
When are stockings like dead men?
When they are men-ded; when their soles are departed; when they are in holes; when they are past heeling; when they are no longer on their last legs.

[9169]
How can you make a tall man short?
Borrow ten dollars of him.

[9170]
What is that a poor man has and a rich man wants?
Nothing.

[9171]
At what time of day was Adam created?
A little before Eve.

[9172]
Why is a great bore like a tree?
Because both appear best when leaving.

[9173]
Why do white sheep eat more than black ones?
There are more of them.

[9174]
What is the color of the winds and waves in a severe storm?
The winds blew (blue), the waves rose.

[9175]
If Old Nick were to lose his tail, where should he go to supply the deficiency?
To a bar-room, for there bad spirits are retailed.

[9176]
What is that which is full of holes and yet holds water?
A sponge.

[9177]
When are true words sweet words?
When they are candid (candied).

[9178]
Why should B come before C?
Because any one must be before he can see.

[9179]
Why should the number two hundred eighty-eight never be mentioned in company?
Because it is two gross.

[9180]
What roof covers the most noisy tenant?
The roof of the mouth.

[9181]
Why was Pharaoh's daughter like a broker?
Because she got a little prophet from the rushes on the banks.

[9182]
How many sides are there to a tree?
Two, the inside and outside.

[9183]
When does a man sneeze three times?
When he can't help it.

[9184]
Why are kisses like the creation?
They are made of nothing and are very good.

[9185]
Why is a soprano like a confectioner?
Because she deals in high screams (ice creams).

[9186]
What is that animal which has the head of a cat, and the tail of a cat, and the ways of a cat, and yet which isn't a cat?
A kitten.

[9187]
Why is the Fourth of July similar to an oyster stew?
Because it's no good without the crackers.

[9188]
Why is a field of grass like a person older than yourself?
Because it's past your age (pasturage).

[9189]
What is the difference between the North and South Pole?
All the difference in the world.

[9190]
Why is dough like the sun?
When it rises it is light.

[9191]
What time is it when the clock strikes thirteen?
Time the clock was repaired.

[9192]
Why is a buckwheat cake like a caterpillar?
Because it makes the butterfly.

[9193]
Why is a drawn tooth like a thing that is forgotten?
Because it is out of the head.

[9194]
What does an artist like to draw best?
His salary.

[9195]

Why do women seek husbands named William?

So they can have a Will of their own.

[9196]

Why is a tin can tied to a dog's tail like death?

Because it's something bound to a cur.

[9197]

Why is a fly taller than most men?

Because he stands over six feet without shoes or stockings.

[9198]

Why is the letter S likely to prove dangerous in argument?

Because it turns words into s-words.

PART XI

HUMOR IN VERSE

COMIC POEMS

[9199]
THE PATTER OF
THE SHINGLE

When the angry passion gathering
in my mother's face I see,
And she leads me to the bedroom,
gently lays me on her knee,
Then I know that I will catch it,
and my flesh in fancy itches
As I listen for the patter of the
shingle on my breeches.

Every tingle of the shingle has an
echo and a sting
And a thousand burning fancies
into active being spring,
And a thousand bees and hornets
'neath my coattail seem to swarm,
As I listen to the patter of the shingle, oh, so warm.

In a splutter comes my father—who
I supposed had gone—
To survey the situation and tell her
to lay it on,
To see her bending o'er me as I
listen to the strain
Played by her and by the shingle in
a wild and weird refrain.

In a sudden intermission, which appears my only chance,

I say, "Strike gently, Mother, or
you'll split my Sunday pants!"
She stops a moment, draws her
breath, and the shingle holds
aloft,
And says, "I had not thought of
that, my son, just take them off."
Holy Moses and the angels! cast
your pitying glances down,
And thou, O family doctor, put a
good soft poultice on.
And may I with fools and dunces
everlastingly commingle,
If I ever say another word when my
mother wields the shingle!
—*Anonymous.*

[9200]
WILLIE THE WEEPER

Listen to the story of Willie the
Weeper.
Willie the Weeper was a chimney
sweeper.
He had the hop habit and he had
it bad;
Listen and I'll tell you of a dream
he had.

He went to a hop joint the other
night,
Where he knew the lights were always shining bright,

881

And, calling for a chink to bring
    him some hop,
He started in smoking like he
    wasn't gonna stop.

After he'd smoked about a dozen
    pills,
He said, "This ought to cure all
    my aches and ills."
And turning on his side he fell
    asleep,
And dreamt he was a sailor on the
    ocean deep.

He played draw poker as they left
    the land,
And won a million dollars on the
    very first hand.
He played and he played till the
    crew went broke.
Then he turned around and took
    another smoke.

He came to the island of Siam,
Rubbed his eyes and said, "I won-
    der where I am,"
Played craps with the king and won
    a million more,
But had to leave the island cause
    the king got sore.

He went to Monte Carlo where he
    played roulette,
And couldn't lose a penny but won
    every bet—
Played and he played till the bank
    went broke.
Then he turned around and took
    another smoke.

Then he thought he'd better be
    sailing for home,
And chartered a ship and sailed
    away alone.
Ship hit a rock. He hit the floor.
Money was gone and the dream
    was o'er.

Now this is the story of Willie the
    Weeper;
Willie the Weeper was a chimney
    sweeper.
Someday a pill too many he'll take,
And dreaming he's dead, he'll for-
    get to awake.
           —*Anonymous.*

[9201]
MY LOVE
(A Patchwork Poem)
I only knew she came and went
               Powell.
    Like troutlets in a pool; *Hood.*
She was a phantom of delight,
               Wordsworth.
    And I was like a fool. *Eastman.*

One kiss, dear maid, I said, and
    sighed,   *Coleridge.*
    Out of those lips unshorn:
               Longfellow.
She shook her ringlets round her
    head,   *Stoddard.*
    And laughed in merry scorn.
               Tennyson.

Ring out, wild bells, to the wild sky,
               Tennyson.
    You heard them, O my heart;
               Alice Cary.
'Tis twelve at night by the castle
    clock,   *Coleridge.*
    Beloved, we must part.
               Alice Cary.

[9202]
THE BLIND MEN
AND THE ELEPHANT
It was six men of Indostan
    To learning much inclined,
Who went to see the elephant
    (Though all of them were
    blind),
That each by observation
    Might satisfy his mind.

The First approached the elephant,
  And, happening to fall
Against his broad and sturdy side,
  At once began to bawl:
"God bless me! but the elephant
  Is nothing but a wall!"

The Second, feeling of the tusk,
  Cried: "Ho! what have we here
So very round and smooth and
  sharp?
  To me 'tis mighty clear
This wonder of an elephant
  Is very like a spear!"

The Third approached the animal,
  And, happening to take
The squirming trunk within his
  hands,
  Thus boldly up and spake:
"I see," quoth he, "the elephant
  Is very like a snake!"

The Fourth reached out his eager
  hand,
  And felt about the knee:
"What most this wondrous beast is
  like
  Is mighty plain," quoth he;
" 'Tis clear enough the elephant
  Is very like a tree."

The Fifth, who chanced to touch
  the ear,
  Said: "E'en the blindest man
Can tell what this resembles most;
  Deny the fact who can,
This marvel of an elephant
  Is very like a fan!"

The Sixth no sooner had begun
  About the beast to grope,
Than, seizing on the swinging tail
  That fell within his scope,
"I see," quoth he, "the elephant
  Is very like a rope!"

And so these men of Indostan
  Disputed loud and long,
Each in his own opinion
  Exceeding stiff and strong,
Though each was partly in the
  right,
  And all were in the wrong!

So, oft in theologic wars
  The disputants, I ween,
Rail on in utter ignorance
  Of what each other mean,
And prate about an elephant
  Not one of them has seen!
      —John Godfrey Saxe.

[9203]
THE HEN

A famous hen's my story's theme,
  Which ne'er was known to tire
Of laying eggs, but then she'd
  scream
    So loud o'er every egg, 'twould
      seem
The house must be on fire.
    A turkey-cock, who ruled the
      walk,
A wiser bird and older,
    Could bear 't no more, so off
      did stalk
Right to the hen, and told her:
    "Madam, that scream, I appre-
      hend,
Adds nothing to the matter;
    It surely helps the egg no whit;
Then lay your egg, and done with
  it!
    I pray you, madam, as a friend,
Cease that superfluous clatter!
    You know not how't goes
      through my head."
"Humph! very likely!" madam said,
    Then, proudly putting forth a
      leg,—
"Uneducated barnyard fowl!
    You know, no more than any
      owl,

The noble privilege and praise
   Of authorship in modern days—
I'll tell you why I do it:
   First, you perceive, I lay the egg,
And then—review it."—*Claudius.*

[9204]
BACHELOR AND BIRD

I met a solemn Toucan
   Within a city Zoo.
"Pray, sober bird, if *you* can,
   Enlighten me a few!
One cannot be contented
   In solitary state;
A man would go demented
   Who lived without a mate.
Who can achieve this, *who* can
   See skies forever blue?
I know one can't; but, Toucan,
   Can two, Toucan, can two?

"I want a tiny cottage
   With roses twining o'er,
And beans and leeks for pottage
   Beside the kitchen door;
And children's childish prattle,
   Their gurgling gulps of glee,
As they wage mimic battle
   Against paternal me.
Few can achieve this, *few* can
   Gain such a happy crew;
I know one can't; but, Toucan,
   Can two, Toucan, can two?

"And yet, I fear, contented
   I could not linger yet,
If some dear she consented;
   For if she were brunette,
I'd long for blonde or Titian;
   If one of these I'd gain,
I'd wilt, from a condition
   Of brunette on the brain.
One dear, I fear, it's true, can
   Not thrill me through and
      through;
What worries me, O Toucan,
   Can two, Toucan, can two?"
                     —*Clement Wood.*

[9205]
A RHYME OF THE CITIES

Said little Johnnie to the Owl:
   "I've heard you're wonderous
      wise,
And so I'd like to question you;
   Now, please, don't tell me lies.

"The first thing, then, I'd have you
      tell,
   My empty mind to fill,
Pray, was it that explosive beef
   That made Chicago, Ill.?

"I've heard it said, yet do not
      know—
   In fact, it may be bosh—
Then, tell me, is it lots of dirt
   That makes Seattle, Wash.?

"When certain things will not go
      straight,
   To right them we should try;
So, maybe, you can say what 'tis
   Sets Providence, R.I.?

"Another thing I wish I could
   Inform my waiting class,
Is just how many priests it takes
   To say the Boston, Mass.

"This is the time of running debts,
   As you must surely know;
This secret, then, impart to me:
   How much does Cleveland, O.?

"In ages, too, you must be learned,
   More so than many men;
So, tell me in a whisper, please,
   When was Miss Nashville,
      Tenn.?

"It takes great heat the gold to melt,
   And iron takes much more;
Then is it true, that way out West,
   The rain melts Portland, Ore?

"Some voices are so strong and full,
    And some so still and small,
That I have wondered oftentimes
    How loud could Denver, Col.?"

The Owl scratched his feathered
    pate:
    "I'm sorry, little man;
Ask some one else. I cannot tell.
    Perhaps Topeka, Kan."
                —*Anonymous.*

[9206]
ANY ONE WILL DO
A maiden once, of certain age,
To catch a husband did engage;
But, having passed the prime of life
In striving to become a wife
Without success, she thought it
    time
To mend the follies of her prime.

Departing from the usual course
Of paint and such like for resource,
With all her might this ancient
    maid
Beneath an oak tree knelt and
    pray;
Unconscious that a grave old owl
Was perched above—the mousing
    fowl!

"Oh, give! a husband give!" she
    cried,
"While yet I may become a bride;
Soon will my day of grace be o'er,
And then, like many maids before,
I'll die without an early love,
And none to meet me there above!

"Oh, 'tis a fate too hard to bear!
Then answer this my humble
    prayer,
And oh, a husband give to me!"
Just then the owl from out the tree,
In deep bass tones cried, "Who—
    who—who!"

"Who, Lord? And dost Thou ask
    me who?
Why, any one, good Lord, will do."
                —*Anonymous.*

[9207]
THE PUN
"A pun is the lowest form of wit,"
It does not tax the brain a bit;
One merely takes a word that's
    plain
And picks one out that sounds the
    same.
Perhaps some letter may be changed
Or others slightly disarranged,
This to the meaning gives a twist,
Which much delights the humorist;
A sample now may help to show
The way a good pun ought to go:
"It isn't the cough that carries you
    off,
It's the coffin they carry you off in."
                —*Anonymous.*

[9208]
A BOSTON TOAST
[Written by Dr. Bossidy for an
alumni dinner of Holy Cross
College.]
And this is good old Boston,
    The home of the bean and the
        cod,
Where the Lowells talk to the Ca-
    bots,
    And the Cabots talk only to
        God.
                —*John C. Bossidy.*

[9209]
CASH PREFERRED
The knot was tied; the pair were
    wed,
And then the smiling bridegroom
    said
Unto the preacher, "Shall I pay
To you the usual fee today,
Or would you have me wait a year
And give you then a hundred clear,

If I should find the married state
As happy as I estimate?"
The preacher lost no time in
 thought,
To his reply no study brought,
There were no wrinkles on his
 brow;
He said "I'll take $3.00 now."
                    —*Anonymous.*

[9210]
HELL IN TEXAS

The devil, we're told, in hell was
 chained,
And a thousand years he there remained,
And he never complained, nor did
 he groan,
But determined to start a hell of
 his own
Where he could torment the souls
 of men
Without being chained to a prison
 pen.

So he asked the Lord if He had on
 hand
Anything left when He made the
 land.
The Lord said, "Yes, I had plenty
 on hand,
But I left it down on the Rio
 Grande.
The fact is, old boy, the stuff is so
 poor,
I don't think you could use it in
 hell any more."

But the devil went down to look
 at the truck,
And said if it came as a gift, he was
 stuck;
For after examining it careful and
 well
He concluded the place was too dry
 for hell.
So in order to get it off His hands
God promised the devil to water
 the lands.

For he had some water, or rather
 some dregs,
A regular cathartic that smelt like
 bad eggs.
Hence the deal was closed and the
 deed was given,
And the Lord went back to His
 place in Heaven.
And the devil said, "I have all that
 is needed
To make a good hell," and thus he
 succeeded.

He began to put thorns on all the
 trees,
And he mixed the sand with mil-
 lions of fleas,
He scattered tarantulas along all
 the roads,
Put thorns on the cacti and horns
 on the toads;
He lengthened the horns of the
 Texas steers
And put an addition on jack rab-
 bits' ears.

He put little devils in the broncho
 steed
And poisoned the feet of the centipede.
The rattlesnake bites you, the scor-
 pion stings,
The mosquito delights you by
 buzzing his wings.
The sand burrs prevail, so do the
 ants,
And those that sit down need half
 soles on their pants.

The devil then said that throughout the land
He'd manage to keep up the devil's
 own brand,
And all would be mavericks unless
 they bore
The marks of scratches and bites
 by the score.

The heat in the summer is a hundred and ten,
Too hot for the devil and too hot for men.

The wild boar roams through the the black chaparral,
It's a hell of a place he has for a hell;
The red pepper grows by the bank of the brook,
The Mexicans use it in all that they cook.
Just dine with a Greaser and then you will shout,
"I've a hell on the inside as well as without."

—*Anonymous.*

[9211]
I HAD BUT FIFTY CENTS

I took my girl to a fancy ball;
It was a social hop;
We waited till the folks got out,
And the music it did stop.
Then to a restaurant we went,
The best one on the street;
She said she wasn't hungry,
But this is what she eat:
A dozen raw, a plate of slaw,
A chicken and a roast,
Some applesass, and sparagrass,
And soft-shell crabs on toast,
A big box stew, and crackers too;
Her appetite was immense!
When she called for pie,
I thought I'd die,
For I had but fifty cents.

She said she wasn't hungry
And didn't care to eat,
But I've got money in my clothes
To bet she can't be beat;
She took it in so cozy,
She had an awful tank;
She said she wasn't thirsty,
But this is what she drank:

A whisky skin, a glass of gin,
Which made me shake with fear,
A ginger pop, with rum on top,
A schooner then of beer,
A glass of ale, a gin cocktail;
She should have had more sense;
When she called for more,
I fell on the floor,
For I had but fifty cents.

Of course I wasn't hungry,
And didn't care to eat,
Expecting every moment
To be kicked into the street;
She said she'd fetch her family round,
And some night we'd have fun;
When I gave the man the fifty cents,
This is what he done:
He tore my clothes,
He smashed my nose,
He hit me on the jaw,
He gave me a prize
Of a pair of black eyes
And with me swept the floor.
He took me where my pants hung loose,
And threw me over the fence;
Take my advice, don't try it twice
If you've got but fifty cents!

—*Anonymous.*

[9212]
A SODDET OD SPRIG

I sig the joys of soft ad suddy sprig;
(I sig them through the dose).
A welcob warb
We tedder to her spilig, verdal charb;
(She deeds the warpth), the robid's od the wig;
The blossobs their cobbigled scet exhale
Upod the air, ad everythig here blows—
The pik adebbodee, the pikker dose.

The Easter boddet id dorth-easter
gale.
    The frogs are id the pod (ad
    id the throat),
The yug sprig labkid id the bea-
dow sprigs,—
    Ah, warb, the all-wool labkid!)
    Od the breeze
    A byriad gerbs of idfluedza
    float;
Ad by the stove, id witter fladdel
thigs,
    I ped this soddet ere by figgers
    freeze!
                    —*Anonymous.*

[9213]
LOGICAL ENGLISH

I said, "This horse, sir, will you
shoe?"
    And soon the horse was shod.
I said, "This deed, sir, will you
do?"
    And soon the deed was dod!

I said, "This stick, sir, will you
break?"
    At once the stick he broke.
I said, "This coat, sir, will you
make?"
    And soon the coat he moke!
                    —*Anonymous.*

[9214]
VARIABLE VERBS

A boy who swims may say he
swum,
But milk is skimmed and seldom
skum,
And nails you trim, they are not
trum.
When words you speak, these
words are spoken,
But a nose is tweaked and can't be
twoken,
And what you seek is seldom
soken.
If we forget, then we've forgotten,

But things we wet are never wot-
ten,
And houses let cannot be lotten.
The goods one sells are always sold,
But fears dispelled are not dispold,
And what you smell is never smold.
When young, a top you oft saw
spun,
But did you see a grin e'er grun,
Or a potato nearly skun?
                    —*Anonymous.*

[9215]
SIMILES

As wet as a fish—as dry as a bone;
As live as a bird—as dead as a
stone;
As plump as a partridge—as poor
as a rat;
As strong as a horse—as weak as a
cat;
As hard as a flint—as soft as a mole;
As white as a lily—as black as a
coal;
As plain as a pike-staff—as rough
as a bear;
As light as a drum—as free as the
air;
As heavy as lead—as light as a
feather;
As steady as time—uncertain as
weather;
As hot as an oven—as cold as a
frog;
As gay as a lark—as sick as a dog;
As slow as the tortoise—as swift as
the wind;
As true as the Gospel—as false as
mankind;
As thin as a herring—as fat as a
pig;
As proud as a peacock — as blithe
as a grig;
As savage as tigers—as mild as a
dove;
As stiff as poker—as limp as a
glove;

As blind as a bat—as deaf as a
post;
As cool as a cucumber—as warm as
toast;
As flat as a flounder—as round as a
ball;
As blunt as a hammer—as sharp as
an awl;
As red as a ferret—as safe as the
stocks;
As bold as a thief—as sly as a fox;
As straight as an arrow—as crooked
as a bow;
As yellow as saffron—as black as a
sloe;
As brittle as glass—as tough as
gristle;
As neat as my nail—as clean as a
whistle;
As good as a feast—as bad as a
witch;
As light as is day—as dark as is
pitch;
As brisk as a bee — as dull as an ass;
As full as a tick—as solid as brass.
—*Anonymous.*

[9216]
THE WEATHER
I remember, I remember,
  Ere my childhood flitted by,
It was cold then in December,
  And was warmer in July.
In the winter there were freez-
ings—
  In the summer there were
  thaws;
But the weather isn't now at all
  Like what it used to was!
—*Anonymous.*

[9217]
THE JAPANESE LOVERS
Fanny Foo-Foo was a Japanese girl,
  A child of the great Tycoon;
She wore her head bald, and her
clothes were made
  Half petticoat, half pantaloon;

And her face was the color of lemon
peel,
  And the shape of a tablespoon.

A handsome young chap was
Johnny Hi-Hi;
  He wore paper-muslin clothes;
His glossy black hair on the top of
his head
  In the shape of a shoe brush
  rose;
And his eyes slanted downward, as
if some chap
  Had savagely pulled his nose.

Fanny Foo-Foo loved Johnny Hi-
Hi,
  And when in the usual style
He popped, she blushed such a
deep orange tinge
  You'd have thought she had
  too much bile,
If it hadn't been for her slant-eyed
glance
  And her charming wide-
  mouthed smile.

And oft in the bliss of their new-
born love
  Did these little Pagans stray
All around in spots, enoying them-
selves
  In a strictly Japanese way,
She howling a song on a one-
stringed lute,
  On which she thought she
  could play.

Often he'd climb to a high ladder's
top,
  And quietly there repose,
As he stood on his head and fanned
himself,
  While she balanced him on her
  nose,
Or else she would get in a pickle
tub,
  And be kicked around on his
  toes.

The course of true love, even in
Japan,
    Often runs extremely rough,
And the fierce Tycoon, when he
heard of this,
    Used Japanese oaths so tough
That his courtiers' hair would have
stood on end'
    If they'd only had enough.

So the Tycoon buckled on both his
swords,
    In his pistol placed a wad,
And went out to hunt for the truant pair,
    With his nerves well braced by
a tod.
He found them enjoying their
guileless selves
    On the top of a lightning rod.

Sternly he ordered the gentle Foo-
Foo
    To "Come down out of that
there!"
And he told Hi-Hi to go to a
place—
    I won't say precisely where.
Then he dragged off his child,
whose spasms evinced
    Unusual wild despair.

But the great Tycoon was badly
fooled,
    Despite his paternal pains,
For John, with a toothpick, let all
the blood
    Out of his jugular veins;
While with a back somersault over
the floor
    Foo-Foo battered out her brains.

They buried them both in the Tycoon's lot
    Right under a dogwood tree,
Where they could list to the nightingale

And the buzz of the bumblebee,
And where the mosquito's sorrowful chant
    Maddens the restless flea.

And often at night when the Tycoon's wife
    Slumbered as sound as a post,
His almond-shaped eyeballs glared
on a sight
    That scared him to death, al-
most:
'Twas a bald-headed spectre flitting
about
    With a paper-muslin ghost.
            —*Anonymous.*

[9218]
NOTHING SUITED HIM
He sat at the dinner table there,
    With discontented frown.
The potatoes and steak were underdone
    And the bread was baked too
brown.
The pie was sour, the pudding too
sweet,
    And the mincemeat much too
fat,
The soup was greasy, too, and salt—
    'Twas hardly fit for a cat.

"I wish you could taste the bread
and pies
    I have seen my mother make;
They were something like, and
'twould do you good
    Just to look at a slice of her
cake."
Said the smiling wife: "I'll improve with age.
    Just now, I'm a beginner.
But your mother called to see me
today
    And I got *her* to cook the din-
ner."
            —*Anonymous.*

[9219]
DARWIN

There was an ape in the days that
  were earlier;
Centuries passed, and his hair grew
  curlier;
Centuries more gave a thumb to
  his wrist,
Then he was a Man and a Positivist.
                —*Mortimer Collins.*

[9220]
KAFOOZALUM

In ancient days there lived a Turk,
A horrid beast within the East,
Who did the prophet's holy work
As Baba of Jerusalem.
He had a daughter sweet and smirk,
Complexion fair and dark blue hair,
With nothing 'bout her like a Turk
Except her name Kafoozalum.

  Chorus:

Oh, Kafoozalum, Kafoozalum, Kafoozalum.
Oh, Kafoozalum, the daughter of
  the Baba.

A youth resided near to she,
His name was Sam, a perfect lamb;
He was of ancient pedigree
And came from old Methusalem.
He drove a trade—and prospered
  well—
In skins of cats and ancient hats,
And, ringing at the Baba's bell,
He saw and loved Kafoozalum.

If Sam had been a Mussulman,
He might have sold the Baba old,
And, with a verse of Al Koran
Have managed to bamboozle him.
But oh dear, no, he tried to scheme,
Passed one night late the Baba's
  gate
And came up to the Turk's harem
To carry off Kafoozalum.

The Baba as about to smoke;
His slaves rushed in with horrid
  din;
"Mashallah, dogs your house have
  broke,
Come down, my lord, and toozle
  'em!"
The Baba wreathed his face in
  smiles,
Came down the stair and witnessed
  there
A gentleman in three old tiles
A-kissing of Kafoozalum.

The pious Baba said no more
Than twenty prayers, then went
  upstairs,
And took his bowstring from the
  door
And came back to Kafoozalum.
The maiden and the youth he took,
And choked them both, a little
  loath,
Together threw them in the brook
Of Kedron in Jerusalem.

And so the ancient legend runs,
When night comes on in Lebanon,
And when the Eastern moonlight
  throws
Its shadows o'er Jerusalem,
Betwixt the wailing of the cats,
A sound there falls from ruined
  walls,
A ghost is seen in three old hats
A-kissing of Kafoozalum.
                —*Anonymous.*

[9221]
THE BRIDEGROOM

Will you take this woman
  For your lawful wedded wife?
Will you honor and obey her
  Throughout your natural life?
Will you let her have her way
  And fulfill her each desire;
Start the breakfast every morning,
  Chop the wood and build the
  fire?

Will you let her drive your car?
  Will you give her all your money,
Go to parties every night?
  Will you always call her honey?
Will you support her mother,
  Father and her brothers,
Uncles, aunts, cousins,
  And a half dozen others?
He gazed queerly at the parson,
  Then he gave his head a tilt,
And hopelessly he raised his eyes,
  And weakly said, "I wilt."
            —*Sundial*

[9222]
BIRTH-STONES
For laundresses, the soapstone;
For architects, the cornerstone;
For cooks, the puddingstone;
For soldiers, the bloodstone;
For politicians, the blarneystone;
For borrowers, the touchstone;
For policemen, the pavingstone;
For stock brokers, the curbstone;
For shoemakers, the cobblestone;
For burglars, the keystone;
For tourists, the Yellowstone;
For beauties, the peachstone;
For editors, the grindstone;
For motorists, the milestone;
For pedestrians, the tombstone.
            —*Anonymous.*

[9223]
TRUTH IN PARENTHESES
I really take it very kind—
This visit, Mrs. Skinner—
I have not seen you such an age—
(The wretch has come to dinner!)
Your daughters, too—what loves of
    girls!
What heads for painters' easels!
Come here, and kiss the infant,
    dears—
(And give it, perhaps, the measles!)

Your charming boys I see are home
From Rev. Mr. Russell's—

'Twas very kind to bring them
    both—
(What boots for my new Brussels!)
What! little Clara left at home?
Well, now, I call that shabby!
I should have loved to kiss her so—
(A flabby, dabby babby!)

And Mr. S., I hope he's well?
But, though he lives so handy,
He never once drops in to sup –
(The better for our brandy!)
Come, take a seat—I long to hear
About Mathilda's marriage;
You've come, of course, to spend
    the day—
(Thank heaven! I hear the car-
    riage!)

What! must you go?—next time I
    hope
You'll give me longer measure,
Nay, I shall see you down the
    stairs—
(With most uncommon pleasure!)
Good-by! Good-by! Remember, all,
Next time you'll take your din-
    ners—
(Now, David—mind, I'm not at
    home,
In future to the Skinners.)
            —*Thomas Hood*

[9224]
METHUSALEH
Methuselah ate what he found on
    his plate,
And never, as people do now,
Did he note the amount of the
    calory count;
He ate it because it was chow.
He wasn't disturbed as at dinner
    he sat,
Devouring a roast or a pie,
To think it was lacking in granu-
    lar fat
Or a couple of vitamins shy.

He cheerfully chewed each species
  of food,
Unmindful of troubles or fears
Lest his health might be hurt
By some fancy dessert;
And he lived over nine hundred
  years.
                    —*Anonymous.*

[9225]
AN EVENING IDYLL
The evening star its vesper lamp
  Above the west had lit,
The dusky curtains of the night
  Were falling over it.
He seized her waist and clasped
  her hand
  And told his tale of love;
He called her every tender name,
  "My   darling,"   "duck,"   and
  "dove."

A tremor shook her fairy form,
  Her eyes began to blink
Her pulse rose to a hundred, and
  She cried: "I think—I think—"

He sighed: "You think you love
  me?" for
  His soul was on the rack;
"Oh, no!" she yelled; "I think a bug
  Is crawling down my back!"
                    —*Anonymous.*

[9226]
THERE WAS A LITTLE GIRL
There was a little girl,
And she had a little curl
  Right in the middle of her fore-
  head.
When she was good
She was very, very good,
  And when she was bad she was
  horrid.

One day she went upstairs,
When her parents, unawares,
  In the kitchen were occupied
  with meals

And she stood upon her head
In her little trundle-bed,
  And then began hooraying with
  her heels.

Her mother heard the noise,
And she thought it was the boys
  A-playing at a combat in the
  attic;
But when she climbed the stair,
And found Jemima there,
  She took and she did spank her
  most emphatic.
                —*H. W. Longfellow.*

[9227]
OWED TO KNEES
Knees to the right of us
Knees to the left of us,
Knees crossed in front of us,
  How they display 'em!

On they go trippingly,
Daintily, skippingly,
Winds biting nippingly
  Fail to dismay 'em.

Round knees and flatter ones,
Thin knees and fatter ones,—
Mostly the latter ones—
  Everywhere listed;

Straight and contorted ones
Queerly distorted ones,
Mates and ill-sorted ones,
  Comically twisted.

Bare knees and boney ones,
Real knees and phoney ones,
Silk-covered toney ones,
  Plump and beguiling,

Pale knees and painted ones,
Nice knees and tainted ones,
Queerly unacquainted ones,
  Onward go filing.

Gay knees and sad ones,
Good knees and bad ones,
Warm, woolen-clad ones
  Taunting the breezes;

Straight knees and bandy ones,
Bum knees and dandy ones,
Awkward and handy ones,
  On go the kneezes.

Knees to the right of us,
Knees to the left of us,
Knees crossed in front of us,
  Often we've seed 'em;

Knees ever passing by,
Styles mounting to the sky,
Seem to exemplify
  Woman's New Freedom.
—*Northwestern Purple Parrot.*

[9228]
THE RETORT

Old Birch, who taught the village
    school,
  Wedded a maid of homespun
    habit;
He was as stubborn as a mule,
  And she as playful as a rabbit.
Poor Kate had scarce become a
    wife
  Before her husband sought to
    make her
The pink of country polished life,
  And prim and formal as a
    Quaker.

One day the tutor went abroad,
  And simple Katie sadly missed
    him,
When he returned, behind her
    lord
  She shyly stole, and fondly kissed
    him.
The husband's anger rose, and red
  And white his face alternate
    grew:

"Less freedom, ma'am!" Kate
    sighed and said,
  "O, dear! I *didn't know 'twas
    you!*"
    —*George Perkins Morris.*

[9229]
WHERE ARE YOU GOING, MY
PRETTY MAID?

"Where are you going, my pretty
    maid?"
"I am going a-milking, sir," she
    said.
"May I go with you, my pretty
    maid?"
"You're kindly welcome, sir," she
    said.
"What is your father, my pretty
    maid?"
"My father's a farmer, sir," she
    said.
"What is your fortune, my pretty
    maid?"
"My face is my fortune, sir," she
    said.
"Then I can't marry you, my pretty
    maid?"
"Nobody asked you, sir," she said.
    —*Mother Goose.*

[9230]
ANOTHER TREE

'Twas Harry who the silence broke:
  "Miss Kate, why are you like a
    tree?"
"Because, because I'm board," she
    spoke.
  "Oh, no, because you're woo'd,
    you see!"

"Why are *you* like a tree?" she
    said.
  "I have a—heart?" he queried
    low.
Her answer made the young man
    red.
  "Because you're sappy, don't you
    know."

"Once more," she asked, "why are
you now
  A tree?" He couldn't quite perceive.
"Trees leave sometimes, and make
a bow,
  And you may also bow,—and
leave."
           —*Anonymous.*

[9231]
LOVE'S ACROBATICS
He went out one lovely night
  To call upon a miss,
And when he reached her resi-
dence

                      this.
              like
          stairs
       up
    ran
He
Her papa met him at the door,
  He didn't see the miss.
He'll not go there again though
—for
He
    ʇuǝʍ
      down
        sɹıɐʇs
          like
            ·sıɥʇ
             —*Anonymous.*

[9232]
LOVE
He struggled to kiss her. She strug-
gled the same
To prevent him so bold and un-
daunted.
But, as smitten by lightning, he
heard her exclaim,
"Avaunt, sir!" and off he avaunted.

But when he returned with a wild
fiendish laugh,
Showing clearly that he was af-
fronted,

And threatened by main force to
carry her off,
She cried "Don't!" and the poor
fellow donted.

When he meekly approached, and
sat down at her feet,
Praying loudly, as before he had
ranted,
That she would forgive him, and
try to be sweet,
And said "Can't you!" the dear girl
recanted.

Then softly he whispered, "How
could you do so?
I certainly thought I was jilted;
But come thou with me, to the parson we'll go;
Say, wilt thou, my dear?" and she
wilted.
           —*Anonymous.*

[9233]
THE EVIDENCE
Maude Muller, on a summer night,
Turned down the only parlor light.
The judge, beside her, whispered
things
Of wedding bells and diamond
rings.
He spoke his love in burning
phrase,
And acted foolish forty ways.
When he had gone Maude gave a
laugh
And then turned off the dicto-
graph.
           —*Anonymous.*

[9234]
THE ULTIMATE JOY
I have felt the thrill of passion in
the poet's mystic book
And I've lingered in delight to
catch the rhythm of the brook;

I've felt the ecstasy that comes
  when prima donnas reach
For upper C and hold it in a long,
  melodious screech.
And yet the charm of all these
  blissful memories fades away
As I think upon the fortune that
  befell the other day,
As I bring to recollection, with a
  joyous, wistful sigh,
That I woke and felt the need of
  extra covers in July.

Oh, eerie hour of drowsiness—'twas
  like a fairy spell,
That respite from the terrors we
  have known, alas, so well,
The malevolent mosquito, with a
  limp and idle bill,
Hung supinely from the ceiling,
  all exhausted by his chill.
And the early morning sunbeam
  lost his customary leer
And brought a gracious greeting
  and a prophecy of cheer;
A generous affability reached up
  from earth to sky,
When I woke and felt the need of
  extra covers in July.

In every life there comes a time of
  happiness supreme,
When joy becomes reality and not
  a glittering dream.
'Tis less appreciated, but it's worth
  a great deal more
Than tides which taken at their
  flood lead on to fortune's shore.
How vain is Art's illusion, and
  how potent Nature's sway
When once in kindly mood she
  deigns to waft our woes away!
And the memory will cheer me,
  though all other passions fly,
Of how I woke and needed extra
  covers in July.
                      —*Anonymous.*

[9235]
THE BRITISH TAR

A British tar is a soaring soul,
  As free as a mountain bird,
His energetic fist should be ready
  to resist
  A dictatorial word.
His nose should pant and his lip
  should curl,
His cheeks should flame and his
  brow should furl,
His bosom should heave and his
  heart should glow,
And his fist be every ready for a
  knock-down blow.

His eyes should flash with an in-
  born fire,
  His brow with scorn be rung;
He never should bow down to a
  domineering frown,
  Or the tang of a tyrant tongue.
His foot should stamp and his
  throat should growl,
His hair should twirl and his face
  should scowl;
His eyes should flash and his breast
  protrude,
And this should be his customary
  attitude!
                      —*W. S. Gilbert.*

[9236]
THE CONTEMPLATIVE
SENTRY

When all night long a chap remains
  On sentry-go, to chase monotony,
He exercises of his brains,
  That is, assuming that he's got
  any.
Though never nurtured in the lap
  Of luxury, yet I admonish you,
I am an intellectual chap,
  And think of things that would
  astonish you.
  I often think it's comical
  How Nature always does
  contrive

That every boy and every gal
That's born into the world
alive
Is either a little Liberal,
Or else a little Conservative!
Fal lal la!

When in that house M. P.'s divide,
If they've a brain and cerebellum
too,
They've got to leave that brain
outside,
And vote just as their leaders
tell 'em to.
But then the prospect of a lot
Of statesmen, all in close prox-
imity,
A-thinking for themselves, is what
No man can face with equanim-
ity.
Then let's rejoice with loud
Fal lal
That Nature wisely does
contrive
That every boy and gal
That's born into the world
alive
Is either a little Liberal,
Or else a little Conservative!
Fal lal la!
—*W. S. Gilbert.*

[9237]
THE POLICEMAN'S LOT
When a felon's not engaged in his
employment,
Or maturing his felonious little
plans,
His capacity for innocent enjoy-
ment
Is just as great as any honest
man's.
Our feelings we with difficulty
smother
When constabulary duty's to be
done;

Ah, take one consideration with
another,
A policeman's lot is not a happy
one!

When the enterprising burglar isn't
burgling,
When the cut-throat isn't occupied in crime,
He loves to hear the little brook
a-gurgling,
And listen to the merry village
chime.
When the coster's finished jumping on his mother,
He loves to lie a-basking in the
sun:
Ah, take one consideration with
another,
A policeman's lot is not a happy
one!
—*W. S. Gilbert.*

[9238]
WOMAN'S WILL
Men, dying, make their wills, but
wives
Escape a work so sad;
Why should they make what all
their lives
The gentle dames have had?
—*John Godfrey Saxe.*

[9239]
ODE TO TOBACCO
Thou who, when fears attack,
Bidst them avaunt, and Black
Care, at the horseman's back
Perching, unseatest;
Sweet when the morn is gray;
Sweet, when they've cleared away
Lunch; and at close of day
Possibly sweetest:

I have a liking old
For thee, though manifold
Stories, I know, are told,
Not to thy credit;

How one (or two at most)
Drops make a cat a ghost—
Useless, except to roast—
    Doctors have said it;

How they who use fusees
All grow by slow degrees
Brainless as chimpanzees,
    Meagre as lizards;
Go mad, and beat their wives;
Plunge (after shocking lives)
Razors and carving knives
    Into their gizzards.

Confound such knavish tricks!
Yet know I five or six
Smokers who freely mix
    Still with their neighbors;
Jones—(who, I'm glad to say,
Asked leave of Mrs. J——)
Daily absorbs a clay
    After his labours.

Cats may have had their goose
Cooked by tobacco-juice;
Still why deny its use
    Thoughtfully taken?
We're not as tabbies are:
Smith, take a fresh cigar!
Jones, the tobacco-jar!
    Here's to thee, Bacon!
        —*Charles Stuart Calverly.*

[9240]
SNEEZING

What a moment, what a doubt!
All my nose is inside out,—
All my thrilling, tickling caustic,
Pyramid rhinocerostic,
    Wants to sneeze and cannot do
        it!
How it yearns me, thrills me, stings
    me,
How with rapturous torment wrings
    me!
    Now says, "Sneeze, you fool,—
        get through it."

Shee—shee—oh! 'tis most del-
    ishi—
Ishi—ishi—most del-ishi!
(Hang it, I shall sneeze till spring!)
Snuff is a delicious thing.
        —*Leigh Hunt.*

[9241]
CASEY AT THE BAT

It looked extremely rocky for the
    Boston nine that day;
The score stood two to four, with
    but an inning left to play.
So, when Cooney died at second,
    and Burrows did the same,
A pallor wreathed the features of
    the patrons of the game.

A straggling few got up to go,
    leaving there the rest,
With that hope which springs
    eternal within the human
    breast.
For they thought: "If only Casey
    could get a whack at that,"
They'd put even money now, with
    Casey at the bat.

But Flynn preceded Casey, and
    likewise so did Blake,
And the former was a pudd'n, and
    the latter was a fake.
So on that stricken multitude a
    deathlike silence sat;
For there seemed but little chance
    of Casey's getting to the bat.

But Flynn let drive a "single," to
    the wonderment of all.
And the much-despised Blakey
    "tore the cover off the ball."
And when the dust had lifted, and
    they saw what had occurred,
There was Blakey safe at second,
    and Flynn a-huggin' third.

Then from the gladdened multi-
    tude went up a joyous yell—

It rumbled in the mountaintops, it
  rattled in the dell;
It struck upon the hillside and re-
  bounded on the flat;
For Casey, mighty Casey, was advancing to the bat.

There was ease in Casey's manner
  as he stepped into his place,
There was pride in Casey's bearing
  and a smile on Casey's face;
And when responding to the cheers
  he lightly doffed his hat,
No stranger in the crowd could
  doubt 'twas Casey at the bat.

Ten thousand eyes were on him as
  he rubbed his hands with dirt,
Five thousand tongues applauded
  when he wiped them on his
  shirt;
Then when the writhing pitcher
  ground the ball into his hip,
Defiance glanced in Casey's eye, a
  sneer curled Casey's lip.

And now the leather-covered sphere
  came hurtling through the air,
And Casey stood a-watching it in
  haughty grandeur there.
Close by the sturdy batsman the
  ball unheeded sped;
"That ain't my style," said Casey.
  "Strike one," the umpire said.

From the benches, black with people, there went up a muffled
  roar,
Like the beating of the storm waves
  on the stern and distant shore.
"Kill him! kill the umpire!" shouted
  someone on the stand;
And it's likely they'd have killed
  him had not Casey raised his
  hand.

With a smile of Christian charity
  great Casey's visage shone;

He stilled the rising tumult, he
  made the game go on;
He signaled to the pitcher, and
  once more the spheroid flew;
But Casey still ignored it, and the
  umpire said, "Strike two."

"Fraud!" cried the maddened thousands, and the echo answered
  "Fraud!"
But one scornful look from Casey
  and the audience was awed;
They saw his face grow stern and
  cold, they saw his muscles
  strain,
And they knew that Casey wouldn't
  let the ball go by again.

The sneer is gone from Casey's
  lips, his teeth are clenched in
  hate,
He pounds with cruel vengeance
  his bat upon the plate;
And now the pitcher holds the ball,
  and now he lets it go,
And now the air is shattered by the
  force of Casey's blow.

Oh, somewhere in this favored
  land the sun is shining bright,
The band is playing somewhere,
  and somewhere hearts are
  light;
And somewhere men are laughing,
  and somewhere children shout,
But there is no joy in Boston:
  Mighty Casey has struck out.
  —*Ernest Lawrence Thayer.*

[9242]
SUSAN SIMPSON
Sudden swallows swiftly skimming,
  Sunset's slowly spreading shade,
Silvery songsters sweetly singing,
  Summer's soothing serenade.

Susan Simpson strolled sedately,
  Stifling sobs, suppressing sighs.

Seeing Stephen Slocum, stately
  She stopped, showing some sur-
    prise.
"Say," said Stephen, "sweetest
    sigher;
  Say, shall Stephen spouseless
    stay?"
Susan, seeming somewhat shyer,
  Showed submissiveness straight-
    way.

Summer's season slowly stretches,
  Susan Simpson Slocum she—
So she signed some simple
    sketches—
  Soul sought soul successfully.

Six Septembers Susan swelters;
  Six sharp seasons snow supplies;
Susan's satin sofa shelters
  Six small Slocums side by side.
          —*Anonymous.*

[9243]
A LIFE'S LOVE
I loved him in my dawning years—
  Far years, divinely dim;
My blithest smiles, my saddest
    tears,
  Were evermore for him.
My dreaming when the day began,
  The latest thought I had,
Was still some little loving plan
  To make my darling glad.

They deemed he lacked the con-
    quering wiles,
  That other children wear;
To me his face, in frowns or smiles,
  Was never aught but fair.
They said that self was all his goal,
  He knew no thought beyond;
To me, I know, no living soul
  Was half so true and fond.

In love's eclipse, in friendship's
    dearth,
  In grief and feud and bale,

My heart has learnt the sacred
    worth
  Of one that cannot fail;
And come what must, and come
    what may,
  Nor power, nor praise, nor pelf,
Shall lure my faith from thee to
    stray.
My sweet, my own—*Myself.*
          —*Anonymous.*

[9244]
ABDULLAH BULBUL AMIR,
OR,
IVAN PETROFSKY SKOVAR
The sons of the Prophet are valiant
    and bold,
  And quite unaccustomed to fear;
And the bravest of all was a man,
    so I'm told,
  Called Abdullah Bulbul Amir.

When they wanted a man to en-
    courage the van,
  Or harass the foe from the rear,
Storm fort or redoubt, they were
    sure to call out
  For Abdullah Bulbul Amir.

There are heroes in plenty, and
    well known to fame,
  In the legions that fight for the
    Czar;
But none of such fame as the man
    by the name
  Of Ivan Petrofsky Skovar.

He could imitate Irving, tell for-
    tunes by cards,
  And play on the Spanish guitar;
In fact, quite the cream of the
    Muscovite guards,
  Was Ivan Petrofsky Skovar.

One day this bold Muscovite shoul-
    dered his gun,
  Put on his most cynical sneer,

And was walking downtown when
    he happened to run
Into Abdullah Bulbul Amir.

"Young man," said Bulbul, "is ex-
    istence so dull
That you're anxious to end your
    career?
Then, infidel, know you have trod
    on the toe
Of Abdullah Bulbul Amir.

"So take your last look at the sea,
    sky and brook,
Make your latest report on the
    war;
For I mean to imply that you are
    going to die,
O Ivan Petrofsky Skovar."

So this fierce man he took his
    trusty chibouk,
And murmuring, "Allah Aklar!"
With murder intent he most sav-
    agely went
For Ivan Petrofsky Skovar.

The Sultan rose up, the disturbance
    to quell,
Likewise, give the victor a cheer.
He arrived just in time to bid
    hasty farewell
To Abdullah Bulbul Amir.

A loud-sounding splash from the
    Danube was heard
Resounding o'er meadows afar;
It came from the sack fitting close
    to the back
Of Ivan Petrofsky Skovar.

There lieth a stone where the
    Danube doth roll,
And on it in characters queer
Are "Stranger, when passing by,
    pray for the soul
Of Abdullah Bulbul Amir."

A Muscovite maiden her vigil doth
    keep
By the light of the pale northern
    star,
And the name she repeats every
    night in her sleep
Is Ivan Petrofsky Skovar.
                        —*Anonymous.*

[9245]
THE COSMIC EGG

Upon a rock, yet uncreate,
Amid a chaos inchoate,
An uncreated being sate;
Beneath him, rock,
Above him, cloud.
And the cloud was rock,
And the rock was cloud.
The rock then growing soft and
    warm,
The cloud began to take a form,
A form chaotic, vast and vague,
Which issued in the cosmic egg.
Then the Being uncreate
On the egg did incubate,
And thus became the incubator;
And of the egg did allegate,
And thus became the alligator;
And the incubator was potentate,
But the alligator was potentator.
                        —*Anonymous.*

[9246]
DRIED-APPLE PIES

I loathe, abhor, detest, despise,
Abominate dried-apple pies.
I like good bread, I like good meat,
Or anything that's fit to eat;
But of all poor grub beneath the
    skies,
The poorest is dried-apple pies.
Give me the toothache, or sore
    eyes,
But don't give me dried-apple pies.
The farmer takes his gnarliest fruit,
'Tis wormy, bitter, and hard, to
    boot;

He leaves the hulls to make us
　　cough,
And don't take half the peeling off.
Then on a dirty cord 'tis strung
And in a garret window hung,
And there it serves as roost for
　　flies,
Until it's made up into pies.
Tread on my corns, or tell me lies,
But don't pass me dried-apple pies.
　　　　　　　—*Anonymous.*

[9247]
ART

The hen remarked to the mooley
　　cow,
As she cackled her daily lay,
(That is, the hen cackled) "It's
　　funny how
I'm good for an egg a day.
I'm a fool to do it, for what do I
　　get?
My food and my lodging. My!
But the poodle gets that—he's the
　　household pet,
And he never has laid a single egg
　　yet—
Not even when eggs are high."

The mooley cow remarked to the
　　hen,
As she masticated her cud,
(That is, the cow did) "Well, what
　　then?
You quit, and your name is mud.
I'm good for eight gallons of milk
　　each day,
And I'm given my stable and grub;
But the parrot gets that much, any-
　　way,—
All she can gobble—and what does
　　she pay?
Not a dribble of milk, the dub!"

But the hired man remarked to the
　　pair,
"You get all that's coming to you.

The poodle does tricks, and the
　　parrot can swear,
Which is better than you can do.
You're necessary, but what's the use
Of bewailing your daily part?
You're bourgeois—working's your
　　only excuse;
You can't do nothing but just pro-
　　duce—
What them fellers does is ART!"
　　　　　　　—*Anonymous.*

[9248]
THE COUNTRY STORE

Far out beyond the city's lights,
　　away from din and roar,
The cricket chirps of summer
　　nights beneath the country
　　store;
The drygoods boxes ricked about
　　afford a welcome seat
For weary tillers of the ground,
　　who here on evenings meet.

A swinging sign of ancient make,
　　and one above the door,
Proclaim that William Henry
　　Blake is owner of the store;
Here everything from jam to
　　tweed, from silks to ginghams
　　bright,
Is spread before the folk who need
　　from early morn till night.

Tea, sugar, coffee (browned or
　　green), molasses, grindstones,
　　tar,
Suspenders, peanuts, navy beans,
　　and homemade vinegar,
Fine combs, wash ringers, rakes,
　　false hair, paints, rice, and
　　looking glasses,
Side saddles, hominy, crockery
　　ware, and seeds for garden
　　grasses.
Lawn mowers, candies, books to
　　read, corn planter, household
　　goods,

Tobacco, salt, and clover seed,
  horsewhips and knitted hoods,
Canned goods, shoe blacking, lime
  and nails, straw hats and carpet slippers,
Prunes, buttons, codfish, bridal
  veils, cranberries, clocks and
  clippers.

Umbrellas, candles, scythes and
  hats, caps, boots and shoes and
  bacon,
Thread, nutmegs, pins and Rough
  on Rats, for cash or produce
  taken;
Birdseed, face powder, matches,
  files, ink, onions and many
  more,
Are found in heaps and stacks and
  piles within the country store.
        —*Anonymous.*

[9249]
THE LAWYER'S INVOCATION
TO SPRING
Whereas, on certain boughs and
  sprays,
  Now divers birds are heard to
    sing,
And sundry flowers their heads
  upraise,
  Hail to the coming on of Spring!

The songs of those said birds
  arouse
  The memory of our youthful
    hours,
As green as those said sprays and
  boughs,
  As fresh and sweet as those said
    flowers.

The birds aforesaid—happy pairs!—
  Love, 'mid the aforesaid boughs,
    inshrines
In freehold nests; themselves, their
  heirs,
  Administrators, and assigns.

O busiest term of Cupid's court,
  Where tender plaintiffs actions
    bring,—
Season of frolic and of sport,
  Hail, as aforesaid, coming
    Spring!
    —*Henry P. Howard Brownell.*

[9250]
IMAGISTE LOVE LINES
I love my lady with a deep purple
  love;
She fascinates me like a fly
Struggling in a pot of glue.
Her eyes are grey, like twin ash
  cans,
Just emptied, about which still
  hovers
A dainty mist.
Her disposition is as bright as a
  ten-cent shine,
Yet her kisses are tender and
  goulashy.
I love my lady with a deep purple
  love.

        —*Anonymous.*

[9251]
TO A LOUSE
On Seeing One on a
Lady's Bonnet at Church
Ha! whare ye Gaun, ye crawlin'
  ferlie?
Your impudence protects you sairly:
I canna say but ye strunt rarely
  Owre gauze an' lace;
Though, faith! I fear ye dine but
  sparely
  On sic a place.

Ye ugly, creepin', blastit onner,
Detested, shunned by saunt an' sin-
  ner,
How dare you set your fit upon her,
  Sae fine a lady?
Gae somewhere else, and seek your
  dinner
  On some poor body.

Swith, in some beggar's haffet
    squattle;
  There ye may creep and sprawl
    and sprattle
Wi' ither kindred, jumping cattle,
  In shoals and nations:
Whare horn nor bane ne'er daur
    unsettle
  Your thick plantations.

Now haud you there, ye're out o'
    sight,
Below the fatt'rels, snug an' tight;
Na, faith ye yet! ye'll no be right
  Till ye've got on it,
The very tapmost tow'ring height
  O' Miss's bonnet.

My sooth; right bauld ye set your
    nose out,
As plump and gray as ony grozet;
O for some rank, mercurial rozet,
  Or fell, red smeddum!
I'd gie you sic a hearty dose o't,
  Wad dress your droddum!

I wad na been surprised to spy
You on an auld wife's flannen toy;
Or aiblins some bit duddie boy,
  On 's wyliecoat;
But Miss's fine Lunardi, fie!
  How daur ye do 't?

O Jenny, dinna toss your head,
An' set your beauties a' abread!
Ye little ken what cursèd speed
  The blastie 's makin'!
Thae winks and finger-ends, I
    dread,
  Are notice takin'!

O wad some power the giftie gie
    us
To see oursel's as ithers see us!
It wad frae monie a blunder free
    us,
  And foolish notion·

What airs in dress an' gait wad
    lea'e us,
  And ev'n devotion!
    —*Robert Burns.*

[9252]
THE DOLLAR AND THE CENT
A big silver dollar and a little
  brown cent,
Rolling along together went;
Rolling along the smooth sidewalk,
When the dollar remarked, for dol-
  lars can talk:
"You poor little cent, you cheap
  little mite,
I am bigger and twice as bright.
I'm worth more than you a hun-
  dredfold.
And written on me in letters bold
Is the motto drawn from the pious
  creed:
'In God We Trust,' which all may
  read."
"Yes, I know," said the cent,
"I'm a cheap little mite, and I know
I'm not big, nor good, nor bright,
And yet," said the cent,
With a meek little sigh,
"You don't go to church as often
  as I."
    —*Anonymous.*

[9253]
ELEGY ON THE DEATH OF
A MAD DOG
Good people all, of every sort,
  Give ear unto my song;
And if you find it wondrous short,
  It cannot hold you long.

In Islington there was a man
  Of whom the world might say,
That still a godly race he ran—
  Whene'er he went to pray.

A kind and gentle heart he had,
  To comfort friends and foes:
The naked every day he clad—
  When he put on his clothes.

And in that town a dog was found,
   As many dogs there be,
Both mongrel, puppy, whelp, and
     hound,
   And curs of low degree.

This dog and man at first were
    friends;
   But when a pique began,
The dog, to gain his private ends,
   Went mad, and bit the man.

Around from all neighboring streets
   The wondering neighbors ran,
And swore the dog had lost his wits,
   To bite so good a man!

The wound it seemed both sore
    and sad
   To every Christian eye:
And while they swore the dog was
    mad,
   They swore the man would die.

But soon a wonder came to light,
   That showed the rogues they
    lied:—
The man recovered of the bite,
   The dog it was that died!
          —*Oliver Goldsmith.*

[9254]
EPIGRAM

Sly Beelzebub took all occasions
To try Job's constancy and patience.
He took his honor, took his health,
He took his children, took his
    wealth,
His servants, oxen, horses, cows—
But cunning Satan did *not* take his
    spouse.
But Heaven, that brings out good
    from evil,
And loves to disappoint the devil,
Had predetermined to restore
Twofold all he had before;

His servants, horses, oxen, cows—
Short-sighted devil, *not* to take his
    spouse!
      —*Samuel Taylor Coleridge.*

COMIC SHORT VERSE

[9255]
Women's faults are many,
   Men have only two:
Everything they say,
   And everything they do.

[9256]
And from the depths of the sedan
   There came a muffled curse
He was trying to fold a road-map
   Same as it was at first.

[9257]
It's easy enough to be pleasant
When life flows round and round,
But the man worth while
Is the man who can smile
When his garter's comin' down.

[9258]
Twinkle, twinkle, movie star,
Out in Hollywood so far;
Don't you hold your head so high—
You'll bump your nose against the
    sky.

[9259]
I eat my peas with honey,
   I have done it all my life;
They do taste kind of funny,
   But it keeps them on the knife.

[9260]
Mary had a little lamb,
   A lobster and some prunes,
A glass of milk, a piece of pie,
   And then some macaroons;
It made the naughty waiters grin
   To see her order so;
And when they carried Mary out,
   Her face was white as snow.

[9261]

I never see my rector's eyes,
He hides their light divine;
For when he prays, he shuts his
    own,
And when he preaches, mine.

[9262]

When Venus vamped Adonis—tried
    to string him as her beau—
He grabbed his hat and left her flat;
    a-hunting he would go.
A wild, wild boar bore down on
    him, and with his dying breath
This clever youth cried, "Ve, for-
    sooth, I'm simply bored to
    death!"

[9263]

Swans sing before they die—'twere
    no bad thing
Should certain persons die before
    they sing.

—Dodd

[9264]

A young lady wishing to entangle
a young man in the meshes of
Cupid, sent him the following invitation:

O, will you come to tea with I,
    And help me eat a custard pie?

To which the young man, with cor-
responding sentiment and grammar, replied:

Another asked me to tea,
And I must go and sup with she.

[9265]

Mary had a little car
    She drove in manner deft,
But every time she signaled right,
    The little car turned left.

[9266]

Alas the poor Hindu,
He does the best he kindu;
He sticks to his caste from first to
    last,
And for trousers makes his skindu.

[9267]

She was leaning on the rail,
    And was looking deathly pale.
Was she looking for a whale?
    Not at all.
She was papa's only daughter,
Casting bread upon the water,
In a way she hadn't oughter,
    That was all.

[9268]

Ruth rode in my new cycle car
In the seat in back of me;
I took a bump at fifty-five,
And rode on Ruthlessly.

[9269]

Twinkle, twinkle, little star,
How I wonder what you are,
Polish, Austrian, Swede or Mex.,
Twinkling with imported sex.

[9270]

Say it with flowers,
    Say it with eats,
Say it with kisses,
    Say it with sweets,
Say it with jewelry,
    Say it with drink,
But always be careful
    Not to say it with ink.

[9271]

Sir, I admit your general rule,
That every poet is a fool;
But you yourself may serve to
    show it,
That every fool is not a poet.

.—Pope

[9272]

No word was spoken when they
    met,
    By either—sad or gay;
And yet one badly smitten was,
    'Twas mentioned the next day.
They met by chance this autumn
    eve,
    With neither glance nor bow;
They often come together so—
    A freight train and a cow.

[9273]
Whene'er a hen lays eggs, with each
She is impelled to make a speech.
The selfsame urge stirs human
  bones
Whenever men lay cornerstones.

[9274]
Lives of master crooks remind us
We may do a bit of time,
And, departing, leave behind us
Thumb-prints in the charts of crime.

[9275]
With Violet cuddling in his arms,
  He drove a car—poor silly.
Where he once held his Violet,
  He now holds a lily.

[9276]
How wisely Nature, ordering all
  below,
Forbade a beard on woman's *chin*
  to grow,
For how could she be shaved (what-
  e'er the skill)
Whose *tongue* would never let her
  chin be still?

[9277]
"My dear, what makes you always
  yawn?"
The wife exclaimed, her temper
  gone,
  "Is home so dull and dreary?"
"Not so, my love," he said, "not so;
But man and wife are *one,* you
  know;
  And when *alone* I'm weary!"

[9278]
Brown has a lovely baby girl,
  The stork left her with a flutter;
Brown named her "Oleomargarine,"
  For he hadn't any but her.

[9279]
You can always tell the English,
You can always tell the Dutch,
You can always tell the Yankees—
But you can't tell them *much!*

[9280]
The saddest words of tongue or pen
May be perhaps, "It might have
  been,"
The sweetest word we know, by
  heck,
Are only these "Enclosed find
  check!"

[9281]
A punning epigram on Dr. Isaac
Lettsom:
If anybody comes to I,
  I physics, bleeds and sweats 'em;
If after that they like to die,
  Why, what care I?—I. LETTSOM.

[9282]
"Harry, I cannot think," says Dick,
"What makes my ankles grow so
  thick."
"You do not recollect," says Harry,
"How great a calf they have to
  carry."

[9283]
When the scrappy plumber died,
  His wife, with humor grim,
Decided, knowing his habits well,
  To bury his tools with him.

[9284]
'Twixt the optimist and the pessi-
  mist
The difference is droll:
The optimist sees the doughnut
  While the pessimist sees the hole.

[9285]
  "Her countenance fell,"
  Writes an author gifted.
  No doubt she went
  And had it lifted.

[9286]
Into the coop the rooster rolls an
  ostrich egg;
  The hens he faces.
"Not to chide or deride, but only
  to show
What's being done in other places."

[9287]

'Tis done beneath the mistletoe,
'Tis done "beneath the rose,"
But the proper place to kiss, you
    know,
Is just beneath the nose.

[9288]

I used to love my garden,
    But now my love is dead,
For I found a bachelor button
    In black-eyed Susan's bed.

[9289]

There was a man in our town
    And he was wondrous wise;
He swore (it was his policy)
    He would not advertise.
But one day he did advertise,
    And thereby hangs a tail,
The "ad" was set in quite small
    type,
And headed "Sheriff's Sale."

[9290]

I often pause and wonder
    At fate's peculiar ways,
For nearly all our famous men
    Were born on holidays.

[9291]

Yesterday upon the stair
I saw a man who was not there.
I saw him there again today;
I wish that man would go away.

[9292]

O, MLE, what XTC
I always feel when UIC,
I used to rave of LN'S eyes,
4 LC I gave countless sighs,
4 KT, 2, and LNR,
I was a keen competitor.
But each now's a non-NTT,
4 U XL them all UC.

[9293]

I crept upstairs, my shoes in hand,
    Just as the night took wing,
And saw my wife, four steps above,
    Doing the same darned thing.

[9294]

The man who calls coupé a "coup"
May be an ignorant sort of goop,
But he often has more jack, I'd say,
To buy than the one who says
    "coo-pay."

[9295]

I envy you little lightning bug,
You worry not a bit,
For when you see a traffic cop,
You know your tail light's lit.

[9296]

'Twas in a restaurant they met,
    Romeo and Juliet.
He had no cash to pay the debt,
    So Romeo'd what Juli'et.

[9297]

That Eve was the first Summer girl
    There is no doubt at all,
For we are plainly told that she
    Arrived before the Fall.

[9298]

The rain is raining all around;
    It rains on roads and streets,
On highways and on boulevards,
    And those in rumble seats.

[9299]

They walked in the lane together,
    The sky was covered with stars;
They reached the gate in silence,
    He lifted down the bars.
She neither smiled nor thanked him
    Because she knew not how;
For he was just a farmer's boy,
    And she—a Jersey cow.

[9300]

Talk about excitement
    To make the people look up,
Wait 'til Gabriel trumpets
    On a nation-wide hook-up.

[9301]

Ten little Commandments spoiling
    lots of fun—
Along came the Younger Genera-
    tion, and then there were none.

[9302]

Beneath the spreading chestnut tree
The smith works like the deuce,
For now he's selling gasoline,
Hot dogs and orange juice!

[9303]

Mary had a little lamb,
It's fleece was white as snow.
She took it to Pittsburgh,
And now look at the damned thing.

[9304]

He rocked the boat,
Did Ezra Shank;
These bubbles mark

O

O

O

O

O

Where Ezra sank.

[9305]

When it freezes and blows, take
care of your nose, that it don't get
froze, and wrap up your toes in
warm woollen hose.

The above, we suppose, was written in prose, by some one who
knows the effect of cold snows.

[9306]

"May I print a kiss on your lips?"
    he asked,
She nodded her sweet permission.
So they went to press,
And I rather guess,
They printed a large edition.

[9307]

Don't worry if your job is small,
    And your rewards are few;
Remember that the mighty oak
    Was once a nut like you.

[9308]

The optimist fell ten stories.
    At each window bar
He shouted to his friends:
    "All right so far."

[9309]

One night in late October,
When I was far from sober,
Returning with my load with manly
    pride,
My feet began to stutter,
So I lay down in the gutter,
And a pig came near and lay down
    by my side;
A lady passing by was heard to say:
"You can tell a man who boozes,
By the company he chooses,"
And the pig got up and slowly
    walked away.

[9310]

On Greenland's icy mountains,
    That's where I want to be,
In weather, when the mercury
    Abides at ninety-three.
For some sweet maiden Eskimo,
I'd swap Bess, Nell or Cora,
And at her daddy's igloo gate
    We'd study the aurora.

[9311]

Little Miss Muffet decided to rough
    it
In a cabin quite old and medieval.
A rounder espied her and plied
    her with cider
And now she's the forest's prime
    evil.

[9312]

A woman is an awful thing.
    I like her.
She'll never pet without a ring.
    I like her.
To some he-man she loves to cling,
Until his sense and roll take wing:
Then you just watch her crown her
    king!
    I like her.

[9313]

A doctor fell in a well,
    And broke his collarbone.
The doctor should attend the sick
    And leave the well alone.

[9314]
Tobacco is a filthy weed—
    I like it.
It satisfies no normal need—
    I like it.
It makes you thin, it makes you
    lean,
It takes the hair right off your bean;
It's the worst darned stuff I've ever
    seen.
    I like it.

[9315]
I sneezed a sneeze into the air;
It fell to ground I knew not where
But hard and cold were the looks
    of those
In whose vicinity I snoze.

[9316]
If kissing were not lawful
    The lawyers would not use it;
And if it were not pious,
    The clergy would not choose it;
And if 'twere not a dainty thing,
    The ladies would not crave it;
And if it were not plentiful,
    The poor girls could not have it.

[9317]
Girls when they went out to swim,
    Once dressed like Mother Hub-
    bard,
Now they have a bolder whim:
    They dress more like her cup-
    board.

[9318]
From yon blue heavens above us
    bent,
The gardener Adam and his wife
Smile at the claims of long descent.
    —Tennyson

[9319]
Blessings on thee, little girl,
With your dimples and your curl,
With your short skirts shorter still
'Spite the blust'ry April chill;
Little fore, and less behind.
Honest, isn't nature kind?

[9320]
Mary had a little lamb,
A little pork, a little jam,
A little egg on toast,
A little potted roast,
A little stew with dumpling white,
A little shad,
For Mary had
A little appetite.

[9321]
She wore her stockings inside out
All through the summer heat.
She said it cooled her off to turn
The hose upon her feet.

[9322]
Divorced are Mr.
    And Mrs. Howell;
He wiped the car
    With her best guest towel!

[9323]
Ladies, to this advice give heed—
In controlling men:
If at first you don't succeed,
Why, cry, cry again.

[9324]
The bathers and the boatmen fly,
    The golfers and the blimps de-
    part;
The fox hunt fills the news-reel eye
    And soon the ski-jump views will
    start.

[9325]
Oh, what a funny bug is a lightning
    bug;
His light is on the wrong end.
He never sees where he is going,
But only where he has been.

[9326]
She took my hand with loving care;
She took my costly flowers so rare.
She took my candy and my books!
She took my eye with meaning
    looks.
She took all that I could buy,
And then she took the other guy.

[9327]

A pair in a hammock
Attempted to kiss,
And in less than a jiffy
They landed like this.

[9328]

Men scorn to kiss among themselves
And scarce will kiss a brother.
Women often want to kiss so much
They smack and kiss each other.

[9329]

According to the styles exposed
In every modiste's shop,
Legs now are worn much longer,
With a girl perched up on top.

[9330]

My name is Ebenezer—
'Tis a name I much despise;
And, oh, how quick I'll drop it
When rich Uncle Ebbie dies!

[9331]

The Mrs. never misses
Any bargain sale,
For the female of the species
Is more thrifty than the male.

[9332]

Love is like an onion
You taste it with delight
And when it's gone you wonder
What ever made you bite.

[9333]

There was onst two cats in Kilkenny,
And aich thought there was one
cat too many;
So they quarrelled and fit,
And they gouged and they bit,
Till, excepting their nails,
And the tip of their tails,
Instead of two cats there wasn't any.

[9334]

To fix the boundaries of earth
Brings nations to the mat,
There are no boundaries to mirth,
Let's all be glad of that!

[9335]

A June bug married an angleworm;
An accident cut her in two.
They charged the bug with bigamy;
Now what could the poor thing
do?

[9336]

He never traveled extensively
And his knowledge of places was
pretty slim—
Oh, all he knew of geography
Was that Edna was all the world
to him.

[9337]

Woman, lovely woman—
Isn't she fair and sweet?
She wears more clothes when she
goes to bed
Than she does upon the street.

[9338]

My tYpust is on hor vacution,
My trypist's awau fpr a week,
My typudt us in hwr vscarion
Wgile thse danm kews plsy hude
and seej.

[9339]

'Twas ever thus, from childhood's
hour
That chilling fate has on me fell;
There always comes a soaking
shower
When I hain't got no umberell.

[9340]

I slept in an editor's bed last night,
When no editor chanced to be
nigh:
And I thought, as I tumbled that
editor's nest,
How easily editors lie.

[9341]

Attend your church, the parson
cries,
To church each fair one goes;
The old go there to close their eyes,
The young to eye their clothes.

[9342]

To a bottle:
'Tis very strange that you and I
    Together cannot pull;
For you are full when I am dry,
    And dry when I am full.

[9343]

Ignoramus:
Whether first the egg or the hen?
Tell me, I pray you, ye learned men.
        First Scribe:
The hen was first, or whence the
    egg?
Give us no more your doubts, I beg.
        Second Scribe:
The egg was first, or whence the
    hen?
Tell me how it could come, and
    when.

[9344]

The fashions come, the fashions go,
    Now longer skirts, now shorter;—
But everything that women wear,
Some prune reformer tears his hair
And says they hadn't orter!

[9345]

I always fly
Into a rage
When some dame chortles:
"Be your age."

[9346]

Wives of great men all remind us,
    As we scan their mien and gait,
That the men who were as blind as
    That, cannot have been so great.

[9347]

Great fleas have lesser fleas,
    And these have less to bite 'em;
These fleas have lesser fleas,
    And so *ad infinitum.*

[9348]

I wish I were a kangaroo,
Despite his funny stances;
I'd have a place to put the junk
My girl brings to the dances.

[9349]

'Tis an excellent world that we live
    in,
To lend, to spend, or to give in;
But to borrow, or beg, or get a
    man's own,
'Tis just the worst world that
    ever was known.

[9350]

If you your lips would save from
    slips,
    Five things observe with care;
Of whom you speak, to whom you
    speak,
    And how, and when, and where.

[9351]

The world of fools has such a store,
    That he who would not see an
        ass,
Must bide at home, and bolt his
    door,
    And break his looking-glass.

[9352]

A fool does never change his mind,
    And who can think it strange?
The reason's clear—for fools, my
    friends,
    Have not a mind to change.

[9353]

"Why can't you hide what ought
    to be hid,
And dress modest and plain, as
    your grandmother did?"
"Dear aunt, so I do—as you may
    perceive,
I dress in the mode of grandmother
    —Eve!"

[9354]

The curfew tolls the knell of part-
    ing day,
    A line of cars winds slowly o'er
        the lea,
A pedestrian plods his absent-
    minded way
    And leaves the world quite un-
        expectedly.

[9355]
You can't fill a man as you fill up
a pitcher;
 He always will hold
 A little more gold
And never so rich that he wouldn't
be richer.

[9356]
He who goes to bed, and goes to
bed sober,
Falls as the leaves do, and dies in
October;
But he who goes to bed, and does
so mellow,
Lives as he ought to, and dies a
good fellow.

[9357]
"I miss my husband so!"
 The woman cried.
'And so just one more shot
 At him she tried.

[9358]
A teacher asked the children to
submit a couplet made to rhyme
with Kelley. Little Willie released
this epic:
There was a likely lad named
 Kelley.
Who waded in the brook up to his
 knees.
"Where is the rhyme?" asked
 teacher.
"Water wasn't deep enough!" replied Willie.

COMIC VERSE CHAINS

[9359]
Oh, shed a tear
 For Luther Stover;
He tried to toot
 Two State cops over.
   —New York Sun.

Please wail one wail
 For Adolph Barr;
He just would drive
 A one-eyed car.
   —Macon Telegraph.

Bill Muffet said
 His car couldn't skid;
This monument shows
 That it could and did.
   —Newark (Ohio) Advocate

[9360]
Behold the pretty cotton plant
 With blossom white and full,
They pick the downy stuff and lo
 They sell us suits of wool.
   —Spokane Review.

Behold the humble alley cat,
 A thing for jests and knocks,
Around my lady's neck his skin
 Is changed to silver fox.
   —Macon Telegraph

Behold the tiny baby steer,
 A cute, though awkward thing.
For him good money we will pay
 As chicken a la king.
   —Buffalo News.

[9361]
Of course, I've learned a lot of
 things
 And a lot of things I've missed;
But why does a flapper lift her foot
 When she is being kissed?
   —Florida Times-Union

To learn you don't know even that
 Has caused me much surprise—
I'll bet you don't know, either, why
 She always shuts her eyes.
   —Buffalo Evening News.

[9362]
He who stops to look each way
Will drive his car another day.
   —Florida Times-Union.
But he who speeds across the "stop"
Will land in some mortician's shop.
   —Tampa Tribune.

And he who starts his car in gear
May end his ride upon a bier.
                    —*Tarpon Springs Leader.*

Who fights a truck for half the road,
Will make pallbearers "tote" a load.
                    —*Waycross Journal-Herald.*

He who crashes through the red
May wake up and find he's dead.
                    —*Buffalo Evening News.*

[9363]

A man who has two wives, of
    course,
  Is always called a bigamist;
But when he has some three or four
  We guess he is a pigamist.
                    —*Florida Times-Union.*

The greedy guy who gets so far
  From being a monogamist
As to have spouses four, I'd call
  A matrimonial hogamist.
                    —*E. B. in the Boston Transcript.*

[9364]

The angler lies in wait with hook
  And line and rod and reel,
And hap at night he brings the cook
  A bullhead or an eel.
                    —*Judge.*

The angler lies forever at
  The mercy of the skeeters,
Of stinging fly and biting gnat
  And other blood depleters.
                    —*Albany News.*

The angler lies, but we surmise
  That this is idle chat.
We'll merely say, "The angler-lies,"
  And let it go at that.
                    —*Boston Transcript.*

[9365]

Now, ladies in a crowded bus
Occasion very little fuss
Because they always cross their
    knees,
Conserving space, a bit like these:
            XXXXXX

But gaze upon a row of men
And blush for shame a little when
You see their spreading, sprawling
    ways
That make them like this row of
    A's:
            AAAAAA
—*Charlie Leedy in the Youngstown
Telegram.*

But only yesterday I rode
Across from one whose legs were
    bowed;
The best she could achieve, poor
    miss,
Was something very much like this:
            VVVVVV
—*Ema Spencer in the Newark
(Ohio) Advocate.*

But I wish you would tell me,
    please,
How they could have been like V's.
Unless my eyes deceive me, miss,
Bow legs in street cars look like
    this:
    ( ) ( ) ( ) ( ) ( ) ( ) ( ) ( )
—*Ed Scanlan in the Buffalo News.*

[9366]

How sweet to waken in the morn
  When sunbeams first begin to
    creep
Across the lea—and then to lie
  Right back again and go to sleep.
                    —*Youngstown Telegram.*

How sweet to waken in the morn
  Without one bit of fear or doubt,
And sudden then to realize
  The furnace fire is all but out.
                    —*Oakland Times.*

How sweet to waken in the morn
  Without a care the mind to
    cumber,
Then hurry to the phone and find
  Some ass is calling the wrong
    number.
                    —*Boston Transcript.*

[9367]
Myrtilla's eyes are blue and bright,
   And mischief in them lies.
Her wavy hair is crisp and light,
   But not so are her pies.
                    —Judge.

She makes a picture, day by day,
   That fairly turns my head.
She also—this I grieve to say—
   Makes ferro-concrete bread.
                    —Boston Transcript.

Her eyes are soft and limpid
   As the blue Italian lakes
And on their sandy bottoms
   Belong the cakes she bakes.
                    —Buffalo Evening News.

[9368]
'Tis better to have loved
   And lost
Than wed and be
   Forever bossed.
                    —Florida Times-Union.

The saddest words
   Of tongue or pen—
Why did I marry
   That old hen?
                    —Oskaloosa Messenger.

For the human race
   (Thus saith a booster)
The hen's more useful
   Than the rooster.
                    —Hendry County News.

[9369]
I hope he tried to cross the sea
   In an old and leaky dory,
The guy who says: "Yes, yes," to
      me
   When I'm telling a story.
                    —Buffalo News.

And with a doodad I could poke
   The everlasting lout
Who, when I'm telling my best joke,
   Gets up and moves about.
                    —Youngstown Telegram.

In front a coming train I'd lay,
   And gladly, too, the bore
Who greets my story with, "Oh, say,
   I've heard that one before!"
                    —Warren (Ohio) Tribune.

[9370]
Beneath this grassy mound now
      rests
One Edgar Oscar Earl,
Who to another hunter looked
Exactly like a squirrel.
                    —Philadelphia Inquirer.

And under this—a lonely pile,
Lies Rufus Rastus Babbitt;
He looked the part, a gunner
      thought,
And shot him for a rabbit.
                    Cincinnati Enquirer.

Beneath this weeping willow tree
Lies Edward Everett Bier,
Who, by another hunter, was
Mistaken for a deer.
                    —Buffalo News.

NONSENSE POEMS

[9371]
A FROG WENT A-COURTING
A frog went a-courting, away did
   ride, huh-huh.
A frog went a-courting, away did
   ride,
Sword and pistol by his side, huh-
   huh.

He rode up to Miss Mousie's door,
   huh-huh.
He rode up to Miss Mousie's door
With his coat all buttoned down
   before, huh-huh.

He took Miss Mousie on his knee,
   huh-huh.
He took Miss Mousie on his knee,
And he said my dear will you
   marry me, huh-huh.

Oh no! kind sir, I can't say that,
huh-huh.
Oh no! kind sir, I can't say that,
You'll have to get the consent of
my uncle rat, huh-huh.

Uncle rat he laughed and shook his
fat side, huh-huh
Uncle rat he laughed and shook his
fat side,
To think that his niece would be a
bride, huh-huh.

Oh, where shall the wedding breakfast be, huh-huh.
Oh, where shall the wedding breakfast be,
Way down in the woods in a hollow
tree, huh-huh.

The first that came was a long-tailed
rat, huh-huh.
The first that came was a long-
tailed rat——
Etc.

—*Anonymous.*

[9372]
BUZ, QUOTH THE BLUE FLY
Buz, quoth the blue fly,
Hum, quoth the bee,
Buz and hum they cry,
And so do we:
In his ear, in his nose, thus, do you
see?
He ate the dormouse, else it was he.
—*Ben Jonson*

[9373]
VAN AMBURGH'S MENAGERIE
Van Amburgh is the man that goes
with all the shows;
He goes into the lion's den, and
shows you all he knows;
He sticks his head in the lion's
mouth, and keeps it there
awhile,
And when he takes it out again, he
greets you with a smile.

Chorus:
For the elephant now goes round,
the band begins to play,
Those boys around the monkey's
cage, they'd better keep away.

This is the Arctic polar bear, oft
called the iceberg's daughter,
Been known to eat three tubs of
ice, then call for soda water;
She wades in the water up to her
knees, not fearing any harm;
You may growl and grumble as
much as you please, but she
don't care a darn.

Next comes baboon Emmeline,
catching flies and scratching
her head,
Weeping and wailing all the day,
because her husband's dead;
Poor weeping, wailing water lily,
of all her friends bereft,
That monkey is thumbing his nose
at her with his right paw over
his left.

Next comes the anaconda boa constrictor, called the anaconda for
brevity;
He can swallow an elephant as well
as a toad, and is noted for his
great longevity,
Can swallow himself, crawl through
himself, come out with great
facility,
Tie himself into a bowknot, snap
his tail, and wink with great
agility.

That hyena in the next cage, most
wonderful to relate,
Got awful hungry the other night,
and ate up his female mate;
Now, don't go near his cage, he'll
hurt you, little boys,
For when he's mad he'll growl and
bite, and make a horrible noise.
Gr-rr-r——

Next comes the condor, an awful
    bird, from the highest moun-
    tain tops:
Been known to eat up little boys
    and then to smack his chops;
This performance can't go on—
    there's too much noise and con-
    fusion;
Those ladies giving those monkeys
    nuts will injure their consti-
    tution.
                    —*Anonymous*.

[9374]
THE CRUISE OF THE "P. C."
Across the swiffling waves they
    went,
    The gumly bark yoked to and fro;
The jupple crew on pleasure bent,
    Galored, "This is a go!"

Beside the poo's'l stood the Gom,
    He chirked and murgled in his
    glee;
While near him, inagrue jipon,
    The Bard was quite at sea.

"Gollop! Golloy! Thou scrumjous
    Bard!
Take pen (thy stylo) and endite
A pome, my brain needs kurgling
    hard,
    And I will feast tonight."

That wansome Bard he took his pen,
    A flirgly look around he guv;
He squoffled once, he squirled, and
    then
    He wrote what's writ above.
                    —*Anonymous*.

[9375]
THE WONDERFUL OLD MAN
There was an old man
    Who lived on a common
And, if fame speaks true,
    He was born of a woman.
Perhaps you will laugh,
    But for truth I've been told

He once was an infant
    Tho' age made him old.

Whene'er he was hungry
    He longed for some meat;
And if he could get it
    'T was said he would eat.
When thirsty he'd drink
    If you gave him a pot,
And what he drank mostly
    Ran down his throat.

He seldom or never
    Could see without light,
And yet I've been told he
    Could hear in the night.
He has oft been awake
    In the daytime, 't is said,
And has fallen asleep
    As he lay in his bed.

'T is reported his tongue
    Always moved when he talk'd,
And he stirred both his arms
    And his legs when he walk'd;
And his gait was so odd
    Had you seen him you'd burst,
For one leg or t' other
    Would always be first.

His face was the drollest
    That ever was seen,
For if 't was not washed
    It seldom was clean;
His teeth he expos'd when
    He happened to grin,
And his mouth stood across
    'Twixt his nose and his chin.

When this whimsical chap
    Had a river to pass,
If he could n't get over
    He stayed where he was.
'T is said he ne'er ventured
    To quit the dry ground,
Yet so great was his luck
    He never was drowned.

At last he fell sick,
  As old chronicles tell,
And then, as folks say,
  He was not very well.
But what was as strange
  In so weak a condition,
As he could not give fees
  He could get no physician.

What wonder he died!
  Yet 't is said that his death
Was occasioned at last
  By the loss of his breath.
But peace to his bones
  Which in ashes now moulder.
Had he lived a day longer
  He'd have been a day older.
                    —*Anonymous.*

[9376]
A SONG ON KING WILLIAM III
  As I walked by myself,
  And talked to myself,
    Myself said unto me,
  Look to thyself,
  Take care of thyself,
    For nobody cares for thee.

  I answered myself,
  And said to myself,
    In the self-same repartee,
  Look to thyself,
  Or not look to thyself,
    The selfsame thing will be.
                    Anonymous.

[9377]
SORROWS OF WERTHER
Werther had a love for Charlotte
  Such as words could never utter;
Would you know how first he met
    her?
  She was cutting bread and butter.

Charlotte was a married lady,
  And a moral man was Werther,
And for all the wealth of Indies
  Would do nothing for to hurt
    her.

So he sighed and pined and ogled,
  And his passion boiled and
    bubbled,
Till he blew his silly brains out,
  And no more was by it troubled.

Charlotte, having seen his body
  Borne before her on a shutter,
Like a well-conducted person,
  Went on cutting bread and butter.
        —*William Makepeace Thackeray.*

[9378]
THREE CHILDREN
Three children sliding on the ice
  Upon a summer's day,
As it fell out they all fell in,
  The rest they ran away.

Now, had these children been at
    home,
  Or sliding on dry ground,
Ten thousand pounds to one penny
  They had not all been drowned.

You parents all that children have,
  And you too that have none,
If you would have them safe abroad
  Pray keep them safe at home.
                    —*Anonymous.*

[9379]
A LOVE-SONG BY A LUNATIC
There's not a spider in the sky,
  There's not a glowworm in the
    sea,
There's not a crab that soars on
    high,
  But bids me dream, dear maid,
    of thee!

When watery Phoebus ploughs the
    main,
  When fiery Luna gilds the lea,
As flies run up the window-pane,
  So fly my thoughts, dear love, to
    thee!
                    —*Anonymous.*

[9380]
CAPTAIN JINKS

I'm Captain Jinks of the Horse
  Marines,
I feed my horse on corn and beans,
And sport young ladies in their
  teens,
  Though a captain in the army.
I teach young ladies how to dance,
How to dance, how to dance,
I teach young ladies how to dance,
  For I'm the pet of the army.

Chorus:

Captain Jinks of the Horse Marines,
I feed my horse on corn and beans,
And often live beyond my means,
  Though a captain in the army.

I joined my corps when twenty-one,
Of course I thought it capital fun;
When the enemy came, of course
  I ran,
  For I'm not cut out for the army.
When I left home, mama she cried,
Mama she cried, mama she cried,
When I left home, mama she cried:
  "He's not cut out for the army."

The first time I went out to drill,
The bugle sounding made me ill;
Of the battle field I'd had my fill,
  For I'm not cut out for the army.
The officers they all did shout,
They all did shout, they all did
  shout,
The officers they all did shout:
  "Why, kick him out of the army."
              —*Anonymous.*

[9381]
THE MOON IS UP

The moon is up, the moon is up!
  The larks begin to fly,
And, like a drowsy buttercup,
  Dark Phoebus skims the sky,

The elephant, with cheerful voice,
  Sings blithely on the spray;
The bats and beetles all rejoice,
  Then let me, too, be gay.

I would I were a porcupine,
  And wore a peacock's tail;
To-morrow, if the moon but shine,
  Perchance I'll be a whale.
Then let me, like the cauliflower,
  Be merry while I may,
And, ere there comes a sunny hour
  To cloud my heart, be gay!
              —*Anonymous.*

[9382]
NONSENSE

Good reader, if you e'er have seen,
  When Phoebus hastens to his
    pillow,
The mermaids with their tresses
    green
  Dancing upon the western billow;
If you have seen at twilight
    dim,
  When the lone spirit's vesper
    hymn
Floats wild along the winding
    shore,
The fairy train their ringlets weave
  Glancing along the spangled
    green;—
    If you have seen all this, and
    more,
God bless me! what a deal you've
    seen!
              —*Thomas Moore.*

[9383]
UNCLE SIMON AND UNCLE
JIM

Uncle Simon he
Clum up a tree
To see what he could see
When presentlee
Uncle Jim
Clum up beside of him
And squatted down by he.
              —*Artemus Ward.*

[9384]
LINES BY A MEDIUM
I might not, if I could;
  I should not, if I might;
Yet if I should I would,
  And, shoulding, I should quite!

I must not, yet I may;
  I can, and still I must;
But ah! I cannot—nay,
  To must I may not, just!

I shall, although I will,
  But be it understood,
If I may, can, shall—still
  I might, could, would, or should!
                    —*Anonymous.*

[9385]
ALONE
Alone! Alone!
I sit in the solitudes of the moon-
  shades,
Soul-hungering in the moonshade
  solitudes sit I——
My heart-lifts beaten down in the
  wild wind-path.
Oppressed, and scourged and beaten
  down are my heart-lifts.
I fix my gaze on the eye-star, and
  the eye-star flings its dart upon
  me.
I wonder why my soul is lost in
  wonder why I am,
And why the eye-star mocks me,
Why the wild wind beats down my
  heart-lifts;
Why I am stricken here in the
  moonshade solitudes.
Oh! why am I what I am,
And why am I anything?
Am I not as wild as the wind and
  more crazy?
Why do I sit in the moonshade,
  while the eye-star mocks me
  while I ask what I am?
Why? Why?
                    —*Anonymous.*

[9386]
SING FOR THE GARISH EYE
Sing for the garish eye, ...
  When moonless brandlings cling!
Let the froddering crooner cry,
  And the braddled sapster sing.
For never and never again,
  Will the tottering beechlings
  play,
For bratticed wrackers are singing
  aloud,
  And the throngers croon in May!
                    —*W. S. Gilbert.*

[9387]
TO MARIE
When the breeze from the blue-
  bottle's blustering blim
Twirls the toads in a tooroomaloo,
And the whiskery whine of the
  wheedlesome whim
Drowns the roll of the rattatattoo,
Then I dream in the shade of the
  shally-go-shee,
And the voice of the bally-molay
Brings the smell of the pale poppy-
  cod's blummered blee
From the willy-wad over the way.

Ah, the shuddering shoe and the
  blinkety-blanks
When the punglung falls from
  the bough
In the blast of a hurricane's hicketty-
  hanks
  O'er the hills of the hocketty-how!
Give the rigmarole to the clangery-
  whang,
  If they care for such fiddlededee;
But the thingumbob kiss of the
  whangery-bang
  Keeps the higglede-piggle for
  me.

It is pilly-po-doddle and aligobung
  When the lollypop covers the
  ground,

Yet the poldiddle perishes plunkety-
    pung
When the heart jimny-coggles
    around
If the soul cannot snoop at the gig-
    glesome cart
Seeking surcease in gluggety-glug.
It is useless to say to the pulsating
    heart,
"Yankee-doodle ker-chuggety-
    chug!"
                —Anonymous.

[9388]
PHILOSOPHY
Across the moorlands of the Not
    We chase the gruesome When;
We hunt the Itness of the What
    Through forests of the Then.
Into the Inner Consciousness
    We track the crafty Where,
We spear the Ego tough, and beard
    The Self within its lair.

With lassos of the brain we catch
    The Isness of the Was;
And in the copses of the Whence
    We hear the think bees buzz.
We climb the slippery Which to see
    The pallid Thusness roll;
And lift the So beside the Why
    Above the Over Soul!
                —Anonymous.

[9389]
SONNET FOUND IN A
MADHOUSE
Oh, that my soul a marrow-bone
    might seize!
For the old egg of my desire is
    broken,
Spilled is the pearly white and
    spilled the yolk, and
As the mild melancholy contents
    grease
My path the shorn lamb baas like
    bumblebees.

Time's trashy purse is as a taken
    token
Or like a thrilling recitation, spoken
By mournful mouths filled full of
    mirth and cheese.

And yet why should I clasp the
    earthful urn?
Or find the frittered fig that felt
    the fast?
Or choose to chase the cheese
    around the churn?
Or swallow any pill from out the
    past?
Ah, no, Love, not while your hot
    kisses burn
Like a potato riding on the blast.
                —Anonymous.

[9390]
THE LOGIC OF IT
If a man who turnips cries
Cry not when his father dies,
'Tis a proof that he would rather
Have a turnip than a father.
            —Samuel Johnson.

[9391]
THE MONKEY'S WEDDING
The monkey married the Baboon's
    sister,
Smacked his lips and then he kissed
    her,
Kissed so hard that he raised a
    blister.
    She set up a yell.
The bridesmaid stuck on some court
    plaster,
It stuck so fast it couldn't stick
    faster,
Surely 'twas a sad disaster,
    But it soon got well.

What do you think the bride was
    dressed in?
White gauze veil and a green glass
    breast-pin,
Red kid shoes—quite interesting,
    She was quite a belle.

The bridegroom swelled with a blue
  shirt collar,
Black silk stock that cost a dollar,
Long false whiskers the mode to
  follow;
He cut a monstrous swell.

What do you think they had for
  supper?
Black-eyed peas and bread and but-
  ter,
Ducks in the duck-house all in a
  flutter,
  Pickled oysters too.
Chestnuts raw and boil'd and
  roasted,
Apples sliced and onions toasted,
Music in the corner posted,
  Waiting for the cue.

What do you think was the tune
  they danced to?
"The Drunken Sailor"—and some-
  times "Jim Crow,"
Tails in the way—and some got
  pinched, too,
  'Cause they were too long.
What do you think they had for a
  fiddle?
An old Banjo with a hole in the
  middle,
A Tambourine made out of a rid-
  dle,
  And that's the end of my song!
                        —Anonymous.

[9392]
THE OWL AND THE PUSSY-
CAT

The Owl and the Pussy-Cat went to
  sea
  In a beautiful pea-green boat:
They took some honey, and plenty
  of money
  Wrapped up in a five-pound note.
The Owl looked up to the stars
  above,
  And sang to a small guitar,

"Oh, lovely Pussy, oh, Pussy, my
  love,
  What a beautiful Pussy you are,
    You are,
    You are!
  What a beautiful Pussy you are!"

Pussy said to the Owl, "You elegant
  fowl,
  How charmingly sweet you sing!
Oh, let us be married; too long we
  have tarried:
  But what shall we do for a ring?"
They sailed away for a year and a
  day,
  To the land where the bong-tree
    frows;
And there in the kood a Piggy-wig
  stood,
  With a ring at the end of his nose,
    His nose,
    His nose,
  With a ring at the end of his nose.

"Dear Pig, are you willing to sell
  for one shilling
  Your ring?" Said the Piggy, "I
    will."
So they took it away and were mar-
  ried next day
  By the Turkey who lives on the
    hill.
They dined on mince and slices of
  quince,
  Which they ate with a runcible
    spoon;
And hand in hand, on the edge of
  the sand,
  They danced by the light of the
    moon,
    The moon,
    The moon,
  They danced by the light of the
    moon.
                        —Edward Lear

[9393]
THE AHKOND OF SWAT

Who, or why, or which, or *what*
       Is the Ahkond of Swat?
Is he tall or short, or dark or fair?
Does he sit on a stool or sofa or
    chair,
           or Squat,
       The Ahkond of Swat?

Is he wise or foolish, young or old?
Does he drink his soup and his cof-
    fee cold
          or Hot,
       The Ahkond of Swat?

Does he wear a turban, a fez, or a
    hat?
Does he sleep on a mattress, a bed
    or a mat,
          or a Cot,
       The Ahkond of Swat?

Does he like to lie on his back in a
    boat
Like the lady who lived in that isle
    remote,
         Shalott,
       The Ahkond of Swat?

Does he beat his wife with a gold-
    topped pipe,
When she lets the gooseberries
    grow too ripe,
         or Rot,
       The Ahkond of Swat?

Does he like new cream, and hate
    mince-pies?
When he looks at the sun does he
    wink his eyes,
         or Not
       The Ahkond of Swat?

Someone, or nobody knows I wot
Who or which or why or what
       Is the Ahkond of Swat?
          —Edward Lear.

[9394]
ELEGY FOR A DEPARTED NOBLEMAN

The noble Earl of Sandwich is de-
    parted,
His lordship is decidedly deceased.
    No man was better bred—
    (Note Sandwich, ergo bread)—
He'd done his duty at the final feast.

His relatives, Count Pumpernickel
    Sandwich,
Duke Matzoth, and the Earl of
    Eirish S'Teu,
    Regret it, as is meet—
    (Note Sandwich, ergo meat)—
Adieu, departed nobleman, adieu!
          —Carveth Wells.

[9395]
FATHER WILLIAM

"You are old, Father William," the
    young man said,
    "And your nose has a look of sur-
        prise;
Your eyes have turned round to the
    back of your head,
    And you live upon cucumber
        pies."
"I know it, I know it," the old man
    replied,
    "And it comes from employing a
        quack,
Who said if I laughed when the
    crocodile died
    I should never have pains in my
        back."

"You are old, Father William," the
    young man said,
    "And your legs always get in
        your way;
You used too much mortar in mix-
    ing your bread,
    And you try to drink timothy
        hay."

"Very true, very true," said the
    wretched old man,
    "Every word that you tell me is
    true;
And it's caused by my having my
    kerosene can
    Painted red where it ought to be
    blue."

"You are old, Father William," the
    young man said,
    "And your teeth are beginning to
    freeze,
Your favorite daughter has wheels
    in her head,
    And the chickens are eating your
    knees."
"You are right," said the old man,
    "I cannot deny,
That my troubles are many and
    great,
But I'll butter my ears on the Fourth
    of July,
And then I'll be able to skate."
                    —*Lewis Carroll.*

[9396]
THE WHITING AND THE SNAIL

"Will you walk a little faster?" said
    a whiting to a snail,
"There's a porpoise close behind us,
    and he's treading on my tail.
See how eagerly the lobsters and
    the turtles all advance—
They are waiting on the shingle—
    will you come and join the
    dance?
Will you, won't you, will you,
    won't you, will you join the
    dance?
Will you, won't you, will you,
    won't you, won't you join the
    dance?

"You can really have no notion how
    delightful it will be
When they take us up and throw us,
    with the lobsters, out to sea!"
But the snail replied, "Too far, too
    far!" and gave a look askance—
Said he thanked the whiting kindly,
    but he would not join the
    dance.
Would not, could not, would not,
    could not, would not join the
    dance;
Would not, could not, would not,
    could not, could not join the
    dance.

"What matters it how far we go?"
    his scaly friend replied.
"There is another shore, you know,
    upon the other side.
The farther off from England the
    nearer is to France—
Then turn not pale, beloved snail,
    but come and join the dance.
Will you, won't you, will you,
    won't you, will you join the
    dance?
Will you, won't you, will you,
    won't you, won't you join the
    dance?"
                    —*Lewis Carroll.*

[9397]
TURTLE SOUP

Beautiful soup, so rich and green,
Waiting in a hot tureen!
Who for such dainties would not
    stoop?
Soup of the evening, beautiful soup!
Soup of the evening, beautiful soup!
    Beau-ootiful soo-oop!
    Beau-ootiful soo-oop!
    Soo-oop of the e-e-evening,
    Beautiful, beautiful soup!

Beautiful soup! Who cares for fish,
Game, or any other dish?
Who would not give all else for
    two p-
Ennyworth of beautiful soup?

Pennyworth of beautiful soup?
　Beau-ootiful soo-oop!
　Beau-ootiful soo-oop!
　Soo-oop of the e-e-evening,
　　Beautiful, beauti-FUL SOUP!
　　　　　—*Lewis Carroll.*

[9398]

Tweedle-dum and Tweedle-dee
Resolved to have a battle,
For Tweedle-dum said Tweedle-
　dee
Had spoiled his nice new rattle.
Just then flew by a monstrous crow,
　As big as a tar-barrel,
Which frightened both the heroes
　so
They quite forgot their quarrel.

[9399]

I went to the animal fair,
The birds and beasts were there.
The big baboon, by the light of the
　moon,
Was combing his auburn hair.
The monkey, he got drunk,
And sat on the elephant's trunk.
The elephant sneezed and fell on
　his knees,
And what became of the monk, the
　monk?

[9400]

We're all in the dumps,
For diamonds are trumps;
The kittens are gone to St. Paul's!
The babies are bit,
The moon's in a fit,
And the houses are built without
　walls.

[9401]

The man in the wilderness asked of
　me
How many strawberries grew in the
　sea.
I answered him as I thought good,
As many as red herrings grow in
　the wood.

[9402]

Thy heart is like some icy lake,
　On whose cold brink I stand;
Oh, buckle on my spirit's skate,
　And lead, thou living saint, the way
　To where the ice is thin—
That it may break beneath my feet
And let a lover in!

[9403]

Behold the wonders of the mighty
　deep,
Where crabs and lobsters learn to
　creep,
And little fishes learn to swim,
And clumsy sailors tumble in.

[9404]

The night was growing old
　As she trudged through snow
　　and sleet;
Her nose was long and cold,
　And her shoes were full of feet.

[9405]

My home is on the rolling deep,
I spend my time a-feeding sheep;
And when the waves on high are
　running,
I take my gun and go a-gunning.
I shoot wild ducks down deep
　snake-holes,
And drink gin-sling from two-quart
　bowls.

[9406]

"If half the road was made of jam,
　The other half of bread,
　How very nice my walks would
　be,"
　The greedy infant said.

[9407]

A centipede was happy quite,
　Until a frog, in fun,
Said, "Pray, which leg comes after
　which?"
This raised her mind to such a pitch
She lay distracted in a ditch,
　Considering how to run.

[9408]

I love to stand upon my head
    And think of things sublime
Until my mother interrupts
    And says it's dinner-time.

[9409]

'Tis midnight, and the setting sun
    Is rising slowly in the west;
The rapid rivers slowly run,
    The frog is on his downy nest.
The pensive goat and sportive cow
Hilarious hop from bough to bough.

[9410]

'Tis sweet to roam when morning's
    light
    Resounds across the deep;
And the crystal song of the wood-
    bine bright
    Hushes the rocks to sleep.
And the blood-red moon in the
    blaze of noon
    Is bathed in a crumbling dew.
And the wolf rings out with a glit-
    tering shout,
    To-whit, to-whit, to-whoo!

[9411]

How very sad it is to think
    Our poor benighted brother
Should have his head upon one end,
    His feet upon the other.

[9412]

A lobster wooed a lady crab,
    And kissed her lovely face.
"Upon my sole," the crabbess cried,
    "I wish you'd mind your plaice!"

[9413]

The sorry world is sighing now,
    The flu is at the door;
And many folks are dying now
    Who never died before.

[9414]

If all the land were apple-pie,
    And all the sea were ink;
    And all the trees were bread and
    cheese,
What should we do for drink?

[9415]

I dreamed a dream next Tuesday
    week,
    Beneath the apple-trees;
I thought my eyes were big pork-
    pies,
    And my nose was Stilton cheese.
The clock struck twenty minutes to
    six,
    When a frog sat on my knees;
I asked him to lend me fifty cents,
    But he borrowed a dollar from
    me.

PARODIES

[9416]

BEAUTIFUL SNOW
(*With a drift*)

Oh! the snow, the beautiful snow
(This is a parody, please, you know;
Over and over again you may meet
Parodies writ on this poem so
    sweet;
Rhyming, chiming, skipping along,
Comical bards think they do noth-
    ing wrong;
Striving to follow what others have
    done,
One to the number may keep up
    the fun.)
Beautiful snow, so gently you scud,
Pure for a minute, then dirty as
    mud!

Oh! the snow, the beautiful snow!
Here's a fine mess you have left us
    below;
Chilling our feet to the tips of our
    toes;
Cheekily landing full pert on our
    nose;
Jinking, slinking, ever you try
'Neath our umbrella to flop in our
    eye;

Gamins await us at every new street,
Watching us carefully, guiding our feet,
Joking, mocking, ready to throw
A hard-compressed ball of this beautiful snow.
—*Anonymous.*
(*After Popular Song*)

[9417]
THE NEWEST THING IN CHRISTMAS CAROLS
God rest you, merry gentlemen!
May nothing you dismay;
Not even the dyspeptic plats
Through which you'll eat your way;
Nor yet the heavy Christmas bills
The season bids you pay;
No, nor the ever tiresome need
Of being to order gay;

Nor yet the shocking cold you'll catch
If fog and slush hold sway;
Nor yet the tumbles you must bear
If frost should win the day;
Nor sleepless nights—they're sure to come—
When "waits" attune their lay;
Nor pantomimes, whose dreariness
Might turn macassar gray;

Nor boisterous children, home in heaps,
And ravenous of play;
Nor yet—in fact, the host of ills
Which Christmases array.
God rest you, merry gentlemen,
May none of these dismay!
—*Anonymous.*
(*After Popular Song*)

[9418]
IF I SHOULD DIE TO-NIGHT
If I should die to-night
And you should come to my cold corpse and say,

Weeping and heartsick o'er my lifeless clay—
If I should die to-night,
And you should come in deepest grief and woe—
And say: "Here's that ten dollars that I owe,"
I might arise in my large white cravat
And say, "What's that?"

If I should die to-night
And you should come to my cold corpse and kneel,
Clasping my bier to show the grief you feel,
I say, if I should die to-night
And you should come to me, and there and then
Just even hint 'bout paying me that ten,
I might arise the while,
But I'd drop dead again.
—*Ben King.*
(*After Popular Song*)

[9419]
THE TALE OF LORD LOVELL
Lord Lovell he stood at his own front door,
Seeking the hole for the key;
His hat was wrecked, and his trousers bore
A rent across either knee,
When down came the beauteous Lady Jane
In fair white draperie.

"Oh, where have you been, Lord Lovell?" she said,
"Oh, where have you been?" said she;
"I have not closed an eye in bed,
And the clock has just struck three.
Who has been standing you on your head
In the ash-barrel, pardie?"

"I am not drunk, Lad' Shane," he
  said:
  "And so late it cannot be;
The clock struck one as I enteréd—
  I heard it two times or three;
It must be the salmon on which I
  fed
Has been too many for me."

"Go tell your tale, Lord Lovell,"
  she said,
  "To the maritime cavalree,
To your grandmother of the hoary
  head—
  To any one but me:
The door is not used to be openéd
  With a cigarette for a key."
           —*Anonymous.*
      (*After Popular Song*)

[9420]
MARY HAD A LITTLE LAMB
Oh, Mary had a little lamb, regarding whose cuticular
The fluff exterior was white and
  kinked in each particular.
On each occasion when the lass was
  seen perambulating,
The little quadruped likewise was
  there a gallivating.

One day it did accompany her to
  the knowledge dispensary,
Which to every rule and precedent
  was recklessly contrary.
Immediately whereupon the peda-
  gogue superior
Exasperated, did eject the lamb
  from the interior.

Then Mary, on beholding such
  performance arbitrary,
Suffused her eyes with saline drops
  from glands called lachrymary,
And all the pupils grew thereat
  tumultuously hilarious,
And speculated on the case with
  wild conjectures various.

"What makes the lamb love Mary
  so?" the scholars asked the
  teacher.
He paused a moment, then he tried
  to diagnose the creature.
"Oh pecus amorem Mary habit
  omnia temporum."
"Thanks, teacher dear," the scholars cried, and awe crept darkly
  o'er 'em.
           —*Anonymous.*

[9421]
TWO GREEN ONIONS
BEHIND THE TRUE
There was a lady lived in a hall,
Large in the eyes, and slim and
  tall;
And ever she sang from noon to
  noon,
Two red roses across the moon.

There was a lady worked in a flat,
Large in the feet, and squat and
  fat;
And ever she sang from three to
  two,
Two green onions behind the truel

There was a man came home to
  dine,
Expecting fish and roast and wine;
And he heard that kitchen lady coo
Two green onions behind the true.

He asked for soup, and he asked
  for fish,
For roast—or, in fact, for any dish:
While the unheeding lady crooned
  anew,
Two green onions behind the true.

I trow he stopp'd, ere he dined
  again,
A new cook-lady for to obtain,
Who would not substitute for stew
Two green onions behind the true.
          —*Carveth Wells.*
    (*After William Morris*)

[9422]
TO SALLY

The man in righteousness arrayed,
  A pure and blameless liver,
Needs not the keen Toledo blade,
  Nor venom-freighted quiver.
What though he wind his toilsome
    way
  O'er regions wild and weary—
Through Zara's burning desert
    stray,
  Or Asia's jungles dreary:

What though he plough the billowy
    deep
  By lunar light, or solar,
Meet the resistless Simon's sweep,
  Or iceberg circumpolar!
In bog or quagmire deep and dank
  His foot shall never settle;
He mounts the summit of Mont
    Blanc,
  Or Popocatapetl.

On Chimborazo's breathless height
  He treads o'er burning lava;
Or snuffs the Bohan Upas blight,
  The deathful plant of Java.
Through every peril he shall pass,
  By Virtue's shield protected;
And still by Truth's unerring glass
  His path shall be directed.

Else wherefore was it, Thursday
    last,
  While strolling down the valley,
Defenseless, musing as I passed
  A canzonet to Sally,
A wolf, with mouth-protruding
    snout,
  Forth from his thicket bounded—
I clapped my hands and raised a
    shout—
  He heard—and fled—confounded.

Tangier nor Tunis never bred
  An animal more crabbed;

Nor Fez, dry-nurse of lions, fed
  A monster half so rabid;
Nor Ararat so fierce a beast
  Has seen since days of Noah;
Nor stronger, eager for a feast,
  The fell constrictor boa.

Oh! place me where the solar beam
  Has scorched all verdure vernal;
Or on the polar verge extreme,
  Blocked up with ice eternal—
Still shall my voice's tender lays
  Of love remain unbroken;
And still my charming Sally praise,
  Sweet smiling and sweet spoken.
      —*John Quincy Adams.*
       (*After Horace*)

[9423]
PARODY ON POPE

Why has not man a collar and a
    log?
For this plain reason,—man is not
    a dog.
Why is not man served up with
    sauce in dish?
For this plain reason,—man is not
    a fish.

      —*Sydney Smith.*

[9424]
THE MUSICAL PITCH

Break, break, break,
  O voice!—let me urge thy plea!
Oh, lower the Pitch, lest utter
  Despair be the end of me!

'T is well for the fiddles to squeak,
  The bassoon to grunt in its play;
'T were well had I lungs of brass,
  Or that nothing but strings give
    way!

Break, break, break,
  O voice! I must urge thy plea,
For the tender skin of my larynx is
    torn,
  And I fail in my upper G!
      —*Anonymous.*
      (*After Tennyson*)

[9425]
BELIEVE ME, IF—
Believe me, if all those adhering
    young charms
    Which I view with admiring dis-
        may,
Are going to rub off on the shoul-
    ders and arms
    Of this suit which was cleaned
        just today,
Thou wilt still be adored with my
    usual zeal,
    My sweetheart, my loved one, my
        own;
But I'll sternly repress the emotions
    I feel
    And love you, but leave you
        alone.

It is not that thy beauty is any the
    less,
    Nor thy cheeks unaccustomedly
        gay;
They are lovely indeed, as I gladly
    confess,
    And I think I should leave them
        that way.
For the bloom of your youth isn't
    on very tight,
    And the powder rubs off of your
        nose,
So my love is platonic, my dear, for
    tonight,
    Since these are my very best
        clothes.
                    —*Anonymous.*
            (*After Thomas Moore*)

[9426]
THE LAST CIGAR
'Tis a last choice Havana
    I hold here alone;
All its fragrant companions
    In perfume have flown.
No more of its kindred
    To gladden the eye,
So my empty cigar-case
    I close with a sigh.

I'll not leave thee, thou lone one,
    To pine; but the stem
I'll bite off and light thee
    To waft thee to them.
And gently I'll scatter
    The ashes you shed,
As your soul joins its mates in
    A cloud overhead.

All pleasure is fleeting,
    It blooms to decay;
From the weeds' glowing circle
    The ash drops away.
A last whiff is taken,
    The butt-end is thrown,
And with empty cigar-case,
    I sit all alone.
                    —*Anonymous.*
            (*After Thomas Moore*)

[9427]
WHEN LOVELY WOMAN
When lovely woman wants a favor,
    And finds, too late, that man
        won't bend,
What earthly circumstances can
        save her
    From disappointment in the end?

The only way to bring him over,
    The last experiment to try,
Whether a husband or a lover,
    If he have feeling is—to cry.
                    —*Phœbe Cary.*
            (*After Goldsmith*)

[9428]
I REMEMBER, I REMEMBER
I remember, I remember,
    The house where I was wed,
And the little room from which
        that night
    My smiling bride was led.
She did n't come a wink too soon,
    Nor make too long a stay;
But now I often wish her folks
    Had kept the girl away!

I remember, I remember,
  Her dresses, red and white,
Her bonnets and her caps and
    cloaks,—
  They cost an awful sight!
The "corner lot" on which I built,
  And where my brother met
At first my wife, one washing-
    day,—
  That man is single yet!

I remember, I remember,
  Where I was used to court,
And thought that all of married life
  Was just such pleasant sport:—
My spirit flew in feathers then,
  No care was on my brow;
I scarce could wait to shut the
    gate,—
  I'm not so anxious now!

I remember, I remember,
  My dear one's smile and sigh;
I used to think her tender heart
  Was close against the sky.
It was a childish ignorance,
  But now it soothes me not
To know I'm farther off from
    Heaven
  Than when she wasn't got!
          —*Phœbe Cary.*
          (*After Hood*)

[9429]
ANNABEL LEE
'T was more than a million years
    ago,
  Or so it seems to me,
That I used to prance around and
    beau
  The beautiful Annabel Lee.
There were other girls in the neigh-
    borhood
  But none was a patch to she.

And this was the reason that long
    ago,
  My love fell out of a tree,

And busted herself on a cruel rock;
  A solemn sight to see,
For it spoiled the hat and gown
    and looks
  Of the beautiful Annabel Lee.

We loved with a love that was
    lovely love,
  I and my Annabel Lee,
And we went one day to gather the
    nuts
  That men call hickoree.
And I stayed below in the rosy
    glow
  While she shinned up the tree,
But no sooner up than down ker-
    slup
  Came the beautiful Annabel Lee.

And the pallid moon and the hectic
    noon
  Bring gleams of dreams for me,
Of the desolate and desperate fate
  Of the beautiful Annabel Lee.
And I often think as I sink on the
    brink
Of slumber's sea, of the warm pink
    link
  That bound my soul to Annabel
    Lee;
And it wasn't just best for her in-
    terest
  To climb that hickory tree,
For had she stayed below with me,
  We'd had no hickory nuts maybe,
But I should have had my Annabel
    Lee.
          —*Stanley Huntley.*
          (*After Poe*)

[9430]
THE MODERN HIAWATHA
He killed the noble Mudjokivis.
Of the skin he made him mittens,
Made them with the fur side in-
    side,
Made them with the skin side out-
    side.

He, to get the warm side inside,
Put the inside skin side outside;
He, to get the cold side outside,
Put the warm side fur side inside.
That's why he put the fur side in-
side,
Why he put the skin side outside,
Why he turned them inside outside.
—*Anonymous.*
(*After Longfellow*)

[9431]
NURSERY SONG IN PIDGIN ENGLISH

Singee a songee sick a pence,
Pockee muchee lye;
Dozen two time blackee bird
Cookee in e pie.
When him cutee topside
Birdee bobbery sing;
Himee tinkee nicey dish
Setee foree King!
Kingee in a talkee loom
Countee muchee money;
Queeny in e kitchee,
Chew-chee breadee honey.
Servant galo shakee,
Hangee washee clothes;
Cho-chop comee blackie bird,
Nipee off her nose!
—*Anonymous.*

[9432]
THE AMATEUR FLUTE

Hear the fluter with his flute,
Silver flute!
Oh, what a world of wailing is
awakened by its toot!
How it demi-semi quavers
On the maddened air of night!
And defieth all endeavors
To escape the sound or sigh
Of the flute, flute, flute,
With its tootle, tootle, toot;
With reiterated tooteling of exas-
perating toots,
The long protracted tootelings of
agonizing toots

Of the flute, flute, flute, flute,
Flute, flute, flute,
And the wheezings and the spit-
tings of its toots.
Should he get that other flute,
Golden flute,
Oh, what a deeper anguish will his
presence institoot!
How his eyes to heaven he 'll
raise,
As he plays,
All the days!
How he 'll stop up on our ways
With its praise!
And the people—oh, the peo-
ple,
That don't live up in the
steeple,
But inhabit Christian parlors
Where he visiteth and plays,
Where he plays, plays, plays
In the cruellest of ways,
And thinks we ought to listen,
And expects us to be mute,
Who would rather have the ear-
ache
Than the music of his flute,
Of his flute, flute, flute,
And the tootings of his toot,
Of the toots wherewith he tooteleth
its agonizing toot,
Of the flute, flewt, fluit, floot,
Phlute, phlewt, phlewght,
And the tootle, tootle, tooting of
its toot.
—*Anonymous.*
(*After Poe*)

[9433]
A PSALM OF LIFE

Life is real, life is earnest,
And the shell is not its pen—
"Egg thou art, and egg remainest"
Was not spoken of the hen.

Art is long and Time is fleeting,
Be our bills then sharpened well,

And not like muffled drums be
    beating
On the inside of the shell.

In the world's broad field of battle,
In the great barnyard of life,
Be not like those lazy cattle!
Be a rooster in the strife!

Lives of roosters all remind us,
We can make our lives sublime,
And when roasted, leave behind us,
Hen tracks on the sands of time.

Hen tracks that perhaps another
Chicken drooping in the rain,
Some forlorn and henpecked brother,
When he sees, shall crow again.
—*Attributed to Oliver Wendell
Holmes.*

(*After Longfellow*)

[9434]
EXCELSIOR
The swampy State of Illinois
    Contained a greenish sort of boy,
    Who read with idiotic joy—
        "Excelsior!"

He tarried not to eat or drink,
    But put a flag of lightish pink,
    And traced on it in violet ink—
        Excelsior!

Though what he meant by that
    absurd,
    Uncouth, and stupid, senseless
    word,
    Has not been placed upon rec-
    ord—
        Excelsior!

The characters were very plain,
    In German text, yet he was fain
    With greater clearness to ex-
    plain—
        Excelsior!

And so he ran, this stupid wight,
    And hollered out with all his
    might,
    (As to a person out of sight)—
        "Excelsior!"

And everybody thought the lad
    Within an ace of being mad,
    Who cried in accents stern and
    sad—
        "Excelsior!"

"Come to my arms," the maiden
    cried;
    The youth grinned sheepishly,
    and sighed,
    And then appropriately replied—
        "Excelsior!"

The evening sun is in the sky,
    But still the creature mounts on
    high
    And shouts (nor gives a reason
    why)
        "Excelsior!"

And ere he gains the topmost crag
    His feeble legs begin to lag;
    Unsteadily he holds the flag—
        Excelsior!

Now P. C. Nab is on his track!
    He puts him in an empty sack,
    And brings him home upon his
    back—
        Excelsior!

Nab takes him to a lumber store,
    They toss him in and lock the
    door,
    Which only makes him bawl the
    more—
        "Excelsior!"
            —*Anonymous.*
        (*After Longfellow*)

[9435]
I KISSED YOU

(Parody on *You Kissed Me,* by
Josephine Slocum Hunt)

I kissed you, I own, but I did not
   suppose
That you, through the papers, the
   deed would disclose,
Like free-loving cats, when on
   ridgepoles they meet—
When their squalls of "You kissed
   me!" disturb the whole street.

I kissed you. The impulse as suddenly came
As that cold-looking cloud is trans-
   formed into flame;
My act was the lightning that
   glances and thrills,
And yours the loud thunder that
   blabs to the hills.

I kissed you. As kissed the poor
   Cyprian boy
In dreams, his Diana, so cold and so
   coy,
And foolishly fancied—encircling
   your charms—
A maid—not a matchbox—was
   clasped in my arms.

I kissed you. The zephyr on tiptoe
   passed by,
The moon with a kerchief cloud
   hid her soft eye;
From the bough that swayed o'er
   us, all silvered with dew,
With a half-smothered titter the
   katydid flew.

I kissed you. All nature to counterfeit sleep,
Half promised our secret so sacred
   to keep;
No ubiquitous press correspondent
   peeped through
The leaves. I was "interviewed"
   only by you.
I kissed you. Then, scared at my
   boldness, I deemed

You had fainted, or else you would
   surely have screamed:
But no, you not only all censure
   forebore,
But, like Oliver Twist, are now asking for "more."

I kissed you. All others may do it
   who choose,
But I to repeat the performance re-
   fuse.
On your lips I will never again
   print a smack;
By the press or by note, you may
   send that one back.
I kissed you. The poetess Sappho
   of old,
Like you, was so warm that her
   Pharon grew cold;
So she ended her love and her life
   in a pet—
I presume there are equal facilities
   yet.

—*Anonymous.*

[9436]
TOWSER SHALL BE
TIED TONIGHT

(A parody on *Curfew Must Not
Ring Tonight*)

Slow the Kansas sun was setting
   o'er the wheat fields far away,
Streaking all the air with cobwebs,
   at the close of one hot day;
And its last rays kissed the fore-
   heads of a man and maiden fair,
He with whiskers short and frowzy,
   she with red and glist'ning hair;
He with jaws shut stern and silent,
   she with lips all cold and white,
Struggled to keep back the murmur, "Towser must be tied tonight."

"Papa," slowly spoke the maiden,
   "I am almost seventeen,
And I've got a real lover, though
   he's rather young and green;

But he has a horse and buggy, and
a cow and thirty hens,
Boys that start out poor, dear Papa,
make the best of honest men;
But if Towser sees and bites him,
fills his heart with sudden fright,
He will never come again, pa:
Towser must be tied tonight."

"Daughter," firmly spoke the
farmer (every word pierced her
young heart
Like a carving knife through
chicken, as it hunts a tender
part),
"I've a patch of early melons, two
of them are ripe today;
Towser must be loose to watch
them, or they'll all be stole away.
I have hoed them late and early,
(in dim morn and evening light)
Now they're grown I must not lose
them. Towser won't be tied tonight."

Then the old man ambled forward,
opened wide the kennel door;
Towser bounded forth to meet him,
as he oft had done before.
And the farmer stooped and loosed
him from the dog chain short
and stout;
To himself he softly chuckled:
"Bessie's fellow must look out."
But the maiden at the window saw
the cruel teeth show white;
In an undertone she murmured,
"Towser must be tied tonight."

Then the maiden's brow grew
thoughtful, and her breath came
short and thick,
Till she spied the family clothesline, and she whispered, "That's
the trick."
From the kitchen door she glided
with a plate of meat and bread;

Towser wagged his tail in greeting,
knowing well he would be fed.
In his well-worn leather collar tied
she then the clothesline tight,
All the time her white lips saying:
"Towser must be tied tonight."

"There, old doggie," spoke the
maiden. "You can watch the
melon patch,
But the front gate's free and open
when John Henry lifts the latch,
For the clothesline tight is fastened
to the harvest-apple tree.
You can run and watch the melons,
but the front gate you can't see."
Then her glad ears heard a buggy,
and her eyes grew big and bright,
While her young heart said in gladness: "Towser, dog, is tied tonight."

Up the patch the young man saun-
ters, with his eye and cheek
aglow,
For he loves the red-haired maiden,
and he aims to tell her so.
Bessie's roguish little brothers, in a
fit of boyish glee,
Had untied the slender clothesline
from the harvest-apple tree;
Then old Towser heard the footsteps, raised his bristle, fixed for
fight.
"Bark away," the maiden whispers.
"Towser, you are tied tonight."

Then old Towser bounded forward,
past the open kitchen door;
Bessie screamed and quickly followed, but John Henry's gone
before.
Down the path he speeds most
quickly, for old Towser sets the
pace,
And the maiden, close behind
them, shows them she is in the
race.

Then the clothesline—can she get
it? And her eyes grow big and
bright,
As she springs and grasps it firmly.
"Towser shall be tied tonight."

Oftentimes a little minute forms
the destiny of men.
You can change the fate of nations
by the stroke of one small pen.
Towser made one last long effort,
caught John Henry by his pants,
But John Henry kept on running,
for he thought that his last
chance;
But the maiden held on firmly, and
the rope was drawn up tight;
But old Towser kept the garments,
for he was not tied tonight.

Then the old man hears the racket;
with long stride he soon is there,
While John Henry and the maiden,
crouching, for the worst prepare.
At his feet John tells his story,
shows his clothing soiled and
torn;
And his face, so sad and pleading,
yet so white and scared and
worn,
Touched the old man's heart with
pity, filled his eyes with misty
light;
"Take her, boy, and make her
happy. Towser shall be tied tonight."

—*Anonymous.*

[9437]
HOME SWEET HOME
You over there, young man with
the guide-book, red-bound, cov-
ered flexibly with red linen,
Come here, I want to talk with you;
I, Walt, the Manhattanese, citi-
zen of these States, call you. . . .
Come with me, I will give you a
good time; I will give you all the

Venice you want, and most of
the Paris.
I, Walt, call to you. I am all on
deck! Come and loaf with me!
Let me tote you around by the
elbow and show you things.
You listen to my ophicleide!
Home! . . .

The brown-stone house; the father
coming home worried from a
bad day's business; the wife
meets him in the marble-paved
vestibule; she throws her arms
about him; she presses him close
to her; she looks him full in the
face with affectionate eyes; the
frown from his brow disappear-
ing.

Darling, she says, *Johnny has fallen
down and cut his head; the cook
is going away, and the boiler
leaks.* . . .
The sound of the husband's voice
on the still night air—he is singing: *We won't go home till morning!*—the wife arising toward
the wood-shed hastily going,
stealthily entering, the voice all
the time coming nearer, inebriate, chantant,
The wood-shed; the club behind
the door of the wood-shed; the
wife annexing the club; the husband appearing, always inebriate,
chantant;
The husband passing the door of
the wood-shed; the club over his
head, now with his head in contact; the sudden cessation of the
song; the temperance pledge
signed the next morning; the
benediction of peace over the
domestic foyer temporarily resting.

—*Henry Cuyler Bunner.*
(*After Walt Whitman*)

[9438]
TREES

I think that I shall never see
A hazard rougher than a tree—
A tree o'er which my ball must fly
If on the green it is to lie;
A tree which stands that green to
    guard,
And makes the shot extremely
    hard;
A tree whose leafy arms extend
To kill the mashie shot I send;
A tree that stands in silence there
While angry golfers rave and swear.
Niblicks were made for fools like
    me,
Who cannot even miss a tree.
                    —*Anonymous.*
                    (*After Kilmer*)

[9439]
THE DAY IS DONE

The day is done, and darkness
    From the wing of night is loosed,
As a feather is wafted downward
    From a chicken going to roost.

I see the lights of the baker
    Gleam through the rain and mist,
And a feeling of sadness comes o'er
    me
    That I cannot well resist:

A feeling of sadness and longing
    That is not like being sick,
And resembles sorrow only
    As a brickbat resembles a brick.

Come, get for me some supper,—
    A good and regular meal—
That shall soothe this restless feel-
    ing,
    And banish the pain I feel.

Not from the pastry bakers,
    Not from the shops for cake;
I wouldn't give a farthing
    For all that they can make.

For, like the soup at dinner,
    Such things would but suggest
Some dishes more substantial,
    And tonight I want the best.

Go to some honest butcher,
    Whose beef is fresh and nice,
As any they have in the city,
    And get a liberal slice.

Such things through days of labor
    And nights devoid of ease
For sad and desperate feelings
    Are wonderful remedies.

They have an astonishing power
    To aid and reinforce,
And come like the "finally, breth-
    ren,"
    That follows a long discourse.

Then get me a tender sirloin
    From off the bench or hook,
And lend to its sterling goodness
    The science of the cook.

And the night shall be filled with
    comfort,
    And the cares with which it be-
    gun
Shall fold up their tents like In-
    dians,
    And silently cut and run.
                    —*Phoebe Cary.*
                    (*After Longfellow*)

[9440]
THE BACHELOR'S
SOLILOQUY

To wed, or not to wed? That is
    the question
Whether 't is nobler in the mind to
    suffer
The pangs and arrows of outra-
    geous love
Or to take arms against the power-
    ful flame
And by oppressing quench it.

To wed—to marry—
And by a marriage say we end
The heartache and the thousand
painful shocks
Love makes us heir to—'t is a con-
summation
Devoutly to be wished! to wed—
to marry—
Perchance a scold! aye, there's the
rub!
For in that wedded life what ills
may come
When we have shuffled off our
single state
Must give us serious pause. There's
the respect
That makes us Bachelors a numer-
ous race.
For who would bear the dull un-
social hours
Spent by unmarried men, cheered
by no smile
To sit like hermit at a lonely board
In silence? Who would bear the
cruel gibes
With which the Bachelor is daily
teased
When he himself might end such
heart-felt griefs
By wedding some fair maid? Oh,
who would live
Yawning and staring sadly in the
fire
Till celibacy becomes a weary life
But that the dread of something
after wedlock
That undiscovered state from
whose strong chains
No captive can get free) puzzles
the will
And makes us rather choose those
ills we have
Than fly to others which a wife
may bring.
Thus caution doth make Bachelors
of us all.

And thus our natural taste for matrimony
Is sicklied o'er with the pale cast
of thought.
And love adventures of great pith
and moment
With this regard their currents turn
away
And lose the name of Wedlock.
                    —*Anonymous.*
                    (*After Shakespeare*)

[9441]
TOOTHACHE

To have it out or not. That is the
question—
Whether 't is better for the jaws
to suffer
The pangs and torments of an aching tooth
Or to take steel against a host of
troubles,
And, by extracting them, end
them? To pull—to tug!—
No more: and by a tug to say we
end
The toothache and a thousand natural ills
The jaw is heir to. 'T is a consum-
mation
Devoutly to be wished! To pull—
to tug!—
To tug—perchance to break! Ay,
there's the rub,
For in that wrench what agonies
may come
When we have half dislodged the
stubborn foe,
Must give us pause. There's the
respect
That makes an aching tooth of so
long life.
For who would bear the whips and
stings of pain,
The old wife's nostrum, dentist's
contumely;

The pangs of hope deferred, kind
  sleep's delay;
The insolence of pity, and the
  spurns,
That patient sickness of the healthy
  takes,
When he himself might his quietus
  make
For one poor shilling? Who would
  fardels bear,
To groan and sink beneath a load
  of pain?—
But that the dread of something
  lodged within
The linen-twisted forceps, from
  whose pangs
No jaw at ease returns, puzzles the
  will,
And makes it rather bear the ills
  it has
Than fly to others that it knows not
  of.
Thus dentists do make cowards of
  us all,
And thus the native hue of resolution
Is sicklied o'er with the pale cast
  of fear;
And many a one, whose courage
  seeks the door,
With this regard his footsteps turns
  away,
Scared at the name of dentist.
                    —*Anonymous.*
                 (*After Shakespeare*)

[9442]
LET DOGS DELIGHT—

A little maid, her hair in braid (up-
  braided by her mother),
Began to bait and pesticate her
  little baby brother.
The mother rare seized daughter's
  hair, upbraiding her with vigor:
"Commit no mayhem, child, I pray,
  until the lad is bigger!

(Chorus)
"Don't pinch your baby brother,
  Don't punch him in the eye;
Don't poke him in the ear-drums—
  It will make our darling cry.
Don't butt his little ribs in,
  Don't carve him with that knife;
If you whittle his arms and legs off,
  He'll look different, all his life!"

The little maid at once obeyed her
  mother's tender chiding.
"It's what I ought to do," she
  thought, "and thus escape a hiding."
She caught his ears, to still his
  fears, and did some quick explaining,
How she'd refrain from causing
  pain—concluding by refraining:

(Chorus)
"Won't pinch my baby brother,
  Won't punch him in the nose,
Won't poke him in the eyeballs—
  It's annoying. I suppose.
Won't twist his little spine out,
  Won't carve him with that knife;
If I whittle his head and trunk off,
  He'd look different, all his life!"
                    —*Alvin Winston,*
                    (*Popular Songs*)

LIMERICKS

[9443]
There was a young man named
  Achilles,
Whose wrongs always gave him the
  willies.
  So he sulked in his tent
  Like a half-witted gent—
Say, wasn't them heroes the sillies!
                    —*E. M. Robinson.*

[9444]

There once was an old anaconda
Who began to read "Daniel De-
  ronda,"
  Which he calmly explained
  Was all that remained
Of a book agent from Tonawanda.

[9445]

There was a young girl of Australia
Who went to a dance as a dahlia.
  When the petals uncurled,
  It revealed to the world,
That the dress, as a dress, was a
  failure!

[9446]

There was a young lady named
  Banker,
Who slept while the ship lay at
  anchor;
  She awoke in dismay
  When she heard the mate say:
"Now hoist up the topsheet, and
  spanker!"

[9447]

A certain young fellow named Bee-
  bee
Wished to wed with a lady named
  Phoebe.
  "But," he said, "I must see
  What the clerical fee
Be before Phoebe be Phoebe Bee-
  bee."

[9448]

The Reverend Henry Ward Beecher
Called a hen a most elegant crea-
  ture.
  The hen, pleased with that,
  Laid an egg in his hat,
And thus did the hen reward
  Beecher!
        —*Oliver Wendell Holmes.*

[9449]

There was an old man of St. Bees,
Who was stung in the arm by a
  wasp.

When asked, "Does it hurt?"
He replied, "No, it doesn't,
I'm so glad that it wasn't a hornet."
        —*W. S. Gilbert.*

[9450]

There was a princess of Bengal,
Whose mouth was exceedingly
  small;
  Said she, "It would be
  More easy for me
To do without eating at all!"
        —*Walter Parke.*

[9451]

There was a young man so be-
  nighted,
He never knew when he was
  slighted;
  He would go to a party,
  And eat just as hearty,
As if he'd been really invited.

[9452]

There once was a person of Benin,
Who wore clothes not fit to be seen
  in;
  When told that he should n't,
  He replied, "Gumscrumrudent!"
A word of inscrutable meanin'.
        —*Cosmo Monkhouse.*

[9453]

There was an old soldier of Bister
Went walking one day with his sis-
  ter,
  When a cow at one poke
  Tossed her into an oak,
Before the old gentleman missed
  her.

[9454]

There was a young man who was
  bitten
By twenty-two cats and a kitten;
  Sighed he, "It is clear
  My finish is near;
No matter; I'll die like a Briton!"
        —*Walter Parke.*

[9455]

A young person of Tomahawk Bluff
Carried pistols to make him look
    tough.
    When they asked, "Do you
    chew?"
    He replied, "Yeth, I do,
I'm a wegular wetch of a wough."

[9456]

A maiden at college, Miss Breeze,
Weighed down by B. A.'s and Lit.
    D.'s,
    Collapsed from the strain.
    Said her doctor, "It's plain
You are killing yourself—by de-
grees!"

[9457]

There once were some learned
    M. D.'s,
Who captured some germs of dis-
    ease,
    And infected a train
    Which, without causing pain,
Allowed one to catch it with ease.

[9458]

There was a young woman named
    Bright,
Whose speed was much faster than
    light.
    She set out one day,
    In a relative way,
And returned on the previous night.

[9459]

A painter, who lived in Great
    Britain,
Interrupted two girls with their
    knitain,
    He said, with a sigh,
    "That park bench—well I
Just painted it, right where you're
    sitain."

[9460]

There was a young man of Cadiz
Who inferred that life is what it is;

For he early had learnt,
If it were what it weren't,
It could not be that which it is.

[9461]

A canner, exceedingly canny,
One morning remarked to his
    granny,
    "A canner can can
    Anything that he can;
But a canner can't can a can, can
    he?"

            —Carolyn Wells.

[9462]

Here's to the chigger,
The bug that's no bigger
Than the point of an undersized
    pin;
But the welt that he raises
Sure itches like blazes,
And that's where the rub comes in!

[9463]

There was a young man from the
    city,
Who met what he thought was a
    kitty;
    He gave it a pat,
    And said, "Nice little cat!"
And they buried his clothes, out of
    pity.

[9464]

A silly young man from the Clyde
In a funeral procession was spied;
    When asked, "Who is dead?"
    He giggled and said,
"I don't know; I just came for the
    ride."

[9465]

There was a young lady of Cork,
Whose Pa made a fortune in pork;
    He bought for his daughter
    A tutor who taught her
To balance green peas on her fork.

[9466]
A maiden who walked on the Corso
Displayed overmuch of her torso.
　A crowd soon collected
　But no one objected,
And some were in favor of more so.

[9467]
A certain young gourmet of Crediton
Took some *pâté de foie gras* and spread it on
　A chocolate biscuit,
　Then murmured, "I'll risk it."
His tomb bears the date that he said it on.
　　　—*Rev. Charles Inge.*

[9468]
There was a young lady of Diss,
Who said, "Now I think skating bliss!"
　This no more will she state,
　For a wheel off her skate
Made her finish up something like this!

[9469]
Endeavored a lady in No. Dak.
To picture a bear with a kodak.
　The button she pressed—
　The bear did the rest;
The lady stopped running in So. Dak.

[9470]
There was an old man who said, "Do
Tell me how I'm to add two and two?
　I'm not very sure
　That it does n't make four—
But I fear that is almost too few."

[9471]
A Mouse in her room woke Miss Dowd.
She was frightened—it must be allowed.

Soon a happy thot hit her—
To scare off the critter,
She sat up in bed and meowed.

[9472]
There was a dear lady of Eden,
Who on apples was quite fond of feedin';
　She gave one to Adam,
　Who said, "Thank you, Madam,"
And then both skedaddled from Eden.

[9473]
Said an envious, erudite ermine,
"There's one thing I cannot determine:
　When a dame wears my coat,
　She's a person of note;
When I wear it, I'm called only vermin!"

[9474]
There was an old maiden from Fife,
Who had never been kissed in her life;
　Along came a cat;
　And she said, "I'll kiss that!"
But the cat answered, "Not on your life!"

[9475]
A canny young fisher named Fisher
Once fished from the edge of a fissure.
　A fish with a grin
　Pulled the fisherman in—
Now they're fishing the fissure for Fisher.

[9476]
A newspaper man named Fling
Could make "copy" from any old thing.
　But the copy he wrote
　Of a five dollar note
Was so good he is now in Sing Sing.

[9477]

A flea and a fly in a flue,
Were imprisoned, so what could
    they do?
  Said the fly, "let us flee!"
  "Let us fly!" said the flea,
And they flew through a flaw in the
    flue.

[9478]

A tutor who tooted a flute
Tried to teach two young tooters to
    toot.
  Said the two to the tutor,
  "Is it harder to toot, or
To tutor two tutors to toot?"
              —Carolyn Wells.

[9479]

A major, with wonderful force,
Called out in Hyde Park for a horse.
  All the flowers looked round,
  But no horse could be found;
So he just rhododendron, of course.

[9480]

There once was a young man named
    Gale
Who cherished the thought of a sail.
  He boarded a yacht,
  But remained on his cot
Except when he hung o'er the rail.

[9481]

There was an old girl of Genoa,
I blush when I think what Iowa.
  She's gone now to rest,
  Which I think's for the best
Otherwise I would borrow Samoa.

[9482]

There once was a dear little gnome
Who arrived at his home on Cape
    Nome.
  Said his mother, "My dear,
  Do you know where you are?"
He looked up and answered, "Why,
    no'm!"

[9483]

There was an old fellow named
    Green,
Who grew so abnormally lean,
  And flat, and compressed,
  That his back touched his chest,
And sideways he couldn't be seen.

[9484]

There once was a lady from Guam
Who said, "Now the ocean's so
    calm
  I will swim, for a lark."
  She encountered a shark.
Let us now sing the 90th psalm.

[9485]

There was a young fellow named
    Hall,
Who fell in the spring in the fall;
  'Twould have been a sad thing
  If he'd died in the spring,
But he didn't—he died in the fall.

[9486]

There was a young girl of West
    Ham,
Who hastily jumped on a tram.
  When she had embarked,
  The conductor remarked,
"Your fare." "Well, they do say I
    am."

[9487]

There was a young lady named
    Hannah,
Who slipped on a peel of banana.
  As she lay on her side,
  More stars she espied
Than there are in the Star-Spangled
    Banner.

[9488]

The Sultan got sore on his harem,
And invented a scheme for to scare
    'em;
  He caught him a mouse
  Which he loosed in the house
(The confusion is called harem-
    scarem.)

[9489]

There was an old man in a hearse,
Who murmured, "This might have
　　been worse;
　　Of course the expense
　　Is simply immense,
But it doesn't come out of my
　　purse."

[9490]

To a person arriving in Heaven
Said St. Peter, "We dine sharp at
　　seven,
　　Then breakfast's at eight—
　　Never mind if you're late,
And there's biscuits and milk at
　　eleven."

[9491]

The poor benighted Hindoo,
He does the best he kin do;
　　He sticks to his caste
　　From first to last,
And for clothes he makes his skin
　　do.

[9492]

There was an old man who said,
　　"How
Shall I flee from this horrible cow?
　　I will sit on this stile
　　And continue to smile,
Which may soften the heart of that
　　cow."

[9493]

There once was a man who said,
　　"How
Shall I manage to carry my cow?
　　For if I should ask it
　　To get in my basket,
'T would make such a terrible row."

[9494]

A nifty young flapper named Jane
While walking was caught in the
　　rain.

She ran—almost flew,
Her complexion did, too,
And she reached home exceedingly
　　plain.

[9495]

"There's a train at 4:04," said Miss
　　Jenny.
"Four tickets I'll take; have you
　　any?"
　　Said the man at the door,
　　"Not four for 4:04,
For four for 4:04 is too many."

[9496]

There's a lady in Kalamazoo
Who bites all her oysters in two;
　　She has a misgiving,
　　Should any be living,
They'd raise such a hullabaloo.
　　　　　　　—William Bellamy.

[9497]

There was a young lady of Kent,
Whose nose was most awfully bent.
　　She followed her nose
　　One day, I suppose—
And no one knows which way she
　　went.

[9498]

There was a young lady of Kent
Who said that she knew what it
　　meant
　　When men asked her to dine,
　　Gave her cocktails and wine.
She knew what it meant—but she
　　went!

[9499]

A scrupulous priest of Kildare,
Used to pay a rude peasant to swear,
　　Who would paint the air blue,
　　For an hour or two,
While his reverence wrestled in
　　prayer.

[9500]
There once were two cats in Kilkenny,
And each cat thought that there was
  one cat too many,
And they scratched and they fit and
  they tore and they bit,
'Til instead of two cats—there
  weren't any.

[9501]
There once was a bonnie Scotch
  laddie
Who said, as he put on his plaidie,
  "I've just had a dish
  Of unco' guid fish."
What had he had? Had he had had-
  die?

[9502]
There was a young salesman of
  Leeds
Rashly swallowed six packets of
  seeds.
  In a month, silly ass,
  He was covered with grass,
And he couldn't sit down for the
  weeds.

[9503]
'Tis said, woman loves not her
  lover
So much as she loves his love of her;
  Then loves she her lover
  For love of her lover,
Or love of her love of her lover?

[9504]
There was a young sailor of Lyd,
Who loved a fair Japanese kid;
  When it came to good-bye,
  They were eager but shy,
So they put up a sunshade and—
  did.

[9505]
There once was an old man of
  Lyme.
Who married three wives at a time:

When asked, "Why a third?"
He replied, "One's absurd!
And bigamy, sir, is a crime."
  —*Cosmo Monkhouse.*

[9506]
There was a young lady of Lynn,
Who was so excessively thin,
  That when she assayed
  To drink lemonade
She slipped through the straw and
  fell in.

[9507]
There was a gay damsel of Lynn,
Whose waist was so charmingly
  thin,
  The dressmaker needed
  A microscope—she did—
To fit this slim person of Lynn.

[9508]
A bookworm of Kennebunk, Me.
Found pleasure in reading Monte.
  He also read Poe
  And Daniel Defoe,
But the telephone book caused him
  pe.

[9509]
A grain broker in New Boston,
  Maine,
Said, "That market gives me a pain;
  I can hardly bear it,
  To bull—I don't dare it,
For it's going against the grain."

[9510]
There was a young lady named
  Maud,
A very deceptive young fraud;
  She never was able
  To eat at the table,
But out in the pantry—O Lord!

[9511]
There was a young lady named May,
Who read a love story each day.
  "It's funny," she said,
  When at last she was wed;
"I didn't think life was this way."

[9512]

There was an old man named Mc-
Guire,
Lost his footing and fell in the mire.
   Said a bland passer-by,
   "Cheer up, never say die!"
"But I must," he replied, "I'm a
dyer!"

[9513]

A trader, named Sandy McVeetie,
With a Cannibal King made a
treaty.
   In a glass of gin-sling
   Mac toasted the king;
And then the king—toasted Mc-
Veetie.
                         —F. J. Smith.

[9514]

There was a young lady of Milton,
Who was highly disgusted with Stil-
ton;
   When offered a bite,
   She said, "Not a mite!"
That suggestive young lady of Mil-
ton.

[9515]

A man and his lady-love, Min,
Skated out where the ice was quite
thin.
   Had a quarrel, no doubt,
   For I hear they fell out:
What a blessing they didn't fall in!

[9516]

There was a young lady of Munich,
Whose appetite simply was unich.
   "There's nothing like a food,"
   She contentedly cooed,
As she let out three tucks in her
tunich.

[9517]

There was an old man of Nantucket
Who kept all his cash in a bucket;
   But his daughter, named Nan,
   Ran away with a man—
And as for the bucket, Nantucket.

[9518]

There was a young person named
Ned
Who dined before going to bed,
   On lobster and ham
   And salad and jam,
And when he awoke he was dead

[9519]

There once was a girl of New York
Whose body was lighter than cork;
   She had to be fed
   For six weeks upon lead,
Before she went out for a walk.
                   —Cosmo Monkhouse.

[9520]

There was a young lady from Niger,
Who smiled as she rode on a tiger.
   They came back from the ride
   With the lady inside,
And the smile on the face of the
tiger.

[9521]

There is a wild tale about Nona,
Who wore a black chiffon kimona.
   Don't think for a minute
   There's anything in it—
That is, anything except Nona.

[9522]

There was a young man from Os-
tend,
Who vowed he'd hold out to the
end;
   But when half way over
   From Calais to Dover,
He did what he didn't intend.

[9523]

There once was a guy named
Othello,
A dark, disagreeable fellow;
   After croaking his wife,
   Then he took his own life—
That bird wasn't black, he was yel-
low!
                   —E. M. Robinson.

[9524]
There was a young fellow named
Paul,
Who went to a fancy dress ball;
They say, just for fun
He dressed up like a bun,
And was "et" by a dog in the hall.

[9525]
A wonderful bird is the pelican!
His mouth can hold more than his
belican.
He can take in his beak
Enough food for a week—
I'm darned if I know how the heli-
can!
—Dixon Merritt.

[9526]
There was a young lady named Per-
kins,
Who just simply doted on gherkins.
In spite of advice,
She ate so much spice,
That she pickled her internal work-
in's.

[9527]
There was an old sculptor named
Phidias,
Whose knowledge of Art was in-
vidious.
He carved Aphrodite
Without any nightie—
Which startled the purely fastidi-
ous.

[9528]
Here lies a young salesman named
Phipps,
Who married on one of his trips,
A widow named Block,
Then died of the shock,
When he saw there were six little
chips.

[9529]
There once was a pious young
priest,
Who lived almost wholly on yeast;

"For," he said, "it is plain
We must all rise again,
And I want to get started, at least."

[9530]
There was a young man of Quebec
Who was frozen in snow to his
neck.
When asked, "Are you friz?"
He replied, "Yes, I is,
But we don't call this cold in Que-
bec."
—Rudyard Kipling.

[9531]
There was a young lady named
Ruth,
Who had a great passion for truth.
She said she would die
Before she would lie,
And she died in the prime of her
youth.

[9532]
The bottle of perfume that Willie
sent
Was highly displeasing to Millicent;
Her thanks were so cold
They quarreled, I'm told,
Through that silly scent Willie sent
Millicent.

[9533]
There was a young person called
Smarty,
Who sent out his cards for a party;
So exclusive and few
Were the friends that he knew
That no one was present but
Smarty.

[9534]
There once was a maiden of Siam,
Who said to her lover, young Kiam,
"If you kiss me, of course
You will have to use force—
But God knows you're stronger than
I am."

[9535]

A railway official of Skewe
Met an engine one day that he
    knew.
    Though he smiled and he bowed,
    That engine was proud;
It cut him—it cut him in two!

[9536]

You might marry Miss Prunella
    Smart,
Whose hair is so scant it won't
    part;
    She's cross-eyed and thin
    And as ugly as sin,
But then, she has such a good heart!

[9537]

A father once said to his son,
"The next time you get off a pun,
    Go out in the yard
    And kick yourself—hard!
And then I'll begin when you're
    done."

[9538]

There once was a lonesome, lorn
    spinster,
And luck had for years been ag'inst
    her;
    When a man came to burgle
    She shrieked, with a gurgle,
"Stop thief, while I call in a min'-
    ster!"

[9539]

As a beauty I am not a star,
There are others more handsome
    by far;
    But my face—I don't mind it,
    For I am behind it;
It's the people in front that I jar.
                —Anthony Euwer.

[9540]

There was a young fellow named
    Strauss
Who got on a terrible sauss;

He had the right key
In the keyhole, you see,
But the keyhole was in the wrong
    hauss.

[9541]

There was a young woman named
    Sue,
Who wanted to catch the 2:02;
    Said the trainman, "Don't hurry
    Or flurry or worry;
It's a minute or two to 2:02."

[9542]

Said a gentle old man, "I suppose
I ought not to wear my best clothes.
    But what can I do?
    I have only two,
And these are no better than those."

[9543]

Said a monk, as he swung by his
    tail,
To the little monks, female and
    male:
    "From your offspring, my dears,
    In a few million years,
May evolve a professor in Yale!"

[9544]

There was a young person named
    Tate,
Who went out to dine at 8:08;
    But I will not relate
    What that person named Tate
And his tête-à-tête ate at 8:08.

[9545]

Augustus Fitzgibbons Moran
Fell in love with Maria McCann.
    With a yell and a whoop
    He cleared the front stoop
Just ahead of her papa's brogan.

[9546]

There was an old man of Tobago,
Who lived on rice, gruel, and sago;
    Till, much to his bliss,
    His physician said this:
"To a leg, sir, of mutton, you may
    go!"

She twirled round and round, till
    she sank underground,
Which distressed all the people of
    Chertsey.

[9571]

There was an Old Person of Ches-
    ter,
Whom several small children did
    pester;
They threw some large stones,
    which broke most of his bones,
And displeased that Old Person of
    Chester.

[9572]

There was a Young Lady whose
    chin
Resembled the point of a pin;
So she had it made sharp, and pur-
    chased a harp,
And played several tunes with her
    chin.

[9573]

There was an Old Man of Coblenz,
The length of whose legs was im-
    mense;
He went with one prance from Tur-
    key to France,
That surprising Old Man of Co-
    blenz.

[9574]

There was an old person of Deal,
Who in walking used only his heel;
When they said, "Tell us why?" he
    made no reply,
That mysterious old person of Deal.

[9575]

There was an Old Person of Dover,
Who rushed through a field of blue
    clover;
But some very large Bees stung his
    nose and his knees,
So he very soon went back to
    Dover.

[9576]

There was a Young Lady whose
    eyes
Were unique as to color and size;
When she opened them wide, peo-
    ple all turned aside,
And started away in surprise.

[9577]

There was an old person of Fife,
Who was greatly disgusted with
    life;
They sang him a ballad, and fed
    him on salad,
Which cured that old person of
    Fife.

[9578]

There was an old lady of France,
Who taught little ducklings to
    dance;
When she said, "Tick-a-tack!" they
    only said, "Quack!"
Which grieved that old lady of
    France.

[9579]

There was an Old Man of the
    Hague,
Whose ideas were excessively
    vague;
He built a balloon to examine the
    moon,
The deluded Old Man of the
    Hague.

[9580]

There was an Old Man of Cape
    Horn,
Who wished he had never been
    born;
So he sat on a Chair till he died of
    despair,
That dolorous Man of Cape Horn.

[9581]

There was an Old Person of Hurst,
Who drank when he was not
    athirst;

When they said, "You'll grow fatter!" he answered "What matter?"
That globular Person of Hurst.

[9582]
There was an Old Man who said,
"Hush!
I perceive a young bird in this
bush!"
    When they said, "Is it small?"
    He replied, "Not at all;
It is four times as big as the bush!"

[9583]
There was an Old Man of Kam-
schatka
Who possessed a remarkably fat
Cur;
    His gait and his waddle
    Were held as a model!
To all the fat dogs in Kamschatka.

[9584]
There was an Old Man of Leghorn,
The smallest that ever was born;
    But quickly snapped up he
    Was once by a Puppy,
Who devoured that Old Man of
Leghorn.

[9585]
There was an Old Man of Molda-
via,
Who had the most curious behavior;
For while he was able, he slept on
a table,
That funny Old Man of Moldavia.

[9586]
There was an Old Man of the
North,
Who fell into a basin of broth;
But a laudable cook fished him out
with a hook,
Which saved that Old Man of the
North.

[9587]
There was an Old Man with a nose,
Who said, "If you choose to sup-
pose
That my nose is too long, you are
certainly wrong!"
That remarkable Man with a nose.

[9588]
There was a Young Lady whose
nose
Was so long that it reached to her
toes;
So she hired an Old Lady, whose
conduct was steady,
To carry that wonderful nose.

[9589]
There was an Old Man of Peru,
Who never knew what he should
do;
So he tore off his hair, and behaved
like a bear,
That intrinsic Old Man of Peru.

[9590]
There was an Old Man of Peru,
Who watched his wife making a
stew;
But once, by mistake, in a stove she
did bake
That unfortunate Man of Peru.

[9591]
There was a young person in pink,
Who called out for something to
drink;
But they said, "O my daughter,
there's nothing but water!"
Which vexed that young person in
pink.

[9592]
There was an Old Person of Sparta,
Who had twenty-five sons and one
"darter";
He fed them on Snails, and weighed
them in scales,
That wonderful Person of Sparta.

[9593]
There was a Young Lady of Swe-
den,
Who went by the slow train to Wee-
don;
When they cried, "Weedon Sta-
tion!" she made no observation,
But thought she should go back to
Sweden.

[9594]
There was an Old Man who sup-
posed
That the street door was partially
closed;
But some very large Rats
Ate his coats and his hats,
While that futile Old Gentleman
dozed.

[9595]
There was an old man of Thermo-
pylae,
Who never did anything properly;
But they said, "If you choose
To boil eggs in your shoes,
You shall never remain in Ther-
mopylae."

[9596]
There was an Old Man in a tree,
Who was horribly bored by a Bee;
When they said, "Does it buzz?"
he replied, "Yes, it does!
It's a regular brute of a Bee."

[9597]
There was an old person of Ware
Who rode on the back of a bear;
When they said, "Does it trot?"
He said: "Certainly not,
It's a Moppsikon Floppsikon bear."

[9598]
There was a Young Lady of Welling,
Whose praise all the world was
a-telling;

She played on the harp, and caught
several Carp,
That accomplished Young Lady of
Welling.

[9599]
There was an old person of Wick,
Who said, "Tick-a-Tick, Tick-a-
Tick,
Chickabee, Chickabaw,"
And he said nothing more,
This laconic old person of Wick.

[9600]
There was an old person of Woking,
Whose mind was percerse and pro-
voking;
He sate on a rail,
With his head in a pail,
That illusive old person of Woking.

[9601]
There was an Old Man of the Isles,
Whose face was pervaded with
smiles;
He sang "High dum diddle," and
played on the fiddle,
That amiable Man of the Isles.

[9602]
There was an Old Person of Cadiz,
Who was always polite to all ladies;
But in handing his daughter, he fell
into the water,
Which drowned that Old Person of
Cadiz.

[9603]
There was an Old Person of Buda,
Whose conduct grew ruder and
ruder,
Till at last with a hammer they
silenced his clamor,
By smashing that Person of Buda.

[9604]
There was an Old Man of Columbia,
Who was thirsty, and called out for
some beer;

But they brought it quite hot, in a
small copper pot,
Which disgusted that man of Columbia.

[9605]
There was an Old Person of Chili,
Whose conduct was painful and
silly;
He sate on the stairs, eating apples
and pears,
That imprudent Old Person of
Chili.

[9606]
There was an Old Person of Tring,
Who embellished his nose with a
ring;
He gazed at the moon every eve-
ning in June,
That ecstatic Old Person of Tring.

[9607]
There was a Young Lady of Bute,
Who played on a silver-gilt flute;
She played several jigs to her
Uncle's white Pigs:
That amusing Young Lady of Bute.

[9608]
There was a Young Lady of Nor-
way,
Who casually sat in a doorway;
When the door squeezed her flat,
she exclaimed, "What of that?"
This courageous Young Lady of
Norway.

[9609]
There was an Old Person whose
habits
Induced him to feed upon Rabbits;
When he'd eaten eighteen, he
turned perfectly green,
Upon which he relinquished those
habits.

[9610]
There was an Old Man of Corfu,
Who never knew what he should
do;

So he rushed up and down, till the
sun made him brown,
That bewildered Old Man of Corfu.

[9611]
There was a Young Lady of Lucca,
Whose lovers completely forsook
her;
She ran up a tree, and said "Fiddle-
de-dee!"
Which embarrassed the people of
Lucca.

[9612]
There was an Old Man of th'
Abruzzi,
So blind that he could n't his foot
see;
When they said, "That's your toe,"
he replied, "Is it so?"
That doubtful Old Man of th'
Abruzzi.

[9613]
There was an Old Person of Philoe,
Whose conduct was scroobious and
wily;
He rushed up a Palm when the
weather was calm,
And observed all the ruins of Phi-
loe.

[9614]
There was a Young Lady of Troy,
Whom several large flies did annoy;
Some she killed with a thump, some
she drowned at the pump.
And some she took with her to
Troy.

[9615]
There was an Old Man of Bohemia,
Whose daughter was christened
Euphemia;
But one day, to his grief, she mar-
ried a thief,
Which grieved that Old Man of
Bohemia.

[9616]

There was a Young Lady of Hull,
Who was chased by a virulent Bull;
But she seized on a spade, and
    called out, "Who's afraid?"
Which distracted that virulent Bull.

[9617]

There was an Old Person of Bangor,
Whose face was distorted with anger;
He tore off his boots, and subsisted
    on roots,
That borascible Person of Bangor.

[9618]

There was a Young Lady of Russia,
Who screamed so that no one could
    hush her;
Her screams were extreme,—no one
    heard such a scream
As was screamed by that Lady of
    Russia.

[9619]

There was an Old Lady whose folly
Induced her to sit in a holly;
Whereon, by a thorn her dress being torn,
She quickly became melancholy.

[9620]

There was an Old Man on whose
    nose
Most birds of the air could repose;
But they all flew away at the closing
    of day,
Which relieved that Old Man and
    his nose.

[9621]

There was a Young Lady of Parma,
Whose conduct grew calmer and
    calmer:
When they said, "Are you dumb?"
    she merely said, "Hum!"
That provoking Young Lady of
Parma.

[9622]

There was an Old Person of Mold,
Who shrank from sensations of
    cold;
So he purchased some muffs, some
    furs, and some fluffs,
And wrapped himself well from
    the cold.

[9623]

There was a Young Lady of Wales,
Who caught a large Fish without
    scales;
When she lifted her hook, she exclaimed, "Only look!"
That ecstatic Young Lady of Wales.

[9624]

There was an Old Man who said,
    "Well!
Will *nobody* answer this bell?
I have pulled day and night, till my
    hair has grown white,
But nobody answers this bell!"

[9625]

There was an Old Person of Ems
Who casually fell in the Thames;
And when he was found, they said
    he was drowned,
That unlucky Old Person of Ems.

[9626]

There was a Young Lady of Clare,
Who was madly pursued by a Bear;
When she found she was tired, she
    abruptly expired,
That unfortunate Lady of Clare.

[9627]

There was an old person of Pinner,
As thin as a lath, if not thinner;
They dressed him in white, and
    roll'd him up tight.
That elastic old person of Pinner.

[9628]

There was an old person of Bromley,
Whose ways were not cheerful or
    comely;

He sate in the dust, eating spiders
and crust,
That unpleasing old person of
Bromley.

[9629]
There was an Old Lady of Prague,
Whose language was horribly vague;
When they said, "Are these caps?"
she answered, "Perhaps!"
That oracular Lady of Prague.

[9630]
There was an old person of Pisa,
Whose daughters did nothing to
please her;
She dressed them in gray, and
banged them all day,
Round the walls of the city of Pisa.

[9631]
There was an old man of Dumblane,
Who greatly resembled a crane;
But they said, "Is it wrong, since
your legs are so long,
To request you won't stay in
Dumblane?"

[9632]
There was a young lady of Green-
wich,
Whose garments were border'd
with Spinach;
But a large spotty Calf bit her shawl
quite in half,
Which alarmed that young lady of
Greenwich.

[9633]
There was an old person of Hyde,
Who walked by the shore with his
bride,
Till a Crab who came near fill'd
their bosoms with fear,
And they said, "Would we'd never
left Hyde!"

[9634]
There was an old man of Thames
Ditton,
Who called out for something to
sit on;
But they brought him a hat, and
said, "Sit upon that,
You abruptious old man of Thames
Ditton!"

[9635]
There was an old man, who when
little
Fell casually into a kettle;
But, growing too stout, he could
never get out,
So he passed all his life in that
kettle.

[9636]
There was an old person of Jodd,
Whose ways were perplexing and
odd;
She purchased a whistle, and sate
on a thistle,
And squeaked to the people of
Jodd.

LITTLE WILLIES

[9637]
Willie, hitting at a ball,
Lined one down the school-house
hall.
Through his door came Dr. Hill.
Several teeth are missing still!

[9638]
Willie's cute as cute can be!
Beneath his brother, only three,
He lit a stick of dynamite.
Now Bubby's simply out of sight!

[9639]
Willie, writing on the bed,
Spilt some ink on Mother's spread.
"Ma," he said, when she came back,
"It will dye a lovely black!"

[9640]
Little Willie, on his bike,
Through the village took a hike.
Mrs. Thompson blocked the walk;
She will live, but still can't talk.

[9641]
Willie and two other brats
Licked up all the Rough-on-rats.
Father said, when mother cried,
"Never mind—they'll die outside."

[9642]
Willie, cunning little creature,
Blew a bean and hit his teacher.
"Most impressive was the scene,"
Willie said, "when bean met bean."

[9643]
Willie saw some dynamite,
Couldn't understand it quite.
Curiosity never pays;
It rained Willie seven days.

[9644]
Willie fell down the elevator—
Wasn't found till six days later.
Then the neighbors sniffed, "Gee
    whizz!
What a spoiled child Willie is!"

[9645]
Willie in the cauldron fell;
See the grief on mother's brow!
Mother loved her darling well;
Darling's quite hard-boiled by now.

[9646]
Making toast at the fireside
Nurse fell in the fire and died;
And, what makes it ten times worse,
All the toast was burned with
    Nurse.

[9647]
Willie, at a passing gent,
Threw a batch of fresh cement
Crying, "Wait until you dry,
Then you'll be a real hard guy."

[9648]
My darling wife was always glum.
I drowned her in a cask of rum,
And so made sure that she would
    stay
In better spirits night and day.

[9649]
Willie, with a thirst for gore,
Nailed the baby to the door.
Mother said, with humor quaint,
"Willie, dear, don't spoil the paint."

[9650]
Little Will, with father's gun,
Punctured grandma, just for fun.
Mother frowned at the merry lad:
It was the last shell father had.

[9651]
Willie split the baby's head,
To see if brains were gray or red.
Mother, troubled, said to father,
"Children are an awful bother!"

[9652]
Little Willie, raising hob,
Laughed at Mother's boyish-bob.
Mercy! how his trousers tingled
When he, later on, was shingled!

[9653]
Willie, as the fire burned low,
Gave it a terrific blow.
Grandpa's beard got in the draft;
Dear me, how the firemen laughed!

[9654]
Pity now poor Mary Ames,
Blinded by her brother James.
Red hot nails in her eyes he
    poked—
I never saw Mary more provoked!

[9655]
Willie caught his sister, Nan,
Being hugged by her young man.
"Gee!" said Willie, with a cackle,
"That guy don't know how to
    tackle."

[9656]
Little Willie, with a rock,
Beaned the cuckoo in the clock.
Father said: "Why don't it tick?"
Willie said: "The bird is sick."

[9657]
Little Willie lit a rocket
Which his Pa had in his pocket.
Next day he told Cousin Dan,
"Papa is a traveling man."

[9658]
Little Willie, in bows and sashes,
Fell in the fire and got burned to
    ashes.
In the winter, when the weather is
    chilly,
No one likes to poke up Willie.

[9659]
Little Willie, home from school,
Where he'd learned the Golden
    Rule,
Said, "If I eat up this cake
Sis won't have a stomach-ache."

[9660]
Father heard his children scream,
So he threw them in the stream,
Saying, as he drowned the third,
"Children should be seen, not
    heard!"

[9661]
Little Willie hung his sister;
She was dead before we missed her.
"Willie's always up to tricks.
Ain't he cute? He's only six!"

[9662]
Willie's Pa, I grieve to state,
Came home from the lodge quite
    late.
When he tottered Willie cried,
"Look at Papa! He's off-side!"

[9663]
Father, I regret to state,
Cut his daughters up for bait.
We miss them when it's time to
    dine,
But father's fish taste simply fine.

[9664]
Willie, whose ideas are strange,
Put some pin-wheels in the range.
When Cook lit the gas next day,
BOY! it was some grand display! ! !

[9665]
Willie, when the wind was strong,
Flew his kite all morning long.
"My," he cried, "just see it dance!
The tail's made out of Papa's pants."

[9666]
Willie poisoned his father's tea;
Father died in agony.
Mother came, and looked quite
    vexed:
"Really, Will," she said, "what
    next?"

[9667]
Willie on the railroad track—
The engine gave a squeal.
The engineer just took a spade
And scraped him off the wheel.

[9668]
Willie playfully poisoned his Ma;
When he'd finished his work,
He remarked with a smirk,
"This will cause quite a family jar."

[9669]
Father nailed his darling wife
Fast against the parquet flooring.
He was loath to take her life,
But he *had* to stop her snoring.

[9670]
Into the cistern little Willie
Pushed his little sister Lily.
Mother couldn't find our daughter:
Now we sterilize our water.

[9671]
Baby sat on the window-seat.
Mary pushed Baby into the street.
Baby's brains splattered the "arey,"
And mother smiled "Tchk, tchk!"
    at Mary.

WESTERN DIALECT VERSE

[9672]
LITTLE BREECHES

I don't go much on religion,
    I never ain't had no show;
But I've got a middlin' tight grip,
        sir,
    On the handful o' things I know.
I don't pan out on the prophets
    An' free-will, an' that sort of
        thing—
But I b'lieve in God an' the angels,
    Ever sence one night last spring.

I come to town with some turnips,
    An' my little Gabe come along—
No four-year-old in the county
    Could beat him for pretty an'
        strong,
Peart an' chipper an' sassy.
    Always ready to swear and
        fight,—
And I'd l'arnt him to chaw ter-
        backer,
    Jest to keep his milk-teeth white.

The snow come down like a blanket
    As I passed by Taggart's store;
I went in for a jug of molasses
    An' left the team at the door.
They scared at something an'
        started—
    I heard one little squall,
An' hell-to-split over the prairie
    Went team, Little Breeches an'
        all.

Hell-to-split over the prairie!
    I was almost froze with skeer;
But we rousted up some torches,
    And s'arched for 'em far an' near.
At last we struck horse an' wagon,
    Snowed under a soft white
        mound,
Upsot, dead beat—but of little Gabe
    No hide nor hair was found.

And here all hope soured on me,
    Of my feller-critter's aid—
I jest flopped down on my marrow-
        bones
    Crotch-deep in the snow, an'
        prayed. . . .
By this, the torches wuz played out,
    An' me an' Isrul Parr
Went off for some wood to a sheep-
        fold
    That he said wuz somewhar thar.

We found it at last, an' a little shed
    Where they shut up the lamb at
        night.
We looked in an' seen them hud-
        dled thar,
    So warm an' sleepy an' white;
An' THAR sot Little Breeches an'
    chirped,
    As peart as ever you see,
"I wants a chaw of terbacky,
    An' that's what's the matter of
        me."

How did he git that? Angels
    He could never have walked in
        that storm.
They jest scooped down an' toted
        him
    To whar it was safe an' warm.
An' I think that savin' a little child,
    An' bringin' him to his own,
Is a derned sight better business
    Than loafin' around The Throne.
            —John Hay.

[9673]
JIM BLUDSO

Wall, no! I can't tell whar he lives,
    Bekase he don't live, you see;
Leastways, he's got out of the habit
    Of livin' like you an' me.
Whar have you been for the last
        three year
    That you haven't heard folks tell
How Jimmy Bludso passed in his
        checks
    The night of the Prairie Belle?

He weren't no saint—them en-
    gineers
Is pretty much all alike—
One wife in Natchez-under-the-Hill
And another one here in Pike;
A keerless man in his talk was Jim,
    And an awkward hand in a row,
But he never flunked, an' he never
    lied—
I reckon he never knowed how.

And this was all the religion he
    had—
To treat his engine well;
Never be passed on the river;
To mind the pilot's bell;
And if ever the Prairie Belle took
    fire,
A thousand times he swore
He'd hold her nozzle agin the bank
Till the last soul got ashore.

All the boats has their day on the
    Mississip',
And her day come at last,—
The Movastar was a better boat,
But the Belle she *wouldn't* be
    passed.
And so she come tearin' along that
    night—
The oldest craft on the line—
With a nigger squat on her safety-
    valve,
And her furnace crammed, rosin'
    an' pine.

The fire bust out as she cl'ared the
    bar
And burnt a hole in the night,
And quick as a flash she turned,
    an' made
For that willer-bank on the right.
There was runnin' an' cursin', but
    Jim yelled out
Over all the infernal roar,
"I'll hold her nozzle agin the bank
Till the last galoot's ashore!"

Through the hot black breath of
    the burnin' boat
Jim Bludso's voice was heard,
An' they all had trust in his cus-
    sedness,
And knowed he would keep his
    word.
And, sure's you're born, they all got
    off
Afore the smokestack fell,—
And Bludso's ghost went up alone
In the smoke of the Prairie Belle.

He weren't no saint—but at Jedg-
    ment
I'd run my chance with Jim,
'Longside of some pious gentlemen
That wouldn't shook hands with
    him.
He seen his duty, a dead-sure
    thing,—
And went for it, thar an' then:
And Christ ain't a-goin' to be too
    hard
On a man that died for me.
                        —*John Hay.*

[9674]
THE MYSTERY OF GILGAL
The darkest, strangest mystery
I ever read, or heern, or see,
Is 'long of a drink at Taggart's
    Hall—
Tom Taggart's or Gilgal.

I've heern the tale a thousand ways,
But never could get through the
    maze
That hangs around that queer day's
    doin's;
But I'll tell the yarn to youans.

Tom Taggart stood behind his bar,
The time was fall, the skies was
    far,
The neighbors round the counter
    drawed,
And calmly drinked and jawed.

At last come Colonel Blood of Pike,
And old Jedge Phinn, permiscus-
  like,
And each, as he meandered in,
Remarked, "A whiskey-skin."

Tom mixed the beverage full and
  far,
And slammed it, smoking, on the
  bar.
Some says three fingers, some says
  two—
I'll leave the choice to you.

Phinn to the drink put forth his
  hand;
Blood drawed his knife, with accent
  bland,
"I ax yer parding, Mister Phinn—
Jest drap that whiskey-skin!"
No man high-toneder could be
  found
Than old Jedge Phinn the country
  round.
Says he, "Young man, the tribe of
  Phinns
Knows their own whiskey-skins!"

He went for his 'leven-inch bowie-
  knife:
"I tries to foller a Christian life;
But I'll drap a slice of liver or two,
My bloomin' shrub, with you."

They carved in a way that all
  admired,
Tell Blood drawed iron at last, and
  fired.
It took Seth Bludso 'twixt the eyes,
Which caused him great surprise.

Then coats went off, and all went
  in;
Shots and bad language swelled the
  din;
The short, sharp bark of Derringers,
Like bull-pups, cheered the furse.

They piled the stiffs outside the
  door;
They made, I reckon, a cord or
  more.
Girls went that winter, as a rule,
Alone to spellin'-school.

I've s'arched in vain, from Dan to
  Beer-
Sheba, to make this mystery clear:
But I end with hit as I did begin:
"WHO GOT THE WHISKEY-
  SKIN?"
                    —John Hay.

[9675]
CLARE DE KITCHEN
In old Kentuck in de arternoon,
We sweep de floor wid a bran-new
  broom,
And arter that we form a ring,
And dis de song dat we do sing:
Oh! Clare de kitchen, old folks,
  young folks,
Clare de kitchen, old folks, young
  folks,
Old Virginny never tire.

I went to de creek, I couldn't git
  across,
I'd nobody wid me but an old blind
  horse;
But Old Jim Crow came riding by,
Says he, old fellow, your horse will
  die.
          So clare, &c.

My horse fell down upon de spot,
Says he, "Don't you see his eyes is
  sot?"
So I took out my knife and off wid
  his skin,
And when he comes to life I'll ride
  him agin.
          So clare, &c.

A jay bird sot on a hickory limb,
He wink'd at me and I winked at
  him;

I pick'd up a stone and I hit his
shin,
Says he, "You better not do dat
agin."
       So clare, &c.

A bullfrog dress'd in soger's close
Went in de field to shoot some
crows;
De crows smell powder and fly
away,
De bullfrog mighty mad dat day.
       So clare, &c.

Den down I went wid Cato Moore,
To see de steamboat come ashore;
Every man for himself, so I pick'd
up a trunk;
"Leff off," said de captain, "or I
burn you wid a chunk."
       And clare, &c.

I hab a sweetheart in dis town,
She wears a yellow striped gown,
And when she walks de streets
around,
De hollow of her foot make a hole
in de ground.
       Now clare, &c.

Dis love is a ticklish ting, you
know,
It makes a body feel all over so;
I put de question to coal-black Rose,
She as black as ten of spades, and
got a lubby flat nose.
       So clare, &c.

Go away says she wid your cow-
cumber shin,
If you come here agin I stick you
wid a pin;
So I turn on my heel and I bid her
good-bye,
And arter I was gone she began to
cry.
       So clare, &c.

So now I'se up and off, you see,
To take a julep sangaree;
I'll sit upon a tater hill,
And eat a little whippoorwill.
       So clare, &c.

I wish I was back in Old Kentuck,
For since I left it I had no luck;
De gals so proud dey wont eat
mush,
And w'en you go to court 'em dey
say, "O hush."
       So clare, &c.
       —*Anonymous.*

[9676]
THE TEXAS COWBOY

I'm the howler from the prairies of
the West.
If you want to die with terror, look
at me!
I'm chain-lightning—if I ain't, may
I be blessed
I'm the snorter of the boundless
peerarie.

(*Chorus*)

He's a killer and a hater;
He's the great annihilator;
He's the terror of the boundless
peerarie.

I'm the snoozer from the upper
trail;
I'm the reveler in murder and in
gore;
I can bust more Pullman coaches
on the rail
Than any one who's worked the
job before.

(*Chorus*)

He's a snorter and a snoozer,
He's the great trunk-line abuser;
He's the man who put the sleeper
off the rail.

I'm the double-jawed hyena from
the West;
I'm the blazing bloody blizzard of
the States;
I'm the celebrated slugger, I'm the
pest;
I can snatch a man baldheaded
while he waits.

(*Chorus*)

He's the double-jawed hyena,
He's the villain of the scena;
He can snatch a man baldheaded
while he waits.
—*Anonymous.*

[9677]
CASEY JONES

Come all you rounders if you want
to hear
A story 'bout a brave engineer;
Casey Jones, that was the rounder's
name,
On a heavy eight-wheeler he rode
to fame.

Casey Jones mounted to the cabin,
Casey Jones, throttle in his hand,
Casey Jones mounted to the cabin,
Took his farewell journey to the
Promised Land.

The caller called Casey about half
past four;
He kissed his wife good-by at the
station door,
He climbed into the cabin, with his
orders in hand,
For his farewell journey to the
Promised Land.

He tore through South Memphis
yards on the fly,
He heard the fireman say to him,
"You've got a white eye";
All the switchmen knew by the
engine's moan
That the man at the throttle was
Casey Jones.

The rain had been a-fallin' for five
or six weeks,
The railroad track was nothin' but
the bed of a creek;
They rated him down to a thirty-
mile gait,
Threw the south-bound mail about
eight hours late.

Fireman said, "Casey, you're runnin' too fast,
You run the block board the last
station you passed."
Casey says, "Yeah, I b'lieve we'll
make it though,
For the engine's steamin' better
than I ever know."

Casey says, "Fireman, don't you
fret,
Keep knockin' at the fire-door,
don't give up yet;
I'm going to run the engine till
she leaves the rail,
Or make it on time with the
southern mail."

Around the curve he saw it comin'
down the dump—
Two locomotives, an' they're bound
to bump!
The fireman hollered, "It is just
ahead—
We might jump an' make it, but
we'll all be dead."

'Twas round this curve he spied a
passenger train;
He roused the fireman, caused the
bell to ring;
The fireman jumped off, but Casey
Jones stayed on—
He's a good engineer, but he's
dead an' gone.

Casey says before he died,
"There are two more lines that I
wish I'd tried."

The fireman said, "What can they
be?"
"Why the Southern Pacific an' the
Sante Fe."

Poor Casey Jones he was all right,
He stuck by his duty both day an'
night,
They loved to hear the whistle an'
ring of No. 3,
As he rode into Memphis on the
old I. C.

Headaches and heartaches and all
kinds of pain
Are not apart from a railroad train;
Tales that are earnest, noble, and
grand,
Belong to the life of a railroad man.

Casey Jones mounted to the cabin,
Casey Jones, throttle in his hand,
Casey Jones mounted to the cabin
Took his farewell journey to the
Promised Land.
—*Anonymous.*

[9678]
PLAIN LANGUAGE FROM
TRUTHFUL JAMES
(Popularly known as *The Heathen
Chinee*)

Which I wish to remark—
And my language is plain—
That for ways that are dark
And for trick that are vain,
The heathen Chinee is peculiar:
Which the same I would rise to
explain.

Ah Sin was his name;
And I shall not deny
In regard to the same
What that name might imply;
But his smile it was pensive and
childlike,
As I frequent remarked to Bill
Nye.

It was August the third,
And quite soft was the skies,
Which it might be inferred
That Ah Sin was likewise;
Yet he played it that day upon
William
And me in a way I despise.

Which we had a small game,
And Ah Sin took a hand:
It was euchre. The same
He did not understand,
But he smiled, as he sat by the table,
With the smile that was childlike
and bland.

Yet the cards they were stocked
In a way that I grieve,
And my feelings were shocked
At the state of Nye's sleeve,
Which was stuffed full of aces and
bowers,
And the same with intent to
deceive.

But the hands that were played
By that heathen Chinee,
And the points that he made,
Were quite frightful to see,—
Till at last he put down a right
bower,
Which the same Nye had dealt
unto me.

Then I looked up at Nye,
And he gazed upon me;
And he rose with a sigh,
And said, "Can this be?
We are ruined by Chinese cheap
labor,"—
And he went for that heathen
Chinee.

In the scene that ensued
I did not take a hand,
But the floor it was strewed,
Like the leaves on the strand,

With the cards that Ah Sin had
been hiding
In the game "he did not understand."

In his sleeves, which were long,
He had twenty-four packs,—
Which was coming it strong,
Yet I state but the facts;
And we found on his nails, which
were taper,
What is frequent in tapers,—that's
wax.

Which is why I remark,—
And my language is plain,—
That for ways that are dark,
And for tricks that are vain,
The heathen Chinese is peculiar,—
Which the same I am free to
maintain.
—*Bret Harte.*

[9679]
THE GOVERNMENT CLAIM

Frank Baker's my name, and a
bachelor I am.
I'm keepin' old batch on an elegant
plan,
You'll find me out West in the
county of Lane,
A-starving to death on a government claim.

My house is constructed of natural
soil,
The walls are erected according to
Hoyle,
The roof has no pitch, but is level
and plain,
And I never get wet till it happens
to rain.

Hurrah for Lane county, the land
of the free,
The home of the grasshopper, bedbug, and flea,
I'll holler its praises, and sing of
its fame,

While starving to death on a government claim.

How happy I am as I crawl into
bed,
The rattlesnake rattling a tune at
my head,
While the gay little centipede, void
of all fear,
Crawls over my neck, and into my
ear;
And the gay little bedbug so cheerful and bright
He keeps me a-going two-thirds
of the night.

My clothes are all ragged, my language is rough,
My bread is case-hardened, both
solid and tough.
The dough it is scattered all over
the room,
And the floor would get scared at
the sight of a broom.

The dishes are scattered all over
the bed,
All covered with sorghum and government bread,
Still I have a good time, and I live
at my ease,
On common sop sorghum, an'
bacon an' cheese.

How happy I am on my government
claim,
I've nothing to lose, I've nothing
to gain,
I've nothing to eat and I've nothing
to wear,
And nothing from nothing is honest and fair.

Oh, here I am safe, so here I will
stay,
My money's all gone, and I can't
get away,

There's nothing to make a man
  hard and profane,
Like starving to death on a government claim.

Now come on to Lane county,
  there's room for you all,
Where the wind never ceases, and
  the rains never fall,
Come join in our chorus to sing for
  its fame
You sinners that're stuck on your
  government claim.

Now hurrah for Lane county, where
  the blizzards arise,
The wind never ceases, and the
  moon never rise,
Where the sun never sets, but it
  always remains,
Till it burns us all out on our
  government claims.

Now, don't get discouraged, you
  poor hungry men,
You're all just as free as the pig
  in the pen,
You stick to your homestead, and
  battle the fleas,
And look to your Maker to send
  you a breeze.

Now, all you poor sinners, I hope
  you will stay
And chew the hard rag till you're
  toothless and gray,
But as for myself, I'll no longer
  remain,
To starve like a dog on a government claim.

Farewell to Lane county, farewell
  to the West,
I'll travel back east to the girl I
  love best,

I'll stop at Missouri to get me a
  wife,
Then live on corn dodgers, the rest
  of my life!
  —*Anonymous.*

[9680]
THE OLD CHISHOLM TRAIL
Come along boys, and listen to my
  tale,
I'll tell you of my troubles on the
  old Chisholm trail,

I started up the trail October
  twenty-third,
I started up the trail with the 2-U
  herd.

O, a ten dollar hoss an' a forty dollar
  saddle—
And I'm goin' to punchin' Texas
  cattle.
I woke up one mornin' on the old
  Chisholm trail.

Rope in my hand and a cow by the
  tail.
I'm up in the mornin' afore daylight
And afore I sleep the moon shines
  bright.

Old Ben Bolt was a blamed good
  boss,
But he'd go see the girls on a sore-
  backed hoss.

Old Ben Bolt was a fine old man
And you'd know there was whiskey
  wherever he'd land.

My hoss throwed me off at the creek
  called Mud,
My hoss throwed me off round the
  2-U herd.

Last time I saw him he was goin'
  'cross the level
A-kickin' up his heels and a-runnin'
  like the devil.

It's cloudy in the West, a-lookin'
    like rain,
And my damned old slicker's in
    the wagon again.

Crippled my hoss, I don't know
    how,
Ropin' at the horns of a 2-U cow.

We hit Caldwell and we hit her
    on the fly,
We bedded down the cattle on the
    hill close by.

No chaps, no slicker, and it's pour-
    ing down rain,
And I swear by God I'll never
    night-herd again.

Feet in the stirrups and seat in the
    saddle,
I hung and rastled with them long-
    horn cattle.

Last night I was on guard and the
    leader broke the ranks,
I hit my horse down the shoulders
    and I spurred him in the flanks.

The wind commenced to blow, and
    the rain began to fall,
Hit looked, by grab, like we wuz
    goin' to lose 'em all.

I jumped in the saddle and grabbed
    holt the horn,
Best blamed cow-puncher ever was
    born.

I popped my foot in the stirrup an'
    gave a little yell,
The tail cattle broke loose and the
    leaders went to hell.

I don't give a damn if they never
    do stop;
I'll ride as long as an eight-day
    clock.

Foot in the stirrup an' hand on the
    horn,
Best damned cowboy ever was born.

I herded and I hollered and I done
    very well,
Till the boss said, "Boys, just let
    'em go to hell."

Stray in the herd and the boss said
    kill it,
So I shot him in the rump with the
    handle of the skillet.

We rounded 'em up and put 'em
    on the cars,
And that was the last of the old
    Two Bars.

Oh, it's bacon an' beans 'most every
    day,—
I'd as soon be a-eatin' prairie hay.

I'm on my best hoss and I'm goin'
    at a run,
I'm the quickest shootin' cowboy
    that ever pulled a gun.

I went to the wagon to get my roll
To come back to Texas, dadburn
    my soul.

I went to the boss to draw my roll,
He had figured it out I was nine
    dollars in the hole.

I'll sell my outfit just as soon as I
    can,
I won't punch cattle for no damned
    man.

Goin' back to town to draw my
    money.
Goin' back home to see my honey.

With my knees in the saddle and
    my seat in the sky,
I'll quit punchin' cows in the sweet
    by an' by.

—*Anonymous.*

MISCELLANEOUS DIALECT VERSE

[9681]
DER WRECK

T'vas der goot shkiff Hezberus
Dot paddled on der pond,
And dere vas she, der skibber's gal,
Of whom he vas zo fond.

Green vos her eyes, like sour grabes
Her sheeks I can't devine,
Her boozum brown, like bretzel
shticks,
Her voice a gentle chime.

Mit dhen foot pibe der skibber sat,
Wrabbed in his schmelly koad,
Und watched his daughter koff und
shneeze
Ven schmoke got down her
throad.

Den up und spoke der paddle man,
"Look mashter, let'z turn pack
A shwan lives 'ere, der peebles zay,
Vot likes to peck und hack."

"So let'z turn pack, mein mashter
dear,
Und from t'iz trip refrain."
Der skibber schmoked his dhen foot
pibe,
Und shmiled mit grim dishdain.

Den near und near der shkiff did
got
To vare dot schwan hung out,
Until at last, mit tellesgobe,
Dey shpied its head und shnout.

Vel, down it schwam und shmote
der shkiff
Mit all its might und main,
Und made it shump dree times its
length,
Und den shump back again.

"Come 'ere mein kin," der skibber
said,
"Und do not tremble zo,

Mein pibe can kill der biggest
schwan
From Kiel to Kokomo."

He wrabbed her in his old pea koad,
His joy, his life, his soul,
Den mid a piece of herring shkin,
He lashed her to a pole.

"Oh, dad, I hear der dinner bell!
I fear ve are der grub."
"Vel, hold yer tongue, dear Mary
Ann,
Und let me shteer der tub."

"Oh, dad, I see dot schwan again!
He'll eat both you und me."
But papa's teeth dey clonkled zo,
Der pibe fell in der zee.

Den Mary Ann she glasped her
hands,
Und through her runnie nose
She shtart to say she vas O. K.,
But den der runny froze.

Und dare, through rain und hurry-
cane,
Und through der schleet und
schnow,
Der maiden prayed und begged der
schwan
To take der pibe und go.

But no! He shwam up to der wreck,
Und den der fun began,
He knocked der scaredies from der
deck,
All but shweet Mary Ann.

He whacked und shmacked der
Hezberus,
Mit it he mopped der place,
Und as he clopped it good und hard,
He shpied her kindly vace.

Und den der schwan felt like a
goose,
He vatched shweet Mary go,
Und as like lead der shkiff vent
down,
He called: "I luff you zo."

At prake of day in Zeider Bay
Shweet Mary Ann vas found,
Her form vas cold un frozen shtiff,
Und to der pibe vas bound. . . .
*Von hand vas cross her empty form
Zerene und calm she lay;
For she vas gone vare she'll t'aw
out,
Und vare you'll all go zomeday.
(Revised by Gerald F. Lieberman,
from a 19th century
uncredited version.)*

[9682]
DER CHARGE
(On der occasion ven a gent van-
dered in a zaloon during a Dutch
vedding und invited der guests to
"valk up." Der nople manner in
vich dey oxcepted his kind offer zug-
gested dis boem.)

A few shdteps, a few shdeps
A few shdteps onvard,
Ub to der bar
Valked a few hundredt.

All dose who vas seated
Got ub vhen dey heard
Dhey vas to be treated;
Ub—ub 'fore a man could vink,
Ub to der bar dey schlink
Quick like der eye der wink
Valked a few hundredt.

Lager in front of dhem,
Lager in back of dhem,
Schnapps all 'round of dhem
Boobled und schbarkled
Lo! to duty dey harckled.

Blenty dhey drank of it
Dhey voodn't leave a bit—
Looking for more to git,
Bellies dhey tunderedt,
Nople few hundredt.

Shone all dheir noses ret,
Conking each odher's het,
Such dhirst you neffer met,
"How could dhey hold it?"
Der bargeeber vondered.

Ober der bar dhey vent,
Right down der shtuff dhey sent;
(Out ducked der buyin' gent)
Dhen to dheir homes dhey vent—
But not all dose few hundredt.

Vhen such a dhing vas done?
Beer-schnapps down by der ton?
All records zundered.
Honor der Dutch Prigade
Oooh, vhat a charge dhey made.
Who saw der tab vas Baid?
(All der vorld vondered.)
Not *dot* few hundredt!
*(Revised by Gerald F. Lieberman,
from a 19th century
uncredited version.)*

[9683]
ZWEI LAGER
Der night vas dark as anydhing,
Ven at mine door two vellers ring,
Und say, ven asked who vas dhere,
"Get up and git"—and den dey
schvear—
"Zwei lager."

I says, "Tis late; shust leaf mine
house,
Und don'd be making such a
towse!"
Dey only lauft me in der face,
Und say, "Pring oudt, 'Old Schweiz-
erkase,'
"Zwei lager."

I dold dem dot der bier vas oudt;
But dose two shaps set oup a shout,
Und said no matter if 'twas late,
Dot dey moost haf "put on der
schlate
"Zwei lager."

"Oh! go avay, dot is goot boys,"
Mine moder says, "und schtop der
noise";
But sdill dem vellers yelt avay,
Und dis vos all dot dey would say:
"Zwei lager."

"Vot makes you gome," mine
   taughter said,
"Ven beoples all vas in der ped?
Shust gome to-morrow ven you're
   dhry."
But dem two plackguards sdill did
   cry,
                        "Zwei lager."

"Vot means you by sooch dings as
   dese?
I go and calls for der boleese,"
Says Schneigelfritz, who lifs next
   door;
Dey only yelt more as pefore,
                        "Zwei lager."

"You shust holdt on a leedle vhile,"
Says mine Katrina mit a schmile;
"I vix dose shaps, you pet my life,
So dey don'd ask off Pfeiffer's vife
                        "Zwei lager."

Den righd avay she got a peese
Of goot und schtrong old Limburg
   sheese,
And put it shoost outside der door;
And den we didn't hear no more
                        "Zwei lager."
                   —*Charles F. Adams.*

[9684]
DER NIGHD
PEHIND GRISDMAS
T'vas der nighd pehind Grisdmas,
   und all ofer der haus,
Non von beobles vas schleeping,
   nix cum arous;
Der sdockings was vlung all ofer
   dose shair,
Vor hopes auf Saind Niglebus nix
   longer was dhere;
Yimmie und Shakey vos tossing
   widoud schleeb in der ped,
Der leeddle stomacks vas pig, wid
   gandy, nuds, bies und pread;
Vhile mudder mit a nighd-dress,
   und I mit a gown,

Vas yust make up our minds ve
   vouldn't lie down;
Ven vrom der haus oud py der
   lawn ve heard somedings glatter;
Like der tuyfle I shumped ofer my
   shair, vonderin' vat vas der mad-
   der;
Righd avay qvick to der vinder I
   vent, with a vlash,
Grapped avay der plinds und shofed
   up der sash;
Der moon, all undressed, vas foolin'
   arount pelow,
Und saying, "Gife us a rest, mid
   dat, 'Peautiful Schnow' ";
Vot vas dose, so heellup me, vidch
   to dhese eyes appear,
But a horse und scleigh, poth vas
   oldt und qveer,
Trawin' a leddle old bump-packed
   rooster, solemn und schlow,
Dot I know'd mit a glance 'tvas
   oldt Toctor Prough,
Vrom der outdside I drew my head,
   und durnt arounts,
Ven up-stairs comes dat rooster, mit
   dwo or dhree pounts;
He vas all govered up mit a pig ofer-
   goat make long pelow,
Und der vhisker py hes schin vas
   vhide like der schnow;
He spoke nix a vord, but straighd
   vend to work,
Velt all der bulses, und gife der
   arms a jerk;
Und making hes vingers on der top
   of hes nose,
Vith a vag auf hes ear, to der schim-
   mney he goes;
"Von sboonful auf oil, oldt vomans,
   und sum prandy
Scheese dose nuts, raisins, bies, und
   der gandy;
Dose dender schmalt stomach vill
   never digest
Der schveets vot dhey got—pretzels
   und krout vas der feast;"

Bud dat makes nodhings out, dose
advise mit vrents,
Ven der gustom auf Grisdmas der
odher vay dends;
All vater und mutters, oldt Schanty
Claws too,
Vas oxceeding plind; vell, a good-
mighd to you;
Und dhese vords ve heard him ex-
claim, as he trofe oud auf sighd,
"Dose bully bics, raisins, und gandy
makes tocdor's bill all righd."
—*Sidney W. Wetmore.*

[9685]
LOOKOUT MOUNTAIN, 1863—
BEUTELSBACH, 1880

"Yah, I shpeaks English a leetle;
berhaps you shpeaks petter der
German."
"No, not a word."—"Vell den,
Meester, it hardt for to be con-
derstandt.
I vos drei yahr in your coontry, I
fights in der army mit Sherman—
Twentiet Illinois Infantry—fightin'
Joe Hooker's commandt."

"So you've seen service in Georgia—
a veteran, eh?"—"Vel, I tell you
Shust how it vos. I vent ofer in
sixty, und landt in Nei-York;
I sphends all mine money, gets sick,
und near dies in der Hospiddal
Bellevue;
Ven I gets petter I tramps to Chee-
cago to look for some vork."

"Preetty young then, I suppose?"
"Yah, svansing apout; und der
beoples
Vot I goes to for to ask for vork
dey have none for to geef;
Efery von laughs; but I holds my
head up just so high as der stee-
ples.
Only dot var comes along, or I
should have die, I belief."

"Ever get wounded? I notice you
walk rather lame and unsteady.
Pshaw! got a wooden leg, eh? What
battle? At Lookout? don't say?
I was there too—wait a minute—
your beer glass is empty already,—
Call for another. There! tell me
how 'twas you got wounded that
day."

"Vell, ve charge ope der side of der
mountain—der sky vas all smoky
and hazy,
Ve fight all day long in der clouds,
but I nefer get hit until night—
But—I don't care to say mouch
apout it. Der poys called me foolish and crazy,
Und der doctor vot cut ofe my leg,
he say, 'Goot'—dot it serf me
shust right.

"But I dinks I vood do dot thing
over again, shust der same, and
no matter
Vot any man say."—"Well, let's
hear it—you needn't mind talking to me,
For I was there, too, as I tell you—
and Lor! how bullets did patter
Around on that breastwork of boul-
ders that sheltered our Tenth
Tennessee."

"So? Dot vos a Tennessee regiment
charged upon ours in de efening,
Shust before dark; und dey yell as
dey charge, und ve geef a hurrah,
Der roar of der guns, it vas orful."
—"Ah! yes, I remember, 'twas
deafening,
The hottest musketry firing that
ever our regiment saw."

"Und after we drove dem back, und
der night come on, I listen,
Und dinks dot I hear somepody a
calling—a voice dot cried,

'Pring me some vater for Gott's
    sake'—I saw his peltbate glisten,
Oonder der moonlight, on der bara-
    pet, shust outside.

"I dhwor my canteen ofer to vere
    he lie, but he answer
Dot his left hand vos gone, and his
    right arm broke mit a fall.
Den I shump ofer, und give him to
    drink, but shust as I ran, sir,
Bang! come a sharpshooter's pullet,
    and dot's how it vos—dot is all."

"And they called you foolish and
    crazy, did they? Him, you be-
    friended—
The reb, I mean—what became of
    him? Did he ever come 'round?"
"Dey tell me he crawl to my side,
    und call till his strength vos all
    ended,
Until dey come out mit stretchers,
    and carry us from der ground.

"But pefore ve go, he ask me my
    name und shays he: 'Yacob Keller,
You loses your leg for me, und some
    day if both of us leefs,
I shows you I don't forget,'—but he
    most have died, de poor feller,
I nefer hear ofe him since. He don't
    get vell, I beliefs.

"Only I alvays got der saddisfach-
    shun ofe knowin—
Shtop! vots der matter? Here, take
    some peer, you're vite as a sheet—
Shteady! your hand on my shoul-
    der? mut gootness! I dinks you
    vos goin'
To lose your senses avay und fall
    right off mit der seat.

"Geef me your handts. Vot! der left
    von gon? Und you vos a soldier
In dot same battle?—a Tennessee
    regiment?—dot's mighty queer—
Berhaps after all you're—"—"Yes,

Yacob, God bless you, old fellow,
    I told you
I'd never—no never forget you. I
    told you I'd come, and I'm here."
                —*George L. Catlin.*

[9686]
MINE KATRINE
You vould't dink mine frau—
If you shust look at her now,
Vhere der wrinkles on her prow
    Long haf been—
Vas der fraulein blump und fair,
Mit der vafy flaxen hair,
Who did vonce mine heart en-
    shnare—
    Mine Katrine.

Der dime seems shord to me
Since we game acrosd der sea,
To der goundry off der free
    Ve'd nefer seen;
But ve hear de beople say
Dhere vas vork und blendy bay,
So I shtarted right avay
    Mit Katrine.

Oh, der shoy dot filled mine house
Vhen dot good oldt Tocter Krauss
Brought us "Leedle Yawcob
    Strauss,"
    Shveet und clean;
Vy, I don't pelief mine eyes,
Vhen I look now, mit surprise,
On dot feller, shust der size
    Off Katrine.

Den "dot leedle babe off mine,"
He vas grown so tall und fine—
Shust so sdrait as any pine
    You efer seen;
Und der beoples all agree
Sooch fine boys dey nefer see
(Dey looks mooch more like me
    As Katrine.)

Vell, ve haf our criefs und shoys,
Und dhere's naught our lofe de-
    stroys,

aud married a man without some
    "soap"—
e vas lazy doo—but she did hope
ot he'd get bedder, when shildren
    came;
ut when dey had, he was yoost der
    same.
nd ofder now dem dears vill come,
s she sits alone ven her day's vork's
    done,
nd dinks of der day Hans called
    her "my dear,"
nd asked her for a glass of bier;
ut she don'd comblain nor efer has,
nd oney says, "Dot coodn't vas."
                    —*Anonymous*.

[9688]
DER MOON

en in der nighd der sun goed
    oud,
And dwinkles in der shky der
    shdars,
nd efery lofer finds his moud
So full of shweedmeads like der
    jars
er ish breserves, dot ish der dime
someding oferhead vill glimb,
t, vhen your eyes ish all in dune,
Vill been der moon.

at ish der moon you can't found
    oud—
Dhere vas a boet vonce did said
vas a sheeze, but dot's aboud
Der only dings dot vills his head,
d yed bisides, of dot vas drue,
r very ding dot he vould do
uld been do glimb der shky ub
    soon,
Und eadt der moon.

anahow, ve didn't care
Of id vas sheeze or anydings,
long id dwinkles oud up dhere,
Und mit der sky some vhitevash
    prings
t makes der night zeem like a
    sharm,

Und hangs your shveedheardt on
    your arm,
Und makes you vish der year vas
    Shune
    Und always moon.

Dots foony vhat a shange idt
    makes—
    Der man mit gommon senses
        villed,
Vonce in der moonlighd, quickly
    vakes
    Und finds dot all his brains vas
        gilled,
Und mit his girl idt vas no use
Dot he vould helb to been a goose,
For brains aint vordt a bicayune
    Benead der moon.

But novhere in der vorld dots vide
    Vill daffy grow so easy yedt
Ash vhen Katrine ish by your side
    Und moonlighd vill your heart
        ubsedt;
Der shugar-blums dot you vould
    shlib
From oud benead your unter lib
Vhen dots der vay you vill gom-
    mune
    Vould fill der moon.
                    —*Wade Whipple*.

[9689]
DER DEMPERANCE BLEDGE

Der man vas dere, I said to him
"Bleeze kindly sign der bledge."
He said, "Vhy shure, I glad to do."
But den his missus hedge.

"You leaf mine Luke der vay he is,"
Her clogs dey tapped der woot.
"Vhen drunk he is a human bearl,
Putt sober he's no goot!"
                    —*Anonymous*.

[9690]
MONSIEUR NOOTON

He sow ze apple downwards fell,
He zought, "Why not fell up as
    well?"

But I miss does leetle boys
    Dot used to been;
Und der tears vill somedine sdart,
Und I feels so sick at heart,
Vhen I dinks I soon must part
    From Katrine.

Old Time vill soen pe here,
Mit his sickle und his shpear,
Und vill vhisper in mine ear,
    Mit sober mien;
"You musd coom along mit me,
For it vas der Lord's decree;
Und von day dose poys you'll see,
    Und Katrine."
      —*Charles F. Adams.*

[9687]
MAUD MULLER
Maud Muller, von summer after-
    noon
Vas dending bar in her fadder's sa-
    loon.
She solt dot bier, und signed "Shoo
    Fly,"
Und vinked at der men mit her lefd
    eye.
But ven she looked oud on her
    shdreed,
Und saw dem gals all dressed so
    shweed,
Her song gifed out on a ubber note,
Cause she had a hoss in her troat;
Und she vished she had shdamps to
    shpend,
So she might git such a Grecian
    Bend,
Hans Brinker valked shlowly down
    her shdreed
Shmilin' at all der galse he'd meed;
Old Hans vas rich—as I been
    dold,—
Had houses und lots, und a barrel of
    gold.
He shdopped by der door, und potty
    soon
He valked righd indo dot bier sa-
    loon.

Und he vinked at Mau[...]
    "My dear,
Gif me, of you pbleas[...]
    bier."
She vend to der pblace [...]
    keg shtood,
Und pringed him a g[...]
    fresh und goot.
"Dot's goot," said Ha[...]
    better drink
As effer I had in mine[...]
He dalked for a vhil[...]
    "Good day."
Und up der shdreet he [...]
Maud hofed a sigh, an[...]
    how
I'de like to been dot ol[...]
Such shplendid close [...]
    vear,
Dot all the gals around[...]
In dot Central Park I'd[...]
Und efery evenin' go [...]
Hans Brinker, doo, [...]
    qweer,
(But dot mike peen [...]
    beer.)
Und he says to himself[...]
    along,
Hummin' der dune [...]
    song,
"Dot's der finest gal I [...]
Und I vish dot she [...]
    be."
But here his solillogw[...]
    end,
As he dinked of der [...]
    might shbend;
Und he maked up his [...]
    for him,
He'd marry a gal mit [...]
So he vent righd off d[...]
Und married a voor[...]
    gray.
He vished now, but al[...]
Dot he was free to m[...]
Free as he vas dot aft[...]
Ven he med Maud [...]
    bier saloon.

Zen in his head zare ring a bell,
Ze more zat fell za more he sell.
He kick ze tree and down zey came,
So Monsieur Nooton he made his
name.
—*Anonymous.*

[9691]
HOME AGAIN

How schweed to dhink of home
Und frendts ve loaf so dear,
Ven ve runned avay from der house
To see der sights so quveer;
'Tis den dot ve look pack
Und vish dot ve vas dhere,
Und be greeded vit dot welcome
home
Und vid der joys to share.
To see der fader und mooder,
Und hear dhem speak vonce
more;
Vhy, id's bedder dan gold or silver
Send from a foreighn shore;
Und you sid down by der fireside
Of dot liddle brown stone frame,
Vhile your fader mit a jack und 9
dails
On you back he vas wriden his
name.
Vell, you don'd care to to runned
avay again
Und see der vorld vonce more;
You had enough, you ain'd no hog,
Ligke you vas dot dime before.
—*Anonymous.*

[9692]
I'M O'ER YOUNG TO
MARRY YET

I'm o'er young, I'm o'er young,
I'm o'er young to marry yet;
I'm o'er young, 'twad be a sin
To tak me frae my mammy yet.
I am my mammy's ae bairn,
Wi' unco folk I weary, sir;
And lying in a man's bed,
I'm fley'd it mak me errie, sir.
I'm o'er young, I'm o'er young,

I'm o'er young to marry yet;
I'm o'er young, 'twad be a sin
To tak me frae my mammy yet.
Hallowmass is come and gane,
The nights are lang in winter, sir.
And you and I in ae bed,—
In trowth, I dare na venture, sir.
I'm o'er young, I'm o'er young,
I'm o'er young to marry yet;
I'm o'er young, 'twad be a sin
To tak me frac my mammy yet.
Fu' loud an' shill the frosty wind
Blaws thro' the leafless timmer,
sir;
But if ye come this gate again,
I'll aulder be gin simmer, sir.
I'm o'er young, I'm o'er young,
I'm o'er young to marry yet;
I'm o'er young, 'twad be a sin
To tak me frae my mammy yet.
—*Robert Burns.*

[9693]
THE FRENCHMAN AND
THE MOSQUITOES

Petite moskeetare, you time it have
come!
Ze frost he have call for you—go
you now home.
All of your buz-ze-buz into my ear—
Now I am ride of it, skeetare, my
dear!
Ven to bed in my garret I go,
Zen viz your moosic you bozaire me
so,
Viz you tin trompit you sing all ze
night;
Mr. Jack Frost now he freeze-a you
tight.
Ah! vat a blessing ze cole vintar be,
Ven he kill all of ze skeetare and
flea!
Zen till ze spring time varm vedder
sail being.
Monsieur Moskeetare, mo more you
vill sing!
—*Anonymous.*

[9694]
DER BABY

So help me gracious, every day
I laugh me wild to see der vay
My schmall young baby dries to
    play—
    Dot funny leetle baby.

Vhen I look on dem leetle toes,
Und saw dot funny leetle nose,
Und heard der vay dot rooster
    crows,
    I schmile like I was grazy.

Und vhen I heard der real nice vay
Dhem beoples to my wife dhey say,
"More like his fater every day,"
    I vas so pround like blazes.

Sometimes dhere comes a leetle
    schquall.
Dot's when der vindy vind vill crawl
Right in its leetle stomach schmall,—
    Dot's too bad for der baby.

Dot makes him sing at night so
    schveet,
Und garrydoric he must eat,
Und I must chumb spry on my feet,
    To help dot leetle baby.

He bulls my nose und kicks my
    hair,
Und grawls me ofer every-where,
Und shlobbers me but vat I care?
    Dot vas my schmall young baby.

Around my head dot leetle arm
Vas schqueezin me so nice and
    varm—
Oh! may dhere never come some
    harm
    To dot schmall leetle baby.
    —*Anonymous.*

[9695]
SAD FATE OF A
SCOTTISH KING
(who fell in wi' lawers)

"O' majesty," sae went their song,
"We ask ye ca' us advocates."

The king said "Nae, 'twould bae too
    wrong,
Ye lawr'd the land, ye'll grab the
    gates."

On kingly ears they beat their plead
That lawer/lyer ring the same,
Though not akin in craft or deed
The soundin' brought their trade
    poor fame.

O' Scottish King, O' mahn o' hate
Ye laid ye doon where winters glean
And wi' ye leave found at the gate
The lyin' lawers o' Aberdeen.
    —*F. Kingston Dane.*

[9696]
TO A FRIEND STUDYING
GERMAN

Vill'st dou learn de Deutsche
    Sprache?
Dou moost eat apout a peck
A week of stinging sauerkraut
Und sefen pfoundts of speck,
Mid Got knows vot in vinegar
Und deuce knows vot in rum:
Dish ish de only cerdain way
To make de accents coom.
Vill'st dou learn de Deutsche
    Sprache?
If a shendleman dou art,
Denn shtrike right indo Deutsch-
    land
Und get a schveetes heart,
Und if you shoost kit married
(Vood mit vood soon makes a fire),
You'll learn to sprech Deutsch, mein
    kind,
Ash fast ash you tesire.
    —*C. G. Leland.*

[9697]
DER POLITITCHEN'S
RUBY YACHTS

Cum, filling der cup mitt der songs
    fum spring,
Und hear der polititchens' sing,

Dair summer songs shmell like der rose,
Dair vinter deeds shmell up der nose.
Der promise gutt like flower dey say,
Putt vhere's der bloomers fum yesterday?
Der roses dat dey shaid dey'd pluck,
De let dry up und fade avay.
Sum for der glory of dis place, und sum
Shpout like prophitz uv Paradize to cum;
Dey take der cash, der credit dey nixsht,
Vhile dey heed da call to a tidy sum.
Und like der booze shtiff umfidel,
Dem crookers crooked yur pants as vell;
Amazing vot dose fakirs buy
Mitt money fum der shtuff dey sell!
—*Gerald F. Lieberman.*

IRISH DIALECT VERSE

[9698]
THE IRISH ECLIPSE
In Watherford, wanst, lived Profissor McShane,
The foinest asthronomer iver was sane;
For long before noight, wid the scoince he knew,
Whereiver wan shtar was, sure he could see two
    Quite plain,
    Could Profissor McShane.
More power to him! ivry clare noight as would pass
He'd sit by the windy, a-shovin' his glass;
A poke at the dipper, that plaised him the laist,
But a punch in the milky way suited his taste
    Small blame
    To his sowl for that same!

Now, wan toime in Watherford, not long ago,
They had what the loike was not heard of, I know,
Since Erin was undher ould Brian Borrhoime;
The sun was ayclipsed for three days at wan toime!
    It's thrue
    As I'm tellin' to you.
'Twas sunroise long gone, yit the sun niver rose,
An' ivry wan axed, "What's the matther, God knows?"
The next day, and next, was the very same way,
The noight was so long it was lasting all day,
    As black
    As the coat on yer back.
The paiple wint huntin' Profissor McShane,
To thry if he'd know what this wondher could mane.
He answered thim back, "Is that so? Are ye there?
'Tis a lot of most iligant gommachs ye air,
    To ax
    For the plainest of facts!
"Ye're part of an impoire, yez mustn't forget,
Upon which the sun'niver able to set;
Thin why will it give yer impoire a surproise
If wanst, for a change, he refuses to roise?"
    Sez he,
    "This is aizy to see!"
    —*Irwin Russell.*

[9699]
LARRY'S ON THE FORCE
Well, Katie an' is this yersilf? An' where was you this whoile?

An' ain't ye dressed! You are the
wan to illusthrate the stoile!
But niver moind thim matters now,
there's toime enough for thim;
An' Larry—that's me b'y—I want to
shpake to you av him.
Sure, Larry bates thim all for luck!
—'tis he will make his way,
An 'be the proide an' honnur to the
sod beyant the say.
We'll soon be able—whist! I do be
singin' till I'm hoorse,
For iver since a month or more, me
Larry's on the foorce!
There's not a proivate gintleman
that boords in all the row
Who houlds himself loike Larry
does, or makes as foine a show;
Thim eyes av his, the way they
shoine—his coat, an' butthons
too—
He bates them kerridge dhroivers
that be on the avenoo!
He shtips that proud an' stately-
loike, you'd think he owned the
town,
An' houlds his shtick convanient to
be tappin' some wan down.
Aich blissed day I watch to see him
comin' up the shtrate,
For, by the greatest bit av luck, our
'house is on his bate.
The little b'ys is feared av him, for
Larry's moighty strict,
An' many's the litthle blagyard he's
arristed, I expict;
The baggyars gits acrass the shtrate
—you ought to see thim fly!—
An' organ-groinders scatthers whin
they see him comin' by.
I know that Larry's bound to roise;
he'll git a sergeant's post.
An' afther that a captaincy widhin
a year at most;
An' av he goes in politics he has
the head to throive—

I'll be an Alderwoman, Kate, afore
I'm thirty-foive!
What's that again? Y'are jokin',
surely—Katie—*is* it thrue?
Last noight, you say, *he—married?*
and Aileen O'Donahue?
O Larry! c'ud ye have the hairt—
but let the spalpeen be—
Av he demanes himsilf to *her,* he's
nothin' more to me,
The ugly shcamp! I always said,
just I'm tellin' you,
That Larry was the biggest fool av
all I iver knew;
An' many a toime I've tould mesilf
—*you* see it, now av course—
He'd niver come to anny good av
he got on the foorce!
—*Irwin Russell.*

[9700]
WINNIE SPEAKS HER WELCOME

Well, Shamus, what brought ye?
It's dead, sure I thought ye—
What's kept ye this fortnight
from callin' on me?
Stop there. Don't be lyin';
It's no use denyin'—
I know ye've been waitin' on
Kitty Magee.
She's ould an' she's homely;
There's girls young an' comely
Who've loved ye much longer
an' better than she;
But, 'deed, I'm not carin',
I'm glad I've no share in
The love of a boy who'd love
Kitty Magee.
Away! I'm not cryin',
Yer charge I'm denyin',
Ye're wrong to attribute such
wakeness to me;
If tears I am showin',
I'd have ye be knowin'
They're shed out of pity—for
Kitty Magee!

For mane, an' consated,
Wid pride overweighted,
   Cold, heartless, an' brutal she'll
   find ye to be;
When ye she'll be gettin',
She'll soon be regrettin'
   She e'er changed her name from
   plain Kitty Magee.
What's that? Am I dhr'amin'?
Ye've only been shammin',
   Just tryin' to test the affection of
   me?
But ye're the sly divil!
There now! Plase be civil—
   Don't hug me to death! I'm not
   Kitty Magee.

Yeh kisses confuse me;
Well, I'll not refuse ye—
   I know ye'll be tinder an' lovin'
   wid me;
To show my conthrition
For doubts an' suspicion,
   I'll ax for first bridesmaid—Miss
   Kitty Magee!
            —*Will Emmett.*

[9701]
THE IRISHMEN'S BALL
"Plans for Irish Ball Thursday in
the Hotel Commodore Now Com-
plete."—*New York Headline.*
There's "Erin Go Bragh" on a ceil-
   ing
   That's daubed with a riot of
   green;
The emerald walls are all reeling
   With "Down with the King and
   the Queen!"
The usher squad practices dealing
   Out bricks and stout sticks for
   them all:
When every young Gael is supplied
   with shillalies,
   They'll start up the Irishmen's
   ball!

There's Finnegan, Flanagan, Kelly,
   O'Neill and O'Sheel and O'Shay,

McMilligan, Mulligan, Skelly,
   O'Reilly, O'Rourke, and O'Day.
There's Harrigan, Burke and
   O'Delly,
There's Garrigan, Gilligan,—all
From attic to basement, St. Patrick
   to Casement,
   On hand for the Irishmen's ball.

Each neighboring paint-shop dis-
   gorges
   Great oceans of emerald paint;
Long banners denounce the Three
   Georges—
   The Lloyd, and the King, and the
   Saint;
Potatoes for regular orgies,
   And good Irish Stew for them
   all—
With corn-beef and cabbage com-
   pleting the grabbage
   On hand for the Irishmen's ball.

O'Brien, O'Ryan, Gilhooley,
   Mullanigan, Brannigan, Coyle,
Maloney, Mahoney, and Dooley,
   O'Grady and Brady and Doyle;
McQuillin, McMillin, Gilluly,
   McNish and McNutt and Mc-
   Call—
O hurry and fix up—we'll have the
   grand Micks-up,
   The peak of the Irishmen's ball!
            —*Alan Dubois.*

[9702]
HOW PADDY STOLE THE
ROPE
There was once two Irish labouring
   men; to England they came over;
They tramped about in search of
   work from Liverpool to Dover.
Says Pat to Mick, "I'm tired of this;
   we're both left in the lurch;
And if we don't get work, bedad,
   I'll go and rob a church."
"What, rob a church!" says Mick to
   Pat; "how dare you be so vile?

There's something sure to happen
as you're treading down the aisle.
But if you go I go with you; we'll
get out safe, I hope";
So, if you'll listen, I'll tell you here
how Paddy stole the rope.

So off they went with theft intent,
the place they wanted finding;
They broke into a country church
which nobody was minding.
They scraped together all they could
and then prepared to slope,
When Paddy cries out, "Hold on,
Mick, what shall we do for rope?
We've got no bag to hold the swag,
and e'er we get outside,
With something stout and strong,
my lad, the bundle must be tied."
Just then he spies the old church
bell, and quick as an antelope,
He scrambled up the belfry high to
try and steal a rope.

Now when Paddy up the belfry got,
"Ah-hah, bedad, but stop;
To get a piece that's long enough,
I must climb up to the top."
So, like a sailor, up he went, and
near the top, says he,
"I think the piece that's underneath
quite long enough will be."
So, holding by one arm and leg, he
drew his clasp knife out,
And right above his big fat head he
cut the rope so stout.
He quite forgot it held him up, and,
by the Holy Pope,
Down to the bottom of the church
fell Paddy and the rope.

"Come out of that," says Mick to
Pat, as he on the floor lay groaning,
"If that's the way you cut a rope, no
wonder now you're moaning.
I'll show you how to cut a rope, so
just lend me the knife."

"Be careful," cries out Pat, "or else
you'll lose your life."
He clambered up the other rope,
and, like an artful thief,
Instead of cutting it above, he cut it
underneath.
The piece fell down and left poor
Mick alone up there to cope;
Says he, "Bad luck unto the day
when we came stealing rope."
Now with Paddy groaning on the
floor and Mick hung up on high,
Says Pat, "Come down." "I can't,"
cried Mick, "for if I do, I die."
The noise soon brought the beadle
round, the sexton and police,
And although they set poor Micky
free, they gave them no release.
They marched them to the county
jail where their conduct now they
rue,
And if they'd got no work before,
they've plenty now to do;
And for their ingenuity they now
have larger scope
Than when they broke into a church
to try and steal a rope.
—*Anonymous.*

[9703]
MISS FOGGERTY'S CAKE
As I sat by my window last evening,
The letterman brought unto me
A little gilt-edged invitation
Saying, "Gilhooley, come over to
tea."
Sure I knew 'twas the Foggertys
sent it,
So I went for old friendship's
sake,
And the first thing they gave me to
tackle
Was a slice of Miss Foggerty's
cake.
Miss Martin wanted to taste it,
But really there weren't no use,
For they worked at it over an hour

And couldn't get none of it loose.
Till Foggerty went for a hatchet
And Killey came in with a saw;
The cake was enough, by the powers,
To paralyze any man's jaw.
In it were cloves, nutmegs and berries,
Raisins, citron and cinnamon, too;
There were sugar, pepper and cherries,
And the crust of it nailed on with glue.
Miss Foggerty, proud as a preacher,
Kept winking and blinking away,
Till she fell over Flanigan's brogans
And spilt a whole brewing of tay.
"O, Gilhooley," she cried, "you're not eating,
Just take another piece for my sake."
"No thanks, Miss Foggerty," says I,
"But I'd like the recipe for that cake."
McNulley was took with the colic,
McFadden complained of his head,
McDoodle fell down on the sofa
And swore that he wished he was dead.
Miss Martin fell down in hysterics,
And there she did wriggle and shake,
While every man swore he was poisoned
By eating Miss Foggerty's cake.
—*Anonymous.*

[9704]
FINIGAN'S WAKE
Tim Finigan lived in Walker street—
An Irish gintleman, mighty odd.
He'd a bit of a brogue, so neat and sweet,
And to rise in the world, Tim carried a hod.
But Tim had a sort of tippling way;
With a love of liquor Tim was born,
And, to help him through his work each day,
Took a drop of the creature every morn.

Chorus:

Whack! Hurrah! Now dance to your partners,
Welt the flure, your trotters shake;
Isn't all the truth I've told ye,
Lots of fun at Finigan's wake?

One morning Tim was rather full,
His head felt heavy and it made him shake;
He fell from the ladder and broke his skull,
So they carried him home, his corpse to wake.
They rolled him up in a nice clean sheet,
And laid him out upon the bed,
With fourteen candles round his feet
And a bushel of 'taters round his head.
His friends assembled at his wake,
Missus Finigan called out for the lunch;
And first they laid in tay and cakes,
Then pipes and tobacky and whisky punch.
Miss Biddy O'Neil began to cry:
"Such a purty corpse did yez ever see!
Arrah! Tim mavourneen, and why did ye l'ave me?"
"Hold your gob!" sez Judy Magee.
Then Peggy O'Connor took up the job:
"Arrah, Biddy," says she, "ye're wrong, in sure."

But Judy gave her a belt in the gob,
And left her sprawling on the
flure.
Each side in war did soon engage;
'Twas woman to woman and man
to man;
Shillelah law was all the rage
And a bloody ruction soon began.

Mickey Mulvaney raised his head,
When a gaslon of whisky flew at
him;
It missed him, and, hopping on the
bed,
The liquor scattered over Tim.
"Och! he revives! See how he
raises!"
And Timothy, jumping from the
bed,
Cries, while he lathers round like
blazes,
"Bad luck ter yer souls! D'ye
think I'm dead?"

—*Anonymous.*

[9705]
JONAH AND THE WHALE

About the year of one B. C.,
A gallant ship set out to sea,
To catch a whale and salt his tail,
To salt the end of his tail.

But when about a mile from shore
The ship began to dance,
Then every son of a sailorman,
Put on his working pants,
His pants, his pants, his working
pants.

And down into the hold they went,
And over the pumps their backs
they bent.
They pumped and pumped,
They thought they would drown,
The deck was too wet to sit down.

Then up spoke Mike O'Flaherty,
There's a Jonah on the boat, sez he;

So off they ran from Mike to Dan,
To find the Jonah Man.

And when upon the deck they came,
His "Nibs" a-smiling sat—
A-lighting a paper cigarette
In the crown of his derby hat,
His hat, his hat, his derby hat.

So they gave a whoop and they gave
a yell
And overboard poor Jonah fell.
Sez Mike to Jim, " 'Tis better for
him—
'Tis certainly better for him."

Just then a monster whale passed
by,
And Jonah's trousers caught his eye.
"As I'm a goat, there's a lunch
afloat,"
And he swallowed him into his
throat.

Just about then the whale felt ill,
Sez he, "That lunch was poor,
For, judging by the way I feel,
I've swallowed a Jonah sure,
A Jonah, a Jonah, a Jonah sure."

Then Mike McGinty gave a call,
And he coughed up Jonah, pants
and all,
'Twas on the spot ('tis not forgot),
McGinty's corner lot.

"Get out of here!" McGinty said;
"You can't stay here unless you're
dead.
You'll hoodoo me and my familee,
My wife and familee."

So then he called his beautiful wife,
A mermaid fat and pale,
Who gave poor Jonah a terrible jag
With the end of her jagged tail,
Her jag, her jag, her jagged tail.
—*Anonymous.*

PART XII

TOASTS FOR ALL OCCASIONS

TOASTS TO MEN

[9706]
Here's to the men, God bless them!
Worst of my sins, I confess them!
In loving them all, be they great or
small,
So here's to the boys! God bless
them!

[9707]
Gentlemen, may you never scold
a wife or wive a scold.

[9708]
May all single men get married,
and all married men be happy.

[9709]
Here's to one and only one,
And may that one be he
Who loves but one and only one,
And may that one be me.

[9710]
Drink to the man who keeps his
head, though he loses his heart.

[9711]
My husband—may he never be
tight; but tight or sober, my husband.

[9712]
To the Bachelor,—who is always
free!
To the Husband,—who, sometime, may be!

[9713]
Here's to the man who loves his
wife,
And loves his wife alone:
For many a man loves another
man's wife
When he might be loving his own.

[9714]
To the model husband: any other
woman's.

[9715]
Here's to that most provoking man,
The man of wisdom deep,
Who never talks when he takes his
rest,
But only smiles in his sleep.

[9716]
Here's to the man who is wisest and
best,
Here's to the man who with judgment is blest.
Here's to the man who's as smart as
can be—
I mean the man who agrees with
me.

[9717]
To the bachelors: may they never
impale their freedom on the point
of a steel pen.

[9718]
The gentlemen—divide our time,
double our cares, and treble our
troubles.

[9719]
A pipe, a book, a fire, a friend,
  A stein that's always full,
Here's to the joys of a bachelor's
    life,
  A life that is never dull.

[9720]
May every man be what he thinks
himself to be.

[9721]
Here's to man:—he is like a kerosene lamp; he is not especially
bright; he is often turned down; he
generally smokes; and he frequently
goes out at night.

TOASTS TO WOMEN

[9722]
Here's to our sweethearts and our
    wives;
May our sweethearts soon become
    our wives,
And our wives ever remain our
    sweethearts.

[9723]
Here's to the woman whose heart
    and whose soul
Are the light and life of each spell
    we pursue;
Whether sunn'd at the tropics or
    chilled at the poles,
If woman be there, there is happi-
    ness too.

[9724]
Here's to the gladness of her glad-
    ness when she's glad,
Here's to the sadness of her sad-
    ness when she's sad;
But the gladness of her gladness,
And the sadness of her sadness,
Are not in it with the madness of
    her madness when she's mad.

[9725]
I fill this cup to one made up
  Of loveliness alone,
A woman, of her gentle sex
  The seeming paragon.
Her health! and would on earth
    there stood
  Some more of such a frame,
That life would be all poetry,
  And weariness a name.

[9726]
Here's to our wives!
They keep our hives
In little Bees and honey;
They darn our socks,
They soothe life's shocks,
And don't they spend the money!

[9727]
To the Ladies
The Ladies, God bless them—that
    time-honored toast,
The one to be drunk and applauded
    the most,
The Ladies, God bless them, don't
    drink it in jest,
For I am toasting tonight the one
    you love best.

The mother that bore you, now
    withered and old,
But dearer by far than all the earth's
    gold.
The sister that followed your foot-
    steps in life,
But what is still dearer, your brave-
    hearted wife.

The Ladies, God bless them, God
    bless every one,
May the eye of the Father and the
    love of the Son
Watch o'er and protect them—keep
    them holy and pure,
With life to sustain and health to
    endure.
The Ladies, God bless them.

[9728]

To ladies' eyes, around boys,—
We can't refuse, we can't refuse,
Their bright eyes so abound, boys
It's hard to choose, it's hard to
    choose.

—*Moore*.

[9729]

Here's to the lasses we've loved, my
    lad;
Here's to the lips we've pressed;
For kisses and lasses, like liquor in
    glasses,
The last is always the best.

[9730]

THE WOMAN THAT'S GOOD

Ho, gentlemen! lift your glasses
    up—
Each gallant, each swain and
    lover—
A kiss to the beads that brim in the
    cup,
A laugh for the foam spilt over!
For the soul is a-tilt and the heart
    beats high,
And care has unloosed its tether;
"Now drink," said the sage, "for
    tomorrow we die!"
So, lets have a toast together.
Swing the goblet aloft, to the lips
    let it fall;
Then bend your knee to address
    her;
And drink, gentle sirs, to the queen
    of us all—
To the Woman that's Good—
    God bless her!

O, Youth is a madcap, and Time is
    a churl!
Pleasure palls, and Remorse fol-
    lows after;
The world hurtles on its pitiless
    whirl,
With its kisses, its tears, and its
    laughter;

But there's one gentle heart, in its
    bosom of white—
Dear Love with the tender eyes
    gleaming,
Who has all the wealth of my
    homage to-night,
Where she lies in her innocent
    dreaming—
And a watch o'er her ever my spirit
    shall keep,
While the angels lean down to
    caress her;
And I'll pledge her again, in her
    beautiful sleep,—
The Woman that's Good—God
    bless her!

Ah, Bohemia's honey was sweet to
    the sip,
And the song and the dance were
    alluring—
(The mischievous maid with the
    mutinous lip
Had a charm that was very en-
    during)
But out from the music and smoke-
    wreaths and lace
Of that world of the tawdrily
    clever,
There floats the rare spell of the
    pure little face
That has chased away folly for-
    ever!
And I pledge my last toast, ere I go
    to my rest—
O fortunate earth to possess
    her!—
To the dear tender heart in the lit-
    tle white breast
Of the Woman that's Good—
    God bless her!

[9731]

A toast of wine, to woman divine,
I would toss off in haste, me think;
To her eyes, to her hair, to her
    beauty so rare—
But I haven't the wine to drink.

[9732]

Then with wine, as is due, let the
　　honors be paid,
Whilst I give my hand, heart and
　　head,
"Here's to her, the fond mother,
　　dear, partner, kind maid,
Who first taught me to love, woo
　　and wed!"
We mutually pledge to each other
　　our lives, our fortunes and our
　　sacred honor.

[9733]

Here's to the Ladies: You can't
live with them and you can't live
without them.

[9734]

To woman: She needs no eulogy;
she speaks for herself.

[9735]

Here's to Woman: A mistress of
arts, who robs a man of his bachelor's degree and forces him by lectures to study philosophy.

[9736]

"Woman—the morning star of
infancy, the day star of manhood,
the evening star of old age; bless
our stars and may they always be
kept at a telescopic distance."
　　　　　　　—Bachelor's toast.

[9737]

The ladies, God bless them,
May nothing distress them.

[9738]

May her voyage through life be as
　　happy and as free
As the dancing waves on the deep
　　blue sea.

[9739]

Drink to fair woman, who, I think,
　　Is most entitled to it;
For if anything ever can drive me
　　to drink,
　　She certainly could do it.

[9740]

To each man's dearest girl, married or single.

[9741]

Here's to the pretty woman,
　　With whom I love to tarry.
But being same and human,
　　Here's to the girl I marry.

[9742]

Here's to the prettiest, here's to the
　　wittiest,
　　Here's to the truest of all who are
　　　true,
Here's to the neatest one, here's to
　　the sweetest one,
　　Here's to them, all in one—here's
　　to you.

[9743]

To our sisters, our cousins and
our aunts.

[9744]

Here's to the halo that crowned her
　　head,
When at her feet I tarried,
And here's to the hats she wears in-
　　stead,
Since she and I were married.

[9745]

If all your beauties one by one,
I pledge, dear, I am thinking
Before the tale was well begun
I had been dead of drinking.

[9746]

Drink, drink, drink!
Drink to the girl of your heart;
The wisest, the wittiest, the bravest,
　　the prettiest,
May you never be far apart.

[9747]

Here's to the girl who's bound to
　　win
Her share at least of blisses,
Who knows enough not to go in
When it is raining kisses.

[9748]

Women, the better half of the Yankee world—at whose tender summons even the stern Pilgrims were ever ready to spring to arms, and without whose aid they could not have achieved the historic title of the Pilgrim Fathers. The Pilgrim Mothers were more devoted martyrs than were the Pilgrim Fathers, because they not only had to bear the same hardships that the Pilgrim Fathers endured, but they had to bear with the Pilgrim Fathers besides.

—*Joseph Choate*.

[9749]

Brew me a cup for a winter's night.
For the wind howls loud and the furies fight;
Spice it with love and stir it with care,
And I'll toast your bright eyes, my sweetheart fair.

[9750]

Here's to women, the sweetheart, or the wife,
The delight of our fireside by night and by day,
Who never does anything wrong in her life,
Except when permitted to have her own way.

[9751]

Here's to the dearest
    Of all things on earth
(Dearest precisely—
    And yet full of worth.)
One who lays siege to
    Susceptible hearts.
(Pocket-books also—
    That's one of her arts!)
Drink to her, toast her,
    Your banner unfurl—
Here's to the *priceless*
    American Girl!

[9752]

Here's to the girls of the American shore,
I love but one, I love no more,
Since she's not here to drink her part,
I'll drink her share with all my heart.

[9753]

Here's to the ladies, the good, young ladies;
But not too good, for the good die young,
And we want no dead ones.
And here's to the good old ladies,
But not too old, for we want no dyed ones.

[9754]

Here's to the girl that strictly in it,
Who doesn't lose her head even for a minute,
Plays well the game and knows the limit,
And still gets all the fun there's in it.

[9755]

Here's to the girl that's good and sweet,
Here's to the girl that's true,
Here's to the girl that rules my heart—
In other words, Here's to you.

[9756]

The Ladies—We admire them for their beauty, respect them for their intelligence, adore them for their virtue, and love them because we can't help it.

[9757]

Here's to the girl I love,
    And here's to the girl who loves me,
And here's to all those who love her whom I love
    And all those who love her who love me.

[9758]

A health to our sweethearts, our
friends and our wives,
And may fortune smile on them the
rest of their lives.

[9759]

Here's to the maiden of bashful
fifteen,
Here's to the widow of fifty;
Here's to the flaunting, extravagant
queen,
And here's to the housewife that's
thrifty!
Let the toast pass.
Drink to the lass.
I'll warrant she'll prove an excuse
for the glass.
　　　　　　　—Sheridan.

[9760]

May these ladies distrust man in
general, but not us in particular.

[9761]

To perfect woman nobly planned,
To warn, to comfort and command.

[9762]

A drink, my lass, in a deep clear
glass,
Just properly tempered by ice,
And here's to the lips mine last
have kissed,
And if they were thine, here's
twice.

[9763]

Here's to the girl who loves me
And here's to the many who
don't;
Here's to the girl who accepts me,
And here's to the many who
won't.

[9764]

Here's to our Wives: May they
be as blissfully trustful as we are
trustfully blissful.

[9765]

Here's to Woman: The fair magician who can turn man into a
donkey and make him think he's
a lion.

[9766]

The ladies—may their virtues exceed the magnitude of their skirts,
and their faults less than their hats.

[9767]

The ladies—may we kiss all the
girls we please, and please all the
girls we kiss.

[9768]

To woman, if she cannot be captain of a ship, may she always command a smack.

[9769]

To woman's heart—to man's it's
not akin,
For her heart is a home while his
heart is an inn.

[9770]

Here's to the love that lies in woman's eyes,
And lies, and lies, and lies.

[9771]

Here's to the girl I love the best,
It ought not to be hard to guess
it;
For I raise my glass and gaze at
one
Who loves me but won't confess
it.

[9772]

The ladies—divide our sorrows,
double our joys, and treble our
expenses.

[9773]

Here's to a Pat Hand of Queens:
Mother, Wife, Sister and Sweetheart; the noblest of all God's crea-
tions—pure, beautiful woman.

[9774]

To our wives—as dear as their clothes.

[9775]

Here's to the Ladies: First in our hearts and first in our pocket-books.

[9776]

To our sweethearts and wives. May they never meet!

[9777]

Woman—the fairest work of creation; the edition being extensive, let no man be without a copy.

[9778]

Here's to the woman, who in our hours of ease,
Uncertain, coy and hard to please,
But seen too oft-familiar with thy face,
First pity, then endure, then embrace.

[9779]

Here is to the bride: May your hours of joy be as numerous as the petals of your bridal bouquet.

[9780]

We've toasted the mother and daughter;
We've toasted the sweetheart and wife;
But somehow we missed her,
Our dear little sister—
The joy of another man's life.

[9781]

Here's to the widows, too dainty to touch,
And here's to their bonnets and suches and such,
And here's to the shy
Little twist of the eye;
A toast to the widows! they all know so much!

[9782]

Here's to the maid who is thrifty,
And knows it is folly to yearn,
And picks out a lover of fifty,
Because he has money to burn.

[9783]

We have toasted our sweethearts,
Our friends and our wives,
We have toasted each other
Wishing all merry lives;
Don't frown when I tell you
This toast beats all others
But drink one more toast, boys—
A toast to—"Our Mothers."

[9784]

Here's to the happiest hours of my life—
Spent in the arms of another man's wife:
My mother!

[9785]

'Tis not the girl with the *raven* locks,
Nor the one with the head of *brown*,
Or the maiden fair with the *auburn* hair,
Or the one with the golden crown.

But the girl I love the best of all,
And the one I toast tonight,
With her smiling face and charming grace,
Wears a crown of gleaming *white*—
My mother!

[9786]

Here's to mothers: The guide-posts to heaven.

[9787]

To our fathers' sweethearts,—our mothers.

[9788]

Here's to the mother-in-law that's the mother-in-equity.

TOASTS TO LOVE, COURTSHIP
AND MARRIAGE

[9789]
I have known many,
Liked a few,
Loved one—
Here's to you!

[9790]
Let's be gay while we may
And seize love with laughter:
I'll be true as long as you,
But not a moment after.

[9791]
May we kiss those we please, and
please those we kiss!

[9792]
Here's to love, the only fire
against which there is no insurance!

[9793]
May the single be married, and
the married happy.

[9794]
May those who love truly be always
believed;
And those who deceive us be always deceived.

[9795]
Here's to those who'd love us
If we only cared,
Here's to those we'd love,
If we only dared.

[9796]
Here's to her eyes, those homes of
prayer.
Ah! how they make me think!
I like them sad.
I like them glad.
I love them when they wink.

[9797]
Drink to life and the passing show,
And the eyes of the prettiest girl
you know.

[9798]
Here's to the wings of love—
May they never moult a feather,
Till my big boots and your little
shoes,
Are under the bed together.

[9799]
Drink to me only with thine eyes,
And I will pledge with mine;
Or leave a kiss within the cup,
And I'll not look for wine.

[9800]
By those we love may we be
loved.

[9801]
May we all have the unspeakable
good fortune to win a true heart,
and the merit to keep it.

[9802]
Health to the bold and dashing
coquette,
Who careth not for me;
Whose heart, untouched by love as
yet,
Is wild and fancy free.

[9803]
Here's health to those I love,
and wealth to those who love me.

[9804]
Drink, for faith and hope are
high—
None so true as you and I—
Drink the lover's litany—
"Love like ours can never die!"

[9805]
There's a beautiful toast
To the feminine host—
There's a swing to "the ladies—
God bless 'em,"
But the women should cry
With their glasses on high,
A toast to the men who dress 'em!

[9806]
The life we love with those we
love.

[9807]

Then fill a fair and honest cup, and
    bear it straight to me;
The goblet hallows all it holds,
    whate'er the liquid be;
And may the cherubs on its face
    protect me from the sin
That dooms one to those dreadful
    words,
"My dear, where have you been?"
             —*Holmes.*

[9808]

A book of verses underneath the
    bough,
A jug of wine, a loaf of bread,—
    and thou
Beside me singing in the wilder-
    ness—
Oh! wilderness were paradise enow!
             —*Omar Khayyam.*

[9809]

Here's to the red of the holly berry,
    And to its leaf so green;
And here's to the lips that are just
    as red,
    And the fellow who's not so
    green.

[9810]

Here's to man—he can afford anything he can get. Here's to woman
—she can afford anything that she
can get a man to get for her.

[9811]

Here's head first, in a foaming glass!
Here's head first, to a lively lass!
Here's head first, for a bit of kiss-
    ing,
For the good don't know the fun
    they're missing!

[9812]

Here's to the sweets that are out
    of sight
    And not on our lawful diet,
To the stolen day and pilfered night,
To each and every dear delight,
    Including the kiss on the quiet.

[9813]

Drink to me only with thine eyes—
    I'll take a little wine.
      The eyes we prize
      Are full of lies,
    I'll none of that in mine.

[9814]

Here's to the pictures on my
desk. May they never meet.
          —*College Man's Toast.*

[9815]

Here's to love—the disease which
begins with a fever and ends with
a pain.

[9816]

Here's to Love; a thing so divine,
    Description makes it but the less.
'Tis what we feel, but cannot
    define—
'Tis what we know, but cannot
    express.

[9817]

May we have those in our arms
that we love in our hearts.

[9818]

While there's life on the lip, while
    there's warmth in the wine,
One deep health I'll pledge, and
    that health shall be thine.

[9819]

Were't the last drop in the well,
    As I gasp'd upon the brink,
Ere my fainting spirit fell,
    'Tis to thee that I would drink.
             —*Byron.*

[9820]

Drink, my jolly lads, drink with
    discerning,
Wedlock's a lane where there is no
    turning:
Never was owl more blind than a
    lover,
Drink and be merry, lads, half seas
    over.
             —*Mulock.*

[9821]
Here's to the Chaperone,
May she learn from Cupid
Just enough blindness
To be sweetly stupid.

[9822]
Here's to the bachelor, lonely and
gay,
For it's not his fault he was born
that way.
And here's to the spinster, lonely
and good,
For it's not her fault—she hath
done what she could.

[9823]
Here's to the bride and the bridegroom,
We'll ask their success in our
prayers,
And through life's dark shadows
and sunshine
That good luck may ever be
theirs.

[9824]
Here's to my mother-in-law's
daughter,
And here's to her father-in-law's
son;
And here's to the vows we've just
taken,
And the life we've just begun.

[9825]
Here's to thee and thy folks from
me and my folks;
And if thee and thy folks love me
and my folks
As much as me and my folks love
thee and thy folks
Then there never was folks since
folks was folks
Love me and my folks as much as
thee and thy folks.

[9826]
May hymen never join those
hands whose hearts are divided.

[9827]
Here's to matrimony, the high
sea for which no compass has yet
been invented.

[9828]
To Marriage—The happy estate
which resembles a pair of shears;
so joined that they cannot be separated; often moving in opposite
directions, yet always punishing
anyone who comes between them.

[9829]
Here's to the stork,
A most valuable bird,
That inhabits the residence districts.
He doesn't sing tunes,
Nor yield any plumes,
But he helps out the vital statistics.

TOASTS TO FRIENDS

[9830]
Then here's to thee, old friend; and
long
May thou and I thus meet,
To brighten still with wine and
song
The short life ere it fleet.

[9831]
To the friend who never had a
hole in his pocket.

[9832]
To old chums with young hearts.

[9833]
A dinner, coffee and cigars,
Of friends, a half a score.
Each favorite vintage in its turn,—
What man could wish for more?

[9834]
May we all travel through the
world and sow it thick with friendship.

[9835]

Here's to the four hinges of Friendship—
Swearing, Lying, Stealing and Drinking.
When you swear, swear by your country;
When you lie, lie for a pretty woman,
When you steal, steal away from bad company
And when you drink, drink with me.

[9836]

Here is to friendship: One soul in two bodies.

[9837]

May we ever be able to serve a friend and noble enough to conceal it.

[9838]

Here's to the tears of friendship. May they crystallize as they fall and be worn as jewels by those we love.

[9839]

May we never see an old friend with a new face.

[9840]

May we have more and more friends, and need them less and less.

[9841]

Here's Champagne to our real friends,
And real pain to our sham friends.

[9842]

Friendship's the wine of life.
Let's drink of it and to it.

[9843]

May we never want a friend, nor a bottle to give him.

[9844]

May the lamp of friendship be lighted by the oil of sincerity.

[9845]

May the bark of friendship never founder on the rock of deceit.

[9846]

May we treat our friends with kindness—and our enemies with generosity.

[9847]

May we have a few real friends rather than a thousand acquaintances.

[9848]

Bread—to feed our friendship,
Salt—to keep it true.
Water—that's for welcome,
Wine—to drink to you!

[9849]

Here's to our friends in adversity, and may we never be in the same fix.

[9850]

May we never have friends who, like shadows, keep close to us in the sunshine, only to desert us on a cloudy day.

[9851]

Here's to our absent friends,—
God bless them.

[9852]

Here's a toast to the future,
A toast to the past,
And a toast to our friends, far and near.
May the future be pleasant;
The past a bright dream;
May our friends remain faithful and dear.

[9853]

Here's a health to our friends and a reprieve for our enemies.

[9854]

May friendship, like wine, improve as time advances, and may we always have old wine, old friends, and young cares.

[9855]

Here's to the friends of tomorrow.

[9856]

May the hinges of friendship never rust, nor the wings of love lose a feather.

[9857]

Friend of my soul! this goblet sip—
'Twill chase the pensive tear;
'Tis not so sweet as woman's lip,
But, O! 'tis more sincere.
Like her delusive beam,
'Twill steal away the mind,
But unlike affection's dream,
It leaves no sting behind.

[9858]

Come charge high, again, boy, nor let the full wine
Leave a space in the brimmer, where daylight may shine;
Here's the friends of our youth— though of some we're bereft,
May the links that are lost but endear what are left.

—*Moore.*

TOASTS TO GOOD FELLOWSHIP

[9859]

Clink, clink, your glasses and drink!
Why should we trouble borrow,
Care not for sorrow,
A fig for the morrow!
Tonight let's be merry and drink!

[9860]

A glass is good, a lass is good,
And a pipe to smoke in cold weather,
The world is good and the people are good,
And we're all good fellows together.

[9861]

Then fill the bowl—away with gloom,
Our joys shall always last;
For hope shall brighten days to come,
And mem'ry gild the past.

[9862]

The good die young—Here's hoping that you may live to a ripe old age.

[9863]

To a short life and a merry one.

[9864]

Fill the goblet again; for I never before
Felt the glow which now gladdens my heart to its core.
Let us drink! Who could not? Since life's varied round
In the goblet alone no deception is found.

—*Byron.*

[9865]

Come friends, come let us drink again,
This liquid from the nectar vine,
For water makes you dumb and stupid,
Learn this from the fishes—
They cannot sing, nor laugh, nor drink
This beaker full of sparkling wine.

[9866]

Here's to beefsteak when you're hungry—
Whisky when you're dry,
All the girls you ever want,
And heaven when you die.

[9867]

Drink! for you know not whence you come, nor why:
Drink! for you know not why you go, nor where.

—*Omar Khayyam.*

[9868]

Here's rest to the weary;
In peace rest his soul;
Good luck to the wanderer
Who's lost the keyhole!

[9869]

Here's to the health of those we
love best—
Our noble selves—God bless us;
None better and many a darn sight
worse,
Drink today and drown all sorrow;
You shall, perhaps, not do it to-
morrow.
—*Beaumont and Fletcher.*

[9870]

Here's to a temperance supper
With water in glasses tall,
And coffee and tea to end with—
And me not there at all.

[9871]

Laugh at all things,
Great and small things,
Sick or well, at sea or shore;
While we are quaffing
Let's have laughing,
Who the devil cares for more.
—*Byron.*

[9872]

Wine and women, mirth and
laughter—
Sermons and aspirin on the day
after.

[9873]

The Frenchman loves his native
wine;
The German loves his beer;
The Englishman loves his 'alf and
'alf,
Because it brings good cheer.
The Irishman loves his "whisky
straight,"
Because it gives him dizziness.
The American has no choice at all,
So he drinks the whole damned
business.

[9874]

Here's to beauty, wit and wine
and to a full stomach, a full purse
and a light heart.

[9875]

Here's to a long life and a merry
one;
A quick death and an easy one;
A pretty girl and a loving one;
A cold bottle—and another one.

[9876]

Come fill a bumper, pass it round,
May mirth, and song, and wit
abound,
In them alone true wisdom lies—
For to be merry's to be wise.

[9877]

The miser may be pleased with
gold,
The sporting beau with pretty
lass;
But I'm best pleased when I behold
The nectar sparkling in the glass.

[9878]

Drink today and drown all sorrow,
You shall perhaps not do't to-
morrow;
Best while you have it, use your
breath;
There is no drinking after death.

[9879]

Here's to champagne, the drink
divine,
That makes us forget our troubles;
It's made of a dollar's worth of
wine
And three dollars worth of bubbles.

[9880]

Fill the bumper fair! Every drop
we sprinkle
O'er the brow of care, smoothes
away a wrinkle.
Wit's electric frame ne'er so swiftly
passes
As when through the frame it
shoots from brimming glasses.

[9881]

Come, fill the bowl, each jolly soul;
Let Bacchus guide our revels;
Join cup to lip, with "hip, hip, hip,"
And bury the blue devils.

[9882]

This night is ours, then strew with
flowers
The moments as they roll:
For if any pain or care remain,
Why, drown it in the bowl.
This lesson oft in life I sing,
And from any grave I still shall
cry,
Drink, mortal, drink, while time
is young,
Ere death has made thee old as I.
—*Moore.*

[9883]

Eat, drink, and be merry, for tomorrow ye diet.

[9884]

A glass is good, and a lass is good,
And a pipe to smoke in cold
weather,
The world is good and people are
good,
And we're all good fellows together.
Let schoolmasters puzzle their brain
with grammar and nonsense
and learning,
Good liquor, I stoutly maintain,
Gives genius a better discerning.

[9885]

Here's to mine and here's to thine!
Now's the time to clink it!
Here's a flagon of old wine,
And here we are to drink it.

[9886]

To drink to-night, with hearts as
light,
To loves as gay and fleeting
As bubbles that swim on the
breaker's brim,
And break on the lips while meeting.

TOASTS ON FORTUNE AND PROSPERITY

[9887]

May the tide of fortune float us
into the harbor of content.

[9888]

May fortune recover her eyesight
and be just in the distribution of
her favors.

[9889]

When climbing the Hill of Prosperity,
May we never meet a friend coming
down.

[9890]

May bad fortune follow you all your
days
And never catch up with you.

[9891]

May you live long and prosper.

[9892]

Here's to our creditors—may they
be endowed with the three virtues,
faith, hope and charity.

[9893]

May poverty always be a day's
march behind us.

[9894]

May Dame Fortune ever smile on
you; but never her daughter—Miss
Fortune.

PATRIOTIC TOASTS

[9895]

The union of lakes, the union of
lands,
The union of states none can sever,
The union of hearts, the union of
hands,
And the flag of our union forever!

[9896]
Here's health to Columbia, the pride
of the earth,
The Stars and Stripes—drink the
land of our birth!
Toast the army and navy, who
fought for our cause,
Who conquered and won us our
freedom and laws.

[9897]
To the land we live in, love and
would die for.

[9898]
Land of the forest and the rock,
Of dark blue lake and mighty
river,
Of mountains reared on high to
mock
The storm's career and lightning
shock,
My own green land forever.
—*Longfellow.*

[9899]
Here's to America, free laws and a
free church,
From their blessing may plotters be
left in the lurch;
Give us pure candidates and a pure
ballot box,
And our freedom shall stand as firm
as the rocks.

[9900]
To Our America: The best land
in the world; let him that don't like
it, leave it.

[9901]
One flag, one land, one heart, one
hand, one nation evermore.
—*Oliver Wendell Holmes.*

[9902]
To her we drink, for her we pray,
Our voices silent never;
For her we'll fight—let come what
may,
The Stars and Stripes forever.

[9903]
The Lily of France may fade,
The Thistle and Shamrock
wither,
The Oak of England may decay,
But the Stars shine on forever.

[9904]
Old Glory: May her stars shine
forever in the eternal blue, and her
stripes reach round the world!

[9905]
Long may our flag in triumph wave
Against the world combined,
And friends a welcome—foes a
grave,
Within our borders find.

[9906]
Here's to the Army and Navy,
And the battles they have won,
Here's to America's colors—
The colors that never run.

[9907]
Our Navy.—May it ever float.

[9908]
Here's to the American Eagle,
That bird so uncommonly hale,
Whom nobody yet could inveigle
When they tried to put salt on his
tail.

[9909]
The American Eagle and the
Thanksgiving Turkey:
May one give us peace in all our
States,
And the other a piece for all our
plates.

[9910]
The American Heart—Quick and
strong in its generous impulses,
firm in its attachments, sound to
the core.

[9911]
May we never seek applause from
party principles, but always deserve
it from public spirit.

[9912]
May all mankind make free to enjoy the blessings of liberty, but never take the liberty to subvert the principles of freedom.

[9913]
May corruption be chained,
And truth maintained.

[9914]
May we never know any difference between our country and others save the oceans which separate them.

[9915]
May the seeds of dissension never find growth in the soil of America.

[9916]
May noise never excite us to battle, or confusion reduce us to defeat.

[9917]
May the blossoms of liberty never be blighted.

[9918]
May the wings of liberty never want a feather.

[9919]
May our counsels be wise, and our commerce increase,
And may we ever experience the blessings of peace.

[9920]
May we be slaves to no party and bigots to no sect.

[9921]
To the highest law, the welfare of the people.

[9922]
May our great men be good, and our good men be great.

[9923]
May the tree of liberty flourish round the globe, and every human being partake of its fruits.

[9924]
O England!—model to thy inward greatness,
Like little body with a mighty heart!
—*Shakespeare.*

[9925]
Here's to the land of the shamrock so green,
Here's to each lad and his darling colleen,
Here's to the ones we love dearest and most,
And may God Bless old Ireland!— that's an Irishman's toast.

TOASTS OF SENTIMENT AND GOOD-WILL

[9926]
Love to one, Friendship to a few, and Good-Will to all.

[9927]
May good humor preside when good fellows meet,
And reason prescribe when 'tis time to retreat.

[9928]
May the most you wish for be the least you get.

[9929]
May wine never prove the cause for strife.

[9930]
May truth and liberty prevail.

[9931]
Here's to the heart that never wanders and the tongue that never slanders.

[9932]
May goodness prevail when beauty fails.

[9933]
To the memory of ourselves, without regret.

[9934]
May good nature and good sense ever be united.

[9935]
May our pleasures be free from the stings of remorse.

[9936]
O, wad some Pow'r the giftie gie us
To see oursels as others see us!
It wad frae monie a blunder free us.
—*Robert Burns.*

[9937]
Here's a health to all who need it.

[9938]
May we grumble without cause,
And may we never have cause to grumble.

[9939]
To each man's best and truest love,—unless it be himself.

[9940]
By deserving success may we command it.

[9941]
As we meet upon the level, may we part upon the square.

[9942]
May we never speak to deceive nor listen to betray.

[9943]
Here's to the men who lose!
It is the vanquished's praises that I sing,
And this is the toast I choose:
"A hard-fought failure is a noble thing!
Here's to the men who lose."

[9944]
May your coffee and slanders against you be ever alike—without grounds.

[9945]
May their joys be as deep as the ocean,
And their misfortune as light as its foam.

[9946]
May we live to learn well, and learn to live well.

[9947]
May the heart that melts at the sight of sorrow always be blessed with the means to relieve it.

[9948]
Good luck till we are tired of it.

[9949]
May our shadows never grow less.

[9950]
May we never feel want or ever want feeling.

[9951]
May we be slaves to nothing but our duty, and friends to nothing but merit.

[9952]
May the sword of justice be swayed by the hand of mercy.

[9953]
May our talents never be prostituted to vice.

[9954]
May virtue be our armor when wickedness is our assailant.

[9955]
May the prison gloom be cheered by the rays of hope, and liberty fetter the arm of oppression.

[9956]
To everyone, I wish love in every breast, liberty in every heart, and learning in every head.

[9957]
May the eye that drops for the misfortunes of others never shed a tear for its own.

[9958]

May our imagination never run away with our judgment.

[9959]

May we never be influenced by jealousy nor governed by interest.

[9960]

May we never be blind to our own errors.

[9961]

May we never be the slaves of interest or of pride.

[9962]

May our pleasures be free from the stings of remorse.

[9963]

May Satan never pay visits abroad nor receive company at home.

[9964]

May we never flatter our superiors or insult our inferiors.

[9965]

May the frowns of fortune never rob innocence of its joys.

[9966]

Riches without pride, or poverty without meanness.

[9967]

Riches to the generous and power to the merciful.

[9968]

May every day be happier than the last.

[9969]

May we distinguish the weeds from the flowers.

[9970]

May the thorns of life only serve to give a zest to its flowers.

[9971]

May we strengthen the weak, give light to the blind, clothe the naked, and be friends to mankind.

[9972]

Success to our hopes and enjoyment to our wishes.

[9973]

May we fly from the temptation we cannot resist.

[9974]

May genius and merit never want a friend.

[9975]

May the pole-star of hope guide us through the sea of misfortune.

[9976]

May you live all the days of your life.

—*Swift.*

[9977]

Here's to the man or woman who speaks well of us to our enemies.

[9978]

To them that love others better than themselves.

[9979]

May the pleasures of youth never bring us pain in old age.

[9980]

May every day bring more happiness than yesterday.

[9981]

May we never know want till relief is at hand.

[9982]

Sunshine and good humor all over the world.

[9983]

May we have the wit to discover what is true and the fortitude to practice what is good.

[9984]

May we e'er mingle in the flowing bowl,
The feast of reason and the flow of soul.

TOASTS TO HOSTS AND GUESTS

[9985]
To Our Host,—the host of hosts.

[9986]
Here's a toast to the host who
carved the roast;
And a toast to the hostess—may she
never "roast" us.

[9987]
Here's a toast to the hostess, a toast
to the host,
May we all meet again, e'er we give
up the ghost.

[9988]
To Our Hosts: Happiness, health
and prosperity.

[9989]
Let's drink to our friend and host.
May his generous heart, like his
good wine, only grow mellower
with the years.

[9990]
Here's to the host and the hostess,
We're honored to be here to-
night;
May they both live long and pros-
per,
May their star of hope ever be
bright.

[9991]
So health and love to all your mansion;
Long may the bowl that pleasures
bloom in,
The flow of heart, the soul's expan-
sion,
Mirth, joy and song your board
illumine.

[9992]
I thank you for your welcome which
was cordial,
And your cordial which was welcome.

[9993]
To Our Guest: A friend of our
friend's is doubly our friend.
Here's to him.

[9994]
You are welcome, my fair guests;
that noble lady,
Or gentleman that is not freely
merry,
Is not my friend: This to confirm
my welcome:
And to you all good health.
—*Henry VIII.*

[9995]
By the bread and salt, by the water
and wine,
You are welcome, friends, at this
board of mine.

[9996]
Come in the evening, or come in
the morning—
Come when you're looked for, or
come without warning;
A thousand welcomes you'll find
here before you,
The oftener you come here the more
I'll adore you!

TOASTS IN GENERAL

[9997]
A little health, a little wealth,
A little house and freedom,
With some few friends for certain
ends,
But little cause to need 'em.

[9998]
Pass me the wine. To those that
keep
The bachelor's secluded sleep
Peaceful, inviolate and deep
I pour libation.
—*Dobson.*

[9999]
Here's to the fellow who smiles
When life rolls along like a song,
And here's to the chap who can
smile
When everything goes dead wrong.

[10000]
I drink it as the fates ordain it,
Come fill it, and have done with
rhymes;
Fill up the lonely glass and drain it
In memory of dear old times.

[10001]
And fill them high with generous
juice,
As generous as your mind,
And pledge me in the generous
toast—
The whole of human kind!
—*Robert Burns.*

[10002]
Here's to us that are here, to you
that are there, and the rest of us
everywhere.

[10003]
Happy are we met, Happy have we
been,
Happy may we part, and Happy
meet again.

[10004]
Here's a health to the future,
A sigh for the past;
We can love and remember,
And hope to the last;
And for all the base lies
That the almanacs hold,
While there's love in the heart,
We can never grow old.

[10005]
Here's to the future, whatever it
brings,
And hoping we'll never swerve
From doing right and thinking
right,
And getting what we deserve.

[10006]
Our drink shall be water, bright,
sparkling with glee,
The gift of our God, and the drink
of the free.

[10007]
A health to our sweethearts,
Our friends and our wives,
And may fortune smile on them
The rest of their lives.

[10008]
Ho! stand to your glasses steady!
'Tis all we have left to prize.
A cup to the dead already,—
Hurrah for the next that dies.
—*Dowling.*

[10009]
Come, love and health to all:
Then I'll sit down. Give me some
wine, fill full,
I drink to the general joy o' the
whole table.
—*Shakespeare.*

[10010]
To the old, long life and treasure;
To the young, all health and pleas-
ure.
—*Ben Jonson.*

[10011]
Here's to merry old world,
And the days be they bright or
blue,
Here's to the fates, let them bring
what they may—
But the best of them all—That's
you.

[10012]
Here's a health to thee and thine
From the hearts of me and mine;
And when thee and thine
Come to see me and mine,
May me and mine make thee and
thine
As welcome as thee and thine
Have ever made me and mine.

[10013]
Here's a toast to all who are here,
No matter where you're from;
May the best day you have seen
Be worse than your worst to come.

[10014]
Long live life, say I—and good fellowship for the future.

[10015]
Here's to friends both near and far;
Here's to woman, man's guiding star;
Here's to friends we've yet to meet,
Here's to those here; all here I greet;
Here's to childhood, youth, old age,
Here's to prophet, bard and sage,
Here's a health to every one,
Peace on earth, and heaven won!

[10016]
Thus circling the cup, hand in hand, ere we drink,
Let sympathy pledge us, through pleasure, through pain,
That, fast as a feeling but touches one link,
Her magic shall send it direct through the chain.

[10017]
Welcome be ye that are here,
Welcome all, and make good cheer,
Welcome all, another year.

[10018]
To you, and yours, and theirs, and mine,
I pledge with you, their health in wine.

[10019]
Here's to man from morning till night;
Here's to the man with courage to fight—
The courage to fight and the courage to live—
The courage to learn, and to love, and forgive.

[10020]
Here's to us all—God bless us everyone.
—*Dickens.*

[10021]
A cheerful glass, a pretty lass,
A friend sincere and true;
Blooming health, good store of wealth
Attend on me and you.

[10022]
Old wood to burn, old wine to drink, old friends to trust, and old authors to read.
—*Bacon.*

[10023]
I drink to the days that are!
—*William Morris.*

[10024]
May the right person say the right thing
To the right person in the right way.
At the right time, in the right place.

[10025]
Here's to another and one other,
Whoever she or he may be.

[10026]
Here's to all the world,—
For fear some darn fool may take offence.

[10027]
May you live as long as you like,
And have what you like as long as you live.

[10028]
Here's to those who love us,
And here's to those who don't,
A smile for those who are willing to,
And a tear for those who won't.

[10029]
Here's to the heart that fills as the bottle empties.

[10030]
Here's to you two and to we two,
If you two love we two
As we two love you two,
Then here's to we four!
But if you two don't love we two
As we two love you two,
Then here's to we two and no more.

[10031]
To the land we love, and the "love"
we "land."

[10032]
Here's to the times we might have
had,
  Here's to the girls we might have
won.
Here's that we do the thing next
time,
  That last time we should have
done.

[10033]
Here's to you as good as you are,
And here's to me as bad as I am;
And as bad as I am, and as good as
you are,
I'm as good as you are, as bad as I
am.

[10034]
At the goblet's brink,
Let us pause and think,
  How they do it in Japan.
First the man takes a drink,
Then the drink takes a drink,
  Then the drink takes the man.

[10035]
Here's to Morpheus: May he let us
sleep like a log but not like a
sawmill.

[10036]
Here's to the joke, the good old
joke,
  The joke that our fathers told;
It is ready tonight and is jolly and
bright
  As it was in the days of old.

[10037]
Here's a toast to great ambition,
About which people rant.
It makes you want to do the thing
That everyone knows you can't.

[10038]
  May the Lord love us but not call
us too soon.

[10039]
Here's to my pipe, a trusty friend
indeed,
Filled with that soothing and rest-
giving weed,
That fills my soul with peace and
joy and laughter—
I'd rather smoke here than in the
hereafter.

[10040]
May you be hung, drawn and quar-
tered,—
Hung in the halls of prosperity,
Drawn by a chariot and four,
And quartered in the arms of one
you love best.

[10041]
  To the ministers who don't
preach, and the preachers who minister.

[10042]
  We haven't all had the good fortune to be ladies; we have not all
been generals, or poets or statesmen;
but when the toast works down to
the babies, we stand on common
ground—for we've all been babies.
                          —Mark Twain.

[10043]
To Home, the place where we
receive the best treatment and
which we appreciate the least.

[10044]
Here's to the ships of our navy,
And the ladies of our land;
May the first be ever well rigged,
And the latter ever well manned.

[10045]
Here's to the soldier who fights and loves—may he never lack for either.

[10046]
Here is to home where a world of strife is shut out and a world of love is shut in.

[10047]
Here's to the soldier and his arms,
Fall in, men, fall in;
Here's to woman and her arms,
Fall in, men, fall in!

[10048]
A toast for three.
I'm as dear to you as he,
He's as dear to me as thee,
You're as dear to him as me,
Here's to 'Three's good company."

[10049]
Here's to our fisherman bold;
Here's to the fish he caught;
Here's to the ones that got away,
And here's to the ones he bought.

[10050]
To mankind we drink:—'tis a pleasant task:
Heaven bless it and multiply its wealth;
But it is a little too much to ask
That we should drink to its health.
—*Physicians' Toast.*

[10051]
Here's wishing good health and long life to you,
And the choice of the girls for a wife to you,
And your land without penny of rent to you:
If these three blessings are sent to you,
Then there'll be peace and content to you.
—*An Irish Toast.*

[10052]
Unto our doctors let us drink,
Who cure our chills and ills,
No matter what we really think
About their pills and bills.

[10053]
Saint Patrick was a gentleman,
Who, thro' strategy and stealth,
Drove all the snakes from Ireland,—
Here's a bumper to his health.
But not too many bumpers,
Lest we lose ourselves, and then
Forget the good Saint Patrick,
And see the snakes again.
—*An Irish Toast.*

[10054]
Here's to de holidays! Bless de hull t'ree hundred and sixty-five of 'em!
—*Hobo's Toast.*

STORIES ABOUT TOASTS

[10055]
In presenting Franklin Delano Roosevelt, the Democratic candidate for the presidency in 1932, to a great audience in Denver, the local presiding officer couldn't resist a highly laudatory reference to the vice-presidents of the meeting on the platform.

"I want you to know, Mr. Roosevelt, that there are sitting with you on this platform men qualified to serve with you in the cabinet, men of United States Senatorship size, men who would bring honor and high attainment to the highest diplomatic posts."

Candidate Roosevelt, upon arising, said:

"Mr. Chairman, members of the

cabinet, distinguished representatives of the nation in the Senate of the United States, and plenipotentiaries extraordinary in foreign lands!"

[10056]
At a dinner of the foreign ministers, following the American Revolutionary war, the British ambassador gave: "England—the sun, whose bright beams enlighten and fructify the remotest corners of the earth." The French ambassador followed with: "France—the moon, whose mild, steady, and cheering rays are the delight of all nations, controlling them in the darkness, and making their dreariness beautiful." Benjamin Franklin then rose, and, with his usual dignity and simplicity, said: "George Washington—the Joshua, who commanded the sun and moon to stand still, and they obeyed him."

[10057]
Senator Spooner of Wisconsin said the best speech of introduction he ever heard was delivered by the German mayor of a small town in Wisconsin, where Spooner had been engaged to speak.
The mayor said:
"Ladies und shentlemens, I haf been asked to indrotoose you to the Honorable Senator Spooner, who will make to you a speech, yes. I haf now done so; he vill now do so."

[10058]
A minister, on the closing night of a church conference prayed:
"Oh Lord, be with the first speaker and give him power to move this people. And be with the second speaker and endue him with Thy spirit. And Lord, Lord, have mercy on the last speaker!"

[10059]
During the war with Great Britain an American officer, who carried a flag over to the British lines, after having dispatched the business of his mission, was invited by the commanding British officer to dine. As usual on such occasions, the wine was circulated, and a British officer being called upon for a toast, gave "Mr. Madison, dead or alive"; which the American drank without appearing to give it particular notice. When it came to the American's turn to give a toast, he gave, "The Prince Regent, drunk or sober."—"Sir," said the British officer, bristling up and coloring with anger, "that is an insult."—"No, sir," answered the American very coolly, "it is only a reply to one."

[10060]
A minister, concerning the volubility of a certain toastmaster, prayed: "Oh, Lord, from all traducers and all introducers, deliver us!"

[10061]
At a political dinner, a workingman, who was called upon for a toast offered the following: "Here is health to poverty; it sticks to a man when all his friends forsake him."

[10062]
A Negro bishop in introducing a white clergyman, said:
"Breddern, it is not often I arise to present a white speaker in this meeting-house. But you can be sure he has a powerful message for you. An' while his skin may be white, his heart is as black as any of us!"

[10063]
An admirer of William Jennings Bryan took so much of the evening

to catalogue the Commoner's uncommon qualities as statesman and speaker, that all Mr. Bryan could give and catch the train was practically his postoffice address.

"Wonderful speech!" exclaimed a listener after it was all over.

"Yep, and the baldheaded feller who spoke last wasn't so bad!" affirmed the man just behind.

[10064]

"It affords me great pleasure," began Chauncey M. Depew in introducing Dr. Vincent to a New York audience, "to present the president of the University of Minnesota, popularly acclaimed as the 'Cyclone of the Northwest.'"

"I appreciate the designation," said Dr. Vincent in arising, "by the most eminent wind authority of the East."

[10065]

"Who was the speaker of the evening?" asked one who did not attend.

"The toastmaster, of course," replied one who did.

INDEX

A

Abbreviation, 3260
Ability, 6314
Abnormal, 3507
Aboard Ships, 1021–1047
Absence, 6315
Absent-minded Professors, 3949–3977
Abstinence, 6316
Accidents, 1003, 1008, 1664, 2405, 4775, 6956
Accommodating, 5501
Accomplishment, 2290, 4241
Accuracy, 1665
Achievement, 3403, 4252, 4273
Acoustics, 5549, 5595
Acquaintance, 7297
Acting, 2619, 7132, 7298
Actors, 5392, 6318. *See* Broadway
Adam, 3675
Adams, John Quincy, 5492
Address, 5315
Ade, George, 5421, 5446, 5513
Adjustment, 3055
Admiration, 6815, 7299
Admission, 4551, 4948
Adult, 7300
Advances, 1960, 4356
Advantages, 4548
Adversity, 6319
Advertising, 522, 575, 1381, 1521, 1980, 2861, 3651, 5621, 6154, 6910, 7210, 7255, 7301
Advice, 535, 2240, 2483, 4765, 4867, 4940, 6320, 7302, 7574, 8006
Affectation, 6321
Affected speech, 6709
After death, 43
After-dinner speaking, 622, 7303, 7769
Age, 266, 307, 339, 527, 773, 1060, 1381, 1739, 1744, 1799, 1811, 1816, 1817, 1842, 2034, 2040, 2043, 2238, 2257, 2430, 2640, 3122, 3128, 3259, 3352, 3489, 3497, 4097, 4993, 5363, 5492, 6322, 7304
Agreement, 2462
Aid, 290, 2816, 2949
Aim, 2077
Aimless, 4178
Alarm clock, 4484
Alibi, 1633
Alien, 2899
Alienist, 1156, 4841
Alimony, 2836, 2839, 2850, 6323, 7306
Alliance, 7307
Allowances, 1938, 2325
Alone, 5682
Alphabet, 3181, 5688
Alumni, 3886, 3980, 4282
Ambiguity, 970
Ambition, 77, 671, 745, 1335, 3861, 4310, 4326, 4816, 5008, 6858
America, 6673
American, 203, 326, 7295, 7308, 7309, 7310
American Scene, The, 1–346
Americans Abroad, 1699–1730
Ancestry, 22, 62, 113, 151, 172, 176, 226, 263, 278, 1775, 2286, 3262, 5486, 6324, 6672, 6951, 6954, 7185, 7985, 7997, 8993
And, 5592
Angels, 2259, 2384, 2636, 2643
Angry, 3702, 7231
Animal, 6325

Anniversary, 2222
Annuity, 4888
Answering letters, 5388
Anticipation, 981
Anti-climax, 1700, 2125, 4187, 5565
Antipathy, 3742
Antiques, 30, 4475, 4500, 7311
Antonyms, 1588
Ants, 3474, 3557, 6290
Apartments, 39, 85, 417, 4566, 7312
Apologetic, 4551, 4582
Apology, 5367, 6404, 7230
Appeal, 6409
Appearance, 18, 1222, 1346, 1361, 2035, 4795, 6326
Appendicitis, 4950, 4964, 4971, 5001, 5004, 7311
Appetite, 1576, 1830, 7181
Applause, 5586, 5600, 5606
Apples, 4957, 5028
Application, 4326
Appreciation, 468, 616
Appropriate remark, 610
Aquisitive, 2043
Arrangement, 2699
Architecture, 1706
Arguments, 1188, 3449, 6300, 7011
Aristocracy, 1724
Arliss, George, 5656
Arm, 4741
Art, 347–391, 3027, 3304, 5356, 5538, 6284, 6328, 7314
Ashamed, 2208, 5623
Asking, 2824
Assessments, 2189
Assistance, 3696
Association of thought, 1620
Astronomy, 3372
Athletics, *See* Sports
Athletics, college, 4220–4238
Attachment, 1655
Attendance, 5594
Audiences, 392, 432
Author, 6329
Authority, 5695
Autographs, 5505, 5656
Automobiles, 784–953
Avarice, 6330
Average Man, 7316
Aviators, 1217, 1514, 5460
Awkward, 4370

B

Babies, 2876–2934, 5412
Bachelors and Spinsters, 2860–2875, 1630, 6331, 7317, 7318
Back-seat drivers, 789, 822, 841, 850, 857, 873, 898, 917, 919, 924, 925, 932, 934, 952, 953
Bacon, Lord, 5350
Bait, 2322, 4704
Balance, 1994, 4506
Baldness, 287, 3005, 3345
Balzac, 5473
Banks, 2702, 2716, 4584–4603, 7097, 7112, 7294, 7319
Barbers, 744–783, 5047, 6878, 7320
Bargaining, 1642, 4745, 7205

Bargains, 3156, 3257, 5519, 7057, 7236, 7321, 7322
Barnum, P. T., 5380
Barrie, J. M., 5451, 5495
Barrymore, John, 5485, 5499, 5589, 5609
Baseball, 6195–6212, 6658, 7323
Bathing, 118, 1797, 1805, 1831, 2408, 3147, 5369, 7170
Bathing suits, 93
Bathroom, 3631
Beans, 3538
Beard, 4490
Beauty, 1812, 1814, 2071, 6332
Beecher, Henry Ward, 5151, 5404, 5408, 5512
Behavior, 1978
Bennett, James Gordon, 5364
Belittling, 1704
Berry, 6775
Bet, 7073
Bible, 811, 3649
Bigamy, 3388, 7324
Big cities, 48
Bigoted, 4791, 7101, 7325
Billboards, 7902
Bill collector, 9, 1796, 6904, 6945, 7343, 7937
Bills, 2306, 2765
Birthday, 1782, 2430, 7326, 7801
Birthplace, 3545
Biscuits, 2422
Black and white, 993
Blackmail, 3265
Blame, 2489, 3485
Blessing, 6334
Blind, 6335
Boarding Houses, 727–743
Boasting, 72, 1066, 1072, 1073, 3155, 4552
Boiled cabbage, 3493
Boners, 33, 47, 121, 209, 260, 328, 571, 1047, 1131, 1701, 1825, 2673, 3494, 5131, 5568, 8504–8622
Books, 114, 1778, 5535, 5573, 6336, 7758, 7766
Boon, 2255
Boosters, 1
Bootlegging, 6337
Bore, 4, 285, 987, 6771, 7327, 8006
Borrowing, 206, 224, 295, 4211
Boss, 2310, 2599, 2738
Boston, 87, 292, 1707, 2903, 3001, 3259, 3543, 7328
Boxing, 6213–6226, 6710
Bragging, 1722, 7184
Brains, 1969, 4625, 4647, 7136
Bravery, 1114, 1121, 2541, 2995, 7035
Breakfast food, 293
Brevity, 847, 1494, 1524, 1556, 2664, 3867, 3985, 4300, 6900, 6929, 7225
Bride, 7740, 7797. See Married Life
Bridge, 3783, 4258, 6087–6105, 7121, 7330, 7754
British, See English
Broadway, 5544–5627, 7331
Bromides, 38
Brooklyn, 276, 972
Brooks, Phillips, 3422, 5504
Brotherly love, 3591
Budget, 1618, 2301, 2331, 2391, 7332
Building, 6275, 6309
Bulls, 66, 272, 1181
Bumpy trains, 1007
Burbank, Luther, 5405
Burning the candle, 3375
Buses and Street Cars, 954–980, 6703, 6709, 6978
Business, 3167, 4285–4732, 6338, 7333
But, 1639, 5592
Butchers and Grocers, 4414–4440
Buyer, 4620

C

Cake, 2307, 2437, 2609, 3136
Calamities, 2505
California, 160, 162, 186, 300, 888, 6310
Calling, 4761, 7969
Calm, 5023
Calmness, 1421
Cameras, 4846
Camping, 164
Canary, 4487, 4493
Cancellation, 4674, 4678, 4690
Candidate, 6339
Cannibalism, 6340
Canvasser, 5076
Capacity, 5704
Capital punishment, 3537, 3847, 4884
Careful, 3042, 3197, 4592, 7173
Careless, 2, 1651, 2357, 2742
Caruso, Enrico, 5940
Cash registers, 4494
Caterpillars, 3073
Cats, 2866, 3471
Caution, 552, 561, 565, 588, 761, 1411, 1488, 1646, 2139
Celebration, 3710
Celebrities, See Famous Men
Censor, 4139
Certain, 1749
Chauffeur, 7336. See Automobiles
Challenge, 5294
Champagne, 5478
Changing times, 4157
Chaperon, 4092
Character, 2173
Charging, 4439
Charitable, 5614
Charity, 402, 1085, 1320, 4613, 6232
Chatter, 5518
Cheating, 1207, 2942, 6011
Checking up, 2854
Chef, 1448
Chesterfield, Lord, 5448, 5526
Chickens, 138
Child of Satan, 3630
Children, 2935–3678, 6343
Chinese, 7116, 7255–7274
Chivalry, 957, 967, 1192, 1274, 1599, 1629
Choate, Joseph, 5375
Choice, 1344, 1627, 1889, 2945, 3043, 3045, 5466, 7068
Choir, 3000
Chorus girl, 7338. See Broadway
Christening, 2933
Christians, 6344
Christmas, 228, 7339, 7662
Christmas cigars, 2559, 7958
Christmas gifts, 2519
Church, 2388, 2946, 3009, 3322, 3623
Churchill, Winston, 5493
Cigarette lighter, 2514
Cigars, 2519
Circumstances, 2029
Circumstantial evidence, 613, 639, 714, 1169, 4848, 4921
Circuses and Show Business, 5688–5706, 7202
City life, 1443
Civilization, 6345, 7340, 7561, 7848
Civilized nation, 7341
Clark, Champ, 5353, 5479
Classroom in colleges, 3815–3948
Clay, Henry, 5432, 5455
Cleanliness, 3732
Clergymen, See Preachers
Clever, 1207, 2004, 2987
Climate, 238, 6310
Clothes, 2900
Clubs, 105, 2755, 2763
Cockney, 973

Co-ed, 7342. *See* College Wit
Coffee, 617, 641, 654, 655, 664, 705, 741, 4997, 5521, 6735
Coincidence, 2148
Cold, 6312
College Wit and Humor, 3815–4284, 7344
Comeback, 96
Comforting, 2875
Comic Dictionary, 7297–7527
Comic Poems, *See* Humorous Verse
Commerce, 1221
Commission, 4637
Committee, 59, 7345, 7346
Commuter, 11, 960, 961, 963, 964, 7347
Companionate, 2841
Company, 3843
Company manners, 3333
Comparisons, 810, 1092
Competition, 1183, 1849
Complaints, 166, 193, 604, 797, 1016, 4503
Compliments, 264, 7146
Compromise, 734, 4367
Conceit, 14, 279, 1868, 1880, 2061, 2064, 2076, 2097, 2102, 2103, 2176, 2804, 6346
Concentration, 1342, 1936, 2109
Concert, 3313
Conference, 4313, 4317, 4384
Confession, 117, 1204, 7184
Confidence, 2666, 4483, 5042
Confidential, 4361
Confusion, 6, 212, 216, 962, 1898, 2153, 2565, 2756, 3364, 4466, 4774, 4798, 6877
Congestion, 4558
Congress, 632, 8010
Conscience, 4497, 4783, 7348, 8013
Consent, 3196
Conservation, 7289
Conservative, 6348, 7349
Consistent, 4856
Conspicuous, 6655
Conspiracy, 463
Constancy, 1048, 2198
Construction, 3348
Consulting, 7976
Contact, 129, 5493
Contagious, 2888
Contempt, 4902, 4920, 8008. *See* Lawyers
Contentment, 635, 645, 1353, 1512, 1657, 2279, 2868, 3479
Contingent fee, 4778. *See* Lawyers
Contradicting, 1908
Contribution, 1527, 5143
Conundrums, 8992–9198
Conversation, 1419, 1777, 1840, 2739
Conversion, 5153
Convert, 5343
Converted, 4438, 4668
Convictions, 2263, 4887
Cooks, 1178, 2413, 2659, 2853, 7549
Cooking, 1641, 2225, 2226, 2319, 2354, 2499, 2608, 6350
Coolidge, Calvin, 5530, 5531, 5541
Cooperation, 1612, 2032, 6278
Copeland, Charles Townsend, 5482
Coppers, 3794
Cold, 6288
Collective nouns, 3895
College athletics, 4220–4238
College classroom, 3815–3948
College humor back home, 170, 4239–4284
College Life, 3978–4024
College Wit and Humor, 3815–4284
Collar button, 2729
Collecting, 4289, 4419, 4426, 4676, 4689, 4808, 5574, 6699
Collection, 3632, 5214, 6860
Coloring, 464
Colors, 2347, 2595
Columbus, 6673

Corn, 6273, 6279
Cornstalk, 6308
Corroboration, 6285
Co-starring, 5589
Cost of living, 153, 183
Counting, 3514
Country club, 7
Courage, 101, 240, 1996, 2939, 6351
Courtesy, 1637, 7263
Courtship, 1870–2216, 7350
Coward, 3, 6354
Cows, 6293
Crafty, 6051
Creation, 7940
Credit, 198, 593, 708, 933, 2025, 5064, 7027
Creditor, 7351
Crime, 6355
Criminal, 7352. *See* Lawyers, and Police and Prisoners
Critics, 360, 445, 6356, 7353
Criticism, 409, 3125
Crossed signals, 2309
Crown, 3629
Crutches, 4742
Crying, 2777, 7607
Cue, 7269
Culture, 413, 488, 1699
Cure, 232
Curfew, 1609
Curiosity, 123, 340, 578, 724, 1406, 1544, 1806, 1857, 2115, 2480, 3102, 4472, 4670, 5631
Custard, 3010
Cynic, 7354

D

Dancing, 324, 2341, 4126, 4127, 4137, 4142, 4181, 4198
Dangerous, 6202
Dared, 5588
Darwin, Charles, 5449
Deaf, 317, 5113, 5117, 6685
Death, 5193, 5562, 6357
Debate, 5294, 5517
Debts, 5, 78, 855, 891, 1476, 1996, 2570, 2589, 2686, 3278, 7152, 7215, 7356, 7945
Deceive, 2789
Decency, 1774
Decision, 1928
Decoy, 5134, 6108
Deduction, 235, 2600, 3900, 5372, 5691, 6742
Definitions, *See* Comic Dictionary
Deliberate, 1664
Democracy, 1708, 6359
Democrats, 5240, 5244, 5246, 5263, 5264, 5332
Democratic headquarters, 5397
Demonstration, 4764
Denomination, 3688
Dentists, 2001, 2177, 3278, 5081–5109, 6908, 7218, 7257, 7357
Dependent, 2802
Depew, Chauncey M., 5464, 5505
Depressed, 1446
Depression, 4591
Description, 2934, 3136, 3343, 4513, 7242, 7261
Destiny, 6360
Detail, 528
Determination, 158, 3232
Devil, 4806, 6361
Devotion, 4441
Diagnosis, 5538
Dialect Verse, *See* Humorous Verse
Diary, 2436
Dickens, Charles, 5543
Diction, 2474

Dictionary, 5135, 5196, 5409
Dictionary, Comic, 7297–7527
Diet, 1329, 1794, 2438, 2705, 2801, 6362, 7533, 7810
Difference, 2171, 3586, 3879, 4900, 5628
Dignity, 3387
Diplomatic, 5466, 7360, 7361
Direction, 949, 1021, 4968, 6166, 7188
Dirty, 6752, 6788
Disability, 804
Disagreement, 2280, 2368, 4742
Disappointment, 5696
Disarmament, 6228
Discipline, 3056
Discouraged, 897, 907, 2870, 5141
Discovery, 675, 6873
Discretion, 640, 1034
Disease, 6364
Dishonesty, 1147, 4231
Disillusionment, 2184
Disraeli, 5389
Distance, 1628, 1662
Distinction, 1866
Distrust, 1195
Disturbing, 5197
Dividends, 2189
Dividing-up, 5352, 7159
Diving, 6283
Division, 2721, 2975, 4771, 4801
Divorce, 523, 2007, 2834–2859, 3199, 5632, 5640, 5653, 6365
Doctors, 4936–5080, 6366, 6863, 6917, 7603
Dogs, 3, 51, 161, 202, 301, 346, 522, 744, 1323, 1519, 2820, 3065, 3081, 3090, 3177, 3339, 3522, 3708, 4470, 5180, 6367, 7061, 7223, 7355
Do it now, 4287
Donkey, 2687
Doubt, 2085, 4828
Doyle, Arthur Conan, 5372
Drafts, 1002
Dressing, 2556
Drinking, 25, 315, 1105, 1439, 1837, 2180, 2783, 2803, 3999, 6368, 6903, 6944, 7058. See Drunks
Drought, 1395, 1495, 1517
Drug Stores, 4394–4413
Drunks, 1232–1309, 7114, 7363. See Drinking
Dumas, Alexandre, 5415
Dumb, 16, 254, 229, 549, 1101, 1126, 1137, 1165, 1810, 2747, 4341
Duncan, Isadora, 5511

E

Early bird, 3390
Eating, 57, 1802, 5704
Echo, 6297, 7365
Economy, 358, 1242, 2099, 2238, 2339, 2389, 2649, 2704, 3013, 3376, 4087, 5517, 7366. See Scotch
Editors and Reporters, 521–546
Education, 1155, 1584, 1603, 1610, 2247, 2657, 3477, 4249, 4654, 6371
Efficiency, 73, 979, 1600, 5076, 7189
Efficiency Experts, 4386–4393
Ego, 6373
Egotist, 2061, 7367, 7368
Eiffel Tower, 5398
Einstein, 5418, 5426, 5463
Election, 6374
Electricity, 5500
Elevator, 201, 3146
Eligible, 1750
Eloquence, 2163
Eliot, President, 5422
Embarrassment, 3842, 4768
Emotional, 579
Empty, 3003

Empty title, 3397
Encouragement, 1871, 1973, 1984, 2865, 4040, 6141
Encore, 5502, 7369
Endorsement, 2598, 4595, 4684, 5638, 7095
Enemies, 6955
Engagement, 7370. See Love and Courtship
Engineers, 784
English, 145, 326, 6654–6845, 7371, 7597
English language, 262, 264, 526, 583, 585, 678, 690, 720, 802, 1378, 1427, 1852, 2935, 2997, 4060, 6691, 6696
Enterprise, 5488
Entertaining, 1500, 1780
Enthusiasm, 648, 7372
Epigrams, 6375, 7528–7620
Epitaphs, 6376, 7373, 8016–8125
    American, 8016–8051
    British, 8052–8118
    Suggested, 8119–8125
Epithets, 5384
Equalizing, 7040
Errors, 546, 2080, 3017, 5111. See Mistakes
Errors in Print, See Humorous Errors
Ethics, 6377
Etiquette, 539, 3025, 7273, 7374
Eugenics, 5511
Evasive, 4827
Eve, 3675
Evidence, 1914, 1985, 2908, 4764, 5075
Evil, 6378
Evolution, 4779
Exaggeration, 86, 943, 1139, 3266, 5465
Example, 2707
Exception, 2477
Exchange, 2107, 2211, 3055, 3089
Excitement, 1421, 1616, 2397
Exclusiveness, 6381
Excuses, 34, 165, 244, 814, 819, 823, 832, 849, 862, 875, 878, 884, 893, 945, 1109, 1372, 1416, 1567, 1663, 2273, 2425, 2555, 2749, 3381, 3775, 4312, 4378, 8011
Exercise, 298, 1351, 2271, 2618
Executives, 4312
Expense account, 4630, 4638
Experience, 1454, 2184, 2406, 2445, 3737, 4672, 7375
Expired, 6665
Explanation, 1763, 2535, 2916, 3051, 3154, 3753, 6303
Explicit, 4402
Exposed, 3863
Expression, 3226
Extravagance, 1317, 6952
Eyesight, 826, 833, 909, 1203
Eyes open, 6030

F

Facts, 3942, 4763, 6380
Fairness, 586
Faith, 531, 1148, 5012, 5060, 6381, 7376
Faithful, 2073, 7547
Fall of man, 3667
Fall, 1400
False reports, 61
Fame, 348, 483, 3865, 5496, 5499, 6382, 7377
Familiarity, 97, 550, 4046, 4767, 5667, 6793, 7143
Family, 6383
Family Humor, 3367–3404, 6383
Famous Men, 5348–5543
Fare, 6022
Farewell, 6981
Farmer, 1380–1624, 3594, 3948, 7772
Farmhand, 1416, 1441, 1463. See Farmer

1011

Farm income, 1415, 1498, 1510, 1536, 1551
Farm relief, 1482, 1537
Fascist, 5401
Fashion, 4505, 6384, 7604. *See* Women's clothes
Fate, 6385
Father, 801, 871, 902, 936, 2149, 2564, 3011, 3399, 3559, 4266, 7901
Fat people 53, 127, 809, 954, 959, 976, 992, 1469, 2913, 5003, 5395, 5684
Faults, 2409, 2571, 3099, 4257
Fear, 1886, 2313, 3242, 3248, 6942
Fees, 4777, 4801, 4903, 4904, 4926, 5049, 5185, 6900
Fiction, 2360, 7378
Field, Eugene, 5465, 5506
Fighting, 1616, 3135, 3145, 3296, 6221, 7229
Filling station, 794, 812, 889, 1493, 6938
Final, 4128
Finance, 856, 1349
Finding, 6126
Firmness, 7379
First aid, 173
Fish, 6291
Fishing, 1710, 3131, 6138-6194, 6305
Fix, 6038
Flaming Youth, 4025-4219
Flattery, 1230, 1316, 1324, 1850, 1915, 2640, 2650, 3142, 4616, 4898, 6976, 7177, 7380
Fleas, 3656
Flies, 6170
Flirting, 1017, 1920, 2757, 2759, 3789, 5210
Flood, 6291
Flowers, 2805, 7274
Food, 6386
Fool, 6387, 7100
Football, 6925, 7381, 7382. *See* Athletics, College
Foreign language, 5505, 7033
Foreigners, 3519, 5236, 7197
Forgiveness, 3075, 3476, 3622, 8001
Force, 2121, 3354
Formal, 5485, 6933
Formal dress, 17
Formula, 2884
Fortune, 1915, 6388
Fountain pen, 309
Francis I, 5370
Francis, Saint, of Sales, 5376
Franklin, Benjamin, 5416, 5458
Frankness, 692, 1036, 2082, 3125, 3203
Fraternities, *See* College Life
Freedom, 6389
Freedom of speech, 58
French, 7205-7221
Friction, 4574
Friends, 23, 56, 126, 185, 1859, 2356, 3874, 6919, 6969, 7384
Friendship, 6390
Fright, 4211
Full, 3103
Fumbling, 1790
Funeral, 2345
Fuss, 2921
Futile, 3881, 4752
Future, 55, 864, 4298, 4250, 6392
Futurism, 355

G

Gags, 5707-6006
Gain, 1993
Gall, 4966
Gallantry, 7127, 7226
Gambling, 6393
Game warden, 6124
Gangster, 1157
Gardening, 280, 1945

Garrick, 5487
Generosity, 124, 231, 1371, 1854, 2629, 2816
Genius, 6394, 7385
Gentility, 7386. *See.* Ancestry
Gentleman, 4534, 4737, 4892
Gentleness, 1456
George III, 5367
George, Lloyd, 5351, 5403
German, 7222-7243
Getting together, 3252
Ghosts, 5051
Gifts, 2929, 3127, 6899, 6965
Gilbert, W. S., 5371
Girls, 7387. *See* Modern Girls
Giving, 3661
Gladstone, W. E., 5388, 5389
Glamour, 4350
Glass, Carter, 5517
Glory, 1138
God, 3451, 3614, 3846, 6396
Going concern, 4529
Gold-digger, 139
Golden rule, 2949, 6397, 7596
Golden Wedding, 7216
Goldfish, 3755
Goldwyn, Samuel, 5454, 5661
Golf, 3634, 4875, 5190, 6007-6086, 6820, 6853, 6910, 7334, 7389, 7390, 7900
Good, 3210, 4845, 5166
Good-bye, 1086
Good deed, 191, 3264
Good guess, 3936
Good listener, 3393
Good luck, 134
Good news, 6220
Goodwin, Nat, 5438, 5533
Gossip, 1771, 1783, 6398
Government, 6399
Government project, 5292. *See* Politicians
Grace, 3016, 3026, 3044, 3174, 4709, 5178
Grades, 3500, 3521, 3572, 4253
Grammar, 3303, 6400
Grant, General, 3263
Grass widow, 2963
Gratitude, 252, 1512, 1813, 2248, 2330, 5068, 6150, 6265, 6401
Gravitation, 3508, 3566
Gravy, 3611
Greeley, Horace, 5435, 5510
Grit, 4785
Grocers and Butchers, 4414-4440
Growing old, 24, 5507. *See* Age
Growth, 6308
Guarantee, 4517
Guessing, 1894, 5695
Guitry, Sacha, 5378

H

Habeas corpus, 4796
Habit, 115, 182, 716, 2142, 2191, 2703, 4749, 4984
Hair, 2060, 2401, 2488, 2496, 2548, 2642, 3257, 4337, 4967
Hamburger, 3506
Hamlet, 3511
Hammerstein, Oscar, 5502, 5540
Handicaps, 2544
Hanna, Mark, 5303
Happiness, 2204, 2230, 7852
Happening, 1571
Hard luck, 2885, 6007
Hard times, 4555, 4617
Harvard, 4147, 4188, 4217, 4263, 4570, 8801
Hash, 619, 703, 730, 2294, 3428
Haste, 2, 2500, 5229
Hate, 4089, 6403
Hats, Women's, 2434, 2453, 2624, 2625, 2743, 2782, 2787, 2795. *See* Women's clothes

Haunted, 6728
Haydn, 5525
Hay-fever, 3613, 4999
Health, 1653, 5492
Hearing, 3152
Heat, 6306
Heaven, 148, 239, 249, 439, 513, 1621, 2389, 2575, 2604, 2800, 2968, 3119, 3175, 3190, 4859, 5519, 6050, 6404, 7079, 7117, 7162, 7276
Hebrew, See Jewish
Height, 6298, 6308
Heirloom, 3731
Hell, 41, 148, 239, 249, 513, 532, 831, 842, 1621, 1659, 1669, 1712, 2230, 2389, 2469, 4426, 4499, 4613, 4859, 5033, 5211, 5229, 5397, 5411, 5519, 6050, 6811, 7162, 7192
Helpful, 3676, 3766
Henpecked, 980, 1172, 1927, 2416, 4454
Henry VIII, 5370
Hepburn, Katharine, 5671
Hereditary, 1971, 4174, 7031
Hero, 1064
Hesitation, 1380
Highbrow, 3810, 7394
High church, 5132
High finance, 19
High pay, 4586
High prices, 1158, 4427
Hiking, 133
Hillis, Newell Dwight, 5519
Hints, 90, 1995, 2017, 2141, 3018, 4359
History, 111, 4245, 6406, 7395
Hitler, Adolf, 5524
Hoax, 5477
Hoboes, See Tramps
Holding our own, 1628
Holidays, 248, 1314, 3236
Hollywood, 5628–5687
Holmes, Justice Oliver Wendell, 5363, 5423, 5518
Home, 2693, 2791, 4178, 6408
Homely, 7978
Home-sickness, 1142, 7214
Honesty, 1518, 1604, 4457, 4703, 6352, 7397
Honeymoon, 2267, 2350, 6409, 7750. See Married Life
Honor, 4769, 6410, 8014
Honor system, 3816
Hope, 501, 3463, 6174, 6411, 7398
Hopeless, 2120, 4787
Horseback-riding, 3298
Horse Racing, 231, 6227–6233, 6873, 7167
Horses, 1426, 1432, 1433, 1476, 1636, 3105, 6292, 6887, 7227
Hospital, 2262, 7400. See Doctors
Hotels, 547–591, 7001, 7401
Hot weather, 135, 143, 237
Hounding, 5574
Housekeeping, 1801, 2964
Howard, Leslie, 5491
Howells, William Dean, 5395
Howlers, 8623–8695
Humanity, 2656
Human nature, 531
Humble, 8012
Humor, 6412
Humorous Errors, 8126–8503
    Announcements, Church, 8351–8362
    Announcements, Varied, 8363–8376
    Newspaper Advertisements, 8377–8415
    Newspaper Headlines, 8126–8173
    Newspaper Stories, 8174–8350
    Newspaper Want Ads, 8416–8484
    Signs, 8485–8503
Humorous Verse, 9199–9705
    Chains, 9359–9370
    Irish Dialect, 9698–9705
    Limericks, 9443–9636
    Little Willies, 9637–9671
    Miscellaneous Dialect, 9681–9697
    Nonsense Poems, 9371–9415
    Parodies, 9416–9442
    Poems, 9199–9254
    Short Verse, 9255–9358
    Western Dialect, 9672–9684
Hunting, 6106–6137, 6305, 6863, 6964
Hurry, 6911, 7008
Husband, 6413
Hypocrisy, 6414
Hypocrite, 7403

I

Ice water, 1705
Ideal, 2130, 4986
Identity, 251, 684, 1407, 1644, 3274, 4218, 7151
Idleness, 1409, 3593
Ignorance, 28, 104, 142, 194, 325, 354, 653, 1157, 1575, 1702, 1760, 3408, 3447, 3452, 4746, 4754, 4770, 5633, 5659, 6415
Ignoring, 3804
Illegible, 5358, 5435, 7404
Illusion, 6416
Imagination, 380, 1828, 4597, 5033
Imitation, 1717, 1768, 1843, 2039, 2297
Impatience, 985
Impersonation, 5555, 5556
Implied, 3226
Impression, 2010, 4890
Impressionism, 382
Improvement, 1215, 3213, 3240
Impunity, 4747
Incentive, 2788
Income, 12, 183, 2148, 2834
Income Tax, 156, 7125, 7644
Inconsistent, 3164
Incredible, 2551, 2677
Incredulity, 106
Independent, 4382
Indians, 1660, 1666, 1667, 1669
Indispensable, 4837
Indulgent, 1751
Inferiority complex, 288
Influence, 3370
Information, 245, 1611
Ingersoll, Robert, 5515
Initiative, 4222
Innocence, 357, 6383
Inquisitive, 2480, 2528
Insane Persons, 1206–1231, 5216, 5261, 7584
Insistence, 2180
Insomnia, 1661
Inspiration, 378, 6421
Installments, 2311, 2403, 2487, 3373, 4451, 4502, 7405, 7805
Insult, 4103, 4958
Insurance, 1833, 2706, 2766, 4574–4583
Intentions, 2128
Interest, 6772
Interpretation, 2670
Interruption, 2251, 3150, 5512
Introduction, 7225
Intuition, 2253, 7406
Investment, 1618
Involuntary, 3701
Involved speech, 4748, 4776, 4872, 4913, 4924, 6877
Irish, 7016–7204
Irish Dialect Verse, 9698–9705
Irony, 7407
Italian, 7802. See Nationalities and Races

J

Jackass, 5353
Janitor, 7408

1013

Jealousy, 6424
Jerrold, Douglas W., 5357, 5366, 5406, 5440
Jewish, 7012, 7192
Johnson, Dr. Samuel, 5377, 5381, 5384, 5390, 5391, 5419, 5436, 5516
Joint account, 7410
Joy, 2723
Judge, 6426
Judgment, 2059, 2771, 2796
Jurisdiction, 2674, 6418
Juries, 4754, 4756, 4758, 4792, 4793, 4800, 4809, 4837, 4855, 4893, 4901, 4929, 6428, 7066, 7171, 7413
Just debt, 4920
Justice, 6429, 7224
Justified, 4879

K

Kahn, Otto, 5469
Keeping on the ground, 7980
Keeping quiet, 7991
Keep it up, 4229
Keepsake, 7414
Kelvin, Lord, 5500
Key to success, 4288
Kibitzer, 7415
Kin, 5350
Kindness, 649, 1422, 1456, 1773, 3516, 4239
Kind words, 5506
Kipling, Rudyard, 5461
Kismet, 7153
Kisses, 334, 1770, 3827, 4169, 4213, 6430, 7416, 7890, 7919
Kittens, 3231
Knock-kneed, 1065
Knowledge, 868, 1145, 1497, 1533, 2292, 2302, 2729, 2962, 3072, 3164, 3366, 4344, 6431, 7291

L

Ladies, The Dear, 1731–1869
Lady, 4864, 6432
Lamb, Charles, 5178, 5412, 5445
Landlord, 4740, 6784, 7069, 7256
Language, 6434
Last Word, 2352, 2593, 2687
Late, 4296, 7746
Latest, 4346
Late trains, 1019, 1468, 1530
Latin, 3484
Laughter, 3444, 3750, 5231, 5526
Laundries, 188, 4446, 4478, 4687, 4712, 6946, 7417
Law 1532, 4763, 6435
Laws, Loony, 1670–1698
Lawsuit, 268, 7418
Lawyers, 1214, 1644, 4733–4935, 6436, 7419
Laziness, 310, 914, 1404, 1409, 1430, 1452, 1462, 1506, 1519, 1546, 1553, 1569, 1586, 1606, 1608, 2507, 2510, 2572, 3473, 3593, 3767, 4428, 4652, 4663
Leadership, 3079
Lear's Limericks, 9563–9636
Lease, 4557
Lectures, 7420, 7421
Legend, 698
Legislator, 5261
Leisure, 2420
Lending, 4602
Letters, 3360, 4306, 4308, 4330, 4444, 4498, 4504, 4521, 4808
Liars, 3283, 4889, 5200, 6143, 6158, 6219, 7589. See Lying
Liberal, 4790, 6438
Liberal Republican, 5297
Liberty, 6439, 7422
Life, 2606, 6441, 7423, 7566

Limericks, 9443–9636
Lincoln Stories, 5556, 7966–8015
Lind, Jenny, 5357
Lindsey, Judge Benjamin B., 5414
Lisp, 2022, 4410
Listening, 306, 2615, 2925
Literal Meaning, 13, 88, 99, 225, 236, 806, 997, 1499, 3464
Literature, 463–520, 6442
Little Darlings–And Devils, The, 2935–3366
Little Devils, 2935–3366
Little Tots, 2935–3366
Little Willies, 9637–9671
Loafing, 2507
Lodges, 103, 149, 2719, 2746, 2943
Lodgers, See Boarding Houses
Logic, 353, 1209, 1516, 1555, 2626, 3214, 3364, 3844, 4277, 6443, 7051
London, Jack, 5402
Longevity, 4962
Longfellow, H. W., 5373
Long, Huey, 5407
Long Sermons, 5112, 5115, 5133, 5180, 5181, 5205, 5219
Long speeches, 5272, 5286, 5529
Loony Laws, 1670–1698
Losing things, 1014
Lost, 3219
Love and Courtship, 1870–2216, 1875, 1944, 1954, 1988, 2033, 2050, 2052, 2086, 2596, 2767, 3081, 6445, 7426, 7534, 7558, 7916, 7924
Love letters, 1903, 1911, 2432, 7893, 7928
Low Church, 5132
Loyalty, 534
Luck, 674, 1489, 1833, 2520, 3317, 3386, 3421, 5080, 6447, 7427
Luxury, 2653, 7428
Lying, 2444, 3513, 4809, 5228, 7973. See Liars

M

Macready, 5358
Magazines, 7935
Mail, 3360, 3713
Majority, 983, 5544
Make-believe, 5587
Making sure, 7974
Man, 6450, 7429, 7755
Man-about-town, 7430
Management, 1490
Manicurist, 2177
Manners, 234, 311, 977, 1486, 2133, 2965, 2974, 2984, 3062, 3645, 5083, 6451
Married Life, 2217–2811, 7431, 7432, 7548, 7585. See Matrimony
Marquis, Don, 6060
Masterpiece, 6897
Mathematics, 1107, 1413, 1420, 1459, 1489, 1574, 1595, 1607, 2043, 2257, 2538, 3041, 3350, 3573, 3583, 3903, 4684, 6020, 6172, 7032
Matrimony, 2227, 3535, 6452, 6633, 7433. See Married Life
Measles, 3033, 3047, 3311, 3625, 4961
Medicine, 6453
Mementos, 2990
Memory, 15, 204, 323, 332, 676, 965, 1752, 1899, 1930, 1974, 2168, 2586, 2658, 3499, 4618, 4635, 4945, 5057, 5325, 5413, 5680, 6009, 6265, 6774, 6821
Men's clothes, 222
Mercenary, 1795
Mercy, 6455
Merger, 2601
Mess, 3045, 3088
Method, 2726, 3736
Meticulous, 657, 689

Michelangelo, 4659
Middle age, 7434
Middle-of-the-road, 5312
Milk, 1492, 1496, 1504, 1604, 3027, 3034, 3481, 3585, 5119
Millionaire, 3416
Military honors, 1106
Mind, 2811
Minding own business, 7091, 7683
Mind-reading, 1928
Minority, 5534
Miscellaneous Stores, 4441–4544
Miser, 6458
Mistakes, 36, 196, 207, 219, 318, 3075, 4835, 4840. See Errors
Mistakes in Print, See Humorous Errors
Mixed Metaphor, 5321
Mix-up, 11
Mob, 6459
Model, 2901
Moderation, 6460
Modern age, 7435
Modern art, 368
Modern children, 270, 2969, 3004, 3113, 3384
Modern girls, 1961, 2159, 2160, 3402, 7436. See Flaming youth
Modern literature, 7437
Modern woman, 7438
Modern youth, 808, 1624. See Flaming youth
Modesty, 1120, 1127, 3069, 5689, 6461
Monarchy, 6462
Money, 23, 1326, 1904, 1913, 1955, 1964, 2092, 2144, 2456, 2638, 3012, 3115, 4688, 6463, 7277, 7439, 7440
Monogamy, 3388
Monologue, 7441
Monopolist, 7442
Monument, 6465
Mood, 5551
Moody, Dwight, 5387
Moore, 5355
Morality, 6466
More light, 7988
Morris, William, 5393
Morrow, Dwight W., 5413
Mortgage, 4571, 6467
Mosquitos, 1241, 1480, 6269, 6281, 7183, 7444
Mother, 7443
Mothers-in-law, 1547, 2812–2833, 4865, 6018
Mother-tongue, 2778
Moths, 2786
Movies, See Hollywood
Motion Pictures, See Hollywood
Moving, 2890
Mozart, 5525
Mud, 6296
Mules, 3501
Multiply, 3467
Murder, 6470
Mutual, 2042, 6417
Music, 392–462, 6471, 7235
Mustache, 6698

N

Names, 200, 548, 739, 785, 807, 859, 942, 994, 1000, 1071, 1118, 1164, 1505, 1581, 1939, 1979, 2203, 2245, 2419, 2469, 2891, 2972, 3438, 3492, 3781, 3888, 4561, 6472, 6681, 7154, 7292
Napoleon, 5420, 5643
Narrow escape, 3986, 6132
Nations and Races, 6654–7296
Nature, 5356, 6473, 7943
Necessity, 6474
Neckties, 4523
Neighbors, 74, 76, 184, 190, 265, 283, 407, 416, 418, 425, 455, 456, 458, 459, 461,

462, 815, 1865, 2299, 2388, 2396, 2407, 2452, 3272, 3409, 4464, 4568, 6475, 7445
Nerve, 5050
Nerves, 4966
Neutrality, 1625
Never satisfied, 4257, 4487
Newly rich, 257, 314, 359, 389, 394, 4447, 4559
Newlyweds, 2256, 2267, 2269, 2285, 2294, 2300, 2307, 2312, 2314, 2320, 2340, 2350, 2354, 2362, 2411, 2422, 2437, 2439, 2447, 2455, 2499, 2509, 2552, 2562, 2591, 2608, 2659, 2688, 2701, 2773, 2799, 4414, 4416, 4707. See Married Life
New models, 899
News, 1571, 2883, 6477
Newspapers, 3295
Newsreel, 2896
New Year, 6478
New York City, 60, 168, 197, 215, 316, 649, 2931, 3447, 4586, 4715
Niagara Falls, 6755, 7075
No, 4029
Noah, 5252
No charge, 4333
Noise, 1016, 5400, 7030, 7602
Nonsense Poems, 9371–9415
Nose, 2947
Notes, 420, 5227, 7095
Nudist, 7447
Numskull, 7039
Nurses, 2717, 4947, 5062, 5063, 5074
Nye, Bill, 5535

O

Oath, 4853, 4899, 4905, 4932, 6479
Obedience, 1082, 2170, 2440, 3391
Obey, 2810
Objection, 4918
Obliging, 4056
Observation, 3607
Obvious, 4989
O'Connell, Daniel, 5368
Office Boys, 4357–4385
Office, 4285–4393
O.K., 4466
Older, 4388. See Age
Old-fashioned, 808
Old maid, 1150. See Bachelors and Spinsters
Old masters, 3726
Old timers, 174
Old times, 324
Omens, 6481
One way, 2794, 6641
Open mind, 5821
Opera, 430, 446, 955. See Music
Operation, 1840
Opinion, 6482
Opportunist, 7449
Opportunity, 2146, 4281, 6483, 7135, 7450
Optimism, 4606, 7451
Optimists, 1614, 3316, 7452
Option, 1878
Oratory, 6484, 7224, 7453
Orders, 1098, 2365, 4627
Organizers, 6933
Originality, 370, 1896, 2889, 3063, 6485
Orphan asylum, 5280
Overcautious, 7996
Overcrowding, 1617
Overselling, 5214
Overzealous, 6671

P

Passen, Pierre van, 5401
Pacifist, 2982, 7454

1015

Paderewski, 5437, 5439, 5452
Page, Walter Hines, 5475
Pain, 6486
Parachute, 112, 116, 128, 169, 504
Paragon, 7456
Parents, 6487, 7457, 7776
Parodies, 9416–9442
Parrot, 139, 4522, 4540, 4541, 4544, 5460, 6035
Partners, 6103, 6488, 6580, 6609
Passage, 5126
Passion, 6489
Password, 7164
Past, 6490
Patience, 601, 626, 630, 946, 1426, 5631, 6176, 6491
Patriot, 7458
Patriotism, 1050, 1111, 6492, 6824
Patton, Francis Landy, 5400
Pay, 2089, 5164
Paying bills, 4689
Payment, 2574
Peace, 4734, 6493, 7090, 7459
Peaceful methods, 3354
Pedestrian, 816, 860, 865, 886, 893, 908, 909, 930, 948, 7460
Pedigree, 5415, 6494, 6736
Penn, William, 5520
Penurious, 89
People, 6496
Pep, 5561
Percentage, 695
Perfection, 221, 2224, 2599, 2882, 3268, 3426
Performance, 5302
Perjury, 6977
Permanent, 6693
Permission, 2823
Perseverance, 527, 6112, 6497
Persistence, 542, 1907, 3677, 6384
Pessimist, 7166, 7461
Peter, the Apostle, 3636
Petty cash, 4365, 4385
Pharisees, 3663
Phelps, William Lyon, 7910
Philanthropist, 3294, 7462
Philanthropy, 6498
Phillips, Wendell, 5411
Philosopher, 7463
Philosophy, 131, 6499, 7464
Phlegmatic, 6688
Phonetic spelling, 3389
Photographers, 7465
Physicians, See.Doctors
Picnic, 110
Pidgin English, 7266, 7271
Pie, 1320, 1339, 1375, 2669
Piety, 6501
Pig, 3206
Pigeons, 137
Pilgrims, 6502
Plagiarism, 6503
Plain citizen, 291
Plain language, 1089
Plans, 1193
Playing, 3296
Playing safe, 35, 3782
Pleasing customers, 4492
Pleasure, 6505
Plumbers, 4655, 4658, 4662
Poems, Humorous, See Humorous Verse
Poets, 472, 478, 480, 482, 484, 491, 495, 496, 506 512, 514, 517, 520, 1949, 3575, 6506, 7215, 7467
Poker, 1057, 1113, 1656, 6239, 6246, 6256, 7468
Poker face, 7469
Police and Prisoners, 1146–1205
Politeness, 1084, 2960, 3208, 5230

Political jobs, 5233, 5238, 5239, 5257, 5259, 5265, 5299, 5307, 5326, 5338, 5347. See Politicians
Politicians, 767, 1650, 1891, 5233–5348, 6507, 7470, 7471
Politics, 6508
Polygamy, 6509, 7473
Pompous, 564, 1011, 1224, 7989
Popular, 1809, 4479, 4643, 7474
Popular songs, 7475, 7646
Population, 3447
Possession, 1895, 1943
Postcards, 1714
Posterity, 6511
Postscripts, 7476
Postmaster, 1424
Poverty, 1185, 1508, 3095, 6512
Power, 6513
Practical, 2267, 2922
Practice, 1141, 2116, 2492, 5130, 6747
Praise, 2806, 4320, 7477
Prayers, 1023, 1032, 1417, 1585, 1625, 2971, 2979, 3019, 3023, 3086, 3124, 3128, 3160, 3185, 3186, 3188, 3204, 3238, 3245, 3267, 3340, 3639, 5202, 5282, 6514, 6675, 6867
Preachers, 1229, 1444, 5110–5132, 6515
Precaution, 1879, 1985, 4000
Precedence, 1579
Precedent, 2369, 7993
Precise, 1548, 5196
Precocious, 3171
Predicament, 2566
Preface, 6516
Preference, 3834
Prejudice, 4870, 6517
Premiums, 167, 4722
Preparedness, 1206, 2989, 3747, 4786, 5184
Presence of mind, 2612
Presents, 1870, 1993
Press, 522, 537, 540, 6519
Prices, 146, 3040, 5515
Pride, 4789, 6127, 6520, 7089, 7091, 8015
Princeton, 4257, 4263, 5400
Principle, 6521
Printing Errors, See Humorous Errors
Prisoners, 1146–1205
Privacy, 1424, 1844, 2827
Production, 1470
Profanity, 144, 166, 786, 1093, 1645, 2879, 2891, 3067, 3098, 3112, 3152, 3159, 3349, 3480, 3634, 4484, 4716, 5211, 6023, 6025, 6035, 6151, 6184, 6885, 7260
Professors, 3815–3977
Proficiency, 1024, 6866
Profits, 2517, 4427, 6920
Progress, 1161, 1410, 1667, 1999, 2250, 5039, 5644, 6264
Prohibition, 6526
Promises, 5302
Promoting, 530, 4820, 7478
Proof, 2953, 3431, 6179, 7037
Property, 6528
Prosperity, 4815, 6529, 7479
Protection, 2441
Proximity, 7143
Psychiatry, 6532
Psychology, 80, 3323, 3383
Public speaking, 7481
Publicity, 4772, 5658, 5669, 6881
Pullman cars, 7226
Punctual, 4297, 7482
Punishment, 6276
Puns, 8696–8945
Puppies, 5240
Puritan, 333
Purpose, 3835, 4509

1016

Q

Quacks, 86
Quakers, 31, 32, 1916, 2192, 2329, 3482
Qualifications, 4081, 4351, 7975
Quality, 2781
Quarrels, 2096, 5694, 6534
Questions, 2429, 3169, 3241, 3323, 3620, 3852, 3858, 4878, 4981, 5298
Quick-thinking, 799, 2642
Quiet, 1571, 3602
Quiller-Couch, 5447
Quotation, 6535
Quotation Dictionary, 6314–7296

R

Rabbits, 1648
Races and Nations, 6654–7296
Rachmaninoff, 5462
Radical, 7483
Radio, 6, 8, 84, 92, 119, 175, 199, 345, 2968, 3026, 3071, 3340, 4698, 7000
Radio gags, 5707–6006
Railroads, 981–1020
Rain, 52, 1529, 1632, 1634, 2364, 6286, 7246
Raising funds, 5127
Ranch, 7244
Randolph, John, 5455
Rascals, 2718, 6537
Reactionary, 329
Ready-made, 4531
Real Estate, 1405, 4545–4573, 6538
Realism, 350, 375, 6284
Reaping, 6702
Reason, 2876, 6539
Rebellion, 6540
Rebuke, 3801
Receipts, 1669, 6620
Reciprocate, 681, 879, 1451, 1592, 2049, 3240
Reciting, 3068, 3172
Recognition, 1950, 4136
Recommendation, 3748, 5608, 6341
Record, 7979
Reducing, 1800, 1853
Reed, Thomas B., 5261
References, 3687, 3727, 7148
Refined, 4251
Reflection, 1440
Reform, 1151, 2250, 5268, 5355, 5387
Rejuvenation, 5031
Related, 227
Relatives, 90, 109, 136, 147, 242, 2542
Relativity, 629, 5463
Relentless, 4934
Religion, 6542, 7630
Remarque, Erich, 5485
Remorse, 2662
Reno, 2216
Repentance, 6233
Reporters, 521–546
Reproof, 3768
Republican, 5240, 5244, 5246, 5264, 5291, 5305, 5322
Reputation, 6544, 7486
Resemblance, 29, 1187, 4819, 5509, 6526
Reserved, 6793
Resistance, 6924
Resourceful, 10, 3608, 3609, 4618, 4631, 6819
Respect, 1124, 3401, 5692, 7487
Responsible, 4383, 5330
Restaurants, 592–726, 7489
Restraint, 337
Retribution, 6545
Revenge, 3745, 6546
Revolution, 6548
Reward, 2936, 2995, 6549, 6663, 6949, 6973, 7146
Rich, 6550

Rights, 4740
Riley, James Whitcomb, 5494
Ring, 1743, 1979, 2021, 2036, 2079
Risk, 2735, 3746
Rivalry, 5562
Rogers, Will, 5468, 5529
Romantic, 304, 858, 1227, 1703, 2012, 2223, 2523, 2776, 4204
Roosevelt, Franklin Delano, 10055
Roosevelt, Theodore, 5393
Rossini, 5431
Rothschild, Baron, 5352
Rouge, 5376
Rumor, 6552
Rural, 1380–1624
Russell, George, 5394
Russian, 3921

S

Sabbath, 6553
Sacrifice, 3338
Safety, 1411, 2951, 3123
Sagacity, 4703
Sailors, 1048–1145
Saint, 6554
Salad, 6555
Salary, 5545, 5562, 5570, 5628, 5630
Sales, 3040, 4516, 4531, 6610
Salesmanship, 782, 2336, 3167, 4432, 4495, 4513, 4547, 4562, 5143
Salesmen, 568, 791, 880, 1002, 1062, 1500, 3647, 4376, 4616–4638, 7275, 7672
Salisbury, Lord, 5365
Salvation Army, 40
Samples, 717, 3687, 4625, 4697, 4758, 6721
Sand, 1991, 2190, 4158
Sanity, 4970
Santa Claus, 46, 2976
Sarcasm, 437, 572, 677, 687, 711, 771, 795, 839, 897, 906, 921, 929, 2031, 2168, 2786
Satisfaction, 543
Saving, 1522, 2929, 3528, 5220, 6119, 7072, 7237
Saxe, John Godfrey, 5428
Scandal, 3460, 4723
Scared, 6386
Scenarios, 5362. See Hollywood
Scenery, 289
Scholar, 6557
School, 6558
School Children and Teachers, 3405–3610
Science, 1201, 3035, 4681, 5039, 6559
Scientific farming, 1392, 1528, 1538
Scotch, 6846–7015, 7493
Sculptor, 7494. See Art
Seasickness, 1027, 1029, 1035, 1038, 1039, 1041, 1043, 1044, 1045, 6487
Seasons, 4508
Second choice, 5334
Secretaries, See Stenographers
Secrets, 1756, 1815, 1820, 1858, 2015, 2221, 2350, 3751, 3891, 6560
Security, 7084
Selection, 7139
Self-confidence, 1798
Self-control, 2410, 2636
Self-defense, 3461, 6130
Self-denial, 3239
Self-made man, 297, 2481, 3107, 5510, 7495
Self-starter, 2681
Sentiment, 1160, 1162, 2610, 2922, 3231, 3233
Servants, 3679–3814, 5410, 6561
Service, 662, 680
Sex, 6562
Shakespeare, 467, 474, 498, 513, 1729, 4818, 5371, 5496, 5622, 5650, 6563
Sharing, 2134, 2622, 3054, 4277, 4771

Shaw, George Bernard, 5480, 5511, 5522, 5534
Sheridan, 5361, 5443, 5444
Shiftlessness, 544
Ships, 1021–1047
Shock, 3770, 4172
Shoes, 1058, 1742, 1764, 7141
Shopping, 2737, 2769, 2991, 4512, 4526, 4533, 6628
Show Business, 5544–5706
Shy, 1881, 1973, 1991
Siddons, Mrs., 5392
Signals, 5139, 5235
Signs, 958, 1076, 1325, 1622, 6182, 8485–8503
Silence, 7158
Silly questions, 989, 990, 1001
Silly stories, 50
Silver lining, 1431, 1517, 1540, 4548, 4591
Similes, 6236
Simplicity, 1740
Sin, 3622, 3638, 3665, 3828, 5128, 5541, 6564, 7496
Sincerity, 6565
Sister, 3182, 3201
Size, 4600, 4753, 5351, 5528, 6289
Skeptic, 1582, 5532
Skill, 4904
Skin game, 1423, 1472
Skinner, Otis, 5595
Slander, 6566
Slang, 82, 1725, 3396
Sleep, 187, 335, 343, 628, 995, 1420, 1661, 3734, 3880, 4978, 7156
Sleeping in church, 5156, 5169, 5179
Slips-of-speech, 20, 27, 79, 3179, 5542
Slow, 2880, 6274
Slow trains, 1004, 1006, 1010, 1012, 1388, 6841
Smiles, 4405, 5231
Smith, Alfred E., 5498
Smiths, 145, 502
Smithson, James, 5399
Smoking, 2454, 3130, 3224, 7497, 7794
Smoot, Reed, 5476
Snakes, 6307
Snobbery, 6567
Snoring, 2366
Snow, 3106, 6284
Socialism, 5352, 7159
Society, 7, 17, 42, 161, 1131, 1649, 1804, 1822, 6570
Soldiers and Sailors, 1048–1145, 6571, 7086, 7164
Solicitude, 3706, 5629
Solitude, 1617
Solomon, 3095
Solution, 2709
Somnambulist, 2153
Soul, 6572
Soup, 598, 620, 621, 624, 625, 627, 633, 636, 653, 654, 669, 670, 702, 709, 722, 727
South, 49, 255, 5305, 5322
Speakers, 64, 65, 155, 204, 269, 286, 312, 2724, 3546, 3672, 3927
Specialists, 4952, 4998, 5036, 5041, 7291
Specific, 1119, 1987, 2011, 2163, 4402, 6678
Speculation, 7600
Speeches, 5497, 6573
Speed, 836, 839, 862, 929, 6200, 6274, 6280, 6311
Spelling, 3539, 4339, 4415
Spending, 2575
Spinach, 3341, 3344
Spinsters, 2860–2875
Splitting hairs, 4836, 4894
Sports, 1357, 1640, 6007–6264
Sporting, 6117, 6261
Spring, 7498

Squandering, 7086
Staël, Madame de, 5466
Stage and Radio Gags, 5707–6006
Statesman, 5243, 6578. See Politicians
Statistics, 1457, 2112, 2393, 3096, 3195, 3925, 4578, 5054, 7718
Status, 6579
Stealing, 2652
Stenographers, 2124, 4331–4356
Stevenson, Robert Louis, 5501
Stingy, 1453, 2140, 2259, 3394, 4613, 5533. See Scotch
Stock Brokers, 4604–4615
Stoic, 6569
Stores, miscellaneous, 4441–4544
Stock, 3113, 3450, 6534
Straight talk, 3082
Strangers, 3132
Strategy, 500, 612, 803, 1080, 1426, 1826, 1850, 2246, 2361, 2374, 2522, 2612, 2682, 2812, 3082, 3221, 3272, 3328, 3713, 5591
Streetcars, 954–980
Strength, 3220, 7499
Stubborn, 2925
Study, 3844
Stupidity, 140, 6582
Stuttering, 37, 1153, 4544, 5702, 6682
Style, 6583
Substitute, 617, 633, 642, 1383, 1414, 3116, 5140, 5174, 5183, 5284, 6664
Suburbs, 960, 961, 963, 964
Subway, 7500
Success, 230, 1668, 4327, 5027, 5495, 6584, 7501, 7938
Succession, 3911
Suggestion, 1338, 1893, 4287, 4432, 7121
Suicide, 6585
Sullivan, John L., 5427
Summer boarders, 1402, 1442, 1448, 1509, 1526, 1541, 1554, 1576
Sunday, 3624, 6162, 6188, 6820
Sunday, Billy, 5532
Sunday Schools, 3611–3678
Sunset, 7196
Superiority of men, 80
Superlative, 2914
Superstition, 134, 308, 3762, 4683, 6586
Support, 2858
Surprise, 2453, 2677, 2782
Surrender, 2342
Survival, 5692, 5694
Suspicious, 7294
Swedish, 7244–7254
Swimming, 3182, 3524
Swing music, 395, 424
Sympathy, 1240, 2970, 4082, 4729, 6670
Synonym, 3845, 7503

T

Table d'hote, 6661
Taciturn, 1647, 2664, 5531, 6933
Tact, 45, 592, 701, 715, 1731, 2265, 2400, 2588, 2697, 2790, 4105, 4495, 6034, 6587
Tactless, 63, 1767
Taft, William Howard, 5369, 5467
Take courage, 6232
Talent, 6588
Talk, 3356, 5245, 5348
Talkative, 981, 5349
Talking shop, 91, 1210, 2142
Tall building, 6304
Talleyrand, 5466
Tall Stories, 1139, 1449, 1460, 6265–6313
Tarkington, Booth, 5453
Taxes, 46, 1848, 6590

1018

Taxis, 971, 1436, 3404, 6909
Teachers, 3405-3610
Technical, 4746, 4877, 7971
Teetotaler, 7091, 7101
Telegram, 2910, 4632, 6915, 6929, 6962, 7169
Telepathy, 2016
Telephone, 179, 206, 277, 882, 2730, 2794, 3119, 3673, 3937, 4328, 4477, 4890, 6694, 7263, 7505
Television, 6592
Temper, 1577, 2018, 2261, 5186
Temperance, 58, 75, 120, 319, 342, 5520, 6591
Temporary, 6362
Temptation, 3109, 3149, 3165, 6593, 7506
Tenacious, 8000
Tenant, 7256
Tennyson, Lord, 5674
Testimony, 7107
Texas, 1659, 1662
Theaters, 6595. *See* Broadway
Thief, 6596
Thin, 7087
Thinking, 1835, 2770, 3039, 4831, 6597, 7132, 7190
Thoughtful, 3233
Thrift, 182, 738, 1397, 1408, 2387, 5354, 6679
Tidings, 5142
Time, 773, 905, 996, 1458, 1776, 1906, 2395, 2576, 3094, 3728, 3822, 4913, 6599, 6733
Timidity, 100, 1170
Tolerant, 8001
Tomorrow, 3029, 6601
Tongue trippers, 68
Toothbrush, 1382
Tips, 577, 6713, 6718, 6890, 6926, 6966, 6975, 7509
Toasts, 9706-10065
    Fortune and Prosperity, 9887-9894
    Friends, 9830-9858
    General, 9997-10054
    Good fellowship, 9859-9886
    Hosts and Guests, 9985-9996
    Love, Courtship and Marriage, 9789-9829
    Men, 9706-9721
    Patriotic, 9895-9925
    Sentiment and Good-Will, 9926-9984
    Stories About, 10055-10065
    Women, 9722-9788
Tobacco, 4938, 7511
Tots, 2935-3366
Tough, 6045
Tourists, 6268
Town booster, 4549, 4677
Tragedy, 3511
Trains, 1005, 1437, 7286
Training, 7601
Traitor, 5343
Tramps, 1310-1379
Travel, 6605
Treating, 6947, 6988, 6996
Tree, Beerbohm, 5601
Trees, 6272, 6301
Triangle, 3505
Trickery, 3371, 4729
Triplets, 2915, 2920, 2930, 3076, 5231
Trouble, 21, 1564, 1568, 2137, 2212, 2616, 2708, 3619, 7223
Trust, 7027
Truth, 539, 545, 547, 1025, 1097, 1127, 1128, 1440, 1604, 1665, 2118, 2157, 2590, 4360, 5262, 5636, 6159, 6608, 6961
Trying, 6138
Turnover, 2362, 5424

Twain, Mark, 5135, 5214, 5349, 5374, 5386, 5417, 5433, 5434, 5459, 5464, 5472, 5481, 5488, 5509, 5527, 5539
Twins, 1959, 2030, 2245, 2475, 2891, 2896, 2918, 2942, 3015, 3020, 3547, 3957, 6878, 7026
Typographical Errors, 538. *See* Humorous Errors
Tyranny, 6609

U

Ugly, 5508
Umbrella, 44, 205, 282, 336
Understanding, 6611
Understatement, 1399
Undertakers, 3484, 5271, 6612
Unequal, 7021
Unexpected, 4191
Union, 6614
Universe, 6615
Unlucky, 1366
Unprepared, 6080
Unreasonable, 682
Uplifters, 83
Urgent, 3771
Useful, 2293
Utopia, 6616

V

Vacation, 1792, 7731
Vaccination, 229
Valor, 6617
Values, 178, 381, 718, 1502, 7990
Van, Billy, 5385
Vanity, 1845, 5548, 5552, 5554, 5580, 5636, 5675, 6618
Vegetarians, 665
Venice, 1710
Veracity, 6180
Verbosity, 193
Verse, Humorous, *See* Humorous Verse
Vestris, Madame, 5382
Vice, 6620
Vice-president, 4590
Victoria, Queen, 5354
Victory, 6621
Vintner, 6622
Virgin, 6623
Virtue, 6624
Vocational guidance, 4525, 4629
Voltaire, 5448
Vote, 6625

W

Wagnerian Music, 403, 428
Wages, 3785, 6626
Waiters, *See* Restaurants
Waiting, 2398
Wall Street, 7877, 7965
Wallace, Edgar, 5362
War, 6627, 7516
Washington, George, 3175, 3495
Wasteful, 7270
Watchdog, 4536, 7222
Watchman, 3462
Water, 6628
Watterson, Henry, 5379
Weakness, 6629
Wealth, 26, 327, 1724, 6630
Weather, 181, 238, 555, 767, 1315, 1730, 4858, 5494, 6631, 6992, 7129, 7187, 7621
Webster, Daniel, 5252, 5430, 5432, 5489
Wedding, 2639, 2756, 3066, 6632, 7517, 7854
Wedlock, *See* Matrimony

1019

Week-end guests, 998
West, 6634
West, Mae, 5671
West Point, 4149
Western, 1625–1669
Western Dialect Verse, 9672–9684
Whim, 2728
Whisper, 4951
Whistler, 5356, 5359, 5424, 5523
Wholesome, 6716
Whoppers, See Tall Stories
Wickedness, 6635, 7518
Widow, 6636
Widower, 1741, 2178, 2375
Wife, 6637
Wild oats, 4192
Wilde, Oscar, 5359, 5360, 5457
Will, 4882
Willies, Little, 9637–9671
Will-power, 2938, 3129, 3729
Wilson, Woodrow, 5396
Wind, 1450, 1638, 6238, 6286, 6638
Wine, 6639
Winner, 3022, 6021
Wisdom, 2863, 3392, 6542, 6640
Wise, 6641
Wisecracks, 7621–7965
Wishes, 2119, 2745, 6761
Wit, 6642
Witness, 6643
Witty retorts, 67, 125, 486, 558, 576, 1054,
    1063, 1112, 1122, 1438, 2291, 7142
Witty Sayings, 7528–7620
Woman driver, 787, 795, 819, 820, 826, 827,
    829, 830, 840, 843, 849, 852, 869, 876,
    883, 885, 887, 892, 900, 901, 915, 916,
    918, 922, 928, 941
Woman hater, 1643
Women, 123, 1808, 2476, 2919, 6644, 7520,
    7940. See Ladies, The Dear

Women's clothes, 214, 379, 1761, 1769, 1819,
    1823, 1824, 2278, 2335, 2603, 7522. See
    Hats, Women's
Work, 189, 211, 1363, 3038, 3462, 4318,
    4323, 4424, 5364, 6813, 7277
Working-men, 4639–4664
World, 3088, 6646, 7530
Worms, 2382, 2568, 2832, 4266
Worry, 189, 1434, 2479, 4666, 4841, 7523
Worse, 5217
Worth, 1441, 3014, 4203, 5164
Writer, 3749
Wrong, 5025, 6649
Wynn, Ed, 5508, 7911

Y

Yale, 4184, 4263, 4265, 7253, 8801
Yankees, 154, 296
Yarn, 2573
Yawn, 7524
Year, 7525
Yes, 5652
Yes-men, 7526
Yesterday, 6650
Young, Brigham, 5474
Younger generation, 70
"You Tell 'Em" Puns, 8946–8991
Youth, 3325, 5363, 5480, 6651
Youth, modern, See Flaming youth

Z

Zanesville, 4677
Zeal, 1149, 7527
Zero, 3851
Zoo, 177, 209, 2631, 2769

A